PRINTED CIRCUITS HANDBOOK

Related Titles

Alvino • PLASTICS FOR ELECTRONICS

Classon • SURFACE MOUNT TECHNOLOGY FOR CONCURRENT ENGINEERING
  AND MANUFACTURING

Ginsberg and Schnoor • MULTICHIP MODULE AND RELATED TECHNOLOGIES

Harper • ELECTRONIC PACKAGING AND INTERCONNECTION HANDBOOK

Harper and Miller • ELECTRONIC PACKAGING, MICROELECTRONICS, AND INTERCONNECTION
  DICTIONARY

Harper and Sampson • ELECTRONIC MATERIALS AND PROCESSES HANDBOOK, 2/E

Lav • BALL GRID ARRAY TECHNOLOGY

Licari • MULTICHIP MODULE DESIGN, FABRICATION, AND TESTING

Sergent and Harper • HYBRID MICROELECTRONICS HANDBOOK, 2/E

Boswell • SUBCONTRACTING ELECTRONICS

Boswell and Wickam • SURFACE MOUNT GUIDELINES FOR PROCESS CONTROL, QUALITY,
  AND RELIABILITY

Byers • PRINTED CIRCUIT BOARD DESIGN WITH MICROCOMPUTERS

Capillo • SURFACE MOUNT TECHNOLOGY

Chen • COMPUTER ENGINEERING HANDBOOK

Coombs • ELECTRONIC INSTRUMENT HANDBOOK, 2/E

Di Giacomo • DIGITAL BUS HANDBOOK

Di Giacomo • VLSI HANDBOOK

Fink and Christiansen • ELECTRONICS ENGINEERS' HANDBOOK, 3/E

Ginsberg • PRINTED CIRCUITS DESIGN

Juran and Gryna • JURAN'S QUALITY CONTROL HANDBOOK

Jurgen • AUTOMOTIVE ELECTRONICS HANDBOOK

Manko • SOLDERS AND SOLDERING, 3/E

Rao • MULTILEVEL INTERCONNECT TECHNOLOGY

Sze • VLSI TECHNOLOGY

Van Zant • MICROCHIP FABRICATION

*To order or receive additional information on these or any other
McGraw-Hill titles, please call 1-800-822-8158 in the United States.
In other countries, contact your local McGraw-Hill representative.*

BC15XXA

PRINTED CIRCUITS HANDBOOK

Clyde F. Coombs, Jr. **Editor in Chief**

Fourth Edition

McGraw-HILL

New York   San Francisco   Washington, D.C.   Auckland   Bogotá
Caracas   Lisbon   London   Madrid   Mexico City   Milan
Montreal   New Delhi   San Juan   Singapore
Sydney   Tokyo   Toronto

Library of Congress Cataloging-in-Publication Data

Printed circuits handbook / Clyde F. Coombs, Jr. — 4th ed.
     p.   cm.
     Includes index.
     ISBN 0-07-012754-9
     1. Printed circuits—Handbooks, manuals, etc.   I. Coombs, Clyde
F.
     TK7868.P7P76   1995
     621.3815′31—dc20   95-25131
                                                                  CIP

McGraw-Hill

A Division of The McGraw-Hill Companies

3 4 5 6 7 8 9 10   FGRFGR   9 9 8 7

ISBN 0-07-012754-9

*The sponsoring editor for this book was Steven Chapman, and the production
supervisor was Suzanne W. B. Rapcavage. It was set in Times Roman by
North Market Street Graphics.*

McGraw-Hill books are available at special quantity discounts to use as
premiums and sales promotions, or for use in corporate training programs.
For more information, please write to the Director of Special Sales,
McGraw-Hill, Inc., 11 West 19th Street, New York, NY 10011. Or contact
your local bookstore.

This book is printed on recycled, acid-free paper containing
10% postconsumer waste.

To Ann

CONTENTS

Chapter 3. Types of Printed Wiring Boards   3.1

Chapter 4. Special-Construction Printed Wiring Boards   4.1

Chapter 5. Introduction to Surface-Mount Technology   5.1

Chapter 8. Base Materials

Chapter 9. Advanced Materials Technology

Chapter 10. Physical Characteristics of the PCB

Chapter 11. The PCB Design Process   **11.1**

Chapter 12. Designing a PCB for Manufacturability   **12.1**

Chapter 13. Electrical and Mechanical Design Parameters   **13.1**

Chapter 14. Multilayer Design Issues

Chapter 15. Manufacturing Information Documentation and Transfer

Part 3   Fabrication Processes

Chapter 16. Fineline Technologies

Chapter 17. Imaging

Chapter 18. Drilling

Chapter 19. Plating

Chapter 22. Machining and Routing

Chapter 23. Multilayer Processing

Chapter 24. Solder Resist Material and Processes   24.1

Chapter 25. Process Characterization and Control   25.1

Chapter 26. Bare Board Electrical Testing   26.1

Part 4   Assembly Processes

Chapter 27. Assembly Processes   27.3

Part 5   Solder and Soldering

Chapter 28. Design for Soldering and Solderability   **28.3**

Chapter 29. Solder Materials and Processes   **29.1**

Chapter 30. No-Clean Assembly Process   30.1

Chapter 31. Fluxes and Cleaning **31.1**

Chapter 32. Assembly Inspection **32.1**

Part 6   Test and Repair

Chapter 33. Loaded Board Testing   33.3

Part 7   Waste Minimization and Treatment

Chapter 34. Process Waste Minimization and Treatment   34.3

Part 8 Quality and Reliability of Printed Circuit Processes

Chapter 35. Acceptability of Fabricated Circuits   35.3

Chapter 36. Acceptability of Printed Circuit Board Assemblies   36.1

Chapter 37. Reliability of Printed Circuit Assemblies 37.1

Chapter 38. Electronic Contract Manufacturing Supplier Selection and Management 38.1

Part 9   Flexible Circuits

Chapter 39. Materials for Flexible Circuits   **39.3**

Chapter 40. Design of Flexible Circuits   **40.1**

Chapter 41. Fabrication and Assembly of Flexible Circuits   41.1

Chapter 42. Rigid-Flex Circuits   42.1

CONTRIBUTORS

Steven M. Allen   *AVEX Electronics* (CHAP. 38)

A. D. Andrade   *Sandia National Laboratories* (CHAP. 35)

Joyce M. Avery   (CHAP. 34)

James P. Block   *Laminating Company of America* (CHAP. 18)

Bruce Bolliger   *Hewlett-Packard Co.* (CHAP. 32)

James Cadile   *NOVA Drilling Service Inc.* (CHAP. 22)

Dr. Edward Duffek   *Adion Engineering Company* (CHAPS. 19, 21)

Natalie B. Feilchenfeld, Ph.D.   *IBM Microelectronics Division* (CHAP. 17)

Robert A. Forcier   *Nelco International Corporation* (CHAP. 9)

Gary M. Freedman   (CHAP. 29)

Smith A. Gause   *Westinghouse Electric Corporation* (CHAP. 8)

Judith Glazer, Ph.D.   *Hewlett-Packard Co.* (CHAP. 37)

Foster Gray   *Texas Instruments* (CHAP. 16)

Howard D. Green   *Micromodule Systems, Inc.* (CHAP. 6)

Steve Gurley   (CHAP. 42)

Philip J. Hallee   *Everett Charles Technologies* (CHAP. 26)

Paul W. Henderson   *Hewlett-Packard Co.* (CHAP. 30)

Charles G. Hennigsen   *Insulectro* (CHAPS. 8, 22)

Ralph J. Hersey, Jr.   *Lawrence Livermore National Laboratory* (CHAP. 13)

Happy T. Holden   *Hewlett-Packard Co.* (CHAPS. 4, 7)

Robert R. Holmes, Ph.D.   *AT&T* (CHAPS. 14, 23)

Rodney Laird   *Acuson Inc.* (CHAP. 5)

George Messner   *Consultant* (CHAP. 1)

Peter G. Moleux, P.E.   (CHAP. 34)

Dr. Hayao Nakahara   *N.T. Information Ltd.* (CHAPS. 3, 20, 24)

Kenneth P. Parker   *Hewlett-Packard Co.* (CHAP. 33)

Clyde Parrish   *PC World* (CHAP. 15)

Lee W. Ritchey   *3Com Corp.* (CHAPS. 10, 11, 12)

Ray D. Rust, Ph.D.   *AT&T* (CHAP. 25)

Sheldahl Technical Staff   *Sheldahl Inc.* (CHAPS. 39, 40, 41)

John W. Stafford   *Motorola Inc.* (CHAP. 2)

Leland Tull   *Contouring Technology* (CHAP. 22)

Laura J. Turbini, Ph.D.   *Georgia Institute of Technology* (CHAP. 31)

Stephan A. Vickers   (CHAP. 27)

Bruce Wooldridge   *DSC Communications Inc.* (CHAP. 36)

PREFACE

The printed circuit (or printed wiring) process continues to be the basic interconnection technique for electronic devices. Virtually every packaging system is based on this process, and will continue to be for the foreseeable future. However, just as the industries which it serves grow and change, the printed circuit technology, and industry, continue to grow and change. This new edition reflects these changes. We have added several new chapters on material not addressed in the previous books, and, in addition, all but a few chapters have been revised extensively to reflect the new demands on the process as well as the new capabilities available to product designers.

Of the several changes that have occurred in the printed wiring field over the years, none have been so profound and pervasive as surface-mount technology. The component package, freed of the constraints of the dual in-line package, has become a true variable in the design equation. Now, not only can the package be almost any shape, but the number of leads on it can be very large—in the hundreds—and the pitch of the centers can be very small—well below 0.010 in. This has created the need for a level of high-density circuitry not commercially available before, including fine geometry lines and traces, ultrasmall holes, high layer counts, and new materials. This, in turn, has created the need for new approaches to processes to mass-produce these boards and assemblies. In addition, the board engineering processes and tools have experienced major developments to allow the product designers to take advantage of these capabilities. As a result, a working knowledge of all aspects of the printed circuit processes is necessary to achieve the results demanded by the marketplace.

Design for manufacturability and concurrent engineering are real needs in the printed circuit industry. Designers must know the process, and the process engineers must know the design needs. Time-to-market and cost issues put pressure on doing it right the first time and coming to volume production rate quickly. The printed circuit can be the controlling element in both. It is the purpose of this book to help all who are involved make the correct decisions based on information about the processes, how they work, and how they are used.

In this edition, we have recognized the needs of the total community of people who work with printed circuits and need to understand areas outside their own specialties. We have updated the traditional process areas to represent the high-density technology demanded by the continuing trend to smaller and denser packaging, and have developed a new emphasis on design processes and tools, materials, quality, testing, and inspection, to help those who design, specify, buy, accept, or use printed circuit boards and assemblies provided by others. In addition, as the trend to specialized suppliers of products and services continues, this provides the information to match the design needs with the production capability at the beginning of the design cycle, and tells what information is needed by manufacturing and how to get it there instantly.

This, therefore, is a new book. We have built on the past material, but it reflects the needs and capabilities of the present and future.

As with all the editions of this book, I want to express special appreciation to the IPC (Institute for Interconnecting and Packaging Electronic Circuits). Over the years, many people there have provided major contributions to the material presented here, and that is true with this edition also. Ray Pritchard, retired Executive Director, continues to be a tremendous source of insight into the industry, as is Dieter Bergman, Technical Director. In addition, Tony Hilvers somehow found time in his busy schedule to provide personal help to several authors. I also wish to acknowledge the continued support of the management and staff of the Hewlett-Packard Company, especially in the Printed Circuit Operation and the Electronic Assembly Development Center.

Clyde F. Coombs, Jr.

P · A · R · T · 1

INTRODUCTION TO PRINTED CIRCUITS

CHAPTER 1
ELECTRONIC PACKAGING AND INTERCONNECTIVITY

George Messner
Consultant, Sea Cliff, New York

1.1 INTRODUCTION

All electronic components must be interconnected and assembled to form a functional and operating system. The design and the manufacture of these interconnections have evolved into a separate discipline called *electronic packaging.* Since the early 1950s, the basic building block of electronic packaging is the *printed wiring board* (PWB) and it will remain that into the foreseeable future. This book outlines the basic design approaches and manufacturing processes needed to produce these PWBs.

This chapter will outline the basic considerations, the main choices, and the potential tradeoffs which must be accounted for in the selection of the interconnection methods for electronic systems. Its main emphasis will be on the analysis of potential effects that the selection of various printed wiring board types and design alternatives could have on the cost and performance of the complete electronic product.

1.2 HIERARCHY OF INTERCONNECTIONS

To have the proper perspective on where PWBs fit into electronic systems, it will be helpful to describe briefly the packaging hierarchy of electronic systems. Some time ago, the Institute for Interconnecting and Packaging Electronic Circuits (IPC)[1] proposed eight categories of system elements in ascending order of size and complexity, which will be used here to illustrate typical electronic packaging structures. These are as follows:

Category A consists of fully processed active and passive devices. Bare or uncased chips and discrete capacitors, resistors, or their networks are typical examples of this category.

Category B comprises all packaged devices (active and passive) in plastic packages, such as DIPs, TSOPs QFPs, and BGAs, as well as those in ceramic packages, such as PGAs, and connectors, sockets, and switches. All of them are ready to be connected to an interconnecting structure.

Category C is substrates which interconnect uncased or bare chips (i.e., the components of category A) into a separable package. Included here are all types of multichip modules (MCMs), chip-on-boards (COBs), and hybrids.

Category D covers all kinds of substrates which interconnect and form assemblies of already packaged components, i.e., those from categories B and C. This category includes all types of rigid PWBs, flexible and rigid-flexible, and discrete-wiring boards.

Category E covers the back planes made by printed wiring and discrete-wiring methods or with flexible circuits, which interconnect PWBs, but not components, from the preceding groups.

Category F covers all intraenclosure connections. Included in this category are harnesses, ground and power distribution buses, RF plumbing, and co-ax or fiber optics wiring.

Category G includes the system assembly hardware, card racks, mechanical structures, and thermal control components.

Category H encompasses the entire integrated system with all its bays, racks, boxes, and enclosures and all auxiliary and support subsystems.

As seen from the preceding list, PWBs are exactly in the center of the hierarchy and are the most important and universally used element of electronic packaging.

The packaging categories F, G, and H are used mainly in large mainframes, supercomputers, central office switching, and in some military systems. Since there is a strong trend toward the use of miniaturized and portable electronic products for the majority of electronic packaging designs, tradeoffs are made in the judicious application and selection among the elements of the first five categories. These will be discussed in this chapter.

1.3   FACTORS AFFECTING SELECTION OF INTERCONNECTIONS

Selection of the packaging approaches among the various aforementioned elements is dictated not only by the system function, but also by the component types selected and by the operating parameters of the system, such as the clock speeds, power consumption, and heat management methods, and the environment in which the system will operate. This section provides a brief overview of these basic constraints which must be considered for proper packaging design of the electronic system.

1.3.1   Speed of Operation

The speed at which the electronic system operates is a very important technical factor in the design of interconnections. Many digital systems operate at close to 100 MHz and are already reaching beyond that level. The increasing system speed is placing great demands on the ingenuity of packaging engineers and on the properties of materials used for PWB substrates.

The speed of signal propagation is inversely proportional to the square root of the dielectric constant of the substrate materials, requiring designers to be aware of the dielectric properties of the substrate materials they intend to use. The signal propagation on the substrate between chips, the so-called *time of flight,* is directly proportional to the length of the conductors and must be kept short to ensure the optimal electrical performance of a system operating at high speeds.

For systems operating at speeds above 25 MHz, the interconnections must have *transmission line* characteristics to minimize signal losses and distortion. Proper design of such transmission lines requires careful calculation of the conductor and dielectric separation dimensions and

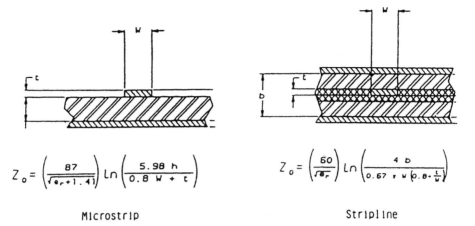

$$Z_0 = \left(\frac{87}{\sqrt{\varepsilon_r+1.41}}\right) \ln\left(\frac{5.98\ h}{0.8\ W + t}\right)$$

$$Z_0 = \left(\frac{60}{\sqrt{\varepsilon_r}}\right) \ln\left(\frac{4\ b}{0.67\ \pi\ W\ (0.8 \cdot \frac{t}{W})}\right)$$

Microstrip   Stripline

FIGURE 1.1   Schematic diagram of stripline and microstrip.

their precise manufacture to ensure the expected accuracy of performance. For PWBs there are two basic transmission line types (see Fig. 1.1):

- Stripline
- Microstrip (For details, see Chap. 9.)

1.3.2 Power Consumption

As the clock rates of the chips increase and as the number of gates per chip grows, there is a corresponding increase in their power consumption. Some chips require up to 30 W of power for their operation. With that, more and more terminals are required to bring power in and to accommodate the return flow on the ground planes. About 20 to 30 percent of chip terminals are used for power and ground connections. With the need for electrical isolation of signals in high-speed systems operation, the count may go to 50 percent.

Design engineers must provide adequate power and ground distribution planes within the multilayer boards (MLB) to ensure efficient, low-resistance flow of currents, which may be substantial in boards interconnecting high-speed chips consuming tens of watts and operating at 5 V, 3.3 V, or lower. Proper power and ground distribution in the system is essential for reducing *di/dt* switching interference in high-speed systems, as well as for reducing undesirable heat concentrations. In some cases, separate bus-bar structures have been required to meet such high power demands.

1.3.3 Thermal Management

All the energy that has been delivered to power integrated circuits (ICs) must be efficiently removed from the system to ensure its proper operation and long life. The removal of the heat from a system is one of the most difficult tasks of electronic packaging. In large systems, huge heat-sink structures, dwarfing the individual ICs, are required to air-cool them, and some computer companies have built giant superstructures for liquid cooling of their computer modules. Some computer designs use liquid immersion cooling. Sill, the cooling needs of large systems tax the capabilities of existing cooling methods.

The situation is not that severe in smaller, tabletop or portable electronic equipment, but it still requires packaging engineers to ameliorate the hot spots and ensure longevity of operation. Since PWBs are notoriously poor heat conductors, designers must carefully evaluate the method of heat conduction through the board, using such techniques as heat vias, embedded metal slugs, and conductive planes. (For details, see Chap. 9.)

1.3.4   Electronic Interference

As the frequency of operation of the electronic equipment increases, many ICs, modules, or assemblies can act as generators of radio frequency (RF) signals. Such electromagnetic interference (EMI) emanations can seriously jeopardize the operation of neighboring electronics or even of other elements of the same equipment, causing failures, mistakes, and errors, and must be prevented. There are specific EMI standards defining the permissible levels of such radiation, and these levels are very low.

The packaging engineers, and especially PWB designers, must be familiar with the methods of reducing or canceling this EMI radiation to ensure that their equipment will not exceed the permissible limits of this interference (for details, see Chap. 9).

1.3.5   System Operating Environment

The selection of a particular packaging approach for an electronic product is also dictated by its end use and by the market segment for which that product is designed. The packaging designer has to understand the major driving force behind the product use. Is it cost driven, performance driven, or somewhere in between? Where will it be used—for instance, under the hood of a car, where environmental conditions are severe, or in the office, where the operating conditions are benign? IPC[2] has established a set of equipment operating conditions classified by the degree of severity, which are listed in Table 1.1.

1.3.5.1 Cost.   The universal digitization of most electronic functions led to the merger of consumer, computer, and communication technologies. This development resulted in the increased appeal of electronics and the need for mass production of many electronic products. Thus, product cost has become the most important criterion in any design of electronic systems. While complying with all the aforementioned design and operation conditions, the design engineer must keep cost as the dominant criterion, and must analyze all potential tradeoffs in light of the best cost/performance solution for the product.

The importance of the rigorous cost tradeoff analysis during the design of electronic products is underscored by the fact that about 60 percent of the manufacturing costs are determined in the first stages of the design process, when only 35 percent of the total design effort has been expended.

Attention to manufacturing and assembly requirements and capabilities (so-called *design for manufacturability and assembly,* or (DFM/A) during product design can reduce assembly costs by up to 35 percent and PWB costs by up to 25 percent. (See also Chap. 6.)

The elements which must be considered for the most cost-effective electronic packaging designs are:

- Optimization of the PWB design and layout to reduce its manufacturing cost
- Optimization of the PWB design to reduce its assembly cost
- Optimization of the PWB design to reduce testing and repair costs

The following sections provide some guidelines on how to approach such optimization of PWB designs. Basically, the costs of the electronic assemblies are directly related to their com-

TABLE 1.1   Realistic Representative-Use Environments, Service Lives, and Acceptable Cumulative-Failure Probabilities for Surface-Mounted Electronics by Use Categories

Use category	Worst-case use environment					Years of service	Acceptable failure risk, %
	T_{min}, °C	T_{max}, °C	ΔT,* °C	t_D, h	Cycles/ year		
1—Consumer	0	+60	35	12	365	1–3	~1
2—Computers	+15	+60	20	2	1460	~5	~0.1
3—Telecomm	−40	+85	35	12	365	7–20	~0.01
4—Commercial aircraft	−55	+95	20	12	365	~20	~0.001
5—Industrial &	−55	+95	20	12	185		
automotive-			&40	12	100	~10	~0.1
passenger			&60	12	60		
compartment			&80	12	20		
6—Military	−55	+95	40	12	100		
ground & ship			&60	12	265	~5	~0.1
7— LEO	−40	+85	35	1	8760	5–20	~0.001
Space GEO				12	365		
8—	a			40	2	365	
Military b	−55	+95	60	2	365	~10	~0.01
avionics c			80	2	365		
			&20	1	365		
9—			60	1	1000		
Automotive	−55	+125	&100	1	300	~5	~0.1
—under hood			&140	2	40		

& = in addition

* ΔT represents the maximum temperature swing, but does not include power dissipation effects; for power dissipation calculate ΔT_e.

plexity and there are a number of measurements relating the effects of various PWB design elements to their costs to guide the design engineer in selection of the most cost-effective approach.

1.4   ICs AND PACKAGES

The most important factors influencing PWB design and layout are the component terminal patterns and their pitches, especially these of ICs and their packages, since these dictate the density of the interconnecting substrates. Thus, this element will be considered first.

Driven by the need for improved cost and performance, the complexity of ICs is constantly increasing. Due to relentless progress in IC technology, the gate density on a chip is increasing by about 75 percent per year, resulting in the growth of IC chip I/O terminals by 40 percent per year, which places ever-increasing demands on the methods of their packaging and interconnection.

As a result, the physical size of electronic gears keeps shrinking by 10 to 20 percent per year, while the surface area of substrates is being reduced by about 7 percent per year. This is accomplished by continuously increasing wiring densities and reducting line widths, which has severely stressed PWB manufacturing methods, reduced processing yields, and increased the costs of the boards.

1.4.1 IC Packages

Since their inception, IC chips have been placed within ceramic or plastic packages. Until about 1980, all IC packages had terminal leads which were soldered into plated-through-holes (PTHs) of the PWBs. Since then, an increasing number of IC packages have their terminals made in a form suitable for surface-mounting technology (SMT), which has become the prevailing method of component mounting.

There has been a proliferation of IC package types, both for through-hole assembly as well as for surface mounting, varying in their lead configurations, placement, and pitches. (See Chap. 2 for details.) Also, IPC-SM-782[3] provides a good catalog of the available SMT packages and of the PWB footprint formats they require for their assembly.

Basic I/O termination methods of IC packages include the following:

- *Peripheral,* where the terminations are located around the edges of the chip or package
- *Grid-array,* where the terminations are located on the bottom surface of the chip or package

Most IC packages have peripheral terminations at their edges. The practical limit on the peripheral lead pitches on packages is about 0.3 mm, which permits locating, at most, 500 I/Os on a large IC package, as shown in Table 1.2. It has also become evident that, in typical board assembly operations, the yields plummet as the lead pitches go below 0.5 mm.

TABLE 1.2   Quad Flat Pack Configurations and Lead Pitches
Shows body size and number of pins for each configuration

QFP configurations		Lead pitches, mm			
		0.65	0.5	0.4	0.3
Reference	Body size (mm × mm)		Pins		
QFP8	28 × 28	160	208	256	336
QFP16	32 × 32	184	240	296	392
QFP19	36 × 36	208	272	344	456
QFP10	40 × 40	232	304	376	504

It is expected that chips with terminal counts below 150 to 200 will continue to use packages with peripheral leads, if these can be soldered within practical assembly yields. But for IC packages with over 150 to 200 I/Os, it is very attractive to use the grid-array terminations, since in such a case, the entire bottom surface area can be utilized for terminations, which makes it possible to place large numbers of I/Os within a limited area.

This consideration has led to the development of a number of area array solder bumping termination methods for IC and multichip module (MCM) packages, variously called pad grid, land grid, or ball grid arrays (BGAs) with terminal grids set at 1 mm (0.040 in.), 1.27 mm (0.050 in) and 1.50 mm (0.060 in), respectively.

Use of grid arrays provides a number of benefits. The most important is the minimal footprint area on the interconnecting substrate, but grid arrays also offer better electrical performance due to low electrical parasitics in high-speed operation, simplified adaptation into SMT component placement lines, and better assembly yields, despite the impossibility of direct visual inspection of the joints.

Due to continuous decrease of the terminal pitches on packages, it is important that PWB designers carefully assess the manufacturing and assembly capabilities of PWB substrates requiring such fine pitch terminations, to ensure the greatest yields and lowest cost of the product.

1.4.2 Direct Chip Attachment

The relentless pressures of size, weight, and volume reduction of electronic products has resulted in a growth in interest in direct chip attachment (DCA) methods, where bare IC chips are mounted directly to the substrate. These methods are extensively used on chip-on-board (COB) and multichip module (MCM) assemblies, as shown in Fig. 1.2.

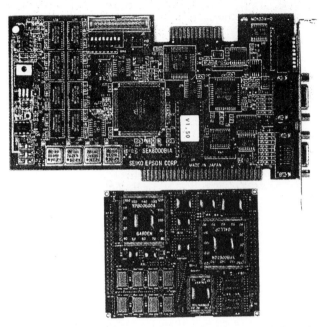

FIGURE 1.2   Illustration of chip-on-board (COB) and multichip module (MCM) assemblies.

Three methods of bare chip attachment to the substrate are as follows:

- *Wire bonding* is the oldest and the most flexible and widely used method. (More than 96 percent of all chips today are wire bonded.)
- *Tape-automated bonding* (TAB) is useful with small I/O pitches and provides the ability to pretest the chips before assembly.
- *Flip chipping* is used for its compactness and improved electricals, typical of which is the C-4 process of IBM.

The problems of thermal coefficient of expansion (TCE) mismatch between silicon chips which are directly flip chipped onto a laminate substrate have been effectively eliminated by using a filled epoxy *underfill* encapsulation technique between the chip and the substrate (see Fig. 1.3). This method distributes stresses over the entire area of the chip and thus significantly improves the reliability performance of this assembly method.

While the chips which need area array or flip-chip terminations—i.e., those with the high pin counts—are the fastest-growing category of ICs, they still represent only a very small percent of all ICs used. Even by the year 2000, the ICs with over 100 I/Os are expected to account for no more than 10 percent of total worldwide IC consumption (see Fig. 1.4). The designers

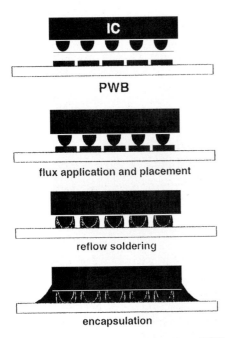

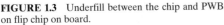

FIGURE 1.3 Underfill between the chip and PWB on flip chip on board.

must, therefore, ascertain which of the DCA methods will be the most cost beneficial for the particular application.

1.4.3 Chip Scale Packages (CSPs)

When mounting unpackaged chips on these interconnecting substrates it is not always possible to ascertain that only properly operating chips have been assembled. By now, there are a number of methods proposed to solve this *known good die* (KGD) problem.

As one of the ways to resolve this problem, a number of manufacturers have developed a set of miniature packages, only slightly larger than the chip itself, which protect the chip and redistribute the chip termination to a grid array. These miniature packages permit testing and burning in of chips prior to their final assembly. A typical example of such chip scale packages is shown in Fig. 1.5. There are a number of such packages on the market.

The designer, however, must analyze the termination pitches of these new CSPs because some use very tight grids, such as 0.5 mm (0.020 in) or less, which need special PWB techniques to permit signal redistribution from these packages to the rest of the board.

In general, the current PWB technology is adequate to provide direct chip terminations if wire bonding or TAB techniques are used for interconnecting bare chips to the substrate. It requires placing suitable bonding pads spaced by the required pitch in one or two rows around the chip site. While this somewhat reduces the packaging efficiency of the board, it is still an effective method for DCA assemblies.

With grid array, the situation is more difficult since the signals from internal rows of area grid terminations must be routed between the terminals located closer to the edge, which do not permit more than one, or at most two, conductors to pass through. In most cases, these signals from internal rows are brought down into internal layers of MLBs.

The conventional PCB constructions today cannot handle any grid arrays with pitches below 0.020 in, while some flip-chip ball grid arrays go below 0.010-in pitch. In cases when grid distances of the area terminations are below 0.50 mm (0.040 in), special redistribution layers are frequently used, which distribute signals to the conventionally made PTHs in supporting MLB.

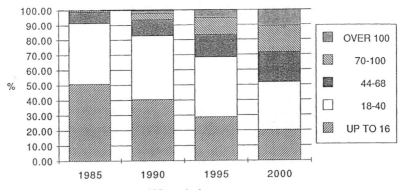

FIGURE 1.4 The distribution of IC terminal counts.

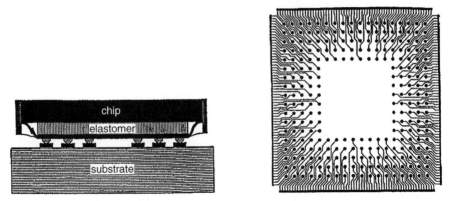

FIGURE 1.5   Chip scale package of Tessera, Inc., San Jose, Calif.

Such layers consist of unsupported dielectric layers where small vias or blind holes are formed by laser or plasma etching or are photoformed, and then plated using additive or semiadditive metallization processes. While this approach requires some extra area beyond the chip perimeter to complete the signal transfer and increases the costs of substrates, it permits the mounting of flip chips and the CSPs on PWBs. A typical method for forming such redistribution layers, called *surface laminar circuit* (SLC),[4] has been developed in IBM's Yasu plant.

1.5   *DENSITY EVALUATIONS*

1.5.1   Component Density Analysis

Since the components and their terminations exert a major effect on the design of the PWB, a number of metrics have been developed to establish the relationships between component density and PWB density. A major analysis of these relationships has been made by H. Holden of Hewlett-Packard[5] and some of his charts and derivations are provided here to guide the design engineers during the development of a rational PWB design.

This information is very useful to determine where the designed product will fit in the component density spectrum and what, therefore, is to be expected for PWB density.

Figure 1.6 provides a generalized view of the relationships among the component density, their terminal density, and the necessary wiring density which will be required to accommodate the selected degree of component complexity. The definition of the wiring connectivity W_f is provided.

1.5.2   PWB Density Metrics

It is essential for the proper design of PWBs to determine the density requirements and then analyze alternative methods of board construction for the most cost-effective design. There are a number of basic terms and equations used for the calculation and analysis of PWB wiring density.

$$W_c = \frac{T*L}{G} \text{ in/in}^2 \tag{Eq. 1.1}$$

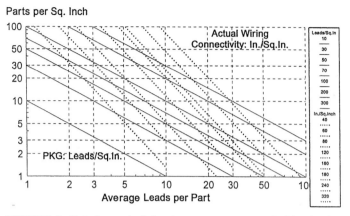

FIGURE 1.6 Plot of general relations between component and wiring density.

where W_c = wiring capacity
T = tracks per channel
L = number of signal layers
G = channel width

But it is more important to determine the required wiring density which will be sufficient to interconnect all the components on the desired board size. There have been a number of empirically developed equations which permit the calculation of such a wiring demand. The simplest has been developed by Dr. D. Seraphim[6]:

$$W_d = 2.25 \, N_t*P \tag{Eq. 1.2}$$

where W_d = wiring demand
N_t = number of I/Os
P = pitch between packages

A more elaborate equation has been developed by Mikhail,[7] which states that if

$$R = k(1 + .1*1n(N))*N^{1/6} \tag{Eq. 1.3}$$

where R = average node length
N = number of modules
k = constant = 0.8 for boards

then the

$$W_{dp} = R\left(\frac{P_n - 1}{P_n}\right)*N_t*P \text{ (in component pitches)} \tag{Eq. 1.4}$$

where W_d = wiring demand
P_n = number of pins per net
N_t = number of I/Os per component
P = spacing (or pitch) between components

To convert W_{dp} to W_d in/in²:

$$W_d = \left(\frac{1}{P^2}\right)*W_{dp} \quad \text{or} \quad W_d = R(P_n - 1)*\frac{N_t}{P}*P_n \tag{Eq. 1.5}$$

In order to evaluate what wiring density must be available on the board to accommodate the required wiring demand, a wiring efficiency factor (W_{eff}) must be accounted for, since it is impossible to use in actual wiring the entire 100 percent of available wiring capacity W_c. Unfortunately, since this wiring efficiency varies with the capabilities of the CAD design systems and with the types of board structures used for component mounting, there are no firm values for this factor. While for most rigid MLBs this efficiency is around 50 percent, in some designs using unreinforced distribution layers in sequential buildup with blind vias, the wiring efficiency can be raised to 70 to 75 percent. In discrete-wiring boards, such as Multi-wire® and Micro-wire®, wiring efficiencies of 60 to 65 percent have been routinely achieved. In most cases, and for ease of preliminary calculations, wiring efficiency of 50 percent has been effectively used. Thus, the actual wiring capacity $W_{c,act}$ necessary for a specific board design is:

$$W_{c,act} = \frac{W_d}{W_{eff}}$$

(Eq. 1.6)

where W_{eff} is 50 percent or the appropriate value in a specific case.

1.5.3   Special Metrics for Direct Chip Attach (DCA)

The assembly of uncased or bare chips on substrates has become popular mostly due to the ability of such assemblies to reduce the area of interconnections. The ideal limit for such assembly would be to place all the chips tightly together, without any space in between. This would result in 100 percent packaging efficiency, a metric measuring the ratio of silicon area to the substrate area. Naturally, such 100 percent efficiency is not achievable, but this metric is still useful in ranking various substrate construction or bare chip attachment methods, as shown in Fig. 1.7.

Packaging efficiency of 100 percent is impossible to achieve because all chip-mounting methods require some space around the chips. Even with flip chips, there must be a distance left between the chips to permit room for the placement tool.

Dr. Charles[8] of Johns Hopkins University has listed the dimensions in Table 1.3 for the necessary spacing between the chips (or the total width of the frame around the chips) for vari-

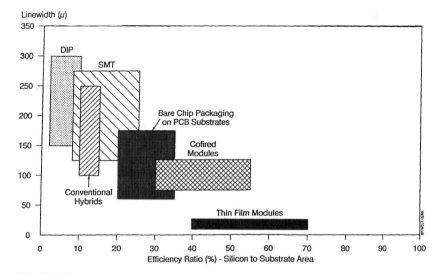

FIGURE 1.7   Packaging efficiency. *(Courtesy of BPA, used with permission.)*

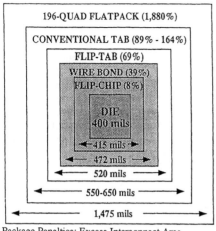

Package Penalties: Excess Interconnect Area

FIGURE 1.8   Chip area required to accommodate bonding methods.

ous chip attachment methods. These or very similar distances have also been cited by a number of other sources.

Even with the flip-chip mounting, packaging efficiency must be derated to about 90 percent, for wire bonding to 70 percent and for TABs to about 50 percent, and in some cases much more. A very similar situation is shown graphically in Fig. 1.8. The packaging efficiency deratings shown in Fig. 1.8 are required to accommodate only the wiring bond pads on the substrates. But the mounting of bare chips on PWBs requires additional signal redistribution area to permit placement of larger-diameter PTHs farther out for communication with internal layers. It is evident that the packaging efficiencies on PWBs could be reduced to the range of only 20 to 30 percent, unless special surface signal redistribution layers (as previously mentioned) are used, which are made of unreinforced dielectric material. In such cases, packaging efficiency and the chip-to-chip distances will again be similar to the values cited in Table 1.3.

It is apparent that direct chip attachment on PWBs will result in the significant reduction of the packaging efficiency of such assemblies, except for the fact that components can be mounted on both sides of the PWB substrate. It has been shown that wire bonding can be done on both sides of a PWB with some special fixturing; also, *outer lead bonding* (OLB) of TABs can be done on both sides of the PWB substrate. Thus, while single-sided bare chip assembly on PWBs reduces its packaging efficiency to about half that of other types of substrate constructions, the ability to place components on both sides of PWBs brings it back to the same packaging efficiency level as others.

1.6   METHODS TO INCREASE PWB DENSITY

There are three basic ways to increase the connectivity or available conductor capacity of PWBs[9]:

- Reduce hole and pad diameters
- Increase the number of conductive channels between pads by reducing the widths of the conductors
- Increase the number of signal planes

The effect of each approach on manufacturing yields, and thus on board costs, will be discussed in sequence. It should be noted that the last option is the simplest but the most costly solution, which thus should be used only after the methods suitable for resolving the first two conditions have been proven inadequate for achieving the desirable board density.

TABLE 1.3   Spacing Required Between Chips

Attachment method	Chip spacing, mils
Flip chip	15–20
Wire bonding	70–80
Flip TAB	100–120
Regular TAB	150–400

1.6.1 Effect of Pads on Wiring Density

The major obstacles preventing increase of conductor channel capacity are large pad diameters around the plated-through-holes (PTHs), since at the present state of technology, PWBs still require pads wider than the conductors at their location. These pads reduce the obtainable connectivity of PWB boards and must be accounted for in a proper analysis of interconnection density I_d. For instance, in one design, the reduction of pad diameters from 55 to 25 mils (by 55 percent) doubled the interconnection density, while the reduction in conductor pitch C_p from 18 to 7 mils (by 61 percent) increases it only by 50 percent. It is obvious that the reduction of pad diameters, or their total elimination, could be a more efficient way to increase the wiring capacity of complex PWBs.

The purpose of copper pads surrounding the drilled holes in PWBs is to accommodate any potential layer-to-layer or pattern-to-hole misregistrations and thus prevent any hole breakout outside the copper area of the pads. This misregistration is caused mainly by the instability and movement of the base laminate during its processing through the PWB or multilayer board (MLB) manufacturing steps.

The base material standards specify that such movement be limited to a maximum of 300 ppm, but the actual base material excursions are closer to 500 ppm, producing 10 mils of layer movement within a 20-in distance. For many applications this tolerance is too wide, as it requires at least a 10-mil-wide annular ring around drilled holes, resulting in considerable conductor channel blockage.

Another cause of material instability in MLBs is the excessive material movement which occurs if the laminating temperature exceeds the glass transition temperature T_g of the laminate resin. On the other hand, if the laminating temperature remains below the T_g of the resin, there is minimal dimensional variation of the base material, as the resin is still in its linear expansion phase. This explains the need for use of high-T_g resins in the PWB industry.

The data obtained from the performance of new, more stable *unidirectional* laminates indicate that the base material movement is reduced, for instance to 200 ppm from 500 ppm, and the requirements for the annular ring width will be reduced to 4 mils from 10 mils.

Table 1.4 illustrates the connectivity gains made possible when a more stable laminate material is used, permitting a reduction in the initial diameters of the pads (as given in the first column) spaced at 2.5 mm (0.100 in), while keeping the conductor pitches constant. The most effective use of the signal plane area is achieved when the pads are eliminated and the z-axis interconnects are confined within the width of the conductors forming the *invisible vias*.

TABLE 1.4   Effect of Pad Diameters on Interconnectivity Density

Pad dia, in	Cond pitch, in	I_d @ 500 ppm, in/in²	I_d @ 200 ppm, in/in²	I_d @ invisible via, in/in²
0.055	0.010	20	37	55
0.036	0.018	30	48	55
0.025	0.009	40	96	100
0.025	0.007	60	130	143

This derivation is based on actual data obtained from the performance of new, more stable, *unidirectional* laminates. While MLBs using these new, more dimensionally stable, unidirectional laminates with reduced pad diameters could be manufactured by conventional manufacturing methods, the production of MLBs with invisible vias requires the use of a sequential manufacturing process similar to the SLC process previously described.

PWB manufacturers are reasonably comfortable with the production of boards with 4- or 5-mil-wide conductors, but they still require large pads around plated holes to ensure against hole breakout. This limits the currently available wiring density to about 40 to 60 in/in² per plane, as seen from Table 1.4. A technology which will permit PWB manufacturers to fabricate invisible vias could increase the connectivity per PWB signal plane from this current range to the level of 100 to 140 in/in². Conductor widths of 0.002 in will offer a PWB of 200 to 250 in/in² per signal plane.

Table 1.5 illustrates the most important result of increased connectivity per layer: a reduction in the number of signal layers needed to provide the same wiring density W_d. Table 1.5 was constructed by applying connectivity data from Table 1.4 to a 50-in² MLB with total wiring length of 10,000 in. Note also that the layer count in Table 1.4 has been brought up to the next-higher full-layer value, i.e., the calculated 1.4 layers have been recorded as 2 layers.

TABLE 1.5   Effect of Increased Connectivity of Reduction Layers

Pad dia, in	Cond pitch, in	I_d @ 500 ppm, layers	I_d @ 200 ppm, layers	I_d @ invisible via, layers
0.055	0.010	10	6	4
0.036	0.018	7	4	4
0.025	0.009	5	2	2
0.025	0.007	4	2	2

The major benefit of such a reduction in the layer count is that it can result in a significant reduction of the manufacturing cost, while providing the same total interconnection length.

1.6.2   Reduction of Conductor Width

An obvious method to increase the connectivity of PWBs is to reduce the widths of conductors and spaces and thus increase the number of available wiring channels on each signal plane, as described previously. This is the direction which has been used in the IC and PWB industries for many years. However, it is impossible to decrease conductor widths or spaces indefinitely. The reduction of the conductor width is limited by the current-carrying capacity of thin, small conductors, especially when these conductors are long, as they frequently are on PWBs. There are processing limits to this conductor reduction, since manufacturing yields may plummet if this reduction stretches the process capabilities beyond their normal limits.

There is also a limit to the reduction of the spaces between the conductors, governed mainly by electrical considerations, i.e., by the need to prevent excessive cross talk, to minimize noise, and to provide proper signal propagation conditions and characteristic impedance.

Still, such conductor reductions, if achieved within the described limits, can be an effective path for increasing the PWB density and the reduction of PWB manufacturing costs. As seen from Table 1.6, constructed from cost data derived from the Columbus program of BPA, the reduction of conductor widths from 6 to 3 mils halves the number of signal layers necessary to assure the same connectivity, (while their yields, interconnection density, and board area were kept constant). This reduction in the number of layers can reduce significantly the manufacturing costs of PWB boards.

1.6.3   Effect of Conductor Widths on Board Yields

It is obvious that any successful increase of conductor density I_d in PWBs would be effective only if the processes exist which permit their manufacture with reasonable yields. Unfortunately, the yields of thin conductors in PWBs fall rapidly as their widths are reduced below

TABLE 1.6 Effect of Conductor Widths on Number of Layers and Board Cost for a 6-in × 8-in MLB, with $I_d = 450$ in/in², 65 to 68 Percent Yields

Line-space	Total no. of layers	No. of signal layers	Board cost, %
3–3	8	4	55
4–4	10	6	64
5–6	12	7	77
5–7	14	8	87
6–6	16	8	90
7–8	20	10	100

5 mils, as shown in Fig. 1.9. Therefore, the understanding of manufacturing yields is very important for analysis of the most cost-effective manufacturing process, because the process yields have a major effect on the cost of interconnection substrates.

A useful empirical equation for calculating the manufacturing cost is:

$$\text{Cost } C = \frac{(\text{material} + \text{process costs})}{\text{Yield } Y} \tag{Eq. 1.7}$$

To establish the effect of the interconnection density I_d on the final yield of substrates, the total processing yield can be split into two components: one that depends on the conductor density, i.e., Y_{Id}, and the second, which is a function of the combined yields of the rest of the manufacturing processes:

$$Y_{\text{total}} = Y_{Id} * Y_{\text{proc}} \tag{Eq. 1.8}$$

In a well-controlled manufacturing operation, the process-dependent yields (such as plating) remain fairly constant for a given technology, permitting the yield function to be based solely on the changes in the conductor widths.

As seen from Fig. 1.10, the defects which affect this density-dependent yield function Y_{Id}, are conductor opens and shorts between them. It would be reasonable to assume that such defects have a Poisson distribution over the total length TL of conductors of a substrate, with an average defect frequency of v. The yield is the probability of zero defects ($n = 0$) in the total conductor length TL. Thus,

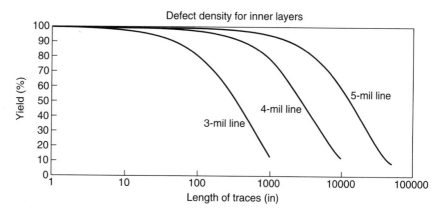

FIGURE 1.9 Board yields vs. conductor width.

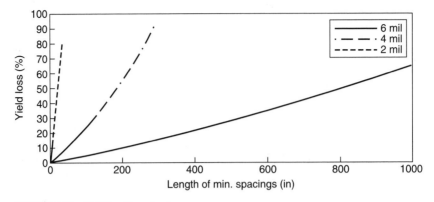

FIGURE 1.10 Yield loss from shorts.

$$Y = (\text{at } n = 0) = e^{(-v \,*\, \text{TL})} \qquad \text{(Poisson distribution)} \qquad \text{(Eq. 1.9)}$$

As seen from Figs. 1.9 and 1.10, the defect frequency v depends also on the widths of lines and spaces, i.e., on the conductor pitch C_p. With a decrease of C_p, v will increase, but for very large C_p, v should be 0, since Y_{ld} will be 100 percent.

For instance, in the case of a design using invisible pads, where $C_p = 2w$, the interconnection density I_d, can be expressed as $I_d = \text{TL}/A$, and I_d is proportional to C_p, i.e., $I_d * C_p = 1$, and $\text{TL} = A/C_p$. Therefore, v in this equation can be empirically expressed as:

$$v = -\ln \frac{Y_o}{\text{TL}_o} * \left(\frac{C_{po}}{C_p} \right)^b \qquad \text{(Eq. 1.10)}$$

where b is an exponent dependent on the technology or process used to form the conductors. This exponent b varies considerably from facility to facility and among various pattern formation methods, and must be empirically determined for each case.

Using the cost model developed at MIT by L. H. Ng and R. Field[10], in 1990 E. van Andel of AKZO Corp. analyzed some manufacturing variations on the substrate costs and plotted a number of yield-dependent cost curves for these processes, one set of which is shown in Fig. 1.11.

These plots show that a steep increase in costs occurs after a certain conductor density value is reached for each type of board construction. It is caused by the rapid deterioration of yields which is brought about by the reduction in the conductor widths needed to provide increased connectivity within a constant number of signal planes.

These plots also show clearly that there are definite tradeoff points between the two ways to provide increased density in substrates—either by increasing the number of layers or by decreasing the conductor pitch on each level. It is evident that decreasing the conductor widths on signal planes is a more economical solution until the line widths reach the dimensions at which layer yields become extremely low, thereby causing a rapid increase in their manufacturing costs. Above the density level where the layer cost intersects the cost of additional signal planes, it will be more cost efficient to increase the overall substrate density by adding layers with a more conservative design of conductor widths and higher yields.

Another important point is also demonstrated by these plots: the strong effect that the size of the boards has on their yields. It is seen that in large boards (dotted lines, for 10- by 10-in boards) the costs increase very rapidly with the increase of conductor density. On the smaller boards (solid lines for 4- by 4-in boards), however, the increase in conductor density per layer

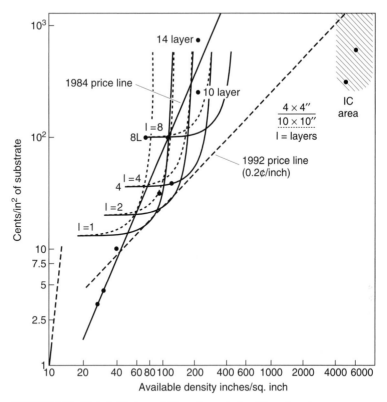

FIGURE 1.11   Plot of effects on yields on the cost of multilayer boards.

remains cost effective for a much wider range, before additional layers are needed to accommodate the increased density of substrates.

1.6.4   Increase in Number of Conductor Layers

This is the simplest and most straightforward solution: When there is insufficient room on existing layers to place all the necessary interconnecting paths, add a layer. This approach has been widely practiced in the past, but when cost effectiveness of the substrates is of paramount importance, a very careful design analysis must be made to minimize layer counts in MLBs, because there is a significant cost increase with every additional layer in the board. As seen from Table 1.6, calculated for 6- by 8-in MLBs produced in large quantity with yields and conductor density kept constant, there is almost a linear relationship between board costs and layer count.

Table 1.6 also shows that any increase in the number of signal layers in boards operating at frequencies requiring transmission line characteristics will double the total number of layers, due to the need to interleave ground or dc power planes between signal planes.

A typical example of the effect of layer count on the finished MLB yield can be seen from Fig. 1.12, prepared some years ago by BPA. We can see that there is a definite decrease in the manufacturing yields with increased number of layers in any of the line-widths categories.

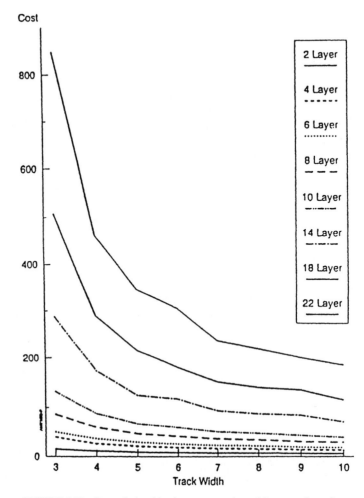

FIGURE 1.12 Cost relationships between number of layers and conductor widths.

This is rather a typical situation in board manufacturing since increased complexity and thickness of MLB with a higher number of layers usually leads to a larger number of problems on the production floor.

1.7 COST/DENSITY PLOTS

All the preceding considerations provide the design engineer with some insight on how a particular design element might affect the cost of manufacturing or assembling the PWBs. But there is a need to have an overall picture of how the density of substrates might affect their cost or their price. It should be noted that in the following the terms *cost* and *price* are used interchangeably, as the selling price of a substrate is usually directly proportional by a constant factor to the cost of its manufacture.

An empirical study of basic relationships between the cost and density of substrates was made in a paper by G. Messner[11] in the *IEEE CHMT Proceedings* of June 1987, where a generalized relationship between the price of the interconnecting substrates and their conductor density per unit area was derived. It relates the log of substrate density, or available *connectivity,* in inches per square inch, on the x axis, to the log of substrate price, in cents per square inch, on the y axis. (See Fig. 1.11.) This plot established a system which permitted a ranking of the cost effectiveness of various interconnection technologies. It was based on a generalized analysis of PWB pricing data, and is only an approximation, but it did reflect fairly accurately the prevalent trends in the past decade of price/density relationships in the PWB and multilayer markets.

It may be useful to elaborate here on the construction of this price/density graph to reduce confusion in its use and content. The x axis values give the total wiring channel capacity of all the *signal* layers of a substrate, but the y axis gives the prices for the *entire* structure, i.e., including the ground and power planes and surface terminal layers. On average, a typical interconnection structure will contain twice as many total layers as signal layers.

The information in this chart is for the total conductive capacity of a substrate but does not address the distribution of conductors on each layer, nor the number of layers required to produce the total required interconnection density.

The difference between the total theoretical wiring capacity obtainable in a substrate (as given by the x axis) and the actually provided interconnection wiring density is the *efficiency* of the wiring achieved in a given system, as was discussed before. From empirical observations by a number of authorities and from actual wiring length calculations of various substrates, the prevailing wiring efficiency is assumed to be around 50 percent, i.e., the theoretically available wiring capacity of 200 in/in^2 on a substrate will, generally, result in 100 in/in^2 of actual wiring length on that substrate.

1.7.1   Effects of Price Lines on Cost Trends

On the graph in Fig. 1.11 the two trend lines are of importance: the solid 1984 price line and the dashed 1992 price line. The 1984 price line shows that in the mid-80s the prices of substrates were increasing approximately as the square of the interconnection density. The graph also indicates that, with time, due to the experience curve effects and general market dynamics, the price/density relationship was constantly changing. As a result, it was expected that at some time, arbitrarily marked in the plot as the 1992 price line, substrate prices would increase only linearly with substrate density.

The analysis of 1994 prices of a variety of PWBs and MLBs indicated that recent technical developments and serious price erosion, experienced in the 1993–94 time frame, have brought the price/density relationships to the levels predicted by the 1992 price line, i.e., that a linear relationship now exists between the density of the substrates and their prices.

A mathematical analysis of the relation between substrate prices and their density was done by Dr. D. Kelemen[12] in a paper at the 1989 IEPS Conference. Starting with the equation developed by Donald Seraphim (see Sec. 1.5.2), defining the wiring length required to interconnect an array of uniform square devices,

$$W_d = 2.25\, N_t {}^* P \qquad\qquad (\text{Eq. 1.2})$$

he defines the area A required for interconnection of such a device, as well as the interconnection density I_d, which permits the following equation to be written:

$$A = P^2 = \frac{W_d}{I_d} = (2.25)^2 * \frac{N_t^2}{I_d^2} = 5 * \frac{N_t^2}{I_d^2} \qquad\qquad (\text{Eq. 1.11})$$

which shows that the packaging area of a device is dependent on the substrate connectivity or interconnection density.

The cost C of that device area on the substrate can be written as:

$$C = k * I_d * A = k * 5 * \frac{N_t^2}{I_d^{(2-x)}}$$

(Eq. 1.12)

where k = constant. If $x = 2$, as has been shown by the quadratic relationship of the 1984 price line in the plot of Fig. 1.11, then the cost C for interconnecting a device becomes:

$$C = k * 5 * N^2$$

(Eq. 1.13)

indicating that, in this case of a quadratic relationship between the price of a substrate and its interconnection density, the price of interconnections for a device depends only on its terminal count. This conclusion is supported by the fact that with the quadratic relationship between price and density, as the connectivity or conductor density of a substrate increases, the area required for device mounting, as well as the pitch between devices decreases, and this area reduction generally compensates for the greater costs of the denser substrates.

The linear relationship between the price and density of substrates, as indicated by the 1992 price line in Fig. 1.11, produces an even more significant effect on substrate costs. When in (Eq. 1.12), x becomes 1 then the price of substrates becomes inversely proportional to connectivity:

$$C = k * 5 * \frac{N_t^2}{I_d}$$

(Eq. 1.14)

REFERENCES

1. The Institute for Interconnecting and Packaging Electronic Circuits, 7380 N. Lincoln Ave, Lincoln-wood, IL 60646

2. Werner Engelmaier, "Alloy 42—A Material to Be Avoided for Surface Mount," *Proceedings NEPCON Conference 1995,* Anaheim, Calif., March 1995, pp. 1730–1741.

3. Publication IPC-SM-782, "Surface Mount Design and Land Pattern Standard," The Institute for Interconnecting and Packaging Electronic Circuits.

4. Y. Tsukada, et al., "A Novel Solution for MCM-L Utilizing Surface Laminar Circuit and Flip Chip Attach Technology," *Proceedings of 2d Int'l Conference on Multichip Modules,* Denver, Colo., April 1993, pp. 252–259.

5. H. Holden, "Metrics for MCM-L Design," *Proceedings IPC National Conference on MCM-L,* Minneapolis, Minn., May 1994.

6. D. Seraphim, "Chip-Module-Package Interface," *Proceedings of Insulation Conference,* Chicago, Ill., September 1977, pp. 90–93.

7. R. Tumala, "Principles of Electronic Packaging," *Microelectronics Packaging Handbook,* McGraw-Hill, New York, 1990, pp. 62–67.

8. H. Charles, "Design Rules for Advanced Packaging," *Proceedings ISHM 1993,* pp. 301–307.

9. G. Messner, "Analysis of the Density and Yield Relationships Leading Toward the Optimal Interconnection Methods," *Proceedings of Printed Circuits World Conference VI,* San Francisco, Calif., May 1993, pp. M 19 1–20.

10. L. H. Ng and F. R. Field, "Technical Cost Modeling for PCB Fabrication," *PC Fabrication,* September 1990, p. 68.

11. G. Messner, "Cost-Density Analysis of Interconnections," *IEEE CHMT Transactions,* vol. 10, June 1987, pp. 143–148.

12. D. G. Kelemen, "Cost Considerations in High Density Packaging," *Proceedings of IEPS Conference,* 1989, pp. 12–16.

CHAPTER 2
SEMICONDUCTOR PACKAGING TECHNOLOGY

John W. Stafford
Motorola Inc.
Semiconductor Products Sector
Final Manufacturing Development Center
Phoenix, Arizona

2.1 INTRODUCTION

A revolution has occurred in the electronics industry due to advances in semiconductor design and manufacturing, packaging of semiconductor die, product physical design, and packaging of electronics systems. Table 2.1 compares the computing capability available over the years. What has occurred is that there has been a constant increase in functionality (i.e., instructions per second) along with continuous decreases in the cost per instruction. One result is that portable communications such as pagers and cellular phones, which have come to market relatively recently, have now become commodity items.

2.1.1 Electronic Packaging Issues

Electronic packaging begins where circuit design leaves off.

2.1.1.1 Physical Design and Packaging Issues. The issues involved in electronic physical design and packaging are as follows:

- Selection of appropriate electronic components (i.e., semiconductors, discrete, and passives)
- Mechanical layout and assembly of components, interconnectors, and cases
- Production engineering/technology
- Electrical parameters of interconnects (controlled impedance design, cross talk, clock skew, signal propagation delay, etc.)
- Thermal conditions (heat dissipation, cooling, etc.)

The driving force in this revolution originates with the advances that have occurred in integrated circuit (IC) technology and the levels of integration obtained. The initial driver to this was the development of a micron-level lithographic capability.[1] This continuing thrust for

TABLE 2.1   Cost Comparison

	Approx. no. of instructions/s	Price	Cents/ instruction
1975 IBM mainframe	10,000,000	$10,000,000	100
1976 Cray 1	160,000,000	$20,000,000	12.5
1979 Digital VAX	1,000,000	$ 200,000	20.0
1981 IBM PC	250,000	$ 3,000	1.2
1984 Sun Microsystems 2	1,000,000	$ 10,000	1.0
1994 Pentium PC	66,000,000	$ 3,000	0.0045

Source: *New York Times,* April 20, 1994.

higher levels of integration has forced an ongoing effort for smaller and cheaper means of packaging these ICs so they can be interconnected in a cost-effective manner that does not degrade the electrical performance of the assembled circuit. As a result, high-performance systems require consideration of both the integrated circuit design and its packaged format and the design of the interconnect that connects the integrated circuits.

2.1.1.2 Digital Circuit Design Considerations.   Digital circuits should be able to do the following:

- Transfer a complete logic swing in shortest time
- Have the interconnect characteristic impedance designed to equal the load impedance
- Have characteristic impedance that is purely resistive to minimize reflections
- Accommodate clock skew

For the interconnection of digital semiconductor devices, a major issue that must be considered is *clock skew,* which results from varying the length of clock lines and is a major design consideration for high-speed products.

2.1.1.3 Analog Circuit Design Considerations.   Analog circuits should be able to do the following:

- Maximize power transferred from input to output
- Have the driver impedance be a complex conjugate of the transmission line

2.1.1.4 Power Issues for Silicon Semiconductors.   The following items are power considerations for silicon semiconductors:

- Transistor-transistor logic (TTL) and complementary metal-oxide semiconductors (CMOS) power dissipation depend on frequency and increase dramatically at high frequencies.
- Drain of an emitter collector logic (ECL) device is independent of frequency for a given load.
- Resistance loading drains the output capacitor of CMOS circuitry.
- Terminating CMOS circuits to control reflection imposes a power penalty.

   Gallium arsenide (GaAs) semiconductors have emerged as a competitive semiconductor technology to silicon,[2] especially for high-speed logic applications. For GaAs logic, power dissipation is independent of frequency and GaAs circuit operation is unaffected by power supply voltages down to about 1 V.

2.1.2 Chip Trends

Semiconductor packaging and printed circuit board (PCB) evolution tracks the advances in IC technology. As a consequence of being able to put more circuitry on a silicon IC, its package size and the number of package input/output (I/O) pins have increased as well as the wiring density required of the medium that interconnects the packaged ICs.

2.1.3 Requirements for Electronic Systems

The requirements for electronics systems and products driven by semiconductor technology developments are as follows:

1. The advances in integrated semiconductor technology mean products will operate at higher speeds and have higher performance and greater functionality.
2. The reliability and quality of products will be givens and are expected to be built in at no cost premium.
3. The volume (i.e., size) of the electronics products is diminishing, which is constrained only by ergonomic requirements and the ability to dissipate heat (i.e., power).
4. The costs of the components and assembly are expected to continuously decrease with time.
5. The time to market impacts all of the preceding items.

2.2 SINGLE-CHIP PACKAGING

Prior to 1980 the semiconductor package which was predominately used was the *dual in-line package* (DIP). The package is rectangular in shape with leads on 0.100-in pitch along the long sides of the package.

Figure 2.1 shows the various semiconductor formats and package trends. The packages on the left of Fig. 2.1 are essentially perimeter I/O packages (i.e., DIPs, quad flat packages [QFPs], plastic leaded chip carriers [PLCCs], tape-automated bonding [TABs], etc.). The package types on the lower right-hand part of Fig. 2.1 represent emerging area array packages

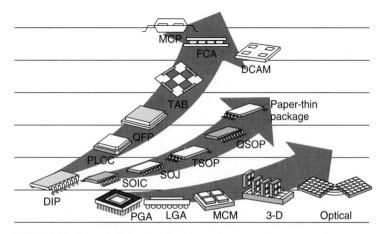

FIGURE 2.1 Integrated circuit packaging trends.

such as pin grid array (PGA) packages (an array of pins attached to the package base for electrical connection), land grid array (LGA) packages (an array of conducting pads on the package base for electrical connection, sometimes called pad array carriers, or PACs), and, when the lands have reflowed solder balls attached, they are called ball grid array (BGA) packages and multichip modules (MCMs). The pitch of the I/Os of DIPs and PGA packages is 0.1 in, while the I/O pitches of the balance of the parts are 0.060 in or less (i.e., 0.050 in, 0.5 mm, 0.4 mm, 0.3 mm). Array-type packaging concepts have emerged to provide higher package electrical performance and/or lower packaging densities (package area/die area).

2.2.1 Dual In-Line Packages (DIPs)

Figure 2.2 shows the configuration of a DIP. DIPs are available with a cofired ceramic body with the leads brazed along the long edges or they come in a post-molded construction where the die is bonded to a lead frame and gold wires interconnect the chip to the lead frame leads prior to molding of a plastic body around the lead frame. DIPs are limited to 64 or fewer I/Os.

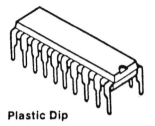

Plastic Dip

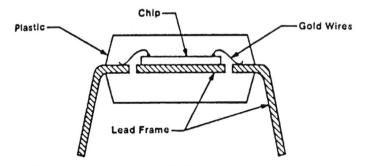

FIGURE 2.2 Dual in-line package (DIP).

2.2.2 Leadless Ceramic Chip Carriers (LCCCs)

To improve the form factor, packages for commercial and military applications were developed called *leadless ceramic chip carriers* (LCCCs), consisting essentially of the cavity portion of the ceramic hermetic DIP (see Fig. 2.3) with solderable lands printed onto the bottom of the LCCC package. These parts were assembled to ceramic substrates and used in both military and telecommunications products. Almost concurrently, leaded versions of the leadless packages begin to appear. The pitches of the leadless parts were 0.040 and 0.050 in, while the

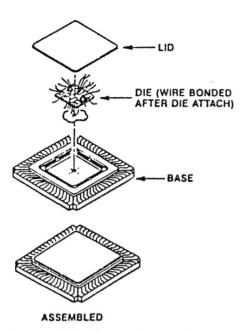

ASSEMBLED

FIGURE 2.3 Leadless ceramic chip carrier (LCCC).

leaded parts were on a 0.050-in pitch. Reference 3 discusses these developments in detail. By 1980, thrust-to-quad surface-mount packaging had begun, with the emphasis on leaded plastic quad packages.

Reference 4 also shows that there is a dramatic swing away from through-hole-mounted parts (i.e., DIPs), to surface-mount packages. In 1993, 50 percent of the semiconductor packages fabricated were DIPs which were through-hole mounted.

2.2.3 Plastic Quad Flat Package (PQFP)

The driver for the surface-mount plastic packages has been the development of the plastic quad flat package (PQFP), which consists of a metal lead frame with leads emanating from all four sides. The lead frame is usually copper, to which the semiconductor die is die bonded (usually epoxy die bonded). The I/Os of the die are connected by wire bonds to the lead frame leads. The conventional method of wire bonding is thermosonic gold ball wedge bonding. A plastic body is then molded around the die and the leads are trimmed and formed. Figure 2.4(*a*) shows the cross-sectional view of a PQFP.

PQFPs have their leads formed in a gull-wing fashion (see Fig. 2.4) while plastic lead chip carriers (PLCCs) have their leads in the shape of a J, which are formed (i.e., folded) underneath the package.

Figure 2.5 shows the lead pitch and pin count limit versus QFP size and lead pitch. QFPs are in production and readily used in the assembly of product with 0.5-mm pitch. Based on molding capability and impact of lead length on electrical performance, a molded body 30 mm on a side is thought to be the practical limit. QFPs with 0.5-mm pitch based on the preceding are limited to around 200 I/Os. QFPs with 0.4-mm pitch have been implemented.

Figure 2.4 also shows the variety of surface-mount plastic packages which have been developed based on plastic quad flat package technology.

Ceramic and plastic quad flat packs (QFPs) as well as plastic leaded chip carriers (PLCCs) are used to package gate array and standard cell logic and microprocessors. Small-outline IC (SOIC) and small-outline J-lead (SOJ) packages are used to package memory (SRAM and DRAM) as well as linear semiconductors. Pin count for all package types is limited only by molding capability and the demand for ever-thinner molded packages.

2.2.4 Pin Grid Array (PGA) and Pad Array Carrier (PAC)

Consider the impact of using a perimeter I/O package versus an area array package. Figure 2.6 illustrates the differences between an area array package (pad array carrier) and a perimeter array package (leadless chip carrier). Figure 2.7 shows the relation between the package area versus I/O for perimeter and area array packages. It is clear from Fig. 2.7, that for semiconductors with I/Os greater than 100, pin grid array (PGA) and pad array carrier (PAC) packages are becoming increasingly attractive for packaging very large scale semiconductor integrated circuits (VLSI) and ultra-large-scale semiconductor integrated circuits (ULSI).

2.2.4.1 Perimeter Array I/O Package Advantages/Disadvantages. Perimeter array I/O packages at 0.050-in pitch can be readily surface-mount assembled. 0.4-mm-pitch perimeter I/O QFPs are now being introduced to manufacture and 0.3-mm-pitch perimeter I/O QFPs

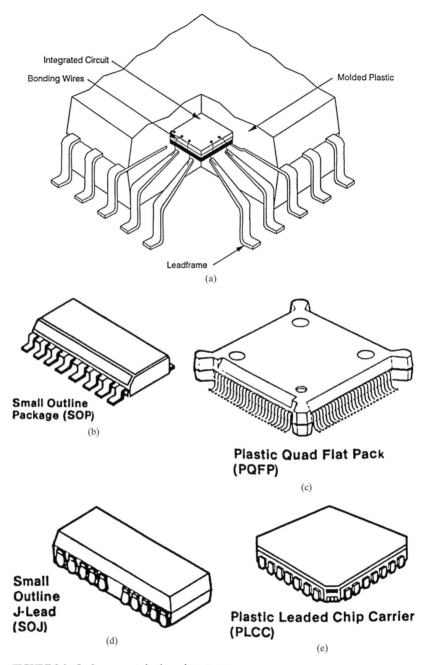

Integrated Circuit

Bonding Wires

Molded Plastic

Leadframe

(a)

Small Outline Package (SOP)

(b)

Plastic Quad Flat Pack (PQFP)

(c)

Small Outline J-Lead (SOJ)

(d)

Plastic Leaded Chip Carrier (PLCC)

(e)

FIGURE 2.4   Surface-mount plastic package types.

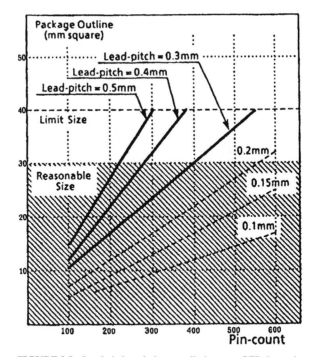

FIGURE 2.5 Lead pitch and pin count limit versus QFP size and lead pitch.

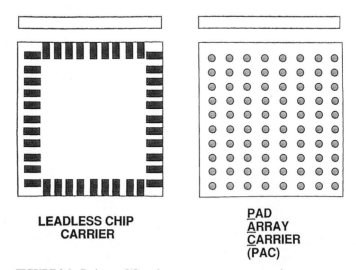

FIGURE 2.6 Perimeter I/O package versus an area array package.

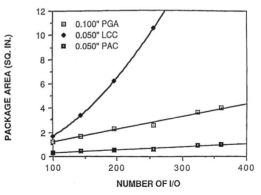

FIGURE 2.7 Pad area carrier (PAC) packaging efficiency

are in development. Reviewing Fig. 2.5, which shows QFP size versus lead pitch and pin count, it is apparent that the usefulness of QFPs is limited to around 400 I/Os. There is a controversy in the packaging and assembly community as to whether 0.3-mm-pitch QFPs, particularly with a large number of I/Os, will ever be a high-throughput, high-assembly-yield part due to the fragility of the lead (0.015 mm wide) and the possibility of solder shorts between leads. Clearly there is a disconnect.

2.2.5 Pad Array and Ball Grid Array Packages

This disconnect is being addressed first by pad array and ball grid array package technology. References 5 and 6 provide details of this emerging technology, particularly as it relates to low-cost plastic array packages with reflowed solder balls attached to the package array I/Os. Figure 2.8 shows a ceramic ball grid array (CBGA) and Fig. 2.9 shows a cross section of the plastic ball grid array (PBGA).

The advantages of ball-grid-array packages (ceramic or plastic) include the following:

- The package offers a high-density interconnect.

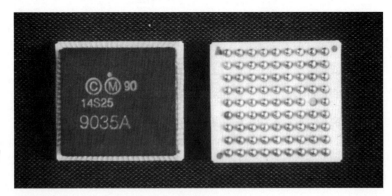

FIGURE 2.8 Ceramic ball grid array (BGA).

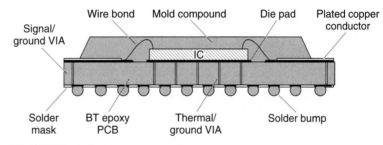

FIGURE 2.9   Ball grid array cross section.

- The packages have achieved six-sigma soldering (demonstrated for 0.060- and 0.050-in I/O pitches) because of the large volume of solder on the I/O pad.
- The package is a low-profile part.
- The package has potential for superior electrical performance in that the total lead length is short, controlled impedance interconnects can be designed in, and low dielectric constant materials can be used for the substrate.
- The package has potential for superior thermal performance.
- The package concept is extendable to multichip packages (MCPs).

2.2.6   Direct Chip Attach (DCA)

The next step down from area array packages is direct chip attach (DCA). The methods of attaching a semiconductor die directly to an interconnect board (PCB, multilayer ceramic, etc.) are:

- Die bond/wire bond
- Tape-automated bonding
- Flip-chip bonding

An exhaustive discussion of wire bond, TAB, and controlled-collapse chip connection (C4) or solder bumped flip chip–to–board interconnect technology can be found in Chap. 6 of Ref. 7. Figure 2.10 illustrates these chip interconnect methodologies.

2.2.6.1   Die Bonding to Printed Circuit.   The preferred method of die bonding and wire bonding is epoxy die bonding to the interconnect (i.e., PCB or multilayer ceramic) and gold ball–wedge wire bonding. One of the advantages of gold ball–wedge wire bonding is that a wedge bond can be performed on an arc around the ball bond. This is not true for wedge–wedge wire bonding.

Wire bonds can be made with wire diameters as small as 0.8 mil. Thermosonic ball–wedge bonding of a gold wire is performed in the following manner: (1) a gold wire protrudes through a capillary; (2) a ball is formed over the end of the wire by capacitance discharge or by passing a hydrogen torch over the end of the gold wire; (3) bonding of the ball is accomplished by simultaneously applying a vertical load to the ball bottomed out on the die bond pad while ultrasonically exciting the capillary (the die and substrate are usually heated to a nominal temperature); (4) the capillary is moved up and over to the substrate or lead bond pad, creating a loop, and under load and ultrasonic excitation, a bond is made; (5) the wire is clamped relative to the capillary, and the capillary moves up breaking the wire at the bond.

Die bond and wire bond attach suffers from the problem that this method of chip attach is difficult to repair, particularly if the chip is encapsulated.

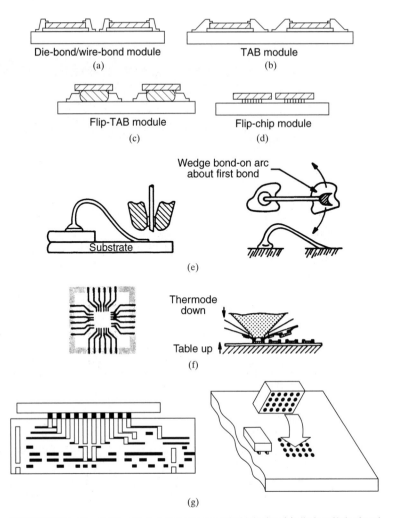

FIGURE 2.10 Direct chip attach interconnect metholdologies: (*a*) die bond/wire bond module; (*b*) TAB module; (*c*) flip TAB module; (*d*) flip-chip module; (*e*) thermosonic gold wire bonding; (*f*) TAB bonding; (*g*) flip-chip bonding.

2.2.6.2 Tape-Automated Bonding (TAB). Tape-automated bonding (TAB) is more expensive than wire bonding and may require a substantial fan out from the die to make the outer lead bond. TAB is a process in which chemically etched, prefabricated copper fingers, in the form of a continuously etched tape of repetitive sites, are simultaneously bonded using temperature and pressure to gold or gold-tin eutectic bumps which are fabricated on the I/Os of the die. The outer leads of the TAB-bonded die are excised and simultaneously bonded to tinned pads on the interconnect, using temperature and pressure.

2.2.6.3 Solder-Bumped Die. The use of solder-bumped die for packaging electronic systems was pioneered by IBM and was called controlled-collapse chip connection (C4) by IBM. The solder bump composition of the C4 die is approximately 95Pb/5Sn. The C4 die in the IBM application were attached to multilayer ceramic substrates by reflow soldering, using a flux which required cleaning after reflow. The initial IBM application of C4 technology was for high-end computer packaging. Flip-chip attach where the die I/Os are solder bumped (usually with 95Pb/5Sn or eutectic Pb/Sn solder) and the chip reflow attached to its interconnect are only now emerging as a viable packageless technology for consumer commercial products. For the direct chip attach (DCA) technology, the PCB flip-chip lands are usually solder-finished with a eutectic Pb/Sn solder. A no-clean flux is used for DCA soldering. References 8 to 10 discuss some of the emerging developments for direct attach of solder-bumped die to PCBs for commercial product applications. Figure 2.11 shows the DCA application discussed in Ref. 10. In this application, the CBGA packaged microprocessor was solder bumped and direct chip attached to illustrate the potential savings in PCB real estate.

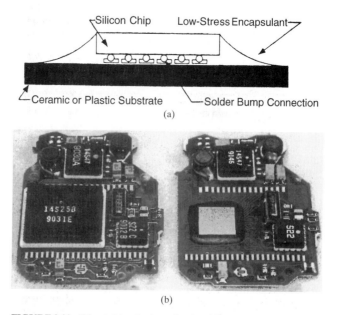

FIGURE 2.11   Direct chip attach application. Microprocesspr on left is in ball grid array while microprocessor on right is attached by solder bumps to show potential area savings.

2.2.7   Packaging Density Comparison and Trends

The packaging density trend lines (package area/die area) are summarized in Fig. 2.12. The area efficiencies of array package concepts are evident and have been maintained over a period of 20 years.

It is apparent then that the trends for new semiconductor chip packaging are increasing package I/Os with the emergence of area array packages for high-I/O semiconductors to minimize package size and enhance package electrical performance (i.e., lower lead inductance). The impact of this will be pressure on PCB fabricators to minimize line width and space in order to escape from high-I/O array packages or DCA semiconductors. In 1986, for PCB interconnects, 10-mil line and spaces were nominal; in 1992, 8-mil line and space was nominal; and in 1995, 6-mil line and space are nominal to meet commercial hand-held electronics products interconnect requirements.

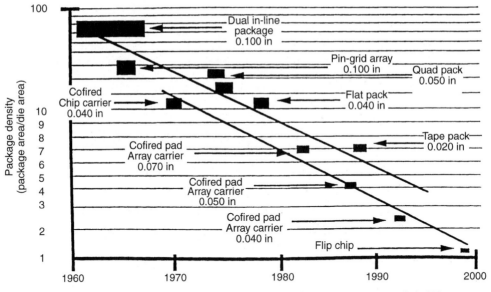

FIGURE 2.12   Packaging trends show the area efficiency of array package concepts over a period of 20 years.

2.3   MULTICHIP PACKAGES

Multichip packages (MCPs) have emerged as a packaging option where performance is an issue or where interconnect area for connecting packaged ICs is at a premium. The performance issue is one of increasing semiconductor performance and the impact of the interconnect medium on the performance of the assembled die. The consequence of this is that the interconnects can no longer be considered to provide an instantaneous electrical connection. It can be shown that for copper conductors on polyimide at a clock frequency of 200 MHz, the maximum allowable length of interconnect is 170 mm or about 6.8 in. As a reference point, the clock speed for the DEC ALPHA RISC microprocessor was 200 MHz or better in 1995.

2.3.1   Multichip vs. Single-Chip Packages

Multichip packages for memory have found broad application in the personal computer (PC) and laptop computer products. Multiple memory die (packaged or unpackaged) are assembled on a rectangular interconnect (PCB or multilayer ceramic) with I/O along one rectangular edge. Such a package is called a *single in-line package* (SIP). The I/Os of the SIP can have DIP leads assembled to them for through-hole attach onto a printed circuit board or they can have lands on the package to mate with a suitable connector. For through-hole-mounted SIPs, the leads are usually on a 0.100-in pitch. Memory packaged in SOP or thin SOP (TSOP) or SOJ packages are assembled onto SIPs whose substrate is a PCB in appropriate multiples to offer enhanced memory capability. Direct chip attach (DCA) of memory die is also possible. Figure 2.13 shows several SIP configurations. The top portion of Fig. 2.13 shows an early version of a SIP using a ceramic substrate and leadless ceramic chip carriers with soldered-on leads. The bottom portion of Fig. 2.13 shows a typical version of a SIP to mate with a SIP-type connector.

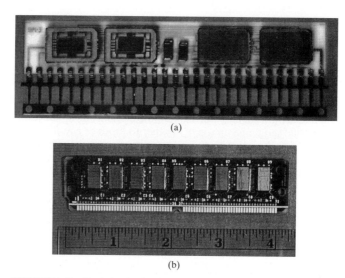

(a)

(b)

FIGURE 2.13   Single in-line (SIP) configurations.

2.3.2   Multichip Packages Using Printed Circuit Technology

Multichip packages using PCB technology, but using leads on the substrate, are also being implemented to provide improved product functionality and board space savings. Figure 2.14 shows the concept of the lead-on-substrate (LOS) multichip package. The leads to the substrate can be fabricated integral with the board during the PCB fabrication or can be soldered on using a suitable high-temperature solder. The LOS multichip packages can be post-molded or cover-coated with a suitable encapsulant.

The LOS multichip package could also be implemented using a cofired ceramic package with the leads brazed on and finished by cover-coating with a suitable encapsulant or hermetic sealing of the assembled ICs. Chapter 7 of Ref. 7 gives a detailed discussion of the cofired multilayer ceramic package manufacturing processes.

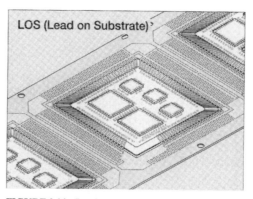

FIGURE 2.14   Lead-on-substrate (LOS) printed circuit board multichip package.

The I/O format for the lead-on-substrate (LOS) packages generally follows the standards for QFP packages.

2.3.3 Multichip Packages Using Organic Substrates

The more prevalent form of multichip packages uses a multilayer organic interconnect built on a substrate such as silicon, alumina ceramic, or metal composite. The dielectric films are patterned serial one on top of another to produce a multilayer interconnect. The dielectric of choice is polyimide with thin-film copper conductors. The technology for the interconnect in question uses processes and manufacturing equipment initially developed for semiconductor manufacture. This technology has a 1-mil line and space capability. The packages can have the cavity face up (facing away from the PCB) or face down (facing the PCB), if a heat sink is required for heat dissipation.

Figure 2.15 shows wire-bonded die on a silicon substrate packaged in a premolded QFP and a ceramic QFP. A premolded QFP is a lead frame about which a plastic body has been molded and which contains a cavity for a die or a substrate. The method of interconnect from the silicon substrate to the package is by wire bonding. As shown in Fig. 2.10, bare die can be attached to the silicon substrate by die/wire bonding, TAB bonding, and flip-chip bonding. As with the lead-on-substrate technology, the I/O format for the QFPs which house the multichip substrate follows the standards for QFP packages.

2.3.4 Multichip Package and Pin Grid Array

Pin grid array (PGA) packages can also be used as MCPs containing the type of substrate shown in Fig. 2.15. The PGA packages can have their cavity face up (facing away from the PCB) or face down (facing the PCB) if the package requires a heat sink for power dissipation. The pitch of the pins on the PGA is usually 0.1 in.

2.3.5 Multichip Package and Known Good Die (KGD)

One of the issues in the application of multichip package technology is the availability of *known good die* (KGD). Clearly considering that for most die, the packaged die test yield after wafer test runs somewhere around 95 percent, the MCPs are limited to perhaps five integrated circuit die per package at best.

2.4 OPTICAL INTERCONNECTS

As the performance of semiconductors increases, as measured by clock frequency, the allowable length of interconnect which does not degrade the device performance decreases.

2.4.1 Advantages of Optical Interconnects

The advantages of optical interconnects are as follows:

- The signal propagation is independent of the bit rate (up to 20,000 Gbits/s).
- The component is immune to electromagnetic interference (EMI) and cross talk.

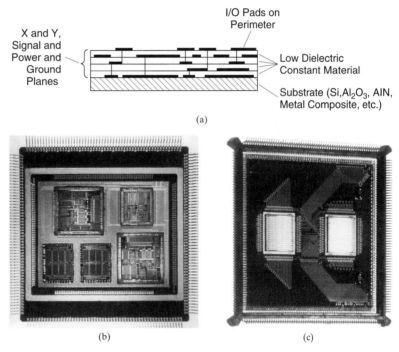

FIGURE 2.15 Multichip package example.

- The optical signals can pass through one another (optical noninteraction).
- The components lend themselves readily to multiplexing.

Advances in optoelectronic devices are leading to active consideration of local optical signal distribution to:

- Reduce the pin count of packages for complex VLSI chips by replacing I/O complexity with band width.
- Carry very high bit rate signals in hybrid circuits and printed circuit board assemblies.
- Allow highly complex interconnections to be achieved without the cost and difficulties of a metal-based back plane.

Where high performance and a high level of interconnects are required, multichip packages (MCPs) and multichip modules (MCMs) have emerged as one packaging idea to provide the performance required. In addition, fiber optic transmitters and receivers are now commercially available to provide high performance offboard optical interconnect in place of a hard-wired backplane interconnect using standard PCB technology and cabling. These fiber optic transmitters and receivers generally use hermetic and nonhermetic custom dual in-line (DIP) package formats for packaging. With advances in optoelectronic semiconductors onboard optical interconnects are also being investigated and demonstrated. Reference 11 discusses one such demonstration of on-board optical interconnects where a polymeric optical waveguide, including branch and cross circuits, was fabricated in the polyimide dielectric of a multilayer copper polyimide silicon substrate.

REFERENCES

1. D. R. Herriott, R. J. Collier, D. S. Alles, and J. W. Stafford, "EBES: A Practical Lithographic System," *IEEE Transactions on Electron Devices,* vol. ED-22, no. 7, July 1975.

2. Ira Deyhimy, Vitesse Semiconductor Corp., "Gallium Arsenide Joins the Giants," *IEEE Spectrum,* Feb. 1995.

3. J. W. Stafford, "Chip Carriers—Their Application and Future Direction," *Proceedings International Microelectronics Conference,* Anaheim, California, February 26–28, 1980, New York, N.Y., June 17–19, 1980. Also published in *Electronics Packaging and Production,* vol. 20, no. 7, July 1980.

4. Ron Iscoff, "Costs to Package Die Will Continue to Rise," *Semiconductor International,* Dec. 1994, p. 32.

5. Bruce Freyman and Robert Pennisi, Motorola, Inc., "Overmolded Plastic Pad Array Carriers (OMPAC): A Low Cost, High Interconnect Density IC Packaging," *Proceedings of the 41st Electronics Components Technology Conference (ECTC),* Atlanta, Ga., May 1991.

6. Howard Markstein, "Pad Array Improves Density," *Electronics Packaging and Production,* May 1992.

7. Rao R. Tummala and Eugene J. Rymaszewski, *Microelectronics Packaging Handbook,* Van Nostrand Reinhold, New York, 1989.

8. Yutaka Tsukada, Dyuhei Tsuchia, and Yohko Machimoto, IBM Yasu Laboratory, Japan, "Surface Laminar Circuit Packaging," *Proceeding of the 42nd Electronics Components and Technology Conference (ECTC),* San Diego, Calif., May 18–20, 1992.

9. Akiteru Rai, Yoshihisa Dotta, Takashi Nukii, and Tetsuga Ohnishi, Sharp Corporation, "Flip Chip COB Technology on PWB," *Proceedings of the 7th International Microelectronics Conference,* Yokohama, Japan, June 3–5, 1992.

10. C. Becker, R. Brooks, T. Kirby, K. Moore, C. Raleigh, J. Stafford, and K. Wasko, Motorola, Inc., "Direct Chip Attach (DCA), The Introduction of a New Packaging Concept for Portable Electronics," *Proceedings of the 1993 International Electronics Packaging Conference,* San Diego, Calif., September 12–15, 1993

11. K. W. Jelley, G. T. Valliath, and J. W. Stafford, Motorola, Inc., Schaumburg, Ill., "1 Gbit/s NRZ Chip to Chip Optical Interconnect," *IEEE Photonics Technology Letters,* vol. 4, no. 10, Oct. 1992.

CHAPTER 3
TYPES OF PRINTED WIRING BOARDS

Dr. Hayao Nakahara
N.T. Information Ltd., Huntington, New York

3.1 INTRODUCTION

Since the invention of printed wiring technology by Dr. Paul Eisner in 1936 several methods and processes have been developed for manufacturing printed wiring board (PWBs) of various types. Most of these have not changed significantly over the years; however, some specific trends continue to exert major influences on the types of PWBs required and the processes that create them:

1. Computers and portable telecommunications equipment require higher-frequency circuits, boards, and materials, and also use more functional components that generate considerable amounts of heat that need to be extracted.
2. Consumer products have incorporated digital products into their design, requiring more functionality at ever-lower total cost.
3. Products for all uses continue to get smaller and more functional, driving the total circuit package itself to become more dense, causing the PWBs to evolve to meet these needs.

These trends have led to the larger use of nonorganic base substrates, such as aluminum and soft iron. In addition, alternate ways to create boards have been developed. These will be discussed in this chapter, along with the traditional board structures and processes. The terms *printed wiring board, PWB,* and *board* will be used synonymously. Also, the words *laminate, substrate,* and *panel* will be used interchangeably.

3.2 CLASSIFICATION OF PRINTED WIRING BOARDS

PWBs may be classified in many different ways according to their various attributes. One fundamental structure common to all of them is that they must provide electrical conductor paths which interconnect components to be mounted on them.

3.2.1 Basic PWB Classifications

There are two basic ways to form these conductors:

1. *Subtractive:*   In the subtractive process, the unwanted portion of the copper foil on the base substrate is etched away, leaving the desired conductor pattern in place.
2. *Additive:*   In the additive process, formation of the conductor pattern is accomplished by adding copper to a bare (no copper foil) substrate in the pattern and places desired. This can be done by plating copper, screening conductive paste, or laying down insulating wire onto the substrate on the predetermined conductor paths.

The PWB classifications given in Fig. 3.1 take into consideration all these factors, i.e., fabrication processes as well as substrate material. The use of this figure is as follows:

• Column 1 shows the classification of PWBs by the nature of their substrate.
• Column 2 shows the classification of PWBs by the way the conductor pattern is imaged.
• Column 3 shows the classification of PWBs by their physical nature.
• Column 4 shows the classification of PWBs by the method of actual conductor formation.

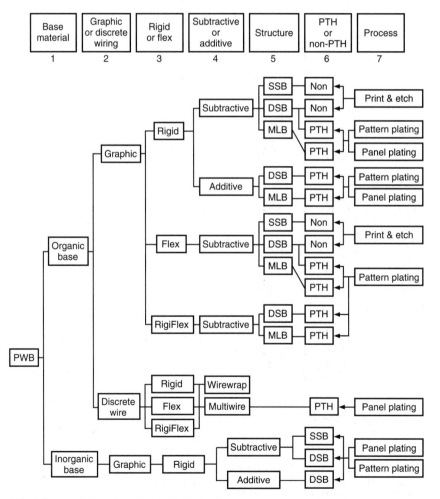

FIGURE 3.1   Classification of printed wirnging boards.

- Column 5 shows the classification of PWBs by the number of conductor layers.
- Column 6 shows the classification of PWBs by the existence or absence of plated-through-holes (PTHs).
- Column 7 shows the classification of PWBs by production method.

3.3 ORGANIC AND NONORGANIC SUBSTRATES

One of the major issues that has arisen with the ever-higher speed and functionality of components used in computers and telecommunications is the availability of materials for the PWB substrate that are compatible with these product and process needs. This includes the stresses on substrate material created by more and longer exposure to soldering temperatures during the assembly process, as well as the need to match the coefficient of thermal expansion for components and substrate. The resultant search has found new materials, both organic and nonorganic based. The details of these materials are explained in Chaps. 8 and 9, but this outlines the basic character of the two types of substrate.

3.3.1 Organic Substrates

Organic substrates consist of layers of paper impregnated with phenolic resin or layers of woven or nonwoven glass cloth impregnated with epoxy resin, polyimide, cyanate ester, BT resin, etc. The usage of these substrates depends on the physical characteristics required by the application of the PWB, such as operating temperature, frequency, or mechanical strength.

3.3.2 Nonorganic Substrates

Nonorganic substrates consist mainly of ceramic and metallic materials such as aluminum, soft iron, and copper-invar-copper. The usage of these substrates is usually dictated by the need of heat dissipation, except for the case of soft iron, which provides the flux path for flexible disk motor drives.

3.4 GRAPHICAL AND DISCRETE-WIRE BOARDS

Printed wiring boards may be classified into two basic categories, based on the way they are manufactured:

1. Graphical
2. Discrete-wire

3.4.1 Graphical Interconnection Board

A *graphical PWB* is the standard PWB and the type that is usually thought of when PWBs are discussed. In this case, the image of the master circuit pattern is formed photographically on a photosensitive material, such as treated glass plate or plastic film. The image is then transferred to the circuit board by screening or photoprinting the artwork generated from the master. Due to the speed and economy of making master artwork by laser plotters, this master can also be the working artwork.

Direct laser imaging of the resist on the PWB can also be used. In this case, the conductor image is made by the laser plotter, on the photoresistive material, which is laminated to the board, without going through the intermediate step of creating a phototool. This tends to be somewhat slower than using working artwork as the tool and is not generally applied to mass production. Work continues on faster resists, as well as exposure systems, and this method will undoubtedly continue to emerge.

3.4.2 Discrete-Wire Boards

Discrete-wire boards do not involve an imaging process for the formation of signal conductors. Rather, conductors are formed directly onto the wiring board with insulated copper wire. Wire-wrap® and Multiwire® are the best known discrete-wire interconnection technologies. Because of the allowance of wire crossings, a single layer of wiring can match multiple conductor layers in the graphically produced boards, thus offering very high wiring density. However, the wiring process is sequential in nature and the productivity of discrete-wiring technology is not suitable for mass production. Despite this weakness, discrete-wiring boards are in use for some very high density packaging applications. See Fig. 3.2 for an example of a discrete-wiring board.

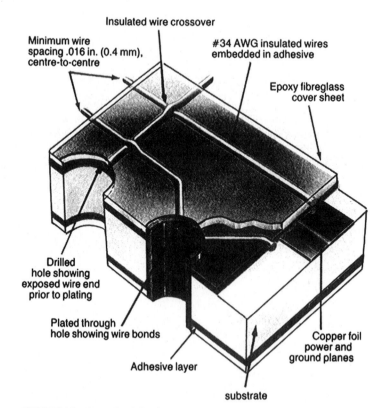

FIGURE 3.2   Example of discrete-wiring board.

3.5 RIGID AND FLEXIBLE BOARDS

Another class of boards is made up of the *rigid* and *flexible* PWBs. Whereas boards are made of a variety of materials, flexible boards generally are made of polyester and polyimide bases. *Rigi-flex boards,* a combination of rigid and flexible boards usually bonded together, have gained wide use in electronic packaging (see Fig. 3.3). Most rigi-flex boards are three-

FIGURE 3.3 Rigi-flex printed wiring board.

dimensional structures that have flexible parts connecting the rigid boards, which usually support components; this packaging is thus volumetrically efficient.

3.6   GRAPHICALLY PRODUCED BOARDS

The majority of boards produced in the world are graphically produced. There are three alternative types:

1. Single-sided boards
2. Double-sided boards
3. Multilayer boards

3.6.1   Single-Sided Boards (SSBs)

Single-sided boards (SSBs) have circuitry on only one side of the board and are often referred to as print-and-etch boards because the etch resist is usually printed on by screen-printing techniques and the conductor pattern is them formed by chemically etching the exposed, and unwanted, copper foil.

3.6.1.1   *Typical Single-Sided Board Materials.* This method of board fabrication is generally used for low-cost, high-volume, and relatively low functionality boards. In the Far East, for example, the majority of SSBs are made of paper-based substrates for lowest cost, with the most popular grade of paper-based laminate being XPC-FR, which is a flame-retardant phenolic material that is also highly punchable. In Europe, FR-2 grade paper laminate is the most popular substrate for SSBs because it emits less odor than XPC-FR when placed in high-voltage, high-temperature environments, such as inside a television set chassis. In the United States, CEM-1 material, which is a composite of paper and glass impregnated with epoxy resin, is the most popular substrate for SSBs. While not as low cost as XPC-FR or FR-2, CEM-1 has gained popularity because of its mechanical strength and also because of the relative unavailability of paper phenolic laminates.

3.6.1.2   *Single-Sided Board Fabrication Process.* Given the emphasis on cost and low complexity, SSBs are generally produced in highly automated, conveyorized print-and-etch lines, using the following basic process flow.

Step 1:   Cut substrate into appropriate panel size by either sawing or shearing.

Step 2:   Place panel in loader which feeds them into the line.

Step 3:   Clean panels.

Step 4:   Screen panel with ultraviolet curable etch-resist ink.

Step 5:   Cure the etch-resist ink.

Step 6:   Etch exposed copper.

Step 7:   Strip the resist.

Step 8:   Apply solder resist.

Step 9:   Screen legend.

Step 10:   Form holes by drilling or punching.

Step 11:   Test for shorts and opens.

The conveyor speed of automated print-and-etch lines ranges from 30 to 45 ft/min. Some lines are equipped with an on-line optical inspection which enables the elimination of the final electrical open/short test.

As previously noted, after the conductor pattern is generated in the print-and-etch line, holes for component insertion are formed on the panel by punching when the panel is made of paper-based substrate, but must be formed by drilling when the panel is made of glass-based substrate.

3.6.1.3 Process Variations.   In some variations, the conductor surface of the PWB gets insulated, exposing only pads, and then conductive paste is screened to form additional conductors on the same side of the board, thus forming double conductive layers on a single side.

Most metal-core PWB consumer applications are made of aluminum substrate, which comes as a copper-clad material. PWBs made of such material do not have through-holes, and components are usually surface-mount types. These circuits are frequently formed into three-dimensional shapes.

3.6.2 Double-Sided Boards

By definition, double-sided boards (DBs) have circuitry on both sides of the boards. They can be classified into two categories:

1. Without through-hole metallization
2. With through-hole metallization

The category of through-hole metallization can be further broken into two types:

1. Plated-through-hole (PTH)
2. Silver-through-hole (STH)

3.6.2.1 Plated-Through-Hole Technology.   PTH technology is discussed in some detail in Sec. 3.7; however, some comments are appropriate here.

Metallization of holes by copper plating has been practiced since the mid-1950s. Since PWB substrate is an insulating material, and therefore nonconductive, holes must be metallized first before subsequent copper plating can take place. The usual metallization procedure is to catalyze the holes with palladium catalyst followed by electroless copper plating. Then, thicker plating is done by galvanic plating. Alternately, electroless plating can be used to plate all the way to the desired thickness, which is called *additive plating*.

The biggest change in the manufacturing process of double-sided PTH boards, and also of multilayer boards (MLBs), is the use of *direct metallization* technologies. (See Chap. 19 for full discussion of electroless and direct metallization for through-hole boards.) Here, simply, it eliminates the electroless copper process. The hole wall is made conductive by palladium catalyst, carbon, or polymer conductive film, then copper is deposited by galvanic plating. The elimination of electroless copper, in turn, allows the elimination of environmentally hazardous chemicals, such as formaldehyde, and EDTA, which are two main components of electroless copper-plating solutions.

3.6.2.2 Silver-Through-Hole Technology.   STH boards are usually made of paper phenolic materials or composite epoxy paper and glass materials, such as CE-1 or CE-3. After double-sided copper-clad materials are etched to form conductor patterns on both sides of the panel, holes are formed by drilling. Then the panel is screened with silver-filled conductive paste. Instead of silver, copper paste can also be used.

Since STHs have a relatively high electrical resistance compared with PTHs, the application of STH boards is limited. However, because of their economic advantage (the cost of

STH boards is usually one-half to two-thirds that of functionally equivalent PTH boards), their application has spread to high-volume, low-cost products such as audio equipment, floppy disk controllers, car radios, remote controls, etc.

3.6.3 Multilayer Boards (MLBs)

By definition, MLBs have three or more circuit layers (see Fig. 3.4). Main applications of MLBs used to be confined to sophisticated industrial electronic products. Now, however, they are the mainstream of all electronic devices, including consumer products such as portable video cameras, cellular phones and audio discs.

3.6.2.3 Layer Count. As personal computers and workstations become more powerful, mainframe computers and supercomputers are being replaced in many applications by these smaller machines. As a result, the use of highly sophisticated MLBs, which have layer counts over 70, are being reduced, but the technology to produce them is proven. At the other end of the layer-count spectrum, thin and high-density MLBs with layer counts between 4 and 8 are mainstream. The drive towards thinner MLBs will continue and is made possible by the continuing concurrent advancement of materials and equipment to handle thin core materials.

3.6.2.4 Via and Via Production Technologies. As PWBs have had to address the issues of higher speed, higher density, and the rise of surface-mount components that use both sides, the need to communicate between layers has increased dramatically. At the same time, the space available for vias has decreased, causing a continuing trend towards smaller holes, more holes on the board, and the decline of the use of holes that penetrate the entire board, which use space on all layers. As a result, the use of buried and blind vias has become a standard part of multilayer board technology, driven by the need for this increased package density (Fig. 3.4).

One of the immediate issues that arise from these trends is the problems of drilling and the associated cost of this fabrication step. Printed wiring boards, which once were stacked three high on a drilling machine, must be drilled individually, and the number of holes per board has risen, to accommodate the need for vias. This has caused a major problem for fabricators, who find that a lack of drilling capacity is creating a big demand on funds for additional machines, while the cost of drilling continues to increase dramatically. Therefore, alternate methods for creating vias are being developed. These pressures will be ongoing, and therefore the process listed here, or some equivalent, will undoubtedly become more important as the drive to miniaturization continues and drilling individual holes becomes less and less practical.

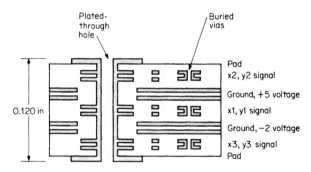

FIGURE 3.4 Cross-section multilayer board with buried via holes. Buried vias are built into each of the double-sided boards that make up the final multilayer structure.

These processes have been developed to mass-produce vias without drills.

Surface Laminar Circuits (SLCs).   The most notable MLB technology developed to form vias is the *sequential* fabrication of multilayers without press operations. This is particularly important for surface blind via holes.

The process for fabricating a board using surface laminar circuits is as follows (see Fig. 3.5):

1. Innerlayer ground and power distribution patterns are formed.
2. Panel receives an oxide treatment.
3. Insulating photosensitive resin is coated over the panel by curtain or screen-coating methods.
4. Holes are formed by photoexposure and development.
5. Panel is metallized by usual copper reduction process (consisting of catalyzing and electroless copper plating or by direct metallization process).
6. Thicker deposition of copper is made by continuation of electroless copper plating or galvanic plating.
7. Circuit patterns are formed by dry film tenting process.

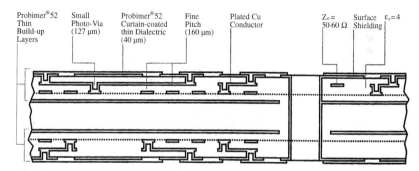

FIGURE 3.5   Example of surface laminar circuit (SLC) board cross section. (*Courtesy IBM Yasu and Ciba-Geigy Limited.*)

DYCOstrate®.   A different approach to small via creation has been taken by Dyconex AG of Switzerland. After ground and power patterns are formed on the panel, and the panel is oxide-treated, polyimide-backed copper foil is laminated on the panel. Holes in the copper are formed by a chemical etching process, and the insulating polyimide material underneath the holes is removed by plasma etching. PWBs made in such a way are called DYCOstrate. In other, similar technologies, different dielectric materials are used, and they are removed by alkaline solutions. The rest of the process is similar to that for SLC; that is, holes are metallized and a thick copper deposition is made by electroless or galvanic plating, and the circuit pattern is formed by a tent-and-etch process (see Fig. 3.5).

Drilled Vias.   In both SLC and DYCOstrate cases, through-holes can also be made by conventional drilling and plating processes, in addition to the surface blind via holes.

Cost Impact.   The manufacturing cost of these sequential technologies is not necessarily directly cheaper than conventional MLB technology, which depends on a laminating press operation. However, since the cost of making standard holes in a board can be as high as 30 percent of the total manufacturing cost, and the creation of holes in these processes is comparatively inexpensive, the overall cost for equivalent functionality can be less. In addition, the fine pattern capability for this process is excellent. For example, an eight-layer conventional structure can often be reduced to a four-layer structure, reducing the total cost for the same packaging density.

3.7   *MOLDED INTERCONNECTION DEVICES*

Three-dimensional circuit technology was of great interest in the early to mid-1980s. The proponents for this technology, however, realized the mistake of trying to make it directly competitive with conventional flat circuits and have developed a niche where the substrate also offers other functional uses, such as structural support for the product.

Manufacturers of three-dimensional circuits prefer to call them *molded interconnection devices* (MIDs). In many applications of MIDs, the number of components to interconnect the electronic and electrical components can be reduced, thus making the total assembly cost cheaper and the final structure more reliable.

3.8   *PLATED-THROUGH-HOLE (PTH) TECHNOLOGIES*

In 1953, the Motorola Corporation developed a PTH process called the *Placir* method,[1] in which the entire surface and hole walls of an unclad panel are sensitized with $SnCl_2$ and metallized by spraying on silver with a two-gun spray. Next, the panel is screened with a reverse conductor pattern, using a plating resist ink, leaving metallized conductor traces uncovered. The panel is then plated with copper by an electroplating method. Finally, the resist ink is stripped and the base silver removed to complete the PTH board. One problem associated with the use of silver is the migration caused by silver traces underneath the copper conductors.

The Placir method was the forerunner of the semiadditive process, which is discussed in Chap. 20.

In 1955, Fred Pearlstein[2] published a process involving electroless nickel plating for metallizing nonconductive materials. This catalyzer consists of two steps. First the panel is sensitized in $SnCl_2$ solution, and then it is activated in $PdCl_2$ solution. This process presented no problem for metallizing nonconductive materials.

At the same time that Pearlstein's paper was published, copper-clad laminates were starting to become popular. Manufacturers of PWBs applied this two-step catalyzing process to making PTHs using copper-clad laminates. This process, however, turned out to be incompatible with the copper surface. A myriad of black palladium particles called *smads* were generated between copper foil and electrolessly deposited copper, resulting in poor adhesion between the electroless copper and the copper foil. These smads and electroless copper had to be brushed off with strong abrasive action before the secondary electroplating process could begin. To overcome this smad problem, around 1960 researchers began attempting to develop better catalysts; the products of their research were the predecessors of modern palladium catalysts.[3]

The mid-1950s was a busy time in the area of electroless copper-plating solutions. Electrolessly deposited nickel is difficult to etch. But since it adheres somewhat better to the base than does electroless copper, research for the development of stable electroless copper-plating solutions was quite natural. Many patent applications for these solutions were filled in the mid-1950s. Among the applicants were P. B. Atkinson, Sam Wein, and a team of General Electric engineers, Luke, Cahill, and Agens. Atkinson won the case, and a patent[4] teaching the use of Cu-EDTA as a complexing agent was issued in January 1964 (the application had been filed in September 1956).

3.8.1   Subtractive and Additive Processes

Photocircuits Corporation was another company engaged throughout the 1950s in the development of chemicals for PTH processes. Copper-clad laminates were expensive, and a major portion of expensive copper foil had to be etched (*subtracted*) to form the desired conductor pattern. The engineers at Photocircuits, therefore, concerned themselves with plating (*adding*) copper conductors wherever necessary on unclad materials for the sake of economy. Their efforts paid off. They were successful in developing not only the essential chemicals for reliable PTH processes but also the fully additive PWB manufacturing technology known as the CC-4* process. This process is discussed in detail in Chap. 20.

With the use of $SnCl_2$-$PdCl_2$ catalysts and EDTA-base electroless copper-plating solutions, the modern PTH processes became firmly established in the 1960s. The process of metallizing hole walls with these chemicals for the subsequent formation of PTHs is commonly called the *copper reduction process.* In the subtractive method, which begins with copper-clad laminates, pattern plating and panel plating are the two most widely practiced methods of making PTH boards. These methods are discussed in the following subsections.

3.8.2 Pattern Plating

In the pattern-plating method, after the copper reduction process, plating resist layers of the reverse conductor image are formed on both sides of the panel by screening resist inks. In most fineline boards, photosensitive dry film is used instead. There are some minor variations in the pattern-plating method (see Fig. 3.6):

1. Catalyzing (preparing the nonconductive surface to cause copper to come out of solution onto that surface)
2. Thin electroless copper (0.00001 in) followed by primary copper electroplating; thick electroless copper (0.0001 in)
3. Imaging (application of a plating resist in the negative of the desired finished circuit)
4. Final electroplating copper
5. Solder plating (as etching resist) 0.0002 or 0.0006 in
6. Stripping plating resist
7. Etching of base copper
8. Solder etching (0.0002-in case); solder reflow (0.0006-in case)
9. Solder mask followed by hot-air solder coater leveler if solder etching is used
10. Final fabrication and inspection

Most manufacturers of DSBs with relatively wide conductors employ thick electroless copper plating. However, thin electroless copper followed by primary electroplating is preferred for boards having fine-line conductors, because a considerable amount of surface is brushed off for better adhesion of dry film. This provides a higher reliability for PTHs. Solder reflow boards had been preferred by many customers, particularly in military and telecommunications applications, until the emergence of hot-air solder coater levelers. Although the solder-over-copper conductors protect the copper from oxidization, solder reflow boards have some limitations. Solder mask is hard to apply over reflowed solder, and it tends to wrinkle and peel off in some areas when the boards go through component soldering. A more serious problem is the solder bridging that occurs when the conductor width and clearance become very small.

In step 9, the entire surface of the board except for the pads is covered by solder mask, and then the board is immersed into the hot-air solder coater leveler, resulting in a thin coating of

---

* CC-4 is a registered trademark of Kollmorgen Corporation.

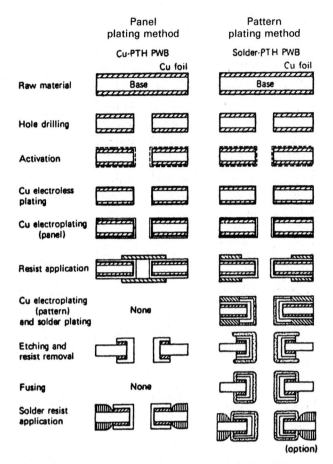

FIGURE 3.6 Key manufacturing steps in panel plating and pattern-plating methods.

solder over the pads and the hole walls. The operation sounds simple, but it requires constant fine-tuning and maintenance of the hot-air solder coater leveler; otherwise, some holes may become heavily clogged with solder and are then useless for component insertion.

One advantage of the pattern-plating method over the panel-plating method is in etching. The pattern-plating method needs to etch only the base copper. The use of ultrathin copper foil (UTC), which is usually ⅛ or ¼ oz thick, offers a real advantage. However, as long as electroplating is used, the pattern-plating method cannot escape from a current distribution problem, regardless of the thickness of the base foils. The panel-plating method by electroplating suffers from the same problem but to a lesser degree. Good current distribution is very difficult to achieve when the boards are not of the same size or type, and particularly if some have large ground planes on the outer faces being plated. When the board has a few holes in an isolated area remote from the bulk of the circuitry, these tend to become overplated, making component lead insertion difficult during assembly. To minimize this current distribution problem, various countermeasures are practiced, such as special anode position, anode masking, agitation, and plating thieves. But none of these offers a decisive solution to the distribution problem, and they are extremely difficult to implement flexibly and effectively in a large plating operation, where a large number of product mixes have to be handled all the time.

Another advantage of the pattern-plating method is its ability to form padless micro-via holes of a diameter ranging from 0.012 to 0.016 in. Micro-via holes enable better usage of conductor channels, thereby increasing the connective capacity of the board.

3.8.3 Panel Plating

In the panel-plating method, there are two variations for finishing the board after the panel is plated with electrolytic copper to the desired thickness. In the *hole-plugging* method, the holes are filled with alkaline-etchable ink to protect the hole walls from being etched; this is used in conjunction with screened etch resist. In the other method, called *tent-and-etch* or simply *tenting,* the copper in the hole is protected from etching by covering the hole or tenting with dry film, which is also used as an etch resist for conductors on the panel surface. The simplified sequence of the panel-plating method is as follows (see Fig. 3.6):

1. Catalyzing
2. Thin electroless copper deposition (0.0001 in)
3. Electroplating copper (0.001 to 0.0012 in)
4. Hole plugging with alkaline-resolvable ink; tenting (dry film lamination)
5. Screen-print etching resist (conductor pattern); photoexpose the panel for conductor pattern
6. Etching copper
7. Stripping etching resist
8. Solder mask
9. Solder coater leveler (optional)
10. Final fabrication and inspection

The panel-plating method is ideal for bare copper board. However, it is a difficult way to make padless via holes, which are becoming more popular. Generally, the conductor width of 0.004 in is considered to be the minimum realizable by this method for mass production.

Although the use of the panel-plating method in the United States and western Europe is limited, nearly 60 percent of the PTH boards in Japan are manufactured by this method.

3.8.4 Additive Plating

Plated-through holes can be formed by additive (electroless) copper deposition, of which there are three basic methods: fully additive, semiadditive, and partially additive. Of these, semiadditive involves pattern electroplating for PTHs with very thin surface copper, but the other two form PTHs solely by electroless copper deposition. The additive process has various advantages over the subtractive process in forming fineline conductors and PTHs of high aspect ratio. A detailed account of the additive process is given in Chap. 20.

3.9 SUMMARY

Modern electronic packaging has become very complex. Interconnections are pushed more into lower levels of packaging. The choice of which packaging technology to use is governed by many factors: cost, electrical requirements, thermal requirements, density requirements, and so on. Material also plays a very important role. All things considered, PWBs still play important roles in electronic packaging.

REFERENCES

1. Robert L. Swiggett, *Introduction to Printed Circuits,* John F. Rider Publisher, Inc., New York, 1956.
2. Private communication with John McCormack, PCK Technology, Division of Kollmorgen Corporation.
3. C. R. Shipley, Jr., U.S. Patent 3,011,920, Dec. 5, 1961.
4. R. J. Zebliski, U.S. Patent 3,672,938, June 27, 1972.

CHAPTER 4
SPECIAL-CONSTRUCTION PRINTED WIRING BOARDS

Happy T. Holden
Hewlett-Packard Co., Loveland, Colorado

4.1 HIGH-DENSITY PRINTED WIRING BOARD TECHNOLOGY ISSUES

The continuous trend towards higher-density printed wiring boards (PWBs) has caused a great deal of strain on the traditional fabrication processes, especially drilling. As holes no longer need to be large enough to accommodate a component lead, and the increasing use of finer pitch on integrated circuit packages creates the need for more holes per unit area, the problems in drilling have become central to the ability to fabricate bare PWBs. As a result, a great deal of research has gone into developing alternatives to traditional drilling. There are several processes available, and they will be described in this chapter, but the selection of any particular one will depend on the end use and the manufacturer's demonstrated capability.

4.2 DRILLED VIA ISSUES

Drilled holes and vias are among the basic structures of PWBs; however, they have significant problems. For example, since the via and pad can block routing channels, each year the via and pad get smaller. Standard technology can produce a via pad size of 0.025 in with a 0.014- to 0.015-in drilled hole. These holes can decrease to as small as 0.008 in, but as they get smaller, they also get more expensive. As a result, small-hole drilling can contribute as much as 30 to 40 percent of the total cost of the PWB. Also, as the holes get smaller for the same thickness board, the aspect ratio increases. This tends to decrease reliability as high-aspect holes have problems of getting sufficient plating solution and solder into the hole.

One response, as shown in Fig. 4.1, is the use of drilled blind vias. This addresses a number of density issues, but does not help the cost of the board.

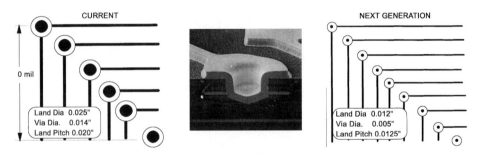

FIGURE 4.1 Current throughhole and blind via compared to next-generation blind vias.

4.3 NONDRILLED VIAS

There are technologies for the replacement of the blind via, in the form of nondrilled blind and buried vias. These vias, shown in Fig. 4.1 as next-generation, are very small compared to those noted as current. For example, these pad diameters range from 0.008 to 0.012 in, with the hole being 0.004 to 0.006 in.

4.3.1 Basic Processes for Nondrilled Vias

Two companies pioneered these nondrilled vias:

- Dyconex of Switzerland has developed a process for drilling vias in polyimide film using plasma. This is called DYCOstrate® and is shown in Fig. 4.2.
- IBM of Yasu, Japan, has developed a process for using their photosensitive solder mask as a dielectric and photodeveloping the vias. This is called *surface laminar circuits,* or SLC. This structure can be seen in Fig. 4.3.

4.3.2 Sequential or Built-up Circuits

From this early work, others have developed such *sequential,* or *built-up* circuits. The methods for forming the vias vary from punching to eximer laser. Of these, we have identified seven additional buildup technologies with enough information to be described here (see also Figs. 4.4 to 4.10). The total list is as follows:

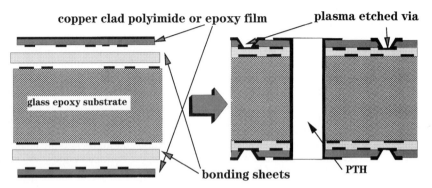

FIGURE 4.2 Cross section of DYCOstrate® type nondrilled via construction.

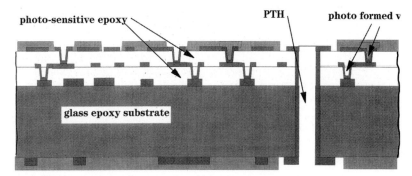

FIGURE 4.3 Cross section of surface laminar circuit type nondrilled via construction.

1. Surface laminar circuits (SLC)
2. Sequential bonded film (DYCOstrate®)
3. Film redistribution layers (FRL)
4. Conductive adhesive bonded flex (Z-link)
5. Built-up structure system (IBSS)
6. Sequential bonded cores (ALIVH)
7. Carrier-formed circuits
8. Roll sheet buildup
9. Sheet buildup

All of these technologies provide approximately the same high-density design rules. A review of these rules and the dielectric constant of the nonglass dielectric material is seen in Table 4.1. These design rules endow buildup technologies with four to eight times the wiring density of conventional all-drilled through-hole vias.

TABLE 4.1 List of Design Rules and Materials for Eight "Buildup" Technologies

Technology	Insulation material, ε	Lines/ spaces	Via/land diameter
Film redistribution layer (FRL)	Epoxy, 4.0	75/75 μm	125/250 μm
Conductive adhesive bonded flex	Polyimide film, 3.8	25/50 μm	25/200 μm
Sequential bonded film (DYCOstrate)	Polyimide film, 3.8	75/75 μm	100/200 μm
Surface laminar circuits (SLCs)	Epoxy, 4.0	75/75 μm	125/250 μm
Build-up structure system (IBSS)	Epoxy + PES, 4.0	75/75 μm	125/250 μm
Sequential bonded cores (ALIVH)	Epoxy aramid, 3.8	100/100 μm	125/250 μm
Carrier formed circuits	Epoxy acrylate, 4.6	100/100 μm	150/400 μm
Roll sheet buildup	Epoxy, 3.2	100/100 μm	150/450 μm
Sheet buildup	Epoxy, 3.2	75/75 μm	100/400 μm

4.4 *SURFACE LAMINAR CIRCUITS (SLCs)*

SLC was the first and most documented of the photoformed vias. A cross section of an SLC board is shown in Fig. 4.3. The main elements of the manufacturing process are outlined here. It is important to emphasize that the process starts with ordinary FR-4 laminate.

1. Start with two-sided copper-clad FR-4 laminate.
2. Circuitize level 1: Photoresist is applied, exposed, and developed, then the copper is etched and the resist stripped.
3. Coat dielectric 1: The photo dielectric is applied to one or both sides, dried, exposed with artwork of the vias, and the vias are developed.
4. Copper plate 1: The dielectric is etched for adhesion, processed through electroless copper, and built up with electroplated copper.
5. Circuitize 2: Photoresist is applied, exposed, and developed, protecting the copper in the vias as the circuitry is etched.
6. Coat dielectric 2: The photo dielectric is applied again to one or both sides, dried, exposed, and the vias developed
7. Drill through-holes: If through-holes are required, they are drilled in now.
8. Copper plate 2: The dielectric is etched, processed through electroless copper, and built up with electroplated copper.
9. Circuitize 3: Photoresist is applied, exposed, and developed, protecting the copper in the vias as the circuitry is etched.
10. Coat solder mask: A final coat of photosensitive solder mask is applied, dried, exposed, and developed. At this point the final metallization or copper protection is applied and the circuit is ready to use.

4.5 *DYCOSTRATE MANUFACTURING PROCESS AND CONSTRUCTION*

The concept of DYCOstrate is relatively simple:

1. Double-sided copper clad (0.5 oz/0.05 oz) polyimide foil (50 mm thick) film is processed or laminated to an FR-4 board.
2. The copper foil is patterned by conventional print-and-etch processing.
3. Exposure to a dry plasma etching process (20 to 25 min) generates all the holes in a parallel process.
4. Electroless copper and panel plating adds an additional 15 to 25 μm of copper. Plating connects top and bottom layers.
5. A second imaging step is necessary to generate the circuitry through subtractive etching.
6. The surface is finished with solder mask.
7. Final application of electroless Ni/au or organic coat protects the PWB for soldering.

The sequential buildup process described here can be repeated to generate substrates with 6, 8, 10, etc., copper layers. It is also possible to laminate all polyimide structures directly to a heat sink by using a standard FR-4 B-stage prepreg.

4.6 OTHER BUILDUP TECHNOLOGY PROCESSES

4.6.1 Film Redistribution Layers (FRL)

FRL is a photosensitive dielectric applied to a finished multilayer board so that small photodefined vias can provide a copper redistribution surface layer to the multilayer. In many cases, this is the only additional high-density layer required to interconnect modern high-density components. (See Fig. 4.4.)

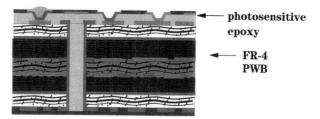

FIGURE 4.4   Film redistribution layers (FRL).

4.6.2 Conductive Adhesive Bonded Flex

Two-sided, high-density flexible circuits are connected in a multilayer by a conductive adhesive of dispersed metal spheres. As pressure and curing takes place, the conductive spheres conduct between the pads of the finished flexible circuits. (See Fig. 4.5.)

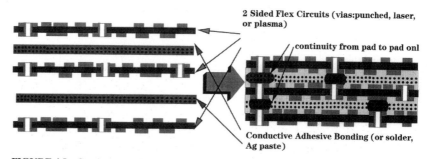

FIGURE 4.5   Conductive Adhesive Bonded Flex.

4.6.3 Built-up Structure System (IBSS)

The IBSS is a photosensitive dielectric with the addition of a thermoset plastic, PES-polyethylene sulfonium. This renders the dielectric with both a higher T_g and better bonding characteristics for electroless copper. The final copper is a full-additive build. (See Fig. 4.6.)

4.6.4 Sequential Bonding Cores (ALIVH)

ALIVH stands for *any-layer inner via hole* and is a buildup technology utilizing the aramid paper laminate and its many excellent properties. One of these is that it laser drills very eas-

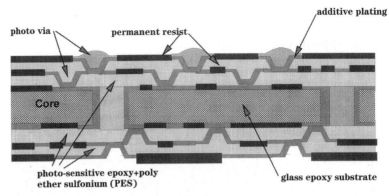

FIGURE 4.6 Built-up structure system (IBSS).

ily. In this process a CO_2 laser is employed to drill the small vias. These vias are then filled with a silver-filled paste. (See Fig. 4.7.)

4.6.5 Carrier-formed Circuits

Separate circuits are prepared on stainless steel carriers with the surface metallization and then copper plated. Vias are plated post on the copper and then covered with liquid epoxy and cured. These separate carriers are then laminated to FR-4 with prepreg and drilled through. Final metallization connects the separate circuits together. (See Fig. 4.8.)

4.6.6 Roll Sheet Buildup

Single-sided epoxy-coated foil is laminated to etched thin core and then vias are chemically etched and metallized. The lamination process is conducted by a rolling heat and pressure. (See Fig. 4.9.)

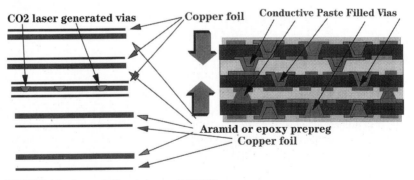

FIGURE 4.7 Sequential bonded cores (ALIVH).

4.6.7 Sheet Buildup

Similar to the roll sheet buildup, individual sheets of prepreg and copper foil are laminated to double-sided or multilayer circuits and laser drilled to produce blind vias. The PWB is finished in the normal fashion. (See Fig. 4.10.)

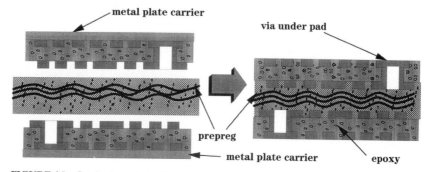

FIGURE 4.8   Carrier-formed circuits.

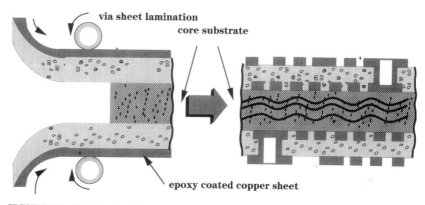

FIGURE 4.9   Roll sheet buildup.

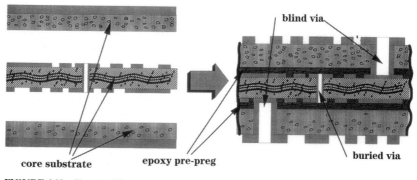

FIGURE 4.10   Sheet buildup.

BIBLIOGRAPHY

Buchwald, Manfred, and Peter Stempfy, "*DYCOstrated*" *Expertise,* the newsletter for Zuken Redac Customers, Winter 1994/1995.

Holden, Happy, "Using Non-Conventional PCB Build-Up Technology To Reduce The Cost And Design Complexity For MCM-Ls," *ISHM Microelectronics,* April 1995.

Moser, Michael, and T. T. Terrier, "Higher Density PCBs For Enhanced SMT And Bare Chip Assembly Applications," *4th International Conference on Multichip Modules,* Denver, Colo., April 19–21, 1995.

Tsukada, Yutaka, and Yohko Mashimoto, "Low Temperature Flip Chip Attach Packaging On Epoxy Base Carrier," *Proceedings of the Surface Mount International Conference & Exposition,* San Jose, Calif., September 1–3, 1992.

———, and Syuhei Tsuchida, "Surface Laminar Circuit, A Low Cost High Density Printed Circuit Board," *Proceeding of the Surface Mount International Conference & Exposition,* San Jose, Calif., September 1–3, 1992.

CHAPTER 5
INTRODUCTION TO SURFACE-MOUNT TECHNOLOGY

Rodney Laird
Acuson Inc., Mountain View, California

5.1 INTRODUCTION

Surface-mount technology (SMT) has grown dramatically in scope and technical complexity since the late 1980s. In SMT, the electrical components are soldered to pads on the surface of the printed circuit board instead of in plated holes drilled through the board. In addition to discrete chip devices, PLCC and QFP packages, SMT now includes ball grid array (BGA), tape-automated bonding (TAB), and direct chip attach (DCA) packages. SMT has emerged as the workhorse component packaging technology and has surpassed through-hole technology (THT) in the percentage of components used in new designs (Fig. 5.1).

The THT dual in-line pin (DIP) package and many of the pin grid array (PGA) packages have been replaced by a myriad of SMT packages. SMT packaging developments have provided a dramatic increase in circuit density and electrical performance while improving cost and quality. Figure 5.2 shows how these new developments have dramatically increased the packaging options available for new designs. The SMT developments, including ball grid arrays (BGA), chip-on-board (COB), flip chip attach (FCA), and multichip modules (MCM), are discussed in more detail later in this chapter and in other chapters.

5.2 BENEFITS OF SMT VS. THT

Surface-mount technology has many benefits over through-hole technology. Some of these benefits include increased component density, double-sided assembly, improved electrical performance, reduced cost, and higher quality. These attributes which make SMT attractive are interrelated. Increased density promotes better electrical performance, decreases required real estate of the bare circuit board, and can reduce the size and cost of the product. The small body size and lead pitch of the components require automation in the design and manufacture of the printed circuit assembly (PCA) which yields a higher-quality, more consistent product.

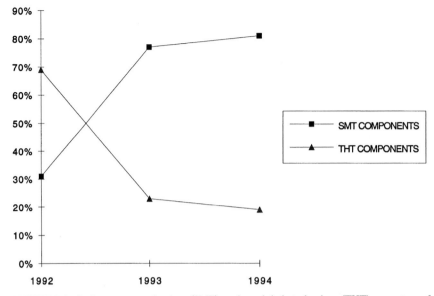

FIGURE 5.1   Surface-mount technology (SMT) vs. through-hole technology (THT) percentage of components placed on printed circuit assemblies in the United States.

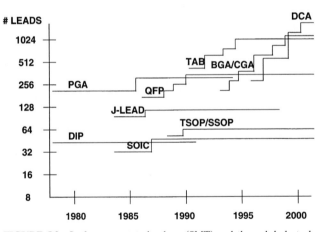

FIGURE 5.2   Surface-mount technology (SMT) and through-hole technology (THT) integrated circuit packaging developments.

5.2.1 Component Size and Density

The reduced component size and the corresponding density improvement with SMT is one of the greatest attributes as compared with THT. Not only are SMT components significantly smaller than through-hole components, they can be attached on both sides of the circuit board for additional density. The higher pin count with SMT components also allows more functionality in each component. The functionality achievable on a single SMT board, therefore, might be equivalent to that of several THT boards. The circuit density possible with SMT allows economical products to be built which were not possible before, such as notebook and pen-based computers, paging and cellular products, consumer electronics, and medical diagnostic devices.

5.2.2 Electrical Performance

Improved electrical performance is another attribute of SMT over THT. The increased density possible with SMT necessitates smaller trace widths and spacing, smaller vias, and decreased trace length. This provides shorter propagation delays, lower via impedance, faster logic edge rates, and thus increased performance. In many cases, SMT is required because acceptable performance levels cannot be attained with THT at the necessary clock speeds. The increased density and performance, however, create challenges in the design and layout of the boards for SMT land pad shape creation, component spacing, trace routing density, PCA layer count, via size/spacing, thermal management, and logic signal integrity. The SMT printed circuit board fabrication process also requires more advanced technology than THT to handle the smaller trace width and spacing, smaller via size, increased layer count, and impedance requirements.

5.2.3 Cost

Cost savings can be achieved with SMT in a number of areas. The cost of the bare circuit board, one of the most expensive components of a PCA, can be significantly reduced for a given level of functionality with SMT because of the decrease in board size resulting from the increase in component density. Even though higher-technology capability is often required to manufacture a bare SMT circuit board, the overall cost can be lower because the boards take less real estate on the PC fabrication process panel, allowing more images per panel.

Component cost for SMT continues to decline rapidly for many packaging styles as the volume of SMT components increases. Plastic quad flat packs (PQFPs) are an excellent example. By the mid 1990s, the cost of SMT was at parity with, or below, THT equivalents in most packaging styles for SMT 1.27-mm(0.050-in) pitch, passive, and discrete packages. SMT can actually be an enormous cost advantage for high-pin-count devices. As SMT volumes increase, the cost differential will become even greater.

5.2.4 Quality

The quality of SMT printed circuit assemblies can surpass that of THT. To achieve this, however, in-depth process development and process control is required. Refinements to all stages of the printed circuit assembly process are required for SMT because of new demands on the materials, such as solder paste and flux, as well as the new demands on the equipment capability. Detailed understanding of the capability and limitations of the materials and processes is the key to developing low-defect-rate processes.

One of the necessary developments in SMT has been the high degree of automation. Automation is a very important aspect of achieving high quality in SMT. Equipment developments have provided unprecedented levels of control for the process-intensive steps. Very high placement accuracy and speed for pick-and-place equipment are also possible. Computer-aided design (CAD) data-driven program generation is another important contribution from the automation of SMT design and assembly processes. Many companies have achieved integrated electronic CAD data flow from the schematic design phase through design and fabrication of the bare PCB to programming of the assembly equipment on the production floor.

The result of all the developments has been optimized SMT processes capable of defect rates below 50 parts per million (ppm) measured by solder joint. Ball grid array (BGA) packages can provide a defect rate at least an order of magnitude lower.

5.3 IMPLEMENTATION OF SMT FOR NEW PRODUCTS

There are many ways to implement SMT on new products. The tradeoffs are very product dependent and require a detailed understanding of both the resources available to commit to SMT and the product requirements. Decisions need to be made concerning which design rules will be used, who will design and lay out the product (in-house, subcontract), who will assemble the product, and what the anticipated volumes will be.

5.3.1 Design for Manufacturability Guidelines

Design for manufacturability (DFM) guidelines are used to specify the implementation of and limitations for the design and physical layout of printed circuit boards. Effective DFM guidelines are critical to achieve manufacturable printed circuit assemblies and to ensure low defect rates. The DFM guidelines should cover a wide range of areas including:

- SMT land pad and stencil geometry
- Component/trace/via spacing and keepout
- Component orientation/pin #1 identification
- Routing and via size/placement rules
- External numbering and labeling
- Manufacturing features (board size, component orientation/numbering, fiducial marks)
- PCA rework requirements

There are numerous places to get DFM guidelines, such as the Institute for Interconnecting and Packaging Electronics Circuits (IPC), a contract assembly house, or one of the many SMT consultants who specialize in documentation and training for all areas of SMT. DFM considerations are discussed in more detail in Sec. 5.6.

5.3.2 CAD Layout Services

The CAD layout of the board is an extremely important step to assure the manufacturability of the printed circuit assembly. CAD layout design is where most of the DFM guideline recommendations are implemented. There are many different options for CAD layout, including in-house or *captive* CAD design services, external CAD design services, and CAD design by the contract board assembly house. In-house or *captive* CAD layout capability provides a number of benefits, such as better opportunity for contact among the electrical designer, manufacturing engineer, and CAD designer during the layout process; uniform implementation across all the board designs (design shape library); better understanding and control over the design implementation; and feedback paths for continuous process improvement. Also required is investment in the CAD tools and personnel training, which can be significant.

External CAD layout services can be beneficial when it is not cost effective to maintain the capability in-house, when sufficient expertise does not exist or is not required in-house, or as an overflow capability when internal capability is exceeded. External CAD design houses can use their own DFM guidelines or implement those provided for the job. Many contract assembly houses also provide CAD layout services which complement their printed circuit assembly capability by incorporating their DFM guidelines and providing a close link to the production floor. Close coordination between the PCB CAD designers and electrical and manufacturing engineers working on a board is very important for the effective design of printed circuit boards.

5.3.3 Printed Circuit Assembly Services

There are three options for assembling the printed circuits: in-house, subcontract, and OEM.

5.3.3.1 In-house Manufacturing.   In-house or *captive* manufacturing offers the ultimate in control over the process and delivery, including the production capacity, assembly process parameters, thermal profiles, and materials. In-house manufacturing can make sense if the product volume is very high, product complexity is high requiring a specialized process or innovation, or if high flexibility in delivery, product ramp, or change implementation is important. In-house manufacturing, however, is a very large commitment because of the capital investment, purchasing support required, production line process and materials management issues, and the personnel management issues.

5.3.3.2 Subcontract Assembly.   The high capital cost of SMT and overhead rates, however, have caused many companies to rely on subcontract assembly vendors rather than develop or continue to maintain captive production capability. There are many subcontract assembly vendors which can accommodate any SMT assembly need from design and prototype to full-volume, turnkey production. The capability of a subcontract assembly vendor must match the product to be built for process capability, volume, and cost. Contract assembly vendors offer many different services, including basic board assembly, design for manufacturability (DFM) analysis, layout, ECO (engineering change order) support, component procurement, in-circuit test (ICT), functional test, and finished box assembly. Mainstream SMT technology for boards up to 14×18 in with 0.5-mm (0.0197-in) minimum component pitch and medium density is readily available with excellent results. Higher-technology assembly capability (high density, large boards, advanced component package types) generally requires additional equipment capability and/or specialized process development and optimization. Engineering support from the customer is often required in these cases to match the assembly process to the needs of the product.

5.3.3.3 Original Equipment Manufacture (OEM).   Original equipment manufacture refers to purchasing a finished product from another manufacturer who is responsible for all aspects of the design and manufacture of the product. This approach can take the form of purchasing a product which is already available on the market or working with a manufacturer to design a new product which can then be purchased as a standard product. This product option allows the purchaser to have minimal involvement in the actual technology used to design and produce the product.

5.4 SMT MATERIALS

Surface-mount technology developments are pushing to extend capabilities of materials used in existing SMT processes to achieve smaller geometry, higher density, and lower defect rates for new designs. A detailed understanding of the material capability, critical parameters, and limitations is very important in reducing defect rates and extending the technology for new packages and new environmental regulations. New requirements are causing material and equipment vendors to work closely with customers to achieve integrated solutions.

5.4.1 Solder Paste

Solder paste consists of small spheres of solder metal (solder powder) mixed with flux to form a paste. Solder paste is the most important material in the SMT process. It is applied to the bare circuit board in the stencil-printing process, using a stencil and squeegee (see Sec. 5.8). There are two basic components of the solder paste:

- Solder powder
- Flux

Mixing the flux and the powder creates the solder paste (Fig. 5.3). This is done by the solder paste manufacturer. The size and shape of the solder powder, the percent metal content, and the flux vehicle including viscosity modifiers have complex interrelationships which determine the characteristics of the solder paste.

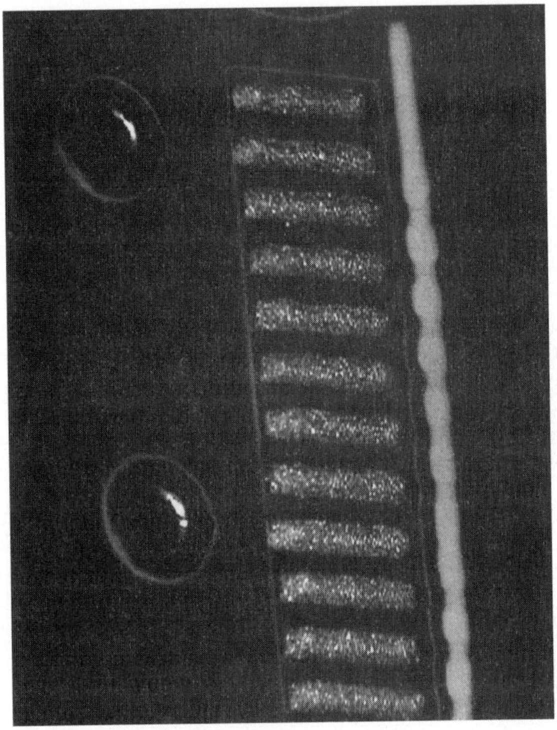

FIGURE 5.3   Fine-pitch solder paste bricks.

5.4.1.1 Solder Powder.   The solder powder is made up of small spherical or irregular shapes of solder. The powder is sorted into ranges of diameters usually by mesh screens. Different solder powder mesh size ranges are used for different minimum lead pitches. The determining factor is the stencil aperture size.

Depending on the powder-forming process parameters, the powder can either be spherical or irregular. Spherical shapes are generally preferred. Irregular shapes can be oblong, crescent, or even clumps of two or more spheres stuck together. A small percentage of irregular balls is allowed and tends to increase the viscosity and thixotropic properties of the solder paste. Powder-processing parameters also affect the amount of oxides on the surface of the balls. Lower levels of oxide on the surface of the solder balls reduce the amount of cleaning required by the flux.

5.4.1.2 Flux.   The flux consists of inert solids (i.e., rosin), activators, viscosity modifiers (i.e., alcohols), and other additives. The inert solids serve two purposes: They provide the solution into which to dissolve the activators and they also act as an oxygen barrier coating to protect the solder joint from further oxidation during the reflow process. The activators are the cleaning agents added to the flux to remove oxidation on the pad, lead, and solder powder to prepare for reflow. The viscosity modifiers are the additives used to adjust the paste viscosity characteristics. Other additives are used to adjust solder paste properties such as flux surface tension or solder paste drying rate. There are four classes of solder paste flux formulations which determine the cleaning technology that can be used for the printed circuit assemblies:

- Rosin flux
- Water-soluble flux
- No-clean flux
- Synthetic flux

Rosin Flux.   Rosin fluxes are made from pine resin and must be cleaned with Freon™-based solvents, alcohol, or semiaqueous solutions. Most rosin-based fluxes are RMA type, which stands for rosin-based, mildly activated flux. Rosin flux has a long history but has been largely phased out due to restrictions on Freon-based cleaning solvents. Semiaqueous cleaning is also an option with rosin flux although this is not a popular alternative due to the complexity of the required cleaning equipment, the expense of the chemicals and equipment operation, the volatility of some of the chemical compositions, and waste disposal of spent flux.

Water-Clean Flux.   Water-clean flux is the most common alternative to rosin flux with chlorinated fluorocarbons (Freon) cleaning. It is made from synthetic, organically activated (OA) compounds and readily dissolves in water. These are generally quite active fluxes and must be removed after soldering to eliminate the opportunity for corrosion. Cleaning is usually accomplished with heated deionized (DI) water.

No-Clean Flux.   No-clean fluxes are defined as fluxes which are inert after soldering and cause no long-term reliability concern if they remain on the PCA during operation. No clean fluxes can be left on the PCA without risk of corrosion or dendritic growth as long as they have gone through the proper heating cycle to render the activators inert. No-clean fluxes have fewer activators in general than other flux types.

No-clean fluxes require a tighter reflow process control window, especially for low-solids fluxes, and often require nitrogen environments to achieve low defect rates. Nitrogen environment can significantly reduce the amount of oxidation during reflow which allows the flux activators to better clean the pads, leads, and solder powder.

5.4.1.3 *Solder Paste Parameters.*   Solder paste must perform three functions:

- Print through the stencil in the appropriate volume, shape, and position to create the solder joint.
- Provide the tackiness to hold the components in place until reflow.
- Provide flux to clean the pad, lead, and solder powder during reflow.

Solder paste must perform effectively in all of the SMT process steps: stencil print, component placement, reflow, and clean. The flux residue must be cleanable after assembly or rendered inert during the solder process. Some of the critical parameters for solder paste are:

- Viscosity
- Percent metal content
- Solder powder size and shape
- Flux activity

- Tack time
- Stencil life
- Cleaning

Viscosity. Solder paste viscosity is a very complex attribute resulting from a combination of many different parameters. Solder pastes are highly thixotropic, non-Newtonian fluids where their viscosity varies depending on the shear rates. Many solder pastes have thixotropic properties which allow the solder pastes to act as a liquid under shear but solidify when left at rest, much like gelatinous soups. Two parameters which directly affect the viscosity characteristics of solder paste are:

Percent metal

Solder powder size and shape

Both of these parameters affect the amount of friction contact between the solder balls in the powder. Higher friction translates to higher viscosity.

Viscosity modifiers, formulated by the solder paste manufacturer, are added to create specific viscosity properties. They are typically high-boiling-point alcohols, which the solder paste vendors must mix together to achieve the proper balance of viscosity, boiling point, and flux volume. The solder paste viscosity properties must provide good printing characteristics yet not allow slumping during reflow. Slumping, where the solder paste brick spreads, sometimes allowing adjacent bricks to touch, can lead to solder bridges and solder balls during reflow. The paste must also be formulated such that the volatiles vaporize in the reflow oven before reflow to prevent boiling and sputtering of the paste.

Percent Metal Content. Solder pastes are typically 88 to 91 percent metal by weight (45 to 65 percent by volume) for stencil-print applications and 60 to 75 percent metal by weight (25 to 45 percent by volume) for dispensing applications. Ninety percent metal by weight, which equates to 60 percent metal by volume, is most commonly used in stencil-printing applications. Ninety-one percent metal is close to the maximum metal loading while still ensuring 100 percent flux fill in the interstitial spaces between the solder balls. A higher percentage of metal leaves less flux in the suspension and thus the solder balls are more tightly packed. When solder balls touch, the friction between the balls makes the viscosity increase markedly.

Solder paste dispensing applications use a much lower percentage of metal content. Seventy percent metal is very common in dispensing applications. The extra flux is required to help the paste flow through the dispensing needles in a smooth, controlled manner. If solder balls clump together, they can clog the needle or make the paste flow unevenly.

Solder Powder Size and Shape. The solder powder is sorted using a series of mesh screens to filter powder into particular ranges. The mesh size distribution directly affects the minimum stencil aperture dimensions. Typically, the maximum solder powder diameter should be no more than 50 percent of the width of the smallest stencil aperture. If the solder powder is too large, the paste can clog the stencil apertures or not fully release onto the board when the stencil is lifted.

Standard 1.27-mm(0.050-in) mil pitch and some 0.65-mm(0.0256-in) pitch apertures work well with −200/+325 mesh powder (60 to 80 μm diameter). Apertures with 0.5-mm(0.0197-in) pitch and some with 0.4-mm(0.0157-in) pitch require −325/+500 mesh (40 to 60 μm diameter) powder. Pitches of 0.4 mm(0.0157 in) and below usually require even finer solder powder (−500/+625 mesh, <40 μm). A very small percentage (<½ percent) of very small diameter powder is allowed in solder paste. These fine balls can spread with the flux during the reflow process, creating a fringe of small balls around the reflowed joint. Some of the balls coalesce to form larger balls which can lodge between leads and cause electrical failure.

The spherical solder powder shape is preferred because it has the lowest surface area per volume for oxides to form. Spheres also move over each other more easily, becoming lubricated by the flux for consistent viscosity. Irregular shapes can be oblong, crescent, or even clumps of two or more spheres stuck together. They can increase the viscosity as well as the thixotropic properties of the solder paste. The irregular shapes, however, can cause difficulty with solder paste release from the stencil apertures.

Flux Activity.   Flux activity refers to the quantity of activators added to the flux to remove oxides and provide a solderable surface on the lead, pad, and solder powder. Flux must not contain bromides because they are highly hydroscopic and can be absorbed into the PCB or flux residues, causing long-term reliability problems.

Tack Time.   Tack time is the length of time the printed paste retains the tackiness to hold components in place. If tackiness is diminished, the paste may not be able to hold components in place during the pick-and-place operation or during handling after placement before the assembly is reflow soldered. Tack time should be above 4 h, with 12 h or more being preferred. Prototype, low-volume, or high-complexity PCAs require long tack time pastes to allow for machine stoppages, program fixes, and other unforeseen delays in the assembly process, whereas high-volume products do not.

Solder Paste Life.   Solder paste life refers to the length of time the solder paste can be used on the stencil while actively printing. The paste life is usually in the range of 8 h but can go as high as 24 h depending on the paste formulation, operating temperature, and humidity. Paste, as it ages, can increase in viscosity as the volatiles evaporate. It can also decrease in viscosity if shear thinning occurs or if the paste absorbs moisture hydroscopically. The vendor specifications should be followed concerning solder paste life.

Stencil Life.   Stencil life refers to the maximum time duration between prints while still allowing consistent deposits of solder paste on the bare board. After this period of inactivity, the paste flux begins to dry along the walls of the stencil aperture, causing the aperture to be reduced in size or totally clogged. The paste brick definition is also diminished. The stencil should be washed to assure high-quality printing. In some cases, the stencil can be used again without washing but it requires several prints to flush out the old paste. The rejected boards must be cleaned and reprinted.

Cleaning.   Flux must be formulated for easy and thorough cleaning (if required) after soldering. The cleaning solvent is dependent on the flux composition. Flux is generally more difficult to clean as time goes on. Lower surface tension of the cleaning solvent helps allow cleaning in tight spaces under components and in through-hole barrels.

Cleanliness is measured in two ways: ionograph and surface insulation resistance (SIR). Ionograph testing consists of submerging the PCA to be tested into isopropyl alcohol while measuring the amount of equivalent NaCl ionic contamination. Measurement is in micrograms of NaCl equivalent per square inch. SIR testing consists of measuring the resistance between two exposed metallization, interleaved comb patterns on the PCB. SIR values are measured in ohms per square where square refers to the unit of open space between interleaved portions of the combs where the unit length equals the separation between two comb fingers. In both tests, the PCA is expected to have been processed in the normal reflow or wave process, followed by cleaning, if required.

5.4.1.4 *Solder Paste Storage and Handling.*   Solder paste is a very critical component of a successful SMT process and must be packaged, stored, and prepared in the proper manner. Packaging of solder paste is usually in a jar or syringe. Solder paste should never be stored with air contact. Solder paste should be stored in a refrigerator above freezing (1 to 6°C). Refrigerating solder paste greatly slows any flux evaporation, tendency for powder to settle leaving liquid flux on top, and flux chemical degradation. Although some solder paste vendors do not specifically recommend that their solder paste be refrigerated, it is a good precautionary measure. When solder paste is needed, it should be removed from the refrigerator and allowed to reach room temperature before being opened to prevent moisture from condensing on the solder paste when it is opened.

5.4.2 Wave Solder Flux

The wave solder flux is very similar to solder paste flux in chemical composition and process function; however, the application method is very different. Wave solder flux is applied usually in one of four ways: foam, wave, pressure spray, and electrostatic spray. The foam-fluxing technique is the most traditional method and uses a pumice stone partially submerged in a bath of flux. Air is pumped from the bottom of the pumice stone, creating a foam of flux which contacts the bottom surface of a PC board as it passes above the stone. Wave fluxing is very similar to wave soldering except using flux instead of solder. Wave fluxing is not common, however, because of the large quantity of flux deposited on the PCA.

Pressure spray and electrostatic spray are two alternative methods of applying flux to the bottom of a wave solder board. Both methods attempt to better control the amount and location of flux applied to a PC board. These methods are commonly used for water-soluble and no-clean fluxes. These methods also attempt to reduce the amount of wasted flux.

5.4.3 Solders

There are many different solder metallizations used in SMT for lead plating, land pad coatings, solder paste powder, and wave solder pots. The most common is tin/lead compositions, such as eutectic alloy of 64 percent tin and 37 percent lead. See Chaps. 28 and 29 for more information on solder compositions.

5.4.4 Conductive Adhesives

Conductive adhesives are epoxies filled with a conductive material to give them conductive electrical properties. They are used to make the electrical connection between the lead and pad as an alternative to soldering. Conductive adhesives are being used in specific applications where either the temperatures for reflow soldering are not acceptable or where the metallurgies of the two materials to be connected are not compatible. Liquid crystal diode (LCD) displays are a common user of conductive adhesives because of the temperature sensitivity of the LCD material.

5.4.5 Solder Paste Stencils

Stencils (also called metal masks) are almost universally used to apply solder paste to the board for mass reflow processes. Stencils are effectively being used for components down to 0.4-mm(0.0157-in) pitch.

5.4.5.1 Stencil Fabrication Techniques. There are numerous methods of creating stencils. Chemical etch stencils are the most common because of the readily available process capability and low cost. The stencil fabrication options include:

- Chemical etch stencils
- Laser-cut stencils
- Additive stencils
- Combinations of plated and etched stencils
- Coatings and texturing for stencils

The different stencil technologies strive for smooth aperture wall texture with vertical or slightly trapezoidal apertures where the wider portion of the aperture contacts the land pad (Fig. 5.4).

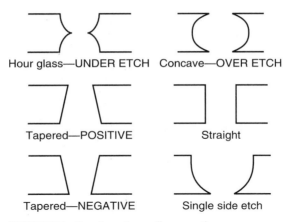

FIGURE 5.4 Stencil aperture wall cross section.

Chemical Etch Stencils.   Chemical etch stencils are etched from both sides simultaneously and meet at the center of the stencil thickness. The etching is continued after the initial break-through to reduce the knife-edge created midway through the aperture (Fig. 5.5). Overetch-ing can cause a concave aperture profile and excessively large apertures. Underetching can cause a significant knife-blade and reduced aperture size. Some of the challenges with chem-ical etching include determining the proper artwork correction to assure the desired final aperture size, aligning the top and bottom film so they create a vertical aperture instead of an offset aperture, controlling the etch bath to assure even, consistent etch rates, and timing the etch process with etchant flow characteristics to provide the correct aperture size while pro-viding a nearly vertical side wall.

Laser-Cut Stencils.   Laser-cut stencils are manufactured by using a laser to cut the desired apertures (Fig. 5.6). The desired apertures must be programmed for the laser using CAD data. The lasers have very good accuracy both in location and size of the apertures. They are also able to provide straight or slightly tapered side walls with smooth wall texture. Lasers, how-ever, are expensive and relatively slow, which pushes the cost of laser-cut stencils significantly above that of chemical etch stencils (approximately two times).

Stepped Stencils.   Stepped stencils have localized regions where the stencil thickness has been reduced (Fig. 5.7). Stepped stencils are usually used for fine-pitch SMT components where the required volume of solder and the stencil aperture aspect ratio necessitate a thin-ner stencil. Stepped stencils are created in a two-stage etching process. First, the stencil must have the step regions chemically etched down to the proper thickness. The typical step stencil uses an 0.008-in stock with 0.006-in step regions. The apertures can then be created using either chemical etch or laser techniques.

Care must be taken to assure that the step region is aligned with the aperture locations. Stepped stencils are more difficult for chemical etching for two reasons:

1. The etch rates vary for different stencil thicknesses.
2. The etch resist adhesion and artwork image transfer resolution are not as good as with sin-gle-level stencils.

Alternative Fabrication Process Stencils.   Various plating and etching options have been tried to create improved stencils but few see any significant usage. One option is a sandwich stencil where nickel is plated on both sides of a core material. In this process the stencil aper-ture pattern is nickel plated onto the stencil core stock, leaving only the apertures unplated. The nickel acts as an etch resist and the base stencil stock is etched away to form the finished

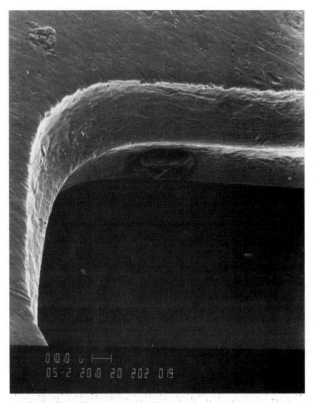

FIGURE 5.5 SEM photograph of chemical etch stencil aperture.
(Courtesy Universal Instruments, Binghamton, N.Y.)

stencil aperture. This option does not give a uniform aperture wall because of the undercut created during the etching of the core material.

Another option that has been tried mostly on an experimental basis is a totally additive stencil. For this option, a base material is chosen which can be plated. An etch resist is then laminated and imaged so that the stencil apertures are the only part of the resist remaining. The base material is then plated to the appropriate thickness, after which the etch resist and base metal are removed, providing a stencil which has been 100 percent plated. A major concern for this procedure is the edge quality of the etch resist because it fully determines the aperture wall surface.

Coatings and Finishes for Stencils.   Coatings can be used as an extra step after chemical etching to improve the paste release characteristics during stencil printing. Nickel and Teflon™ have been plated on stencils to provide a more uniform side-wall surface and to decrease the side-wall friction. Chemical polish techniques are also used at times to improve the side-wall texture and smooth the knife-edge from chemical etching. Care must be taken with chemical polishing, however, because it can also round the corners on the lip of the stencil aperture. Chemical polishes are not recommended for laser-cut stencils because the crystal structure along the aperture walls is changed during the laser-etching process and etches unevenly along the grain boundaries.

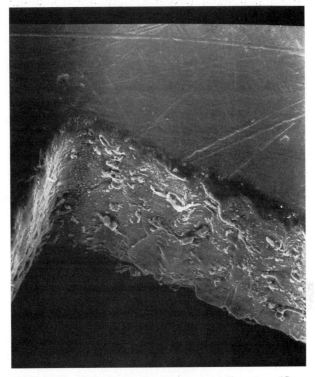

FIGURE 5.6 SEM photograph of laser-cut stencil aperture. *(Courtesy Universal Instruments, Binghamton, N.Y.)*

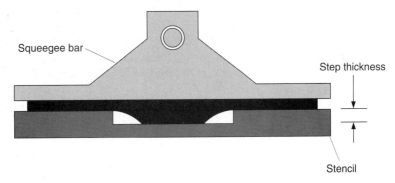

FIGURE 5.7 Stepped stencil cross section showing squeegee deflection.

5.4.5.2 Stencil Material.   Many different metals are used to create stencils. The most common stencil material is stainless steel, although beryllium copper, alloy 42, and molybdenum are also used. The issues in choosing the stencil material have to do with cost, ease of etching, durability, and aperture-wall quality. Copper alloys are the easiest to etch, but they are also easily damaged. Stainless steel alloys are more difficult to etch and require a tighter control on the etch bath, but they provide very good wear and damage resistance and are not affected by fluxes or solvents. Molybdenum has wonderful etch properties and can provide extremely vertical side walls but requires very toxic chemicals for etching.

Stencil material must be flexible, but not sustain plastic deformation. This means that the yield curve should be broad yet maintain a high yield strength. Stainless steel #304 meets these requirements very well for most applications. Extremely fine apertures—0.4-mm (0.0157-in) pitch and less—require higher stencil yield strength properties because of the very thin webs between apertures and the large deformation at the stencil aperture lip–to–SMT pad contact.

5.4.5.3 Stencil Mounting. Stencils are mounted to a frame using a stretched mesh border (Fig. 5.8). The mesh border provides the elastic tension on the stencil to maintain a taught stencil yet allows compliance for the stencil to deflect under the pressure of the squeegee during the stenciling process. This deflection is required for stencil snap-off during the stencil-print cycle. The border can either be nylon or stainless steel. The stainless steel mesh border provides a higher tension capability and maintains that tension better than nylon. But the nylon mesh allows more total deflection without deforming the mesh and is less expensive. The edge of the stencil should be perforated to provide a better mechanical hold for the glue at the stencil-to-mesh interface.

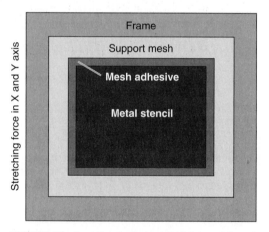

FIGURE 5.8 Stencil mounting to stencil frame with mesh border.

5.4.5.4 Stencil Fiducial Marks. Most stencil printers used for fine-pitch printing require fiducials for optical alignment of the stencil to the board. In order to do this, fiducials must be etched into the stencil. Fiducials are half-etched (etched from one side only) and then filled with black epoxy to provide the visual contrast. Stencil printers require the fiducials to be either on the top or bottom surface of the stencil depending on their configuration. Typically, only two or three fiducials are used by the stencil printer, although more may be etched on the stencil to allow for localized alignment optimization for fine-pitch dense areas of the board. Descriptive text is also half-etched into the stencil.

5.4.6 Squeegees

There are several types of squeegees for stencil printing. There are rubber (polyurethane) squeegees of varying hardness and geometry, and metal squeegees. Both rubber and metal squeegees are used widely.

5.4.6.1 Squeegee Configuration.   Rubber squeegees can be square with one corner contacting the stencil, vertically mounted with a V-shaped tip, or square-nosed and mounted at an angle depending on the stencil printer configuration (Fig. 5.9). Metal squeegees are made from a straight, thin strip of metal mounted at an angle. Metal blades are coated to reduce friction between the stencil and the blade. In all cases, the straightness and sharpness of the blade is very important to maintain a uniform and repeatable print. Rubber squeegees must be sharpened or replaced regularly.

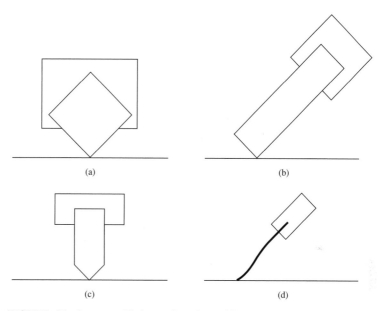

(a)

(b)

(c)

(d)

FIGURE 5.9   Squeegee blade configurations: (*a*) diamond tip; (*b*) square tip; (*c*) pointed tip; (*d*) metal blade.

5.4.6.2 Squeegee Material.   Squeegees can be made of rubber (polyurethane) of varying hardness or they can be made of metal. There are two major considerations in choosing a squeegee blade: maximum aperture width and whether a step-down stencil is used. The aperture width helps determine the squeegee hardness for polyurethane squeegees because of the scooping phenomenon. With scooping, the squeegee blade deflects into an aperture and reduces the print thickness. The phenomenon is most prevalent when the apertures are large, long, and parallel to the blade. A harder blade has less deflection, thus reducing the amount of scooping in the aperture. Step-down stencils, however, may require a slightly softer squeegee to conform to the step cavity. Squeegee hardness is usually 85 to 90 durometer for nonstep stencils and 70 to 85 for step stencils.

Metal squeegees are generally used only with nonstep stencils. Metal squeegees do not conform well for step stencils and require a large keepout area around step regions to allow deflection into the step region. Metal squeegees, however, virtually eliminate the scooping problem and make the printing process much less dependent on the squeegee pressure parameter. Metal squeegees, however, are more expensive than rubber squeegees.

5.5 SMT COMPONENTS

It is the availability of component packages for surface mounting that has allowed the dramatic move from through-hole technology to surface-mount technology. Since the early 1990s, most types of components have been offered in surface-mount packages, and as such, these components are often referred to as surface-mount devices (SMD). Some representative packages are shown in Fig. 5.10.

As can be seen, there are many different packaging families. In addition, there are many variations within each family. Component vendor recommendations need to be used with caution because they are often designed without knowledge of the assembly process to be used and are often tailored to one specific design and are not transferable to multiple component vendors.

There are two governing bodies which ratify standard specifications for component types and sizes: the Joint Electronic Device Engineering Council (JEDEC) and the Electronic

FIGURE 5.10   Typical surface-mount component packages.

Industries Association of Japan (EIAJ). These standards are converging with many package styles already matching; however, there are still a number of component packaging types which are not. Care must be taken in dealing with these specifications because, being a compilation of input from many vendors, they have a fairly wide specification window to meet many needs. Significant variation among vendors is possible while still meeting the specifications. Descriptions of the different component types can be found in Chaps. 1 and 2.

In order to achieve optimum solderability, each component must be matched with an appropriate land or pad shape when the printed circuit board is layed out. Otherwise, defects such as shown in Fig. 5.11 can occur frequently. Lists and sample shapes of the land patterns can be obtained from the Institute for Interconnecting and Packaging Electronics Circuits (IPC) document IPC-SM-782, from various consultant publications, or from other companies. A short list is provided in Chap. 15 of this book.

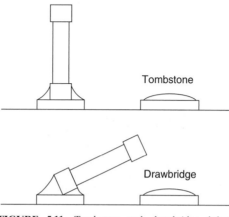

FIGURE 5.11 *Tombstone* and *drawbridge* defects occur when landpad geometry is not matched with the reflow process. This is most common when vapor phase reflow is used.

5.6   *DESIGN FOR MANUFACTURABILITY*

Design for manufacturability (DFM) is the discipline of evaluating and enhancing the manufacturability of a product during the design process within a concurrent engineering environment. The design phase is the key point where DFM concerns need to be considered: 80 percent of the cost of a product is determined during the design phase. Only minor reductions in cost are possible once a product is ready for production. DFM is one of the many considerations that must be included in the design of printed circuit assemblies. Other considerations include the design feature list, performance, cost, layout/density, and procurement issues. To be most effective, these tradeoffs must be made as a concurrent effort between manufacturing engineers, test engineers, electrical designers, component engineers, CAD designers, purchasing, and others.

In order to assure a manufacturable design, there are a number of considerations that must be addressed:

- DFM guidelines
- CAD design implementation
- CAD shapes

- Component spacing
- PCB layer stack-up
- PCB/component TCE
- Dimensional stability
- Stencil design
- Electrical performance requirements
- Other manufacturing features

5.6.1   DFM Guidelines

DFM guidelines provide a reference document where manufacturability requirements are documented. They are critical to implementing a cost-effective, consistently manufacturable product. DFM guidelines are available from a number of sources including the IPC (IPC-D-330, IPC-SM-782), contract assembly houses, and private consultants. They may need to be reviewed and modified to match the particular product to be manufactured.

5.6.2   CAD Design Implementation

Printed circuit computer-aided design (CAD) is the design implementation phase where the physical layout of the board is determined. CAD layout is the point at which the DFM guidelines, schematic design, and circuit electrical property requirements converge.

There are four basic stages in the design of the circuit board. They provide good checkpoints where the design progress can be reviewed and verified. The four design stages are:

- Board outline creation, including standard features
- Component placement
- Trace routing
- Postprocessing

5.6.2.1   Board Outline Creation.   Board outline creation is where the board size and form is determined as well as the layer stack-up. Many of the standard board features are also added at this point, such as tooling holes, mounting holes, fiducial registration marks, board labeling, and keepout locations. Global parameters are included with most CAD systems for the trace routing and spacings between pads, traces, and planes. Many of the DFM requirements can be incorporated into these keepout, routing, and spacing rules which define the CAD system constraints or through design rule checks (DRCs).

5.6.2.2   Placement.   Placement is the point at which the basic component positioning or "floor planning" takes place. Component shapes are placed to group the circuitry for a given functionality together and so that the signals and buses flow smoothly. Manufacturing issues for component spacing, component orientation, and thermal mass distribution must be addressed at this point.

5.6.2.3   Trace Routing.   Trace routing is usually accomplished by first manually routing critical signals such as clocks, then autorouting the bulk of the signals, followed by manual cleanup of the last few unrouted nets. Tools for autorouting the board can be simple or very sophisticated, with signal properties which allow control of trace width, trace spacing, and parallelism of nets. The trace width and spacing requirements are initially defined by the manufacturing constraints for the board stack-up.

5.6.2.4 *Postprocessing.* Postprocessing is where all of the layout cleanup and final feature implementation is accomplished. Some of the features that need to be implemented include reference designator numbering and positioning, test point assignment, regional fiducial assignment, and bare-board fabrication and assembly drawings. Artwork plots and fabrication and assembly drawings are generated and verified at this stage.

5.6.3 CAD Shapes

CAD shapes define the features needed to create a physical CAD representation of an object such as a component, plated-through-hole, or tooling hole. Most CAD systems support a library for shapes which allows standard land pad geometries for different package types to be generated and maintained. CAD shapes encompass the features for all layers of the board, including SMT land pads, stencil apertures, signal and plane layer pads, hole sizes, solder mask clearance, plane layer antipads, thermal clearance/ties, silkscreen, and pin one markers. CAD shapes play an important part in implementing the manufacturability, testability, and reliability of the PC assembly.

5.6.3.1 *Component Shapes.* SMT land patterns and stencil apertures are the most important part of an SMT component shape. They impact the defect rate and reliability of a PCA by defining the solder fillet shape and volume. The component shape defines the area onto which the lead is placed, the relative position of the lead foot to the land pad, and the volume and position of the solder paste.

There are many sources to obtain standard land patterns. The IPC (SM-782), contract manufacturers, and private consulting firms can all provide adequate land pattern shapes. 1.27-mm(0.050-in) pitch land patterns are very robust, and there is little variation from one source to another. Fine-pitch patterns, however, have more variability and often require custom designs to match the component vendors or meet board density requirements.

The length and separation of fine-pitch land pads for gullwing leads should provide a 0.5-mm (0.020-in) fillet for both the heel and toe at the inner- and outermost lead variances. The width of the land pad should be 0.002 to 0.003 in wider than either the stencil aperture or the maximum lead width. Wider land pads allow more side fillet on the solder joint and provide gasketing around the stencil aperture. Gasketing improves print quality and reduces the opportunity for paste to get under the stencil at the periphery of the stencil aperture.

Component shapes encompass more than just the SMT land pad sizes and stencil apertures. They also include the solder mask clearance, the keepout area around the part, and the silk screen outlines and reference designators. The solder mask clearance for liquid photoimageable (LPI) materials is generally 0.002 to 0.003 in per side. The placement, route, and plated-through-hole (PTH) keepouts around or under the component shape must be determined for each component type.

5.6.3.2 *Plated-Through-Holes.* The plated-through-holes (PTH) are the drilled and plated holes in the bare PCB. PTHs are used to provide electrical connections between layers (vias) or for soldering THT components. PTH via connections are designed as small as possible to save real estate on the board and improve routing density. PCB thickness to via diameter aspect ratios up to 6:1 are common. Higher aspect ratios often command a cost premium and require PCB fabrication vendors with more advanced technology capabilities.

The CAD shape features that must be specified are the finished hole size, pad diameter, antipad for power/ground plane clearance, and thermal connections to plane layers. Finished hole size refers to the diameter of the PTH after copper plating of the barrel plus any solder coating.

The antipad refers to the clearance around the vias on the plane layers to ensure that no connection will be made between a signal via and the plane layer. Thermal connections are used to connect vias to plane layers. A reduced thermal connection is often required on plane layers to ensure PTH solder fill during wave and to ensure reworkability of THT components. Thermal connections consist of an antipad with three or four ties from the plane to the via pad to create the electrical connection.

5.6.3.3   *Other Shapes.* CAD shapes can be created for any number of other features, including fiducials, heat sinks, test patterns, test points, tooling holes, and mounting holes.

5.6.4   Component Spacing

Component spacing requirements have a direct effect on the density of a PCB design and, therefore, the manufacturability of the board. The spacing requirements need to be well specified and communicated to the PCB CAD designers, including relative orientations of packages with corresponding minimum spacing rules. Spacing rules in general refer to the land pad to land pad spacing. Any component body overhang needs to be accounted for in the land pad spacing values. There are a number of considerations in determining the required component spacing:

- Rework
- Process considerations (i.e., shadowing)
- Inspection
- Placement equipment
- Thermal layout

Rework spacing considerations include the ability to access solder joints with rework tools and equipment without damaging the assembly or exceeding the maximum adjacent component temperature (see Sec. 5.16.3). Process considerations include minimizing shadowing of solder joints which could lead to incomplete soldering. Inspection considerations concern the ability to inspect the solder joint fillets to assure adequate solder volume and reflow conditions. Placement equipment considerations include assuring that the assembly step sequence does not allow components to be placed which could interfere with later placement operations.

5.6.5   PCB Layer Stack-up

The layer stack-up refers to the specification of the number of power/ground and signal layers, the order of those layers, the line width and spacing for the different types of signals to be routed, the board construction material and dielectric constant, the distance between layers, and the resulting transmission line impedance. PCB layer stack-up must be done either during schematic design or as a first step in the CAD layout process. Many things are determined when the layer stack-up is chosen, such as minimum trace width and spacing, trace impedance, board thickness, and number of routing layers.

5.6.6   PCB/Comp TCE

The printed circuit laminate thermal coefficient of expansion (TCE) directly affects the reliability of solder joints and vias and must be fully understood to assure a reliable product. The TCE mismatch between a component and the board creates one of the greatest sources of reliability problems. As an assembly thermally cycles, the board and components expand and contract at different rates causing localized microscopic stresses on the solder joints. Repeated thermal cycles cause crack growth and eventual fracture of the solder joints. The z-axis TCE is also important and affects the reliability of the via barrels. Repeated reflow temperature thermal cycles can cause radial circumferential cracks leading to intermittent connections.

TCE problems can be minimized in three ways: selecting materials with similar TCEs, providing adequate compliance in the solder joint (usually with lead form), or reducing the geometry of the component so the TCE differences do not create large stresses. In the case of vias, thinner boards and lower z-axis TCE can minimize barrel cracking problems.

5.6.7   Dimensional Stability

Dimensional stability refers to the ability of the bare circuit board to maintain its CAD design dimensions through printed circuit fabrication and assembly thermal cycles. Dimensional stability problems increase linearly with board size. Typical PCB stretch specifications (IPC-A-600) allow 0.1 percent distortion, inch per inch.

The board-to-stencil alignment problem is a major concern for larger boards with fine-pitch devices (<=0.065 mm). The stencil and boards are produced by different vendors using the same CAD data. If they do not match, the solder paste can be applied with misalignment in opposite directions at the edges of a board and the stencil alignment cannot fix the problem. There are two approaches to resolve this problem: minimize the variation at the board vendor by characterizing the materials and making artwork corrections to scale the image, or laying out the board so that the most sensitive fine-pitch components are placed near the center of the board to minimize the effect.

5.6.8   Other Design Considerations

There are many other design considerations which affect manufacturing features and consistency including:

- Fiducials
- Reference designators
- Board features
- Component orientation
- Panelization

5.6.8.1   Fiducials.   Fiducials are needed on PCBs to permit vision alignment of the stencil and components to the board. There are two types of fiducials: global and local. Global fiducials are placed in at least three corners of the board. They should be placed so that the fiducials are nonsymmetric to prevent the board from being processed upside down or backwards. Three fiducials provide better alignment by allowing independent x- and y-axis distortion correction.

Local fiducials are used to eliminate component placement variation due to localized PCB pattern distortion. Local fiducials should be placed within 4 in of all fine-pitch devices.

5.6.8.2   Reference Designators.   Reference designators should be numbered in a logical, ordered flow. The common methodology is to start at one corner and number in rows across the board. Different types of components have different alphanumeric designations, i.e., U100, R100, C100 for ICs, resistors, and capacitors, respectively. The important point is to create a standard numbering scheme so any part can be found quickly by reference designator.

5.6.8.3   Board Features.   There are several board features that are required on all boards. Some of these include component and routing keepouts, tooling holes, board part number, revision box, regulatory markings, and place of origin marking. Keepouts need to be specified at the beginning of the PCB layout process. Other features are used when needed, such as serial number, barcode label, and mounting holes. Many of these features do not have a required position so they can be placed either where space permits in the usable area of the board or in the component keepout area along the edges of the board.

5.6.8.4 *Component Orientation.* Wave-soldered SMT components have a distinctly preferred component orientation. This preferred orientation is very important for defect rate reduction. Reflow-soldered components, however, do not have an inherently preferred orientation. For reflow-soldered components, it is important that the orientation of the components be easily recognizable to assist placement verification and to assure that rework or hand-load components are placed correctly. The preferred method for reflowed components sets pin number one on components in a standard direction. Pin one must be marked clearly with arrows, dots, numbers, notches on component outlines, or some other recognizable mark.

5.6.8.5 *Panelization.* Panelization refers to creating a multiple-image panel for PC assembly. The method of depanelization is a critical decision. The individual images can be routed with connecting tabs or left fully connected to the process panel. Connecting tabs can be of several different types: solid, which require routing or shearing after assembly; perforated holes, which are manually broken but can leave a rough edge; and scored with a V-cut, which are also manually broken but provide a smoother edge.

5.7 ASSEMBLY FLOW

There are different flows for the printed circuit assembly process depending on what type of components are loaded on the board and which side they are placed on. The standard processes are:

- Single-sided SMT (Type I: SMT components on the top side of the board; see Fig. 5.12*a*)
- Mixed SMT, through-hole (Type II: SMT and through-hole components; SMT possible on bottom side, wave solder of bottom-side SMT, and through-hole components; see Fig. 5.12*a* plus Fig. 5.12*b*)
- Double-sided reflow (Type III: SMT on both sides of the board; reflow process used for both sides; see Fig. 5.12*c*)
- Additional processes (additional assembly process steps usually performed after the standard SMT reflow/wave processes such as TAB, DCA; see Fig. 5.12*a* plus Fig. 5.12*d*)

5.8 STENCIL PRINTING

Stencil printing is the SMT process step where solder paste is applied to the bare circuit board using a stencil and squeegee. Traditional screen printing of solder paste has been almost totally replaced by stencil printing because of the ease of use, decreased process variability, and improved consistency. The squeegee pushes a bead of paste across the top of the stencil which is positioned above the bare circuit board, forcing the solder paste into apertures in the stencil (Fig. 5.13). When the stencil is lifted from the board, solder bricks are left on the individual SMT land pads.

The stencil-printing process is one of the most critical process steps in surface-mount technology. The solder paste variables must be optimized with the stencil and machine variables to assure a high-yield process. Well-formed and -aligned solder bricks are the prerequisite for

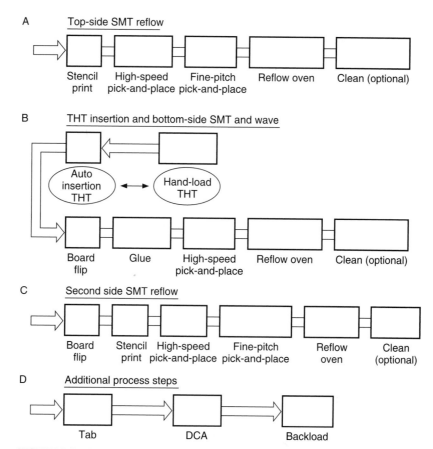

FIGURE 5.12   Surface-mount technology (SMT) process flow: (*a*) single-sided SMT; (*b*) mixed SMT, through-hole technology (THT) backside wave solder; (*c*) double-sided SMT; (*d*) additional process steps.

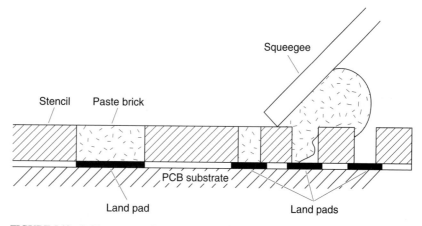

FIGURE 5.13   Solder paste application with stencil printing.

a low-defect-rate assembly process. The stencil-printing process requires optimization of a number of parameters:

Machine Control Parameters

- Squeegee pressure
- Squeegee speed
- Print cycle
- Stencil snap-off
- Stencil lift-off speed
- Squeegee angle
- Stencil alignment

Other Process Parameters

- Stencil aperture and thickness dimensions
- Stencil washing and wiping
- Temperature/humidity
- Reprinting boards
- Support fixture/tooling plates

5.8.1 Squeegee Pressure

Squeegee pressure, along with squeegee speed, are the most important stencil-print machine parameters. The squeegee pressure determines the downward hydraulic force pushing the solder paste into the stencil apertures. The squeegee pressure must be enough to wipe the stencil cleanly around all stencil apertures. If a step stencil is used, the squeegee must deflect into the recessed area and wipe cleanly around the fine-pitch pads. The ledge around the perimeter of the step area will still accumulate some paste.

The relationship of the squeegee pressure to the solder paste volume is complex. One aspect of the squeegee pressure is the contact angle of the squeegee to the stencil surface. Higher squeegee pressure causes more deflection of the squeegee tip and a more acute angle of contact. The more acute angle of contact creates a higher downward hydraulic pressure, pushing paste into the stencil aperture and resulting in a better volume fill.

Another aspect of squeegee deflection is the amount of compliancy of the squeegee tip. A compliant squeegee can scoop into a stencil aperture and reduce the total volume of solder paste deposited in the aperture (Fig. 5.14). Higher squeegee pressure results in more deflection and therefore more scooping in the stencil apertures. Harder squeegee blades can minimize this effect because they are less compliant and deflect less into the apertures. Metal blades create very little scooping and have a much reduced effect of squeegee pressure on the print volume.

5.8.2 Squeegee Speed

Squeegee speed is also a very important stencil-print parameter. Squeegee speed is usually set at the high end of the acceptable range to decrease stencil print cycle time. Typical squeegee speeds are in the 25- to 50-mm/s range. Squeegee speed has a complex relationship with the paste viscosity, squeegee pressure, and squeegee angle.

For any given paste viscosity, there must be enough downward force and time to allow the solder paste to fill the stencil aperture and push all the air out of the cavity. Higher squeegee

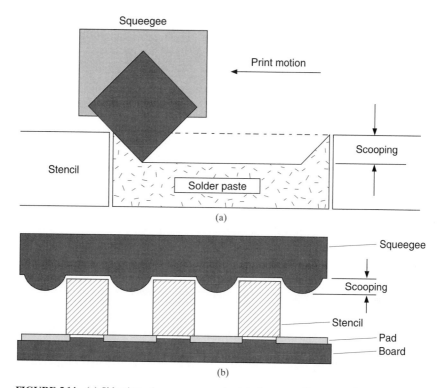

FIGURE 5.14   (*a*) Side view of squeegee scooping into large stencil aperture; (*b*) scooping with squeegee perpendicular to fine-pitch stencil apertures.

speed creates lower dynamic paste viscosity, which makes the solder paste easier to push into the stencil apertures. Increasing the squeegee speed also increases the hydraulic forces at the tip of the squeegee blade, pushing the solder paste into the stencil apertures. If the squeegee speed is too fast, however, the paste will not have time to completely fill the stencil cavity and push out all of the air, and the solder paste brick will have insufficient volume.

The squeegee pressure and squeegee angle also have an effect. A more acute squeegee angle causes higher hydraulic forces on the solder paste at the squeegee tip. If the squeegee speed increases such that the hydraulic forces are greater than the squeegee pressure at the tip, the squeegee will hydroplane and give excessive printed solder volume.

5.8.3   Stencil Snap-off

Stencil snap-off refers to the separation between the stencil and the printed circuit board during the printing process. High snap-off (>0.020 in) is used to help peel the stencil away from the PC board during the printing process. The squeegee pushes the stencil down to contact the bare PC board and push paste into the stencil apertures. As the squeegee passes over a portion of the board, the tension from the mesh border pulls the stencil back off the board, leaving the solder paste brick on the PC board. A well-tensioned stencil is required to make this work.

Setting the snap-off distance low (<0.005 in) keeps the stencil effectively contacting the PC board until the end of the stencil printer cycle, at which time the whole stencil is lifted off the

PC board in one motion. Low snap-off helps prevent any print shift due to the squeegee pulling the stencil in one direction. Low snap-off can also be a problem if a vacuum tooling plate is used to hold the PCB. Any vacuum leakage can pull flux and solder balls under the stencil between the stencil and board and cause solder balls and print degradation.

5.8.4 Stencil Liftoff Speed

Stencil liftoff speed control is available on many automated stencil printers. This parameter allows the machine to lift the stencil off the printed board (or lower the board away from the stencil) in a very controlled manner. This motion is intended to allow the solder paste to pull away from the stencil slowly so that the solder paste has time to release from the walls in the stencil aperture. Machines without this capability have an abrupt separation between the board and stencil which can cause a significant portion of the paste to remain in the stencil aperture if the paste is very viscous or if the stencil aperture side-wall texture does not allow easy release of the solder paste.

5.8.5 Squeegee Angle

Squeegee angle refers to the contact angle between the squeegee and the stencil surface. This parameter is usually a hardware adjustment and is not changed from one setup to the next. The typical squeegee mounting angles are 45 or 60°. A more acute squeegee angle increases the hydraulic forces pushing the solder paste into the stencil apertures. The squeegee angle must be set to give the solder paste enough downward hydraulic force to fill the stencil apertures yet not allow the squeegee to hydroplane with the given squeegee pressure, resulting in an excessively thick brick deposit. The pressure of the squeegee can also cause the squeegee to deflect and make the contact angle more acute.

5.8.6 Stencil Alignment

Alignment of the stencil to the printed circuit board is critical to achieve proper placement of the solder paste brick on the SMT land pads. Stencil alignment requirements are dependent on the board size, the component pitch, and the stencil and printed circuit board variances. Proper stencil alignment is made difficult because the stencil and printed circuit board are manufactured by separate vendors with different tolerances. The stencil alignment cannot make up for the mismatch of the PCB to the stencil but it can split the mismatch so that the center is most perfectly aligned and both ends have half of the total variance but in opposite directions. The combined tolerance stack-up should, at minimum, assure that the paste brick and the entire length of the lead foot have contact.

Most stencil printers used for components with 0.65-mm(0.0256-in) pitch and smaller have automatic vision alignment of the stencil to the board. The vision-aligned stencil printers require fiducial alignment targets on the board and the stencil to use for alignment. Many systems use two fiducials, although three-fiducial systems are superior because they allow stencil alignment to be optimized in both x and y axes instead of a combined average.

5.8.7 Stencils

The stencil material requirements and fabrication process options are discussed in detail in Sec. 5.4.5. There are several decisions that must be made in selecting the proper stencil for the product and process. These decisions concern:

- Stencil thickness (step-down)
- Stencil material
- Aperture size
- Aperture profile
- Fiducial/text etch, mounting

5.8.7.1 *Stencil Thickness.*

Stencil thickness is determined by the smallest stencil aperture size for the finest-component pitch. The minimum aperture width–to–stencil thickness aspect ratio should not be less than 1.5:1 for a robust printing process. Stencils are most commonly 0.005, 0.006, or 0.008 in thick with the 0.005-in thickness reserved for ultrafine pitch (0.4 mm [0.0157 in] pitch). Stencils that are 0.006 or 0.008 in can be used for 1.27-mm (0.050-in) pitch; however, the stencil aperture dimensions may need to be adjusted to provide the correct solder volume. Hot-air (solder) leveled (HAL or HASL) boards require less solder deposited in the form of paste than organic coated boards or gold boards because they have a solder coating in the range of 100 to 2000 μin. Finer-pitch products (down to 0.5-mm [0.0197-in] pitch) most commonly use 0.006-in-thick stencils to improve the stencil aperture aspect ratio and also provide a more appropriate volume of solder paste.

Step-down stencils can also be used to allow the larger-pitch areas to maintain higher paste thickness and volume while the fine-pitch areas use a thinner stencil for a better aspect ratio and more appropriate printed paste volume. Step-down stencils have the fine-pitch areas etched down from 0.008 to 0.006 in or 0.006 to 0.005 in, depending on the component pitch. More than 0.002 in is generally considered to be too large of a step. There are a number of negatives for step stencils, however, because they:

- Require a large component keepaway around components in the step-down region to allow for the squeegee deflection into the stepped region during printing. The keepaway for rubber squeegee blades is approximately 0.200 in minimum and 0.400 in maximum for metal squeegee blades.
- Require an additional etching step to reduce the step region before the stencil can have the apertures etched.
- Are more difficult to etch because of reduced etch-resist adhesion, artwork distortion in the step region, and differing etch factors because of the different stencil thickness.
- Are more susceptible to handling damage.

5.8.7.2 *Stencil Aperture Size and Profile.*

The stencil aperture size can be adjusted to provide the appropriate solder paste volume, optimize the stencil printing process, or accommodate multiple vendors for a particular package. In general, 1.27-mm(0.050-in) pitch and discrete passive components use a 1:1 stencil aperture–to–land pad match. Pitch components of 0.65 mm (0.0256 in) and smaller require a smaller stencil aperture than land pad. The reason is twofold: (1) The finer-pitch components do not require a full land pad size paste brick volume, and (2) a slightly narrower stencil aperture provides a gasket effect around the stencil aperture so that solder paste and flux do not have the opportunity to flow into the gap between the fine-pitch pads. This gasket effect greatly extends the number of prints possible before the stencil must be wiped or washed and also reduces the number of bridges by assuring a better separation between the printed paste bricks. One formula sometimes used to select the proper stencil aperture is the land pad minus 20 percent for both width and length.

The etched size tolerance is very important to maintain a controlled stencil-print process and provide the proper solder volume for reflow. The size tolerance for stencil apertures should be ±0.001 in for 0.65-mm (0.0256-in) pitch and smaller apertures and ±0.002 in for 1.27-mm (0.050-in) pitch apertures and larger.

The stencil aperture profile is also very important. The ideal stencil aperture has vertical side walls or slightly tapered (0.0005 to 0.00075 in/edge) with the bottom wider than the top. There are many manufacturing options for stencils, as discussed in Sec. 5.5.5. The most common stencil is chemically etched (304) stainless steel. Care must be taken with chemically etched stencils, however, because the knife-edge at the center of the aperture can cause the solder paste not to release from the stencil onto the board during stencil print. The knife-edge should be no more than 0.0005 in per edge for 0.65-mm (0.0256-in) pitch and smaller apertures. Laser-cut stencils are a very good alternative which eliminates the knife-edge with chemical etch and provides a very good aperture size tolerance as well. Laser stencils, however, are more expensive and have a longer lead time.

5.8.8   Stencil Washing and Wiping

Stencils must be cleaned regularly to maintain good print definition and print volume. Cleaning can be in the form of wiping the bottom of the stencil or removing the stencil from the stencil printer and washing the whole stencil. Wiping the bottom side of the stencil is usually done to remove solder paste balls and flux that have collected on the bottom side of the stencil. Solder balls on the bottom of the stencil can hold the stencil off the board and cause more balls and flux to push under the stencil. This leads to poorly defined solder paste bricks and solder balls around the pads after reflow.

Washing the stencil is recommended any time the stencil print quality has degraded such that it deposits less than 80 percent of the target volume of solder paste or when the stencil will not be used for a long period of time (usually more than ½ to 1 h). Washing stencils is usually done with a dedicated stencil-washing machine. The solvent can be DI water, water with a saponifier, or, in special cases, alcohol. Freon has been virtually eliminated as a solvent because of the environmental concerns. Stencils must be completely dry before mounting on the stencil printer.

5.8.9   Reprinting Boards

Stencil-print rejects can be wiped, washed, and reused as long as the wash cycle is sufficient to remove all of the solder balls. Solder balls pick up static charge and can cling to the PC board in inconvenient places such as via holes, solder mask pockets (especially corners), and near special plating areas. Solder balls left on a reprinted board will reflow and can contaminate gold pads or edge connectors and can coalesce into larger balls which must be washed off during the cleaning cycle. PC boards must be completely dry before reprinting.

5.8.10   Temperature and Humidity

Solder paste viscosity can vary dramatically when the temperature in the factory or stencil printer rises above 28 or below 20°C or when the relative humidity is above 60 percent. In these cases, environmental control on the stencil printer is recommended. The solder paste vendor recommendations for operating environment should be followed.

5.8.11   Support Fixture and Tooling Plate

Stencil printing requires some form of support fixture or tooling plate to hold and support the printed circuit board. Support fixtures and tooling plates utilize various types of hold-down mechanisms, such as vacuum, tooling pins, and edge grips. Any of these methods will work if implemented properly. Vacuum tends to be the most difficult to use because of the need for gasketing around the vacuum points and the changeover required to accommodate different board via and through-hole patterns. With improper gasketing the solder paste can also be drawn through the stencil apertures and underneath the stencil, leaving a fringe of solder paste around the pads and poor print definition. The stencil will then need to be washed or wiped much more frequently.

Tooling pins and edge grips both hold the printed circuit board well. Tooling pins are most accurate for systems without vision alignment. Edge grips provide the most flexibility for board setup and changeover. A flat plate or any kind of area support can be used to support the board during the printing process for single-sided SMT boards. Two-sided boards, however, require uniquely placed supports to hold the board or a tooling plate with cavities for bottom-side components.

5.8.12 Cycle Time

Stencil-print cycle time is usually much shorter than the component placement time. The cycle time of the stencil-print process is usually dictated by the speed of the squeegee. Only in high-volume production lines where the component count is low or the component placement capacity is dramatically increased does the stencil-print cycle time become a concern. Stencil printers can usually print with a cycle time under 30 s, depending on the size of board. The cycle time is generally 60 to 70 percent squeegee travel and 30 to 40 percent board handling and associated print cycle operations.

5.9 SOLDER PASTE DISPENSING

Solder paste dispensing is an alternative to stencil printing. Dispensing is a much more time-intensive process than stencil printing and is also not as consistent. Dispensing has two niches where it is ideally suited: rework and fast-turn prototypes. Dispensing is used in rework to add solder and flux to pads where a new part is to be placed. These systems are usually hand operated. Fast-turn prototypes can also use dispensing to eliminate the tooling costs with stencils and allow quick-turn application of solder paste. Dispensing, however, is not widely used for prototyping because of the predominance of stencil-printing expertise, the mass application capability, and the more uniform shape and volume with stencils.

5.10 COMPONENT PLACEMENT

Component placement equipment development has made great strides over the last five to seven years. There are many models of equipment available which provide high-accuracy and high-speed placement capability with very good reliability. The optimal solution for any factory or product line depends on many things, including the component styles, total number of feeders on-line, capital budget, and speed requirements. Placement equipment comes in two general categories: high-speed machines for smaller component sizes and high-accuracy, large-component machines with package size flexibility for fine-pitch and larger-body-size components.

5.10.1 Placement Speed

SMT placement speed has improved steadily. The rated placement speeds for high-speed placement machines are commonly in the 24,000 to 28,000 placements/h range with some equipment rated at 38,000 placements/h. High-accuracy, large-component placement equipment speed is much lower at 5000 to 8000 placements/h, but they have the capability to handle fine-pitch and large-body-size components, which often require picking from component trays. These quoted speeds must be derated to account for the type of components being placed, the layout of the board, and the board-handling time to get the expected placement time for a real board. Actual achievable placement rates are typically 50 to 70 percent of the advertised speed.

5.10.2 Equipment Programming

SMT placement equipment is almost universally programmed using the board CAD data for each component. There are usually two components to the placement program: CAD data for a particular board and component description information by package type. The board CAD data provides the *x-y* position, rotation, part number or feeder number, package type, and top-versus-bottom information. The component description information is usually in a database library and includes information about feeder size, feeder pitch, pickup point, vacuum nozzle size, placement speed, component dimensions, standard orientation, placement pressure, and, sometimes, fiducial location.

Many companies have attained automated data transfer from the schematic design, through the CAD design phase, all the way to the production floor. With the size and complexity of many of the board designs, manual manipulation of CAD data is impractical and can lead to many errors and production delays. There are a number of software packages available which will take CAD data from most any board CAD design system and create a machine program for the most common placement equipment brands. These software programs can determine the optimal feeder setup for a single board or set of boards and also optimize the placement sequence to minimize cycle time.

5.10.3 Component Feeders

There are many different types of feeders to handle the many different geometries of components. The four types of feeders are

- Tape and reel
- Tray
- Tube
- Bulk

Tape and reel feeders use a reel of components which have been loaded into an embossed plastic or paper tape. The tape has cavities for the components and a plastic film cover over the cavities to hold them in place. When the plastic film is pulled back, the component can be picked out of the pocket and placed onto the board. Used tape is then sheared off as the new portion of the tape advances. Tape and reel feeders are the preferred method for the delivery packaging of most electrical components because of the ease of handling, the large number of parts on a single reel, the feeder speed and reliability, and the protection provided for the components. They can handle a wide range of components from the smallest passives to the 84-pin PLCC, including some fine-pitch components.

Tray feeders are used for fine-pitch components and very large components which cannot fit in tape and reel. Trays are stackable and have a matrix of cavities which support and position the components while protecting the leads from contact and damage.

Tube feeders are very common and use gravity, vibration, or forced air to slide the component down into the pickup position. Tube feeders are easy to use but require frequent replenishing in production. Tube feeders are used either for components with leads on two opposing sides so that the bodies of the components are butted together and the leads do not risk damage or for four-sided leaded components with robust leads such as PLCCs.

Bulk feeders are used for small, inexpensive components which are not easily damaged. These components are usually cheaper in bulk. Bulk feeders are often vibratory feeders.

5.11   *REFLOW SOLDERING*

Reflow soldering is the SMT assembly process where solder paste, which has already been deposited on the board, is reflowed (melted) to form an electrical and mechanical connection between the printed circuit board and the individual component leads. There are four general types of reflow technologies:

- Vapor phase
- Infrared
- Natural convection
- Forced-air convection

Convection reflow ovens, particularly forced-air convection reflow ovens, have become the technology of choice for most SMT needs.

5.11.1   Reflow Process

The reflow profile has four distinct sections (Fig. 5.15):

- Preheat temperature ramp sections
- Stabilize or flux activation sections

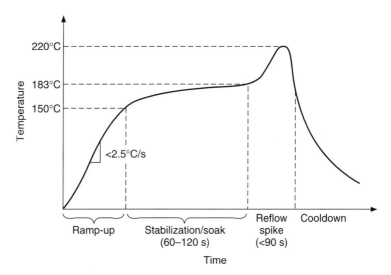

FIGURE 5.15   Typical infrared (IR) oven reflow temperature profile.

- Reflow temperature ramp sections
- Cool-down sections

5.11.1.1 Preheat Temperature Ramp.   The first portion of the reflow profile, the preheat temperature ramp, brings the board up to the flux activation temperature. The ramp rate must not be so fast that the ceramic components crack, but it must be fast enough to satisfy the production rate requirements. The maximum ramp rate generally quoted by most passive component vendors is 3°C/s. Most reflow profiles use ramp rates in the 2 to 2.5°C/s range. The preheat ramp takes components from ambient up to the flux activation temperature (130 to 150°C).

5.11.1.2 Stabilization Region.   The stabilization region (sometimes called the *soak* region) serves three purposes:

- To allow the temperature variations across assembly to stabilize before reflow
- To provide time at an elevated temperature for the activated flux to clean the component leads, land pads, and solder powder before reflow
- To allow flux volatiles to evaporate before reflow

Flux activation temperature is typically in the 140 to 160°C range. The stabilization region time is typically 30 to 45 s.

5.11.1.3 Reflow Temperature Ramp.   The reflow temperature ramp region quickly raises the solder temperature above the melting point to allow all joints to reflow smoothly and uniformly. The typical maximum reflow temperature for various locations on the assembly is in the 200 to 220°C range, depending on the component type and location on the board.

Low-thermal-mass regions need to be profiled as well as high-thermal-mass regions. All regions of the assembly should have peak reflow temperatures in the 200 to 225°C range. Higher than this, and the flux may become baked on the board and difficult to clean, component damage can occur, and the epoxy material in the printed circuit board can become degraded. Lower than this, and the joints may not reflow fully.

5.11.1.4 Cool-down Region.   The cool-down region of the profile must lower the temperature of the PCA below the melting point of the solder quickly enough to prevent the creation of excessive nonsolderable intermetallics on the pads. Bringing the temperature down below the melting point quickly minimizes the oxidation of the leads and joints and provides a smaller crystal structure within the solder joint for greater reliability and strength. The assembly must exit the reflow oven with solidified joints, or joint integrity may be sacrificed. Oxidation of unloaded land pads (for secondary side soldering) and through-hole pads must also be minimized. The ideal time above reflow is 60 s, although up to 90 s is considered acceptable.

5.11.2 Reflow Profiling

Reflow soldering requires in-depth understanding and control of the critical process parameters. There are many machine parameter combinations which can create a workable profile. Optimization of the process parameters needs to be done for the particular product being built. Size, distribution, and thermal mass of both the bare PC board and the components can vary significantly between product types. The equipment parameters must be set up for each product to achieve the desired optimal profile. It is important to note that the equipment setup parameters may change from one assembly to the next but the resulting thermal profile experienced by any assembly should not.

5.11.2.1 *Inert Atmosphere Soldering.* Many ovens have options for inert atmosphere (nitrogen) soldering. Nitrogen atmosphere is not required in many applications to achieve acceptable reflow results, but it does improve the defect rate significantly and also provides much shinier and more aesthetically pleasing solder joints. Nitrogen is used extensively for no-clean applications.

Another large benefit with nitrogen soldering is that the SMT land pads and through-hole pads which are not soldered in the first-pass assembly operation have significantly less oxidation created during the first pass through a nitrogen reflow oven. Nitrogen concentrations are effective in the 100 to 300 ppm oxygen range. Ultra-high-purity systems (0 to 20 ppm oxygen) provide marginally better results at much higher nitrogen consumption rates.

5.11.2.2 *Vapor Phase Reflow.* Vapor phase reflow technology utilizes a high-boiling-point (approximately 213°C), inert, CFC-based material which, when vaporized, condenses on the printed circuit assembly and heats the board to the melting point of the solder. When the solder is melted, the solder joint is formed.

Vapor phase technology has advantages in that it cannot overheat the PCA and it has a very large capacity to transfer heat to the assembly. Vapor phase technology is still used in situations where very high thermal masses must be soldered.

There are a number of disadvantages, however, with vapor phase technology. The inert material is very expensive and the drag-out of the material in and under components can make the production costs quite high. The most common formulations, also, are being phased out because they contain chlorofluorocarbons (CFC).

5.11.2.3 *Infrared Reflow.* Infrared (IR) reflow uses blackbody radiation to heat the assembly (Fig. 5.16). Quartz lamps are commonly used as the primary IR radiation source with a reemitting back panel to stabilize the air temperature and broaden the radiation emission spectrum. IR ovens usually have no more than 50 percent IR heat transfer with the other 50 percent being natural convection from the air in the heating chamber. The highest IR transfer rate is achieved in the preheat and reflow ramp zones. The stabilization zone, however, is virtually 100 percent convection. IR ovens are being phased out in favor of forced-air convection ovens, which have higher heating capacity and provide more uniform profiles.

5.11.2.4 *Natural Convection Reflow.* Natural convection reflow equipment, usually just called convection reflow, has been the dominant reflow technique for many years. Natural convection equipment uses heated panels to control the bulk temperature of the air inside the oven and thus control the heat transfer to the PCA (Fig. 5.17). Heat transfer occurs through natural convection. The equipment layout is very similar to IR convection reflow, except that they use heated panels instead of IR lamps as a heat source. Also, response to heavy board loading is slow and spacing must be controlled.

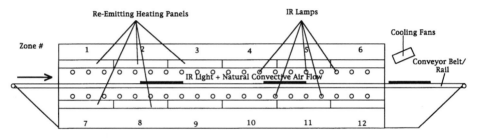

FIGURE 5.16 Infrared (IR) reflow equipment.

Profile changeover time is also a problem with natural convection. Because of the high thermal mass and the slow heat dissipation of the natural convection equipment, changing from a hotter profile to a cooler profile requires a lengthy stabilization period. Loading of the oven can be a concern if many high-thermal-mass components are processed in quick succession. A highly loaded oven can create a significantly different profile for the board than a lightly loaded oven, given the same setup parameters because of the response time of the heaters and the bulk air temperature. Profiling is recommended to characterize the loading conditions of the oven as well as the thermal mass of the assembly.

5.11.2.5 Forced-Air Convection Reflow.

Forced-air convection reflow utilizes pressurized hot air impinging on the printed circuit assembly to reflow the board. The hot air flows through holes in the backing plates both above and below the board (Fig. 5.18). The forced air helps to increase the heat transfer rate and disperse the heat energy evenly across the assembly.

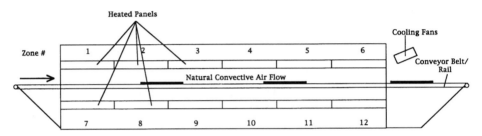

FIGURE 5.17 Natural convection reflow equipment.

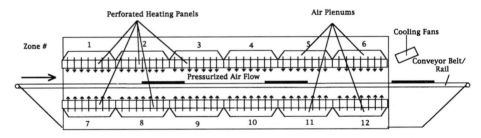

FIGURE 5.18 Forced-air convection reflow oven.

Forced-air convection reflow is the technology of choice at present. It offers a number of advantages over other reflow techniques:

- More uniform heating
- Less profile variation between products
- Higher heat transfer capability
- Higher throughput of larger-mass assemblies

The main advantage of forced-air convection reflow as compared with natural convection or IR reflow stems from the superior heat transfer produced by the air flow impinging on the printed circuit assembly. The forced-air convection oven provides a uniform temperature air blanket which heats the board evenly and produces a constant air flow which ensures maximum heat transfer.

The uniform heating allows boards with a wide distribution of thermal mass to be processed without creating large temperature variations across the board. This uniform heating also allows boards with similar thermal density to be processed with the same reflow setup parameters. The high heat transfer rate allows boards with a higher overall thermal mass to be processed without excessively slowing the machine belt speed.

The forced-air convection ovens have a lower temperature set point than natural convection ovens due to the efficiency of heat transfer. This then reduces the risk of overheating a low-density section of the board.

5.12   ADHESIVE ATTACHMENT OF COMPONENTS

SMT components on the secondary side of the printed circuit assembly are often attached with adhesive to hold components in place during the reflow or wave-solder processes. In reflow processes, the adhesive is used for components which will be on the bottom of the board, i.e., upside down, during the second pass through the SMT reflow process. Surface tension of the solder is not a reliable means to hold larger-mass (>32-pin PLCC) components onto the bottom of the board while the board, components, and solder are above reflow temperature.

The most common use of adhesive attachment of components, however, is for bottom-side wave solder of SMT components. After the normal SMT top-side assembly process, the board is flipped, the glue is applied to the PCB, the SMT components are placed, and the PCA assembly is heated or exposed to UV light to cure the glue. The through-hole components are then loaded and the assembly is passed through the wave solder equipment to form the THT and SMT solder joints.

The adhesive must be able to bridge the gap between the board and the component and hold the component firmly in place. The shear strength is typically 3 to 4 lb for passives and 4 to 5 lb for plastic body components. The epoxy must be deposited underneath the component but must not get onto the solder joint pads. Epoxies are normally removable after heating with heat guns or soldering irons.

5.13   WAVE SOLDERING

Wave soldering was designed for mass soldering of through-hole components on a PCA. It has been extended to include soldering of select SMT components on the bottom side of the circuit board. In the wave-solder process, printed circuit boards loaded with components, which have their solderable leads and pads accessible on the bottom of the board, are passed over a flux applicator which coats the bottom of the board and component leads with flux, followed by a heating section which preheats the board and activates the cleaning agents in the flux. The boards are then passed over one or two waves of molten solder to create a solder connection between the component lead and the PCB pad (Fig. 5.19).

5.13.1   Wave-Soldered Components

The types of parts that are wave soldered are through-hole components of all types, SMT passives and discretes, and SMT ICs. Passive SMT devices and discrete transistors and diodes are the predominant types of SMT components that are wave soldered onto the bottom of PCAs. Discrete resistors and capacitors of 1812 body size or larger are not recommended for wave-soldering applications because of their tendency to crack due to the thermal shock when the solder wave contacts the components.

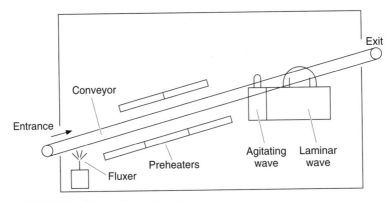

FIGURE 5.19   Wave-solder equipment.

ICs are not commonly wave soldered onto PCAs. The problems with wave soldering ICs are due to the thermal shock during wave soldering causing cracks, mold-seam splits, and delamination between the molded plastic and the lead frame. Some of the crack defects show up only after a period of use and can cause premature failure of products in the field. With careful process control, however, small ICs (SOICs <0.300-in body width) can be successfully wave soldered.

5.13.2   Layout Considerations

Wave-soldered components must be positioned on the PC board with the correct orientation and spacing to assure high yield during wave soldering. Components should be oriented so the solder wave is not required to go over the body of the component to reach the solder joints. For discrete passives, this means that the solder wave should contact both leads of the component at the same time. For small-outline components (SOIC, SOT), the solder wave should contact the leads along both sides of the component at the same time (Fig. 5.20).

Components should also be placed so that they do not shadow other components. Components which block access of the wave to other component leads (does not apply to same-size components which are in line) must have spacing distance at least twice the height of the tallest component. This spacing will allow adequate access for the wave to contact any shielded solder joint.

5.13.3   Equipment Operation

Wave-solder equipment performs three basic operations:

- Flux application to leads and pads
- Board and component preheat
- Mass soldering of joints to create an electrical and mechanical connection

5.13.3.1   Flux Application.   Flux is applied in one of four ways: foam, pressurized spray, electrostatic spray, and wave fluxing. Foam flux has historically been the method of choice. New flux formulations and application methods, however, have greatly diminished the use of foam fluxing. Foam fluxing uses a porous stone (pumice) resting in a pan of flux. Pressurized air forced through the bottom of the stone creates a foam which coats the bottom of the circuit board as it passes over the stone. Foam fluxing applies a uniform, thick layer of flux to the board.

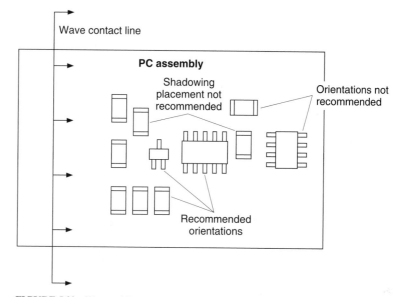

FIGURE 5.20   Wave-solder component orientation and placement.

Spray fluxing is becoming the predominant method of flux application. It uses a high-pressure sprayer along with a motorized carriage to coat the bottom of the board and components with flux. The spray fluxer moves in an axis across the conveyor width, while the board passes above on the conveyor. Spray pressure, belt speed, and sprayer travel speed can be used to apply a controlled amount of flux.

Electrostatic spray is similar to regular spray fluxing except for the electrostatic charge given to the fine flux droplets as they are being sprayed. Electrostatic fluxing gives less overspray and a more controlled deposition. This method is commonly used, although it is not staged to replace other application methods.

5.13.3.2   *Board and Component Preheat.* Preheating the board and components is required to minimize the temperature spike when the board enters the molten wave of solder and to activate the cleaning agents in the flux. Preheating is done after fluxing and consists of bottom-side board heaters as well as optional top-side heaters positioned under or over the conveyor belt. The board is heated as it passes through the preheater section of the machine. Various heating elements are employed, such as convective panel heaters or infrared (IR) lamp heaters.

5.13.3.3   *Wave Soldering.* The solder wave consists of a pot of molten solder which is pumped through a manifold or nozzle spanning the full width of the conveyor belt to form a solder fountain. The wave width is defined by the height of the solder pot, the position of solder dams, and the volume of solder being pumped. The height of the solder wave is determined by the vertical position of the manifold and solder dams. The molten solder is maintained at a set temperature.

There are two different types of solder waves: turbulent and laminar. The turbulent wave is often used in addition to the laminar wave for bottom-side SMT components to provide an agitating motion for the solder. The turbulent wave is created either by oscillating the solder nozzle or by setting up standing waves on the wave surface. The turbulent wave is used to help remove air pockets around SMT components and leads which can keep SMT leads from soldering. Turbulent waves are quite narrow waves (approximately ½-in width).

The laminar wave is a much broader wave (2 to 6 in) with a smooth, laminar flow. The laminar wave provides the contact time with the board to allow solder to wick up the vias and THT leads. The laminar wave provides a smooth, consistent-volume solder joint.

5.13.4 Wave-Solder Profile

The wave-solder profile consists of three regions: preheat ramp, wave contact, and cooling (Fig. 5.21).

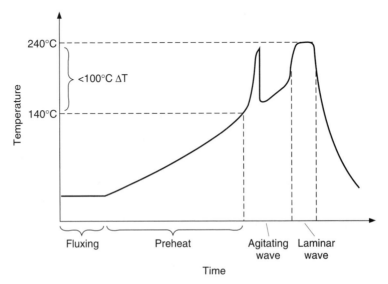

FIGURE 5.21   Wave-solder profile.

The preheat region is used to preheat the bare board, preheat the SMT components, and activate the flux before entering the wave. If the board is too cool, the vias connected to plane layers (high thermal mass) will not fill with solder and the SMT components may experience thermal shock which could cause cracks. Bottom-side SMT components must not experience more than a 100°C temperature delta going into the wave solder.

Wave-solder pot temperatures are maintained between 240 and 260°C. The PCA bottom-side board temperature very quickly reaches the wave-solder pot temperature and stays there until it exits the wave. Wave-solder contact time should not be longer than 4 s in either wave. The wave contact time is one of the critical parameters determining the amount of heat transferred to the board.

Double reflow during wave solder is an important failure mode where the top-side SMT solder joints achieve reflow temperatures during the wave-solder process. The result is a greatly weakened or fractured solder joint for the top-side SMT component. Fine-pitch components are the most dramatically affected because of their low-thermal-mass leads and solder joints. Double reflow is caused by thermal heat transfer through the vias, along the traces to the SMT land pads. This phenomenon can be controlled by proper PCB layout to minimize thermal conduction paths and proper profiling to control the solder-wave contact time.

5.13.4.1   Cooling.   There are usually no cool-down zones in wave-solder equipment. The PCAs cool in ambient air as the assembly travels on the exit conveyor. The PCAs should be allowed to cool below the glass transition temperature T_g of the PCB before being removed from the solder pallet or put into the cleaner.

5.14   DOUBLE-SIDED REFLOW

Double-sided reflow is very similar to single-sided reflow except that the process is used for both sides of the assembly. The secondary side refers to the side of the board which does not contain the bulk of the IC components and often has a larger proportion of passives, discretes, and small ICs. Many of the smaller components rely on the surface tension of the solder joints to hold the parts in place during the second reflow process. Double-sided reflow usually requires the secondary side to be reflowed first. Fewer parts need to be glued in place on the secondary side, and the effect of a second reflow thermal cycle is less of a concern for smaller components. The opportunity for handling damage of critical ICs is also diminished by processing the secondary side first.

Differential heating profiles for top vs. bottom are also used for double-sided reflow. With differential heating, the top side of the PCA reaches reflow temperatures while the bottom side is kept cooler to prevent reflow of the solder joints and possible dropping of components. Specialized profiles are developed for this application and must be closely controlled. Epoxy to hold components in place is no longer needed for bottom-side components with differential heating profiles.

Double-sided reflow requires custom fixturing to support the assembly during the second SMT process. The fixturing can be either a dedicated tooling plate with recesses for the previously loaded components or configurable supports in each of the process machines.

5.15   ELECTRICAL TEST

Electrical testing of printed circuit assemblies is used to verify that the performance of the printed circuit assembly meets the required standards before it is shipped to customers. It can also be used to isolate problems when they occur. Electrical testing can be done at a number of different levels during the assembly process. Levels of testing of the assembled board include in-circuit test (ICT), functional test, and environmental stress screening (ESS). These different tests verify progressively higher levels of performance and help isolate corresponding failures. In order to facilitate testing, there are a number of design-for-test (DFT) techniques that can be applied during the electrical design and layout phases to make tests easier to conduct and failure isolation faster and less cumbersome.

5.15.1   Design for Test (DFT)

Design for test (DFT), like design for manufacturability (DFM), requires consideration during the early stages of the design phase of the PCA. DFT seeks to develop test capability built into the schematic and component design which facilitates isolation of component and board level failures as early as possible. Layout considerations which make test points accessible and fixturing reliable must also be included. The end goal is to find defects as early as possible, decrease failure isolation time, increase outgoing quality, and reduce overall production and support costs of a product.

There are a number of realities that make board layout and fixturing for electrical test more difficult with SMT assemblies. These include dramatically increased lead (and test point) density, leads which are accessible from only one side, and components on both sides of the PCB which can block test via access. There are also some techniques which help make electrical testing easier, including signal isolation, test vector generation, and boundary scan. Some of the testing techniques require implementation in the schematic, the design of the components, or the programmable logic devices (PLDs).

5.15.1.1   Signal Isolation.   There are many techniques which allow signals to be isolated so that component functionality can be tested. It is important not to have output enables tied directly to power or ground in order to simplify ICT. There are a number of ways to do this using pull-up and pull-down resistors and tri-state buffers. Each of these techniques requires implementation in the schematic. Signal isolation requires each net to be tested to have an individual test point. Optimal testability would provide a test point for every net in the circuit.

5.15.1.2   Boundary Scan.   Boundary scan is a method of verifying basic digital IC functionality and solder joint integrity of input/output (I/O) pins where verification of all the internal chip functionality is difficult or impossible otherwise. Boundary scan must be implemented into the functionality of the component and requires some number of pins to control the chip and write test vectors.

Components with boundary scan have a read/write register at every pin or *boundary* of the component. Values can be loaded into the pin registers and either clocked in from or clocked out to other boundary scan components or test probe points, depending on the I/O configuration of the pins. The set of values loaded or retrieved is called a *vector.* Proper transfer of vectors into or out of a component verifies basic chip functionality and solder joint electrical integrity.

Boundary scan components can be connected to allow multiple component testing at the same time. Boundary scan provides a means of testing components without requiring test points at every lead and without requiring detailed understanding of the functionality of the IC.

IEEE Specification 1149.3 was created by the Joint Test Action Group (JTAG) and defines a standard boundary scan specification. JTAG defines a unique serial bus for test vectors plus control and clocking capability using four extra pins for each component. Many processors and other high-complexity components are now offered with JTAG capability. PLDs can also be designed to include JTAG capability.

5.15.1.3   Test Points.   Test points are typically designed for 1.27-mm (0.050-in), 1.78-mm (0.070-in), or 2.54-mm (0.100-in) minimum pitch spacing. There are different probe designs for each of these minimum pitches. 2.54-mm (0.100-in) probes are the most robust and are the best choice when the test point density allows their use. 0.070-in probes are also quite robust, although they sometimes do not have the vertical travel of 0.100-in probes. 1.27-mm (0.050-in) probes present a number of additional challenges because they are much more fragile, they are difficult to insert at the required pitch, they usually require soldered lead tails, and they are more expensive.

Test point pads need to be the correct size to account for tolerances of the tooling pins, test point hole angle, PCB stretch or shrinkage, and a number of other tolerances.

5.15.1.4   Layout Considerations.   There are many considerations at the board layout stage. The placement and spacing of the test points is critical. The test points must be spaced from components so that the test point cannot contact a neighboring component, given the tolerances for the test pin–to–test point alignment tolerance. Probing SMT leads is not recommended, but through-hole leads can be probed. Test points can be special pads, vias, or even the ends of SMT pads as long as the pads have been extended to prevent lead contact with the test probe.

Test points can be on either the top or bottom of the PCB. Bottom-side test points are preferred because there are usually less components on the bottom and a single-sided test fixture can be generated. Test points can be placed on both top and bottom, but a clamshell-style fixture is required in order to test the board. Clamshell fixtures are more expensive, more difficult to use and maintain, and can require more alignment tolerance margin for the top-side probing.

Test points need to be marked in the design to minimize their movement in any revisions of the assembly. Relatively few changes are allowed in test fixturing before a new fixture is required. Test fixtures can be expensive and require several weeks lead time for complex boards.

5.15.2   Model Generation

Test models must be generated to permit verification of IC functionality. Test models consist of a series of input test vectors (set of values to be loaded into input registers) which exercise the functionality of an IC in a known manner. The component functionality can be verified by measuring the corresponding output vectors (set of values presented by the output registers) and comparing them to the expected response.

The test vector models can be generated by breaking down the logic used inside the chips (for less complex components), obtaining test vector models from the component vendor, stimulating an actual component to measure the desired response, or using boundary scan (JTAG). The coverage, or percent of functionality verified, depends on the complexity of the IC, extent of the development of the vectors, and the number of test vectors required to exercise the different levels of functionality. The test model for each component can be stored in a library and used as building blocks when ICT or functional test programs are generated.

5.15.3   In-Circuit Test (ICT)

In-circuit test (ICT) refers to the testing done directly after the printed circuit assembly. ICT is used to verify connectivity between test points, verify component value, and check basic logic functionality. ICT does not typically test operation at the actual clock speed.

ICT uses dedicated ICT machines which have built-in multimeters, current sources, and programmable I/O. ICT equipment is available for up to 7000 nets. The equipment typically uses a bed-of-nails test bed in either a single-sided or clamshell configuration which is connected through an interface plate to the I/O, power and multimeter connections.

5.15.3.1   In-Circuit Test Program Generation.   ICT programs are generated from the schematic design and component library test models. The ICT program can perform a number of different functions including component value testing, frequency response characteristics measurement, and logic testing. All of these tests require a working knowledge of the schematic in order to control and measure the correct nets. Tests using test vectors from library models can be incorporated into the program. Testing with JTAG can also be incorporated into the program.

ICT test coverage refers to the percentage of the electrical functionality that is exercised by an ICT test program or the percentage of lead/trace opens or shorts that are detectable. The generation of the test program determines the test coverage. More extensive test coverage requires more extensive testing, which can be expensive both for model or program generation as well as actual testing time each time a PCA is tested.

There are two parts of ICT testing: Shorts testing and the ICT program.

Shorts Testing.   The lowest level of ICT testing is for shorts between nets. This type of testing requires only a simple ICT program, without knowledge of the schematic interconnectivity. Shorts testing looks for low-impedance connections between any two test points and is very good for picking up solder shorts from the assembly processes.

ICT Program Testing.   The ICT program measures component values and schematic functionality. The multimeter capabilities of the ICT equipment allows verification of passive device values as well as characteristic impedance from other functions on the board. ICT programs are usually performed at much slower speeds than those at which the system actually operates because of the analysis that must take place simultaneously. Defects are logged by the ICT equipment and can be fed into data-tracking systems for later analysis.

5.15.3.2 Fixturing.   A unique fixture must be created for each printed circuit assembly. The fixture must connect from the probe points on the PCA to be tested to the I/O, power, and multimeter connections on the ICT machine. Many simple boards use wire wrap to create the connection, although many newer, complex boards use a separate PCB to do the mapping.

5.15.4 Functional Test

Functional test consists of testing a printed circuit assembly as part of the complete system in which it will be used. Functional test can be done by individual assembly for designs which have a high degree of stand-alone capability or as part of the whole system. It may be more efficient for stand-alone assemblies to dispense with ICT and use strictly functional test.

Assemblies which are part of a larger system usually require a mock-up of the complete system to exercise all of the required functionality.

Functional test is quite different in approach from ICT. Functional test exercises operational functionality as part of a system rather than individual components and nets. Integrated functionality, including different modes of operation, are tested with different test patterns and the results are written to memory. Results are usually verifiable without requiring test probe measurement of nets, although some calibration operations may require specific test point measurement.

5.14.5 Environmental Stress Screening (ESS) Test

Environmental stress screening (ESS) refers to the testing of an assembly in a working system at its operational margins or beyond in order to find weak components which are ready to fail.

There are several ways that ESS can be used. ESS can be used to validate that an assembly or system works at its specification margins for voltage, temperature, or humidity. It can also be used to stress the assembly beyond its normal specification range in order to force weakened components to fail. Finally, ESS can be used as a diagnostic and continuous process improvement tool to increase the operational envelope until a substantial number of failures occur in order to find weaknesses in the design.

ESS attempts to exercise the assembly long enough to find the majority of the infant mortality failures but not so long as to significantly decrease the life of the product. ESS is a non-value-added step which should be eliminated if the design and components can be made sufficiently robust.

5.16 *REPAIR AND REWORK*

Repair and rework in this section refer to any soldering technique used to repair or replace any SMT component on a previously assembled or partially assembled printed circuit assembly. The cause of the rework can be either SMT process related (opens, bridges, misaligned, misoriented, missing components, etc.) or component related (defective component).

5.16.1 Design for Rework (DFR)

Design for rework (DFR) is a subcategory of design for manufacturability (DFM). DFR is predominantly incorporated into the component spacing specifications. The spacing between components must be large enough to allow soldering iron and rework station nozzle access. The spacing must also be large enough to keep the adjacent component temperature during rework below approximately 150°C. The adjacent component temperature specification is dependent on the rework equipment type and the tools used.

5.16.2 Equipment Options

There are many equipment options for performing SMT rework. There are many hand tools for doing individual solder joint repairs or manual component replacement or rework. There are also many automatic equipment options which, when characterized and programmed, can automatically remove components as well as semiautomatically replace them. Hand tools are often used for 1.27-mm (0.050-in) pitch components and larger because of their versatility and ease of use. Automated equipment is often used for fine-pitch components (0.65-mm [0.0256-in] pitch and lower) where process control is needed to assure reliability of the reworked solder joints. Hand tools can also be used for fine-pitch components, but they require an experienced operator and, thus, the rework quality is dependent on operator skill.

5.16.2.1 Hand Tools.   The hand tools come in four basic varieties:

- Soldering irons
- Thermal tweezers
- Thermodes
- Hot-air tools

Soldering Irons.   Soldering irons are the most common hand tools. There are many different size tips for soldering irons to accommodate the variety of lead size and thermal masses. Soldering irons should have closed-loop feedback for temperature to assure that the solder joints and the flux will not be overheated (solder joint tip temperature <700°F). Soldering irons must also be calibrated regularly to assure proper temperature operation.

Thermal Tweezers.   A variation of the soldering iron is the thermal tweezers. Thermal tweezers use two soldering tips with special tip shapes to fit different types of components. The two soldering tips are connected and spring-loaded in a tweezer-like configuration. There are thermal tweezer tips to remove discrete passives, SOICs, and PLCCs of varying sizes.

Thermodes.   Thermodes are used infrequently as hand tools. Thermodes use a flat bar to heat all of the component leads simultaneously so that the component can be lifted off the pads in one operation. Thermodes must have individual tools to fit each of the different configurations of components. Gullwing components are the only package styles that use thermodes. The thermode must put pressure on the lead against the land pad to provide the thermal contact. Leads which are underneath the component body, like J leads, are not accessible by thermodes.

Hot-Air Tools.   Hot-air tools are very common and use forced hot air impinging on the component and leads to melt the solder. Care must be used with hot-air tools to assure that adjacent component leads do not reach 150°C (Sec. 5.8.3).

There are several sizes of hot-air tools, such as the hot-air blower for larger applications and the hot-air pencil for more detailed uses. There are many types and sizes of nozzles, also, which can be attached to the hot-air source. There are nozzles for many of the different component types which fit over the component and direct the hot air onto the leads. Specialized nozzles for every type of component can be quite costly as well as difficult to change while they are still hot.

5.16.2.2 Automatic Equipment.   Automating the rework process is done to remove the operator-dependent aspects of the rework process which can affect the solder joint quality and reliability or lead to damage of the PCA. There are many different rework equipment vendors who can provide rework solutions to automatically remove and replace components on printed circuit assemblies.

Automatic rework equipment allows standard heating profiles to be developed and stored to assure controlled and repeatable heating processes during production use. Automating the rework process relies heavily on characterizing the process for each component type and bare PCB thickness and layer count. The equipment also provides alignment capability to accurately realign SMT components during the replacement process.

Automated equipment vendors provide an alignment fixture to hold and position the PCA, a programmable heating cycle, a vacuum chuck to lift the components, and a component alignment system using a stereo microscope or video camera. Alignment of components to be replaced is usually done manually with the assistance of a stereo microscope or video camera.

For component removal, the automated rework equipment controls the heating cycle and then lifts the rework component off the board. The rework profile must be sufficient to fully melt the solder joints before lifting the component; otherwise, SMT land pads could be pulled off the bare board. The heating cycle should be similar to the reflow profile where the maximum temperature should be in the 205 to 220°C range and the dwell time above reflow should be less than 120 s. Stabilization or soak regions are not required with rework because of the localized nature of rework.

During the component replacement process, the rework equipment provides an optical lead-to-pad alignment process (operator dependent) followed by the controlled heating cycle and component placement. An automated rework process is most beneficial for large components and fine-pitch components where there are many leads which must experience the same heating process.

5.16.3   Heating

There are three basic types of heat transfer used in rework of PCAs: convection, radiant, and conductive heating. Each method has advantages and disadvantages.

The temperature of adjacent components must be kept below 150°C to maintain the reliability of the adjacent component leads. Solder joints become significantly weaker above 150°C and can fracture under the stress of the localized board bowing during the rework heating process.

5.16.3.1   Convection Heating.
Hot-air convection is the most common heating method for removing and replacing components with gullwing or J-leads. Hot-air convection allows a whole component or a whole region to be heated at once. The air temperature is easily controlled with temperature feedback systems. Hot-air convection provides a smooth temperature ramp rate.

Care must be given when reworking with hot air because hot-air convection heats everything in the vicinity where it is applied. The adjacent component leads must not reach more than 150°C. To do this the hot air can be precisely directed using customized nozzles, the neighboring component leads can be shielded, or ample component placement spacing can be designed into the board to minimize adjacent component heating effects.

Custom nozzles can be difficult because they often need to be changed while they are still hot, many different nozzles are required for the multitude of package styles, and it can be very expensive and not very timely to procure nozzles for new component styles. Some equipment vendors use configurable jets which heat only the areas required and do not require tool changeout.

5.16.3.2   Radiant Heating.
Radiant heating is accomplished using infrared (IR) lamps to reflow the solder joints. IR rework systems do not have a problem with adjacent component temperature because they focus the light energy only on the component leads to be reworked.

IR rework systems use a view plate with cutouts to direct the IR light to the localized areas to be heated. The view plates are easy to fabricate and change for different component styles. IR rework systems work well with gullwing leads but are not very effective with hidden leads such as J-leaded components or BGAs. IR lamp heating is usually used with automated rework systems. Hand tools rarely use IR heating.

5.16.3.3 Conductive Heating. Conductive heating is utilized by a wide range of soldering tools from single-point soldering irons to thermal tweezers to fine-pitch, hot bar thermode bonders. Conductive heat transfer is used to convey heat to the solder joints. Conductive heat transfer relies on good thermal contact between the soldering tool and the component lead or pad either by solder wetting to the tool and lead/pad or by pressure contact.

To maintain good thermal heat transfer, soldering irons rely on solder wetting to the tool and the lead/pad. Therefore, the tool must be cleaned regularly of oxidized solder and flux residue to promote good wetting. Thermode bonders, however, rely on pressure contact rather than solder wetting onto the tool for heat transfer. Thermode bonders must maintain a very straight contact surface to assure uniform thermal pressure with all the leads to be heated.

5.16.4 Component Removal and Replacement

This section describes the steps required to remove and replace many leaded components, such as integrated circuits, which can benefit from automatic rework processes. Two to four leaded devices such as discrete ICs and passive components are usually done with a soldering iron and solder wire and are not covered in this section.

5.16.4.1 Number of Rework Operations. The number of rework operations that can be performed on a single location is limited. Excessive numbers of rework operations can cause delamination of the printed circuit board, through-hole barrel cracks, and excessive inter-metallic formation at the copper/tin interface on the land pads. All of these failure modes can show up as intermittent and early life failures but rarely as hard failures during production tests. Single solder joint repair is not counted as a rework thermal cycle.

The number of rework operations is limited by the total number of thermal cycles that a component location experiences. A typical recommended maximum number of thermal cycles is five. This allows for two to four rework operations, depending on the PC board fabrication technology and the assembly process steps. A typical board may see one thermal cycle with hot-air leveling (HAL), one with the top-side reflow process and one with bottom-side reflow or wave soldering. This would allow two additional rework processes. More than two rework operations in this case could lead to early life (infant mortality) failures. For other boards where organic coated copper pads are used and there is only a single top-side reflow thermal cycle, the number of reworks could be four before reliability is compromised. Additional thermal cycles are counted for a component when an adjacent component is reworked and the component experiences a thermal cycle above 150°C.

Boards using alternative laminate materials such as polyimide, cynate ester, and BT resin can survive more thermal cycles (up to 7 to 10) before failure is imminent. These more exotic dielectric materials have a number of benefits; however, they cost three to four times more than epoxy glass (FR-4) laminates. Benefits include:

1. Less z-axis expansion which lowers the risk of barrel cracking, pad lifting, and post separation

2. Higher glass transition (T_g) temperature which provides more resilient lamination integrity

3. Better dimensional stability

4. Lower dielectric constant

5.16.4.2 Replacing Components.   There are four steps in replacing components: reconditioning pads, solder/flux application, component placement/alignment, and heating.

Reconditioning Pads.   Reconditioning the pads before reattaching a component is important to remove solder tails or spikes protruding from the pads and the variations in the remaining solder volume on the pad after component removal. Reconditioning can consist of reheating the pads to level the solder, using solder wick to remove remaining solder, or adding solder to provide enough solder volume for a new component solder joint.

Solder and Flux Application.   There must be enough solder either remaining on the pad or added in the reattachment process to create a new solder joint. If additional solder is required, the solder can be either applied to the pad as part of the reconditioning step or deposited as part of the component replacement process. Solder can be deposited in three forms in the replacement process:

- Solder paste—dispensed with a syringe or printed with a ministencil

- Solder preforms—applied as a solder ribbon along the leads

- Bumped pads—solder applied directly to the pads (part of reconditioning process)

Solder paste dispensing is a very efficient method of applying additional solder. For components of 0.64 mm (0.025 in) pitch and above, a bead of solder paste across all the pads can be used to provide the necessary solder. During reflow, the paste bead will divide and wick onto the individual pads with little or no bridging as long as the paste bead is of the appropriate width and volume. Ministencils, where small stencils are used to print solder paste bricks on individual pads, are currently being investigated but are not in widespread use due to the spacing required around the components.

Solder preforms come in various geometries. Some have alignment combs which help align the part and eliminate bridging between leads. Solder preforms are not widely used, however, because of the time-consuming two-step manual alignment process for the preform and the component, the high cost of the preforms, and the necessity to stock several different preform pitches/lead counts.

Component Placement and Alignment Methods.   Components can be aligned either using rework station optical alignment aids or by hand. Optical alignment tools often have optical parallax problems and require operator training and skill to achieve success. Manual methods which also require skill and agility provide an iterative method which some operators find easier.

Many different methods are used for aligning components from placing components into solder paste using optical alignment tools to tacking corner pins with a soldering iron.

Heating Cycle.   The heating cycle for reworked components is critical for good rework reliability. As in reflow, the solder joints need to be heated sufficiently to reflow all of the joints, yet not overheated such that the flux is baked onto the board and is difficult to clean. An automatic rework station that has been characterized for all the board/component combinations is the preferred method for heating fine-pitch rework components. Components reworked with a controlled profile can have the same strength and reliability as the originally reflowed solder joint.

Liquid or paste flux will need to be applied if it is not already present in solder paste or solder preforms. Flux is usually applied using a squeeze bottle with a needle applicator. Flux should be used sparingly to prevent it from becoming entrapped under the component.

Other methods such as heating the solder joints individually with a soldering iron or hot-air blower produce a highly variant heating cycle which relies on the operator's *feel* and experience. Components reworked in this manner have a much higher defect rate than the standard reflow process and can contribute significantly to failures in the field.

5.16.5 Cleaning

Cleaning for reworked components should be done after the board has had all rework completed. The boards can be cleaned in a production-quality in-line cleaner or in a batch cleaner. Spray solvent or brush cleaning of a localized area is not acceptable because flux can flow under the component, leaving potentially corrosive deposits.

No-clean fluxes can be used in rework, but they must be rendered inert through the proper heating cycle. The amount of flux used is also a concern with no-clean because excessive deposits can be cosmetically unacceptable or the flux residue can make test probing at that location difficult.

CHAPTER 6
MULTICHIP MODULES

Howard D. Green
MicroModule Systems, Inc., Cupertino, California

6.1   INTRODUCTION

Multichip modules (MCMs) are a specialized integrated circuit (IC) design and packaging technology with many applications in high-volume products and assemblies. Originally developed to enable high-speed performance applications and solve board signal quality problems, MCMs are implemented by product designers who require:

- Smaller form factors than those readily achieved using single-chip surface-mount (SMT) or ball-grid-array (BGA) packaging.
- Higher chip-to-chip signal quality than is generally available using other interconnect and packaging technologies. Selected electrical characteristics that can be dramatically improved by MCM implementation include reduced time of flight, improved rise and fall times, and lower system noise.
- Faster product delivery times than those available using custom ICs.

Multichip modules (a typical workstation MCM design is shown in Fig. 6.1) take advantage of many standard IC packaging and printed circuit board (PCB) manufacturing technologies, and offer a range of alternatives for the designer. This chapter provides a general overview of multichip modules, including MCM technologies, selection criteria, design, and manufacturing.

6.1.1   Definition of Multichip Modules

From the inception of the electronics industry, semiconductor and passive devices were attached through DIP packages and, later, pin grid arrays using through-hole assembly processes. In the mid-1980s the DIP package began to be displaced in selected applications by surface-mount packages, as shown in Fig. 6.2. Surface mount brought the advantages of much higher pin counts and interconnect densities into widespread use. SMT adapted readily to dense, multilayer printed circuit boards, and readily supported pin counts in excess of 300 leads per package. A variety of SMT packages reached adoption by the JEDEC and EIAJ

FIGURE 6.1 A six-chip multichip module used in a workstation. 125-MHz device consists of CPU, cache controller, and four high-speed SRAMs in a ceramic pin grid array. Four-layer thin-film substrate size is 33 mm by 33 mm. Copper signal traces are 16μ wide on a 50-μ pitch. Die are connected using wire bond with surface-mount capacitors inside a 131-pin ceramic pin-grid-array package. MCM implementation resulted in approximately a 30 percent performance increase over conventionally packaged devices due to the ability to run all the devices at a full 125 MHz.

standards bodies, including quad flat packs, thin small-outline packages, plastic leadless chip carriers, and many others. For a more complete discussion of surface-mount technology, please refer to Chap. 5.

By the mid-1990s, selected SMT applications were being displaced by a combination of chip-on-board (COB) and MCM technologies. Both COB- and MCM-based products shared the common advantage of consuming minimal board space and offered the potential for higher subsystem performance, due to the elimination of at least one layer of interconnect (the IC package). COB and MCM technology also provided the designer with reduced switching noise and the ability to achieve higher system clock rates.

MCMs were initially developed and implemented by large companies in the defense, telecommunications, and mainframe systems industries. The technology was developed as an extension of earlier hybrid integrated circuits, like those shown in Fig. 6.3. Like MCMs, hybrids combined a board space savings with higher subsystem performance as compared to ICs and passive devices in single-chip packages. The performance increase was primarily derived by removing the individual IC packages, eliminating a layer of interconnect structure, and attaching the bare silicon (or gallium arsenide) ICs and passive components to an interconnect substrate.

6.1.2 Hybrid Integrated Circuits (Hybrids)

Hybrid integrated circuits (hybrids) are a precursor to multichip modules and application-specific integrated circuits (ASICS). Hybrids commonly integrate both packaged and unpack-

1970's Plated Through Hole Technology, 200 pin PGA

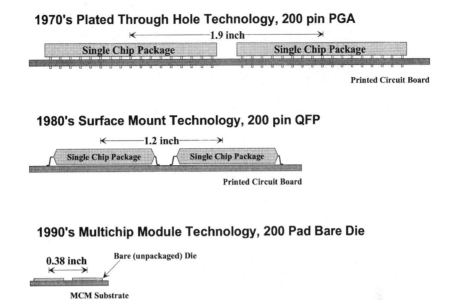

|←————————1.9 inch————————→|

Single Chip Package   Single Chip Package

Printed Circuit Board

1980's Surface Mount Technology, 200 pin QFP

|←———1.2 inch———→|

Single Chip Package   Single Chip Package

Printed Circuit Board

1990's Multichip Module Technology, 200 Pad Bare Die

Bare (unpackaged) Die

0.38 inch
|←——→|

MCM Substrate

FIGURE 6.2 Interconnect levels on PCB. From top to bottom: ICs in single-chip dual in-line (DIP) package; ICs in PQFP; multiple ICs in bare die format on MCM.

FIGURE 6.3 Thick-film hybrid. Device is 2 in by 2.2 in in a ceramic QFP. Pin pitch is 0.040 in. Device consists of a bit slice CPU, four 4K ASICS, and a bipolar prom, among other components. *(Photo: Hughes Aircraft Company.)*

aged active and passive components on the substrate, while an MCM will typically contain only bare die. As summarized in Table 6.1, hybrids share many of the attributes of multichip modules: They combine multiple electronic components into a single function, are roughly the size of a large single-chip package, and integrate electronics from a variety of suppliers. Typical hybrid applications include digital signal processing, mixed-signal military and telecommunications applications, and often power management. Substrate materials are most commonly thick films of metals and ceramic combined to form a multilayer ceramic substrate.

TABLE 6.1   Comparison of Hybrids vs. Multichip Modules

	Hybrid	Multichip Module	Comments
Substrate material	Thick-film ceramic substrate	PWB, ceramic, silicon, glass, or metal substrate	MCMs are built on a variety of substrate starting materials, depending on cost, reliability, hermeticity, wiring density, thermal conductivity, and other requirements
Device types	Packaged ICs, bare die, packaged passive components	Multiple bare die, some packaged passive components	Most MCMs are composed primarily of multiple bare ICs with some passives—most nonessential passives are to be found outside the MCM
Typical applications	Hermetic military, power management, RF applications	CPU chipsets, device controllers, memories	Aside from some high-end telecom applications and limited automotive use, hybrids are typically mil/aerospace products, while MCMs have more widespread commercial application

6.1.3 Origins of Multichip Modules

By the mid-1980s, multichip modules were in widespread use in high-performance applications like mainframe computer systems. The modules proved to be more reliable than large numbers of soldered-in ICs with several hundred I/O each and supported higher clock rates (1 GHz or more in some instances)—which were difficult to achieve cost effectively using single-chip packages and multilayer printed wiring boards. MCMs were also able to sustain high thermal requirements when compared to the system assembly technologies available at that time.

Early multichip modules were built in fairly low (few tens of thousands of units per year) quantities, were highly complex devices operating at 500-MHz-plus clock rates, and dissipated 100 W or more. In their large metal housings, early high-performance MCMs were extremely expensive and were prone to rework due to the limited availability of die test technologies. Unit prices in excess of $10,000 were fairly common. Since the product goal in most cases was "performance at (almost) any price," and the computer systems business generated high profit margins in the late 1980s, these costs were accepted.

It became a strong belief within the electronics industry that MCM technology would remain a high-cost, exotic option usable only when it was necessary to squeeze the absolute maximum performance from a given set of ICs. This belief was reinforced by the circumstances common to most early implementors of the technology—nearly all MCM applications were built inside large, vertically integrated systems companies that designed and manufactured their own silicon, developed custom interconnect and die attach technologies for module assembly, and built their own design and test systems.

For many years the potential infrastructure that would have enabled the low-cost emergence of MCM technology remained captive inside the systems, telecommunications, and aerospace companies. By the early 1990s, a merchant infrastructure began to form, driven by the increasing demand for the benefits of MCMs throughout the electronics industry. The MCM infrastructure is composed of semiconductor manufacturers willing to sell their products in bare die form; MCM foundries that design, assemble, and test MCMs; manufacturers of substrates and packages; and providers of design tools, test services, process equipment, and fixturing.

The emergence of this infrastructure helped to drive the cost of MCMs below $10 for many applications, and enabled the development and successful marketing of commercial MCM-based products.

6.1.4 Benefits of MCMs

The advantages derived from implementing MCMs include the following:

- The total product form factor can be up to 10 times smaller than the same function implemented in single-chip packages and multilayer PCBs. This allows additional functionality to be added in a given space, or allows the product form factor to be reduced.
- Routing layers on the PCB can be reduced by implementing an MCM. A design that must be implemented in an 8- to 12-layer board can often be built using 4 to 6 layers. Fewer PCB layers means PCB manufacturing and test costs are lower and manufacturing yields are higher.
- ICs which are developed for use in MCMs can be designed with tighter noise margins, smaller output drivers, and in smaller die sizes. These characteristics translate directly to higher performance, lower IC manufacturing costs, and reduced power consumption.
- In some cases, a cost savings can be realized by eliminating the cost of multiple high-performance single-chip packages. While elimination of the plastic molding compound for a quad flat pack (at $0.20/chip) is unlikely to justify implementing an MCM, the elimination of two $12.00 ceramic pin grid arrays may provide sufficient justification for an MCM.

Additional features and benefits of MCM technology are summarized in Table 6.2.

6.1.5 Choosing MCMs over Single-Chip ICs

Generally, the designer looking to create an integrated function for a new or upgraded system will specify a microprocessor, an appropriate amount of memory, and some form of custom or semicustom logic—either an ASIC, FPGA (field-programmable gate array), or PLD (programmable logic device). When packaged as single chips, these devices are appropriate choices for many applications.

Many product designs require form factors smaller than the aggregate surface area of the packaged components required for implementation. By implementing the same design in one or more MCMs, the product can be up to an order of magnitude smaller.

Some cases exist where a straight tradeoff must be made between an MCM and an IC. Table 6.3 summarizes selected attributes that should be taken into account early in the design

TABLE 6.2   Multichip Module Features and Benefits

Feature	Benefit
MCM-based products can be up to 12 times smaller than identical product built using single-chip packages on PCB.	Smaller board space—lower cost, higher PCB manufacturing yield. Including additional functionality in the same board space can provide an opportunity to add additional functionality and provide a differentiated product, gaining a market advantage.
MCMs can help solve board routing problems by enabling chip-to-chip interconnects to remain inside the module, reducing the number of wiring layers on multilayer PCB.	Fewer board wiring layers = lower PCB cost, high manufacturing yield; simpler board.
Since many ICs can be packaged within a single MCM the size of one packaged IC, PCB designs can often be reduced from dual-sided to single-sided.	Single-sided SMT operations have higher assembly yields and lower costs compared to dual-sided designs.
Packaging multiple die in a single SMT package can reduce assembly costs by elimination of multiple surface-mount operations.	Fewer component attachments = higher reliability, lower manufacturing cost, smaller board footprint.
Thin-film MCM substrate technology provides an excellent electrical signal propagation medium, with lower dielectric constant, shorter traces, and controlled impedance.	MCM-based designs can run at higher clock rates than equivalent designs built using single-chip packages.
Bare die can be purchased pretested and burned-in, for costs below the cost of packaged ICs.	Lower-cost components with higher initial quality levels reduce rework and component costs.

cycle. Since applications have differing levels of complexity, different cost targets, and varying implementation goals, choosing between different types of ICs and MCM technologies requires careful analysis to make appropriate tradeoffs. The MCM should be considered for applications where:

- The time to design and build the custom semiconductor and reach acceptable yields for volume manufacturing exceeds the time required to design and build a multichip module integrating existing IC designs. MCM substrates, even when built using the semiconductor-like MCM-D process described in Sec. 6.2.3 are much simpler to design and faster to ramp into production than an ASIC of even moderate complexity, containing perhaps a few hundred thousand gates.

- The functions to be integrated cannot be found in the same cell libraries using complementary technologies. Many designs have analog *and* digital components, or a GaAs clock with CMOS gate arrays, cache, and microprocessors. Other designs have a requirement for devices (fast cache memory, programmable logic, signal processing, or microprocessor, for example) that generally are built using different semiconductor manufacturing processes.

- The design is changing rapidly but cannot be customized in part with a single PLD. Many such applications exist where a core function requires modest tailoring over time. An MCM offers many advantages for such an implementation, because the board space will be the same (or less) than a CPU alone in a traditional single-chip package, and building a custom ASIC may cause the design to miss its market window. Moreover, by tailoring a PLD or FPGA within an MCM, the board space will be reduced and the application's flexibility will increase.

TABLE 6.3 Costs and Features of Varieties of Custom Silicon vs. Multichip Modules

Attribute	ASIC/gate array	FPGA	PLD	MCM
Gates/cells	50K–1000K or more	2000–40,000	2000–40,000	N/A—typically contains 2–20 ICs
Engineering charges	$20K and up	Few $K	Few $K	$20–$50K
Design time	6 months	Few days	Few days	2–5 weeks
Reprogrammability	N	Y	N	Y (with FPGA)
Board space	1	1	1	≥10 (varies with IC complexity)
Cost/qty 100	Few $1000	$20–$50	$20–$50	Few $1000
Cost/qty 100,000	$10–200	$20–$50	$20–$50	$10–$200 (plus die cost)
First prototype	1–4 months	1–2 weeks	1–2 weeks	1–4 weeks
Fully custom	Y	N	N	Y
Combination of analog and digital logic	Y (limited avail.)	N	N	Y
Maximum I/O	Hundreds—in BGA and other complex single-chip packages ASICs can be built supporting well over 700 I/O	<300	<300	Thousands (although typically an MCM will have far fewer peripheral I/O than the sum of the die inside the module. Thus, an 18-chip MCM with over 2000 die bonds from the ICs to the MCM substrate may still have only a few hundred I/O.

- ASIC nonrecurring engineering (NRE) charges may be higher than the equivalent charges to implement an MCM. Particularly with a PWB-based (MCM-L, described in Sec. 6.2.1) substrate, NRE charges can be quite low.

6.1.6 Low-Power MCMs

Multichip modules (particularly MCM-Ds) have inherently good signal integrity qualities (see Table 6.6). This allows low power/low voltage (below 3.3 V) to be specified for lightweight, high-performance hand-held and battery-powered applications. Low-power MCMs also dissipate less heat than multiple components in single-chip packages, allowing higher-clock-rate devices to be employed without forcing the use of exotic and expensive cooling technologies, which are generally impractical in most low-cost portable applications.

6.2 MCM TECHNOLOGIES

Multichip modules are composed of three core technologies: MCM-L, MCM-C, and MCM-D. Subsequent sections will outline the details surrounding their fabrication and use. The naming convention was developed to describe the interconnect substrate material for the MCM, rather than any operating characteristics or packaging of the modules.

6.2.1 MCM-L

MCM-L (the name is derived from the use of a laminate or PWB-based substrate material) is an MCM technology with a large installed base and a very large potential manufacturing infrastructure, since every PCB board manufacturer has the potential to build laminate substrates. Due to the low cost per square inch of simple printed wiring boards, MCM-L technology is often portrayed as the lowest-cost MCM alternative—and for many (but not all) applications, it is.

MCM-L applications are often packages of two to four bare die, wire bonded to a dense PWB substrate, then molded into a plastic package like a plastic leadless chip carrier (PLCC) or plastic quad flat pack (PQFP) for surface mounting onto a larger board. A typical MCM-L module is shown in Fig. 6.4. MCM-L substrates are also frequently used in ball-grid-array (BGA) multichip packages. Key parameters of MCM-L substrates are virtually identical to printed wiring boards, as detailed in Table 6.4.

When compared to other MCM technologies, MCM-L is limited in its wiring and via geometries, its ability to build structures with integrated passive components, and its thermal performance. Finally, flip-chip (a die attach technology defined in Sec. 6.5.3) implementations may be limited by the inherent TCE (thermal coefficient of expansion) mismatch between silicon and NEMA grade FR4 or similar substrate materials.

6.2.1.1 Chip-on-Board.
Chip-on-board (COB) is differentiated from MCM-L as follows: COB is a die interconnect technology that features bare die mounted on a printed wiring board. Many products use COB technology in combination with standard surface-mount processes, whereas a multichip module (including MCM-L) is generally a smaller PWB con-

FIGURE 6.4 Multichip module built using laminate (MCM-L substrate) for embedded PC application. Device consists of a 4-Mbit DRAM, graphics controller, RAMDAC, and some discrete components.

TABLE 6.4 MCM-L Substrate Characteristics

Parameter	Impact	Typical value
Std. flow prepreg thickness	Characteristic impedance	0.06 mm
Via drill	Bond pad-to-bond pad distance	0.2 mm
Via FHS	Bond pad-to-bond pad distance	Drill .050/.075 mm (0.15 mm)
Via pad size (drill plus outer layer)	Limits routing density	Drill +0.254 mm (0.454)
Via pad size (inner layer)	Limits routing density	Drill +0.254 mm (0.454)
Via antipad	Cuts up power plane	Drill +0.6–0.8 mm (0.8)
Trace width (base)	Limits routing density	0.1 → 0.050 mm
Trace width (top)	Limits routing density; 2 mil descramble—yield impact; amount of overetch of trace at top drives increased trace resistance	base—25 μ–20 μ
Bond finger width	Die bond pad pitch is decreasing high I/O die require fanout in the substrate design to match 4-mil pitch IC bond pads	0.1 mm
Trace space	Routing density, crosstalk	0.1–0.075 mm
Minimum pitch	Limits routing density	0.15–0.125 mm
Die attach supported	Rework; backside bias	Wirebond, TAB, flip chip

TABLE 6.5 Selected MCM-C Substrate Characteristics

Parameter	Impact	Typical value
Via pitch	Fanout, footprint size	0.2 mm
Via diameter	Routing pitch, line density, mfg. yield	0.050
Line width	Routing density (generally via density) will limit	0.1 mm
Line capacitance	Attenuation	2.4 pF/cm
Line resistance	Delay	0.5 Ω/cm 5.2 mΩ/$\square$
Standard line impedance X signal		45 Ω
Standard line impedance Y signal		45 Ω
Decoupling capacitance		1.0 pF/cm
Via capacitance		2.8 pF/cm
Via resistance		18 mΩ/mm
Dielectric constant	Electrical performance limited to lower clock rates	9.5–10.3

taining only bare die which is assembled and tested as a single discrete function before attachment to a more complex subsystem or board.

6.2.2 MCM-C

Multichip modules built on a cofired ceramic substrate (MCM-C) were initially designed for high-performance mainframe applications and are the closest point of MCM evolution pointing back to hybrid circuits. In cofired substrates, multiple layers are fired simultaneously, while thick-film hybrids are fired one layer at a time. This technology is based on a variety of different materials and firing temperatures. (High-temperature cofired substrates are fired at 1500°C, while low-temperature substrate firing temperatures range from 850 to 900°C.) Traditionally, MCM-C has been the best MCM technology for embedding large numbers of passive devices, including capacitors, resistors, RF couplers, filters, and power dividers. An overview of the electrical characteristics of MCM-C is provided in Table 6.5. The technology has been part of mainframe and many military computer systems since the late 1970s and has many automotive applications as well.

MCM-C's advantages include a high degree of ruggedness and hermeticity (operating environments up to 350°C are supported in some cofired technologies). MCM-C supports many layers of interconnect structure, although the advantage of multiple layers is offset by the relatively modest routing pitch of the ceramic technology. Due to substrate material characteristics, for some applications MCM-C forces the designer to choose between relative levels of thermal and electrical performance—high-temperature cofired has excellent thermal performance with modest electrical characteristics, while LTCC reverses these attributes. MCM-C is built in generally larger substrate or module form factors than MCM-L or MCM-D, and large numbers of ICs and passives are often built into ceramic MCMs. MCM-C is fired in large multilayer sheets or panels. These panels are then cut into individual MCM substrates. Bare die and any passive components are attached to the substrates, and the substrates are assembled into packages, forming a module like that shown in Fig. 6.5.

6.2.3 MCM-D

MCM-D (the name is derived from *deposited* thin film) is a multichip module technology built using thin films of metal and dielectric on a substrate or decal. MCM-D was developed for use in mainframes and high-volume telecommunications applications where system clock rates exceeded 500 MHz, board space was extremely limited, and thermal challenges were in the 10- to 100-W (and greater) range. Although sometimes viewed as silicon on silicon—because bare die are attached directly to a silicon substrate—MCM-D technology is also built in volume using ceramic, glass, and metal substrates.

MCM-D is manufactured in processes that closely resemble semiconductor manufacturing. Some MCM-D foundries use copper conductors with an organic (polyimide or similar) dielectric, while other MCM-D manufacturers use a process even closer to the semiconductor industry, and employ aluminum conductors and a silicon dioxide (or other inorganic) dielectric material. A sample cross section of an MCM-D structure is shown in Fig. 6.6.

Costs in MCM-D are extremely volume-sensitive, due to the investment required to operate a wafer fabrication facility. For this reason, some MCM-D manufacturers have developed large area panel technologies for MCM-D substrates, using process technology similar to that originally developed for the flat panel display (FPD) industry.

MCM-D should generally be chosen for high-volume applications requiring very small form factors and thermal performance of 0.24 to 1.5°C/cm^2/W, as well as interconnect routing densities above 300 pads/in^2. Additional characteristic parameters of MCM-D are detailed in Table 6.6.

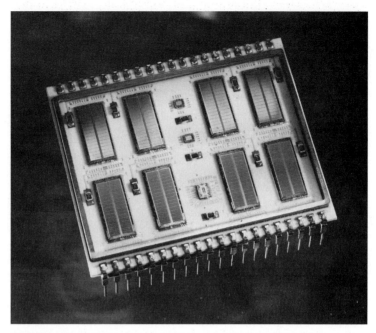

FIGURE 6.5 Cofired ceramic multichip module (MCM-C). *(Photo courtesy National Semiconductor Corporation.)*

6.2.4 Mixed MCM Technologies

Companies specializing in MCM-L or MCM-C often support design and/or manufacturing processes which deposit a few layers of high-density interconnect structure on the surface of their substrates, thus taking advantage of the line density offered by MCM-D. Other MCMs which combine technologies and manufacturing processes are also available—MCM-L with plasma-etch vias provides interconnect densities close to MCM-D within a PWB-cost structure and MCM-C with a thin-film layer or two provides a way to integrate large numbers of passives and ICs with very dense signal-routing requirements. Finally, MCM-D in combination with laminate or ceramic technology produces products with the performance of MCM-D and pricing structures virtually identical to traditional PWB or cofired implementations. This mixing of technologies is roughly equivalent to the many PCB designs that integrate through-hole, surface-mount, and COB components in a single board.

6.2.5 Other MCM Technologies

Specific design issues have led to a number of alternative MCM technologies. These MCMs are built to address unique form factor or electrical performance requirements. Many standard and custom MCMs have been introduced using these MCMs in the workstation and aerospace markets.

6.2.5.1 Chips First.   One alternative MCM technology uses a manufacturing process whereby the ICs are placed at the bottom of the MCM, with the interconnect layers built (or placed) over the bare die. This chips-first process has the advantage of thin-film geometries

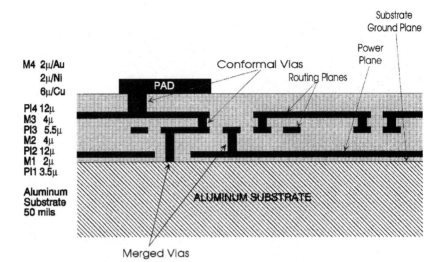

FIGURE 6.6 Cross section of MCM-D multichip module. Layers shown in the drawing are defined as follows (starting from the base substrate at the bottom of the module): PI1 is the first layer of polyimide, and provides a 3.5-μm layer of insulation between the ground plane and the power plane. The first layer of deposited metal (M1) is a 2-μm layer of copper which functions as the power plane. PI1 is a 12-μm layer of polyimide between the power plane and the first routing plane. M2 is the first of two 4-μm copper routing planes. PI3 is a 5.5-μm dielectric layer between the M2 and M3 (4 μm of copper) routing layers. PI4 is a final dielectric layer between the routing layers and the pad layer, where the signal traces are attached to the bare die. The pad layer (M4 on the drawing) is composed of 6 μm of copper, 2 μm of nickel, and 2 μm of gold, as is the top layer of this thin-film substrate structure. When MCM-D is built on a silicon or ceramic substrate, one additional metal deposition step (traditionally referred to as Metal 0 [M0] is used for a ground plane. The layers of polyimide between the copper planes also allow the MCM-D substrate designer to build in some decoupling capacitance, reducing the needed for some added decoupling capacitors in the MCM design.

with manufacturing costs similar to panel-based MCM-D, since the substrate is built as a sheet rather than a spin/sputter/plate process. Chips first also provides excellent electrical performance—in some cases even better signal qualities than more traditional MCM-D. The major disadvantage of this process is an absolute requirement for fully tested bare die, since in most cases rework or die replacement is problematic.

6.2.5.2 3-D MCMs. A second alternate MCM technology stacks multiple bare die together, achieving silicon/package densities in excess of 1–1 in the x/y direction. So-called 3-D memory products, like the example shown in Fig. 6.7, are the most successful of this type of MCM architecture, although microprocessor and DSP-based 3-D MCMs have been implemented in very high performance aerospace applications. 3-D technology works best with devices like DRAMs or SRAMs, which can be easily postprocessed to route all their I/O to one or more sides of the die. Using 3-D technology, very large memory configurations can be built in PCMCIA, SIMM, or other industry-standard package form factors.

6.3 SELECTING AN APPROPRIATE MCM TECHNOLOGY

Each individual MCM technology can be configured as a workable solution to a specific problem. Short of multiple parallel product implementations, it can be difficult to make the initial

TABLE 6.6 Selected MCM-D Technology Characteristics

Parameter	Impact	Typical value
Line width	Interconnect density	10–20 µm
Line pitch	Smallest footprint, pitch	75–50 µm
Via width	With geometries smaller than those available by drilling, MCM-D has high routability for very complex designs, supporting a smaller board footprint than other MCM technologies and a higher silicon/substrate ratio	30–50 µm
Number of layers	Cost, wiring density	1–6
Die attach technology	Mechanically compatible with volume assembly infrastructure and processes	Wirebond, TAB, flip chip
Thermal resistance	Better thermal performance than ceramic or laminate	1.62–0.24°C/cm^2/W
Characteristic impedance	Better electrical performance/higher clock rate	50–60 Ω ±5%
1-sided near-end crosstalk	Electrical performance	1.9–3.2%
Dielectric constant	Electrical performance—lower delay	2.7–3.5
Line resistance	Electrical performance	4.5 mΩ/□ 2 Ω/cm
Line capacitance	Electrical performance—reduced attenuation	1.02–0.82 pF/cm
Line inductance	Electrical performance	3.41–3.02 nH/cm

technology decision for a specific application. Some flexible rules and/or guidelines exist for first-order technology selection and are outlined in Table 6.7.

6.4 MCM DESIGN

Unlike most PCB designs, where the interface is fairly well defined and where an average PCB designer can get predictable output (boards) without knowing many of the details of the fabrication process, MCM design requires close communication between the design team and the personnel who will be performing substrate fabrication, substrate test, module assembly (die attach and die-to-substrate interconnect), module functional test, and module qualification.

Due to the history of large R&D expenditures for MCM development, many different technologies and methodologies exist. As a result, almost any MCM design is achievable in any given technology—and the most important consideration is designing a cost-effective solution to meet a given set of product pricing and performance targets.

6.4.1 Determining the Designer

An important first step is determining who will perform the MCM design. Many first-time MCM implementations are designed successfully by OEMs with no in-house MCM design

FIGURE 6.7 New memory wafer stacking technology. The new 128-Mbyte memory wafer stack in center of picture holds as much information, equal to approximately 100 novel-length books, as the 64 standard memory chips surrounding it. Cubic Memory, Inc., of Scotts Valley, Calif., announced that it has developed a new technology for stacking semiconductor wafers, multidice segments, and individual dice. The patented technology enables the production of new memory and storage solutions with very high density that can be easily manufactured at a reasonable cost. *(Photo courtesy Cubic Memory, Inc.)*

expertise. They are able to perform this due to the availability of sophisticated MCM design software, by the support available from design software vendors and MCM manufacturers, and the availability of technology files customized for specific MCM foundries, which facilitate the transfer of specific design rules into a generic design platform.

However, MCM design software and foundry-specific technology files are no substitute for the level of support provided by a proven manufacturer. Extra time for the inevitable learning curve should be added to the product schedule for the MCM design if the choice is made to proceed independently.

An alternative design strategy is to take advantage of a third-party design service. These organizations are prepared to evaluate a specific set of product requirements and undertake the design of a relatively unbiased solution. The only disadvantage to this strategy is the risk that this approach, through flexible, will not result in a design as optimized as one undertaken by a design team dedicated to a particular foundry and technology.

The third option is to allow a foundry's design team to understand your requirements, and optimize the use of their technologies to meet your program requirements.

Since MCM manufacturers have all realized that not every MCM design can be developed for optimal results using any specific technology, many have aligned themselves with strategic alliances and partnerships to offer a full range of MCM technologies based on laminate, cofired, and thin-film substrate processes.

TABLE 6.7   MCM Technology Selection Advisor

Application	Most appropriate MCM technology	Factors driving technology selection
Few ICs, 3 W or less, under 200 I/O on module	MCM-L	For MCM of low complexity, if via geometries do not form extremely fine line PCB, a laminate MCM is appropriate.
Embedded passives	MCM-C, MCM-D	Typically, MCM-C processes have best results in embedded passives; MCM-D characteristics may eliminate some passives.
High clock rate (150 MHz+)	MCM-D	Thin-film MCMs offer best signal quality.
Form factor 2 in² or less	MCM-D	Thin-film MCMs offer smallest form factor.
Modest board space available	MCM-L	Where size reduction is not a program goal, the design should default to MCM-L.
High power (10 W or more)	MCM-D, MCM-C	High-power chip-on-board designs are highly likely to face difficult routing, and cause difficulties in manufacturing (CTE mismatch between PCB and die).
BGA	MCM-L, MCM-C, MCM-D	BGA packages are available using all MCM substrate technologies. Choosing the type of BGA is purely driven by the substrate criteria.
Hermetic package	MCM-C, MCM-D on ceramic	While PCB substrates could be placed in a hermetic package, the default decision should be to use a ceramic substrate.
Multiple, high I/O ICs	MCM-D	Wiring and pad density highest using MCM-D.
Very low power (1 V)	MCM-D	MCM-D offers best signal quality.
Low-medium I/O count	MCM-L	Routing density is adequate, no requirement for staggered leads.
MIL STD	MCM-C, MCM-D on ceramic	Driven by military qualification standards.
Low power, very low cost	MCM-L	Watch cost crossover with thin film, higher pad pitches may drive preference for MCM-D.
Low z-axis	MCM-D, MCM-L	Thinnest substrate materials.
Large number of ICs, low silicon integration	MCM-L	Chip-on-board (MCM-L) best fit for large PWB-based substrates.

6.4.2   Design Tradeoffs

The MCM design effort requires an iterative process wherein cost tradeoffs and analysis are required when a product design is started. The decision matrix to follow in reaching a conclusion to implement an MCM design using a particular substrate technology includes at least the steps in Table 6.8, drawn from a workstation design.

6.4.3   MCM Design Process

The MCM design process is outlined in Fig. 6.8. Typically the process starts off with the collection or derivation of the requirements for the new module. Information that must be available includes that detailed in Sec. 6.10. Typical design issues are summarized in Table 6.9, and include the following items:

TABLE 6.8 Technology Selection Process for a RISC Workstation
Default design eliminated MCM-L quickly.

Problem	Implementation choice
Existing SMT layout gating performance of . workstation	Evaluate impact of MCM.
Components consist of CPU, bus interface, five cache RAMS, ASIC, small number of passives.	20-W CPU requires heat sink. Rule out COB, MCM-L.
Critical path on workstation is from the CPU to the bus interface and cache RAMs.	No need to incorporate new ASIC or other silicon in design; model MCM performance to understand impact of improved signal quality on system performance.
Wiring and via density very high.	Rule out MCM-C. Evaluate MCM-D.
Passives key to design.	Examine impact of keeping passives off MCM.
Need to keep mfg. cost same or less due to competitive market.	Reduce size of MCM-D substrate; integrate CPU, bus interface, SRAMs on module.

- Choice of substrate technology
- MCM and program cost goals
- Testability requirements including availability of boundary scan or built-in self-test (BIST) on the ICs
- Thermal load
- Bill of materials
- Top view of the module showing proposed component placement
- Cross section showing the assembly method and connection scheme from the components to module pins
- Preliminary thermal analysis
- Preliminary electrical analysis

Die data are used to generate a physical template of the die, which will allow the substrate pad location to be determined in relation to the die pads. The netlist (if supplied by the MCM customer) is used to determine connectivity between components.

Once the quotation has been reviewed by the MCM customer, it is merged with any new technical requirements, and the MCM design cycle moves into the design capture phase. Here the detailed analysis required to complete the quotation is merged with any design information developed independently by the customer (more detailed schematics, netlists, and similar items). These data are merged into the design database and referenced throughout the rest of the design cycle.

The next phase includes the detailed engineering analysis, in which critical electrical, mechanical, and thermal elements are merged into the design. Electrical analysis focuses on meeting the noise and time-of-flight budgets specified for the product. Noise analysis ensures the integrity of the signals under dynamic conditions (simultaneous switching.) Time-of-flight analysis compares the interconnect delay against a customer-defined budget.

An optimal placement is chosen based on routing constraints, which can include the ability to achieve 100 percent routability of the design on the preferred substrate technology, but also the minimization of clock skew or delay on critical nets. Placement is also driven by ther-

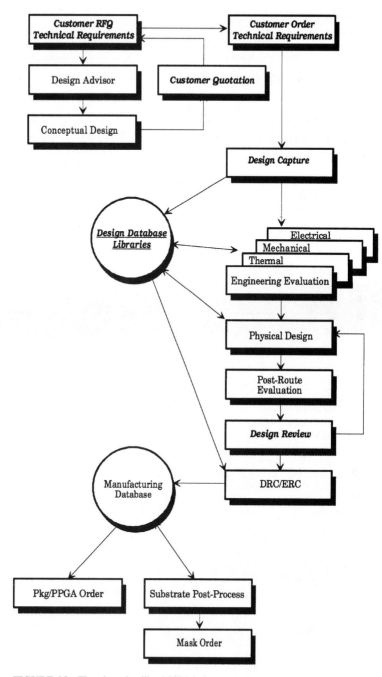

FIGURE 6.8   Flowchart detailing MCM design process.

TABLE 6.9   Early Decisions Critical to MCM Program Success
Careful analysis at this stage will help ensure a cost-effective implementation that meets program goals.

Multichip module attribute	Impact on MCM design process
Preferred substrate technology	Routability, cost
Environment for module	Package type, reliability constraints, form factor available
Cost goals	Substrate selection, package type
Lifetime product volume	Substrate selection, interconnect selection, test methodology, manufacturing ramp. Ask MCM foundry where price breaks occur before determining your purchasing strategy—you may choose a one-time-buy for a specific design.
Thermal environment	Package type, substrate type, routing density, number and type of vias
Number of bare die required	Substrate size, MCM technology
Number and type of passives required	Substrate technology
Die attach methodology	Test methodology, pad selection
Die cost/rework goals	Test method, die pads required
Test methodology	Rework or discard test failures

mal simulation, which takes as its inputs the thermal conductivity and heat spreading of the substrate materials, as well as other environmental attributes and mechanisms for removing heat from the MCM. The goal here is to ensure that the maximum junction temperatures specified for the die are not exceeded by the module and package design. Lowering T_{jmax} (maximum junction temperature of the individual ICs) has a direct impact on MCM (and total system) reliability.

A power supply analysis should be performed to ensure that there is a sufficient number of power and ground pins to minimize inductance (and therefore ground bounce), especially in the worst case with all outputs switching simultaneously. Since overcoming signal quality problems may be the reason an MCM is being specified, this analysis requires careful consideration. Normally full planes are dedicated to both ground and power supply; when this is not the case (as in a low-cost design in which ground, power, and routing traces are merged onto fewer layers), a full dc and ac power supply analysis must be performed.

Physical design comprises four major steps:

- Packaging the design
- Designing the components
- Placement
- Routing

Packaging involves creating a netlist and bill of materials for the design. Component design completes (or imports from the design library) a template for each of the ICs used in the MCM. Placement locates the components on the substrate, and routing connects each of the component pins or pads using connectivity information in the netlist.

Nets are normally routed in a series of passes. First, a test route is used to determine whether 100 percent routability is achievable given other constraints, such as thermal vias; next critical nets could be routed by special net rules, or even by hand; finally, the rest of the routing can be completed, usually by autorouting software.

Postroute analysis could include any or all of: electrical, thermal, mechanical, power supply integrity, or reliability analysis.

Following the postroute analysis, systematic design verification (see the DRC/ERC design rule check/electrical rule check stage in the design process overview) should be performed, where electrical opens and shorts are detected, and where metal trace and via size and spacing violations, if any, are detected. Finishing details, such as alignment marks and test structures used during the manufacturing process, are then added.

6.4.4 MCM Design Software

Multichip modules are designed using software that is derived from the design tools used by the PCB and semiconductor industries. This software runs on high-end PCs and workstations and is capable of importing and exporting files in standard formats such as Gerber and GDS II that are tailored to the requirements of MCM and PCB manufacturers.

Beyond basic MCM design software, the most important additional software for the MCM designer is an MCM technology (or design) toolkit. Toolkits are software products consisting of libraries of design rules, primitives, and manufacturability guidelines and are developed by MCM manufacturers to allow a commercial software platform to be tailored to a specific MCM foundry. This speeds implementation of the design by assuring that any constraints in the targeted process are accurately reflected in the design software.

The MCM designer will require specialized tools for module layout, routing, thermal and electrical modeling, design rule checking, as well as libraries of pads, vias, and die. Top-layer metallization information is critical for MCM designs, since a designer must know the function and location of each bond pad or other next-level interconnect structure on the die—details that are not required when designing with traditionally packaged ICs. It will be necessary to work closely with the IC manufacturer to ensure that pad changes and changes in die size are incorporated in the library of die used to support any particular MCM design.

6.4.5 Designing in MCMs

When an MCM has been properly designed, it should present no more challenge to a product designer than any other packaged integrated circuit. In fact, the board designer has to accommodate fewer components, since ICs that would otherwise require routing resources are contained inside the MCM. In general, the specific number of ICs inside an MCM should not be a consideration for the board designer. Some MCMs may, however, require multiple supply voltages, and MCMs may be larger than some single-chip packages.

6.4.6 Impact of MCMs on Product Design

Multichip modules can provide a number of cost and improved time-to-market benefits to any program. These benefits are most readily derived when the decision to implement a product based on MCM technology is made early enough to influence the design of all the critical system components. Design stages of special importance include the following.

6.4.6.1 IC Design.   Where a designer can influence IC design tradeoffs, it is possible to optimize the interaction between the semiconductor devices in the module. This optimization can also permit the IC designer to specify less robust drivers, reducing the buffer setup times (which translates into faster IC performance) and also reducing the power levels required for the drivers, which translates into lower power requirements and less heat that must be dissipated through the MCM.

6.4.6.2 PCB Design. By moving all the routing complexity inside the MCM and simplifying the PCB design, the board designer can reduce the number of layers and fanout required to support the multichip module, and can make board-level test simpler. COB-based system designs must make careful tradeoffs when specifying ICs with 4-mil or smaller pad pitches—the cost impact of additional layers and the fanout required to support the die pad pitch may make the PCB cost prohibitive and will certainly add to the test complexity. Above 4-mil pad pitches, board designs for COB and MCM-L applications are relatively straightforward and have few cost or test performance penalties.

6.4.6.3 Thermal Challenges. Reliability is directly related to the junction temperature of operating ICs. Many traditional board designs attempt to address thermal problems in high-power designs by placing high-wattage ICs as far apart as possible. This practice has a number of drawbacks for high-speed designs, in which designers optimize performance by increasing the number of routing layers on the board and reducing chip-to-chip trace lengths. In an MCM, the ICs are located within a single package, making thermal management a localized problem. Ensure that you understand the thermal models driving the performance of the MCM, and also make sure that the cabinet thermal characteristics can support the MCM's requirements for cooling.

Frequently, the PCB designer is able to plan for the electrical characteristics involved in MCM implementation, but overlooks two other criteria: the MCM is very likely to be larger than a single-chip package and the thermal challenge of an MCM may be substantially different from that of a single-chip component. For high reliability, boards must be designed with the maximum operating temperature of all the ICs inside the MCM in mind.

6.5 MCM DIE INTERCONNECT TECHNOLOGIES

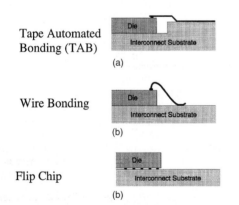

Tape Automated Bonding (TAB)

(a)

Wire Bonding

(b)

Flip Chip

(b)

FIGURE 6.9 Common MCM die interconnect technologies: (*a*) tape-automated bonding (TAB), in which the die is attached to the substrate using a carrier (see Fig. 6.10 for another view of a TAB device); (*b*) side view of wire bond, which is described in Sec. 6.5.2. Wire-bond die interconnect attaches a single gold or aluminum wire from the die pad to a corresponding structure on the surface of the substrate; (*c*) an alternate die interconnect technology, flip chip, in which the die makes contact with the substrate through solder balls or other interconnect structures in an area array structure on the surface of the die.

All multichip modules require the attachment of bare die to the substrate. Since the die are unpackaged, care must be taken during assembly to avoid damaging the unencapsulated silicon. Figure 6.9*a–c* shows three main die attach technologies: tape-automated bonding (TAB), wire bonding, and flip chip. Table 6.10 provides a summary of the attributes of each die interconnect technology. Typically, flip chip offers the lowest assembly cost and highest reliability, followed by wire bond, then TAB. The flip-chip and wire-bond assembly infrastructures are far more robust, while TAB often adapts readily to use on PCB substrates.

6.5.1 Tape-Automated Bonding (TAB)

TAB processes package the individual die in a plastic frame, permitting some test operations to be performed on the die prior to module assembly. Both epoxy- and solder-based processes are in use, and TAB frames can support a variety of die bonding pad orientations, including some formats where the bonding pads are in the center of the die in an array. TAB processes are readily automated (as are the other die attach technologies).

TAB's main limitation is the availability of TAB-packaged die, the costs associated with tooling, and the risk

TABLE 6.10   Overview of Commercial MCM Bare Die Interconnect Technologies

Attribute	TAB/tape	Wire bond	Flip chip
Supports ac test	Y	Y	Y
Supports die burn-in	N	Y	Y
Die-to-die spacing	Low	Med	Best
IC postprocessing	Y	N	Depends on supplier
Reworkable/replaceable	V good	Moderate	Moderate
Cost/lead	HI	Med	Low
Widespread availability	N	Y	N
Staggered leads	Y	Y	N/A
Area array pads	N	N	Y
Perimeter pads	Y	Y	Y

that different IC manufacturers (if they support TAB at all) might not support incompatible metallurgies, formats, bonding pitch, and the like. Figure 6.10 shows a small die in a TAB frame prior to assembly. A TAB'd die requires substrate real estate roughly equivalent to that required for the fanout of a bare die on a laminate substrate. Both wire-bond and flip-chip die attach technologies make more efficient use of a substrate, allowing smaller, lower-cost MCM implementations.

FIGURE 6.10   SEM (scanning electron microscope) photograph shows bare die in TAB frame. Outer lead bond pitch is 8 mil, and inner lead bond pitch is 4 mil. Die-to-die spacing with tab can be as low as 250 mil, depending on the fanout required.

6.5.2   Wire Bond

Wire bond is a die attach methodology characterized by an extremely mature technology, a large, low-cost infrastructure, and an ability to support large numbers of ICs. An example of a bare IC interconnected to a substrate using wire bond is shown in Fig. 6.11. Since large numbers of single-chip packages rely on wire-bond processes to attach the IC to the lead frame or other package component, most ICs have metallurgy and pad pitches which readily adapt to wire bond. In an MCM, the bond wires are either gold or aluminum. The process itself is reworkable and low cost, with pricing in commercial volumes under $0.01 per lead.

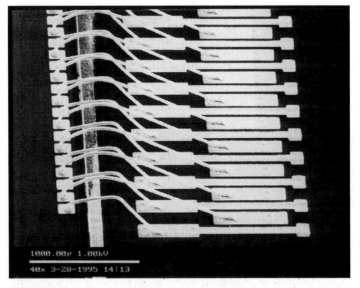

FIGURE 6.11   SEM photograph shows wire-bond die attach. Pad pitch for wire bond can be below 4 mil. Die-to-die spacing with wire bond can be as low as 45 mil.

6.5.3   Flip Chip

Flip-chip die attach processes have been developed to support pad-limited IC designs, allowing semiconductor designers to take advantage of this packaging technology to place pad sites in an array on the surface of the die, rather than just around the perimeter. Figure 6.12 shows a RISC microprocessor with solder balls on the die, ready for flip-chip die attach.

Among other advantages, flip-chip technology often permits the use of shorter trace lengths within the IC, allows the device to be made smaller, and also allows the MCM designer to support minimal die-to-die spacing (within thermal and rework constraints) in an MCM, since no space around the die is required for bond pads. Flip chip is also used to design die for optimum silicon performance in leading-edge applications. Flip-chip technology does have a few drawbacks: Not every IC design is built using this process, so a decision to use flip chip for all the devices in an MCM may require postprocessing the die to put solder bumps on the pads. Finally, differing thermal expansion coefficients between bare die and the substrate material may require alternate substrate starting materials.

For some applications, PCB-based substrates may be effective when using wire bond or TAB but unable to support flip chip. Before specifying a flip-chip implementation, ensure that the thermal properties of the substrate and die attach material will be compatible.

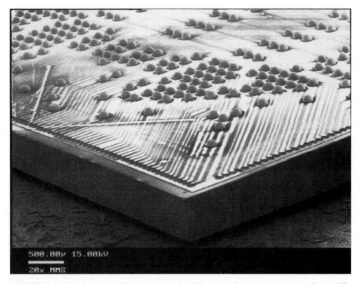

FIGURE 6.12   Bumped die prepared for flip-chip die attach process. Some ICs
are configured for either wire bond or flip chip—the perimeter wire-bond pads are
visible in this SEM photograph, as well as the solder balls required for the IBM C4
flip-chip process. Flip-chip die-to-die spacing can be under 40 mil and is gated only
by assembly and rework fixturing and the thermal performance of the MCM.

A number of different flip-chip processes are supported. Gold-based, solder-based, and
epoxy-based flip-chip technologies have reached the market.

6.6   MCM PACKAGES AND TRADEOFFS

Multichip modules can take advantage of almost every type of package technology developed
for the single-chip packaging industry. MCMs are built in hermetic ceramic QFPs, in pin grid
arrays, and in a variety of low-cost plastic packages, including ball grid arrays (BGAs), plastic
leadless chip carriers (PLCCs), and plastic quad flat packs (PQFPs). The MCM designer will
choose a package type based on the number of I/O required for the module, the thermal performance required, and any environmental constraints (especially those requiring hermeticity). MCMs adapt readily to ball grid array (BGA) and other package technologies, and they
integrate readily into high-volume assembly processes when built into industry-standard footprints and form factors.

Since almost any IC packaged in a single-chip package is much smaller than the package outline, many die can be placed in a standard form factor like a 28-mm molded PQFP, for instance.

6.7   OVERVIEW OF MULTICHIP MODULE MANUFACTURING

All multichip modules contain a number of common steps: design and manufacture of an
interconnect substrate, substrate test, die attach, packaging or encapsulation, and module test.
All MCM manufacturing processes are reworkable to some degree, depending on the stage of
manufacture and the die-to-die spacing inherent in the design.

Multichip modules and substrates are typically manufactured and assembled in Class 10,000 clean rooms, although substrate fabrication (especially MCM-D) may take place in Class 100 environments. Contamination and other environmental controls (especially humidity) must be in place to at least the same level as in single-chip package assembly processes, since the same die attach technologies are used in MCM manufacturing. Furthermore, plastic-packaged MCMs share the same reliability parameters as plastic single-chip packages. Steps must be taken to maintain a low-moisture environment to limit "popcorning" and other process defects inherent in plastic packages.

6.7.1 MCM-L

Laminate-technology MCMs are built on a PCB substrate, using identical manufacturing processes common to fineline PCB designed for surface-mount manufacturing (see Part 3). MCM-L substrates can be configured to support wire bond (chip-on-board), flip chip, or TAB-mounted ICs, subject only to the limitations of via density and thermal and TCE capabilities required for the MCM. COB-based MCM-L designs may be protected by glob top, although many MCM-L designs are packaged in QFP, BGA, or other plastic packages and then attached using standard SMT processes to the next level of interconnect. The only difference in MCM-L or COB substrates and traditional board manufacturing processes is the requirement that metal pads be built under the die site to permit die replacement.

6.7.2 MCM-C

Cofired ceramic substrates are built in multiple layers, then fired together. Initially the ceramic is milled and mixed, then rolled into sheets and dried. Once the material is dry, the interconnect for each layer is built. First vias are punched, then the conductor traces are built using a screened-on paste. This process is repeated for the number of layers required by the design, which can support 30 or more layers. When complete, the substrate layers are stacked and laminated, then singulated, or cut to their final size.

Once singulated, the substrates are fired at a temperature set for the ceramic technology in use (high- or low-temperature ceramics have different thermal and electrical properties based on their starting material). The fired substrates are plated, then pin brazing is performed.

Following the brazing operation, the MCM moves into assembly, where bare die are attached and a metal lid is placed over the die cavity to protect the MCM. Typically, these lids are hermetically sealed.

The resulting module is an extremely robust structure with good thermal and electrical properties. A particular advantage of cofired ceramic MCMs is the ability of the technology to permit many different passive devices into the substrate layers. This capability has been used extensively in automotive, telecommunications, power management, and many military and aerospace modules.

6.7.3 MCM-D

Deposited multilayer thin-film modules (MCM-D) are built on processing lines that have traditionally resembled semiconductor manufacturing. Thin-film technology shares many attributes with semiconductor manufacturing and is often performed at former semiconductor fabrication facilities.

MCM-D manufacturing begins with the deposition of a layer of metal used for the ground plane. Technologies based on metal substrates may not require this step, since the base substrate material will itself provide the ground plane. However, large numbers of MCM-D substrates are built on silicon, ceramic, or other structures.

Following the deposition of the ground plane, a layer of dielectric material is deposited, either spun on, extruded, sprayed on, or placed in a sheet of material. Metal for conductive traces is then sputtered onto the water. Depending on the nature of the dielectric (if photo-sensitive materials are used, these steps are unnecessary), a thin photoresistive coating is applied, then the wafer is exposed through a semiconductor-like mask, and the interconnect layer is developed.

Following development, the image is etched into the dielectric, then plated up to the appropriate thickness. The process is repeated through each layer of interconnect, including signal traces and plasma-etched vias, until (generally four) layers have been deposited on the substrate. Typically, MCM-D substrates have a power plane, ground plane, two or more routing planes, and a pad layer which supports interconnection to the ICs.

6.8   TESTING MULTICHIP MODULES

MCM test strategies and technologies have evolved from two parallel directions: module-level functionality testing similar to that defined in Chap. 33 (testing PCB boards) and IC-level testing. MCM test strategies must be closely coupled with an understanding of the costs and resource tradeoffs to be encountered during manufacturing. At minimum, MCM test strategies fall into roughly three different segments: prototype, low volume, and high volume.

6.8.1   Prototype and Low-Volume MCM Test

Testing of multichip module prototypes (prototype lot sizes range in quantity from 1 to 100 units) is typically focused on checking for opens and shorts in the module. This may extend to boundary scan, in which the individual ICs are run through their scan chain. During prototype build test coverage is quite limited, but the tradeoff is the determination if the design is viable. Per-unit tests can take up to a half hour, using capital equipment that is in the $100,000 range. Development of the test routines can take anywhere from a few days to a week or more.

6.8.2   QV Testing for Medium-Volume MCMs

Modules whose lifetime build will be in the thousands adapt most readily to a test strategy built around quick-verify (or QV) test equipment. This test approach is based on technologies used in module-level testing—a custom set of hardware is developed, along with a set of test vectors. Test time is typically a few minutes for a fairly complex module, and the test routines normally take a few labor-weeks to develop. Test coverage is much better than boundary scan and net integrity test, at the cost of application or product-specific test fixture development, along with development of the test routines themselves.

6.8.3   High-Volume MCM Test Strategy

For very high volume MCMs (100,000 or more units), it is cost-effective to migrate the test strategy to a modified IC tester. Test equipment costs can range from $500,000 to over $2,000,000, accompanied by a labor-year or more of test vector development, but the payback is very thorough test coverage of all the ICs in a module in seconds. Due to the cost of the test equipment and the engineering effort required to develop the test routines for a specific application, it is critical that very high throughput and tester utilization be achieved.

TABLE 6.11   Attributes Required for Specifying Multichip Modules

MCM attribute	Impact on program/product goals
Delivery schedule	When parts are needed, resource loading, qualification plans, rush charges may apply
Program volume	Need to ask foundry where price breaks occur
Maximum module dimensions (x, y)	Substrate size, cost, thermal performance
z axis	Thermal impact, ability to implement dual-sided MCM
Airflow in cabinet	Thermal, lifetime reliability
Number of power-on/lifetime	Important for determining MCM reliability
MTBF	Package type, IC testing required
Next-level interconnect	Package type, assembly cost
Die sizes $(x/y,$ thickness)	Substrate size, die attach technology
Netlist availability	Design time
Netlist format	Compatibility with foundry
Number of die	Substrate size, thermal load, assembly cost, substrate technology
JTAG or BIST on die	Built-in self test allows ICs to be tested without proprietary test vectors—JTAG and BIST reduce test costs in prototype and volume
Electrical rules/net topology—differential pairs, minimum delay rules, etc.	Substrate selection, degree of modeling required to ensure design acceptance, also may drive use of product-specific design rules
Critical nets	May require manual placement, different geometries in the case of specific signals
Number and type of passive components	Substrate technology, module size, assembly cost
Hermeticity requirements	Substrate technology—hermetic packages invariable are larger and more expensive
Total number of connectors from the MCM (signal, ground, power)	Substrate technology, package type
Pad, ball, or pin pitch to next level of interconnect	Assembly technology, module assembly yield
Die bond pad size	Determines assembly technology, reworkability
Die bond pad pitch	Determines pad pitch on substrate
Die bond pad metallurgy	For compatibility with die interconnect process
Perimeter or area array pads	Die attach technology
Die supply format (TAB, tape, wafer, gel-pak)	Tooling
Die test vectors available	May have yield impact if unavailable and if die not functionally tested prior to shipment
Module block diagram format/availability	Reduces design time for foundry
Path length restrictions	Drives design rules for specific MCM technology
Module noise margin	Assists with simulation requirements
Minimum rise time	"
Minimum pulse width	"
Maximum clock rate	"

TABLE 6.11 (*Continued*)   Attributes Required for Specifying Multichip Modules

MCM attribute	Impact on program/product goals
Loading or termination	Can drive layout of MCM, help determine if terminating resistors required (additional passive components = additional surface mount attachments, translating to higher assembly cost)
SPICE models available	Required for simulation
System cooling medium	Heat-sink design/requirements
System temperature and velocity	"
Junction temperature	Technology tradeoffs/reliability modeling
Operating temp range	"
Storage temp range	"
Allowable package thermal resistance	If customer-specified package

6.9   PURCHASING MULTICHIP MODULES

The MCM implementer will face some design and supplier management hurdles immediately. Early issues which must be decided in partnership with the chosen MCM supplier include the following.

Die supply is a critical determinant of MCM implementation success. If particular components are unavailable in bare die form, or available only for a prohibitive premium, the MCM may require redesign. Die availability is the most critical early issue for the MCM implementer. While the situation in bare die availability, pricing, and quality levels has improved greatly, and IC suppliers have announced known good die programs, this is early homework for both the OEM and their MCM partner.

An important consideration when entering the MCM design cycle is to specify that the MCM be compatible with standard assembly fixturing, to keep manufacturing and test tooling charges to a minimum. This is done by working within the design rules of MCM manufac-

TABLE 6.12   Key Points When Selecting a Source for Custom MCMs

Semiconductor partnerships	The ability to source, test, and handle bare die from multiple suppliers is critical for most custom MCMs. Most MCMs have ICs from at least three different suppliers (a microprocessor, additional custom logic, and some cache [DRAM or SRAM]). Securing a low-cost, reliable die supply is essential when building MCMs.
Test (die, module, system) capability	Choose an MCM partner who can work with you on both prototype and volume test at all levels—bare die, substrate, and MCM. IC partnerships and test equipment partnerships are critical here.
MCM and PCB design processes and software compatible with your operations	Most MCM manufacturers have multiple design entry points and can import designs from multiple platforms. Ensure that your design process and tools are compatible early in the product cycle.

turers who offer their products in EIAJ or JEDEC-standard form factors. Ensure that (in-house or contract) assembly partners understand the physical dimensions and interconnect structure whereby your MCM(s) will be assembled onto the final product.

A common misperception of some MCM customers is to focus on substrate cost reduction—when the substrate (and package) cost is outweighed by the cost and quality level of the silicon to be integrated into the module. Many MCMs contain $100 to $1000 of bare die, making all but the most expensive packaging a tiny fraction of the die cost. If the die yield percentage shows any signs of dropping below the high 90s, the cost both in rework and die replacement can rapidly erode any incremental savings elsewhere in the module. The best strategy here is to work with IC suppliers selling bare die tested to the quality level of packaged parts, or make use of bare die burn-in and test technology to keep assembly and rework costs down and module yields high.

6.9.1 MCM Customer Checklist

1. Reduce the number of ICs and passives to be included in the MCM. Module size is a key cost driver in MCM manufacturing (in any MCM technology), as are the number of die. If large quantities of passives are required within the MCM, this should immediately indicate that a cofired ceramic or specialized thin-film solution may be required. Resistor networks may help, and most thin-film technologies may greatly reduce any requirements for decoupling capacitors on the MCM. Also, since combined IC yields will rapidly impact assembly and test yields for the module, it is generally useful to reduce the number of ICs to those which must remain on the MCM. By keeping noncritical components outside the module and on the board, substrate size is reduced, the package can be smaller, and MCM costs become much lower.

2. Keep high-I/O devices *inside* the MCM. A balance will need to be struck in the MCM design whereby reducing the I/O count outside the MCM (by integrating additional high-pin-count silicon inside the module) is weighted against the increase in MCM form factor. Building MCMs that have silicon with relatively low levels of integration is best left to a follow-on product generation—single-chip ASICs are a much better solution if the application requires a very large number of basic ICs.

3. Match the package type required to your application. If the application dictates the MCM package type, it may also dictate the type of MCM required. Hermetic packages typically require either MCM-C or MCM-D. Choose the lowest-cost package your design can sustain reliably. Pin grid arrays, PLCCs, and other nonhermetic solutions can permit more flexibility in the MCM technology. Plastic packages typically call for MCM-L, although some manufacturers have built MCM-D in plastic as well.

4. Understand the application's thermal requirements. An MCM with a demanding thermal load (over about 4 W) requires additional system design considerations. MCM-L generally is not the best choice for these applications, unless the form factor restrictions are relatively loose. To keep junction temperatures within acceptable limits, an MCM-L design may require cutting into the substrate in order to provide a direct thermal path to the back of the die, robbing the substrate of the routing channels that alternative substrate technologies normally will place under the die. MCM-C and MCM-D generally are best at handling dense modules with high junction temperatures.

5. High clock rates (over 150 MHz) and demanding signal quality requirements are the domain of MCM-D, with its aggressive line widths (typically in the 1- to 20-μm range.) MCM-C has been used as well for high-performance applications, especially if the MCM has a simultaneous requirement for a large number of die and the use of embedded passives. A small, high-performance MCM with many simultaneously switching outputs will generally be best implemented using thin film (MCM-D.) Thin-film technology is also the domain of low-power applications (below 3.3 V), since its signal quality is better than that of standard laminate or ceramic devices.

TABLE 6.13   Matrix of Organizations and Functional Responsibilities for Implementing a Custom Multichip Module

Function	MCM program responsibilities
MCM design	Substrate design, thermal and electrical modeling
Assembly and package engineering	MCM package design, assembly process development
Quality	Quality and reliability plan
Product engineering	Productization plan, yield forecast, manage technical risks, manage all development activities, interface to process development/process engineering organization
IC/die engineering	Technical interface to silicon vendor
Production planning	Die supply, inventory control, production planning, manage phase review process for product
Test engineering	Manage die test strategy and programs, develop and manage component (substrate and MCM) test plans
Manufacturing	Build product, manage to program cost goals

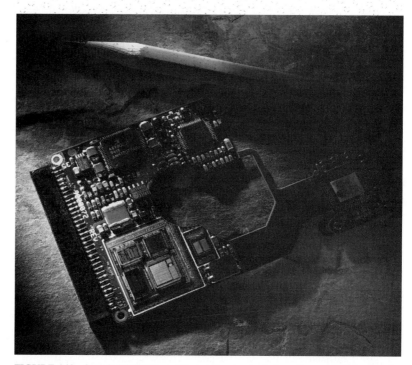

FIGURE 6.13   Sample PCMCIA card design shown prior to bare die encapsulation. Device contains one 600-I/O multichip module, a flash die attached using COB, and 100 surface-mount components.

6.9.2   Creating an MCM Specification

Some foundries may require a large number of details, others can deliver a budgetary quotation with minimal information, but a basic overall checklist includes the data highlighted in Table 6.11. Where this information is not immediately available it must be obtained or derived early in the request-for-quotation (RFQ) process. In selected circumstances, the MCM customer may be charged for the engineering resources required to complete critical items prior to the start of the MCM design process.

When preparing an RFQ for an MCM, the schedule and basic design information provided in Table 6.11 will help any foundry determine the feasibility of the design, including the best technology, which types of packages are appropriate, and whether the design as submitted is likely to meet the stated cost targets. Normally, a review will be held early in the RFQ process that will include representation from the customer and foundry organizations involved in the project, including substrate fabrication, module assembly, MCM, IC, and substrate test, and quality.

6.9.3   Comparison with PWB Sourcing

When identifying any manufacturing partner for a strategic component, there are some general requirements to consider, such as the ability to demonstrate robust quality and reliability, and sufficient capacity to meet product requirements. When choosing an MCM manufacturing partner one should additionally look for the attributes outlined in Table 6.12—namely, semiconductor partnerships, test capability, and design tools and procedures compatible with your environment.

Procuring a standard component based on MCM technology will require fairly standard levels of integration between the customer and the MCM supplier. However, a full-custom MCM requires a higher degree of interaction between the end customer, semiconductor manufacturer, and MCM foundry than would be the case in a simple contract manufacturing relationship using a high-volume PWB contract assembly service and single-chip-packaged ICs. Table 6.13 details some of the technical and business functions that must be involved when sourcing a custom MCM.

6.10   PC CARD (PCMCIA) IMPLEMENTATION OF MULTICHIP MODULES

PC cards, originally known as PCMCIA cards (the name is derived from the Personal Computer Memory Card International Association) are small peripheral devices designed for the notebook and hand-held computing market. Originally the exclusive domain of IC devices (typically memory), a wide variety of applications has been developed in card form factors,

TABLE 6.14   Overview of Standard PC Card Geometries and Typical Applications

Attribute	Types of PC cards		
	Type I	Type II	Type III
Height	3.3 mm	5 mmz	10.5 mm
Width	54 mm	54 mm	54 mm
Raised area	N/A	48 mm wide	51 mm wide
Typical applications	Flash memory	Network interfaces, disk drives	Disk drives
I/O count	68	68	68
I/O pitch	1.27 mm	1.27 mm	1.27 mm

from FLASH memory card drives to network and communications devices and disk drives, as well as a number of more exotic applications such as global positioning systems.

PC cards represent an area of opportunity for the MCM designer, since the cards are small, ideally draw low power (since they are often inserted into battery-operated computing devices), have no airflow, and must be extremely rugged in order to support a variety of operating environments and extensive handling at the hands of end users. Typically, PC cards have been built on MCM-L substrates, although specific applications (like the one shown in Fig. 6.13) have used MCM-D to integrate multiple ICs into the space normally allocated for one traditionally packaged component. See also Table 6.14.

ENGINEERING AND DESIGN OF PRINTED CIRCUITS

CHAPTER 7
PLANNING FOR DESIGN, FABRICATION, AND ASSEMBLY

Happy T. Holden
Hewlett-Packard Company, Loveland, Colorado

7.1 INTRODUCTION

Advances in interconnection technologies have occurred in response to the evolution of component packages, electronic technology, and increasingly complex functions. Therefore, it comes as no surprise that various forms of printed wiring remain the most popular and cost-effective method of interconnections.

Manufacturing, assembly, and test technologies have responded by improvements in their technologies. These increased capabilities have made selection of technologies, design rules, and features so complex that a new function has developed to allow for the prediction and selection of design parameters and performance-vs.-manufacturing costs. This is planning for design, fabrication, and assembly. This activity has also been called *design for manufacturing and assembly* or sometimes *predictive engineering*. It is essentially the selection of design features and options that promote cost-competitive manufacturing, assembly, and test practices.

Popular electronics today is competitive because of its cost. The need for cost reduction to remain competitive is a principle responsibility of product planning. On the average, 75 percent of the recurring manufacturing costs are determined by the design drawing and specifications.[1] This was one of the conclusions found by an extensive study General Electric conducted on how competitive products were developed. Manufacturing typically determines production setup, material management, and process management costs (Fig. 7.1), which are a minor part of the overall product cost.

Time-to-market along with competitive prices can determine a product's ultimate success. The first of a new electronic product in the market has the advantages. By planning the PWB layout and taking into consideration aspects and costs of PWB fabrication and assembly, the entire process of design and prototyping can be done with minimum redesigns (respins).

Electronics is one of the biggest enterprises there is globally. It is common for design to be done in one hemisphere and manufacturing in another. It is also common for manufacturing to be done in a number of different places simultaneously. An integrated approach must be adopted when the intention is to rationalize fabrication and assembly as part of the entire production system and not as individual entities, as shown in Fig. 7.2. This dispersed manufacturing must be taken into consideration during the design planning and layout process. No finished product is ever better than the original design or the materials it is made from. The purpose of this chapter is to provide information, concepts, and processes that lead to a

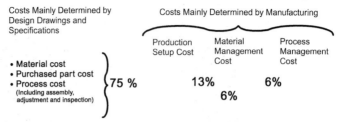

FIGURE 7.1 Typical product manufacturing costs. Design determines the majority of the cost of a product.

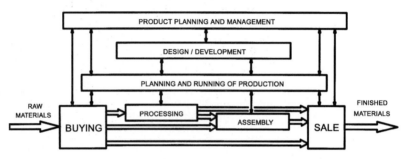

FIGURE 7.2 Fabrication and assembly rationalized by planning, manufacturing, and design.

thoughtfully and competitively designed printed circuit, ensuring that all pertinent design and layout variables have been considered.

7.2 GENERAL CONSIDERATIONS

The planning process central focus will be the tradeoffs between the loss and gain in layout, fabrication, assembly, and test vs. the costs in these domains. Therefore, some major considerations will be the following:

1. New product design process (Secs. 7.3.1, 7.3.2)

2. The role of metrics (Secs. 7.3.3, 7.3.4)

3. Layout tradeoff planning (Sec. 7.4)

4. PWB fabrication tradeoff planning (Sec. 7.5)

5. Assembly tradeoff planning (Sec. 7.6)

6. Tools for design advising and manufacturing audits (Sec. 7.7)

7.2.1 Planning Concepts

What is planning for design, fabrication, and assembly (PDFA)? It is a methodology that addresses early in the development process all those factors that can impact production and customer satisfaction. The central idea of PDFA is to make design decisions to optimize particular domains, such as producibility, assemblability, testability, and fit to a product family, in manufacturing. Planning takes place continuously in the electronic design environment (Fig. 7.3). The data and specifications flow in one direction, from product concept to manufacturing. During the design process, 60 percent of the manufacturing costs are determined in the first stages of design when only 35 percent of the design engineering costs have been expended. The typical response is shown in Fig. 7.4.[1]

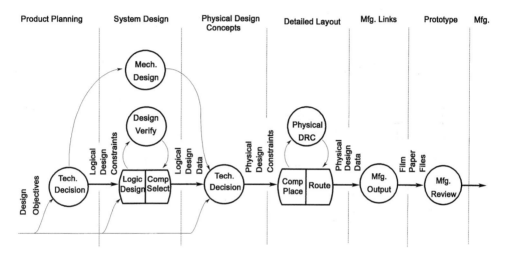

FIGURE 7.3   Today's electronic design environment.

7.2.2 Producibility

Producibility is now regarded as an intrinsic characteristic of a modern design. Like the concept of quality in manufacturing, it must be built in, not inspected in. So also producibility must be designed in; it cannot be a checkpoint in the design process or inspected in by tooling. Later in this chapter, we will offer a process to define producibility unique to each design or manufacturing process.

7.3 NEW PRODUCT DESIGN

The key to superior producibility in new product design is an expanded design process and the role of metrics or data-based analysis in planning tradeoffs.

7.3.1 Expanded Design Process

The new, expanded design process that incorporates planning, tradeoffs, and manufacturing audits is shown in Fig. 7.5. This differs from the more conventional design process (as seen in Fig. 7.3) by the inclusion of four important steps:

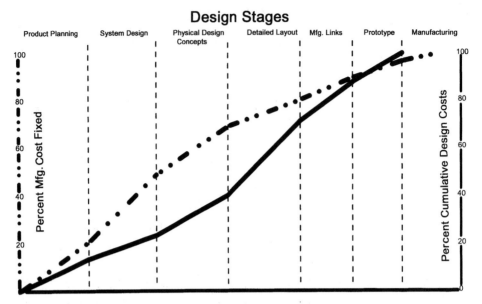

FIGURE 7.4   Design cost accumulation versus intrinsic manufacturing costs.

1. The formal *technology tradeoff analysis* during specifications
2. Detailed tradeoff selection of features for layout, fabrication, and assembly
3. Design advice during component placement and routing to carry out the plan
4. Manufacturing audits to review the finished layout for producibility, time-to-market, and competitiveness

7.3.2   Product Definition

The first new step in the expanded design process is specification and product definition. This key step takes ideas, user requirements, opportunities, and technologies and formulates the executable specifications of a new product, or in other words, partitions the design. During this operation, the ability to predict what will happen in manufacturing by technologists that may not have any manufacturing expertise can affect both time-to-market and ultimate product costs. Figure 7.6 shows the technology tradeoff analysis that requires the balance of loss and gain in the performance of various domains versus costs. Size and partitioning for IC and ASIC must be balanced with overall packaging costs and the resultant electrical performance. All of these factors affect the manufacturability and product cost.

Another definition of this process could be called a *verified design.*[2] This is compared to the traditional approach, which is a *nonverified design.* This is diagrammed in Fig. 7.7. The advantage of the verified design can be significant reduction in time by eliminating many redesigns in order to achieve the original product objectives.

7.3.3   The Role of Measures

Metrics are data and statistically backed measures—for example, wiring demand W_d (Sec. 1.3.2). These measures can be density, connectivity, or, in this context, producibility. These

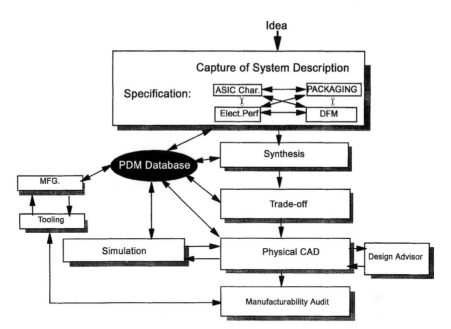

Specification:	- user supplied constraints and ideas formulate executable specifications
Capture of System Description	Technology Tradeoff Analysis: Balance of loss and gain in various domains' performance vs cost.
Synthesis	- generation of a netlist from the executable specifications.
Trade-off	- Selection of layout, fab and assy features vs. cost,
Physical CAD	- conversion of netlists to system & module layouts.
Simulation	- detailed analysis of design structures to support all other design (CAD) activities.
Design Advisor	- continuous display of design rated by performance rules
Manufacturability Audit	- check of design to mfg design rules and capabilities
Tooling	- conversion of module layouts to panel layout
MFG.	- conversion of module layouts to physical products
PDM Database	- Enterprise wide database to validate, store and control all product related information

FIGURE 7.5   The expanded electronics design process.

Specification:

- user supplied constraints and ideas formulate executable specifications

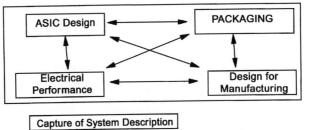

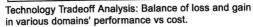

Technology Tradeoff Analysis: Balance of loss and gain
in various domains' performance vs cost.

FIGURE 7.6 Specifications determine product partitioning and producibility.

metrics are the basis for predicting and planning. When used in the design process, there are
four categories of measures applied to a product:

- *Metrics:* Both the product and the process are measured by physical data using statistical
  process control (SPC) and total quality management (TQM) techniques (predictive engineering process).
- *Figure of merit:* Both the product and the process are scored by linear equations developed by consensus expert opinion (expert opinion process).
- *Opinion:* Opinion, albeit from an expert, is applied after or concurrent with design (manufacturing engineering inspection process).
- *No opinions:* No attempt to inspect or improve the design is done during the specification,
  partitioning, or design stage (over-the-wall process).

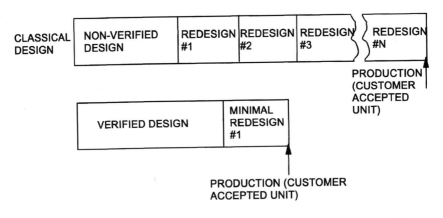

A Verified Design is accomplished with predictive models that include producibility,
performance and cost estimates.

FIGURE 7.7 Design incorporating tradeoffs vs. traditional design.

It is always preferable to have metrics when discussing producibility. But if metrics are not available, then opinions are better than nothing. The problem with opinions is that they are difficult to defend and explain and, when used in conjunction with producibility, many times they vary with each person. That is why the figure-of-merit process is so popular. For a small amount of work by experts it produces a scoring procedure that can be used and understood by all.

Metrics also establish a common language that links manufacturing to design. The producibility scores form a nonopinionated basis that allows a team approach that results in a quality, cost-competitive product (Fig. 7.8).

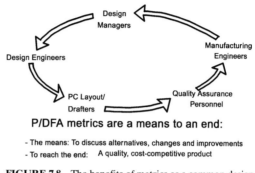

P/DFA metrics are a means to an end:

- The means: To discuss alternatives, changes and improvements
- To reach the end: A quality, cost-competitive product

FIGURE 7.8   The benefits of metrics as a common design language.

The strategy in applying these measures is shown in Fig. 7.9. The analysis process is unique to every individual and company, but certain conditions have to be met and considered if the product is going to be successful. If the score meets producibility requirements, then select this approach; if not, then evaluate other opportunities and repeat the process. In the rest of this chapter, measures and metrics will be introduced that provide insight for layout, fabrication, and assembly planning.

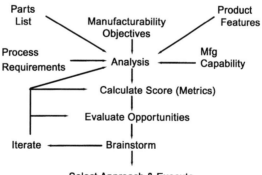

FIGURE 7.9   Process using measures and metrics to obtain a producible product.

7.3.4   Figure of Merit (FOM)

Metrics are the preferred measures for design planning, but their availability for predicting producibility are limited today. Metrics also can take many months to develop and the amount of experimentation may make them costly. The measure that is much more cost effective and quicker to develop is the *figure of merit.* The figure of merit is the result of one or two days' work by a group of design and manufacturing experts. The process is an eight-step procedure as shown in the flowchart seen in Fig. 7.10.

This procedure uses classical TQM techniques to brainstorm, rank, and formulate an equation that will score producibility, assemblability, or any other measure that can be used in design planning. The two factors used in the producibility score are made up of (1) the *coefficient* C_x and (2) the factor weighting FW_x.

7.3.4.1 *Coefficient* C_x.   The coefficients in the producibility score are the result of brainstorming all the possible contributors to producibility that can affect the product (Fig. 7.11*a*). These are grouped into common ideas or factors by techniques such as *clouds of affinity* or *Kay-Jay.* (Fig. 7.11*b*). These factors are ranked by voting or other pareto techniques such as paired-ranking, as seen in Fig. 7.11*c*. The actual voting scores form the coefficients C_x.

7.3.4.2 *Factor Weightings* FW_x.   Each factor that emerges from the ranking process is calibrated by assigning values from one 1 to 100, as seen in Fig. 7.11*d*. The 1-factors are easy to manufacture and the 100-factors are impossible today but will be merely very difficult in a few years.

The resulting scoring equation will look like the following linear equation:

$$\text{Score} = (C_1)\,(FW_1) + (C_2)\,(FW_2) + (C_3)\,(FW_3) + (C_n)\,(FW_n) + \ldots$$

For example, assuming the producibility of a bare PWB may be scored with the preceding equation if the following factors were established by the FOM. process:

1. Size of the substrate $C_1 = 1.5$

2. Number of drilled holes $C_2 = 3.0$

3. Minimum trace width $C_3 = 4.0$

Where the proposed PWB design has:

1. Size of the substrate $FW_1 = 36$

2. Number of drilled holes $FW_2 = 18$

3. Minimum trace width $FW_3 = 31$

The producibility SCORE would equal

$$1.5 \times 36 + 3.0 \times 18 + 4.0 \times 31 \ (\text{or } 54 + 54 + 124) = 232$$

This is compared to alternatives, with the highest number indicating least producible.

7.4 LAYOUT TRADEOFF PLANNING

Predicting density and selecting design rules is one of the primary planning activities for layout. The actual layout of a PWB is to be covered in Chaps. 10, 11 and 12. The selection of design rules not only affects circuit routing but profoundly affects fabrication, assembly, and test.

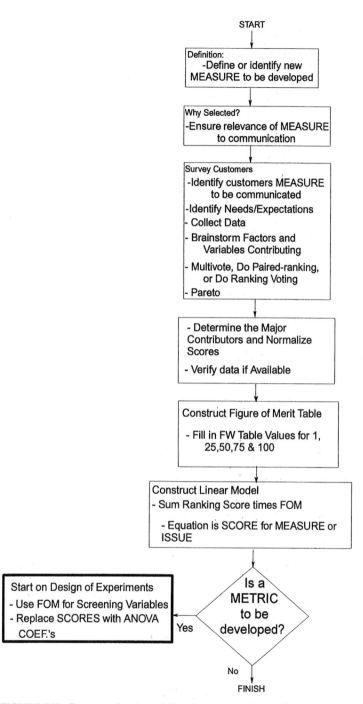

FIGURE 7.10   Process to develop a figure of merit as a substitute for metrics.

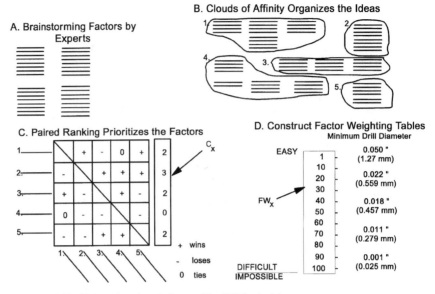

FIGURE 7.11   Figure-of-merit techniques utilize TQM principles.

7.4.1   Selecting Design Rules

Connectivity and density equations were introduced in Chap. 1. As a recap, they are:

- Wiring capacity W_c is the maximum wiring density of a PWB or its design rules, defined as

$$W_c = \frac{T \times L}{G} \text{ (in cm/cm}^2 \text{ or in/in}^2)\qquad\text{(Eq. 7.1)[3]}$$

where T = number of traces per wiring channel
L = number of signal layers
G = wiring channel width

- PWB layout efficiency E is the ratio of the density used by wiring features (traces, pads) divided by maximum density available for the board.[3]
- Wiring demand W_d is the actual wiring density that occurs when connecting all components, defined as

$$W_d = W_c \times E \text{ (in cm/cm}^2 \text{ or in/in}^2)\qquad\text{(Eq. 7.2)[3]}$$

where W_c = wiring capacity
E = PWB layout efficiency

7.4.2   Layout Efficiency

Layout efficiency is the ratio of the actual wiring density it takes to wire up a schematic vs. the maximum wiring density, or W_d divided by W_c. Layout efficiencies, typically, for ease of calculations are assumed to be 50 percent. Table 7.1 provides a more detailed selection of efficiencies.

TABLE 7.1 Typical Layout Efficiencies

Design scenario	Conditions	Efficiency, %
Through-hole, rigid	Gridded CAD	45
Surface-mount/mixed	w/wo backside passives, gridless CAD	50–55
Surface-mount/mixed	w/backside actives, gridded CAD	35–45
Surface-mount only	w/wo backside passives, gridless CAD	up to 60
Surface-mount/mixed	1-sided blind vias, gridless CAD	up to 65
Surface-mount/mixed	2-sided blind vias, gridless CAD	up to 70
Built-up technologies[3]	2-sided microblind vias, gridless CAD	up to 80

7.4.3 Other Layout Metrics

Other layout metrics in typical use are *equivalent ICs* (EIC) and *equivalent ICs per square centimeter* (equivalent ICs per square inch). An EIC is the total number of leads of the components divided by 14 or 16, the old number of pins on a DIP. Many people also use 20 as a divisor. The EICs/cm^2 (EIC/in^2) is EIC divided by the top surface of the PWB.

Another metric is the *design density index* (DDI). It is a calibration technique of the design rules for a PWB compared to the DD index. Equation (7.3) gives the DDI, and a typical calibration chart looks like Fig. 7.12.

$$DDI = 13.6 \times [EIC/in^2]\ \hat{}\ 1.53 \qquad\qquad (Eq.\ 7.3)$$

This chart gives a good visual record of how efficient a company has been in PWB layout. As various PC boards are charted, their DDIs form a distribution. This distribution is a form of

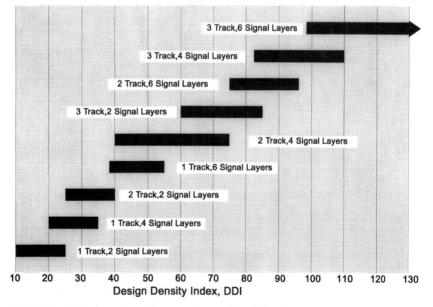

FIGURE 7.12 Design rules and layer count for various design density indexes.

layout efficiency E, since at the bottom of the distribution more EICs are connected than at the top of the distribution.

7.4.4   Packaging Technology Map

The packaging technology map[4] is a simple technique to predict a PWB, COB, or MCM-L wiring demand and its assembly complexity. By plotting components per square inch (or components per square centimeter) against average leads per component on a log–log graph (Fig. 7.13), the wiring demand in in/in^2 (or cm/cm^2) and assembly complexity in $leads/in^2$ (or $leads/cm^2$) can be calculated. The equations for these two metrics are as follows.

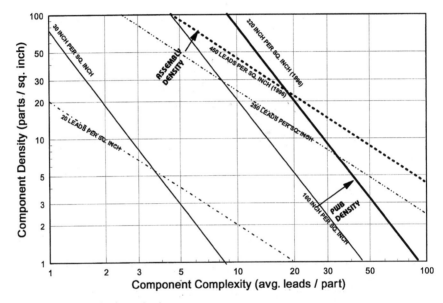

FIGURE 7.13   Packaging technology map.

$$W_d = 3.5 \times (COMP) \char`^ 0.5 \times I \qquad\qquad \text{(Eq. 7.4)}$$

where $COMP$ = components/cm^2 (in^2)
I = average leads/component

$$\text{Assembly complexity} = COMP \times I \qquad\qquad \text{(Eq. 7.5)}$$

where $COMP$ = components/cm^2 (in^2)
I = average leads/component

Using these two equations, Fig. 7.14 shows lines of constant wiring demand (in cm/cm^2 or in/in^2) and assembly complexity (in leads per cm^2 or in^2) that can be plotted on the chart in Fig. 7.13.

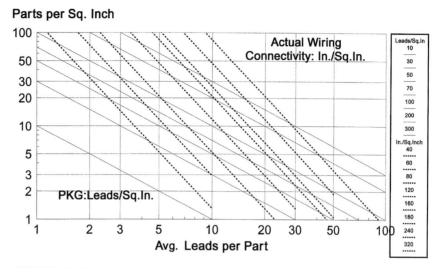

FIGURE 7.14 Wiring and assembly density.

7.4.5 Typical Example

As an example, take a typical printer formatter board with these characteristics:

Components	86
Leads	1540
Size	7.6 in. × 7.5 in. = 57 in²

$$\text{EIC/in}^2 = \frac{110}{57} \text{ in}^2 = 1.93$$

$$\text{DDI} = 13.6 \times (1.93)^{\wedge}1.53 = 37.7 \sim$$

The result is rounded to the next higher multiple of 10, in this case 40. Entering Fig. 7.12 at the line for 40, the first combination suggested as acceptable is for 2 tracks 2 signal layers.

7.5 *PWB FABRICATION TRADEOFF PLANNING*

The metrics for PWB and COB fabrication deal with tradeoffs between the performance objectives and the PWB price. This is where producibility comes in, since prices need manufacturing yields before they can be estimated accurately. Three items are required to predict these factors:

1. Fabrication complexity matrix
2. Prediction of producibility and first-pass yield
3. Relative price as a function of a price index

7.5.1 Fabrication Complexity Matrix

The fabrication complexity matrix is supplied by a PWB fabricator that relates the various design choices on a PWB to design points. These points are based on the actual costs a fabricator will charge for these features. Typical factors that fabricators can use to cost a PWB are:

- Size of the board and number that fit on a panel
- Number of layers
- Material of construction
- Trace and space widths
- Total number of holes
- Smallest hole diameter
- Solder mask and component legends
- Final metallization or finish
- Gold-plated edge connectors
- Factors specific to design, etc.

Once the fabricator has collected the factors that influence pricing, actual costs are determined and assigned to these factors, then the figures are normalized with the smallest nonzero amount. The fabrication complexity matrix would look like Table 7.2.

TABLE 7.2   Example of a Fabrication Complexity Matrix

Factors	Pts.	Highest	Pts.	High middle	Pts.	Low middle	Pts.	Lowest
No. of layers	95	8	75	6	50	4	25	2
Trace width (mils)	8	4	5	5–6	3	7–8	1	10
No. of holes	40	5000–8000	25	3000–5000	15	1000–3000	5	>1000
Min. hole dia. (mil)	40	8	25	12	15	16	0	<20

7.5.2 Predicting Producibility

The simple truth about printed circuit boards, multichip modules, and hybrid circuits is that the design factors, such as those listed previously, can have a cumulative effect on manufacturing yield. These factors all affect producibility. Specifications can be selected that individually may not adversely affect yields but cumulatively can significantly reduce yields. A simple algorithm is available[5] that collects these factors into a single metric, in this case called the *complexity index* (CI). It is given in Eq. (7.6).

$$\text{Complexity index} = A \times H \times T \times L \times \text{TO} \qquad \text{(Eq. 7.6)}$$

where A = area of board with 100% yield
H = number of holes in this board
T = minimum trace width on this board
L = number of layers on this board
TO = minimum tolerance, absolute number, for this board

Where area, number of holes, minimum trace width, number of layers, and minimum tolerance (absolute number) are the factors of the board being designed.

7.5.2.1 First-Pass Yield.   The first-pass yield equation is derived from the Wiebel probability failure equations.[5] This equation is a more general form of the equation typically used to predict ASIC yields by defect density and is as follows:

$$FPY\% = \frac{100}{e^{[(\log \, CI/A)^B]}} \qquad \text{(Eq. 7.7)}$$

where   FPY = first-pass yield
         CI = complexity index
         A, B = constants

To determine the constants A and B in Eq. (7.7), a fabricator will need to characterize his manufacturing process. This is done by selecting a number of printed circuits currently being produced that have various complexity indexes, hopefully some low, medium, and high. The first-pass yield (at electrical test without repair) of these printed circuits for several production runs are recorded. A statistical software[6] program that has a model-based regression analysis can now determine A and B from this model:

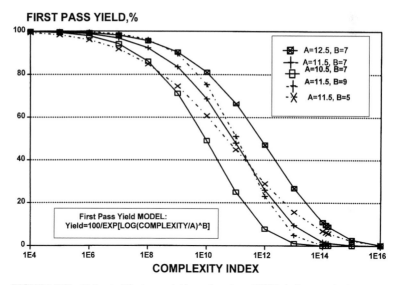

FIGURE 7.15   Estimated first-pass yield as a function of PWB design complexity.

$$FPY \text{ estimate} = f(x) = \frac{100}{e^{[\log \, (\text{complexity}/\text{PARM}_1)]^{\text{PARM}_2}}}$$

where $\text{Parm}_1 = A$
         $\text{Parm}_2 = B$

The first-pass yield will follow the examples in Fig. 7.15. Constant A determines the slope of the inflection of the yield curve and constant B determines the x-axis point of the inflection.

7.5.3   Typical Example

One company approached this planning process as part of its PWB design for manufacturing program in 1988. This continued a long tradition of design for manufacturing and assembly (DFM/A) that started with the Dewhurst-Boothroyd Design For Assembly in 1986.[7,8]

7.5.3.1   PWB Fabrication Complexity Matrix (FCM).   The PWB fabrication complexity matrix that this company developed is shown in Table 7.3. This FCM is based on a per-panel basis of 18 in by 24 in and does not use per-board. Also, volume is assumed to be in a preset amount.

TABLE 7.3   Example of One Company's Fabrication Complexity Matrix

Fabrication factors	Pts.	Highest	Pts.	High middle	Pts.	Low middle	Pts.	Lowest
Material of construction	147	Polyimide	88	Cyanate ester	49	FR-4	40	CEM III
No. of layers	196	8 layers	137	6 layers	89	4 layers	36	2-sided
No. of holes/panel	270	<20,001	180	10,001–20,000	90	3001–10,000	27	>3000
Min. trace/spacing	25	>4 mil	10	4–5 mil	6	6–8 mil	1	<8 mil
Gold tabs	48	3 sides	32	2 sides	16	1 side	0	none
Annular ring	30	>2 mil	21	2–4 mil	7	4–6 mil	1	<6 mil
Solder mask	25	2 S dry film	17	2 S LPI	10	1 S LPI	5	screened
Metallization	75	Reflowed tin/lead	69	Selective solder coat	46	Electroless Ni/Au	29	SMOBC /organic coat
Min. hole dia.	166	=>8 mil	84	9–12 mil	69	13–20 mil	5	<20 mil
Controlled impedance tolerance	105	±5%	62	±10%	30	±20%	0	None

Points are per panel. For board, divide by number per panel.

7.5.3.2   PWB Complexity.   Figure 7.15 shows this company's first-pass yield. The curve with $A = 11.5$ and $B = 9.0$ was current for the last six months of 1989. Price index is the total points from the complexity matrix divided by the first-pass yield.

7.5.3.3   Relative Costs.   The price index data for this company is shown in Fig. 7.16. The price index (PI) can vary from 150 which corresponds to a 70 percent price reduction to a PI of 1000 which corresponds to a 275 percent increase in price.

7.6   ASSEMBLY TRADEOFF PLANNING

The metrics of assembly tradeoffs relate factors of process, component selection, and test-to-assembly prices. Yields and rework are factored into the points of the assembly complexity matrix. The point total provides an estimation of the relative prices of assembly and test.

7.6.1   Assembly Complexity Matrix

The assembly complexity matrix is a matrix supplied by the PCB assembler. It relates various process assembly and test choices that the assembler provides along with various component size, orientation, complexity, and known qualities to the costs of providing for these design choices. Typical factors that may affect assembly costs are:

- One- or two-pass IR reflow
- Wave solder process
- Manual or automatic parts placement
- Odd-shaped parts
- Part quality level
- Connector placement
- Test coverage
- Test diagnosability
- Assembly stress testing
- Repair equipment compatibility

By collecting all the costs associated with assembly, test, and repair and then normalizing these costs with the smallest nonzero value, a matrix such as that shown in Table 7.4 can be produced.

TABLE 7.4   Example of an Assembly Complexity Matrix

Factors	Pts.	Highest	Pts.	Middle	Pts.	Lowest
Solder process	35	1-pass IR	20	2-pass IR	0	IR & wave solder
Placement	8	100% auto	5	99–90% auto	0	>90% auto
Digital test coverage	9	<98%	3	98–90%	0	>90%
Manual attachment	8	100% Auto	25	Brackets	0	Postsolder assembly

7.6.2   Typical Example

An example of the assembly complexity matrix is the *assembly report card* created by IBM-Austin.[9] This complexity matrix has 10 factors that range in points from 0 to 35. The total points can affect the prices from a 30 percent discount to a 30 percent penalty. Table 7.5 illustrates this assembly complexity matrix.

7.7   TOOLS FOR ADVISING AND AUDITS

Chapters 10, 11, and 12 will go into the details of designing and laying out a printed circuit board. Part of that process will be to execute the planning factors developed in this chapter. The other is checking the design to see if the planned goals are achieved. Tools that assist in executing that plan are design advice software, and those that check the finished layout are manufacturability audit software.

7.7.1   Design Advice[10]

A new generation of software has been developed that can advise a PCB designer on how close the design is to a prescribed set of standards. These standards and rules can cover various domains such as DFMA, EMC, high-frequency controlled impedance, and others.

TABLE 7.5 Assembly Complexity Matrix

Assembly factors	pt	A	pt	B	pt	C	pt	D
Assembly process	35	2 pass IR	25	IR/wave B/S passives	20	IR/wave <=5 B/S actives	0	IR/wave >5 B/S actives
Stress tests	15	0 h	12	<=3 h insitu	6	<=6 h insitu & <=3 h static	0	>6 h
Parts SPQL	10	No high hitters	7	<2 high hitters	4	<4 high hitters	0	>5 high hitters
ICT digital test coverage	9	>98% coverage	6	>95% coverage	3	>90% coverage	0	<90% coverage
Diagnosibility	9	<=10 min.	6	<=20 min	3	<=30 min	0	>40 min
Placement/ insertion	6	100% auto	4	>=95% auto	2	>=90% auto	0	<90% auto
Manual attachment	6	100% auto	4	Simple BKT	2	Diff BKT	0	Post-solder assembly
Connector selection	4	Auto ASM + retention + keyed	2	Manual + retention + keyed	1	Manual + retention	0	manual
Handling damage exposure	3	No handling list violations	2	<3 handling list violations	1	<5 handling list violations	0	>6 handling list violations
Repair	3	100% auto	2	>=90% auto	1	<90% auto	0	<90% auto + difficult

The rules can be coded by the user or purchased from vendors. Each rule is weighted according to its relative importance and that weight is taken into account in calculating the result for the rule category and design. There are 10 category meters (histogram and numeric) of rules and an overall design meter. These meters are:

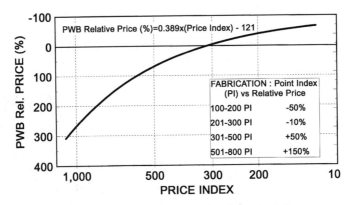

FIGURE 7.16 PWB relative price as a function of the price index.

- Measure the compliance with each rule from 0 to 100 percent compliance.
- Indicate the location of problems in a simple and direct manner within the PCB layout software.

FEATURES	CHECKLIST
CAD netlist compare	
Annular ring error	
Padstack checklist	
Plane clearance error	
Manufacturability analysis,DRC	
Thermal leg count violation	
Circuit checklist	
Unterminated lines	
Resist slivers	
Copper islands	
Solder mask checklist	
Solder short violation	
Mask coverage	
Mask to via check	
Teardrop pad addition	
Solder paste check	
Silkscreen clipping	
Part to part clearance/automation	
Quality parts	
Hole audit / lead diameter	
Part density	
Height clearance	
Allowable machine span	
Part spacing	
Drill optimization	
Automatic solder mask generation	
Bare board test points	
In-circuit test point analysis	
In-circuit test checklist	
Boundary scan audit	
Test point management	
Design profile	
Registration generator	
Keepout audit	

FIGURE 7.17 A checklist for items to review to assure PWB producibility.

- For each type of problem, indicate how the problem can be eliminated.
- Perform its analysis on-line without the need for batch processing.

7.7.2 Manufacturability Audits Performed by the Designer

These tools provide checklists, audit rules, and design rules to assure a correct design file and rapid introduction to PWB fabrication and through-hole/SMT assembly.

7.7.2.1 Design Rule Checks (DRCs). The design rules that these audit tools use are more detailed than those typically provided with CAD programs. Design rules can be stored by project, function, or application.

7.7.2.2 Machine, Component, and Producibility Checks. The features these tools provide for producibility checks and audits are:

- Fabrication manufacturability and artwork audit
- Metal sliver clearance, shorts, solder shorts, copper islands, and unattached metal checks
- Checks for unconnected nets and subnets, loose ends, and nonfunctional vias
- Audits that compare drilling with manufacturability requirements
- Annular ring, padstack, plane clearance, resist slivers, and silkscreen clipping
- Solder paste, solder mask coverage, mask to via, and other SMT checks
- Producibility enhancements like teardrop additions

A sample checksheet for a manufacturing audit is shown in Fig. 7.17.

REFERENCES

1. General Electric, "Review of DFM Principles," Internal DFM Conference Paper, Charlottesville, Va., 1982.
2. Robert Hawiszczak, "Integrating Design for Producibility into a CAE Design Environment," *NEPCON EAST,* June 1989, pp. 3–14.
3. D. P. Seraphim, R. C. Lasky, and C. Y. Li, *PRINCIPLES OF ELECTRONIC PACKAGING,* McGraw-Hill, New York, 1989, pp. 39–52.
4. H. T. Holden, "Segmentation of Assemblies: A Way to Predict PWB Characteristics," *IPC T/MRC Conference,* New Orleans, La., Dec. 8–10, 1993.
5. H. T. Holden, "PWB Complexity Factor: CI," *IPC Technical Review,* March 1986, p. 19.
6. Statgraphics, Ver. 2.6, Statistical Graphics Corp., 2115 East Jefferson St., Rockville, MD 20852, 301-984-5123.
7. G. Boothroyd, and P. Dewhurst, *Design for Assembly,* Dept. of Mechanical Engineering, University of Massachusetts, Amherst, Mass., 1983.
8. Douglas Daetz, "The Effect of Product Design on Product Quality and Product Cost," *Quality Progress,* June 1987, pp. 63–67.
9. H. Hume, R. Komm, and T. Garrison, IBM, "Design Report Card: A Method for Measuring Design for Manufacturability," *Surface Mount International Conference,* Sept. 1992, San Jose, Calif., pp. 986–991.
10. John Berrie and Andy Slade, "Knowledge Based Design Analysis for EMC," *Publication of Zuken-Redac Systems Ltd.,* Tewkesbury, Gloucestershire, UK, 1995.

CHAPTER 8*
BASE MATERIALS

Charles G. Henningsen
Insulectro, Mountain View, California

Smith A. Gause
Westinghouse Electric Corporation, Hampton, South Carolina

8.1 OVERVIEW

It is important to understand the types of copper-clad laminates that are available, how they are made, where they are used, and the advantages and disadvantages of each before selecting the material most suitable for the intended application.

Many types of copper-clad materials are available (see Fig. 8.1). The copper-clad laminates most widely used in the manufacture of printed circuit boards, however, are FR-2, CEM-1, CEM-3, FR-4, FR-5, and GI. These are the materials that are primarily discussed in this chapter.

The FR-2 laminates are composed of multiple plies of paper that have been impregnated with a flame-retardant phenolic resin. The major advantages of FR-2 are their relative low cost and their good electrical and punching qualities. FR-2 is typically used in applications where tight dimensional stability is not required, such as in radios, calculators, toys, and television games.

FR-3, the other all-paper base laminate, is also made of multiple plies of paper that have been impregnated with an epoxy-resin binder. The FR-3 laminate has higher electrical and physical properties than the FR-2 but lower than those of epoxy laminates that have woven glass cloth as a reinforcement. FR-3 is used to manufacture printed circuits used in consumer products, computers, television sets, and communication equipment.

CEM-1 is a composite material having a paper core impregnated with epoxy resin. Woven glass cloth impregnated with the same resin covers the two surfaces. This construction allows the material to have punching properties similar to those of FR-2 and FR-3, with electrical and physical properties approaching those of FR-4. CEM-1 is used in smoke detectors, television sets, calculators, and automobiles as well as in industrial electronics.

CEM-3, a composite of dissimilar core material, uses an epoxy-resin-impregnated nonwoven fiberglass core with epoxy-resin-impregnated woven glass cloth surface sheets. It is higher in cost than CEM-1, but it is more suitable for plated through-holes. CEM-3 is used in applications such as home computers, automobiles, and home entertainment products.

FR-4 (military-type GF) laminates are constructed on multiple plies of epoxy-resin-impregnated woven glass cloth. It is the most widely used material in the printed circuit board

---

*Adapted from Coombs, *Printed Circuits Handbook* 3d ed. McGraw-Hill, New York, 1988, Chap. 6.

Laminate designations and materials

Grade	Resin			Reinforcement				Flame retardant
	Epoxy	Polyester	Phenolic	Cotton paper	Woven glass	Mat glass	Glass veil	
XXXPC			•	•				
FR-2			•	•				•
FR-3	•			•				•
FR-4	•				•			•
FR-5	•				•			•
FR-6		•					•	•
G-10	•				•			
CEM-1	•			•	•			•
CEM-2	•			•	•			
CEM-3	•				•	•		•
CEM-4	•				•	•		
CRM-5		•			•	•		•
CRM-6		•			•	•		
CRM-7		•				•	•	•
CRM-8		•				•	•	

FIGURE 8.1   Laminate designations and materials. (*Reprinted from* Electronic Packaging and Production *magazine.*)

industry because its properties satisfy the electrical and mechanical needs of most applications. Its excellent electrical, physical, and thermal properties make it an excellent material for high-technology applications. It is used in aerospace, communications, computers and peripherals, industrial controls, and automotive applications.

FR-5 types (military-type GH) are laminated using multiple plies of woven glass cloth impregnated with mostly polyfunctional epoxy resin. The glass transition temperature T_g is typically 150 to 160°C, as compared with an FR-4 with a glass transition temperature of 125 to 135°C. FR-5 is used where higher heat resistance is needed than is attainable with FR-4 but not where the very high thermal properties of GI-type materials are needed.

GI-type materials are composed of multiple plies of a woven glass cloth impregnated with a polyimide resin. The materials have a glass transition temperature in excess of 200°C, which virtually eliminates "drill smear" caused by heat during the drilling process. It also exhibits excellent mechanical properties and z-axis dimensional stability at high temperatures. GI materials have a lower interlaminar bond strength than the epoxy systems; therefore, care should be taken when drilling and routing.

8.2   GLASS TRANSITION TEMPERATURE

The T_g has become a measure of how well a laminate resin system resists softening from heat. When the T_g temperature is reached, the resin changes from its "glassy" state and causes changes in the laminate's properties. The T_g is not a measure of the resin's melting point, but rather a point at which molecular bonds begin to weaken enough to cause a change in physical properties (dimensional stability, flexural strength, etc.), and its value is determined by the intersection of the two slopes of the temperature-property-change curve (Fig. 8.2a). FR-4 epoxy exhibits a T_g of 115 to 125°C and polyimide 260 to 300°C.

Although the T_g value is a measure of the toughness of a material under heating, it is not meant for comparison purposes once the T_g is exceeded. For example, materials with a higher T_g are desirable because they maintain their stability over a wider temperature range up to the T_g. However, once the T_g is exceeded, the material properties of a high-T_g resin could

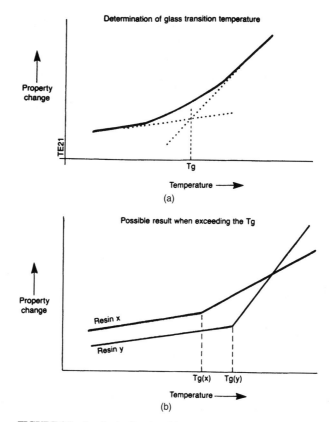

FIGURE 8.2   Laminate glass transition temperature is the point where properties exhibit significant change: (*a*) T_g is calculated by determining the intersection of the rate of change of the material at low temperature, and the rate of change at higher temperatures; (*b*) The higher the T_g, the more dimensionally stable the laminate. (However, when the T_g is exceeded, the ability to predict material performance is essentially lost.) (*Reprinted from* Electronic Packaging and Production *magazine.*)

change much more rapidly than a material with a low T_g. At a higher temperature, the lower-T_g material may often exhibit superior properties (Fig. 8.2*b*).

8.3   LAMINATE MANUFACTURING PROCESS

8.3.1   Treating the Base Material

The base raw material—paper, glass matte, woven glass cloth, quartz, or Kevlar®—is impregnated or coated with resin. The resin is then polymerized to a point suitable for storage and final pressing. A machine called a *treater* or *coater* is used for treating the material. First the material passes through a dip pan of resin, where it is impregnated, and then through a set of metering rollers (squeeze rollers) and a drying oven. The oven is air-circulating or infrared and can be up to 120 ft long. Most of the volatiles such as solvents in the resin are driven off in the oven, and the resin is polymerized to what is called a *B-stage*. This semicured material is also known as *prepreg*.

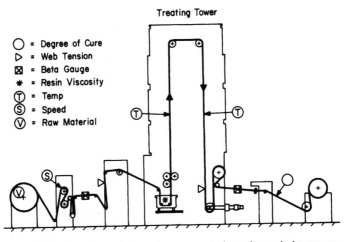

FIGURE 8.3   Location and type of process controls on the vertical tower processing system. (*Westinghouse Electric Corp.*)

The prepreg is dry and nontacky. The treater illustrated in Fig. 8.3 is a vertical treater that runs principally glass cloth; horizontal treaters impregnate mainly paper and glass matte.

Rigid process control is applied during treating so that the ratio of resin to base material, the final thickness of the prepreg, and the degree of resin polymerization can be monitored. Beta-ray gauges may compare the raw material with the final semicured product and automatically adjust the metering rollers above the resin dip pan so that the proper ratio of resin to base material is maintained. The degree of polymerization of the resin is controlled by the treater air temperature, air velocity, and speed at which the material passes through the treater.

The prepreg material is usually stored in an area where the temperature is controlled below 70°F and below 35 percent humidity until the time of the pressing operation. Each roll or stack of prepreg is tagged with the processing date and the test results for resin content, gel time, resin flow, cured thickness, and volatile content.

8.3.2   Copper Inspection

Besides the base material and resin, the other principal component of copper-clad laminates is copper foil. Today, almost all copper is electrodeposited rather than rolled. Each roll of copper is inspected by the laminator for visual surface quality and pinholes, and a sample is taken for trial pressing. The trial pressing sample is tested for copper peel strength, solder blister resistance, copper oxidation after heat exposure, and general surface quality. The side of the foil to be pressed against the prepreg is treated with an alloy to improve adhesion of the copper to the laminate. The alloy is a proprietary coating, usually of zinc or brass, in a controlled ratio to enhance the chemical bond between the copper and the resin.

8.3.3   Laminate Buildup

Most laminators build up their sheets in clean room facilities with filtered air-conditioned systems to control the temperature and humidity as well as to keep dust particles from the copper and prepreg during buildup. Electrostatic attraction of dust particles to the treated material and copper before pressing is a source of contamination in the laminate and a source of pits and dents on the copper surface of the finished laminate. During the buildup operation, the copper foil is first laid against a large polished stainless steel press plate. Then a number of sheets of prepreg are laid on top of the copper. The number of layers depends on the desired thickness of the laminate and the characteristics of the prepreg material. Some of the art of laminating comes in balancing all of these variables to produce a final dense material to relatively close tolerances. The final sheet of copper foil is placed on top of the prepreg if the material is to have copper on both sides. If copper is desired on only one side of the laminate, a release film such as Tedlar® replaces one of the sheets of copper.

8.3.4 Laminate Pressing

The press plates, with the material, are removed from the buildup room and stacked in a large, multiopening press. Several sheets are pressed into each press opening, with typical presses being capable of molding 80 sheets 36×48 in to 250 sheets 48×144 in, $\frac{1}{16}$ in thick. The presses, which are hydraulic, are capable of developing pressure in excess of 1000 lb/in^2. Steam is a typical heat source. It is released into the press platens until the platens reach the uniform laminating temperature. The packs or books of material are then loaded into the press, and the desired pressure is applied so that the material is cured into a final homogeneous sheet. To ensure that all of the sheets in the pack or book receive the desired state of cure, thermocouples are placed in several sheets in the press. A timer automatically records time against a preset cure cycle. When the desired stage of cure is achieved, the steam is automatically cut off and cold water pumped through the press platens until the material is at approximately 80°F. The material is then removed from the press, and the edges are trimmed from the sheet to remove the irregular resin flow areas.

8.3.5 Laminating Quality Control System

Statistical process control methods are used to verify that each step in the manufacturing process is controlled. Figure 8.4 outlines laminate traceability. Each press load is tested according to the appropriate sampling plan to ensure that the material will meet customer requirements. Each sheet is then identified as to manufacturer, appropriate specification, and load or lot number. Most manufacturers retain samples of material from each load for at least one year to enable them to effectively check any processing problems or questions which may result from the use of that lot in the field. Periodically, laminators are required to run a complete set of physical and electrical tests as set forth by NEMA or MIL-P-13949.

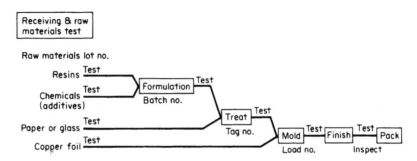

FIGURE 8.4   Laminate flowchart for laminate quality control.

8.4   LAMINATE EVALUATION, SPECIFICATION, AND QUALITY CONTROL

Various types of manufacturers of copper-clad laminate must be evaluated before the criteria necessary for design and fabrication process control can be established. Too often the evaluation is based on one sheet or sample submitted by each manufacturer. Generally, electrical and mechanical design and the particular fabrication process will demand that the final material have certain features and controls. It is, therefore, imperative that evaluation tests and specifications be determined by the demands on the finished product. Standards often are set unrealistically high in many areas that have no relationship to the fabrication process requirements of the final product. Some of the tests most commonly used today to determine the pertinent areas for test and evaluation are described in the following sections.

8.4.1   Surface and Appearance

Probably the most difficult test to define adequately has been that of surface and appearance standards. Perhaps more laminate has been rejected for pits and dents in the copper than for any other reason. This is particularly frustrating to the laminator, who has used a great deal of technical skill to build a consistent insulating material only to find it rejected by the user for cosmetic reasons. Most laminators believe that surface and appearance standards must be applied in light of the finished boards. Some purchasers of laminate require copper surface standards only on critical areas, such as the areas for tips inserted into edge connectors. In those cases, the user usually provides the laminators with an overlay of the critical copper areas to be inspected on each sheet of material before it is shipped. Thus the surface standard is applied only to areas that are pertinent to the finished board. With more than 90 percent of the copper being ultimately removed, the chance of a pit or dent affecting a critical area is small indeed. Nevertheless, many customers will pay premium prices by requiring the laminator to use special techniques or special selection to provide pit-free copper-clad material.

8.4.2   Copper Surface

Copper pits and dents are best defined in the surface standards established in MIL-P-13949. The specification defines the longest permissible dimension of a pit or dent and supplies point values for rating all pits and dents.

1. *Grade A:*   The total point count shall be less than 30 for any 12- × 12-in area.
2. *Grade B:*   The total point count shall be less than 30 for any 12- × 12-in area.

   There shall be no pits or dents with the longest dimension greater than 0.015 in. Pits with the longest dimension greater than 0.005 in shall not exceed three in any square foot.
3. *Grade C:*   The total point count shall be less than 100 for any 12- × 12-in area. The point system is as follows:

Longest dimension, in	Point value
0.005–0.010, inclusive	1
0.011–0.020, inclusive	2
0.021–0.030, inclusive	4
0.031–0.040, inclusive	7
Over 0.040	30

Scratches are permitted that have a depth less than 140 μin, or a maximum of 20 percent of the foil thickness, when measured with a Johannson surface finish indicator N533. Foil thickness is specified in MIL-F-55561 and is as shown in Table 8.1. The scratches to be tested should be located visually using 20/20 vision.

TABLE 8.1   Copper Foil Thickness and Tolerance

Nominal weight, oz/ft^2	Tolerance, wt %		Nominal thickness, in*	Tolerance, in*
	Class 1	Class 2		
⅛	±10	±5	0.00020	—
¼	±10	±5	0.00036	—
⅜	±10	±5	0.00052	—
½	±10	±5	0.0007	±0.0001
¾	±10	±5	0.0010	±0.0002
1	±10	±5	0.0014	±0.0002
2	±10	±5	0.0028	±0.0003
3	±10	±5	0.0042	±0.0004
4	±10	±5	0.0056	±0.0006
5	±10	±5	0.0070	±0.0007
6	±10	±5	0.0084	±0.0008
7	±10	±5	0.0098	±0.0010
10	±10	±5	0.0140	±0.0014
14	±10	±5	0.0196	±0.0020

* Derives by weight test method 2.2.12 of IPC-CF-150.

8.4.3 Color

Color variance from lot to lot on any particular grade of laminate is usually caused by variation in color of batches of resin, types of paper used, or variation of alloy coating on the copper. All the raw materials are supplied to the laminator, and only by careful inspection of incoming raw materials can a laminator be in complete control of their final effect on color. If coloration must be specified in copper-clad laminate, it should be done by working closely with the laminator. A set of samples that will illustrate the acceptable color extremes must be established.

8.4.4 Punchability and Machinability

The test for punchability and machinability has been subject to much debate among laminators and users. As of this writing, no universally accepted test method exists for either characteristic, and research has found little correlation with values such as Rockwell or Barcol hardness.

8.4.4.1 Drilling.   Each laminator should be consulted on recommended drilling speeds and feeds prior to any evaluation. Sometimes, poor drilling from one material to another occurs because each laminator was not given the benefit of recommendations for the material. Sectioning the board will help in evaluating the type of hole being obtained and is particularly important on plated-through applications. Often sectioning will show that the material has been heated by drilling to such an extent that the surface is smooth and not platable, is smeared with resin, or is so roughened that glass fibers protrude and will inhibit continuous plated through-holes.

8.4.4.2 Punching. Punchability can be measured in a die that simulates the conditions used in the fabrication process. Various hole sizes, spacings, and configurations should be incorporated in the test die. Many paper-base grades will tend to vary in punchability from lot to lot, so care must be taken to measure a wide range of sample panels. Careful physical inspection and sectioning of the holes will tell what type of punching is being obtained. The material must be carefully inspected to ensure that no cracking occurs and that there is no lifting of copper around the hole. Each laminator should be consulted as to the recommended die tolerance and punching temperatures.

8.4.5 Peel Strength

8.4.5.1 Before the Soldering Operation. The basic test pattern for testing peel strength or copper-bond strength specified in MIL-P-13949 and by NEMA standards is illustrated in Fig. 8.5. The pattern should be processed by the same fabrication techniques as in the user's final process, with the exception of exposure to various plating solutions or solder which will also be tested. When being tested for peel strength, the specimen should be mounted on a flat, horizontal surface. The wide copper end of each trace should be peeled back approximately 1 in so that the line of peel is perpendicular to the edge of the specimen. The end of the peeled strip should then be gripped by a clamp which is attached to a force indicator or tensile tester adjusted to compensate for the weight of the clamp and connecting chain. The copper foil is then pulled from the material at a rate of 2 in per minute, and the minimum load of the force indicator is recorded.

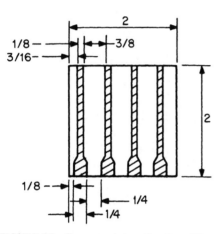

FIGURE 8.5 Copper peel strength pattern. Dimensions are in inches.

Peel strength of a ⅛-in trace is converted to pounds per inch width of peel by dividing the indicated force by the measured width of the strip. The peel strength test pulls the adhesion area directly under the radius formed between the copper being peeled at right angles and the material. Since 2-oz copper forms a larger radius than 1-oz copper, a greater area of adhesion is being pulled. As a consequence, peel strength for 2-oz copper is increased. For that reason, it is always important to maintain a peeling force that is 90° to the copper surface so that the radius of the peel is constant. Generally, a 5° deviation from perpendicular is acceptable; if a large enough distance is allowed between the specimen and force indicator, the 5° variance will not be exceeded during the source of the test. However, many users and laminators have found it desirable to use a testing machine which moves the force indicator along the test specimen as the copper is being pulled, thus keeping the angle of pull constant.

8.4.5.2 During Soldering. As circuit traces and pads have become smaller, the problem of bond strength retention at dip-soldering or solder-touchup temperatures has become increasingly important. At an elevated temperature, the NEMA test uses the same test pattern. The test sample, if G-10 or FR-4, is immersed in silicone oil for 6 min at 125°C and if G-11 or FR-5 at 150°C. Peeling is done, as in the preceding, while the sample is submerged in oil, and the average peel retention is noted.

The long immersion is required to bring both the specimen and the test jig to a constant temperature; shorter periods of immersion can result in extremely inconsistent test data. Specimens can also be placed in an air-circulating oven for 60 ± 6 min. The peel test can then be run in the oven at the appropriate elevated temperature. Underwriters Laboratories has also developed a test to determine long-term effects of heat aging on bond strength. The test is the normal peel test after the sample has been aged at 125°C for 1344 h.

8.4.5.3 After Soldering. It is usually important to test for peel strength after the dip-soldering cycle. The specimen should be floated on the solder pot at 550°F for 5 to 20 s, depending on the material being used. No flux should be used on the copper, and all excess solder must be removed. Any solder on the specimen will result in extremely irregular peeling. Sometimes, petroleum jelly may be applied to the copper before soldering to prevent any solder wetting. After excess solder is removed, the specimens should be visually examined for evidence of blistering and delamination of the metal foil.

8.4.5.4 After Plating. Plating solutions, particularly cyanide gold, can affect adhesion on some copper-clad laminates. Therefore, it is recommended that a peel test be considered after exposure to a normal plating operation. MIL-P-13949 recommends that the pattern illustrated in Fig. 8.6 be used if peel tests are to be run after plating. The procedure recommended is as follows:

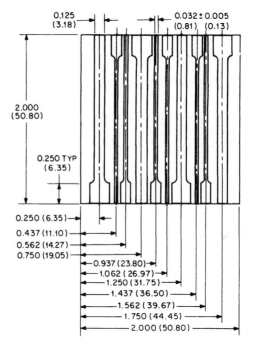

FIGURE 8.6 MIL-P-13949 peel strength test pattern. Dimensions are in inches; numbers in parentheses are metric equivalents in millimeters.

1. Immerse in methylene chloride for 75 ± 15 s at 20 to 25°C (68 to 77°F).

2. Dry specimens 15 ± 5 min at 105 to 148.9°C.

3. Immerse in a solution of 10 g/L sodium hydroxide at 85 to 95°C for 5 ± 1 min.

4. Rinse in hot water at 50 to 55°C for 5 ± 1 min.

5. Immerse for 30 ± 5 min in a solution of 10 g/L sulfuric acid (sp gr 1.836) and 30 g/L boric acid solution at 55 to 65°C.

6. Rinse in hot water at 50 to 55°C for 5 ± 1 min.

7. Dry for 30 ± 5 min at 105 to 148.9°C.

8. Immerse in hot oil at 215 to 225°C for 40 ± 5 s.

9. Immerse in 1,1,1-trichloroethane at 20 to 25°C for 75 ± 15 s to remove hot oil.

10. Air-dry and inspect specimens for such defects as delamination, wrinkles, measling, warping, twisting, blisters, and cracks.

The ½2-in lines shall be used. The peel strength shall be calculated using the actual width of each line tested.

8.4.6 Bow and Twist

Bow and twist in manufactured sheets with either or both dimensions 18 in or over is determined by suspending the sheet so that the horizontal level plane touches both corners. No pressure shall be applied to the straight edge of the sheet. The bow or twist is calculated as follows:

$$C = \frac{36D}{L^2} \times 100\%$$

where C = bow and twist for 36-in dimension
D = maximum deviation from horizontal straight edge
L = length in inches along the horizontal straight edge

Cut-to-size panels should be placed unrestrained on a flat surface, with the convex surface of the panel upward and measuring the maximum vertical displacement.

The deviation is expressed in inches per inch rather than in terms of a 36-in dimension.

8.4.6.1 Bow and Twist Variation—Cut Panels.   Bow and twist of cut panels with either dimension less than 18 in are per MIL-P-13949. See Table 8.2. For intermediate thickness, the next greater thickness value applies.

TABLE 8.2   Bow or Twist of Cut-to-Size Panels

		Total variation, maximum, %			
		Laminate—Class C			
		All weights of foil, one side		All weights of foil, two sides	
Thickness,* in	Panel size (maximum dimension), in	All other types	Types GP, GR, GT, GX, GY	All other types	Types GF, GR, GT, GX, GY
0.02 and over	8 or less	2.0	—	1.0	—
	8–12	2.0	—	1.5	—
	>12	2.5	—	1.5	—
0.030 or 0.031	8 or less	1.5	3.0	0.5	3.0
	8–12	1.5	3.0	1.0	3.0
	>12	2.0	3.0	1.0	3.0
0.060 and over	12 or less	1.0	1.5	0.5	1.5
	>12	1.5	1.5	0.5	1.5

* For nominal thicknesses not shown in this table, the bow and twist for the next-lower thickness shown shall apply.

8.4.7 Solder Resistance

Solder resistance should be measured and evaluated according to the NEMA grade for the laminate. When the laminate is to be used for military applications, MIL-P-13949 should be followed. Solder resistance is measured by horizontally floating specimens on a solder bath for a time dependent on the laminate grade and specification temperature given. The specimens are then visually evaluated for blistering, measling, delamination, and weave exposure.

NEMA specification LI-1-1983 requires both clad and etched specimens cut 2×2 in to be floated at 500°C for 5 to 10 s for paper-base laminates, epoxy, and paper phenolic, respectively, and 20 s for all other laminate grades. MIL-P-13949 does not recognize any paper-reinforced laminates or glass with paper composites. MIL-P-13949 requires clad and etched specimens 2×2 in to be floated at 550°F for 10 s. Etched specimens are tested with and without solder flux of type R or RMA.

Some fabricators specify other test requirements to further guarantee the integrity of laminate for its specific application.

For many laminates, the NEMA and MIL-spec requirements are only minimal, and the actual solder resistance is greater.

8.4.8 Autoclave

The autoclave, often referred to as the *pressure cooker test,* is used to select laminates of high moisture resistance which offer improved yields of printed wiring boards through infrared fusing and wave soldering.

Specimens are etched and sheared to size (1×5 in to 4×6 in), set vertically into a metal rack, and placed into a pressure cooker or steam autoclave and held at 15 lb/in² for 30 min. The samples are removed to cool for 5 min and are then dipped vertically into a solder bath at 500°F for 20 s. The specimens are then inspected for the presence of blisters, measling, crazing, or weave texture, which are reasons to suspect irregularity in the laminate. In some instances, more strenuous autoclave conditions, such as 550°F solder and autoclave exposure up to 75 min, are used to further screen materials for critical applications.

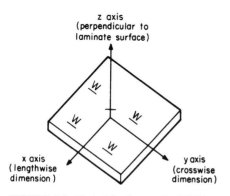

FIGURE 8.7 Typical laminate axis definition. Note that *x* (lengthwise) direction is defined by a specific part of the manufacturer's watermark.

8.4.9 Dimensional Stability

The need for circuit board dimensional stability has increased with increased circuit density. In general, the dimensional stability in the lengthwise or crosswise dimension *x, y* illustrated in Fig. 8.7 is a function of the laminate reinforcement (glass or paper). The thickness expansion *z* is generally a function of the resin system or resin matrix. It is important to recognize which is the lengthwise direction of the treated material going into laminate construction. The laminator usually identifies the lengthwise dimension by the vertical direction of the watermark, as shown.

To measure dimensional stability, one specimen should be taken from the lengthwise edge and one from the center of each sample sheet. Specimens should conform to Fig. 8.8, which is taken from MIL-P-13949F military specification.

8.5   *DEGREE OF CURE*

The curing of epoxy-resin-based printed circuit boards is directly related to the quality and performance of the boards. Methods for monitoring the curing process and of defining the extent of cure are needed to ensure that the circuits will meet design requirements. One method of defining cure is by measuring the glass transition temperature of the epoxy resin. Such measurements have been made in several ways and related to curing parameters via automatic dielectrometry. Based on these results, incoming inspection routines for materials have been defined, board pressing cycles established, and in-process controls fixed.

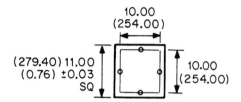

FIGURE 8.8 Dimensional stability specimen. Dimensions are in inches. Metric equivalents (to the nearest 0.01 mm) are given for general information only and are based on 1 in = 25.4 mm. Millimeters are in parentheses.

The extent of cure of epoxy resins can be measured by determining the glass transition temperature T_g, which is the temperature at which a polymer changes from a rigid, brittle, glasslike material to a softer, rubberlike product. At high temperatures, polymer molecules can move slightly, relative to one another. As temperature is decreased, a point T_g is reached where the thermal energy supplied is no longer enough to encourage this movement. Since the relative motion of the molecules in an epoxy resin also is dependent on the amount of cross-linking (cure), T_g and cross-linking are related.

Certain properties of epoxy resins have been found to be different above and below T_g. These include the heat content, the volume expansion coefficient, dielectric losses, refractive index, stiffness, and hardness. Of these, the heat capacity, the expansion, and the electrical losses are easily measured and are excellent tools with which to measure T_g and, hence, the degree of cure.

Limiting our discussion to epoxy-glass laminates and the methods suitable for those not having extensive laboratory facilities, the following techniques are suggested.

8.5.1   Thermal Analysis

Use a differential scanning calorimeter to determine the residual caloric value of the cured sample. The instrument measures heat from the exothermic reaction, caused by the resin curing, as a caloric value. When a laminate is fully cured, some residual caloric value always remains. Measurement of that value in a differential scanning calorimeter usually gives low numbers compared to the very high exothermic reaction measured when uncured samples are tested. Therefore, the measured amount of residual caloric values on acceptable standard laminates will provide a working reference for residual values and for the high exotherm of uncured samples.

8.5.2   Spectral Analysis

In some instances, spectral analysis is applicable, but it has some inherent drawbacks. Sample extraction and determination of weight loss during the extraction plus the spectral analysis of the extractables can sometimes provide a measure of the degree of cure.

8.5.3   Dip-Soldering Techniques

Many users determine relative degree of cure by inserting a 6- × 6-in sample with a 1-in strip of copper etched on it into a 500°F solder pot at a 45° inclination. Measurement of deflection as well as warp and twist will often give a measure of the relative degree of cure if enough data have been gathered to determine the basic working range of a particular resin system.

8.5.4 Dielectric Analysis

Dielectric analysis[1] consists of the dynamic measurement of dielectric properties of a material during its cure and postcure. Properties measured are dissipation factor and capacitance. They represent the response of polar groups in the material to a changing ac electric field. The response depends principally on the temperature and frequency of measurement, the number of polar groups per unit volume, and the mobility of the polar groups. It is the latter property that is of greatest concern in dielectric analysis, because it directly reflects the curing process.

The equipment used for dielectric analysis consists of a capacitance bridge with a frequency range of 0.1 to 1.0 kHz. Support equipment consists of a pneumatic press test cell with temperature control capability of $\pm 1°C$ and a three-channel recorder to record sample temperature, capacitance, and dissipation factor. This equipment has been used in production presses by attaching its sample leads to aluminum foil electrodes placed on either side of a prepreg sheet. Usually one electrode is separated from the sample by an inert film. Generally 0.001-in-thick polyimide film is used.

8.5.5 Microdielectrometry

An improved dielectric measuring technique known as *microdielectrometry* is available to monitor the cure of epoxy resins.[2] Integrated circuit technology is used to develop a miniaturized probe that combines a small size with built-in amplification to measure dielectric properties of polymers at frequencies as low at 1 Hz. The integrated circuit device consists of a planar interdigitated electrode structure with a pair of matched field-effect transistors. The electrode geometry does not change during cure and is reproducible from device to device.

The system, in essence, takes the relative gain and phase of the sensor output compared with sensor input (imposed sinusoidal voltage under command from a programmed computer) and, using an internally stored calibration, converts the data into permittivity ε', loss factor ε'', and their ratio, the loss tangent or dissipation factor $\tan \delta = \varepsilon''/\varepsilon'$. Thus ε' and ε'' can be measured for any material that is on the surface of the integrated circuit chip or sensor. The sensor consists of a 2- $\times$ 4-mm integrated circuit mounted in a flat cable package. Both electrodes used in the dielectric measurement are placed on the same surface to form an interdigitated capacitor, and on-chip amplification produces high signal-to-noise ratios.

8.5.6 Dynamic Dielectric Analysis

Dynamic dielectric measurements made over a wide range of frequency provide a sensitive and convenient technique for monitoring the cure process, and onset of flow, the onset of the reaction, changes in resin age, and changes in resin composition. This technique has been used to study the imidization and addition reactions of a polyimide dielectrically.[3]

8.6 INSULATION RESISTANCE

The insulation resistance between two conductors or holes is the ratio of the voltage to the total current between the conductors. Insulation resistance is composed of both the volume and surface resistance in a copper-clad laminate. Results of insulation resistance tests can vary widely if careful control of environmental conditions and process techniques of the test samples is not exercised. Although the actual value of insulation resistance may be important initially, the change in resistance under a specified environmental condition is usually more significant. The insulation resistance test is of greatest value when the test specimen is subjected to the same environment as will be required in the final application.

8.6.1 Parameters and Test Conditions

The insulation resistance of copper-clad laminates decreases both with increasing temperature and with increasing humidity. Volume resistance is particularly sensitive to temperature changes, and surface resistance changes widely and very rapidly with changes in humidity. Since extended periods of conditioning are required to determine the effects of humidity on surface resistivity, it is recommended, for example, that 96 h at 35°C in a 90 percent relative humidity environment be used. Test data also show that some materials will recover from humidity conditioning much more rapidly than others. Therefore, it may be desirable to cycle humidity and temperature in accordance with Method 106 of MIL-STD-202 (except steps 7a and 7b shall be omitted). Measurement shall be made at high humidity.

For consistent results to be obtained, extreme care must be taken in processing and handling the test boards. Etching of the pattern must leave well-defined lines, with no cracked or ragged areas. Rubber gloves—preferably surgical—must be used at all times while handling the test boards. Fingerprints can reduce the value of surface resistivity by as much as three decades. The following procedure for cleaning test specimens is recommended before any testing proceeds.

1. Place specimens from etch bath immediately in racks in running water at 60°F for 5 min.
2. Place specimens in 10 percent oxalic acid with agitation for 10 min.
3. Scrub with fine pumice.
4. Place specimens in running water at 60 ± 5°F for 30 min.
5. Scrub with demineralized water (1 MΩ minimum). Rinse with fresh demineralized water. Remove with gloves.
6. Stand specimens on rack in oven at 80°C for 1 h (use double clip).
7. Remove with rubber gloves (washed with alcohol), and put into desiccator used as dust-free container.
   a. Wash gloves in alcohol and store in same dust-free container.
   b. Touch only sample edges or clip leads; wear rubber gloves.

8.6.2 Specimen Preparation

Either the metal foil of the specimen may be completely removed by etching, or metal foil outlines may be left on the specimen to form the edges of the electrodes. The electrodes are generally completed with an application of a porous, conductive silver paint to both sides of the specimen. However, for comparative purposes, copper electrodes may be used rather than the conductive paint.

8.6.2.1 Surface Resistance.
The surface resistance between two points on the surface on any insulation material is the ratio of the dc potential applied between the two points to the total current between them. One of the most commonly used surface resistance patterns is the ASTM pattern illustrated in Fig. 8.9. This is a circular pattern with a three-electrode arrangement for measuring the surface resistance parallel to the laminate. The third electrode is a guard conductor which intercepts stray currents that might otherwise cause error. For measurement of surface resistance, the resistance of the surface gap between electrodes 1 and 2 is measured. The measured current flows between electrodes 1 and 2, while stray current flows between electrodes 1 and 3, as shown in Fig. 8.10.

Dimensions						
Thickness (t)	D_1 dia	D_2 dia	D_3 dia	D_4	D_5	Length of one side of specimen (L)
0.031 or less (.79)	1.000 (25.40) ± 0.005 (.13)	1.020 (25.91) ±0.005 (.13)	1.375 (34.93) ±0.005 (.03)	0.010 (.25) ±0.001 (.03)	0.177 (4.50) ±0.005 (.13)	2.000 (50.80) ±0.015 (.38)
.137 (3.48) or less	2.000 (50.80)	2.500 (63.50)	3.000 (76.20)	.250 (6.35)	.250 (6.35)	4.000 (101.60)
.138 (3.51) to 0.250	3.500 (88.90)	4.500 (114.30)	5.500 (139.70)	.500 (12.70)	.500 (12.70)	6.500 (165.10)

FIGURE 8.9   Electrode configuration of volume resistivity and surface resistivity test. Dimensions are in inches; numbers in parentheses are metric equivalents in millimeters.

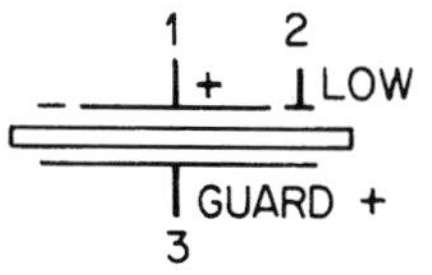

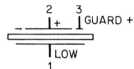

FIGURE 8.10   Guarding circuit for surface resistance parallel to the laminate.

Measurements should be made after 500 V_{dc} has been applied to the specimens for 60 s + 5 − 0 by means of a megohm bridge having an accuracy of ±6 percent at 10^{11} Ω. Measurements are to be made at the end of the prescribed conditioning time and condition.

Surface resistivity is calculated as follows:

$$r's = \frac{R'P}{D}$$

where VRw = surface resistivity, mΩ
R' = measured surface resistance, MΩ
P = measured perimeter of the guarded electrode, cm
D = distance between inner circle and outer guard ring, cm

8.6.2.2   Volume Resistance.   Volume resistance is the ratio of the dc potential applied to electrodes embedded in a material to the current between them. It is usually expressed in ohm-centimeters. The ASTM test pattern shown in Fig. 8.9 can also be used for volume resistance. For the measurement of volume resistance, the measured current flows between electrodes 1 and 3 while stray current flows between electrodes 2 and 3, as shown in Fig. 8.11.

FIGURE 8.11   Guarding circuit for volume resistance.

8.6.2.3   Steps

Comb Patterns.   Comb patterns such as the one illustrated in Fig. 8.12 have also been commonly used in surface-resistance tests. The patterns may simulate the final configuration of most copper-clad laminate boards, since the lines on the pattern approximate trace spacing in the board. Because of the narrow, close pattern, care must be taken to achieve clean, well-defined lines with no ragged areas.

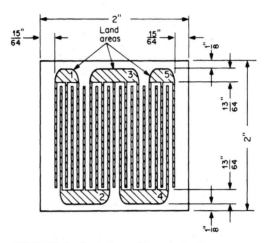

FIGURE 8.12   Insulation resistance test pattern.

Specimen Preparation.   Tinned terminals should be soldered to the land areas on the pattern using a 25- to 40-W soldering iron. The solder or resin should not spread beyond the land areas.

Removal of Fingerprints and Flux.   Thoroughly clean and dry the specimens as follows and, until completion of treating, handle them by the edges only. Brush with a bristle brush under running tap water that is between 15.5 and 25.5°C (60 and 80°F). The hardness of the tap water should not exceed 175 ppm (expressed as calcium carbonate). Deionized water may be employed. Dry with oil-free compressed air. Brush while submerged in isopropyl alcohol, removing all excess resin. Dip into fresh isopropyl alcohol and dry with oil-free compressed air. Dry in an oven for 2 h between 49 and 60°C (120 and 140°F), remove from the oven, and then condition for 24 h before testing at 23°C (73.4°F) and 50 percent RH.

Note that the preceding cleaning procedure does not replace the rinse after etching but supplements it.

Specimen Conditioning.   Condition the specimen in the chamber for 96 h at 35°C in a 90 percent RH environment. Afterwards, apply a potential of 100 to 500 V_{dc} measurement to be made at preceding temperature and humidity. Take measurements between the following terminals: 1 and 2, 2 and 3, 3 and 4, 4 and 5.

Take the readings after an electrification time of 60 s + 5 – 0 by means of a megohm bridge having an accuracy of ±6 percent at $10^{11}\Omega$.

8.6.2.4   Properties of Copper-Clad Laminates.   To establish the design parameters necessary for any copper-clad printed board application, one must know the principal laminate properties. Listed in this section are the characteristics that are most readily required in both electrical and mechanical design applications. Some of the tests involving those properties are described in the section on laminate evaluation.

8.7   GRADES AND SPECIFICATIONS

See Tables 8.3 to 8.5.

TABLE 8.3 Standard Materials

NEMA grade	Military designation MIL-P-13949F	Resin system	Base	Color	Description
XXXPC	None	Phenolic	Paper	Opaque brown	Phenolic paper with punchability at or above room temperature
FR-2	None	Phenolic	Paper	Opaque brown	Phenolic paper, punchable, with flame-resistant (self-extinguishing) resin system
FR-3	PX	Epoxy	Paper	Opaque cream	Epoxy resin, paper base with flame-resistant resin system, cold punching, and high insulation resistance
CEM-1	None	Epoxy	Paper-glass composite	Opaque tan	Epoxy resin paper core with glass on the laminate surface, self-extinguishing, economic fabrication of paper base, mechanical characteristics of glass
CEM-3	None	Epoxy	Glass matte	Translucent	Epoxy resin nonwoven glass core with woven glass surfaces, self-extinguishing, punchable with properties similar to FR-4
FR-6	None	Polyester	Glass matte	Opaque white	Polyester, random glass fiber, flame-resistant, designed for low-capacitance or high-impact applications
G-10	GE	Epoxy	Glass	Translucent	Epoxy-glass, general purpose
FR-4	GF	Epoxy	Glass	Translucent	Epoxy-glass with self-extinguishing resin system
G-11	GP	Epoxy	Glass	Translucent	High-temperature epoxy-glass with strength and electrical retention at elevated temperatures
FR-5	GH	Epoxy	Glass	Translucent	High-temperature epoxy-glass with flame-resistant resin system with strength and electrical retention at elevated temperatures
None	GI	Polyimide	Glass	Translucent dark brown	Polyimide resin, glass laminate with high continuous operating temperature and high property retention at temperature, low-z dimensional expansion

TABLE 8.4   Materials for High-Frequency Application

NEMA grade	Military designation MIL-P-13949	Resin system	Base	Color	Description
GT	GT	TFE	Glass	Opaque brown	Glass fabric base, PTFE (Teflon) resin, controlled dielectric constant
GX	GX	TFE	Glass	Opaque brown	Glass fabric base, PTFE (Teflon) resin dielectric constant with closer controlled limits than GT
		Polystyrene	Glass	Opaque white	Polystyrene cast-resin base for low-dissipation-factor applications
		Cross-linked polystyrene	Glass	Opaque white	Polyethylene cast base, radiation cross-linked for low dissipation factor

TABLE 8.5   Materials for Additive Circuit Processing

NEMA grade	Military designation MIL-P-13949	Resin system	Base	Color	Description
			Adhesives		
XXXPC	None	Phenolic	Paper	Opaque brown	These laminates are designed for use with additive processes using adhesive bonding techniques.
FR-2	None	Phenolic	Paper	Opaque brown	
FR-3	None	Phenolic	Paper	Opaque brown	
FR-4	None	Epoxy	Glass	Translucent	
			Seeded and coated		
XXXPC	None	Phenolic	Paper	Opaque brown	These laminates are used in the patented seeded and coated processes. They are seeded with a small percentage of the catalytic seeding agent dispersed throughout the resin system and are coated with a catalyzed adhesive.
FR-2	None	Phenolic	Paper	Opaque brown	
FR-3	None	Phenolic	Paper	Opaque brown	
FR-4	None	Epoxy	Glass	Translucent	
CEM-1	None	Epoxy	Paper-glass composite	Opaque tan, blue, white	
CEM-3	None	Epoxy	Glass-matte composite	Translucent	
			Sacrificial aluminum-clad		
FR-2	None	Phenolic	Paper		These laminates are the patented sacrificial additive process. They are clad on two sides with a specially anodized aluminum foil. The sacrificial aluminum cladding makes the laminate surface acceptable for the additive process.
FR-3	None	Phenolic	Paper		
FR-4	None	Epoxy	Glass, glass-paper composite		
			Swell and etch		
FR-4	None	Epoxy	Glass	Translucent	This laminate is used in the commercially available swell-and-etch additive process. The epoxy-glass laminate has a 0.0015-in-thick resin-rich surface and a specially designed surface for swell-and-etch chemicals.

8.7.1 Material Designations

The most common method of designating copper-clad materials is described in MIL-P-13949 and illustrated in Fig. 8.13. As an example, GFN-0620-CN/CI-A-2-A means no coloring in flame-retardant glass-epoxy laminate, 0.062 in thick, ½-oz/ft² copper, drum side out, on one side, and 1-oz/ft² copper, drum side out, on the other side, grade A pits and dents, class 2 thickness tolerance, and class A warp and twist.

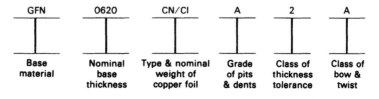

GFN	0620	CN/CI	A	2	A
Base material	Nominal base thickness	Type & nominal weight of copper foil	Grade of pits & dents	Class of thickness tolerance	Class of bow & twist

FIGURE 8.13   Designation of copper-clad laminates.

8.7.2 Conditioning Designations

The conditioning designations used to describe the environment in which tests were run are as follows:

Condition A: As received; no special conditioning
Condition C: Humidity conditioning
Condition D: Immersion conditioning in distilled water
Condition E: Temperature conditioning
Condition T: Test condition

Conditioning procedures are designated in accordance with the following:

1. First, a capital letter indicates the general condition of the specimen to be tested, i.e., as received or conditioned to humidity, immersion, or temperature.
2. A number indicating the duration of the conditioning, in hours, follows.

8.8 MECHANICAL PROPERTIES OF LAMINATES

The principal characteristics usually required in the mechanical design of printed boards are outlined here. If a specific test is required, the test is listed under a particular heading. Whenever they are available, the minimum standards set forth in MIL-P-13949 or NEMA standards for industrial laminates are used.

FIGURE 8.14   Flexural strength test.

8.8.1 Flexural Strength

Method: ASTM D 790. Unit of value: lb/in². This test is measure of load that a beam will stand without fracture when supported at the ends and loaded in the center, as shown in Fig. 8.14. See Table 8.6.

TABLE 8.6 Flexural Strength—Condition A, Minimum Average lb/in^2

Material	Lengthwise	Crosswise
XXXPC	12,000	10,500
FR-2	12,000	10,500
FR-3	20,000	16,000
FR-4	60,000	50,000
FR-5	60,000	50,000
FR-6	15,000	15,000
G-10	60,000	50,000
G-11	60,000	50,000
CEM-1	35,000	28,000
CEM-3	40,000	32,000
GT	15,000	10,000
GX	15,000	10,000
GI	50,000	40,000

8.8.2 Weight of the Base Material

Unit of value: oz/ft^2 (add 1 or 2 oz/ft^2 per side for the weight of copper). See Table 8.7.

TABLE 8.7 Base Material Weight, oz/ft^2

Material	$\frac{1}{32}$ in	$\frac{1}{16}$ in	$\frac{3}{32}$ in	$\frac{1}{8}$ in
FR-2	3.3	6.7	10	13.4
FR-3	3.6	7.2	11	14.5
CEM-1	4.0	7.6	11.6	14.7
CEM-3	—	9.2	—	—
G-10	4.5	9.9	14.7	19.5
G-11	4.5	9.8	13.4	19.6
FR-4	5.0	10.0	15.0	20.0
FR-5	5.2	10.2	15.4	20.4

8.8.3 Thickness Tolerance

Nominal thicknesses and tolerances should be specified below per MIL-P-13949. At least 90 percent of the area of a sheet should be within the tolerance given, and at no point should the thickness vary from the nominal by a value greater than 125 percent of the specified tolerance. Cut sheets less than 18 × 18 in should meet the applicable thickness tolerance in 100 percent of the area of the sheet. Class of tolerance is as specified in the type designation. For nominal thicknesses not shown in this table, the tolerance for the next-greater thickness shown applies. The nominal thicknesses include the metal foil except microwave materials, which are without foil. See Table 8.8.

8.8.4 Bow and Twist Percent Variation

Bow and twist values are per MIL-P-13949. The values apply only to sheet sizes as manufactured and to cut pieces having either dimension not less than 18 in. For intermediate thickness, the next-greater thickness value applies. See Tables 8.2 and 8.9.

TABLE 8.8 Nominal Thickness and Tolerances* for Laminates, per MIL-P-13949F

| Thickness, in × 10⁻³ | Class 1 | | Class 2 glass-reinforced | Class 3 glass-reinforced | Class 4 for microwave application |
	PX paper base only	Glass-reinforced			
0010 to 0045	—	±0010	±00075	±0005	—
0046 to 0065	—	±0015	±0010	±00075	—
0066 to 0120	—	±0020	±0015	±0010	—
0121 to 0199	—	±0025	±0020	±0015	—
0200 to 0309	—	±0030	±0025	±0020	—
0310 to 0409	±0045	±0065	±0040	±0030	±002
0410 to 0659	±0060	±0075	±0050	±0030	±002
0660 to 1009	±0075	±0090	±0070	±0040	±002
1010 to 1409	±0090	±0120	±0090	±0050	±0035
1410 to 2400	±0120	±0220	±0120	±0060	±0040

* These tighter tolerances are available only through product selection.

TABLE 8.9 Bow and Twist, per MIL-P-13949

Total variation, maximum, % (on basis of 36-in dimension)*

| Thickness, in† | Class A | | | Class B | | |
| | All types, all weights, metal (one side) | All types, all weights, metal (two sides) | | All types, all weights, metal (one side) | All types, all weights, metal (two sides) | |
		Glass	Paper		Glass	Paper
0.20 and over	—	5	—	—	2	—
0.030 or 0.031	12	5	6	10	2	5
0.060 or 0.062	10	5	6	5	1	2.5
0.090 or 0.093	8	3	3	5	1	2.5
0.120 or 0.125	8	3	3	5	1	2.5
0.240 or 0.250	5	1.5	1.5	5	1	1.5

* These values apply only to sheet sizes as manufactured and to cut pieces having either dimension not less than 18 in.
† For nominal thicknesses not shown in this table, the bow or twist for the next-lower thickness shown shall apply.

8.8.5 Maximum Continuous Operating Temperature

See Table 8.10.

8.8.6 Peel Strength

Method: See Sec. 8.4.6. Unit of value: lb/in of width. See Table 8.11.

8.8.7 Coefficient of Thermal Expansion

Method: ASTM D 696 (at 130°F). Unit of value: in/°C. The coefficient of thermal expansion, Table 8.12, is the change in length per unit of length per degree change in temperature. The coefficient may vary in different temperature ranges, so the temperature range must be specified.

TABLE 8.10   Operating Temperature

Materials	Temp., °C, for	
	Electrical factors	Mechanical factors
Ordinary applications		
XXXP	125	125
XXXPC	125	125
FR-2	105	105
FR-3	105	105
CEM-1	130	140
CEM-3	130	140
FR-6	105	105
G-10	130	140
FR-4	130	140
G-11	170	180
FR-5	170	180
GI	260	260
High-frequency applications		
GT	220	220
GX	220	220
Polystyrene	110	110
Cross-linked polystyrene	100	100

8.8.8 Water Absorption

Unit of value: Percent water absorption is the ratio of weight of water absorbed by the material to the weight of the dry material. See Table 8.13.

8.8.9 Copper Bond Strength Retention

See Table 8.14.

8.8.10 Flammability

According to Underwriters Laboratories, materials tested for flammability are classified 94V-0, 94V-1, 94V-2. For material flame ratings, see Table 8.15. Definitions of those classifications, as tested by the Underwriters Laboratories flammability procedure, are outlined as follows.

94V-0: Specimens must extinguish within 10 s after each flame application and a total combustion of less than 50 s after 10 flame applications. No samples are to drip flaming particles or have glowing combustion lasting beyond 30 s after the second flame test.

94V-1: Specimens must extinguish within 30 s after each flame application and a total combustion of less than 250 s after 10 flame applications. No samples are to drip flaming particles or have glowing combustion lasting beyond 60 s after the second flame test.

94V-2: Specimens must extinguish within 30 s after each flame application and a total combustion of less than 250 s after 10 flame applications. Samples may drip flame particles, burning briefly, and no specimen will have glowing combustion beyond 60 s after the second flame test.

TABLE 8.11 Peel Strength

| | Ordinary applications | | | |
| | Condition A, oz | | Condition E-1/150, oz | |
Materials	1	2	1	2
XXXP	6	7		
XXXPC	6	7		
FR-2	6	7		
FR-3	8	9	5	6
CEM-1	8	10	5	6
CEM-3	8	10	5	6
FR-6	7	8		
G-10	8	10	5	6
FR-4	8	10	5	6
G-11	8	10	5	6
FR-5	8	10	5	6
GI	9	10	8	9
	High-frequency applications			
GT	8	10	2	3
GX	8	10	2	3
Polystyrene	6.0	7.0		
Cross-linked polystyrene	6.0	7.0		

| | Additive (typically processed) | | |
Adhesive-coated	Condition A, 1 oz	Sacrificial aluminum	Condition A, 1 oz
XXXPC	9	FR-2	9
FR-2	9	FR-3	9
FR-3	9	CEM-1	9
FR-4	9	FR-4	9
CEM-1	9		
CEM-3	9		

Seeded and coated	Condition A, 1 oz	Swell and etch	Condition A, 1 oz
XXXPC	11	FR-4	9
FR-2	11		
FR-3	11		
FR-4	12		
CEM-1	12		
CEM-3	12		

94HB: Specimens are to be horizontal and have a burning rate less than 1.5 in/min over a 3.0-in span. Sample must cease to burn before the flame reaches the 4-in mark.

8.8.11 Fungus Resistance

See Tables 8.16 and 8.17.

TABLE 8.12 Coefficient of Thermal Expansion

Material	Coefficient, $\times 10^{-5}$	
	Lengthwise	Crosswise
Ordinary applications		
XXXP	1.2	1.7
XXPC	1.2	1.7
FR-2	1.2	2.5
FR-3	1.3	2.5
CEM-1	1.1	1.7
CEM-3	1.0	1.5
FR-6	1.0	1.0
G-10	1.0	1.5
FR-4	1.0	1.5
G-11	1.0	1.5
FR-5	1.0	1.5
GI	1.0	1.2
High-frequency applications		
GT	1.0	2.5
GX	1.0	2.5
Polystyrene	7.0	7.0
Cross-linked polystyrene	5.7	5.7

TABLE 8.13 Water Absorption, Condition D 24/23

Material	$\frac{1}{32}$ in	$\frac{1}{16}$ in	$\frac{3}{32}$ in
Ordinary applications			
XXXP	1.3	1.0	0.85
XXXPC	1.3	0.75	0.65
FR-2	1.3	0.75	0.65
FR-3	1.0	0.65	0.60
CEM-1	0.50	0.30	0.25
CEM-3	0.50	0.25	0.20
FR-6		0.40	
G-10	0.50	0.25	0.20
FR-4	0.50	0.25	0.20
G-11	0.50	0.25	0.20
FR-5	0.50	0.25	0.20
GI		1.0	
High-frequency applications			
GT	0.20	0.10	0.09
GX	0.20	0.10	0.09
Polystyrene		0.05	
Cross-linked polystyrene		0.01	

TABLE 8.14 Copper Bond Strength Retention

Material	%	Material	%
XXXP	50	G-11	50
FR-2	50	FR-4	50
FR-3	50	FR-5	50
G-10	50	CEM-1	50
		CEM-3	50

TABLE 8.15 Flammability Classifications

Grade	UL classification	Grade	UL classification
XXXPC	94HB	G-10	94HB
FR-2	94V-1	FR-4	94V-0
FR-3	94V-0	G-11	94HB
CEM-1	94V-0	FR-5	94V-0
CEM-3	94V-0	FR-6	94V-0

TABLE 8.16 Fungus Resistance Tests

Test organism	Culture no.	Military specification
Aspergillus niger	WADC 215-4247	MIL-F-8261
Aspergillus favus	WADC 26	MIL-F-8261
Trichoderma T-1	WADC T-1	MIL-F-8261
Chaetomium globosum	USDA 1042.4	MIL-E-4970
Aspergillus niger	USDA tc 215-4247	MIL-E-4970
Penicillium luteum	USDA 1336.1	MIL-E-4970
Aspergillus flavus	WADC 26	MIL-E-4970
Memnoniella echinata	WADC 37	MIL-E-4970
Myro-thecium verrucaria	ATCC 9095	MIL-E-5272
Aspergillus terreus	ATCC 10690	MIL-E-5272
Penicillium	ATCC 9849	MIL-E-5272

TABLE 8.17 Fungus Resistance Test Results

Material	Construction	Military specifications		
		MIL-F-8261	MIL-E-4970	MIL-E-5272
XXP	Paper-phenolic	Not resistant	Not resistant	Not resistant
XXXPC	Paper-phenolic	Not resistant	Not resistant	Not resistant
FR-3	Paper-epoxy	Resistant	Resistant	Resistant
FR-4	Glass-epoxy	Resistant	Resistant	Resistant
FR-5	Glass-epoxy	Resistant	Resistant	Resistant

8.9 ELECTRICAL PROPERTIES OF LAMINATES

8.9.1 Relative Humidity on Surface Resistivity of Glass-Epoxy

The effect of humidity on surface resistance of glass-epoxy was measured by using the ASTM three-electrode circular pattern, starting with 97.5 percent RH at 40°C and decreasing the humidity to 64 percent. The results, shown in Fig. 8.15, indicate that the surface resistivity decreases logarithmically with an increase in humidity at approximately the rate of one decade per 20 percent humidity change.

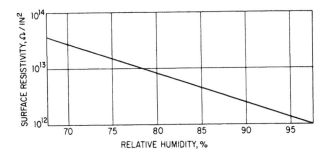

FIGURE 8.15   Surface resistivity vs. relative humidity.

8.9.2 Thermal Conductivity of Base Materials Without Copper

See Table 8.18.

TABLE 8.18   Thermal Conductivity of Base Materials

Material	Conductivity	Material	Conductivity
XXXP	1.7	G-11	1.8
FR-2	1.8	FR-4	1.8
FR-3	1.6	FR-5	1.8
G-10	1.8	CEM-1	1.8
		CEM-3	1.8

8.9.3 Dielectric Strength

(Perpendicular to the laminations at 23°C.) Method: ASTM D 149. Unit of value: V/mil. Dielectric strength is the ability of an insulation material to resist the passage of a disruptive discharge produced by an electric stress. A disruptive discharge is measured by applying 60-Hz voltage through the thickness of the laminate, as shown in Fig. 8.16. All the tests are run under oil. In the short-time test the applied voltage is increased at a uniform rate of 0.5 kV/s. In the step-by-step test, the initial voltage is 50 percent of the short-time breakdown voltage; thus, the voltage is increased in increments according to a predetermined schedule of 1-min intervals. The test values for dielectric strength vary with the thickness of the material, the form and size of electrodes, the time of application of the voltage, the temperature, the frequency and wave shape of

FIGURE 8.16   Dielectric strength test.

the voltage, and the surrounding medium. Step-by-step data for $\frac{1}{16}$-in-thick material are as shown in Table 8.19.

TABLE 8.19 Dielectric Strength Data

Material	V/mil	Material	V/mil
XXXP	740	G-10	510
FR-2	740	G-11	600
FR-3	550	FR-4	500
CEM-1	500	FR-5	500
CEM-3	500	GI	750

8.9.4 Dielectric Breakdown

(Parallel to the laminations at 23°C.) Method: ASTM D 149. Unit of value: kV. Condition D 48/50. Dielectric breakdown is the disruptive discharge measured between two electrodes (Pratt and Whitney No. 3 taper pins) inserted in the laminate on 1-in centers perpendicular to the laminations. All tests are run under oil. The short-time and step-by-step tests are performed as in the test for dielectric strength perpendicular to laminations. Step-by-step data on $\frac{1}{16}$-in-thick material are given in Table 8.20.

TABLE 8.20 Dielectric Breakdown Data

Material	kV	Material	kV
XXXPC	15	G-10	40
FR-2	15	FR-4	40
FR-3	30	G-11	40
FR-6	30	FR-5	40
CEM-1	40	GT	20
CEM-3	40	GX	20

FIGURE 8.17 Dielectric constant test.

8.9.5 Dielectric Constant (Permittivity)

Method: ASTM D 150. Unit of value: dimensionless. Dielectric constant is the ratio of the capacitance of a capacitor with a given dielectric to the capacitance of the same capacitor with air as a dielectric, as illustrated in Fig. 8.17. The dielectric constant is a measure of the ability of an insulating material to store electrostatic energy. It is calculated from the capacitance as read on a capacitance bridge, the thickness of the specimen, and the area of the electrodes. It varies with temperature, humidity, and frequency. See Table 8.21.

FIGURE 8.18 Dissipation factor test.

8.9.6 Dissipation Factor

(Average at 1 MHz.) Method: ASTM D 150. See Fig. 8.18. Unit of value: dimensionless. In an insulating material, the dissipation factor is the ratio of the total power loss, in watts, in the material to the product of the voltage and current in a capacitor in which the material is a dielectric. It varies over a frequency range. See Tables 8.22 and 8.23.

TABLE 8.21 Permittivity

Materials	Permittivity at 1 MHz condition D 24/23
Ordinary applications	
XXXPC	4.1
FR-2	4.5
FR-3	4.3
CEM-1	4.4
CEM-3	4.6
FR-6	4.1
G-10	4.6
FR-4	4.6
G-11	4.5
FR-5	4.3
GI	4.8
High-frequency applications	
GT	2.8
GX	2.8
Polystyrene	2.5
Cross-linked polystyrene	2.6

TABLE 8.22 Dissipation Factors

Materials	Dissipation factor at 1 MHz	
	Condition A	Condition D 24/23
Ordinary applications		
XXXP	0.028	0.03
XXXPC	0.028	0.03
FR-2	0.024	0.026
FR-3	0.024	0.026
CEM-1	0.027	0.028
CEM-3	0.020	0.022
FR-6	0.020	0.028
G-10	0.018	0.019
FR-4	0.018	0.020
G-11	0.019	0.020
FR-5	0.019	0.028
GI	0.020	0.030
High-frequency applications		
GT	0.005	0.006
GX	0.002	0.002
Polystyrene	0.00012–0.00025*	0.00012–0.00066*
Cross-linked polystyrene	0.0004–0.0005[†]	0.0005–0.0005

* Condition A, 10 MHz.
[†] Condition A, 10 GHz.

TABLE 8.23 Permittivity and Dissipation Factor of FR-4, Condition D 24/23

Frequency	Dielectric constant	Dissipation factor
100 Hz	4.80	0.009
1,000	4.75	0.012
10,000	4.70	0.015
100,000	4.65	0.018
1 MHz	4.60	0.020
10	4.55	0.022
100	4.50	0.024
1,000	4.45	0.025
10,000	4.40	0.025

8.10   *LAMINATE PROBLEMS*

8.10.1   Traceability

It is impossible to build circuit boards in any quantity without having some difficulties that will be blamed principally on the copper-clad laminate material. Too often, the base material appears to be the cause of trouble, when actually the fabrication process is out of control. Even a carefully written and executed laminate specification will fail to specify the tests necessary to help identify the laminate as a cause of or a contribution to a process problem. Listed in this section are some of the most common laminate problems and how to recognize them.

Once a laminate problem is encountered, it should be considered for addition to the material specification. Often the addition, if not made, allows continuing variations and subsequent rejections. Usually any material problem traced to laminate variations will occur in discrete raw material or press load batches manufactured by the laminator. Few users keep records extensive enough to permit identification, in any processing area, of a particular press load or batch of material. So usually the boards continue to be manufactured and loaded; warpage in the solder pot, for example, may continue, and a large amount of labor and expensive components will be lost. If the load number is immediately known, the laminator can check resin batches, copper lots, cure cycles, etc. If the user does not provide continuity with the laminator's quality control system, the user is penalized in the long run. The common problems associated with base material in the fabrication process are discussed in the following sections.

8.10.2   Measling and Blistering

Cause	Corrective action
Entrapped moisture	Check drill hole quality. Check for delamination during drilling.
Excessive exposure to heat during fusing and hot-air leveling	Monitor equipment for proper voltage regulation and temperature.
Laminate weave exposure	Ensure that you have sufficient butter coat. Be sure all wet processes are checked when materials are changed.
Measles related to stress on boards with heavy ground planes	Postbake panels prior to drilling. Be sure laminate has balanced construction. Use optimum preheat conditioning before IR fusing or hot-air leveling.
Handling when laminate temperature exceeds its glass transition temperature	Allow boards to cool to ambient temperature before handling.
Measling when large components or terminals are tight enough to cause excessive stress when heated	Check tooling for undersized holes. Loosen tight terminals.

8.10.3   Dimensional Stability

Cause	Corrective action
Undercured laminate	Check laminate vendor for glass transition temperature.
Distorted glass fabric (FR-4)	Examine etched panels for yarns parallel to warp and fill direction.
Dense hole patterns with fine lines and spaces	Prebake laminate in panel form before drilling.
Dimensional change parallel to grain differs from that of cross grain	Have laminator identify grain direction.

8.10.4   Warp and Twist

Cause	Corrective action
Improper packing	Assure that packing skids are flat and have sufficient support.
Storage	Stack material horizontally rather than vertically.
Distorted glass fabric (FR-4)	Examine etched panels for yarns parallel to warp and fill direction.
Excessive exposure to heat	Maintain proper temperature and exposure times in all heat-related fabricating processes (IR fusing, hot-air leveling, and solder mask applications).
Improper handling after exposure to heat applications	Cure solder mask horizontally. Use proper cooling techniques after IR fusing and hot-air leveling.
Unbalanced laminate construction	Work with laminator to get balanced construction.

8.10.5   Copper Foil

Cause	Corrective action
Fingerprints due to improper handling	Handle copper cladding with gloves.
Oils from punching, blanking, or drilling	Degrease with proper solvent.
Poor solderability on print-and-etch boards	Degrease to remove contaminates. Use highly activated flux. Check laminator for procedure to remove excessive antistaining compound.

8.10.6   Copper Bond Strength

Cause	Corrective action
Pad or trace lifting during wave soldering	Check for undercut due to overexposure during etch. Check with laminator to be sure solvents used in the circuit manufacturing process are compatible with the laminate.
Pad or trace lifting during hand soldering	The hand-soldering device is too hot or wattage is too high for the application. The device operator is applying heat too long to the soldered pad.
Pad or trace lifting during processing	Check laminate supplier for bond strength properties of the lot of material in the process. Check for undercut during etch. If pads lift after solder leveling, check fuser voltage or hot-air leveling equipment temperature.

REFERENCES

1. Z. N. Sanjana and R. N. Sampson, "Measuring the Degree of Cure of Multilayer Circuit Boards," *Insulation/Circuits,* April 1981, pp. 89–92.

2. S. D. Senturia, N. F. Sheppard, H. L. Lee, and S. B. Marshall, "Cure Monitoring and Control with Combined Dielectric Temperature Probes," *SAMPE,* vol. 19, no. 4, 1983, pp. 22–26.

3. D. E. Kranbuehl, S. E. Belos, and P. K. Jue, "Dynamic Dielectric Characterization of the Cure Process: LARC-160," *SAMPE,* vol. 19, no. 4, 1984, pp. 18–21.

CHAPTER 9
ADVANCED MATERIALS TECHNOLOGY

Robert A. Forcier
Nelco International Corporation, Tempe, Arizona

9.1 INTRODUCTION

Advanced materials play a vital role in the manufacture of thinner, smaller, and faster interconnects. In fact, certain new materials enable miniaturization to occur at a higher rate when compared to normal FR-4 materials. Developments in advanced materials provide new degrees of freedom in properties such as thermal resistance, ultrathin dielectrics, and small-hole formation. More importantly, they provide the foundation for MCM-L, PCMCIA, smart cards, and high-density multilayer technologies.

Advanced materials can be selected for particular applications by examining each of the component parts of the system:

1. Carrier system
2. Copper foil technology
3. Resin system which binds the copper foil and the carrier

Cost effectiveness is the key to the selection of the different combinations of the carrier, the copper foil, and the resin system. FR-4 laminates still remain the most cost-effective solution to many packaging disciplines. In more complex designs, advanced materials such as BT/epoxy and cyanate ester are required. These systems have higher T_gs which provide more heat resistance to the multilayer interconnect and, in some cases, lower D_k/D_f polymers which provide electrical properties that are improved over FR-4 in high-speed applications. Of course, the farther away from FR-4 technology, the more cost involved. Therefore, the best selection of advanced materials is always one of a balance of properties depending on the application requirements.

Before examining the possible advanced material options in reinforcement, copper foils, and resin technology, it is valuable to define the technical drivers that are transforming the multilayer interconnect industry. There are two major categories of product drivers for advanced materials:

- *Miniaturization.* This is the driver for lighter, smaller, and denser interconnects.
- *Speed.* This is the driver for interconnects that provide faster processing speeds and greater signal integrity with high-speed computing and signal processing.

These drivers are key for the selection of the proper advanced material technology. They also provide the basis for most of the development of even more advanced materials. The semiconductor device and its package is the primary source of interconnect drivers, since the semiconductor is the primary component of any system. Multilayer interconnect technology is evolving as the semiconductor complexity is evolving.

9.1.1 Miniaturization Drivers

Miniaturization of interconnects provides value by providing more interconnect density in the same size package or more interconnect density in a smaller package. Cellular phones, personal digital assistants, PC cards, and automotive electronics represent products which are transported from location to location or are integrated into moving vehicles for vehicle control and communication. It is obvious that these products will benefit directly from being lighter, smaller, and thinner due to reduced space and weight.

In addition to the need for miniaturization for weight and space savings, there is a simultaneous driver for more functionality of components to complement these new products. Desktop computers obviously have a need for more functionality in the same space with each new model introduction. This increase in complexity coincides with the advances in the density and complexity of semiconductors. As the I/O count of the semiconductor increases, so does the necessity of finer lines and spaces on the multilayer substrate. Tables 9.1 and 9.2 provide a semiconductor technology roadmap for both the device itself and for the associated package.

TABLE 9.1 The National Technology Roadmap for Semiconductors*

	1995	1998	2001	2004	2007
Memory	64M	256M	1G	4G	16G
Chip I/Os, high perf	900	1350	2000	2600	3600
Chip frequency, MHz	150	200	250	300	375
Chip size (mm²)	250	300	360	430	520
Power, high perf, W	80	100	120	140	160
Logic power, W/cm²	5	7	10	10	10
Battery, W	2.5	2.5	3.0	3.5	4.0

Source: Semiconductor Industry Association.

TABLE 9.2 State of Assembly and Packaging Technology

	Present technology	Process development	Advanced development
Power, cost/perform, W	14	22	37
Chip size, cost/perform, mm²	140	240	340
Performance, MHz	100	150	200
Junction temp T_j, automotive, °C	150	165	175
Packaging thickness, mm	1.0	0.8	0.5
Pin count QFP*	208	340	464
Pin count BGA*	225	324	576
Pitch QFP, mm	0.5	0.4	0.3
Pitch BGA, mm	1.5	1.27	1.0
Pad pitch wire bond, μm	115	100	70

Source: Semiconductor Industry Association.

Table 9.1 defines a clear trend toward higher I/Os from today to the year 2007. Each I/O added to a semiconductor increases the complexity of the interconnect and defines the necessity for miniaturization for any given state of technology. Table 9.1 also defines a clear trend towards higher frequencies. As more functionality of the semiconductor is designed in, a greater need for higher signal speeds to communicate between components and other devices becomes paramount.

The evolution of the package for the semiconductor is defined in Table 9.2. The most important driver for miniaturization is the pitch of the predominant two-chip packages, the QFP and the BGA. The pitch (separation of leads) in these two packages is dropping dramatically. This is also the case with the pitch for wire bond, as is also indicated in Table 9.2.

The pad pitch for wire bonding is important because some miniaturization techniques involve removal of the semiconductor package altogether. These techniques are flip chip and direct chip attach. In both cases, the pitch required is substantially less (usually more than 50 percent) than traditional packages. These technologies place significant demands on the multilayer interconnect for even finer lines and spaces.

Table 9.3 provides a technology roadmap for the multilayer interconnect.

TABLE 9.3   PCB Characteristics, Parameters, Trends

Parameter	Unit	Standard	Leading edge	Projected
T_g	°C	130	170	250
Material		FR4/glass	PI,BT,CE,TF . . .	Application dependent
Dielectric constant		4.5	3.5	2.8
$T_{CE}(z$ dir.$)$	ppm/K	190	135	50
Line width	μm	150	100	70
Line space	μm	250	150	100
Land diameter	μm	750	300	LL
Line height	μm	50	30	15
PTH	μm	1000	300	200
Drill diameter				
Blind via	μm	400	250	250
Diameter				
Buried via	μm	N.A.	250	200
Diameter				
Micro via	μm	150	100	75
Diameter				
Dielectric surf	μm	N.A.	50	40
Thickness, core	μm	250	150	100
Thickness, card	mm	1.5	0.7	0.4
Thickness, layer count		6	10	25
Solder mask		Print screen	Curtain coating	Application dependent
Surface		ASL	Au/Ni	Org./Sn
Finish				Plat.
SMT pitch	μm	625	500	400
BGA grid	μm	2500	1000	625
PIH grid	μm	2500	1000	625
Wire bond pitch (die)	μm	150	100	75
FCA pitch	μm		250	2

Source: Dr. Theis zur Nieden, STP Electronic Systems, Sindelfingen, Germany.

It is clear from Table 9.3 that, as the interconnect package pitch decreases, the corresponding multilayer interconnect density increases with smaller hole diameters and finer lines and spaces. This is a well-defined miniaturization trend in multilayer printed circuits that follows directly from the advances in the density and complexity of semiconductors. As I/O counts increase, so does the necessity of finer lines and spaces on the multilayer substrate. Of particular interest in this table are the impacts on advanced materials. The trend in materials is towards higher T_gs which are projected in the final column to be 250°C with an intermediary step of 170°C. Higher T_gs are required for the assembly of the more complex devices for the following reasons:

- Higher yields in multiple heat assembly processes
- Compatability with gold wire bond processes
- Better reliability for applications with significant thermal cycling
- Improved rework of such devices as BGA
- Higher product operating temperatures
- Structural integrity of ultrathin PCMCIA-type devices

In addition to T_g trends in advanced materials, notice the substantial drop in thickness of both core and the final board thickness of the interconnect. An average core thickness of 250 μm in standard FR-4 technology drops substantially to 100-μm technology in the projected years. Many product designs require materials to be thinner and thinner for miniaturization. This is especially true in the multilayer interconnects that provide the solution for notebook computers, cellular phones, PDAs, and PCMCIAs.

9.1.2 Frequency Drivers

As computers and modules obtain processing speeds above 100 MHz, signal speed and integrity become paramount. Generally, FR-4 materials can be designed in systems running above 100 MHz, but the design becomes very difficult. As processing speeds continue to accelerate as indicated by the recent PowerPC™ and Pentium™ chip products now on the market, the pressure will continue to lower the dielectric constant.

Figure 9.1 illustrates the ever-increasing clock speeds of types of computer technologies and it also illustrates the threshold for the impact on materials (50 MHz). At this level, both signal speed and signal integrity become issues. Advanced material technology can provide

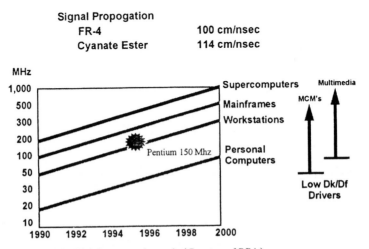

FIGURE 9.1   High frequency demands. (*Courtesy of BPA.*)

robust solutions from a variety of polymer and carrier systems which often utilize low-thermal-setting polymers. For example, cyanate ester provides signal transmission speeds of 114 cm/ns compared to 100 cm/ns compared to normal FR-4 epoxy materials. Lower D_k and lower D_f provide the following solutions when selecting advanced material technologies.

Lower dielectric constant D_k benefits:

- Faster conductor speed
- Thinner interconnects for the same conductor geometries

Lower dissipation factor D_f benefits:

- Improved signal integrity with high frequencies
- Less signal loss at high frequencies

9.2 COPPER FOIL TECHNOLOGY

Advanced multilayer technology relies fundamentally on copper being the primary conductor medium. The main process for producing the copper foil for advanced materials technology is the process of electrodeposition on a drum. Usually this drum is either stainless steel or titanium. After the plating process, the foil is removed and then treated with a variety of post-plating processes that provide a robust surface for bonding during the multilayer lamination step. The technology of manufacturing copper foil is mature and the supply of good-quality foil is available throughout the global marketplace.

9.2.1 Class 1 and Class 3 Electrodeposited Foils

IPC-MF-150 delineates the most common types of electrodeposited foils. The two primary types listed in Table 9.4 are Class 1 and Class 3 foils. The difference between the two foils is in a property called *high-temperature elongation*. Class 3 values for the property of high-temperature elongation are higher than those of Class 1, and usually Class 3 carries a cost premium for this extra ductility.

TABLE 9.4   IPC-MF-150 Typical Properties
Class 1, Class 3

Type	Copper weight	Tensile strength		Elongation, min	
		@ room temperature	@ 180°C	@ room temperature	@ 180°C
Type E, Class 1 standard ED	1 oz	30,000 lb	N.A.	3%	N.A.
	2 oz	30,000 lb	N.A.	3%	N.A.
Type E, Class 3 high-temp ED	1 oz	N.A.	20,000 lb	N.A.	2%
	2 oz	N.A.	25,000 lb	N.A.	3%

It is common in higher-technology materials and their associated multilayers to utilize Class 3 foils because they provide an extra margin of safety in reliability and yields when compared to Class 1 foils. The higher elongation at temperature provides more resistance to copper cracking of the foil during thermal cycling and/or thermal shock of the board. Foil crack-ing is more predominant on thicker boards, especially when they are built with low-T_g resin systems. A simple switch to Class 3 foils can prevent this defect from occurring and allow more of a process window for manufacturing. As miniaturization continues, the importance of copper foil grows for two reasons:

1. Copper foils become a higher percentage of the finished laminate when compared to resin and glass as the dielectrics become thinner, therefore contributing more to dimensional stability and other key characteristics of the multilayer materials.
2. Copper foils have a distinct impact on the ability to etch fine lines.

For example, 1 oz copper is only 22 percent of the total thickness of a 0.010-in laminate, while copper is 41 percent of a 0.002-in ultrathin ½-oz laminate, which is a significant difference. Fig-ure 9.2 illustrates copper percent of the multilayer thickness for various core laminates, which is a good reference to understand the impact of copper technology on thinner cores.

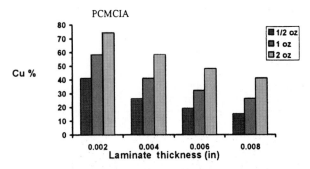

FIGURE 9.2 Copper percent of multilayer thickness.

As copper becomes a higher percentage of the laminate, its importance in fine-line etching is critical to high-process yields. Multilayer interconnects continue to drop their line width designs as mentioned in Sec. 9.1, and with each lowering of the fine-line hurdle, better mate-rials and processes are required to achieve good yields. The newer technologies of flip chip and direct chip attach will require even finer external and internal line widths. From a design standpoint, finer lines are easier to achieve with thinner coppers. Three-mil lines and spaces are much easier to fabricate with ½-oz copper than with 1-oz copper. However, movement towards thinner coppers is not always possible from a design standpoint. Therefore, to address this issue of fine-line generation, two new copper foil technologies are specifically engineered for fine-line resolution. These two technologies are *fine-grain foils* and *reverse-treated foils*. In each case, these foils are available in Class 1 and Class 3 type electrodeposited foils.

9.2.2 Fine-Grain Foils

Fine-grain foils are part of a new copper foil technology that meets the requirements of IPC-ML-150, while providing a base material that improves the yields of the etching process. The main metallurgical difference of fine-grain foils when compared to traditional foils is non-columnar grain structure. Standard foils have large grain boundaries and are columnar in shape. By adjusting the process of electrodeposition, the copper foil manufacturers have achieved a unique metallurgy. In addition to a fine-grain structure that enhances etching, these foils have a much lower profile geometry on the treatment side of the foil. In general, the lower the profile in treatment, the more precise the line definition during the etching process. This in turn allows a more robust fine-line control and, therefore, impedance control.

Part of this technology incorporates the benefits of Class 3 technology foils. Fine-grain foils typically have high fatigue resistance to foil cracking because they have higher tensile strength and higher elongation compared to standard foils. This imparts some extra stiffness. Fortunately, this is a benefit for multilayer manufacturing because extra stiffness allows for easier handling during the fabrication process. The advantages of fine-grain foils are:

- Improved etching due to small grain structure
- Improved etching due to lower profile treatments
- High-temperature fatigue resistance due to improved toughness
- Improved handling ability due to stiffness

In Table 9.5, some of the benefits and properties of fine-grain foils are provided. These benefits are compared to the properties of the other new copper technology, reverse-treated foils.

TABLE 9.5   Reverse-Treated Foils and Fine-Grain Foils

Type foil	Designation	Value engineering processes	Elongation, min	Tensile, Kpsi	Treatment
Reverse-treated	Double treat	Oxide, preclean	5%	55	Both sides
Reverse-treated	MLS	Preclean, microetch	5%	55	Both sides
Fine-grain	SQ VLP JTCAM	Etching/fine-grain metallurgy	5–8%	70–100	Single side
Fine-grain	VLP	Fine-grain/Low-profile	8–9%	27–70	Single-sided or double-treated

9.2.3 Reverse-Treated Foils

In Table 9.5, two reverse-treated foil technologies are listed. The first of the two technologies is double-treat copper foil. This foil technology is well established in the industry. Laminates manufactured with double-treat foil have a light tannish color and are manufactured by placing a secondary treatment on the drum side of the copper foil in addition to the normal secondary treatment on the matte side of the copper. In this manner, the foil has both a topside and a bottomside treatment. The advantage of this technology, even though it costs more, is the elimination of the black oxide process at the multilayer user. A laminate made with double-treat copper does not need the black oxide process. The disadvantage of this copper foil is that the process window for photoresists is somewhat limited compared to standard coppers. Therefore, the total cost benefits of double-treat are not readily apparent.

A rediscovered technology of the second type of reverse-treated foil is the lower-cost MLS or RTF system. This system is differentiated by the elimination of one of the secondary treatments on the foil (matte-side). This type of system has many of the benefits of double treatment with a smaller cost differential.

9.3 ADVANCED CARRIER SYSTEMS

The structure of the copper-clad laminates is provided by the carrier system. The carrier system basically provides this structure through mechanical strength of fibers which are part of the carrier system. Traditionally, this structure has been achieved with woven E-glass fabrics of various weave styles and various filament diameters.

As technology progresses in MCMs and associated designs, these woven fabrics are evolving to finer weaves and thinner and smoother fabrics to facilitate higher yields in the multilayer process. In addition to woven fabrics, random fiber fabrics are seeing a resurgence in activity for both cost and technology reasons. Random fiber products couple low cost and facilitate microvia generation with the new technologies of laser ablation, plasma ablation, micropunching, and chemical milling.

9.3.1 Advanced Glass Filaments

Glass filaments are the basis of woven and nonwoven glass fabrics. Table 9.6 lists the physical and electrical properties of three basic systems that are used in advanced multilayer interconnects. E-glass comprises the vast majority of all applications because of its general properties and its low cost. S-glass and D-glass are very specialized E-glass fibers that have two important properties that differ from E-glass: lower dielectric constant and lower expansion rates. Designers can utilize the lower dielectric constant to build either faster circuits or multilayer boards with thinner overall thickness, depending on the design need. The lower expansion rates can be utilized for applications which require a very controlled x-y CTE because of the surface-mount components. Usually, high-technology surface-mount components are more compatible with substrates that have x-y CTEs that are closer to the CTE of the silicon die inside them. S-glass and D-glass have been utilized for sophisticated multilayers that combine cyanate ester with the associated woven fabrics. The finished multilayers are reliable for ceramic chip carrier mounting with no loss in reliability.

TABLE 9.6 Comparative Properties of Glass Fibers

	E	S	D
Specific gravity	2.54	2.49	2.16
Tensile strength, lb/in^2	500,000	665,000	350,000
Modulus of elasticity @ 72°F			
lb/in^2 × 106, as draw	10.5	12.4	7.5
After annealing	12.4	13.5	Not measurable
Elongation @ 72°F %	4.8	5.7	4.7
Thermal expansion coefficient in/in/°F × 106	2.8	1.6	1.7
Strain point, °F	945	1400	890
Annealing point, °F	1215	1490	970
Dielectric constant @ 1 MHz	5.80	4.53	3.56
Dielectric constant @ 10 MHz	6.13	5.21	4.00
Power factor, 1 MHz	0.001	0.002	0.005
Power factor, 10 MHz	0.0039	0.0068	0.0026
Refractive index	1.547	1.523	1.47

Both the S-glass and the D-glass are available in few glass styles, and the availability of these fabrics is poor. Typically the two glass styles used are 6080 (similar to 1080) and 6116 (similar to 2116). Therefore, unless the application has very specialized requirements, E-glass is the fabric of choice.

9.3.2 Single-Ply Woven E-Glass Fabrics

One of the most exciting technologies that improves the price and performance in multilayer systems is the increased use of single-ply woven E-glass fabrics. Traditionally, FR-4 systems have required a minimum of two plies of bond ply/prepreg between each copper layer, due to concerns about the integrity of the dielectric; therefore, the extra ply was insurance. With the advent of advanced vacuum lamination techniques, improved resin systems, and advanced technology in woven E-glass fabrics, single-ply fabrics provide more flexibility to the designer.

There are several advantages to single-ply fabrics for MCM-Ls and other associated technologies:

- Lower cost compared to multiple ply
- Thinner dielectrics are possible
- More consistency for the fabricator in dimensional stability

Table 9.7 lists several single-ply fabrics and their associated weaving information. Generally, heavier fabrics have tighter weaves and larger filaments; therefore, heavier fabrics are harder to drill. On the positive side, heavier fabrics are very cost effective in providing the most thickness for the least amount of fabric plies.

TABLE 9.7   Single-Ply E-Glass Fabrics

Mils per ply	Style number	Warp yarn	Filling yarn	End count	Filling count	Fabric thickness	Fabric weight, oz/yd^2
1.0	14498	D1800 1/0	D1800 1/0	74.0	74.0	0.0008	0.51
1.5	106	D 900 1/0	D900 1/0	56.0	56.0	0.0013	0.72
3.0	1280	D 450 1/0	D 450 1/0	60.0	60.0	0.0022	1.58
3.5	2113	E 225 1/0	D 450 1/0	60.0	56.0	0.0029	2.31
4.0	2313	E 225 1/0	D 450 1/0	60.0	64.0	0.0032	2.38
4.5	2116	E 225 1/0	E 225 1/0	60.0	58.0	0.0038	3.22
5.0	1652	E 150 1/0	E 150 1/0	52.0	52.0	0.0045	4.18
6.0	1500	E 110 1/0	E 110 1/0	49.0	42.0	0.0052	4.95
7.0	7628	G 75 1/0	G 75 1/0	44.0	32.0	0.0068	6.00
7.5	7629	G 75 1/0	G 75 1/0	44.0	34.0	0.0070	6.25
9.0	7635	G 75 1/0	G 50 1/0	44.0	29.0	0.0080	6.90

Figure 9.3 shows a SEM micrograph of a 106 fabric weave structure. The filament diameter in this case is 0.00026 in. Each filament is placed in a bundle and the bundle is woven into this particular style. As fabrics become thinner, it is normal to see open spaces in the weave pattern.

In addition to cost advantages, dimensional stability of single-ply laminates meets or exceeds the dimensional stability of two-ply constructions. Because of the cost and DS advantages, single-ply laminates are quickly becoming the advanced material technology of choice.

FIGURE 9.3   SEM micrograph of 106 weave structure

9.3.3   Nonwoven Aramid Reinforcement

The technical trend in MCM-L materials is away from the woven-type materials and towards random-fiber carriers. The reason for this technology switch is the search for higher yields as the geometries in MCM-L and other technologies continue to miniaturize. Certain random-fiber materials have the unique capability of microvia generation by either plasma or by laser ablation. In addition, random-fiber carriers are lower in cost when compared to woven fabrics for a given fiber type.

The random-fiber material Thermount® is characterized in Table 9.8. Since the Aramid fiber is an organic fiber and not a mineral fiber as E-glass is, it also has the unique property of lower density. Boards manufactured with Thermount as a base material are essentially lighter than conventional boards by at least 15 percent.

TABLE 9.8   Thermount Fabric Properties*

Property	E-210	E-220	E-230
Basis weight, oz/yd	0.91	1.60	2.00
Thickness, mils	1.70	2.87	3.55
Density, g/cm^3	0.75	0.75	0.75
Break strength, lb/in			
Machine	6.0	9.0	11.0
Transverse	5.0	9.0	11.0
Laminate thickness	0.0018 ± 0.0004 in	0.0032 ± 0.0004	0.004 ± 0.0005

    * At 51 percent resin content.

9.4   ADVANCED RESIN SYSTEMS

Resin systems provide the bond between the copper and the substrate in the multilayer system and have a strong influence on the final electrical, mechanical, and physical properties of the multilayers. More important, they play a large part in the total cost of the system which includes the processability issues normally encountered in the traditional printed circuit facilities. In general, resin systems are moving towards higher T_gs and improved electrical properties. Nearly every multilayer system can benefit from higher T_gs. Newer advanced polymer systems allow for improved processing windows at the printed circuit board manufactured compared to earlier resin technologies.

9.4.1   180 T_g Multifunctional Epoxies

The highest growth area for advanced multilayer materials centers around the 180-T_g point, which is somewhat of a sweet spot because a significant amount of heat resistance is obtained in a cost-effective manner. The T_g of 180°C is proving to be a very cost effective balance for high-technology boards which demand good thermal resistance for wire bonding and assembly. Advancements in multifunctional epoxies now allow excellent performance with little impact to processing characteristics. For all intents, the 180-T_g systems process very closely to the parameters of previous 140-T_g systems.

The higher T_g provides several thermal benefits. The reliability of a 180-T_g epoxy board is improved over a 140-T_g board during reliability thermal cycling. In addition, during multiple thermal shocks, a 180-T_g plated through-hole survives with less impact to the hole from the solder. Pad lifting and various other defects such as voiding in zones A and B (IPC test methodology) are greatly reduced.

From the packaging side, the processes of wire bonding, direct chip attach, BGA mounting, and BGA rework are more robust with multifunctional epoxies. Table 9.9 illustrates the higher-temperature hardness values possible with high-T_g multifunctional epoxies as compared to traditional multifunctional epoxies. This improvement in hardness at high temperatures allows gold wire bonding processes to be robust. Figure 9.4 illustrates a wire bond on a 180-T_g multifunctional epoxy laminate with no coining or depressions due to inadequate hardness at temperatures.

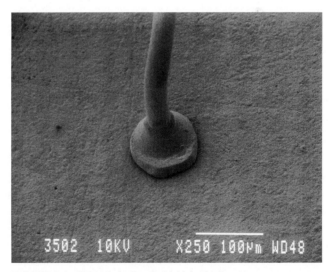

FIGURE 9.4   SEM of wire bond with high-T_g substrate.

TABLE 9.9   High-Temperature Hardness Testing

Resin system	Rockwell superficial hardness ASTM E18, room temperature	Rockwell hardness 150°C	% Retention
140 °C epoxy	52.5	35.8	68.1
180 °C high T_g epoxy	57.5	47.1	81.9
180 °C BT/epoxy	57.4	50.2	87.4
180 °C epoxy/Thermount	67.9	59.2	87.2

9.4.2 BT/Epoxy Resins

BT/epoxy resin systems are primarily used in semiconductor packaging applications such as the internal interconnect of BGAs and MCM-Ls. BT stands for bismaleimide triazine and represents a high-performance resin system with good electrical properties and good thermal properties. Normally, epoxy is blended into this system to provide good toughness. BT/epoxies have a nominal T_g of 180°C.

These systems are utilized when improved electrical performance is required in addition to 180-T_g performance. With this higher performance, some sacrifice in processability at the board manufacturer is required. Usually BT/epoxies have a smaller process window than 180-T_g multifunctional epoxies. The primary reasons for the popularity in semiconductor applications is the compatibility with different wire-bonding processes combined with more specialized electrical characteristics. In addition, BT/epoxies have a good sound history in their resistance to ionic conductive growth (CAF) and the popcorn test (moisture + heat cycle), which are two important semiconductor tests for semiconductor packaging.

9.4.3 Polyimide Resins

Polyimide and toughened polyimide systems have the most heat resistance of all the advanced resin systems. They are utilized in applications where heat resistance is critical, such as burn-in boards, oil exploration electronics, military avionics, and certain MCM-Ls. The standard polyimide systems have a T_g of 260°C and the toughened polyimide systems have a T_g of 220°C. Most applications are moving towards the toughened systems because they are more compatible with traditional printed circuit processes and are slightly lower in cost. Toughened polyimide systems have a wider process window because they are less brittle and allow for easier drilling and routing.

9.4.4 Cyanate Ester Resins

The premier resin system for advanced applications is cyanate ester because it combines the properties that are crucial to miniaturization: low D_k/low D_f combined with excellent thermal resistance (T_g of 250°C). Cyanate ester has excellent thermal and electrical properties and is used in very high end applications such as high-speed switchgear and backplaces. Cyanate ester materials have a somewhat narrow process window, and specialized printed circuit processing is required. However, when this is performed, cyanate ester boards produce a superior advanced multilayer board. Because it is possible with lower-D_k materials to reduce the overall thickness of a board for the same impedance, cyanate esters are often selected in applications where the overall thickness needs to be contained for either cost or technology. Backplanes, for example, can be designed with reduced thicknesses of up to 25 percent when compared to standard FR-4 systems.

9.5   ADVANCED MATERIALS DESIGN GUIDE

By combining various combinations of resin technology, carrier technology, and copper technology, excellent choices are available for advanced interconnect technologies. Proper selection always requires a careful balance of cost, properties, and application requirements. Therefore, it is important that the end application be carefully defined.

9.5.1   Advanced Woven Composites

Proper selection of the correct woven multilayer technology for each application will ensure optimum yields and cost/performance characteristics. In most cases, a balance of properties must be decided on that optimizes the mechanical and electrical characteristics vs. the cost of the different types of engineered materials. Overspecified materials or underspecified materials will cause extra costs through either lower yields or wasted materials. Table 9.10 lists an application description guide that helps narrow the application and material options available. Table 9.11 further defines the options by their properties.

TABLE 9.10   Application Description Guide

Application & description	Resin	T_g (TMA)	Cost (x)*
High-volume, medium & high technology, low-cost, PCMCIA	Multifunctional epoxy	140	1.0
Thick M/L, backplanes, DCA, ball grid array, underhood, PCMCIA, pin grid array	Multifunctional epoxy	170	1.2–1.4
MCM-L, CA, ball grid array, high-speed computing, pin grid array	BT/epoxy	180	1.4–1.6
Military hardware, high reliability, avionics	Polyimide	260	2.2–2.4
High reliability, avionics, medium cost profile	Toughened Polyimide	220	2.0–2.6
Controlled CTE MCM-Ls, laser microvia MCM-Ls, PCMCIA	Thermount polyimide	220	TBD
High-speed computing telecommunications hardware, high-frequency electronics, high reliability	Cyanate ester	250	2.3–2.6

* Based on six-layer bill of materials.

9.5.2   Woven Mechanical and Electrical Properties

A closer look at the mechanical and electrical properties allows the designer further options in cost reduction and optimum performance for each particular appication. Figures 9.5, 9.6, and 9.7 are comparison graphs that illustrate electrical, x-y CTE and z-axis CTE values of several material and substrate options. Notice again that each material has several different properties and each application will require a different balance.

9.5.3   PCMCIA, Smart Card, and MCM-L Ultrathin Materials

Certainly, the major market trends towards lighter, smaller, and faster are being led by PCMCIAs, smart cards, and MCM-Ls. Ultrathin materials are absolutely essential for the success of these technologies and form the foundation of process capability. Laminates with very thin

TABLE 9.11   Advanced Material Technology Comparative Properties

	140°C epoxy	170°C epoxy	170°C BT/epoxy	260°C polyimide	220°C polyimide	220°C Thermount	250°C CE
Peel strength, 1 oz cu, lb/in							
After stress, min	9	9	6.5	7.5	7.5	6.0	8.0
After thermal cycling, min	9	9	6.5	8.0	8.0	6.0	8.0
At elevated temps., min	7	7	6.0	6.0	6.0	5.0	7.5
After solutions exposure	9	9	5.0	7.0	7.0	5.0	8.0
Volume resistivity, min							
C-96/35/90, MΩ/cm	10^8	10^8	10^7	10^7	10^7	10^7	10^7
E-24/125, MΩ/cm	10^7	10^7	10^7	10^7	10^7	10^7	10^7
Surface resistivity, min							
C-96/35/90, MΩ	10^7	10^7	10^6	10^7	10^7	10^7	10^7
E-24-125, MΩ	10^7	10^7	10^7	10^7	10^7	10^6	10^7
Arc resistance, min.	65	65	118	136	100	125	160
Electric strength, V/mil min.	1250	1300	1200	1350	1200	970	1650
Flammability UL94	V-0	V-0	V-0	V-1	V-0	N.A.	V-0
Glass transition temp., °C TMA	140	170	180	260	220	220	250
Z-axis expansion, %	4.5	3.7	3.7	1.7	2.9	—	2.4
Dk, 1 MHz 50% r.c.	4.3	4.3	4.1	4.5	4.5	4.10	3.8
Moisture absorption, %	0.10	0.10	<0.50	0.35	0.35	0.78	<0.50

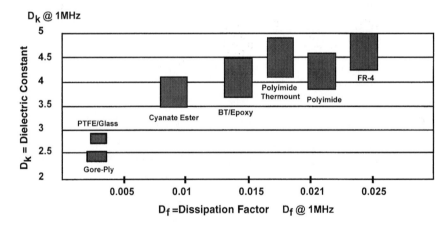

FIGURE 9.5   Advanced material technology electrical properties.

coppers and dielectrics must retain all of the characteristics of normal multilayer materials, such as dimensional stability and heat resistance, while carrying the extra burden of maintaining an excellent dielectric, with thickness less than 50 μm. Advanced materials technologies have allowed significant breakthroughs in this area with prepreg and copper-clad laminates commercially available below 50 μm in thickness.

9.5.3.1   Sub-50-μm Laminate.   Table 9.12 defines several constructions of copper-clad laminates that are commercially available in an ultrathin format. Special manufacturing techniques are utilized to manufacture these laminates. Extra precautions for purity and cleanliness and low-profile coppers are necessary as the raw material precursors to the laminate manufacturing. Low-profile coppers are necessary for two reasons: (1) dimensional stability

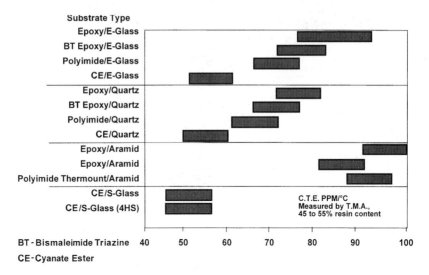

FIGURE 9.6 *z*-axis expansion comparison (+50 to 285°C).

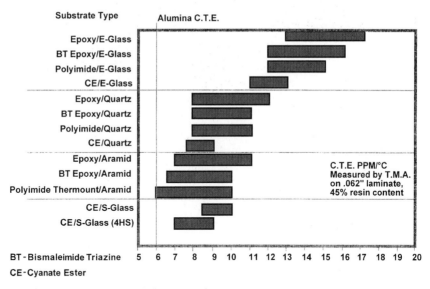

FIGURE 9.7 *x*- and *y*-axis CTE (−55 to 95°C).

and (2) dielectric control. If the copper profile is too rough, there is risk that the dielectric will be compromised by a protruding copper tooth.

9.5.3.2 PCMCIA Constructions.   PCMCIA constructions typically are exclusively single-ply and utilize all ultrathin materials and ultrathin bond plys/prepregs. Figure 9.8 illustrates a six-layer PCMCIA construction consisting of a single-ply 106 copper-clad laminate and a single-ply 1080 prepreg. This type of construction is possible with virtually any resin system, including 180-T_g multifunctional epoxies, BT/epoxies, and polyimides.

TABLE 9.12 Ultrathin Laminate Properties

Multifunctional 140 & 180°C T_g					
Thickness	Tolerance	Constr.	RC%	D_k	Copper
0.0015	±0.00025	(R&D)	61	4.2	12–30
0.0020	±0.003	1-ply 106	63	4.2	12–35
0.0022	±0.003	1-ply 1080	50	4.4	12–35
0.0025	±0.003	1-ply 1080	55	4.2	12–35
0.0030	±0.005	1-ply 1080	63	4.2	12–35
0.0040	±0.005	1-ply 106/1080	53	4.3	12–35
0.0044	±0.005	1080/1080	52	4.4	12–35

Typical Board Build-Up
6 Layer TLC 0.014" Total Thickness

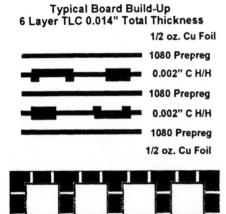

1/2 oz. Cu Foil
1080 Prepreg
0.002" C H/H
1080 Prepreg
0.002" C H/H
1080 Prepreg
1/2 oz. Cu Foil

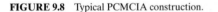

FIGURE 9.8 Typical PCMCIA construction.

9.5.4 Advanced Nonwoven Laminates

The random Aramid materials such as Thermount have several unique properties. Table 9.13 describes the advantages of an Aramid material impregnated with two advanced resins. Since Aramid fibers have a negative fiber CTE, copper-clad laminates manufactured with Thermount have the ability to have significantly lower x-y CTEs. These CTEs are 7 to 9 ppm/°C compared to a standard epoxy-glass laminate with CTEs as high as 16 ppm. Since multilayer boards have varying amounts of copper as a percentage of their volume, the designer should be aware of the relationship of copper content to the board volume. Table 9.13 illustrates a clear advantage of Thermount nonwoven materials for reduced x-y parameters.

Prior to random-fiber Aramid materials becoming available, two other technologies were utilized extensively to reduce x-y CTE: copper-invar-copper and woven Aramid. These two technologies are being superseded by the cost-effective nonwoven Aramid fibers.

TABLE 9.13 Thermount Laminate Comparative Properties

Properties	E-glass/high-T_g epoxy	Thermount/high-T_g epoxy	Thermount/ polyimide
Dimensional stability, %	±0.05	±0.02	±0.02
In-plane CTE, ppm	16–19	7–9	7–9
Dielectric constant	4.5	3.9	3.6
Density, g/cm³	1.7	1.3	1.3
Glass transition temperature, °C	180	180	220
Laminate smoothness, A	4200	2200	2200
Laser ablation	Deep UV Yag	All	All

With the trend towards microvias, Thermount has the additional advantage of enabling the designer and manufacturer to use two processes that are incompatible with glass-based substrates: plasma ablation and laser ablation. Both plasma etching and laser ablation of microvias allow for cost-effective hole generation when the holes are very small in diameter.

9.5.5 Low-Cost Mixed Dielectrics

In many designs, more than one material system is combined within the same multilayer board to improve the cost/performance ratio. Since the internal core provides mostly structural support, the core can remain low cost. It would not be uncommon to select a standard FR-4 epoxy multifunctional system or a 180-T_g multifunctional epoxy system for the internal core.

On the outside of the multilayer board, a high-performance material can be efficiently laminated. Since the outside can carry the most density and must be chip compatible, it is not unusual to select high-T_g materials, such as Thermount, for capping the multilayer board.

9.5.5.1 Microvia Enabling Materials.   An advantage to the mixed dielectric approach is the use of microvia enabling materials on the exterior surface of the board. Figure 9.9 depicts one possible scenario for mixed dielectrics and microvia formation. Table 9.14 illustrates possible options for different via formations and the compatibility with different materials. Since these technologies are changing rapidly, it would be difficult to maintain an up-to-date listing of the latest advances. Suffice it to say, there are several options for compatibility between newer via formation technologies and advanced materials.

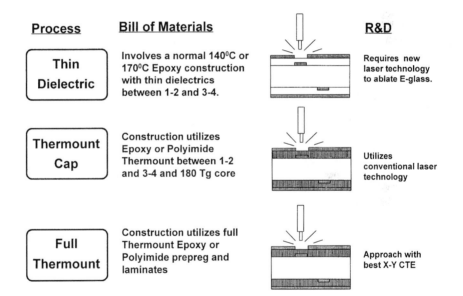

FIGURE 9.9   Possible mixed dielectric approaches to interstitial via hole formation (IVH).

TABLE 9.14   Interstitial Via Hole Material Compatibility Chart

	Copper	E-glass	Thermount	Liquid crystal polymer	Speedboard® e-PTFE
Plasma	No	No	Yes	Yes	Yes
YAG laser	Yes	Yes	Yes	Yes	Yes
CO_2 laser	No	No	Yes	Yes	Yes
Excimer laser	No	No	Yes	Yes	Yes

CHAPTER 10
PHYSICAL CHARACTERISTICS OF THE PCB

Lee W. Ritchey
3Com Corp., Santa Clara, California

10.1 CLASSES OF PCB DESIGNS

Printed circuit boards (PCBs) or printed wiring boards (PWBs) can be divided into two general classes which have common characteristics based on their end functions. These two classes have very different materials and design requirements and functions and, as a result, need to be treated differently throughout the design and fabrication processes. The first class contains analog, RF, and microwave PCBs such as are found in stereos, transmitters, receivers, power supplies, automotive controls, microwave ovens, and similar products. The second contains digital-based circuitry such as is found in computers, signal processors, video games, printers, and other products that contain complex digital circuitry. Table 10.1 lists many of the characteristics of each class of PCBs.

TABLE 10.1 Characteristics of RF/Analog vs. Digital-Based PCBs

RF, microwave, analog PCB	Digital-based PCB
Low circuit complexity	Very high circuit complexity
Precise matching of impedance often needed	Tolerant of impedance mismatches
Minimizing signal losses essential	Tolerant of lossy materials
Small circuit element sizes often essential	Small circuit element sizes desirable
Only 1 or 2 layers	Many signal and power layers
High feature accuracy needed	Moderate feature accuracy needed
Low/uniform dielectric constants needed	Dielectric constant secondary

10.1.1 Characteristics of Analog, RF, and Microwave PCBs

As can be seen from Table 10.1, the materials, design, and fabrication needs of this class of PCBs are markedly different from those of PCBs commonly referred to as digital.

- Circuit complexity is low because most components used have two, three, or four leads. This is due to the high usage of resistors, transistors, capacitors, transformers, and inductors.

- Traces, pads, and vias often act as inductors, capacitors, and coupling elements in the actual circuit. Their shapes may have a material effect on overall circuit performance. For example, the lead inductance and capacitance in a transistor collector circuit wire may act as the resonant components for an RF amplifier or it may degrade performance if it is unwanted. Figure 10.1 shows the impedance of traces as a function of their capacitance.

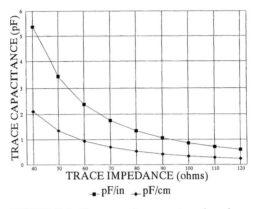

FIGURE 10.1 Trace capacitance vs. trace impedance, based on $L_0 = 8.5$ nH/in. (*Prepared by Ritch Tech, 1992.*)

- Two traces running side by side may be used to couple a signal from one circuit to another as is done in directional couplers of microwave amplifiers. (This same coupling in a digital circuit may result in a signal getting into a neighboring circuit causing a malfunction.)
- A series of conductors running side by side may function as a band-pass filter. Proper performance of filters, as well as most other wideband RF circuits, depends on all frequencies traveling with equal speed through the structures. To the extent that this is not true, frequencies that arrive later distort the signal being processed. This is called *phase distortion*.

Figure 10.2 illustrates the dielectric constant of various PCB materials as a function of frequency. Notice that some materials exhibit a dramatic decline in dielectric constant as frequency increases. The speed with which a signal travels through a dielectric is a function of the dielectric constant. Figure 10.3 illustrates signal velocity as a function of dielectric constant. From these two graphs it can be seen that using a dielectric material with a nonuniform dielectric constant in RF applications may result in severe phase distortion because the higher-frequency components arrive at the output before the lower frequencies.

- A trace in a power supply circuit may be expected to carry several amps without significant heating or voltage drop. Its resistance may even be used as a sense element to detect current flow. Similarly, handling large currents with insufficient copper in a trace may result in a voltage drop that degrades circuit performance. Figure 10.4 illustrates trace resistance of a copper trace as a function of its width and thickness. Figures 10.5 and 10.6 illustrate conductor heating as a function of width, thickness, and current flow.
- PCBs used in consumer electronics tend to share lower circuit complexity with RF and analog PCBs. However, the performance demands are far lower. The need for the lowest possible cost offsets this. To achieve the cost objectives, every effort is made to keep all connections on a single side and to form all holes in a single operation by punching. This

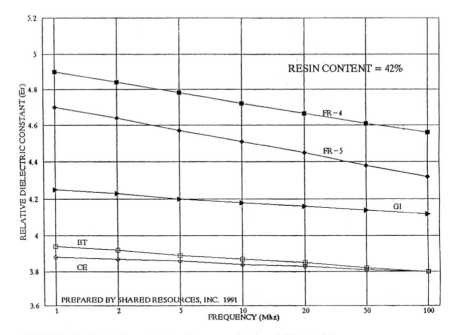

FIGURE 10.2   Dielectric constants vs. frequency of various PCB materials.

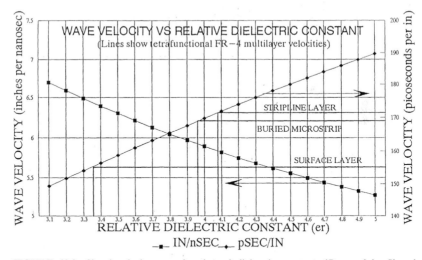

FIGURE 10.3   Signal velocity as a function of dielectric constant. (*Prepared by Shared Resources, Inc., 1991*)

eliminates both drilling and plating. The substrate material system is often resin impregnated paper, the lowest-cost substrate system for electronic packaging.

Summarizing, successful RF and analog design depends heavily on the properties of the materials used and on the physical shapes of the conductors and their proximity to each other

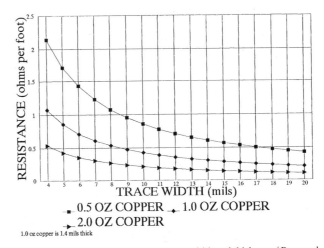

FIGURE 10.4 Trace resistance vs. trace width and thickness. (*Prepared by Ritch Tech.*)

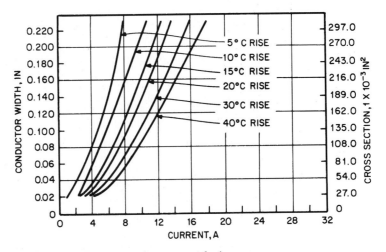

FIGURE 10.5 Temperature rise vs. current for 1-oz copper.

rather than on the ability to handle very large numbers of circuits simultaneously. Hand routing or connecting of the individual parts coupled with manipulating the shapes of individual copper features are essential parts of this design process. For these reasons, the design tools and design team must be chosen to meet these needs. Physical layout tools that provide convenient graphical manipulation of PCB shapes are a must.

10.1.2 Characteristics of Digital-Based PCBs

Compared to RF and analog PCBs, digital-based PCBs have complex interconnections, but are tolerant of rather wide feature size and materials variations.

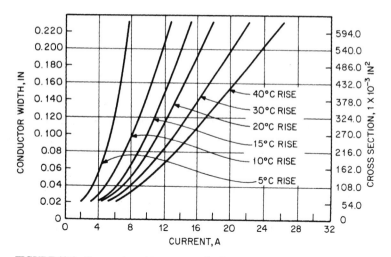

FIGURE 10.6   Temperature rise vs. current for 2-oz copper.

- They are characterized by very large numbers of components, often numbering in the hundreds and sometimes the thousands.
- Digital components often have large numbers of leads, as high as 400 or more. This high lead count stems from logic architectures that have data and address buses as wide as 128 bits or more. To connect PCBs with these wide data buses, digital systems often contain board-to-board connectors with as many as 1000 pins.
- Digital circuits have increasingly fast edges and low propagation delays to achieve faster performance. Edge rates as fast as 1 ns are now encountered in devices destined for products as common as video games. Table 10.2 lists edge speeds of some commonly used logic families, edge rate being the time required for a logic signal to switch from one logic level to the other (switching speed). Propagation delays, the time required for a signal to travel through a device, are decreasing along with edge rates.

TABLE 10.2   Typical Logic Family Switching Speeds

Logic family	Edge speed, ns	Critical length, in
STD TTL	5.0	14.5
ASTTL	1.9	5.45
FTTL	1.2	3.45
HCTTL	1.5	4.5
10KECL	2.5	7.2
BICMOS	0.7	2.0
10KHECL	0.7	2.0
GaAs	0.3	0.86

- These fast edges and short propagation delays lead to transmission line effects such as coupling, ground bounce, and reflections that can result in improper operation of the resulting PCB. Table 10.2 illustrates the degree to which a fast switching signal will couple into a neighboring line as a function of the edge-to-edge separation and the height of the signal pair above the underlying power plane. The critical length listed in Table 10.2 is the length of parallelism between two traces at which the coupling levels in Fig. 10.7 are reached.

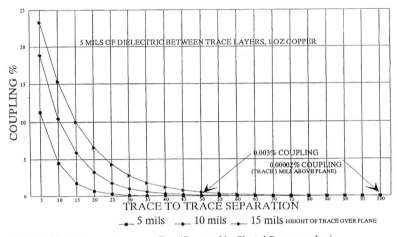

FIGURE 10.7 Trace-to-trace coupling. (*Prepared by Shared Resources, Inc.*)

The digital circuits themselves are designed to function properly with input signals that vary over a relatively wide range of values. Figure 10.8 illustrates the signal levels for a typical logic family, in this case ECL. The smallest output signal from an ECL driver is the difference between VOL_{max} and VOH_{min} or 0.99 V. The smallest input voltage to a device at which the logic part is designed to work properly is the difference between VIL_{max} and VIH_{min} or 0.37 V. The difference between these two levels, the noise margin of 0.62 V is available to counteract losses in the wiring and the dielectric and from other sources such as coupling and reflections. From this it can be seen that digital logic has a high tolerance of losses and higher immunity to noise.

This tolerance of noise and losses makes it possible to have trace features and base materials that introduce substantial losses and distortion while still achieving proper operation. It is this relatively high tolerance of distortion that makes it possible to manufacture economical digital PCBs.

Summary. The large number of connections in digital PCBs generally requires multiple wiring layers to successfully distribute power and interconnect all the devices. As a result, the design task is heavily weighted on the side of successfully making many connections in a limited number of routing layers while obeying transmission line rules. The base materials need to have characteristics that result in a PCB that is economical to fabricate and able to withstand the soldering processes while preserving high-speed performance. Compared to RF PCBs, losses in the dielectric tend to be of little concern for digital PCBs. The actual shapes of conductors, pads, holes, and other features have little effect on performance. (For detailed treatment of these topics, see Howard W. Johnson and Martin Graham, *High Speed Digital Design: A Handbook of Black Magic,* Prentice Hall, New York, 1993.)

The PCB design system and the design skill set for digital PCBs must be optimized to ensure accuracy in making large numbers of connections while successfully handling the high speed requirements of the system. Achieving this in a reasonable amount of time demands the use of a CAD system that contains an automatic router for use in connecting the wires.

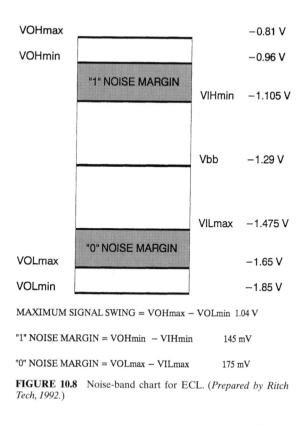

TYPICAL 10K ECL LOGIC VOLTAGE LEVELS

MAXIMUM SIGNAL SWING = VOHmax − VOLmin 1.04 V

"1" NOISE MARGIN = VOHmin − VIHmin   145 mV

"0" NOISE MARGIN = VOLmax − VILmax   175 mV

FIGURE 10.8 Noise-band chart for ECL. (*Prepared by Ritch Tech, 1992.*)

10.2 TYPES OF PCBs OR PACKAGES FOR ELECTRONIC CIRCUITS

The range of choices for packaging electronic circuits is quite broad. Some of the parameters that influence the choices are weight, size, cost, speed, ease of manufacture, repairability, and function of the circuit. The more common types are listed as follows with a brief description of their characteristics.

Levels of packaging are often used when referring to how electronics circuits are packaged. The first level of packaging is the housing of an individual component. This is usually an encapsulating coating, a molded case, or a cavity-type package such as a PGA (pin grid array). The second level of packaging is the PCB or substrate on which individual components are mounted. Third-level packaging is any additional packaging beyond these two. Most often third-level packaging takes the form of a multichip module (MCM) that has bare components mounted in it which is itself mounted on a PCB along with other components.

10.2.1 Single- and Double-Sided PCBs

These PCBs have conductor patterns on one or both sides of a base laminate with or without plated through-holes to interconnect the two sides. These are the workhorses of consumer electronics, automotive electronics, and the RF/microwave industry. They are the lowest-cost choice for consumer products. Laminate materials range from resin-impregnated paper for consumer electronics to blends of low-loss Teflon™ for RF applications.

10.2.2   Multilayer PCBs

These PCBs (see Fig. 10.9) have one or more conductor layers (usually power planes) buried inside in addition to having a conductor layer on each outside surface. The inner layers are connected to each other and to the outer layers by plated through-holes or vias. These are the packages of choice for nearly all digital applications ranging from personal computers to supercomputers. Numbers of layers range from 3 to as many as 50 in special applications. Laminate materials are nearly always some type of woven glass cloth impregnated with one of several resin systems. The resin system is chosen to satisfy requirements such as the ability to withstand high temperatures, cost, dielectric constant, or resistance to chemicals.

10.2.3   Discrete-Wire or Multiwire PCBs

This class of PCBs is a variation of the multilayer package. A circuit board is constructed by etching a pair of power layers back to back on a laminate substrate. A layer of partially cured, still sticky laminate is bonded to each side of this power plane structure. Discrete wiring is rolled into this sticky adhesive in patterns that will connect leads or serve as access to surface-mount component pads.

Once all of the wires have been rolled into place, a second layer of laminate is placed over the wires, followed by copper foil sheets. This sandwich is then laminated, drilled, and processed like any multilayer PCB. The resulting PCB has outer layers and power planes much like any multilayer PCB. The principle difference is the printed wiring signal layers have been replaced by discrete wiring layers. In some cases of very high wiring density, alternating layers of power planes between wiring layers serve as isolation.

Designing a discrete-wiring PCB (see Fig. 10.10) involves adding a special discrete-wiring router to a standard PCB design system to generate the files for the machine that rolls the wire into the dielectric. Discrete wiring once provided a faster prototyping alternative to multilayer fabrication. At the present time, both technologies are equally rapid and cost effective during prototyping. However, for modest to high-volume production, multilayer technology is more cost effective than discrete wiring.

10.2.4   Hybrids

These circuits are usually single- or double-sided ceramic substrates with a collection of surface-mount active components and screened-on resistors made from metallic pastes. They are most often found in hearing aids and other miniature devices.

10.2.5   Flexible Circuits

These circuits are made by laminating copper foil onto a flexible substrate such as Kevlar® or Kapton®. They can range from a single conductor layer up to several layers. They are most often used to replace a wiring harness with a flat circuit to save weight or space. Often, the flexible circuit will contain active and passive components. Common applications are cameras, printers, disk drives, avionics, and video tape recorders.

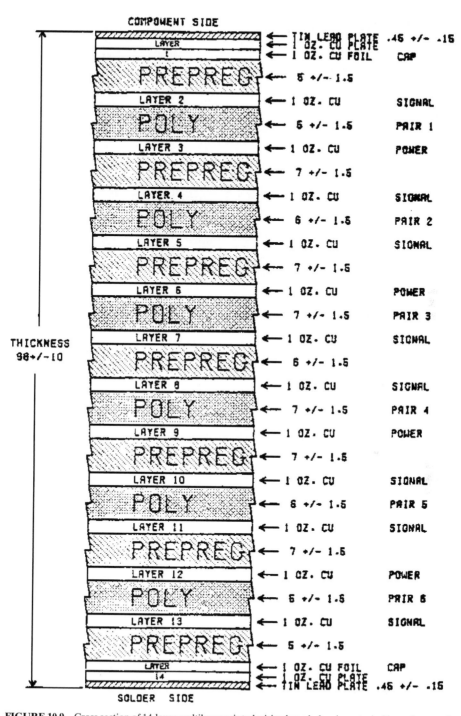

FIGURE 10.9 Cross section of 14-layer multilayer printed wiring board, showing a typical inner layer and prepreg material relationship. In this case, to reduce z-axis expansion, the innerlayers are polyimide, while the prepreg material is semicured polyimide. Typical signal, power, and ground layers are also indicated, as well as the thickness of the copper foil for each layer.

FIGURE 10.10   Cross section of a discrete-wire PCB. (*Courtesy of Icon Industries.*)

10.2.6   Flexible Rigid or Flex-Rigid

As the name suggests, these are combinations of flexible PCBs and rigid PCBs in a single unit. The flexible portion of the circuit is made first and included in the lamination process of the rigid portion of the assembly. This process eliminates wiring harnesses and the associated connectors. Applications include avionics and portable equipment such as laptop computers. As a rule, a flex-rigid assembly is more expensive than an equivalent combination of PCBs and cables.

10.2.7   Backplanes

Backplanes are special cases of multilayer PCBs. They tend to contain large quantities of connectors that have been installed using press fit pins. In addition, backplanes are used to distribute large amounts of dc power to the system. This is accomplished by laminating several power planes inside the backplane and by bolting bus bars onto the outside surfaces. Some applications require that active components, such as surface-mount ICs, be soldered to their surfaces. This greatly increases the difficulty of assembly as a result of the need to solder fine-pitch parts to a large, thick PCB.

10.2.8   MCMs (Multichip Modules)

Multichip modules are essentially miniature PCBs. Miniaturization is achieved by removing components such as ICs from their packages and mounting them directly to the substrate using wire bonds, flip chip, TAB or flip TAB. The motivation for using an MCM is miniaturization, reduction in weight, or a need to get high-speed components as close to each other as possible to achieve high-speed performance goals. MCMs usually represent a third level of packaging in a system between packaged components and the carrier PCB. As a result, this additional level of packaging virtually always results in a more expensive, more complex assembly than the equivalent circuits in standard packages. There are several types of MCM package.

10.2.8.1 *MCM-L, Multichip Module, Laminate.* This version of an MCM is manufactured from very thin laminates and metal layers using the same techniques employed in the manufacture of standard PCBs. Features such as holes, lands, and traces are much finer and require tooling similar to that used to manufacture semiconductors. This is the least expensive MCM type to design, tool, and manufacture. The same design tools and methodologies used for PCBs can be used.

10.2.8.2 *MCM-C, Multichip Module Ceramic.* This version of an MCM is manufactured by depositing conductor layers on thin layers of uncured ceramic material, punching and backfilling holes for vias, stacking the layers, and firing the total to create a hard ceramic multilayer substrate. This is the second least expensive MCM type to design, tool, and manufacture. It has been the workhorse of IBM's large mainframe computers for at least two decades. The same design tools and methodologies used for PCBs can be used.

10.2.8.3 *MCM-D, Multichip Module Deposited.* This version of an MCM is manufactured by depositing alternating thin films of organic insulators and thin films of metal conductors on a substrate of silicon, ceramic, or metal. The design and manufacturing techniques used for this technology resemble that used to create integrated circuit metallization. The thermal conductivity of the substrate is quite good. Design and fabrication support for MCM-D is limited.

10.2.8.4 *MCM-D/C, Multichip Module Deposited and Cofired.* This version of an MCM is a combination of a cofired, multilayer ceramic substrate containing the common wiring for a family of modules and deposited conductor and insulation layers containing the personality wiring. It has all of the problems of each technology it uses plus problems related to mismatches in temperature coefficient of the two materials systems.

10.2.8.5 *MCM-Si, Multichip Module Silicon.* As the name implies, this MCM technology starts with a silicon substrate like that used to make integrated circuits. Conductor patterns are formed using silicon dioxide (glass) as an insulator and aluminum or a similar metal for the wiring patterns in the same manner as is employed to build an integrated circuit. In fact, the same design tools and fabrication tools used to build ICs are used to build MCM-Si modules.

A significant advantage of MCM Si is the fact that the substrate is the same material as the ICs that will be attached to it. Therefore, it is thermally matched to the ICs, ensuring reliable contacts over extremes of temperature.

10.2.8.6 *Summary of MCM Technologies.* MCM packaging may be seen as a way to achieve higher performance from a collection of high-speed ICs than can be accomplished by mounting them onto a PCB or as a way to reduce size and weight. In reality, higher levels of integration nearly always result in a more economical solution. For all but low-volume, specialty applications, such as aerospace electronics and specialty processors for very high performance equipment, this has proven to be true for quite some time. This is likely to continue to be so for some time as semiconductor technology continues to improve the density of functionality that can be placed on a single IC. One need only examine the progression of microprocessor performance to see this phenomenon at work.

When a high-performance product requires integrated circuits made with different processing technologies, such as analog and CMOS or ECL and CMOS, integration does not represent a reasonable alternative to MCMs. Examples of this type of product are high-performance graphics products and video signal processing equipment.

10.3 METHODS OF ATTACHING COMPONENTS

A wide range of methods has evolved for attaching components to PCBs. The methods chosen as well as the combinations of methods chosen for a product have a substantial impact on the final cost, ease of assembly, availability of components, ease of test, and ease of rework. The five basic attachment combinations are: through-hole only, through-hole mixed with surface-mount on one side, surface-mount one side only, surface-mount both sides, and surface-mount both sides with through-hole.

10.3.1 Through-Hole Only

All component leads attach to the PCB by being inserted into holes that pass through the PCB. The components may be secured by wave soldering or by pressing into holes that result in an interference fit (press fit). Assembly involves a component placement operation followed by a wave-soldering operation. This method is still the workhorse of the low-cost consumer electronics industry.

10.3.2 Through-Hole Mixed with Surface-Mount

Components such as connectors and PGAs are attached to the PCB with through-hole technology. All other components are mounted using surface-mount packages. This is the most common method used to assemble electronics products. Assembly is a two-step process that involves placing all surface-mount parts and soldering them in place with a solder reflow system, then inserting all through-hole parts and soldering them in place in a wave-soldering operation. Alternatively, the through-holes may be hand-soldered if the quantity is small.

10.3.3 Surface-Mount, One Side Only

This type of package is made up of only surface-mount parts all mounted on the same side of the PCB. Assembly is a one-step process that involves placing all components and soldering them in place using some form of solder reflow.

10.3.4 Surface-Mount, Both Sides

This type of package contains surface-mount components on both sides. Assembly is a two-step process that involves placing all components on one side and reflow soldering them, followed by placing all components on the other side and reflow soldering them. In addition to more complex assembly operations, designing and testing this type of assembly is much more complex, as parts often share the same area on opposite sides of the PCB, causing conflicts when trying to locate vias and test points.

10.3.5 Surface-Mount, Both Sides with Through-Hole

As the name implies, this package type contains surface-mount parts on both sides, as well as through-hole parts such as connectors. In most cases, the surface-mount components on one side are passives, such as bypass capacitors and resistors that can withstand being passed through wave soldering. Assembly is a three-step process that involves placing the surface-mount components on the primary side and reflow soldering them. Once this is complete, the secondary-side surface-mount components are glued in place, the through-hole components are inserted, and the PCB is sent through wave soldering.

Because of the extra operations and exposure of components on the secondary side to molten solder, this type of assembly is prone to many assembly defects. It is important to note that soldering fine-pitch parts on the secondary side using wave soldering results in excessive solder bridging and should be avoided. In addition, active components, such as ICs, may be damaged by exposure to excessive heating.

10.4   COMPONENT PACKAGE TYPES

Over time, a wide assortment of packages has been developed to house components. Selecting the correct package type for each component is one of the most important parts of the design process. Package types chosen affect ease of design, assembly, test, and rework, as well as product cost and component availability.

10.4.1   Through-Hole

This class of component is characterized by parts that have wire or formed leads. These leads pass through holes drilled or punched in the PCB and are soldered to lands on the back side or to plating in the holes. This is the original package type used for electronic components. A major benefit of through-hole components is the fact that every component lead passes all the way through the PCB. Because of this, there is automatic access to any PCB layer to make connections. Further, every lead is available on the bottom of the PCB, so test tooling is easy to construct. With the advent of surface-mount components, through-hole is used primarily for connectors and pluggable devices such as microprocessors mounted in PGA packages.

Through-hole packages are often preferred for ICs and other components that dissipate large amounts of heat, because of the relative ease with which heat-sinking devices can be fitted to them. In addition, it is much easier to provide a socket for a through-hole device. This eases the task of changing programmable parts and microprocessors when it is necessary to upgrade a system.

Caution: Integrated circuits in through-hole packages are becoming difficult to find as they are displaced by surface-mount equivalents and should be avoided in new designs unless a secure supply of components is available for the production life of the design.

10.4.2   Surface Mount

This package type is the mainstream choice for packaging electronic components of every type, including connectors. Its principle characteristic is that all connections between a component lead and the PCB or substrate is made with a lap joint to a pad on the surface of the PCB. This has both advantages and disadvantages. On the advantage side, since there are no holes piercing the PCB, wiring space on inner layers and on the reverse side is not consumed with component lead holes. Because of this, it is usually possible to wire a PCB in fewer layers than would be true with through-hole parts. Another and larger benefit is the fact that surface-mount components are always smaller than their through-hole equivalent, making it possible to fit more parts in a given area.

The main disadvantages of surface-mount components stem from the fact that there are no leads to easily grip with instrumentation probes and that there may not be access to the leads from the reverse side for purposes of production testing. This gives rise to the need to add a test pad to most nets on the back side in order to perform production test. It also gives rise to the need for very expensive, complex adapters in order to provide access to leads on processors and other complex devices to probe their inputs and outputs when performing diagnostic work.

Yet another disadvantage of surface-mount parts stems from their small size. It is more difficult to remove heat from SMT packages than it is for their through-hole equivalent. In some cases, such as high-performance processors, the heat generated by the IC is too high to permit proper operation in an SMT package.

10.4.3   Fine Pitch

Fine pitch is a special class of surface-mount components. This class is characterized by lead pitches lower than 0.65 mm (25 mils). These fine lead pitches are usually driven by very high lead count ASICs (160 pins and up) or by the extreme miniaturization requirements of PCM-CIA (Personal Computer Memory Card Industry Association) cards, PDAs (personal digital assistants), and other small, high-performance products. The motivation for designating a special fine-pitch-component class of surface-mount parts is the extra difficulty of successfully testing, assembling, and reworking these parts on PCBs, as well as in building PCBs with accurately formed patterns and solder masks to mate with the leads of fine-pitch parts. Fine-pitch parts are the source of most manufacturing defects in a well-run SMT assembly line. The defects stem from lack of coplanarity of the leads, bent leads, insufficient solder on the joints, and poor alignment of the leads to the patterns on the PCB.

Successful manufacture using fine-pitch components involves very tight cooperation among the PCB designer, the PCB fabricator, the component manufacturer, and the PCB assembler/tester. It almost always involves specialized assembly, test, and rework tooling. Design is most often done by convening a series of meetings of the engineering personnel of all these groups to evolve a set of rules, processes, equipment, tooling, and components. These meetings need to start at the product development stage and continue to be held until the proper pad shapes and sizes have been established and the production process is stable.

10.4.4   Press Fit

Press fit is a special form of through-hole technology. Components are fastened to the PCB by deliberately designing an interference fit between the component lead and the plated through-hole in the PCB. The principle application of press-fit technology is the attachment of connectors into backplanes. The reason for this is that early backplanes were built by wire wrapping the signal connections onto the connector pins extending out the back of the backplane. Trying to solder the connector pins to the backplane through this field of pins proved difficult, if not impossible. The solution was press fit.

Successful assembly of a press-fit backplane rests in designing a hole size small enough to create a solid connection with the pins while ensuring that the hole is large enough to permit the insertion of the pin without fracturing the hole barrel.

Caution: Hot-air leveling the solder on a backplane results in a hole with irregular diameter. This irregularity will almost certainly result in damaged hole plating when the insertion operation is done. Be sure to note on the fabrication drawing of a press-fit backplane that hot-air solder leveling is prohibited. Solder must be plated onto the backplane traces and pads and fused using IR reflow or hot-oil reflow to fuse the lead and tin into a solder alloy.

10.4.5   TAB

TAB stands for tape-automated bonding, which is a technique for attaching bare IC die to a printed circuit board. It uses a subminiature lead frame that attaches directly to the bonding pads of an IC at one end, spreads out to a much larger pitch, and attaches to pads on a PCB. The tape in the title describes the method for carrying the parts prior to assembly, which is a tape with the TAB lead frame and IC built into it. The tape is wound onto a reel for handling. The principle application of TAB components is products such as pagers and portable phones that are made in very high volume and can justify the automation involved in attaching TAB parts to substrates.

10.4.6 Flip Chip

Flip-chip technology involves plating raised pillars of metal on the bonding pads of ICs, turning them upside down, and attaching them to a matching pattern on a substrate. The substrates are most often silicon and precision ceramics. From this description, it can be seen that this is a very specialized packaging method. To succeed, a source of tested good bare die with plated-on pillars must be available. This situation occurs almost exclusively in very high performance supercomputers where the ICs have been specially designed for the application or in very high volume applications such as pagers and cellular phones.

10.4.7 BGA

BGA or ball grid array is a relatively new technology that is a cross between pin grid arrays and surface mount. High-pin-count IC die are mounted on a multilayer substrate made from ceramic or organic material. The die are connected to the substrate using standard wire-bond techniques and encapsulated in epoxy or another form of cover. The bottom side of the substrate contains an array of high-melting-point solder balls which connect to the wire-bond pads through the multilayer substrate. These balls mate with a matching array of pads on the PCB and are reflow soldered during the same operation as all other surface-mount parts. (See Fig. 10.11.)

The appeal of BGA technology is as an alternative to high-pin-count, fine-pitch SMT ICs. As mentioned earlier, assembling high-pin-count, fine-pitch SMT parts is very difficult, owing to the fragile nature of the component leads. BGAs represent a much more robust package during component-level test and during assembly.

As with most technologies, there are some disadvantages to BGAs. Among these are:

- The solder joints are hidden from view, so inspecting them requires x-rays.
- The solder joints are not accessible for rework, so the soldering process must have a very high success rate.
- Part removal requires special tooling.
- The pattern on the PCB surface is an array of pads that require one via each all the way through the PCB, hampering routing.
- All component leads are concentrated in a much smaller area than the equivalent part in a fine-pitch SMT package. This concentrates the wiring in a small area pierced with many vias. As a result, the BGA PCB will likely have more wiring layers than the equivalent SMT PCB.
- The BGA package is more expensive than the equivalent fine-pitch SMT package, by as much as three times.

10.4.8 Wire-Bonded Bare Die

As the name implies, this method of assembly involves attaching bare IC die directly to a substrate using an adhesive or reflowing solder and connecting the bonding pads to pads on the

FIGURE 10.11 Typical ball grid array package. (*Courtesy of Icon Industries.*)

PCB using wire-bond techniques. Virtually all digital watches and many other similar consumer products use this assembly technique. It is very inexpensive when used in very high volume products with only a single IC to connect.

10.5 MATERIALS CHOICES

A wide variety of materials has been developed for use in packaging electronic circuits. These can be divided into three broad classes: reinforced organics, unreinforced organics, and inorganics. These are used primarily for rigid PCBs, flexible and microwave/RF PCBs, and multichip modules, respectively. The following treatment of the available materials concentrates on the principle materials systems used in PCB design along with the properties that warrant their use. See Chaps. 13 and 14 in this handbook for detailed data provided on loss tangents, temperature of coefficient of expansion, glass transition temperature, and other electrical properties.

IPC, the Institute for Interconnecting and Packaging Electronic Circuits, publishes a comprehensive series of standards that list in detail the properties of all types of laminates, resins, foils, reinforcement cloths, and processes that are candidates for the manufacture of PCBs. These standards start with IPC-L-108B and run up to IPC-CF-152. It is recommended that copies of the applicable standards be obtained at the start of a program in order to ensure a thorough understanding of all important characteristics of the materials being considered for a design.

Properties important to the manufacture of PCBs include:

- *Glass transition temperature T_g*—The temperature at which the coefficient of thermal expansion in a resin system makes a sharp change in rate from a slow rate of change to a rapid rate of change. A high T_g is important for PCBs that are very thick to guard against barrel cracking or pad fractures during the soldering operation.

- *Coefficient of thermal expansion T_{CE}*—Surface-mount assembly process subjects the printed wiring assembly to more numerous temperature shocks than typical through-hole processes. At the same time, the increase in lead density has caused the designer to use more and more layers, making the board more susceptible to problems concerned with the base material's coefficient of thermal expansion T_{CE}. This can be a particular problem with regard to the z-axis expansion of the material, as this induces stresses in the copper-plated hole, and becomes a reliability concern. Figure 10.12 shows typical z-axis expansion for a variety of printed circuit base laminate materials.

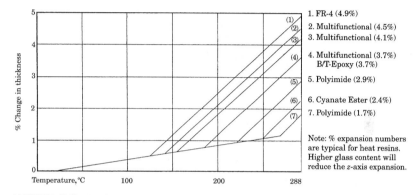

FIGURE 10.12   Typical z-axis expansion via thermal mechanical analysis. (*Courtesy of Nelco International Corp.*)

- *Relative dielectric constant e_r*—This characteristic measures the effect that a dielectric has on the capacitance between a trace and the surrounding structures. This capacitance affects impedance as well as the velocity at which signals travel along a signal line. (See Figs. 10.3 and 10.4) Higher e_r produces lower impedance, higher capacitance, and lower signal velocity.

- *Loss tangent, tan (f), or dissipation factor*—A measure of the tendency of an insulating material to absorb some of the ac energy from electromagnetic fields passing through it. Low values are important for RF applications, but relatively unimportant for logic applications.

- *Electrical strength or dielectric breakdown voltage DBV*—The voltage per unit thickness of an insulator at which an arc may develop *through* the insulator.

- *Water absorption factor WA*—The amount of water an insulating material may absorb when subjected to high relative humidity, expressed as a percent of total weight. Absorbed water increases relative dielectric constant as well as reduces DBV.

10.5.1   Reinforcement Materials

The principal reinforcement for PCB substrate materials is cloth woven from glass fibers. A variation of this glass is cloth made from quartz fibers. The resulting material has a slightly lower dielectric constant than ordinary glass, but at a substantial cost premium and a more difficult drilling cycle. Kevlar is an alternate woven reinforcement that results in a lower-weight material system with a lower dielectric constant, also at a higher cost and higher difficulty in processing.

TABLE 10.3   Properties of Some Common PCB Materials Systems*

	T_g	e_r	tan (f)	DBV, V/mil	WA, %
Std. FR4 epoxy	125C	4.1	0.02	1100	.14
Multifunctional epoxy	145C	4.1	0.022	1050	.13
Tetrafunctional epoxy	150C	4.1	0.022	1050	.13
BT/epoxy	185C	4.1	0.013	1350	.20
Cyanate ester	245C	3.8	0.005	800	.70
Polyimide	285C	4.1	0.015	1200	.43
Teflon	N.A.	2.2	0.0002	450	0.01

* All with E-glass reinforcement, except Teflon.

The original reinforcement material for PCBs was paper or cardboard in some form. Paper impregnated with a resin system is still in use in consumer applications where lowest possible cost is necessary and where performance is not an issue.

10.5.2 Polyimide Resin Systems

Polyimide resin-based laminates are the workhorse of electronics that must withstand high temperatures in operation or in assembly or repair. Common applications include down-the-hole well-drilling equipment, avionics, missiles, supercomputers, and PCBs with very high layer count. The principle advantage of polyimide is its ability to withstand high temperatures. It has approximately the same dielectric constant as epoxy resin systems. It is more difficult to work with in fabrication, is more costly than FR4 systems, and absorbs more moisture.

10.5.3 Epoxy-Based Resin Systems

Epoxy resin-based laminates are the workhorse of virtually all consumer and commercial electronic products. There are several variations of this pervasive laminate family, each developed to answer a special need. Among these are standard FR4, multifunctional epoxy, difunctional epoxy, tetrafunctional epoxy, and BT or bismaleimide triazine blends. Each of these was developed to answer the need for a resin with a successively higher T_g or glass transition temperature. Multifunctional epoxy is the most commonly used form.

10.5.4 Cyanate Ester-Based Resin Systems

This resin system is a recent entrant into the high-performance resin system category. It is said to offer processing characteristics superior to those of the FR4 blends while offering a higher T_g.

10.5.5 Ceramics

A wide variety of ceramic or alumina substrate materials have been developed for use in hybrids and multichip modules. These materials are the subject of specialized manufacturing processes beyond the scope of this handbook. The reader needing information on this group of materials is advised to contact a major manufacturer of ceramic materials.

10.5.6 Exotic Laminates

Kevlar, Kapton, Teflon, and RO 2800 are materials developed for specialty applications. The first two, in the form of thin films, are commonly used as substrates for flexible circuits. The latter two are the principal dielectrics for microwave and RF circuits. All of these materials can be used with or without reinforcements.

10.5.7 Embedded Components Materials

Specialized materials have been developed to allow construction of passive components such as resistors and capacitors into the PCB structure itself. Most of these materials are patented and available from a very small supplier base.

10.5.7.1 Embedded Resistors. These are formed by plating a very thin film of nickel or other metal onto a copper foil layer and laminating this foil, plated side in, to an FR4 or other substrate material. To form a resistor, a window is opened in the copper foil, exposing the underlying nickel resistor layer. A resistor of the appropriate value is formed in the resistance material layer. Contact is made with the resulting resistor by etching connecting pads in the copper foil layer and drilling holes through these pads and plating the holes.

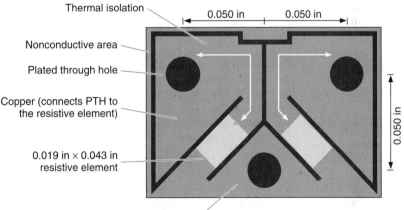

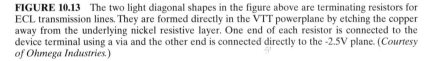

FIGURE 10.13   The two light diagonal shapes in the figure above are terminating resistors for ECL transmission lines. They are formed directly in the VTT powerplane by etching the copper away from the underlying nickel resistive layer. One end of each resistor is connected to the device terminal using a via and the other end is connected directly to the -2.5V plane. (*Courtesy of Ohmega Industries.*)

Resistive material is available in 25- and 100-Ω/square values. The principal application of embedded resistor technology is as terminating resistors for ECL transmission lines and as resistors on flexible circuits in products such as cameras and portable tape and CD players. Practical resistor values range from about 10 to 1000 Ω.

10.5.7.2 Embedded Capacitance. This is formed by placing two copper planes close to each other using very thin dielectrics (1.5 to 2.0 mils). The principal application is in the creation of very high quality, high-frequency capacitance between two power planes. This does indeed result in high-quality capacitance, but usually at a high cost resulting from the need to add a pair of extra planes to a PCB in order to create the capacitance (see Fig. 10.14).

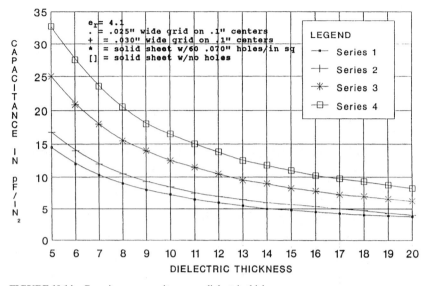

FIGURE 10.14   Capacitance per unit area vs. dielectric thickness.

10.6   FABRICATION METHODS

A wide variety of fabrication methods has been developed to meet the needs of the electronics industry. The following descriptions are quick summaries of each method intended to acquaint the reader with their advantages and disadvantages and likely applications. Detailed treatments are presented elsewhere in this book.

10.6.1   Punch Forming

Punch forming is used in the manufacture of very low cost, single-sided PCBs such as are used in many consumer electronic products. The process involves printing and etching the conductor patterns on one side of a laminate substrate, usually paper-reinforced epoxy. All holes are punched in a single stroke by a die containing a pin and opening for each hole. The PCB outline is formed in a second die that "blanks" it from the panel in which it is processed.

Often, several PCBs will be contained in a single panel sized to travel through the assembly process. After a PCB is punched out of the panel, it is forced back into the vacant hole and is held in place by interlocking fibers along the edges of the PCB. After assembly and testing is complete, each PCB is pressed from the panel. This is known as *crackerboarding* and is aimed at reducing overall manufacturing costs.

10.6.2   Roll Forming

Roll forming is a process used to manufacture flexible circuits in very large quantities. This is the lowest-cost method for the manufacture of flexible circuits. However, it involves substantial tooling, so it is applicable only for very high volume products. Examples of PCBs manufactured using this method are printer head connections, disk drive head connections, and the circuits used in cameras and camcorders. The PCBs can be single- or double-sided.

Roll forming resembles newspaper printing in that the process starts with a large roll of copper-clad laminate that is fed through a long process line containing stations which perform each operation on a continuous basis, starting with printing the conductor pattern, etching it, forming the holes, testing, and blanking from the roll itself. The process can include lamination of a cover insulator layer over the conductors as well.

10.6.3 Lamination

Lamination is the process by which PCBs of more than two layers are formed. The process begins by etching the conductor patterns of the inner layers onto thin pieces of laminate called *details*. These details are then separated by partially cured laminate called *prepreg* and stacked in a *book* with layers of prepreg on the top and bottom and foil sheets on the outside. This stack is placed into a press capable of heating the combination to a temperature that causes the prepreg resin to reach the liquid state. The liquefied resin flows into the voids in the copper patterns to create a *solid* panel upon cooldown. Once cooled, the panel is sent through the drilling and plating operations much like a two-sided PCB.

Note that some materials, such as polyimide, do not have a prepreg form to act as the glue during lamination. In these cases, a special glue sheet must be used during lamination to fasten the individual layers together.

10.6.4 Subtractive Plating

Subtractive plating is a method of forming traces and other conductive patterns on a PCB by first covering a sheet of laminate with a continuous sheet of copper foil. A layer of etch resist is applied such that it covers the copper pattern that is desired. The panel with protective coating is passed through an etcher that removes (subtracts) the unwanted copper, leaving behind the desired patterns. This is the dominant, almost only, method in common usage in the printed circuit industry today.

10.6.5 Additive Plating

As the name implies, this method of forming conductor patterns involves beginning with a bare substrate and plating on the conductor patterns. There are two methods for doing this: electroless plating on areas sensitized to accept electroless copper and electroplating by first applying a very thin coating of electroless copper over the entire surface to act as a conductive path, followed by electroplating to full thickness.

Additive plating is seen as a method for reducing the amount of chemicals required to manufacture PCBs, and this is true. However, the process does not yield copper sufficiently robust to withstand the handling of normal assembly and rework. As a result, it is not commonly available in production.

10.6.6 Discrete Wire

Discrete wire is a method for forming the wiring layers by rolling round wire into a soft insulating material coated onto the outsides of power plane cores. This method is often referred to as *multiwire*. It is available from only a very small number of manufacturers and offers few advantages over conventional multilayer processing. It is described more fully in Sec. 10.2.3.

10.7   CHOOSING A PACKAGE TYPE AND FABRICATION VENDOR

A key part of arriving at a successful design is choosing PCB materials, component-mounting techniques, and fabrication methods that meet the performance needs of the product being designed while achieving the lowest possible costs. Among the decisions that are part of this process are deciding whether to package a product on one large PCB or several smaller PCBs, whether to spread components out to hold the layer count down or increase layers, move components closer together, and design a smaller PCB, whether to package some components in a multichip module that is then mounted on the PCB, as well as other issues.

Part of this decision-making process is arriving at an overall package choice that can be manufactured by the mainstream fabricators and assemblers. Failure to do this will result in excessively high prices and long lead times stemming from the lack of a competitive supplier base from which to choose. At the extreme, where some of the more exotic materials systems are used, there may be as few as one supplier to turn to. In markets where there is substantial price pressure, such as with disk drives and PCs, it imperative that the design choices be made such that the PCBs can be manufactured at offshore fabricators. Not doing this will place the product at a competitive disadvantage.

10.7.1   Trading Off Number of Layers Against Area

Cost of the bare PCB is often a significant contributor to the overall cost of an assembly. As the number of layers in a PCB increases, the cost increases. A standard practice is to spread components out to make room for the connecting wiring as a way to avoid adding additional wiring layers. As might be expected, there is a point at which PCB size grows to where a smaller PCB with more layers yields a more economical solution. Determining where this breakpoint is requires some knowledge about the PCB fabrication process.

Table 10.4 shows typical costs of four-, six-, and eight-layer 18 in by 24 in standard process panels built at offshore manufacturers. This table can be used to calculate the relative cost of PCBs as layer count is increased to reduce area. While the absolute costs in the table are based on Spring 1995 pricing for Pacific Rim fabricators, the percentage relationships between the costs of panels of various layer counts are a good indicator of relative costs for deciding when to increase layer count and reduce area.

10.7.1.1   Background Information.   Multilayer PCBs of six or more layers are normally built on standard 18 in by 24 in panels using pin lamination. Many four-layer PCBs are built offshore using a process called mass lamination with panels sizes of 36 in by 48 in (four times a "standard" panel). The pricing of individual PCBs is based on how many PCBs fit on a stan-

TABLE 10.4   PCB Panel Process Cost vs. Layer Count
Price per panel, $ U.S., Spring 1995

Number of layers	Panels per mo. 100	Panels per mo. 250	Panels per mo. 1000	Panels per mo. 5000
4 mass lam*	$260	$250	$240	$231
4 pin lam†	84	80	77	74
6 pin lam†	113	108	104	100
8 pin lam†	147	140	135	130

To determine the number of PCBs that will fit onto a panel, allow 0.125 in between PCBs and allow 0.75-in margin on all four sides. Net areas are 34.5 in by 46.5 in and 16.5 in by 22.5 in.
For gold plating on connector tips, add up to $2 per PCB.
* 36 in × 48 in panel.
† 18 in × 24 in panel.

dard panel. Therefore, designers need to choose finished PCB sizes with this in mind (assuming the size is negotiable).

The pricing matrix in Table 10.4 is in price per panel based on the following:

- Solder mask over bare copper, silk screen one side only
- Standard multifunctional FR4 laminate
- 1-oz copper inner layers, ½-oz outer layer foil plated up to 1.5 oz nominal
- Thickness accuracy: ±10% overall, ±1.5 mil any dielectric layer
- No controlled impedance requirement or testing
- 1-mil minimum copper plating in holes
- No vias smaller than 13 mils
- Traces and spaces: 7 mil, 7 mil
- Standard delivery: (no acceleration premium)
- Fabrication site: **Pacific Rim Fabricators**
- No gold plating
- Tested to CAD netlist

Since PCB fabrication is based on standard panels, the cost of each PCB is affected by how much of each panel is used to form the PCBs built on it and the amount of the panel that is scrapped. Clearly, the more of each panel that is usable, the lower the average cost of each PCB will be. As one chooses the size and form factor of each PCB, attention should be paid to how many will fit onto a standard panel in order to minimize the scrap material created.

10.7.2   One PCB vs. Multiple PCBs

One way to keep individual PCB layer counts down is to divide the circuitry among several smaller, simpler PCBs. There is a hidden cost associated with doing this. The hidden cost is spread across several organizations, ranging from the design activity, through manufacturing, and into the sales and service organization. The costs are those associated with handling multiple assemblies, such as managing multiple designs and their documentation, managing the procurement, inventory, testing and stocking of multiple assemblies, and the cost of interconnecting the multiple assemblies. In almost all cases, these costs exceed any savings that might be realized by the creation of multiple assemblies.

CHAPTER 11
THE PCB DESIGN PROCESS

Lee W. Ritchey
3Com Corp., Santa Clara, California

11.1 OBJECTIVE OF THE PCB DESIGN PROCESS

The objective of the PCB design process is to engineer a PCB, including all of its active circuits, that functions properly over all the normal variation in component values, component speeds, materials tolerances, temperature ranges, power supply voltage ranges, and manufacturing tolerances and to produce all of the documentation and data needed to fabricate, assemble, test, and troubleshoot the bare PCB and the PCB assembly. Doing less than this in any area exposes the manufacturer and user of the PCB assembly to excessive yield losses, excessively high manufacturing costs, and unstable performance.

Achieving the objective involves carefully designing a process that matches the end product, selecting design tools with controls and analytical utilities, and selecting a materials system and components that match.

11.2 DESIGN PROCESSES

Figure 11.1 is a flowchart of the major steps in a complete PCB design process, beginning with specification of the desired end product and continuing through to archiving or storing away the design database in a form that permits subsequent design modifications or regeneration of documentation as necessary to support ongoing production. This process takes advantage of all the computer-based tools that have been developed to assure a "right the first time" design. The basic process is the same for either analog or digital PCBs. The differences in the design process for the two classes of PCBs center around the differences in complexity of these two types of circuits, as mentioned in Chap. 10.

11.2.1 The System Specification

The design team begins a new design by creating a *system specification*. This is a list of the functions the design is to perform, the conditions under which it must operate, its cost targets, development schedule, development costs, repair protocols, technologies to be used, weight and size, and other requirements as are appropriate. A rough definition of each of these variables is necessary at the start to permit proper choices of materials, tools, and instrumentation. For example, a project may involve the design of a portable computer that must weigh less

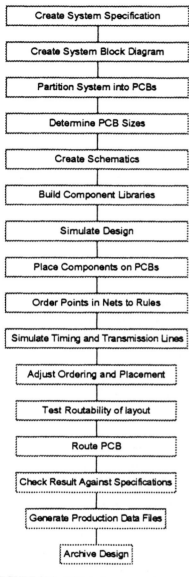

FIGURE 11.1 PCB design process steps.

than 5 lb, fit into a briefcase, operate on batteries for two hours, have a mean time between failures (MTBF) of 200,000 hours or more, cost less than $2000, have 4 Mbytes of memory, 240 Mbytes or more of mass storage, and be MS-DOS compatible. This specification serves as the starting point for a new design.

11.2.2 System Block Diagram

Once the system specification has been completed, a block diagram of the major functions is created, showing how the system is to be partitioned and how the functions link or relate to each other. Figure 11.2 is an example of this partitioning.

11.2.3 Partitioning System into PCBs

Once the major functions are known and the technologies that will be used to implement them are determined, the circuitry is divided into PCB assemblies, grouping functions that must work together onto a single PCB. Usually this partitioning is done where data buses link functions together. Often these buses will be contained on a backplane into which a group of daughter boards are plugged. In the case of a PC (personal computer), partitioning often results in a mother board and several smaller plug-in modules such as memory, display driver, disk controller, and PCMCIA interface.

11.2.4 Determining PCB Size

As soon as the amount of circuitry and the technology that each PCB must contain is known, the area and size of each PCB may be estimated. Often, the PCB size is fixed in advance by the end use. For example, a system based on VME or multibus technology will have to use the PCB sizes defined by the standard. In this case, system partitioning and component packaging technology will be dictated by what will fit onto these standard PCB sizes.

The finished cost of a PCB often turns on the number of layers and the quantity that will fit onto the standard manufacturing panel sizes. (For most PCB fabricators, this size is 18 in by 24 in with a usable area of 16.5 in by 22.5 in.) Sizing PCBs to utilize all or most of the panel area results in the most cost-effective bare PCB. (See Table 10.4.)

11.2.5 Creating the Schematic

Once the system function, partitioning, and technologies have been determined, the schematic or detailed connections between components can take place. Schematics and block diagrams are normally created on CAE (computer-aided engineering) systems. These systems allow the designer to draw the schematic on a CRT screen or terminal. The data needed by all of the following steps in the design process is generated by the CAE system from this schematic.

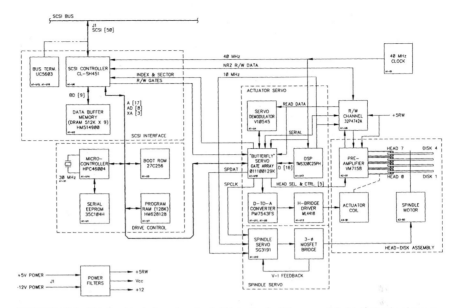

FIGURE 11.2   This is a block diagram of a digital device (in this case a disk drive) that has been seg-
mented to its assembly levels. The dashed lines represent initial partitioning of the entire product to
printed circuit assemblies and also shows the expected interface (connector) requirements.

11.2.6 Building Component Libraries

The tools used in the PCB design process must be supplied a variety of information about
each part in order to complete each step. This information is entered into a library or set of
libraries, one entry per component. Among the pieces of data needed are:

- Type of package that houses the component, e.g., through-hole, QFP, DIP
- Size of component, lead spacing, lead size, pin-numbering pattern
- Function each pin performs, e.g., output, input, power pin
- Electrical characteristics of each pin, e.g., capacitance, output impedance

11.2.7 Simulating Design

To be sure a design will perform its intended function over the intended range of conditions,
some form of design verification must be done. These conditions may include component
value accuracies, range of component speeds, operating and storage temperature ranges,
shock and vibration conditions, humidity ranges, and power supply voltage range. Historically,
this has been done by building breadboards and prototypes and subjecting them to rigorous
testing. As systems and their operation software have grown more complex, this technique has
proved to be inadequate. To solve this problem, simulators have been developed that allow a
computer to simulate a function without having to build it. These simulators make it possible
to perform tests far quicker, more rigorously, and more completely than any breadboard or
prototype could ever be expected to.
    Defects discovered by a simulator can be corrected in the simulation model with ease and
the tests rerun before any commitment to hardware is made.

11.2.8   Placing Components on PCBs

Upon successful completion of the logical and gross timing simulation process, the actual physical layout can begin. It begins by placing the components of the design on the surface of the PCB in patterns that group logical functions together. Once this is done, the groups of components are located on the PCB surfaces such that functions that interact are adjacent, components that generate heat are cooled properly, components that interface to the outside world are near connectors, and so on. This placement operation can be done manually by the designer using graphics-based tools or automatically by the PCB CAD system.

11.2.9   Sequencing Nets to High-Speed Rules

Most logic families have sufficiently fast rise and fall times and short enough propogation delays to be subject to high-speed problems such as coupling and reflections. To ensure that these high-speed effects do not result in malfunctions, it is necessary to arrange the connections between the loads, terminations, and drivers to control these high-speed phenomena. This arranging of nodes or points in a net is referred to as *sequencing* or *scheduling*. Once the components have been placed on the surface of the PCB, the spatial arrangement of all the nodes on each net is known. At this point, it is possible to determine how to connect the driver to the loads and terminators to form proper transmission lines, ensuring that improper stubs are not created and that the terminator is at the end of the net.

11.2.10   Simulating Timing and Transmission Lines Effects

Upon completion of component placement and sequencing the nodes in each net, it is possible to estimate the length and characteristics of each net. This is possible because the x-y location of each point in a net is known, the order of connections is known, and the fact that the actual wiring must be done in either the x or y direction is also known. This length information can be used to model the high-speed switching characteristics of each net and predict the presence of excessive noise and reflections as well as to estimate the length of time required for signal to travel the length of each line, all before actually routing or building the PCB.

This simulation step makes it possible to detect potential malfunctioning signals prior to routing and take steps to fix the problem while the time invested in the design is still modest.

11.2.11   Adjusting Sequencing and Placement

If the simulations done in sec. 11.2.10 reveal excessive time delays or reflection problems, the placement may need to be adjusted to move critical parts closer together or add terminations to nets with excessive reflections. By doing this simulation and adjustment, a design can be assured of meeting the "right the first time" goal so important to high-performance designs.

11.2.12   Testing Routability of Placement

At this point, enough analysis has taken place to know that the design will function correctly if routed. However, it may not route in the number of signal layers required by the cost goal. Most CAD systems have tools, such as rats-nest analyzers, that help the designer determine if the design will fit into the allowed signal layers. If it will not, the routability analyzer may give clues on how to revise the component placement to achieve a successful route. Once the placement has been adjusted, the timing and transmission line simulation steps must be repeated to ensure that the set of goals has been met.

11.2.13 Routing PCB

This step involves fitting all the connections into the signal layers in the form of copper traces, following spacing and length rules. It usually involves a combination of hand routing special signals and automatically routing the rest.

11.2.14 Checking Routed Results

After all the connections have been routed into the signal layers, the actual shape and length of each wire is known, as is the layer(s) on which the wires have been routed and which nets are neighbors. This physical data can be loaded into the timing and transmission line analyzers to do a final check that all design goals have been met. Any violations that are detected can be repaired by hand rerouting as necessary. Once this set of checks has been completed and any adjustments made, the final routed result is checked against the schematic netlist to ensure that there are no discrepancies. A final check is performed on the Gerber data to ensure that the line width and spacing rules have been complied with and that there is no solder mask of silk screen on any pad, as well as that traces and other features that must be protected from solder are covered by solder mask.

11.2.15 Generating Manufacturing Files

This step involves generating the photoplotting files, pick-and-place files, bare and loaded board test files, drawings, and bills of material needed to do the actual manufacturing. Typical lists of these files are shown in Tables 12.3 and 12.4.

11.2.16 Archiving Design

Once all the manufacturing data has been created, the design database and all of the manufacturing data files are stored on a magnetic tape or other storage media for future use to incorporate changes and for backup in the event that the files and drawings created for manufacturing are lost or destroyed.

11.3 DESIGN TOOLS

From the definition of the objective of the PCB design process it can be seen that the process extends from concept all the way through fabrication to assembly and test. Computer-based tools have evolved to automate or improve the speed and accuracy of every step in the process. These tools can be divided into three major groupings based on where they are used:

- CAE (computer-aided engineering) tools
- CAD (computer-aided design) tools
- CAM (computer-aided manufacturing) tools

It is apparent from the names of the tools that they are used in circuit design, physical layout of the PCB, and manufacture of the bare PCB and the PCB assembly.

11.3.1 CAE Tools

CAE tools is the name generally used to refer to the computer-based tools and systems that are employed in the stages of design before the physical layout step or to analyze and evaluate the electrical performance of the final physical layout. These include:

11.3.1.1 Schematic Capture Systems. As the name implies, these tools are used by the design engineer to draw a schematic or circuit diagram. The simplest systems are graphical replacements for the classical drawing board, allowing the engineer to place logic and electronic symbols on the surface of the drawing and connect their terminals with lines. More advanced systems perform substantial error checking such as guarding against multiple uses of the same pin or net name. Failure to connect critical pins such as power pins can be done by using information contained in their component libraries about each part. In addition, these systems can generate netlists to be used by simulators and PCB routers and bills of material for use in the manufacture of the PCB assembly.

11.3.1.2 Synthesizers. Synthesizers are specialized CAE tools that allow a designer to specify the logic functions that a design is expected to perform in the form of logical operations such as dual full adder, 16-bit-wide register, or other macro functions. The synthesizer will extract the equivalent logic circuit functions from a function library and connect them together as specified by the designer to arrive at a complete logic diagram. This synthesized circuit can then be used as part of a bigger design. Some advantages of synthesizers are that all functions of a given type will be implemented the same way and be error free and that time needed to compose a system schematic is reduced by eliminating the labor required to design repeating circuits.

11.3.1.3 Simulators. Simulators are software tools that create computer-based models of a circuit and run them with input test patterns to verify that the circuit will do the intended function when implemented in hardware. Even when run on very large computers, simulators usually run at only a tiny fraction of the speed of the actual circuit. When circuits grow complex, as in a 32-bit microprocessor or digital signal processor, the time required to perform a complete simulation can be very long, sometimes so long that this method of circuit verification becomes impractical. Typical simulation speeds are 1 or 2 s for each machine cycle. A machine cycle may be as little as 2ns or 500 million/s for a system with a 500-MHz clock. This is a 500 million-to-1 slowdown! As circuits have grown more complex and simulation times have become excessive, engineers have been forced to build physical models of a proposed circuit and run actual code against the model as a method of ensuring that the design is accurate. Clearly, this adds both time and cost to the development cycle, both by adding the time needed to build the model and the time needed to locate design errors and fix them. The solution to this problem is circuit emulation.

11.3.1.4 Emulators. Emulators or circuit emulators are collections of programmable logic elements, such as PLAs (programmable logic arrays), that can be configured to represent almost any kind of logic circuit. These emulators are commercially available as standard products from several EDA (electronic design automation) companies. The resulting hardware emulation of a circuit can be operated much faster than a software simulation, sometimes as fast as 1/100th of actual final operating speed. Due to this increased speed, the verification of a circuit can take place much faster. In some cases, the emulations are used as substitutes for the actual circuit to verify that the software created to run with the circuit is error free before any commitment is made to final hardware. This technique is used extensively in the design of complex ICs such as microprocessors and custom ASICs. In fact, the Intel Pentium™ microprocessor and its operating system was completely emulated and run successfully on a large hardware emulator prior to making the first silicon.

The use of emulation technology has eliminated the need to iterate or modify designs as errors are detected, saving very large sums of development money as well as development time. In some cases, it has made circuits practical that would not be without it. For example, most supercomputers and other advanced products are built with multilayer ceramic PCBs and MCMs. These packaging technologies do not lend themselves to modification with external wiring to correct errors. As a result, it is necessary to produce entirely new assemblies in order to correct design errors. The same is true for the integrated circuits in the system as well.

11.3.1.5 Circuit Analyzers.   Circuit analyzers are tools that examine circuits to ensure that they will perform properly over the range of timing variations in circuits and tolerances of components that are expected to be encountered in normal manufacturing. These analyzers do this by constructing mathematical models of each circuit and then varying the values of each component over their expected tolerance ranges. The behavior of the circuit is calculated by its model and the result compared to preestablished limits. Violations are flagged to alert the design engineer. Among the conditions checked for are freedom from excessive signal coupling from neighboring circuits and that transient behavior such as reflections, overshoot and undershoot, and ringing are within proper limits. This type of analysis is often referred to as worst-case tolerance and timing analysis. It can be run on a design before physical layout begins as well as after layout is completed.

Some examples of circuit analyzers are SPICE and PSPICE. SPICE and PSPICE build mathematical models of each circuit and then perform thousands of complex calculations to predict how the circuit will respond to input signals. Most suppliers of CAD systems also offer their own adaptations of these analysis tools.

11.3.1.6 Impedance Predicting Tools.   These tools are used to examine the cross section, trace sizes, and materials properties of a PCB to ensure that the resulting circuit impedance is within allowable limits or to interactively adjust these parameters to achieve a desired final impedance. This is an essential step in the design of the PCB itself. Most suppliers of CAD systems intended for high-speed design supply some form of on-line impedance analysis tools as part of their systems.

11.3.2 CAD Tools

CAD tools are used to turn the electrical circuit described by the schematic into a physical package or PCB. CAD tools are typically operated by PCB designer specialists who are skilled in the areas of PCB manufacture and assembly rather than by electrical engineers. These tools are fed netlists, component lists, wiring rules, and other layout information by schematic capture or CAE tools. In their simplest form, they allow the designer to create the pad patterns for the component leads and PCB shape and then manually connect the component leads with copper traces. The most sophisticated CAD tools can automatically determine the optimum location of each component on the PCB (autoplacement) and then automatically connect (autorouting) all leads while following high-speed layout rules. This is accomplished by providing the CAD tool with a table of rules specifying which components must be located in groups or near connectors as well as by specifying how much space must be maintained between neighboring traces, the maximum length allowed between points on a net, etc.

The outputs of CAD tools are the information files needed to fabricate, assemble, and test the PCB assembly. These are test netlists, photoplotting files, bills of materials, pick-and-place files, and assembly drawings. CAD tools are made up of circuit routers, placement tools, checking tools, and output file generation tools.

11.3.2.1 Placement Tools.   Placement tools are used to arrange the components on a PCB surface. Placement tools tend to be part of a complete CAD system rather than a module purchased separately. The inputs to a placement tool are:

• Component list or bill of material

• Netlist or manner in which the components connect to each other

- Shapes, sizes, and spacial arrangement of the component leads
- Shape of the PCB with areas into which components cannot be placed (keepouts)
- Instructions concerning fixed locations for components, such as connectors
- Electrical rules, such as maximum and minimum distance between points on a net
- Thermal rules, such as which parts must be kept apart or near sources of air flow

Placement tools range from completely manual to fully automatic. All have some form of graphical feedback to the designer that assesses the quality of the placement in terms of its ability to be routed or connected in the desired number of signal layers. Most have spacing rules that ensure that the components have enough room between them for successful assembly, rework, and testing.

11.3.2.2 Routers.   Routers are the part of a CAD system that makes the physical connections between the components as specified by the netlist. A router operates on the PCB netlist and placement after the placement step has been completed. Routers range from the completely manual, in which case the designer specifies where wires are to be located by using a graphical display and a mouse or light pen, to fully automatic, where a specialized software program takes the netlist, the placement, the spacing rules, and the wiring rules and makes all the decisions necessary to completely connect all components. The principal advantage of manual routing lies in the fact that the designer can tailor every connection to his liking. The principal disadvantage of manual routing is the fact that it is slow and time consuming, often taking several minutes to completely route and check a single net. Automatic or autorouters solve this speed problem. However, the ability to control the detailed shape of each net is limited by the ability of the autorouter to follow wiring rules. Some advanced autorouters are able to comply with very complex wiring rules. A significant problem with autorouters lies in the fact that they may not find ways to successfully route all of the wires. When this occurs, the designer must add more wiring space in the form of more layers or attempt to complete the routing manually. An important feature of a good autorouter is its manual routing option, as it substantially affects the ease with which this often necessary "finishing" operation is completed. Nearly all routers have a suite of checking tools that ensure that the final route matches the netlist and that all of the spacing rules have been followed.

Routers come in several forms and can be purchased as an integral part of a CAD system or as modules to add onto CAD systems. Some router types are:

Gridded Router.   This type of router operates by placing wires on a predefined grid pattern. The routing surface is divided into a uniform grid that provides a proper gap between traces when wires are routed on every grid line. It is the first form of both manual and autorouter offered with CAD systems. The primary disadvantages of gridded routers are that it is difficult to manage more than one trace width without losing wiring density and it requires end points of nets to be on the routing grid in order to connect to them successfully. Offgrid component connections typically have to be made by hand and checked by hand.

Gridless Router.   This form of router does not depend on a grid to locate wires on a surface. Instead, it places as many wires in a space as will fit and still maintain the spacing rules established by the design engineer to ensure proper electrical performance while optimizing manufacturability. Multiple trace widths on the same layer are handled easily by this type of router. Once the routing job is completed, the router divides up any unused space equally. The advantage of this technique lies in its ability to optimize manufacturability by keeping spaces as large as possible. The disadvantage of this type of router lies in the fact that it usually depends on a given wiring layer being all horizontal or all vertical—a real disadvantage in SMT applications where components do not need through-holes to connect them but a very powerful router for designs with a very regular array of high-pin-count parts, such as big CPUs and massively parallel processors. This router type is the workhorse of very high complexity digital designs where there is a great deal of regularity and a need to achieve predictable spacings and trace lengths for speed and performance reasons.

Shape-based Router. This type of router recognizes shapes already placed in a wiring surface and routes wires to avoid them. Spacing between wires and other objects, such as vias, used to change layers and component pads is maintained as the router places a wire in a space. This router is becoming the workhorse of SMT-based designs.

11.3.2.3 Checking Tools. These tools verify that the routed PCB complies with rules such as spacing between traces and trace and holes by comparing the actual spacings found in the finished artwork to rules provided by the designer. They also ensure that all nets are completely connected and are not connected to objects they should not be, such as other nets and mechanical features on the PCB, by comparing the routed results to data supplied by the CAD system. Some checking tools also check to ensure that transmission line rules are followed and that coupling from neighboring traces is within limits. Checking tools are usually an integral part of a CAD system.

11.3.2.4 Output File Generators. Once a PCB has been routed and all connectivity verified as accurate, the CAD system holds this information in a neutral form specific to the way in which its operating system is built. For this data to be useful in manufacturing, it must be converted into forms usable by other equipment such as photoplotters, testers, assembly equipment, and MRP systems. Output file generating routines do this conversion. Most CAD systems are equipped with a limited set of these when shipped. Additional generators or converters must be ordered as add-ons.

11.3.3 CAM Tools

CAM tools are CAD systems tailored to the needs of the fabrication process. The output of the PCB design process is a set of CAD files that describes each artwork layer of a PCB, the silk screen requirements, drilling requirements, and netlist information. This information must be modified before it can be used to build a PCB. For example, if a fabricator needs to build several copies of a PCB on a single panel, the fabricator will need to add specialized tooling patterns to the artwork and alter trace widths in order to compensate for etching. Initially, these operations were done manually with a high potential for error and significant labor costs. CAM stations or tools allow the fabricator to do all of these operations automatically and rapidly.

CAM stations can check artwork against spacing rules, breakout rules, and connectivity rules and make corrections if necessary. CAM stations can synthesize netlists (the manner in which points in a design are connected) from the Gerber data for use at bare PCB test, in those cases where no netlist was provided by the customer. In cases where a netlist was provided by the customer, the Gerber synthesized netlist can be compared to the CAD generated netlist as a final way of verifying that the artwork does, in fact, match the schematic—one more safeguard against data corruption anywhere in the translation processes.

11.4 SELECTING A SET OF DESIGN TOOLS

The task of selecting the proper set of CAE, CAD, and CAM tools for a project or company is often one of the most critical steps in determining project success. To reduce the problems associated with interfacing tools to each other, it is desirable to choose all of the tools from a single vendor. However, very few vendors are able to offer best-in-class tools for every phase of the design process. Further, it is very difficult for a single CAD/CAE system to handle the wide variety of design types that may be required across a very large process or across an entire company. For example, a CAD system with a powerful autorouter is of very little use to a design team laying out single-sided PCBs with many irregular parts such as transformers and power transistors. Conversely, a system tailored to do power supply layout well will fare very poorly on a CPU design with many high-speed buses. Knowing this, how does one select the "right" tool set?

11.4.1 Specification

The first step in the tool selection process is to characterize the types of design that the tool set will be required to handle. Next, the level of simulation and design rule checking required to ensure "right the first time" designs must be determined in order to select the right level of simulation and checking tools. For example, performing transmission line analysis on a stereo PCB may be an elegant step but it is a waste of resources. Choosing not to do this level of analysis on a high-speed disk drive PCB may result in a design that is unstable throughout its product life.

Key to success with any tool is the availability of designers qualified to operate it. This pool of designers needs to be assessed for each type of candidate system. If a system or tool is chosen that does not have a pool of qualified operators from which to draw, the result will likely be substantial delays while the necessary expertise is developed or designs that are substandard if the learning time is too short.

11.4.2 Supplier Survey

Once these facts are known, a survey of potential tool suppliers must be conducted. Basic elements include:

1. Determining how closely each tool candidate comes to meeting the need and its cost to acquire, set up, and maintain
2. Assessing the long-term viability of the supplier to ensure that the tool does not become an "orphan" should the supplier fail
3. Making a check with other users of the candidate tools to ensure that they perform as advertised

11.4.3 Benchmarking

Representative benchmark designs need to be made on each candidate system to assess how well they are done. Depending on the size of the potential sale and the size of the benchmark design, a vendor may do the benchmark free of charge. If not, one should be prepared to pay for this valuable step in the evaluation process. Only after completing all of these evaluation steps is it possible to make an informed selection. Doing less, such as relying on an outsider to recommend tools or taking a vendor's word for it, carries the risk of owning a tool that delays development or, worse, having to repeat the selection process in the middle of a project.

11.4.4 Multiple Tools

Knowing the wide variety of designs that may be encountered and the fact that virtually all CAD and CAE tools have been designed to be very good at some subset of design types, it is unrealistic to expect that a single set of tools from a single vendor will be able to deal with all problems equally well. A company with a wide range of design types, such as a company engaged in the design of computers and instrumentation, should expect to own more than one set of tools, each set optimized to its set of tasks. Trying to force one set of tools onto all types of problems is certain to result in overtooling simple designs and undertooling complex ones.

11.5   INTERFACING CAE, CAD, AND CAM TOOLS TO EACH OTHER

A major argument for buying all of the CAE, CAD, and CAM tools from a single vendor is to ensure that they all play together. In the past, this was a major concern because each vendor had proprietary data formats and there were no industry standard data formats. IPC, IEEE, and other trade associations have evolved standard forms of data interchange between systems. These have been adopted by suppliers, such that it is relatively easy to interface best-in-class tools from different vendors to each other.

11.6   INPUTS TO THE DESIGN PROCESS

11.6.1   Libraries

Each CAE and CAD tool uses a series of libraries that contain information describing each component that may be used in a design. These range from a simple description of the physical size of the pads and their relative positions to a full logical model that can be exercised in a simulator. Libraries do not usually come as part of a system. They must be purchased separately or developed one part at a time by the user. Libraries in mature systems can be quite large and represent a substantial investment in time to develop them. Unfortunately, libraries are usually unique to a given tool and cannot be transferred easily should a new tool be chosen.

11.6.1.1   Pad Shapes and Physical Features.   The most basic library used by a CAD system describes the physical characteristics of a part in a manner that allows the CAD system to create its mounting holes pattern and pads as well as its silk screen outline and solder mask pattern. This library entry will contain a *pad stack* that describes how large the component lead holes are and the size and shape of the pads that will appear in each type of PCB layer. For example, an outer layer pad will need to be large enough to ensure adequate annular ring, an antipad will be needed in a power plane to ensure that the plated-through-hole barrel does not touch the power plane, or a thermal pad will be necessary to make a connection to the plane in a manner that still allows reliable soldering. These library entries may contain the unique part numbers used by a company to build a bill of materials, in which case, the CAD system will be able to produce a bill of material in ready-to-use form.

Some physical feature libraries also contain information about the nature of a pin, such as whether it is an input, output, or power pin. This data is used by the checking programs to ensure that the points in a net are ordered properly for high-speed performance or to ensure that a net has the correct kinds of pins in it.

11.6.1.2   Functional Models.   CAE tools that simulate the operation of a PCB require a library of models that describe how each part operates logically. These are functional models. Functional models do not contain information about propagation delay or rise times needed to verify that timing rules are complied with. Functional models are often used to configure emulators.

11.6.1.3   Simulation Models.   Simulation models are extended versions of functional models. They contain all the functional information as well as detailed information about path delays through a part and rise and fall times. They are used to ensure that worst-case timing conditions result in a properly operating design.

11.6.2 PCB Characteristics

One of the sets of data required by the physical layout system is a description of the PCB or its physical characteristics. This includes its size, number and kinds of layers, thicknesses of insulating layers, copper thicknesses, and areas that are not available for parts or traces.

11.6.3 Spacing and Width Rules

To ensure compliance with manufacturing and transmission line rules, the trace widths and trace spacings for each layer must be entered into the CAD system. This is typically done in tabular form.

11.6.4 Netlists

Netlists describe to the CAD system how the pins of each device connect to each other. Systems that manage routing or layout to high-speed design rules will require netlists that contain instructions on how to handle each net, such as what impedance to use, what spacing to preserve with respect to neighbors, and whether terminations or special ordering is needed.

11.6.5 Parts Lists

Parts lists tell the CAD system what type of library entry to use for each part in the design.

CHAPTER 12
DESIGNING A PCB FOR MANUFACTURABILITY

Lee W. Ritchey
3Com Corp., Santa Clara, California

12.1 DESIGN FOR MANUFACTURABILITY

Design for manufacturability or DFM is the process of ensuring that a design meets the needs of each step in the manufacturing process from the outset, rather than revising a design after it has entered the manufacturing process and been found to have manufacturing problems. DFM has traditionally meant ensuring that a PCB is easy to fabricate and assemble. This definition has grown too narrow for the high-speed, high-complexity printed circuit board assemblies (PCBAs) of today. DFM needs to extend to include design for testability, worst-case component tolerances, and worst-case component timing.

12.1.1 Fabrication

Optimizing the cost of a bare PCB is done by choosing spacing, materials, and clearances that meet the design goals of the PCB while holding the demands on the fabricator for accuracy to a level that fits the fabricator's standard process. Table 12.1 lists key tolerance areas in the fabrication process as a function of standard process, leading edge, and state of the art for industry leading fabricators, both in the United States and worldwide. *Standard process* represents tolerances that will result in the lowest possible cost PCB. *Leading edge* represents an accuracy level that a good fabricator can meet, but only with some special handling. *State of the art* represents an accuracy that only a very few fabricators can achieve and then only with substantial extra care and extra cost.

The information in Table 12.1 should be used to guide both the determination of design rules for a class of PCBs and as an indicator of a given fabricator's capabilities. For example, to maintain the lowest possible PCB cost, a designer of consumer electronic PCBs must select tolerances and spacings that are as generous or more generous than in the "standard" column. A designer of PCBs for high-performance file servers will need to use tolerances and spacings in the leading edge column in order to accommodate the very high pin count, fine-pitch components necessitated by this type of product. As might be expected, the cost of a PCB will be higher as the tighter tolerances are added. This is a necessary consequence of striving for high performance in a design. The type of PCB that would warrant the use of state-of-the-art tolerances and their related higher cost are products where weight is at a premium or where performance is more important than everything else. Examples are space hardware and supercomputers, respectively.

TABLE 12.1   Fabrication Capabilities

	Standard	Leading edge	State of the art
Minimum outer line width	0.005	0.003	<0.003
Minimum inner line width	0.004	0.003	<0.003
Minimum outer space width, trace/trace	0.005	0.003	<0.003
Minimum inner space width, trace/trace	0.005	0.003	<0.003
Minimum outer space, trace/pad	0.004	0.003	<0.003
Minimum inner space, trace/pad	0.004	0.003	<0.003
Minimum space PCB edge to conductor	0.025	0.025	0.010
Layer-to-layer registration	0.005 f/b	0.005 f/b	
Maximum overall PCB thickness	0.200	0.225	>0.225
Minimum PCB thickness tolerance, %	±10	±7	±5
Dimensions, hole location	±0.002	±0.002	±0.001
Dimensions, fab OD	±0.005	±0.005	±0.005
Fabrication radius	0.031 min.	0.031 min.	
Warp, in/in	0.010	0.007	0.005
Minimum component pitch	0.008	0.008	0.006
Minimum dielectric thickness	0.002	0.002	0.002
Maximum number of layers	24	32	unknown
Pad to hole size			
Minimum, plated hole size	0.010	0.008	0.003
Tolerance, plated hole size	±0.003	±0.003	±0.002
Minimum inner pad (min. hole + amount)	0.021	0.019	process dependent
Plane relief over drilled hole	gap + nom + 0.019	nom + 0.017	
Minimum outer pad (1 mil annular ring)	nom hole + 0.019	+0.017	process dependent
Minimum outer nonplated hole to trace	0.010	0.010	
Minimum inner nonplated hole to trace	0.010	0.010	
Maximum number of holes per in^2	490	750	1000
Drilling			
Minimum drill size	0.010	0.008	0.003
Maximum aspect ratio	7:1	16:1	16:1
Testing capability			
Minimum component lead pitch	0.008	0.008	
SMT minimum pad spacing	0.005	0.003	<0.003
Line to SMT pad minimum spacing	0.005	0.003	<0.003
Minimum core thickness	0.002	0.002	0.0015
Electrical characteristics			
Impedance, %	±10	±5	<±5

All dimensions in inches.
SOURCE: Courtesy of Hadco Corporation.

The data in Table 12.1 are also useful in selecting fabrication vendors. For example, if a company is designing industry-standard PCBs such as those found in personal computers, the vendors chosen should be capable of manufacturing PCBs to the specifications shown in that column. Similarly, if a company is designing PCBs of the complexity found in high-performance workstations and file servers, the vendors chosen should be able to manufacture PCBs to the specifications shown in the leading edge column. As vendors are selected, care must be exercised to ensure that vendors with the proper capability are selected. Chosing vendors with capability that is too low will result in quality problems that will likely interfere with just-in-time (JIT) and dock-to-stock programs as well as expose the product to reliability problems in the field. Chosing vendors with too high a capability may result in PCB costs that are too high to allow competitive pricing of the final design.

12.1.2 Assembly

As a result of the growth in complexity of components, especially high-pin-count ICs, printed circuit board assembly has evolved into an equally complex task. From the discussions in Chap. 10 of the types of packages that can be chosen from and the fact that it is possible to mount components on both sides of a PCB, it can be seen that care must be exercised in the design process to ensure that a design has been optimized for assembly. The need to use automatic equipment (pick-and-place machines) to load components onto the PCB places restrictions on how parts are oriented and how much space must be allowed between components for the placement equipment. While most pick-and-place equipment and solder paste application equipment has similar requirements for pad spacing and sizes, each has some special needs. Prior to launching the final design, it is imperative that the manufacturers of this equipment be consulted to ensure that the optimum spacings and pad sizes have been chosen.

As SMT parts have grown to contain more and more leads at finer and finer pitches, the ability of pick-and-place equipment to accurately locate a part on its PCB pad pattern has become increasingly challenged. To solve this problem, optical scanners have been added to pick-and-place equipment that use optical pattern recognition to locate the pattern on the PCB, pinpoint the exact location of a part on the placement head, and do real-time corrections for minor errors. The scanning equipment needs to find some standard pattern on the surface of the PCB that it recognizes as a reference point against which to do the alignment. This standard pattern is called a *fiducial*. It is a small diamond or dot that is clear of solder mask, placed near each fine-pitch part to serve as an accurately known reference point. The pick-and-place machine uses this fiducial to accurately locate the pad pattern on the PCB. The number, size, and shape of these fiducials needed for each kind of fine-pitch part may vary with the brand of pick-and-place equipment. Some small parts need only one fiducial, while very large, fine-pitch, high-pin-count parts may require as many as three fiducials located near the package corners and in the center of the pattern. Because of this varying requirement, it is essential to consult the potential assemblers of the finished PCB to be sure that the correct fiducial patterns are being used.

12.1.3 Loaded Board Test

The objective of loaded board test is to ensure that each finished PCBA is accurately assembled and performs its function properly and when it does not, to quickly locate the source of the failure so it can be repaired. There are two principal methods for performing loaded board test. These are in-circuit test and functional test. Each has its advantages and disadvantages. Table 12.2 compares the capabilities of circuit test to functional test. A successful production test has two functions. The test must first detect a defect and then quickly and accurately guide the tester to its location so it can be fixed. From Table 12.2 it can be seen that using only one form of test carries with it the risk of missing some types of failures in the case of in-circuit test or a very difficult or impossible task of locating a defect, so it can be repaired.

12.1.3.1 In-Circuit Test (ICT). This is a test method that relies on making a contact with both ends or all leads of every component on a PCB. The in-circuit tester has *pin electronics* that make it possible to measure component values and voltage values as well as to drive the pin with a logic signal or examine the logic signal on a pin that is being driven by a circuit on the PCB. Contact is made by pressing the PCBA down onto a bed-of-nails fixture that has a nail or test point that contacts each net or circuit on the PCB. Because a contact is made to

TABLE 12.2 Comparison of Capabilities of In-Circuit to Functional Test to Detect and Locate Defects

Defect type	In-circuit test	Functional test
Solder short	Detect—excellent Locate—excellent	Detect—good Locate—poor
Open circuit	Detect—excellent Locate—excellent	Detect—good Locate—poor
Resistor value	Measure—excellent	No capability
Capacitor value	Measure—good	No capability
Inductor/transformer value	Measure—fair	No capability
Missing component	Detect—excellent	Detect—fair
Diode in backward	Detect—excellent	No capability
Logic failure	Detect—fair	Detect—excellent
Speed problem	Detect—poor	Detect—good

every net, it is possible to perform a wide variety of parametric tests to determine if components are the right value, whether nets are shorted to each other or to power planes, whether component leads are continuously connected right up into the die, and, to a limited degree, how well each part functions. Shorts and opens testing, as well as component value testing and testing to ensure that components are not installed backwards or missing, is done without power being applied to the PCB. Because of this, many defects, such as short circuits that would cause damage, can be detected and cleared before power is applied. Once shorts, opens, and component assembly problems have been cleared, power is applied to the PCB and functional testing is done.

In-circuit test is a very efficient—and the most cost effective—method for locating manufacturing defects and is commonly used across the electronics industry. However, in-circuit testing has some limitations as a result of how the testers are constructed and how the fixturing is done. These limitations are the inability to test a PCBA at speed and to thoroughly test the functionality of complex digital devices such as microprocessors and ASICs. The per-pin drive electronics that permit an in-circuit tester to accurately locate manufacturing defects is not capable of running at speeds needed to detect speed problems or to exhaustively exercise complex logic devices. Because of this limitation, a second functional test is needed following in-circuit test.

Successful fixturing of a PCBA for in-circuit test depends on access to every net from one side of the PCBA, usually the bottom or noncomponent side. This is normally done by locating the nails or probes so they contact component leads. With the advent of surface-mount parts, many component leads do not pass through the PCB. As a result, the designer must place special test pads on the bottom of the PCB for every net that does not have a component lead passing to the bottom side of the PCBA. Many users have evolved the practice of attaching a test pad to every net, even when a component lead is accessible as a way to ensure uniformity of contacts.

12.1.3.2 Functional Test.
This amounts to running the PCBA through an exhaustive set of operations at normal speed in order to locate logic problems and speed problems. This testing is done after in-circuit test has detected and removed shorts, opens, and other manufacturing defects, so this testing can concentrate on speed and logic faults. It is normally done in a test setup that simulates the final product or on the final product itself.

Functional testing is quite good at determining whether or not a PCBA functions correctly. However, it is very difficult to determine the nature and location of a fault from the clues functional test can provide, because the tester must deduce the nature and location of a defect from these clues. These clues most often are a wrong answer to a calculation or a complete failure to respond to the input test pattern. From these limited clues, the tester must work backwards or forwards to see where the PCBA is failing and then perform measurements to determine the reason. In fact, it is often the case that some simple defects that ICT finds rapidly in complex assemblies are never located using functional test. Without in-circuit test to prescreen PCBAs for functional test, it is likely that many assemblies would land in a "bone pile" and never be repaired or that an excessive amount of very expensive test technican labor would be consumed locating defects that ICT finds in seconds.

Successfully debugging assemblies at functional test requires highly skilled technicians, while success at locating and repairing defects at ICT can be accomplished with medium-skill operators. Clearly, a well-designed test suite must include both ICT and functional test.

12.1.4   Worst-Case Tolerance Analysis

This involves analyzing a design in such a way, with analog simulators, that one is assured that for all combinations of component values within their normally encountered tolerance ranges the design will meet its specifications. For example, a mathematical model of a servo feedback loop might be constructed and values of resistors, capacitors, and gain elements varied over all possible combinations of their normal ranges of accuracy to determine if response and set-tling times remain within proper operating ranges. This analysis must take place before final PCB layout to be most efficient. A variety of CAE tools exist for performing this task.

12.1.5   Worst-Case Timing Analysis

Like worst-case tolerance analysis, this involves some form of simulation that tests to make sure that for all combinations of edge speed and propagation delay that are normally encoun-tered in production ICs, the design will not be unstable. As clock rates have continued to increase, it is becoming necessary to include the time delays in the wiring on the PCB as part of this analysis. Again, a wide variety of CAE tools exists for performing this level of analysis.

12.2   DEVELOPING A DESIGN RULE SET

"Successful the first time" design relies on developing a set of design rules that balances or accounts for the needs of all the steps in the design and manufacturing process. The rule set size varies with the complexity of the design and its performance objectives. A rule set that is necessary for success with a supercomputer running with a 500-MHz clock rate would surely burden a consumer product with costs that would prevent it from being competitive in its marketplace. Conversely, a rule set that would make a consumer product successful would be woefully inadequate for the supercomputer. Evolving a rule set with the requisite level of completeness is a complex engineering task involving participation from all members of the design and manufacturing team.

The following is a list of some of the major categories that must be considered as part of the rules development process.

- Coupling
- Impedance matching
- Power distribution
- Ground bounce

- IR drops in traces and power lines
- Noise budget
- Pad geometries
- Lines and spaces
- Clearances
- Dielectric thickness
- Copper/conductor thickness
- Testability
- Assembly requirements

12.3   OUTPUTS OF THE DESIGN PROCESS

The end purpose of the design PCB process is to provide manufacturing with the drawings and files needed to successfully fabricate, assemble, and test the PCBA and deliver it to its end user. The following is a list of these outputs:

- Photoplotting data files
- Fabrication drawings
- Drill files
- Bare PCB test files
- Assembly files
- Loaded PCBA test files
- Assembly drawings
- Design archive files
- Bills of materials

12.3.1   Photoplotting Data Files

These files are a collection of NC (numerical control) data files generated by the PCB CAD system. They are used in the creation of film images of each copper layer in a PCB. Also included are files that represent the solder masks and silk screens for each side of the PCB. These film images are used in the PCB fabrication processes such as etching and plating.

The common name for these files is Gerber data or Gerber files. This name has its origin with the Gerber Instrument Company, first manufacturer of NC-controlled photoplotters used to create artwork. Photoplotting files are organized following the standards created by the Gerber company. This form has evolved into a de facto standard that is used throughout the PCB design industry. IPC-D-350 defines this data format.

12.3.2   Fabrication Drawings

A fabrication drawing describes the materials to be used, the order of stacking of the layers, the hole-drilling sizes and plating information, surface-plating requirements, overall PCB size, dimensional accuracy, and other data needed to fabricate and inspect the finished PCB. Like other CAD-generated documents and data, these drawings can be communicated and stored electronically. The standard formats commonly used for this are called IGES, .DXF, HPGL, and .DWG.

12.3.3   Drill Files

Drill files contain the precise *x-y* locations and sizes of all the holes to be drilled through a PCB. Also included is information about whether a hole is to be plated with copper or not. Several formats have evolved in which drill data can be organized. Among these are Excellon™, a format devised by the drill machine manufacturer Excellon, that has evolved into an industry standard. Others include formats defined by IPC-D-356, a more generic or universal format.

12.3.4   Bare PCB Test Files

As PCBs have become more complex, the possibility of a short or open forming between circuits on a PCB has increased. To guard against shipping a PCB with defects of this type, fabricators have acquired special testers that make contact with the end points of every circuit on a PCB. These testers compare the actual connections in the PCB under test to the connections in the CAD system schematic. Bare PCB test files are the data files generated by the CAD system for this purpose.

Each vendor of bare board testers has evolved a format for the bare board test data that is compatible with its tester's internal processor. This has forced designers of PCBs to create several different versions of the test files in order to ensure that the proper version was available to purchasing. To solve this problem, the IPC has evolved a standard format for bare board test data that has been adopted by the industry. This format is IPC-D-356.

12.3.5   Assembly Files

In order to assemble a PCB, information about the components used on a PCB and their location must be communicated to the manufacturing facility. This information includes quantities and types of components used, their *x-y* locations and their orientation, which side of the PCB each component is to be mounted on, and photoplotting data to be used to create solder paste masks.

Assembly data files can be created in a variety of forms, depending on the manufacturing facility being served. However, a standard form has been developed that is usable by virtually all assembly operations. The creation of this form has dramatically simplified the creation and transmittal of assembly data files by CAD departments. This standard format is defined in IPC-D-356.

12.3.6   Loaded PCB Test Files

The most efficient way to detect defects in assembled PCBs is with the technique known as in-circuit test. This form of test is done by creating a bed-of-nails fixture onto which the assembled PCB is mounted, component side up. A spring-loaded "nail" is loaded into the fixture for each net or circuit on the PCB. These nails contact component leads protruding through the bottom of the PCB or special test pads added to the bottom side of the PCB for this purpose.

The loaded PCB test files contain the location of each test point, the name of the net connected to the test point, and the nature of the components connected to the net. Using this data, the in-circuit tester can detect whether the right parts are present, whether a net is shorted to another structure in the PCB, whether the active components function correctly, and, in some cases, it can load EPROMS, flash memory, and other firmware.

Loaded board test files are created in formats specific to the tester that will be used. Most CAD systems have drivers that convert the CAD data into the form required by the tester that will be used.

12.3.7   Assembly Drawings

An assembly drawing contains instructions on how to assemble a PCB. It is used in conjunction with the assembly data files. It contains information that is not present in the electronic pick-and-place file, such as hardware that must be mounted or microcode that must be loaded into flash memory. Assembly drawings may be stored and transmitted along with the other electronic using one of the standard formats previously discussed.

12.3.8   Design Archive Files

Design archive files are a collection of all the design files created in the design process. They are organized onto a single backup tape or other storage media in such a manner that they can be retrieved to generate new copies of drawings and files or so that modifications can be made to the design. Design archive files are an insurance policy against loss of the hard-copy drawings usually stored in document control.

12.3.9   Bills of Materials

Bills of materials contain a complete listing of all the parts, labels, microcode, and other items needed to build a PCB assembly. They contain the generic part names, the manufacturing part numbers, part reference designators, revision levels of microcode, and other information needed to assemble the PCBA.

12.3.10   Typical Collection of Manufacturing Files

Fabricators and assemblers of PCBs require a combination of the files and drawings in order to do their job. These files and drawings or often sent to the manufacturing operation electronically. Tables 12.3 and 12.4 are typical lists of the files and drawings that are sent to fabricators and assembler, respectively. These listings contain typical file names and their contents. These are the files likely to be posted to a bulletin board to be accessed by the manufacturing activity or sent by a data link such as a modem or data network.

TABLE 12.3   A Typical Collection of Design Files Sent to a PCB Fabricator

File name	File contents
BBBBpCCC.arc*	Arc file of Gerber files containing:
applist.p	List of photoplot apertures for artwork
ly1 thru lyx.ger	Gerber photoplot data for x PCB layers
topmsk.ger	Gerber photoplot data for top solder mask
botmsk.ger	Gerber photoplot data for bottom solder mask
topslk.ger	Gerber photoplot data for top silk screen
botslk.ger	Gerber photoplot data for bottom silk screen
pc_356.out	IPC 356 data for blank PCB netlist testing
name0.rep	Drill allocation report for plated holes
name0.prf	Excellon drill file for all plated holes
name1.rep	Drill allocation report for all nonplated holes
XX.XX.fab	Fabrication drawing in HPGL format, sheet XX of XX

* BBBBpCCC is the part number of the PCB.

TABLE 12.4   A Typical Collection of Design Files Sent to a PCB Assembler

File name	File contents
BBBBaCCC.arc*	Arc file of all assembly data containing:
applist.a	Aperture list for plotting paste mask
readme.asy	Readme file describing assembly
tpstmsk.ger	Gerber photoplot data for top paste mask
bpstmsk.ger	Gerber photoplot data for bottom paste mask
BBBB-CCC.dbg	Mfg. output, data format info.
BBBB-CCC.dip	Mfg. output, x-y loc. dip components
BBBB-CCC.log	Mfg. output, component log.
BBBB-CCC.man	Mfg. output, x-y loc. manual insert components
BBBB-CCC.smt	Mfg. output, x-y loc. top smt components
BBBB-CCC.smb	Mfg. output, x-y loc. bottom smt components
BBBB-CCC.unp	Mfg. output, parts not mounted
BBBB-CCC.vcd	Mfg. output
XX_XX.asy	Assembly drawing in HPGL format, sheet XX of XX
XX_XX.fab	Fabrication drawing in HPGL format, sheet XX of XX

  * BBBBaCCC is the part number of the assembly.

12.4 STANDARDS GOVERNING PCB DESIGN, MATERIALS, FABRICATION, ASSEMBLY, AND TEST

12.4.1 MIL Specifications

MIL specs have been developed by joint agencies of the major U.S. armed services to cover the design and construction of PCBs used in the equipment they procure. Among these are MIL-P-55110D, Military Specification, Printed Wiring Boards, General Specification for, and MIL STD-275E, Military Standard, and Printed Wiring for Electronic Equipment. Both of these specifications cover design, materials, quality, and testing topics and duplicate each other in many areas. They are available from U.S. Army Electronics Research and Development Command, Fort Monmouth, NJ 07703.

These specifications cover many of the design and fabrication requirements for PCBs destined for use on equipment that will ultimately be used by many U.S. government agencies. They are somewhat dated documents that are gradually being superseded by equivalent documents generated and maintained by the IPC.

12.4.2 IPC Specifications

The IPC (Institute for Interconnecting and Packaging Electronic Circuits) is an organization sponsored by both government and commercial manufacturers of PCBs and materials and users of PCBs. Its mission is to develop and maintain specifications governing all aspects of the PCB industry, from materials through assembly and test. Specifications also include standards for exchanging design, fabrication, and test information in electronic form.

The list of specifications maintained by the IPC is too long to list here. A partial list is printed elsewhere in this handbook. These specifications are revised at frequent intervals, so they reflect the state of the art in PCBs and will usually be of more value to designers than the corresponding MIL specs. Copies of these specifications can be obtained from IPC, 7380 Lincolnwood Ave., Lincolnwood, IL 60646.

12.4.3   PCMCIA Specs or PC Specs

The Personal Computer Memory Card Industry Association has evolved a set of standard PCB designs that are approximately the size of a normal credit card for use in portable computers and palmtop devices. This family of cards or packages has evolved into a very broad collection of adapter cards, ranging from FAX modems to flash memories to disk drives. To more accurately reflect the fact that this has evolved from memory card applications only to more general-purpose interface solutions, the association has elected to shorten the designator to *PC cards*. A set of design standards has evolved, governing the design of PCMCIA-compatible products. These standards can be obtained from PCMCIA Headquarters, 1030 East Duane Avenue, Suite G, Sunnyvale, CA 94086.

The IPC is in the process of converting the PCMCIA design specification to an IPC specification number, IPC-2220-4. When this has been completed it will replace the PCMCIA Association specification.

12.4.4   ANSI Standards

The American National Standards Institute, based in Washington, D.C., maintains a wide variety of standards governing metal composition, drawing symbols, and other matters related to the design of electronic products. Most are of secondary importance to the design of PCBs.

12.5   ASSOCIATIONS RELATED TO THE PCB INDUSTRY

12.5.1   IPC

The IPC is the principal global agency responsible for creating and maintaining specification of all kinds related to the manufacture and use of both rigid and flexible PCBs. Its membership includes most manufacturers of materials, equipment, supplies, and chemicals used in the manufacture of PCBs as well as assemblers, and users of PCBs. Its specifications include workmanship and inspection standards.

The IPC has two conventions per year at which training sessions are held and plans are made to update specifications and create new ones as needed. In addition, the IPC conducts a wide variety of training sessions throughout the year. The address of the IPC is listed in Sec. 12.4.2.

12.5.2   PCMCIA

The PCMCIA was formed by manufacturers of memory ICs and personal computers to develop form factor and interface standards for credit-card-size memory PCBs for use in personal computers. This form factor has rapidly evolved into a standard for a very wide variety of interface cards for personal computers. The address of the PCMCIA is listed in Sec. 12.4.3.

CHAPTER 13
ELECTRICAL AND MECHANICAL DESIGN PARAMETERS

Ralph J. Hersey, Jr.
Lawrence Livermore National Laboratory, Livermore,
California

13.1 PRINTED CIRCUIT DESIGN REQUIREMENTS

The electrical characteristics of printed board and multichip electrical connection substrates have become a critical functional product definition, and design requirement, for many electrical and electronic products. Until the late 1980s, most printed board designs were printed wiring designs, in that, with the exception of power and ground distribution, component placement and the arrangement of conductive and nonconductive patterns were not critical for functional electrical requirements. This was particularly true for most digital applications. However, since the late 1980s, electrical signal integrity has become a more serious design consideration in order to meet both functional performance and regularatory compliance requirements.

13.2 INTRODUCTION TO ELECTRICAL SIGNAL INTEGRITY

Electrical signal integrity is a combination of frequency and voltage/current, depending on the application. In low-level analog, very small leakage voltages or currents, thermal instabilities, and electromagnetic couplings can exceed acceptable limits of signal distortion. In a similar manner, most digital components can erroneously switch by application of less than 1 V of combined dc and ac signals.

13.2.1 Drivers for Electrical Signal Integrity

Analog and digital signals are subject to many issues that can cause signal distortion and degrade signal integrity. Some of these concern the transmission of the signal, and some the return paths.

13.2.1.1 Signal Integrity Terms for Both Analog and Digital Signals. Table 13.1 provides a listing of many of the issues that affect the signal transmission.

TABLE 13.1 Representative List of Issues for Both Analog and Digital Signals

Rise time	Thermal offset voltage
Fall time	Thermal offset current
Skew	Low-level amplifier
Jitter	High-impedance amplifier
High skew rate	Charge amplifier
Intermodulation distortion	Integrating amplifier
Harmonic distortion	Wideband amplifier
Phase distortion	Video amplifier
Crossover distortion	Precision amplifier

13.2.1.2 Return Paths. All electrical signals have a signal conductor and a signal return path. Very frequently, the signal conductor is shown on the schematic and the return conductor is neither shown nor mentioned on the schematic/logic drawing. This can also present a problem with PB CAD (computer-aided design) tools. Some CAD tools are "dumb" in that they will automatically route a transmission line as one of the signal conductors but will not route the necessary signal ground on one of the adjacent conductive pattern layers.

13.2.2 Analog Electrical Signal Integrity

The design of some analog printed circuits is a critical balance of all of the known parameters and characteristics of the complete design-through-use product development, manufacturing, assembly, test, and use processes. Analog designs cover all or portions of the complete electromagnetic spectrum, from dc all the way up into the GHz range of frequencies. Active and passive electrical/electronic components and materials have various levels of sensitivity to operating environments and conditions, such as temperature, thermal shock, vibration, voltage, current, electromagnetic fields, and light. In particular, the signal input terminals, voltage connections, and especially analog signal grounds are critical to analog signal integrity.

13.2.2.1 Sensitive Circuitry Isolation. One of the key methods to improve analog signal integrity is to isolate or separate the more critical or sensitive portions of the design. Sensitive circuitry may be susceptible to one or more external forces, such as electromagnetic, voltage, and grounding systems, mechanical shock/vibration, and thermal. Sometimes the more sensitive circuitry is repackaged into a separate function module that provides its own isolation and separation from the offending condition. Isolation and separation can be provided by physical separation, electromagnetic and thermal barriers, improved ground practices and design, power source filtering, signal isolators, shock and vibration dampeners, and elevated or lowered temperature controlled environment.

13.2.2.2 Thermal Electromotive Force. Below a few millivolts, thermal electromotive forces (EMFs) can have a significant impact on low-level analog signal integrity. Thermal EMFs of a nonsymmetrical sequence of various metal junctions (conductors) or symmetrical sequences of various metal junctions operating at different temperatures will generate and inject undesirable voltage (or induce unwanted currents) into the electrical signal path. This thermocouple effect is desirable in the case of temperature measurements. However, in the case of other low-level measurements it is an undesirable characteristic. Therefore, the requirement for low-signal-level PCDs is to ensure that all components and electrical interconnection networks and corresponding electrical terminations (such as soldered, welded, wire-bonded, or conductive adhesive) are symmetrical and isothermal. Electrical components, such as thin/thick-film resistors of different values (resistance), may have resistor elements manufactured from different formulations or compositions of materials and will have a designed-in thermal EMF error due to component selection.

13.2.3 Digital Electrical Signal Integrity

Each digital logic family of integrated circuits has manufacturer-specified electrical operating parameters and signal transfer characteristics, many of which have become industry standards due to multiple sourcing (manufacturing) of the family of components. The electrical signal integrity requirements for digital ICs are primarily the high and low electrical (voltage/current) requirements for the output, input, clock, set, reset, clear, and other signal names; the signal rise/fall times, clock frequency(s) and setup/hold times; and the voltage and ground connections as are necessary for the control and operation of the IC.

The input, output, and electrical signal transfer parameters and characteristics for digital ICs vary from logic or microprocessor family to family. Signal ICs are a large matrix of components, consisting of the semiconductor substrate materials, such as silicon, silicon/germanium, and gallium arsenide, that make up the various types of transistors. As shown in Table 13.2, the large number of digital IC families available create a complex matrix of design issues and requirements.

TABLE 13.2 Typical Digital Logic Rise and Fall Times

Logic family	Typical rise/fall time, ns	Logic family	Typical rise/fall time, ns
STD TTL	5	H	6
L	6.5	HCT	8
S	3.5	AC	3
ALS	1.9	ACT	
FTTL	1.2	10K ECL	0.7
BiCMOS	0.7	100ECL	0.5
		GaAs	0.3

The electrical signal integrity of the rise and fall times of electrical signals is a major driver and concern for high-speed and high-frequency printed circuits. Table 13.2 lists some of the typical rise and fall times of some of the popular digital logic families.

13.3 INTRODUCTION TO ELECTROMAGNETIC COMPATIBILITY

Electromagnetic compatibility (EMC) is a serious design requirement for both functional performance to design and regulatory compliance requirements. EMC encompasses the control and reduction of electromagnetic fields (EMF), electromagnetic interference (EMI), and radio frequency interference (RFI) and covers the whole electromagnetic frequency spectrum from dc to 20 GHz. Worldwide, the electronics industry has had to pay increasing attention to EMC to comply with both national and international standards and regulations. EMC involves major design considerations that ensure proper function within the electronic component, assembly, or system in order to:

1. Limit the emission (radiative or conductive) from one electronic component assembly, or system, to another.
2. Reduce the susceptibility of an electronic component, assembly, or system to external sources of EMF, EMI, or RFI.

There are three keys to EMC:

1. Design the product so that it produces less stray electromagnetic energy.
2. Design the product so that it is less susceptible to stray electromagnetic energy.
3. Design the product to prevent stray electromagnetic energy from entering or leaving the product.

13.4 NOISE BUDGET

Good design requires up-front determination of a *noise budget,* which should be included in the product definition requirements. The noise budget is the summation of all of the dc and ac voltages (or currents) that form a boundary within which the component, assembly, or system is designed to function.

$$e_{noise} = e_{dc} + e_{ac} \qquad (13.1)$$

where e_{dc} = dc electrical noise
e_{ac} = ac electrical noise

The *dc noise budget* consists of the voltage settings (preset) of the power supplies, the operating tolerance of the power supply, and the series dc voltage drops of the voltage distribution system.

The *ac noise budget* consists of the effectiveness of the local bypass capacitor, the amount of decoupling between the load, the bulk decoupling capacitor, and the power distributions system, the local voltage drops in the component's voltage/ground conductors, and the component's input voltage tolerance.

As mentioned in Sec. 13.5.3, many of the operating electrical, mechanical, thermal, and environmental parameters and conditions can have a major influence on the noise budget. With a limited focus on digital designs, additional noises that may need to be considered are EMC radiated and conducted emissions from other electromagnetic equipment and thermally generated voltages (thermocouple effect) due to electrical connections with differing layers of metals operating at different temperatures. The following is a list of most of the electrical voltages that should be considered for a noise margin analysis:

Switching noise*	Changes in supply voltage
Cross talk*	Changes in junction temperature
Impedance mismatch*	Changes in die ground voltage (IR)
Component wire bond (IR)[†]	Component lead (IR)

13.5 DESIGNING FOR SIGNAL INTEGRITY AND ELECTROMAGNETIC COMPATIBILITY

13.5.1 High Speed and High Frequency

Higher operating speeds and frequencies have had a dramatic effect on electronic packaging technology as a whole, but in particular on PBs and PBAs. Higher operating speeds have

---

* For digital circuits these three may amount to about 50 to 60 percent of the noise budget.
[†] (IR) voltage drop (current X resistance).

forced an evolutionary change from traditional PWD methods and practices, which were suitable for lower operating speeds, into the realm of serious PCD. Many of the technical design practices for most digital designs have had to adopt high-frequency analog techniques for design, synthesis, and analysis. In addition, component packaging densities have increased, functional electronic packaging densities have increased, more digital components are of the CMOS family design, and CMOS power dissipation increases with operating frequency, the end result being that thermal management has become more of a concern to PBD and other electronic packaging design personnel.

13.5.2 Leakage Currents and Voltages

Input guarding for stray leakage currents and voltages can be an important design consideration, in particular for some analog but also for some digital designs (especially CMOS). Many analog design requirements are based on thermal, pressure, force, strain, and other sensor technologies that have very low levels and ranges of electrical output voltages or currents. In addition, many of the requirements are for measurement accuracy and precision of a few percent or less. In combination, these requirements can present a challenge to electronic and PBD personnel. Very few sensors are robust in terms of their electrical output parameters; most of them have what is termed in the analog world "low-level" signal output for voltage and/or current. Therefore, many of these sensors require signal conditioning and amplifier circuits to improve the integrity of the electrical signal(s). Many of these signal conditioning and amplifier circuits have high-input-resistance characteristics which cause them to be more susceptible to erroneous signals. As a result, "guarding," as described later, becomes necessary to control stray voltages and currents.

Small, undesired, and unintended leakage currents and voltages can have a significant impact on the electrical signal integrity of some analog, as well as digital, applications. Leakage currents of a few nA or less, and leakage voltages of a few µV or less, can affect the designed functional performance of an electronic assembly. It is nearly impossible, from a practical point-of-view, for a high-input-resistance circuit to distinguish between a desired and undesired electrical signal. Thus, extreme care must be used in the design, manufacturing, and assembly processes of high-input-resistance products. Therefore, suitable PBD concepts must be included in the design to reduce and control the leakage currents and voltages. The following list identifies some of the common causes for leakage currents and voltages in PBAs.

- Insufficient (surface or volume) insulation resistance of base laminate
- Environmental contamination, fingerprints and skin oils, human breath, residual manufacturing and processing chemicals, improperly cured materials, solder fluxes, and surface moisture, such as humidity.
- Surface and subsurface contamination, such as can be found:

  On or in the assembled component

  Between conformal coatings and the surfaces they are protecting

  On, in, or under the solder resist

  Between conductive patterns on or in the electrical interconnection substrate

13.5.2.1 Design Concepts to Control Leakage Currents and Voltages. The primary concept for input guarding is to limit and control undesirable leakage currents and voltages or to prevent their formation in the first place. In theory, the principal is very simple: There are no leakage currents or voltages if there are no differences in electrical potential. In practice this is difficult to achieve and may not be a viable solution. However, by minimizing (the goal being to eliminate) the differences of potential between the critical electrical interconnection networks and components (leads and/or bodies) and all other materials, the formation of undesired leakage currents and voltages can be controlled (minimum effect) or eliminated (maximum effect).

- Form a *Faraday cage* around the critical conductive patterns and components using a combination of conductive patterns (frequently called *input guarding* and *guard rings*) and shielding enclosures.
- Keep all unguarded voltages out of the Faraday cage or protected area.
- Electrically connect the Faraday cage to a low-impedance voltage source that follows the critical (protected) voltage.

13.5.2.2 *Guard Rings—A Design Method to Control Leakage Currents and Voltages.*
The control of electrical leakage to the more critical signal terminals/leads can be optimized through the selection of components, various levels of implementing input guarding into the design, and the selection of the materials for the electrical interconnection substrate.

Some components provide unconnected, unused, or guard terminals/leads adjacent to the input terminals. Care must be exercised for the balance or trim terminals/leads, as in most cases these terminals are connected (internally) in the component directly into the input differential amplifier circuitry of the component; thus, any undesirable leakage currents or voltages to these terminals/leads may result in undesired operation. Some linear operational amplifiers (op-amps) and other linear components are more suitable for input guarding than others; some have two (or more) unused terminals/leads that are used to improve electrical isolation between the protected terminals/leads in the component itself, as well as the component land pattern and electrical interconnection substrate.

The simplest method for providing input guarding to control input leakage currents and voltages is through the use of guard rings of conductive patterns *on all layers of PB conductive patterns* that surround the terminals/leads and associated circuitry. The guard ring is attached to a low-impedance voltage source that best follows the input signal or, as recommended by some analog IC manufacturers in their application notes, to the metal case of the component. As a result, the input terminals of high-input-resistance, low-bias-current, low-offset-voltage Op-amps can be guarded from stray electrical leakage currents and voltages.

13.5.3 Voltage and Ground Distribution Concepts

There are a few main concepts for the distribution of voltage(s) and ground in PBs, their assemblies, and other electronic assemblies. In general, most serious PCDs use one or more ground planes for the common electrical connection(s), for the source(s) of electrical power, and for the reference or return electrical signal path. The keys to good voltage and ground distribution systems are:

- Providing a low-impedance voltage and ground distribution system
- Meeting functional performance product definition design requirements
- Optimizing EMC

Depending on the design, the ground system may also be used for the grounding conductor interconnection(s) for the electrical safety and similar compliance requirements. For electrical signal integrity considerations, it is generally desirable to have separate but parallel electrical interconnection networks for the grounded (signal and power) and grounding (electrical safety) conductors. Like ground, voltage distribution for serious PCDs generally consists of one or more voltage planes (or portions thereof), although for some designs routed conductive patterns or buses may be a functionally acceptable option. A bused voltage and ground system may be acceptable for some designs, but they are generally limited to the PCD with lower operating frequencies and slower rise and fall times. The voltage and ground distribution and the location and type of bypass capacitors can have a significant impact on EMC and electrical signal integrity.

13.5.3.1 *Grounding Concepts.*   Electrical grounding is one of the most important concepts and probably the least understood aspect of electrical signal integrity and EMC. All electrical conductors, including ground, form very subtle, but active, electrical interconnection network that can significantly compromise the product definition's requirements for electrical signal integrity and EMC. In particular, the grounding system is critical to ensure compliance to functional performance and regulatory requirements. Grounding (and voltage distribution) concepts are a matrix of requirements, concepts, concerns, considerations, and practices. In general, there is no universal solution suitable for all applications. Grounding is considered by some to be an art, which can be supported in that some grounding systems are completely unstructured and the reasons that some systems work, while others do not, are not clear. As a result, there has been an ongoing search to find a set of rules that can be used for the design of grounding systems and, unfortunately, many of the rules are conflicting. For example, a modular modem PCMCIA electronic assembly may have a suitable grounding system for normal telecom line operation. Yet, this may be totally inadequate if a 100-1kA electrical current, coupled through the PCMCIA assembly into the personal computer's electrical grounding system, is induced in the telecom line due to a nearby lightning strike or fallen power line. Similarly, a suitable electrical safety grounding system for power line frequencies may not be suitable near a high-power, high-frequency radio, television, or telecommunications transmitter. The following are some of the major concerns and considerations that are involved in good grounding practices:

- Integration of analog and digital signal converters, especially with more than 12 bits of resolution—ground loops and noise
- High-speed and high-frequency operation—ground pull-up and EMC
- High-speed and high-frequency bus line drivers and receivers—major ground pull-up and EMC concerns
- Low-signal-level analog sensors (transducers)
- Length of the conductors in the voltage/grounding system as a considerable portion of the electrical wavelength of one of the frequencies of the signal range of EMC
- When designing a grounding system, consideration of developing a grounding map that identifies all grounding requirements and voltage/current/frequency requirements

13.5.3.2 *Grounding Systems.*   The following is an introduction to several grounding and voltage distribution systems and their electrical characteristics.

Single-Point and Point-Source Grounding Concepts.   Single-point grounding is a method whereby the grounding electrical interconnection network is connected to ground at a single point at either the source or load end of the electrical interconnection network. The voltage drops between the various grounding nodes is a function of the interconnection network impedances, operating frequency, and current. Point-source or *star* grounding systems have a single-point grounding location for all electrical loads. The point-source grounding point is connected to another grounding point using a low-impedance bus or grounding conductor.

Multiple-Point Grounding Concepts.   A multiple-point grounding system may be in the form of a loop or tree-like structure. In a loop grounding system the voltage drops around the loop may vary, depending on the electrical characteristics of each of the loads attached to the grounding loop. In a tree, the grounding system has good voltage regulation and allows leads to be independently attached or removed from the tree without a significant impact on the remaining loads.

Ground Planes.   Ground planes are the grounding system of choice for most serious PCD requirements. Ground planes can improve the electrical signal integrity of the grounding system and EMC, provided all critical conductors are buried (lands only) on outer layer(s) of the printed board assembly.

Separation of Grounds. The identification and separation of natural groupings of grounds into similar requirements increases the assurance of conformance to product definition requirements. Some of the natural groupings are as follows:

- Electrical safety ground
- Power supply ground
- Low-level analog ground
- High-level analog ground
- Digital ground
- I/O ground
- Pulsed power/energy ground

When defining the printed circuit design requirements for a particular assembly, results of an analysis of the grounding elements necessary for proper functional performance must be included.

13.5.3.3 Bypass Capacitors. The selection, location, number, and value of the bypass capacitor(s) for PCDs can affect functional circuit performance. The purpose of the bypass capacitor is to provide the necessary electrical energy to minimize the effect of a component's normal transient switching and load currents during functional operation. The selection, location, and placement of the bypass capacitor can have a significant impact on EMC and a lesser impact on functional performance. One of the keys to EMC management is to prevent or minimize the generation and subsequent radiation of electromagnetic fields in the first place.

13.5.3.4 Voltage and Ground Buses. As operating frequencies and speeds increase, voltage and ground bus distribution systems may function as lump constant shock-excited oscillators. The frequency of oscillation is dependent on the series inductances of the voltage and ground bus system and shunt capacitors. One of the worst cases is when the voltage and ground buses are placed as railroad rails with the bypass capacitors, and digital integrated circuits are alternated in position like railroad ties bridging between the rails.

13.5.3.5 Voltage and Ground Planes. Voltage and ground planes can be an effective means to provide a relatively low resistance and impedance[1] to distribute voltage and ground within a PBD. However, maximum effectiveness—solid metal, with no holes or cutouts for plated through-holes or other necessary features—is an unobtainable condition. Therefore, voltage and ground planes are a compromise in design and requirements due to the necessary holes in the planes for electrical interconnections and component mounting.

Voltage and Ground Plane Resistance. The sheet resistance of solid copper voltage and ground planes is relatively low for most copper foil thicknesses. For 35-μm-thick copper foil, the dc (solid) sheet resistance is less than 1 mΩ/sq. The dc resistance of copper foil is shown in Eq. (13.2). The (solid) sheet resistance for selected copper foils is shown in Table 13.3. Due to the almost infinite number of possible variations in the size, placement, and shape of perforated mesh planes, the following data are presented for informational and comparative purposes only.

$$R_{DC} = \frac{17.2}{t_{\mu m}} \text{ m}\Omega/\text{sq} \tag{13.2}$$

t_{mm} is in μm

TABLE 13.3 Solid Area Copper Foil Sheet
Resistance

Copper thickness, μm	Sheet resistance, mΩ/sq
5	3.44
9	1.911
12	1.433
17	1.012
26	0.662
35	0.491
70	0.246

Resistance models for periodic mesh grid planes[2] is of interest for *uniform* grids, but is of limited use for grid planes that are not periodic and for ac electrical network analysis.

Voltage and Ground Plane Impedance.   The impedance of perforated mesh voltage and ground planes is difficult to perform due to the number of variations in the size, placement, and shape of perforated mesh planes.

13.6   *MECHANICAL DESIGN REQUIREMENTS*

The design intent of PBs and their assemblies is primarily to mount and lend mechanical support to components as well as to provide all of the necessary electrical interconnections. However, PBAs should not be used as a (major) structural member.

There are three general forms of PBAs:

1. *Functional module*—A plug-in and a mechanically mounted PBA. The functional module is in the form of a component, whereby leads or other types of electrical terminals provide both electrical interconnections and mechanical mounting of the module to the next higher level of electronic packaging.

2. *Plug-in module*—This provides all of the necessary electrical interconnections at one or more edge-board connectors. A plug-in module typically plugs into a mother board, or sometimes electrical cables are used. The plug-in module is mechanically supported on one edge by the edge-board connector and on one or more edges by card guides, rails, or a mounting frame.

3. *Mechanically mounted PBA*—This is mounted and/or supported in a mechanical assembly or housing with a number of mechanical fasteners around its periphery (and internally to the PBA for additional support, if required). The most common mechanically mounted PBA is the mother board, such as is frequently used in personal computers. Mechanically mounted PBAs are one of the members of an electrical/electronic assembly and are physically mounted in the assembly using one or more mechanical fasteners, such as screws, clips, and standoffs. A common example of a mechanically mounted PBA is a modular power supply.

All forms of PBAs have many common requirements necessary to meet their product definition requirements, although there will be significant variations in the product definition requirements for PBAs due to their specific form and application requirements. For example, the requirement for PBA flatness due to bow and twist may be different for a plug-in than for a mechanically mounted PBA. The requirements for the number and location of mounting fasteners for a mechanically mounted PBA will be different for a relatively thick MLB with low-mass components than for a simpler PB with high-mass components.

The following list of factors, based primarily on Ginsberg,[3] must be considered and evaluated in the design of a PB and its assembly:

- Configuration of the PB, size, and form factor(s)
- Need for mechanical attachment, mountings, and component types
- Compatibility with EMC and other environmental
- PBA mounting (horizontal or vertical) as a consequence of other factors such as dust and environment
- Environmental factors requiring special attention, such as thermal management, shock and vibration, humidity, salt spray, dust, altitude, and radiation
- Degree of support
- Retention and fastening
- Ease of removal

13.6.1 General Mechanical Design Requirements

The general mechanical design requirements for PBs and PBAs include the methods of dimensioning, mounting, guiding during insertion and removal of plug-in components or assemblies, retention, and extraction. Frequently, the PBA mounting method is predetermined as a design requirement to an established compatibility with existing hardware. In other cases, the printed board designer has a choice in determining which PB mounting method is more suitable after considering such design factors as the following:

- PB size and shape based on form, fit, and function requirements
- Input/output terminations and locations
- Area and volume restrictions
- Accessibility requirements
- Ease of repair/maintenance
- Modularity requirements
- Type of mounting hardware
- Thermal management
- EMC
- Type of circuit in its relationship to other circuits

13.6.1.1 Dimensioning and Tolerancing.   The dimensioning and tolerancing system for PBs and PBAs must ensure that the product is appropriately defined for all of the product form, fit, and function requirements for the complete product life cycle, from definition through manufacturing to end use. Dimensioning and tolerancing are critical at least for the design, manufacturing, assembly, inspection, test, and acceptance phases.

Regardless of the dimension and tolerance standards that are used to establish and document the product definition's mechanical design and acceptance requirements,[4] there should be at least two (primary) data reference features in every PBD (see Fig. 13.1). The purpose is to ensure the integrity of a PB's and PBA's datum reference throughout the production and acceptance process. In general, it should be a nonfunctional hole (in the case of PBs) or a surface feature that is used as the primary datum reference for final dimensional measurements and acceptance of the product. The datum reference should not be a machined edge that is formed in the last phases of the manufacturing, fabrication, or assembly process in a secondary machining operation.

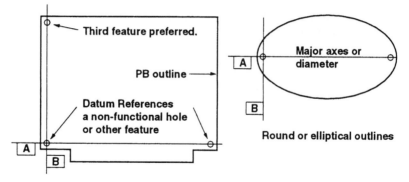

Rectangular and square outlines

FIGURE 13.1   All printed boards and their assemblies should have their datum references included into the design to ensure the integrity of the mechanical datum references throughout a product's production and acceptance cycles.

13.6.1.2   *Mechanically Mounted Printed Board Assemblies (PBAs).* PBAs should be mounted to ensure their mechanical (and sometimes electrical grounding) integrity throughout their product life cycle. The following are some of the generally accepted requirements and practices for mechanically mounted PBAs:

- PBAs should be supported within 25 mm of the edge of the PBA on at least three sides.
- As good practice, fabricated printed boards (PBs) having a thickness of about 0.7 to 1.6 mm should be mechanically supported on 100-mm or lower intervals, and PBs thicker than 2.3 mm on less than 1.3-mm intervals.
- Fasteners should not be located on less than the PBs thickness or the fastener's head diameter (whichever is lower) from the edge of the PB.

13.6.1.3   *Guides for Printed Board Assemblies.* A major advantage of using plug-in printed board assemblies rather than other electronic packaging techniques is the suitability of PBAs for use with mechanical PBA card guides for ease of maintenance, changing configuration, and up-grading function or performance. There are many PBA guide hardware systems that are available either commercially, as industry standard, or proprietarily. The PBA may be predetermined as a design requirement or may be developed based on the size and shape of the PBA, *the degree of dimensional accuracy needed to ensure proper mating alignment with the mating connector system,* and the desired degree of sophistication. Some PBA guide systems contain a built-in locking system that provides mechanical retention and thermal management (conductive).

   Caution: Some PBA card guide systems have become somewhat of industry standards and can be obtained or assembled to fit most PBAs. However, not all of the industry-standard-like PBA guide systems are compatible or interchangeable for retaining or extracting PBAs.

13.6.1.4   *Retaining Printed Board Assemblies.* Quite often, shock, vibration, and normal handling requirements necessitate that the PBA be retained in the equipment by mechanical devices. Some PBA retaining systems are attached as hardware to the PB during assembly; other retaining systems are built into the PBA mounting hardware frequently called a *cage.* The selection of a proper PBA retaining system is important, since the retaining devices may reduce the amount of PB area available for component mounting and interconnections, and can add significantly to the cost of the electronic equipment.

13.6.1.5   Extracting Printed Board Assemblies.   A number of unique principles have been developed and applied to solve the various problems of extracting PBAs from their plug-in enclosures. The result has been a proliferation of proprietary and a few industry-standard-like extraction systems. The most common industry-standard extractor is injection-molded plastic hardware that is free to partially rotate when attached to the PBA with a pressed-in pin. Many of these PBA extraction tools use a minimum of PB space, thereby maximizing available PB area for components and conductor routing. They also protect both the PBA and the associated mating connector(s) from damage during the extraction process.

The following should be considered when selecting among the many different types of PBA extraction tools:

- The area of the PBA available for attachment
- The extractor's effect on the PBA-to-PBA mounting pitch
- The need for special provisions in the PBD, such as mounting holes, mounting clearance holes, and notches
- The size of the extractor, especially if the extractor is to be stored in the equipment with which it is used
- The need for an extraction device that is permanently attached to the PBA, usually by riveting
- The need for specially designed considerations, such as load-bearing flanges, in the PBA mounting chassis or cage hardware
- The suitability of the extractor to be used with a variety of PB sizes, shapes, and thicknesses
- The cost of using the extractor, both in piece price and added design costs
- The degree of access required inside the equipment to engage and use the extraction tool

13.6.2   Shock and Vibration

Shock, vibration, flexing, and bowing can be functional performance and reliability concerns for PBAs—more so for larger PBAs. For many PBAs, the worst-case exposure to shock and vibration occurs in nonfunctional or operational usage, during shipping and other forms of transportation from one location to another, or possibly in functional use when the functionally operating product containing PBAs is inadvertently dropped on the floor. Other PBAs are designed to withstand specified levels of shock and vibration in transportation and in use. The design requirements for shock and vibration vary, depending on each family of general requirements. For example, there are nonoperating shock and vibration withstand requirements for vehicular, train, ship, and air transportation for domestic and international shipment for Level 1, 2, or 3 products, which include various procedures and requirements for packaging. The shock and vibration functional design requirements are many and varied, and are very dependent on the application. Some sources of shock and vibration are very obvious, while others are very subtle. The levels and duration of shock and vibration vary significantly in each application: An electronic sensor mounted on a vehicle's axle is different from the radio mounted on the dashboard. There are the differences among ground-based, rack-mounted, industrial control equipment, aircraft, aerospace, and munitions applications. Some vibrations are subtle, low-level continuous, and are frequently caused by electric or gas motor-driven rotating machinery and equipment. Continuous low-level vibrations can induce *mechanical fatigue* in some electrical/electronic equipment.

13.6.2.1   Shock.   *Mechanical shock* can be defined as a pulse, step, or transient vibration, wherein the excitation is nonperiodic.[5] Shock is a suddenly applied force or increment of force, by a sudden change in the direction or magnitude of a velocity vector. With few exceptions, shocks are not easily transmitted to electronic equipment by relatively light mounting frames and structures. Most shocks to electronic equipment in the consumer, commercial, and industrial markets are due to dropping during handling or transportation, the exceptions being electronic sensors or equipment mounted to heavier mounting frames, such as vehicle axles and punch-press-like equipment, or military equipment subjected to air dropping or to explosive forces, such as munitions. Most shock impact forces result in a transient type of dampened vibration which is influenced by the natural frequencies of the mounting frame. Generally, shock either results in instantaneous failure or functions as a stress concentrator by reducing the effective strength of the connection or lead for subsequent failure due to additional shock(s) and vibration.

13.6.2.2 *Vibration.*

Vibration is a term that describes oscillation in a mechanical system, and is defined by the frequency (or frequencies) of oscillation and amplitude. PBAs that are subjected to extended periods of vibration will often suffer from fatigue failure, which can occur in the form of broken wires or component leads, fractured solder joints, cracked conductive patterns, or broken contacts on electrical connectors. The frequency(s) of vibration, resonances, and amplitude(s) all influence the rate to failure.

Flexing and bowing in PBAs is the result of induced shock and vibration into the PBA. Different PBA mounting methods have differing susceptibilities to shock and vibration. In general, most small PBA functional modules are manufactured as components and are frequently encapsulated with a polymeric potting material into a solid mass, and they therefore have minimal shock and vibration requirements within the module. The plug-in PBA is restrained on one edge by the edge-board connector(s), and to some extent along the two sides of the PBA by mechanical guides. This leaves only one edge of the PBA free to flex from shock and vibration or to bow from residual manufacturing or assembly stress in the PBA. However, a handle along the free edge of the PBA or a restraining bar can be located across the center of the free edge of the PBA and mechanically attached for support at the ends of the restraining bar to the PBA mounting hardware (card cage). Generally, the mating edge-board connector has a molded-plastic body that provides mechanical support to the mated edge-board connector and has sufficient compliance in the electrical contacts to maintain good electrical connections within the connector's performance specifications. Mechanically mounted PBAs can be more of a shock and vibration concern for three main reasons:

1. The PBA can be very large, sometimes as large as 600 mm². More frequently, the maximum width is 430 mm (the width of a standard electronic chassis) and less than 600 mm long. Although most are less than 300 mm², this still creates a large area and can be a problem if unsupported.

2. The PBA is misused as a mechanical support structure for high-mass components, such as magnetic components (iron-cored transformers and inductors), power supplies, and large (in physical size) function modules.

3. The PBA is not included in the mechanical design definition.

13.6.2.3 *Major Shock and Vibration Concerns.*   These include the following:

- Flexing between PBAs may cause shorts between adjacent PBAs or to the enclosure.

- The fundamental mode is the primary mode of concern because it has the large displacements that cause fatigue damage to solder joints, component leads, and connector contacts.

- Continuous flexing of a PBA will fracture component leads and, more important, surface-mounted component solder joints, due to mechanical fatigue failure. (Mechanically induced flexing or vibration in assembled PBs is used under controlled conditions to induce failures in solder joints for quality and reliability studies.)

- Movement of a PBA within its mechanical guides will be amplified due to shock and vibration resonance or harmonic resonance.

- Fatigue life modeling for PBA mounted components has become significantly more complex due to in-use simultaneous application of both vibration and thermal cycles. Vibration strains and thermal strains should be superposed for more representative modeling.

13.6.2.4 Types of Edge Mounting. The problems, methods of analysis, and minimization of the effects of shock and vibration on PBAs are the same as in other engineering applications, and similar solutions can be used. PBAs are designed and manufactured in a wide range of shapes and sizes, with rectangular being the most common because of the shape of most electrical/electronic equipment, especially for plug-in PBAs. Though PBAs are a multi-degree-of-freedom system, the fundamental mode is of primary importance because it has the large displacements that are the primary cause of fatigue failure in solder joints, component leads, wires, and connector contacts.[6] Most vibrational fatigue damage occurs at the fundamental or natural frequency because displacement is highest and stress is maximized. Edge or boundary conditions are terms that are used to define the method of attachment of the PBA (or, more generically, a panel) to its mounting frame. The term *free edge* is used to define those edges that are not restrained and are free to move and/or rotate along the edge of the PBA out of their normal mounting plane. The terms *supported edge* or *simple support* used to define an edge that is restrained in out-of-plane movements but is allowed rotational movement around the PBA's edge. The terms *fixed edge* or *clamped edge* are used to define an edge that is restrained in both out-of-plane and rotational movements. Illustrations of the definitions for fixed edge, supported edge, and free edge, and their applications to plug-in mounted PBAs, are shown in Fig. 13.2.

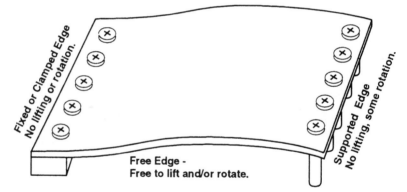

FIGURE 13.2 The method of mounting PBAs contributes to shock and vibration concerns, but can be reduced by good design practices.

13.6.2.5 Board Deflection. The amount of strain on a PBA component is a function of the maximum deflection of the PBA when subjected to shock and vibration. Those components mounted closest to the center of the assembly are subjected to the greatest strain, as illustrated in Fig. 13.3.

A set of empirical maximum deflection (δ) calculations has been developed by Steinberg, and his latest equation[7] has more parameters than previous equations, reflecting the sophistication and requirements for modern PBDs (units adjusted from inches to mm).

$$\delta = \frac{k\,0.00022\,B}{ct\sqrt{L}}$$

(13.3)

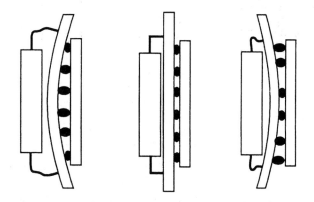

FIGURE 13.3 The PB bends in a PBA during shock and vibration, with the most severe stresses applied to the components mounted centermost on the assembly.

where k = units conversion coefficient; for inches $k = 1$, for mm, $k = \sqrt{25.4}$

B = length of PB edge parallel to component located at center of board (worst case), mm

L = length of component, mm

t = thickness of PB, mm

c = 1.0 for standard DIP

   = 1.26 for DIP with side brazed leads

   = 1.0 for PGA with four rows of pins (one row extending along the perimeter of each edge)

   = 2.25 for CLCC

Analysis of the maximum deflection calculation formula reveals (as expected) that components with some compliance built into their component mounting and electrical terminations (such as the DIP and PGA) can be subjected to about twice the vibrational deflection as an SMT CLCC, provided component size, PB size, and PB thickness are equivalent. The latest equation for maximum deflection calculations is rated for 10 million stress reversals when subjected to harmonic (sinusoidal) vibration, and 20 million stress reversals when subjected to random vibration. It must be understood that this equation is a first approximation for predicting solder joint life. There are many factors that must be included for a more rigorous analysis and prediction. A more thorough discussion is found in Barker.[6]

13.6.2.6 Natural (Fundamental) Resonance of Printed Board Assemblies. The mechanical mounting of PBAs and their components is a key design consideration in the ability of the PBA to withstand shock and vibration. The overall size of the PBA is not a major factor, provided a suitable mechanical support structure is included as a part of the PBA's product definition requirements. There is a large matrix of ways to mount panels (PBAs) using various combinations of free edges, supported edges, fixed edges, and point supports and by calculating fundamental resonance. The following four examples compare the fundamental natural resonances of the same rectangularly shaped PBA using different edge-mounting techniques. Additional formulas for calculating other natural resonances are found in Barker,[6] Steinberg,[7] and others.

In the following examples—demonstrations of the sensitivity of PBAs to their methods of mounting—the same PBA is used for direct comparative purposes (see Fig. 13.4). The following are the design requirements and material parameters that were used for the calculations:

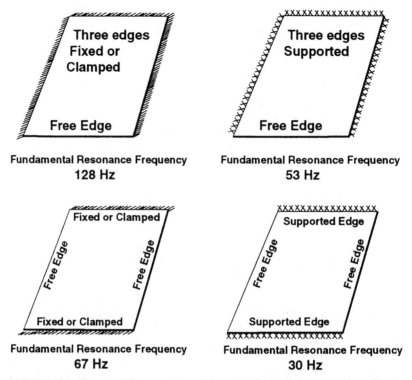

FIGURE 13.4 The same PBA can have a wide range of natural resonances depending on the mounting method, which is why shock and vibration concerns are a critical design consideration.

E	Modulus of elasticity (type GF epoxy-glass)	1.378×10^4 MPa
μ	Poisson's ratio	0.12 (dimensionless)
a	Longer dimension of the PBA	200 mm
b	Narrower dimension of the PBA	150 mm
t	Thickness of the PBA	1.6 mm
W	Weight of the PBA including components	0.25 kg

$$D = \frac{Et^3}{12(1 - \mu^2)} \tag{13.4}$$

where D is the plate bending stiffness.

$$M = \frac{W}{g} \tag{13.5}$$

$$f_n = C_0 P_0 \sqrt{\frac{Dab}{M}} \text{ Hz} \tag{13.6}$$

where f_n is the natural resonant frequency.

13.6.3 Methods of Reinforcement and Snubbers

Printed board assemblies are stiffened using one or more methods to raise the natural resonant frequency sufficiently above the shock and vibration threat. The most obvious is to change the method of retaining or mounting the PBA in the next higher level of assembly. Frequently, though, this may not be an acceptable option due to the resources and schedule changes that may be necessary for extensive redesign. However, some simpler modification in the design may meet requirements. Sometimes changing the plug-in PBA guide from a loose supportive guide to a tighter spring-loaded or clamping-type guide may be sufficient. Other methods are to add ribs or stiffeners, additional single-point mounting locations, or *snubbers* across the surfaces of the PBAs.

REFERENCES

1. Donald R. J. White and Michel Mardiguian, "EMI Control, Methodology and Procedures," *Interference Control Technologies, emf-emi Control,* 4th ed., Gainsville, Va., pp. 5.5–5.6.

2. Ruey-Beei Wu, "Resistance Modeling of Periodically Perforated Mesh Planes in Multilayer Packaging Structures," *IEEE Transactions on Components, Hybrids, and Manufacturing Technology,* vol. 12, no. 3, September 1989, pp. 365–372.

3. G. L. Ginsberg, "Engineering Packaging Interconnection System," Chap. 4 in Clyde F. Coombs, Jr. (ed), *Printed Circuits Handbook* 3d ed., McGraw-Hill, New York, 1988 pp. 4–17.

4. ANSI-YI4.5 "Dimensioning and Tolerancing," American National Standards Institute, New York, (date of current issue).

5. Cyril M. Harris and Charles E. Crede (eds.), *Shock and Vibration Handbook,* vol. 1, McGraw-Hill, New York, 1961, p. 1–2.

6. Donald B. Barker, Chap. 9, in *Handbook of Electronic Packaging Design,* Michael Pecht (ed.), Marcel Dekker, Inc., New York, 1991, p. 550.

7. Dave S. Steinberg, *Vibration Analysis for Electronic Equipment,* 2d ed., John Wiley, New York, 1988.

CHAPTER 14
MULTILAYER DESIGN ISSUES

Robert R. Holmes, Ph.D.
AT&T, Richmond, Virginia

14.1 RELIABILITY ISSUES

A multilayer board is a complex structure and it can have a wide variety of defects. Defects that actually prevent the board from working are called *functional defects*. Nonfunctional defects do not prevent the board from working, but they present a potential reliability threat. Functional defects, such as opens and shorts, are relatively easy to detect and are a clear cause for rejection. Some nonfunctional defects are very likely to cause future failures and must be avoided. For example, ionic contamination, although difficult to find, will almost certainly cause a future electrochemical activity and must never be tolerated. Other nonfunctional defects are cosmetic, affecting appearance but not reliability. Specifications vary widely on acceptance criteria for nonfunctional defects. Some specifications require only functionality. The IPC Class 1 specification for consumer products approaches this limit. Other specifications, such as the IPC Class 3 specification for high-reliability products, prohibit virtually all flaws.

Occasionally a fabricator will discover an entire production lot of MLBs with a nonfunctional defect, and the designer will be asked to accept boards on a one-time nonconforming basis. Often, there is little risk in agreeing to this request. If the nature of the flaw is understood and there is no serious reliability consideration, they can be accepted. However, caution is always required in giving approval, because even purely cosmetic flaws can be a sign of poor workmanship and may be a symptom of more serious problems. The goal of this chapter is to help the designer understand the nature of many common flaws so that an informed decision is possible.

Some defects are caused by poor design choices, while others are caused by poor processing. This section will review some common defects, describing each in enough detail to distinguish it from the others. The discussion will review potential reliability concerns, causes of the defect, and recommended corrective action. For the purposes of the discussion, defects are grouped into five broad categories:

1. *Substrate flaws:* Defects affecting MLB substrate integrity
2. *Surface damage:* Defects located on surface of copper features
3. *Mechanical problems:* Thickness and warp
4. *Internal misregistration:* Alignment of internal features to drilled holes
5. *Interconnection issues:* PTH and circuit flaws

14.1.1   Substrate Flaws

In a perfect laminate, the dielectric is uniform and free of flaws. In a real laminate, this is often not the case, and an entire lexicon has been developed to describe substrate flaws. Among the terms used are *blisters, delaminations, voids, silver streaks, tennis racket, weave exposure, weave texture, measles, foreign material,* and *pink ring.* Some specifications allow a minimum level of some of these flaws. Others allow none.

14.1.1.1   Blisters and Delaminations.

Blisters and delaminations arise when there is an adhesive or cohesive failure in the dielectric. This failure can occur at a copper-to-dielectric interface, at a B- to C-stage interface, or within a dielectric layer. If the failure occurs during lamination, it is called a *blister,* otherwise it is a *delamination.* They appear as whitish areas often associated with a slight raised area on the board surface. In some cases, they are deep inside the board and can be detected only in microsection. Size varies from barely visible to several inches in diameter.

The internal void associated with a blister or delamination is very undesirable and is prohibited by most specifications. The void can grow with time. If it is cut by a drilled hole, it can trap process chemicals. If the board operates in a humid environment, it can become saturated with moisture due to diffusion. In any case, the internal surface of the void is an excellent site for electrochemical activity leading to internal shorts.

Blisters can be caused by poor design. For example, if a high-layer-count board has a region on several layers with no copper, the lamination pressure in this region may be inadequate to assure B-stage adhesion. The solution is to include dummy copper areas to equalize pressure. Another bad situation occurs when low-density signal layers have a solid copper border. The solution here is to replace the solid border with some type of stripe or dot pattern.

The most common cause of delamination is moisture. A fabricated board can absorb more than 1 percent water (by weight). At levels above 0.5 percent, boards can delaminate during soldering. The solution to moisture blisters is to store boards in low humidity or to bake before soldering. If neither solution is practical, there are materials such as the epoxy-PPO blends that have very low moisture absorption.

Another cause of blisters and delamination is poor processing. Out-of-tolerance B-stage or an out-of-control press can easily give poor adhesion. Trapped debris, such as pieces of release material, will cause delamination or blisters. Contaminated innerlayers will blister during lamination or delaminate during soldering. Failures of the B-stage to copper adhesion can be caused by a poor adhesion treatment. In the case of black oxide or silane treatments, an out-of-control bath may have been used. In the case of a reduced oxide treatment, there may be an excessive hold time between treatment and lamination (a 48-h maximum is recommended). In the case of double treated copper layers, the treated surface may be contaminated with photoresist debris.

14.1.1.2   Voids.

The term *void* describes a variety of conditions. These include isolated voids that look like blisters, as well as clouds of small voids that give the laminate a hazy appearance. The primary distinction between a blister and an isolated void is the way they form. A blister is an adhesion failure, whereas a void is a failure of the resin to completely fill a space.

Like blisters, voids are a reliability risk due to the potential for moisture saturation and electrochemical activity. Unlike blisters, voids are not due to an adhesion failure, and they are unlikely to propagate. Under many specifications, voids are a cause for rejection, but if they are in an area with no circuitry or plated holes, they can be safely tolerated. Care must be exercised to assure that voids never span internal circuits.

Voids result from trapped air or volatiles and are found where the local lamination pressure is low. One such place is a panel edge. During B-stage flow, the panel perimeter is a boundary where the hydrostatic pressure in the liquid B-stage is zero. Near the perimeter, the pressure is too low to dissolve air and other volatiles, leading to voids. Generally the outer 0.5 in or so of any panel is subject to severe voiding. Insufficient B-stage flow arising from defective B-stage or an improper press cycle can greatly increase the size of the voided area. Using high lamination pressure or vacuum-assisted lamination reduces the width of the voided region, but does not eliminate edge voids altogether.

One cause of voids is a design feature requiring B-stage fill, coupled with B-stage that has poor flow characteristics. This condition is aggravated if the feature requiring fill is repeated on every layer. In this case, local pressure is low, reducing resin fill. A prevacuum may be of some help in preventing feature-related voids, but the real solution is to select a B-stage and press cycle combination that produces flow and fills all features before the cure is too far advanced.

14.1.1.3 *Silver Streaks and Tennis Racket Appearance.*

Occasionally an MLB shows streaks in the dielectric that follow individual glass bundles and are easily confused with voids. When they run preferentially in one direction, they are called *silver streaks.* Less frequently, they run in both directions, producing a tennis racket–like appearance.

SEM micrographs of silver streaks generally fail to find voids. The source of the streaks appears to be refraction or scattering of light at the interface between glass fibers and resin. The apparent cause of this optical discontinuity is poor wetting of the glass by the resin. Since there is no physical separation between the resin and the glass, silver streaks are not a serious reliability threat. Nevertheless, silver streaks and voids are easily confused, and, in serious cases, silver streaks are a cosmetic problem. Some specifications treat them like voids and prohibit them. Others allow a limited amount of silver streaking. One compromise is to allow them as long as they do not cross isolated conductors. In any case, silver streaks are evidence of marginal materials and should be avoided when possible.

Silver streaks often occur with one B-stage lot and then vanish with another. They affect glass running in one direction, but not both. Although most common near the panel edges, they often run many inches into the panel itself. Silver streaks can be reduced, but not eliminated, by adjusting the press cycle to increase resin flow. These observations suggest that the root cause of silver streaks is the glass yarn, probably an inconsistent application of the silane treatment used to enhance adhesion. Although the silver streak effect can be minimized by lamination process changes, the best solution is to work with the material vendor to obtain material not subject to silver streaks.

14.1.1.4 *Weave Exposure and Weave Texture.*

In a good laminate, glass is well encapsulated by resin and the surface has a uniform resin layer. In some laminates, the glass cloth is very close to the surface and an obvious weave texture is apparent. In the worst-case condition, glass yarn is actually exposed.

On innerlayers, exposed glass bundles are encapsulated during lamination. If the innerlayer process includes adequate cleaning, exposed glass is not a cause for concern. Process cleanliness should be verified by surface insulation resistance and extract conductivity tests. On finished MLBs, exposed glass provides a path for flux penetration and is a cause for rejection. Although weave texture does not expose glass and is generally accepted, it is a cosmetic problem that reduces assembly margin, and it is a sign of poor MLB lamination conditions. Corrective action should be taken when weave texture is observed.

Weave exposure and weave texture are signs that the surface dielectric has too little resin. This can occur if a very low resin content B-stage is used for the cap layer. A more likely cause is that the press cycle caused too much resin flow. In either case, the solution is to optimize the press cycle and materials to produce the correct surface conditions.

14.1.1.5 *Measles.*

Measles are tiny white spots that appear on or near the board surface. They correlate with the glass weave, occurring where horizontal and vertical yarns cross. They often appear after a mechanical or thermal shock. Measles generally do not propagate unless the board is subjected to additional thermal or mechanical abuse.

Books could be written about measles. There is great controversy about their cause and the risk they bring to an MLB. Although there is no real evidence for a reliability risk from measles, they are an undesirable cosmetic condition and most specifications limit them. One common limit is to prohibit overlap of adjacent measles. Another is to allow overlap so long as the measles do not bridge between two conductors. Some conservative specifications try to prohibit measles altogether.

Measles appear to be evidence of stress fractures at the resin–glass interface. Carefully prepared microsections often find evidence of this damage. Measles are most common with heavy glass yarns and with resin-poor surfaces. The best solution is to select a B-stage resin and press cycle combination that produces a resin-rich surface. If this approach is inadequate, then the outer-layer B-stage glass should be limited to the fine yarns such as type 106 or 1080.

14.1.1.6   Foreign Material.   There are many types of foreign material. The most common is organic. Laminates and B-stage are occasionally found with hairs or bugs trapped in the resin. MLB lamination can trap pieces of the plastic bag used to ship B-stage, or fragments from gloves and clean room garments. Sometimes, foreign material is visible through the board surface and can be detected by a careful visual inspection, but often it is hidden in the board and impossible to detect. The only real protection against foreign material is well-controlled clean rooms. Organic foreign material is a symptom of poor workmanship and a cause for rejection, but it is not always a serious reliability concern. Well-encapsulated organic material that does not lead to blisters or delamination is generally relatively harmless.

Another type of foreign material is metal slivers. Metal slivers are a much more serious problem than organic material because they often produce very small clearances, resulting in a serious reliability risk. The copper foil used for outerlayers is one source of metal slivers. Foil is cut to size and punched for tooling before it is used. If these mechanical operations are not carefully done, slivers are created. All copper foil used in MLB fabrication must be cleaned and inspected to ensure that it is completely free of copper slivers. Another source of slivers is the etched circuit lines themselves. When one innerlayer slides over another, tiny copper slivers are torn off the edges of the circuit lines. These slivers are a few tenths of a mil in diameter, and up to an inch long. The best way to avoid this source of slivers is to never stack etched layers without a protective separator.

14.1.1.7   Pink Ring.   Pink ring is a cosmetic defect in which a white or pink area is seen on an internal copper feature surrounding a plated hole. This appearance is caused by the presence of clean copper, free of the dark copper-oxide coating used as an adhesion promoter. Pink ring can extend 40 mil or more beyond the perimeter of the hole, but it never extends beyond the edges of the internal copper feature. In a worst case, pink rings from adjacent holes overlap. They are never seen on the vendor-treated side of a copper layer, and they can be hidden by large surface lands. To be detected in a finished board, an oxide-treated copper innerlayer must be visible. A microsection through a pink ring area often shows no evidence of a defect, but in some cases a small separation is visible between the copper layer and the adjacent B-stage.

There is considerable controversy on the reliability issues associated with pink ring, and most specifications tolerate limited amounts. Thermal shock studies show no evidence that the pink ring can propagate. The pink ring never spans isolated conductors, so there is no possibility of electrochemical activity. The crack is generally very narrow, and there is no evidence of significant chemical absorption. On the other hand, sometimes a large crack occurs and the resulting gap inhibits PTH plating, leading to severe neck-down in the PTH barrel. This creates a risk of a future PTH failure. Pink ring represents poor process conditions. There may be little risk in accepting a limited amount of pink ring, but the board fabricator should be held responsible for implementing root-cause solutions.

Pink ring occurs when a weak oxide bond is combined with aggressive drilling, resulting in a failure of the B-stage to copper bond during drilling. If the drill also heats the epoxy above T_g, it will pull epoxy upward during drill withdrawal, opening a small crack. During hole cleaning and electroless plating, acids dissolve the black oxide, leaving a pink ring.

One fix for pink ring is to bake the board after drilling. This allows the deformed epoxy around the hole to relax and seal the crack. Baking is not a root-cause solution for pink ring;

it is a repair operation that introduces a new process step. A better solution is to replace the black oxide surface treatment with a reduced oxide treatment. This increases adhesion and provides a surface resistant to acid attack, potentially hiding the problem. The best solution is to use less aggressive drilling conditions combined with an optimized reduced-oxide treatment. Less aggressive drilling includes fewer hits on a drill before it is changed and drilling fewer panels in a stack. Drilling is also improved if the designer omits nonfunctional lands. These lands reduce drill life and increase the heat that is generated by the drill.

14.1.2 Copper Surface Damage

A second class of MLB defects is dents and epoxy spots involving copper surfaces. For this discussion, dents include scratches and other forms of mechanical damage. Dents cause lifted photoresist, leading to shorts and clearance problems. Large dents in a conductor compromise conductor integrity. Dents in gold fingers are particularly serious because of the possibility of contact failures. Epoxy spots affect circuit yield by inhibiting plating and etching, leading to defective circuits. To avoid these problems, the MLB fabricator must strive to eliminate large dents and reduce smaller dents and epoxy spots to an absolute minimum.

14.1.2.1 Causes of Surface Damage. Whenever an MLB is handled, there is a risk of damage to the copper surface. The risk of damage during machine loading and unloading is generally recognized, and most fabricators carefully train operators on the need to handle panels with care. Well-designed automation will limit damage during handling steps.

Galling is a less well known source of surface defects. Whenever two clean metal surfaces come together, it is possible to form a small cold weld. Galling is the damage that occurs when the surfaces are separated, fracturing the cold weld. This is a well-known problem in relay contacts, but it also occurs between copper surfaces on MLB panels and between steel separators. In both cases, the solution is to keep the surfaces separated. The best way to do this is to use release sheets or slotted racks.

Poor cleanliness during lamination is another major source of surface defects. The separator sheets, which serve as a mold surface during lamination, must be clean. Foreign material trapped between the separator sheet and the MLB surface copper will cause dents. Epoxy dust will cause epoxy spots. Most fabricators make an effort to establish clean room conditions during stackup. However, their best efforts are frustrated by epoxy debris. Some solutions for epoxy debris are discussed in following sections.

14.1.2.2 Preventative Measures for Surface Damage. Epoxy dust that falls on internal layers is not a problem, because it melts into the B-stage during lamination, but dust falling on a surface copper sheet or on a separator leads to dents and epoxy spots. It is difficult to avoid this dust, because the stack-up operation uses dusty B-stage sheets. Among the techniques used to control epoxy dust are the following:

- Laminar flow air over the stack up area
- Ion sources in the incoming air stream to prevent static electricity
- Two operators at stack-up, one for B-stage and the other for Cu and separators
- Storage of B-stage on a low shelf below separators and copper
- Positive air flow over the B-stage storage shelf

Cured chunks of epoxy often find their way into the stack-up room, causing dents. One source is the resin that flows onto the separator sheet and into the tooling holes during lamination. If separator sheets are not completely cleaned after each use, cured epoxy will be carried into stack-up. One solution to this problem is to use a mold release on the separator. This inhibits epoxy sticking and eases cleaning. Lamination tooling pins and reusable compliant materials are another source of cured epoxy. Cured epoxy is shaved off dirty pins when separator sheets are added to the stack. The best practice is careful cleaning of anything that goes into the stack-up area and the use of mold release on pins and separators.

One way to minimize dents and epoxy spots is to preseal the copper foil to the separator sheet in a clean environment. A commercial product known as CAC™ does this. Figure 14.1 shows a cross section of a CAC sheet.

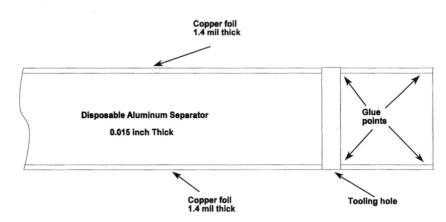

FIGURE 14.1   Diagram showing configuration of a CAC disposable separator.

The core of the CAC sandwich is a sheet of aluminum that serves as a disposable separator sheet. Copper foil is glued to each side of the aluminum, and tooling holes are punched through all three. As indicated, the glue joint connecting the copper foil to the aluminum is restricted to a small ring around each tooling hole and around the perimeter of the plate. The glue effectively seals out all foreign materials. In a standard stack-up, the operator completes an MLB by placing a sheet of copper foil, a steel separator, and another sheet of foil to start the next MLB. In a CAC stack-up, the separator and both sheets of foil are placed as a single part. This reduces stack-up labor and eliminates the possibility of anything getting trapped between foil and separator.

14.1.3 Mechanical Problems

A good MLB must be flat, satisfy a nominal thickness requirement, and be free of waviness and other types of thickness nonuniformity. These conditions are all difficult to achieve, and most specifications allow some deviation.

14.1.3.1 Warp.   The curvature of an MLB is called *warp.* This includes cylindrical curvature along one axis, as well as saddle shapes and spherical shapes in two axes. Warp is measured by supporting the board at three points and measuring the maximum deviation from the plane defined by these three points. The warp is the magnitude of this deviation divided by the greatest dimension of the board. For example, a board that measures 8 in by 16 in and has a 0.160-inch mil deviation from planarity is described as having a 1 percent warp (0.160 ÷ 16). Figure 14.2 shows an example of a board with a simple cylindrical warp and how warp is defined in this case.

Warped boards are a serious problem during assembly, and as device pitches decrease, the need for flat boards has grown. Older specifications allowed as much as 1.5 percent warp. Today most limit warp to 1.0 percent and some restrict it to as little as 0.5 percent.

Warp = D/L x 100%

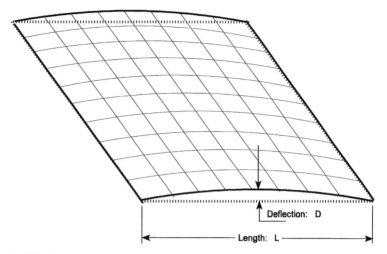

Deflection: D

Length: L

FIGURE 14.2 Example of stack-up asymmetry leading to warp.

The most common cause of warp is uneven cooling. This may occur during lamination, during board fabrication operations, or during assembly. The root cause is a large thermal gradient across the board as it cools through T_g. For example, when a board perimeter cools faster than its interior, the perimeter becomes rigid while the center is still rubbery. The perimeter then acts like a rigid band, producing out-of-plane distortions. This type of warp is called *extrinsic* to emphasize the fact that it is induced into an otherwise flat board. Extrinsic warp can be eliminated by heating the board above T_g and then cooling it slowly and uniformly.

Intrinsic warp is caused by a lack of symmetry in board design or materials. It does not disappear when the board is heated and cooled in a stress-free state. The only way to reduce intrinsic warp is to heat and cool the board under pressure. This "repair" is not advised, since the warp will generally return in subsequent thermal cycles.

For best results, MLB designs must be symmetrical with respect to a center plane. Asymmetric stack-ups often have intrinsic warp because differences in the coefficient of thermal expansion (CTE) cause internal stresses when the MLB is cooled from lamination. These stresses lead to warp. For best results, layer thicknesses and power planes placement must be symmetric. If this is not possible, a flat board can still be obtained if attention is given to the CTE values of the materials on the opposite side of the center plane.

Figure 14.3 shows two designs, each containing four innerlayers. The design on the left is asymmetrical. It has two 14-mil cores followed by two 5-mil cores. The arrangement of planes is also asymmetrical. The top four planes are S-P-S-P, while the bottom four are S-S-S-S. This MLB will show a large intrinsic warp. The design on the right stacks the same layers symmetrically. In this design the two 5-mil cores are on the outside and the two 14-mil cores are in the center. The planes are arranged symmetrically (SSPSSPSS). This structure will produce a flat MLB.

Material problems can cause random intrinsic warp. MLB materials are made by impregnating resin in a woven glass cloth. Warp can be caused by misalignment in the glass weave or when resin impregnation is heavier on one side of the cloth than the other. The weaving process is not symmetric and the two in-plane directions, called the *machine* and the *fill* directions, have different mechanical properties. If a sheet of glass is inadvertently rotated 90° it will cause severe warp. Some fabricators consciously cross-ply the B-stage material, but they maintain symmetry with respect to the center plane of the board.

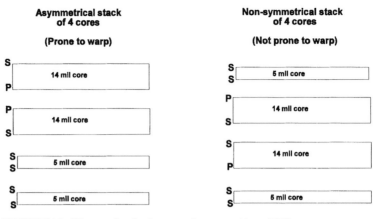

FIGURE 14.3   Diagram showing how warp is measured in an MLB.

14.1.3.2   *Incorrect Thickness.*   The nominal thickness of an MLB is an important parameter for many designs. An incorrect thickness is not a reliability problem, but it may affect system performance. The thickness of individual layers affects cross talk and impedance. Overall board thickness affects the proper function of connectors and latches. In some systems, excessively thick boards cause mechanical interferences. As a practical matter ±20 percent is a standard thickness tolerance. Tighter tolerances are possible, but they introduce design and manufacturing complexity.

The first step to thickness control is proper design. The B- and C-stage materials used to make an MLB come in discrete thicknesses. Often there is a conflict between a desired board thickness and the materials available. In this case, the design must be examined. Generally, a minor change in design parameters will allow the desired thickness to be achieved. As a rule of thumb, for a ±20 percent thickness tolerance, the design nominal must be within 5 percent of the target board thickness.

Material and process variations have a major impact on board thickness. During MLB lamination, resin flows out of the MLB. The final board thickness is determined by the initial resin amount, the glass thickness, and the resin flow. The first two parameters are controlled by the material vendor and are specified in terms of the treated weight of the B-stage. Resin flow is determined by lamination press parameters (temperature and pressure) and by B-stage rheology. The lamination process is generally well controlled and most flow variation comes from rheology variations.

B-stage rheology can be directly measured in a viscometer or indirectly determined by parameters such as gel time, resin flow, and scaled flow. Gel time and resin flow are not well correlated to press performance and are not recommended as material control parameters. The scaled flow test is a laboratory simulation of the lamination process. It uses an isothermal lab press operated at a pressure designed to give the same flow as the production press. Flow observed in this test is well correlated to the flow occurring during lamination. Many B-stage specifications include scale flow test limits.

14.1.3.3   *Nonuniform Thickness.*   Closely related to incorrect thickness is nonuniform thickness. This, too, causes mechanical problems with connectors, latches, card guides, etc. It is less of an issue for performance because the performance of a circuit is relatively insensitive to local thickness variations.

The root cause of nonuniform thickness is poor pressure distribution. MLBs are laminated in stacks of up to 12 panels. Separators are inserted between each board to isolate them from each other. However, even 0.062-in-thick steel is not completely effective, and a thinner separator, especially the aluminum used in CAC, is relatively ineffective. If a stack is all the same code, features can print through the entire stack. For the internal boards in a stack, this gives a slight dent on one side and a corresponding bump on the opposite. The resulting undulations of the surface are barely noticeable and there is little thickness variation. However, the top and bottom board in a stack are pressed against a rigid plate that prevents deflection. The compliant material used at the top and bottom of the lamination stack is designed to equalize pressure, but it is rarely completely effective and significant pressure variations occur over the area of a typical panel. Areas corresponding to a high copper density experience high pressure, resulting in thin spots in the panel. Areas corresponding to low copper density experience low pressure and are thick. This effect is particularly bad in areas adjacent to solid copper features such as panel borders or stiffeners. In this case, the stiffener region is thin and the adjacent board area is thick. This phenomenon is often described as a *wavy panel*.

Wavy panel problems can be reduced by using stiffer separators, thicker compliant materials, and lower lamination pressures. Unfortunately, these solutions increase costs and lower productivity. Another solution is to mix codes in a stack. This prevents the buildup of areas of high and low pressure. The problem with mixed codes is the difficulty in separating mixed lots. The best solution is to avoid sharp variations in copper density in the design. Noncircuit areas of a panel should be filled with a broken copper pattern such as dots or stripes. One approach uses a 50 percent density of 100-mil-wide dots of diamonds. Another approach uses a pattern of rays radiating from the panel center. The rays are about 1 in wide at the panel border and shrink to about 100 mil in the center. These rays fill any region not occupied by a board. In both cases, features on adjacent layers are staggered so that they do not fall on top of each other. Designs using these fillers have relatively uniform copper density and rarely give wavy panels.

14.1.4 Internal Misregistration

One of the greatest challenges in MLB manufacture is to obtain adequate innerlayer registration. All internal features must be registered accurately to each other, and they must all be accurately registered to the drilled holes. Hole-to-innerlayer misregistration creates two potential reliability problems: failure of the hole to line connection and shorts between holes and isolated conductors.

14.1.4.1 Breakout.   When a misaligned hole breaks out of its associated land, the area of connection becomes less than 360°. In an extreme case, where a misaligned hole cuts into a connecting circuit line, the connection area is reduced to the width of the line. When breakout occurs, poor drilling can cause land tearout. Many MLB users believe that these conditions represent a significant reliability hazard and prohibit hole breakout. Some even require a minimum annular ring as a margin of safety. Other users believe that tearout can be prevented by proper drilling, and allow breakout if the design includes *keyholes* to extend the land in the direction of connecting lines. Still others believe that a connection equal to the line width is adequate and allow unlimited breakout. The correct answer may depend on the PTH process used. In a well-controlled process with good drilling, hole cleaning, and plating, the metallurgical bond between an internal line and a barrel is as good as the line itself. There is no real reason to require a greater copper cross section at the barrel than elsewhere in the line. Indeed, technologies such as Multiwire™ that depend on a landless connection between a plated hole and an embedded wire are believed to be quite reliable. The only real reason for prohibiting breakout is to compensate for a poor PTH process. The real interconnection risk in a PTH comes from smear, and even a 360° connection is risky when covered with smear.

If breakout is allowed, a minimum clearance must be specified between a drilled hole wall and isolated internal features. A significant amount of substrate damage surrounds each drilled hole, and this region is affected by processing chemicals. If an isolated feature is too close to a hole wall there is a potential for shorts to develop when bias is applied. The minimum allowed clearance varies between specifications, but it generally falls in the range of 2 to 5 mil.

14.1.4.2   Region of Influence of a PTH.   If the process capability for the registration of a drilled hole to an internal feature is given by a value D, then for a drilled hole of diameter H there is an imaginary circle of diameter $H + 2D$ centered at the nominal center of the hole that defines all possible locations for hole wall. This is called the *region of influence* of the drilled hole. Figure 14.4 shows the relationship between the region of influence and the nominal location of the hole.

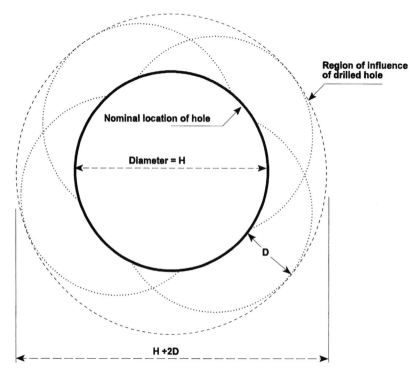

FIGURE 14.4   Region of influence of drilled hole with location uncertainty of D.

If breakout is prohibited, the size of all internal lands must be bigger than the region of influence of the hole. Figure 14.5 shows the relationship between minimum land size and the region of influence in the case where breakout is not allowed. As indicated by Fig. 14.5, the requirement of no breakout leads to rather large internal lands with a corresponding impact on internal routing density.

When breakout is allowed, the minimum land size can be reduced and the routing density increased. Unfortunately, the gain is relatively small because a minimum clearance is still needed between hole walls and isolated internal features. Figure 14.6 shows the situation for a hole of diameter H with a region of influence of diameter $H + 2D$ and a minimum hole to line spacing of C.

In this case, the designer must provide a spacing of at least $D + C$ between the nominal hole wall location and all isolated internal features. For example, a 13-mil hole may have a location

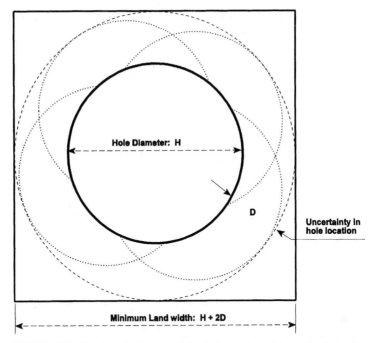

Hole Diameter: H

D

Uncertainty in
hole location

Minimum Land width: H + 2D

FIGURE 14.5 Region of influence of the hole and the minimum land size (no break out).

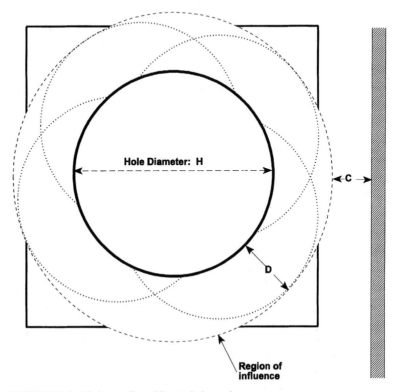

Hole Diameter: H

C

D

Region of
influence

FIGURE 14.6 Minimum allowed line-to-hole spacing.

uncertainty of 7 mils and require a minimum 5-mil isolation. The result is that each 13-mil diameter hole actually excludes routing from a circle 37 mil in diameter $(13 + 2 \times 7 + 2 \times 5)$. Replacing this hole with an 8-mil hole reduces the excluded region to 32 mil. The same gain can be achieved by reducing the location uncertainty from 7 to 4.5 mil. This emphasizes the importance of improving internal layer registration capability.

14.1.4.3   Mathematics of Registration.
The registration between drilled holes and the features on a layer can be described in terms of the superposition of two patterns. One pattern, the drilled holes, is considered to be accurate. The other pattern, representing the features on the layers, is treated as shifted and distorted.

Shifts can be represented as a combination of a rigid movement in *x*, a rigid movement in *y*, and a rotation. Figure 14.7 shows schematically how each of these affects the alignment between two patterns. The solid lines can be viewed as representing a hole pattern and the dotted lines a printed pattern. In the general case, all three components of rigid shift are combined.

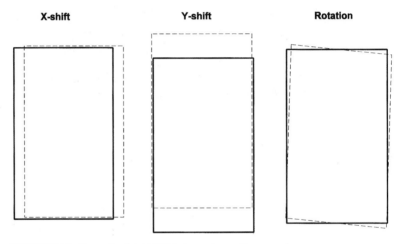

FIGURE 14.7   Example of rigid shift between two patterns.

Shifts can be caused by tooling errors at print, postetch punch (if used), stack-up, or drill. If only one layer is shifted, the problem is either print or artwork. If both sides of an innerlayer show the same shift, a problem probably occurred at postetch punch or at stack-up. If all layers are shifted with respect to the drill pattern, the most likely problem is a drill offset. Generally, careful diagnostics will determine the root cause.

Distortions observed in an MLB are generally linear. This means that size of the distortion is proportional to the *x* or *y* distance from the panel center. Any linear distortion can be represented as a combination of the following four deformations:

x growth   *x* deformation proportional to *x* distance from panel center
y growth   *y* deformation proportional to *y* distance from panel center
x shear   *x* deformation proportional to *y* distance from panel center
y shear   *y* deformation proportional to *x* distance from panel center

In reality, *x* shear, *y* shear, and rigid rotation are not independent, and it is often convenient to ignore rotation and capture it, as a combination of *x* shear and *y* shear.

Figure 14.8 shows schematically how each of the four linear distortions affects the alignment between two patterns. The solid lines can be viewed as representing a perfect pattern and the dotted lines a distorted pattern. In the general case, all four components of rigid shift are combined.

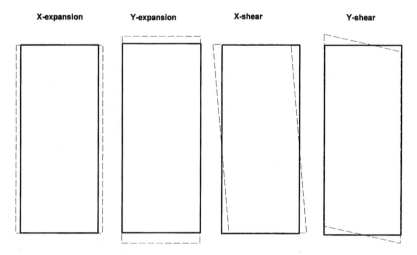

FIGURE 14.8   Example of the four linear pattern deformations.

One source of expansion is the laminate material. The innerlayer C-stage substrate shrinks when copper is etched. The etched panel shrinks further when its internal stresses are relaxed by heating above T_g. Another source of expansion is artwork which grows when heated or exposed to humidity. Careful environmental control is needed to avoid problems in this area. A third source of expansion is the lamination process. Although all three sources of expansion are important, the largest is the pattern shrinkage that occurs in lamination. Most fabricators compensate for this shrinkage by printing a slightly oversized image.

Shear deformation is generally small for symmetrical tooling. One source of shear deformation is a misalignment between the x and y axis on the drill machine. This will appear as a reproducible combination of x shear and y shear.

14.1.4.4 *Lamination Effects on Registration.*   With the exception of the lamination process, most of the contributors to misregistration can be minimized by paying attention to process details such as tooling accuracy, environmental control, and setups. Lamination effects are more complicated and account for most of the internal layer misregistration seen in a typical MLB process.

CTE Difference (C-Stage vs. B-Stage).   The CTE difference between B-stage and C-stage causes C-stage shrinkage during lamination. B-stage has more resin and a higher CTE than C-stage, so during the heat-up portion of the lamination cycle the B-stage expands more than the C-stage. After bonding, the two materials contract together with the result that the C-stage ends up in compression and the innerlayer pattern shrinks.

Resin Effects.   Resin cure and flow effects also contribute to misregistration. Epoxy shrinks slightly when it cures, causing some innerlayer shrinkage. The viscous drag associated with resin flow has a tendency to stretch the innerlayer, and if the flow is not perfectly centered, viscous drag will produce large lateral forces on an innerlayer, leading to innerlayer shifts.

CTE Difference (MLB vs. Tooling Plate).   Tooling pins are used to ensure layer-to-layer alignment. In most processes, the pins are locked to steel caul plates or to steel separator plates. If the CTE of the steel does not exactly match the CTE of the MLB, the pins will induce stresses in the MLB. Some fabricators try to combat this problem by using an overdetermined tooling system that locks the MLB to the steel at many points. Other fabricators use a pin-in-slot approach that allows some relative movement between the steel and the MLB.

Lamination Tooling Effects.   Some tooling systems use 20 or more pins. The hope is that by locking the MLB to steel, it will resist the lateral forces that tend to move the layers, thereby minimizing random shifts. It is also argued that the MLB will be constrained to expand and contract at the same rate as steel, giving a predictable lamination shrinkage. In reality, the forces associated with CTE mismatches are large, and even with 20 pins, innerlayer tooling holes tear slightly, resulting in unpredictable results. This approach also locks strains into the MLB that relax later, leading to unpredictable postlamination movement of tooling holes and internal features.

The four-slot system allows for thermal expansion mismatches during the heat-up portion of the lamination cycle. Unfortunately, resin flow fills the slots and prevents independent movement of the MLB during the cool-down cycle. One major weakness of the four-slot system is that it provides little resistance to lateral forces caused by uneven resin flow. Both overdetermined and four-slot systems have strong supporters. However, it is faster for an operator to stack on four pins, and the industry trend seems to be moving in that direction.

Insufficient Retained Copper.   Another area of disagreement among fabricators is the benefit of retained copper. One school of thought says that copper will stabilize a layer and give a smaller, more predictable shrinkage factor. Adherents to this theory avoid signal–signal layers and use heavy copper borders around all board images. Other fabricators report little advantage from added copper and avoid solid copper borders because of the connection between substrate defects and abrupt changes in copper density. The best compromise is to replace solid copper borders with a dot or stripe pattern. This provides adequate stability for lamination without causing blisters or voids.

14.1.4.5 Registration Tests.
Most innerlayer features are hidden in a finished MLB, so special coupons are needed to measure internal registration. The linear model previously discussed predicts a maximum misregistration at one corner of a board, so a good test must examine all four corners. Some specifications allow sample testing on a few boards per lot, while others require registration testing on all boards. Sample testing identifies systematic errors such as incorrect compensation or tooling errors; but it misses board-specific problems such as layer shifts or shrinkage variations.

Microsection, x ray, and electrical test are all used to measure registration. The microsection method requires a coupon with a pair of holes and internal lands at every layer. The lands are sized so that the hole falls outside of the land when misregistration exceeds its allowed limit. To fully test a board, eight microsections are required, one in the *x* direction and one in the *y* direction for all four corners. If any one microsection shows breakout, the board is rejected. Figure 14.9 shows the appearance of a test hole with unacceptable breakout. This method has the advantage of providing specific feedback on the nature of the registration failure, but it is slow and costly.

X ray is a popular way to measure registration. Several varieties of x-ray coupon are used. One approach is to use a copper feature with a clearance hole on every layer. A test hole is drilled through the feature. If any layer is improperly registered, the test hole will hit the copper feature. A collimated x-ray beam can be used to determine if any layer contacts the hole. An alternative coupon has a solid copper land on each layer. The x ray is then used to look for evidence of breakout on any layer. The major drawback of x-ray methods is poor resolution. This is a particular problem for high-layer-count boards where it is very difficult to resolve a single layer.

An electrically readable registration test coupon is a fast and unambiguous way to find misregistration. Figure 14.10 shows one configuration for an electrically readable registration

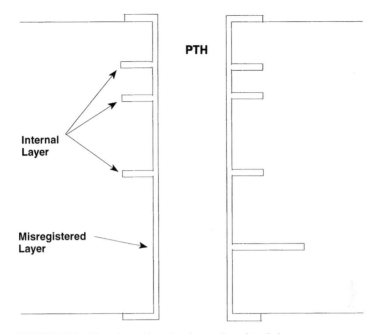

FIGURE 14.9 Misregistered layer in microsection of test hole.

Copper feature repeated on each layer

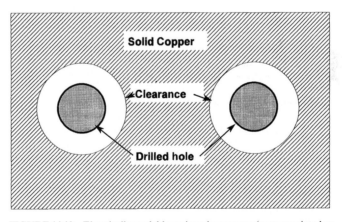

FIGURE 14.10 Electrically readable registration coupon (pattern printed on each innerlayer).

coupon. Each layer of this coupon has a copper feature with a clearance for two drilled holes. The size of the clearance is selected so that the nominal clearance between the edge of the feature and the hole wall is equal to the registration tolerance for that layer. On a properly registered layer, both holes pass through a clearance and are electrically isolated. However, if any layer is misregistered, the two holes short. This coupon is small and can be placed within a board image or on the MLB panel close to a board. The coupon is easy to test manually with an inexpensive continuity tester, or it can be tested automatically as part of final board electrical test.

14.1.5 Connection Flaws

Connection flaws are defined as flaws in the circuit or the PTHs. These include improper circuit width, nicks, reduced clearances, ionic contamination, and PTH flaws such as barrel cracks, epoxy smear, and innerlayer separation. None of these prevent the board from actually working, but if bad enough, all will cause future failure. Most specifications have limits on these flaws, and the limits are generally conservative. If specification limits are met, there is little reliability concern. The problem is that these defects are difficult to detect, and they often find their way into finished boards, leading to field failures. The answer is not to tighten specifications; rather it is to insist on root-cause solutions that will prevent the defects.

14.1.5.1 *Improper Circuit Width.* Improper circuit width is caused by etching, plating, or artwork problems. On controlled-impedance boards, improper circuit width will cause impedance errors that compromise functionality. Wide circuits cause narrow clearances and the risk of electromigration failures. Narrow circuits limit current-carrying ability. If a narrow circuit is designed to carry a high current, perhaps for a short time during a fault condition, the circuit will function until the fault condition occurs. It then overheats, damaging the MLB.

Circuit width problems can be detected by impedance measurements and by dc resistance measurements. Most causes of improper width affect an entire lot, so a sample test on a few test circuits is a good screen for the lot. The root-cause solution is good statistical process control (SPC) during manufacture. Problems are generally caused by processes operating outside normal limits. A well-controlled MLB process will deliver 10 percent control on line width at a very high confidence level, and should be able to achieve 5 percent control with limited screening.

14.1.5.2 *Nicks.* A nick in a circuit is defined as a local region where the circuit width is reduced. Nicks are caused by handling damage, artwork flaws, foreign material, and substrate dents. In practice, the length of a nick can vary from a few mil up to 100 mil, but is rarely any longer. It is not unusual to see nicks that reduce the circuit width to a few mil or less.

A nick is an alarming cosmetic feature, but unless it reduces circuit width to almost zero it is not a cause for failure. Since nicks are short they have no effect on high-frequency operation until the frequency approaches the 100-GHz range, which is well above the operating range of standard MLB materials. The high thermal conductivity of copper makes it a poor fuse, and even very deep nicks will carry high currents. The dc resistance added to a circuit by a nick is very small. As an example, a 1-oz copper circuit that is 10 mil wide by 3 in long has a dc resistance of about 300 mΩ. If that circuit has a nick that reduces its width to 1 mil over a distance of 20 mil (an extreme nick), the circuit resistance is increased by 20 mΩ (less than extending the circuit length by 0.2 in or reducing average width by 0.7 mil).

The major risk associated with nicks is the potential for circuit opens during mechanical handling or thermal cycling. This risk is minimized if the circuit is encapsulated by solder mask or, in the case of innerlayers, by cured epoxy. Nevertheless, nicks are a concern and most specifications limit them.

Automatic optical inspection (AOI), which is used on innerlayers, is a good screen for nicks, but it is rarely used on outerlayers. Most fabricators depend on human inspectors to find outerlayer nicks. Nicks occur at random, are very small, and are isolated. Human inspectors have difficulty finding them. The best defense against outerlayer nicks is a high-yield outerlayer process. Nicks and opens are caused by the same conditions, so any process with few opens also has few nicks. In fact, given their relatively low risk and the ineffectiveness of visual inspection, it may be cost effective to waive inspection for nicks in any process with a low frequency of opens.

14.1.5.3   Reduced Clearances.   Although clearance violations can be caused by wide circuits, they are more likely to be caused by unetched copper protrusion from a circuit line. Like nicks, protrusions are generally small and are caused by poor handling, damaged artwork, foreign material, and substrate dents. They can easily reduce clearances to a few mil or less.

The risk associated with narrow clearances is that electrochemical activity may produce dendrites bridging the gap. For clean boards operating at the voltages used in most electronic circuits, there appears to be little risk of this failure. The proof of this is that high-density boards perform reliably at a design ***nominal*** of 3 mil or less, and thin boards perform reliably with a single 2.8-mil-thick sheet of B-stage separating layers. In spite of this experience base, some specifications set a minimum line-to-line spacing of 5 mil or greater and require two sheets of B-stage for layer-to-layer spacings below 5 mil. This is very conservative.

For standard MLBs, the inspection situation for protrusions and clearance flaws is similar to that for nicks. AOI is an excellent screen for innerlayers, and the best defense against outerlayer defects is a high-yield process. A process with few shorts will also have few clearance faults, and it may be cost effective to waive inspection for clearances in a process with a low frequency of opens.

One situation in which a narrow space is very undesirable is in a circuit operating at high voltage. In circuits that must withstand high voltage for short periods, such as an occasional fault condition, dielectric breakdown across small clearances can lead to severe dielectric damage. Fortunately, the dielectric strength of epoxies and solder mask exceeds 1000 V/mil, and dielectric breakdown between completely encapsulated circuits is rarely an issue. Breakdown occurs at much lower voltages when a narrow clearance is combined with a dielectric void or a solder-mask skip. Voids and solder-mask skips are also a problem for circuits that must operate continuously at high voltage. In this case, the void is an excellent site for dendritic grown. In other words, *narrow clearances coupled with voids or solder-mask skips are a reliability problem for MLBs that must operate at high voltage.* The best approach for high-voltage applications is to test all high-voltage nets with an applied voltage of 750 to 1000 V. This will produce breakdown at potential failure sites.

14.1.5.4   Ionic Contamination.   Many MLB process steps include exposure to strong ionic chemicals. Any residue from these processes that contaminates innerlayers or finished boards is a serious reliability threat. Ambient moisture will produce ionization that will support leakage currents leading to dendritic growth. To prevent this failure, boards must be clean. The most effective way to ensure clean boards is good process controls coupled with regular process monitoring.

Two types of tests are used to monitor ionic contamination. One measures *insulation resistance* (IR) and the other uses extraction methods to measure ionic material. There are several variations of the IR test, all using a test coupon containing parallel lines. The coupon is exposed to a high humidity and the leakage current between the lines is measured. High leakage current is taken as a sign of contamination. The IR test is sensitive to small islands of contamination and it detects contaminants that have low solubility. On the other hand, it is slow to perform and requires a special coupon.

In the extraction method, the board is soaked in a mixture of alcohol and water to dissolve any ionic contaminates. The average density of ionic material on the board can be calculated from the change in conductivity of the bath and the area of the board. The extraction method is quick and can be performed on an actual board. However, it can miss insoluble salts, and it is not sensitive to small isolated spots of contamination.

For best results, both IR and extraction monitors should be used. A good strategy is to do extract conductivity tests once every shift at the following process points:

- Innerlayer prior to laminate
- MLB panel prior to solder mask
- Finished MLB

IR test coupons should be run through the entire process including soldering operations at least once a week.

14.1.5.5 PTH Flaws. The plated hole is the heart of an MLB. A modern MLB may contain more than 10,000 holes, and if one hole fails, the board fails. One type of PTH failure is the loss of barrel integrity. Incomplete plating can cause pinholes and ring voids. Thin or brittle plating leads to stress cracking during soldering or system operation. A second class of failure is related to connection integrity. Epoxy smear or poor copper adhesion can lead to marginal joints that separate in a thermal shock. All of these conditions raise serious reliability concerns.

With thousands of holes per board there is no way to inspect quality into plated holes. Even if a coupon is tested on every board, the sampling rate is low on a per-hole basis, and in a poor process there is no guarantee that boards with passing coupons are significantly better than boards with failing coupons. The only way to ensure reliable plated holes is to establish a robust process that produces no failures.

One way to maintain a robust process is to establish SPC limits for all critical variables at drill, electroless plate, and electrolytic plate. The process should never be operated if any variable falls outside limits.

Another safeguard is frequent PTH testing with immediate corrective action when any evidence of process drift is seen. As a minimum, metallurgical cross sections would be taken from the plated product hourly. If any evidence is seen of poor drilling, poor plating, voids, barrel cracks, epoxy smear, or interface cracks (postseparation), immediate corrective action must be taken. In addition, regular product samples should be tested for the same conditions. A good process should be able to pass these tests with few if any failures.

14.2 ELECTRICAL PERFORMANCE

MLB conductor layers can be described as either signal (S) or power/ground (P/G). As the names imply, S layers interconnect signals and P/G planes distribute power and ground. In addition, P/G planes provide impedance reference, shield cross talk, and control electromagnetic interference (EMI). These functions add design complexity and place demands on the dielectric properties of materials.

At low speed, the signal transit time is much less than its rise time, or in the case of analog signals, the transit time is much less than the period of the signal. In this limit, the signal line is an equipotential surface. The most significant signal loss is a small voltage drop due to the ohmic resistance of the trace. Other than isolating circuits, the properties of the insulator are unimportant.

At high speeds, the circuit can no longer be viewed as operating at one voltage, and the electric fields in the insulator become important. The conductor becomes a transmission line and the PCB a waveguide. Reflections occur at impedance discontinuities, and signal loss occurs through skin effect and dielectric loss. Signals couple through cross talk and radiate to the environment through EMI effects.

As a rule of thumb, low speed limits apply until the time of travel of a signal approaches half the signal rise time of a digital signal or half the period of an analog signal. When the travel time approaches these limits, voltage gradients along the signal path become important and the time for signal transmission adds significant delay time to the circuit.

The velocity of the signal is the speed of light divided by the square root of the dielectric constant. For epoxy MLBs, transmission speed is approximately 6 in/ns. This means that in a 6-in-long circuit, transmission line effects become important at a rise time of 2 ns, and for analog signals, at a frequency of 500 MHz. In low dielectric materials, transmission speeds increase to 8.5 in/ns and transmission line effects become important in a 6-in circuit at 1.4 n/s rise time and 708 MHz analog frequencies—not a big change.

14.2.1 Controlled Impedance (CI)

Characteristic impedance Z_0 is an important transmission line parameter. If the impedance of different parts of a circuit are mismatched, high-speed signals reflect at the discontinuity, much as light reflects at the surface of a pool of water. The result is a loss of signal strength and reflected pulses that cause timing problems and false triggers. For CI applications, the Z_0 of critical circuits must be within 10 percent of nominal for reliable performance.

The Z_0 of a circuit is equal to the square root of L/C, where L is the circuit self-inductance and C is the capacitance to ground. The parameters L and C are determined by the circuit geometry and the properties of the dielectric. Figure 14.11 shows three possible transmission line configurations. When the signal line is on the board surface and there is one buried P/G plane, the configuration is called *surface microstrip*. A *buried microstrip* configuration is identical to the surface microstrip except the signal line is covered by dielectric. In the *stripline* configuration, one or two signal layers are sandwiched between two P/G planes. For all three configurations, impedance is increased by increasing the dielectric spacing or decreasing line width. Analytical expressions for Z_0 have been published for these configurations.*

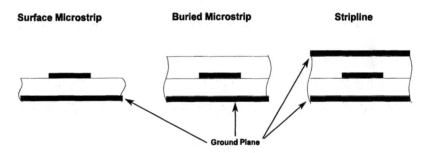

FIGURE 14.11   Comparisons of three transmission line configurations.

For standard epoxy, the dielectric thickness and the line width needed to achieve 50 Ω are approximately equal. For material systems with a lower dielectric constant, 50 Ω corresponds to line widths that slightly exceed the dielectric thickness. As a rule of thumb, the CI tolerance will be met if the percent tolerance on both line width and dielectric thickness are as good as the percent tolerance on CI. For example, in a design with 10-mil lines and a 10 percent CI tolerance, the required tolerances on both line width and dielectric thickness are approximately 1 mil. For 5-mil lines, the tolerance shrinks to 0.5 mil.

Tight tolerances present a severe challenge in manufacturing CI boards. Imaging processes must be carefully controlled to hold line width tolerances of 10 percent on fine lines. Some fabricators inspect innerlayers to ensure that line width tolerances are achieved. It is likely that successful manufacture of fine-line CI products will require new specifications on raw material to ensure tighter control of properties such as C-stage thickness, B-stage flow properties, and resin content. Dielectric constant variation is generally small, but care must be taken to account for changes in resin content that might be associated with material substitutions.

14.2.2 Signal Attenuation at High Frequency

At very high frequency, dielectric loss and skin effect become important. For analog circuits, these effects attenuate the signal strength. For a digital signal, they attenuate the high-frequency components of a pulse, resulting in an increase in the rise time.

---

* *Electronics Material Handbook,* vol. 1, Packaging ASM International, Materials Park, Ohio, 1989, pp. 601–603.

14.2.2.1   Dielectric Loss.   Dielectrics contain dipole molecules that are capable of absorbing energy from a high-frequency signal. This is how a microwave oven heats organic materials. In a transmission line, the amount of energy absorbed is proportional to the length of the line, the frequency of the signal, and a property of the dielectric called *tan* δ. For standard MLB materials, tan δ is 0.02. This gives serious signal losses at frequencies above 1 GHz. For circuits operating at 1 GHz or higher, a material like PTFE (tan δ = 0.001) is preferred.

14.2.2.2   Skin Effect.   The skin effect is the result of self-inductive effects that force high-frequency currents to the surface of a conductor. As the frequency of the signal increases, the thickness of the conducting "skin" decreases and the dc resistance increases. The skin effect resistance is proportional to the square root of the frequency and is independent of dielectric constant.* As an example, at a frequency of 0.1 GHz, the skin depth is 0.25 mil and the dc resistance of a 5-mil-wide, 1-mil-thick copper conductor doubles from 0.13 to 0.26 Ω/in. At a frequency of 10 GHz, the skin depth drops to 25 μin and the effective resistance increases to 2.6 Ω/in. This means that in the GHz frequency range, power losses due to the skin effect are important and wide traces are required.

14.2.3   Signal Coupling at High Frequencies

High-frequency electrical signals generate electric fields that radiate energy. When energy is coupled to a nearby circuit, it is called *cross talk*. When the energy is radiated to the environment, it is called *electromagnetic interference* (EMI). Both effects have a serous implication for high-speed MLBs.

14.2.3.1   Cross Talk.   When two electrical circuits are sufficiently close to each other, a signal in one induces a spurious signal in the other. This effect, called cross talk, is a serious problem for the high-speed, high-density circuits. Cross talk is measured by a coupling coefficient that gives the magnitude of the signal induced in the "quiet" or nondriven line as a function of the magnitude of the signal applied to the driven line. Coupling increases with signal speed and with proximity between nets.

Cross talk can occur between circuits on different layers (interlayer) or between circuits on the same layer (intralayer). Interlayer coupling is high for parallel, overlapping paths, but it is completely screened by intervening P/G planes Most designs are routed on layer pairs, using orthogonal routing rules, with circuits on one layer going in the *x* direction and circuits on the other going in the *y* direction. Layer pairs are isolated from other layer pairs by a P/G plane. The result is that there are no parallel circuits on adjacent layers and very little interlayer cross talk.

The quantitative details of the intralayer coupling coefficient are complex and are given elsewhere.† Qualitatively, intralayer cross talk is minimized by keeping a wide space between parallel lines and by avoiding long runs of parallel circuits. Unfortunately, these solutions reduce interconnection density, requiring a tradeoff between cross talk and interconnection density. Intralayer coupling is also reduced by nearby P/G layers. Coupling is not directly affected by the dielectric constant, but for any specified impedance, a lower dielectric constant allows a reduced line-to-layer spacing, giving lower cross talk for the same lines and spaces. This option is very important for high-speed designs and is one of the reasons for using low-dielectric-constant materials.

In summary, orthogonal routing on adjacent layer pairs prevents excessive interlayer cross talk. Intralayer cross talk is minimized by selecting the maximum line-to-line spacing consistent with routing needs, and by using low-dielectric-constant materials. Design audits must be used to minimize the length of parallel runs on the same layers.

---

* *Electronics Material Handbook,* vol. 1, Packaging ASM International, Materials Park, Ohio, 1989, p. 603.

Electronics Material Handbook, vol. 1, Packaging ASM International, Materials Park, Ohio, 1989, pp. 35–41.

14.2.3.2 Electromagnetic Interference (EMI). A high-speed circuit radiates electromagnetic energy to the environment and can produce unacceptable interference in nearby electronics. Often, entire systems must be shielded to minimize EMI. Unfortunately, shielding is not 100 percent effective, and it is best to reduce EMI at its source. Outer ground planes effectively screen emissions coming from internal signal layers. One way to reduce EMI is to make the outermost innerlayer a P/G layer, and to restrict outerlayer routing to short fanout patterns.

EMI from RF circuits will also cause interference in circuits on the same board. One solution is to isolate RF circuits on a separate, well-shielded board. This works for some applications but is not always practical. Another solution is to isolate RF circuits in a well-shielded part of the board. If the board is large enough, this can be accomplished by dedicating one part of the board to RF and the rest to non-RF circuits. The RF portion is then totally enclosed by a metal shield. For applications like cellular phones, this approach makes the board too large. In this case, RF circuits can be restricted to one side of the board and non-RF to the other. This works well if the RF region is completely screened by a surface enclosure and a buried ground plane, and *no PTHs connect the two regions.* The restriction on PTHs leads to the use of blind holes for these applications.

CHAPTER 15

MANUFACTURING INFORMATION DOCUMENTATION AND TRANSFER

Clyde Parrish
PC World, Division of Circuit World Corp., Toronto, Canada

15.1 INTRODUCTION

The manufacturing of printed circuit boards (PCBs) begins with the soft-tooling process. This process is the transformation of customer computer-aided design (CAD) data into the necessary tools required for manufacturing the bare printed circuit board. The typical tools required for manufacturing printed circuit boards include artwork for photoprinting of inner conductive layers, outer conductive layers, and solder mask patterns. Artwork is also created for screen printing patterns for nomenclature and via-plugging layers. Additional tools required include drill and routing numerical controlled (NC) programs, electrical testing netlists and fixtures, and CAD reference soft-tools. During the tooling process, the bill of materials (BOM) and process routing are also defined.

During the tooling process, the customer part numbers are analyzed to determine the compatibility of the design features with the manufacturing process capabilities. Additionally, attempts to optimize the manufacturing of the product at the lowest cost is a primary goal. However, the majority of the costs have been defined before the design is transmitted to the manufacturing site by the PCB designer. An early investment in time by the PCB design team and the manufacturing tooling team can result in the most significant savings in overall product cost.

This chapter describes the PCB tooling process, as defined in Fig. 15.1, including the transfer of information, design reviews, optimization of materials, definition of BOM and routings, tool creation, and additional processes that are required.

15.2 INFORMATION TRANSFER

The tooling process begins with the receipt of information from the customer. This information historically has been transferred via mail or overnight delivery. Increasingly over the past 10 years the communication between design site and manufacturer has been via electronic means to reduce lead times. Unfortunately, although the time required to send information to the manufacturer has decreased to minutes or hours from day(s), a significant issue with the provision of packages to manufacturers is the completeness of the information provided.

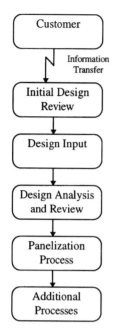

FIGURE 15.1   The soft-tooling process.

The following sections define the basic information required to transmit and methods for communication.

15.2.1   Information Required

Timely tooling of a part number depends on having the correct information. All features required to exist on the PCB must be defined to the manufacturer. The information is defined via design data, drawings, and textual information. The information and common data formats required to permit the tooling of the PCB include the following:

- Part number information

  Information: This information defines the part number to be built, including revision number, releases, dates, etc.

  Format: This information is typically provided in the part drawing or may be provided as an additional text file.

- Part drawing

  Information: This drawing may contain specific design requirements such as material requirements, controlled impedance requirements, solder mask type, nomenclature color, and dimensional tolerances.

  Format: Common formats for drawings are HP-GL and PostScript.

- Drill drawing

  Information: Although the drill data is provided via data files, this information typically contains only the location of holes and the tool number. The tool number is referenced against the drill drawings to determine the required sizes, plating status, size tolerances, and the total count for verification.

  Format: Common formats for drawings are HP-GL and PostScript.

- Subpanel drawing

  Information: Many assembly operations require boards to be provided in a subpanel form (many parts on one shippable unit). The drawings will define the orientation and position of each part, the subpanel dimensions, tooling hole information, special markings, and specific manufacturing processes and tolerances.

  Format: Common formats for drawings are HP-GL and PostScript.

- Artwork data

  Information: This data consists of files for each circuitry, coating (e.g., solder mask), or marking (i.e., nomenclature) layer.

  Format: The data required is usually RS-274, commonly called *Gerber data.* Gerber data is provided as a standard output from most PCB CAD systems.

- Aperture list files

  Information: The definitions of the shapes used for drawing are required for each layer provided of artwork data. Special shapes like thermal pads should specifically define its method of construction.

  Format: This information is usually provided as a text file, although the information may also be defined in the beginning of the individual artwork files, including constructions of complex apertures.

- Drill data

  Information: This information may consist of a single or multiple file(s), and defines the location and tool number used for each hole in the PCB. The files required should define all plated, unplated (can be combined with plated if fully defined), buried via, and blind via layers.

  Format: Common data files provided are Excellon format.

- Drill tool files

  Information: This information describes the size, plating status, layer-from and layer-to (in the case of buried and blind vias), and file names. This information is referenced against the drill drawing.

  Format: This information is usually provided as a text file, although the information may also be defined in the beginning of the individual drill files.

- Special requirements information

  Information: The drawing or a file should describe any special requirements not defined in other information. It is important for the PCB designer not to assume that requirements are understood, but to refer to specifications or clearly define the requirements.

  Format: This information is typically provided in the part drawing or may be provided as an additional text or drawing file.

- Netlist data

  Information: Netlist data defines the connectivity of the circuitry.

  Format: This information can be provided from the CAD systems in various formats, or it can be extracted from the drill and artwork data. Contact the PCB manufacturer for compatible formats, if the netlist data is to be provided directly. The Institute for Interconnecting and Packaging Electronic Circuits (IPC) has defined a neutral format, IPC-356, which provides all the information necessary for netlist and electrical test fixture creation.

The IPC has defined an alternative neutral format for most of the previously defined data which provides simpler processing at the manufacturer, IPC-350. This format can be generated by most PCB CAD systems and processed by most PCB CAM/tooling systems. The PCB customer should review the compatibility of this format with the PCB manufacturer prior to sending.

15.2.2 Modem Transmission

Currently, the most popular means for transmitting data from design site to manufacturing site is via personal computer modem transmission. Two popular methods for communications are:

1. Dedicated connection to waiting compatible software

2. Bulletin board–type service

Method 1 is the simplest means to initiate communication. Almost any communication package can provide the capability, for example, X-Modem or Windows terminal. Method 2 provides a more robust environment similar in concept to CompuServe. Each user has an individual account logon and password.

15.2.3 Internet Transmission

Several methods are available for connecting to the Internet, depending upon the volume of data, the interactiveness required, and the budget. Typically, a company will utilize a UNIX-based machine for accessing the Internet. UNIX-based computers are used to provide multi-user/multitasking capabilities (i.e., two or more people may be performing a task at the same time). Personal computers can also provide access depending on the functionality and interactiveness desired. The following describes some of the alternatives available:

- *User-Account on Internet Provider's Computer.* This is the least expensive method for gaining access to the Internet. The account is accessed via dial-up modem connection, running a terminal emulation program. Many Internet providers offer this service. Monthly account fees are available for a minimal charge for each account, depending on disk storage requirements. Individual accounts may be maintained for each customer to provide security between customers. Transmission of data from the provider's machine may be provided via popular transfer protocols (e.g., X-Modem), dependent on your Internet provider. The communication speed is limited to modem speed, typically 14,400 baud.

- *Interactive Dial-Up.* This method provides direct communication to customers, through prior contact and the internal initiation of the connection. The communications between the internal computer and the Internet provider computer is typically via Serial Line Internet Protocol (SLIP) or Point-to-Point Protocol (PPP) software. These software packages provide the continuation of network communication from internal systems to the Internet provider. This service can cost less than $100 per month.

- *Dedicated Dial-Up.* Dedicated dial-up lines are similar to the interactive dial-up, except that a dedicated phone number is provided. The connection to the Internet can be used either for interactive or for continuous-connection dial-up service. This service will cost slightly more than the interactive dial-up service, due to the dedicated line costs at the Internet provider.

- *Leased Lines.* Leased lines provide continuous, high-speed communications between a company and its Internet provider. They are also the most expensive, ranging from several hundred to several thousand dollars per month.

Security of the machines connected to the Internet is of prime importance. Any direct connections (i.e., not the user account just described) to the Internet are usually handled by dedicated machines acting as a firewall to prevent unauthorized entry into a firm's network, as outlined in Fig. 15.2.

There are numerous books available about the Internet and how to connect to it. There are also numerous consulting firms available to assist in the process, which is nontrivial, to prepare a secure connection.

15.3 INITIAL DESIGN REVIEW

The purpose of the initial design review is to determine the potential fit of the product to the manufacturing facility, determine general cost information, and prepare for tooling. Proper upfront analysis of a product prior to manufacturing or tooling, results in a reduction in waste of time and materials.

It is the responsibility of the manufacturing site to determine the fit of a given product to its capabilities. PCB manufacturing sites should monitor and maintain a list of manufacturing capabilities and a technology roadmap of where the facility is developing additional process capabilities. This list of capabilities will define the acceptability of a product for manufacturing, or whether the product is a research and development project.

15.3.1 Design Review

Reviewing the incoming package for design requirements (e.g., line width and spacing) versus the PCB manufacturing capabilities will define the capability for manufacturing, and provide

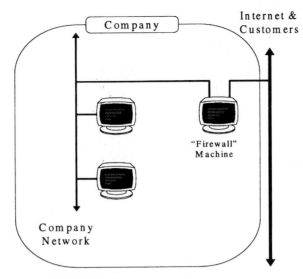

FIGURE 15.2 Typical Internet connection.

a prediction of the resulting yield. Among the design characteristics that should be reviewed against process capabilities are the following:

Item	Issue
Maximum number of layers	Higher-layer-count products require greater control of processes and tooling tolerances.
Board thickness	Some process or handling equipment may have limitations on board thickness (either too thin or too thick).
Minimum feature width	Finer line widths require better control of artwork and process tolerances. In addition, the relationship of line width to copper weight is significant in providing a well-defined line. Fine lines with lower copper weights are easier to manufacture than fine lines with higher copper weights.
Minimum feature spacing	Finer feature spacing requires better control of artwork and process tolerances. In addition, the relationship of feature spacing to copper weight is significant. Fine spaces with lower copper weights are easier to manufacture than fine spaces with higher copper weights.
Minimum finished hole size	Smaller holes require higher manufacturing process capabilities and imply (due to design characteristics) finer tolerances on tooling and internal registration systems.

Maximum aspect ratio	Small holes and thick boards result in difficulty during the plating processes and can result in defective products that may or may not pass electrical testing. Plating high-aspect-ratio holes requires chemistry and process parameter enhancements.
PCB dimensional tolerances	Fine PCB profile or cutout tolerances may result in punching/blanking requirements versus routing, or changes in the routing parameters or programming.
Feature-to-feature tolerances	Location of features on the PCB to other features may require alternative materials or process changes to reduce the tolerances.
Hole size tolerances	Consistency in the plating process versus selected drilling hole size and plating densities have significant impact on the capability to control hole tolerances. Adjustments to the PCB design, drill hole size selection, or process parameters may be required to produce an acceptable product with tighter tolerances.

15.3.2 Material Requirements

Determination of the bill of materials is required during the initial analysis of the design. The determination of the BOM and other material-processing requirements will define the manufacturing facility's capability to produce and its material cost structure. In addition, the definition of the material requirements will be the basis for the generation of the process traveler requirements.

The primary materials requiring definition are those included in the BOM, including laminates, prepregs, copper foil, solder mask, and gold. The materials may be explicitly defined by the PCB customer (e.g., usage of a specific solder mask), or may be implied in the drawings or specifications provided with the tooling package.

Several factors impact the selection of the raw materials, including the following:

- Customer-defined physical constraints, for example, the definition of the physical dimensions between conductive layers
- Customer specification of electrical properties, for example, the definition of the impedance requirements on certain layers
- Manufacturing process capabilities related to lamination thicknesses and tolerances
- Specification of material dielectric requirements, for example, the usage of FR-4 or polyimide
- Specifications of physical operating parameters, for example, the minimum requirements of the glass transition temperature

The determination of the laminates, prepregs and copper foils are based upon the following:

- Standard constructions for the PCB manufacturer of a defined PCB layer count, final thickness, copper weight, and dielectric spacing.
- Custom constructions based on defined physical constraints (e.g., minimum dielectric spacing). These custom constructions are defined through knowledge of the lamination pressing

thickness of materials vs. copper circuitry densities, and the availability of materials from suppliers.

* Custom constructions based on defined electrical property constraints. These custom constructions are typically defined via equations or software models provided with certain product parameters.

The determination of solder mask is based on the customer specifications and drawings. Once the acceptability of the solder masks is defined, the selection of the acceptable masks by the PCB manufacturer is based on either preferred process (due to volume or cost) or the design characteristics' interaction with the solder mask. These design characteristics include the following:

* *Tenting of vias*—A dry film solder mask may be preferred over liquid photoimageable solder mask with a secondary via plugging process.
* *Platable area densities/higher external copper weights*—Thin solder masks may not be able to ensure coverage of high plating.
* *Secondary processes*—Post-solder-mask processes may chemically or mechanically alter the appearance of certain solder masks.

The determination of gold requirements are based on the thickness and area of the gold. These factors can be used to calculate the requirement of gold per PCB product.

15.3.3 Process Requirements

The selection of the proper product routing (or traveler) is critical to the upfront analysis of the product acceptability to manufacturing. Considering a typical multilayer PCB product, the product routings can be broken into two parts: the innerlayer pieces and the outerlayer piece.

The product routings of the innerlayer pieces are fairly standard, and are typically as follows:

Step	Typical process requirements
Layer cleaning	Cleaning of the laminate surface via either mechanical or chemical cleaning processes
Imaging	Coating of the laminate with photoresist material and the exposure of the photoresist with artwork defining the innerlayer pattern
Develop-etch-strip (DES)	Developing of the photoresist, etching of the exposed copper, and stripping of the remaining photoresist
Innerlayer inspection	Inspection of the innerlayer piece to the PCB design intent
Oxide	Coating of the innerlayer piece with an oxide layer prior to lamination

One of the few decision points in innerlayer manufacturing is whether the product will require inspection. This decision can be based on the manufacturing facility's process capabilities and the design of the specific innerlayer piece. For example, if the process capability for innerlayer manufacturing of designs at 0.008-in lines and spaces is 100 percent yield, and the product has been designed at or above 0.008-in lines and spaces, then the product may not require inspection. Typically, the design package will identify the design technologies (e.g., line width and spacing), however, these should be confirmed during the design analysis and review stage.

The product routings of the outerlayer pieces define the finished product appearance and, as a result, are more complex. Assuming a pattern plating process, the typical outerlayer process routings for a SMOBC/HASL (solder mask over bare copper/hot-air solder level) product is as follows:

Step	Typical process requirements
Lamination	Lamination of innerlayer pieces with prepreg and copper foils to create the outerlayer piece
Drilling	Addition of the holes providing pathways for electrical conductivity between outer layer and innerlayer pieces, and other PCB design purposes
Electroless copper plating	Deposition of copper on the surface and in the holes of the product, providing the conductivity necessary for electroplating
Imaging	Coating of the panel with photoresist material, the exposure of the photoresist with artwork defining the outerlayer pattern, and the developing of the outerlayer pattern
Electroplate copper	The plating of the final circuitry of the product
Tin plating	Sacrificial plating over the final circuitry of the product
Strip-etch-strip (SES)	Stripping of the remaining photoresist, etching of the exposed copper, and stripping of the sacrificial plating
Solder mask	Coating of the bare copper product with either dry film or liquid photoimageable solder mask, exposing of the panel with the PCB customer-supplied artwork pattern, developing of the pattern (exposing the sites requiring solder), and curing of the solder mask
Nomenclature	Screening of the nomenclature onto the panel and curing
HASL	Coating the exposed copper sites with solder, leveling to the customer's requirements of thickness
Depanelization	NC routing of the PCB products from the manufacturing panel
Electrical testing	Electrical testing of the product for conformance to the PCB design
Inspection	Verification of product conformance to specifications prior to shipment to the PCB customer

After the electroplate copper operation, the process may change to meet the surface finish requirements. Some of the alternative steps affecting the outerlayer product routing include the following:

Item	Typical process requirements
Selective gold plating	Before the SES process, the panel is coated with additional resist and the selective sites are exposed. These exposed sites are then plated with nickel and gold. The panel will then proceed through the SES process. The HASL step would be omitted.
NPTH in planes without annular ring	A secondary drilling operation will be required to drill the holes, if the hole is to be located through the copper or the hole/feature size is beyond the process capabilities of tenting. This step may occur at the depanelization step.
Scoring	Additional tooling holes may be required to register the panel to the scoring machine blades. Programming of the scoring machine will be required to set the locations and depth of the cuts. This step may occur prior to NC routing of the product.
Countersink holes	The countersinking process is normally performed prior to depanelization.
Gold finger plating	Plating of nickel and gold over the finger area on connectors. This process typically requires shearing/NC routing separation of the panel to place the fingers at the edge of the remaining pieces, taping the product to expose only the fingers, stripping of the solder, plating nickel, and plating gold, and removal of the tape. These operations occur prior to the depanelization process. Finger plated products usually require chamfering of the fingers.
Via plugging	Plugging of vias may occur prior to solder mask or after the HASL operations.
Chamfer	After depanelization of the products from the manufacturing panel, the PCB products are processed through a machine to add an angle to the edge of the part or fingers.
Organic coating	Products requiring organic coating would omit the HASL step and be coated prior to inspection.

15.3.4 Panelization

The selection of the manufacturing panel is one of the most important steps in achieving product profitability. Several factors affect the selection of panel sizes to produce a specific product. These include:

- Material utilization
- Process-specific constraints
- Process limitations

All of these factors will impact the selection of the manufacturing panel size and the profitability of the product.

15.3.4.1   Material Utilization.   The material manufacturing costs, which correspond to 30 to 40 percent of total costs, are directly related to the square inches of material processed. The material costs can include the following: laminate, prepreg, copper foil, solder mask, photoresists, drill bits, chemicals, etc. Generally, these materials are consumed relative to the panel area manufactured.

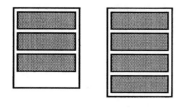

60%   75%

FIGURE 15.3   Selection of the best panel to increase the material utilization of the shippable product.

The appropriate manufacturing panel size (refer to Fig. 15.3) should be selected such that the shippable product consumes the highest percent of the manufactured panel as possible, thus reducing waste material and product costs.

During the design phase of the PCB, the board profile is defined. The impact of designing the profile, which results in poor manufacturing panel utilization, significantly impacts the cost of the product. During the definition of the PCB board profile, the PCB designer should consult with his manufacturing site to provide DFM feedback. Odd-shaped PCB profiles can still result in good material utilization, through nesting of the PCB on the panel.

General limitations in the selection of the appropriate panel sizes include the following: minimum spacing between products for depanelization processes (typically 0.100 in) and minimum panel border-to-product spacing to permit tooling and registration systems (typically 0.600 in).

15.3.4.2   Product Process-Specific Constraints.   In the selection of manufacturing panel sizes, there may be processing constraints which restrict the usage of specific panels or limit the method of placing the shippable product on the panel. For example, the manufacturing of products with gold tab plating may require additional spacing between products and restrictions on the rotation and nesting of products. These constraints may force the usage of panel sizes below the optimal material utilization.

15.3.4.3   Process Limitations.   Process limitations may require the usage of nonoptimal panel sizes. For example, due to a product's registration requirements, additional tooling may be required, thus reducing the available area for shippable product and reducing the material utilization. Another example is the limitations of some processes to permit larger panel sizes due to the physical processing constraints of the equipment.

15.3.5   Initial Design Analysis

After the initial design review, the basics of the design are known and a decision on whether to manufacture the design has to be made, and if so, the cost must be determined. Once the cost has been determined, the product price can be provided to the PCB customer.

The material and process requirements with the manufacturing panel selection define the basics of the product costs. These factors, combined with the prediction of yield based on the design review, will allow the product to be costed.

15.4 *DESIGN INPUT*

The input of the design into the CAM system is primarily performed by the loading of Gerber data into the PCB CAM system, after defining the apertures and shapes to be used. Alternatively, most PCB CAM systems accept the IPC-350 format.

The information loaded into the PCB CAM systems includes all artwork layers (e.g., circuitry layers and solder mask layers) and the drill files. Although some PCB CAM systems can accept NC routing files (i.e., board profiling), these files are normally not part of the PCB design system's capabilities to create, and therefore are not provided to the PCB manufacturer.

Prior to the loading of the PCB design files, the aperture codes within the design file need to be related to physical shapes within the PCB CAM system. These shapes are usually round, square, and rectangular, but may also include complex shapes (e.g., thermal relief pads for innerlayer planes). The complex shapes may need to be created on the CAM system from information provided by the PCB designer. The complete definition of these complex shapes by the PCB designer is critical to the success of the resulting design. Incomplete descriptions could result in nonfunctional designs.

During the loading process of the design files, it is important to review any log files and screen messages for missing aperture definitions or damaged design files.

After loading the files, the design should be reviewed for any problems with the interpretation of the data or apertures while aligning the data for further processing.

The PCB CAM operator must ensure that the apertures match those defined by the PCB designer and that the design input process has proceeded without failure, since subtle errors could result in nonfunctional designs that may not be determined within the manufacturing site but only at the PCB customer site.

15.5 *DESIGN ANALYSIS AND REVIEW*

The design analysis and review step is a refinement of the initial design review performed earlier by focusing on the actual design data. The design analysis and review consists of the following steps:

- Design rule checking
- Manufacturability analysis
- Single image edits
- DFM (design for manufacturability) enhancements

These steps provide the final checking of the PCB design requirements against the capabilities of the PCB manufacturer and preparation of the design for manufacturing.

15.5.1 Design Rule Checking

Design systems lay out circuits to defined rules; however, these systems may fail to adhere to these rules, because of either system failure or manual intervention. The purpose of reviewing the data package, in addition to reviewing the documented design constraints, is to confirm that the product can be produced at the manufacturing site and to the expected manufacturing yields. The analysis of the provided data describing the circuitry of the PCB to the manufacturing facility's production capabilities is critical to the success of the product.

The following information defines typical design rule checking that is performed, the reasons for checking, and the method of checking. Also, see Fig. 15.4.

DRC item	Purpose of check	Method of checking
Drill layer duplicate coordinates	Duplicate drill holes consume manufacturing capacity and may result in broken drill bits.	Most PCB CAM systems have an explicit check for this problem, provided a given radius of tolerance.
Minimum drill hole-to-hole spacing	Drill holes too close may result in broken material between the holes.	Most PCB CAM systems have an explicit feature spacing check.
NPTH-to-board edge minimum spacing	Drill holes too close to the board edge may result in broken material at the board edge.	Merge routing profile onto a copy of the NPTH layer and execute a spacing check of the pad to trace (the route layer would appear as a trace).
Missing drill holes	Missing holes may result in nonfunctional designs or products that cannot be used due to missing mounting or tooling holes.	Pad registration checking against a circuit reference layer, with verification of pads without PTH holes.
Extra drill holes	Extra drilled holes could result in nonfunctional designs from cutting of traces or shorts (if the holes become plated).	Pad registration checking against a circuit reference layer, with verification of PTH holes without pads.
Board edge-to-board edge minimum spacing	Routing cuts leaving minimal material may result in fractured or broken material between routing.	Feature spacing checking of the routing layer as a design layer, without considering electrical connectivity.
Copper-to-board edge minimum spacing	Tolerances of the routing operation may result in copper exposed at the edges of the product.	Feature spacing checking of the routing layer as a design layer against the circuitry layer.
Minimum annular ring	Most customer specifications define the minimum acceptable annular ring on PCB products. Annular ring is dependent on the design and the registration tolerances of the manufacturing processes.	Most PCB CAM systems have an explicit annular ring check.
Minimum pad-to-pad spacing	In addition to feature spacing and potential shorts, pad spacing affects the capability to electrically test products.	Most PCB CAM systems have an explicit feature-to-feature spacing check.
Minimum pad-to-track spacing	Feature spacing below manufacturing capabilities could result in shorts and poor product yields.	Most PCB CAM systems have an explicit feature-to-feature spacing check.
Minimum track-to-track spacing	Feature spacing below manufacturing capabilities could result in shorts and poor product yields.	Most PCB CAM systems have an explicit feature-to-feature spacing check.
Copper-to-NPTH minimum spacing	NPTH locations too close may prevent proper tenting of holes and require secondary drilling operations. NPTH too close may result in damaged features (e.g., cut traces).	Feature minimum spacing against a copy of the design layer merged with the NPTH layers.
Minimum line width	Line widths below manufacturing capabilities could result in poor product yields.	Some PCB CAM systems have an explicit check for this problem, others may require review of the apertures used and highlighting of the apertures for visual inspection.
Track termination without pad	Although this may be design intent, missing pads may be the result of poor design information or loading failures. These problems can result in nonfunctional designs.	Most PCB CAM systems have an explicit check for this problem.
Pad stack alignment	Misaligned pad stacks may result in unpredictable annular ring results, incorrect compensations of registration, and product scrap.	Most PCB CAM systems have an explicit pad registration check.

DRC item	Purpose of check	Method of checking
Minimum solder mask pad clearance	Solder mask pad clearances below manufacturing capabilities could result in solder mask on the pads, and poor product yields.	Check solder mask layer (as a circuit layer) against the circuitry layer using an annular ring check.
Minimum solder mask edge-to-feature spacing	Solder mask edge to feature spacing below manufacturing capabilities could result in exposed features and poor product yields.	Feature minimum spacing against a copy of the design layer merged with the solder mask layer.
Minimum solder mask annular ring for NPTH	NPTH solder mask clearances may need to be larger to prevent ghosting of the solder mask from light diffraction through the product.	Check solder mask layer (as a circuit layer) against the NPTH layer, verify for no matches of the NPTH to solder mask layer.
Solder mask-to-board edge minimum clearance	PCB edge clearances may need to be larger to prevent ghosting of the solder mask from light diffraction through the product.	Feature minimum spacing against a negative copy of the solder mask layer merged with the routing layer.
Solder mask minimum web	Solder mask webs below manufacturing capabilities could result in solder mask breakdown and poor product yields. This problem potentially results in the PCB assembler with solder bridging defects.	Use minimum feature-to-feature spacing on the solder mask layer.
Plane-to-board edge minimum clearance	Spacing below the tolerances of the routing operation may result in copper exposed at the edges of the product.	Feature spacing checking of the routing layer as a design layer against the plane.
Minimum plane layer annular ring	Annular ring below manufacturing registration and tolerance capabilities could result in open connections, and poor product yields.	Most PCB CAM systems have an explicit annular ring check.
Minimum plane layer clearance	Plane clearances below manufacturing registration and tolerance capabilities could result in shorts and poor product yields.	Most PCB CAM systems have an explicit annular ring check.
Plane-to-plane isolation	Plane layer isolation typically results from either incorrect designs or interpretation of aperture lists; the result is a nonfunctional product.	Most PCB CAM systems have an explicit layer-to-layer isolation check.
Nomenclature-to-NPTH minimum spacing	Nomenclature spacing below manufacturing capabilities may result in nomenclature in the hole from misregistration or bleeding of the nomenclature ink.	Feature minimum spacing against a copy of the nomenclature layer merged with the NPTH layers.
Nomenclature-to-solder mask minimum spacing	Nomenclature spacing below manufacturing capabilities may result in nomenclature on product features from misregistration or bleeding of the nomenclature ink.	Feature minimum spacing against a copy of the nomenclature layer merged with each solder mask layer.
Nomenclature-to-feature minimum spacing	Nomenclature spacing below manufacturing capabilities may result in nomenclature on product features from misregistration, bleeding of the nomenclature ink or skipping of the screen over features resulting in illegible markings.	Feature minimum spacing against a copy of the design layer merged with the nomenclature layer.
Nomenclature minimum feature sizes	Nomenclature sizes below manufacturing capabilities could result in illegible nomenclature and poor product yields.	Some PCB CAM systems have an explicit check for minimum line width, others may require review of the apertures used and highlighting of the apertures for visual inspection.

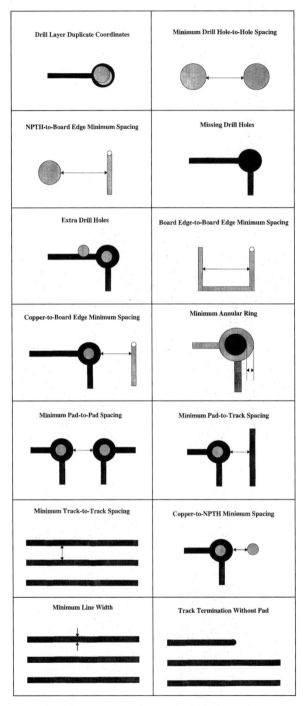

FIGURE 15.4 Examples of design rule check elements.

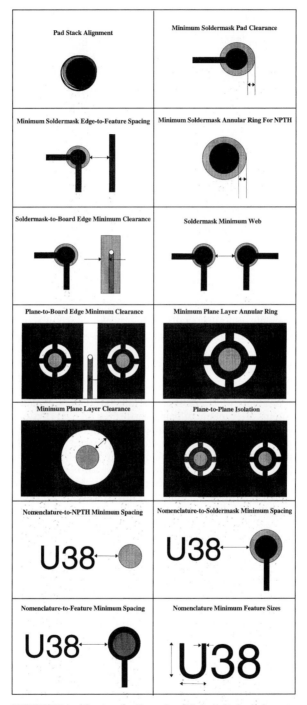

FIGURE 15.4 (*Continued*)   Examples of design rule check elements.

15.5.2 Manufacturability Review

The design rule checking results are reviewed against the PCB manufacturing capability matrix, with dispositions being made to the acceptability of violations. The PCB customer may be contacted regarding design violations for corrected designs to be retransmitted or to permit design changes to be performed by the PCB manufacturer.

Additionally, the factors reviewed during the initial design review are revisited to confirm the results based upon design actuals. If differences are noted, product yields and/or cost predictions may need to be altered.

15.5.3 Single Image Edits

In general, all designs have information which must be removed before the design can be manufactured. Most of these features are used as references during the PCB layout phase to assist the designer in understanding the available real estate. However, these references must be removed or modified to manufacture the board to design intent. Among these typical items are the following:

Item	Impact if not removed/modified
NPTH pads on outerlayers	Plated holes
Routing crop marks	Copper at board edge
Direct contact plane markings of drilled holes	Open circuits
Clip nomenclature with solder mask data	Nomenclature on pads/in holes

15.5.4 DFM Enhancements

The manufacturability of the PCB can be improved through design enhancements. Many of the enhancements are capable of being performed on CAD systems only (or through specialized post-CAD software); other enhancements can be performed at the manufacturing site.

Ideally, all design enhancements would be performed at the design site to maintain the consistency of products from multiple manufacturers; however, some of the DFM enhancements can impact the CAD system's capability to provide further design changes. Specifically, the optimization of track-to-feature spacing could result in blocked routing channels, preventing an autorouter from performing. The following are typical DFM enhancements (see Fig. 15.5a–e):

Item	Result from enhancement
Copper balancing	The balancing of copper on the surface of the design will improve the distribution of plating (in the pattern-plating process), preventing areas of overplating due to the isolation of features. This improvement is noticed in the ability to control the plated hole diameters to tolerances and the reduction of plating heights which impact solder mask coverage. (See Fig. 15.5a.)
Teardropping	As annular rings decrease due to tighter design specifications, the capability to have defects due to registration/annular ring failures increases. The addition of teardropping increases the pad-to-trace junction size, improving the reliability of

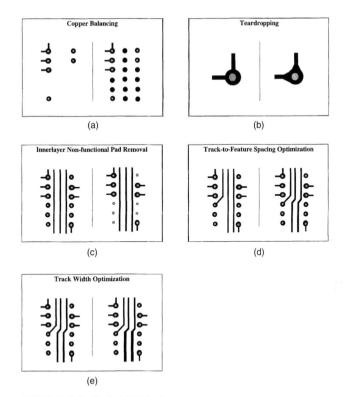

FIGURE 15.5 Typical DFM enhancements.

the connection and improving product yields. (See Fig. 15.5*b*.)

Removal of nonfunctional pads on innerlayers   Innerlayer shorts result from several factors, among them the proximity of circuitry to other circuitry. The occurrence of shorts can be correlated to the running length of the circuitry versus the running length at some minimum spacing between circuitry (at the process capability of the operation). Reducing the total distance at minimum spacing will reduce the probability of shorts, resulting in improved yields. (See Fig. 15.5*c*.)

Optimization of track-to-feature spacing   As defined in the nonfunctional pads discussion, the occurrence of shorts can be correlated to the running length of the circuitry versus the running length at some minimum spacing between circuitry (at the process capability of the operation). Reducing the total distance at minimum spacing will reduce the probability of shorts, resulting in improved yields. (See Fig. 15.5*d*.)

Track width optimization	The occurrence of opens can be correlated to the running length of the circuitry versus the running length at minimum track width (at the process capability of the operation). Reducing the total distance at minimum track width will reduce the probability of opens, resulting in improved yields. (See Fig. 15.5e.)

15.6 PANELIZATION PROCESS

The panelization process results in the placement of the PCB single images in the locations defined in the panelization definition step during the initial design review. In addition to the placement of the PCB single images, the following features may be added to the panel for manufacturing.

Item	Purpose
Customer coupons	Provided to the customers for their inspection of the PCB product. These coupons are typically treated as separate PCB single images.
Internal coupons	During the manufacturing process, destructive testing may be required to confirm product quality. These coupons are typically treated as separate PCB single images.
Tooling holes	Holes used for registration of manufacturing panels to artwork, drilling, or routing operations are added to the panel borders.
Outerlayer thieving patterns	Plating thieving patterns are sometimes needed to balance the platable area across the panel.
Innerlayer venting patterns	The addition of copper to innerlayers outside the PCB single image provides for more consistency in the lamination process.
Textual markings	Operator aides may be provided outside the PCB single image to improve manufacturing quality.

15.7 ADDITIONAL PROCESSES

An important step in all the processes already defined is the necessity for proper information management. Archival of PCB customer-supplied information and the files generated from the tooling process are critical for disaster recovery. Archiving systems exist in the market that also provide for centralized data management and distribution of the information to the various departments within an organization.

In addition to the basic tooling steps already defined, most PCB manufacturing sites require the following information to be created:

- CAD reference files
- Electrical test netlist and fixture creation files

The CAD reference files, if required, are generally created within the PCB manufacturing site. These files prepare *automated optical inspection* (AOI) systems with data that confirms that manufactured pieces match, within tolerances, the PCB design.

Electrical test netlist files may be either created internally or sent to an outside contractor to prepare the files and the resulting fixture. These files use as input either the Gerber or IPC data provided by the PCB customer.

P · A · R · T · 3

FABRICATION PROCESSES

CHAPTER 16
FINELINE TECHNOLOGIES

Foster Gray
Printed Circuits Resources, Defense System Equipment Group,
Texas Instruments, Austin, Texas

16.1 THE NEED FOR HIGH-DENSITY INTERCONNECTS

The printed wiring board (PWB) design is driven by the type of semiconductor component packages used in the design, the package lead pitch, and the maximum number of leads on the packages.

16.1.1 Higher-I/O Components

The Semiconductor Research Industry Roadmap[1] shows the trends for silicon CMOS device lead count for various market applications. These markets for electronics products include commodities, hand-held, cost/performance, high-performance, and automotive ICs. The expected I/O count is shown in Fig. 16.1. These systems make up most of the electronic products being built today. Many of these products require high-density packaging. Today the revenue center of gravity for device I/O is 208 to 225 leads. If we assume that the commodity and hand-held markets will continue to represent the revenue center of gravity for semiconductor packages, then we can expect to need 600 I/O by the year 2001. The increases depicted in lead count (or I/O) are directly related to the large increase in the functions per chip which has come about by the shrinking line width on the silicon devices. The SRI forecast indicates that the packaging interconnect structure for cost/performance products must be able to interconnect up to 1125 I/O by the year 1998, 1700 by the year 2001, and 4000 by the year 2010. The I/O count drives the via count on the PWB, since each lead requires a surface layer connection to its neighbor component, or that it be connected by a via using an internal layer on the PWB.

16.1.2 I/O Drives Wiring Length

The component I/O also drives the wiring length required by the packaging interconnect substrate (P/I substrate). Higher I/O will require more wiring to interconnect the device leads. Therefore, an increased wiring capability will be required in the PWB. The power and ground pins make up about 20 to 35 percent of the device leads and connect directly to an internal power or ground layer by a via without additional wiring. The remainder of the leads need wiring to complete the interconnect. The cost of the P/I substrate, such as a multilayer PWB, is almost directly proportional to the number of layers and, to a lesser degree, the width of the

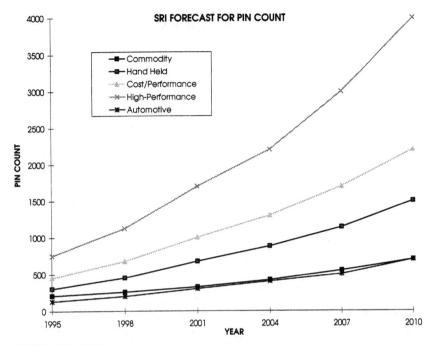

FIGURE 16.1   SRI forecast for pin count.

lines and spaces, as long as the line and space size is within the capability of the PWB manufacturing process. Higher I/O will require that more wiring be placed on each layer, or the layer count and cost will increase. What are the factors that control the wiring on the P/I substrate? They are:

1. Number and size of the via lands

2. Width of the lines

3. Spacing between lines

The line and space in this analysis are set to be equal so there are only two factors that control wiring length. For high-performance designs the space is governed by electrical characteristics such as cross talk and is independently determined. The width of the line, and therefore the need for fine lines, is only one of the two factors that affect wiring length. We will look at each of these factors.

16.1.2.1   Wiring Length.   The wiring length required can be estimated by an empirical analysis by Dr. D. Seraphim of IBM[2] who showed that the wiring length required to interconnect multiple devices is directly proportional to the number of component terminals and the pitch between terminals. Therefore, wiring length is minimized by putting the devices closer together and making the lead pitch smaller. The Seraphim equation is:

$$L_{ideal} = \frac{1.5\,D\,(1.5\,N_t)}{2} \tag{14.1}$$

where

L_{ideal} = ideal wiring length per chip site
D = distance between chip sites
N_t = number of terminals on the chip

Dr. Seraphim empirically established that at best there is a 50 percent efficiency in actual versus the ideal wiring length. This would make the required wiring length twice the ideal value or:

$$L_{\text{act}} = 2.25 \; D \; N_t \qquad (14.2)$$

16.1.2.2   Wiring Length on the P/I Structure.   A method was developed by George Messner of Interconnection Decision Consulting[3] to estimate the conductor routing capability of the PWB based on the number of conductors which can be placed between PTHs or vias. His definition is as follows:

$$\text{Connectivity} = \text{conductors per cm per unit length}$$
$$\qquad (14.3)$$
$$= \text{cm of conductor wiring/cm}^2$$

This connectivity definition describes the total conductor channel capacity per layer which is provided by a particular design. The method requires a count of the number of conductors that can be placed between PTH or via lands on a single internal layer located in 1 cm^2. Figure 16.2 shows a drawing of two lines between plated-through-hole lands which are 2.54 mm (0.100 in) apart. This design has two lines per 2.54 mm (0.100 in) or 7.9 lines per cm (20 lines per 2.54 cm). The tracks have unit length for an area of 1 cm^2. For the 7.9 lines, each 1.0 cm long, this would

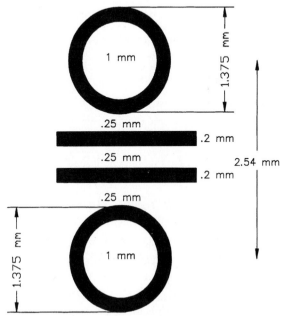

DIP PACKAGING — 2 CHANNELS PER 2.54 mm

FIGURE 16.2   Pin-in-hole layer routing limited by PTHs and via lands. Square grid = 100 vias/in^2.

be 7.9 cm/cm². The number of conductors is usually stated in tracks or conductors per cm². Therefore one, two, or three tracks between lands would equate to 3.9 cm/cm², 7.9 cm/cm² or 11.8 cm/cm². This metric gives the wiring density per layer so the total wiring density is found by multiplying the layer wiring density by the number of layers. This analysis applies only to internal layers. In Fig. 16.2 the land takes up 55 percent of the space between adjacent holes. The need to reduce the space taken up by the land is the main driver for using surface-mount components which do not have large leads going through the PWB, resulting in large lands.

Top and bottom layers on boards with surface-mount components have land patterns to which the surface-mount components are mounted which also limits surface routing. Pin-in-hole components have the leads inserted in the PTH lands and, although the leads do not block routing, the PTH lands are much larger than the via used for surface mounting and take up much of the routing space. This limits the number of lines per channel that can be achieved on external layers.

16.1.3 Device Package Drives Via and Wiring Requirements

Both pin-in-hole (PIH) and surface-mount (SMT) packages are in general use for the electronics made in the world. Most commercial PWBs have both component types.

16.1.3.1 Pin-In-Hole Trends.   The dual in-line package (DIP) has limited I/O capability since the leads are on 2.54-mm (100-mil) spacing. The trend today is that the DIP will continue to be used where relatively low lead count is required and through-hole mounting is employed.[4] The DIP package will limit the wiring density to one to two lines per 2.54 mm as seen in Fig. 16.2. The single in-line package (SIP) which has leads on 1.27-mm (50-mil) spacing is also a pin-in-hole package and is widely used for resistor arrays and memory arrays because it uses very little PWB real estate. The SIP also is available in an SMT package. The SIP package with its single row of leads will restrict routing between the pins to one line per channel. The pin grid array (PGA) package is widely used because it has the capability for high pin count in a pin-in-hole package. The typical high-I/O package on a computer PWB, such as the microprocessor chip, will often be in a ceramic PGA. The PGA has an array of pins designed for through-hole insertion. The pins are typically on a 2.54-mm (100-mil) grid. PGAs can be assembled on standard PWBs at high yield. The PGA can also be socketed, which makes it very easy to replace. This package, however, has a number of drawbacks:

1. The package is expensive.

2. The package is leaded and requires relatively large through-holes.

3. The through-holes limit the routing density in the PWB.

All of the pin-in-hole packages put additional demands on the PWB due to the requirement for large holes and associated lands.

16.1.3.2 Surface-Mount Trends.   Surface-mounted semiconductor packages have two types of package attachment methods:

1. Peripheral leads which solder attach to rectangular top surface lands

2. Round lands in an array pattern which solder attach directly to the device package

Peripheral Leaded Packages
Quad Flat Pack.   The quad flat pack (QFP) peripheral leaded package is shown in Fig. 16.3. The lead pitch on peripheral lead packages has decreased as the lead count has increased to keep the package to a reasonable size. Over the last few years, the QFP pitch has decreased from 1.27 mm (50 mil) to 0.50 mm (20 mil) in standard packages in the United States, cover-

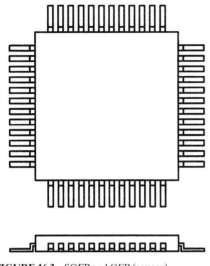

FIGURE 16.3 SQFP and QFP (square).

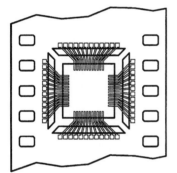

(a)

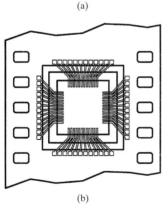

(b)

FIGURE 16.4 Typical TAB tape: (*a*) annular ring supported by tie bars at each corner; (*b*) free-floating annular ring supports leads.

ing the lead count range from 24 to 432. Japanese manufacturers are using 0.4-mm-pitch QFP packages in production with mass reflow and with fine-pitch QFP packages down to 0.3-mm (12-mil) centers with lead count up to 576. Lead pitch will need to decrease to 0.2 mm to meet the >1000-I/O need shown in Fig. 16.1.

Tape-automated bond (TAB). The tape-automated bond (TAB) package is shown in Fig. 16.4. These packages are peripheral leaded packages similar to the QFP except the lead attachment to the die does not use wire bonding but uses the copper TAB tape inner leads to make the die attachment. The outer leads on the tape are attached to the packaging interconnect structure by thermodes which solder attach all the leads at one time. The tape is either in a 35- or 70-mm-wide sprocketed format depending on the die size and can be handled in a fully automatic manner. TAB lead pitches go from 0.50 to 0.20 mm, covering the lead count range from 84 to greater than 1000.

Fan-Out and Fan-In Patterns. Peripheral leaded packages need fan-out and/or fan-in patterns to connect the leads to the PWB vias. Typical patterns for fan-in and fan-out patterns for QFPs are shown in Fig. 16.5. As the device I/O has increased, however, the package size and area occupied on the PWB has become very large due to multiple factors:

1. The package gets larger to accommodate more leads.

2. The PWB fanout area required increases to interconnect the land to the via for each signal I/O. As the package lead pitch gets smaller, the lead fan-out to a land occurs both under the package and outside the package as in Fig. 16.5.

3. The wiring required to connect the package land to the via is limited by the surface wirability and the vias which interfere with the land pattern. Observe from Fig. 16.5 that the surface attach lands block positions that the via would occupy. This further limits routability due to via starvation.

Peripheral Leaded Surface Wiring. The surface patterns block routing of lines between lands on the surface layers. At or below 1.27 mm land spacing, no lines are usually routed between lands on the surface layer. Surface routing is controlled by land spacing on the SMT components. The pitch of the SMT land determines how many lines can be placed between lands. It can be seen from Fig. 16.6 that one line between lands can be accommodated for 1.27-mm (50-mil) pitch components while two lines between lands requires a 125-μm (micrometer) (5-mil) line on the plated outer layer. Small line widths on the outer layers can substantially increase the PWB cost due to the etching of fine lines with plated copper. Usually no more than one line is run between 1.27-mm-pitch SMT lands. At 0.63-mm (25-mil) pitch, only one 0.1-mm (4-mil) line is run between lands, but the possibility of bridging at assembly is very great. A good design rule is to run no lines between 0.63-mm-pitch or closer-spaced lands. It may be concluded that fewer and fewer lines

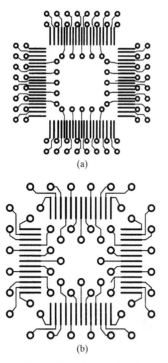

FIGURE 16.5 Fan-in and Fan-out patterns: (*a*) 0.4-mm pitch FQFP; (*b*) 0.63-mm pitch QFP.

will be routed on outer layers as the lead pitch continues to decrease. This does not include two-sided PWBs where all the lines run on surface layers.

Via Grid and Internal Wiring Capacity.   The decreasing land pitch requires more vias in the interconnect structure. To accommodate more vias, the via pitch has decreased from 2.54-mm (100-mil) square grid (15.5 vias per cm^2), to a 2.54/1.27-mm stagger grid pitch (31 vias per cm^2), to 1.27-mm square grid pitch with (62 vias per cm^2). The 2.54-mm square grid was quite adequate for pin-in-hole parts with a maximum lead count of 64 pins. However, with SMT parts, the lead count can exceed 30 per cm^2, so more via sites are necessary. The 2.54/1.27-mm stagger grid shown in Fig. 16.7 provides 31 vias per cm^2 while at the same time not blocking internal routing channels in either the *x* or *y* direction. The 1.27-mm (50-mil) square grid shown in Fig. 16.8 provides 62 vias per cm^2 for high-pin-count devices. However, the extra lands use valuable routing space. The 1.27-mm square grid has 50 percent less wiring capacity than the stagger grid and requires a 50 percent smaller line and space but twice the number of vias. For this reason, a tradeoff between via density and wiring density must be made. Figures 16.7 and 16.8 illustrate the wiring densities available with these via patterns. As the device package I/O has increased, the trend is to use the 1.27-mm square grid.

Ball Grid Array (BGA) Packages.   The BGA package is similar to the pin grid array package except the pins are replaced by a solder ball attached to a land on the package.

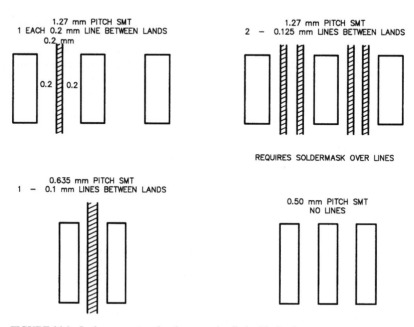

FIGURE 16.6 Surface-mount surface layer routing limited by lands.

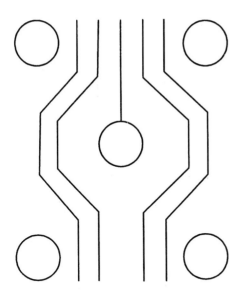

TYPICAL

5 lines/channel
0.15 mm lines/spaces
0.75 mm land
0.4 mm drill
31 vias/sq cm
Wiring Density = 19.7 cm/cm²

FIGURE 16.7 PWB via density—2.54/1.27-mm stagger grid.

Figure 16.9 shows both a fully populated and perimeter array BGA package. Since no through lead is used, the via is sized based on manufacturing and reliability considerations. The package is available with both a ceramic and plastic body. The multilayer ceramic package body has both ball and column solder joints. The typical ceramic package family covers the I/O range from 120 to 500.[5] The plastic packages are available with a two-sided PWB interconnect substrate and a multilayer PWB interconnect substrate. A family of overmolded two-sided printed circuit pad array carrier packages called OMPAC is available for I/O up to 220.[6] Figure 16.10 shows package size as a function of lead and pad spacing for a variety of area array and peripheral leaded packages. For I/O count greater than 350, the area array package has a significantly lower area than the QFP package with 0.3-mm pitch. Tape-automated bond (TAB) peripheral leaded packages with pitch of 0.25 and 0.20 mm have area requirements similar to the BGA packages up to 500 leads. The BGA package would seem to be the package of choice above 500 leads.

16.2 FINELINE IMPACT ON INTERCONNECT SUBSTRATE

16.2.1 Plated Surface Layers

The formation of fine lines on surface layers can be done by electroplating and etching the surface pattern or by forming the surface pattern by fully additive copper plating. Copper electroplating presents a unique problem due to plating thickness variations related to the plating process. The surface layer may be either panel plated or pattern plated. Figure 16.11 shows the sequence for panel plating and Fig. 16.13 for pattern plating. These sequences are for double-sided rigid and multilayer rigid PWBs. Both start with an initial metalization of the plated-through-holes.

16.2.1.1 Panel-Plate Process. In the panel-plate process shown in Fig. 16.11 the total panel is plated with the full thickness of copper. This plating method gives the most uniform plating across the complete panel surface since the high-current-density areas are at the panel edges. A typical acid copper-plating machine should be able to maintain a copper thickness variation of ±12 μm (0.5 mil) over a 457- × 610-mm (18-in × 24-in) panel. Figure 16.12 shows the shape and undercut for the various conductor formation processes. Panel plating gives the most line width narrowing due to etch undercut, while the fully additive copper gives an almost ideal line shape. Table 16.1 shows the amount of copper that must be etched for a 35-μm (1-oz) copper foil and a 17-μm (½-oz) copper foil outerlayer panel-plated surface assuming 25 μm of copper is required in the hole. This table shows that the surface copper to be etched with 1-oz copper foil is 70 ±13.4 μm. The ½-oz copper foil surface has 55 ± 13.1 μm of copper to be etched. The metal etch resist which protects the copper in the holes and on the surface features is usually plated 8 to 20 μm thick. A dry film resist as thin as 25 μm can be used on the surface without overplating. Overplating will cause the plating to "mushroom" over the resist and make stripping very difficult. The etcher is set up to completely etch across the entire panel and thus must etch to the high side of the copper thickness. This would require about 83 μm (3.3 mil) of copper to be etched for the 35-μm foil layer and 68 μm (2.7 mil) for the 17-μm foil layer. An ideal

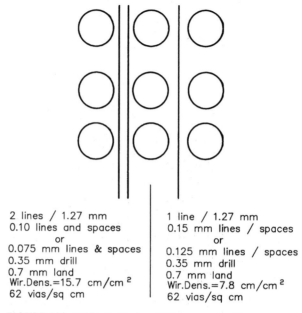

2 lines / 1.27 mm	1 line / 1.27 mm
0.10 lines and spaces	0.15 mm lines / spaces
or	or
0.075 mm lines & spaces	0.125 mm lines / spaces
0.35 mm drill	0.35 mm drill
0.7 mm land	0.7 mm land
Wir.Dens.=15.7 cm/cm ^{2}	Wir.Dens.=7.8 cm/cm ^{2}
62 vias/sq cm	62 vias/sq cm

FIGURE 16.8 PWB via density—1.27-mm square grid.

isotropic etch would etch the top of the conductor in under the resist as much as the thickness of copper to be etched on both sides of the line. In fact, for a metallic etch resist like tin lead the undercut for each side of the line is equal to 30 to 50 percent of the copper thickness to be etched. The lines on the surface can be expected to be narrowed by at least 85 µm for the 35-µm foil surface layer and 70 µm for the 17-µm foil layer during the etch process. If the surface copper line widths for panel plating are set at 152 µm (6 mil) minimum this should yield a 67-µm (2.7-mil) line with 35-µm foil outers and 84 µm (3.3 mil) for 17-µm foil outers. In either case,

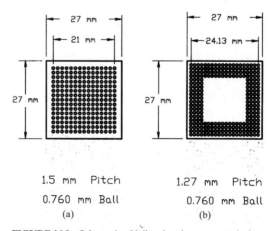

FIGURE 16.9 Schematic of full and perimeter array devices: (*a*) full grid BGA, 225 I/O; (*b*) perimeter BGA, 225 I/O.

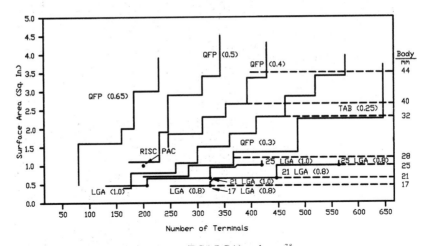

FIGURE 16.10 Effectiveness of array (BGA/LGA) packages.[7,8]

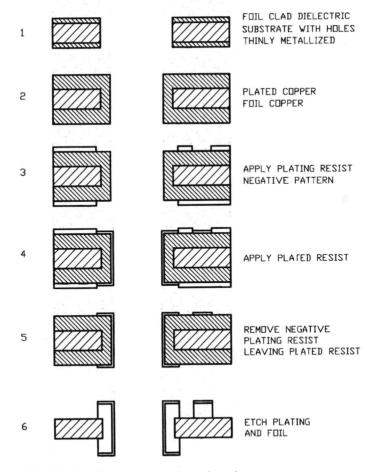

1	FOIL CLAD DIELECTRIC SUBSTRATE WITH HOLES THINLY METALLIZED
2	PLATED COPPER FOIL COPPER
3	APPLY PLATING RESIST NEGATIVE PATTERN
4	APPLY PLATED RESIST
5	REMOVE NEGATIVE PLATING RESIST LEAVING PLATED RESIST
6	ETCH PLATING AND FOIL

FIGURE 16.11 Panel plate, print, plate resist, etch.

Panel Electroplate

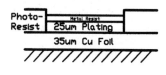
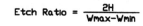
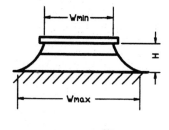

$$\text{Etch Ratio} = \frac{2H}{Wmax - Wmin}$$

Pattern Electroplate

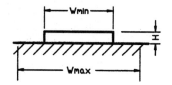

$$\text{Etch Ratio} = \frac{2H}{Wmax - Wmin} > 1.0$$

Fully Additive Copper

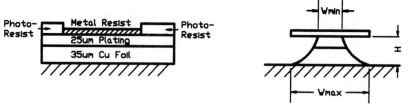

Wmax-Wmin

FIGURE 16.12   Fineline conductor formation.

TABLE 16.1   Panel Plate Copper

	Thickness 35-μm foil, μm	Tolerance 35-μm foil, μm	Thickness 17-μm foil, μm	Tolerance 17-μm foil, μm
Base copper	32	3.5	17	1.7
Copper strike	0	0	0	0
Panel plate	38	13	38	13
Thickness & RMS value	70	±13.4	55	±13.1

lines on panel-plated surface layers are significantly reduced from the design values. Compensation of the lines for etch undercut should be done by growing the lines. The spacing should not be reduced below 76 µm (3 mil) where the etching capability begins to decrease. Compensation factors will depend on the particular manufacturing process and equipment being used.

16.2.1.2 Pattern-Plate Process. The pattern-plate process is designed to minimize the amount of copper to be etched and therefore allow finer lines on the surface. Figure 16.13 shows the pattern-plate process. There are two ways to process step 1. The thinly metallized panel can be "struck" with 7 to 8 µm of panel-plated copper, like in Fig. 16.11. The process then follows the rest of the sequence. Figure 16.13 shows the more typical way to pattern plate. The resist is used to form the plating pattern so the copper to be etched is minimized. When a strike is not used, the copper to be etched in pattern plating is 36 µm with 35-µm outerlayer foil and 19 µm with 17-µm foil outers. This decreased copper to be etched will result in a significant reduction in the etch narrowing of the surface circuits with pattern plating, so 125-µm (5.0-mil) to 150-µm (6.0-mil) circuits are common. The disadvantage of pattern plating is that isolated circuits may significantly overplate, causing plated-through-holes to be undersized and isolated lines to overplate. This plating thickness variation can create problems at assembly. Surface plating robber bars can decrease the overplating problem but not completely eliminate it. If all surface-mount components are used, then vias can usually be undersized without a consequence. Tables 16.2 and 16.3 show the advantages of pattern plating (with and without a strike) to decrease the amount of copper which must be etched and thus increase the etched line surface width.

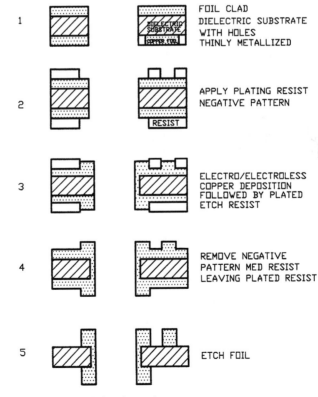

FIGURE 16.13 Print-plate-etch process sequence.

TABLE 16.2   Pattern Plate Copper with Strike

	Thickness 35-μm foil, μm	Tolerance 35-μm foil, μm	Thickness 17-μm foil, μm	Tolerance 17-μm foil, μm
Base copper	32	3.5	17	1.7
Copper strike	8	0.8	8	0.8
Pattern plate copper	0	0	0	0
Thickness & RMS value	40	±3.6	25	±1.9

TABLE 16.3   Pattern Plate Copper—No Strike

	Thickness 35-μm foil, μm	Tolerance 35-μm foil, μm	Thickness 17-μm foil, μm	Tolerance 17-μm foil, μm
Base copper	32	3.5	17	1.7
Copper strike				
Pattern plate copper	0	0	0	0
Thickness & RMS value	32	±3.6	17	±1.9

16.2.1.3 *Additive Plate Process.*

Fully additive plating is capable of near absolute plating uniformity, independent of panel surface design and hole size dimensions. It is capable of high-aspect-ratio (>20:1) small-hole plating and elimination of metal etch plating resists; it does not require plating thieving, is insensitive to the mixing of simple and complex designs, is highly solderable, and eliminates all etching to provide conductor definition.[9] Additive plating is widely practiced in Japan and to a much lesser extent in the United States. The capabilities of the process have been well known in the United States but a variety of reasons have kept the technique from wider acceptance.

Barriers to Use of Fully Additive Plating.   Until the last few years the process required a license and the charging of royalties for use. A significant commitment to process control was necessary since the process was not very stable. The process required a screen-printed epoxy-based permanent resist or a solvent-based dry film permanent additive resist. There was no available aqueous dry film resist which could withstand the bath chemistry. Since most PWB manufacturers have only aqueous resist available, this has been a major barrier. Laminates for the fully additive process have also been a problem.

Two approaches were used to provide adequate peel strength of the plated copper. One used a sacrificial laminated foil that was etched off to form a textured surface. The second used a modified epoxy which was coated on the unclad catalyzed laminate surface. The coated laminate required a chemical etch of the surface to get good adhesion to the additive copper deposit. The laminates were available from only a few laminators and were expensive. The metallurgical properties of the original fully additive bath left much to be desired since the copper deposit was embrittled due to entrapped hydrogen. The additive process requires a significant capital investment. Historically, the PWB industry has been underfunded since it is a low-profit-margin business. There are no small U.S. PWB manufacturers who use fully additive plating.

The Promise of Additive Plating.   Additive processes can produce lines and spaces down to the resolution limit of the resists used, which for a 35-μm-thick dry film resist is about 50 μm. The fully additive plating baths on the market today actually have superior metallurgical properties to the typical electroplating baths as demonstrated in testing by IPC members and reported in Ref. 10. Two new approaches have been developed that eliminate most of the barriers.

Feature Plate.   Figure 16.14 shows the process steps for a semiadditive process called Envision™[11] where standard laminate clad with thin copper (i.e., 17 μm or less) is drilled, cat-

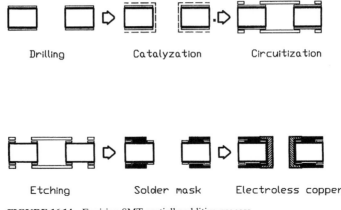

FIGURE 16.14   Envision SMT partially additive process.

alyzed, circuitized with a tenting dry film resist, etched, and solder masked with a pattern which acted as the plating resist in the additive bath. The holes are plated with the additive copper and coated with a copper protectant. Dinella[9] calls this *feature plate*.

Semiadditive.   A second semiadditive method uses a laminate with a thin copper foil and an organic nonpermanent plating resist. Aqueous-developable resists for fully additive plating are now available. The part is drilled, catalyzed, circuitized with a positive resist pattern, pattern plated with additive copper to form the circuits and plate the holes, and pattern plated with an electroless metal etch resist such as immersion tin. It is resist stripped, the background copper is flash etched, and it is solder masked and coated with a copper solder protectant.

16.2.2 Surface Layer Routing

The routing of surface layers of PWBs is limited by the land size required by the SMT component, wire-bond sites, direct chip attach pads, PTH pads required for the component lead inserted in the plated-through-hole or via, and the thickness of the plated copper. Surface routing was discussed in Sec. 16.1.3 under "Peripheral Leaded Surface Wiring." Direct chip attach requires surface features to shrink by almost an order of magnitude: DCA lands on 0.25- to 0.6-mm pitch, with 0.070-mm lines on 0.16-mm pitch.[12] Another level of circuit density has to be achieved on surface layers of PWBs to meet the need for direct chip attach.

16.2.2.1 Via Land Size.   The via land size on the surface is controlled by the drill size, the panel size, and the drill location tolerance. The outerlayer land is usually smaller than the internal via land since the laminate dimensional instability does not need to be included in the land size calculation. The via hole pattern is drilled in the panel after lamination and prior to any high-temperature thermal processing which causes dimensional changes. For greater wiring density, the surface land size must also decrease. Holes can be mechanically drilled down to 100 μm (4 mil) or less. A number of companies are drilling 150-μm (6-mil) diameter holes but not in production. However, mechanically drilled holes begin to add cost to the PWB below about 0.3 mm (12 mil) due to a number of considerations:

1. Fewer hits/min are obtained with small drills due to decreased chip load.
2. The flute length on the small drill limits the number of panels which can be stacked together.
3. The small drill tends to wander more from entry to exit.

4. The cost of a 0.1-mm drill can increase by a factor of 7 times over the cost of 0.35-mm and larger drills.

Smaller holes can be formed with lasers, punched, plasma etched, and formed photographically. It is not within the scope of this chapter to discuss these hole formation methods. All of these techniques will allow a significantly smaller via land size.

16.2.3   Internal Layer Fineline Formation

The ability to form internal layer circuitry with fine lines and with high first-pass yields is critical to increasing the wiring density of printed wiring boards. Until recently, there has been no quantitative method to measure what yields can be achieved in production except by electrical testing the particular layer or by using a semiquantitative automatic optical test method. There has also been no way to predict what the yields should be. An electrical test of each layer is not practical due to the cost of the fixtures or the time and cost to perform the test with a flying probe electrical tester.

16.2.3.1   Conductor Analysis Technology.   AT&T has developed a method to measure the innerlayer process capability.[13,14] The approach provides a way to improve fineline manufacturing capability by providing a method to measure current performance and by establishing targets to strive for in the future. When used with the *Electrical Test Method to Characterize Printed Board Conductor Formation Capability*,[13] the model predicts the capability of new equipment (or the present manufacturing equipment), materials, and processes used to manufacture printed wiring board innerlayers. Two types of conductor patterns are available. The first is called the *Multiple-Pitch Serpentine Test Pattern* which has features that range in width from 51 to 305 μm, and the second is called the *Single-Pitch Serpentine Test Pattern*, which has one line width and one space which are 76/76 (76-μm line and 76-μm spaces), 102/102, and 127/127 feature sizes on 457-mm × 610-mm (18 × 24-in) panels. Conductors on one side of the panel are predominately parallel to the long side of the panel, while conductors on the other side of the panel are parallel to the short dimension. The patterns are multiple up on the panel. A flying probe two-point electrical tester is used to measure the resistance of each circuit with a two-point probe. The data which can be extracted from the resistance measurement includes conductor yield, percent opens, percent shorts, defect map on the panel, line width probability distribution, line width capability index, and copper thickness. Recently a bed-of-nails electrical test system has become available commercially for testing all points on the test patterns at one time.[15] This greatly speeds up the test and analysis process and makes the process available to all PWB fabricators and suppliers of materials and equipment to improve their products.

16.2.3.2   Industry Capability for Conductor Formation.   Reference 14 describes studies conducted to evaluate dry film photoresists and liquid photoresists, and PWB manufacturers' capability to produce fineline conductors. Designed experiments were performed to determine the proper expose conditions for dry film resist to maximize the yield of 76-μm (3-mil) lines on the 51-μm (2-mil) to 305-μm (12-mil) Multiple-Pitch Test Pattern. When the best process conditions were determined, the 76/76-μm (152-μm pitch) Single-Pitch Serpentine Test Pattern panels were processed. The author developed a defect density model based on a Poisson probability. Figure 16.15 shows the predicted panel yield vs. defect density for 6-, 8-, and 10-mil pitch designs. Table 16.4 shows the authors' calculated values for the characteristics of single-pitch patterns for 76/76-μm (6-mil), 102/102-μm (8-mil), and 127/127-μm (10-mil) pitch lines and spaces.

The dry film studies were performed at the AT&T Bell Laboratories while the data from liquid photoresists were acquired from experiments conducted at β-site installations or at the photoresist supplier's location. Five major PWB suppliers manufactured the single-pitch density test patterns during the 1990–1991 time frame by suppliers who claimed 76/76-μm capa-

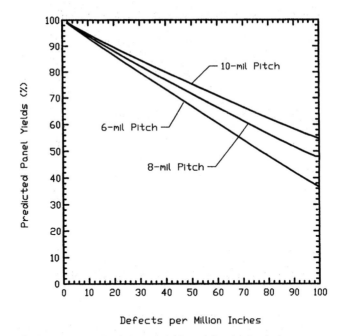

FIGURE 16.15 Predicted panel yields vs. defect density. Active area per panel side: 300 in^2 at 10% coverage. Curves for 6-, 8-, and 10-mil pitch designs.

TABLE 16.4 Characteristics of Single-Pitch Test Patterns

Pattern ID	Number of modules per side	Number of conductors per module	Total conductor length perpanel, m
127/127	4	35	18.0
102/102	4	35	24.2
76/76	4	35	31.8

bility. Figure 16.16 is the summary of the dry film and liquid photoresists and the benchmark studies. The data was censored to remove repeating defects. The goal was 90 percent first-pass yield which is equivalent to 10 defects per million inches of conductor for the 152-μm (6-mil) pitch pattern. The best liquid resists were better than the best dry film resists but none approached the 10 defect per million inches. The tool that AT&T has developed will allow PWB manufacturers and suppliers to measure the defect level in their facility and understand how to improve the first-pass yields.

16.2.4 Via Requirements

The routing on internal layers is limited by the pad size and the line and space dimension.

16.2.4.1 Internal Layer Wiring. What strategy can we use to increase the wiring density of PWBs? There are a number of factors that influence wiring density. Some of these are:

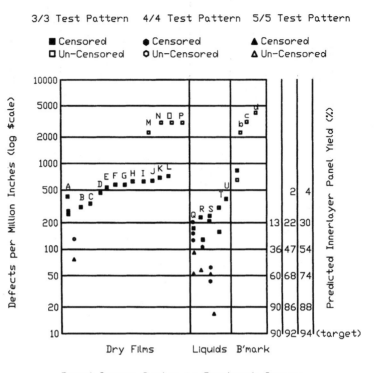

FIGURE 16.16   Photoresist system and benchmark evaluations. All data from print/etch processing on 1-oz copper.

1. PTH via grid

2. Via land size and number of vias

3. Line width and space width

PTH Via Grid.   The plated-through-hole via grid was discussed in Sec. 16.1.3, "Via Grid and Internal Wiring Capacity."

Via Land Size.   The via and associated land represents the major limit to achieving high wiring density. A through-via is almost always formed mechanically by drilling. The minimum via size that can be mechanically drilled is related to the aspect ratio of the hole since very small drills are deflected by the glass bundles in the laminate with heavy glass cloth.

Very thin laminates use lightweight glass cloth and do not appear to cause as much deflection of the drill bit. Furthermore, electroplating of vias becomes difficult when the PWB thickness is more than five times the drill diameter. With today's technology the minimum drill size for a typical 1.50-mm-thick or thicker SMT PWB would be 0.25 mm (8 mil) to 0.4 mm (16 mil). Land sizes are selected based on the drill registration capability of the PWB manufacturer and the specification requirement for annular ring. For a 457-mm × 610-mm (18 × 24-in) panel size, the drilled hole can be misregistered by 0.075 mm (3 mil) or more in any direction due to machine and tooling hole accuracy. The laminate dimensional stability of 0.0003 to 0.0005 mm/mm creates the largest misregistration since it affects the pad location on the internal layer. Layer artwork compensation is designed to limit the misregistration but predicting the value for all circuit configurations is difficult. If the via land is made 0.30 mm (12 mil) larger than the drilled hole size, then the hole could be expected to be at any location within the $D + 0.30$-mm land area. A good design rule is to keep a minimum guard band of 0.125 mm (5 mil) from the PTH hole wall to the nearest noncommon conductor. Therefore, add 0.125 mm (5 mil) to the land radius as a keepout area. It should be noted that it does not matter whether an actual land is present or not. This is the case with a landless hole. The land is actually the locus of points that the drilled hole will occupy. The additional clearance above must be added to the drilled hole locus of points as a guardband for shorting. Therefore, the effective routing space available is:

$$\text{Routing space} = \text{routing grid dim} - (D_L + (2 \times \text{keepout})$$
$$= \text{routing grid dim.} - (D_D + 0.3 + 0.25) \qquad (14.4)$$
$$= \text{routing grid dim.} - D_D + 0.55 \text{ mm}$$

where D_L = land diameter, mm
D_D = drill diameter, mm

Figure 16.17 shows the model for routing space. The land size D_L assumed in this example is designed at $D_L + 0.15$ mm. With this design rule for drill size versus land size, no annular ring is assumed and for larger misregistration than 0.15 mm, hole breakout may occur.

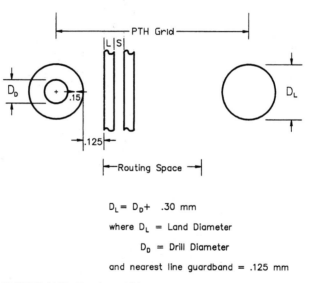

$$D_L = D_D + .30 \text{ mm}$$

where D_L = Land Diameter

D_D = Drill Diameter

and nearest line guardband = .125 mm

FIGURE 16.17   Routing model.

16.3   *WIRING COMPARISONS*

Table 16.5 was developed for a PWB model with a design rule for the land size to be 0.3 mm larger than the drill size and a minimum of 0.125 mm space between the land and the nearest line. The land size chosen represents the typical capability for PWB panel in the 457×610-mm (18×24-in) size. The 0.3 mm (12 mil) was chosen based on a basic dimensional instability of PWB laminates of about 0.0003 mm/mm. The panel has a 762-mm (30-in) diagonal and thus can have a 0.23-mm (9-mil) dimensional change due to the laminate material alone. Table 16.5

shows the track densities for various line/space width with a 1.27-mm (50-mil) via grid pattern. The important effect that can be seen from Table 16.5 is the importance of making the hole and land as small as possible. A typical PWB today would have a 125-μm line and space and a 0.45-mm (18-mil) via drilled hole diameter. The number of lines per channel can be doubled by using a 0.25-mm (10-mil) drill diameter with the same 125-μm line. The wiring density can be tripled by a combination of a 100-μm line and a 0.15-mm (6-mil) drill diameter. With the 0.45-mm (18-mil) drill and 0.75-mm land, the wiring density is the same for a 150/150-μm, 125/125-μm, and 100/100-μm line and space design. A 75/75-μm line and space must be used to get two lines per channel. For large panel sizes, the innerlayer yield for a 150-μm line could be 98 percent while a 75-μm line might be 50 percent or less.

The number of lines can be further increased by using a smaller design rule for drill land size.

TABLE 16.5   Wiring Density Comparison*
Diameter of land = drill diameter + 0.3 mm

	1.27-mm square grid (62 holes/cm²)						
Hole dia. D_D, mm	0.15	0.20	0.25	0.3	0.35	0.40	0.45
Land dia. D_L, mm	0.45	0.50	0.55	0.6	0.65	0.70	0.75
Keepout, mm	0.125	0.125	0.125	0.125	0.125	0.125	0.125
$D_D + 0.55$ mm	0.7	0.75	0.8	0.85	0.9	0.95	1.0
Routing space = $1.27 - D_D + 0.55$ mm	0.57	0.52	0.47	0.42	0.37	0.32	0.27
	Tracks between vias						
Line/space, μm							
76/76, μm	4	3	3	3	3	2	2
102/102, μm	3	3	2	2	2	2	1
127/127, μm	2	2	2	2	2	1	1
152/152, μm	2	2	2	1	1	1	1
	Wiring density cm/cm² per layer						
Line/space, μm							
76/76, μm	31.5	19.1	19.1	19.1	19.1	15.7	15.7
102/102, μm	19.1	19.1	15.7	15.7	15.7	15.7	7.8
127/127, μm	15.7	15.7	15.7	15.7	15.7	7.8	7.8
152/152, μm	15.7	15.7	15.7	7.8	7.8	7.8	7.8

* For different sizes of drilled holes, and for given line widths, this shows the number of tracks that can be placed between vias.

REFERENCES

1. "National Technology Roadmap for Semiconductors," *Workshop Working Group Reports,* Semiconductor Industry Association, 1994

2. Donald Seraphim, "Chip-Module-Packaging Interfaces," IBM Corporation, *Proceedings of the Electronic Insulation Conference,* Sept. 1977.

3. George Messner, "Derivation of Uniform Interconnection Density Analysis," *Printed Circuit World Convention V,* June 1987.

4. "Status of the Technology, Industry Activities and Action Plan 1992," EIA/IPC Surface Mount Council, presented at *Surface Mount International,* August 1992.

5. Vernon L. Brown, "A New Land Grid Array Package Family," *Proceedings of the 1992 Surface Mount International Conference,* Sept. 1992, pp. 105–125.

6. B. Freyman, and R. Pennesi, "Overmolded Plastic Array Carriers (OMPAC): A Low Cost, High Interconnect Density IC Packaging Solution for Consumer and Industrial Electronics," *41st ECTC,* May 11, 1991, pp. 176–182.

7. Sigliano, *Advanced Packaging,* March/April 1994, IPC-SM-782.

8. J. H. Lau, et al., vol. 1 of *Electronic Materials Handbook: Packaging,* ASM International Handbook Committee, pp. 274–296.

9. Don Dinella, "Additive Process Technology For the Future PWB Market," *Printed Circuit World Convention,* PCWC VI-P17, San Francisco, Calif., May 11–14, 1993.

10. IPC-TR-578, *Leading Edge Manufacturing Technology Report,* September 1984.

11. Kathy Nargi-Toth, "Additive Processing on the Upswing," *Electronic Packaging & Production,* December 1994, pp. 38–39.

12. Yutaka Tsukada, and Syuhei Ttsuchida, "Surface laminar Circuit, A Low Cost High Density Printed Circuit Board," *1992 Proceedings, Surface Mount International,* San Jose, Calif. Aug. 30–Sept. 3, 1992, pp. 537–542.

13. Ronald J. Rhodes, "Description of an Electrical Test Method to Characterize Printed Wiring Conductor Formation Capability," *The IPC Technical Review,* vol. 33, no. 2, March 1992, pp. 24–34.

14. Ronald J. Rhodes, and David Au, "Predicting Printed Wiring Board Innerlayer Panel Yield," *Proceedings of the IPC Printed Circuits EXPO,* Paper No. P5-2, April 1994.

15. Timothy A. Estes, and Ronald J. Rhodes, "An Electrical Test System for Conductor Formation Process Analysis," *Proceedings of the IPC Printed Circuits EXPO,* Paper No. P5-3, April 1994.

CHAPTER 17
IMAGING

Natalie B. Feilchenfeld, Ph.D.
IBM Microelectronics Division, Endicott, New York

The imaging process comprises several sequential steps which together allow for the metal interconnect pattern to be formed on a bare substrate. The steps themselves are interactive and it is a balance between them that allows for the reproduction of a master pattern into a metal pattern with high fidelity. The success of the steps in the sequence are dependent on the materials or chemicals used, but also to a large extent on the equipment utilized. Thus, again there is a balance of various factors in order to obtain a stable, reproducible, and high-yield/low-cost process. The details of the chemistry and the equipment used to perform it will be outlined, and as often as possible the tradeoffs of various choices will be highlighted so that both the inexperienced process engineer and the designers and procurers of PWBs who need an overview of the process considerations will be able to proceed in their work to obtain a manufacturable product.

The process sequence for imaging is given in Fig. 17.1 where the resulting pattern is used for either subtractive or additive metal pattern transfer. The details of these processes are given in the subsequent chapters. In a generic sense the process involves the coating of a polymeric material onto the substrate of interest, patterning the material either by depositing the initial layer in a patterned fashion (screen printing) or by the use of a master of the pattern desired and a photographic sequence of expose and develop for copying the master to the polymer coating. The choice between these patterning sequences is governed by the feature size desired. Larger features (8 mil and greater) can be very economically formed by screen printing. Feature sizes smaller than 8 mil are formed using a photolithographic process. For further details on the screen printing process, the previous edition of this handbook and Chap. 24 on solder mask processing in this edition are recommended.[1]

17.1 PHOTOSENSITIVE MATERIALS

The photosensitive polymeric systems used in the PWB industry are used either as liquids directly or as dry films of an initial liquid solution. Both types of materials are used widely and are excellent solutions for a variety of processing requirements. In addition, these materials may function in a photographic sense in a positive or negative tone. The difference is illustrated in Fig. 17.2 and arises from the distinct chemical compositions and in the photoinitiated reaction within the film itself. The key factor to the functioning of these materials is that their solubility in the developing solution changes on exposure to light. In the case of the common negative acting systems, the photoreaction provides a polymer network that is less soluble in

Clean Surface

⇓

Apply Photoresist

⇓

Expose Photoresist

⇓

Develop Photoresist Image

⇓

Pattern Transfer Image
(plating or etching)

⇓

Strip Photoresist

FIGURE 17.1 The photolithographic process sequence.

the develop solution by promoting cross-linking between one or more of the components in the polymeric matrix. The resulting molecular weight change in the exposed region of the film reduces the material's solubility, and it is these regions which remain after development of the image. In the positive-acting systems, the chemistry is very often that of the novalac resin-based materials utilized by the semiconductor industry. Upon irradiation, the material becomes more soluble than the original, and it is these exposed regions that are removed in the developer solution. There are many reports of the inherent differences in product yield associated with either positive- or negative-acting material.[2] Positive-acting materials are often considered to provide for a higher yield process. This could be due to the division of lines and spaces on the phototool; spaces are a greater area than lines. For a positive-acting material, the spaces are clear and these large areas are less sensitive to defect-causing debris. In contrast, for negative phototools, a small size and amount of contaminant will be reproduced as an open in the conductor. It is unfortunate that there are few materials that don't have some other obvious attribute such as thickness, coating method, etc., which will alter the yield other than their photographic tone.

There is a large variety of materials commercially available, but how does one determine which one is likely to perform best for a given application? There are several key factors to consider—several technical and many economic, the latter of which are unique to each manufacturing facility. The technical decision sequence is summarized in Fig. 17.3. The foremost consideration is the end use of the pattern; the material must have chemical compatibility with the subsequent pattern transfer steps. The chemical nature of these steps, especially the solution pH, must be distinct from the photoresist's unique solubility. Only then can the photoresist perform as an accurate mask for pattern transfer. Another key factor is the nature of the substrate itself in terms of topography and surface features; i.e., is the mask required to cover or tent plated-through-holes or tooling features, and must it conform to existing circuitry? This consideration will dictate if dry film or liquid materials are appropriate and, in some instances, the required tone of the photoresist material.

Equally important is the required product feature dimension and allowable variation. This is usually specified in terms of line width and spacing with a given allowable variation on the nominal. Since these product parameters are for the final conductor features, some estimate of the photoresist processing contribution to this value must be established. Each material has its inherent contrast or ability to switch from exposed to unexposed. This, along with the resist thickness, phototool, and light source used for exposure, govern the feature dimensions that can be defined with a given material. For the materials used in the PWB industry, the following rule usually holds: The minimum line width definable in production is usually 0.5 to 1.0 mil greater than the photoresist thickness. New process sequences demonstrated improvements beyond this traditional barrier.[2,3,4,5] Of a more practical nature, the material chosen must have adhesion to the underlying substrate. There are many approaches to promoting adhesion between dissimilar materials, but there must be an inherent compatibility.

17.1.1 Dry Films

Dry film photoresist materials are commonly used for pattern formation prior to both plating and etching of underlying metals. They are available in a range of film thickness from 0.5 to

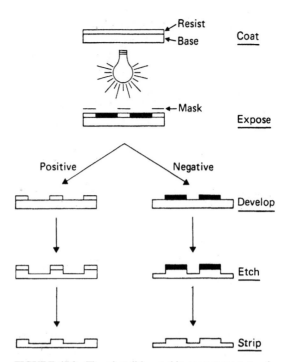

FIGURE 17.2 The photolithographic process sequence for positive and negative tone photoresists. (*Reprinted by permission of C. G. Willson*, Introduction to Microlithography, Theory, Materials and Processing, *ACS Symposium Series 219, Washington, D.C., 1983, p. 89.*)

3.0 mil, typically. These free-standing films are laminated using hot rollers and pressure to the PWB substrate. They are purchased as a three-film sandwich, where the outer polyester has optical properties, the photosensitive material is found in the middle, and there is an outer backer sheet of polyethylene (see Fig. 17.4). The optical clarity of the polyethylene sheet is important with respect to the dimensions of the features to be formed. For 4- to 5-mil features, all available grades can be used with good success; for dimensions less than 4 mil, optical-grade materials enhance the image quality and, therefore, the product yield. Most thin dry films of 1-mil thickness and less are routinely produced on this high-quality covering material. The purpose of this coverlay is two-fold: (1) to protect the photoactive material from damage and from adhering to the phototool during hard contact printing, and (2) to limit the amount of oxygen migrating into the film during the exposure step.

Oxygen is a very efficient quencher of the radical reaction portion of the imaging reaction and, although components are added to most commercial formulations to overcome the quenching which results from oxygen present within the film, this outer film provides a diffusion barrier to further addition of oxygen.

The chemical and mechanical properties of these materials have been tailored to various subsequent processing requirements, i.e., to withstand either acidic (cupric chloride/hydrochloric acid $CuCl_2$-HCl etching) or basic (ammoniacal etching) solutions and are also further specialized for either acid-based plating or etching. Given the variety of materials available, they will be described here in terms of the photolithographic processing chemistry used

CONSIDERATIONS

POSSIBILITIES

_____

_____

Process Application?

                                Etch   Plate

Chemistry?

                                 Acid   Alkaline

Product Features?

                  Topography   PTH   No Features

Resolution?

                    2   3   4   5   6   mils

_____

_____

Possible Conclusions (for example)

Etch/Acid/Topography/ 2 mil features   Electrodepositied resist
Etch/Acid/ Topography/ 5 mil features   Dry film or
                                         curtain coated liquid

FIGURE 17.3 Criteria for selection of photoresist materials.

for developing the image. Three types are utilized: aqueous, semiaqueous, and solvent-developable systems (see Table 17.1). With the agreement to the Montreal Protocol eliminating the use of chlorinated hydrocarbons, the usage of the solvent-developable materials has decreased dramatically and the predominate material type is the aqueous-processable. The dry film materials vary in their exact chemical compositions, but all comprise the following components: photoactive compound, monomer, polymer backbone, dye, and additives.[6] The light is absorbed by the photoactive compound which subsequently reacts with the monomer to alter the solubility of the film in the irradiated area of the film. The polymer sets the fundamental solubility of the system and this is modified by the photoreaction. The dye changes color to provide a latent image of the master pattern in the film. This manufacturing aid actually decreases the efficiency of the desired photoreaction, since it consumes a portion of the incident radiation to proceed. The additives often promote adhesion, lend flexibility to the film, or aid in another desirable property. But all components function together to provide a versatile processing option.

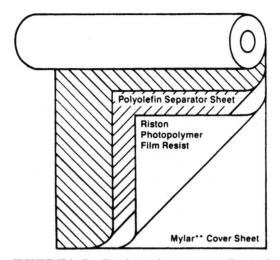

FIGURE 17.4   Dry film photoresist components. *(Reprinted with permission of Du Pont Electronics, Du Pont Technical Literature.)*

TABLE 17.1   Summary for Dry Film Photoresist Types and Chemistries

Photoresist type	Develop solution	Strip solution	Application
Aqueous-processable	Sodium/potassium carbonate	Sodium/potassium hydroxide	Acidic solution: etching, plating Limited alkaline solutions: alkaline etch
Semiaqueous-processable	Sodium tetraborate/ Butyl cellusolve	Ethanolamine or Butyl carbitol/ Butyl cellusolve	Alkaline solutions: etching, precious metal plating
Solvent-processable	(Methyl chloroform) Alternate to CFCs	(Methylene chloride) Alternate to CFCs	Strong alkaline: Full-build electroless Cu plating

17.1.2   Aqueous-Processable Dry Films

The majority of materials used today are based on an acrylate polymer with various forms of photoreaction initiation. The initiator's absorption is designed to coincide with the major emission wavelength of the mercury arc lamps in the ultraviolet region of the spectrum at 365 nm. Many are based on the use of Michler's ketone and its subsequent sensitization of a triplet state promoted radical chain polymerization. This also explains the material's sensitivity to oxygen, an efficient triplet quencher. These materials are also very efficient at converting the light energy into a chemical reaction due to the radical chain reactions; absorption of one photon of light results in many cross-links in the polymer matrix. Usual exposure doses as measured as the irradiance from 330 to 405 nm to functionally cross-link these materials vary from 25 to 90 mJ/cm^2 depending on the exact chemistry used and the thickness of the materials which compares favorably to positive-acting materials used for conventional optical lithography in semiconductor (IC) production where doses of 200 to 500 mJ/cm^2 are common.

The images in these materials are developed in alkaline solutions of 1% or less by weight of sodium or potassium carbonate. The complete removal of the photoresist after pattern transfer is accomplished in 1M or greater solutions of sodium or potassium hydroxide at elevated temperatures, often with the addition of an antitarnishing additive to limit the oxidation of the copper. Thus, in general these materials exhibit excellent stability in acidic solution, but they do have varying stability to more strongly acid and alkaline solutions. In fact, there are three subclasses of materials: for acid etching of copper, for acid plating of copper, and for alkaline (ammoniacal usual) etching of copper. Increased acid stability is required for use in acid copper plating where the pHs of the solutions often are below 1. For ammoniacal copper etching at pH 8 to 9, increased alkaline stability is required. This latter capability illustrates the flexibility in tailoring these materials to their end use since these materials are imaged using similar alkaline chemicals: Develop at pH 10.3 and strip at pH 13. Often these "alkaline" stable materials are developed at high temperatures.

In the past, several novel materials were formulated to be exposed at a visible wavelength, 450 nm, instead of the 365 nm usually used. These materials were especially designed to be used with specialized exposure equipment—either visible lasers or magnified projection printing. Laser direct imaging has progressed and utilizes the Ar^+ ion laser output clustered around 360 nm. Conventional materials can be used, although improvements in the photospeed are desirable. Several specialized materials are available where the required exposure dose is close to 20 mJ/cm^2. This faster exposure time is required for economic viability of this system.[7] The remainder of their processing is identical to that of conventional materials.

Another distinctive family of aqueous-developable materials are those that are processed in dilute acidic media. At first they were available as electrophoretic depositable materials stemming from the similar chemistry used in the electrophoretic coating of automobiles. A dry film version of this type of material was formulated and characterized to have excellent stability in alkaline solutions. This material would be utilized in strong alkaline etching solutions as are used for polyimides and for full-build electroless copper plating.[8]

17.1.3 Semiaqueous-Developable Dry Films

These materials are very similar in composition to the aqueous-developable materials. The polymer back bond is less alkaline-soluble and probably contains fewer acrylic acid pendant groups. The developer chemistry is slightly alkaline (sodium tetraborate) and also typically contains an organic assist of butyl cellusolve. The process control for this mixture is more complicated than that used for aqueous-processable materials.

Semiaqueous-developable photoresists are used when increased stability to chemical attack is required. Often they are used for image transfer steps in highly alkaline solutions such as polyimide etching or gold and precious metal plating applications. This increased stability can take two forms: the surface and side walls of the material remains intact and underplating is limited, both of which allow for accurate image transfer.

17.1.4 Solvent-Developable Dry Films

Solvent-developable dry films were the first commercially produced materials. They are based on methyl methacrylate polymers and a similar Michler's ketone initiation system as currently used for aqueous-developable materials. As imaging materials, they can have a very high contrast, the photolithographic measure of how little energy is required to change from image formation to image washout. Despite this measured property, these materials, in practice, are prone to scumming where residues remain in the spaces between exposed photoresist features after develop. Often, slight etching of the underlying substrate is required to have a clean image transfer step, especially for pattern-plating applications. The majority of the uses for these materials are again for instances where increased stability for subsequent processing is required. In many instances these materials are the only ones that can withstand harsh conditions and, therefore, substitute materials have not been found for these chemical processing sequences.

Traditionally these materials are developed in trichloroethane and stripped in methylene chloride. In a practical sense, these solvents were easy to use in a manufacturing mode: single component and nonflammable for large-batch operations in either a spray or immersion tool set. In the past few years, the use of chlorinated hydrocarbons (CFCs) has been sharply reduced and will be eliminated, according to the provisions of the Montreal Protocol. This has forced the use of alternative develop and strip chemistries.[9]

17.1.5 Aqueous-Processable Liquids

These materials come from a variety of sources and in many respects are a thinner and liquid-coatable form of the dry film materials. The thin coatings have superior resolution. The resolution is approximated to the thickness of the material and, therefore, a coating of less than 1 mil will have resolution on that order. They find their main use for innerlayer imaging, where they are coated using roller, spray, curtain, and electrostatic apply methods. These methods will be discussed later in the chapter (with equipment). The cleanliness of the substrate and the coating and drying operation is critical for a high-yield process with these materials. There is evidence of superior adhesion of these materials to the copper or substrate due to their drying on the surface with excellent conformation.[10] The films are dried to allow for hard contact with the phototool used during exposure. If soft or off contact only can be used, then the resolution and the yield, especially in 5-mil and less features, is severely compromised. For the majority of the materials, the develop and stripping conditions of these materials are similar to that of aqueous-developable films, mild alkaline sodium carbonate, and strong alkaline sodium hydroxide. Exceptions to this are positive-acting novolac type and negative acid-developable ones.

The chemistry of the typical materials is similar to that of the aqueous-developable dry films. They depend on a radical chain reaction to promote cross-linking in the acrylate polymer material. Their sensitivities differ depending on the initiator system chosen. The materials are available with minimal solvent content and a few are diluted with water.[11,12] This reduces the emissions from coating and drying that must be contained and treated.

There are two other types of liquids that can be utilized, depending on the chemical compatibility required for subsequent processing. The acid-developable materials are mentioned in the dry film aqueous section and again in the following section on electrophoretic depositable materials. They are materials with high contrast, good resolution, and chemical stability, which are developed in aqueous acid solutions. The other alternative is a positive tone novolac resin-based system that finds its application most usually in the semiconductor industry for imaging integrated circuits. They have excellent resolution and chemical stability in acid and a large number of basic solutions (precious metal plating). The chemistry involves the conversion of a base-insoluble diazonaphthalquinone to the base-soluble indene acid. Thus, this photo-driven conversion alters the solubility of the base material in alkaline solutions, allowing for image formation.

17.1.6 Electrophoretic Depositable Materials

These materials are the newest arrival for PWB imaging with the introduction in the late 1980s and early 1990s of several electrophoretic depositable (ED) materials.[13–15] The early materials were modifications of those used for the coating of automobiles and appliances. These fast coating processes provide a defect-free film of high durability on conductive substrates and are well suited to large-volume production. A far greater variety of materials is now available, including both anodically and cathodically deposited materials that are both positive and negative acting. They will be discussed here in those terms.

The common processing sequence is as follows: preclean, coat, rinse, protective coat (optional), dehydration bake, expose, develop, pattern transfer, and strip. The early portion is unique, although similar to that required for more conventional liquids. The best results are obtained with the preclean and coating processes within the same equipment, which resembles a batch electroplater. Often the boards are not dried between these steps. The coating material wets the clean substrate surface very well and this is key to obtaining a defect-free coating. The bake after coating removes the residual water in the film and allows the film to coalesce and harden for hard contact exposure. Sometimes it is necessary to coat a protective film in addition to the photoresist to improve this hardness and to provide an oxygen diffusion barrier.

The composition of the photoresist coating solution is actually a microdispersion, or emulsion, or micelle, depending on the exact stability and size of the organized components. The photoresist constituents are found within the vesicle (hydrophobic) and the outer shell is charged (hydrophilic) (see Fig. 17.5). The charged vesicle migrates under the influence of an electrical field (applied voltage in a plating cell) to either the cathode (ammonium ion, cathodic material) or anode (carboxylic acid anion, anodic material), with the counter ion migrating to the opposite electrode. There are, therefore, two distinct types of plating reactions, as represented in Fig. 17.6. In practical terms, there are other differences. Copper dissolves in the anodic case; the substrate is cleaned, but often copper is incorporated into the films. The cathodic deposition reaction produces more gas and, therefore, some form of agitation is required for pin-hole-free coatings.

The coating reaction is self-limiting and proceeds until the substrate is insulated. The absolute thickness is a function of the chemistry and the deposition conditions: applied voltage or current density and temperature. There is little adjustability. In one case, a wide range from approximately 0.3 to 1.0 mil can be deposited with the same chemical composition (see

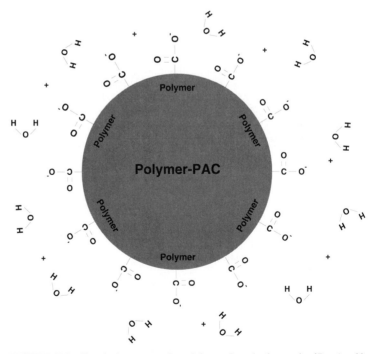

FIGURE 17.5 Chemical representation of electrophoretic photoresist. (*Reprinted by permission of J. Dubrava, et al., "Development of a Novel Positive-Working Electrodeposited Photo Resist Process for the Production of High Density PWB Outerlayers,"* Presentation at the IPC Conference Spring 1995, *San Diego, Calif.*).

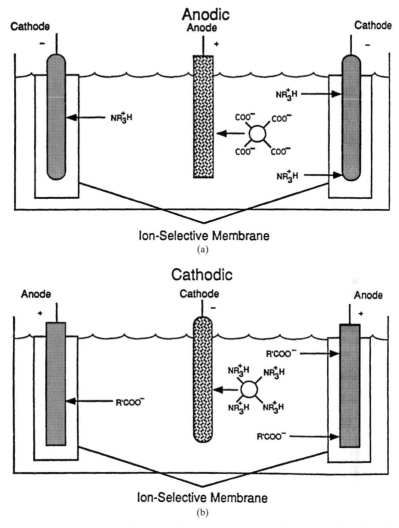

FIGURE 17.6 Plating reactions occurring during electrodeposition of cathodic and anodic materials. *(Reprinted with permission of Du Pont Electronics, Du Pont Technical Literature.)*

Fig. 17.7), by varying the solution temperature.[16] The typical thickness from 0.3 to 0.5 mil extends below the current manufacturable limit for dry film materials and is comparable to conventional liquid-coated materials. Therefore, again these materials have excellent resolution—less than 1 mil—and are an extension to more conventional lithographic techniques. The additional feature of obtaining coverage on all exposed conductive surfaces is an advantage for substrates with topography and represents a unique capability.

17.1.6.1 Cathodic-Deposited Materials.   The cathodically depositable materials are microdispersions or emulsions based on the ammonium salt of methacrylic acid. Lactic acid anion is used as the counter ion. In addition, the main polymeric components are acrylates or epoxies or a mixture of both functionalities with different resulting film properties. The devel-

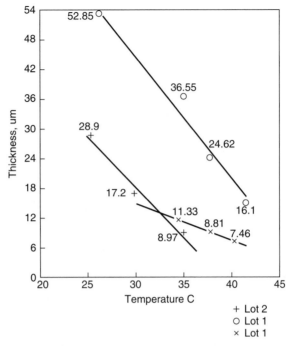

FIGURE 17.7 Deposited film thickness as a function of temperature for Eagle® electrodepositable photoresist.

oper of dilute lactic acid is different from that used for other aqueous-processable dry films and liquid-coatable materials.

Despite their acid developing chemistry, their acid solubility is selective to organic acids so that these materials do withstand the etching in $CuCl_2/HCl$ and $FeCl_3/HCl$ solutions. They have unique stability in alkaline solutions, such as those used for electroless plating and alkaline etching. With a thickness of approximately 0.5 mil, they have a limited application as a material for patterning plating except for a material with adjustable thickness which is compatible with precious metal plating (Au, Pd). These materials require a change to a distinct but manageable chemistry for develop and strip, but they are unique in their adhesion to the substrate and chemical stability for pattern transfer processes.

17.1.6.2 Anodically Deposited Materials. One example of electrophoretically depositable photoresist is analogous to an aqueous-developable dry film and liquid coatables since similar photochemistry occurs and they are processed in identical chemicals. Their clear advantage is that fewer changes are required to obtain the advantages of an electrophoretic deposited material: they have good resolution due to the thin coating and good substrate coverage.

The majority of these materials are positively acting and are distinct in chemistry from traditional PWB materials but are very similar to semiconductor materials based on diazonaphthalquinone chemistry with a novolac resins backbone. The novolac hydroxyl group is ionized and it is responsible for the deposition reaction. These materials typically have a longer deposition time than the cathodic systems for comparable thickness.

The use of these materials is for applications where the resist must remain, but there is no possibility of exposing it (negative tone cannot be used). Thus it is used as a replacement for tent and etch for outerlayer conductor formation.

17.2   EQUIPMENT ALTERNATIVES

The process steps to obtain a usable image are all interactive and, therefore, the equipment plays a very large role in the success of the overall process. For each step there are numerous options and the choice between them is governed by the product specifications with respect to layer thickness and feature size and, in some instances, by the chosen photoresist, in addition to the economic factors which are unique to each installation. The alternative equipment for each process step will be described with criteria with which to compare them.

17.2.1   Cleanliness Considerations

Cleanliness is of concern for the entire photolithography process. This includes yellow room contamination level (cleanliness class), solution filtration, equipment cleanliness class, and product handling. The relative importance of each of these must be established for the product feature dimensions. The sensitivity of the photolithographic sequence to the size and location of contamination can be determined, and then the appropriate level of cleanliness can be instituted and maintained.[17-19] In addition, equipment to remove contamination from flat surfaces—either panels or equipment—can be used throughout the processing sequence. These *sticky rollers* are available as free-standing equipment and as hand-held items.

17.2.2   Preclean

This step provides the foundation for all the others since only an appropriately cleaned substrate allows for good adhesion between the photoresist and the substrate and for the remainder of the process to be successful. All laminates arrive at the imaging area dirty and, depending on the type of contamination, the exact process sequence is chosen. Contamination—epoxy dust—from trimming and processing the laminate itself is removed by mechanical cleaning. The surface copper is either foil or foil with electroless or electroplated copper. The foil has been treated with an antitarnishing agent of chromium and zinc, which is removed for reproducible imaging results. Not only are contaminants removed, but also the texture or surface roughness of the copper is altered to promote mechanical adhesion between the base copper and the photoresist. The extent of this texturing is measured by the usual parameters for surface roughness where the height and spacing of the topography is quantified by profilometer measurements (see Fig. 17.8).

Chemical cleanliness can be determined in a variety of ways. Wetting is often tested using a *water break test* or more analytically in terms of contact angle where a low value is desirable. In addition, analytical techniques can be used to evaluate the chemical composition of the surface (Auger and X-ray Photoelectron Spectroscopies), Table 17.2.[20,21]

17.2.2.1   Mechanical Cleaning.   Most mechanical cleaning equipment utilizes a slurry of particles either directly (scrubbing or vapor blasting) or impregnated into brushes to physically abrade the copper surface. Both pumice and aluminum oxide are used as slurry materials. The differing final surface texture is grooved after using brushes and an even texture after scrubbing (see Fig. 17.9). In both instances the boards must have a sufficiently thick layer of copper so that a loss of 50 μin does not impact the final conductor height. Many advances have been made, but it remains difficult to mechanically clean very thin or flimsy panels.

The texture of the resulting surface provides for mechanical adhesion between the photoresist and the copper. The resist conforms to the topography and, thus, the extent and type of texture is tailored to the type of photoresist. If the gouges are too deep, a dry film with traditional lamination will have difficulty in conforming to the surface. The conductor wiring will be defective: near or full opens after etching and underplating or shorts after pattern

R $_a$ Arithmetic mean of all departures from the mean line

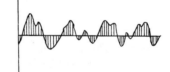

R $_{max}$ Maximum peak to valley height within sampling area

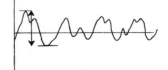

S $_m$ Mean spacing between peak measured at the mean line

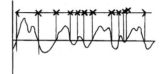

FIGURE 17.8   Surface roughness parameters.

TABLE 17.2   Copper Surface Chemical Composition as Measured by X-Ray Photoelectron Spectroscopy (XPS)

Sample	% Cu	% O	% C	% N	% Zn	% Cr
Initial		46	24		16	12
Preclean 1	12	19	68			
Preclean 2	6	10	70	14		

plating. Thus, the process must be matched with the materials and apply method to be used subsequently.

The equipment itself is conveyorized, with the boards passing through the brushes or slurry and then to rinse chambers before exiting through a dryer section. Residual pumice can remain on the copper surface due to insufficient rinsing. The upkeep on this equipment is very important since the brushes deteriorate with use and the slurry also will degrade. The proper functioning of the mechanical parts that come in contact with the product is key. Equipment which isolates the abrasive from the majority of the tool will be more durable.

17.2.2.2   Chemical Cleaning.   Chemical cleaning can comprise several solutions since each type of contaminant has its own solubility (see Table 17.3). Grease and fingerprints require a soap solution or solvent to dissolve them. The antitarnish treatment is removed and copper is roughened with mild etchants for the copper, such as ammonium or sodium persulfate, or peroxide/sulfuric acid. Often there is an induction time for copper removal which depends on the oxidation level of the surface and the amount of antitarnish treatment. Com-

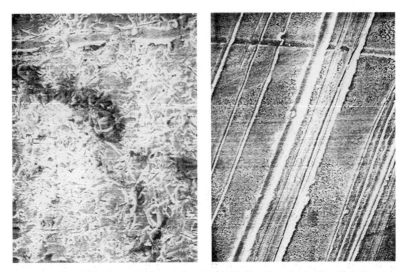

FIGURE 17.9 Comparison of the pumice cleaned (*left*) and mechanically abraded copper surfaces (*right*), 1200X. (*Reprinted with permission of D. P. Seraphim, R. C. Lasky, and C-Y Li,* Principles of Electronic Packaging, *McGraw-Hill, 1989, p. 383.*)

TABLE 17.3 Cleaning Solutions Used to Remove Various Contaminants

Cleaning technique	Process chemistry	Contaminant removed
Abrasion	Pumice, Al oxide	All
Plasma	CF_4/O_2, O_2/H_2O	Organic
Chemical solutions (aqueous etchants)	H_2SO_4, HCl, etc.	Inorganic
Chemical solutions (nonaqueous)	Alcohols, etc.	Organic
Thermal	N_2	H_2O

Source: Adapted from *Introduction to Microlithography*, 1st ed., L. F. Thompson and M. J. Bowden, *American Chemical Society Symposium Series 219*, Washington, D.C., 1983, p. 184.

mon solutions are used both directly and as trade chemistries where surfactants and other proprietary additives have been included. Alternatively, the oxide and antitarnish treatment can be removed initially, followed by a surface roughening. The oxide removal is accomplished with mild acidic cleaning solutions such as sulfuric acid.

The selection of the cleaning solution also depends on the thickness of the copper; for thin "seed" layers used for electrolytic pattern plating, very little etching can be tolerated. In this instance, extremely dilute solutions or dry methods are used. Thus, chemical adhesion can be more important than mechanical. A review of adhesion considerations is found in Ref. 22. Selection of the process chemicals and sequence depends again on the photoresist to be used subsequently and the overall conductor formation process.

These cleaning sequences are often contained in conveyorized spray equipment with rinsing between each step. Batch processing in a tank system with a hoist for basket movement between solutions is also used. The uniformity of the etching of panels within a basket must be measured, although with short immersion times, the uniformity is quite good and reproducible if the bath's chemical composition is consistent.

17.2.2.3 Electrolytic Cleaning.   A unique approach to cleaning is built by Atotech which utilizes electrolytic cleaning to remove the antitarnishing agent.[23,24] The overall sequence is contained within an in-line conveyorized tool. The antitarnishing agents are removed electrolytically along with oils and fingerprints. Very little to no copper is removed in an inherently uniform process. The surface texture is then altered by microetching and then passivated prior to dry film photoresist lamination or other coatings.

17.2.3 Photoresist Apply

The numerous choices for applying the photoresist are tied in most instances to the photoresist choice. The discussion here will be divided between liquid and dry film methods. Irrespective of the method chosen, the cleanliness of the operation—both the equipment and the clean room—and the handling of the product are important. It is also advisable to minimize the handling at this stage with the use of automated operation. Specifically, in-line equipment, with the preclean step, and automatic loading and unloading are advised.

17.2.3.1 Dry Film Hot Roll Lamination.   This process is utilized for dry film materials where both temperature and pressure are used to coat the photoresist on the panels. At the point of contact, the photoresist is heated above its T_g and simultaneously pressed onto the substrate. The material flows to conform to the irregularities of the copper surface. For aqueous-developable materials, the use of wet lamination has been shown to increase the flow and greatly improve the resulting conductor formation yield.[25-28] This process is not always possible with drilled holes and, therefore, heating the panels prior to lamination is often used to improve photoresist conformation to the surface. Both heated rollers and infrared heaters are used. To maximize the flow of the material, the key process parameters are conveyor speed, temperature set point for the cure rolls, and rigidity of the cure rolls with respect to the core material and rubber durometer.

Both automatic and manual tools are available for film lamination (see Fig. 17.10). In the latter instance, the operator places the panel in the nip of the rollers and it is pulled through by the rotation of the cure rollers. The continuous film of photoresist must be trimmed for each panel on at least two sides. This technique is labor intensive and extremely dirty due to the chips of resist generated by trimming, but is ideal for very thin materials and nonstandard-size panels in small lot sizes.

The automatic equipment is a conveyorized system where the panel can enter from an automatic loader or a conveyorized preclean tool directly into and through the dry film laminator. The photoresist can be placed within the board edge by choosing the film width and tool metering appropriately. This is a relatively clean operation where the panels require little handling. The available equipment is able to convey very thin and nonrigid panels. The panels are often heated, wetted (wet lamination), or cleaned ahead of the actual lamination.

17.2.3.2 Dry Film Vacuum Lamination.   This method of applying the photoresist is a modification of the hot roll lamination; temperature and pressure are used to adhere the photoresist to the part with a heated vacuum platen instead of cure rolls. This method is useful for products where the photoresist has difficulty conforming to either tall features or closely spaced ones. This method will "pull" the material into tight spaces and provide conformal coverage. This equipment is also used for material that will deform nonuniformly under the pressure of the cure rolls, such as thin unreinforced polyimides; in vacuum lamination, the pressure is distributed evenly over the piece for improved dimensional stability control.

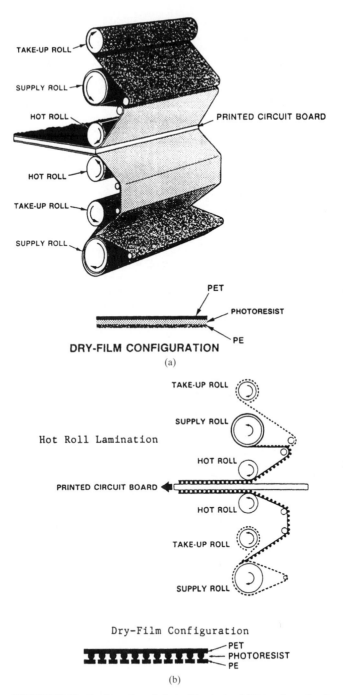

FIGURE 17.10   Configuration of a hot roll laminator: (a) three-dimensional schematic; (b) two-dimensional schematic. (*Reprinted with permission of E. S. W. Kong,* Polymers for High Technology, *ACS Symposium Series 346, Washington, D.C., 1987, p. 280.*)

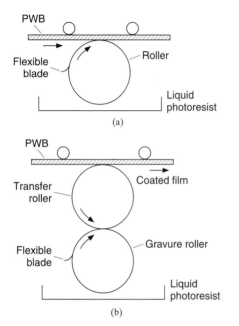

FIGURE 17.11 Configuration of a roll coater: (*a*) direct coating; (*b*) indirect coating.

17.2.3.3 Liquid Coating. The great variety of methods are distinguished by being single- or double-sided, where curtain and screen coating are single-sided, requiring processing the panels twice through the equipment operation, with a slight drying between coatings. There is obviously a difference in the solvent content of the two sides. The remaining techniques discussed here—roller, spray, electrostatic, and electrophoretic coating—are double-sided and are well suited to high-volume manufacturing. In all instances, the cleanliness of the surroundings, equipment, and solutions is important for high-yield processing. Most equipment has means of conserving the materials by trapping excess liquid for filtering and reapplying.

17.2.3.4 Roller Coating. This method places liquid films on the board by transferring the liquid from one set of rollers to another (see Fig. 17.11). The exact physical configuration of the rollers, the number of rollers, the surface of the rollers, and metering of the material all vary. Often, gravure roller coating is used where the rollers that contact the panel have grooves or cross hatches which dictate the amount of liquid deposited on the substrate and are set with a measured overlap or interference so that the board is squeezed between the rollers.[29] A range of viscosity also influences the range of coating thickness. Improvements in the handling of panels and in the ability to confine the solution to the center of the board allows for two-sided simultaneous "postage stamp" coverage similar to that obtained with dry film materials. The tooling and location holes are clear of material. In the commercial systems, the coater is a conveyorized system with the panels entering a clean oven immediately after coating. The throughput of these systems can be as high as 240 panels/h.

17.2.3.5 Electrophoretic Coating. This method requires specially formulated materials which are characterized by the deposition type: anodic or cathodic. The equipment schematic in Fig. 17.12 illustrates the process sequence through preclean, coat, permeate rinse, rinse, and dry.[30] The parts are placed in the photoresist solution wet or are often sprayed with solution to ensure wetting, especially if the parts have blind or through-vias. Voltage is applied and within 20 s to 3 min an insulating film forms. Rinsing removes loosely bound material which is returned to the plating cell after ultrafiltration to separate the photoresist and the counter ion. This aids in maintaining the ionic balance. After a final water rinse, the panel is dried to remove any incorporated water and to consolidate the film. The film is now tack-free and can be imaged.

The exact specifications for the equipment components vary with the chemical composition of the photoresist; some can tolerate PVC while others require polypropylene or polyethylene. The electrodes are made of stainless steel and encased in an ion-selective membrane which is flushed to prevent the buildup of the counterion migrating there during deposition. The permeate and ultrafiltration unit is important for long-term stability of the coating solution. The coating unit is often enclosed in a clean environment to reduce the amount of particles found in solution or resting on the part as the process proceeds.

17.2.3.6 Spray Coating. This method is rarely used since it wastes much of the coating material. To obtain a uniform coating, the spray head traverses a larger area than the substrate to be coated. The overspray can be 50 to 80 percent of the total material utilized. Very thin and uniform coatings are possible. The spray head configuration, along with the droplet size, con-

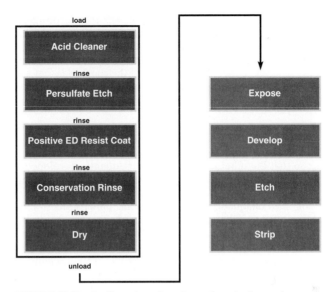

FIGURE 17.12 Configuration of an electrophoretic photoresist coater. (*Reprinted with permission of J. Dubrava, et al., "Development of a Novel Positive-Working Electrodeposited Photo Resist Process for the Production of High Density PWB Outerlayers,* Presentation at the IPC Conference Spring 1995, *San Diego, Calif.*)

veyor speed, and the nozzle backpressure, dictate the exact characteristics of the coating with respect to thickness and topographical coverage.[31]

17.2.3.7 Electrostatic Coating.   This method is similar to spray coating except that the rotating spray head is charged and the panel is grounded. The photoresist is atomized and attracted to the substrate. Often used for solder mask coating, it provides for a uniform coating with less material waste than with conventional spraying.[32–35] There is good coverage of conductor sidewalls and rough surfaces, but sharp corners such as those found on the rim of a plated-through-hole (PTH) get a thicker coating while the interior of a PTH will receive none. Thus, this restricts the use to innerlayers.

17.2.3.8 Curtain Coating.   This method is also commonly used to coat liquid solder mask materials. The panel is conveyed through a vertically falling curtain of the photoresist at high speed. The coating can be defined spatially so that the edges are not covered. Again a postage stamp coating results. The thickness of the coating is controlled by the size of the slot through which the liquid falls and the pressure that is exerted across the slot.[36] This coating is one-sided, and for two-sided panels the material is partially dried and then coated on the reverse side. The material in the curtain is returned to the sump and is reused for very efficient utilization of the material. The temperature and viscosity are controlled for reproducible coatings. This method is limited since very thin panels cannot be conveyed through the curtain at high velocity and extra handling is required to coat one side at a time.

17.2.3.9 Screen Coating.   This is another common method for coating solder mask with either a pattern or flood coverage. The screen differs in mesh size and this, along with the liquid solution viscosity, will dictate the wet coating thickness. The screen is placed above the panel to be coated and the material is pushed through the openings in the screen onto the panel surface. The film will form from the discrete deposits. For double-sided applications, the coating is partially dried and the reverse side is coated. There is a difference in the solvent content of the sides, which would result in nonuniformity for very precise lithography. In addition, the sequential nature of the coating will allow debris and contaminants to be embedded into the first coating. The advantage of this method is that a coater is inexpensive to purchase and operate. A postage stamp coating is possible, and the waste is minimized.

17.2.4 Expose

In this key step for image formation, the master pattern is aligned to and exposed in the product so that the relief image can be subsequently developed. The elements of the process are the phototool, the registration of the phototool to the panel, and the light source used for exposure. The choices for phototools, of either film or glass, differ as to sharpness of the transition from opaque to clear, the patterns' dimensional stability, and the substrate absorption of the exposing light. The panel is aligned either mechanically with pins holding the phototool with respect to the product or optically with alignment features dictating the movement of the phototool and product. The alignment requirements are interrelated to those achieved at composite lamination and drilling. The registration scheme is contained within the exposure equipment. The light source alternatives include contact printing with either a collimated or uncollimated light source, proximity printing, projection printing, and laser direct imaging. The latter three methods separate the phototool from the substrate and are expected to have an increased product yield due to reduced contamination. No phototool is used in laser direct imaging since the laser beam exposes the image based on the design data.

17.2.4.1 Registration.   The image is placed on the panel with respect to a point of reference so that the image is well aligned to previous and future features. In multilayer construction the innerlayer images are aligned front to back for successful lamination and drilling of the PTHs. The outerlayer image is then aligned to the drilled holes. The same considerations are relevant for single-layer boards. Thus, accurate alignment is clearly part of the imaging process and also depends on knowledge and control of the dimensional stability of the product. The image must be scaled to match the dimension of the board at the exposure step; for multilayer structures with several photolithographic steps, a series of dimensional measurements are required prior to product manufacture.

Mechanical registration entails the use of fixed pins or other mechanical devices to hold the phototool and the panel in place during exposure. The actual configuration of the pins and their shape varies. Both two- and three-point systems are used. The three-point systems well define the center location since they are located at the extremes of the area to be patterned. The shapes of the pins are either round or elongated with one flat side. In the latter case, the flat side defines the edge, while round pins center within the hole in the panel and phototool. Film artwork alignment holes are punched with respect to the product pattern by plotting alignment targets as part of the product pattern and optically aligning and punching a slot or hole. The edges of the punched feature wear and registration will deteriorate with use. For glass artwork the glass is drilled at the alignment locations and a bushing is placed at the center of the hole. The pin is then inserted through the bushings in top and bottom artwork and through the panel. With use, the bushings do move and must be reset for maximum reproducibility.

Optical alignment systems operate either manually or automatically. In both instances the phototool is plotted with alignment targets—usually an opaque dot that is smaller than a drilled or punched hole in the panel. With backlighting, the dot (phototool) is aligned to the center of the hole (product). Often, three locations at the edges of the panel are used. For manual systems, micrometers move the part or artwork, while for automatic schemes, a vision system will calculate the movement necessary, and motors move either the phototool or the product into alignment. There is no wear on the phototool when it is optically registered and therefore the accuracy is maintained with usage. The absolute accuracy achieved with optical methods is superior to mechanical means with the best accuracy and reproducibility obtained with automatic optical systems. The extra expense is warranted only to meet stringent product requirements.

17.2.4.2 Exposure Control and Measurement.   The role of exposure is to functionally cross-link the material, which will not be 100 percent cured chemically. The appropriate energy dose is determined experimentally on the product of interest—the combination of dose and develop to produce features with straight sidewalls. Contrast curves, which plot the log of the exposure dose versus the thickness of the film remaining when the exposure is done from the backside of the material coated on an optical clear substrate, identify the functional cure point: The thickness loss is less than 10 percent (see Fig. 17.13). Exposure in the region of stability ensures that the base of the material has reacted. Step wedges, film strips with a series of neutral density filters, are also used to determine appropriate exposure doses. The dose is varied to obtain photoresist residue on the area with the manufacturer's recommended step value. The success of this technique depends on the appropriate choice and consistency in the developer conditions. Step wedges are often used to control the expose or expose-and-develop processes.

The measurement of the dose can be obtained by two techniques. The energy incident on the photoresist is expressed as the product of the lamp intensity and the time of exposure:

$$\text{Energy} = \text{intensity} \times \text{time} \tag{17.1}$$

Thus, the exposure dose can be measured directly by the use of an integrating radiometer or measurement of both the light intensity with a radiometer and exposure time. The radiome-

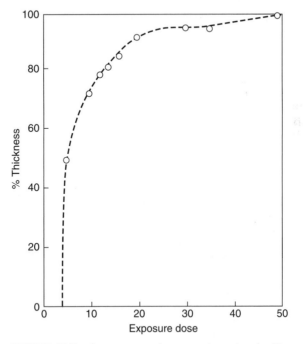

FIGURE 17.13 Contrast curve for a negative-acting dry film photoresist, percent film thickness remaining versus exposure dose (mJ/cm^2).

ter response must be matched to the spectral output of the light used so that representative measurements are made (see Fig. 17.14). Most exposure equipment provides the option of using either direct energy or time measurement. With a stable light source, they are equally reproducible.

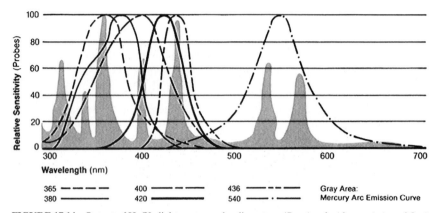

FIGURE 17.14   Output of Hg/Xe light source and radiometers. *(Reprinted with permission of Optical Associates, Inc., Milpitas, Calif., Technical Literature.)*

17.2.4.3   Contact Exposure Tools.   This equipment places the phototool and the panel in direct contact and for "hard" contact draws a vacuum between the pieces. A range of wavelengths of light is used, often from a mercury or mercury/xenon light source, which is stable and has a high-intensity output at ultraviolet and visible (UV/Vis) wavelengths (see Fig. 17.15). The light from the lamp is spread over the area of the board to be exposed by placing the board at a distance from the source, noncollimated, or with the use of optical elements, collimated as shown in Fig. 17.15. The lamp intensity for noncollimated sources is greater and therefore less time is required to expose the panel. The process throughput is noticeably enhanced for those materials requiring a large dose and there are suggestions that greater intensity does improve line definition.[37] Collimation refers to the angle of incidence for the light and is important for fineline definition. Exposure under the opaque areas cannot be tolerated when defining fine spaces in the photoresist, which is the challenge for both additive and subtractive conductor formation.

In addition to collimation, good contact between the phototool and the panel is the most important factor to control in fineline formation. Any gap will result in exposure under the opaque and poor line width control in addition to reduced resolution. Since the lamp's output degrades with time and spectral output is altered, the photoprocess will change with time if the lamp is not routinely replaced. The exact limits required depend on the line and space definition required, but the lamp life is typically 1000 h. Failure to replace a lamp can result in it exploding and damaging the optical elements in the exposure unit, which is far most costly than routine maintenance.

17.2.4.4   Noncontact Exposure Equipment.   Semiconductor imaging demonstrated the yield limitation to using contact exposure equipment and developed noncontact methods to increase the conductor yield with the continual requirements for smaller features. The PWB industry is following this evolution, driven by the increased demand for products with fine features of 3 mil and less. The semiconductor tool concepts cannot be used directly, since there are important differences between the IC and PWB products: the physical size of the substrate and product pattern to be imaged and the flatness of that substrate. The key to noncontact methods is the use of appropriate optics for clear image placement in the photoresist (Fig. 17.16), even if the image transfer function has degraded. In the PWB instance, this includes the depth of focus to allow for panel warpage and the resolving power, given the contrast of the resist. The following approaches address these concerns and are viable alternatives to contact printing.

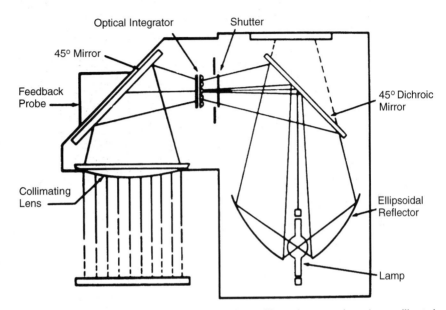

FIGURE 17.15   Configuration of lamp and optics for a collimated contact printer. A noncollimated source is identical except for the collimation lens in the lower right. *(Reprinted with permission of Optical Associates, Inc., Milpitas, Calif., Technical Literature.)*

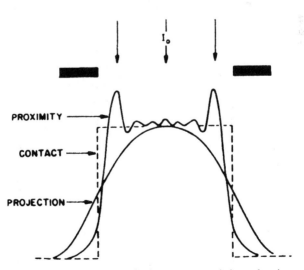

FIGURE 17.16   Image transfer for contact, proximity, and projection printing.

Proximity Printing. The oldest method for off-contact printing, which requires no modification to the equipment optics, is proximity printing. The phototool is held out of contact from 5 to 20 mil, typically. The image in the photoresist suffers due to the distance between the mask and the part, which allows exposure under the opaque area of the mask. Debris on the mask is likely imaged since there is little distance between the artwork and panel surfaces. Nevertheless, resolution to 3 mil is claimed with thin coatings of liquid resist and proximity printing.[38]

Laser Direct Imaging. This method of exposure does not require a phototool and therefore is expected to provide the ultimate in flexibility with respect to customized pattern compensation factors and engineering changes to the product design. The visible optics of the 1980s have changed to a UV system that does not require a specialized photoresist, although a faster version of a conventional material will enhance the tool throughput. The illumination is a frequency multiple of the Ar^+ laser at 350 to 360 nm. Differing optics are used for either single- or multiple-beam operation. The multiple-beam operation decreases the time required for exposure, and this method is more economically feasible for large-volume manufacturing; exposure times for an 18-in × 24-in panel are on the order of 30 s. The beam spot size and addressability of the beam determine the resolution of the equipment (see Fig. 17.17). Thus, depending on the product mix, the equipment specification and resulting cost can be tailored to each producer's requirements.

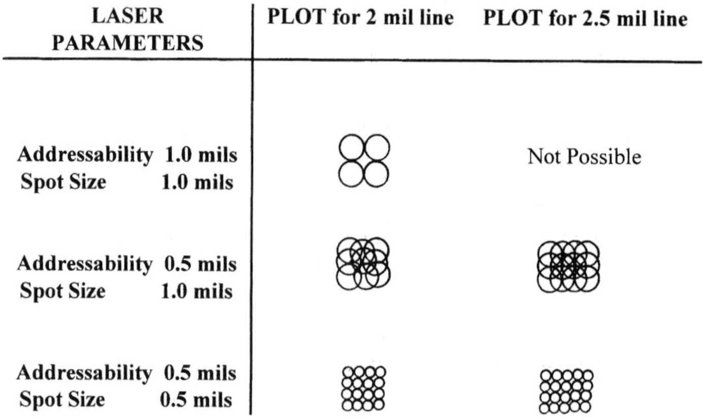

LASER PARAMETERS		PLOT for 2 mil line	PLOT for 2.5 mil line
Addressability 1.0 mils Spot Size 1.0 mils			Not Possible
Addressability 0.5 mils Spot Size 1.0 mils			
Addressability 0.5 mils Spot Size 0.5 mils			

FIGURE 17.17 Final image dimension as governed by spot size and addressability of a laser plotter or laser direct exposure tool.

Projection Printing. Three approaches are possible for this technique: scanning, stitching, and magnified projection printing. Scanning and stitching evolved from semiconductor and multichip modules deposited type, MCM-D, thin-film technology, where smaller, flatter substrates are used. They require movement of the phototool and/or the substrate during exposure. Magnified projection imaging is unique to the PWB application and has no moving optical components. A schematic of all three systems is given in Fig. 17.18.

The scanning printer requires the synchronized movement of the part and the phototool during exposure. The precise alignment of the two pieces must be maintained during the motion. Periodic adjustment for flatness is possible and usually required since this equipment has a small depth of focus. For typical PWB formats, a large phototool is required; glass phototools are expensive to manufacture and pattern, but film phototools do not have the required flatness, rigidity, and sharp line definition. This exposure technique is suited for and demon-

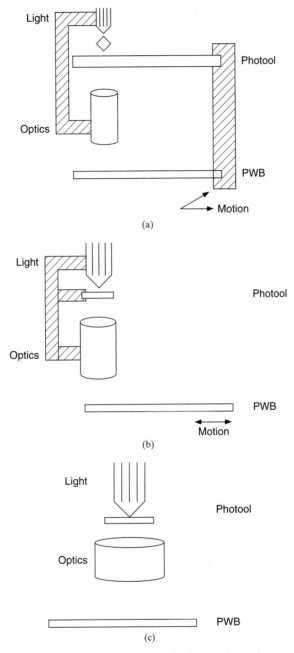

FIGURE 17.18 Configuration for projection imaging equipment: (*a*) scanning, (*b*) stitching, and (*c*) magnified.

strated for high resolution over a large, relatively flat area with a high contrast resist.[39, 40] For flat panel display manufacture, these criteria are met, but few PWB applications exist.

The stitcher projection printers are step-and-repeat tools that use a repeating image or "stitch" together several images. The artwork generation and management in the equipment is complicated and this has hampered its widespread use for large panels. The usual active area size as defined by the optics is approximately 6-in × 6-in. Thus, for a standard 18-in × 24-in panel, 12 artwork changes are required to expose one side. These systems have very high resolving capability and large depth of focus. Again, glass artwork is used, although these smaller plates are easier to generate and use than in a scanning projection printer.

The magnified projection imaging concept was first realized in the SeriFLASH™ exposure tool in the late 1980s, which utilized a liquid crystal display as the phototool and 436-nm illumination. The phototool was 5-in × 5-in, with the image magnified six times to expose an 18-in × 24-in panel. The liquid crystal features were one-sixth of the final conductor width. The demonstrated photoresist definition was limited to 5 mil. The equipment was modified for 365-nm exposure and a glass phototool; the resolution improved to 4-mil line and 4.5-mil spacing.[41, 42] Further work has resulted in 2-mil line and 2.5-mil space resolution.[43] The exposure time required is similar to that of contact exposure equipment. With optimized optics, this may become a high-resolution tool that utilizes conventional photoresist and phototools.

17.2.4.5 Phototools.   Two base materials are used: polyethylene and glass, which differ in their optical properties, their dimensional stability with respect to temperature and humidity, and their durability. A plot of their optical transmission is given in Fig. 17.19 and its impact on the exposure time is given in Table 17.4. Thus, the less expensive materials have poorer transmission properties, although for most applications except those requiring high intensity, this property is not limiting. The edge definition is probably the largest difference between the options. A comparison is given in Fig. 17.20.[44] This is also affected by the pixel size of the plotter used to expose the master and the spot's addressability (see the section on Laser Direct Imaging). From the photos, the edge definition is sharpest for chromium on glass and worst for silver halide on polyethylene. With a low-contrast photoresist, poor light collimation, these differences are not measurable on the printed photoresist image or in the patterned conductor, but for finer feature definition there is a difference. In addition, glass and film dimensions change differently with respect to temperature, and only film dimensional stability is affected by humidity (see Table 17.5). Again, the requirements of the product dictate which material is required.

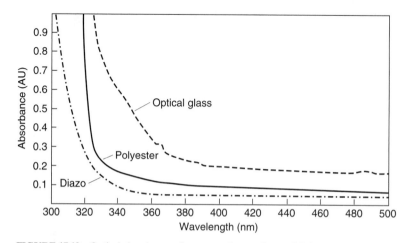

FIGURE 17.19   Optical absorbance of common phototool materials in the spectral region of PWB photoresist exposure.

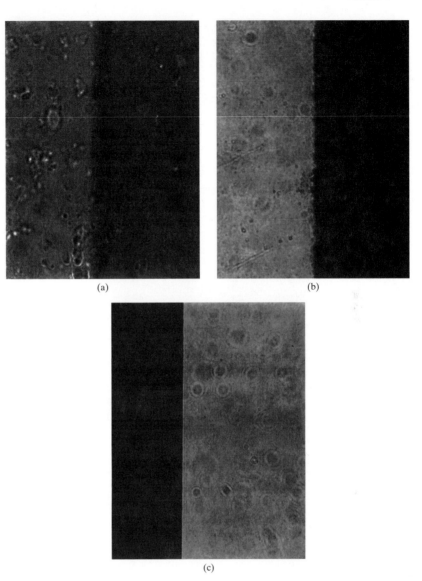

FIGURE 17.20   Optical micrograph of the image edge of common phototool materials, 1600×: (*a*) diazo; (*b*) polyester; (*c*) Cr on glass.

In a practical sense, the phototools have differing durability, which is important for use in a manual contact printer. The damage is very product and expose tool dependent, but, commonly, glass artwork is usable for 100 to 400 contacts, with repair and film artwork usable for 20 to 50. Thus, the cost differential for large numbers of the same part number may actually favor the glass artwork, while for model parts the film artwork is ideal. The majority of the panels are fabricated with film artwork and finer-line single-chip modules; laminate type, SCM-L, and MCM-L applications are beginning to require glass artwork.

TABLE 17.4   Comparison of the Optical Transmission of Various Phototool Materials

Property	Diazo	Polyester	Glass
Absorbance at 365 nm	0.271	0.107	0.047
Transmission at 365 nm	54%	78%	90%
% increase in exposure time vs. glass	40	13	0

TABLE 17.5   Phototool Substrate Materials Dimensional Stability with Respect to Temperature and Relative Humidity

Substrate	Expansion coefficient, ppm/°C	Expansion coefficient, %RH/°C
Soda lime glass	9.2	0
Low-expansion glass	3.7	0
Pyrex	3.2	0
Quartz	0.5	0
Polyester	18	9

Source: Kodak Technical Literature (ACCUMAX 2000) for Polyester film; *Tables of Physical and Chemical Constants,* Longman, London, 1973, p. 254, and *Formulas, Facts and Constants,* H. J. Fischbeck and K. H. Fischbeck, Springer-Verlag, Berlin, 1987, for glass data.

17.2.5   Develop

In this process step, the solubility difference between the exposed and unexposed portions of the photoresist is realized. Immersion in an appropriate solvent results in a relief image of the master pattern. The process conditions are adjusted to alter the clearing time for dissolving the unexposed for negative materials or exposed for positive ones. The total dwell time is set to approximately double the time to clear, commonly called a 50 percent breakpoint. Additional variables include the solution temperature, agitation, and concentration. The resulting photoresist images should be distinct with vertical sidewalls. Failure to accomplish this is an indication that the previous process step set points require adjustment. Images larger than the phototool dimension result from incomplete development, overexposure, or poor contact at expose. If the images are smaller than expected, then the expose dose is too low or development is too aggressive. Distorted images can be caused by problems with preclean, apply, or expose.

The common equipment for developing is spray conveyorized, either horizontally or vertically. Additives to the developer solution are required in many instances to prevent foaming. The solution is filtered to remove resist particles and either replenished with fresh solution to maintain a consistent dissolved resist value and solution concentration or operated continuously for a certain amount of product and replaced. Waste developer solution is treated (aqueous and semiaqueous) or distilled and reused (solvent). Rinsing is also important to stop the dissolution reaction. In addition, water with a high mineral content often improves the aqueous photoresist resist image and the conductor yield. Tank systems can also be used, especially for materials with a wide process latitude. Often, ultrasonic agitation is used to aid in the dissolution.

There are additional steps which improve the resist removal in the line channels and the conductor formation yield. Plasma treatment has been used effectively to improve product yield, especially with respect to shorts in a print-and-etch process.[2] In addition, for some aqueous-developable dry films, a heat treatment after exposure has improved the space definition, and spaces equal to or smaller than the resist height have been resolved.[3-5] Thus, these process steps ensure that tight resolution requirements can be met.

17.2.6 Strip

The photoresist is removed from the substrate after it has functioned in the pattern transfer step. The equipment used for this process step is identical to that used for developing. The removal is accomplished by swelling and dissolving the material. Some materials are removed in sheets or as small particles and, depending on the equipment design, can be accommodated. Often brushes and ultrasonic agitation is added to aid in the resist removal. As with developing, filtration is important to keep fresh solution reaching the part and the nozzles of a spray tool clean. For stripper chemistries that oxidize the copper, an antitarnishing agent is often added either to the stripping solution or as part of the rinsing.

17.3 DESIGN FOR MANUFACTURING

A high-yield conductor formation process can be enhanced by the optimization of several design features. These concern the conductor dimensions and the process used to form them. Specifically, these are the process sequence to be used (etched or plated metal), the division of conductor pitch between line and spacing, and the PTH capture land size and shape.

17.3.1 Process Sequence: Etch vs. Plate Considerations

For a given product conductor dimension, there is often a question of the appropriate process sequence. Although the capabilities of imaging and the pattern transfer step dictate the overall limitations, the decision depends on the unique capabilities of the manufacturing line to be used. Some general considerations can clarify the true issues for most production situations.

The photoresist patterning for plating and etching are very distinct. For etching, a thin photoresist is desirable to maximize the etchants' attack in the line channel. Thus, the resolution of the photoresist does not limit the process, since very small spaces can be resolved in liquid-coated materials. The challenge for conductor formation resides with the etching. Depending on the metal thickness and the etching equipment, it can be very difficult to remove the copper in tight spaces. Therefore, the key criteria defining the capabilities of the print-and-etch process is the minimum spacing cleared as constrained by the final conductor height and the etchant chemistry and equipment.

For plated products, the photoresist thickness must be greater than or equal to the final thickness of the conductor wire and it must be possible to clear a photoresist space equal to the final conductor width. These fine spaces are challenging when the conductor height increases. The photoresist resolution is on the order of its thickness, so that for 1-mil-thick plating, it would be difficult to resolve smaller than a 1.5-mil photoresist space, irrespective of the final conductor spacing. Thus, the challenge for plating is to resolve the fine spaces in thicker photoresist materials and then to ensure that the plating solution wets the bottom of the narrow photoresist channels.

Thus, to choose the conductor formation process, the thickness of the conductor and the line width and spacing are the key parameters. A generalized relationship between them is found in Fig. 17.21. It is important that this type of plot is known for the production area before the process sequence is determined.

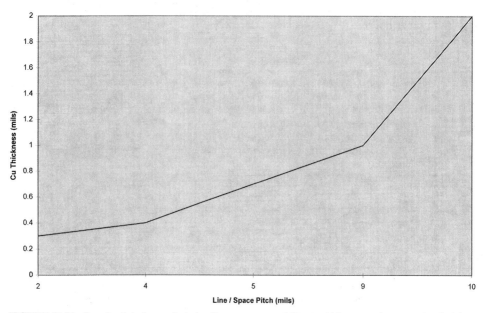

FIGURE 17.21 Sample plot of manufacturing line process capability to aid in processing sequence decisions. Feature dimensions above the line would be processed with pattern plating while those below the line with print and etch.

17.3.2 Line and Space Division for a Fixed Pitch

It is common for product designs to have a fixed pitch, whether it refers to the I/Os for direct chip or packaging attachment or to the spacing between PTHs. This space is often divided equally between conductors and spacing. As mentioned previously, for either additive or subtractive processing, the photoresist and pattern transfer process yield can be enhanced by avoiding the resolution limitations of each sequence.

In subtractive conductor formation, an etch factor is used to obtain straighter sidewalls and improved line width control. If lines and spaces are equally allocated, then the photoresist must resolve a smaller space than a line. This is difficult, except for very thin coatings and by using one of the enhancement schemes.[2–5] Thus, it is a higher-yielding process to have a larger space than line.

For additive processing, the spacing in the photoresist is the limiting factor. After pattern transfer, this will become the line. In this instance, equal line and space is more acceptable, but based on the photoresist concerns, a wider final line than space is preferred. At the same time, it is desirable to increase the spacing for reduced incidence of line shorting which translates to a wider "line" in the photoresist. The former is usually more important. Therefore, for both process sequences there is preferably balance between line width and spacing.

17.3.3 PTH Capture Pad Size and Shape for Optimum Line Formation

Just as the conductor line and spacing can be optimized, so can the PTH capture pad shape and size be altered to further increase the yield. The absolute dimension of the feature is dictated by the placement accuracy of the drilling process and the overall dimensional stability of the product. The feature is sized to ensure that the PTH and conductor are connected. There are varying specifications as to the extent of capture that is required.

Depending on the direction and magnitude of the dimensional stability and the drill wander and accuracy, the shape required to capture the PTH can be changed. This would reduce the size of this feature in at least one direction. In consequence, the spacing between the line and pad increases. Since this location is a change to the nominal line-to-line spacing, the narrowing of the channel results in shorting between the features in both a print-and-etch process and additive processes. In the former case, it is more difficult to clear the space, and in the latter, the narrower resist width is often underplated. Thus, when possible, an elongated pad will benefit the final conductor yield.

REFERENCES

1. L. R. Wallig, "Image Transfer" in Clyde Coombs (ed.), *Printed Circuits Handbook,* 3d ed., McGraw-Hill, New York, 1988, pp. 11.2–11.3.

2. T. A. Estes, and R. D. Rust, "Photoresist Residue Removal Using Plasma," *Presentation at the IPC Fall 1993 Conference,* Washington, D.C.

3. R. Stoll, "High Definition Imaging for High Yield/High Resolution Printed Circuit Board Manufacturing," *Presentation at the IPC Spring 1994 Conference,* Boston, Mass.

4. R. Stoll, "High Definition Imaging," *PC Fab* vol. 17, no. 6 June 1994, p. 31.

5. T. A. Estes, and L. O. Connolly, "Thermally Enhanced Imaging," *Presentation at the IPC Fall 1994 Conference,* Los Angeles, Calif.

6. E. Hayes, "An Overview of Dry Film Imaging Chemistry," *PC Fab,* May 1988, p. 74.

7. J. H. Choi, "Some Fundamental Aspects of UV Laser Direct Imaging," *Presentation at the IPC Spring 1995 Conference,* San Diego, Calif.

8. J. H. Choi, "Chemistry and Photoresist for Electroless Deposition," *Presentation at the IPC Spring 1992 Conference,* Bal Harbor, Fla.

9. U.S. Patent 5,268,260, Nov. 7, 1993.

10. Artaki, et al., "Surface Preparation Requirements for Fine Line Processing, *PC Fab,* April 1990, p. 55.

11. R. J. Almond, M. E. Goewey, and B. F. Jobson, "Lowering Innerlayer Fabrication Cost with Liquid Resists," *IPC Spring 1995,* San Diego, Calif.

12. M. Gurian, and N. Ivory, "Performance Requirements of Primary Liquid Resists," *Electronics Packaging & Production,* March 1995, p. 49.

13. Trademark™ of Du Pont Electronics; registered trademark® of Shipley Co., Inc.; registered trademark® of PPG Industries, Inc., respectively.

14. J. Murray, "ED Processes Revisited," *PC Fab,* May 1992.

15. H. Nakahara, "Electrodeposition of Primary Photoresists," *Electronic Packaging & Production*, February 1992, p. 66.

16. W. Wilkins, and S. J. Fuerniss, IBM Microelectronics, unpublished results.

17. L. Hecht, and M. Cibulsky, "Particle Collection Using a Cascade Impactor," *PC Fab,* May 1992, p. 34.

18. M. Wisnosky, "Modeling of Defects in the Print and Etch Process of Printed Circuit Board Manufacturing," *IEEE Proceedings of Electronics Components Conference,* 1986, p. 520.

19. W. Moreau, *Semiconductor Lithography,* Plenum Press, New York, 1989, pp. 267–281.

20. N. B. Feilchenfeld, and L. J. Matienzo, IBM Microelectronics, unpublished results.

21. K. H. Dietz, "Surface Preparation for Primary Imaging," *Presentation and paper at IPC Spring 1992 Conference,* Bal Harbor, Fla., p. TP-1025.

22. W. Moreau, *Semiconductor Lithography,* Plenum Press, New York, 1989, pp. 651–664.

23. S. Crum, "Surface Preparation Process Improvements," *Electronic Packaging & Production,* July 1993, p. 24.

24. Atotech technical information.

25. J. D. Ganjei, "Statistical Study of the Inner Layer Imaging Process Using Dry Film Photoresist and Wet Lamination," *Proceedings of the Technical Program, NEPCON East '89,* 611, Cahners, Des Plaines, Ill.

26. G. E. Homan, "Yieldmaster Wet Lamination System for Improving Fine Line Innerlayer Yields," *Proceedings of the Technical Program, NEPCON East '89,* 115, Cahners, Des Plaines, Ill.

27. G. E. Homan, and K. S. VanLandingham, "Wet Lamination System for Improving Fine Line Inner-layer Yields," *IPC Paper TP-826,* 1989.

28. E. Hayes, and J. Carraway, "Improving Conformance and Yields with Wet Lamination," *PC Fab,* April 1990, p. 63.

29. R. Patel, and H. Benkreira, "Gravure Roll Coating of Newtonian Liquids," *Chem Eng Sci* vol. 46, no. 3, 1991, p. 751.

30. J. Dubrava, D. Pai, J. Rychwalski, and J. Steper, "Development of a Novel Positive-Working Electrodeposited Photoresist Process for the Production of High Density Outerlayers," *Presentation at the IPC Spring 1994 Conference,* Boston, Mass.

31. C. Young, "The In Line Spray Conformal Coat Process," *Proceedings of the Technical Program NEPCON West '89,* p. 1676, vol. 2, Cahners, Des Plaines, Ill.

32. D. Marks, and T-C. Lee, "Electrostatic Applications of Resists and Solder Masks," *PC Fab,* September 1991, p. 100.

33. K. Grah, "Electrostatic Coating of Photosensitive Resists," *Proceedings of the Technical Program, NEPCON West '89,* p. 885, vol. 1, Cahners, Des Plaines, Ill.

34. E. Pscheidt, "Electrostatic Application of Liquid Photoimageable Solder Masks," *Proceedings of the Technical Program SMTA Exposition and Conference 1989,* San Jose, Calif., p. 837.

35. W. R. Grace & Co., ACCUSPRAY, Technical Information.

36. J. Nguyen, "Curtain Coating in Soldermask Application," *Proceedings of the Technical Program NEPCON West '89,* p. 869, vol. 1, Cahners, Des Plaines, Ill.

37. D. J. Heden, "Improving Fine Line Resolution with High Intensity Exposure," *PC Fab,* December 1987, p. 48.

38. W. R. Grace & Co., ACCUTRACE®, Technical Information.

39. H. G. Muller, Y. Yuan, and R. E. Sheets, "Large Area Fine Line Patterning by Scanning Projection Lithography," *Proceeding of the 3rd International Conference and Exhibition Multichip Modules* (SPIE Vol. 2256), Denver, Colo., April 1994, p. 100.

40. H. G. Muller, Y. Yuan, and R. E. Sheets, "Large Area Fine Line Patterning by Scanning Projection Lithography," *IEEE Transactions on Components, Packaging and Manufacturing Technology Part B: Advanced Packaging,* vol. 18, no. 1, 1995, p. 33.

41. N. G. Bergstrom, "Projection Direct Imaging of High Density Interconnection and Printed Circuit Manufacture," *International Conference on Advances in Interconnection and Packaging,* SPIE Vol. 1390, 1990, p. 509.

42. G. B. Fefferman, R. K. Kovacs, R. J. Rhodes, and R. D. Rust, "Magnified Image Projection Printing for Resist Exposure," *Presentation at the IPC Fall 1993 Conference,* Washington, D.C.

43. N. B. Feilchenfeld, P. J. Baron, R. K. Kovacs, D. T. W. Au, and R. D. Rust, "Further Progress with Magnified Image Projection Printing for Fine Conductor Formation," *to be presented at the IPC Fall 1995 Conference,* Providence, R.I.

44. S. J. Fuerniss, M. Wozniak, and N. B. Feilchenfeld, IBM Microelectronics, unpublished results.

CHAPTER 18
DRILLING

James P. Block
Laminating Company of America, Garden Grove, California

18.1 INTRODUCTION

The purpose of drilling printed circuit boards is twofold: (1) to produce an opening through the board which will permit a subsequent process to form an electrical connection between top, bottom, and, sometimes, intermediate conductor pathways; and (2) to permit through-the-board component mounting with structural integrity and precision of location.

The quality of a drilled hole through a printed circuit board is measured by its interface with the following processes: plating, soldering, and forming a high-reliability nondegrading electrical and mechanical connection. It is possible to drill holes meeting these requirements with high productivity, consistency, and yield.

The elements of this process are materials, such as laminates, drill entry, and backup, and drills; processes including machine parameters, techniques, and operating personnel; and control evaluation of hole quality, drills, and process machinery. When all these elements are properly developed and implemented, high-quality printed circuit board holes are a natural result. Such holes can be plated directly, eliminating remedial processes of deburring, desmearing, and etchback, and resulting in process simplification, higher yields, and lower costs.

The interaction and practice of elements shown in Fig. 18.1 can optimize the drilling process for the fabrication of printed circuit boards. While all of the elements shown are interdependent, it is hole quality and its location accuracy that ultimately steer decisions on feeds and speeds, material choices, and productivity.

18.2 DRILLS

Drills for making holes in printed circuit boards are usually made of tungsten carbide. This is due to interrelated needs of cost, wear properties, machinability, and handling properties. No other material has proved to be as suitable.

The design of a drill is just as important as the materials used. The design and the wear of the drill affect its drilling temperature, ability to remove chips, tendency to create entry and exit burrs, and smoothness of the hole wall (all directly related to hole quality).

Figure 18.2 shows a typical drill bit geometry. The point angle is usually between 90 and 110° for paper-base materials and between 115 and 130° for glass-base materials. By far the most common point angle used in drilling is 130°.

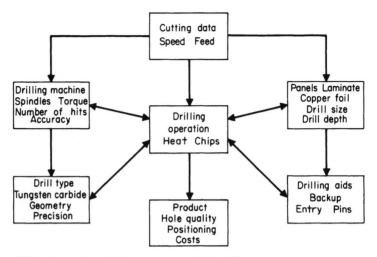

FIGURE 18.1 Essential elements in good PWB drilling.

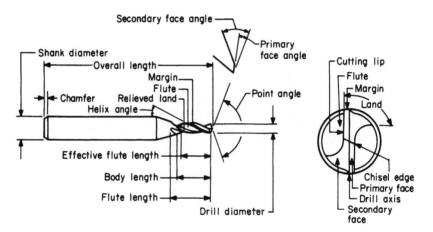

FIGURE 18.2 Typical drill bit geometry.

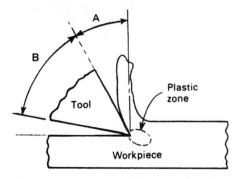

FIGURE 18.3 Drill bit, section view of the cutting process.

The flute or helix angle determines the drill's ability to remove chips from the hole. Helix angles vary from 20 to 50°. A 20° angle provides fast chip removal with poor cutting efficiency. A high helix angle (50°) creates a smaller material plastic zone but yields slower chip removal, as shown in Fig. 18.3, angle A. A helix angle of 30° is a good compromise between a small plastic zone and quick chip removal. This compromise minimizes drilling temperature.

Figure 18.2 also shows an important characteristic of high-performance drills described as a "relieved land." Increases in temperature during drilling can also be caused by the amount of drill surface area in direct contact with the hole wall. To minimize this surface area, most manufacturers remove material just behind the margin or cutting area to reduce friction and thus lower the temperature of drilling. Other geometries being equal, the narrower the margin, the cooler the drilling temperature.

The length of the margin relieved area also affects the drilling temperature. Figure 18.4 shows the relief area in a partially relieved (*a*), fully relieved (*b*), and spade head (*c*) drill. A drill design with a larger relief area will drill cooler because of the smaller drill surface area in contact with the hole wall. Other factors being equal, the partially relieved design will drill hotter than the fully relieved design and the spade head design will drill cooler than the fully relieved design.

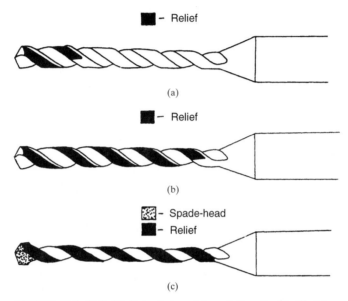

FIGURE 18.4 Drill bit flute designs: (*a*) partially relieved; (*b*) fully relieved; (*c*) spade-head.

The surface finish of the drill is important; that is, the smoother the surface, the cooler the drilling. Surface finishes lower than 4 μin should be used. The volume of empty space in the drill flutes is another important design consideration. The greater the open volume, the higher the capacity of the drill to remove chips efficiently. Conversely, greater volume (thinner center web) implies a weaker drill which is more prone to breakage. Figure 18.5 shows a standard micro drill (*a*) and a step design (*b*) that strengthens the drill without increasing the web thickness by adding a step in the diameter reduction between the drill shank and the fluted area. The added step strengthens the drill bit by reducing the abruptness of the transition between the flute and the shank of the drill bit.

In general, the best drill designs are those that drill with the lowest drill temperature. Drills which drill cooler have a good surface finish, thin webs, no geometrical defects or chips, sharp cutting edges, and durable carbide. In addition, the best operating parameters for drills are those which also minimize drill temperatures. Finally, as drills wear, they drill hotter and hole quality decreases. Run length must be carefully determined.

It should not be assumed that all manufactured drills are of equal quality. Differences in design, manufacturing processes, surface finish, raw materials, and consistency vary widely and should be evaluated prior to the purchase of production quantities of drills.

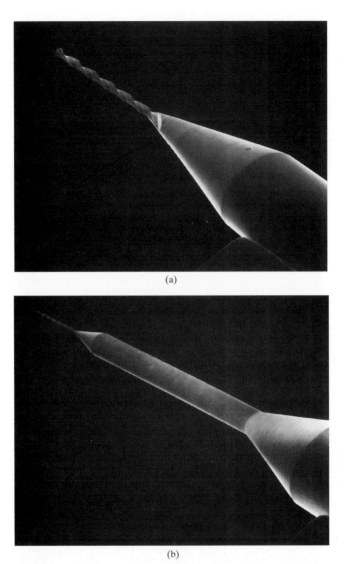

FIGURE 18.5 Micro drill bit designs: (*a*) standard micro drill bit; (*b*) step design micro drill bit.

18.3 HANDLING OF DRILLS

Cutting edges are all important. Drill-handling procedures which do not damage these cutting edges must be used.

Cutting edges or points should never be pressed against metallic or hard surfaces. Drill bits should never touch one another.

18.4   *DRILL BIT INSPECTION*

Drills should be cleaned upon receipt. Approximately ⅛ of each drill's flute should be worked into an orange stick (wood commonly used to clean instruments). This applies a slight pressure to the drill's tip and loosens and removes inadequately bonded carbide and other substances from the drill's surface.

Geometric tolerances in drill dimensions (length and diameter) should be measured by a contactless method. Micrometer techniques can easily damage the cutting points and should never be used. Laser and other optical measuring devices are available that permit higher accuracy and contactless measurement.

A good inspection program is important for both new and repointed drill bits. Micrograin carbide drills are fabricated to industry standards, but variations from those standards produce drill bits of varying quality. Drill inspectors should use a 40 to 140 magnification microscope to examine the quality of the drills. Drills should be held in a fixture like that shown in Fig. 18.6.

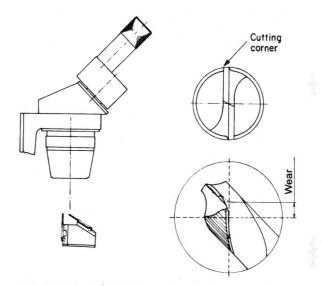

FIGURE 18.6   Drill bit fixture, in place on microscope stage.

Each drill should be inspected for flaws with a stereooptical microscope. Rejection parameters for chips are based on the observation of chips within the cutting points of a drill at the magnification power listed in Table 18.1.

TABLE 18.1   Rejection Parameters for Drills with Chips

Drill size, in	Magnification
<0.0135	50×
0.0135–0.0625	40×
0.0625–0.125	30×
0.125–0.25	20×

Other flaws (layback, overlap, offset, gap negative, flair, and hook) can be observed by comparison to the examples shown in Fig. 18.7. An inspection magnification of 140 is required for drill diameters 0.020 in and smaller.

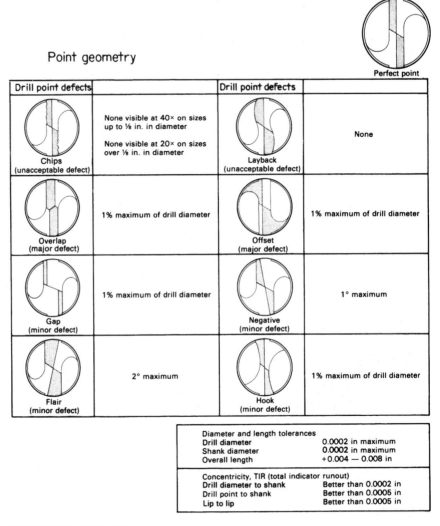

FIGURE 18.7   Drill point flaws.

Drill wear should be determined by measuring the land wear and corner rounding of the cutting edge (as shown in Fig. 18.8). Total wear is the sum of corner rounding and land wear. Total wear for each process can be plotted as a function of the number of holes drilled.

Drills which have geometric defects, chips, poor surface finish, excessive wear, and poor design *do not* give good hole quality. In addition, rapid drill wear may be a sign of poor, fast-wearing carbide.

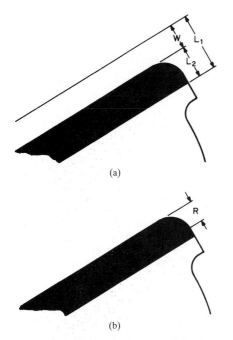

(a)

(b)

FIGURE 18.8 (*a*) Measurement of drill land wear. L_1 = new drill land, L_2 = used drill land, W = land wear, $L_1 - L_2$. (*b*) Measurement of corner rounding. R = corner rounding.

18.5   REPOINTING OF DRILLS

Prior to repointing, drills are required to be cleaned to remove all foreign substances.

When drills of good quality are used, three repointing operations are often possible. The guide to repointing is for the total drill length removed by the repointing operations never to exceed 15 percent of the drill diameter.

Following the repointing operation, all drills should be inspected as previously described for new and stored in a container that will prevent any contact with another drill or hard surface.

If definite signs of wear and resin buildup occur quickly during a run, or if drill bits break frequently, use higher-quality drill bits or better repointing techniques.

Since drill bit quality is only one of the factors essential to good drilling, other factors may be involved when contaminated or quickly dulled drill bits are found. These factors may be improper feeds and speeds, improper entry and backup materials, or poor laminates.

18.6   DRILL ENTRY

Entry materials are flat, thin sheets placed on the drill entry side of the laminate during the drilling operation. They should prevent damage to the top copper laminate surface from the machine's pressure foot, reduce entry burrs, and minimize drill wander. They also should not cause drill damage or excessive wear and should not contaminate holes or increase drilling temperatures.

Smooth, flat surfaces are important attributes for entry materials. They should not be warped or twisted or become distorted during drilling.

It is important for entry materials to center the drill and prevent burr formation on the entry side of the top laminate. It is also important that entry materials do not contain contaminants such as organic resins with oils that could be deposited or smeared on the hole wall.

Entry materials which contribute to rapid drill wear cause poor hole quality. Entry materials which contribute to higher drilling temperatures cause greater amounts of smear.

Table 18.2 lists the available entry materials in order of performance. The best entry material provides for accurate drill entry, burr reduction, and laminate protection. It also is very easy to drill, exerts low torque on the drill, decreases drill temperature, and is void of contaminants affecting the plating processes.

TABLE 18.2   Commercially Available Entry Materials

Designation	Description
Aluminum-clad	Two thin Al alloy skins bonded to a noncontaminating core
Solid aluminum	5–30 mil thick, various alloys
Phenolic, resin-based	12–22 mil thick
	60% + resin, balance paper
Phenolic, paper-based	15–22 mil thick
	60% + paper, balance resin

The worst entry materials have combinations of problems caused by soft surfaces, abrasives, hole contaminants, or hard-to-drill substances that heat the drill and cause resin smear.

Contaminants can often be observed on the drill's point or margin relief areas, following a long drill run. Phenolic entry causes excessive temperatures and can build resin deposits on the drill. Worse yet, they can directly increase the level of smear on the hole wall. Solid aluminum entry can be problematic if it is thick and soft, which builds drill residues, decreases cutting efficiency, and increases temperatures.

Entry materials should always be used. The choice of material is dependent on the cost-performance tradeoff desired. It is always good practice to choose materials that have the lowest probabilities of causing downstream failures.

18.7 DRILL BACKUP

Backup is a material placed under the bottom laminate to terminate the drill at the bottom of its stroke and to prevent an exit burr from forming. Although simple in concept, the backup has surprising and profound effects on the quality of the hole. Given good drilling practice in all other areas, the backup can be the difference between holes ready for plating and holes that need additional processing to accept plating or perhaps those that can never be plated. The reasons are easy to understand.

When a drill terminates in the backup material, the hole is usually cut cleanly and smoothly. All the material that has been cut from the volume of the backup is then carried up through the newly formed holes, where it bangs, scrapes, slides into, and sometimes gouges the hole wall. The choice of this material can have a substantial effect on the resultant hole-wall quality.

It is known that 90 percent or more of drill breakage occurs on the drill retraction after the hole has been formed. It was previously assumed that this occurred because of table movement. If that were the case, all drills on a multiple-spindle machine would break simultaneously, but this is not found in practice. The real answer lies in the binding or seizing action of particulate or resin debris wedging between the drill sides and the hole wall during the retraction.

Two separate phenomena occur. The first involves solid particulate debris from the backup or lower laminates collecting and binding. The second is caused by friction of the drill in the backup material increasing the drill temperature beyond the T_g (softening point) of resins within the system. When this happens, the softened resins smear on the hole wall between the wall and drill, building excessive friction and drag, which can lead to drill seizure and breakage.

It is clear that the drilling process need not deteriorate to that level before substantial damage is done to the hole walls by the chips or materials removed from the backup.

Aside from the direct frictional effects of the drilling process, the temperature problems are compounded even further by the very poor thermal conductivity of the drill's tungsten carbide. Heat from drilling friction remains at the drill's cutting edges and at the point of the drill. Because the heat cannot be conducted away, temperatures rise rapidly, softening and melting the organic resins. This greatly increases drill bit contamination problems and reduces hole quality through smearing.

Because of these factors, the proper backup material must be devoid of low-temperature melting organic resins, cut into easily transportable and soft chips that will not damage the hole wall, free of hole-wall contaminants, and soft enough to reduce friction on the drill tip during the dwell time at the end of the stroke. In addition, the backup must have a surface hard enough to prevent burrs from forming as the drill bit exits the copper-clad laminate.

Meeting these requirements is not an easy task. Correct backups are almost restricted to laminated composite structures and necessitate an exacting choice of raw materials to permit the drilling of quality holes and reliable interconnections. Nevertheless, a broad range of backup materials is currently available. They are shown in Table 18.3 in order of performance.

The best drilling backup structures meet the overall requirements previously outlined with the best tradeoffs. Evaluation of various backups must be performed under rigorously controlled conditions and must use hole quality as the dependent variable. Hole defects such as smearing, gouging, torn glass fibers, hole debris, delamination, nailheading, and burr height must be carefully monitored to understand differences in backups.

TABLE 18.3   Commercially Available Backup Materials

Designation	Description
Vented aluminum	Aluminum structure permitting the drill to terminate in air
Aluminum-clad	Two thin aluminum skins bonded to a noncontaminating core
Paper-clad	Paper bonded to a wood core
Phenolic-clad	Two thin phenolic resin impregnated paper bonded to a wood core
Phenolic	60%+ phenolic resin, balance paper*
Hardboard	Pressed wood fibers with resins and oils*

* Major problem with these products is warpage.

Easily observable performance failures of low-end backups are higher drill breakage, obvious hole-wall smearing, large exit burrs, burned and contaminated drill bits, and burned blind holes in the backup. Down the process line, poor backups usually increase the percentage of blowholes after soldering, which can be directly monitored with statistical quality control (SQC) process control.

Differences in backups have been observed to cause a factor-of-10 difference in the number of blowholes on a multilayer printed circuit board. Other obvious differences are that poor backups are not flat and do not offer enough support to the laminate, which causes burrs. Good backups of any type should be dimensionally stable and uniform in thickness and density. They should not be warped, twisted, or bowed.

Drilling depth into the backup should be set to provide a drill lip penetration depth into the backup of 0.005 to 0.015 in. Figure 18.9 shows a drill terminating in the backup after drilling through the laminate and entry material.

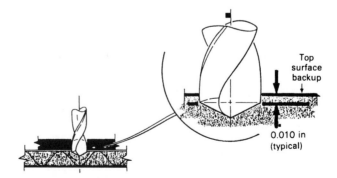

FIGURE 18.9   Setting drill termination depth in the backup.

18.8 *LAMINATES*

All laminates are manufactured to specifications which take into account electrical and physical properties. Ease of drilling ordinarily is not considered by the laminate engineers. It is left up to the printed wiring board fabricator to develop the correct parameters to drill laminates for the best hole quality.

The various types of laminates are formed from several resins and supporting materials. These vary from common to exotic types that differ in the ease with which they may be drilled. From easiest to most difficult to drill, some commonly available laminates are G-10 epoxy-glass, FR-4 epoxy-glass, multifunctional epoxy, polyimide-glass, phenolic-paper, Teflon-glass, polyimide-quartz, and exotics.

Where cloth is used, the of weave and the fiber thickness affect drill wander. The finer the fiber, the less drill wander. In addition, laminate is produced with various thicknesses of copper, either in double-sided laminates or in multilayers. The ratio of the copper thickness to total thickness of the laminate changes the optimum drilling parameters so that feeds and speeds should be adjusted based on the ratio of copper to substrate.

Dimensional stability, warping, bow, and twist specifications are important to the drilling operations. For example, laminates which are not flat drill with high burrs.

The thickness of the laminate to be drilled is controlled by the smallest drill diameter to be used. The controlling factor is 10 times the drill diameter. For example, the maximum material thickness for a 0.020-in-diameter drill is 0.200 in.

As drill depth increases, the drill's deviation from true center increases. For minimum-sized drills, the deviation increases by 0.001 in for each 0.0625 in of laminate thickness. For example, a 0.020-in-diameter drill drilling through 0.200-in laminate provides deviations of 0.005 in. If this is unacceptable, laminate thickness must be reduced.

Good multilayers and double-sided laminates should not require prebaking before drilling to fully cure the laminate. Uncured laminate is unacceptable from the supplier. Prebaking is often practiced to stress-relieve the laminate.

Edges of laminate panels for drilling should be free of burrs so that stacking can occur with good interlaminate contact.

To produce quality holes for each series or type of laminate, the following generalities can be stated:

1. The higher the T_g of the laminate, the better.

2. The laminate should be flat, uniform in thickness, and smooth, and it should exhibit high copper peel strength.

3. Prebaking the laminate before drilling helps dimensional stability but does not "correct" uncured resin.

4. The storage of laminate under controlled conditions of temperature and humidity is necessary. These conditions should be the same as the ambient conditions surrounding the drilling machine.

5. The more glass cloth layers and the higher the glass to resin ratio, the more drill wear is obtained per hole drilled.

6. The thicker the glass cloth diameter, the greater the drill wander.

7. Laminates that are not flat will cause interlaminate entry and exit burring.

8. The more abrasive the supporting fibers (quartz, for example), the greater the drill wear and the shorter the drilling run per drill.

9. Harder and thicker copper shortens the life of the drill.

18.8.1 Stack Preparation

Laminate panels are normally stacked three high between entry and backup materials for 0.062-in-thick double-sided laminates and one or two high for multilayers. They are placed in a pinning machine which drills a minimum of two holes and inserts tooling pins to hold the stack firmly.

Foreign materials and burrs on the laminate must be removed. This is true for entry and backup materials as well. The stack must be tight. Loose pinning causes burrs and poor registration. Poor pin alignment can cause bowed stacks. Pins and bushings should be checked for wear, and drilling machine operators should be instructed on the importance of cleanliness when handling laminates and entry and backup materials.

18.9 DRILLING MACHINES

Drilling machine types vary over a wide range, from single-spindle, manually operated, bottom-drilling types, using templates for locating holes, to multiple-drill-station, CNC, automatic machines that accept stacks of laminate, eject laminate, and change tools automatically.

Machines are designed to accept laminate panels of various sizes, up to 24 × 24 in. Costs range from $10,000 at the low end to $500,000 for the largest and most automated machines. The type of machine needed depends on production capacity and the type of process design.

Whatever the type, it is important to prepare and design the machine's environment. Machines should be located in temperature- and humidity-controlled, dust-free environments. Floors should be adequately designed to carry the machine weight. Machines should be isolated from any external vibrations. Isolated electrical power and grounding are necessary.

Plan on hiring machine operators who are experienced machinists. Machinists with jig-boring experience often make the best PWB drilling operators.

Rigorous and well-planned maintenance programs are important. The items in the following list are most important, but the list is not inclusive.

1. The actual revolutions per minute and feed rate of the machine should be determined by an independent method. Do not rely on the machine readout.
2. Vacuum systems should be maintained at high flow rates and full efficiency. It is better to overdesign this function. Filters should be replaced regularly.
3. Spindle cooling systems, coolant, and heat exhangers should be checked and kept clean so that they work efficiently.
4. Spindles and collets should be kept clean at all times, using noncorrosive cleaners that keep thin protective films on the metallic parts.*
5. Spindle runout should be kept to less than 0.0005 in for heart of the range drilling and to less than 0.0002 in for small hole drilling.
6. Drill bars, springs, and air-pressure seals should be carefully checked and maintained.
7. Pressure foot pressures should remain as high as the laminate will allow.
8. The z-axis alignment should be checked often.

Machine manufacturers' instructions regarding warmup before use should be followed carefully. Machines should be kept scrupulously clean. Dirt, chips, and debris left on machine

---

* Often a dirty or worn collet or a dirty collet seat will increase the total indicated runout (TIR) or cause the runout to be excessive. Before replacing a spindle due to excessive runout, it is wise to first clean or replace the collet, then remeasure the TIR.

tables should be removed with a vacuum cleaner. *Never blow surfaces with compressed air to remove dirt.*

There are two aspects to drill wander: precision and accuracy. Only accuracy is affected by machine performance. The machine accuracy can be checked by drilling a square matrix of holes. The lines of holes can be defined in the *x* and *y* directions by comparing the mean lines to reference holes via regression analysis. These best-fit lines are compared with the desired lines which the machine was instructed to place. From the slopes, the orthogonality of the machine can also be determined.

Precision of drilling is dependent on many factors. One of these is spindle runout. The less the spindle runout, the greater the precision of drilling. With good spindles and a well-maintained machine, precision and accuracy are about equal for 0.0135-in-diameter drills. These calculations are based on drilling 0.100 in of laminate.

Precision is also affected by chip load, roughness of laminate surface, entry material roughness, entry material construction, drill bit diameter, glass weave, glass thickness, drill design, and drill concentricity.

18.10   FEEDS AND SPEEDS

Feed rate in inches per minute is converted to chip load (CL) by using this formula:

$$CL = \frac{\text{feed rate, in/min}}{\text{r/min}}$$

Table 18.4 gives the best surface speeds and chip loads for FR-4 laminate with 1-oz copper on both sides. This table is an example of drilling parameters for double-sided 1-oz copper laminate. If the ratio of copper to substrate changes, the drilling parameters must change.

Notes for Table 18.4:   (1) It is assumed that 80,000 is the maximum r/min of many drilling machines. If your machine can exceed this r/min, use higher values, but limit the surface feet per minute (sfm) to 200 for drill diameters less than 0.015. (2) Chip loads are kept low to prevent drill breakage.

For drilling multilayers, sfm and chip loads are reduced to about 550 and 0.002 to 0.003 in per revolution, respectively, for 0.035-in-diameter drills because of the increase in the ratio of copper to substrate. Corresponding reductions in chip load and sfm are used for all drill sizes.

Exotics are drilled with different parameters, depending on type. These must be determined by each driller on the basis of hole quality and drill durability. As an example, optimum parameters for other types of laminates are shown in Table 18.5.

TABLE 18.4   Typical Parameters for FR-4 Laminates

Drill size	Diameter, in	Laminate thickness, in	Laminate construction	Stack height	Surface speed, ft/min	Chip load, mil/rev	Retraction, in/min
#65	0.0350	0.062	Double-sided	3	550	3.25	1000
		0.062	4-layer ML	3	550	3.00	1000
		0.062	6-layer ML	2	550	2.50	1000
		0.062	8-layer ML	2	500	2.00	1000
#77	0.0180	0.062	Double-sided	2	350	1.60	750
		0.062	4-layer ML	2	350	1.40	750
		0.062	6-layer ML	2	350	1.20	750
		0.062	8-layer ML	2	350	1.00	750
#80	0.0135	0.062	Double-sided	1	275	1.20	500
		0.062	8-layer ML	1	275	1.00	500
#97	0.0059	0.030	Double-sided	1	125	0.50	200

TABLE 18.5 Typical Parameter for Various Laminates

Drill size	Diameter, in	Laminate thickness, in	Laminate construction	Stack height	Surface speed, ft/min	Chip load, mil/rev	Retraction, in/min
#65	0.0350	0.041	4-layer polyimide	2	400	2.00	1000
#80	0.0135	0.041	4-layer polyimide	2	300	0.75	500
#80	0.0135	0.010	Randon glass/Teflon	10	225	1.00	750
#80	0.0135	0.060	Randon glass/Teflon	2	240	1.50	750
#70	0.0280	0.048	8-layer Kevlar	1	400	2.50	500
#70	0.0280	0.024	D.S. molybdenum	1	300	0.25	20

18.11 INSPECTION AND GRADING HOLES

It is extremely helpful to follow a drilling run by plotting hole quality against the number of hits or holes drilled. This can be done to optimize drilling parameters for a new product or laminate, or to decide which drills, entry and backup system, or feeds and speeds are best. This type of plot is also important to determine how long a drill can be run.

To do this correctly, methodology is all important, since the methods used and the grading scale must be adequate in defining hole quality. The best method available is called the *hole-quality standard.*

The method works as follows: The bottom laminate is always used for analysis of hole quality. Either the bottom laminate is sacrificed, or coupons are designed into the laminates so that two holes are drilled in the *x* direction and two holes in the *y* direction for each hit region of interest (see Fig. 18.10). For example, for each drill size, at the beginning of the drilling run, hit 1000, hit 2000, and so on to the end of the run, two holes are drilled in each coupon after each hit region has been completed.

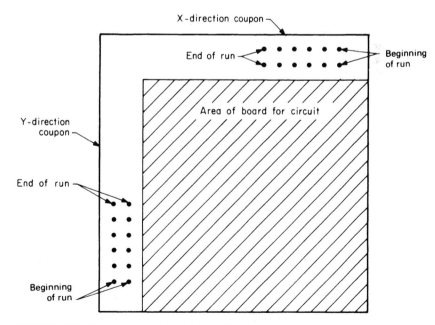

FIGURE 18.10 Coupon method of obtaining holes for sectioning.

The burr height is measured before sectioning with a profilometer or is examined after sectioning with a microscope.

Ordinary light microscope examination is then performed on the sections. If possible, three to five hole sections are used for each hit region to avoid statistical anomalies. If SEM and EDX are available, these can help to make a determination, but they are not absolutely necessary.

Hole quality is defined by separating defects of drilling into copper defects and substrate defects. Each defect is given quantitative and qualitative factors. Table 18.6 lists the defects, the qualitative factors (a), and the quantitative factors (b).

This method takes its perspective from the plating operation. How badly does each defect interfere with plating? If the defect is severe, then the qualitative and quantitative factors are larger.

TABLE 18.6   Defects in Holes: Qualitative and Quantitative Factors*

Defects	Definition	Weighting factor (a)	Extent factor (b)
Copper defects:			
Delamination	Minimum magnification needed to clearly see the defect:	50.0	
	140×		0.01
	100×		0.08
	60×		0.30
	20×		1.20
Nailheading	Nailhead width:	1.5	
	0.00012 in		0.01
	0.00032 in		0.08
	0.00062 in		0.30
	0.00102 in		1.20
Smear	% of copper area covered with smear:	1.5	
	1%		0.01
	11%		0.08
	26%		0.30
	36%		1.20
Burr	% of hole diameter	1.0	
	0.23%		0.01
	0.62%		0.08
	1.19%		0.30
	1.96%		1.20
Debris	% of copper area covered with debris:	0.3	
	1%		0.01
	11%		0.08
	26%		0.30
	36%		1.20
Roughness	Minimum magnification needed to clearly see the defect:	0.2	
	140×		0.01
	100×		0.08
	60×		0.30
	20×		1.20

TABLE 18.6 Defects in Holes: Qualitative and Quantitative Factors* *(Continued)*

Defects	Definition	Weighting factor (a)	Extent factor (b)
Substrate defects:			
Delamination	Minimum magnification needed to clearly see the defect:	20.0	
	140×		0.01
	100×		0.08
	60×		0.30
	20×		1.20
Voids	Minimum magnification needed to clearly see the defect:	0.8	
	140×		0.01
	100×		0.08
	60×		0.30
	20×		1.20
Debris pack	% of substrate area covered with debris pack:	0.8	
	1%		0.01
	11%		0.08
	26%		0.30
	36%		1.20
Loose fibers	% of substrate area covered with loose fibers:	0.3	
	1%		0.01
	11%		0.08
	26%		0.30
	36%		1.20
Smear	% of substrate area covered with smear:	0.3	
	1%		0.01
	11%		0.08
	26%		0.30
	36%		1.20
Plowing	Minimum magnification needed to clearly see the defect:	0.2	
	140×		0.01
	100×		0.08
	60×		0.30
	20×		1.20
Rifling	Minimum magnification needed to clearly see the defect:	0.2	
	140×		0.01
	100×		0.08
	60×		0.30
	20×		1.20

* *Qualitative:* weighting factors relating defects to plating problems. *Quantitative:* values of the defects measured.

This method asks these questions: Which defects are present? How much of each defect is present? How badly does each defect interfere with plating?

Using the qualitative and quantitative (a and b) factors, an empirical equation defines hole quality:

$$\text{Hole quality} = 10(0.2^{\Sigma a_i b_i})$$

This equation gives results between 0 and 10, where 10 is a perfect hole and 0 is an atrocious hole. The a and b factors are arranged so that a hole quality of 7 or higher can go to plating without deburring or desmearing.

Figures 18.11 and 18.12 show two examples of this rating process. Figure 18.13 shows a worksheet that can be used with the microscopic examination, and Fig. 18.14 shows a plot of hole quality versus the number of holes drilled.

Figure 18.14 shows that the dependent variable, hole quality, can be followed as a function of chip load, surface feet per minute, drill bit, number of hits, or entry and backup material. Thus, rational decisions can be made about drilling. Factors can be introduced, logically, to achieve optimum drilling runs reproducibly.

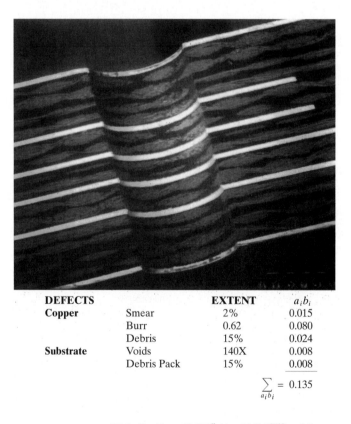

DEFECTS		EXTENT	$a_i b_i$
Copper	Smear	2%	0.015
	Burr	0.62	0.080
	Debris	15%	0.024
Substrate	Voids	140X	0.008
	Debris Pack	15%	0.008
			$\sum_{a_i b_i} = 0.135$

$$\text{Hole Quality} = 10\,(0.2^{\Sigma a_i b_i}) = 10\,(0.2^{0.135}) = 8.0$$

FIGURE 18.11 High-quality hole. Note: The dark material on the copper is loose drilling debris.

DEFECTS		EXTENT	$a_i b_i$
Copper	Nailheading	0.0012 in	0.015
	Smear	30%	0.450
	Burr	0.17%	0.010
	Debris	15%	0.024
	Roughness	140X	0.002
Substrate	Voids	140X	0.008
	Debris Pack	15%	0.064
	Loose Fibers	2%	0.003
	Smear	25%	0.024
	Plowing	140	0.002

$$\sum_{a_i b_i} = 0.135$$

$$\text{Hole Quality} = 10\,(0.2^{\Sigma a_i b_i}) = 10\,(0.2^{0.135}) = 3.8$$

FIGURE 18.12   Poor-quality hole.

18.12 ACCURACY AND PRECISION

It is important to understand how to produce not only high hole quality but also accurate, precisely drilled holes. *Accuracy* can be defined as how well the hole location agrees with the correct or target value. *Precision* is defined as how reproducible the hole location is.

Accuracy problems are usually due to drilling machine problems. Machine problems are due to mechanical wear, loss of computer data, and electromechanical error.

Precision problems are due to poor entry material, laminate thicknesses that are too great for the drill diameter, excessive chip loads, drill resonance, and excessive spindle runout.

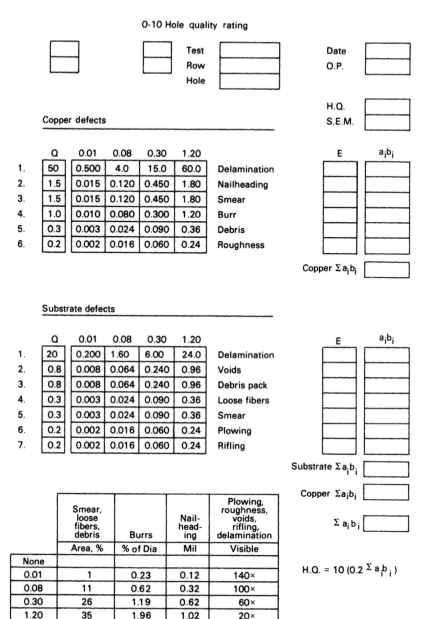

FIGURE 18.13 Worksheet used to determine hole quality.

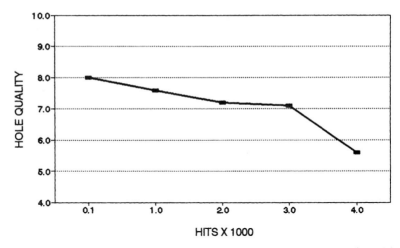

FIGURE 18.14   Plotting hole quality versus the number of hits drilled for a #72 (0.020-in) drill bit in a two-high stack.

18.13   QUALIFYING DRILLING MATERIALS

18.13.1   General Test Procedures

These general test procedures used for entry, backup, and drill evaluations are standard procedures applicable to any drilling evaluation and can be used on a day-to-day basis in a production environment to achieve consistent and quality drilling.

Cut all laminates and backup panels to the same size and keep the grain direction identical in all panels. Entry panels are punched or notched to clear the tooling pin and cut short in both dimensions to prevent buckling when the entry is taped to the top panel. Make the stacks identical by cutting all of the panels from larger sheets of entry, backup, and laminate. For example, if a backup evaluation will use several three-high stacks, cut all of the top laminates for the stacks from one sheet of laminate, all the middle laminates from a separate sheet, and all the bottom laminates from a third sheet. If the same entry will be used in the stacks, cut all the entry panels from a single sheet.

Determine and record the general condition and thickness of each panel. Select panels with minimal variations and matching thickness and identify each panel with location, date, test number, and any other pertinent information. Mark the information directly on the panels in an areas outside of the drilled pattern. Do not apply tape or stickers with information to the panels; they will cause separation resulting in burrs. Condition all test material in the drilling room environment for 24 h prior to testing.

Deburr all edges of the panels to ensure tight and flat stacks. Verify that the tooling pins are not worn and inserted with the tapered end first, and the tooling holes are perpendicular to the stack. Pins ⁵⁄₆₄ in in diameter are recommended because thinner pins allow too much stack movement which can cause drill breakage and hole misregistration. Inspect the pinned stack to ensure intimate contact between laminates and between bottom laminate and backup. Any separation can result in burring.

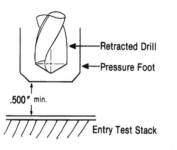

FIGURE 18.15   Minimum height above the stack for accuracy evaluations.

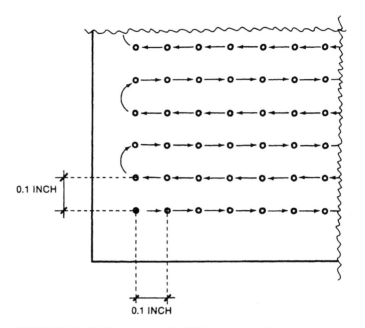

FIGURE 18.16   Drilling pattern with 0.100-in on center grid.

18.13.2   Qualifying the Drilling Machine

For any drilling evaluation, a properly maintained drilling machine is absolutely essential. Start with the machine's maintenance log. If there is a history of problems with the machine, select a different machine. After verifying that the machine has been properly maintained and is free of any major problems, begin the inspection of the machine.

Examine the tooling plate surface for smoothness, removing any surface imperfections or broken drill bits, which would prevent the stack from lying flat. Inspect the tool table pin bushing for wear. A worn bushing will not provide the close tolerance fit required to prevent stack movement. Verify that there is no separation between stack and tool table.

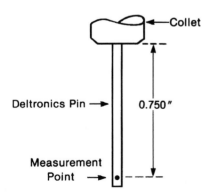

FIGURE 18.17   Spindle runout measurement.

After a routine spindle and table warm-up, check the pressure foot for the correct insert and wear and damage and verify adequate vacuum including inspecting vacuum hoses for tear and cracks. Set and record the height above the stack. The up-stroke setting will be different when the total heights of the stacks vary. A minimum of 0.500 in as shown in Fig. 18.15 is recommended to allow the table motion to stop before the next drill stroke when evalauting hole location accuracy.

Verify the desired feeds, speed, and retraction rates programmed into the CNC controller. Typical drilling parameter for common laminates are listed in Tables 18.4 and 18.5. Indicate the drilling pattern start, end, and total number of hits on the top panel of each drilled stack. The 0.100 in on center grid in Fig. 18.16 is a pattern that allows several consecutively drilled holes near a desired hit location to be cross-sectioned and examined in a single coupon.

With multiple tests, use the same spindle for all testing if it is possible. This will eliminate the spindle as a variable. If two spindles must be used, repeat the tests, switching the stacks under the two spindles. This will cancel the effects of the individual spindles.

With either a stroboscope or a tachometer, verify the spindle r/min for the range of r/min in the testing plan. Using a known concentric pin, such as a Deltronics pin certified to within 0.000050 in of concentricity, measure the static TIR (true indicated runout) with a 0.0001-in or better resolution dial indicator at 0.750 in from the collet, as shown in Fig. 18.17.

If a dynamic runout instrument is available, measure the TIR at the spindle speed to be used in the testing. To eliminate adding the runout from the plastic ring to the spindle, collet, and pin runout, make the measurement on a pin without a plastic ring. Spindle runout generally increases as r/min is raised, except for about 70,000 to 80,000 r/min where the harmonic vibrations of the spindle and pin can cause either a sharp peak or dip in the runout. Excessive TIR will cause poor hole registration and drill breakage. Most drilling machine manufacturers specify a 0.0005-in or better for heart-of-the-range drilling and 0.0002-in or better for small hole drilling. If the TIR is excessive, clean the collet and collet seat, then remeasure the TIR. If the TIR is still out of tolerance, replace the spindle or select another spindle for the tests.

18.13.2.1 Posttest Condition.   After the drilling is completed, remeasure the spindle r/min and TIR to verify that these are the same as the starting conditions.

Inspect the stack to verify that it remained flat on the tool table and that no gaps between the panels developed during drilling. Carefully take the stack apart, inspecting all the surfaces for drilling debris or random burring, which would indicate pinning or pressure foot problems.

Careful examination of the drill can reveal important information about the drilling conditions. For example, when there is heavy buildup of fused resin in the margin relief of the drill, smear will be in the holes. A chipped or damaged drill would be expected to produce a rough hole wall.

If drill breakage occurred during drilling, note the circumstances and number of hits. If the broken part can be retrieved, save it along with the drill and test number. Record whether breakage occurred during drilling or retraction. This information as well as microscope inspection of the broken drill is invaluable in determining the cause.

18.13.3 Qualifying Drill Bits

Drill bits are the most expensive consumable raw material for drilling and are the most essential part of any drilling qualification. The number of rejected drill bits and their defects are an important part of assessing the quality and consistency of the drill bits. Do not assume that new drills are good.

Before starting the qualification, carefully place an identifying mark on the shank of the drill or on its plastic ring. This will facilitate recording the defects and separating defective drill bits during the qualification procedure.

Clean the drill bits by carefully twisting the drill bit in an orangewood stick. This will remove any oil or loose debris that can obscure a defect. The force of the wood will also remove any loose carbide from defective material or from damage due to improper handling.

Visually inspect the drill bits according to the procedure in Sec. 18.4, removing from the wallet or box and setting aside any drill bit that has an unacceptable or major defect listed in Fig. 18.7. Chips and layback can generate excessive drilling temperatures, causing heat-related hole defects; overlap and offset can cause hole location centering problems. Drills with major defects will not produce quality holes. For evaluations, drills with the minor defects listed in Fig. 18.7 should also be removed because these defects will make drill wear measurements more difficult, even though they will not cause poor hole quality.

If the drill bits were not supplied with plastic rings, set the rings on acceptable drill bits and reinspect each bit for damage. If the drills were ringed by the supplier, verify the proper setting according to the drilling machine specifications and reinspect the drill bits. Remove any drill bit that was damaged. Drill bits can easily be damaged during ring setting, especially with ring setters that touch the tip of the drill bit.

Verify the integrity of the drill bit's carbide with a special preconditioning step whereby 100 hits for a 0.013-in diameter or 50 hits for a drill bit smaller than 0.013-in diameter are drilled in a separate stack of entry material, double-sided laminates, and backup. To compare preconditioning wear for a group of drill bits of the same diameter, it is important to use the same stack and same machine parameters for the group of drill bits. This will eliminate variation in drill bit wear from materials and machine parameters as a variable. After the preconditioning step, reinspect the drill bits for any unusual buildup of loose debris that would indicate a problem with chip removal, which would could affect drilling temperatures. Remove the loose debris from the drill bit with clean, dry compressed air and reinspect the drills bits for chipping, wear, and resin buildup. Reject and set aside any drill bits that have chipping or excessive wear. The remaining drill bits would be expected to exhibit normal wear in an evaluation.

If equipment is available for measuring drilling temperatures during the preconditioning step, temperature profiles can be used to select matching drills for comparing entry and backup materials, laminates, or machine parameters. Such a system consists of an Infrared (IR) detector that senses the temperature of the drill bit in the pressure foot as the drill exits the stack on retraction. The signal is sent through a fiberoptic to the detector where it is processed and passed to the display unit and strip chart. The average and range of temperature readings of the drills recorded during the evaluation can be used for comparisons.

18.13.4 Qualifying Entry Materials

The purpose of an entry material is to:

- Protect the product being drilled
- Control laminate entry burring
- Not raise drilling temperature
- Not degrade the hole quality
- Promote drill self-centering
- Not cause excessive drill wear

Burr heights, hole wall quality, drill bit wear, and drilling temperature can be evaluated using a normal test stack for each entry. The drill self-centering test requires a separate test method and a special stack.

The normal test stacks consist of the entry material, laminates, and backup. When testing, if possible use either doubled-sided or multilayer laminates with solid copper innerlayers to make inspecting and rating the cross-sectioned hole easier. The test stack height depends on the number of copper layers and the drill's effective flute length. Multilayer laminates with eight layers and more are normally drilled two high. Double-sided, four- and six-layer laminates can be drilled in a three-high stack if the drills have sufficient flute length. To ensure that all of the test stacks are identical except for the entry material, prepare the stacks of laminates and backup as described under Sec. 18.13.1. For evaluating burring, hole quality, and drill bit wear, use a regular pattern like Fig. 18.16. This will make it easier to follow the sequence of holes drilled and to locate regions of specific hit counts (i.e., start, 500, 1000 hits, etc.).

The hole size for testing depends on the thickness of the entry. Entry materials can be divided into two groups, one less than 10 mil thick for drilling micro holes and the other greater than 10 mil for larger-size holes. Common size drill bits for qualifying entry materials are #80 (0.0135 in) for the thin entry and #76 (0.020 in) for the thicker entry.

Inspect the entry material for pits, dents, edge burrs, and flatness, recording the results as part of the entry material evaluation. Replace any entry material panel having an obvious flaw that could affect drilling. Either cut the entry material shorter than the laminates or notch the entry material panel to clear the tooling pins. After the pinned stack has been mounted on the tooling table and the stack flatness verified, secure the entry material to the top laminate with two small pieces of tape. This will allow the entry material to expand, relieving stress induced during drilling. Be careful not to extend the tape into the area that will be drilled, as the tape can contaminate the holes and cause drill breakage. Do not tape the stack to the tooling table. If the stack does not lie flat on the table, replace it. Tape will not prevent a warped stack from moving during drilling.

The procedure for preconditioning drill bits is described in the previous section on qualifying drill bits. Before starting the test, examine the drills that have been preconditioned to establish a pretest baseline for drill wear. If possible, document the observations with either light photographs or scanning electron micrographs. During drilling, stop at regular intervals—for example, every 500 hits—remove the drill bit from the collet, and carefully examine the bit under 40 to 140 magnification for drill wear and for buildup of fused resin in the margin that would indicate excessive drilling heat. Again, if the equipment is available, document the observations with photos or micrographs. Since it is important to evaluate the performance of entry material over the life of the drill bit, the test should continue long enough to show definite signs of wear without pushing the drill bit to the breaking point. If the drill breaks during the test, repeat the test for that entry material. The number of hits varies depending on the abrasive characteristics of the laminate and wear characteristics of the drill's carbide. Normally the number of hits to show significant wear beyond normal usage is 1500 to 2000 for #80 drill bits and 2500 to 3000 for #76 drill bits.

After drilling is completed and the stack is inspected, to verify that the entry material and laminates are still lying flat on the table, carefully take the stack apart. Determine if the entry material protected the laminates by examining the top surface of the laminate for marks from debris picked up by the pressure foot that have telegraphed through the entry material onto the laminate surface.

Drilling temperature can be monitored during the drilling if the equipment is available. One method is to mount an infrared detector in the pressure foot and focus it on the drill bit point. If stacks are identical except for the entry materials, the difference in drilling temperatures is due to the entry materials. The higher the drilling temperature, the greater the hole wall heat-related defects. If IR monitoring equipment is not available, excessive resin buildup on the drill bit can indicate excessive drilling temperatures.

In an entry material evaluation, burr heights are measured on the entry surface of the top laminate, which is the surface that was next to the entry material. Burr heights are estimated either by inspecting the surface with a stereo microscope or by measuring the burrs with a scanning profilometer. Burrs less than 1 percent of the hole diameter are considered acceptable. When utilizing a mechanical deburring process, burrs greater than 1 percent can be rolled into the hole rather than removed, resulting in blown holes after plating.

After examining burring, remove coupons for unencapsulated hole wall examination from the regions of interest in the bottom laminate and prepare them for the evaluation. The bottom laminate is used for hole wall inspection; since it is closer to the bottom or dwell point in the drill cycle, it will have more heat-related defects than the middle or top laminates in the stack. Comparing hole quality versus the number of hits for the entry materials can determine how many hits can be drilled with each entry material before the hole quality drops below an acceptable level. Boards with a hole quality of 7.0 or greater are considered acceptable for normal printed circuit board processing. With normal drill wear, hole quality decreases with the number of holes drilled as shown in Fig. 18.14. A sudden decrease in hole quality can indicate that damage or severe wear has occurred to the drill or that the margin and flutes have become packed with resin and debris.

Measuring the drill wear, as illustrated in Fig. 18.8, is another important area of entry material evaluation. The extent of drill bit damage and wear from the entry material not only directly affects the life of the drill bit, but, more importantly, they affect hole quality. Chipped or damaged cutting edges on the drill bit can cause glass tearouts from the hole

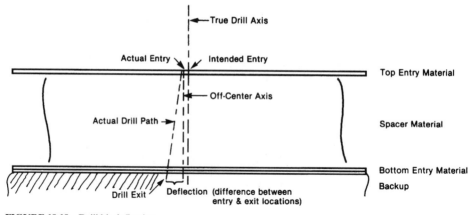

FIGURE 18.18   Drill bit deflection.

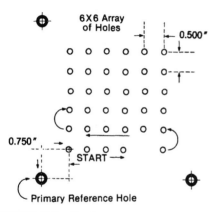

FIGURE 18.19   Small array pattern for measuring drill deflection.

walls and heavy drill wear can raise drill bit temperature, which will increase resin smearing and plowing in the hole wall.

Entry materials require a special test method and a special stack to measure off-center drilling (see Fig. 18.18). The stack consists of two pieces of entry material, one on top of the stack and another on top of the backup at the bottom of the stack. Since a drill bit that enters off the target will be deflected at the top of the stack, and will continue to drill at an angle during the infeed stroke, deflection will be the difference between the top and bottom hole location, as illustrated in Fig. 18.18. Using the same material as the top and bottom panels cancels any difference in thermal expansion that would occur if dissimilar materials were used. The two pieces of entry material are separated by spacer material that does not have a grain structure that could contribute to drill bit deflection. A good choice for a spacer is an aluminum or paper-clad wood core backup. Laminates are a poor choice because of their glass weave, which can deflect the drill bit.

If possible, use the same drill bit for all of the off-center drilling tests. This will eliminate the drill bit as a variable. The matrix in Fig. 18.19 is a good example of a small 6-by-6 matrix for measuring hole location accuracy. Measurements are made on the 36 small holes. The larger-diameter holes are used for reference holes because there is less deflection with larger-diameter drill bits. Drilling the series of patterns twice, once in reverse sequence, will cancel out any differences in drill bit wear for the patterns. For example, if there are three stacks, drill the stacks first in a 1-2-3 order for the first pass and in a 3-2-1 order for the second pass. If possible, drill without removing the drill bit from the spindle collet to eliminate difference of runout caused by reinserting the drill bit (drill bits can pick up dirt during tool changes). If the drill bit is removed for inspection, recheck the runout as described in Sec. 18.13.2.

When the measurements are made and the data collected for all of the criteria, one entry material seldom excels in every category evaluated. Most entry materials have some strong and weak points. Select the entry material judged best for overall performance with emphasis on the most important items in the criteria list by priority in the beginning of Sec. 18.13.4.

18.13.5 Qualifying Backup Material

The main purpose of a backup is to provide a medium to terminate the drill, in addition to the following items.

- not raising drilling temperature
- not contaminating the hole
- not degrading the hole quality
- Control laminating exit burring
- not causing excessive drill wear

These five items are listed in order of importance. Drilling temperature and hole wall contamination are listed first and second because these two areas can have the greatest impact on the quality of the hole and the reliability of the printed circuit board. The effects of the other items are less dramatic.

When qualifying any material, it is always important to eliminate as many variables as possible. With backup evaluations, the use of an entry material is not recommended. This will eliminate one of the main variables and make it easier to compare the effects of the backups.

The normal test stacks for backup evaluation consist of the laminates and backup. For testing, use either doubled-sided or multilayer laminates with solid copper innerlayers to ensure that all holes drilled contain the same amount of copper. The test stack height depends on the number of copper layers and the drill's effective flute length. Multilayer laminates with eight layers and more are normally drilled two high. Double-sided, four- and six-layer laminates can be drilled in a three-high stack if the drills have sufficient flute length. To ensure that all of the test stacks are identical except for the backup, prepare the stacks of laminates and backup as described in Sec. 18.13.1.

It is important to measure the thickness of the backup to determine the correct machine setting for the proper drill penetration (see Fig. 18.9). If several backups are being compared, it is important to keep the penetration depth constant. Drilling deeper into the backup increases the amount of material drilled and therefore increases drill wear and decrease hole quality. When comparing backups of different thicknesses, the height above the stack must be keep constant. Decreasing the height above the stack will raise drilling temperatures and increase heat-related drilling defects.

Inspect the backup for cleanliness, edge burrs, and flatness, recording the results as part of the backup evaluation. Replace any backup material panel having an obvious defect that could affect drilling. Pin the laminates and backup together and inspect the stack to ensure that all panels are flat and in good contact with each other.

A standard drilling pattern like Fig. 18.16 will make it easier to locate and remove consecutive holes at each region of interest. The number of hits should be sufficient to extend drill wear beyond the normal life of the drill bit. For example, if the normal drill life is 1500 to 2000 hits before repointing, the test should be at lest 3000 to ensure sufficient wear.

It is important to eliminate defective drills that would adversely influence the backup evaluations and to verify carbide integrity of the drills selected for the evaluation. This step for preconditioning drill bits is described in Sec. 18.3.3. Before starting the backup evaluation, examine the drill bits after they have been preconditioned to establish a pretest baseline for comparing drill wear that occurs during the test. If possible, document the baseline wear with either light photographs or scanning electron micrographs.

Drilling temperature burr heights, hole wall quality, and drill wear for backup can be evaluated using the same procedures discussed in the entry material qualification, except that no entry material is used and burring is measured on the exit surface of the bottom laminate.

During drilling, monitor drilling temperature with the same method described for qualifying drill bits. Most of the damage to the hole wall caused by the backup is related to heat. The higher the drilling temperature, the greater the hole wall heat-related defects. If IR monitoring equipment is not available for measuring the drill bit temperature during drilling, some information can be indirectly inferred from the examination of the drill bit and hole wall. Excessive resin smear on the drill bit and hole wall indicate high drilling temperatures, assuming the resin in the laminates and backup are fully cured. Undercured resin in either the backup or laminates will also cause heavy smearing.

To collect data for determining drill condition versus the number of hits, stop at regular intervals, during the drilling—for example, every 500 hits—remove the drill bit from the spindle collet, and carefully examine the bit under 40 to 140 magnification for buildup of fused resin in the margin that would indicate excessive drilling heat and for drill wear. Again, if the equipment is available, document the observations with photos or scanning electron micrographs. Since it is important to evaluate the performance of the backup over the life of the drill, the test should continue long enough to show definite signs of wear without pushing the drill bit to the breaking point. If the drill breaks during the test, repeat the test for that backup. The number of hits needed to show definite sign of wear will vary depending on the abrasiveness of the laminate and the wear resistance of the drill's carbide. Normally the number of hits to show significant wear beyond normal usage is 1500 to 2000 for #80 drill bits and 2500 to 3000 for #76 drill bits.

After completing the drilling, inspect the stack to verify that the laminates and backup are still lying flat on the table and that there is no separation between the laminates and the backup. Carefully take the stack apart and determine if the backup material provided proper support for the laminates by examining the exit surface of the bottom laminate for heavy burring and debris that would indicate a lack of support by the backup.

Before the inspection coupons are removed from the bottom laminate, measure the burr heights at each region of interest with a profilometer or estimate the burr heights with a stereo microscope. The laminate surface to examine in a backup evaluation is the exit surface of the bottom laminate, which was the surface in contact with the backup. Burrs less than 1 percent of the hole diameter are considered acceptable. When utilizing a mechanical deburring process, burrs greater than 1 percent can be rolled into the hole rather than removed, resulting in blown holes after plating.

After examining burring, remove coupons from the regions of interest in the bottom laminate for unencapsulated hole wall examination. For example, if the test was 2000 hits, inspecting a coupon every 500 hits would produce five data points, including the first hit of the test. The bottom laminate is used for hole wall inspection since it is closest to the backup and to the dwell point at the bottom of the drill cycle where the drill reaches its highest temperature.

Examine the laminate holes for drilling debris from the backup deposited in the holes by the drill. The laminate holes can be easily contaminated if the backup contains undercured resins, salts, or extending oils. Even cured resins from the backup can be softened by frictional heat, picked up by the drill, and transferred to the hole walls. These resins may be very difficult to remove by etchback and desmearing systems which are designed for the laminate resins.

The backup can also indirectly affect the hole quality by wearing the drill bit and raising the drilling temperature, which can increase hole wall roughness and resin smear. Rating the hole quality in the coupon and plotting hole quality versus the number of hits will determine how many hits can be drilled with a particular backup before the hole quality drops below an acceptable level. Figure 18.14 is an example of a hole quality versus the number of hits. Boards with a hole quality of 7.0 or greater are considered acceptable for normal printed circuit boards processing. A sudden decrease in hole quality in the backup evaluation can indicate the point in the evaluation where the margin and flutes became packed with resin and debris or a point where significant damage occurred to the drill bit.

In the beginning of this section on qualifying backup materials, five items stated as the purpose of a backup were listed in the order of importance. Selecting the backup based on overall results and on the relative importance of these five items is the best way to determine which backup to use.

18.14   *TOTAL DRILLING COST*

In evaluations of consumable materials for drilling it is important to know not only the difference in performance, but how the purchase price affects the total drilling cost. The following method is a simple way of calculating the cost of drills, entry materials, or backups based on a constant 1 ft^2 area. This example illustrates the steps involved by comparing the drilling cost for two backups: backup A at $0.80/ft^2 and backup B at $0.40/ft^2. Since only the material costs will vary, the following factors will be held constant.

1. The drill size is #72 (0.0250 in), which is midrange for the drills used today.

2. The number of holes drilled with a new #72 drill is 6000. Holes need to remain constant and are not to be confused with hits. If drilling laminates two high in a stack, there are 6000 holes with 3000 hits. With four-high stacks of laminates there are only 1500 hits with 6000 holes. Therefore, 6000 holes are kept constant.

3. The machine time to drill 6000 holes is 0.75 h.

4. To simplify calculations the area will remain a constant 1 ft^2.

Utilizing the preceding values and adding examples of rates for labor and machine burden, the following costs are required to drill the 6000 #72 holes.

18.14.1   Labor Cost to Drill

Machine operator cost per hour	$12.00
Machine burden cost per hour	$12.00
	$24.00
Multiply by 0.75 h drill time	$18.00

Since most machines have four stations, the labor is divided by 4, while the material per square foot and drill costs remain the same.

Divide labor by 4 for the number of drill stations	$4.50	$4.50
Cost for a new #72 drill	1.90	1.90
Cost for one resharp	0.25	0.25
Cost for entry material	0.50	0.50
Cost for backup A (used twice)	0.40	
Cost for backup B (used twice)		0.20
Total cost for 6000 holes	$7.55	$7.35

The difference between utilizing the two backups is 2.6 percent of the total drilling cost. If the decision is whether to switch from backup A to backup B, this 2.6 percent saving must be evaluated against the difference in backup performance and the possibility of loss or needed rework of printed circuit boards.

Computer programs can separate and define the accuracy and precision elements in drill wander. It is important to do this to check out new machines, materials, and processes. The method uses a 100-hole square drilling program, reference holes, and use of a comparator to measure location.

18.15 DRILLING PROBLEMS

Common drilling problems, probable causes, and solutions are as follows:

Copper defects	Causes	Solutions
Delamination of copper	Poor laminate	Replace laminate.
	CL too high	Check in-feed.
	Drill slippage	Check drill shank, diameter, and collet tension.
Nailheading	Voids in laminate	Replace laminate.
	Improper drill bits	Check and replace drill bit.
	sfm too high	Check and modify sfm.
	Stack height too high	Reduce stack height.
	Laminate too thick	Reduce sfm.
	Poor entry and backup system	Replace entry and backup with cooler drilling materials.
Smear	Poor backup or entry	Change to higher-quality backup or entry.
	Uncured laminate	Replace laminate.
	Worn drill bit	Check and replace drill bit.
	sfm too high	Check r/min and drill size.
Entry burrs	Poor entry	Change to higher-quality entry.
	Loose stacking	Tighten stack.
	Loose pins	Replace pinning drill.
	Pinning hole burrs	Deburr pinning holes.
	Dirt between surfaces	Clean laminate surfaces.
	Nonperpendicular pins	Repair worn fixture.
	Uncured laminate	Obtain better laminate.
	Low pressure foot pressure	Check springs, seals, and line pressure.
	Chip load too high	Reduce in-feed rate.
	Chipped drill	Check and replace drill.
Exit burrs	Poor backup	Change to higher-quality backup.
	Loose stacking	Tighten stack.
	Loose pins	Replace pinning drill.
	Pinning hole burrs	Deburr pinning holes.
	Dirt between surfaces	Clean laminate surfaces.
	Nonperpendicular pins	Repair worn fixture.
	Low pressure foot pressure	Check springs, seals, and line pressure.
	Chip load too high	Check for drill slippage.
Debris on copper	Retraction rate too high	Check and reduce retraction rate.
	Vacuum system weak or inoperative	Check and improve vacuum system.
	Drill's helix angle improper	Check drill against specs.
	Pressure foot channels plugged	Replace pressure foot.
Roughness of copper	Chipped drill	Check and replace drill.
	Worn OD margin	Check and replace drill.
	Excessive spindle runout	Check and clean spindle, collet, and collet seat.

Substrate defects	Causes	Solutions
Delamination of substrate	Poor laminate	Replace laminate.
	CL too high	Check in-feed rate.
	Drill slippage	Check drill shank diameter and collet tension.
Voids	Poor laminate	Replace laminate.
	Chipped or flawed drills	Check and replace drills.
Debris on substrate	Retraction rate too high	Check and reduce retraction rate.
	Vacuum system weak or inoperative	Check and improve vacuum system.
	Drill's helix angle improper	Check drill against specs.
	Pressure foot channels plugged	Replace pressure foot.
Loose fibers	Worn drill	Check and replace drill bit.
	Uncured laminate	Replace laminate.
	sfm too high	Check r/min and drill size.
Smear	Poor backup or entry	Change to higher-quality backup or entry.
	Uncured laminate	Replace laminate.
	Worn drill bit	Check and replace drill bit.
	sfm too high	Check r/min and drill size.
Plowing	Worn drill	Check and replace drill bit.
	Uncured laminate	Replace laminate.
	sfm too high	Check r/min and drill size.
Rifling	Chipped drill	Check and replace.
	Excessive spindle runout	Check and clean spindle, collet, and collet seat.

Drill wander	Causes	Solutions
Hole locations off target	Poor machine	Check spindle runout and machine accuracy.
	Precision poor	Reduce CL, replace entry material, check drill concentricity, reduce stack height.
	Drill resonance	Drill at different r/min.
	Dirty or worn collets	Clean or replace spindle collets.

CHAPTER 19
PLATING

Edward F. Duffek, Ph.D.
Adion Engineering Company, Cupertino, California

19.1 INTRODUCTION

A major part of manufacturing printed circuit boards involves *wet process* chemistry. The plating aspects of wet chemistry include deposition of metals by electroless (metallization) and electrolytic (electroplating) processes. Topics to be described here are multilayer processing, electroless copper, direct metallization, electroplating of copper and resist metals, nickel and gold for edge connector (tips), tin-lead fusing, and alternative coatings. Specific operating conditions, process controls, and problems in each area will be reviewed in detail. The effects of plating on image transfer, strip and etching are also described in this chapter. See printed circuit plating flowchart in Fig. 19.1.

Two driving forces have had major influence on plating practices: the precise technical requirements of electronic products and the demands of environmental and safety compliance. Recent technical achievements in plating are evident in the capability to produce complex, high-resolution multilayer boards. These boards show narrow lines (3 to 6 mil), small holes (12 mil), surface-mount density, and high reliability. In plating, such precision has been made possible by the use of improved automatic, computer-controlled plating machines, instrumental techniques for analysis of organic and metallic additives, and the availability of controllable chemical processes. Mil-spec-quality boards are produced when the procedures given here are closely followed.

19.2 PROCESS DECISIONS

Process and equipment needs dictate the physical aspect of the facility and the character of the process, and vice versa. Some important items to consider are the following.

19.2.1 Facility Considerations

1. *Multilayer and two-sided product mix:* Need for lamination presses and inner layer processes.
2. *Circuit complexity:* Need for dry film, photoimageable resist, and clean room.
3. *Level of reliability (application of product):* Need for extra controls and testing.

4. *Volume output:*   Need for equipment sizing and building space.

5. *Use of automatic versus manual line:*   Need for productivity, consistency, and workforce.

6. *Wastewater treatment system:*   Need for water and process control capability.

7. *Environmental and personnel safety; compliance to laws.*

8. *Costs.*

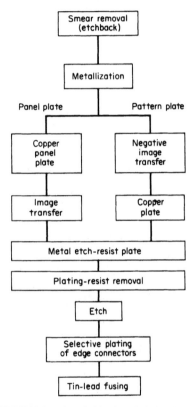

FIGURE 19.1   Printed wiring board plating flowchart.

19.2.2   Process Considerations

1. *Material:*   The principal printed board material discussed will be NEMA grade FR-4 or G-10, i.e., epoxy-fiberglass clad with ½-, 1-, or 2-oz copper. Other materials will be briefly mentioned because they can significantly alter plating and related processes.

2. *Standard:*   Plated-through-hole (PTH) is the current standard of the industry. The following purposes, objectives, and requirements apply to both multilayer and two-sided boards.
   a. Purposes
      Increased circuit density
      Double-sided circuitry
   b. Objectives
      Side-to-side electrical connection
      Ease of component attachment
      High reliability
   c. Requirements
      Complete coverage
      Even thickness
      Hole-to-surface ratio
      0.001 in minimum
      No cracks
      No voids, nodules, inclusions
      No pullaway
      No epoxy smear
      Minor resin recession
      Optimum metallurgical structure
      M/L compatibility

3. *Image transfer.*   Photoimageable, dry film or screening of plating resists will depend on board complexity, volume, and labor skills.

4. *Electroless copper.*   The type chosen will depend on the method of image transfer as well as on the need for panel plating. These processes are readily automated. Currently, 95 percent of printed circuit board manufacturers worldwide rely on the electroless copper method for hole metallization.

5. *Direct metallization technology (DMT).*   Some of the remaining printed circuit board manufacturers have eliminated the electroless copper step and converted to DMT. Developed in the 1980s, DMT methods produce a conductive surface on the nonconductive through-hole surfaces. Electroless copper baths contain formaldehyde and chelators. In addition, the baths use large volumes of water and are difficult to control and waste treat.[1] DMT claims include increased productivity, ease of control, and lower hazardous material involvement. Because of these characteristics, DMT will probably become the principal

method in the next 5 to 10 years.[2] At this time, acceptance of the DMT process has been delayed by the high cost of conveyorized equipment and chemicals.

DMT primary technologies include:
   a. Palladium
   b. Carbon-graphite
   c. Conductive polymer
   d. Other methods

See Sec. 19.6 for further information.

6. *Electroplating processes.*   Deposit requirements are as follows:

   Electrical conductivity

   Mechanical strength

   Ductility and elongation

   Solderability

   Tarnish and corrosion resistance

   Etchant resistance

   Compliance to Mil-specification

   Details emphasizing operation, control and mil-spec plating practices are given in Sec. 19.9. Metal plated structures of completed PC boards are as follows:

   Copper/tin-lead alloy

   Copper/tin (SMOBC)

   Copper/tin-nickel (nickel)/tin-lead

   Copper/nickel/tin

   Nickel/silver

7. *Strip, etching, tin-lead fusing.*   Methods required by these steps are determined by the preceding processes and by the need for automation.

19.3   PROCESS FEEDWATER

19.3.1   Water Supply

Printed circuit board fabrication and electronic processes require process feedwater with low levels of impurities. Large volumes of raw water must be readily available, either of suitable quality, or else treatable at reasonable cost. New facilities must consider water at an early stage of the site selection and planning process. Zero discharge, although a desirable goal, is very costly and difficult to achieve.

19.3.2   Water Quality

Highly variable mineral content causes board rejects and equipment downtime, as well as reduced bath life, burdened waste treatment, and difficult rinse water recovery. Many water supplies contain high levels of dissolved ionic minerals and possible colloidals that can cause rejects in board production. Some of these impurities are calcium, silica, magnesium, iron, and chloride. Typical problems caused by these impurities are copper oxidation, residues in the PTH, copper-copper peelers, staining, roughness, and ionic contamination. Problems in the equipment include water- and spray-line clogging, corrosion, and breakdown. The best plating practices suggest good-quality water for high yields. The need for water low in total dissolved solids (TDS), calcium hardness, and conductivity is well known. Good water eliminates the concern that the water supply may be responsible for rejects. Although water quality is not well defined for plating and PC board manufacturing, for general usage, some guidelines can be assigned as follows. Where high-purity water is required, see Sec. 19.3.3.

Typical quantities are:

Total dissolved solids (TDS)	4 to 20 ppm
Conductivity	8 to 30 µS/cm
Specific resistance	0.12 to 0.03 MΩ
Carbonate hardness ($CaCO_3$)	3 to 15 ppm

Somewhat higher values are acceptable for less-critical processes and rinses.

19.3.3 Water Purification

Two processes widely used for water purification are reverse osmosis and ion exchange. In the reverse osmosis technique, raw water under pressure (1.4 to 4.2 MPa or 200 to 600 lb/in^2) is forced through a semipermeable membrane. The membrane has a controlled porosity which allows rejection of dissolved salts, organic matter, and particulate matter, while allowing the passage of water through the membrane. When pure water and a saline solution are on opposite sides of a semipermeable membrane, pure water diffuses through the membrane and dilutes the saline water on the other side (osmosis). The effective driving force of the saline solution is called its *osmotic pressure.* In contrast, if pressure is exerted on the saline solution, the osmosis process can be reversed. This is called the *reverse osmosis process* (RO), and involves applying pressure to the saline solution in excess of its osmotic pressure. Fresh water permeates the membrane and collects on the opposite side, where it is drawn off as product. Reverse osmosis removes 90 to 98 percent of dissolved minerals and 100 percent of organics with molecular weights over 200, as shown in Table 19.1.

A small quantity of dissolved substances also facilitates deionized (DI) water production, wastewater treatment, and process rinse water recovery, since it makes recycling less costly and more feasible. An RO system will result in lower costs for DI water preparation and for process water recycling. The setup for recycling requires additional equipment for polymer addition, filtration, and activated carbon treatment.

TABLE 19.1 Purified Water Supply Values
Typical in/out RO values

TDS, ppm	SiO_2, ppm	Conductivity, µS	Hardness-$CaCO_3$, ppm
170/4	30/1	130/8	24/1
240/7	45/2	200/14	35/2
300/10	60/2	250/20	45/3

Deionized (DI) water purification is used when high-purity water is required, for example, in bath makeups, rinses before plating steps, and final rinses necessary to maintain low ionic residues on board surfaces. Mil-spec PC boards must pass the MIL-P-28809 test for ionic cleanliness. This is done by final rinsing in DI water. Deionized water is made by the ion exchange technique. This involves passing water containing dissolved ionics through a bed of solid organic resins. These convert the ionic water contents to H^+ and OH^-. Deionized water systems are more practical when using feedwater low in ionic and organic content.

Other requirements are:

pH	6.5–8.0
Total organic carbon	2.0 ppm
Turbidity	1.0 NTU
Chloride	2.0 ppm

19.4 MULTILAYER PTH PREPROCESSING

Two-sided printed circuit boards are usually processed by first drilling and deburring, followed by the through-hole metallization. Multilayers require treatment involving resin smear removal and etchback prior to the electroless copper or DM.

19.4.1 Smear Removal

Drill smear refers to the epoxy resin that coats the innerlayer copper surface in the drilled hole and is due to heating during the drilling operation. Control of this smear is difficult due to variability in dielectric materials, inconsistency in curing stage, and poor drill quality. This smear must be removed before metallization to get full electrical continuity from the innerlayer copper to the PTH. The innerlayer connections will be flush with the drilled hole after smear removal. See Figs. 19.2 to 19.4.

19.4.2 Etchback

This term refers to the continuation of the smear removal process to expose 0.5 mil on the top and bottom surface of the innerlayer copper. Physically, the innerlayer copper will now protrude from the drilled hole three-point connection for copper bonding, which is required on some mil-spec boards (see Fig. 19.5.)

19.4.3 Smear Removal/Etchback Methods

The four methods commonly used utilize hole-wall epoxy or dielectric oxidation, neutralization-reduction, and glass etching.

19.4.3.1 Sulfuric Acid. This process has been used extensively for many years because of its ease of operation and reliability of results. A major disadvantage is a lack of control, which leads to hole-wall pullaway and rough holes. Operator safety is crucial since concentrated sulfuric must be used.

19.4.3.2 Chromic Acid. This method provides more control and longer bath life. However, problems with copper voids due to Cr^{+6} poisoning, wastewater pollution, and contamination of plating processes must be considered. Etchback is possible by double processing.

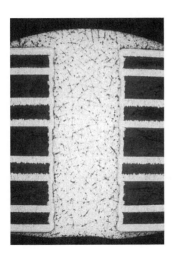

Inner-layer pad

PTH

Optimum inner-layer connection

FIGURE 19.2 PTH vertical and horizontal cross sections illustrating optimum innerlayer connection and smear removal.

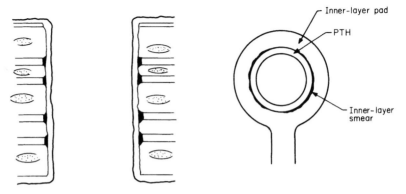

FIGURE 19-3 PTH vertical and horizontal cross sections illustrating innerlayer smear.

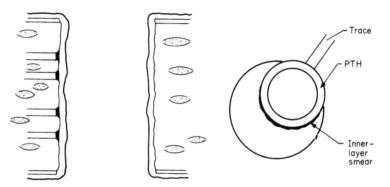

FIGURE 19.4 PTH vertical and horizontal cross sections illustrating innerlayer smear and misregistration.

19.4.3.3 Permanganate. This method is rapidly gaining acceptance due to improved copper adhesion to the hole-wall (less pullaway), smoother PTHs, and better control.[3] Problems result from sludge by-product formation, dark copper holes, and the operators' lack of experience. Permanganate is also used as a second step in conjunction with the other methods to enhance hole quality.[4]

19.4.3.4 Plasma. This is a dry-chemical method in which boards are exposed to oxygen and fluorocarbon gases. Persistent problems with the process are nonuniform treatment of holes—that is, higher etch rates on the edges—and the high cost of equipment. This process has few steps and eliminates the use of large quantities of chemicals. Controls must be provided to prevent air pollution.

19.4.4 Process Outline: Smear Removal and Etchback

The four common methods for smear removal and etchback are given in the following table. Combinations of these methods are also in use because of added reliability to both process and product.

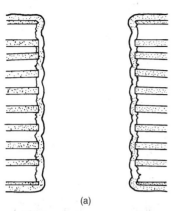

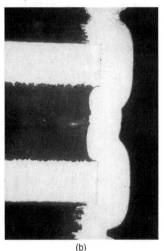

(a)

(b)

FIGURE 19.5   PTH vertical cross section illustrating optimum innerlayer connection and etchback.

19.4.4.1   *Smear Removal and Etchback Processes**

Sulfuric Acid	**Chromic Acid**
Rack panels	Rack panels
Sulfuric acid, 96% 20-s dwell, 15-s drain, room temperature	Chromic acid 3 min, 140°F
Neutralizer 8 min, 125°F	Reducer 3 min, room temperature
Ammonium bifluoride 3 min, room temperature	Ammonium bifluoride 3 min, room temperature
Unrack panels	Unrack panels
High-pressure hole cleaning	High-pressure hole cleaning
Release to electroless copper/DM	Release to electroless copper/DM

Permanganate	**Plasma Etch**
Solvent conditioner 90°F, 5 min	Plasma Oxygen, CF_4, 30 min
Alkaline permanganate 170°F, 10 min	Glass etch (optional)
Neutralizer-120°F, 5 min	High-pressure hole cleaning
Glass etch-4 min, room temp	Release to electroless copper/DM
High-pressure hole cleaning (optional)	
Release to electroless copper/DM	

Polyimide and polyimide-acrylic systems are processed in chromic acid or plasma. Teflon® and R T Duroid®† materials are treated (before operations) in sodium-naphthalene mixtures to yield void-free, high-bond-strength copper in the PTH.

19.5   ELECTROLESS COPPER[5–10]

19.5.1   Purpose

This second series of chemical steps (after smear removal) is used to make panel side-to-side and innerlayer connections by metallizing with copper. The process steps needed include racking, cleaning, copper microetching, hole and surface catalyzing with palladium, and electroless copper. Typical steps are as follows:

---

* Water rinses after each step are not shown.
† Teflon is a registered trademark of E. I. Du Pont de Nemours & Co. R T Duroid is a registered trademark of Rogers Corporation, Chandler, Ariz.

1. *Cleaner-conditioner.* Alkaline cleaning is used to remove soils and condition holes.

2. *Microetch.* This slow acid etching is used for removal of copper surface pretreatments, oxidation, and presentation of uniformly active copper. Persulfates and sulfuric acid-hydrogen peroxide solutions are commonly used.

3. *Sulfuric acid.* Used for removal of persulfate residues.

4. *Predip.* Used to maintain balance of the next step.

5. *Catalyst (activator).* Neutral or acid solutions of palladium and tin are used to deposit a thin layer of surface active palladium in the holes and on the surface.

6. *Accelerator (postactivator).* Used for the removal of colloidal tin on board surfaces and holes.

7. *Electroless copper.* Alkaline chelated copper reducing solution that deposits thin copper in the holes (20 to 100 μin) and surfaces.

8. *Antitarnish.* This is a neutral solution that prevents oxidation of active copper surfaces by forming a copper conversion coating.

19.5.2 Mechanism

Equations 19.1 and 19.2 illustrate the process.

$$Pd^{+2} + Sn^{+2} \rightarrow Pd + Sn^{+4} \tag{19.1}$$

$$CuSO_4 + 2\ HCHO + 4\ NaOH \xrightarrow{Pd} Cu + 2\ HCO_2Na + H_2 + 2\ H_2O + Na_2SO_4 \tag{19.2}$$

19.5.3 Electroless Copper Processes

Selection from several types available depends on the type of image transfer desired. Operation and control of three bath types and the function of constituents are given in Tables 19.2 and 19.3.

TABLE 19.2 Electroless Copper Processes
Operation and control

	Low deposition	Medium deposition	Heavy deposition
Copper	3 g/l	2.8 g/l	2.0 g/l
HCHO	6–9 g/l	3.5 g/l	3.3 g/l
NaOH	6–9 g/l	10–11 g/l	8 g/l
Temperature	65°–85°F	115° ± 5°F	115° ± 5°F
Air agitation	Mild	Mild/moderate	Moderate
Filtration	Periodic	Continuous	Continuous
Tank design	Static	Overflow, separate sump	Overflow, separate sump
Heater	Teflon	Teflon	Teflon
Panel loading	0.25–1.5 ft²/gal	0.1–2.0 ft²/gal	0.1–2.0 ft²/gal
Replenish mode	Manual	Manual or continuous	Automatic
Idle time, control	70–85%	Turn off heat	Turn off heat
Deposition time	20 min	20 min	20–30 min
Thickness	20 μin	40–60 μin	60–100 μin

TABLE 19.3 Electroless Copper
Function of constituents

	Constituent	Function
Copper salt	$CuSO_4 \cdot 5\,H_2O$	Supplies copper
Reducing agent	HCHO	$Cu^{+2} + 2e \rightarrow Cu^0$
Complexer	EDTA, tartrates, Rochelle salts	Holds Cu^{+2} in solution at high pH; controls rate
pH controller	NaOH	Controls pH (rate) 11.5–12.5 optimum for HCHO reduction
Additives	NaCN, metals, S, N, CN organics	Stabilize, brighten, speed rate, strengthen

The problems encountered with this system are as follows:

1. *Uncoppered holes.* This may appear as dark, hazy, or voided copper in the holes. To correct this, check the operation of the smear remover, cleaner, catalyst, accelerator, and the items listed in Table 19.2. Voids may also be due to copper plate precleaner attack.

2. *Hole wall pullaway.* This refers to copper pulling off the PTH, and is observed either as large blisters or by cross sectioning. This may be due to spent sulfuric acid smear removal, or to items given above. Pullaway is controlled by maintaining copper plating smooth and over 1-mil thickness. This may also be observed on solder mask on bare copper (SMOBC) boards due to shock of hot solder immersion.

3. *Bath decomposition.* This is rapid plating out of the copper. Common causes are bath imbalance, overloading, overheating, lack of use, tank wall initiation, or contamination.

4. *Electroless copper to copper-clad bond failure.* Review initial step in process and items in 1.

5. *Staining.* Copper oxidation is due to moisture or contamination on the copper surface. Corrective action involves dipping boards in antitarnish or hard rinsing in DI water.

19.5.4 Process Outline

This outline presents the typical steps in an electroless copper process:

1. Rack
2. Clean and condition
3. Water rinse
4. Surface copper etch (microtech)
5. Water rinse
6. Sulfuric acid (optional)
7. Water rinse
8. Preactivator
9. Activator (catalyst)
10. Water rinse
11. Postactivator (accelerator)
12. Water rinse
13. Electroless copper

14. Rinse

15. Sulfuric acid or antitarnish

16. Rinse

17. Scrub (optional)

18. Rinse

19. Copper flash plate (optional)

20. Dry

21. Release to image transfer

19.6   DIRECT METALLIZATION TECHNOLOGY* †

For 40 years the PTH process of choice has been palladium followed by electroless copper, but there have been at least 12 DMT processes challenging that established process, with several hundred installations, a significant percentage of the total number of PCB shops. The basic idea for the palladium systems dates back to the Radovsky patent of 1963,[11] which claimed a method of using an electrically nonconductive film of palladium in a semicolloidal form to directly metallize through holes in printed circuit boards. Radovsky's invention was never commercialized. The basic idea for the carbon/graphite systems dates back to the very early days of eyelet boards when Photocircuits was experimenting with graphite, silver, and other media to turn their single-sided PCBs into reliable double-sided boards.

19.6.1   Direct Metallization Technologies Overview

From the many media and technical variations, some common elements have evolved.

19.6.1.1   Direct Metallization Technologies Common Elements.   There are two elements common to all DMT:

1. Holes must be conditioned more specifically and thoroughly than for electroless copper.

2. Conductive media must be removed from the copper foil in a majority of the techniques (an exception is DMS-E).

It is understood that additional desmear steps are necessary or advisable when processing multilayer PCBs. Common elements to all horizontal conveyorized DMT systems are:

- Throughput is typically 6 to 15 min for a panel, with the next panel following 1 in behind
- Tremendous economies in rinse water use
- Lower consumption of chemicals
- Fewer steps than in its vertical mode
- Panel-to-panel uniformity

Many DMT processes work better than electroless copper on substrates with "difficult" resin systems such as PTFE, cyanate ester, or polyimide.

---

* Material in this section is the contribution of Dr. Hayao Nakahara, and John Dennis-Browne.
† All proprietary names are trademarked by their respective owners.

19.6.1.2 Direct Metallization Categories.   DMT falls into four broad categories:

1. Palladium-based systems
2. Carbon or graphite systems
3. Conductive polymer systems
4. Other methods

19.6.2 Palladium-based Systems

19.6.2.1 Palladium/Tin Activator with Flash Electroplating.   EE-1[12], the first commercialized direct metallization technique was invented in 1982 at Photocircuits and PCK. It uses a palladium/tin activator followed by mandatory flash electroplating. The flash-plating bath contains a polyoxyethylene compound to inhibit the deposition of copper on the foil surface without inhibiting deposition on palladium sites on nonconductive surfaces (holes, edges, substrate). Deposition occurs by propagation from the copper foil and grows epitaxially along the activated surface of the hole. Coverage takes about 5 to 6 min. This flash is pattern- or panel-plated subsequently to full thickness in any electroplating bath. Microetching is incorporated in the accelerator to remove palladium sites and nail heads from innerlayers. A special cleaner/conditioner is used. This process has never been adapted to horizontal equipment. (See Fig. 19.6.)

19.6.2.2 Palladium/Tin Activator with Vanillin.   DPS,[13] was invented in Japan in the late '80s. This method uses a palladium/tin activator with vanillin, followed by pattern or panel electroplating. It employs a special cleaner/conditioner and a carbonate accelerator. The three key solutions—cleaner/conditioner, activator, and accelerator—all operate at elevated temperatures. DPS has recently been adapted to horizontal equipment, but works well in the vertical mode, both manual and automatic. Following the last step, the *Setter,* DPS yields a stable, grayish conductive palladium film in the holes. It is believed that the cleaner/conditioner slightly solubilizes the activator, attracting it to the nonconductive surface, and that the vanillin lines up the palladium molecules, and directs them towards the work, hence giving lower electrical resistance and better adhesion to nonconductive surfaces. It is also claimed that there is little palladium/tin left on the copper foil, so it is easily soft-etched away in the normal electroplating preplate cycle. (See Fig. 19.7.) DPS was the first DMT process to suggest an Ω meter as the standard quality assurance (QA) tool.

19.6.2.3 Converting Palladium to Palladium Sulfide.   Crimson,[14] invented by Shipley, employs a conversion step after the activator where palladium is changed to palladium sulfide, which is claimed to be more conductive for subsequent electrolytic copper plating. The *enhancer* stabilizes the conductive film so that it is chemically resistant to imaging steps. The *stabilizer* neutralizes residues from the enhancer, thereby preventing contamination of subsequent steps. The *microetch* selectively removes activator from copper surfaces to achieve optimum copper-to-copper bond and reliable dry film adhesion. The process works best in conveyorized horizontal equipment and can be followed by pattern or panel electroplating. (See Fig. 19.8.)

19.6.2.4 Process Variations.   ABC,[15] invented in Israel by Holtzman et al., is similar to EE-1. It has been adapted to conveyorized horizontal equipment, but must be followed by a flash electroplating in a proprietary bath.

Conductron, from LeaRonal, is similar to DPS with the addition of a special cleaner/conditioner and a glass-etch step. It has been adapted to conveyorized horizontal equipment and can be followed by pattern or panel electroplating.

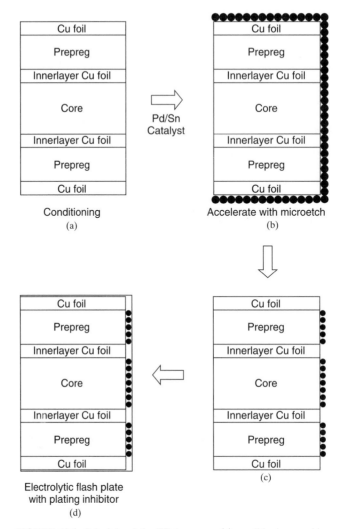

FIGURE 19.6 Principle of the EE-1 process: (*a*) conditioning—making glass and epoxy surfaces receptive of Pd catalyst sites; (*b*) palladium catalyst sites; (*c*) acceleration removes excess tin and microetch removes catalysts from the surface of Cu foil; (*d*) flush Cu plate coppers enter surface in drilling hole walls.

Envision DPS, from Enthone-OMI, and Connect, from M & T (now Atotech), are fairly similar to each other, and to DPS, though each has a specific cleaner/conditioner and modified accelerator. No adaptation has been made to horizontal processing. Both processes can be followed by pattern or panel electroplating.

Neopact,[16] from Atotech, uses a tin-free palladium activator in colloidal form. The subsequent postdip removes the protective organic polymer from the palladium, leaving it exposed and with increased conductivity. It has been adapted to conveyorized horizontal equipment, works well in vertical, and can be followed by pattern or panel electroplating. (See Fig. 19.9.)

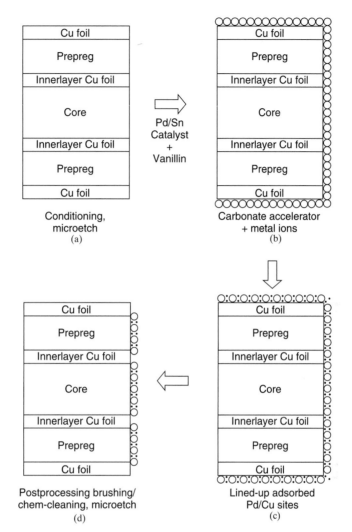

FIGURE 19.7 Principle of the DPS process: (*a*) conditioning for receptive surface; (*b*) catalysts adhering to the surface; (*c*) stronger adhesion; (*d*) ready to plate.

19.6.3 Carbon/Graphite Systems

19.6.3.1 Carbon Suspensions. Black Hole,[17] the second direct metallization technique, was patented by Dr. Carl Minten in 1988 and pioneered by Olin Hunt, who sold their technology to MacDermid in 1991. MacDermid improved the process considerably and called it Black Hole II. Instead of palladium activator, Black Hole II uses carbon suspensions as its conductive medium. Polyelectrolyte conditioned nonconductive surfaces absorb carbon sites, and they "line up" after heating. To ensure sufficient conductivity, the carbon treatment is performed twice. Residues of carbon sites must be removed from the copper foil surface by a

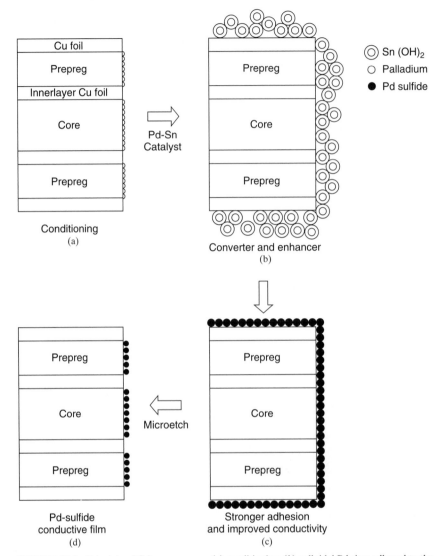

FIGURE 19.8 Principle of Crimson process: (*a*) conditioning; (*b*) colloidal Pd sites adhered to the surface; (*c*) Pd-sulfide (stronger adhesion of Pd catalysts); (*d*) microetch to remove Pd from Cu surface for better Cu-Cu adhesion.

microcleaning step. Black Hole II has been well adapted to conveyorized horizontal equipment and can be followed by pattern or panel electroplating. (See Fig. 19.10.)

19.6.3.2 Graphite. Shadow[18] is from Electrochemicals (division of LaPorte Industries, UK) and uses graphite as its conductive medium. The process sequence of Shadow is very simple and involves fewer steps than most DMTs. Electrochemicals and one of their fabricators, Eidschun Engineering, made the breakthrough in inexpensive, compact, conveyorized horizontal equipment, and the Shadow process is well adapted to this mode. It can be followed by pattern or panel electroplating.

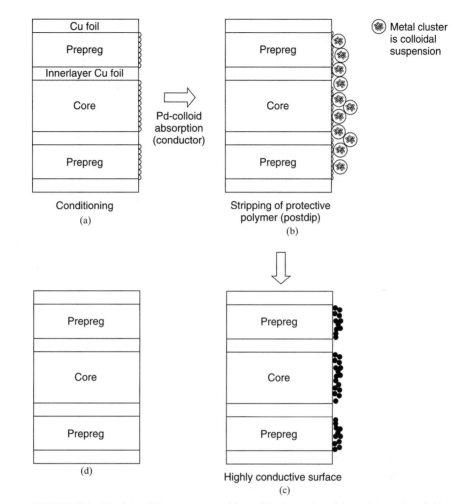

FIGURE 19.9   Principle of Neopact process: (*a*) conditioning surface; (*b*) metal cluster in colloidal suspension adhered to the hole wall; (*c*) stripped Pd adhering to the hole wall; (*d*) Cu reduced.

19.6.4   Conductive Polymer Systems

19.6.4.1   DMS-E.   DMS-E[19] from Blasberg is a second-generation DMS-2 process with which they pioneered in this field. DMS-1 was similar to EE-1. After microetch and conditioning, a potassium permanganate solution forms a manganese dioxide coating in the holes which acts as an oxidizing agent during subsequent synthesis reaction. In the catalyzing step, an EDT* monomer bath wets the manganese dioxide surfaces especially well. During the sulfuric acid fixation step, a spontaneous oxidative polarization takes place, forming a black conductive poly-EDT film on the nonconductive areas of the PCB. This technique is very suitable for use in conveyorized, horizontal equipment, since the oxidative conditioning step is very hot (80 to 90°C), and there are solvents involved. It can be followed by pattern or panel electroplating. (See Fig. 19.11.)

---

* EDT = 3,4 Ethylendioxythiophene.

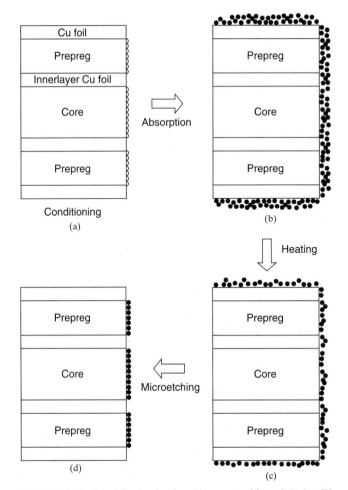

FIGURE 19.10 Principle of carbon/graphite process: (*a*) conditioning; (*b*) carbon particles adhered to the surface; (*c*) dense more conductive carbon conducting film; (*d*) removal of conduction film from Cu surface resulting in stronger Cu-Cu interface.

19.6.4.2 Compact CP. Compact CP[20] was developed by Atotech in 1987 and is essentially similar to DMS-E, except that it combines the catalyzing and fixation steps, it uses an acid permanganate, and the conductive film is a polypyrrole. The technique is very suitable for use in conveyorized, horizontal equipment. It can be followed by pattern or panel electroplating.

19.6.5 Other Methods

There are several other novel ways to metallize holes in PCBs, such as Phoenix and EBP from MacDermid, Schlötoposit from Schlötter. There are conductive ink and laser scribing/filling techniques; there are sputtering and sequential plating, to name a few, but they do not fall within the scope of this chapter.

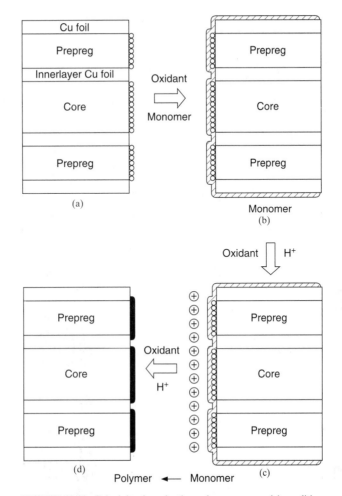

FIGURE 19.11 Principle of conductive polymer process: (*a*) conditioning; (*b*) monomer created on the surface; (*c*) oxidant reduces monomer to polymer yielding highly conductive surface; (*d*) further improved conductive surface.

19.6.6 Comparative Steps of DMT Process

19.6.6.1 DMT.1: Palladium-based Systems. All vertical modes only, for comparison purposes, are shown in Table 19.4.

19.6.6.2 DMT.2: Carbon/Graphite Systems—Conveyorized Horizontal. Conveyorized horizontal systems are shown in Table 19.5.

19.6.6.3 DMT.3: Conductive Polymer Systems. Conveyorized, horizontal systems with optional electrolytic flash are shown in Table 19.6.

TABLE 19.4 DMT.1

Palladium-based systems—all vertical mode only

EE-1	DPS	Crimson	ABC	Conductron	Envision DPS	Neopact
Cleaner conditioner	Cleaner conditioner	Cleaner conditioner	Cleaner conditioner etch	Glass conditioner	Conditioner	Etch cleaner
Rinse	Rinse	Rinse	Rinse	Rinse	Rinse	Rinse
Microetch	Microetch	Predip	Activator	Cleaner conditioner	Carrier	Conditioner
Rinse	Rinse	Activator	Rinse	Rinse	Activator	Rinse
Predip	Predip	Rinse	Salt remover	Microetch	Rinse	Predip
Activator	Activator	Accelerator	Rinse	Rinse	Generator	Conductor
Rinse	Rinse	Rinse	Dry	Predip	Rinse	Rinse
Accelerator	Accelerator	Enhancer	Microetch	Activator	Stabilizer	Postdip
Rinse	Rinse	Rinse	Rinse	Rinse	Rinse	Rinse
EE-1 electrolytic flash	Setter	Microetch	Reactivator	Accelerator	Microetch	Dry
Rinse	Rinse	Rinse	Rinse	Rinse	Rinse	
Dry	Dry	Dry	ABC electrolytic flash	Acid Dip	Dry	
			Rinse	Rinse		
			Dry	Dry		

TABLE 19.5 DMT 2

Carbon/graphite systems—conveyorized horizontal

Black Hole II	Shadow
Cleaner	Cleaner conditioner
Rinse	Rinse
Black Hole I	Shadow bath
Dry	Heated dry
Rinse	Inspection chamber
Condition	Microetch
Rinse	Rinse
Black Hole II	Antitarnish
Heated dry	Dry
Microclean	
Rinse	
Antitarnish	
Rinse	
Dry	

TABLE 19.6   DMT 3
*Conductive polymer systems—conveyorized,
horizontal, shown with optional electrolytic flash*

DMS-E	Compact CP
Microetch	Microetch
Rinse	Rinse
Conditioner	Cleaner/conditioner
Rinse	Rinse
Oxidative conditioning	Permanganate
Rinse	Rinse
Catalyzing	Polyconductor
Fixation	Rinse
Rinse	Soft-etch
Acid dip	Rinse
Electrolytic copper	Acid dip
Rinse	Electrolytic copper
Dry	Rinse
	Dry

19.6.7   Horizontal Process Equipment for DMT

Although many DMTs fit easily into existing electroless copper lines, whether manual or automatic, and perform well in a vertical mode, DMT is becoming inextricably linked to horizontal processing in a conveyorized machine. Like so many inventions, necessity was its mother. Certain DMT processes are marginal in the vertical/basket mode, and handling each panel individually was the only solution. The advent of compact and inexpensive horizontal DMT equipment has been a catalyst. Although Atotech pioneered horizontal electroplating equipment with their Uniplate system, until the development of horizontal DMT machines it was not feasible to engineer a horizontal PTH machine. Now, however, for those who want only flash plating, or even full electroplating, the entire process—both PTH and galvanic—may be horizontal, conveyorized, and automated with the advantages of reduced chemical consumption; radically reduced use of rinse water; panel-to-panel uniformity, reliability, and quality; reduction in operating personnel; reduction of handling; a fully enclosed operating environment; and JIT delivery. Stackers/accumulators further minimize handling and optimize efficiency.

19.6.8   DMT Process Issues

Anything brand new experiences some "teething problems" at the beginning, and DMT is no different. But most of the processes referred to in this chapter are in at least their second generation and some are already in their third, so there are no serious contraindications to the use of DMT. However, there are a few caveats:

1. Esoteric base material does not run well with all DMT.
2. Not all DMT performs as well in the vertical mode as in the horizontal.
3. Certain DMT is better suited to the rigors of multilayer production.
4. Some performs better than others with very small holes.
5. Some processes are cleaner than others.
6. Certain DMT is more sensitive than electroless copper to organic contamination in electrolytic copper plating.

7. Rinsing is important, and some DMT needs special rinsing.

8. Rework is simple in most DMT, but it can be abused, i.e., it changes the cost structure.

9. Quality assurance tools for DMT (how do you know that holes will plate void-free?) are being developed, but at the moment, the only absolutely certain method is to flash electroplate, because, unlike electroless copper, there is not much to see in the hole after DMT.

10. Some DMT analyses and operating controls are rudimentary.

19.6.9 DMT Process Summary

Strong ecological and health reasons will drive the use of DMT for the manufacture of PTH boards. Since the cost of PTH metallization constitutes only 2 to 3 percent, at most, of the total process cost of a PCB, the direct saving resulting from DMT is very small. However, the fringe benefits of this technology are rather significant: water conservation, no noxious chemicals, minimal panel handling, reduced waste treatment, lower labor costs, fewer rejects, etc.

19.7 PANEL VS. PATTERN PLATING

At this point, the copper conductive coating over the insulating material (the epoxy-glass holes) bridges the plated-through-hole with the copper cladding on both sides of the board. The two standard routes to get metal buildup into the holes and the circuit traces are referred to as *panel plating* and *pattern plating*. Refer to Fig. 19.1.

Panel plating is the process wherein the entire surface area and the drilled holes are copper plated, stopped off with resist on the unwanted copper surfaces, and then plated with the etch-resist metal. *Pattern* (or *selective*) *plating* is the process where only the desired circuit pattern and holes receive copper buildup and etch-resist metal plate. A small amount of copper, 20 to 100 µin, and in some cases, an additional 0.2 mil of electroplated copper, remains on the entire panel plus base copper (foil).

During pattern plating, the circuit lines and pads increase in width on each side about as much as the surface thickness during plating. An increase of 0.001 in of the surface thickness results in pad and conductor line-width increase of up to 0.002 in. Allowance for this must be made on the master artwork. Both processes have advantages and disadvantages. In choosing between them, it is important to consider the specific needs and the facilities available. Table 19.7 lists the differences.

TABLE 19.7   Panel vs. Pattern Plating

	Panel	Pattern
Copper plating	Before imaging	After imaging
	Fast plating (high CD)	Fewer steps
	Thickness control	Less power, fewer materials
	Cathode fixturing	Resist contamination
Image transfer	Thinner resists	
Metal etch resist	Optional	Thinner deposits
	Thicker deposits	
	More steps	
Etching	Double etching time	Less etching
	More chemicals	Less undercut
	More pollution	Greater circuit density

19.7.1 Panel Plating—Typical Process

- Receive boards directly from electroless copper/DM.
- Rerack.
- Clean, using acid or alkaline solution.
- Water rinse using spray or counter flow.
- Acid dip using sulfuric acid.
- Copper plate, 1 mil in PTH.
- Drag rinse.
- Water rinse spray or counterflow.
- Dry.

Photoresist	**Screen resist**
(liquid and dry film)	(alkaline ink)
Transfer image	Transfer image
Rack	Rack
Clean, using acid solution	Clean, using acid solution
Water rinse, spray, or counterflow	Water rinse, spray, or counterflow
Microetch	Acid dip (optional)

Water rinse using spray or overflow
Acid dip in sulfuric acid
Water rinse using spray or overflow
Acid dip in fluoboric acid
Tin-lead plate
Drag rinse
Proceed to strip and etch

19.7.2 Pattern Plating—Typical Process

Screen resist	**Photoresist**
(alkaline ink)	(liquid and dry film)
Electroless copper (20 μin)	Electroless copper (60 μin)
Scrub (optional)	Scrub (optional)
Transfer image	Transfer image
Rack	Rack
Clean, using acid	Clean, using acid
Water rinse, spray/counterflow	Water rinse, spray/counterflow
Acid dip (optional)	Microetch

Water rinse, spray or counterflow
Dip in sulfuric acid
Rinse in DI water (optional)
Copper plate, 1 mil in PTH
Drag rinse
Water rinse, spray, or counterflow

>Dip in fluoboric acid
>
>Tin-lead plate, 0.3 to 0.8 mil
>
>Drag rinse
>
>Proceed to strip and etch

19.8   IMAGE TRANSFER AND EFFECTS ON PLATING

Photoimageable liquid, photosensitive dry film, and screened resist inks are the most commonly used resist materials. Photoresists are selected for boards with narrow lines and spaces (3 to 7 mil), whereas screened resists are used on boards with wider lines and spaces (≥8 mil). The processes of plating and image transfer depend on each other for success in the production of quality PC boards. Thus, in the preceding pattern-plating examples, photoresist is needed to produce a narrow-line (6-mil) board but requires a thicker electroless copper (60 μin). This is due to the need for microetching prior to copper plating. In using alkaline-soluble screened resist for a wider line (12-mil) board, a thin electroless copper (20 μin) is suitable since preplate cleaning is done in an acid solution with minimal (if any) copper microetching. Direct metallization offers processing without the electroless copper step.

Problems in plating due to unsatisfactory image-transfer processing include copper-copper peeling, uneven plating, breakdown, and lifting. Strip and etching problems from plating are mainly overplating on the resists, over- and underetching, and slivers.

19.9   ELECTROPLATING: PATTERN BUILDER OF PRINTED CIRCUIT BOARDS

Electroplating is the production of adherent deposits of metals on conductive surfaces by the passage of an electric current through a conductive metal-bearing solution. The rate of plating depends on current and time, as expressed by Faraday's law:

$$W = \frac{I \, t \, A}{n \, F} \tag{19.3}$$

where W = metal, g
  I = current, A
  t = time, s
  A = atomic weight of the metal
  n = number of electrons involved in metal ion reduction
  F = Faraday's constant

Plating occurs at the cathode, the negative electrode. Accordingly, deposit thicknesses are determined by time and by the current impressed on the surface being plated; for example, 0.5 mil (0.0005 in) of tin-lead alloy is plated at 17 A/ft² for 15 min. Section 19.2.2 gives the features of electroplating. See references on electrochemistry and electroplating.[21–29]

Since most plating solutions are similar in nature, their use and the quality of the resulting deposits depend on the processing variables involved. Increasing the concentration, temperature, and agitation will enable faster plating rates and higher cathode efficiencies, but will decrease the throwing power (surface-to-hole ratio) and the bath stability. Most plating solutions require proprietary additives that are either organic or metallic.

The rate of electroplating is limited by the supply of metal ions at the cathode surface. This is of concern in high-speed plating and PTH uniformity and is expressed by the limiting current density given by the following equation:

$$I_L = \frac{n \, F \, D \, C}{\partial} \tag{19.4}$$

where D = metal ion diffusion constant
C = metal ion concentration in solution bulk
∂ = diffusion layer thickness

Smooth bright electroplating cannot be achieved at I_L. Reduced diffusion layer thickness, as achieved by rapid solution agitation systems, allows increased plating speed. In addition, the electrodeposition of alloys presents other factors in addition to those in single element plating.[26] Conditions must be controlled so that uniform composition is maintained over a wide range of operating variables. Table 19.8 gives selected properties of deposits.

TABLE 19.8 Properties of Electrodeposits

	Cu	SnNi	Ni	Au	SnPb	Sn
Melting point, °F	1980	2200	2600	1945	361	450
Hardness, VHN	150	650	250	150	12	4
Coefficient of thermal expansion, 10^{-6}, in/°F	9.4	9.5–10.0	8.0	8.2	12.2	12.8
Conductivity, % IACS	101	32	25	73	11.9	15.6
Electrical resistivity, $\mu\Omega$/cm	1.67	5.4	6.8	2.19	14.5	11.1
Thermal conductivity, CGS, °C	0.97	0.3	0.25	0.71	0.12	0.15

For our purposes, multilayer and the two-sided, plated-through boards are similar in most processing respects. Highly reliable, mil-spec-quality circuit boards can be produced following good plating practice and the standard procedures described later. The flowchart in Fig. 19.1 illustrates the subtractive processes. Pattern plating is the preferred method for manufacturing PC boards. Standard thicknesses are as follows: 1 mil copper, 0.5 mil tin-lead traces, pads, and holes, 0.2 mil nickel, and 50 μin of gold on the connector tips. A 1-mil copper deposit in the PTH is specified in MIL-STD-275 and provides the following:

1. High electrical conductivity
2. Good solderability
3. High ductility and mechanical strength to withstand pulling of component terminal
4. Full copper coverage from surface into PTH
5. Repeated component replacements

19.10 COPPER ELECTROPLATING

Because of its high electrical conductivity, strength, ductility, and low cost, copper is the most commonly used metal for the structure of a printed circuit board. In addition, copper is readily plated from simple solutions and is easily etched. MIL-STD-275 states that electrodeposited copper shall be in accordance with MIL-C-104550, and shall have a minimum purity of 99.5 percent as determined by ASTM E 53. The minimum thickness shall be 0.001 in (1 mil). Requirements for good soldering also indicate the need for 1 mil of copper and smooth holes.[30] Copper plating is generally regarded as the slow step in manufacturing PC boards. New methods which cut plating times by as much as 50 percent include high-speed additives, pulse plating, and rapid solution-impingement machines.[31–35]

19.10.1 Key Factors for Uniform Plating

To have day-to-day control and to achieve ductile, strong deposits and uniform copper thickness, the following controls are required:

1. Maintain equipment following best practices, such as uniform air agitation in the tank, equal anode/cathode distances, rectifier connection on both ends of tank, and low resistance between rack and cathode bar.
2. Maintain narrow range control of all chemical constituents, including organic additives and contaminants.
3. Conduct batch carbon treatment regularly.
4. Control temperature at 70 to 85°F.
5. Eliminate contaminants in tank from preplate cleaners, microetchants, and impure chemicals.
6. Plate at one-eighth to one-half of the conventional cathode current density when using thick boards (0.100 in) with small holes (0.015 in) and fine lines (6 to 8 mil).

19.10.2   Acid Copper Sulfate

The preferred industrial process uses an acid copper sulfate solution containing copper sulfate, sulfuric acid, chloride ion, and organic additives. Using the proper additives, the resultant copper is fine-grained with tensile strengths of 50,000 lb/in² (345 MPa), a minimum of 10 percent elongation, and 1.2 surface-to-hole thickness ratio. Table 19.9 gives acid copper properties.

19.10.2.1   Operation and Control.   See Table 19.9.

19.10.2.2   Agitation.   Air (vigorous) from oil-free source, at 70 to 80°F.

19.10.2.3   Filtration.   Continuous through 3 to 10μ-filter to control solution clarity and deposit smoothness.

19.10.2.4   Carbon Treatment.   New baths do not require activated carbon purification. Occasional circulation through a carbon-packed filter tube can be used to control organic contamination, but is advised only after consultation with supplier. The need for batch carbon

TABLE 19.9   Acid Copper Sulfate
Operation and control

	Conventional	High-speed
Operating variables:		
Copper	2–3 oz/gal	3–4.5 oz/gal
Copper sulfate	8–12 oz/gal	12–18 oz/gal
Sulfuric acid	22–28 oz/gal	24–36 oz/gal
Chloride	40–80 ppm	40–80 ppm
Additives	As required	As required
Temperature	70–85°F	75–100°F
Cathode current density	20–40 A/ft²*	40–150 A/ft²
Anodes:†		
Type	Bars or baskets	
Composition	Phosphorized 0.04–0.06% P	
Bags	Closed-napped polypropylene	
Hooks	Titanium or Monel	
Length	Rack length minus 2 in	
Anode current density	10–20 A/ft² conventional; 25–50 A/ft² high speed	
Properties:		
Composition	99.8% (99.5% min, ASTM E 53)	
Elongation	10–25% (6% min, ASTM E8 or E 345)	
Tensile strength	40–50 kpsi (36 kpsi min, ASTM E 8 or E 345)	

* A/ft² refers to amperes per square foot and is sometimes expressed as ASF.
† Operating anodes should have a thin, brown or black, easily removed film.

treatment is indicated by corner cracking after reflow, dull, pink deposits, haze, haloing, or comet trails around the PTH. Carbon treat about every 1500 (Ah) per gal.

19.10.2.5 Procedure for Batch Carbon Treatment

1. Pump to storage tank.

2. Clean out plating tank.
   a. Rinse and clean tank.
   b. Leach with 10% H_2SO_4.
   c. Adjust agitators.
   d. Clean anodes.

3. Heat solution to 120°F.

4. Add 1 to 2 qt of hydrogen peroxide (35% per 100 gal of solution). Dilute with 2 pt water, using low stabilized peroxide.

5. Air-agitate or mix for 1 h.

6. Maintain heat at 120 to 140°F.

7. Add 3 to 5 lb powdered carbon per 100-gal solution. Use Supercarb,* Norit SGII[†], or Darco.[‡] Mix for 1 to 2 h.

8. Pump back to plating tank promptly or within 4 h.

9. Analyze and adjust.

10. Dummy plate at 10 A/ft^2 for 6 h. Panels should be matte and dull. Replenish with additive.

11. Follow supplier instructions for electrolyzing and startup.

19.10.2.6 Contaminations.
In general, acid copper tolerates both organic and metallic contaminants. Organic residues may come from cleaners, resists, and certain sulfur compounds. Dye systems usually are more resistant than dye-free systems with respect to certain cleaner constituents. Metals should be kept at these maximums: chromium, 25 ppm; iron, 500 ppm; tin, 300 ppm; antimony, 25 ppm. Nickel, lead, and arsenic may also cause roughness, etc.

19.10.2.7 Process Controls
19.10.2.7.1 Bath Composition.   Copper sulfate is the source of metal. Low copper will cause deposit "burning"; high copper will cause roughness and decreased hole-to-surface thickness ratios (wider lines). Sulfuric acid increases the solution conductivity, allowing the use of high currents at low voltages. However, excess sulfuric acid lowers the plating range, whereas low acid reduces hole-to-surface ratio (throwing power). It is important to control the chloride ion (Cl$^-$) at 60 to 80 ppm. Below 30 ppm, deposits will be dull, striated, coarse and step-plated. Above 120 ppm, deposits will be coarse-grained and dull. The anodes will get polarized, causing plating to stop. Excess chloride is reduced by bath dilution or by electrolysis. Excess or insufficient additive will cause deposit "burning" and corner cracking. This condition can be judged by metallographic cross-sectioning and etching.

Optimum-quality plated metal shows no laminations or columnar patterns. The use of DI water and contamination-free materials such as low chloride and iron will give added control and improved deposit quality. Proper analysis and control of the additive components are critical for consistent product quality. Methods available use cyclic voltammetry stripping (CVS)[36–38] and liquid chromatography (LC).[39,40]

19.10.2.7.2 Temperature.   Optimum throwing power and surface-to-hole ratios are obtained by operating at room temperature, i.e., 70 to 80°F. Lower temperatures cause brittleness, "burning," and thin plating. Higher temperatures cause haze in low-current-density areas

---

* Product of M&T Chemicals, Rahway, N.J.

† Product of American Norit Company, Jacksonville, Fla.

‡ Product of ICI Americas, Inc., Wilmington, Del.

and reduced throwing power. Cooling coils may be necessary during a hot summer or under heavy operation.

19.10.2.7.3   Deposition Rate.   A thickness of 0.001 in (1.0 mil) of copper deposits in 54 min at 20 A/ft^2, in 21 min at 50 A/ft^2.

19.10.2.7.4   Hull Cell.   Operation at 2 A will show the presence of organic contamination, chloride concentration, and overall bath condition. However, an optimum Hull cell panel is only a small indication that the bath is in good operating condition, since test results are not always related to production problems. More reliable results are obtained by adjusting bath before Hull cell testing. See Sec. 19.25.4 for procedures on Hull cell and cross-sectioning.

19.10.2.7.5   Cross-sectioning Results.   Sectioning with etching provides information on the plated copper that explains PTH quality in terms of processing factors. Besides showing the overall quality, cross-sectioning gives information on thickness and on possible problems such as drilling, cracking, blowholes, and multilayer smear. Copper deposits with columnar or laminar patterns indicate inferior copper properties. Cross sections of optimum copper deposits show very small nongranular particles (structureless) upon etching.

19.10.2.7.6   Inferior Copper Deposits.   These may be caused by any of the following:

Either low or excess additives

Chloride out of range, i.e., too high or too low

Organic, metal, or sulfur (thiourea) contamination

Excess dc rectifier ripple (greater than 10 percent)

Low copper content with bath out of balance

Roughness in drilling, voids in electroless steps, or other problems introduced in earlier processing

19.10.2.7.7   Cracking and Ductility.   Resistance to cracking is tested by the following:

- *Solder reflow or wave soldering and cross sectioning*
- *Elongation:*   2-mil copper foil should exceed 6 percent elongation. Acid copper elongation should range between 6 and 25 percent. Frequent testing gives more meaningful results.
- *Float solder test:*   This test includes prebaking and flux, using a 5- to 20-s float in a solder pot (60:40) at 550°F, followed by cross-sectioning for evaluation.
- *Copper foil bulge test:*   This test measures tensile strength by puncturing copper at high pressure.
- *Board aging:*   Evidence indicates that ductility and surface properties change with the time elapsed after plating. Boards should not be tested immediately after plating.[41]
- *DC ripple:*   High values of rectifier ripple (8 to 12 percent) may cause inferior copper deposits and poor distribution of thickness.

19.10.2.7.8   Visual Appearance.   As plated, copper has a semibright appearance at all current densities. Unevenness, hazy or dull deposits, cracking and haloing around the PTH, and low-current-density areas indicate organic contamination. Carbon treatment is required if these conditions persist. "Burned," dull deposits at *high* current densities indicate low additive content, contamination, solution imbalance, or low bath temperatures. Dull, coarse deposits at *low* current densities mean that the chloride ion is not in balance.

When chloride is high or bath temperature too low, anodes may become heavily coated and polarized (current drops). Decreased throwing power (surface-to-hole ratio), reduced bath conductivity, or poor-quality plating may also indicate contamination and are corrected by:

1. Maintaining solution balance and chloride content at 60 to 80 ppm.
2. Circulating solution through filter continuously, passing through a carbon canister periodically, or by batch carbon treatment.
3. Analyzing organic additives by CVS, liquid chromatography (LC), or Hull cell.

4. Checking metal contaminations every three months.

5. Controlling temperature between 70 and 85°F.

6. Checking anodes daily and replacing bags and filters (rinsed in hot water) every 3 to 4 weeks.

19.10.2.7.9 Problems.   Table 19.10 lists problems that appear after copper plating. Two groups are listed, with the first group readily correlated to the copper-plating process. Thin, rough copper plating in the PTH may also be exhibited by outgassing and blowholes during wave soldering.[30,42–45] Figures 19.12 to 19.21 illustrate some of these effects.

19.10.3 Copper Pyrophosphate

Once the standard of the industry,[24,46] pyrocopper has been almost entirely replaced by acid copper, except in military and special applications. Pyrocopper continues to be used because of its resistance to cracking, high throwing power, and purity of deposits. The use of organic addi-

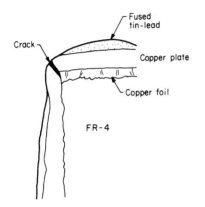

FIGURE 19.12   PTH vertical cross section illustrating copper corner cracking.

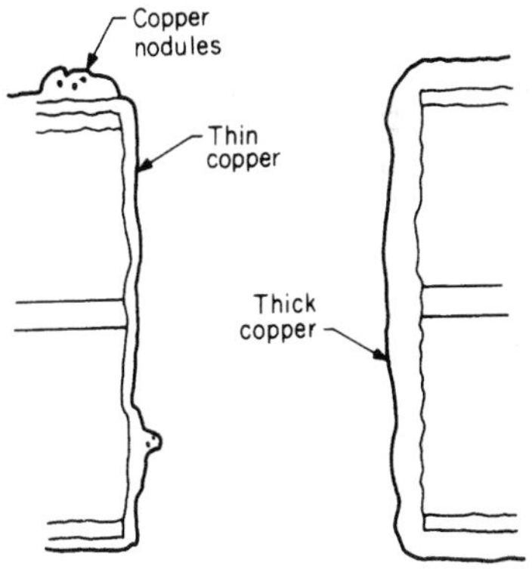

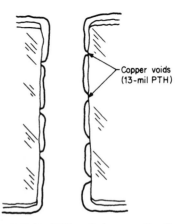

FIGURE 19.13   PTH vertical cross section illustrating uneven, thick/thin copper plating. Nodules due to particle contamination are also shown.

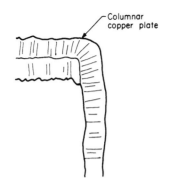

FIGURE 19.14   PTH vertical cross section illustrating columnar copper deposit structure.

FIGURE 19.15   PTH vertical cross section illustrating copper voids.

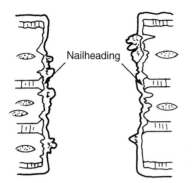

FIGURE 19.16   PTH vertical cross section illustrating rough, nodular copper plating due to drilling roughness and residues. Nailheading is also shown.

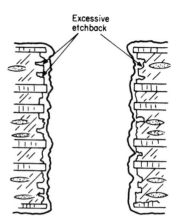

FIGURE 19.17   PTH vertical cross section illustrating hole roughness due to excessive etchback.

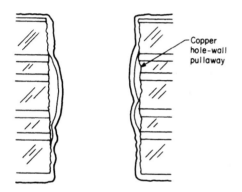

FIGURE 19.18   PTH vertical cross section illustrating copper hole wall pullaway.

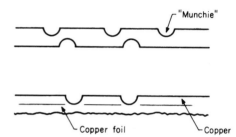

FIGURE 19.19   Trace surface view and vertical cross section illustrating "munchies" and pitting.

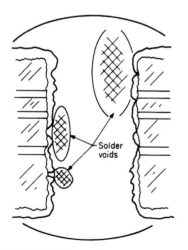

FIGURE 19.20   PTH vertical cross section illustrating wave-soldering blowholes and thin, rough copper plating.

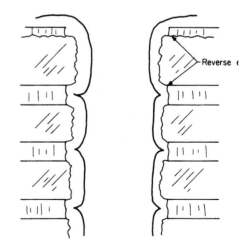

FIGURE 19.21   PTH vertical cross section illustrating reverse etchback.

TABLE 19.10 Printed Wiring Board Copper Plating Defects

Defect in copper process	Cause
Corner cracking	Excess additive, organic contamination in solution; also uncured laminate
Nodules	Particulate matter in solution; also drilling, deburring residues
Thickness distribution	See Sec. 19.10.1.
Dullness	Off-balance solution, organic contamination
Uneven thickness in PTH	Organic sulfur (thiourea) contamination
Pitting	Additive malfunction, also previous steps in electroless copper and preplate cleaning
Columnar deposits	Low additive, rectifier malfunction
Step plating, whiskers	Excess or defective additive
Defect, overall manufacturing process	**Cause**
Voids	Malfunction of electroless copper steps, also preplate cleaner etching
Innerlayer smear	Drilling or malfunction in smear removal
Roughness	Drilling or drilling residues
Hole-wall pullaway	Malfunction of smear removal or electroless copper steps
Copper-copper peeling	Surface residues from image transfer; also off-balance copper-plating process, i.e., low air agitation and high CD
Soldering blowholes	Drilling roughness, voids, and thin plating

tives with pyrocopper is optional,[47,48] but it is preferred because such additives provide wider tolerance of cracking control and improve deposit quality.[49–52] The additive PY-61H,* identified as dimercaptothiadiazole, is effectively controlled in production by CVS.[53–55] See Table 19.11.

19.10.3.1 Process Controls

19.10.3.1.1 Appearance. The film on the operating anodes should be easily removed and appear light tan or golden in color.

19.10.3.1.2 Agitation. Vigorous air agitation between anode and cathode should be maintained, using an oil-free source, at a rate of 1.5 ft^3/min/ft^2.

19.10.3.1.3 Orthophosphate. Heat should be reduced when air is turned off.

19.10.3.1.4 Filtration. Smoothness of deposit may be controlled by the continuous use of a 3- to 5-μ polypropylene filter, with four solution turnovers per hour. A 1-μ (or less) second-stage filtration may be required if PY 61-H is not used. Filters are changed frequently.

19.10.3.1.5 Carbon Treatment. All pyrophosphate baths, regardless of age and with or without additives, require activated carbon purification. This is evidenced by either extremely dull or excessively bright deposits on a Hull cell, by PTH corner cracking, brittleness, or hazy or banded plating. A batch carbon treatment will control organic contamination and thus ensure the best deposits and ductility. This treatment is recommended every six months, or more often if needed. Clearly, shop facilities should be designed to conduct carbon treatment easily without causing downtime. Though continuous or occasional circulation through a carbon-packed filter tube is sometimes used, this method is not reliable because of poor maintenance and the ineffectiveness of carbon. The proper method for batch carbon treatment is described under Sec. 19.10.2.4.

* Product of M&T Chemicals, Rahway, N.J.

TABLE 19.11   Copper Pyrophosphate
Operation and control

Operating conditions:	
pH	8.1–8.5 copper
Copper	2.7–3.5 oz/gal
Pyrophosphate	19.4–26.3 oz/gal
Orthophosphate	8 oz/gal max
Ammonia (NH_3)	0.2–0.3 oz/gal
Ratio (pyro/Cu)	7.5–8.0/L
Temperature	115–125°F
Cathode C.D.	20–35 A/ft^2
Aqua ammonia	As needed; about 1–2 qt/day
PY 61-H*	0.25–0.75 ml/(Ah)
	Control with CVS
Anodes:[†]	
Type	Bars or baskets
Composition	OFHC copper
Bags	Optional, none required
Current density	20–30 A/ft^2
Hooks	Titanium
Length	Rack length minus 2 in

* Product of M&T Chemicals, Rahway, N.J.
[†] Operating anodes should have a thin golden or light tan film.

19.10.3.1.6 Contaminations.   Impurities harmful to pyrocopper are the following.

Organic: These come from additive breakdown, resists, cleaners, and oil. To remove haze and dullness, filter through a carbon pack prior to batch carbon treatment. If haziness persists, add 60 ml of hydrogen peroxide per 100 gal of solution.

Metals: The maximum allowable by atomic absorption are: lead, 10 ppm; iron, 50 ppm; nickel, 50 ppm. To control this contamination, dummy (plate) on scrap panels or corrugated sheets at 5 A/ft^2 for 2 to 6 h, once a week.

Nonmetals.   Maximum levels allowable are: chloride ion (Cl^-), 40 ppm; cyanide (CN^-), 0 ppm; and sulfur (as S^{2-}), 0 ppm.

19.10.3.2 Solution Controls

Copper Pyrophosphate.   This is the source of metal. Low copper (below 2.5 oz/gal) will cause deposit "burning." High copper (above 4.0 oz/gal) will cause roughness and decreased hole-to-surface ratio (decreased line spaces).

Potassium Pyrophosphate. $K_4P_2O_7$ is the complexing agent for copper. A pyrophosphate-to-copper weight ratio of 7.5:1 to 8.0:1 is required for optimum plating control. A low ratio (<7.0:1) causes roughness, reduced throwing power, and banded deposits. A high ratio (>8.5:1) promotes orthophosphate (K_2HPO_4) formation and decreases bright plating range (dullness).[47,49]

pH Range.   The best pH range is 8.1 to 8.5, but remains satisfactory up to 8.8. Higher pH (>9.0) will cause CD range decrease (dullness), roughness, and poor anode corrosion. Low pH (<7.0) causes orthophosphate buildup and reduced throwing power.

Ammonium Hydroxide.   This is added to increase deposit luster and anode corrosion. Low ammonia (<0.1 oz/gal as NH_3) causes dullness, poor anode corrosion, and roughness. High ammonia (>0.4 oz/gal) may cause attack of resist, and may reduce adhesion.

PY 61-H.   This is needed for deposit leveling, copper ductility, roughness (nodule) control, and providing some brightening. A typical addition per 100 gal is about 150 to 200 ml/day, or as required for uniform plating. The amount added can vary somewhat and can be judged either visually, by CVS analysis, by a Hull cell, or by metallographic cross-sectioning and etching of the PTH. Excess PY 61-H causes step plating and corner cracks.[33]

Current Density.   This requires plating at 20 to 35 A/ft^2. One ml (0.001 in) will be deposited in 42 min at 25 A/ft^2.

Hull Cell.   Hull cell.   This is widely used in evaluating bath condition and process problems. A Hull cell run at 2 A will indicate organic contaminants and overall bath condition. An optimum Hull cell will generally mean that the bath is in proper operating condition. See Sec. 19.25.4 for Hull cell and cross-sectioning procedures.

Cross-Sectioning Results.   Besides indicating overall quality, thickness, and other problems such as drilling, cracking, and blowholes, this method gives information on the plated copper and PTH that will tie the copper structure to improvements in processing. Copper deposits plated from balanced baths with the correct amounts of PY 61-H show laminar patterns. PY 61-H is present at suitable concentrations if the PTH corner radius is slightly less than the surface thickness or the hole copper thickness, as shown in Figs. 19.22 to 19.24.[56]

Cracking and Deposit Ductility.   Resistance to cracking is determined by the same tests as for acid copper. The physical properties of pyrophosphate copper deposits are as follows:

Tensile strength, lb/in^2 (avg.)		Elongation percent (avg.)
Organic-free	43,000	3–8
PY 61-H	87,000	5–18

Visual Observation of Plating.   As plated, copper has a matte-to-satin appearance. When PY 61-H is used, the copper should appear semibright-to-satin at all current densities. Nodule formation (roughness) generally indicates particulate matter in the solution and the need for improved filtration and improved maintenance. Common causes of nodule formation are also related to anode control (low anode CD), surface contamination, high copper, high pH, low ratio, and low PY 61-H. Some indications of organic contaminations are hazy, dull deposits; extremely dull or else bright zones on the Hull cell or the work; PTH corner cracking; brittleness; haloing around the PTH holes; and streaky deposits. This applies to baths with or without additives.

Dull deposits may also be caused by low ammonia and foreign metals (lead > 10 ppm). Reduced throwing power (increased surface-to-hole ratio) and poor-quality plating may indicate metal or chloride contamination, which may also reduce bath conductivity. In general,

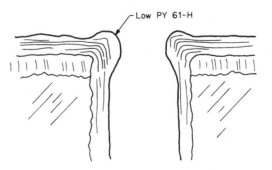

FIGURE 19.22   PTH vertical cross section illustrating low additive (PY 61-H) concentration in copper pyrophosphate.[56]

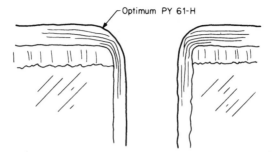

FIGURE 19.23   PTH vertical cross section illustrating optimum additive concentration in copper pyrophosphate.[55]

FIGURE 19.24   PTH vertical cross section illustrating excessive additive concentration in copper pyrophosphate.[55]

peelers are due to faulty precleaning steps. To correct these conditions, the following may be done:

1. Monitor pH, temperature, and anode filming daily.

2. Make daily additions of ammonia and additive.

3. Dummy plate daily if baths are not used.

4. Analyze solution twice per week.

5. Circulate solution continuously through a well-maintained filtration system.

6. Analyze additive weekly by CVS or Hull cell.

7. Monitor metal contaminants monthly.

8. Batch carbon treat every six months.

19.11   SOLDER (TIN-LEAD) ELECTROPLATING

Solder plate (60 percent tin–40 percent lead) is widely used as a finish plate on printed circuit boards. This process features excellent etch resistance to alkaline ammonia, good solderability after storage, and good corrosion resistance. Tin-lead plating is used for several types of boards, including tin-lead/copper, tin-lead/tin-nickel/copper, SMOBC, and surface-mount (SM). Fusing shall be required on all tin-lead plated surfaces. Thickness minimums are not specified.

The preferred composition contains a minimum of 55 percent and a maximum of 70 percent tin. This alloy is near the tin-lead eutectic, which fuses at a temperature lower than the melting point of either tin or lead, and thus makes it easy to reflow (fuse) and solder. (The composition of the eutectic is 63 percent tin, 37 percent lead with a melting point of 361°F.) Fusing processes include infrared (IR), hot oil, vapor phase, and hot-air leveling for SMOBC. Plating solutions currently available include the widely used high-concentration fluoboric acid-peptone system, as well as low-fluoboric, nonpeptone, and a nonfluoboric organic aryl sulfonic acid process. These processes are formulated to have high throwing power and give uniform alloy composition.[57] The sulfonic acid process has the advantage of using ball-shaped lead-tin anodes but is difficult to operate. Table 19.12 gives details of operation and control of two high-throw tin-lead (solder) baths.

TABLE 19.12 Tin-Lead Fluoborate
Operation and control

	High HBF$_4$/peptone	Low HBF$_4$/proprietary
Lead	1.07–1.88 oz/gal	1.4–2.0 oz/gal
Stannous tin (Sn^{+2})	1.61–2.68 oz/gal	2.8–4.0 oz/gal
Free fluoboric acid	47–67 oz/gal	15–25 oz/gal
Boric acid	Hang bag in tank	Same
Additive	Use as needed by Hull cell and Ah usage.	
Temperature	60–80°F	70–85°F
Cathode current density	15–18 A/ft^2	10–30 A/ft^2
Agitation	Solution circulation	Mechanical and solution circulation
Anodes:		
Type	Bar	
Composition	60% tin–40% lead	
Purity	Federal Specification QQ-S-571[30]	
Bags	Polypro	
Hooks	Monel	
Length	Rack length minus 2 in	
Current density	10–20 A/ft^2	

19.11.1 Agitation

The solution is circulated by a filter pump, without allowing air to be introduced.

19.11.2 Filtration

A 3- to 10-μ polypro filter is needed to control solution cloudiness and deposit roughness.

19.11.3 Carbon Treatment

Solution is batch-treated at room temperature every 4 to 12 months. If clear and colorless, additive is added as for new bath makeup. Do not use Supercarb or hydrogen peroxide.

19.11.4 Contaminations

Organic: Comes from peptone or additive breakdown and plating resists. Periodic carbon treatment is needed.

Metallic: Copper is the most serious of these contaminations. It causes dark deposits at low current densities (in the plated-through-hole) and may coat the anodes. The maximum levels of metallic contaminants allowable are copper, 15 ppm; iron, 400 ppm; and nickel, 100 ppm.

Nonmetallic: The maximum levels allowed are chloride, 2 ppm; sulfate, 2 ppm.

Dummy: Copper is removed by dummy plating at 3 to 5 A/ft^2 several hours each week. (Dummy plating is plating at low current density, using corrugated metal sheets or scrap panels.) Other metals such as iron and nickel in high concentrations may contribute to dewetting and cannot be easily removed.

19.11.5 Solution Controls

Stannous and lead fluoborates are the source of metal. Their concentrations and ratio must be strictly maintained, as they will directly affect alloy composition. Fluoboric acid increases the conductivity and throwing power of the solutions. Boric acid prevents the formation of lead fluoride. Additives promote smooth, fine-grained, tree-free deposits. Excess peptone (3 to 4 times too much) may cause pinholes (volcanoes) in deposit when reflowed. Testing by Hull cell and periodic carbon treatments is indicated. The peptone-add rate is about 1 to 2 qt per week for a 400-gal tank. Only DI water and contamination-free chemicals should be used, for example, <10 ppm iron-free and <100 ppm sulfate-free fluoboric acid. A clear solution is maintained by constant filtration.

19.11.6 Deposition Rate

A layer of 0.5-mil tin-lead is deposited in 15 to 17 min at 15 to 17 A/ft^2. The best practice is to plate at 10 to 25 A/ft^2 (2/3 copper current). Higher currents lead to coarse deposits and more tin in alloy. Excessive current causes treeing and sludge formation.

19.11.7 Deposit Composition

The composition should be 60 percent tin to 40 percent lead. Variations are not a problem, since monitoring is maintained by solution analysis. However, the composition should be confirmed with a deposit assay. Alloy composition is determined by the ratio of tin and lead in the solution; thus

$$\text{Sn (oz/gal)} \div \text{total Sn} + \text{Pb (oz/gal)} = \% \text{ Sn}$$

19.11.8 Hull Cell

This test shows overall plating quality and the need for peptone, additives, or carbon treatment, as well as the presence of dissolved copper in the solution.

19.11.9 Visual Observation of Plating

As plated, solder has a uniform matte finish. The deposit should be smooth to the touch. A coarse, crystalline deposit usually indicates the need for additives or peptone or too high a current density. Peeling from copper is generally related to procedure. The fluoboric acid predip should not be used as a holding tank (for more than 5 min) prior to solder plating. Acid strength and cleanliness are also important in this case. Load the tank with some residual current (5 to 10 percent). Rough, dark, thin, or smudged deposits may be due to organic contamination and may require carbon treatment. Dark deposits, especially in low-current-density areas and in the plated-through-hole, are due to copper contamination or to thin plating. A Hull cell test will confirm deposit, and dummy plate will remove copper.

19.11.10 Corrective Actions

1. Keep bath composition in balance.
2. Use contaminant-free chemicals.
3. Dummy plate once a week at 3 to 5 A/ft^2.

4. Circulate solution through filter continuously.

5. Maintain additives by Hull cell and by analysis.

6. Analyze for copper, iron, and nickel every three months.

7. Carbon treat on schedule.

19.12   COPPER/TIN-LEAD PROCESS STEPS

1. Receive panels from image transfer.

2. Rack panels.

3. Soak clean in acid cleaner for 5 min at 125°F.

4. Rinse in cold water (CWR) with spray and overflow.

5. Optional: Dip in 10% HCl for 2 min at room temperature.

6. Rinse in cold water (CWR) with spray and overflow.

7. Dip in 10% sulfuric acid for 5 min at room temperature.

8. Copper plate using acid sulfate at 25 A/ft^2 for 1 h.

9. Drag out with CWR.

10. Rinse with CWR; spray and overflow.

11. Dip in 15% fluoboric acid for 5 min at room temperature.

12. Tin-lead plate, using high-throw fluoborate at 17 A/ft^2 for 15 min.

13. Drag out.

14. Rinse with CWR; spray and overflow.

15. Unrack panels.

16. Release to stripping and etching.

19.13   TIN-LEAD FUSING

Fusing (or reflow) is the process of melting the plated tin-lead deposit after etching or edge-connector plating. The purposes of this step are to remove the tin-lead etching overhang (sliver), to cover exposed copper trace edges, to improve appearance and solderability (especially after storage), and to enhance corrosion resistance. Several methods are used.

1. *Infrared.*   The principle of this technique is to melt the tin-lead with nonfocused IR rays. This method is widely used, since it may be conveyorized, giving consistent quality with high productivity and safety. Machines operate by fluxing, preheating, and melting of tin-lead, followed by cleaning and drying. The melting point of eutectic solder (63 percent Sn, 37 percent Pb) is 361°F (183°C). If either the tin or the lead varies widely from this composition, reflow will not take place in the IR. Equipment has been developed to fuse multilayers with large ground planes, which have given problems in the past.

2. *Hot oil.*   This method was much used in earlier printed board production due to its ease of setup and its high tolerance for all types of boards and surface preparations. Hot oil is not currently preferred due to safety and fire hazards and slow productivity.

3. *Vapor phase.*   This process uses the principle of condensation heating. It involves immersion of a board in a saturated vapor which condenses on the board, causing heating and subsequent tin-lead melting. The heat transfer liquids used are very costly.

4. *Hot-air leveling.* This process is used extensively to produce SMOBC boards. The principle involves dipping a board in pure molten solder and blowing off excess between air knives. Single-unit and high-production conveyorized machines are available. Surface activation with microetching and low copper (<0.30 percent) in solder must be controlled for solderability.

19.13.1   Problems in Tin-Lead Fusing

1. *Dewetting.* This refers to very uneven, thick-thin areas on the surface of solder, on the surfaces of pads, or on the traces after reflow. The most common cause of this problem is tin-lead contamination from etching residues. Solder must be cleaned after etching by chemical or mechanical means, followed by baking and fusing. Other causes of dewetting and nonwetting are underplate copper contamination, exhausted hot oil, and contaminated or inadequate circulation of the tin-lead plating solution.

2. *Outgassing during fusing.* This refers to pinholes, nodules, or small "volcano eruptions" on the tin-lead surface after fusing. This is due to codeposition of organic additives and is corrected by bath carbon treatment. Exhausted reflow oil may also cause this effect.

3. *Nonfusible tin-lead.* This refers to a condition where the tin-lead deposit will not fuse on heating. The cause may be thin plating (less than 0.25 mil), excess peptone, additives, or the need for carbon treatment of plating solution.

4. *Gritty or granular deposits.* These may be due to etching residues, embedded abrasives, soiled surfaces, or additive problems.

5. *Hole plugging.* This refers to closure of the PTH and is due to excessive tin-lead plating.

6. *Poor solderability.* The fused tin-lead deposit is not usually the cause of poor solderability of components. More likely, the causes are contamination and moisture buildup after storage. Correct by cleaning and baking boards at 250°F for 4 h and soldering immediately. Blowholes (gassing) during soldering may be due to thin, rough copper in the PTH.[30,43,44]

19.14   TIN VS. TIN-LEAD ALLOY COMPARISON OF USAGE

Although tin and tin-lead alloy are often equally regarded for finish-plate applications, there are many differences to be considered before a choice is made. For example, tin plate is not suitable for fusing and leaves overhang etch slivers; however, it is rigid under solder mask during wave soldering. Tin-lead is fused but will flow on traces under solder mask when wave soldered. This causes distortion and flaking of the solder mask. Tin is free of water-polluting lead; tin-lead is not. Tin may form whiskers; fused tin-lead will not. Both tin and tin-lead can be used to produce SMOBC boards, but tin may be a better choice, since both are stripped off after etching. Tin will not add to wastewater pollution.

19.15   TIN ELECTROPLATING

Tin is used extensively for plating electronic components and PC boards due to its solderability, corrosion resistance, and metal etch-resist properties. The current MIL-STD-275 does not include tin plating, although earlier versions stated a required thickness of 0.0003 in. Specifications covering tin plating are MIL-T-10727 and MIL-P-38510, which say that tin must be fused on component leads.

19.15.1 Acid Tin Sulfate

This is the most widely used system. Among the many processes available, some produce bright deposits for appearance and corrosion resistance; others give matte deposits which can be fused as well as soldered after long-term heating. Tin sulfate baths are somewhat difficult to control, especially after prolonged use.[58,59] Operation and control are given in Table 19.13.

TABLE 19-13   Acid Tin Sulfate
Operation and control

Operating conditions:	
Tin	2 oz/gal
Sulfuric acid	10–12% by volume
Carrier, additives	Replenish by Ah usage and spectrophotometry
Temperature	55–65°F preferred
	65–85°F hazy
Cathode current density	20–35 A/ft^2
Current efficiency	100%
Solution color	Milky, white
Plating rate	0.3 mil @ 25 A/ft^2 for 10 min
Anodes:	
Type	Bars
Composition	Pure tin
Bags	Polypropylene
Length	Rack length minus 2 in
Hooks	Monel or titanium
Current density	5–20 A/ft^2

19.15.1.1   Process Controls

1. *Agitation.*   Solution is circulated by filter pump without allowing air to be introduced. Cathode rod agitation is also useful for a wider range of plating current densities.

2. *Filtration.*   A 3- to 10-μ polypropylene filter is needed to control excess cloudiness and sludge formation.

3. *Temperature.*   The preferred temperature for deposit luster and visual appearance is 55 to 65°F. Use cooling coils. Baths can operate up to 85°F, but may result in smokey, hazy deposits.

4. *Carbon treatment.*   Batch treatment at room temperature removes organic contaminations. New baths are also made up if problems continue with deposit quality, solderability, thickness control, and cost effectiveness.

5. *Contaminations*
   a. *Organics.*   These come from additives and breakdown of resist.
   b. *Metallic.*   The effects of metallic contaminants on the plated deposits and the maximum levels allowable are as follows:

Copper	Stress	5–10 ppm
	Dullness	150 ppm
Cadmium	Dullness	50 ppm
Zinc	Dullness	50 ppm
Nickel	Streaks	50 ppm
Iron	Dullness	120 ppm

c. *Nonmetallic.*   The maximum level allowable is 5 ppm of chloride.

6. *Anodes.*   Remove when bath is idle to maintain tin content.

19.15.1.2 Solution Controls

1. *Bath constituents.*   Stannous sulfate and sulfuric acid are maintained by analysis; additives by spectrophotometry, Ah usage, Hull cell, and the percentage of sulfuric acid additions. Electronic-grade chemicals must be used to control metallic contaminations of cadmium, zinc, iron, etc.

2. *Control additive.*   Low levels of additives must be maintained.

3. *Hull cell.*   This test is useful for control of additive levels and plating quality. See Sec. 19.25.4 for procedure.

4. *Rinsing after plating.*   Adequate rinsing after plating is important to control white or black spots on tin surfaces. See Sec. 19.16.

5. *Visual observation.*   As plated, tin has a uniform lustrous finish. The deposit should be smooth to the touch.

19.15.2 Problems with Tin Electroplating

1. *Dull deposits.*   These are due to an out-of-balance condition of the main solution constituents, i.e., low acid (<10%), high tin, (>3 oz/gal), improper additive levels, contamination by metals or chlorides, or high temperatures (>65°F).

2. *Peeling tin.*   This comes off due to low acid (<10%).

3. *Slivers.*   These are caused by overetching. A review of etching practice is indicated, as well as the use of ½-oz copper foil.

4. *Pitting.*   If substrate is not the cause, check precleaning, solution balance and contaminants, current efficiency, and current densities. High current densities may cause pitting.

5. *Strip and etching residues.*   Tin is attacked by strong alkaline solutions. To control residues and spotting, use mild room-temperature stripping and alkaline-ammonia etching.

6. *Poor solderability.*   This may be caused by excess additives or contaminations in the bath, poor rinsing, bath age, or excessive thicknesses (>0.3 mil).

19.16   SMOBC PROCESS STEPS

1. Receive panels from image transfer.

2. Rack panels.

3. Soak clean with acid cleaner for 5 min at 125°F.

4. Rinse with cold water (CWR), using spray and overflow.

5. *Optional:* Microetch using sulfuric acid-hydrogen peroxide for 1 min at 100°F.

6. Rinse with cold water (CWR), using spray and overflow.

7. Acid dip in 20% sulfuric acid for 5 min at room temperature.

8. Copper plate, using acid sulfate at 25 A/ft^2 for 1 h.

9. Drag out and rinse in cold water (CWR).

10. Rinse with cold water (CWR), with spray and overflow.

11. Acid dip in 10% sulfuric acid for 5 min at room temperature.

12. Rinse with cold water (CWR), using spray and overflow.
13. Tin plate with acid sulfate for 7 min at 20 A/ft^2.
14. Rinse with warm water.
15. Unrack.
16. Etch copper.
17. Strip tin.
18. Release to hot-air leveling.

19.17   COPPER/NICKEL/TIN PROCESS STEPS

1. Receive panels from image transfer.
2. Rack panels.
3. Soak clean with acid cleaner for 5 min at 125°F.
4. Rinse with cold water (CWR), using spray and overflow.
5. *Optional:* Microetch, using sulfuric acid-hydrogen peroxide for 1 min at 100°F.
6. Rinse with cold water (CWR), using spray and overflow.
7. Acid dip in 20% sulfuric acid for 5 min at room temperature.
8. Copper plate using acid sulfate at 25 A/ft^2 for 1 h.
9. Drag out and rinse in cold water (CWR).
10. Rinse with cold water (CWR), using spray and overflow.
11. Acid dip in 10% sulfuric acid for 5 min at room temperature.
12. Rinse with cold water (CWR), using spray and overflow.
13. Nickel plate with sulfamate for 10 min at 25 A/ft^2.
14. Drag out.
15. Rinse with cold water (CWR), using spray and overflow.
16. Dip in 10% sulfuric acid for 5 min at room temperature.
17. Rinse with cold water (CWR), using spray and overflow.
18. Tin plate with acid sulfate for 10 min at 20 to 30 A/ft^2.
19. Rinse twice with warm water, using overflow.
20. Unrack panels and release to etching.

19.18   NICKEL ELECTROPLATING

Nickel plating is used as an undercoat for precious and nonprecious metals. For surfaces such as contacts or tips that normally receive heavy wear, the uses of nickel under a gold or rhodium plate will greatly increase wear resistance. When used as a barrier layer, nickel is effective in preventing diffusion between copper and other plated metals. Nickel-gold combinations are frequently used as metal etch resists. Nickel alone will function as an etch resist against the ammoniacal etchants.[60] MIL-STD-275 calls for a low-stress nickel with a minimum thickness of 0.0002 in. Low-stress nickel deposits are generally obtained using nickel sulfamate baths in conjunction with wetting (antipit) agents. Additives are also used to reduce stress and to improve surface appearance.

19.18.1 Nickel Sulfamate

Nickel sulfamate is commonly used both as undercoat for through-hole plating and on tips. Conditions given in Table 19.14 are applicable for through-hole and full board plating.

TABLE 19.14 Nickel Sulfamate
Operation and control

Operating conditions:	
pH	3.5–4.5 (3.8)
Nickel	10–12 oz/gal
As nickel sulfamate	43 oz/gal
Nickel chloride	4 oz/gal
Boric acid	4–6 oz/gal
Additives	As required
Antipit	As required
Temperature	130 ± 5°F
Cathode current density	20–40 ASF
Anodes:	
Type	Bars or chunks
Composition	Nickel
Purity	Rolled depolarized, cast, or electrolytic; SD chips in titanium basket
Hooks, baskets	Titanium
Bags	Polypro, Dynel, or cotton
Length	Rack length minus 2 in

19.18.1.1 Process Controls

1. *pH.* With normal operation, pH increases. Lower with sulfamic acid (not sulfuric acid). A decrease in pH signals a problem; anodes should be checked.

2. *Temperature.* The preferred temperature is 125°F. Low temperature causes stress and high CD "burning." Higher temperatures increase softness of nickel deposit.

3. *Agitation.* Solution circulation between panels is done by filter pump and/or cathode rod agitation.

4. *Filtration.* This is done continuously through 5- to 10-μ polypro filter, which is changed weekly.

5. *Deposition rate.* For 0.5 mil, plate 25 to 30 min at 25 A/ft². For 0.2 to 0.3 mil, plate 15 min at 25 A/ft².

6. *Contaminations*
   a. *Metals.* Maximum allowable by atomic absorption: iron, 250 ppm; copper, 10 ppm; chromium, 20 ppm; aluminum, 60 ppm; lead, 3 ppm; zinc, 10 ppm; tin, 10 ppm; calcium, 0 ppm. These metal contaminants lower the deposition rates and cause nonuniform plating. Copper and lead cause dark, brittle deposits at low CD. Dummy at 3 to 5 A/ft². Iron, tin, lead, and calcium cause deposit roughness and stress.
   b. *Organics.* These cause pitting, brittleness, step plating, and lesser ductility.
   c. *Sulfates.* These cause solution breakdown and should not be added.

7. *Carbon treatment.* Circulate through carbon canister for 24 h, or batch treat to remove organics. The basic method to batch carbon treat is as follows:
   a. Heat to 140°F.
   b. Transfer to treatment tank. Do not adjust pH.

c. Add 3 to 5 lb carbon per 100 gal of solution. Premix outdoors.
d. Stir 4 h at temperature.
e. Let settle 1 to 2 h.
f. Filter back to cleaned tank.

19.18.1.2 Common Problems.   Pitting, stress (cracking), and burned deposits are common problems.

1. *Pitting.*   This is caused by low antipit, poor agitation or circulation, boric acid imbalance, or the presence of organics. In testing for antipit, the solution should hold bubble for 5 s in a 3-in wire ring and for less than 5 s in a 5-in ring. In the case of severe pitting, cool to room temperature, add 1 pt/200 gal hydrogen peroxide (35%), bubble air, and reheat to 140°F. Carbon treat as above. Filter quickly.

2. *Stress.*   This refers to the cause of deposit cracking. While low nickel chloride causes poor anode corrosion (rapid decrease in nickel content), high chloride causes excess stress. To prevent this, maintain pH, current density, and boric acid for control below 10 kpsi.

3. *Burns.*   A low level of nickel sulfamate causes high current density "burns."

4. *Hull cell.*   Plate at 2 A, 5 min with gentle agitation. This test is useful for bath condition and contaminants.

5. *Visual observation.*   The plated metal has a matte, dull finish. "Burned" deposits are caused by low temperature, high current density, bath imbalance, and poor agitation. Rough deposits are due to poor filtration, pH out of spec, contamination, or high current density. Pitting is due to low antipit, poor agitation, bath imbalance, or organic contamination. Low plating rates are due to low pH, low current density, or impurities. Gassing at the cathode is a sign of low plating rates.

19.18.2 Nickel Sulfate

This is typically plated with an automatic edge connector (tip) plating machine. Table 19.15 gives the operating conditions that apply to these systems. For additional instruction, follow details in Sec. 19.18.1.

TABLE 19.15   Nickel Sulfate
Operation and control

Operating conditions:	
pH	1.5–4.5
Nickel	15–17 oz/gal
Nickel chloride	2–4 oz/gal (with soluble anodes)
Boric acid	3–4 oz/gal
Stress reducer	As required
Antipit	As required
Temperature	$130 \pm 5°F$
Cathode current density	100–600 A/ft^2
Current efficiency	65%
Anodes:	
Composition	Nickel or platinized titanium

Nickel anodes are preferred in tip machines because the pH and the metal content remain stable. The pH will decrease rapidly when insoluble anodes are used. The pH should be maintained at 1.5 or higher with additions of nickel carbonate. Stress values are higher than in sulfamate baths with values of about 20 kpsi.

19.19 TIN-NICKEL ALLOY

Printed circuit boards produced with tin-lead over tin-nickel[61] and solder masking over tin-nickel (with tin-lead-plated pads and holes) show major improvements over the standard methods of solder masking over tin-lead or copper.[62] When compared with the standard solder mask on copper/tin-lead board, improvements are noted in solder mask stability, reduced entrapment of fluxes, fineline processing, absence of tip line, and reduced need for touchup after wave soldering.[62] When compared with SMOBC, improvements are seen in resistance to hole-wall pullaway and corrosion and ease of component replacement. Surface-mount boards also benefit from the tin-nickel (or nickel) process because of improvements in solder pad thickness control and flatness, terminal strength, repeated component replacement, and reduced touchup. Terminal pull tests gave the following results when component lead wires soldered into a series of PTHs and pulled with a tensile tester were used.

	Pull, lb/in^2	
Board thickness	Copper/tin-lead	Copper/tin-nickel/tin-lead
0.060 in	65	87
0.093 in	71	93
Mil-P-55110	50	50

Tin-nickel alloy also finds uses for burn-in boards and high-temperature applications due to its ability to provide a scratch-, thermal-, and corrosion-resistant barrier on the copper traces. Tin-nickel alloy is commonly plated from a fluoride-chloride electrolyte without additives. This solution has exceptional throwing power and deposits a 1:1 atomic tin-nickel alloy of 65 percent tin and 35 percent nickel. Operating conditions are listed in Table 19.16.

TABLE 19.16 Tin-Nickel Alloy
Operation and control

Operating conditions:	
pH	2.0–2.5 (pH paper)
Nickel	10–12 oz/gal
Stannous tin	3.5–4.2 oz/gal
Fluoride (total)	4.5–6.6 oz/gal
Additives	None
Temperature	$160 \pm 5°F$
Cathode current density	5–17 A/ft^2
Anodes:	
Type	Bars
Composition	Nickel
Purity	Rolled depolarized or cast
Bags	Nylon
Hooks	Monel
Length	Rack length minus 2 in
Deposit composition:	65% Sn, 35% Ni (by weight)

19.19.1 Process Controls

1. *Agitation.*   Solution is slowly circulated by filter pump, without introducing any air. The agitation is turned off during plating.

2. *Filtration.*   A 5- to 10-μ polypro filter is used to remove solids, keeping the outlet under solution.

3. *Carbon treatment.*   Circulate the solution through the carbon canister periodically. This is best done when the bath is not in use. Batch treatment is generally not required, unless there is known organic contamination, like resist leaching or hazy, pitted plating. A poor Hull cell will also indicate the need for carbon treatment.

4. *Contaminations*
   a. *Organic.*   These come from the resist and are carbon treated.
   b. *Metals.*   Maximum allowable by atomic absorption: copper, 25 ppm; iron, 50 ppm; lead, 10 ppm.
   c. *Dummy.*   Plate at 5 A/ft^2, several hours per week to remove metal contaminants.

5. *Solution controls.*   Stannous and nickel chloride provide metal ions. Total fluoride, added as ammonium bifluoride, must be equal to or higher (oz/gal) than the sum of the stannous (Sn^{2+}) and the stannic^{4+} content. The bath pH is very critical and should be maintained at 2.0 to 2.5 (tested by pH paper). Low pH reduces the plating current density range and causes stressed, cracked plating under solder after reflow. The general tendency is for pH to decrease. Add aqua ammonia (ammonium hydroxide) to adjust. Low fluoride causes dull, black plating and should be maintained at 6.5 oz/gal minimum. Use only DI water and contaminant-free chemicals.

6. *Temperature.*   Temperature control is essential for optimum deposits. Below 150°F, the plating range will be reduced, causing cracked white deposits at higher current densities.

7. *Deposition rate.*   Rate at 5 to 17 A/ft^2. A thickness of 0.0002 in (0.2 mil) is plated in 15 min at 15 A/ft^2. Excessive current density may cause cracked deposits after solder reflow.

8. *Deposit composition.*   This is 65 percent tin, 35 percent nickel. Composition remains constant over a wide range of operating conditions.

9. *Hull cell.*   When run at 1 A for 5 min at 160°F, this useful test will give indications of pH control, copper and iron contamination, organic contamination, and overall bath conditions. Hull cell testing has proven to be a valuable aid in solution and process adjustment.

10. *Visual observation of plating.*   As plated, metal is bright over a wide current-density range. Cracked, stressed deposits seen after solder IR reflow are due to low temperature, low pH operation, or high current density. Dull, hazy plating is due to bath imbalance or to organic or metal contaminants. Black plating indicates a need for fluoride. Dark plating in low-current-density areas is caused by copper contamination. White, cracked deposits in high-current-density areas indicate iron contamination or bath imbalance. The corrections needed are as follows:
   a. Check and maintain pH and temperature daily. Stir well.
   b. Maintain fluoride content. Add stannochlor twice weekly.
   c. Test solution with Hull cell once a week. This is important for tin-nickel control.
   d. Analyze for lead, copper, and iron contamination every month. Check Sn^{4+} every 3 months.
   e. Dummy plate once a week.
   f. Check deposit integrity by immersion in tin-lead stripper.

Newer processes are available which use amine additives and operate at lower temperature and higher pH.[63]

19.20 COPPER/TIN-NICKEL/TIN-LEAD PROCESS STEPS

1. Receive panels from image transfer.
2. Rack panels.
3. Soak clean with acid cleaner for 5 min at 125°F.
4. Rinse with cold water (CWR), with spray and overflow.
5. *Optional:* Dip in 10% sulfuric acid for 5 min at room temperature.
6. Rinse in cold water, using spray and overflow.
7. Dip in 10% sulfuric acid for 5 min at room temperature.
8. Copper plate, using acid sulfate at 25 A/ft^2 for 1 h.
9. Drag out and rinse in cold water (CWR)
10. Rinse in cold water (CWR), with spray and overflow.
11. Acid dip, using 10% HCl for 5 min at room temperature.
12. Rinse in cold water (CWR), using spray and overflow.
13. Tin-nickel plate, using chloride-fluoride, pH 2.2, at 160°F and 15 A/ft^2 for 15 min.
14. Drag out and rinse in cold water.
15. Rinse in cold water, with spray and overflow.
16. Dip in 15% fluoboric acid for 5 min at room temperature.
17. Tin-lead plate at 17 A/ft^2 for 15 min.
18. Drag out and rinse in cold water.
19. Rinse in cold water with spray and overflow.
20. Unrack panels.
21. Release to strip and etch.

19.21 GOLD ELECTROPLATING [28]

Early printed circuit board technology used gold extensively. In addition to being an excellent resist for etching, gold has good electrical conductivity, tarnish resistance, and solderability after storage. Gold can produce contact surfaces with low electrical resistance. In spite of its continued advantages, the high cost of gold has restricted its major application to edge connectors (tips) and selected areas, with occasional plating on pads, holes, and traces (body gold). Both hard alloy and soft, pure gold are currently used. Plating solutions are acid (pH 3.5 to 5.0) and neutral (pH 6 to 8.5). Both automatic plating machines for edge connectors and manual lines are in use.

19.21.1 Edge Connectors

19.21.1.1 Acid Hard Gold. To a large extent, acid golds are used for compliance to MIL-STD-275, which states that gold shall be in accordance with MIL-G-45204, Type II, Class 1. The minimum thickness shall be 0.000050 in (50 μin); the maximum shall be 0.000100 in in areas that are to be soldered. A low-stress nickel shall be used between gold overplating and copper. Nonmilitary applications require 25 to 50 μin. Type II hard gold is not suited for wire bonding. These systems use potassium gold cyanide in an organic acid electrolyte. Deposit hardness and wear resistance are made possible by adding complexes of cobalt, nickel, or iron to the bath makeup. Automatic plating machines are being used increasingly because of the enhanced thickness (distribution) control, efficient gold usage, productivity, and quality. A comparison of automatic versus manual plating methods for edge connectors is given in Table 19.17.

TABLE 19.17   Acid Gold-Cobalt Alloy
Operation and control

	Manual	Automatic
Gold Content, troy oz/gal	0.9–1.1	1–3
pH	4.2–4.6	4.5–5.0
Cobalt content	800–1000 ppm	800–1200 ppm
Temperature	90–110°F	100–125°F
Solution density	8–15 Be	12–18 Be
Replenishment per troy oz gold	8 Ah	6.5 Ah
Current efficiency	50%	60%
Agitation	5 gal/min	50 gal/min
Anode to cathode distance	2–3 in	¼ in
Anodes, composition	Platinized titanium	Platinized titanium
Cathode current density	1–10 A/ft^2	50–100 A/ft^2
Thickness	40 ± 10 µin	40 ± 2 µin
Deposition rate for 40 µin	3–6 min	0.3–0.6 min
Deposition composition	99.8% gold, 0.2% cobalt	99.8% gold, 0.2% cobalt
Hardness	150 Knoop	150 Knoop

Gold solution contaminants

Metal	Maximum ppm	Metal	Maximum ppm
Lead	10	Iron	100
Silver	5	Tin	300
Chromium	5	Nickel	300–3000
Copper	50		

Organics: Tape residues, mold growth, and cyanide breakdowns.

19.21.1.2   *Process Controls*

1. *Analysis.*   Gold content, pH, and density should be maintained at optimum values. Operation at very low gold content causes early bath breakdown with loss of properties, less current efficiency, and less cost savings. The pH is raised by using potassium hydroxide and is lowered with acid salts. Solution conductivity is controlled by density, which is adjusted with conductivity salts. Hull cell is not recommended for this purpose.

2. *Anodes.*   Platinized titanium should be replaced when operating voltages are excessive or when thick coatings develop on the anode surfaces.

3. *Recovery.*   Plating solutions should be replaced when contaminated, when plating rates decrease, or after about 10 total gold content turnovers.

19.21.1.3   *Problems.*   Difficulties can be controlled by proper gold bath and equipment maintenance. Some typical situations are the following:

1. *Discolored deposit.*   This may be due to low brightener; to metal contaminants such as lead, low pH, low density, or organic contaminations; or to leaking from tape. Gold plate is stripped to evaluate nickel. For these problems, first try to lower pH, raise density, or increase brightener before replacing bath or using decreased current densities.

2. *Gold peeling from nickel.*   This is generally due to inadequate solder stripping, leaky tape, or to poor activation. Methods to increase nickel activation include increasing acid strength after nickel plating and using fluoride activator, cathodic acid, or gold strike. A gold strike is available which is compatible with gold plate and has low metal content and low pH. Its main purpose is to maintain adhesion to the nickel substrate.

3. *Wide thickness range.*   To narrow thickness range, improve solution movement between panels; clean, adjust, or replace anodes; and adjust or replace solution.

4. *Low deposition rate.*   This is characterized by excessive gassing and low efficiencies. To correct this condition, adjust solution parameters and check for contaminants such as chromium.

5. *Pitting.*   Strip gold and evaluate nickel and copper by cross-sectioning.

6. *Resist breakdown.*   Low current efficiencies cause this condition. Use solvent-soluble screened or dry film for best results.

19.21.2 Microelectronics

19.21.2.1 Pure 24-Karat Gold.   High-purity 99.99 percent gold processes are used for boards designed for semiconductor chip (die) attachment, wire bonding, and plating solder (leaded) glass devices, for their solderability and weldability. These qualities comply with Types I and III of Mil-G-45204. The processes are neutral (pH 6 to 8.5) or acid (pH 3 to 6). Pulse plating is frequently used. Table 19.18 gives typical conditions for a neutral bath.

TABLE 19.18   Neutral Pure Gold
Operation and control

Gold content	0.9–1.5 troy oz/gal
pH	6.0–7.0
Temperature	150°F
Agitation	Vigorous
Solution density	12–15 Be
Replenishment	4 Ah/troy oz
Current efficiency	90–95%
Cathode current density	1–10 A/ft^2
Deposition rate for 100 μin, 5 A/ft^2	8 min
Deposit composition	99.99% + gold
Hardness	60–90 Knoop

19.21.2.2 Alkaline, Noncyanide Gold.   Various processes for alloy and pure gold deposits are available. Solutions are based on sulfite-gold complexes and arsenic additives and operate at a pH of 8.5 to 10.0. A decision to use this process is based primarily on the need for uniformity (leveling), hardness (180 Knoop), purity, reflectivity, and ductility. PC board use is limited to body plating, since wear characteristics of the sulfite-gold are not suitable for edge connector applications. The microelectronics industry uses these processes for reasons of safety and gold purity. Semiconductor chip attachment, wire bonding, and gold plating on semiconductors are possible applications and are enhanced by using pulse plating, without metallic additives.

19.21.2.3 Gold Plate Tests.   Several routine in-process and final quality control tests are performed on gold.

1. *Thickness.* Techniques are based on beta-ray backscattering and x-ray fluorescence. Thickness and area sensitivity are as low as 1 μin with 5-mil pads.

2. *Adhesion.* Standard testing involves a tape pull test.

3. *Porosity.* Tests involve nitric acid vapor and electrographics.[64]

4. *Purity.* Lead is a common impurity that must be controlled to <0.1 percent.

Other tests include discoloration by heating, electrical contact, and wear resistance.

19.22 *PLATINUM METALS*

Interest in these systems usually soars in a climate of high gold prices, even though plating results are not always as dependable as those obtained when using gold.

19.22.1 Rhodium

Deposits from the sulfate or phosphate bath are hard (900 to 1000 Knoop), highly reflective, extremely corrosion-resistance, and highly conductive (resistivity is 4.51 μΩ/cm). Rhodium plate is used where a low-resistance, long-wear, oxide-free contact is required. In addition, rhodium as a deposit on nickel for edge connectors has been replaced by gold. This is due to difficulty in bath control, problems with organic and metallic contaminants, and cost. Table 19.19 shows details of rhodium plating.

TABLE 19.19   Rhodium Sulfate
Operation and control

Rhodium	4–10 g/l
Sulfuric acid	25–35 ml/l
Temperature	110–130°F
Agitation	Cathode rod
Anodes	Platinized titanium
Anode-to-cathode ratio	2:1
Cathode current density	10–30 A/ft^2
Plating rate	At 20 A/ft^2, 10 μin will deposit in 1.4 min, based on 70% cathode current efficiency

19.22.2 Palladium and Palladium-Nickel Alloys

Deposits of 100 percent palladium, 80 percent palladium-20 percent nickel, and 50 percent palladium-50 percent nickel find use as suitable deposits for edge connectors. Deposits are hard (200 to 300 Knoop), ductile, and corrosion-resistant. A palladium-nickel undercoat for gold shows good wear and electrical properties.[65]

19.22.3 Ruthenium

Deposits of ruthenium are similar to rhodium but are plated with easier control, greater bath stability, and high current efficiency at lower cost. Deposits are usually stressed.

19.23   SILVER ELECTROPLATING

Silver is not widely used in the PC industry, although it finds applications in optical devices and switch contacts. Thicknesses of 0.0001 to 0.0002 in (0.1 to 0.2 mil) in conjunction with a thin overlay of precious metal are specified.

Silver plating should not be used when boards are to meet military specification. The reason for this is that, under certain conditions of electrical potential and humidity, silver will migrate along the surface of the deposit and through the body of insulation to produce low-resistance leakage paths. Tarnishing of silver-gold in moist sulfide atmospheres also produces electrical problems on contact surfaces due to diffusion of the silver to the surface.

Another reason for the lack of acceptance of silver is that silver is plated from an alkaline cyanide bath, which is highly toxic. Bright plating solutions produce deposits with improved tarnish and corrosion resistance, relative freedom from porosity, and greater hardness. Plating troubles are usually related to *black anodes* and are due chiefly to solution imbalance, impurities in anodes, or solution roughness and pitting. Most metals to be plated, particularly the less noble metals, require a silver strike prior to silver plating to ensure deposit adhesion.

19.24   IMMERSION, DISPLACEMENT, AND ELECTROLESS PLATING*

Interest in these methods has increased due to their ability to produce coplanar (flat and even pad-to-pad) surfaces required for fine-pitch, surface-mount devices (SMDs). In effect, these systems offer alternatives to hot-air solder leveling and tin-lead alloy plate fusing. These processes are nonelectrolytic.

19.24.1   Tin Immersion

Immersion tin remains in widespread use to clean boards after etching, to cover copper trace edges with tin, and to act as a soldering aid. Self-limiting by nature, immersion tin processes work by displacement of the copper substrate. Deposits are thin, about 30 μin, and must be processed immediately for effective results. Aging and thermal excursions cause the growth of the copper-tin-intermetallics which degrade solderability.[66] In addition, tin readily forms a thick oxide when exposed to high temperatures and humidity.[67]

19.24.2   Tin-Lead Displacement Plating[68]

A tin-lead alloy displacement process has been developed with deposition rates up to 0.6 mil in 30 min. The tin-lead coating is porous, thereby allowing lead and tin ions to diffuse back to the copper substrate.

These systems are proposed for application after solder mask on high-density circuitry and very fine pitch SMD. Key features are uniform thick deposits in holes and pads and maintained solderability. Deposits are fusible. The process is difficult to control, requiring on-line, continuous instrumental analysis, bath heating, frequent adjustments, and filtration. Other drawbacks include plating rate slowdown, alloy composition change during deposition, and deposit porosity.

* M. Carano, Electrochemicals, Inc., Minneapolis, Minn., contributed to this section.

19.24.3 Electroless Nickel[69]

Electroless nickel (EN) followed by immersion or electroless gold also provides coplanar pad surfaces for SMDs. Electroless nickel is an autocatalytic process utilizing a reducing agent such as hypophosphite or borohydride. Hypophosphite is the preferred choice for printed circuits. Deposition rate from a bath at pH 4.4 to 5.2 is ½ to 1 mil/h. The deposit contains 9 to 13 percent phosphorus. EN provides wear resistance, hardness, and excellent uniformity. Thicknesses of 50 to 250 μin are specified when EN is used as a diffusion barrier between gold and copper.

19.24.4 Immersion Gold[70,71]

Immersion gold systems deposit a maximum of 4 to 12 μin of gold over nickel. Additional gold thickness must be applied by an electroless gold system.

19.24.5 Electroless Gold[70,72,73]

Processes are reported capable of depositing 0.5 to 4 mil gold on immersion gold and gold-isolated circuitry by true electroless (autocatalytic) means. These systems contain organic amine boranes and borohydride reducing agents and cyanides and operate at a high pH and temperature. Deposition rate is 80 μin/h. Deposits meet the requirements of MIL-G-45204, Type III, Grade A with 99.9 percent purity and hardnesses of 90 KHN. They are suitable for edge connectors, semiconductor wire bonding, and die attachment.

19.24.6 Electroless Nickel/Electroless Gold Process Steps[74]

1. Acid cleaner
2. Water rinse
3. Acid rinse
4. Microetch
5. Acid rinse
6. Catalyst
7. Postdip
8. Electroless nickel
9. Rinse
10. Immersion gold
11. Rinse
12. Electroless gold
13. Dry

19.24.7 Organic Solderability Preservatives (OSPs)

The OSP processes (also known as prefluxes) are applied to bare copper surfaces after solder mask. Generally, these flat surfaces provide reliable solderability after thermal excursions such as adhesive curing, solder past reflow, and wave soldering, and provided they are adequately protected from oxidation. The OSP must be thermally stable and provide corrosion protection.

Options for OSP systems include chemistry based on substituted azoles[75] and rosin/resin bases.[76] The coatings can generally be applied in immersion, spray, or flood mode. The coatings must bind to copper, preventing humidity and high temperatures from degrading solderability, and must be compatible with no-clean assembly fluxes. Proper surface preparation of the boards is required for OSP coatings to be effective. An alternative to this process is the use of benzotrizole. However, this is an extremely thin coating which gives very limited protection against oxidation and moisture. Improved protection can be achieved by following the benzotrizole step with a posttreatment of a preflux. The preflux will prevent moisture penetration.[77] Both solvent-based and water-based prefluxes are available.

19.24.8 Comparison of Coatings

The following points should be considered when deciding on alternative coatings previously described.

1. *Ease of assembly.*   Fine-pitch technology may require immersion tin or other electroless plating systems. Mixed technology boards may be better suited for OSP coatings.

2. *Rework and Handling.*   OSP coatings are the easiest to rework but are the most fragile compared to metallic systems. OSPs can be removed with organic solvents or with 5% hydrochloric acid if the OSP is a water-based structure.

3. *Shelf life.*   The shelf life of immersion, electroless plated, and OSP coatings is not as long as that of leveled or fused solder surfaces. Storage time should be kept to a minimum for alternative coatings.

19.25 LABORATORY PROCESS CONTROL

19.25.1 Conventional Wet Chemical Analysis

The traditional wet chemical methods for metals and nonmetal plating solution constituents are available from suppliers and in the literature.[78,79] These methods also make use of pH meters, ion electrodes, spectrophotometers, and atomic adsorption. The composition of liquid concentrates for plating solutions is shown in Table 19.20.

19.25.2 Advanced Instrumental Techniques

New techniques have been developed for the control of organic additives in copper plating. Continued development is in progress in the area of measurement of such additives in nickel, gold, and tin solutions. Methods used include liquid chromatography, ultraviolet/visible (UV/VIS) spectrophotometer, cyclic voltametry stripping (CVS), ion chromatography, UV-persulfate oxidation, and polarography. These techniques can detect contaminations in various processes, and they show the need for an effectiveness of carbon treatment. Table 19.21 lists and references these techniques, which are having a major influence on plating process capabilities. Literature references list 136 entries on these techniques.[80]

19.25.3 Metallographic Cross Sectioning[85,86]

A method for cross sectioning PC boards is as follows:

1. *Bulk cutting.*   Removal of manageable-size piece of board or assembly by shearing or abrasive cutting.

TABLE 19.20 Composition of Liquid Concentrates

Chemical	Formula	Weight, lb/gal	Percent	Metal, oz/gal
Acids				
Sulfuric	H_2SO_4	15.0	96	—
Hydrochloric	HCl	9.8	36	—
Fluoboric	HBF_4	11.2	49	—
Alkaline				
Sodium hydroxide	NaOH	12.8	50	—
Ammonium hydroxide	NH_4OH	7.5	28	—
Metals				
Copper sulfate	$CuSO_4 \cdot 5H_2O$	9.7	27	9
Copper fluoborate	$Cu(BF_4)_2$	12.9	46	25.4
Stannous fluoborate	$Sn(BF_4)_2$	13.3	51	44.3
Lead fluoborate	$Pb(BF_4)_2$	14.4	51	65.0
Nickel sulfate	$NiSO_4 \cdot 6H_2O$	11.0	44	17.8
Nickel sulfamate	$Ni(NH_2SO_3)_2$	12.9	50	24
Nickel sulfamate	$Ni(NH_2SO_3)_2$	12.3	43	20
Nickel chloride	$NiCl_2 \cdot 5H_2O$	11.2	54	23.7

TABLE 19.21 Advanced Instrumental Analysis Techniques

Technique	Constituent	References
Cyclic voltammetry stripping	Organics and inorganics	36–38, 53–55
Liquid chromatography with UV/VIS	Organics and inorganics	39, 40
Ion chromatography	Ionic species	81
Polarography	Organics and inorganics	22, 29, 80
Ion selective electrode	Ionic metals, nonmetals	82, 83
Atomic absorption (AA)	Metals, nonmetals	84
UV oxidation	Total carbon	40

2. *Precision cutting.* Low-speed sawing with a diamond wafer blade to produce vertical sections about $1 \times \frac{1}{2}$ in, and horizontal sectioning cut next to PTH pads.

3. *Mounting.* Vertical and horizontal encapsulation of sections in epoxy resin.

4. *Fine grinding.* Hand grinding using 240-, 320-, 400-, and 600-grit silicon carbide papers. Rinse sample between grits.

5. *Polishing.* Diamond polishing (6 μ) on nylon cloth and alumina polishing (0.3 μ) on nap cloth on a rotating wheel. To polish sample, place it on the rotating wheel polisher and move it slowly in the opposite direction. Polish for four min, if using a 6-μ diamond on nylon, and 1 min on 0.3-μ alumina on nap cloth. Clean and dry between polishing compounds.

6. *Etching.* Apply cotton swab for 2 to 5 s, soaked in a solution of equal parts of ammonium hydroxide and 3% hydrogen peroxide. Rinse in water and dry carefully.

7. *Documenting.* Observe and photograph sample with microscope at 30 to 1500× magnification.

19.25.4 Hull Cell

Although the advanced techniques previously discussed provide precise control of plating solutions, Hull cell testing is still widely used in the industry. Its advantages are low cost, simplicity of operation, and its actual correlation with plating production. Its main disadvantage is that defects in copper plating frequently are not shown by this method. For example, Hull cell testing will not help in detecting dull plating, roughness, or pitting. The procedure starts with brass panel preparation, in the following order:

1. Remove the plastic film.
2. Treat with cathodic alkaline cleaner.
3. Soak in 10% sulfuric acid.
4. Rinse.

Repeat these steps until panel is water-break free. Proceed with the Hull cell as follows:

1. Rinse with test solution.
2. Fill to mark.
3. Adjust temperature and agitation.
4. Attach panel to negative terminal.
5. Plate.

Agitation should be similar to tank operation—that is, vigorous air bubbling for copper, gentle stirring for tin and tin-lead, and none for tin-nickel. Plate copper and nickel at 2 A and other metals at 1 A. The effects of bath adjustment, carbon treatment, dummy plating, etc., are readily translated from the Hull cell to actual tank operations. See previous sections on metal plating for Hull cell results, and consult supplier for test equipment.

REFERENCES

1. M. Carano, *Proceedings 16th AESF/EPA Pollution Prevention & Control Conference,* 1995, p. 179.
2. K. Nargi-Toth, *Printed Circuit Fabrication,* vol. 15, no. 34, September 1992.
3. C. A. Deckert, E. C. Couble, and W. F. Bonetti, "Improved Post-Desmear Process for Multilayer Boards," *IPC Technical Review,* January 1985, pp. 12–19.
4. G. Batchelder, R. Letize, and Frank Durso, *Advances in Multilayer Hole Processing,* MacDermid Company.
5. F. E. Stone, *Electroless Plating—Fundamentals and Applications,* Chap. 13, G. Mallory and J. B. Hajdu (eds.), American Electroplaters and Surface Finishers Society, Inc., Fla. 1990.
6. C. A. Deckert, "Electroless Copper Plating," *ASM Handbook,* vol. 5, 1994, pp. 311–322.
7. J. Murray, "Plating, Part 1: Electroless Copper," *Circuits Manufacturing,* vol. 25, no. 2, February 1985, pp. 116–124.
8. F. Polakovic, "Contaminants and Their Effect on the Electroless Copper Process," *IPC Technical Review,* October 1984, pp. 12–16.
9. K. F. Blurton, "High Quality Copper Deposited from Electroless Copper Baths," *Plating and Surface Finishing,* vol. 73, no. 1, 1986, pp. 52–55.
10. C. Lea, "The Importance of High Quality Electroless Copper Deposition in the Production of Plated-Through Hole PCBs," *Circuit World,* vol. 12, no. 2, 1986, pp. 16–21.
11. Radovsky, U.S. Patent 3,099,608, 1963.
12. Morrissey, et al. (Amp/Akzo), U.S. Patent 4,683,036, July 1987.

13. Okabayashi (STS), U.S. Patent 4,933,010, June 1990.

14. Gulla, et al. (Shipley), U.S. Patent 4,810,333, March 1989.

15. Holtzman, et al. (APT), U.S. Patent 4,891,069, January 1990.

16. Stamp, et al. (Atotech), PCT WO 93/17153, September 1993.

17. Minten, et al. (MacDermid), U.S. Patent 4,724,005, February 1988.

18. Thorn, et al. (Electrochemicals), U.S. Patent 5,389,270, February 1995.

19. Blasberg, Europatent 0489759.

20. Bressel, et al. U.S. Patent 5,183,552, 1993.

21. S. Glasstone, *Introduction to Electrochemistry,* D. Van Nostrand, New York, 1942.

22. E. C. Potter, *Electrochemistry,* Cleaver-Hume Press, Ltd., London, 1961.

23. E. Raub and K. Muller, *Fundamentals of Metal Deposition,* Elsevier, Amsterdam, 1967.

24. F. A. Lowenheim, *Modern Electroplating,* 3d ed., J. Wiley and Sons, New York, 1974.

25. W. H. Safranek, *The Properties of Electrodeposited Metals and Alloys,* 2d ed., American Electroplaters and Surface Finishers Society, Florida, 1986.

26. A. Brenner, *Electrodeposition of Alloys,* vols. I and II, Academic Press, New York, 1963.

27. J. W. Price, *Tin and Tin Alloy Plating,* Electrochemical Publications Ltd., AYR, Scotland, 1983.

28. Frank H. Reid and William Goldie, *Gold Plating Technology,* Electrochemical Publications Ltd., AYR, Scotland, 1974.

29. A. J. Bard and L. R. Faulkner, *Electrochemical Methods, Fundamentals and Applications,* J. Wiley and Sons, New York, 1980.

30. E. F. Duffek, "Soldering Process vs. the PC Board," *Printed Circuit Fabrication,* vol. 6, no. 10, 1983, pp. 62–70.

31. N. M. Osero, "Overview of Pulse Plating," *Plating and Surface Finishing,* vol. 73, no. 3, 1986, pp. 20–23.

32. P. P. Pellegrino, "Apparatus for Electroplating, Deplating or Etching," U.S. Patent 4,174,261, 1979.

33. D. A. Luke, "Electroplating Copper for Printed Circuit Manufacture," *Circuit World,* vol. 13, no. 1, 1986, pp. 18–23.

34. M. Carano, "High Speed Copper Plating for Printed Wiring Boards," *Printed Circuit Fabrication,* vol. 6, no. 7, 1983.

35. B. Sullivan, "Electroplating Theory and the High Speed Copper Debate," *Printed Circuit Fabrication,* vol. 8, no. 8, 1985, pp. 35–54.

36. R. Haak, C. Ogden, and D. Tench, "Cyclic Voltametric Stripping Analysis of Acid Copper Sulfate Plating Baths, Part I: Polyether-Sulfide-Based Additives," *Plating and Surface Finishing,* vol. 68, no. 4, 1981, p. 52; "Part II: Sulfonium-alkane-sulfonate-Based Additives," *Plating and Surface Finishing,* vol. 69, no. 3, 1982, p. 62.

37. M. Carano and T. Barringer, "Optimization of an Acid Copper Plating Bath for Through-hole Plating," *Proceedings of the 12th AES Plating in the Electronics Industry Symposium,* Orlando, Fla., January 1985.

38. P. Bratin, "New Developments in the Use of Cyclic Voltametric Stripping for Analysis of Plating Solutions," *Proceedings of AES Analytical Methods Symposium,* Chicago, March 1985.

39. T. R. Mattoon, P. McSwiggen, and S. A. George, "Printed Circuit Plating Bath Process Control," *Metal Finishing,* vol. 83, Parts I, II, and III, 1985.

40. K. Heikkila, "Selection and Control of Plating Chemistry for Multilayer Printed Wiring Boards," *ElectriOnics,* August–September 1985.

41. P. J. Darikh, "Electro-deposited Copper for Hi-Rel PCs," *Electronic Packaging and Production,* vol. 17, no. 3, 1977, pp. 61–65.

42. M. W. Jawitz, "Trouble Shooting Manual for Printed Circuit Production," *Insulation/Circuits,* vol. 22, no. 4, 1976, pp. P-5–P-36.

43. C. Lea, F. H. Howie, and M. P. Seah, "Blowholing in the PTH Solder Filets," *Circuit World,* vol. 12, no. 4, 1986, Parts 1–3, pp. 14–25.

44. C. Lea, F. H. Howie, and M. P. Seah, "Blowholing in the PTH Solder Filets," *Circuit World,* vol. 13, no. 3, 1986, Part 8, pp. 11–20.

45. B. F. Rothschild and R. P. McCluskey, "Plated-through Hole Cracking: Causes and Cures," *Electronic Packaging and Production,* vol. 10, no. 5, 1970, pp. 114–124.

46. G. R. Strickland, "Pyrophosphate Copper Plating in Printed Circuit Manufacture," *Product Finishing,* no. 4, 1972, pp. 20–24.

47. B. F. Rothschild, "The Effect of Ortho-phosphate in Copper Pyrophosphate Plating Solutions and Deposits," *Metal Finishing,* vol. 84, no. 1, 1978, pp. 49–51.

48. J. W. Dini, H. R. Johnson, and J. R. Helms, "Effect of Some Variables on the Throwing Power and Efficiency of Copper Pyrophosphate Solutions," *Plating,* vol. 54, no. 12, 1967, p. 1337.

49. B. F. Rothschild, "Copper Electroplating Systems: An Evaluation," *Electronic Packaging and Production,* vol. 15, no. 8, 1975, pp. 102–107.

50. C. J. Owen, H. Jackson, and E. R. York, "Copper Pyrophosphate Plating without Additives," *Plating,* vol. 54, 1967, pp. 821–825.

51. L. E. Hayes, "Organic Additives for Pyrophosphate Copper: Panacea or Poison?" *Electronic Packaging and Production,* no. 17, 1977, pp. 102–104.

52. D. E. Sherlin and L. K. Bjelland, "Improve Electrodeposited Copper with Organic Additives and Baking," *Insulation/Circuits,* vol. 24, no. 9, 1978, pp. 27–32.

53. D. Tench and C. Ogden, "A New Voltametric Stripping Method Applied to the Determination of the Brightener Concentration in Copper Pyrophophate Plating Baths," *Journal of the Electrochemical Society,* vol. 125, 1987, p. 194.

54. C. Ogden and D. Tench, "New Methods for Understanding and Controlling Plating Systems Applied to Circuit Board Plating from Copper Pyrophosphate Baths," *Proceedings of 7th AES Symposium on Plating in Electronics Industry,* San Francisco, January 1979.

55. C. Ogden and D. Tench, "On the Mechanism of Electrodeposition in the Dimercapto-thiadiazole/Copper Pyrophosphate System," *Journal of the Electrochemical Society,* vol. 128, 1981, p. 539.

56. B. F. Rothschild, J. G. Semar, and H. K. Omata, "Carbon Treatment of Pyrophosphate Copper Baths for Improved Printed Wiring Board Production, *Proceedings of the Printed Wiring and Hybrid Circuits Symposium,* Fort Worth, Tex., November 1975.

57. B. F. Rothschild, "Solder Plating of Printed Wiring Systems," *Proceedings of the Printed Circuit Plating Symposium,* California Circuits Association, Nov. 5–6, 1969, pp. 10–21, and Nov. 12–13, 1968, pp. 61–65.

58. G. F. Jacky, "Soldering Experience with Electroplated Bright Acid Tin and Copper," *Circuit Technology Today,* California Circuits Association, October 1974, pp. 49–74.

59. P. E. Davis and E. F. Duffek, "The Proper Use of Tin and Tin Alloys in Electronics," *Electronic Packaging and Production,* vol. 15, no. 7, 1975.

60. R. G. Kilbury, "Producing Buried Via Multilayers: Two Approaches," *Circuits Manufacturing,* vol. 25, no. 4, 1985, pp. 30–49.

61. E. Armstrong and E. F. Duffek, "Tin-Nickel Increases PC Reliability," *Electronic Packaging and Production,* vol. 14, October 1974, pp. 125–130; *Electronic Production Methods and Equipment,* (G.B.), vol. 4, no. 2, 1975, pp. 41–42.

62. E. F. Duffek, "P.C. Processing Using Solder Mask Over Tin-Nickel," *Electronic Packaging and Production,* vol. 19, no. 6, 1979, pp. 71–74.

63. M. Carano, "Tin-Nickel Plating: An Alternative," *Printed Circuit Fabrication,* vol. 7, no. 7, 1984.

64. J. W. Dini, Chapter 8, "Porosity," *Electrodeposition: The Material Science of Coatings and Substrates,* Noyes Publications, New Jersey, 1993.

65. R. G. Baker and R. Duva, "Electrodeposition and Market Effect of Palladium and Its Alloys," *Plating and Surface Finishing,* vol. 73, no. 6, 1986, pp. 40–46.

66. R. J. Klein Wassink, *Soldering in Electronics,* 2d ed., Electrochemical Publications LTD, AYR, Scotland, 1989, pp. 155–159.

67. I. Artaki, et al., "Solderability Preservation Coatings: Electroless Tin vs. organic Azoles," *SMI International Conference,* San Jose, Calif., 1993.

68. Beam Solder PC, Uyemura International Corporation, Ontario, California, 1992.

69. E. F. Duffek, D. W. Baudrand, and J. G. Donaldson, "Electroless Plating: Fundamentals and Applications," Chap. 9, G. Mallory and J. B. Hajdu (eds.), American Electroplaters and Surface Finishers Society, Inc., Florida, 1990.

70. Y. Okinaka, *Ibid.,* Chap. 15.

71. F. Simon, "Deposition of Gold Without External Current Source," *Gold Bulletin, World Gold Council,* vol. 26, no. 1, 1993, pp. 14–23.

72. *Ibid.*

73. H. O. Ali and R. A. Christie, "A Review of Electroless Gold Deposition Processes," *Circuit World,* vol. 11, no. 4, 1985, pp. 10–16.

74. KAT Process, Uyemura International Corporation, Ontario, California, 1994.

75. J. L. Parker Jr., S. and R. B. Banes, U.S. Patent No. 4,373,656, 1983.

76. B. J. Costello, J. Langan, and R. Hawkins, U.S. Patent No. 5,176,749, 1993.

77. P. Goldman, et al., "Enhanced SMT Solderability with No HASL: Proprietary Treatments for Copper Pads," *IPC Technical Review,* December 1990.

78. D. G. Foulke, *Electroplaters' Process Control Handbook,* rev. ed., R. E. Krieger Publishing Company, Huntington, N.Y., 1975.

79. K. E. Langford and J. E. Parker, *Analysis of Electroplating and Related Solutions,* 4th ed., R. Draper Ltd., Teddington, England, 1971.

80. See Ref. 64, Chapter 7, "Additives."

81. K. Haak, "Ion Chromatography in the Electroplating Industry," *Plating and Surface Finishing,* vol. 70, no. 9, 1983.

82. M. S. Frant, "Application of Specific Ion Electrodes to Electroplating Analyses," *Plating,* vol. 58, no. 7, 1971.

83. W. C. McDonnell, "Ion Selective Electrodes for Analysis in Metal Finishing," *Plating and Surface Finishing,* vol. 73, no. 11, 1986, pp. 32–35.

84. W. Slavin, *Atomic Absorption Spectroscopy,* Interscience Publishers, New York, 1968.

85. J. A. Nelson, "Basic Steps for Cross Sectioning," *Insulation/Circuits,* 1977.

86. P. Wellner and J. Nelson, *High Volume Cross Sectional Evaluation of Printed Circuit Boards,* IPC WC-4B-1, Evanston, Ill., 1981.

CHAPTER 20
PWB MANUFACTURE USING FULLY ELECTROLESS COPPER

Dr. Hayao Nakahara
N.T. Information Ltd., Huntington, New York

20.1 FULLY ELECTROLESS PLATING

Fully electroless plating has been recognized as a viable technology for some time. It is especially useful for the formation of fineline conductors and considered excellent for plating small, high-aspect-ratio holes because of its high throwing power when compared with that of galvanic plating (see Fig. 20.1). However, its use was limited to the manufacture of double-sided and simple multilayer printed wiring boards (PWBs) for some time after the commercial introduction of the additive process called CC-4 began at Photocircuits Corporation in 1964. This was due to some relatively poor physical properties of electrolessly deposited copper, such as elongation of 2 to 4 percent, compared to 10 to 15 percent achieved by galvanically deposited copper.

The view on electroless plating technology began to change in the mid-1970s when IBM decided to utilize the technology for the fabrication of multilayer boards (MLBs) to package its then top-of-the-line mainframe computers.[1] IBM and other PWB makers using fully electroless copper plating have continuously improved the properties of electrolessly deposited copper since the early 1980s. IBM has continued to use the technology for the fabrication of more advanced MLBs for mainframe and supercomputers.[2,3] Stimulated by IBM's work, and because of technical necessity, NEC Corporation and Hitachi Ltd. of Japan also applied electroless plating technology for the fabrication of MLBs for their mainframe and supercomputers.[4,5]

Today, electrolessly deposited copper is considered as reliable as galvanically deposited copper, and fully electroless plating technology is finding its way to many applications.[6–20] In this chapter, we will discuss various methods of PWB fabrication by means of fully electroless copper-plating technology.

PWB fabrication technology using electroless plating is often referred to as *additive technology*. Therefore, throughout this chapter, the words *electroless* and *additive* will be used interchangeably. Electroless copper plating for through-hole metallization, which deposits a thin film of copper on the wall of plated-through-holes (PTHs), typically from 0.3 to 3 μm thick, is a technology different from the one under consideration and will not be discussed in this chapter (see Chap. 19, "Electroplating").

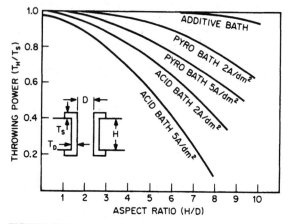

FIGURE 20.1 Ability of electroless bath to plate hole of high aspect ratio without reducing throwing power.

20.2 THE ADDITIVE PROCESS AND ITS VARIATIONS

There have been many variations to additive processes,[20,21] but there are three basic additive processes commercially practiced, as illustrated in Fig. 20.2:

1. Pattern-plating additive
2. Panel-plate additive
3. Partly additive methods

20.3 PATTERN-PLATING ADDITIVE

Pattern-plating additive methods can be classified further into three different approaches, as described in the following sections, depending on the base substrates used.

20.3.1 Catalytic Laminate with CC-4®*[22]

CC-4 stands for *copper complexer number 4,* EDTA, the fourth complexing agent successfully tried by Photocircuits in the early 1960s for full-build electroless copper-plating solution. Over time, the term CC-4 has been used frequently as an adjective, such as in "CC-4 process" or "CC-4 bath."

20.3.1.1 Process Steps. The CC-4 process starts with catalytic laminates coated with catalytic adhesive. The process sequence is as follows:

1. Catalytic base laminate coated with catalytic adhesive (both sides)
2. Hole formation

---

* CC-4 is a registered trademark of AMP-AKZO Corporation.

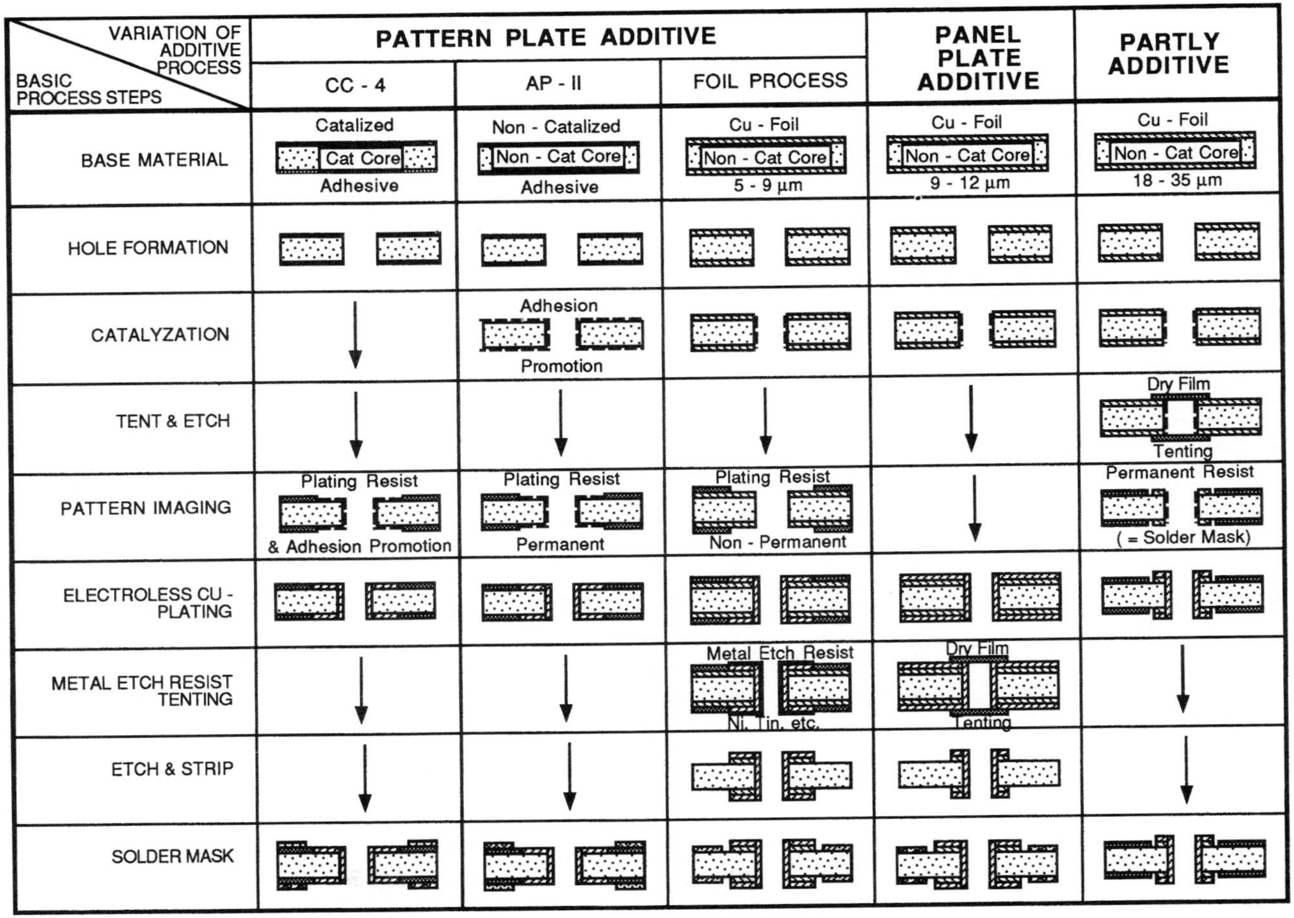

FIGURE 20.2 Variation of additive process.

20.3

3. Mechanical abrasion of the adhesive surfaces for better adhesion of plating resist
4. Application of plating resists (screening ink or dry film resist)
5. Formation of microporous structure of exposed adhesive surfaces by chemical etching in acid solution (CrO_3/H_2SO_4 or CrO_3/HBF)
6. Fully electroless copper deposition on the conductor tracks and hole walls
7. Panel baking
8. Application of solder mask and legends
9. Final fabrication and test

20.3.1.2 Resist Issues. When the conductor width is 8 mil (0.2 mm) or wider, image transfer (step 4) for a majority of CC-4 boards is still done by screen printing with thermally curable or UV-curable ink, since the cost of imaging by screening method is less than one-third that of dry film imaging. The plating resist is permanent; that is, it stays permanently as an integral part of the board. UV-curable ink is preferred because of its shorter curing time that tends to minimize lateral ink flow while being cured. Lateral ink flow narrows the conductor width since the conductor is formed in the trench between plating resists. See Fig. 20.3.

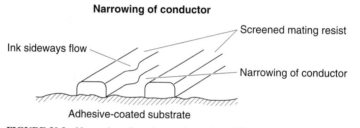

Narrowing of conductor

Ink sideways flow

Screened mating resist

Narrowing of conductor

Adhesive-coated substrate

FIGURE 20.3 Narrowing of conductor due to lateral flow of plating resist after application.

20.3.1.3 Typical Plating Conditions. Although the practical limitation of screen printing conductor pattern is 8 mil (0.2 mm), in a mass production environment, 6-mil (0.15 mm) conductor patterns have been successfully screened, but such a pattern is confined to a limited area of the panel. Therefore, a conductor pattern which is less than 6 to 7 mil is normally formed by dry film resist. E.I. du Pont de Nemours & Co. and Hitachi Chemical Co., Ltd., are two major suppliers of permanent dry film plating resists which withstand the hostile plating bath environment. Typically, additive bath temperatures range from 68 to 80°C and pH from 11.8 to 12.3, and panels must stay in the bath for more than 10 h with plating speed of typically 2.0 to 2.5 μm/h.

Since the use of solvent such as 1-1 trichloroethane is being banned, semiaqueous-developable permanent dry film resist has been developed by Hitachi Chemical to withstand the plating condition as previously described and is used extensively in Japan.

Since paper-based laminates are still the dominant materials in Japan (although CEM-3 and FR-4 laminates have been used increasingly in recent years), some allowance for this material in the plating solution is made. Therefore, plating baths for paper-based laminates are usually maintained at the lower end of the operating temperature (68 to 72°C) in order not to delaminate them.

20.3.1.4 Permanent Plating Resist. The use of a permanent plating resist creates a flush surface, where the copper and resist are at the same height from the base laminate. This offers two distinct benefits. In the board fabrication process, after the conductors are formed, the chance of their destruction due to scratch is minimized. (See Fig. 20.4.) In addition, the flush surface makes the application of solder mask easier and reduces the consumption of solder resist by as much as 30 percent when compared to that incurred in a conventional subtractive, etched foil process. In the board assembly process, a permanent plating resist acts as the solder resist and tends to minimize solder bridges during the soldering operation, particularly for fine-pitch devices.

FIGURE 20.4   Flush surface resulting from additive plating with permanent plating resist. *(Photo courtesy of Ibiden Co. Ltd.)*

20.3.2 Noncatalytic Laminate with AP-II[22]

AP-II is an abbreviation of Additive Process II developed by Hitachi Ltd. This process also makes use of permanent plating resist. However, unlike the CC-4 process, it starts with noncatalytic laminate coated with noncatalytic adhesive. Its process sequence is as follows.

20.3.2.1 *Process Steps*

1. Noncatalytic laminate coated with noncatalytic adhesive
2. Hole formation
3. Mechanical abrasion of adhesive surfaces followed by chemical roughening (adhesion promotion)
4. Catalyzation of the surfaces and hole walls
5. Application of plating resists

The rest of the process is essentially the same as the CC-4 process (steps 6 through 9).

20.3.2.2 *Advantages/Disadvantages.*   This catalyzing version of the pattern-plating additive process has one advantage over the CC-4 process, that is, the use of noncatalytic base laminates which are cheaper than catalyzed laminates. On the other hand, this process has a disadvantage also in that pattern repair before plating is not possible because resist which

protrudes sideways and makes the conductors narrower cannot be removed since the Pd catalyst underneath the protruding part of the resist tends to be removed as well if repair is attempted, resulting in plating voids. However, in a really fineline conductor case such as 4 mil (0.1 mm) or below, repair attempts will not be made; hence, this disadvantage does not usually impede this catalyzing version of the pattern-plating additive process.

20.3.2.3   AP-II Variation AAP/10.   A variation of the AP-II process called the AAP/10 process has been developed and practiced by Ibiden Co., Ltd., of Japan to fabricate high-layer-count MLBs with fineline conductors down to 3 to 4 mil.[23,24] The AAP/10 process is essentially the same as AP-II except that the adhesive used for the AAP/10 process has better insulation characteristics, suitable for higher performance.

20.3.3   Foil Process

Although an adhesive-coated surface provides adequate insulation characteristics for most applications, some boards, such as ones used for mainframe computers, require higher insulation resistance than adhesives can render. When IBM decided to use fully electroless plating to form fineline conductors on innerlayers of high-aspect-ratio MLBs in the mid1970s, it took an approach different from the adhesive system.[1]

20.3.3.1   Process Steps.   The process developed at IBM is as follows:

1. Copper-clad laminate (5-μm copper foil).
2. Drill holes.
3. Treat copper surface with benzotriazol.
4. Catalyze the panel.
5. Dry film laminate for conductor pattern (reverse pattern).
6. Do fully electroless copper deposition on the conductor track.
7. Metal overplate as etch resist (tin-lead, tin, nickel, etc.).
8. Strip dry film and etch copper.
9. Strip metal etch resist.
10. Do oxide treatment for subsequent lamination.

20.3.3.2   Process Issues.   This foil process requires strong adhesion of dry film plating resist on copper surface. Benzotriazol treatment of the copper surface improves adhesion of dry film. However, the most crucial step is cleaning the copper surface (virgin copper) to obtain an optimum pH for best reaction between copper and benzotriazol.

Hitachi Ltd. found that the use of compounds having amino and sulfide groups is effective in suppressing delamination between copper surface and plating resist.[21] It uses dry film resist which contains a trace of benzotriazol rather than treating the copper surface with the chemical. Baking the panel after exposure/development of dry film at about 140°C for 1 h is found to improve the adhesion between copper surface and dry film during plating operation and at the same time prevents this chemical from breaching out into the plating bath, which could poison the bath.

Table 20.1 shows representative high-tech MLBs fabricated by means of additive technology. Innerlayer patterns of all MLBs listed in the table are made by the foil process. The outerlayer patterns are formed by the panel-plate additive process, which is the subject to be discussed in the following section.

TABLE 20.1 Large-Scale MLBs

Computer	IBM ES-9000	NEC ACOS-3900	Hitachi M-880
Materials	Brominated epoxy glass	Polyimide glass	Maleimide styryl
Dielectric C	NA	4.6	3.6
Size, mm	$600 \times 700 \times 7.4$	$446 \times 477 \times 8.0$	$534 \times 730 \times 7.1$
No. layers	22	42	46
Cond. width, μm	81	70	70
Cond. height, μm	43	30	65
PTH dia., mm	0.46	0.6/0.3	0.56/0.3
Aspect ratio	16/1	27/1	23/1
No. of PTHs	42,000	17,000	100,000
No. of IVHs	8,000	11,000	NA
Innerlayer	Additive pattern	Additive panel	Additive pattern
cond. formation	5-μm copper	12-μm copper	12-μm copper
Outerlayer	Additive panel	Additive panel	Additive panel
formation			
Impedance, Ω	80 + 10, −9	60 ± 6	NA

Source: N.T. Information Ltd.

20.4 *PANEL-PLATE ADDITIVE*

Maintaining uniform thickness on the panel surface in a galvanic plating operation is difficult. As the aspect ratio becomes higher, maintaining uniform thickness on the hole wall is also a problem.

Electroless plating offers two distinctively superior features in this respect:

1. Its excellent throwing power for high-aspect-ratio holes (Fig. 20.5)

2. Its ability to deposit copper film of even thickness over the entire circuit panel.

FIGURE 20.5 Excellent hole coverage is achieved by fully additive plating. This shows the cross section of a hole with a 27:1 aspect ratio. *(Photo courtesy of Hitachi Ltd.)*

These features of fully electroless plating are ideal for the fabrication of high-tech MLBs, as described in Table 20.1. All signal conductors of the MLBs are formed on innerlayers and the outerlayer surfaces provide pads only for through-holes and some bonding pads for decoupling capacitors. The process steps of the panel-plate additive method are essentially the same as those of the galvanic panel-plate method:

20.4.1 Process Steps

1. Copper clad laminate (thin copper foil is preferred).

2. Perform hole formation.

3. Catalyze holes.

4. Perform fully electroless copper deposition (panel plate).

5. Perform dry film tent-and-etch.

20.4.2 Process Issues

Tenting with dry film becomes difficult when annular rings are very small or in some cases when there are no annular rings at all. In such cases, a positive electrodeposition system may be applied to overcome this difficulty.

It should be cautioned, however, that there is a limitation to this panel-plate additive approach, even though the thickness of deposited copper film is much more even across the panel. If very fine conductors are to be formed by this method, the conductor cross section becomes intolerably distorted from the ideal rectangular shape as the ratio of the width to the height of the conductor approaches unity, as shown in Fig. 20.6.

FIGURE 20.6 Formation of fineline conductors by etching process results in undesirable, nonrectangular conductor cross section. *(Photo courtesy of Ibiden Co., Ltd.)*

20.5 PARTLY ADDITIVE

As in the case of the panel-plate additive method, the partly additive process starts with copper-clad laminate.[11–14] The essence of this process is to minimize the problem encountered in etching fineline conductors through thick copper which results from through-hole plating (in the conventional etched foil process, through-hole is plated first), by forming conductors first, prior to through-hole plating.

20.5.1 Process Steps

1. Copper-clad laminate.
2. Perform hole formation.
3. Catalyze hole walls and remove catalyst sites from the surfaces by brushing.
4. Perform image transfer by screen print or dry film tenting.
5. Form conductor pattern by etching and stripping the resist.
6. Apply plating resist over the entire surface, but leaving pads and holes uncovered.
7. Perform electroless copper deposition onto the pads and hole walls.

20.5.2 Process Issues

By proper selection of catalysts and etching solutions, the catalyst on the hole walls survives during the etching operation, posing no problem in the subsequent plating step.

In step 6, plating resist can be applied by screen printing when the circuit density is not so high. When the density becomes higher, dry film or liquid photoimageable resist can be used. Liquid resist can be applied by open screen coating, roller coating, or curtain coating.

In some cases, step 6 can be bypassed when sideways line growth is not a problem (Fig. 20.3). In such a case, the plating speed is reduced by 20 to 30 percent, from the normal speed of 2.0 to 2.5 μm, in order to avoid copper deposition on unwanted areas (bare laminate areas). Conductors must be made narrower than the intended final width at the design stage to compensate for the side growth.

20.5.3 Fine-Pitch Components

As the lead pitch of multipin devices becomes narrower than 20 mil (0.5 mm), bridging between adjacent pads during plating can occur even when plating resist is placed between them. As a result, the practitioners of the partly additive process are abandoning this process and converting to the panel-plate additive method based on the experiences they gained from practicing partly additive technology.

20.6 CHEMISTRY OF ELECTROLESS PLATING

Chemical reactions which take place in electroless plating have been treated well in the literature.[4,21] However, they are discussed again here because some of the due comments are relevant to the chemistry of electroless plating.

20.6.1 Electroless Plating Solution Chemical Reactions

Main ingredients of most electroless plating bath formulations consist of

NaOH	pH adjustment
HCHO	Reducing agent (formaldehyde)
$CuSO_4$	Source of copper iron
EDTA	Cheleting agent

20.6.1.1 Copper Deposition. The chemical reaction of copper deposition may be represented by

$$Cu(EDTA)^{2-} + 2HCHO + 4OH^- \rightarrow$$
$$Cu^\circ + H_2 + 2H_2O + 2CHOO^- + EDTA^{4-} \qquad (20.1)$$

Under the alkaline pH condition, the cupric ions would normally combine with OH^- to produce cupric hydroxide $[Cu(OH)_2]$, a useless precipitate. When a cheleting agent such as EDTA is added, it prevents cupric hydroxide formation by maintaining the Cu^{2+} in solution. Once the deposition of metallic copper starts through catalytic sites, the reaction in Eq. (20.1) continues because of the autocratic nature of the reaction.

20.6.1.2 Cannizzaro Reaction and Formaldehyde Concentration. While this main reaction, represented by Eq. (20.1), takes place, other undesirable side reactions proceed, also in competition with the reaction. One of the major difficulties is the lowering of formaldehyde concentration in the solution due to its disproportionate consumption in alkaline solution. This is known as the *Cannizzaro reaction,* which may be characterized by

$$2HCHO + OH^- \quad CH_3OH + HCOO^- \tag{20.2}$$

This reaction continues independently. Fortunately, methanol (CH_3OH) one of the by-products of the Cannizzaro reaction, tends to shift the equilibrium of the reaction in Eq. (20.2) to the left and thus prevent the decrease of formaldehyde concentration by an unproductive reaction. By controlling the plating conditions properly, the wasteful consumption of form-aldehyde by the Cannizzaro reaction can be retained within 10 percent of the consumption in the reaction in Eq. (20.1).

20.6.1.3 Fehlings-Type Reactions.   In addition to the Cannizzaro reaction, the following side reaction also competes for formaldehyde:

$$2Cu^{2+} + HCHO + 5OH^- \quad Cu_2O + HCOO^- + 3H_2O \tag{20.3}$$

20.6.1.4 Other Formaldehyde-Related Reactions.   Under conditions which would favor the Fehlings-type reaction [Eq. (20.3)], spontaneous decomposition of uncatalyzed plating solutions produces precipitation of finely divided copper with attended vigorous evolution of hydrogen gas. The finely divided copper produced is due to the disproportionate quantity of Cu_2O under alkaline conditions:

$$Cu_2O + H_2O \quad Cu^\circ + Cu^{2+} + 2OH^- \tag{20.4}$$

Furthermore, formaldehyde may act as a reducing agent for the cuprous oxide to produce metallic copper:

$$Cu_2O + 2HCHO + 2OH^- \quad 2Cu^\circ + H_2 + 2HCOO^- + H_2O \tag{20.5}$$

20.6.1.5 Filtering.   The Cu° nuclei thus produced according to Eqs. (20.4) and (20.5) are not relegated to deposition on substrate but are produced randomly throughout the solution and become the catalytic sites for further undesirable copper deposition. Continuous filtration with a filter of pore size 20 μm or smaller can improve extraneous copper due to these catalytic sites.[25] The use of continuous filtering also improves the ductility of copper by eliminating codeposition of impurities. In most mass production facilities of PWBs by additive technology, two or three stages of filtering with filters of pore sizes down to 5 μm are common.

20.6.2 Use of Stabilizers

Since the reaction represented in Eq. (20.3) indicates the greatest degree of instability of the plating bath, various measures are taken to counteract this reaction. Alkaline cyanide has been a popular stabilizer used for the CC-4 bath, since cyanide forms strong complexes with Cu^+ ($Cu^+ + 2CN^- \; Cu(CN)_2^{2-}$), but relatively unstable complexes of Cu^{2+}. However, since cyanide also reacts with HCHO, it is difficult to control. 2,2′-dypiridil also chelates Cu^+ and does not react with HCHO. Hence, it is a more favored stabilizer, particularly for those baths used in Japan. On the other hand, a dypiridil bath deposit begins to have less ductility after several plating cycles and weekly bath makeup may be necessary.

Aeration of the plating bath is known to stabilize the solution, and vigorous aeration is commonly used to operate modern full-build electroless baths.

20.6.3 Surfactant

Reduction in surface tension assures that the plating solution is in intimate contact with the catalyst nuclei and permits thorough surface solution interaction. For this reason, a wetting agent or surfactant is included in bath formulations. Polyethelene oxide, polyethelene glycol (PEG), etc., are popular surfactants. Proper usage of surfactants also prevents the accumulation of gaseous material (air and hydrogen bubbles) on the surface of the board, particularly around the entrances of holes, which would also tend to lower the surface-solution interaction and thus seriously impair proper metal deposition.

20.6.4 Reliability of Deposited Copper and Inorganic Compounds

Generally, copper film with high elongation and reasonable tensile strength is preferred for through-hole reliability, although the relation between through-hole reliability and ductility and tensile strength is still not understood clearly.

The use of inorganic compounds containing vanadium or germanium as a part of chemical ingredients in plating baths enhances the quality of deposited copper.[13] Most full-build electroless baths used today contain either V_2O_5 or G_2O_5 to improve the physical properties of deposited copper.

20.6.4.1 Typical Copper Properties. Typical physical properties of reliable electrolessly plated copper are (as plated):

Elongation	8 to 10 percent
Tensile strength	35 to 45 kg/mm^2

After annealing the copper, elongation increases to 12 to 18 percent and tensile strength decreases slightly. These properties are equivalent to the ones resulting from acid copper. Since all panels are baked at about 140 to 160°C for 30 to 60 min during the course of the production process after plating, deposited copper gets annealed, thus assuring high through-hole reliability.

20.6.5 Removal of Impurities

Use of continuous filtering has been mentioned to remove some of the impurities. In addition there are other methods.

20.6.5.1 Electrodialysis. Electrodialysis[26,27] is effective to remove formate ions, sulfate ions, and carbonate ions which are by-products of reactions defined in Eqs. (20.1), (20.2), (20.3), and (20.5).

20.6.5.2 Overflow Method. Another very effective way to remove these unwanted by-products is the *overflow* method. Since essential components of the plating solution are consumed continuously, they must be replenished to maintain desirable plating conditions. In so doing, a considerable amount of the solution overflows because of the addition of water. The overflow also contains the reaction by-products as well as chelated copper ions.

After a certain amount of overflow solution is accumulated, sodium hydroxide and formaldehyde are added to the overflow solution and heated to promote spontaneous decomposition of the plating solution to precipitate copper metal. Addition of copper powder accelerates the precipitation. This so-called *chemical bomb-out* recovery method can be operated in bulk or continuously. The remaining solution can be treated with sulfuric acid to recover over 95 percent of the EDTA in the solution. Usually, the purity of EDTA thus recovered is higher than that of purchased EDTA.

Ninety-eight percent of the solution is recovered as permeate and is used in such processes as rinsing. The concentrate, the other two percent, is high in salt content (Na_2SO_4 and $HCOONa$) and may be evaporated to produce a small amount of solid waste or discharged into the ocean, if the plant is located near the ocean and locally approved.[6] This chemical bomb-out method can achieve two objectives at once: removal of unwanted impurities and recovery of chemicals. With this system, it is easy to maintain Baume at the desired 9°.

20.6.6 Environmental Issues of Formaldehyde

Formaldehyde is considered to be a carcinogen. If exposed to formaldehyde fumes of certain concentration for a long time, it can cause allergy conditions and perhaps cancer, although cancer due to long-time exposure to formaldehyde in the PWB industry has never been reported.

With a good exhaust system and scrubbing through water and peroxide solution, formaldehyde can be made quite harmless. It is a matter of economy. EDTA can be treated as previously mentioned.

Reducing agents alternative to formaldehyde such as glyoxylic acid[27] and hypophosphite (M_3PO_2)[28] have been suggested and tried, but they have not been able to replace formaldehyde as an effective reducing agent at this stage.

20.7 FULLY ELECTROLESS PLATING ISSUES

20.7.1 Efficiency of Electroless and Galvanic Plating

PWB manufacturers which are not familiar with electroless plating often have the misconception that electroless plating takes "too long." On the contrary, electroless plating is faster than galvanic plating, and its volumetric efficiency is twice as much as galvanic plating.

Electroless plating baths operate at the speed of 2.0 to 5.0 μm/h, 2.5 μm being the medium speed. Because of its high throwing power, a deposition thickness of 25 μm on the panel surface also assures 25 μm in the hole. That is, 10 h are needed to plate this thickness. The loading factor in electroless plating can be maintained at 4 dm^2/liter. A 2500-gal (10,000-l) tank can plate about 400 m^2 (4000 ft^2) of panels in one shot in 10 h. That is, 400 ft^2/h, or approximately 130 (18-in × 24-in) panels/h from a 10-m^3 tank. This is equivalent to twice the speed of galvanic plating from the same volume of plating solution. When small, high-aspect-ratio holes are involved, this figure becomes more favorable to electroless plating because the current density of galvanic plating must be reduced to 10 to 12 A/ft^2, which requires more than 2 h of plating for 25 μm in the hole.

Figure 20.7 shows the plating racks filled with panels waiting to be placed in electroless plating tanks. In large-volume operations, the panel-racking operation is fully automated.

20.7.2 Photochemical Imaging Systems

Various photochemical imaging systems have been developed and tried to be put into practice.[6] However, no photochemical imaging systems are used for real production today. They are all unstable and the lateral growth of conductors poses a problem for the fineline applications for which they are intended.

20.7.3 Molded Circuit Application

A handful of three-dimensional molded circuit manufacturers (or, the preferred identification, *molded interconnection device* or MID) have continued their quest for market with this

FIGURE 20.7 Plating racks filled with panels to be plated. *(Photo courtesy of Adiboard, Brazi.)*

product and have met with some success. (See Fig. 20.8.) There are several alternative methods to manufacture MIDs, of which the *two-shot* molding method can produce the most sophisticated three-dimensional interconnection devices.

A part which is to be metallized (circuitized) is molded first. Then, a portion of the first mold which is not desired for metallization is surrounded by the second molding, exposing

FIGURE 20.8 An example of a three-dimensional molded circuit application, in this case a light pen for computer input. *(Photo courtesy of Mitsui Pathtek.)*

only the portion desired to be metallized. This two-shot molding method can be classified further into two alternative methods, which are similar to CC-4 and AP-II.

One is to use catalyzed engineering plastic for the first molding and noncatalyzed plastic for the second molding. Adhesion promotion consists of a swell-and-etch step followed by chromic acid etch. The other alternative is to mold the first part with noncatalyzed plastic materials and expose the molded part to an adhesion promotion process and catalyze. The second part is then molded, as in the first case.

These parts are placed in an electroless plating bath for circuitization. A high rate of growth is expected for MIDs, with the automotive market being the most promising application area.

REFERENCES

1. W. A. Alpaugh and J. M. McCreary, IPC-TP-108, Fall Meeting, 1976.
2. R. R. Tummala and S. Ahmed, "Overview of Packaging for the IBM Enterprise System 9000 Based on the Glass-Ceramic Copper/Thin Film Thermal Conduction Module," *IEEE Trans. on Comp., Hybrids and Mfg. Tech.,* vol. 14, no. 4, Dec. 1991, pp. 426–431.
3. L. E. Thomas, et al., "Second-Level Packaging for the High End ES/9000 Processors," *IBM J. of Research & Development.*
4. H. Murano and T. Watari, "Packaging Technology for the NEC SX-3 Supercomputers," *IEEE Trans. on Comp., Hybrids and Mfg. Tech.,* vol. 15, no. 4, Aug. 1992, pp. 411–417.
5. A. Takahashi, et al., "High Density Multilayer Printed Circuit Board for HITAC M-880," *op. cit.,* pp. 418–425.
6. Clyde F. Coombs, Jr. (ed.), *Printed Circuits Handbook, 3d ed.,* McGraw-Hill, New York, 1986, Chap. 13.
7. U.S. Patent 2,938,805, 1960.
8. U.S. Patent 3,628,999, Dec. 1971.
9. U.S. Patent 3,799,802, Mar. 1974.
10. U.S. Patent 3,799,816, Mar. 1974.
11. U.S. Patent 3,600,330, Aug. 1971.
12. Japanese Patent 43-16929, July 1968.
13. Japanese Patent 58-6319, Feb. 1983.
14. H. Steffen, "Additive Process," Ruwel Werke GmbH, private communication.
15. K. Minten and J. Toth, "PWB Interconnect Strategy Using a Full Build Electroless Plating System: Part I," *PC World Conference V,* Paper No. b-52, Glasgow, Scotland, June 1990.
16. K. Minten, J. Seigo, and J. Cisson, "Part 2: Etch Characteristics," *Circuit World,* vol. 18, no. 4, Aug 1992, pp. 5–12.
17. K. Minten and J. Cisson, "Part 3: Characterization of a Semi-Additive Naked Palladium Catalyst," *Circuit World,* vol. 19, no. 2, Jan. 1993, pp. 4–13.
18. K. Minten, K. Kitchens, and J. Cisson, "Part 4: The Future of FBE Process," private communication.
19. N. Ohtake, *Electronics Technology* (Japanese), 27(7), June 1985, pp. 55–59.
20. N. Ohtake, "New Printed Wiring Boards by a Partly Additive Process," *PC World Conference IV,* Tokyo, Paper No. 44, June 1987.
21. S. Imabayashi, et al., "Partly-Additive Process for Manufacturing High-Density Printed Wiring Boards," *IEEE Trans.* 0569-5503/92/0000-1053, 1992.
22. H. Akaboshi, "A New Fully Additive Fabrication Process for Printed Wiring Boards," *IEEE Trans. on Comp., Hybrids and Mfg. Tech.,* vol. CHMT-9, no. 2, June 1986.
23. R. Enomoto, et al., "Advanced Full-Additive Printed Wiring Boards Using Heat Resistant Adhesive," *PC World Conf V,* Paper No. B6-1, Glasgow, Scotland, June 1990.

24. K. Ikai, "Full Additive Boards," *Electronic Materials* (Japanese), Oct. 1993, pp. 58–63.

25. H. Honma, K. Hagihara, and K. Kobayashi, "Factors Affecting Properties of Electrolessly Deposited Copper," *Circuit Technology* (Japanese), vol. 9, no. 1, 1994, pp. 31–36.

26. T. Murata, "Chemistry of Electroless Plating," *Circuit Technology* (Japanese), vol. 8, no. 5, 1993, pp. 357–362.

27. J. Darken, "Electroless Copper—An Alternative to Formaldehyde," *PC World Conf V,* Glasgow, Scotland, Paper B/6/2, June 1990.

28. J. P. Pilato and Joe D'Ambrisi, "Process for Metallization by Copper Deposition Without the Use of Formaldehyde," MacDermid paper, private communication.

29. R. E. Horn, *Plating and Surface Finishing,* Oct. 1981, pp. 50–52.

30. A. Iwaki, et al., *Photographic Science & Engineering,* vol. 20, no. 6, 1976, p. 246.

CHAPTER 21
ETCHING

Edward F. Duffek, Ph.D.
Adion Engineering Company, Cupertino, California

21.1 INTRODUCTION

One of the major steps in the chemical processing of subtractive printed boards is etching, or removal of copper, to achieve the desired circuit patterns. Etching is also used for surface preparation with minimal metal removal (microetching) during innerlayer oxide coating and electroless or electrolytic plating. Technical, economic, and environmental needs for practical process control have brought about major improvements in etching techniques. Batch-type operations, with their variable etching rates and long downtimes, have been replaced with continuous, constant-etch-rate processes. In addition, the need for continuous processing has led to extensive automation along with complete, integrated systems.

The most common etching systems are based on alkaline ammonia, hydrogen peroxide-sulfuric acid, and cupric chloride. Other systems include persulfates, ferric chloride, and chromic-sulfuric acids. Process steps include resist stripping, precleaning, etching, neutralizing, water rinsing, and drying. This chapter describes the technology for etching high-quality, fineline (0.004 to 0.006 in) circuits in high volume at a lower cost, as well as closed-loop continuous processing, constant-etch rates, control at high dissolved-copper capacities, regeneration-recovery, less pollution, and increased safety. Problems of waste disposal and pollution control have been minimized by adapting these principles.

Typical procedures are given for etching organic (i.e., dry film) and metal-resist boards, and for innerlayers. Strippers and procedures for resist removal are described, based on resist selection, cost, and pollution problems. The properties of available etchants are also described in terms of finish plate compatibility, control methods, ease of control, and equipment maintenance. Other considerations include chemical and etchant effects on dielectric laminates, etching of thin-clad copper and semiadditive boards, solder mask on bare copper (SMOBC), equipment selection techniques, production capabilities, quality attained, and facilities.

21.2 GENERAL ETCHING CONSIDERATIONS AND PROCEDURES

Good etching results depend on proper image transfer in both organic innerlayer print-and-etch and plated-metal etch resists. Etch personnel must be familiar with screened, photosensitive, and plated resists commonly used. The etching of printed boards must begin with suitable cleaning, inspection, and pre-etch steps to ensure acceptable products. Plated boards also require a careful and complete resist removal. The steps after etching are important because they are necessary to remove surface contaminations and yield sound surfaces. This discussion considers the various types of resists and outlines typical procedures use to etch printed boards using organic and plated resist patterns.

21.2.1 Screened Resists

Screen printing is a common method for producing standard copper-printed circuitry on metal-clad dielectric and other substrates. The etch-resist material is printed with a positive pattern (circuitry only) for copper etch-only boards or with a negative image (field only) when plated-through-holes and metal resist are present.

The type of resist material used must meet the requirements for proper image transfer demanded by the printer. From the metal etcher's point of view, the material needs to provide good adhesion and etch-solution resistance; be free of pinholes, oil, or resin bleed-out; and be readily removable without damage to substrate or circuitry.

Typical problems are excessive undercut, slivers, unetched areas, and innerlayer shorts in multilayer boards. In addition, conductor line lifting may occur when the copper-to-laminate peel strength is below specification.

21.2.2 Hole Plugging

Plugged-hole, copper-only boards use alkaline-soluble screen resists in a unique manner. The technique, called *hole plugging*, makes the SMOBC board possible.

21.2.3 UV-Cured Screen Resists

Ultraviolet-cured solventless systems are available for print-and-etch and plating applications. These products are resistant to commonly used acidic plating and etching solutions. Stripping must be evaluated carefully.

21.2.4 Photoresists

Dry film and liquid photoresist materials are capable of yielding fineline (0.004 to 0.006 in) circuits needed for production of surface-mount circuit boards. Like screened resists, photosensitive resists can be used to print either negative or positive patterns on the metal-clad laminate. Although dry film and liquid materials differ in both physical and chemical properties, they will be considered together for our purpose.

In general, both positive- and negative-acting resists offer better protection in acidic rather than alkaline solutions; however, negative-acting types are more tolerant of alkaline solutions. Negative resists, once exposed and developed, are no longer light-sensitive and can be processed and stored in normal white light. The positive resists remain light-sensitive even after developing and must therefore be protected from white light. Liquid photoresists, although less durable, are capable of finer line definition and resolution.

Positive-acting resists are subject to the same problems as are negative-acting resists, although they are easier to remove cleanly, after exposure, from areas to be etched or plated. Problems related to plating photoresist-coated boards are reviewed in Chap. 19.

21.2.5 Plated Etch Resists

At present, the most extensive use of metal-plated resists is found in the production of double-sided and multilayer plated-through-hole circuit boards. The most commonly used resists are solder plate (60 percent Sn, 40 percent Pb), tin, nickel, tin-nickel, and gold. Silver is used to some extent for light-emitting and liquid crystal applications. Details concerning the deposition of these metals are given in Chap. 19. The use of these resists is described in the following paragraphs.

21.2.5.1 Solder Plate.   Tin-lead solder (0.0003 to 0.001 in thick) is the most commonly used plated etch resist. The 60 Sn-40 Pb alloy offers good etchant resistance with few problems. Increased reliability is achieved by the use of solder plate over tin-nickel.[1] Thin solder deposits (0.0002 in) can be used for the SMOBC process. The most suitable etchants are alkaline ammonia, sulfuric acid-hydrogen peroxide, chromic-sulfuric acid, and ammonium persulfate-phosphoric acid. Ferric and cupric chloride acid etchants cannot be used because of solder plate attack. Post-etch neutralization rinses are needed, especially with alkaline systems, to rinse away etchant residues and to maintain optimum surface properties.

21.2.5.2 Tin Plating.   Tin plating (directly over barrier layers of nickel or tin-nickel) is used because of its optimum solderability. Other etchants, such as sulfuric acid-hydrogen peroxide, chromic-sulfuric acid, alkaline ammonia, and ammonium persulfate-phosphoric acid, have been especially formulated for bright tin. Thin tin deposits (0.0002 in) are used to make SMOBC boards. Follow the procedure given previously for solder plate.

21.2.5.3 Tin-Nickel and Nickel.   Tin-nickel alloy (65 percent Sn, 35 percent Ni) and nickel-plate, used as is or overplated with gold, solder, or tin, are also preferred metal resists for etching copper in alkaline ammonia, sulfuric acid-hydrogen peroxide, and persulfates.

21.2.5.4 Gold.   Gold with an underplate of nickel or tin-nickel provides excellent resistance to all the common copper etchants. Some etchants have a slight dissolving effect on gold.

21.2.5.5 Precious Metals and Alloys.   Rhodium has been described as being a suitable resist for edge connectors on boards; however, the plating process is difficult to control. When plated over nickel, rhodium tends to be thin and porous and to lift during etching. Because of varying surface properties, 18k-alloy gold and nickel-palladium must be evaluated carefully when used as substitutes for pure-gold systems.

21.2.5.6 Silver.   Although silver is not used on most printed boards (Mil-STD-275 states that it shall not be used), it has found some application for camera, light-emitting, and liquid crystal devices. Copper etching using silver as resist can be done with alkaline ammonia solutions. Silver loss is about 0.0001 in/min.

21.2.5.7 Etching Procedure: Recommendations for Plated-Metal Resists.   Etching of the metal-resist-plated boards begins with removal of the resist using commercial solvents and strippers. Gold, solder, and tin resists must be handled carefully because they scratch very easily. Tin-nickel alloy and nickel plate, however, are very hard and resistant to abrasion.

The procedure after etching includes thorough water rinsing and acid neutralizing to ensure removal of etchant residues on the board surface and under the traces. Alkaline etchants are followed by treatment with proprietary ammonium chloride acidic solutions, ferric and cupric chloride with solutions of hydrochloric or oxalic acid, and ammonium persulfate with sulfuric acid. Alkaline cleaning is used for tin-lead boards etched in chromic-sulfuric acid. Etchant residues not removed before drying or reflow result in lowered electrical resistance of the dielectric substrate and in poor electrical contact and soldering on the conductive surfaces.[2]

A problem common to etching printed boards is not having the entire area etch clean at the same time. This occurs when etch action is more rapid at the edges of printed areas than in a board expanse of copper. If very fine patterns and lines are required, the result can be loss of the pattern due to undercut, especially when the board is left in the etcher until all the field copper has etched away. Fineline boards in high-volume production require special fineline etchants, dry film photoresist, thin-clad laminate, controlled plating distribution, spray etching, and fully additive or semiadditive processing.

21.3   RESIST REMOVAL

The method used for resist stripping is important when a resist is selected. The effect on board materials, cost and production requirements, and compliance with safety and pollution standards must be taken into account. Both aqueous and solvent stripping systems are widely used.

21.3.1   Screen Resist Removal

Alkali-soluble resist inks are generally preferred. Stripping in the case of thermal and UV-curable resists is accomplished in 2% sodium hydroxide or in proprietary solutions. The resist is loosened and rinsed off with a water spray. Adequate safety precautions must be taken, since caustics are harmful.

Conveyorized resist-stripping and etching machines use high-pressure pumping systems which spray hot alkaline solutions on both sides of the boards. Single-sided boards and certain laminate materials such as the polyimides may be attached by alkaline strippers. Measling, staining, or other degradation is noted when strippers attack epoxy or other substrates.

Screened vinyl-based resists are removed by a dissolving action in solutions of chlorinated, petroleum, or glycol ether solvents. Methylene chloride and toluene are used extensively in cold stripper formulations.[3] Commercial cold strippers are classified according to their pH in a 10% stripper-water mixture. The most common strippers are acidic formulations which contain copper brighteners and swelling, dissolution, and water-rinsing agents. The usual procedure for static tank stripping involves soaking the coated boards in at least two tanks of stripper. Excessive time in strippers is to be avoided because of attack on the "butter" (top epoxy) coat, especially on print-and-etch or single-sided boards. Water is a contaminant in most cold strippers.

Solvent stripping machines are commercially available. High-volume users save costs by using conveyorized systems equipped with reclamation and pollution-control facilities. Distillable cold strippers generally contain methylene chloride or trichloroethylene (TCE). Some heating may be used, but only in closed systems because of health and fire hazards. In all cases, proper safety, ventilation, pollution control, and certified waste disposal must be provided. Methylene chloride, toluene, and TCE are priority pollutants (TTO) regulated by the EPA. Alternatives to methylene chloride are available as glycol ethers.

21.3.2   Photoresist Removal

21.3.2.1   Dry Film.   Dry film resists have been formulated for ease of removal in both aqueous-alkaline and solvent solutions. Strippers of each type are available for both static tank and conveyorized systems. Cold stripper solvent-type formulations are similar to those used on vinyl screen inks in which the primary solvent is methylene chloride.[4] Aqueous-alkaline stripping results in undissolved residues of softened resist films. These residues can be captured in a filter system and disposed of in accordance with waste-disposal requirements.

21.3.2.2   Negative-Acting Liquid Photoresist Removal.   Negative-acting, liquid-applied photoresist can be readily removed from printed boards that have not been baked excessively. Baking is critical to removal because it relates to the degree of polymerization. Since over-baking is also damaging to the insulating substrates, processes should stress minimal baking—only enough to withstand the operations involved.

The negative-acting resists are removed by using solvents and commercial strippers. In this case, the resist does not dissolve; instead, it softens and swells, breaking the adhesive bond to the substrate. Once that has taken place over the entire coated area, a water spray is used to flush away the film.

21.3.2.3   *Positive-Acting Photoresist Removal.*

Positive-acting photoresists are removed by dissolving in acetone, ketone, cellusolve acetate, or other organic solvents. Commercial organic and inorganic strippers are suitable if baking has not been excessive. Removal by exposure to UV light and subsequent dipping in sodium hydroxide, TSP, or other strong alkaline solutions is also effective. Overbaking also makes removal difficult.

Machine stripping is done in a solution of $0.5N$ sodium hydroxide, nonionic surfactants, and defoamers.

21.4   ETCHING SOLUTIONS

This section is a survey of the technology and chemistry of the copper etching systems in common use. Changes from batch-type operation to continuous constant-rate systems with increased process automation represent major innovations in etching practices. Factors that account for these changes are as follows:

1. Fineline board design
2. Thin-innerlayer handling
3. Compatibility with resist
4. Control of etch rate
5. Etch rate (speed)
6. Dissolved copper capacity
7. Ease of process control
8. Ease of equipment maintenance
9. Costs and economics
10. High yield
11. Regeneration and replenishment
12. By-products
13. Operator and environmental protection
14. Disposal and pollution control

All the preceding factors serve to evaluate copper etchants to be used. Introduction, chemistry, properties, and problems are given in this section, along with suggestions for selection and control.

Problems encountered in the control of equipment and etchant solutions are frequently difficult to separate. Often, the utmost in performance and life of the etchant is not attained. A current understanding is needed in the areas of fineline production, regeneration and recycling of materials, and pollution control.

21.4.1   Alkaline Ammonia

Alkaline etching with ammonium hydroxide complexing is increasingly used because of its continuous operation, compatibility with most metallic and organic resists, minimum undercut, high capacity for dissolved copper, and fast etch rates. Both batch and continuous (closed-loop) spray machine systems are in use. Continuous operation provides constant etch rates, high work output, ease of control and replenishment, and improved pollution control. However, costs are relatively high, neutralization after etching is critical, and the ammonium ion introduced to the rinses presents a difficult waste-treatment problem. Complete regeneration with chemical recycling is not routinely practiced.

21.4.1.1   Chemistry.   The main chemical constituents function as follows:

1. Ammonium hydroxide, NH_4OH, acts as a complexing agent and holds copper in solution.
2. Ammonium chloride, NH_4Cl increases etch rate, copper-holding capacity, and solution stability.
3. Copper ion, Cu^{2+}, is an oxidizing agent that reacts with and dissolves metallic copper.
4. Sodium chlorite, $NaClO_2$, is also an oxidizing agent that reacts with and dissolves metallic copper.
5. Ammonium bicarbonate, NH_4CO_3, is a buffer and as such retains clean solder holes and surface.
6. Ammonium phosphate, $(NH_4)_3PO_4$, retains clean solder and plated-through-holes.
7. Ammonium nitrate, NH_4NO_3, increases etch rate and retains clean solder.

Some batch formulations require mixing two solutions just before etching, since oxidizers and complexers are kept separate for stability. Continuous-process operations consist of single-solution makeup buffered to a pH of 7.5 to 9.5.

Alkaline etching solutions dissolve exposed field copper on printed boards by a chemical process of oxidation, solubilizing, and complexing. Ammonium hydroxide and ammonium salts combine with copper ions to form cupric ammonium complex ions [$Cu(NH_3)_4{}^{2+}$], which hold the etched and dissolved copper in solution at 18 to 30 oz/gal.

Typical oxidation reactions for closed-loop systems are shown by the reaction of cupric ion on copper, and air (O_2) oxidation of the cuprous complex ion:

$$Cu + Cu(NH_3)_4{}^{2+} \rightarrow 2Cu(NH_3)_4{}^+ \tag{21.1}$$

$$4Cu(NH_3)_2{}^+ + 8NH_3 + O_2 + 2H_2O \rightarrow 4Cu(NH_4)_4{}^{2+} + 4OH^- \tag{21.2}$$

and for batch-operating systems by chlorite ion on copper:

$$2Cu + 8NH_3 + ClO_2{}^- + 2H_2O \rightarrow 2Cu(NH_3)_4{}^{2+} + Cl^- + 4OH^- \tag{21.3}$$

The calculated copper capacity achieved in batch etching with chlorite is 6 oz/gal of dissolved copper (Table 21.1, no. 1). Air oxidation (O_2) or a temperature increase is needed for higher copper capacity.

Closed-loop etching can be continued with the formation of $Cu(NH_3)_4{}^{2+}$ oxidizer from air during spray etching and as long as the copper-holding capacity is not exceeded.

21.4.1.2   Properties and Control.   Early versions of alkaline etchants were batch-operated. They had a low copper capacity, and the etch rates dropped off rapidly as copper content increased.[5,8,9] It was found to be necessary to add controlled amounts of dissolved oxidizing agents to speed up the rate and increase copper capacity at a constant temperature. Batch operation is still practical for low-volume production.

Etching solutions are operated at 120 to 130°F and are well suited to spray etching. Efficient exhaust systems are required because ammonia fumes are released during operation.[10] Etching machines must have a slight negative pressure and moderate exhausting to retain

TABLE 21-1   Composition of Alkaline Etchants

Component	1[5]	2[6]	3[7]
NH_4OH	3.0 mol/L	6.0 mol/L	2–6 mol/L
NH_4Cl	1.5–0	5.0	1–4.0
Cu (as metal)		2.0*	0.1–0.6
$NaClO_2$	10.375		
NH_4HCO_3	0–1.5		
$(NH_4)_3PO_4$		0.01	0.05–0.5
NH_4NO_3	0–1.5		

* Starter solution only.

the ammonia necessary for holding dissolved copper in solution. Currently available solutions offer constant etching of 1-oz copper in 1 min or less, with a dissolved copper content of 18 to 24 oz/gal.

21.4.1.3   Closed-Loop Systems.   A practical method of maintaining a constant etch rate with minimal pollution uses automatic feeding controlled by specific gravity or density.[9] The process, which is generally referred to as *bleed and feed,* is illustrated in Fig. 21.1. As the printed boards are etched, copper is dissolved, and the density of the etching solution increases. The density of the etchant in the etcher sump is sensed to determine the amount of copper in solution. When the density sensor records an upper limit, a switch activates a pump which automatically feeds replenishing solution to the etcher and simultaneously removes etchant until a lower density is reached.

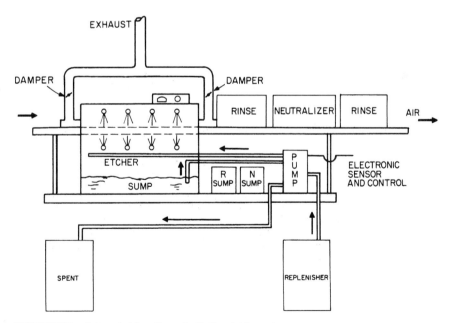

FIGURE 21.1   Automated flow-through alkaline etching system.

A typical operating condition is as follows:*

Temperature	120 to 130°F (49 to 50°C)
pH	8.0 to 8.8
Specific gravity at 120°F (49°C)	1.207 to 1.227
Baumé, Be°	25 to 27
Copper concentration, oz/gal	20 to 22
Etch rate, 0.001 in/min	1.4 to 2.0
Chloride level	4.9 to 5.7 mol/L

A study of the etching rate of copper versus dissolved copper content shows the following effects:

0 to 11 oz/gal	Long etching times
11 to 16 oz/gal	Lower etch rates but solution control difficult
18 to 22 oz/gal	Etch rates high and solution stable
22 to 30 oz/gal	Solution unstable and tends toward sludging

All work must be thoroughly rinsed with water immediately upon leaving the etching chamber. Do not allow the boards to dry before rinsing. Etched circuitry with plated tin-lead solder resist also requires an acid neutralization and application of solder brightener. The main purposes are to remove etchant from under circuit edges and to clean and brighten the circuit surfaces and plated-through-holes. This operation is critical for good solder reflow. Thorough clean-water rinsing and air knife drying result in clean, stain-free surfaces (see Table 21.1).

21.4.1.4   *Regeneration.*   True regeneration requires the following:

1. Removal of portions of the spent etching solution from the etcher sump under controlled conditions.

2. Chemical restoration of spent etchant, i.e., removal of excess by-products and adjustment of solution parameters for reuse.

3. Replenishing of etchant in the etching machine. Constant etching conditions are achieved when regeneration is continuous. Regeneration by these methods is expensive and is thus limited to large printed circuit facilities. The principal methods of regeneration are crystallization, liquid–liquid extraction, and electrolytic recovery.
   a. Recrystallization reduces the copper level in the etchant by chilling and filtering precipitated salts. That is followed by refortification and adjustment of operating conditions.
   b. Liquid–liquid extraction[11,12] is gaining acceptance because of its continuous and generally safe nature. The process involves mixing spent etchant with an organic solvent (i.e., hydroxy oximes) capable of extracting copper. The organic layer containing copper is subsequently mixed with aqueous sulfuric acid, which extracts copper to form copper sulfate. The copper-free etchant is restored, and the copper sulfate is available for electroless copper, acid copper plating, or copper recovery. Closed-loop regeneration systems reduce chemical costs, sewer contamination, and production downtime.
   c. Electrolytic recovery of copper directly from an ammonia complexed copper sulfate etchant. Possible benefits include reduced waste shipments and cost savings.[13,14]

---

* P.A. Hunt Chemical Corporation, West Paterson, N.J.

21.4.1.5 Special Problems Encountered during Etching[15]

1. *Low etch rate with low pH, <8.0:* This is caused by excessive ventilation, heating, downtime, and spraying when the solution is hot, under conditions of adequate replenishment or low ammonia. The pH must be raised with anhydrous ammonia. Automatic replenishment equipment must be checked.

2. *Low etch rate with high pH, >8.8:* This is caused by high copper content, water in etchant, or underventilation.

3. *Low etch rate with optimum pH:* This is due to error of copper thickness, oxygen starvation in etcher, or contamination of etchant.

4. *Solder attack:* This is caused by having excess chloride in etchant, or by the tin-lead deposit not being in compliance.

5. *Residues on solder plate, holes, and traces:* These may be caused by etchant solution imbalance or by spent finisher.

6. *Under- or overetching:* This may be due to improper pH.

7. *Sludging of etch chamber with low pH, <8.0:* See special problem 1. Sludge will be gritty and dark blue. This may be corrected by the addition of anhydrous ammonia.

8. *Sludging of etch chamber with high pH, >8.8:* See special problem 2. Sludge will be light blue and fluffy. This may be due to the copper concentration exceeding the capacity of the chloride concentration. It may be corrected by adding ammonium chloride.

9. *Presence of ammonia fumes:* The cause of this is leaks in the etcher. Ventilate for operator safety.

10. *Pollution:* This results when water coming from the etchers contains dissolved copper. If so, it must be chemically treated and separated from ammonia-bearing rinses. Thin-clad copper laminates present a further problem because the faster movement through the etcher increases the transport of etchant into the rinses.

21.4.2 Sulfuric Acid-Hydrogen Peroxide

Sulfuric-peroxide systems are used extensively for copper surface preparation (microetching), i.e., for oxide coating of inner layers, and for electroless and electrolytic copper plating.[16,17] The reasons for this wide acceptance are the ease of replenishment, simple waste treatment needed, closed-loop copper recovery, and optimum surface texture of the copper. In addition to these advantages, the compatibility of these systems with most organic and metallic resists, their steady etch rates, and the optimum undercut they provide make them especially suited to be used as final etch step.[16–21] Both tank immersion and etching systems are commercially available. Continuous-processing equipment is also available for the electroplating-through-etching operations.

21.4.2.1 Chemistry. Typical constituents of both immersion and spray etchants and their functions are as follows:

1. Hydrogen peroxide is an oxidizing agent that reacts with and dissolves metallic copper.

2. Sulfuric acid makes copper soluble and holds copper sulfate in solution.

3. Copper sulfate helps to stabilize etch and recovery rates.

4. Molybdenum ion is an oxidizing agent and rate exaltant.[22]

5. Aryl sulfonic acids are peroxide stabilizers.[23]

6. Thiosulfates are rate exaltants and chloride-ion controllers which permit lower peroxide content.[24]

7. Phosphoric acid retains clean solder traces and plated-through-holes.[17,25]

The etching reaction is as follows:

$$Cu + H_2O_2 + H_2SO_4 \rightarrow CuSO_4 + 2H_2O \tag{21.4}$$

21.4.2.2   Properties and Control.   The earlier technical problems of slow etch rates, peroxide decomposition, and foaming in spray systems have been solved, but critical concerns still remain. Among these are process overheating, etchant composition balance with by-product recovery, etchant contamination, and the dangers in handling concentrated peroxide solutions. Table 21.2 compares typical composition and operating conditions of immersion and spray-etching systems.

TABLE 21.2   Sulfuric-Peroxide Final Etchants

	Immersion*	Spray†
Makeup:		
Sulfuric acid, 96%	10% by volume	17–20% by volume
Hydrogen peroxide, 50% (200 vol.)	6–8% by volume	10–12% by volume
Copper sulfate	16–20 oz/gal	16–20 oz/gal
Stabilizers	As needed	6–8%
Other additives	As needed	6–8%
Operating conditions		
Copper	4–5 oz/gal	4–5 oz/gal
Etch rate	6–8 min	1.5 min
Temperature:		
Etching	115°F	130°F
Recovery	50–70°F	50–70°F

* Shipley Co., Newton, Mass.
† Electrochemicals, Youngstown, Ohio.

21.4.2.3   Closed-Loop Systems.   Production facilities require continuous recirculating of the etchant through the etching tank or machine and the copper sulfate recovery operation. Etchant replenishment is controlled by chemical analysis and by additions of concentrates.

Copper sulfate recovery is based on lowering the solubility of $CuSO_4 \cdot 5H_2O$ by decreasing the etchant temperature to 50 to 70°F. See Fig. 21.2 and Table 21.2 for method and operating conditions.

21.4.2.4   Problems Encountered with Peroxide Systems

1. *Reduced etch rates:*   This problem can be caused by operating conditions, solution imbalance, or chloride contamination.

2. *Under- and overetching:*   A review of etching conditions, solution control, and the resist-stripping process may show deviations from normal. In the case of immersion etching, the solution and panel agitation may need to be increased. When spray etching, a check of nozzles and line clogging is indicated.

3. *Temperature changes:*   Recirculating water rates and thermostats need to be examined regularly. Overheating may be due to high copper content, contamination, and rapid peroxide decomposition.

4. *Solder attack:*   Review tin-lead process for copper contamination, and etchant for excess chlorides.

5. *Copper sulfate recovery stoppage:*   Examine solution balance, heat exchanger, and other recovery equipment.

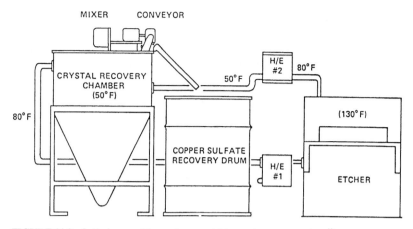

FIGURE 21.2   Sulfuric-peroxide continuous etching and recovery system.[18]

6. *Pollution:*   Examine etcher for leaks, and rinsewater for excess copper.

7. *High equipment costs:*   The need for customized etchers, etching machines, heat exchangers, and recovery units adds considerably to equipment costs.

21.4.3   Cupric Chloride

Cupric chloride systems are typical of the innovations to achieve closed-loop regeneration, lower costs, and a constant, predictable etch rate. Steady-state etching with acidic cupric chloride permits high throughput, material recovery, and reduced pollution. Regeneration in this case is somewhat complex but is readily maintained. Dissolved copper capacity is high compared with that of batch operation. Cupric chloride solutions are used mainly for fineline multilayer inner details and print-and-etch boards.[26] Resists are screened inks, dry film, gold, and tin-nickel. Solder and tin boards are not compatible with cupric chloride etchant.

21.4.3.1   Chemistry.   The etching reaction is as follows:

$$Cu + Cl_2 \rightarrow Cu_2Cl_2 \tag{21.5}$$

Chloride ions, when added in excess as hydrochloric acid, sodium chloride, or ammonium chloride, act to solubilize the relatively insoluble cuprous chloride and thereby maintain stable etch rates. The complex formation can be shown as

$$CuCl_2 + Cl^- \rightarrow CuCl_3^{2-} \tag{21.6}$$

The etchant can be regenerated by reoxidizing the cuprous chloride to cupric chloride as illustrated by the following equations:

1. *Air:*

$$2Cu_2Cl_2 + 4HCl + O_2 \Leftrightarrow 4CuCl_2 + 2H_2O \tag{21.7}$$

This method of regeneration is not used because the oxygen reaction rate in acids is slow and the solubility of oxygen in hot solution is low (4 to 8 ppm). Spray etching induces air oxidation.

2. *Chlorination:*

$$Cu_2Cl_2 + Cl_2 \rightarrow 2CuCl_2 \tag{21.8}$$

3. *Electrolytic:*

$$Cu^+ + e^- \rightarrow Cu \text{ (cathode)} \tag{21.9}$$

$$Cu^+ \rightarrow Cu^{2+} + e^- \text{ (anode)} \tag{21.10}$$

Refer to Table 21.3 for typical formulations.

TABLE 21.3 Cupric Chloride Etching Solutions

Component	Solution 1[27]	Solution 2[28]	Solution 3[29]	Solution 4[30]
$CuCl_2 \cdot 2H_2O$	1.42 lb	2.2 M	2.2 M	0.5–2.5 M
HCl (20° Be)	0.6 gal	30 mL/gal	0.5 N	0.2–0.6 M
NaCl		4 M	3 M	
NH_4Cl				2.4–0.5 M
H_2O	*	*	*	*

* Add water to make up 1 gal.

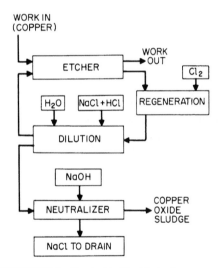

WORK IN
(COPPER)

FIGURE 21.3 Cupric chloride chlorination regeneration system.[29,34]

21.4.3.2 Properties and Control.
Early cupric chloride formations had slow etch rates and low copper capacity and were limited to batch operation.[27–33] Regenerable continuous operation using modified formulations has brought useful improvements. Etch rates of 50 to 55 s for 1-oz copper are obtained from cupric chloride-sodium chloride systems operated at 130°F with conventional spray-etching equipment. Copper capacities are maintained at 15 to 20 oz/gal.

21.4.3.3 Closed-Loop Etching and Regeneration.
Systems in use include chlorination, chlorate, and electrolytic regeneration.

Chlorination. Direct chlorination is the preferred technique for regeneration of cupric etchant because of its low cost, high rate, efficiency in recovery of copper, and pollution control. The cupric chloride-sodium chloride system (Table 21.3, no. 3) is suitable. Figure 21.3 shows the process. Chlorine, hydrochloric acid, and sodium chloride solutions are automatically fed into the system as required. Sensing devices include redox and colorimeter (Cu oxidation state), density (Cu concentration), etch rate monitor, level sensor, and thermostats. Chlorination is reliable and controllable. Other factors are safety and solution control.

1. *Safety:* Use of chlorine gas requires adequate ventilation and leak-detection equipment.

2. *Solution control:* An increase in pH will cause the copper colorimeter to give erroneous readings caused by the turbidity in the solution. Excess NaCl at 18 to 20 oz/gal copper causes coprecipitation of salts when the solution is cooled.

Chlorate Regeneration. This method uses sodium chlorate, sodium chloride, and hydrochloric acid and is an alternate method similar to chlorination.

Electrolytic Regeneration. The electrochemical reversal of the etching of copper shown in Eq. (21.5) is claimed to be effective and economical. Descriptions of this system are given in the literature.[27] On a large scale, electrolytic regeneration requires a high investment in equipment and materials, as well as high-power consumption.

The etchant is a solution of cupric chloride and hydrochloric acid (Table 21.3, no. 1). Etchant flows continuously between spray-etching machines and a plating tank. In the plating machine, two processes take place simultaneously: Copper is plated at the cathode, and regeneration of the spent etchant occurs at the anodes.

21.4.3.4 Batch Regeneration

Oxidizing Agent Treatment. As shown by Eq. (21.7), chemical regeneration is possible with oxygen. Similarly, it is possible with faster, more active oxidizing agents in batch processing, as shown by Clark[32] using hydrogen peroxide or sodium hypochlorite. Equations (21.11) and (21.12) show the oxidation steps:

$$Cu_2Cl_2 + 2HCl + H_2O_2 \rightarrow 2CuCl_2 + 2H_2O \tag{21.11}$$

$$Cu_2Cl_2 + 2HCl + NaOCL \rightarrow 2CuCl_2 + NaCl + H_2O \tag{21.12}$$

Solution Replacement. Black and Cutler[33] have also shown that the reaction given in Eq. (21.7) can be used in principle to regenerate a cupric chloride etching solution.

21.4.3.6 Problems with Cupric Chloride Systems

1. *Slow etch rate:* This is frequently due to low temperatures, insufficient agitation, or lack of solution control. If temperature and agitation are under control, an increase of etching time and a dark green solution may result from a decrease in the cupric iron content. If etching time doubles, the solution should be renewed or regenerated. Acid must also be added to clarify cloudy solutions. In regenerative systems, the source of oxidation may be depleted.

2. *Sludging:* This occurs if acid is low or if water dilution occurs.

3. *Breakdown of photoresists:* This may occur with excess acid and elevated temperatures.

4. *Yellow or white residues on copper surface:* The yellow residue is usually cuprous hydroxide. It is water-insoluble and is left when boards are etched and alkali-cleaned. A white precipitate will probably be cuprous chloride, which can remain after etching in solutions that are low in chloride ion and acid. To eliminate both conditions, the solution in which the board is rinsed just before final water-spray rinsing should be 5% by volume hydrochloric acid.

5. *Waste disposal:* Spent etchant can be sold for its copper content.

21.4.4 Persulfates

Ammonium, sodium, and potassium persulfates modified by certain catalysts have been adopted for the etching of copper in PC manufacturing. Continuous regenerative systems and a batch system using ammonium persulfate are common. Wide use is made of persulfates as a microetch for innerlayer oxide coating and copper electroless and plating processes. Persulfate solutions allow all common types of resists on boards including solder, tin, tin-nickel, screened inks, and photosensitive films. Persulfate solutions are not suitable etchants for gold because of excess undercut and low etch factors.

Formulations of ammonium persulfate catalyzed with mercuric chloride have etch rates comparable to those of the chloride etchants and are preferred for solder, print-and-etch, and tin-nickel boards. Formulations with proprietary additives other than mercury catalysts are available and have been improved to give good etch factors.[35] Regenerative systems have made possible higher copper capacities and constant etch rates. In general, persulfate etchants are unstable and will exhibit decomposition, lower etch rates versus copper content, and lower useful copper capacity. The use of persulfate etching systems has declined recently because of high costs and other improvements in alkaline ammonia etchants.

21.4.4.1 Chemistry.   Ammonium, potassium, and persulfates are stable salts of persulfuric acid ($H_2S_2O_8$). When these salts are dissolved in water, the persulfate ion ($S_2O_8^{2-}$) is formed. It is the most powerful oxidant of the commonly used peroxy compounds. During copper etching, persulfate oxidizes metallic copper to cupric ion as shown:

$$Cu + (NH_4)_2S_2O_8 \rightarrow CuSO_4 + (NH_4)_2SO_4 \tag{21.13}$$

Persulfate solutions hydrolyze to form peroxy monosulfate ion (HSO_5^{1-}) and, subsequently, hydrogen peroxide and oxygen. This hydrolysis is acid catalized and accounts for the instability of acidic persulfate etching solutions.

Ammonium persulfate solution, normally made up at 20%, is acidic. Hydrolysis reactions and etchant use cause a reduction of the pH from 4 to 2. The persulfate concentration is lowered, and hydrated cupric ammonium sulfate [$CuSO_4 \cdot (NH_4)_2SO_4 \cdot 6H_2O$] is formed. This precipitate may interfere with etching.

Solid persulfate compounds are stable and do not deteriorate if stored dry in closed containers. Solution composition is catalyzed by various agents, including organic matter and transition metals (Fe, Cr, Cu, Pb, Ag, etc.). Materials for storage must be chosen carefully. Persulfates should not be mixed with reducing agents or oxidizable organics.[36]

21.4.4.2 Properties and Control.   Etchant compositions are given in Table 21.4. Solution 1 is used for organic and tin-nickel resists. Composition 2 is used for solder-plated circuits. Phosphoric acid (1 to ½% by volume) is added to eliminate the incomplete etching of copper next to the solder conductors (runoff) and to minimize solder darkening.[25]

TABLE 21.4   Composition of Persulfate Etch Solutions

	Solution 1[35,37]	Solution 2[25,35]	Solution 3[25,35]
$(NH_4)_2S_2O_8$	2 lb/gal	2 lb/gal	
$Na_2S_2O_8$			3 lb/gal
$HgCl_2$	5 ppm	5 ppm	15 ppm
Additive	1 g/gal	1 g/gal	1 g/gal
H_3PO_4		57 mL/gal	57 mL/gal

The useful capacity of the etchant is about 7 oz/gal copper at 100 to 130°F. Above 5 oz/gal of copper, it is necessary to keep the solutions at 130°F to prevent salt crystallization. The etch rate of a solution containing 7 oz/gal of dissolved copper is 0.00027 in/min at 118°F.

21.4.4.3 Batch Operation.   Composition 3 is used for batch-type spray etching.[37] Sodium persulfate is preferred because it has minimal disposal problems and somewhat higher copper capacity and etch rates. Etch rates vary throughout bath life and range from 0.0018 to 0.0006 in/min for copper content of 0 to 7 oz/gal. Prepared solutions must be aged for 16 to 72 h before etching when proprietary additives are used.

21.4.4.4 Problems with Persulfates

1. *Low etch rates:*   Since the solution may decompose, it will be necessary to replace the bath. If solution is new, add more catalyst, and check for iron contamination.

2. *Salt crystallization:* Salts crystallize on the board and cause streaks, damage the solder plate, and plug the spray nozzles or filters. When copper content is high, blue salts may precipitate.

3. *White films on solder surface:* This may occur normally, or when the lead content in the solder plate is too high.

4. *Black film on solder:* This condition can result when the solder alloy is high in tin. If solder reflow or component soldering is to follow, activate by tin immersion or with solder brighteners. Adjust phosphoric acid content in etchant and solder-plating conditions.

5. *Spontaneous decomposition of etch solution:* This breakdown is due to contaminated, overheated, or idle solutions. Ammonium persulfate etchants are unstable, especially at higher temperatures. At about 150°F, the solution decomposes quickly. Use it soon after mixing.

6. *Disposal:* The exhausted etchant consists mainly of ammonium or sodium and copper sulfate with a pH of about 2. Two methods for disposal are suggested:

    a. Electrolytic disposition of the copper on the surface of passivated 300 series stainless steel. The spent etchant is acidified with sulfuric acid prior to electrolysis. Once the copper has been removed, the remaining solution can be diluted, neutralized, checked, and discarded. The copper can be removed from the cathode. Spent sodium persulfate can be treated with caustic soda.

    b. Addition of aluminum or iron machine turnings to a slightly acidified solution is another practical but possibly more difficult means of removing the dissolved copper. The reaction, especially in the presence of chloride ions, will be violent, and considerable heat will be given off if the solutions are not diluted.

21.4.5 Ferric Chloride

Ferric chloride solutions are used as etchants for copper, copper alloys, Ni-Fe alloys, and steel in PC applications, electronics, photoengraving arts, and metal finishing. Ferric chloride is used with screen inks, photoresist, and gold patterns, but it cannot be used on tin-lead or tin-plated boards. However, ferric chloride is an attractive spray etchant because of its low cost and its high holding capacity for copper.

The composition of the etchant is mainly ferric chloride in water, with concentrations ranging from 28 to 42% by weight (see Table 21.5). Free acid is present because of the hydrolysis reaction.

$$FeCl_3 + 3H_2O \rightarrow Fe(OH)_3 + 3HCl \qquad (21.14)$$

This HCl is usually supplemented by additional amounts of HCl (up to 5%) to hold back the formation of insoluble precipitates of ferric hydroxide. Commercial formulations also

TABLE 21.5 Composition of FeCl$_3$ Solutions*

	Low strength	Optimum		High strength
Percent by weight	28	34	38	42
Specific gravity	1.275	1.353	1.402	1.450
Baumé	31.5	38	42	45
lb/gal	3.07	3.9	4.45	5.11
g/L	365	452	530	608
Molarity	2.25	2.79	3.27	3.75

* Data taken at 68 to 77°F (20 to 25°C). Photoengraving FeCl$_3$ 42° Baumé has 0.2 to 0.4% free HCl. Proprietary etchants contain up to 5% HCl.

contain wetting and antifoam agents. The effects of ferric chloride concentration, dissolved copper content, temperature, and agitation on the rate and quality of etching have been reported in the literature.[38,39] Commercial availability includes lump $FeCl_3 \cdot 6H_2O$ and aqueous solutions with and without additives. Ferric chloride with additives has the advantage of low foaming (reduced odor and fuming), fast and even etching (due partly to added strong oxidizers and surface-wetting properties), and reduced iron hydroxide precipitate formation, owing to the slight acidity and to the chelating additives. The useful life of ferric chloride etchants and uniformity of etching rates have been greatly improved by the manufacturers of proprietary solutions.

21.4.6 Chromic-Sulfuric Acids

These etchants for solder- and tin-plated boards were preferred for many years. More recently, their use has been limited drastically because of the difficulty in regeneration, inconsistent etch rate, the low limit of dissolved copper (4 to 6 oz/gal), and especially the pollution concerns. Chromic acid etchant is suitable for use with solder, tin-nickel, gold, screened vinyl lacquer, and dry or liquid film photoresists. Although chromic acid etchants are strong oxidizing agents, they do not attack the solder, since insoluble lead sulfate is formed. Undercut is seen less with solder-plated patterns than with gold and organic resists. Proprietary etchants are made with chromic and sulfuric acids. The reaction between copper and chromate is:

$$3Cu + 2HCrO_4^- + 14H^+ \rightarrow 3Cu^{2+} + 2Cr^{3+} + 8H_2O \qquad (21.15)$$

Potassium chromate and potassium dichromate are also used as starting materials. Equations (21.16) and (21.17) show the reaction with sulfuric acid to produce the hexavalent Cr^{6+} oxidizing agent.

$$K_2CrO_4 + H_2SO_4 \rightarrow K_2SO_4 + H_2CrO_4 \qquad (21.16)$$

$$K_2Cr_2O_7 + H_2SO_4 + H_2O \rightarrow K_2SO_4 + 2H_2CrO_4 \qquad (21.17)$$

Compositions of chromic acid etchants are given in Table 21.6. Sulfuric acid is normally used as the source of hydrogen ions. Concentrations of 10 to 13% by volume are used to achieve optimum etchants[42] and maximum holding capacity for copper. The use of other acids has been successful. Nitric acid increases the etch rate but causes attack on the solder plate, phosphoric acid decreases the etch rate, acid fluorides attach titnanium etcher parts and solder, and organic acids are decomposed by chromates. Hydrochloric acid must not be added to this etchant because of toxic chlorine gas[10] formation:

$$2HCrO_4^- + 6Cl^- + 14H^+ \rightarrow 2Cr^{3+} + 3Cl_2 + 8H_2O \qquad (21.18)$$

TABLE 21.6 Composition of Chromic-Sulfuric Acid Etch Solutions*

	Formulation 1[40]	Formulation 2[41]
CrO_3	240 g/L	480 g/L
Na_2SO_4	40.5 g/L	
H_2SO_4 (96%)	180 g/L	31 mL/L
Copper		4.9 g/L

* Proprietary agents contain wetting, antifoaming, and chelating agents, and catalysts.

Chromic-sulfuric mixtures etch copper slowly, and additives are needed to increase the etch rate. For example, sodium sulfate is used in formulation 1 of Table 21.6, and iodine compounds are used in formulation 2.[43]

21.4.6.1   Properties and Control.   Increases in temperature and agitation generally increase the etch rate. However, air agitation of tank solutions results in a much slower etch rate than other methods such as vibration, spray, or splash etching. In addition, air produces a mist or spray which is toxic. These fumes are very corrosive and contaminate plating solutions. Proprietary solutions contain antimisting agents.

A hydrometer is used to control the Baumé value of the solution. The density should be maintained at 30° Baumé at 68°F, and 28° Baumé at 80°F. Water is used to decrease high Baumé solutions. Colorimetric standards made up by adding known quantities of copper to fresh 30° Baumé etchant are used to estimate copper content.

21.4.6.2   Regeneration.   Commercial systems for regeneration of chromic-sulfuric acids are not in common use because of the corrosive nature of the products, the handling hazards, and the pollution restrictions. Other methods in use include electrolytic deposition of copper[42] and electrodialysis.[44]

21.4.6.3   Problems with Chromic-Sulfuric Acid Systems

1. *Solder attack:*   The protective value of solder depends on the formation of insoluble compounds on the surface. Solder is attacked if the sulfate content of the bath becomes very low or contains chloride or nitrates. The solder plate composition can also cause etchant attack. When the lead content becomes low, the sulfate film protection is lowered, and protection is lost.

2. *Slow or no etching of copper:*   This can be caused by low chromic content, low temperature, insufficient acid, or high copper content. The solution is maintained as close as possible to 30° Baumé (pH about 0.1, temperature 80 to 90°F) and should be discarded when copper metal content exceeds 5.5 oz/gal.

3. *Staining of board materials:*   The surfaces of dielectric substrates such as paper-based phenolics are attacked by chromic acid etchants. Removal is difficult, and the boards are generally rejected.

4. *Disposal:*   Spent chromic acid etchants present a serious disposal problem. Disposal must comply with pollution standards and approved practice.

5. *Safety hazards:*   Chromic acid is an extremely strong oxidizing agent. It will attack clothing, rubber, plastics, and many metals. Safety measures require adequate ventilation to keep fumes out of room air, synthetic rubber gloves, aprons, face and eye shields, and storage away from combustible materials. Dermatitis and nasal membrane damage are possible dangers.[10]

21.4.7   Nitric Acid

Etchant systems based on nitric acid have not found extensive application in PC manufacture. Copper etching is very exothermic, which may lead to violent runaway reactions. Problems with this system include solution control, attack on resists and substrates, and toxic gas fuming. However, nitric acid has certain advantages. These include rapid etching, high dissolved copper capacity, high solubility of nonsludging products, availability, and low cost.

21.4.7.1   Chemistry.   Reaction in strong acids is shown by the following equation:

$$3Cu + 2NO_3^- + 4H^+ \rightarrow 3Cu^{2+} + 2NO_2 + 2H_2O \qquad (21.19)$$

Recent work shows that process improvements are possible.[45,46] Controlled etching has been attained in solutions containing 30% copper nitrate, water-soluble polymers, and surfactants. Dry film resists work well in this etchant. An important finding was that straight wall trace edges were achieved using nitric. This could result in higher yields and density of fineline boards.

21.5 OTHER MATERIALS FOR BOARD CONSTRUCTION

Printed board laminates are usually composed of copper bonded to organic dielectric materials, to ceramics, or to other metals.

1. *Organic dielectrics:* These are thermosetting or thermoplastic resins usually combined with a selected reinforcing filler. *Thermoset*-reinforced materials used for rigid and flexible boards provide overall stability, chemical resistance, and good dielectric properties. *Thermoplastic* materials are also used for flexible circuit applications. A factor in material selection is the effect of process solutions, etchants, and solvents on the material. In addition, the adhesives used in laminating metal to substrate can be softened, loosened, and attacked by some solutions.

2. *Thin-clad copper:* Etched printed boards with epoxy laminate of ¼-oz copper or less show minimal overhang and slivers.

3. *Semiadditive copper:* A copper thickness of 0.000050 to 0.000200 in with subsequent copper and resist metal plating shows no overhang or sliver formation.

21.6 METALS OTHER THAN COPPER

21.6.1 Aluminum

Aluminum-clad flexible circuits find use in microwave stripline[47] and radiation-resistance applications. Aluminum and its alloys have good electrical conductivity, are lightweight, and can be plated, soldered, brazed, chem-milled, and anodized with good results. Laminate dielectrics include PPO,[47] polyimide,[48] epoxy-glass, and polyester.

Precleaning for resist application includes nonetch alkaline soak, water rinsing for 5 to 10 s in chromic-sulfuric acid, rinsing, and drying. Preferred etchants include ferric chloride (12 to 18° Baumé), sodium hydroxide (5 to 10%), inhibited hydrochloric acid, phosphoric acid mixtures, solutions of HCl and HF, and ferric chloride-hydrochloric acid mixture.

Screen-printed vinyl resists and dry film photoresist are the most durable for deep etching or chem-milling. A dip in a 10% nitric or chromic acid solution will remove residues from the surface or edges of conductor lines which may be left on some alloys. Dilute chromic acid has also been used for this purpose. Spray-rinse thoroughly with deionized water after etching.

21.6.2 Nickel and Nickel-Based Alloys

Nickel is increasingly used as a metal cladding, electroplated deposit or electroformed structure for printed wiring because of its welding properties. Nichrome- and nickel-based magnetic alloys are other examples of materials requiring special etching techniques.

The methods previously described are adaptable to image transfer and etching of nickel-base materials. Etching uses ferric chloride, 42° Baumé, at about 100°F. Other etchants include solutions made from one part nitric acid, one part hydrochloric, and three parts water, or one part nitric, four parts hydrochloric, and one part water.

21.6.3 Stainless Steel

Alloys of stainless steel are used for resistive elements or for materials with high tensile strength. Etching of the common 300 to 400 series can be done with the following solutions:

1. Ferric chloride (38 to 42° Baumé) with 3% HCl (optional).
2. One part HCl (37%) by volume, one part nitric acid (70%) by volume, one to three parts water by volume. Etch rate is about 0.003 in/min at 175°F, useful for high 300 to 400 series alloys.
3. Ferric chloride + nitric acid solutions.
4. One hundred parts HCl (37%) by weight, 6.5 parts nitric acid by weight, 100 parts water by weight.

21.6.4 Silver

Silver, the least expensive precious metal, has excellent properties, including superior electrical and thermal conductivity, ductility, visible-light reflectivity, high melting point, and adequate chemical resistance. As such, it is widely used throughout the electronics industry. Flexible circuit structures with silver are used in electronic cameras and LED products.

Standard image-transfer methods are suitable. Pre-etch cleaning should include a dip in dilute nitric acid. Mixtures of nitric and sulfuric acids are effective etchants. With silver on brass or copper substrates, a mixture of 1 part nitric acid (70%) and 19 parts sulfuric acid (96%) will dissolve the silver without adversely attacking the substrate. The solutions should be changed frequently to prevent water absorption and the formation of immersion silver on the copper.

Etching can be done with a solution containing 40 g chromic acid, 20 mL sulfuric acid (96%), and 2000 mL water.[49] This is followed by a rinse in 25% ammonium hydroxide. Thin films of silver are etched in 55% (by weight) ferric nitrate in water or ethylene glycol. Solutions of alkaline cyanide and hydrogen peroxide will also dissolve silver. Use extreme caution. Electrolytic etching is also possible with 15% nitric acid at 2 V and a stainless-steel cathode.

21.7 UNDERCUT, ETCH FACTOR, AND OVERHANG

During etching, as the depth of etch proceeds vertically, the sidewalls tend to etch sideways and produce an undercut action. The degree to which this occurs is known as the *etch factor*, defined as the ratio of depth to side attack (see Fig. 21.4). In practice, controlled spray etching vertical to the copper surfaces with selected etchants leads to high etch factors. Immersion etching generally results in low etch factors. Fineline etching with a minimum of undercut is best achieved with copper foil of ½ oz or less and is carried out by removing the board from the etching machine exactly at the time of completion, using fineline etchants. Compensation for line-width reduction and undercutting should be designed into the artwork, especially for panel-plated boards, thick metal cladding, and dense, fineline inner- and outerlayer patterns. The etch factor can be minimized on metal parts by resist patterning and then etching both sides at once.

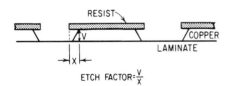

FIGURE 21.4 Etch factor in printed board etching.

Undercut and overhang for resists are shown in Fig. 21.5. Excess overhang may fall loose as metallic slivers and cause electrical shorting, and thus they present reliability problems.

After etching, removal requires soft-brass brushing, ultrasonic agitation and rinsing, or fusion in the case of solder-plated resists.

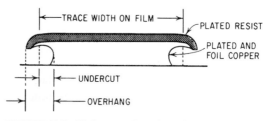

FIGURE 21.5   Undercut and overhang for a plated-metal-resist pattern.

21.8   EQUIPMENT AND TECHNIQUES

Etching techniques and the equipment used today have evolved from four basic etching methods: immersion, bubble, splash (paddle), and spray etching. Spray etching is the most common method, since it is fast, well suited to high production, and capable of very fine line definition.

21.8.1   Spray Etching

Spray techniques include single- and double-sided etching with either horizontal or vertical positioning of the boards. These techniques yield high etch factors and short etching times, due in part to high solution controls and to the introduction of high quantities of air.[50-53] As in all etching procedures, however, the highest definition (fineline patterns) or the use of thicker copper foils requires control of the undercutting by careful selection of equipment and etchants.

Spray-etching machines have evolved simultaneously with the availability of chemical-resistant metals and plastics essential to their construction (PVC and titanium alloys). Titanium is suitable for constant use in all common etchants except sulfuric acid-hydrogen peroxide, which requires stainless steel materials. Polycarbonate, polypropylene, and Hastelloy C alloys are also used.

21.8.1.1   Automatic Vertical Etching.   This type of machine is designed for higher production rates. A mechanism carries a loaded rack through the etch chamber, where it is sprayed on one or both sides by oscillating banks of spray nozzles. The rack goes through water (spray-rinse) and neutralizing chambers. Cooling coils are available for sulfuric-peroxide etchants. Control of pressure to each bank of spray nozzles and on-off valves provide additional versatility.

The etchant sump has a larger volume of etchant than drawer-type vertical etchers, as well as a capability for continuous replenishment.

Fineline etching is attainable when spray nozzles, pressure, speed, and other variables are working optimally.

21.8.1.2   Horizontal Etching.   Double-sided horizontal etchers are generally preferred in PC manufacturing, since the majority of the boards are two-sided. The etcher is available with a drawer-type holding rack and also has a built-in sink at the left of the chamber. The etch operation proceeds and automatically pushes the rack into the rinse area after a timed cycle. Etching is done from independently controlled spray-nozzle banks at the top and bottom. Desirable features in horizontal etching machines include the following:

1. Double-sided etch capability.

2. Single-side (face-down) etching for very fine line work.

3. Built-in rinse area and automatic control; top and bottom water spray which flushes both sides at once and avoids drying of etchant on board and overetching. Handling is eliminated.

4. Sealed-in etch chamber, preferred because it requires no venting even when heated to 100°F.

5. Automatic cooling coils that prevent overheating and maintain constant temperature (for sulfuric acid-hydrogen peroxide and persulfate).

6. Independent gauges, pressure valves, and switching that allow compensation for differences between top and bottom etching.

7. Oscillating action and a large number of spray nozzles that result in even etching over the entire area.

8. Built-in transfer pump with intake going into the etchant sump and output into rinse tank, allowing for filling or emptying without spillage, damage, or hazard. The pump should be electrically reversible for both filling and emptying.

9. Minute- and second-timer switches for careful control of etch time.

10. Titanium heaters that withstand shock cracking.

11. Filters at intake side of spray pumps that prevent solids from damaging or clogging pump and spray nozzles.

12. Screen insert tray for placing thin metal sheet prior to etching. Two screens are sometimes desired.

21.8.1.3 Automatic Horizontal Etching Machines. Made for high-volume production, these machines incorporate the features previously listed for horizontal machines, plus the advantages of conveyorized loading and handling of boards up to 36 in wide and indefinite length, as well as built-in rinsing and neutralizing. In operation, machines are loaded by laying boards flat on an open horizontal conveyor belt which carries them progressively through the etch chamber and subsequent rinses. Rollers on conveyor belts are spaced so as to allow the bottom spray to reach the board. Automatic equipment is available for flow-through solution replenishment, which gives constant etch rates (see Fig. 21.6).

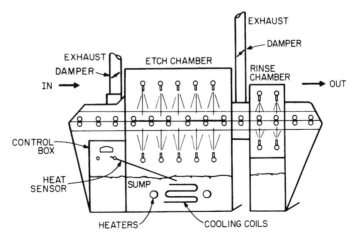

FIGURE 21.6 Horizontal conveyorized spray etcher design.

REFERENCES

1. E. Armstrong and E. F. Duffek, *Electronic Packaging and Production,* vol. 14, no. 10, October 1974, pp. 125–130.
2. W. Chaikin, C. E. McClelland, J. Janney, and S. Landsman, *Ind. Eng. Chem.,* vol. 51, 1959, pp. 305–308.
3. L. Fullwood, *Proceedings of the California Circuits Association Symposium,* San Francisco, May 1971.
4. S. Deforest, *Photoresist Materials and Processes,* McGraw-Hill, New York, 1975.
5. J. Slominski, U.S. Patent 3,466,208, 1969.
6. J. Sykes, E. Papaconstantinou, and K. Murski, U.S. Patent 3,868,485, February 1975.
7. G. Poor and G. F. Hau, U.S. Patent 3,753,818, August 1973.
8. E. Laue, U.S. Patent 3,231,503, 1966.
9. E. King, U.S. Patent 3,705,061, 1972.
10. I. Sax, *Dangerous Properties of Industrial Materials,* rev. ed., Reinhold Publishing Corp., New York, 1957, p. 464.
11. W. Spinney, U.S. Patent 3,440,036, 1966.
12. *Solvent Extraction Technology,* Center for Professional Advancement, Somerville, N.J., 1975.
13. Galvano Organo, *Printed Circuit Fabrication,* vol. 16, no. 1, Jan. 1993, pp. 42–47.
14. Atotech USA, Inc., State College, Pa.
15. K. Murski and P. M. Wible, "Problem-Solving Processes for Resist Developing, Stripping, and Etching," *Insulation/Circuits,* February 1981.
16. F. Good, "Surface Preparation of Circuit Boards for Plating—A New Approach," *Proceeding of the 1975 Spring Meeting of the Institute of Printed Circuits, Inc.,* Washington, D.C., 1975.
17. A. Luke, *Printed Circuit Fabrication,* vol. 8, no. 10, October 1985, pp. 63–76.
18. W. Kear, *Proceedings of the California Circuits Association,* Newport Beach, October 1979, pp. 20–26.
19. Shipley Company, *Printed Circuit Fabrication,* vol. 5, no. 2, February 1982, pp. 79–83.
20. G. Steger, *Printed Circuit Fabrication,* vol. 6, no. 10, January 1983, pp. 33–387.
21. Tate, *Printed Circuit Fabrication,* vol. 7, no. 4, April 1984, pp. 22–30.
22. U.S. Patent 4,130,454, B. Dutkewych, C. Gaputis, and M. Gulla, 1978.
23. U.S. Patent 3,801,512, C. Solenberger, 1974.
24. U.S. Patent 4,130,455, L. Elias and M. F. Good, 1978.
25. U.S. Patent 3,476,624, J. Hogya and W. J. Tillis, 1969.
26. C. Swartzell, *Printed Circuit Fabrication,* vol. 5, no. 1, January 1982, pp. 42–47, 65.
27. G. Parikh, E. C. Gayer, and W. Willard, *Western Electric Engineer,* vol. XVI, no. 2, April 1972, pp. 2–8; *Metal Finishing,* March 1972, pp. 42, 43.
28. L. Missel and F. D. Murphy, *Metal Finishing,* December 1969, pp. 47–52, 58.
29. F. Gorman, "Regenerative Cupric Chloride Copper Etchant," *Proceedings of the California Circuits Association Meeting,* 1973; *Electronic Packaging and Production,* January 1974, pp. 43–46.
30. U.S. Patent 3,306,792, W. Thurmal, 1963.
31. L. H. Sharpe and P. D. Garn, *Ind. Eng. Chem.,* Vol. 51, 1959, pp. 293–298.
32. J. O. E. Clark, *Marconi Rev.,* vol. 24, no. 142, 1961, pp. 134–152.
33. O. D. Black and L. H. Cutler, *Ind. Eng. Chem.,* vol. 50, 1958, pp. 1539–1540.
34. Anonymous, *Circuits Manufacturing Magazine,* April 1972, pp. 55–57.
35. *Etching Metals with Ammonium Persulfate,* Food Machinery and Chemical Corporation, Princeton, N.J. See also *Tech. Bulletins III,* 52, 54, 55; *112,* 4, 29, 1, 35.
36. *Ibid., Tech. Bulletin 110.*
37. U.S. Patent 2,978,301, P. A. Margulies and J. E. Kressbach, 1961.
38. E. B. Saubestre, *Ind. Eng. Chem.,* vol. 51, 1959, pp. 288–290.

39. W. F. Nekervis, *The Use of Ferric Chloride in the Etching of Copper,* Dow Chemical Co., Midland, Mich., 1962.

40. T. D. Schlabach and B. A. Diggory, *Electrochem. Tech.,* vol. 2, 1964, pp. 118–121.

41. Anonymous, *Photoengravers Bull.,* vol. 36, no. 11, 1947, pp. 19–24.

42. S. Gowri, K. S. Indira, and B. T. Shemol, *Metal Finishing,* vol. 64, 1966, pp. 54–59.

43. U.S. Patent 3,322,673, L. J. Slominski, 1967.

44. F. Steward, *Proceedings of the California Circuits Association Symposium,* San Francisco, October 1974.

45. U.S. Patent 4,482,425, J. F. Battey, 1984.

46. U.S. Patent 4,497,687, N. J. Nelson, 1985.

47. F. T. Mansur and R. G. Autiello, *Insulation,* March 1968, pp. 58–61.

48. H. R. Johnson and J. W. Dini, *Insulation,* August 1975, p. 31.

49. P. F. Kury, *J. Electrochem. Soc.,* vol. 103, 1956, p. 257.

50. R. W. Lay, *Electronic Packaging and Production,* March 1982, pp. 65–83.

51. D. Ball and R. Markle, *Electronic Packaging and Production,* June 1983, pp. 74–76.

52. R. Keeler, *Electronic Packaging and Production,* November 1983, pp. 126–132.

53. H. Markstein, *Electronic Packaging and Production,* February 1985, pp. 168–171.

CHAPTER 22
MACHINING AND ROUTING

James Cadile
NOVA Drilling Service Inc., Santa Clara, California

Leland E. Tull
Contouring Technology, Mountain View, California

Charles G. Henningsen
Insulectro, Mountain View, California

22.1 INTRODUCTION

Laminate machining consists of the mechanical processes by which circuit boards are prepared for the vital chemical processes of image transfer, plating, and etching. Such processes as cutting to size, drilling holes, and shaping have major effects on the final quality of the printed board. This chapter will discuss the basic mechanical processes which are essential to producing the finished board.

22.2 PUNCHING HOLES (PIERCING)

22.2.1 Design of the Die

It is possible to pierce holes down to one-half the thickness of XXXPC and FR-2 laminates and one-third that of FR-3 (Fig. 22.1). Many die designers lose sight of the fact that the force required to withdraw piercing punches is of the same magnitude as that required to push the punches through the material. For that reason, the question of how much stripper-spring pressure to design into a die is answered by most toolmakers: "as much as possible." When space on the dies cannot accommodate enough mechanical springs to do the job, a hydraulic mechanism can be used. Springs should be so located that the part is stripped evenly. If the board is ejected from the die unevenly, cracks around holes are almost certain to occur. Best-quality holes are produced when the stripper compresses the board an instant before the perforators start to penetrate. If the stripper pressure can be made to approach the compressive strength of the material, less force will be required and the holes will be cleaner.

If excessive breakage of small punches occurs, determine whether the punch breaks on the perforating stroke or on withdrawal. If the retainer lock is breaking, the cause is almost certain to be withdrawal strain. The remedy is to grind a small taper on the punch, no more than

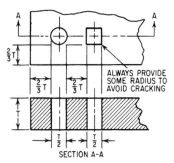

FIGURE 22.1 Illustration of the proper sizing and locating of pierced holes with respect to one another and to the edge of paper laminates. Minimum dimensions are given as multiples of laminate thickness *t*.

1½ in and to a distance no greater than the thickness of the material being punched. If the grinding is kept within those limits, it will have no measurable effect on hole quality or size. The other two causes of punch breakage are poor alignment, which is easily detected by close examination of the tool, and poor design, which usually means that the punch is too small to do the job required.

22.2.2 Shrinkage of Paper-Base Laminates

When paper-base laminates are to be punched, it must be remembered that the materials are resilient and that their tendency to spring back will result in a hole slightly smaller than the punch which produced the hole. The difference in size will depend on the thickness of the material. Table 22.1 shows the amount by which the punch should exceed the print size in order to make the holes within tolerance. The values listed should not be used for the design of tools for glass-epoxy laminates, the shrinkage of which is only about one-third that of paper-base materials.

TABLE 22.1 Shrinkage in Punched Hole Diameters, Paper-Base Laminates

Material thickness	Material at room temp.	Material at 90°F or above
¹⁄₆₄	0.001	0.002
¹⁄₃₂	0.002	0.003
³⁄₆₄	0.003	0.005
¹⁄₁₆	0.004	0.007
³⁄₃₂	0.006	0.010
⅛	0.010	0.013

22.2.3 Tolerance of Punched Holes

If precise hole size tolerance is required, the clearance between punch and die should be very close; the die hole should be only 0.002 to 0.004 in larger than the punch for paper-base materials (Fig. 22.2 and Table 22.2). Glass-base laminates generally require about one-half that tolerance. Dies have, however, been constructed with as much as 0.010 all-around clearance between punch and die. They are for use where inspection standards permit rough-quality holes.

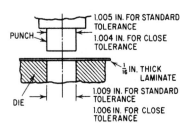

FIGURE 22.2 Example of proper tolerance of a punch and die.

A die with sloppy clearances is less expensive than one built for precision work, and wide clearance between punch and die causes correspondingly more break and less shear than a tight die will cause. The result is a hole with a slight funnel shape that makes insertion of components easier. Always pierce with the copper side up. Do not use piercing on designs with circuitry on both sides of the board, because lifting of pads would probably occur.

TABLE 22.2   Tolerances for Punching or Blanking Paper-Base Laminate

Material thickness	Base material	Tolerance on hole size, in	Tolerances, in, on distance between holes and slots, 90°F				Tolerances for blanked parts, overall dimension, in
			Up to 2 in	2 to 3 in	3 to 4 in	4 to 5 in	
To and including ¹⁄₁₆ in	Paper	0.0015	0.003	0.004	0.005	0.006	0.003
Over ¹⁄₁₆ in to and including ³⁄₃₂ in	Paper	0.003	0.005	0.006	0.007	0.008	0.005
Over ³⁄₃₂ in to and including ¹⁄₈ in	Paper	0.005	0.006	0.007	0.008	0.009	0.008

22.2.4   Hole Location and Size

Designs having holes whose distance from the edge of the board or from other holes approaches the thickness of the material are apt to be troublesome. Such designs should be avoided; but when distances between holes must be small, build the best die possible. Use tight clearance between punch and die and punch and stripper, and have the stripper apply plenty of pressure to the work before the punch starts to enter. If the distance between holes is too small, cracks between holes may result even with the best of tools. If cracks between holes prove troublesome, plan the process so that the piercing is done before any copper is etched away. The reinforcing effect of the copper foil will help eliminate cracks. Most glass-epoxy laminates may be pierced, but the finish on the inside of the holes is sometimes not suitable for through-hole plating.

22.2.5   Warming Paper-Base Material

The process of punching paper-base laminates will often be much more trouble-free if the parts are warmed to 90 or 100°F. That is true even of the so-called cold-punch or PC grades. Do not overheat the material to the point at which it crumbles and the residue is not ejected as a discrete slug. Overheated material will often plug the holes in the die and cause rejects. Opening the taper on the takeaway holes will reduce plugging, but the most direct approach is to pierce at a lower temperature. Glass-epoxy is never heated for piercing or blanking.

22.2.6   Press Size

The size of the press is determined by the amount of work the press must do on each stroke. The supplier of copper-clad sheets can specify a value for the shear strength of the material being used. Typically, the value will be about 12,000 lb/in^2 for paper-base laminate and 20,000 lb/in^2 for glass-epoxy laminate. The total circumference of the parts being punched out multiplied by the thickness of the sheet gives the area being sheared by the die. If all dimensions are in inches, the value will be in square inches. For example, a die piercing 50 round holes, each 0.100 in in diameter, in 0.062-in-thick laminate will be shearing, in square inches:

$$50 \times 0.100 \text{ in} \times 3.1416 \times 0.062 \text{ in} = 0.974 \text{ in}^2$$

If the paper-base laminate has 12,000-lb/in^2 shear strength, 11,688 lb of pressure, or about 6 tons, is required just to drive the punches through the laminate. Bear in mind that, if a spring-loaded stripper is used, the press will also have to overcome the spring pressure, which ought to be at least as great as the shear strength. Therefore, a 12-ton press would be the minimum which could be considered. A 15- or 20-ton press would be considerably safer.

22.3 BLANKING, SHEARING, AND CUTTING OF COPPER-CLAD LAMINATES

22.3.1 Blanking Paper-Base Laminates

When parts are designed to have shapes other than rectangular and the volume is great enough to justify the expense of building a die, the parts are frequently punched from sheets by using a blanking die. A blanking operation is well adapted to paper-base materials and is sometimes used on glass-base ones.

In the design of a blanking die for paper-base laminates, the resilience, or yield, of the material previously discussed under Piercing applies. The blanked part will be slightly larger than the die which produced it, and dies are therefore made just a little under print size depending on the material thickness. Sometimes a combination pierce and blank die is used. The die pierces holes and also blanks out the finished part.

When the configuration is very complex, the designer may recommend a multiple-stage die: The strip of material progresses from one stage to the next with each stroke of the die. Usually in the first one or two stages, holes are pierced, and in the final stage, the completed part is blanked out.

The quality of a part produced from paper-base laminates by shearing, piercing, or blanking can be improved by performing the operation on material which has been warmed. Caution should be exercised in heating over 100°F because the coefficient of thermal expansion may be high enough to cause the part to shrink out of tolerance on cooling. Paper-base laminates are particularly anisotropic with respect to thermal expansion; that is, they expand differently in the x and y dimensions. The manufacturer's data on coefficient of expansion should be consulted before a die for close-tolerance parts is designed. Keep in mind that the precision of the manufacturer's data is probably no better than ±25 percent.

22.3.2 Blanking Glass-Base Laminates

Odd shapes that cannot be feasibly produced by shearing or sawing are either blanked or routed. Glass blanking is always done at room temperature. Assuming a close fit between punch and die, the part will be about 0.001 in larger than the die which produced it. The tools are always so constructed that a part is removed from the die as it is made. It cannot be pushed out by a following part, as is often true when the material has a paper base. If material thicker than 0.062 in is blanked, the parts may have a rough edge.

The life of a punch, pierce, or blank die should be evaluated with reference to the various copper-clad materials that may be used. One way to evaluate die wear caused by various materials is to weigh the perforators, or punches, very accurately, punch 5000 pieces, and then reweigh the punches. Approximately 5000 hits are necessary for evaluation, because the initial break-in period of the die will show a higher rate of wear. Also, of course, the quality of the holes at the beginning and end of each test must be evaluated. Greatly enlarged microphotos of the perforator can be used for visual evaluation of changes in the die.

22.3.3 Shearing

When copper-clad laminates are to be sheared, the shear should be set with only 0.001 to 0.002 in clearance between the square-ground blades (Fig. 22.3). The thicker the material to be cut, the greater the rake or scissor angle between the top and bottom shear blade. The converse also is true: The thinner the material, the smaller the rake angle and the closer the blades. Hence, as in many metal shears, the rake angle and the blade gap are fixed; the cutoff piece can be twisted or curled. Paper-base material can also exhibit feathered cracks along the edge that are due to too wide a gap or too high a shear angle. That can be minimized by supporting both piece and cutoff piece during the shear operation and decreasing the rake angle. Epoxy-glass laminate, because of its flexural strength, does not usually crack, but the material can be deformed if the blade clearance is too great or the shear angle is too large. As in blanking, the quality of a part produced from paper-base laminates by shearing can be improved by warming the material before performing the operation.

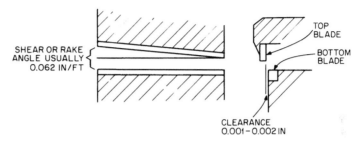

FIGURE 22.3 Typical adjustable shear blades for copper-clad laminates.

22.3.4 Sawing Paper-Base Laminates

Paper-base laminates are much harder on sawing tools than are the hardest woods, and therefore a few special precautions are necessary for good saw life. Sawing paper-base laminates is best accomplished with a circular saw with 10 to 12 teeth per inch of diameter at 7500 or 10,000 ft/min. Hollow-ground saws give a smoother cut; and because of the abrasive nature of laminated materials, carbide teeth are an excellent investment. (See Fig. 22.4 for tooth shape.)

When a saw does not last long enough between sharpenings, use the following checklist. (These steps could have a cumulative effect and change saw life by a factor of 4 to 5.)

1. Check the bearings for tightness. There should be no perceptible play in them.
2. Check the blade for runout. As much as 0.005 in can be significant.
3. When carbide teeth are used, inspect them with a magnifying glass to make sure a diamond tool no coarser than 180 grit was used in sharpening them.
4. If the saw has a thin blade, use a stiffening collar to reduce vibration.
5. Use heavy pulleys with more than one V belt. Rotating parts of the system should have sufficient momentum to carry the sawtooth through the work smoothly and without variation of speed.
6. Check the alignment of the arbor and the motor mounting.

All these steps are intended to reduce or eliminate vibration, which is the greatest enemy of the saw blade. If vibration is noticed, find the source and correct it.

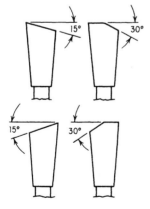

FIGURE 22.4 Commonly used sawtooth designs for paper and cloth laminates. At left, two successive teeth on a 15° alternate-bevel saw. At right, two successive teeth on a 30-ft alternate-corner-relieved (AC-30) saw.

22.3.5 Sawing Glass-Base Laminates

When glass-base laminates are to be sawn, carbide-tooth circular saws can be used; but unless the volume of work is quite low, the added investment required for diamond-steel-bonded saws will be paid for in future savings. The manufacturer's recommendation of saw speed should be followed; usually it will be for a speed in the neighborhood of 15,000 ft/min at the periphery of the saw blade. When economics dictate the use of carbide-tooth circular saws for cutting glass, use the instruction previously given for paper-base laminates (see Fig. 22.4 for tooth shape) and remember that each caution regarding runout, vibration, and alignment becomes more important when glass-reinforced laminates are sawn.

22.4 ROUTING

Modern circuit board fabricators rely principally on routing to perform profiling operations. The high cost and extended lead times for blanking dies, combined with the problem of design inflexibility of hard tooling, limit the punching operation generally to very high volumes or designs specific to die applications. Shearing or sawing are limited to rectangular shapes and generally are not accurate enough for most board applications.

In the modern circuit board fabrication industry, rapid response to customer lead times and economies of universal process application are well served by routing, especially multiple-spindle *computer numerically controlled* (CNC) routing

Routing consists of two similar, yet vastly different fabrication processes:

1. CNC multiple-spindle routing
2. Manual pin routing

The similarities consist of the use of high-speed spindles, utilizing carbide cutting tools, and generating high cutting rates.

22.4.1 Pin Routing

Pin routing is a manual routing process utilizing a template which has been machined of aluminum, FR-4 laminate, or a fiber-reinforced phenolic. The template is made to the finished board dimensions and has tooling pins installed to register to the board's tooling holes. The package (which can have up to four pieces in a stack) is routed by tracking the template against a pilot pin protruding from the router table. The pin height is less than the template thickness. Usually, the machine pilot pin is the same diameter as the router bit and can be offset adjusted to give the operator flexibility in optimizing dimensions. Work should be fed against the rotation of the cutter to prevent the cutter from grabbing.

Pin routing can be an economical process when a small generation of boards is profiled, or if the shapes required are relatively simple. For pin routing to be effective, generally a very skilled operator is required to fabricate the template and to route the boards. Outside machine shops can build aluminum route fixtures for each customer application; however, lead times and costs per order must be considered. Pin routing is usually used by small shops not able to invest in the CNC equipment and its associated support, or as a specialty process, off-line from CNC routing.

In the best pin-routing operations, the volumes produced cannot be compared with multiple-spindle routing.

22.4.2 CNC Routing Applications

The applications of NC routing extend well beyond merely cutting board profiles. The ability to produce boards in multiple-image modules reduces handling, not only in the board shop, but in every subsequent operation from packing, component assembly, wave solder, and test. This is of special value when dealing with a postage-stamp-size part or wire-bondable gold surfaces. Where handling must be minimized, the module acts as a pallet throughout these operations. In addition, unusual or irregular shapes, small or large, can be palletized to simplify handling and conveyance. In Fig. 22.5, examples of tab-routed, or multiple-image, modules are shown.

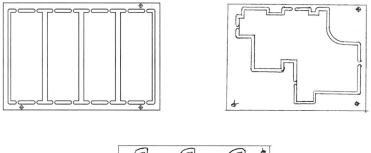

FIGURE 22.5   Examples of tab-routed, or multiple-image, modules.

In Fig. 22.6, each part is shown attached to the frame with breakable or removable tabs and can include features permitting tab removal below the board edge of the image periphery. Note on Fig. 22.6 the use of a score line to ease tab removal. Scoring, alone or in concert with routing (as discussed in Sec. 22.5) can play a large role in board and pallet separation.

Beyond multiple-image palletization, as shown in Fig. 22.7, CNC routing can provide a variety of board requirements including:

1. Internal cutouts
2. Slots
3. Counterbores
4. Board edge conditioning for plating

There are many benefits available through CNC routing beyond those of efficient part profiling. A little planning before the release to production can improve manufacturability as well as provide many no-cost benefits to assembly, soldering, etc.

22.4.3   Computer Numerical Controlled (CNC) Operation

CNC router equipment has the ability to process high volumes of circuit boards very accurately and economically, yet it is coupled with features to enable quick program and setup. This coupling enables the same processing used for high volume to be utilized for prototypes and short-lead-time production.

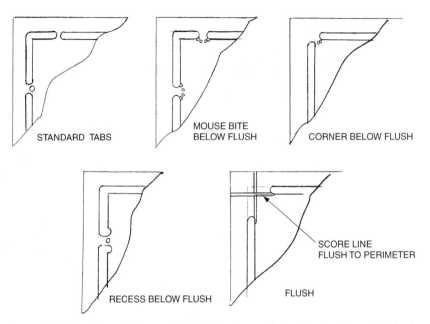

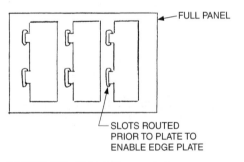

FIGURE 22.6 Each part is shown attached to the frame with breakable or removable tabs. A variety of breakable tabs is shown. Also shown is a score line for ease of tab removal.

FIGURE 22.7 Multiple-image palletization.

With circuit board data files so universally available, the part programming time has dropped to a few minutes, as opposed to the hours it once took, while setups remain at about 15 to 20 minutes, plus cutter labyrinth and first article routing.

Router operation consists of multiple spindles (2 to 5), capable of operating from 6,000 to 36,000 r/min, or more. The router path (x-y table movement and spindle plunge and retract) is determined by program. This permits any number of paths and any location.

The preferred method of registration of the panel to the machine table is to use the full panel and the tooling holes previously drilled. Tooling holes internal to the part provide for the highest accuracy, although manufacturing panel tooling may be used if considered earlier in the process.

22.4.4 Cutter Offset

Since the cutter must follow a path described by its centerline, it must be offset from the desired board edge by an amount equal to its effective radius. This is the basic cutter radius, and it will vary with the cutter tooth form. Most newer-generation equipment will automatically adjust for the cutter radius. However, either manually or automatically, this is a basic element of routing planning. Since the cutters deflect during the routing operation, it is necessary to determine the amount of deflection to be added to the basic cutter radius before expending large amounts on programming parts (Fig. 22.8). Cutter compensation values can be varied.

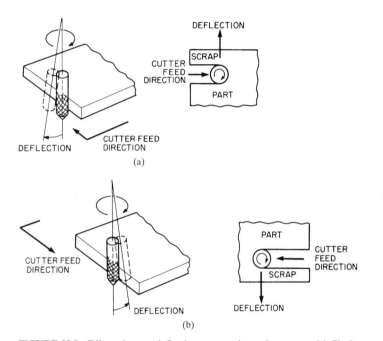

FIGURE 22.8 Effect of cutter deflection on part size and geometry. (*a*) Clockwise cutting (recommended for outside cuts) deflects cutter away from part. That leaves outside dimensions large on first pass unless compensated for in programming. (*b*) Counterclockwise cutting (recommended for inside cuts and pockets) deflects cutter into scrap. Therefore, inside dimensions of holes or cutouts will measure small unless compensated for in programming.

Variables which affect deflection are thickness, type of material, direction of cut, feed rate, and spindle speed. To reduce those variables, the manufacturer should:

1. Standardize on cutter bit manufacturer, selected diameters, tooth form, and end cut.
2. Fix spindle speed (24,000 r/min recommended for epoxy-glass laminates).
3. Rout in clockwise direction on outside cuts, counterclockwise on inside cuts.
4. Standardize on single or double pass.
5. Fix feed rates for given materials. (Note that higher rates will increase part size and slower feed rates will decrease part size.)
6. Develop documented process controls after experimenting with varied parameters.

22.4.5   Direction of Cut

A counterclockwise direction of feed (climb-out) will leave outside corners with slight projections and inside corners with small radii. A clockwise direction of feed (rake cut) will give outside corners a slight radius, and perhaps give inside corners a slight indentation. These irregularities may be minimized by reducing the feed rate or cutting the part twice.

22.4.6   Cutter Speed and Feed Rate

The variables affecting cutter speed are usually limited to the type of laminate being cut and the linear feed rate of the cutter. A cutter rotation of 24,000 r/min and feed rates up to 150 in/in may be used effectively on most laminates, although cutter feed direction may require a lower feed rate. Teflon-glass and similar materials, the laminate binder of which flows at relatively low temperatures, require slower spindle speeds (12,000 r/in) and high feed rates (200 in/in) to minimize heat generation. The graph in Fig. 22.9 shows recommended feed rates and cutter offsets for most standard laminates at various stack heights. The cutter used is a standard ⅛-in-diameter burr type.

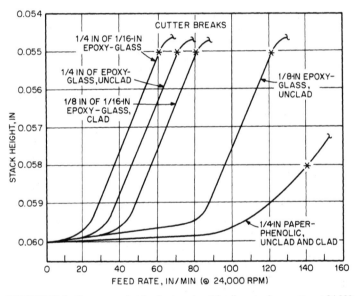

FIGURE 22.9   Recommended feed rate, using ⅛-in-diameter burr cutter at 24,000 r/min, for varying stack heights of specific thickness of material.

22.4.7   Cutter Bits

Because of the precise control of table movement in NC routing, cutter bits are not subjected to shock encountered in pin routing and stylus routing, and therefore small-diameter cutters may be used successfully. However, the fabricator would do well to standardize on ⅛-in-diameter cutters because they are suitable for most production work and are readily available from a number of manufacturers in a variety of types. The resulting 0.062-in radius on all inside corners is usually acceptable if the board designer is aware of it.

Cutter tooth form is more important in NC than in other routing. Because of the faster feed rates possible, it is important that a cutter have an open tooth form that will release the chip easily and prevent packing. Many standard diamond burrs available on the market will load with chips and fail rapidly. The carbide cutting bit will normally cut in excess of 15,000 linear inches of epoxy-glass laminate before erosion of the teeth renders the cutter ineffective or too small.

If extremely smooth edges are required, a fluted cutter may be used. Single- or two-flute cutters with straight flutes should be used when cutting into the foil if minimum burring is desired. It should be noted that such cutters will be more fragile than a standard serrated cutter, and feed speeds should be adjusted accordingly. When a slightly larger burr can be tolerated, two- and three-flute left-hand spiral cutter bits should be used because of their greater strength. The left-hand spiral will force the work piece down rather than lift it, assuming a right-hand turning spindle.

22.4.8 Tooling

To simplify tooling and expedite loading and unloading operations, effective hold-down and chop-removal systems should be provided as part of the machine design. Various methods may then be devised to mount the boards to the machine table while properly registering them to facilitate routing the outline. Some machine designs will have shuttle tables available so that loading and unloading may be accomplished while the machine is cutting. Others will utilize quick-change secondary tooling pallets or subplots that allow rapid exchange of bench-loaded pallets with only a few seconds between boards.

22.4.8.1 Tooling Plates.   Tooling plates utilize bushings and a slot on the centerline of the active pattern under each spindle. They are doweled to the machine table (Fig. 22.10). The plates may be made by normal machine shop practice, or the router may be used to register and drill its own tooling plate. Mounting pins in the tooling plate should be light slip fit.

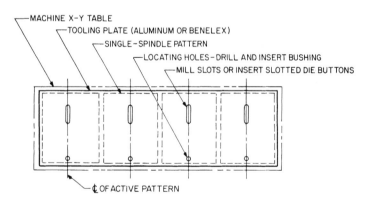

FIGURE 22.10   Typical tooling of numerically controlled routing.

22.4.8.2 Subplates.   Subplates should be made of Benelax, linen phenolic, or other similar material. Subplates should have the pattern to be routed cut into their surfaces. The patterns act as vacuum paths and aid in chip removal. Part-holding pins should be an interface fit in subplates and snug to loose fit in the part, depending on cutting technique used (Fig. 22.11).

It is recommended that the programmer generate the tooling and hold-down pinholes in addition to the routing program. That will provide absolute registration between the tooling holes and the routing program.

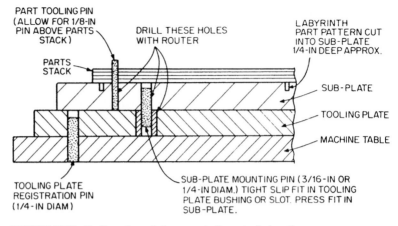

FIGURE 22.11   Tooling schematic for numerically controlled routing.

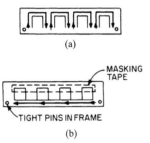

FIGURE 22.12   No-internal-pin method. Step 1: Cut three sides (*a*). Step 2: Apply masking tape (*b*). Step 3: Cut parts away.

22.4.9   Cutting and Holding Techniques

Since the precision required for cutting board outlines, as well as the placement of tooling holes for registering boards, will vary, a number of different cutting and holding methods may be used. Three basic methods are illustrated here. Experimentation will determine which method or combination of methods is most applicable to a particular job. With all methods, the minimum dimension for board separation with a 0.125-in cutter is 0.150 in.

1. *No-internal-pin method:*   If no internal tooling pins are used, the procedure of Fig. 22.12 may be employed, but it is normally used only when no other method is possible. Characteristics of this method are as follows:

Accuracy: ±0.005 in

Speed: Slow (best used with many small parts on a panel)

Load: One panel high for each station

2. *Single-pin method:*   The single-pin method is illustrated in Fig. 22.13. Characteristics of this method are as follows:

Accuracy: ±0.005 in

Speed: Fast (quick load and unload)

Load: Multiple stacks

3. *Double-pin method:*   In the two-pin method, there is a double pass of cutter offset; see Fig. 22.14. Make two complete passes around each board, the first pass at a recommended feed rate and the second at 200 in/min. Remove scrap after the first pass. Characteristics of this method are as follows:

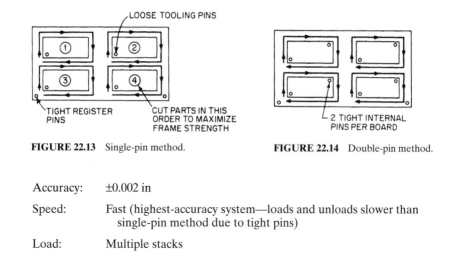

FIGURE 22.13 Single-pin method. **FIGURE 22.14** Double-pin method.

Accuracy: ±0.002 in

Speed: Fast (highest-accuracy system—loads and unloads slower than single-pin method due to tight pins)

Load: Multiple stacks

22.5 SCORING

Scoring is a circuit board fabrication method used to make long, straight cuts quickly, and therefore is often used to create rectangular profile board shapes. More commonly, however, it is used in concert with CNC routing for complex shapes, enabling each tool to be used to its unique advantage. When used with routing, scoring has a much wider application and can provide simple breakaway for complex profiles (Fig. 22.15).

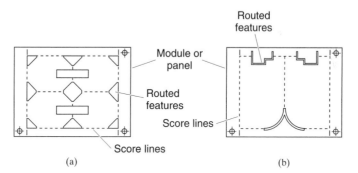

(a)   (b)

FIGURE 22.15 Scoring processes: (*a*) shows module or panel with typical scoring lines and routed corners; (*b*) shows scoring lines and routed complex features.

22.5.1 Scoring Application

Scoring is accomplished by machining a shallow, precise, V-groove into the top and bottom surfaces of the laminate, generally with the use of CNC equipment. The two most significant elements of the score line are as follows:

1. The positional accuracy from the reference feature (usually the registration hole)

2. The depth of the score, which determines the web thickness

The final edges of a scored circuit board are yielded by breaking the panel, or border, at the score line (Fig. 22.16). The angle of the cutting tool is reflected in the V-groove geometry, and limiting this angle to 30 to 90° will minimize the score line intrusion into traces near the edges of the circuit board. The score line exposes the laminate glass fibers and resin. Measurements from these surfaces will vary greatly, even though the score line is precisely machined (Fig. 22.13). These irregular surfaces will be noticed as dimensional growth and should be considered in design or planning when designated as a scored edge.

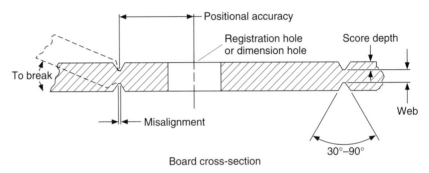

FIGURE 22.16 Cross section of board, showing finished V-groove and break.

The dimensional accuracy of the final board is determined by the degree of precision with which the following are performed:

1. Misalignment within ±0.003 in of the score line from the desired location
2. Web thickness within ±0.006 in of the designated dimension

Typically, a nominal web thickness is 0.020 in for 0.060-in-thick FR-4 boards and 0.014 in for 0.030-in-thick FR-4 laminate. For CEM-1 or CEM-3 materials, 0.040 in and 0.024 in nominal web thickness apply, respectively. These web thickness values enable sufficient module strength to avoid accidental or premature score separation, while providing simple breaking efforts without excessive edge roughness or growth.

22.5.2 Operation

Two major types of panel scoring systems are available:

1. Dedicated CNC scoring machines utilizing high-speed carbide or diamond-embedded cutter blades, operating as a pair, one on each side of the board. This generates the V-groove on each side simultaneously

2. Drills or driller/routers equipped with scoring software and spade type carbide bits, generating score lines on one side of the panel at a time (Fig. 22.14).

22.5.2.1 Dedicated Scoring Equipment. The dedicated CNC scoring machines are high-production, precision computer-driven machines. With an exception or two, they utilize blade-type cutting tools of all-carbide or with carbide inserts, as well as diamond-embedded varieties, and are designed to self-center the panel.

The panel feed rate is high due to the blade's ability to operate at high-surface-feet cutting rates. Scoring both sides simultaneously with one pass contributes greatly to elevated production processing. This equipment utilizes pin or edge registration, with positioning of score lines and steps by programmed instructions. The vertical adjustment of the cutter blades permits variation in V-groove depth and on many models *jump scoring* is available. The ability to do jump scoring, or score/no-score segments along a simple line at desired points is programmable.

22.5.2.2 Multiple-Role Machines.   Scoring with CNC drillers or driller/router machines equipped with scoring software produces score lines only on one side of the panel per machine cycle, although each spindle can be used. The panel and program data must be flipped to score the second side. The panel registration method is similar to that of routing, using existing tooling holes to pin the panel to the machined tooling plates. The tooling plates must be machined flat to assure uniformity of score depth. Brush-type spindle pressure foot inserts should be used to apply downward pressure during score line cutting. Spade-type carbide tools of various angles and configurations are used in the spindles. Typically, multiple passes (two or three) may be required to produce a clean, uniform score line.

CHAPTER 23
MULTILAYER PROCESSING

Robert R. Holmes, Ph.D.
AT&T, Richmond, Virginia

23.1 INTRODUCTION

The fine-pitch surface-mount devices that are now used in many designs have high I/O densities and high operating speeds. In addition, some designs such as cellular telephones have circuits that operate in the radio frequency range (1 GHz and higher). The multilayer boards used in these designs must provide a high interconnection density as well as superior electrical and thermal performance. These conflicting requirements place serious demands on the MLB designs, materials, and processes.

This chapter reviews the design options and materials available to make a high-performance MLB. This leads to a discussion of the MLB manufacturing processes required to make these designs and use these materials. The design discussion reviews MLB design options and discusses ways to meet density and performance needs. The materials discussion focuses on critical electrical and thermal-mechanical needs of a modern system, and the materials available to meet these needs. The sections on MLB manufacturing review the basic process steps for making an MLB and the impact of new material and design options.

23.2 MULTILAYER CONSTRUCTION

A standard multilayer board (MLB) contains internal and external circuits, interconnected by plated through-holes (PTHs) drilled through the entire board. Very dense MLBs may also contain holes connecting adjacent layers. These holes are called *buried* when they are completely inside the MLB and *blind* or *semiburied* when they connect interior layers to the surface. Figure 23.1 shows process sequences for making an MLB.

As shown in Fig. 23.1, the MLB is fabricated by gluing together (laminating) prepatterned, double-sided innerlayer panels, called *components*. The components include one or more board images. Standard MLB (nonburied via) components are undrilled so circuits are patterned using a print-and-etch process. In a buried-via MLB, drilled layers are fabricated like a double-sided board, using a print-plate-etch process. The starting material used to make the component is called C-stage to indicate that it is fully cured prior to lamination. The glue layer is called B-stage to indicate that it is partially cured prior to lamination. After lamination, the composite panel is drilled, patterned, and finished like a standard double-sided panel.

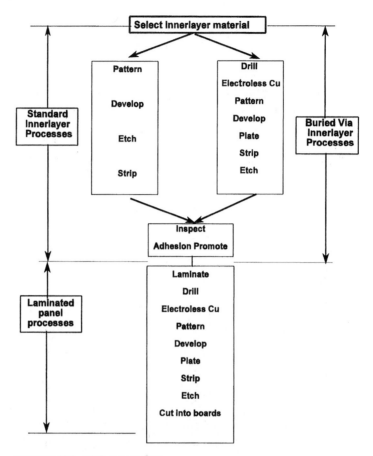

FIGURE 23.1 MLB process flow.

In many MLB constructions, the outerlayers are formed by laminating copper foil along with the component layers. This construction is called *foil capped*. The alternative stack-up, using component boards for the outerlayer, is called *component capped*.

23.2.1 Foil-Capped Stack-up

A foil-capped board is fabricated from one or more patterned innerlayer components and two copper sheets. The copper sheets form the outerlayers of the fabricated MLB. This stack-up is the least expensive way to fabricate an MLB and is by far the most popular design option. Figure 23.2 shows a typical stack-up for a foil-capped eight-layer MLB.

As can be seen in Fig. 23.2, the eight-layer foil-capped board contains three component boards, four glue layers, and two sheets of copper. The copper layers are numbered from 1 to 8, beginning with the top foil layer. In the design pictured, layers 2, 4, 5, and 7 represent signal layers. Layers 3 and 6 represent power/ground layers. When patterned, the outerlayers generally provide additional signal layers; however, on dense designs, the surface may be limited to device footprints and their associated fan-out patterns.

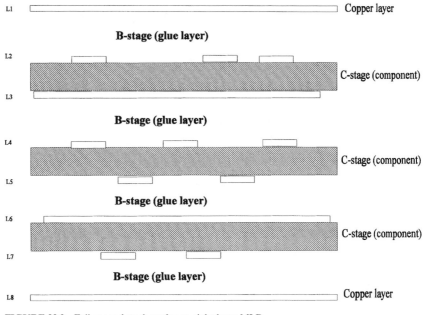

FIGURE 23.2   Foil-capped stack-up for an eight-layer MLB.

23.2.2 Component-Capped Stack-up

A component-capped MLB uses no copper foil. It is fabricated from innerlayer components and B-stage. Figure 23.3 shows an eight-layer component capped board. Note that the eight-layer component-stacked MLB (Fig. 23.3) requires four components, as compared to three for the foil-stacked board (Fig. 23.2). This makes the component-capped board more expensive than the more commonly used foil-capped design. The increased cost is partially offset by savings in B-stage and copper foil and the fact that the outer component board is patterned on only one side prior to lamination.

One reason to use component-capped designs is to avoid fabricating components with signals on both sides. Such a layer is difficult to handle and often has poor dimensional stability. The foil-capped example (Fig. 23.2) has one signal–signal component (layers 4 and 5) and the component-stacked one (Fig. 23.3) has none.

Another reason for using component construction is to take advantage of better C-stage thickness tolerances of material to control critical layer-to-layer spacings. For example, in the foil-stacked design (Fig. 23.2), layers 4 and 5 are separated from the nearest ground plane by a B-stage layer, while in the component-stacked design (Fig. 23.3) this spacing is provided by C-stage. A word of caution: It is generally not possible to improve the thickness control on all layers simultaneously. In the examples, the component-capped structure has better control on layers 4 and 5, but worse on layers 2 and 7.

A third reason that component-capped designs are used is surface quality concerns. When a coarse glass with low resin content is used for the exterior B-stage in a foil-capped stack, the surface copper will exhibit the weave pattern. In addition, the board will exhibit small white spots called measles when subjected to thermal or mechanical stress. Both of these problems can be avoided by a proper selection of B-stage and lamination cycle. The important point is to avoid the use of low-resin-content, heavy glass B-stage in a foil-capped board.

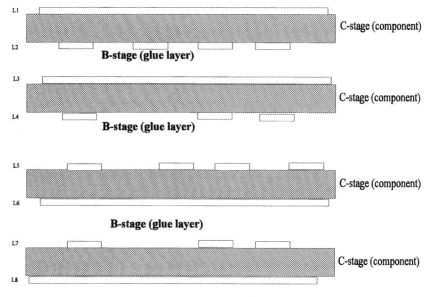

FIGURE 23.3   Component-capped stack-up for an eight-layer MLB.

23.2.3   Controlled Impedance

The signal lines in an MLB have a characteristic impedance. Active devices, connectors, and transmission lines also have characteristic impedances. In a high-speed circuit, signal energy is reflected, rather than transmitted, at any interface with an impedance discontinuity. This means that, to avoid signal losses due to reflections, all impedances must be matched.

The physical relationship between a signal line and the surrounding power/ground layers determines the impedance of that signal line. Two configurations are recognized: *microstrip* and *stripline*. In the eight-layer example (Figs. 23.2 and 23.3), layers 4 and 5 are located between two power/ground planes. This is a stripline configuration. Layers 1, 2, 7, and 8 have a power/ground layer on one side only. This a microstrip configuration. A microstrip circuit may be inside the board (layers 2 and 7) or on the board surface (layers 1 and 8). In all these configurations, the circuit impedance can be calculated from equations that depend on the dielectric constant of the substrate, the width of the signal line, the thickness of the signal line, and the signal line–to–ground plane separations.

Dielectric layer thickness has a major impact on circuit impedance. Not only is the nominal thickness important, but the variability must be minimized. Both the B- and C-stage dielectric layers are generally made of one or more layers of woven glass cloth which has been impregnated with an epoxy resin. The nominal thickness can be adjusted by changing the thickness of the glass cloth or the number of sheets of glass cloth used. Standard glass cloth thickness varies from fine weaves such as type 106 that give approximately 2 mil per sheet to heavy weaves such as type 7628 that give 8 mil or more per sheet. For a given thickness, lowest cost is achieved by using the heaviest glass. For example, one sheet of 7628 is a significantly cheaper way to achieve 8 mil than four sheets of 106. However, heavy glass may give process problems such as uneven surfaces and excessive drill deflection. Dielectric thickness can also be varied by changing the amount of impregnated resin. As a practical matter, the limits on resin content are between 40 and 60 percent (by weight). Best results are achieved with resin contents in the range of 45 to 50 percent. Outside this range, problems may be encountered with poor resin fill, thickness variation, and dimensional instability. Thickness control is one of the many cases in MLB manufacture where cost performance tradeoffs are needed.

23.2.4 Buried Vias

To avoid hopelessly complex routing, each signal net is generally routed using only one pair of layers with what is called *Manhattan geometry*. This means that diagonal routing is avoided and all signal lines run in a horizontal or a vertical direction. To avoid blockage and side-to-side cross-talk problems, horizontal lines run on one layer and vertical lines on the other. This means that, in addition to a via at each end of the net (I/O via), most nets need one or two additional vias (routing via) to change direction from horizontal to vertical. Figure 23.4 shows an example of Manhattan geometry.

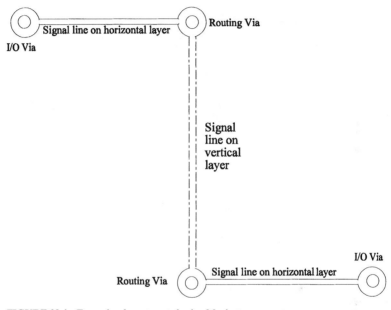

FIGURE 23.4   Example of a net routed using Manhattan geometry.

The net shown in Fig. 23.4 has two I/O vias and two routing vias. The I/O vias connect the signal lines to the board surface where the net connects to an input or output point of an active circuit. The routing vias are used to change directions from horizontal to vertical. With through-hole vias, the routing vias pass through all layers, consuming valuable routing space. A high-layer-count board, with many signal layer pairs, can run out of via sites. In this case, additional layers will not improve routing completion and we say the board is *via-starved*.

One solution to a via-starved board is to use buried vias. The buried via connects two adjacent signal layers and provides routing vias without affecting routing on other layers. Figure 23.5 shows an eight-layer board with two buried-via layers.

Buried vias do not pass through the board, so they do not congest the routing on other layers. In addition, the same via site can be used simultaneously on different layer pairs. Since buried vias are drilled and plated in the thin laminate prior to lamination, they can be very small and positioned very accurately, saving additional routing space. In some applications, buried vias are placed where needed with no reference to a predetermined grid. This gridless routing approach gives very high automatic completion.

To benefit from buried vias, signal layer pairs must be routed on opposite sides of the *same* C-stage component. In Fig. 23.2, layers 4 and 5 are the only buried-via candidates. In Fig. 23.3,

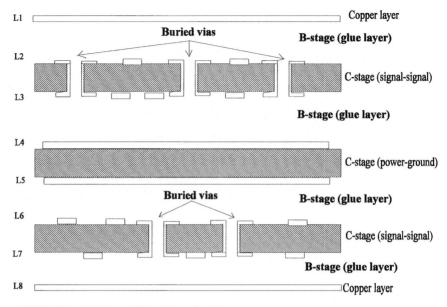

FIGURE 23.5 Eight-layer MLB with two buried-via components.

no signal layers can benefit from buried vias. The design shown in Fig. 21.5 is able to use buried vias on two-layer pairs because a power/ground layer pair separates them. Nonburied-via designs use one power/ground plane between each signal layer pair. This gives cross-talk isolation and impedance reference. A buried-via design uses a second redundant layer to force the next signal layer pair onto the same component. In other words, for a high-layer-count design to use buried vias on all signal layer pairs, *power/ground pairs* must be inserted between each signal layer pair. This increases the number of layers in the board and increases cost. Another disadvantage of buried vias is cost associated with the extra drill and plate operations.

Buried vias are not recommended for most applications unless there is no other alternative or they reduce overall design cost by eliminating a more expensive alternative. For example, in some designs, buried vias may reduce routing congestion so much that the design can be routed on fewer layers, providing a net cost saving. Another exception is the very high layer count boards used on some mainframe computers. These designs often have 40 or more layers, and cannot be routed without buried vias. In general, buried-via designs are specialty products, not a general solution to high interconnection demand.

23.2.5 Blind Vias

Another via option is the blind via which connects the surface layer to one or more internal layers. Figure 23.6 shows an example of a complex eight-layer MLB with both blind and buried vias. The design shown contains buried vias between layers 3 and 4 and between layers 5 and 6. Blind vias connect layers 1 and 2, layers 7 and 8, and layers 5, 6, 7, and 8. The buried vias are fabricated in the component layers as previously described. The blind vias can be fabricated by controlled depth drilling or by sequential lamination. These fabrication options will be discussed in more detail later.

Blind vias may become very important in very dense, double-sided surface-mount designs where there is an interference between I/O vias from opposite sides on the board. This is par-

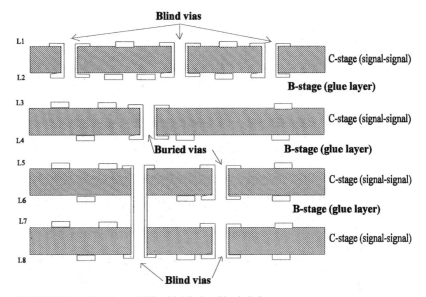

FIGURE 23.6 Eight-layer MLB with blind and buried vias.

ticularly troublesome if the via-in-pad (VIP) approach is used. The VIP is placed directly in the device I/O pad, and with through-vias, device placement is constrained so that pads are nonoverlapping. The way to solve this problem is to use each via site twice. Blind vias make this possible.

A second application for blind vias is to assure complete side-to-side electrical isolation. This is particularly important in wireless designs where the RF circuits must be shielded from other circuits. Through-holes allow RF electric fields to escape from a shielded region. A blind via eliminates this problem and allows RF functions, located on one side of the board, to be totally isolated from logic and control circuits on the opposite side of the same board.

The ultimate use of blind vias is to effectively convert a dense, two-sided surface-mount design to a pair of less dense, one-sided designs. To see how this is possible, visualize an MLB with fine-pitch SMDs on both sides as two separate boards with some level of side-to-side interconnection. The board is designed as two separate subassemblies, with the routing for each side restricted to layers on that half of the board. The I/O connections from one side do not interfere with the I/O connections on the other side. The only through-holes required in this design are the relatively few that provide side-to-side interconnection. Since each via site is used twice, a 100-mil grid may replace a 50-mil grid, providing a significant increase in inner-layer routing resources.

23.2.5.1 Controlled Depth Drilling.   One way to make blind vias is controlled depth drilling. In this case, blind holes are drilled at appropriate locations after lamination. This approach suffers from one serious problem: hole plating. If the depth of a blind hole exceeds its diameter, plating is nearly impossible. This restriction limits the use of blind drilling to layers close to the surface. It also prevents the use of very small blind holes. In addition, uncertainties in the location and depth of internal features requires rather generous design tolerances to assure that a blind hole hits its intended target and no other.

Blind drilling is commonly used when the blind vias are only required to connect through a single thin dielectric layer. A common example is a design that uses the surface layer for fanout to blind vias that lead to the first buried layer, which is a high-density signal layer. For deeper vias, sequential lamination is required.

23.2.5.2 Sequential Lamination.   In the sequential lamination process, two or more sub-assemblies are fabricated, and then relaminated to make the final board. For example, consider a 16-layer board fabricated as two 8-layer subassemblies. The subassemblies are laminated, drilled, plated, and patterned like a standard MLB, with the exception that the sides that will become the final board exterior are blanket-metallized. After patterning, the two subassemblies are laminated together and then processed as a standard MLB.

Blind vias and sequential lamination have been around for some time and do not present any major technical challenges. The major issue is the modification of the automatic router to take advantage of blind vias. A second problem is cost. The manufacturing process involves processing three different assemblies through lamination, drilling, plating, and patterning, so the cost of the board could be as much as double that of a conventional board of similar design.

23.3 MLB MATERIALS

23.3.1 Critical Properties

Many substrate materials are used to fabricate MLBs. By far the most common material is epoxy, including the difunctional and multifunctional systems discussed in Sec. 23.3.2. The specialty materials, discussed in Secs. 23.3.3 and 23.3.4, are used in high-performance MLBs. These include polyimide, cyanate ester, epoxy/cyanate ester blends (BT), epoxy, poly-phynolene-oxide (PPO) blends, and Teflon™ (PTFE) based.

In addition to providing circuit interconnection, the MLB substrate is the electrical and mechanical platform for the system, so the substrate properties are very important for the proper functioning of the system. Among the properties of importance are dielectric constant D_k, dielectric loss (tan δ), glass transition temperature T_g, degradation temperature T_x, and moisture absorption. The following sections will discuss the importance of these and other properties of an MLB substrate. Table 23.1 shows typical values of these properties for some important commercial materials.

TABLE 23.1   Typical Values of MLB Material Properties

Material	D_k, 1 GHz	tan δ, 1 GHz	T_g, °C	T_x, °C	Moisture,* %
Difunctional	4.40	0.020	123	277	1.4
Multifunctional	4.43	0.018	134–178	280–295	1–1.5
Polyimide	4.06	0.006	>250	>300	1.0
Cyanate ester	3.65	0.005	>200	>300	—
BT	2.94	0.011	181	295	0.6
PPO-epoxy	3.85	0.012	179	311	0.6
PTFE-glass	2.60	0.001	†	>300	—
PTFE mat-CE	2.79	0.003	†	>300	—
PTFE-ceramic	4.06	0.002	†	>300	0.4

  * Percent weight gain for 0.062-in-thick sample after 24 h at 100°C; 100% RH (live steam).
  † PTFE is a thermal plastic that melts without a well-defined T_g.

23.3.1.1 Dielectric Constant $\mathbf{D_k}$.   Impedance and transmission speed are both affected by D_k. As previously discussed, impedance must be matched throughout a high-speed circuit. This means that the required impedance of a circuit line is determined by the impedance of other circuit elements. The designer can use standard equations to select values of line width, dielectric thickness, and dielectric constant that will achieve the desired impedance (often 50

Ω). However, factors such as interconnection density and MLB imaging capability generally determine the line width. This means that the tradeoff available to the designer is dielectric thickness versus dielectric constant, with lower values of D_k, allowing thinner dielectrics.

Thinner multilayer boards provide several advantages to the designer. Generally, thin boards have better PTH reliability and fit better into connectors and latches. In addition, a decrease in ground-to-signal spacing will reduce stray electric fields around a conductor and lessen the cross talk to adjacent conductors. Since thinner layers have lower cross talk and give thinner, more reliable MLBs, there is a serious need for low-D_k materials.

Transmission speed is important because the signal transit time affects device timing and determines at what circuit length transmission line effects become important. The transmission speed of an electromagnetic wave in a dielectric medium is the speed of light divided by the square root of D_k. Air has a D_k of 1.0 and electromagnetic waves travel at the speed of light (12 in/ns). At 1 GHz, standard MLB materials have a D_k of 4.4 and the transmission speed is reduced to 6 in/ns. With low-D_k materials, transmission speeds reach 8 in/ns.

23.3.1.2 *Dielectric Loss (tan δ).*

The dielectric constant of a material is a complex quantity with a real and imaginary parts (ϵ' ϵ''). The real part (ϵ') determines the velocity of a transmitted electric signal. It is commonly called D_k. The energy loss per wavelength from the transmitted signal is proportional to tan δ, where δ is the angle between the real and imaginary parts of the complex dielectric constant. For standard MLB materials, tan δ is 0.02 which translates to serious losses at frequencies above 1 GHz. For circuits operating at 1 GHz or higher, a material such as PTFE with a tan δ of 0.001 is preferred.

23.3.1.3 *Moisture Absorption.*

Moisture is the enemy of an MLB. Absorbed water raises D_k, expands the board, and causes thermal defects such as substrate blisters and barrel cracking during soldering. Increases in D_k are generally small, but the resulting impedance drift can be a problem in a circuit with a critical impedance requirement. In-plane expansion can approach 1 mil/in and cause registration problems during stenciling and device placement. Thermal defects during assembly and rework soldering can cause serious yield problems. The severity of these problems depends on storage condition prior to soldering. If storage times are short or if the humidity is low, moisture will not be a serious issue. However, if the MLB is subjected to high humidities for several months or more, special care must be taken. This can include the use of moisture-resistant materials, baking prior to assembly, or storage with a desiccant.

23.3.1.4 *Thermal Stability.*

The important thermal properties of a laminate are the glass transition T_g and the degradation temperature. These properties measure how well the material performs in the assembly soldering and in high-temperature use conditions.

The T_g of a resin is the temperature at which the resin *reversibly* changes from a glassy state to a rubbery state. This loss of modulus creates an effective limit on the operating temperature of the system. T_g also affects the thermal fatigue life of the plated holes in the MLB. Higher values of T_g translate into greater thermal cycle life.

The degradation temperature is a measure of the temperature where the epoxy begins to degrade *irreversibly*. This is generally much higher than T_g. One measure of degradation is the length of time at 260°C (called the T_{260} time) before a rapid expansion due to delamination is detected by a *thermal mechanical analyzer* (TMA). This test is useful for predicting soldering performance, since the test temperature is near soldering temperature. For common materials, the T_{260} varies from a few minutes to hours.

One drawback of the T_{260} test is that high-temperature materials degrade very slowly at this temperature. Another test that is more useful for high-temperature materials is the temperature T_x where a 50 percent weight loss is seen in a TMA scan operating at 2°C/min. Generally, the T_{260} time and T_x are correlated with each other but are not correlated to T_g.

23.3.1.5 *Coefficient of Thermal Expansion.*

The CTE for FR-4, 14 to 20 ppm/C, is higher than that of ceramic and silicon. The resulting thermal expansion mismatch between an MLB and assembled devices can lead to solder joint fatigue failures when the system undergoes multiple heat cycles during power-up and power-down. The best solution is to use packages with compliant leads that can accommodate the CTE mismatch. This allows the system to use standard MLB material systems.

In cases where the device package is incompatible with the CTE of an FR-4 MLB, a low-expansion substrate must be used. This can be achieved in several ways. One possibility is to replace the woven glass in standard FR-4 with woven quartz or organic Aramid (Kevlar™) fibers. Although this reduces the expansion of the substrate, both materials are expensive and difficult to process. A slightly better solution is to use a chopped Aramid mat impregnated with epoxy resin. This material solves the processing problems associated with woven Aramid, but it is still quite expensive. A third approach is to laminate a low-expanding metal such as Invar into the MLB. This plane can double as a heat sink or a power/ground plane.

23.3.2 Standard FR-4 Properties

The most common material for making MLBs is known as FR-4. This is a highly cross linked brominated epoxy resin reinforced with woven glass cloth. The bromine is reacted with the epoxy matrix and is used to provide fire retardancy. Most FR-4 materials satisfy the UL classification of V0 for fire retardancy. FR-4 materials are sold by many suppliers and have become essentially commodity materials.

Two resin systems are used to make FR-4 laminate: *difunctional* and *tetrafunctional*. These systems are distinguished by the nature of the epoxy cross linking. In a difunctional system, the epoxide molecule has two cross-linking sites, and the cured epoxy contains long linear molecular chains. Pure difunctional laminates have excellent physical properties and for many years were the mainstay of the industry. They have a T_g of 120°C which is adequate for most use environments, but is low for some applications.

The epoxide molecule of a tetrafunctional epoxy has more than two cross-linking sites. This allows a high cross-link density and a high T_g. A pure tetrafunctional system is expensive and difficult to work with. To meet the need for a T_g above 120°C, laminators blend difunctional and tetrafunctional resins, producing a mixture referred to as *multifunctional*. Around 1985, some laminators began selling multifunctional epoxy blends with a T_g between 130 and 145°C. This blend was called tetrafunctional, even though it actually contained both di- and tetrafunctional epoxies. Today this blend is available at little or no price premium over a difunctional laminate. Laminators also sell laminates with a higher fraction of tetrafunctional resin. These systems, which are called multifunctional, have values of T_g in excess of 170°C and are sold at price premium of approximately 10 percent over difunctional systems. Multifunctional blends often have lower moisture absorption and a higher thermal degradation temperature than difunctional systems. However, in some multifunctional systems these properties are not improved. Care must be taken in selecting a multifunction system to assure that all properties of importance are enhanced.

23.3.3 Materials with Enhanced Thermal Properties

Modern MLBs often operate at elevated temperatures due to the heat output from devices. When the system is turned off, the board sees a large thermal cycle. As boards become thicker and holes smaller, these thermal cycles result in an increasing threat to the reliability of plated holes. For example, small holes have been shown to fail in 100 or fewer cycles when subjected to multiple thermal cycles up to temperatures near the T_g of the MLB. These cycles can occur when a high-power device is turned on and off. The best solution for systems subjected to such stresses is to use materials with a higher T_g.

Today's MLBs often have surface-mount devices on both sides of the board and they receive three or more solder operations during the assembly of connectors and devices. Furthermore, because of the value of a completed assembly, the board must be able to withstand additional soldering operations needed for occasional removal and replacement of defective devices. Boards made with standard difunctional FR-4 can suffer from lifted lands, cracked PTH barrels, or substrate blisters during these multiple soldering operations. The solution is to use materials with low moisture absorption and a high thermal degradation temperature.

As previously indicated, multifunctional epoxy is emerging as an inexpensive way to enhance thermal performance. With a value of T_g in excess of 170°C, multifunctional epoxy boards have excellent PTH fatigue life when subjected to thermal cycles up to 150°C. However, as noted, some multifunctional epoxies offer little or no improvement in moisture absorption or thermal degradation. For applications requiring thermal properties superior to those available from multifunctional epoxies, there are three alternate resin systems commonly available: polyimide (PI), cyanate ester blends, and poly-phenelene-oxide (PPO) blends.

23.3.3.1 Polyimide.   Probably the best thermal stability is provided by materials in the PI family. This family of materials has a T_g in excess of 250°C, a high thermal degradation temperature, and a CTE less than epoxy. Polyimide resins can be coated on glass fabric to produce an MLB substrate that processes like epoxy FR-4. With a high T_g and high thermal degradation temperature, polyimide MLBs provide high-temperature reliability. For systems that must operate at temperatures above 200°C, polyimide is a good choice. The combination of a high T_g and a relatively low CTE results in excellent fatigue life for plated holes. This makes polyimide a good candidate for very thick boards and for applications where the system must survive multiple thermal cycles over a wide temperature range.

Polyimides have several disadvantages. Early versions used a solvent called MDA that is widely viewed as carcinogenic. Although there was no evidence of MDA release during MLB fabrication or use, many fabricators refused to process MDA-based polyimide. Fortunately, material suppliers have formulated MDA-free versions of polyimide, and most polyimide on the market is MDA-free. A second disadvantage of polyimide is fast moisture uptake. This leads to the problems previously discussed in the section on moisture sensitivity. Generally, polyimide users combat moisture by including multiple bakes in the board fabrication and assembly processes. The third disadvantage of polyimide is cost. The cost of a polyimide laminate is up to four times that of FR-4, and MLB fabrication requires a high-temperature lamination.

Polyimide material has been used in low volume since the 1970s. Broad acceptance has always been limited by cost and fabrication issues. This material family should only be specified for systems that must operate with high reliability in an extreme environment, such as a high ambient temperature or extremes in thermal cycling. This includes some military applications and potentially some consumer applications such as under-hood automotive electronics. For most commercial applications, the lower-cost materials described here are a better choice.

23.3.3.2 Cyanate Ester Blends.   The second most stable resin system in general use is the triazine or cyanate ester family. In its pure form, the cyanate ester resin is brittle and difficult to drill without cracking. In addition, cyanate ester is an expensive resin system. As a result, cyanate ester resin is often blended with epoxy and a small amount of polyimide. This blend—called BT after its two ingredients, bismaleimide and triazine—can be coated on conventional glass cloth to produce a laminate.

BT laminates have a T_g of 180°C and a high degradation temperature. For most high-temperature applications, they are a direct substitute for polyimide. They have the added advantage that the moisture sensitivity and processibility of BT are much closer to conventional epoxy than to polyimide. Other than a high-temperature postlamination bake required for a full cure, the BT process is the same as an epoxy process. The major drawback of the BT laminate is cost. Although BT is much less expensive than polyimide, it is still up to two times the cost of epoxy-based FR-4. The result is that BT is a popular replacement for polyimide, but its use is limited to specialty applications. The trend for most high-temperature, commercial applications is either multifunctional epoxies or poly-phynolene-oxide/epoxy blends.

23.3.3.3   *Poly-Phynolene-Oxide (PPO)/Epoxy Blends.*   The most recent entry to the competition for a cost-effective high-temperature laminate is a material based on the PPO-epoxy blend. This material has a T_g of 180°C and a T_{260} of an hour or more. When coated on glass, the PPO blend processes like epoxy. The only exception is the need for a high-temperature bake to achieve full cure. The major advantages of this new laminate family are a very low moisture absorption and a cost that is only 20 to 50 percent higher than conventional epoxy. The disadvantage of the PPO blend is that it has a broad glass transition temperature with softening beginning well below 150°C. This has an adverse effect on the ultimate fatigue life of high-aspect-ratio holes.

PPO blends were introduced in the early 1990s, and they have the potential to capture much of the demand for high-temperature materials, including some that is now being met by multifunctional epoxy systems. They are an excellent candidate for any application requiring high operating temperatures or moisture resistance. Care should be taken in using this material in applications where the system must operate over a very large number of thermal cycles that include temperatures in excess of 130°C.

23.3.4   Materials with Enhanced Electrical Properties

The D_k and tan δ of a composite material are determined by both the resin and the reinforcement used. Standard FR-4, made up of epoxy resin and woven glass, has a D_k in the range of 4.4 and tan δ of 0.02. This may be reduced somewhat by replacing some or all of the epoxy resin with PPO, cyanate ester, or PTFE. Further reductions require replacing the glass reinforcement.

23.3.4.1   *Cyanate Ester Blends.*   Both the tan δ and the D_k of the cyanate ester resin system are much lower than epoxy. The best results are achieved with pure cyanate ester. However, as mentioned earlier, this resin is brittle and difficult to drill. The BT blend provides an excellent compromise. BT has a D_k of 2.94 and a tan δ of 0.01. This improvement is useful in some applications; however, it is inadequate for many high-performance applications, and the approximately 100 percent cost penalty for BT has prevented its broad acceptance.

23.3.4.2   *PPO Blends.*   As with cyanate ester, both the tan δ and D_k of the PPO resin are lower than epoxy. For processibility and cost reasons, a blend of approximately 50 percent PPO and 50 percent epoxy is generally used. This gives electrical performance similar to BT, but with a cost penalty of only 20 to 50 percent above standard FR-4. It is likely that PPO will find wide use in those applications such as for high-performance workstations that need a small improvement in electrical performance. Unfortunately, the characteristics of a PPO/epoxy blend are often inadequate for very high speeds, such as for supercomputers and wireless (RF) applications.

23.3.4.3   *PTFE-Based Laminates.*   This resin system is commonly known under the trade name Teflon. Of all resin systems in common use, the best electrical performance is provided by PTFE. The D_k of PTFE is close to 2.0 and tan δ is less than 0.001. This is a significant improvement over all other materials. In addition to excellent electrical properties, PTFE has excellent thermal properties. It is a thermal plastic that can operate at temperatures above 300°C without softening, oxidation, or other form of degradation. It is naturally fire retardant so it does not need bromine addition to achieve the UL rating of V0. It has very low moisture absorption. One major drawback of PTFE-based laminates is cost. They are often 100 times more expensive than epoxy-based FR-4. This makes it difficult to justify the use of PTFE if any alternative exists.

Another drawback of PTFE laminates is process complexity. PTFE is a high-temperature thermoplastic that requires a high-temperature lamination cycle, not achievable in conventional lamination presses. The use of special cycles can be avoided by using a low-temperature adhesive, but this leads to compromises with electrical and thermal properties. Although PTFE is relatively easy to drill, it smears over the inner copper layers. This smeared PTFE is difficult to remove and requires aggressive chemical treatment. In addition, PTFE is very hydrophobic, making it difficult to wet in the plating operation. Generally, plating must be immediately preceded by a special fluoride etch (Tetra-etch™) that activates the hole wall and enhances wetting. As an alternative, some PTFE systems can be activated in a plasma etch; however, this does not work with all PTFE materials.

At least three types of laminate systems are available are with PTFE resin.

PTFE Resin Coated on a Conventional Glass Mat.   Although the construction of this laminate is most like standard FR-4, it is not recommended for MLB applications. The large CTE of PTFE coupled with the in-plane strength of the glass reenforcement leads to a very high out-of-plane expansion that can easily fracture a plated hole during soldering. In addition, the glass cloth raises the D_k of the composite. This material is commonly used in applications such as antennas or RF microstrip cables where the circuit is placed on one side of the substrate and a ground plane on the other. Plated holes are not needed, and a very low D_k is not critical.

PTFE Film Impregnated with Cyanate Ester or Epoxy Resin.   PTFE can be formed into a textile-like film full of tiny pores. This cloth can be impregnated with a low-D_k resin like CE to give an MLB substrate with no glass cloth reinforcement. The resulting increase of in-plane CTE reduces the out-of-plane CTE, improving PTH reliability. Although the non-PTFE resin impregnating the PTFE film increases D_k and tan δ over a pure PTFE layer, this composite is at least as good as glass-reinforced PTFE. The conventional resin surface of this material means that it can be laminated using conventional methods and materials, allowing the fabrication of MLBs containing a mixture of PTFE and epoxy layers. The resulting hybrid board can contain any symmetric mix of epoxy and PTFE layers.

The high in-plane CTE of the PTFE layer leads to severe warp in any nonsymmetric stack-up. Hybrid boards are less expensive than pure PTFE boards because they are laminated in a conventional press and they minimize the use of costly PTFE layers. However, the high cost of PTFE and the need for a fluoride etch still makes these boards expensive. The major application for this material is in supercomputer designs that have high-speed circuits requiring enhanced electrical properties mixed with others that will operate on FR-4. This approach will not work in applications where a mixture of RF signals and digital logic requires a nonsymmetric design with low-loss material on one side and standard material on the other.

PTFE Mixed with a Low-D_k Ceramic.   A third approach, in which up to 60 percent ceramic (by weight) is combined with PTFE resin, results in a very interesting material. This material has a low CTE, low tan δ, and low D_k, and by a proper choice of the ceramic it is possible to have an in-plane CTE that matches FR-4. This allows the fabrication of an unbalanced hybrid structure without excessive warp. The high ceramic loading typical of this material minimizes PTFE use and reduces costs. A commercial version of this material is now available with a cost in the range of four to five times standard FR-4, rather than the 100 times typical of other PTFE options. The only serious drawback of this material is the use of a special process such as plasma etch to ensure hole wall wetting.

23.3.5 Materials Summary

Substrate properties affect MLB performance in many important ways. The preceding discussion focused on thermal and electrical properties. The use of small high-aspect-ratio holes, thick boards, and high-power devices drives the need for materials with improved thermal properties. The use of high-speed devices, including RF circuits for wireless applications drives the need for improved electrical performance. In addition to these issues, there are other problems that become critical in high-density designs, but for which there are no effective solution. This includes the need for low warp and extreme flatness to facilitate solder stenciling. Another need is for very good dimensional stability. Registration tolerances often limit interconnection density, and there is a real need for a material with significantly better capability.

Materials exist with improved properties, but the ideal material that combines low cost with improvements in both thermal and electrical properties does not exist. Therefore, the designer must consider the needs of each design before selecting a cost-effective material.

The need for improved thermal properties includes the following three requirements: High T_g, high thermal decomposition temperature, and low moisture absorption. Polyimide meets the first two needs at the expense of increased moisture absorption and high cost. BT satisfies all three needs, but cost remains an issue. The most economical solutions are the multifunctional epoxies and the epoxy-PPO blends. Multifunctionals are relatively inexpensive, provide a significant improvement in T_g, and, in some cases, offer small improvements in thermal degradation temperature and moisture absorption. The PPO blends provide significant improvement in all three areas at a slightly higher cost. If moisture absorption is an issue, the PPO blend may be the best choice; otherwise, the multifunctional epoxies are likely to be the lowest-cost option.

Both BT and PPO-epoxy boards provide small improvements in electrical properties. If the real need is to reduce D_k so that the board thickness can be reduced, these materials may be useful. However, if dielectric loss is a serious problem, the only real solution is to use PTFE. Unfortunately, PTFE is very expensive and difficult to process, so it should be specified only where absolutely necessary. For example, RF circuits will nearly always require PTFE. The ceramic-PTFE blends used in a hybrid construction may be the most cost-effective solution for these applications.

In addition to these issues, there are other problems that become critical in high-density designs, but for which there are no effective solutions. These include the need to assure low warp to facilitate solder stenciling and the need for extreme flatness across the device footprint. Another need is for a material with very good dimensional stability. Registration tolerances often limit interconnection density and there is a real need for a material with significantly better dimensional stability.

23.4   *INNERLAYER PROCESSING*

23.4.1   Innerlayer Materials

The innerlayer process starts with a clad dielectric laminate. Layers without buried or blind vias are not plated, so the thickness of the final circuit is determined by the thickness of the starting copper. For most applications this means a thickness of 1.4 mil (1 oz/ft^2 of copper) or 2.8 mil (2 oz). Both thicker and thinner coppers are used for special applications. For example, backplanes that provide large currents to high-power daughter boards use copper weights up to 5 oz. High-density circuits with low current demands may work well with 0.5-oz copper. With buried and blind vias, additional copper is plated on the traces, so the starting copper thickness is generally 0.5 oz.

Copper foil is fabricated in a plating process that produces a coarse-grained columnar copper. One property of importance is the elongation where fracture occurs. High-elongation foil is generally believed to reduce foil cracks due to thermal cycling Standard copper foils fail at an elongation of 3 to 5 percent. High-elongation foil, called HTE, will stand a minimum elongation of 5 percent. Foil vendors also sell special foils that are fine grained. These foils generally have very high elongation and are advertised to give superior etch performance for fineline boards.

Standard foils are made with a rough surface called the *tooth* on one side and a smooth or shiny surface on the other. The rough side is treated with an adhesion promoter and then laminated against the C-stage dielectric to ensure good adhesion. Since the shiny side of the copper has poor adhesion characteristics, the MLB fabricator must include adhesion promotion steps prior to resist lamination and prior to final board lamination. Double-treated copper foil has a tooth and an adhesion promoter applied to both sides. Although double-treated foil requires no further adhesion-promoting treatments, it has several disadvantages that have prevented its broad use:

- It is expensive, with a cost that often offsets the savings from the eliminated processes.
- It is somewhat fragile so it is difficult to rework.
- Complete resist development is difficult, leading to a high incidence of shorts.
- It is not compatible with the plating processes used to make buried and blind vias.

An alternative approach offered by some laminators is called *shiny side down*. In this approach, the foil vendor makes a standard foil but applies the adhesion promoter to the shiny side, leaving the rough side untreated. The material vendor laminates the smooth side against the dielectric. With a tooth side up, the MLB fabricator can skip the adhesion promotion step prior to print and minimize the adhesion promotion step prior to MLB lamination. The advantage of this approach is that it has the same cost as standard foil and provides some innerlayer processing advantages. The preroughened surface enhances photoresist adhesion and the smooth bottom surface improves fineline etching. The disadvantages of this approach include problems with complete resist development and with buried-via plating processes.

23.4.2 Innerlayer Process Sequences

An innerlayer is essentially a thin double-sided printed circuit. Standard innerlayers which contain no plated holes are made using a print-and-etch process. Blind- and buried-via layers contain holes that must be plated in either a pattern-plate or panel-plate process. Figure 23.7 shows flowcharts for four common innerlayer process options: two for standard innerlayers and two for buried-via innerlayers. All four processes start with a bare copper-clad laminate and end with a patterned double-sided circuit. The patterned circuit must be inspected and treated to enhance adhesion prior to MLB lamination. All four of these sequences work equally well with any of the materials discussed in the materials section.

Processes 1 and 2 are variations of the print-and-etch process used to produce a standard layer with no plated holes. In process 1, the artwork is aligned to predefined tooling holes. These tooling holes are also used for test and laminate. Although Fig. 23.7 shows a variation of process 1 that uses single-sided printing, this process can just as well be done with double-sided printing. In either case, the image is registered to preexisting tooling holes. Process 2 does not use innerlayer tooling holes for artwork alignment. Rather, the innerlayer is edge aligned in a double-sided printer. Side-to-side image registration is achieved by preregistering the two pieces of artwork. Tooling holes are punched, using optical registration, after the panel is etched. Process 1 must be used for any single-sided print process such as one based on wet photoresist. Process 2 will provide the best innerlayer registration because it compensates for panel distortion that occurs during etch.

Processes 3 and 4 are plating processes used for blind- and buried-via layers. In these processes, the printed image is registered to tooling holes that are drilled at the same time as the via holes. This assures optimum alignment between drilled holes and printed features. Process 3 is a pattern-plate process in which the main plating is done after imaging. This process uses a sacrificial metal etch resist, such as tin, that is stripped after etch. Process 4 is a panel-plate process that uses print-and-etch techniques to produce an image on a blanket-plated substrate. Print-and-etch processes have slightly better resolution than print-plate-etch processes, but in plated-hole products, they suffer from problems with voided holes. To avoid voided holes, the printed image can have no hole breakout and the photoresist tents protect-

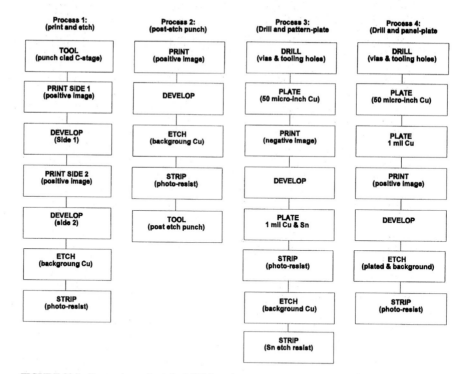

FIGURE 23.7   Processing options for MLB innerlayers.

ing the holes must not lift. In addition, to realize the resolution potential of this method, the blanket-plate layer must be very uniform.

23.4.3 Tooling Hole Formation

Three common methods are used to make tooling holes in innerlayers: prepunch, postetch punch, and drilling.

23.4.3.1   Prepunch.   Prepunch uses a fixed punch-and-die set to cut tooling holes prior to any other fabrication step. The bare panel is edge aligned in the punch press and all tooling holes are punched in one stroke. This has the advantage of high productivity and very reproducible tooling. It has the disadvantage that any panel deformation occurring during innerlayer processing will cause the tooling holes to move.

23.4.3.2   Postetch Punch.   Postetch punching uses an optically aligned punch to cut tooling holes after the pattern is etched. Fabricated innerlayers are edge aligned in the punch; a pair of video cameras image the printed fudicials; a servo-system aligns the panel, minimizing alignment errors due to panel distortion; and tooling holes are punched. This process places an optimized set of tooling holes in the layer just prior to lamination. Postetch punch can be automated so it has high productivity, but it is slower than a simple punch and die. However, the productivity gain achieved by printing without tooling may offset any productivity loss from using postetch punch.

23.4.3.3 Drilled Tooling Holes.   In process sequences 3 and 4, tooling holes are drilled at the same time as the vias. Like prepunch, this method has the disadvantage that process deformations cause the tooling holes to move. If this is a serious concern it is possible to drill the tooling holes used for print and then use a postetch punch to optimize the lamination tooling holes. It is unlikely that this extra process step is cost effective for most MLB designs.

23.4.4 Tooling System

There are almost as many innerlayer tooling systems as there are fabricators. Some fabricators use as few as four tooling pins, others as many as 20. In addition to easy stacking, the four-pin system minimizes problems arising from material growth and shrinkage in an overdetermined tooling system. On the other hand, users of systems with a large number of pins believe that by firmly anchoring the MLB to steel tooling, better stability is obtained. Figure 23.8 shows three possible tooling systems.

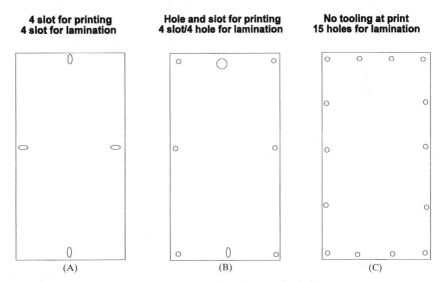

FIGURE 23.8   Three common arrangements of innerlayer tooling holes.

Diagram A in Fig. 23.8 shows a four-slot tooling system. This is an excellent system, because it is not overdetermined, and it allows for growth and shrinkage of the layers during processing. Errors from growth or shrinkage are measured from the panel center rather than an edge or corner. This halves the magnitude of these maximum errors.

The four slots may be used for print, inspect, and laminate, or if postetch punch is used, the slots are used for test and lamination only. Diagram B shows a system in which a prepunched hole and slot are used for print and six additional holes are used for lamination. This system is overdetermined, so material deformation during etch may make layers difficult to stack. Diagram C shows an overdetermined tooling system punched in a postetch punch process. This minimizes stacking problems, but it is still overdetermined during lamination.

23.4.5 Imaging

23.4.5.1 Surface Preparation.   The first step of the imaging operation is surface preparation to enhance photoresist adhesion. Double-treated foils and foils laminated with the tooth side up require minimum surface preparation. Generally, a water rinse to remove foreign material is adequate. For standard innerlayers, a more aggressive treatment is needed. Common options include chemical clean and pumice scrub. If a scrubbing operation is used, care must be taken to avoid mechanical deformation (stretching) of the thin layer.

23.4.5.2   Dry Film Photoresist.   Photoresist is supplied in both dry film and liquid forms. Dry films (See Chap. 17) are a popular choice because of the simplicity of application. For buried-via innerlayers, dry films are preferred since liquids are difficult to use with through-holes. The major weakness of dry film resists is a sensitivity to surface flaws and a tendency to lift on poorly prepared surfaces.

23.4.5.3   Liquid Photoresists.   Liquid resists work well in a print-and-etch process. They have excellent adhesion, a tolerance for surface flaws, and are relatively low cost. The disadvantage of a liquid photoresist is the need to produce a perfect coating. Foreign material, skips, thin spots, and dewetting all cause serious image problems. The use of a wet coating can also cause problems due to resist contamination of the transport system.

Roller Coating.   The least expensive and most popular way to coat liquid resists is with a roller coater consisting of a pair of pinch rollers in which one or both rollers are used for coating. The coating roller has a closely spaced precisely cut spiral grove. Liquid is metered onto this roller and then transferred to the panel. A good roller coater produces an extremely uniform coating. By carefully selecting coater parameters, it is possible to achieve a coating thickness control of 0.1 mil. Some roller coaters use the top roller as a coating roller, allowing the panel to be transported on a clean conveyor system. In these systems, the resist can be dried or the panel can be printed wet. Other roller coaters use both the top and bottom rollers for coating. These roller coaters require a handling system that holds the panel by its edge until the resist is dry. The coating roller is the weak link in a roller coating. Alignment problems result in nonuniform coatings. Flaws produce repeating defects in the coating. Worn or improperly cut grooves result in a low-quality coating.

Curtain Coating.   Liquids can also be applied by curtain coating. The curtain coater operates by pumping a "waterfall" of liquid through a narrow slot. By careful control of the slot width, pumping pressure, and viscosity, a well-controlled curtain of liquid is created. When a panel moves through the curtain, a thin coating is applied to one side. Curtain coaters produce a good-quality coating, but not all photoresists have the proper viscosity for curtain coating. Curtain coaters are more expensive than roller coaters, and they are generally used for processes such as solder mask where the coating must be applied to an uneven surface.

Electrodeposition.   In electrodeposition, a polymer is deposited on a biased metal surface submerged in a liquid medium by a process that is analogous to plating. It gives a well-controlled, high-quality coating. Electrodeposition is expensive and is not widely used for MLB processing.

23.4.5.4   Photoprint.   The third step in imaging is to photoprint the resist. Most printers use hard contact between the film and the innerlayer. This allows good image reproduction without collimated light. The drawbacks of contact printing are defects associated with poor contact, poor productivity due to the time required to establish hard contact, and the potential for artwork damage. The alternative, off-contact printing, holds the film a small distance above the innerlayer surface and prints with collimated light. It permits a high degree of automation. Off-contact printing is absolutely necessary for printing wet layers. The disadvantage of off-contact printing is a loss of resolution due to incomplete collimation and a great sensitivity to dust and scratches on the artwork.

23.4.6   Develop, Etch, and Strip

All modern innerlayer photoresists are aqueous soluble. This means they develop in a mild caustic solution. Resists that use solvent developing are rarely used because of environmental and health concerns.

From the point of view of etching, the four processes shown in Fig. 23.7 can be viewed as two. Processes 1, 2, and 4 use the cured photoresist as an etch resist, and process 3 uses a sacrificial metal layer as an etch resist. The former process sequence is called print and etch, while the latter is called print, plate, and etch.

The print-and-etch process follows standard etching procedures (Chap. 21), but it differs in some details. The most important difference is that the etch resist is a cured photoresist rather than a metal, and the preferred etch is cupric-chloride. Cupric-chloride is easier to control than the ammoniacal etch used with finished boards, and it can be regenerated. Another difference is the degree of automation possible in the print-and-etch process. Since there is no plating step, it is possible to feed printed panels directly into an in-line conveyorized machine that develops the resist, etches the circuits, and strips the resists. These machines, called DES (develop, etch, strip) lines, improve productivity and reduce the defects caused by handling.

The print-plate-etch process is identical to the process for finished boards (Chap. 3). The use of a metal etch resist requires ammoniacal or acid etch. Resist developing is separated from etch by a plating step, so a stand-alone resist developer is required.

23.4.7 Drill and Plate

Buried-via innerlayers are drilled and plated prior to lamination using the same procedures as a finished MLB (Chaps. 18 and 19). However, buried-via innerlayers are thin, and it is easy to drill very small holes. Whereas an 8-mil hole is difficult to drill and plate in a 62-mil-thick MLB, it is relatively easy in a 5- or 10-mil-thick innerlayer. Some manufacturers report success with holes as small as 4 mil. However, very small bits are expensive and easy to break. Special handling is required to load the bits and the drill machine must be vibration free with very low runout. For most MLB shops, 8 mil is a practical lower limit for buried and blind vias. At 8 mil, it is generally possible to drill thin layers in stacks up to 100 mil thick, greatly increasing drill productivity.

The major challenge in buried-via processing is handling. Care must be taken in mechanical operations such as deburr to avoid mechanical damage or distortion. Often, a frame is used to stiffen the layer during plating.

Blind vias may be fabricated like buried vias and drilled prior to lamination, or controlled depth drilling may be used after lamination. Controlled depth drilling has the advantage that standard innerlayer processing is used, including foil stacking (Fig. 23.2). Controlled depth drilling has several limitations:

- Blind holes cannot be stack drilled, severely limiting drill productivity.
- It is difficult to plate a blind hole whose depth exceeds its diameter, limiting maximum hole depth.
- Drill depth tolerances make it easy to under- or overdrill a blind hole, producing a reliability risk.

All of these limitations are avoided when the blind vias are drilled prior to lamination. In this case, the process sequence for a blind-via layer is identical to the sequence for a buried-via layer. Layers can be stack drilled. There is no aspect-ratio limitation, and the need for controlled depth drilling is completely eliminated. To be able to drill blind vias prior to lamination, a component-capped stack-up is required. One side of the outer component layer is patterned prior to lamination, while the other is patterned after lamination. This means that when the blind via is metallized, the unpatterned side is blanket-metallized. This will be true for either pattern plate or panel plate. This outside layer is metallized again when the holes in the finished MLB are metallized. The result can be very thick plating on the exterior of a blind-via board. To minimize this problem, the blind-via innerlayer should be plated with the minimum possible current density on the blanket-metallized side.

The complex MLB structure shown in Fig. 23.7 requires two lamination steps but no new innerlayer process sequence. In the first lamination, layers 5 and 6 are laminated to layers 7 and 8. Both of these innerlayers are standard blind-via innerlayers. The resulting four-layer subassembly is processed like a blind-via layer. In the second lamination, the four-layer subassembly is laminated to a blind-via layer (layers 1 and 2) and a buried-via layer (layers 5 and 6). No special processing is required.

23.4.8 Inspect

Once innerlayer etching is complete, the innerlayer must be inspected. The purpose of inspection is to identify flaws before the layer is laminated into an expensive MLB. In addition, for controlled impedance layers it may be necessary to gauge line widths. Inspection is a necessity on dense signal layers, but is optional for power/ground layers. The two most popular inspection tools are electrical test and automatic optical inspection (AOI).

23.4.8.1 Electrical Test. Electrical test has the advantage that the escape rate due to opens and shorts is very low. It has the disadvantage of not detecting near opens and shorts. In addition, double-sided testing and off-grid testing are generally not practical due to the cost of large specialty fixtures. For designs where nets begin and end on a fixed grid such as 0.1 in, a universal test fixture can be used. In this case, electrical test is very cost effective. Such disciplined designs are often used for backplanes but are relatively rare for circuit packs.

23.4.8.2 Automatic Optical Inspection (AOI). The alternative, AOI, is rapidly becoming a standard. AOI uses a vision system to capture an image of the circuit. By comparing this image to an expected image and/or to a set of design rules, image errors are detected. AOI has the advantage of being able to detect nicks and protrusions. The weakness of AOI is selecting a proper failure criterion. If the criterion is very strict, the machine will identify a large number of possible flaws. This will require excessive verification time. On the other hand, if the criterion is not strict enough, the machine can miss actual flaws that look like acceptable features. As AOI technology matures, both of these problems are being minimized. For example, systems that compare the circuit image to the design data have a lower escape rate than earlier "design rule" systems that only looked for unusual circuit geometry.

Two methods are used to image the circuit. In one, the innerlayer is scanned with a tiny laser spot that causes the substrate to fluoresce. The circuit is seen as a dark image against the light emitted from the substrate. Alternatively, the circuit is illuminated with a bright light so that its image appears bright against the dark background of the substrate. Both methods have strengths and weaknesses. The florescent method is blind to surface flaws and it can be confused by substrate flaws. The top light method is oversensitive to the surface appearance of the copper. Modern AOI machines often use a combination of both image acquisition methods and detect flaws by a combination of design rule checks and comparison to design data.

23.4.9 Adhesion Promotion

Epoxy does not adhere well to untreated copper surfaces. This means that some type of treatment must be applied to the innerlayer before lamination. One option is to use double-treated copper as previously discussed. Double-treated copper has a rough surface with a treatment supplied by the material vendor. Many MLB fabricators report excellent results with double-treated copper. Others report problems with contamination and difficulty with rework. The alternative to using pretreated copper foil is to use a chemical treatment after etching. Two basic chemistries are used for this process: copper-oxide and silane.

23.4.9.1 Copper-Oxide. There are many variations of the copper-oxide treatment, but they all work by producing a rough surface topology that enhances adhesion. Depending on the exact nature of the treatment, the color varies from a light brown to a velvet-like black appearance. These treatments are often called black, brown, or red, depending on their exact color. All are essentially the same surface, with the major difference being the density of the copper-oxide crystals and the ratio of cupric-oxide to cuprous oxide.

All copper-oxide treatments are applied by dipping the innerlayer in a hot (85 to 95°C) caustic bath for 1 min or more. The copper-oxide process is difficult to do in a conveyorized machine, so it generally uses a batch process that requiring racking and unracking. This can lead to innerlayer damage and contamination. The copper-oxide process uses very harsh chemicals that can cause marginal circuit traces to fail. Since the copper-oxide treatment is done after inspection and immediately prior to lamination, it can be the source of quality problems if improperly done.

The copper-oxide surface treatment is very soluble in acids. If the epoxy-copper interface is damaged during drilling, the dark copper-oxide will dissolve during the plating process, leaving a distinct pink ring around holes. Although this is not a serious reliability threat, it is a cosmetic problem and often a cause for rejection. One way to minimize pink ring problems is to use a copper-oxide reduction step after copper-oxide formation. This step converts the copper-oxide crystals back to copper metal, preserving their topology. This reduced copper-oxide surface has limited shelf life, so lamination should follow this process within 48 h.

Copper-oxide treatments are not recommended for material systems that require processing temperatures significantly above 180°C. This includes Teflon and some polyimide materials. Copper-oxide reduction begins to occur spontaneously above this temperature, reducing adhesion. The use of a thin brown copper-oxide or a reduced copper-oxide will reduce the risk of this failure mode. Another problem with polyimide is that it is soluble in strong caustics, so if the treatment time in the oxidation process is excessive, significant substrate damage can occur.

23.4.9.2 *Silane-Based Adhesion Promotion.*

Silane can be used to bond epoxy to other materials. One end of the silane molecule bonds to epoxy. If the other end of the molecule is modified to bond to the second material, the silane can serve as a bridge, greatly enhancing adhesion. It is commonly used in this mode to enhance the adhesion of epoxy to glass. It can also be used to enhance the adhesion of epoxy to copper.

This silane process attaches a thin silane layer to the copper surface. In lamination, the active epoxy molecules bond to the silane, making it a glue layer holding the epoxy to the copper. The trick is to achieve a stable coupling between the silane and the copper. This can be done be precoating the copper with a metal such as tin that reacts with the silane. When properly applied, the silane treatment is very stable and is resistant to chemical attack and delamination. This silane process has the advantage that it can be applied in an in-line conveyorized system. The major weakness of the process is that silane layers can absorb water and fail in some environments. Early forms of silane adhesion promoters occasionally showed this failure.

23.5 LAMINATION PROCESS

23.5.1 Stack Lamination

The lamination process is the key to making a good MLB. In the lamination process, the board is subjected to heat and pressure that melts the B-stage (sticker sheets) and causes it to flow. This encapsulates the circuits and fills any buried vias. The B-stage then cures, establishing a good mechanical bond to the component layers. With the exception of press temperatures, all of the special materials discussed earlier in this chapter can be laminated in standard press cycles.

For productivity reasons, MLBs are usually laminated in a stack of up to 12 boards, called a *book*. Figure 23.9 shows the configuration of a typical book, in which the outermost item is a caul plate or carrier plate. These are thick oversized metal plates, generally steel but sometimes hardened aluminum. The purpose of the caul plate is to provide a stable base to transport the book. The next element in the book is a compliant spacer. The purpose of the compliant material is to provide thermal lagging and to assure that pressure is uniformly applied. Among the materials used for this purpose are multiple sheets of kraft paper, silicone rubber pads, expanded paper-mat paper, and composite board. Kraft paper has the advantage of low cost, but it produces an odor that some press operators find objectionable. Silicone rubber pads have the advantage of being reusable, but they have limited success in controlling edge voids. Excellent results are reported with expanded paper mat, and there are commercial sources for this paper that provide a release sheet which allows several reuses.

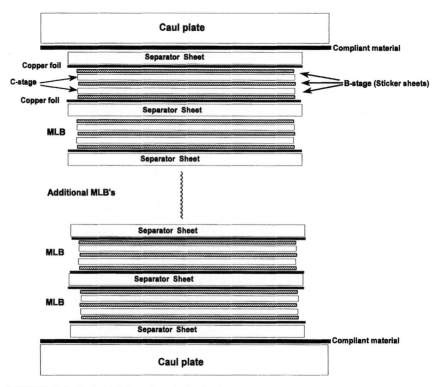

FIGURE 23.9   Typical MLB stack-up for lamination.

The multilayer boards in the book are isolated from each other by metal separator sheets. The separator sheets provide a mold surface for the laminated MLB. It is extremely important that the separator sheets be clean and free of debris. Both aluminum and steel separator sheets are used. The most common type of steel is one of the 400 series stainless steels that have a very durable surface. Hardened 300 series steels are also occasionally used. Separator sheet thicknesses range from as thin as 0.015 in to as thick as 0.062 in. The thicker plates are more rigid and resist the tendency of internal layer features to print through from one MLB to another. Thin aluminum plates have the advantage of being disposable, eliminating the need for cleaning.

Most fabricators use tooling pins that go from caul plate to caul plate, passing through each board and all of the separator sheets. Since the CTE of stainless steel roughly matches the in-plane CTE of a multilayer board, a tight fit to the pin is possible. Aluminum has a much higher CTE, so if aluminum is used, a loose fit to the tooling pin is required.

23.5.2 Types of Lamination Processes

23.5.2.1 Mass Lamination.   The layer-to-layer registration of the MLB is generally maintained by tooling pins. The exception is called *mass lamination.* In a mass lamination process, the MLB tooling holes are drilled after lamination using x-ray or spot facing to locate internal features. With a four-layer, foil-capped MLB, no tooling is needed during lamination. For higher-layer-count boards, the mass lamination process uses rivets to align the cores.

23.5.2.2 Standard Hydraulic Lamination.   A standard hydraulic press has a top or bottom ram and several floating platens that create multiple press openings. Typical presses have four to eight openings. An eight-opening press that laminates 12 high books of MLBs produces 96 MLBs per press cycle. Hydraulic presses are heated by steam, hot oil, or electrical resistance heaters. The steam and hot-oil presses have the advantage of fast heating rates, but their maximum temperatures are limited by the temperature of the heating fluid. For steam this is generally below the lamination temperature needed for high-temperature materials. If a steam press must be used, polyimide, PPO, and cyanate esters can be oven baked to complete their cure. However, the thermal plastic adhesive layers used with Teflon are not compatible with a steam press.

23.5.2.3 Vacuum-Assisted Hydraulic Lamination.   Many hydraulic presses use vacuum to eliminate volatiles. Users of vacuum presses report a reduction of edge voiding and the ability to laminate at a lower pressure. Almost all hydraulic presses sold since 1990 are equipped with a vacuum chamber. In a typical process, the caul plate is loaded onto a spring-loaded rail that holds it off the press platen and limits the heat transfer to the book. The vacuum chamber is closed and a vacuum is drawn and held for up to 15 min. This gives the vacuum time to pull air, moisture, and other volatiles out of the book. At the completion of this prevacuum process, the press is closed, compressing the spring-loaded rails and establishing good thermal contact with the press platens. It is possible to retrofit old presses for vacuum operation through the use of bags or vacuum frames that enclose the caul plates, but the lack of rails means that the prevacuum cycle is done outside the press.

23.5.2.4 Autoclave.   The autoclave is a sealed cylindrical chamber that subjects the book to a high-pressure heated gas. The book is sealed in a vacuum bag, and the hydrostatic pressure from the gas produces the force necessary for lamination. In principle, the autoclave is an excellent machine for producing a void-free lamination. Since the pressure is hydrostatic, it eliminates the problem of low pressure at the panel edge. This results in void-free panel borders and increases the usable area on a panel. In practice, an autoclave requires a long prevacuum cycle and has a slow heat-up rate. It is also vulnerable to problems with vacuum bag failures. The result is that autoclaves have not found broad acceptance.

23.5.3 Critical Lamination Variables

Since hydraulic presses are by far the most common type of press, the following discussion will focus on that process. The quality of the MLB lamination is affected by both the pressure ramp and the temperature ramp. There are almost as many unique cycles as there are fabricators. However, in general, the lamination cycle can be divided into four regions: B-stage melt, B-stage flow, B-stage cure, and cool-down. Figure 23.10 shows a typical lamination cycle with some of the critical variables identified.

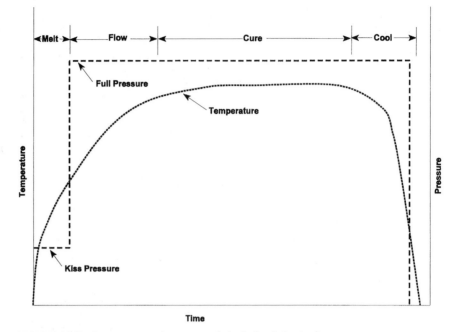

FIGURE 23.10 Temperature and pressure cycle for hydraulic lamination.

23.5.3.1 B-Stage Melt. At the beginning of the melt portion of the lamination cycle, the B-stage is solid and the pressure should be low. Excessive pressure during this portion of the cycle will damage the glass cloth and exaggerate problems with image print-through. Most press cycles start with a low pressure known as a *kiss pressure*. The kiss pressure is high enough to assure good thermal contact without damaging the MLB. The length of the kiss cycle depends on the heating rates and the cure kinetics of the B-stage. In a hot-press cycle, the book is loaded into a preheated press, and the heating rate approaches 20°C/min. In such a cycle, the kiss cycle should be limited to a few minutes, or the B-stage will begin to cure before flow is complete. At the opposite extreme, the press is loaded cold, and the heating rate is determined by the heating ramp of the press. For a slow heating rate of 5°C/min, a kiss cycle of 15 min is appropriate.

23.5.3.2 B-Stage Flow. The second portion of the cycle begins when the B-stage liquifies but before its viscosity begins to rise due to curing. In this region of the cycle, the liquid B-stage flows and encapsulates the circuitry. As long as the internal features are surrounded by liquid B-stage, print-through is not an issue. The key to good results is to select a pressure that will allow reproducible resin flow but which does not squeeze out all available resin before the flow is stopped by the progressing cure. Once again, the exact pressure depends on the temperature cycle, the B-stage viscosity characteristics, and the B-stage cure kinetics. For a fast-curing B-stage and a fast temperature ramp, pressures as high as 600 lb/in^2 may be needed to assure complete circuit encapsulation. On the other hand, with a slow ramp and a long B-stage working time, high pressures give excessive flow and best results are obtained at 200 lb/in^2.

23.5.3.3 B-Stage Cure. In the third part of the cycle, flow has stopped and the resin cure is proceeding. The temperature is held at its maximum value to minimize the time to obtain full cure. For a standard epoxy system, this is generally 170 to 180°C for 60 to 90 min. For high-temperature materials such as polyimide and Teflon, the cure temperature can be significantly higher.

23.5.3.4   Cool-Down.   The last part of the cycle is the cool-down cycle. In Fig. 23.10, it is suggested that the pressure is released after some cooling has occurred but before the book reaches room temperature. In many modern systems, the book is transferred hot to a low-pressure cooling press. It is important to control the cooling rate to minimize warpage. It is generally desirable to cool through T_g in a stress-free state without any significant thermal gradients present. A properly designed cooling press will meet these conditions.

23.5.4   Critical B-Stage Variables

During a typical lamination cycle, the B-stage undergoes several significant changes. At the beginning of the cycle, the B-stage is a solid with a low cross-link density and a melt temperature near 90°C. As the temperature rises, the B-stage melts and becomes a high-viscosity liquid. As the press heats further, the viscosity of the liquid drops. When the B-stage begins to cure, viscosity reaches a minimum and begins to rise. The region around the viscosity minimum is called the *region of maximum flow*. The wider this region and the lower the minimum viscosity, the more flow occurs. Figure 23.11 shows a schematic viscosity curve for a typical cure cycle.

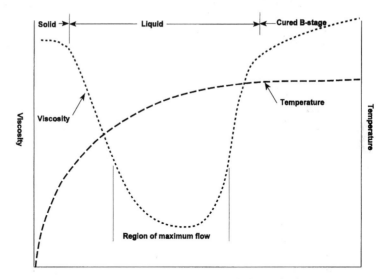

FIGURE 23.11   Typical viscosity curve for B-stage during lamination.

In a high-flow B-stage, the initial cure level is low. This results in a longer time at temperature before the B-stage viscosity rises due to cure. This is often described as a long gel time. In terms of Fig. 23.11, a high-flow B-stage has a low minimum viscosity and a wide region of maximum flow. A low-flow B-stage has a higher degree of initial cure and may include flow restricters to increase the minimum viscosity. High-flow B-stages are useful in presses with a high heating rate where the resin may begin to cure before flow is complete. They give excessive flow if used in a press cycle with a very slow heat rate.

23.5.5 Special Designs

Buried vias are generally relatively small, so the amount of resin that it takes to fill them is not significant. Therefore, the use of buried vias has minimal impact on the lamination cycle. Blind vias create a special problem. They provide a direct path for the melted resin to the board surface. For best results, a low-flow B-stage minimizes the resin flow onto the board surface. In this case, normal deburr and hole clean processes will remove the resin.

In a sequentially laminated MLB, a subassembly containing several layers is laminated, drilled, and plated like a finished MLB. This subassembly is then used in place of a more typical innerlayer in a subsequent lamination. None of these operations require any special lamination procedures.

23.5.6 Lamination Quality Issues

The result of a good lamination cycle is a flat MLB with a void-free substrate and fully cured epoxy layers. All layers must be well registered and the MLB must be free of warp. Each of these requirements puts special demands on the lamination cycle.

23.5.6.1 Poor Thickness Control (Print-Through). One cause of poor thickness control is *print-through* of features from one MLB onto others. When this occurs, the problem is most severe on the outer panels in the book. This problem is generally seen when a group of boards laminated in the same book have the same pattern and that pattern has a clearance area surrounded by copper. Print-through happens in spite of the use of steel separator plates to isolate adjacent panels. One cure for this problem is to use thicker separator sheets. Another is to use a kiss cycle that delays the application of pressure until the B-stage has melted. A third solution is to avoid stacking identical codes in the same press opening.

23.5.6.2 Voids and Moisture. Substrate voids are a serious problem in many lamination processes. One source of these problems is moisture. B-stage is very hygroscopic and must be stored in a low-humidity environment to avoid serious void problems. C-stage components also have a tendency to absorb water and many fabricators use bake to dry layers prior to lamination. However, for a fast innerlayer line with a good dryer in the copper-oxide line, an innerlayer bake is not necessary. Voids generally cluster in the low-pressure regions near the edge of the panel. This effect is minimized by the use of vacuum lamination. Voids can also be reduced by increasing the lamination pressure. However, the use of high pressures with high-flow materials can result in excessive flow, which leads to other substrate flaws such as measles.

23.5.6.3 Blisters and Delamination. Blisters and delamination are also caused by trapped volatiles that collect in the low-pressure regions associated with print-through. If a board has wide copper borders on every layer, blisters are often found in the lower-pressure circuit areas adjacent to the borders. The best solution to this problem is to avoid areas of heavy copper adjacent to low-density circuit areas by replacing solid borders with a dot or stripe pattern.

23.5.6.4 Undercure. The requirement of full cure is relatively easy to obtain if proper cure time and temperature are used. However, material problems or press problems can lead to undercure. The best way to detect this problem is to use a TMA to measure T_g. The TMA measures the z-axis coefficient of expansion which changes at T_g. Periodic measurements of T_g can be used as the basis of a control chart to flag changes in the material or the processes. Another way to check cure is to make two consecutive TMA runs to 180°C. If the values of T_g determined from the two runs differ by more than 5°C, the epoxy is undercured.

23.5.6.5 *Postlamination Bakes.* Many fabricators bake MLBs at 150°C for up to 4 h after lamination. One purpose of this bake is to assure a complete cure. Although a bake will advance the cure, it is unnecessary if a proper lamination cycle is used. As previously discussed, this can be verified by T_g measurements. Additional baking beyond full cure degrades the material and reduces T_g. A second purpose of the bake is to reduce warp often seen in the outer boards of a book. Although a postlamination bake will flatten panels, it is more of a repair than a root-cause solution. If the panels are cured in the press in a way that assures they go through T_g in an isothermal stress–free state, warpage should not occur. The warpage seen in the outer boards of a book are generally a symptom of nonuniform cooling. The third purpose of a bake is to relax internal stress and improve registration. Internal stresses are a symptom of an overdetermined tooling system. If such a system is used, a bake may improve registration. If the more popular four-pin system is used, a bake is unnecessary.

23.5.7 Lamination Summary

The standard hydraulic vacuum press cycle is flexible and has very high productivity. Through the use of multiple openings and stacked lamination, up to 96 panels can be produced in a single 90-min cycle. Hydraulic lamination works effectively with all of the materials and designs discussed in this chapter.

MLB fabricators use many different press cycles, and there are B-stage formulations available for each. The most significant difference among press cycles is in the heating rate. At one extreme, the MLBs are loaded into a cold press. This gives a very slow heating rate, and a B-stage with a low flow is needed to avoid excessive flow. This material works well at low pressures, minimizing print-through and innerlayer distortion. A vacuum cycle is recommended, to minimize voiding in low-pressure regions near the panel edge.

The other extreme is a hot-loaded press with a very fast temperature rise. This cycle needs a high-flow material and a high pressure to complete the resin flow cycle before the onset of cure. Although a vacuum is less important with this cycle, it will minimize edge voids.

Some fabricators use bakes both before and after lamination. The bake before lamination is designed to assure dry layers, but is only needed if innerlayers are stored at high humidity for several days prior to lamination. Other fabricators use a bake after lamination to complete the cure, reduce warp, and relieve stress. Although a postbake will achieve these goals, it is unnecessary in a well-designed lamination process. In the case of high-temperature materials such as polyimide, cyanate ester, and PPO, a postbake is a useful way to achieve a full cure in a process where the maximum press temperature is limited.

CHAPTER 24*
SOLDER RESIST MATERIAL AND PROCESSES

Dr. Hayo Nakahara
N.T. Information, Ltd., Huntington, New York

24.1 INTRODUCTION AND DEFINITION

IPC-T-50[†] b defines a solder resist (mask) as "a coating material used to mask or to protect selected areas of a printed wiring board (PWB) from the action of an etchant, solder, or plating." A somewhat more useful working definition for a solder resist is as follows: a coating which masks off a printed wiring board surface and prevents those areas from accepting any solder during reflow or wave soldering processing (see Fig. 24.1).

24.2 FUNCTIONS OF A SOLDER RESIST

The prime function of a solder resist is to restrict the molten solder pickup or flow in those areas of the PWB, holes, pads, and conductor lines that are not covered by the solder resist. PWB designers, however, often expect more functionality out of the solder resist than just a means to restrict the solder pickup. Table 24.1 lists the functions of a solder resist.

24.3 DESIGN CONSIDERATIONS FOR SOLDER RESISTS

24.3.1 Design Goals

The design goals for the selection and application of a solder resist should be carefully considered. As with all design goals, one should try to achieve maximum design flexibility, reliability, and functionality at a cost consistent with the required level of system performance.

---

* Sections 24.1 to 24.9 have been adapted from Lyle R. Wallig, "Solder Resist," in Coombs (ed.), *Printed Circuits Handbook,* 3d ed., McGraw-Hill, New York, 1988, Chap. 16. Sections 24.10 to 24.12 were prepared specifically for this edition by Dr. Nakahara.
† Institute for Interconnecting and Packaging Electronic Circuits (IPC), Lincolnwood, Illinois.

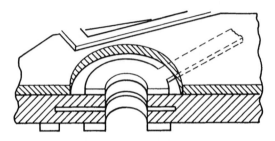

FIGURE 24.1 Important factors of solder resist on a printed wiring board: (*a*) mask should be away from plated-through-hole and its associated land or pad; (*b*) trace should be covered; (*c*) laminated area should be completely covered; (*d*) adjacent conductors should not be exposed.

TABLE 24.1 Functions of a Solder Resist

Reduce solder bridging and electrical shorts.
Reduce the volume of solder pickup to obtain cost and weight savings.
Reduce solder pot contamination (copper and gold).
Protect PWB circuitry from handling damage, i.e., dirt, fingerprints, etc.
Provide an environmental barrier.
Fill space between conductor lines and pads with material of known dielectric characteristics.
Provide an electromigration barrier for dendritic growth.
Provide an insulation or dielectric barrier between electrical components and conductor lines or via
   interconnections when components are mounted directly on top of the conductor lines.

24.3.2 Design Factors

The system's performance and reliability requirements are the keys in determining the selection process for a solder resist. Critical life-support systems will require different materials and standards than a less critical system such as a VCR.

Table 24.2 outlines some of the factors to consider in the design process when selecting a solder resist.

It is not very likely that a single solder resist material or application technique will satisfy all the design considerations that are viewed as necessary. It should also be noted that not all the design factors listed in Table 24.2 carry the same weight or value, so the designer needs to prioritize those design factors, analyze the necessary tradeoffs, and then specify the solder resist material and process that gives the best balance of properties or characteristics.

24.4 ANSI/IPC-SM-840 SPECIFICATION

In an effort to aid PWB and systems designers who wanted to know what performance properties or characteristics they would receive when they asked for a solder resist (mask), an IPC industry group developed the first solder resist specification in 1979. This specification is IPC-SM-840, entitled *Qualification and Performance of Permanent Polymer Coating (Solder Mask) for Printed Wiring Boards.*

The IPC-SM-840 specification calls out three classes of performance which the designer can specify:

TABLE 24.2 Design Factors

Criticality of system's performance and reliability
Physical size of PWB
Metallization on PWB, i.e., SnPb, copper, etc.
Line and space (density) of the PWB
Average height of conductor line (amount and uniformity of the metallization)
Size and number of drilled plated-through-holes (PTHs)
Annual ring tolerance for PTHs
Placement of components on one or both sides of PWB
Need to have components mounted directly on top of conductor line
Need to tent via holes in order to keep molten solder out of selected holes
Need to prevent flow of solder up via holes, which may have components sitting on top of them
Likelihood of field repair or replacement of components
Need for solder resist to be thick enough to contain the volume of solder needed to make good
    solder connections
Choice of specifications and performance class that will give the solder resist properties that are
    necessary to achieve the design goals

Class 1: Consumer—noncritical industrial and consumer control devices and entertainment electronics

Class 2: General industrial—computers, telecommunication equipment, business machines, instruments, and certain noncritical military applications

Class 3: High reliability—equipment where continued performance is critical; military electronic equipment

In addition to calling out the performance classes, the specification assigns responsibility for the quality of the solder resist to the materials supplier, the PWB board fabricator, and, finally, the PWB user.

Responsibilities per IPC-SM-840

Role	Responsibility
Materials supplier	The solder material and the appropriate data on the chemical, electrical, mechanical, environmental, and biological testing. Data are gathered on the standard IPC-B-25 test PWB.
PWB fabricator	The entire PWB fabrication and production process. This includes the application and curing of the solder resist material. The fabricator is also responsible for determining the end use application and the conformance of the PWB and the solder resist to the specification class call-out on the PWB fabrication print.
PWB user	Monitoring of the acceptability and functionality of the completed PWBs.

24.5 SOLDER RESIST SELECTION

The solder resists available are broadly divided into two categories, i.e., permanent solder resists and temporary resists. The breakdown of the solder resist types is shown in Fig. 24.2.

The permanent solder resist materials are classified by the means used to image the solder resist, i.e., screen printing or photoprint. In addition, the screen-printed resists are fur-

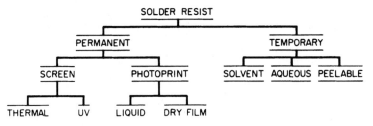

FIGURE 24.2   Solder resist selection tree.

ther classified by the curing technique, i.e., thermal or ultraviolet (UV) curing. The photo-print solder resists are distinguished from each other by whether they are in the form of liq-uid or dry film. The temporary resist materials are classified by chemistry or means of development.

24.5.1   Temporary Resists

A distinction is made between permanent and temporary solder resists. The temporary resists are usually applied to a selected or limited area of a PWB to protect certain holes or features such as connector fingers from accepting solder. The temporary resist keeps solder out of the selected holes and thus allows for certain process- or temperature-sensitive components to be added manually at a later time.

The temporary solder resists usually consist of a latex rubber material or any of a variety of adhesive tapes. These materials can be applied by an automatic or manual dispenser. Some of the temporary mask materials dissolve in the solvents or cleaning processes that are used to clean off the soldering flux residues. This is really a benefit, since it eliminates the need for a separate manual removal and/or cleaning step for the temporary resist.

24.5.2   Permanent Resists

Permanent solder resists are not removed and thus become an integral part of the PWB.

The demand for permanent solder resist coatings on PWBs has greatly increased as the trend toward surface mounting and higher circuit density has increased. When the conductor line density was low, there was little concern about solder bridging, but as the density increased, the number and complexity of the components increased. At the same time, the sol-dering defects, such as line and component shorts, greatly increased. Inspection, testing, and rework costs accelerated as effort went into locating and repairing the offending solder defects. The additional cost of the solder resist on one or both sides of the PWB was viewed as a cost-effective means to offset the higher inspection, testing, and rework costs. The addi-tion of a solder resist also had the added value for the designer of providing an environmen-tal barrier on the PWB. This feature was important and dictated that the materials considered for a permanent solder resist should have similar physical, thermal, electrical, and environ-mental performance properties that are in the laminate material. See Table 24.3 for a com-parison of properties for permanent solder resist types.

24.5.3   Selection Factors

General considerations are as follows:

- Reliability and performance data on the solder resist material

TABLE 24.3 Permanent Solder Resist Selection Guide

Feature	Screen print		Dry film		Liquid photoresist
	Thermal	UV	Aqueous	Solvent	
Soldering performance	1	1	1	1	1
Ease of application	1	1	2	2	2
Operator skill level	2	2	2	2	2
Turnaround time	2–3	2–3	2	2	2
Inspectability	2–3	2–3	3	3	3
Feature resolution	3	3	1	1	1
Adhesion to SnPb	1	3	1–2	1–2	1
Adhesion to laminate	1	1–2	1	1	1
Thickness over conduct or lines	3–4	3–4	1–2	1–2	2
Bleed or residues on pads	3–4	3	1	1	1
Tenting or plugging of selected holes	4	4	1	1	4
Handling of large panel size with good accuracy	3	3	1	1	1
Meeting of IPC-SM-840 Class 3 specification	3–4	3–4	1–2	1	1
Two-sided application	4	4	1	1	3–4
Capital equipment cost	4	4	1–2	1–2	1

Key: 1 = good or high; 2 = moderate; 3 = fair; 4 = poor or low.

- Cost effectiveness
- Past experience
- Vendor reliability and technical support
- Number of panels required
- Appearance and cosmetics of solder resist
- Number of sources for application and supply

Material considerations are as follows:

- IPC-SM-840 class designation call-out
- Cost and availability of materials
- Lot-to-lot consistency record
- Setup and cleanup times
- Working time and shelf life of solder resist
- Safety concern for release of noxious or toxic fumes during processing or curing steps
- Degree of workability

Process considerations are as follows:

- Operator skill level requirement
- Need for special applications or curing equipment
- Cleaning requirements for PWB before and after application
- Size of PWB
- Need for solder resist on one or both sides of PWB

- Number of panels to be processed
- Turnaround time required
- Machinability
- Need to tent selected holes
- Touchup or rework limitations
- Inspectability and conformance to specification

Performance considerations are as follows:

- Testing to IPC-SM-840 specification requirements
- Adhesion after soldering and cleaning
- Bleed-out of resist onto pads or PTHs
- Solvent resistance to flux and flux cleaners
- Ionic contamination levels
- Integrity of resist after soldering and thermal cycling

24.6 SOLDER MASK OVER BARE COPPER (SMOBC)

A major solder resist application technology is called SMOBC. This name stands for the application of *solder mask over bare copper.* A problem for conventional copper-tin-lead electro-plated PWBs is the flow of tin-lead solder under the solder resist during the wave or vapor phase or infrared soldering. This flow of molten metal underneath the resist can prevent the resist from adhering to metal or laminate. If the resist fractures because of this hydraulic force, the surface integrity is lost and the effectiveness of the resist as an environmental or dielectric barrier can be severely impaired. In fact, such breaks in the resist can actually trap moisture, dirt, and soldering flux and serve as a conduit to direct liquids down to the resist-laminate interface. This solder resist situation could lead to serious reliability and/or performance concerns.

The SMOBC process addresses the tin-lead flow problem by eliminating the use of tin-lead electroplating on the conductor lines under the solder resist. An all-copper PTH printed wiring board is often produced by a tent-and-etch process. This process is one in which the PWB is drilled and plated with electroless copper, which is immediately followed by copper panel plating with the full-thickness copper required for the PTHs. A dry film resist process is often used with a negative phototool (clear conductor lines and pads) to polymerize the resist in only those clear areas of the phototool. This polymerized resist will now protect the lines and PTHs during a copper-etching process which will remove all the unwanted background copper. The photoresist is then stripped off, and the solder resist material is applied and processed through curing. Tin-lead is next added to the open component pads and PTHs by the hot-air leveling process.

An alternative process uses conventional procedures to create a pattern-plated board. After etching, however, the metal etch resist is removed chemically, leaving the underlying copper bare. Subsequent process steps are the same as SMOBC.

The primary function of tin-lead in the PTHs and on the component pads is to improve solderability and appearance. It is important to demonstrate the solderability of the holes and pads on the SMOBC panel. This is accomplished by a hot-air leveling process which places a thin coating of molten tin-lead on only those copper areas of the PTH that have not been covered by the solder resist. This hot-air leveling process proves the ability of the copper surface to be soldered and also improves the appearance and solderability after longer-term storage of the PTHs and pad surfaces.

Since there is no flowable metal under the solder resist during the hot-air leveling step or later during component soldering, the resist maintains its adhesion and integrity.

The lower metallization height of the conductor lines allows the use of a thinner dry film resist and also makes the liquid and screen-printing application somewhat easier.

One variation on the basic SMOBC process is to make the PWB by the conventional pattern-plate copper and tin-lead process followed by etching of the background copper. Then another photoresist step is used to tent the holes and pads so that the tin-lead can be selectively stripped from the conductor lines. This would be followed by infrared or oil reflow, cleaning, and application of solder resist. A second process variation strips off the tin-lead plating completely and is followed by cleaning, solder resist application, and hot-air leveling. There are still other PWB fabricators who do not like either of these processes and are opting to use a nonflowable, copper-etchant-resistant metal like tin-nickel under the solder resist. The major shortcoming to tin-nickel is that it is considered more difficult to solder with low-activity soldering fluxes.

24.7 CLEANING AND PWB PREPARATION PRIOR TO SOLDER RESIST APPLICATION

Optimum solder resist performance and effectiveness can be obtained only if the PWB surfaces are properly prepared prior to the application of the resist.

Surface preparation usually consists of a mechanical brush scrubbing for the non–tin-lead PWBs followed by an oven-drying step. The tin-lead PWBs should not be scrubbed and require less aggressive cleaning procedures. The cleaning options prior to solder resist application are shown in Table 24.4.

TABLE 24.4 Preparation for Solder Resist

	Panel metallization		
Operation	Copper	Tin-lead	Other
Mechanical brush	Yes	No	Yes
Pumice	Yes	No	Yes
Solvent degrease	Yes	Yes	Yes
Chemical cleaning	Yes	Yes	Yes
Oven drying	Yes	Yes	Yes

24.7.1 Surface Preparation

Dry-film and liquid-photopolymer resists applied to meet the IPC-SM-840 Class 3 requirements are particularly sensitive to the cleaning processes and baking step used to remove volatiles prior to the application of the resist.

Tin-lead-coated PWBs should not be mechanically brush-scrubbed because of the smearing potential of such a malleable metal as tin-lead. Scrubbing can cause a thin smear of the metal to be wiped across the substrate, leaving a potentially conductive path or, at a minimum, a decrease in the insulation resistance between the conductor lines. Pumice scrubbing is also unacceptable for tin-lead circuitry, since the pumice particles may become embedded in the soft metal, which can lead to poor soldering performance.

Solvent degreasing with Freon* or 1,1,1-trichloroethane cleaners is necessary with tin-lead PWBs in order to remove the light process oils from the solder reflow step, dirt, and finger-

---

* Registered trademark of E. I. du Pont de Nemours & Company.

prints that are usually found on the PWB at the solder resist step. Solvent degreasing will not remove metal oxides or contaminates that are not soluble in the degreasing media.

The last step prior to the application of a solder resist to the PWB should be an oven-drying step in which absorbed surface moisture and low boiling volatiles are removed. This drying step should immediately precede the resist application step in order to minimize the reabsorption of moisture.

The most stringent performance specifications will in turn require the most stringent cleaning procedures prior to the resist application. Not all resists and performance specifications require the same degree of cleaning. In certain cases, where performance requirements are less stringent, some screen-printed resists may be used successfully without any particular cleaning or oven-drying steps.

24.8   SOLDER RESIST APPLICATIONS

Permanent solder resists may be applied to the PWB by any of several techniques or pieces of equipment. Screen printing of liquid solder resists (ink) is the most common; with regard to photoprint solder resists, the dry film solder resists are applied to one or both sides of the PWB by a special vacuum laminator, and the liquid-photoprint solder resists are applied by curtain coating, roll coating, or blank-screen-printing techniques.

24.8.1   Screen Printing

Screen printing is typically carried out in manual or semiautomatic screen-printing machines using polyester or stainless steel mesh for the screen material. If solder resist is required on two sides, the first side is coated and cured or partially cured and then recycled to apply the solder resist on the second side using the screen pattern for that side, and then the entire PWB is fully cured.

24.8.2   Liquid Photoprint

For some liquid-photoprint solder resists, a screen-printing technique is used to apply the resist in a controlled manner to the surface of the PWB. The screen has no image and serves only to control the thickness and waste of the liquid solder resist. There is no registration of the screen, since there is no image. The actual solder resist image will be obtained by exposing the coated PWB with ultraviolet light energy and the appropriate phototool image. The unexposed solder resist areas defined by the phototool are washed away during the development step.

Some liquid-photoprint solder resists require a highly mechanized process (roller or curtain coating) and therefore, because of the equipment costs and the setup, cleanup, and changeover costs, are best suited to high-volume production.

The liquid solder resists do not tent holes as effectively as the dry film solder resist materials.

24.8.3   Dry Film

Dry-film solder resists are best applied using the vacuum laminators that have been designed for that purpose. The equipment removes the air from a chamber in which the PWB has been placed. The solder resist film is held out of contact from the PWB surface until atmospheric pressure is used to force the film onto one or both sides of the PWB.

The roll laminators that apply the dry film resists for plating or etching are usually found to be unacceptable for solder resist application. The roll laminators were designed to apply a resist to a smooth, flat surface such as copper foil, and not to a three-dimensional surface such as an etched and plated PWB. Air is usually trapped adjacent to the conductor lines as the lamination roll crosses over a conductor line running parallel to the lamination roll. Entrapped air next to the conductor lines can cause wicking of liquids, which in turn causes reliability and/or performance concerns.

The dry film resist thickness, as supplied, is usually 0.003 or 0.004 in and will meet the requirement of the Class 3 specification for a 0.001-in minimum thickness of solder resist on top of the conductor lines. The resist thickness chosen depends on the expected thickness of the copper circuitry to be covered, allowing for filling of the spaces between circuit traces with resist.

24.9 CURING

Once the solder mask has been applied to the PWB, it must be cured according to the manufacturer's recommendations. Typically, curing processes are thermal curing by oven baking or infrared heating, UV curing, or a combination of the two processes. The general objective of the curing process is to remove any volatiles (if present) and to chemically cross-link and/or polymerize the solder resist. This curing toughens the resist to help ensure that it will maintain its integrity during the chemical, thermal, electrical, and physical exposure the PWB will see during its service life.

Undercuring, or an out-of-control curing process, is usually the prime cause for solder resist failure. The second leading cause for failure is inadequate cleaning prior to solder resist application.

Special Note—Inspection before Curing.   All PWBs should be carefully inspected for defects prior to curing. Once a solder resist has been cured, it is usually impossible or impractical to strip the resist for rework without seriously damaging the PWB.

24.10 LIQUID PHOTOIMAGEABLE SOLDER RESIST (LPISR)

With the advent of surface-mounting technology (SMT) in the early 1980s, the requirements for tighter registration of solder mask to circuit features have become ever more demanding. As lead pitch of SMT components became finer as illustrated in Table 24.5, conventional thermal and UV curable screen resists could no longer satisfy the requirements to deposit material completely and consistently between the board features, such as adjacent traces or traces and pads. Although dry film solder resist (DFSR) is able to satisfy many of these tighter tolerance requirements, it is expensive and sometimes it has difficulty in coverage of spacings between tightly formed fineline conductors at their base area, leaving small air pockets which tend to erupt during the soldering operation. Therefore, the use of DFSR has declined as SMT has proliferated and liquid photoimageable solder resist (LPISR) has gained acceptance. The usage of DFSR seems to be confined to some special cases when requirements such as hole tenting, small lot size, and thicker mask (3 mil or more) are present.

When Ciba-Geigy introduced the Probimer 52 liquid photoimageable solder resist (LPISR) system in 1978, SMT was not yet in place and most of the printed wiring board (PWB) manufacturers were reluctant to adopt it because the cost of the Probimer system was expensive compared to what they were then using. However, some PWB manufacturers catering to the telecommunication industry started to adopt it because of its excellent corrosion

TABLE 24.5 Standard Design Rules for Surface-Mounted Device (SMD) Pad
(Unit: mm)

Kind of SMD	Number of pins	Pad			Solder mask		Pattern wiring diagram
		Pitch A	Width B	Space C	Clearance D	Width E	
SOP (PLCC)	8 ~ 28	1.27	0.5 ~ 0.6	0.77 ~ 0.67	0.1 ~ 0.15	0.37 ~ 0.57	
			0.6 ~ 0.7	0.67 ~ 0.57	0.1 ~ 0.15	0.27 ~ 0.47	
QFP	64	1.0	0.6	0.4	0.135	0.2	
	80	0.8	0.5	0.3	0.085	0.13	
	100	0.65	0.35	0.3	0.085	0.13	
	48	0.5	0.3	0.2	0.05	0.1	
	224	0.4	0.22	0.18	0.05	0.08	
	300	0.3	0.15	0.15	0.04	0.07	

Source: NEC Corporation.

resistance; then, as SMT started to gain momentum in the mid1980s, other solder resist ink makers saw the value of LPISR and followed Ciba-Geigy into the marketplace. Today, there are a great number of LPISR manufacturers, offering material and process alternatives, and nearly all SMT boards are coated with LPISR.

This section discusses the scope of these LPISR technologies, particularly from the viewpoint of coating methods.

24.10.1 LPISR Makers and Products

Table 24.6 shows a list of major LPISR makers and their representative product line-ups. The reader should be aware, however, that there are many variations to the listed products and they are continuously changing; therefore, this list is presented as a set of examples, rather than a current exhaustive set of alternatives.

After Probimer 52 became successful in the marketplace, many LPISR products were developed. Initially, most of LPISRs were the solvent-developable type (1,1,1-trichloro-ethane) to match the performance of Probimer 52 in corrosion and electrical characteristics. Because of the environmental concerns, however, the use of trichloroethane is discouraged. As a result, nearly all LPISRs marketed today are the aqueous-developable type, with the exception of Probimer 52, 61, and 65, which are solvent-developable (a mixture of nonchlorinated, biodegradable solvents).

At some time, there were nearly 40 LPISR makers worldwide, but only a dozen seem to remain in the business as listed in Table 24.6. Improvements have been made continuously on these products, as mentioned previously. All products in the table satisfy IPC-840B, Class 3, MIL-P-55110D, and Bellcore requirements. Some makers list only a few products in their gen-

TABLE 24.6 Major LPISR Makers and Their Product Line-up

Maker	Trade name	Products	Coating method	Comments
Ciba-Geigy Ltd	PROBIMER	Probimer 52,61,65	Curtain	Nonchlorinated solvent-developable
		Probimer 71,77	Curtain	Aqueous-developable
		Probimer 74	Screen	Aqueous-developable
Coates Circuit Products	IMAGECURE	AQ-XV500	Screen	Aqueous-developable
		AQ-XV501	Curtain	Aqueous-developable
Dexster	HYSOL	SR-8100-01	Screen	Aqueous-developable
Electra Polymers & Chemicals	CARAPACE	EMP 110	Screen	Aqueous-developable, also curtain and spray-coatable
Enthone-OMI	ENPLATE	DSR-3241 A-G	Screen	US Version of DSR-2200, green
		DSR-3241 A-U	Screen	*ibid.,* clear
		DSR-3300	Screen	*ibid.,* matte finish
Lackwerke Peters	ELPEMER	GL-2461 SM, SM-G	Curtain	"G" designates green
		SD-2461 SM, SM-G	Screen	"G" designates green
		SD-2431 SM	Screen	Red-transparent
		SD-2451/2461	Screen	Blue-transparent
		ES-2461 SM	Spray	Electrostatic or conventional spray
Morton Electronic Material	EPIC	EPIC 200	Screen	Aqueous-developable
		EPIC CC-100	Curtain	Aqueous-developable
		LSF 60	Screen	Former Hoechst products
		LSF 60 MATT	Screen	*ibid.,* matte finish
Taiyo Ink Mfg	PHOTO FINER	PSR-4000 H,Z	Screen	Aqueous-developable
		PSR-4000 CC	Curtain	Aqueous-developable
		PSR-4000 SP	Spray	Airless spray
Tamura Kaken	FINEDEL	DSR-2200 (C,F,G)	Screen	Clear, fineline, and green
		DSR-2200 K	Curtain	
		DSR-2200 SP-AL	Spray	Airless
Tokyo Ohka (Lea Ronal)	OPSR	OPSR-5600	Spray	Electrostatic
Toyo Ink	SOLDEREX	SOLDEREX	Curtain	
		D14,D43,D44	Screen	Fast exposure
		SC 40	Spray	
W.R. Grace	ACCUMASK	CM 2001	Spray	Curtain and spray-coatable versions available

eral catalogs, but they offer extensive variations. All of them offer screen-coatable, curtain-coatable and spray-coatable versions.

24.10.2 Coating Methods

It is a standard practice for users of LPISR to select a coating method and the associated equipment, and then select the LPISR, rather than the other way around. Characteristic differences among various LPISRs being small, the selection of a coating method for the requirements of the individual user's goal dictates the success of the LPISR operation.

Once a PWB manufacturer selects a coating method and related equipment, it tends to be locked up with the method, preventing the selection of other options because of the heavy capital investment involved. Therefore, the initial selection of a coating method is very important. For this reason, the focus in this chapter is on the coating method rather than the resist ink itself.

24.10.3 Panel Preparation

Before proceeding with the topic of coating method, a discussion of panel preparation is appropriate because it is the starting point of all processes.

When cleaning copper circuitry for solder mask application, it is important to remove all intermetallic compounds, oxides, and organic and ionic contaminants. A typical cleaning process may consist of the following steps:

- Acid spray rinse (5% hydrochloric acid, for example)
- Water spray rinse
- Mechanical abrasion (jet scrub, pumice scrub, brush scrub, etc.)
- High-pressure water and deionized water rinse
- Dry and optional bake at about 160 to 180°F for 30 min

Mechanical abrasion ensures better adhesion of solder resist to copper and helps resist ink to flow into spacings more naturally by removing sharp conductor edges which sometimes block the smooth flow of resist ink.

24.10.4 Screen Coating

Open screen coating is the simplest entry-level method for most PWB manufacturers, although screen coating can be very sophisticated when the process is to be automated.

24.10.4.1 Single-Sided Screen Coating. On a worldwide basis, the most popular coating method by far is single-sided open screen coating because it is relatively easy to do successfully and has a low entry cost. By its nature, however, screen coating tends to remove resist ink at the conductor edge that makes the first contact with the squeegee and leave spacings between densely spaced conductors uncovered, whether it is a single-sided or simultaneous double-sided coating to be explained in the next subsection. (Figure 24.3 shows this weakness.) To overcome this weakness, the users of the screen-coating method normally screen the panel twice or even three times to ensure sufficient coverage at conductor edges and spacings, particularly at their bottom area. Users of PWBs usually demand that the thickness of the solder resist be about 0.6 mil (or 0.15 mm) at the edges of the conductors.

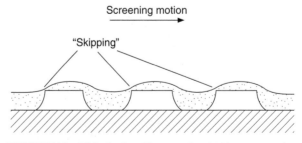

FIGURE 24.3 "Skipping" problem associated with screen coating of LPISR.

Multiple Screening. When the panel is screened more than once, holes tend to be filled with ink at their entrance, which can cause problems later in the process. Earlier, when LPISR was first introduced, PWB manufacturers used to blot the screen with a piece of paper after two or three panels were screened to eliminate excessive ink buildup around holes. Alternatively, the screen or the table (panel) was moved slightly on the second screening to offset the positions of holes in relation to the previous locations of holes on the screen. These practices made the LPISR process very slow and expensive due to the poor productivity. Modern screening machines for LPISR coating are equipped with various features which minimize ink falling into holes. These include elements such as scrapers, which scrape off excess ink buildup at hole locations at the bottom side of the screen while the squeegee returns to the starting position.

Tent-and-Etch Process Application. Some high-volume manufacturers make plated-through-hole (PTH) boards with a panel-plate/tent-and-etch process. This tends to yield a flusher surface than the pattern-plating process, using a patterned screen, which totally prevents ink from going into the holes. In such cases, the speed of screening can be as fast as 10 s per panel or 360 panels per hour. Screening the panel twice or three times naturally slows down the process time to 20 to 25 s per panel, resulting in throughput of only 120 to 150 panels per hour at most.

High-Volume Screening. In high-volume applications, two screening stations are connected in series. After the first side is coated, the panel is semicured for tack-free operation through a convection oven, and the other side is coated and tack-free cured again before exposure.

Screened Ink Curing. Most resist makers recommend the first-side tack-free cure at about 160°F (70°C) for 15 to 25 min and the second side at about the same temperature for 25 to 30 min.

Some manufacturers screen coat one side, tack-free cure, expose, develop, and repeat the same process for the other side of the panel, and then give a final cure to the panel.

Exposure Alternatives. Japanese PWB manufacturers prefer exposure of a single side at a time for better registration, while the rest of the world seems to prefer double-side simultaneous exposure. Energy required for exposure ranges from as low as 200 to upward of 1000 mJ, averaging 450 mJ. High-pressure mercury lamps of 5-, 7-, and 8-kW power are popularly used for photoexposure. Depending on the products and lamp intensity, exposure time ranges from 8 to 60 s.

Development of Exposed Material. Development is done in aqueous solution of 0.8 to 1.2% Na_2CO_3 at a temperature in the vicinity of 85°F (30°C) for all the products except Probimer 52, 61, and 65 which are developed in a nonchlorinated solvent.

Postcure Bake. Postcure bake is done at about 300°F (150°C) for 30 to 60 min in a convection oven. LPISR makers also recommend IR bump at about 340°F (170°C) for 5 min. Some high-volume producers using fully automated line screen legends right after drying the panel, following the final rinse and before the final cure, and combine the final LPISR cure with the legend ink cure in one shot.

Dealing with Warped Material. The panel is usually warped after the conductor pattern is formed. Some screening machines are equipped with a clamping mechanism to hold down the warped panel on the screening table.

Screen Coating Advantages/Disadvantages. The advantage of screen coating over other methods is its ability to block the four peripheral edges of the panel from being coated, thus minimizing the ink waste. However, unlike other methods, the screen must be changed for each different part number and, therefore, setup tends to be time consuming.

24.10.4.2 *Simultaneous Double-Sided Screen Coating.*

This method was conceived by a Japanese PWB manufacturer, Satosen, and the hardware implementation was made by another Japanese company, Toshin Kogyo. Depending on the models, double-sided screening equipment can coat between 120 and 180 panels per hour. These screening machines are equipped with back-side scrapers to prevent resist ink from falling into holes.

There is another maker of double-sided screening equipment: Circuit Automation. The equipment made by this company is essentially the same as the Japanese machine. However, the Circuit Automation machine, sold under the trade name of DP series, avoids ink getting into holes by moving the screen slightly and changing the skew angle of the squeegee on the second screening.

Double-Sided Screen Coating Advantages/Disadvantages. One major advantage of the double-sided simultaneous screening method is that the panel receives tack-free curing only once, and therefore the degree of cure on both sides of the panel is equal while single-sided screening makes the first-side cure more than the second side, and, in some extreme cases, the colors of the two sides may become different.

Double-sided screen coating has one weakness in that it is difficult to screen thin panels. To overcome this problem, the makers of such equipment provide a special frame to mount thin panels, which gives tension to the panel and makes screening possible. However, the throughput by the thin-panel version is somewhat reduced with such a scheme due to the more-intricate panel-mounting scheme.

Basic Process. The conditions for tack-free curing, exposure, development, and final bake in the case of double-sided screening are essentially the same as for single-sided screening. Over 300 double-sided screen coaters have been installed worldwide.

24.10.5 Curtain Coating

Ciba-Geigy introduced the first curtain coating system, Probimer 52, in 1978. Coates Circuit Products of the United Kingdom followed. Years later, Maas of Germany started to offer curtain-coating equipment, but no resist ink. Figure 24.4 shows a typical fully automated configuration of a curtain-coater line.

The speed of the belt conveyor under the curtain of resist ink determines the thickness of the coating. One pass is sufficient to secure the required coating thickness. The quality of coverage by curtain coating is excellent. Curtain coating can accommodate mixed panel sizes of different thicknesses without any setup change, but it can coat only one side of the panel at a

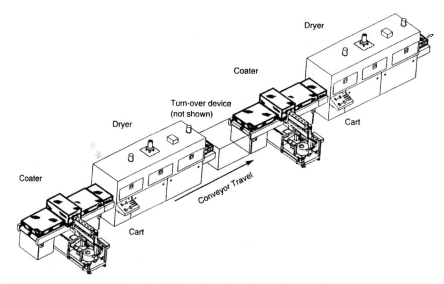

FIGURE 24.4 Typical fully automated configuration of a curtain-coater line.

time. Because of the nature of coating, the entire panel surface gets coated. To provide room for tooling holes and test coupons, 15 to 25 percent of the panel area is used as trimming, and resist ink coated on this trimming area is wasted in curtain coating. That is, "useful" ink utilization in curtain coating is usually between 75 and 85 percent. However, the newer curtain coaters have the provision to block two edges of the panel from being coated, thus improving resist ink utilization.

In the early days of curtain coaters, it was difficult to coat thin panels since the leading edge of a thin panel tends to droop down at the end of the fast conveyor belt under the curtain. However, this problem is overcome by a flipping mechanism provided at the end of the conveyor belt.

To avoid the "lap-around" effect of resist ink at the leading edge of the panel, the panel is usually fed into the curtain at a slightly skewed angle. Curtain coating can process typically 180 panels per hour; a high-productivity model can handle in excess of 300 panels per hour.

The process after coating is more or less the same as in screen coating. Newer types of tack-free curing ovens are made much shorter than the original one and the entire length of a fully automated line with two curtain coaters in series is no more than 60 to 70 ft.

24.10.6 Spray Coating

Spray coating is practiced in three different modes:

1. Electrostatic spray
2. Airless spray
3. Air spray (very small amount of air is mixed with ink)

There are two variations to spray coating:

1. Vertical spray
2. Horizontal spray

24.10.6.1 Vertical Spray Systems. When it comes to the arrangement of spray guns (atomizers), there are also a few variations. In one variation, a single gun sways sideways back and forth, perpendicular to the direction of panel travel. In a second single-gun system, the gun is stationary. In other coaters, two stationary guns are arranged in staggered position. Each one of these gun arrangements has its strength and weaknesses.

In electrostatic spray systems, effective grounding is essential for good results. Also, it is important to keep a distance of about half an inch between adjacent panels. If the adjacent panels get closer than this clearance, sparks may be induced at the edges of these panels, leaving uncoated spots.

In such a system, the typical coating speed is about 240 panels per hour.

24.10.6.2 Horizontal Spray Systems. All horizontal systems coat one side at a time. In most such systems, the panel is tack-free cured before being coated on the second side. In some systems, however, the panel is carried on V belt. After the first side is coated, the panel is flipped and the other side gets coated. In this case, tack-free curing is done only once, but it is difficult to process thin panels in such a system. Thin panels are usually spray coated vertically.

24.10.6.3 Overspray. Unlike screen and curtain coating, spray coating creates an overspray. There are various ways to treat oversprayed ink. In one system, a roll of paper, 800 to 1000 yards long, is used to absorb oversprayed ink. When the entire length of paper is used up, it is removed and treated for waste disposal. In other systems, a container tank is provided underneath the carrying belt to collect oversprayed ink. When the tank gets filled to a certain level (about once every two to three months), chemicals are added to coagulate the ink, and the coagulated ink is carted away for waste disposal.

Curtain-coating and spray-coating methods can process panels of different sizes and shapes without special setup, which is an advantage in dealing with small lot sizes. On the other hand, when panels of mixed sizes are passed through a spray coater, ink utilization can be very poor—as low as 40 percent. Some resist ink manufacturers claim oversprayed ink can be used again by adding solvent, but in reality, reutilization of oversprayed ink is not done because such solvents are not a part of ink formulation and are not compatible with the main ingredients.

Spray coating gives the best conformal coverage on the peaks and valleys of the panel surface. Because of this, however, spray coating can create skips in subsequent legend screening when valleys are too low, as illustrated in Fig. 24.5. After years of struggle, ink makers have now corrected this "skipping" problem by formulating spray inks to fill the valleys high.

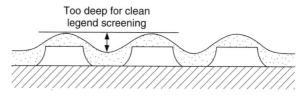

FIGURE 24.5 Spray coating can create good conformity with circuits, which, however, can cause skipping problems in legend screening.

24.11 TENTING HOLES

All coating methods described so far have one problem in common. None of the methods can effectively and reliably tent holes. Closely placed feed-through holes can cause bridging at the time of soldering. Flux can be entrapped in small holes. Therefore, some users of PWBs demand that the holes be tented or filled with solder mask.

Dry film solder mask can provide tenting, but it is usually expensive and often fails to fill the narrow valleys between tightly spaced conductors. To overcome this difficulty, Du Pont came up with a solution with the VALU system, in which the panel is first coated thinly with LPISR and then dry film solder mask is laminated on top of it.

When hole tenting is required in conjunction with screen, curtain, or spray coating, holes are filled with epoxy-based ink by screening after the panel is coated with LPISR. Some PWB manufacturers fill the holes first before coating with LPISR. Such processes add extra cost, but there seems to be no better alternative way to accomplish hole tenting.

24.12 ELECTROLESS NICKEL/GOLD PLATING ISSUES FOR SOLDER RESISTS

Hot-air leveling (HAL) is the most popular surface finish for SMT. As the density of SMT boards becomes higher, first-pass assembly yields tend to be poorer and repair is very costly and error prone. In recent years, electroless nickel/gold finish has been gaining popularity as an alternative finish to HAL. MLBs for cellular telephone applications and a large portion of PCMCIA cards (now called PC cards) are finished with electroless Ni/Au plating, which provides excellent protection against oxidation before the soldering operation. Boards with Ni/Au finish can withstand a few soldering cycles without oxidation. Initially, some LPISRs could not withstand the electroless Ni/Au plating operation. Improvements have been made on most LPISRs available in the market to accommodate electroless Ni/Au plating. If not suitable for electroless Ni/Au plating, LPISR makers offer versions of their resist inks that can satisfy the plating requirement.

CHAPTER 25
PROCESS CHARACTERIZATION AND CONTROL

Ray D. Rust, Ph.D.
AT&T Bell Laboratories, Richmond, Virginia

25.1 INTRODUCTION

The integrated circuit industry drives the requirements for interconnection density of printed wiring boards (PWBs). Each year integrated circuit manufacturing technology decreases feature size and increases functionality. As a result, clock speeds have increased and package size has decreased with higher pin counts.[1] These interconnection density demands have continued to move the printed wiring board industry towards circuitry with smaller and smaller dimensions. The majority of PWB products today have features in the 5- to 8-mil range, although some leading-edge computer technology requires features as small as 1.6 mil.[2] Future interconnection technology projections predict that 2.5-mil features will be commonly required.[3]

As features become smaller and the density of circuitry increases, the cost to manufacture PWBs increases[4,5] due to the more stringent processes and controls required. Accordingly, the cost of repair and scrap also go up.[6] If manufacturers are to profitably enter the fineline, high-density PWB market, high-yield, high-quality conductor formation capability is a necessity. In addition to the fine feature and high density requirements, the integrated circuits' higher clock speeds add controlled impedance requirements on the size and shape of conductors.[5]

For the finished conductor and the processes used to form the conductor during the manufacture of printed wiring boards, a generic definition of high-quality conductors could be that they are formed in the proper locations on the PWB for each board manufactured so that the finished board performance is consistent and reliable. With this definition, a minimum level of quality would require that the conductors are neither open nor shorted to a neighbor (i.e., 100 percent yield) and, in terms of reliability, the conductors are neither nearly open (mouse bites) nor nearly shorted to adjacent conductors (copper spots or residue). A higher level of quality might include control of the size and shape of the conductor (cross-sectional shape) within set limits leading to controlled impedance.[7,8]

25.1.1 Conductor Quality

Clearly, the quality of conductors on a finished printed wiring board depends on the materials and processes used to form the conductors. From a manufacturing perspective, the best processes are ones that are easily controlled and have a broad parameter latitude without changing their characteristics. Choosing among available conductor formation processes and then optimizing the chosen process to obtain the best quality of the finished conductors requires a reliable procedure which can assess differences in the finished product.

From a user's perspective, the selection of a PWB supplier includes non-process-dependent factors, such as cost and delivery, but ultimately depends on the quality of the product supplied. Choosing among the available suppliers to obtain the best-quality product requires a set of measures and standards against which each supplier may be compared. Finished conductor quality is an important subset of the quality measures for any PWB product. Typically, size and shape of the conductors on a finished PWB vary over the surface of the board, from side-to-side on the board, and from board-to-board. Usually the amount that the conductors' shapes and sizes vary within real product is not well known, let alone understood. However, the user does know that in many cases the finished conductors are not of the quality desired.

25.1.2 Conductor Quality Evaluation Methods

There are three commonly used methods to evaluate the finished conductor quality:

1. Physical measurements from cross sections
2. Optical inspection
3. Conventional electrical testing for opens and shorts

Each of these methods has disadvantages.

25.1.2.1 Physical Measurements. Using physical measurements from cross sections is time consuming in both the sample preparation and the actual measurements. Improper sample preparation can cause wider and thicker measurements of the conductors than the actual values due to smearing of the copper during preparation. At best, physical measurements from cross sections provide a measurement of the conductor at one particular point along the conductor which may not be characteristic of the entire panel.

25.1.2.2 Optical Inspection. Optical inspection is used to find faults in conductors, such as opens, shorts, and near opens and shorts. Optical inspection is prone to false alarms and typically does not provide physical width and height measurements. Although there are automatic machines which provide physical width and height measurements from a panel, they are expensive and provide limited information over the panel surface.

25.1.2.3 Conventional Electrical Testing. Conventional electrical testing is used as a pass or fail technique which provides no information about the good conductors.

25.1.3 Conductor Quality Criteria

Few manufacturers or users of PWBs have a sensitive and reliable set of measures and standards against which they can measure finished conductor quality. For high-density, fineline product, a universal methodology to establish measures and standards for finished conductor quality is a necessity. Any method used must have at least five characteristics:

1. The parameters measured must be sensitive to variations in major processing steps.
2. The methodology must challenge the most stringent product requirement.
3. The methodology must provide consistent and repeatable results.
4. The methodology must provide a variety of finished conductor metrics which can be related back to the manufacturing processes.

5. The methodology must be readily available to all PWB manufacturers and PWB users to establish a universal set of measures and standards.

A methodology now exists which contains within it the preceding five characteristics. This methodology has been tested extensively by Imaging Team members (Allied Signal, AT&T, IBM, TI, and Sandia National Laboratories) of the National Center for Manufacturing Science (NCMS) PWB consortium to improve their own processes and to benchmark commercial PWB manufacturers' conductor formation processes.

25.2 METHODOLOGY

Electrical testing to determine opens and shorts has been used for many years to electrically qualify finished PWBs. R. Olson of DuPont[9] and D. Ball of Chemcut[10,11] both extended the use of electrical testing to look at defects over the surface of panels.

25.2.1 Background and Development

Building on and adding to the early work previously described, in 1989, AT&T developed a methodology utilizing electrical testing to characterize printed wiring board conductor formation capability.[12] The AT&T methodology was adopted by the Imaging Team of the NCMS Printed Wiring Board Consortium, funded jointly by industry and the National Institute of Standards and Technology (NIST), U.S. Department of Commerce, as the common technique to benchmark existing processes and new ones under development.

AT&T gave unrestricted use of the test patterns and data processing software to NCMS Team Members for the PWB consortium program research. The NCMS PWB Consortium was created to promote U.S. economic growth and enhance the competitiveness of U.S. PWB businesses by accelerating the development and commercialization of precompetitive, generic technologies and by refining manufacturing practices. In 1993, Sandia National Laboratories (one of the Imaging Team member companies) developed a prototype electrical test system capable of quickly, accurately, and precisely measuring the resistance of conductors formed on PWB substrates.[13] As a result of the NCMS and Sandia National Laboratories developments, Conductor Analysis Technologies, Incorporated (CAT, Inc.), was formed to provide testing and analysis services to the PWB industry. CAT, Inc. offers a complete line of test patterns, electrical test equipment, and analysis software in addition to its testing and analysis service.[14] With commercial availability of the technology and interest shown from PWB trade organizations in creating specifications and standards based on the analytical results, the methodology has the potential to become a universal standard for evaluating conductor formation processes.

25.2.2 Key Methodology Elements

Key elements of the test methodology are:

1. Specially designed test patterns

2. A high-speed electrical test system

3. Analysis software that generates conductor formation metrics from the test data

25.2.2.1 Test Patterns. Three types of test patterns have been developed: single-pitch, defect-density test patterns, multipitch test patterns, and uniformity multipitch test patterns.[12,15]

Single-Pitch Defect-Density. As the name suggests, these patterns are used to evaluate the impact that the materials, equipment, and processes under investigation have on conductor defect density.[16] These patterns have been used in 1-mil line and 1-mil space through 7-mil line and 7-mil space designs (see Table 25.1). The conductor circuitry covers an 18-in × 24-in panel in four modules. Each module consists of 35 conductors that form a serpentine-shaped pattern over an 8-in × 10-in area. Pads at each end of the conductor are probed for a four-wire electrical resistance measurement. The conductors on the top side of the panel are predominantly parallel to the 24-in dimension of the panel, while the conductors on the bottom side of the panel are predominantly perpendicular to the 24-in panel dimension.

TABLE 25.1 Artwork Patterns

Pattern	Design	Conductor width, mil	Space width, mil	Number of conductors per panel side
Single pitch	DD11	1	1	140
	DD22	2	2	140
	DD33	3	3	140
	DD44	4	4	140
	DD55	5	5	140
	DD66	6	6	140
	DD77	7	7	140
Multipitch	MP212	2–12	2.5–11.5	220
Uniformity multipitch	UMP2_5	2–5	2.5–4.5	1408
	UMP3_6	3–6	3.5–5.5	1408
	UMP4_7	4–7	4.5–6.5	1408
	UMP5_8	5–8	5.5–7.5	1408

Multipitch. The multipitch test pattern has 20 four-in^2 modules on each side of an 18-in × 24-in panel. Each module has 11 conductors that terminate in pads for electrical test. The conductor widths range from 2 to 12 mil in 1-mil increments. The spaces between the conductors are the average of the adjacent conductor widths: 2.5 mil between the 2- and 3-mil-wide conductors, etc. (See Table 25.1.) These modules are placed in five columns and four rows over the panel surface. Adjacent modules have the conductors running perpendicular to each other. Each conductor is approximately 81 in long. This design can be used as a conductor formation screening pattern to determine which single-pitch patterns to process, as well as a conductor width and height uniformity measure over the panel.

Uniformity Multipitch. The uniformity multipitch pattern consists of 352 one-in^2 modules, arranged in 22 columns and 16 rows over the 18-in × 24-in panel surface. (Figure 25.1*a* illustrates the module layout and row and column identification for the uniformity multipitch pattern.) Each module has four conductors that terminate in pads for electrical test. These conductors form a serpentine-shaped pattern over the area of the module. Adjacent modules have conductors that are primarily perpendicular to each other (see Fig. 25.1*b* for the arrangement of four modules of the uniformity multipitch pattern).

This pattern has been used in four designs: a 2- to 5-mil design (2-mil, 3-mil, 4-mil, and 5-mil-wide conductors in each module), a 3- to 6-mil design, a 4- to 7-mil design, and a 5- to 8-mil design (see Table 25.1). In all cases, the space width between conductors is the average of the adjacent conductor widths. Patterns for both sides of the panel have identical module placement, but different nomenclature, and special pattern-design identification lines and pads. These test patterns were designed to evaluate process uniformity over a panel surface, from side to side on a panel, and from panel to panel. Because the modules are smaller, this

UNIFORMITY MULTIPITCH ARTWORK
PANEL LAYOUT

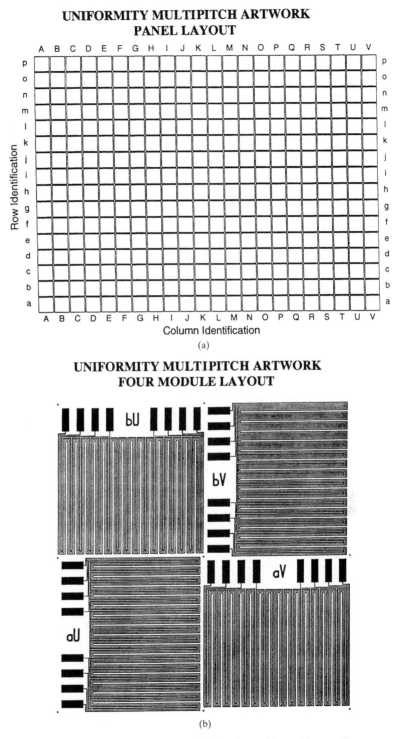

(a)

UNIFORMITY MULTIPITCH ARTWORK
FOUR MODULE LAYOUT

(b)

FIGURE 25.1 Uniformity multipitch pattern: (*a*) panel layout; (*b*) four-module layout.

pattern provides better spatial resolution than the 2- to 12-mil multipitch pattern and is better suited to this task.

25.2.2.2 Electrical Test Systems. During the development of the electrical testing methodology, several types of electrical testers were used: an AT&T-designed two-probe tester (Fig. 25.2), a modified commercial two-probe tester, a custom-designed and -built, commercial fixed-head (bed-of-nails) tester, the Sandia National Laboratories prototype fixed-head tester,[13] and, finally, the CAT Inc., fixed-head tester (Fig. 25.3). The requirement for the electrical tester is the capability of four-wire precision resistance measurement, with accuracy, precision, and speed over an 18-in × 24-in panel. Table 25.2 is an attribute comparison for each of these five electrical test systems. As a part of the development which led to the commercial availability of the electrical testing methodology, the electrical test system design evolved to the CAT Inc., dedicated tester.

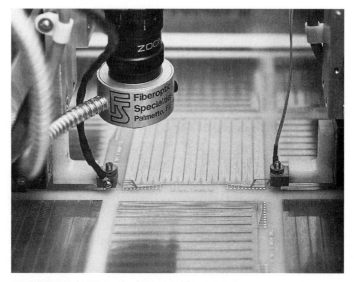

FIGURE 25.2   AT&T two-probe tester panel and probes.

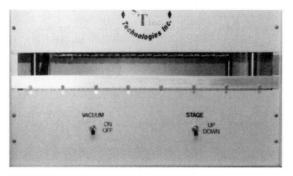

FIGURE 25.3   CAT, Inc., tester panel on platen.

TABLE 25.2   Comparison of Electrical Test Systems

Tester	Precision	Artwork test design capability	Tester use and capability comments
AT&T 2-probe	Good	Single-pitch Multipitch Uniformity multipitch	Slow; some reliability problems
Commercial 2-probe	Poor	Single-pitch Multipitch Uniformity multipitch	Slow; accuracy and precision problems
Commercial bed-of-nails	Excellent	Multipitch	Requires drilled registration holes; cannot test thin material; designed for multipitch pattern only
Sandia National Labs bed-of-nails	Excellent	Uniformity multipitch	Best performance in terms of accuracy, precision, and speed; will test only 12-in × 12-in patterns
CAT Inc. bed-of-nails	Excellent	Uniformity multipitch	Matches best performance in terms of accuracy, precision, and speed; designed for uniformity multipitch pattern only

25.2.2.3   Analysis Software.   A critical element of the electrical test methodology is the ability to obtain, in a timely manner, meaningful information from the electrical test system that can be related in a direct way to the chemical and mechanical parameters of the processes under study. This was accomplished early in the development of the methodology by the evolution of Conductor Analysis Test Software (CATS), a system of DOS executables which analyzes the electrical test data acquired from panels made using any of the specially designed test patterns: single-pitch, multipitch, or uniformity multipitch. The software is menu driven, and creates PostScript® files of tables, graphs, maps, and 3-D plots. When these files are sent to a PostScript printer, they create high-quality outputs that are suitable for technical reports and presentations. Figure 25.4 is a flowchart of the primary metrics available from CATS. Notice that the conductor width and height are determined from the analysis of the electrical test data. As shown in the figure, the data is first separated into good and bad conductors. A good conductor is neither open nor shorted to adjacent conductors. Bad conductors can be open, shorted to a neighbor, or both. From this separation, the conductor yield metric for each line width is generated. The data analysis further separates the bad conductors into opens and shorts (two conductors where the space between them is bridged by a conducting path). The number of opens and shorts metric, as well as the percent opens and shorts metric for each line width is generated in this separation. Finally, a defects map is created, indicating the type and position of defects on the panel(s) surface.

If there are good conductors on the panel, additional, completely independent information is available about the conductor formation process from statistics of the conductor resistance. The geometry of the conductors and the repeatability of the formation process over the panel, from side-to-side on a panel, and from panel-to-panel can be expressed in a variety of metrics, as shown in Fig. 25.8. Further details concerning CATS output will be illustrated in Sec. 25.6.

25.3   MANUFACTURING USE OF THE METHODOLOGY

25.3.1   Procedure for Making and Analyzing Test Panels

To use the methodology, test panels must be made with finished conductors formed from the specially designed test pattern phototools. The procedure for making these panels involves six steps:

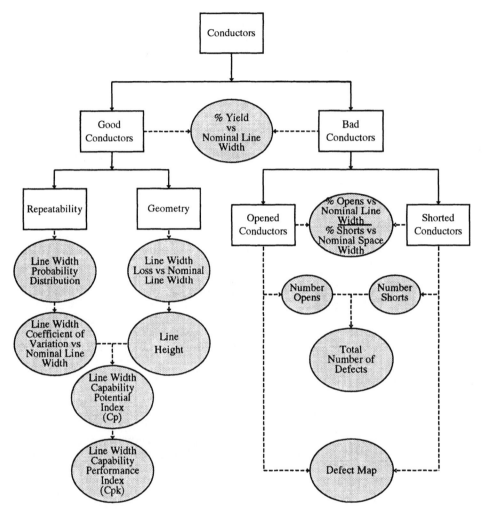

FIGURE 25.4 CATS software output flowchart.

1. Select the appropriate test pattern.
2. Select the panel size and type of laminate.
3. Process the panels.
4. Test the panels.
5. Analyze the test results.
6. Review and act on the results.

25.3.1.1 Select the Appropriate Test Pattern. The test pattern design is chosen by the type of information wanted and the capability of the process used to manufacture the panels. If general information of the process's capability to make a range of feature sizes is wanted, then a uniformity multipitch pattern with the next to the smallest of the four conductors chosen at the nominal process capability conductor width will supply the most information. In this case, there is one conductor width smaller and two conductor widths larger than the nominal. As this pattern is processed, weakness and nonuniformity in the process will show up in the smaller conductor statistics. If all the feature sizes have nearly 100 percent yield, then the conductor and space widths chosen were not small enough. However, if all the feature sizes have very low yields, then the conductor and space widths chosen were too small. The best choice is a test pattern which has high yields for the largest of the features and a moderate drop off in yield as the conductors or spaces become smaller. In general, a good choice for PWB manufacturing is the 2- to 5-mil or 3- to 6-mil uniformity multipitch pattern. Feature sizes in these test patterns challenge most PWB manufacturing processes and provide the best sensitivity for conductor formation capability. However, if the pattern features are too small for the process under investigation and most of the smaller features are shorted, then no statistical information is obtained from the good conductors and a larger feature size pattern must be used. These test patterns are excellent for improving and optimizing processes. If a process is optimized and the purpose of the test is to benchmark the process for a given conductor width, then the single-pitch test patterns supply the best defect-density information.

Once the test pattern has been chosen, the photomask should be made of the same material as used in production processing. A typical photomask would be first-generation silver halide on polyester. Regardless of the material, the photomask should not be compensated. Depending on the photoresist material, negative tonality (conductor pattern is transparent) masks are typically used for print-and-etch processes and positive tonality (conductor pattern is opaque) are typically used for print-plate-etch processes.

25.3.1.2   Select the Panel Size and Type of Laminate.   Most processes are configured to accommodate a specific size panel. All the test pattern designs are available for a variety of panel sizes. Choose the largest test pattern size that can fit on the panel size used in the process to be studied. The laminate should be FR-4 or the equivalent, typically between 3 and 15 mil thick and clad on both sides with copper.

25.3.1.3   Process the Panels

1. Prior to processing, assign a unique identification number on the top side of each panel, in the copper margin area. This identification number should indicate the order that the panels will be processed. When marking the panel, be careful not to obliterate or damage the registration fiducials.

2. Precise side-to-side registration of the top and bottom patterns is not necessary. However, the patterns, including borders (and especially the registration fiducials), must be within the panel edges.

3. *The orientation of the panels through all processing steps is important!* To aid in keeping track of panel orientation, the artwork is identified as TOP and BOTTOM sides. Additionally, the TOP side artwork has LEADING EDGE marked on it to assist in keeping track of the panel's orientation through subsequent processing. Care must be taken to obtain the most information from each process run.

4. Setup panels, used to establish process parameters, should be identified. Once the process parameters are established, all panels processed should be tested.

5. A minimum of 10 panels, processed sequentially at constant parameters, is required to obtain representative data.

6. Do not make any repairs.

25.3.1.4   Test the Panels.   The resistance measurements made during testing of the good conductors are used to calculate the conductor width, conductor height, and conductor cross-sectional area. For best results, the measurements should be acquired automatically, using four-wire Kelvin probes and a precision ohmmeter. Speed, precision, and accuracy are important factors to consider.

If the panels are shipped for testing, it is important to pack the panels carefully so that damage does not occur during shipment. Most laminate suppliers shipping boxes provide adequate protection during shipping, if the test panels are separated by plastic or paper and the empty space in the box is packed with cardboard filler pieces the size of the box.

25.3.1.5   Analyze the Test Results.   The electrical test data can be analyzed for type and position of defects. Two types of defects can be detected: an open in a conductor and a short between two adjacent conductors. Repeating defects that occur in the same feature from panel to panel can be removed from the database and the remainder of the defects can be used to predict yield on product. The results can be presented in tabular and graphical forms.

The electrical resistance data from the good conductors are used as a basis to calculate width, height, and area of individual conductors. Statistical analysis of the conductor dimensions provides minimum, mean, maximum, standard deviation, coefficient of variation,[17] capability potential C_p, and capability performance C_{pk} indices,[18] which can be presented in tabular and graphical forms.

The data can be treated as a single, complete set from the tested panels, or it can be partitioned into subsets. As an example, variation in conductor width can be evaluated over the surface of each panel, from side to side on the panels and from panel to panel. Additional analysis could reveal differences in conductor width dependent on conductor orientation or panel processing direction. These results are the basis for the next step: review and act on the results. CAT Inc.,[14] provides the only commercially available conductor analysis package at the time of this writing.

25.3.1.6   Review and Act on the Results.   Once the electrical test data has been measured and analyzed, and the written report received, it should be carefully reviewed. The process capability should be compared with benchmark data (supplied in the report). If the process under study does not compare favorably with the benchmark data, areas of improvement in cleanliness and control should be considered and discussed with those responsible for the process. If uniformity is not as good as expected, the metrics should be studied for changes in the process parameters and mechanical design of the equipment that could improve the uniformity. Examples of these and other uses of the analyzed data will be given later in the chapter.

25.3.2   Process Characterization and Control

For process characterization and control in manufacturing, the electrical test methodology can be applied in a variety of ways. Figure 25.5 illustrates three primary applications of the methodology which have been used extensively by the member companies in the NCMS consortium.

25.3.2.1   Benchmarking.   Process capability benchmarking has not been available on an industrywide basis. The use of the electrical testing methodology allows the formation and continual update of a universal database for capability benchmarking. Combined within a clearinghouse testing service, an anonymous, continually updated spot plot of process capability benchmarks for a variety of feature sizes can be made available to the industry. For the first time, a PWB manufacturing company can directly compare the performance of its own fineline manufacturing capability with an anonymous database of other manufacturers.

As Fig. 25.5a shows, process benchmarking is a one-time characterization of a process. Benchmarking provides a snapshot-in-time of the particular process sequence. Snapshots of different processes can be compared to show relative differences between the test data. However, it must be remembered in these comparisons that the results are only relative performance and not ultimate capability. Benchmarking of a process is the instantaneous capability

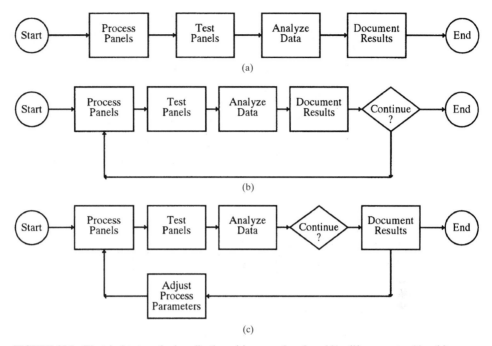

FIGURE 25.5 Electrical test method applications: (*a*) process benchmarking; (*b*) process tracking; (*c*) process optimization.

of that process which depends on many variables and typically will not be the ultimate capability of the process. Consistency and repeatability of a process cannot be determined using one-time benchmarking; instead, a process tracking test method must be used.

25.3.2.2 *Process Tracking.*   Once a manufacturer has determined the in-house circuit formation capability and has compared that capability with other manufacturers' processes by benchmarking, process consistency and control can be addressed through process tracking or monitoring. Figure 25.5*b* illustrates the sequence involved in the process tracking application. The difference between benchmarking and process tracking is that the test method is repeated with established time intervals between the processing of the panel sets. If process tracking reveals poor consistency in the data from run to run, then the control procedures for the process variables—such as conveyor speed, chemical composition, cleanliness, exposure energy—need to be reviewed and explored for adequacy. On the other hand, if the process tracking results show consistent repeatability, then the process control procedures are providing adequate control. Even though a process may show consistency from the tracking data, the measured values from the analysis output may be lower than or not as uniform as desired, either by comparison with other processes or by internal standards. In this case, a third application of the test method, process optimization would be used to determine the ultimate capability of the process.

25.3.2.3 *Process Optimization.*   As equipment and processes are improved, manufacturers are continually purchasing and installing new equipment and processes or modifying existing equipment and processes. The quickest and most efficient way of starting up new equipment and processes is to use the electrical test method for process optimization through a series of designed experiments.

Fig. 25.5c illustrates the sequence involved in the process optimization application. This application differs from process tracking in that the feedback loop for processing additional sets of panels contains a step to adjust the process parameters. If the adjustments are made according to a controlled experimental design, a substantial amount of information can be obtained with a small number of processing runs.[19,20,21]

Process optimization can be applied to an entire processing sequence or to a specific process step within the processing sequence. An example of process optimization for an entire process sequence is a complete print-and-etch line where the variables could be different manufacturers or types of equipment. Remaining with the same example of a print-and-etch line, rather than varying equipment, different chemistries could be evaluated within the same equipment. For the start-up of a new line or new process, a range of parameters for a fixed set of equipment and chemistry can be used to establish operating procedures and parameters.

25.4 USE OF THE METHODOLOGY BY SUPPLIERS OF MATERIALS AND EQUIPMENT TO THE PWB INDUSTRY

Suppliers of materials and equipment to the PWB industry should find this methodology invaluable. Just as manufacturers of PWBs are continually under pressure to build higher-density circuits with finer lines, the suppliers must offer products with greater capability to manufacture finelines at competitive prices. The electrical testing technology can be used to speed the development of new products or improve the performance of existing ones by providing performance feedback in a timely manner. Prior to releasing new products to the industry, suppliers can run extensive tests to establish the performance point of their product, based on a universal testing method, and use this information to advertise expected capability. Thus, the development cycle for new products could be reduced and the expected performance established prior to introduction, allowing suppliers to offer higher-quality products.

25.4.1 Materials Suppliers

Suppliers of photoresists, for example, formulate new materials for a variety of reasons and a variety of applications. Dry film resists have been the mainstay in the industry for many years, but during the past few years there has been a renewed interest in liquid resists, primarily for cost and performance reasons. Early in the material formulation process, photoresist suppliers typically rely on small-area images of test patterns to evaluate resolution. SEM photomicrographs of line-pair patterns formed in the photoresist are used to examine the quality of the edges, etc. However, once the formulation process has progressed to evaluating a few of the best formulations, large-scale tests are often performed at a customer beta site. These tests require a huge investment by both the photoresist supplier and the PWB manufacturer acting as a beta site. The tests are typically performed by selecting one or more products being manufactured (a "real board"), trying them on the new process, and comparing the results to the conventional process. It is difficult to determine the performance of a new resist with this technique because the real board is not a standard, is not designed to determine defect density or uniformity, and probably won't provide important information needed to optimize the process.

A more effective approach for photoresist suppliers to follow, is to install a manufacturing line at their own facility and optimize the production process in-house, prior to releasing it to industry. Several photoresist suppliers have chosen this approach.[22] With this in-house capability, the resist suppliers can now use the electrical test method to characterize conductor formation, improve their formulation and process prior to releasing the product, and, ultimately, provide higher-quality products to the industry.

25.4.2 Equipment Suppliers

Manufacturers of equipment, such as etchers and developers, can use the electrical test method to verify that their equipment is operating properly, and they can use the test results as documentable capability performance levels in their advertisements. The test results can provide important feedback to designers and development engineers of new equipment in their effort to offer new and improved products for the future.

Whenever equipment is purchased by a PWB manufacturing facility, the engineering staff's primary concern is that the equipment will be installed and operating properly as quickly as possible. The equipment supplier is asked to provide technical support for the new equipment during installation and start-up. Using the electrical test method, the equipment supplier can define, with the PWB manufacturer, a mutually acceptable set of metrics from the CATS output which, when achieved, defines the point in time when the supplier's start-up support is complete. Etching equipment manufacturers can also use the electrical test method to set specifications for conductor line-width variation across the surface of a panel, from top to bottom on a panel and from panel to panel for their equipment. Once the equipment is installed, it can be tested to see if it performs to specification.

In addition to verifying when their equipment is operating properly, manufacturers of imaging systems can optimize exposure and developing conditions for fineline, high-density product using the electrical test method.

25.5 USE OF THE METHODOLOGY BY PWB CUSTOMERS

Customers of PWB products are continually faced with the question of choosing a PWB supplier. This important decision is predicated on many factors, some process dependent and some not. Although price, delivery, and reputation are important factors, these qualities alone tell nothing about the manufacturer's process capability to meet the finished board requirements. Ultimately, the selection of a supplier depends on the quality of the product produced and its ability to meet the customer's specifications. Most manufacturers know very little about the conductor size and shape variation within the product they produce.

The electrical test method may be used by customers to qualify PWB manufacturers' conductor formation capability by requiring the manufacturers to supply benchmark data on their processes. Then, by comparing the resulting metrics from the benchmark electrical test method of potential suppliers, internal standards (which could vary from customer to customer) would be set for supplier qualification. Of course, this qualification technique does not test many of the other important processes besides conductor formation that go into manufacturing PWBs, such as through-hole quality, lamination, and registration between layers of multilayer boards. The quality of these processes would need to be evaluated in some other way. However, if the electrical test method data were to be updated periodically (extended time interval process tracking), the consistency and control of each supplier's conductor formation process could be tracked. Using the electrical testing method for standards setting and tracking would help both the customer and the supplier and improve the quality of conductor formation within the industry.

25.6 EXAMPLES OF USE AND INTERPRETATION OF RESULTS

The electrical test methodology can be used to characterize, optimize, and control any equipment, material, and process which influences the formation of conductors on a surface. Using the electrical test methodology:

- Manufacturer's processes have been benchmarked.

- Process performance has been tracked.

- Processes have been improved through optimization.

- Photoresists have been characterized.

- Etching equipment has been characterized and optimized.

- New processes have been started.

- Daily processing parameters have been set up for equipment.

The power of this technology lies in the analysis software which creates tables, graphs, maps, and 3-D plots. Table 25.3 is a listing of the standard, most frequently used outputs available from CATS. However, the standard outputs are only a partial listing of the possible outputs from CATS. Those outputs listed in Table 25.3 provide a glimpse of the scope and variety of conductor formation output metrics available. Although this visual, numerical, and statistical output is a powerful tool, its usefulness lies in the ability to relate it to the physical, optical, chemical, and mechanical parameters of the process under study. Benchmarking PWB manufacturing processes will be used as an example of comparative information obtained from the electrical test methodology and its interpretation in terms of equipment and process parameters. Other, alternative, uses are listed below:

- Tracking of process variation

- New process start-up

- Etcher equipment comparison and optimization

TABLE 25.3 Conductor Analysis Test Software Output

Metric	Type output
Yield (defects)	Feature yield and defect density table
	Feature yield plotted vs. feature width
	Map of opens in conductors over panel surface
	Map of shorts between conductors over panel surface
	Conductor yield plotted vs. panel number
	Conductor yield plotted vs. conductor width loss
	Conductor yield plotted vs. row identification
	Conductor yield plotted vs. column identification
Uniformity (conductors with no defects)	Conductor width and height C_p, C_{pk} table
	Conductor width C_p, C_{pk} graph
	Conductor width histogram
	3-D plot of average width loss for all panels
	3-D plot of width loss for individual panels
	Conductor width plotted vs. panel number
	Conductor width standard deviation vs. panel number
	Conductor width plotted vs. row identification
	Conductor width standard deviation plotted vs. row
	Conductor width plotted vs. column identification
	Conductor width standard deviation plotted vs. column

25.6.1 Benchmarking PWB Manufacturing Processes

CATS output data is available for each side of each test panel and the combination of the two sides. Since actual product usually requires features to be defined and processed on both sides of the panel simultaneously, manufacturing process capability is more accurately reflected in the average of all panel sides. The yield metrics, conductor line yield plotted versus nominal line width and the conductor line defects per panels side for 3-mil and larger features, and one uniformity metric, the conductor line width coefficient of variation (the standard deviation of the conductor line width × 100 divided by the mean value of the conductor line width)[17] plotted versus nominal conductor line width, are two of many metrics which can provide a measure of a given manufacturing process capability when compared with other processes.

Figures 25.6, 25.7, and 25.8 are typical CATS output data from six companies' benchmarked processes on 18-in × 24-in panels. The data are plotted together for comparison. For

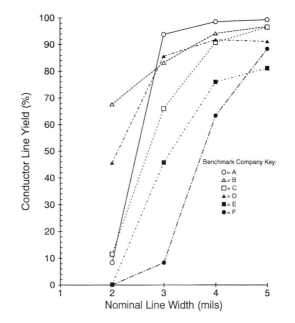

FIGURE 25.6 Benchmark companies' conductor line yield vs. nominal line width.

purposes of interpretation, consider that our company's process for making innerlayers is process C, represented by the clear box in Fig. 25.6. For illustration purposes, five other manufacturers' innerlayer processes are also shown and are labeled A, B, D, E, and F. How can we interpret the information in Fig. 25.6 for our company? First, assume that our company typically makes 5-mil and larger conductors but we are beginning to get requests for some 4-mil product designs and inquiries for 3-mil designs. From Fig. 25.6, at 5-mil conductor sizes, our company ranks second or third highest in yield of the six companies shown (one company is better, one ties our company). This indicates that our process for the feature sizes we commonly make is comparatively quite good (but could be improved; we are not number 1). Note that three other companies, D, E, and F, have substantially reduced yield (below 90 percent)

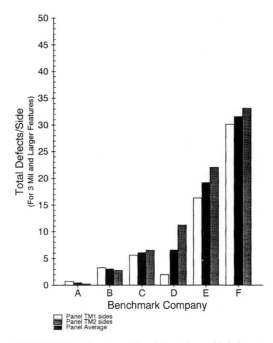

FIGURE 25.7 Conductor line defects for multipitch pattern vs. benchmark process.

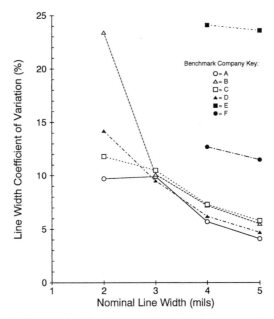

FIGURE 25.8 Line-width coefficient of variation vs. nominal line width.

at 5-mil conductor size. For the 4- and 3-mil conductor size, our company falls in the middle of the other companies' capabilities but is showing a significant drop in yield—down to 90 percent for the 4-mil conductors and around 66 percent for 3-mil conductors. To enhance our 3- and 4-mil conductor capability, we should optimize our process using the smaller features.

The data in Fig. 25.7 show that our process has approximately six defects per panel side for 3-mil and larger features. Exceptional processes (such as manufacturer A's process) have less than one defect per panel size for 3-mil and larger features. We should look at ways to improve this metric and lower the defects per panel side.

In Fig. 25.8, our process has the third-largest line-width coefficient of variation for the 4- and 5-mil features. This graph implies that our ability to make conductors with a consistent line width is not as good as it could be, and we should look for the source of the nonuniformity. To do this, we would need to look at the more detailed information available from the CATS output to determine whether it is a problem of top-to-bottom sides, from panel to panel, or over the surface of a panel side. This detailed information can tell us explicitly what type of changes need to be made in our process. A summary of our benchmarking from Figs. 25.6, 25.7, and 25.8 would be:

1. For 5-mil and larger conductors, our process is the second or third best of the six processes shown.

2. For 3- and 4-mil conductors, we need to optimize our process using these conductor sizes.

3. Our total number of defects per panel side for 3-mil and larger features is too high and we need to consider ways of reducing the defects.

4. The present process does not produce conductors with a consistent line width. We need to identify the source of the nonuniformity and take corrective action.

REFERENCES

1. E. Clark, "Status Report: The Global Multilayer Industry," *Printed Circuit Fabrication,* vol. 15, no. 4, April 1992, pp. 34–39.

2. H. Nakahara, "Fine Line Conductor Formation," *Circuit World,* vol. 18, no. 2, 1992, pp. 42–46.

3. M. O. Flatt, H. Holden, "What Will a World-Class PWB Shop Look Like in the Year 2000?," *Printed Circuit Fabrication,* vol. 14, no. 8, Sept. 1991, pp. 48–50.

4. T. Donnelly, "Discovering the Costs of PCB Fabrication," *Printed Circuit Fabrication,* vol. 15, no. 2, Feb. 1992, pp. 62–67.

5. R. Daniels, "Cost: The Complexity Factor," *Printed Circuit Fabrication,* vol. 13, no. 9, Sept. 1990, pp. 30–36.

6. D. J. McCue, "Survey of Fine-Line Yields," *Printed Circuit Fabrication,* vol. 13, no. 9, Sept. 1990, pp. 98–99.

7. This particular concept of quality was developed by R. J. Rhodes, formerly with AT&T Bell Laboratories, presently President of Conductor Analysis Technologies, Inc. (See also Ref. 12).

8. K. Ritz, "Manufacturing Tolerances for High Speed PCB's," *Circuit World,* vol. 15, no. 1, 1988.

9. G. Sidney Cox and R. A. Olson, "The Optimum Resist Thickness," *PC Fab,* Oct. 1992.

10. D. Ball and R. Campbell, "Fine Lines: How to Evaluate Developing and Etching," *PC Fab,* vol. 10, no. 8, Aug. 1987, p. 20.

11. C. Dessenberger, J. Melonas, and D. Ball, "Converting Fine-Line Images to Fine-Line Circuits," *Printed Circuit Design,* Jan. 1991, pp. 24–30.

12. R. J. Rhodes, "Description of an Electrical Test Method to Characterize Printed Wiring Board Conductor Formation Capability," *The IPC Technical Review,* vol. 33, no. 2, March 1992, pp. 24–34.

13. T. A. Estes and R. J. Rhodes, "An Electrical Test System for Conductor Formation Process Analysis," *Proceedings of the IPC Fall Technical Conference, P5-3,* Boston, Mass., April 24–27, 1994.

14. Conductor Analysis Technologies, Inc. (CAT Inc.), 8500 Menaul Blvd., NE, Suite B270, Albuquerque, NM 87112. Telephone: (505) 294-6936 (1-800-984-CATS).

15. R. J. Rhodes, D. T. W. Au, M. Vyas, and G. B. Fefferman, "NCMS PWB Imaging Team Methodology for Assessing Conductor Formation Processes," *IPC Technical Paper TP-1061,* presented at the IPC Fall Technical Conference, Minneapolis, Minn. Oct. 12–15, 1992.

16. R. J. Rhodes, and D. T. W. Au, "Predicting Printed Wiring Board Innerlayer Panel Yield," *IPC Technical Paper P5-2, presented at the IPC Spring Technical Conference,* Boston, Mass., April 25–27, 1994.

17. I. Miller and J. E. Freund, *Probability and Statistics for Engineers,* Prentice-Hall, Inc., Englewood Cliffs, N.J., 1977, p. 153.

18. D. J. Sober and W. Love, "Understanding Relationships Between Process Control Indices," *PC FAB,* March 1989, pp. 97–100.

19. G. E. P. Box, W. G. Hunter, and J. S. Hunter, *Statistics for Experimenters,* John Wiley and Sons, New York, 1978.

20. G. Taguchi, *Introduction to Quality Engineering,* UNIPUB/Quality Resources, White Plains, N.Y., 1987.

21. G. Taguchi, *System of Experimental Design,* UNIPUB/Kraus International, White Plains, N.Y., 1987.

22. As of March, 1995, the photoresist suppliers, MacDermid Co., Du Pont Electronics, and Shipley had installed in-house print-and-etch manufacturing lines.

CHAPTER 26
BARE BOARD ELECTRICAL TESTING

Philip J. Hallee
Everett Charles Technologies, Pomona, California

26.1 INTRODUCTION

Electrical test has evolved into a process within the process of printed wiring board fabrication. Advances in technology such as surface mount, fine lines and spaces, and increasing pressures to improve cost and economies put significant pressures on the electrical test area. Quality programs requiring netlist testing, surface mount's demands on fixturing, and volume and quick-turn requirements for speed impact electrical test in a variety of ways. This chapter is devoted to the why, what, where, when, and how of electrical test.

26.2 WHY TEST?

Better yet, why pay for test? Why do we need to test? The answer has several components. The primary assumption is that not all boards produced are good. If we could look at the yields in similar-technology printed wiring boards through the history of the industry, we would see exponential improvements in the percentage of good boards produced. Process improvements, scrap reduction, and a wide variety of quality improvement programs have had and are continuing to make a difference. There are several reasons to test, any one of which is sufficient to do it, but, combined, leave no alternative.

26.2.1 The Rule of 10s

First we need to look at the printed wiring board as a component of a completed assembly. A commonly accepted relative measure of the cost of faults in a completed electronic assembly can be expressed by the Rule of 10s (see Fig. 26.1). The idea is that the earlier a fault is caught, the less it will cost. An example might be an open in a bare board that is not found at bare-board test. The faulty bare board is now loaded with components, soldered, and tested. If the fault is found at the loaded-board level, repair or scrap of the assembled board is much more expensive than repair or scrap at the bare-board level. There are situations where the assembler of the board charges back to the manufacturer of the bare board some portion of the cost of the scrapped components, assembly labor, and/or the production cost. The costs can easily exceed the margin on the bare board and even the total cost of materials and production. There is also the risk for the board manufacturer of losing the customer. If the fault were to pass through or escape to the next level of test, which may well be a system-level test, the

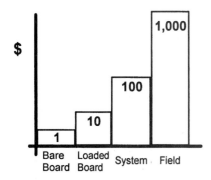

FIGURE 26.1 Cost of a found fault.

repair or scrap cost to diagnose and tear down a computer, automobile, telephone system, etc., can be quite high, especially if it is holding up or slowing the entire assembly line. A fault that passes a system-level test and makes it to the field or the purchaser of the end product—like the government, a corporation, or a consumer—has an even higher cost. Some of these costs are very tangible in the form of field service personnel, parts, and labor. Other costs are counted in lost business and reputation.

26.2.2 Customer Requirement

Where the Rule of 10s is a logical big-picture approach to the necessity to test, a requirement from a customer is quite the opposite. The board user has already determined that electrical test is appropriate and necessary and has made it a requirement as part of supplying the board. It is the obligation and responsibility of the bare-board manufacturer to meet this requirement.

26.2.2.1 Generic or 100 Percent Electrical Test. Unfortunately, this requirement may be nothing more than the words "100 percent electrical test" appearing somewhere in a purchase order or a larger package of documentation. Not only is such a specification relatively meaningless, but the issuer of such a requirement is led to believe that the boards will be tested to the most stringent requirements—that it will not be possible for a single bad board to be delivered. Nothing could be farther from the truth. Such a spec allows for very wide interpretation of what a 100 percent test would consist of by the bare-board manufacturer. The purchaser of the bare board will certainly be dissatisfied when he or she receives a bad board. Although the specific fault on the bare board in question may have a perfectly viable explanation, the 100 percent test specification implies that no explanation is acceptable. In many cases, this is combined with a limitation on acceptable test cost or board cost that the customer has imposed on the bare-board manufacturer, which in turn required cost-driven limits on the thoroughness of electrical test.

26.2.2.2 Written Spec. It is the responsibility of both the bare-board manufacturer and the purchaser or end user of the bare board to develop a test spec that is very specific in terms of test thresholds and method of testing, while keeping in mind the appropriateness to the application for the bare-board design. Some limits on test thresholds and test methodology may be due to equipment and capabilities of the manufacturer. It is the responsibility of the bare-board manufacturer to educate the end user as to the implications of test specifications in thoroughness and cost of test. A menu of test options and costs associated should be presented to the end user with clear explanations as to what fault types are found by specific selections and what fault types could escape from the agreed-upon test specifications. It is the responsibility of the end user to work with the bare-board manufacturer to develop specifications appropriate to the bare board being produced and to accept and plan for any test compromises imposed by cost or spec limits. Areas that should be covered in the specification are:

- Data-driven testing, source of data, format, and integrity
- Test thresholds for voltage, current, isolation, and continuity
- Fixturing method and simultaneous access of all test points
- Test point optimization
- Electrical test board marking
- Resolution of discrepancies in process (contacts and procedures)
- Resolution of escapes

Such agreements make for good communication, clear understanding, happy customers, good reputation, and good business.

26.2.3 Process Monitor

While the previously mentioned reasons for testing are fairly externally focused (external to the manufacturer), monitoring processes would be very inwardly focused. To raise yields, reduce scrap, or generally improve quality, there must be a measure or baseline at which to express results of changes. One of the best areas to collect data is at electrical test. This usually requires an integration of test and repair data. While the test system can identify a bad board and the location of a fault, a repair operator can further classify the fault to associate it with a specific process (imaging, plating, etch, solder mask, etc.). These data can be quantified and analyzed in a variety of ways, and actions may be required on one or more of the following levels:

26.2.3.1 Faults Specific to the Operation. As a company or bare-board manufacturer, there may be fault types experienced in the operation that are not typical of the industry or competition. This is a difficult level to analyze, as much of what would be considered normal or acceptable is perception, based on customer, vendor, or published data and may be highly biased. It may be better to analyze fault types specific to an operation in terms of cost or profitability. Are certain product types profitable to manufacture? What would be the cost to make them profitable?

26.2.3.2 Faults Specific to a Process. Such an analysis of fault data may lead to a specific process that regularly induces faults onto a wide variety of part numbers. This may point to requirements for new settings, procedures, materials, personnel, equipment, etc.

26.2.3.3 Faults Specific to a Part Number. Fault data on a specific part number is useful in improving processes for future part numbers or future runs of the same part number. In some situations where a single part number may run for a considerable period of time and in considerable quantity, it may be possible to feed back electrical test data in a type of real-time mode. In this situation, results from electrical test may help drive some adjustments or quick changes in the process that will improve the yield and reduce scrap or the requirement for repair and retest.

26.2.4 Quality Control

Analysis of fault data is only a piece of what needs to already be in place: that is a quality control system or process. Electrical test data used as process monitoring is only going to be as good as the quality control framework making use of it. Electrical test data can serve as a drive to create a quality control system that provides the communication and means to implement appropriate change. It can also serve as a significant data source in a system that is already in place.

26.3 WHAT WILL YOU FIND?

Faults. More specifically, faults that give the test system measurement results other than those programmed to be representative of a good board. The faults measured may or may not impact the functionality of the circuit board; in most cases, they will. The huge variety in design and application of the printed wiring board would invalidate general statements made about the end result of a certain fault type making its way to the board's completely assembled end use. The IPC has made efforts to distinguish between different classes of board applications with some minor differences in required test specs, recognizing different levels of criticality in test. Obviously, gross shorts and opens in an interconnect will cause problems.

Will an electrical test system find all the faults? No. The definition of "all the faults" is too subjective. The electrical test system clearly could not detect all faults related to aesthetics, annular ring, layer-to-layer registration, etc., that do not effect test system measurable interconnect. Further, the type of test method, fixturing, test programming method, and specifications vary too widely to say that electrical testing will of itself find *all* the faults.

26.3.1 Fault Types

It is worth mentioning briefly the distinction between a defect and a fault. A fault is a test system designation for an item that does not meet the expected criteria. A defect refers specifically to the board and a defect in its design, fabrication, appearance, etc. Not all defects can be detected by the test system. For example, a defect such as narrowing of a trace as in a *dishdown* or *mouse bite,* as long as the connection is still in place, will usually go undetected as a fault. Not all faults are defects. A pin missing in the fixture or removable foreign matter on the surface of a board will be identified by the test system as a fault. Other defects such as delamination are well outside the realm of electrical test faults.

Some clarifications are in order to distinguish types of tests from types of faults. See Table 26.1.

TABLE 26.1   Test and Fault Types

Test type	Fault type identified
Continuity	Open
Isolation	Short and leakage

26.3.1.1 Shorts.   *Definition:* an erroneous connection between two or more networks or isolated points that should not be connected to each other. Shorts are produced in a variety of ways, from overexposure to underetching to slivering to solder leveling. There are many more sources for shorts, but the sources are more appropriate to a board fabrication discussion.

26.3.1.2 Opens.   *Definition:* a discontinuity or nonconnection within a network so that the network is split or divided into two or more erroneous networks. Opens are produced in a variety of ways, from overetching to underplating to contamination to underexposure to misregistration.

26.3.1.3 Leakage.   *Definition:* a type of short sometimes referred to as a high-resistance short, usually defined as a partial connection between two or more nets that exhibits a resistance value between the thresholds defined for an acceptable continuity and an acceptable isolation. A few leakage sources are ionic contamination and moisture. They are very closely related in the sense that both are contaminants and both can and do exhibit conductive characteristics. Ionic contamination can occur at many stages in board fabrication at innerlayer, lamination, plating, solder mask, any handling, etc., and is usually made up of deposits of metal salts. Metal salts are typically conductive and may be widespread in a thin layer in or on a circuit board. The resistive characteristic exhibited by this contamination can be a hard short but is often a high-resistance short. With the addition of moisture, the resistance of a high-impedance short will usually decrease and can eventually become a hard short. The nature of board materials is such that they can absorb moisture relatively easily, and they do over time.

With a leakage path present on a board, metal migration from one trace to another while the board is in operation will further build the path to a hard short. As such, it is important to find leakage faults before they make it to the end product.

26.3.2 Test Methods

With a description in hand of fault types that can be found at bare-board test, we can now look at methods for finding them.

26.3.2.1 *Visual Inspection.* Visual inspection is a very manual approach in that it makes use of people, good lighting, and some type of training on what is acceptable and what is not. Usually a comparison to a known good product or the artwork is made. If the inspection person has seen the board often, he or she becomes more skilled at finding faults and looking in likely locations for faults. This would require high volumes of a single part number. Also, the simpler the product, the higher the percentage of faults that can be found. There are products suited to visual inspection. As technology progresses, the complexity and detail that are contained in a single circuit board of even low to medium technology far outstrip the ability of the inspection person to find even a significant percentage of the faults or potential faults. This, in general, is not an acceptable method for determining whether a board is good.

Visual inspection may be appropriate for the aesthetic or visual appearance of the board. Aesthetics can be checked by a human. There is no question that what appears as poor solder mask application or scratches on a product may be a latent defect that will later lead to failure of what is presently a good board. This falls outside the realm of electrical test. Defects of this type are not detectable or appropriate to a discussion of electrical test.

26.3.2.2 *Automatic Optical Inspection.* Other than the human eye, there are computer-based visual inspection methods, referred to as *automatic optical inspection* or AOI. AOI equipment checks the board or its innerlayers against dimensional parameters that have been programmed into it. These can be generally accepted or design rule–based parameters, or they can be programmed to recognize a window of acceptable dimensions for features on the board. Like manual visual inspection, faults found with this method can imply that there may be an impact on the board's functionality, but the board's functionality and interconnect are not actually tested. Distinctions between the aesthetics of the board's features and its fitness for use are difficult to differentiate. As such, AOI is typically used for innerlayer testing but does not serve as final test.

26.3.2.3 *Electrical Test.* Electrical testing is the most common methodology used to determine if a board is good or bad. To electrically test a board requires that the board come into physical contact with a measurement system. While the measurement system is in physical contact, two test types are performed.

Continuity. Continuity testing checks for the continuous path or appropriate interconnect of pads, traces, and through-holes. This is typically done in a series of point-to-point measurements within a network. For example, the network with test points labeled A through D, shown in Fig. 26.2, would have the test algorithm shown in Fig. 26.3. This algorithm would run internal to the test system and results would be postprocessed before presentation. For a network with four test points, the minimum number of tests would be three to determine if all the points are connected. The number of continuity tests n required to test a network with x test points can be expressed as

$$n = x - 1$$

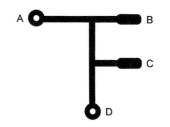

FIGURE 26.2 Sample network.

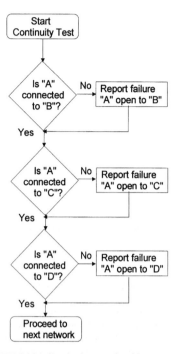

FIGURE 26.3 Continuity test algorithm.

Therefore, to determine how many continuity tests would be required to test a board, it is not enough to know the number of networks or the total number of test points but rather the number of test points in each network. The circuit diagram for the continuity measurement is shown in Fig. 26.4.

Switches are activated to close the connection to the appropriate test points. Current I is driven through the selected points on the board under test and the resultant voltage V is measured. The continuity resistance R is then determined using the relationship $R = V/I$. The circuit diagram in Fig. 26.4 represents a Kelvin or four-wire continuity measurement. This is the most accurate means of taking a continuity measurement. Although we are measuring the resistance of a trace on the board under test, a significant error resistance is present in the measurement system switching. This error resistance can be regularly learned or calibrated and then subtracted from the measurement, but this is less than ideal for accuracy and speed. In a four-wire Kelvin measurement, the current is sourced through one pair of switches and the voltage is measured through another pair in which there is no current flow. With no current flow there is no error resistance.

The measurement of continuity is in ohms (Ω), a unit of resistance to current flow or, more commonly, just *resistance*. While resistance measurements can be made quite easily with hand-held meters into the megohm range, they are not practical on manufacturing test systems that contain large numbers of semiconductor switches in the measurement path. Typical programmable continuity resistance parameters are in a range from 1 to 10 kΩ. There are a few standards in existence for specifying continuity resistance, as summarized in Table 26.2.

The lower the continuity threshold, the more stringent the test of the board. Traces that exhibit resistances of 5, 10, or 25 Ω, although rare when using copper, can significantly impact the functionality of precision measurement instruments or high-speed computer product. There are limitations to how low continuity test thresholds can be set. Part of the limitation comes from the test system's measurement and switch matrix capabilities and, to a greater part, from the type of test fixturing used (see Sec. 26.5.3). A 10-Ω continuity resistance test

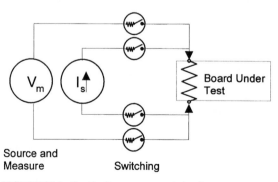

FIGURE 26.4 Continuity measurement circuit.

TABLE 26.2 Continuity test parameter standards.

	IPC-ET-652	MIL-55110D (production)
Maximum continuity resistance test threshold	Class 1: General electronic 50 Ω Class 2: Dedicated service 20 Ω Class 3: High reliability <20 or 10 Ω	10 Ω

threshold is the general practical lower limit for production testing at the time of this publication and represents a good stringent test.

Continuity test current is not addressed in IPC-ET-652 nor in MIL-55110D, and is addressed only as minimal current in MIL-STD-275. We are trying to test the traces and not damage them. If a large amount of current is used, the trace will act as a fuse and will be blown out or burned out, especially in areas where the traces are fine, underplated, or overetched. This blowout may occur after the test system has already determined that there is a connection and is ramping down the measurement. This would produce a board that has tested good, but is bad. The continuity test should not be invasive or destructive. It should determine only what is or is not there and report it. For typical trace geometries, a rough rule of thumb would be that any test current over 100 mA has the potential of damaging circuitry or modifying the condition of a failing trace.

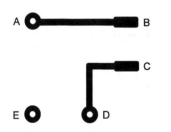

FIGURE 26.5 Three isolated networks.

Isolation. For isolation testing, we are trying to determine if networks or traces are separated or isolated from each other. In Fig. 26.5, A and B represent one two-point network (AB), C and D represent another two-point network (CD), and E represents a single-point network. AB, CD, and E are separate or isolated networks.

In isolation testing, only one point per network is required for the measurement. This assumes that the networks have already passed the continuity test. When testing for isolation, each network is tested against all other networks on the board. This method helps detect distributed contamination and leakage that will be discussed later. To determine if AB is isolated, AB would be switched to one side of the measurement instruments; CD and E would be switched to the other side. To determine if CD is isolated, CD would be switched to one side of the measurement instruments; AB and E would be switched to the other side. The two measurements are represented in Fig. 26.6.

A third measurement would, of course, be required to determine if E was isolated. Therefore, the number of isolation tests required to determine if all the networks on a board are iso-

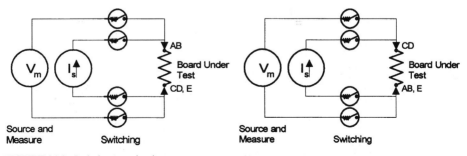

FIGURE 26.6 Isolation test circuits.

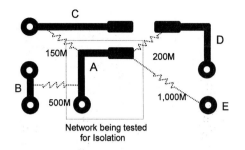

FIGURE 26.7 Leakage due to distributed contamination.

lated is equal to the number of networks on the board and is independent of network size.

A network that fails to be isolated from another network is considered to be shorted. There are also shorts called high-resistance shorts or leakage failures. These are shorts with resistance values above the continuity resistance threshold but below the isolation resistance threshold. This leakage failure condition can occur between two networks or it can occur between a combination of networks. Leakage between multiple networks is usually the result of distributed contamination and presents a special case for the test system.

If the isolation resistance threshold is 100 MΩ and a series of networks exists like those in Fig. 26.7, it is possible for the distributed contamination from one network to one other network to have a resistance value above 100 MΩ and therefore appear to be acceptable or passing isolation. But the board in operation will see isolation from other networks in parallel. Therefore, a complete isolation test must measure one network to all other networks. In the case of the network configuration in Fig. 26.7, the resultant parallel resistance R_A would be as follows:

$$R_A = \frac{1}{((1/R_{AB}) + (1/R_{AC}) + (1/R_{AD}) + (1/R_{AE}))}$$

$$= \frac{1}{((1/500 \text{ M}) + (1/150 \text{ M}) + 1/200 \text{ M}) + (1/1{,}000 \text{ M}))}$$

$$= 68 \text{ M}\Omega$$

Network A would then fail isolation for leakage as it should. It is likely that some of the other networks would fail as well, because the combined parallel resistance would also fall below the isolation resistance threshold of 100 MΩ.

Networks are defined as being isolated from each other if the resistance between them exceeds a specified value. This resistance is expressed in ohms (Ω), a unit of resistance to current flow or, more commonly, just resistance. The resistance threshold for isolation is typically in the MΩ range. While MΩ and even GΩ resistance measurements can be made quite easily with a megohm-capable ohmmeter, there are some special considerations in manufacturing test systems that contain a large number of semiconductor switches as part of the measurement path. When turned off, semiconductor switches are not totally off. They leak some minute amount of current. The amount depends on the size and design of the semiconductor chosen for the switch. Low-leakage switches will exhibit excellent accuracy at high isolation values. Probably the most obvious sign of a good low-leakage design is the relative speed of the isolation test at high isolation values.

Typical isolation resistance parameters are in a range from 1 to 100 MΩ. Some industry standards exist for specifying isolation resistance as summarized in Table 26.3.

These thresholds are fairly easy to implement and, by today's standard, are not a stringent test. Typical minimum commercial specification for isolation resistance is 10 MΩ and requirements for 20, 50, and 100 MΩ are common. All are practical thresholds for testing medium- to high-technology product and are well within the range of the test system. The higher the threshold, the more stringent the test.

There are some other considerations when testing at high isolation values (megohm range). The first is the environment. Water typically contains salts and other molecules that make it conductive. Therefore, humid air has some degree of conductivity. When testing at high isolation values, the test must be performed in an environment that is not too humid

TABLE 26.3 Isolation Test Parameter Standards

	IPC-ET-652	MIL-55110D (production)
Minimum isolation resistance test threshold	Class 1: General electronic 500 Ω Class 2: Dedicated service >2 MΩ Class 3: High reliability >2 MΩ	>2 MΩ

(typically less than 50 percent RH). The measurement of the wet or conductive air will distort the test results. Second, because the measurement current used in high-isolation testing is so small (microamps and often nanoamps), the measurement is slower. The measurement system needs some extra time to wait for such a small current to stabilize before measuring it. Therefore, there is some impact on the speed of the test. If the test speed is unacceptable or the environmental requirements cannot be met, some compromise of the isolation resistance test threshold is necessary.

Voltage.   Voltage is a parameter often discussed and specified as part of the test specification for a board or piece of test equipment. The test voltage value is pertinent to isolation testing only as the voltage used for continuity testing is small (10 V or less). For continuity testing, we are expecting to find a connection; therefore, very low currents and voltages are used to protect the board from damage.

In the case of isolation testing, we are expecting to find the test points isolated or not connected and, as such, higher voltages are typically used to determine the degree of isolation. Standards for test voltage can be found in Table 26.4.

TABLE 26.4 Test Voltage Standards

	IPC-ET-652	MIL-55110D (production)
Isolation test voltage	High enough to provide sufficient current for the measurement in question, but low enough to prevent arc-over	40 V, or twice the maximum rated voltage of the board, whichever is greater

Higher voltage values (500 V and as high as 1000 to 1500 V) have been used in the past to ensure adequate test currents at high impedance. Modern test systems, although still requiring elevated voltages (100 to 250 V), can make the measurements accurately at significantly lower current and voltage levels.

The voltage specified for a test has little to do with the level of stringency that the board is tested to. The continuity and isolation resistance thresholds are paramount. The IPC spec states that fairly well. Voltage selection should therefore be made based on the selected continuity and isolation levels and the speed and accuracy of the measurement. Typical commercial specifications for voltage are 40, 100, and 250. Usually, 100 to 250 V are required for isolation resistance thresholds over 10 MΩ.

A similar situation as described in the continuity current discussion relative to destructive testing can occur with isolation testing. That is that minimal current should be used to limit the possibility of modification or damage to the board. In the case of isolation testing, the risk falls more in the potential to blow out shorts or leakage paths. In this case, the potential risk lies in that the destruction may occur when the test is ramping up, with the result that the test system will then pass the fixed or modified circuit board before causing damage in the rampdown. The board is usually far from fixed. Although a network may exhibit the appropriate level of isolation after having a leakage path or short blown out, contamination, crystallization, metal migration, and moisture absorption will all lead to the eventual reformation of the short or leakage path. A latent defect will have been induced where a defect should have been detected. Again, it is important that the board be tested without being modified. The same or even more restrictive current limitations should apply to the isolation test (10 mA or less).

26.4 DATA PREPARATION

While the hardware and test techniques implement the bare-board test, another element is responsible for directing the hardware to test a board particular to its design. There are several methods for developing the program to which the board will be tested. These methods vary from simple to complex and from escape-prone to very sound. The most common terms used in the language of bare-board test for the test program development are *self-learn* and *netlist testing*. Netlist test is a misnomer that confuses CAD outputs with tester inputs and implies that there is not much in between. For this text we shall use the term *data-driven test program* to indicate the file that is to be loaded into the test system and provides a test derived from the board's design data. The test program is one of several important elements to be developed at data prep. Accepting and formatting input and generating drill, load, and assembly files for the test fixture are the most time consuming tasks and are themselves significant.

Procedurally, a step that takes place before the placement of a board on a fixture is *fixture verification.* In this step, the fixture is compressed with a nonconductive material of similar thickness to the board being tested. An isolation routine is run on the board to verify that the fixture does not contain any shorts. The fixture is then compressed again with a shorting plate on it. In this step, a shorts program is either learned, generated by the test system, or downloaded from the fixturing software. The intent is verification of the correct number of test points, and that under multiple compressions or closures, all points are present and remain in contact with the shorting plate.

26.4.1 Self-Learn

The original, and very common method for developing a test program for a bare board is to self-learn it. The self-learn method requires only that a known good board (preferably) or the first board in the lot requiring test be placed on the test system's fixture. After a few parameter selections and the engagement of the fixture, the test system will run through an algorithm that will detect or learn the interconnect and isolated points of the board requiring test. The next few boards in the lot are tested with this test program and, if the results appear consistent, the test program is accepted; otherwise, another self-learn is performed. This method provides a usable test program and often will yield good test results. But the drawbacks of this method are many. A self-learn test program determines that all the boards are the same, not that they are good. Here are some of the specific potential pitfalls:

- A pin or probe missing in the fixture will not be included in the test program. Shorts or opens that require that point to be detected will pass the test area and escape.
- A consistently open or consistently shorted contact between the test system and the fixture or the fixture and the board will not be included in the test program. Shorts or opens that require the test point(s) to be detected will pass the test area and escape.
- A fault on the board used to self-learn that is consistent throughout the lot to be tested, will be self-learned and used as the test program. All the boards in the lot will pass this fault, yet all the boards in the lot will be bad and will escape from the test area.

Although virtually all test systems contain self-learn capability, it is not considered a good test programming method when working under a quality control framework due to the number of opportunities for escapes.

26.4.2 Data-Driven Test or Netlist Test

The preferred alternative to self-learning is the netlist test, which we shall refer to as a *data-driven test program* (DDP). The basic idea of data-driven test programming is to test the board to the data it was designed to. The power and speed of software and workstations allow us to take the data the board was designed to and perform several functions and produce several outputs that are of great benefit to the electrical test area. There are several steps, and the following should provide a useful understanding.

The fixture and DDP development process can be divided into two stages, the first being the preparation and processing of the various possible input sources into a format usable by the second stage. The second stage is fixture, test program, and repair file creation. Often they are equally time consuming. Factors such as data quality and completeness and fixture design can significantly reduce software processing and engineering time. Board technology, size, and complexity tend to increase time requirements.

26.4.2.1 *Input/Extraction.*   There are a variety of input sources. They can be grouped and summarized as follows.

Drill File.   The use of a drill file only for data preparation is typically associated with self-learn test programming. The board would likely have only through-hole components on it. If SMT were present, then pad locations would have to be digitized and added to the drill file. Digitizing or "bomb siting" is a relatively inaccurate method of determining test pad centers. The drill file would also normally be stripped of via holes. The vias are usually all one tool size or at least a different tool size than the through-holes and are thus readily removed. This drill file can be used directly to create a fixture or can run through a fixturing software package to generate fixture drill data.

This method is used primarily for through-hole and very low technology test applications. It is error prone due to digitizing error, the hazards of self-learn, and the primitive nature of the associated fixture style.

CAD Data.   This typically takes the form of a netlist (related to but not the same as a netlist test program). This is a data file, usually in a format specific to the CAD system used, that contains information useful for the creation of a fixture and test program. Some typical CAD systems are Mentor, Valid, PCAD, PADS, and SciCards. A full data set from a CAD system would contain the following:

- Signal ID, net name, or net number
- Reference designator or pin number (e.g., U14.12, R1.1)
- *x-y* of pad center*
- Pad dimensions and hole size
- Resistor values (if appropriate and not usual)

Often this data set is converted to a standard like IPC-D-356 (see later) by means of a converter. These software converters, although simple, are usually customized for each individual CAD system. A converter must be updated or modified with any output changes made by a CAD vendor due to a CAD system software update or new product introduction. The number of converters that an independent PWB manufacturer would require could be quite high. Fortunately, many of the CAD vendors offer a IPC-D-356 output.

Gerber Data.   Gerber data is a format not intended for usage in test at all. It is a format produced by CAD systems for downloading to photoplotters. The data format directs the photoplotter where to draw and what feature types to expose. This data is contained in a very large set of files. The appropriate information for generation of fixture and test program files

---

* Minimum data set requirement if grouped as connected.

is contained in them, but a considerable amount of processing is necessary. Although Gerber is defined as a standard, it is a standard data format for photoplotters. Designers have a great degree of freedom in how they design and how features are represented in Gerber. This can be seen in the wide variety in form of data found in the Gerber format. This variety leads to some level of error, because it is difficult for a Gerber extraction routine to be capable of handling all possible permutations. A Gerber data file set for fixture and program generation would contain the following:

- All layers and solder mask
- Legend or silk screen*
- Aperture file
- Drill file

IPC-D-350/356.   There are two data formats that fall under the heading of IPC data. The first is an all-encompassing format, IPC-D-350. The IPC-D-350 format contains all data necessary to build the board from bare printed wiring board to fully assembled with components. This large quantity of data presents two difficulties. The first is that the data set is very large, rivaling that of Gerber data. The second is that that much data in a single format is perceived by many end users or designers as a security risk. There is enough data in that file to completely duplicate the board. Many companies hold their designs and technologies too close to allow such a data set to be released. But IPC-D-350 presently represents the only complete and uniform data format for use with electrical test. All other available data sources provide some level of compromise in missing data or lack of standardization.

The second format is specific to electrical test: IPC-D-356. This data set includes enough data to build the fixture and produce a data-driven test program. There is no trace data in the format. Therefore, Gerber or D-350 must be made use of to provide trace data to the test area—usually Gerber and specifically for computer-aided repair. IPC-D-356 is a common output of CAD systems and is a common input to fixturing software packages. CAD netlist and Gerber data is often converted to D-356 to provide the input to the fixturing software.

IPC-D-356 format contains the following basic information:

- Net name
- *x-y* of pad or hole center
- Hole size (plated or unplated), pad size, and rotation
- Reference designation pin number (U1.1, R2.1, etc.)
- Point designation (midpoint, endpoint, etc.)
- Point accessibility layer or side of board (layer number, covered by solder mask, etc.)

26.4.2.2 Fixturing Software.   The following is a generic description of the fixturing software process.

The first step with the input data is to orient it. The toughest side of the board in terms of test centers is usually faced down. This may require flipping or inverting the data.

Test Point Optimization.   The next step entails optimizing the data file. Not all of the points require testing. Figure 26.8 shows a net with a midpoint B that does not need to have a test point on it. Test points at A and C would be all that are necessary to determine whether this net is isolated and contains no opens. Test point optimizing can reduce the number of points in a fixture by 10 to 50 percent, thereby

FIGURE 26.8   Optimizing a net.

---

* Required for computer-aided repair.

reducing the cost of the fixture and the time to test the board. Although optimization provides some economic and minor throughput benefits, they must be offset against the impact at repair and fault coverage risk.

Midpoints as part of the test system failure data are very helpful at the repair function in isolating and speeding the repair of faulty boards. Although most optimization algorithms are very effective, there often is operator intervention required to help the fixturing software determine what is capable of being optimized. This human element adds the inevitable human error in which points may be optimized out that are required for a complete test of the board. Thus, many times optimization is not performed. This speeds data preparation, reduces the chance of errors, and increases fault coverage, while adding some increment of cost to the fixture build and time to the test.

Pin Assignment.   Once the test sites have been identified, test pins can be assigned to the features to be tested. Different pin types are required for different features. For example, a through-hole would require a large head or larger-diameter pin than an SMT pad on 0.025-in centers. There is usually a table of feature types to pin types that the fixturing software references for this assignment. This table is usually standard for the fixture style being built but can be modified for special conditions.

Different Grids.   Although we have not yet discussed fixture types, the fixture in a universal grid system requires assignment to a grid of uniform centers. Please reference later sections of this chapter for fixture and system types. For the sake of a discussion of the test area in order of how a board type would be tested, we must continue a discussion of data preparation withholding coverage of systems and fixtures.

Figure 26.9 shows three of the most common grid configurations available. Single-density, 100 points/in^2, or 0.100-in grid, is the most common. The job being processed must now be assigned to the appropriate grid. Keep in mind that, although a job may have been designed for a certain grid, it is not necessarily exactly on a grid when it gets to electrical test. Therefore, the fixturing software must determine where each on-product location will be assigned on grid. Several factors must be taken into consideration:

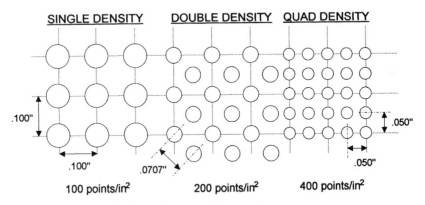

FIGURE 26.9   Single-, double-, and quad-density grid patterns.

- No two points can be assigned to the same grid location.
- No assignments can allow the pins to touch each other (cross pins).
- Drilled holes cannot break out into another assigned location.
- No assignment can extend beyond the predetermined deflection limit (determined by the fixture and pin design).

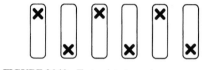

FIGURE 26.10   Test point staggering.

• Points that are too close together must be staggered (see Fig. 26.10).

Pin staggering offers several benefits, including testing finer centers than if pins are assigned in line. Also, staggering can help limit the number of pin diameters in a given fixture. The fewer pin diameters used, the less inventory is required, and the simpler and easier the fixture is to build.

Hole Compensation.   An additional consideration in the generation of the fixture drill files is the hole diameter relative to the pin diameter and pin deflection. Ideally, a pin is assigned a hole diameter some number of mils over its shaft diameter. This clearance allows for ease of pin loading and accurate location or pointing accuracy during test. In practice, a single pin diameter in a fixture will be found to be displaced to a variety of different angles depending on its assignment in the fixture. As such, a pin that is relatively straight up and down will be rather loose in the selected hole diameter, reducing pointing accuracy. A pin deflected to the maximum allowable value will be rather tight, possibly binding in the hole and increasing the chances that contact will not be made with the board (false open). The fixturing software can compensate the hole diameter, depending on the amount the pin is deflected. This improves pointing accuracy and reduces pin binding. The result is a better, more reliable, more repeatable test fixture.

The last step in data preparation requires the marrying of the job being processed with the tooling. The tooling includes tooling to the test system and tooling for the specific fixture design utilized.

26.4.2.3 Output.   Once all the preparation steps and processes have been performed, there are several outputs generated.

Test File.   A data-driven test program or netlist test is an appropriate and useful output file. This file allows the test system to test the board to interconnect specified in the board design, which is an important quality and process control tool.

The data-driven test program can be formatted so that it supports a graphical representation of the fixture and/or board on the test system monitor. On-system graphical views are those of the fixture that can be seen while the system is in operation. They can be used to debug the fixture and/or system during setup, as well as, graphical editing of the test program and on-system performance of repair or verification functions (see Fig. 26.11).

Fixture Files.   Probably the most significant output—the drill files, one for each plate or pass required by the fixture design—are needed in drilling to start the fixture build.

Although most of the discussion of data preparation has centered on the production of universal grid fixturing, a subset of the preceding steps is also required to produce a dedicated or hard-wired fixture, with the exception that a dedicated fixture requires a road map or wiring file. The road map is used at repair or verification to locate failing points. The file itself is an assignment of *x-y* location to test point number. The fixturing software can make use of this file to generate a data-driven program. A load file is also a necessary part of building a dedicated fixture. It indicates where specific probe types are loaded in the fixture. Probes in dedicated fixtures, like pins in universal grid fixtures, must be assigned to match the board feature being tested.

Repair/Verification.   Files can also be output that support the repair or verification function. These files usually require trace data and, as such, require some Gerber inputs. The repair files are generated by a combination of Gerber data and the outputs of the fixturing software.

26.5   TEST EQUIPMENT

The center of the electrical test area is the test system. The type of test equipment appropriate to an operation will vary with the type of boards produced, level of test required, business

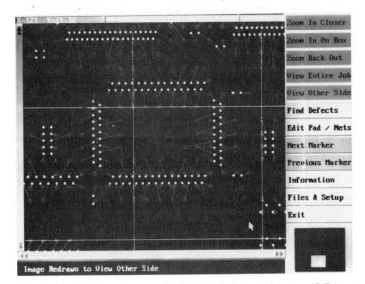

FIGURE 26.11 On-system graphical view of fixture. *(Courtesy of Everett Charles Technologies.)*

direction, and a variety of other influences. We shall look at the types of test equipment available and their basic operation, putting special emphasis on the fixtured test systems, with some depth of discussion given to the fixturing itself. Guidelines for matching test requirements to equipment type, as well as special considerations for high technology SMT testing, are also covered.

26.5.1 Moving Probe

Moving probe, flying probe, and *x-y prober* are all names for the type of test equipment that we shall call a *moving probe test system* (see Fig. 26.12). Moving probe test systems make use of two or more test points that can be accurately and rapidly moved around the board area by means of a computer-controlled motion system. The motion system provides very accurate locating of the probe and thus makes it well suited to testing very fine center SMT. Also, because the moving probe moves, it is not as subject to limitations due to test point density as other test approaches. Issues related to test point density will be discussed later. Test of product with features on both sides requires the use of a double-sided moving probe. For the remainder of this discussion, the term "moving probe" means a double-sided moving probe test system. The moving probe test system is subject to the same techniques and issues related to making measurements as found in fixtured test systems with some additional methodology.

Continuity tests are accomplished by means of point-to-point measurements (see Fig. 26.13). For the sample network used in Fig. 26.2, One of the moving probes would contact point A and the other would contact point B, and a continuity measurement would be made. The second probe would then move to point C, and so on, until the entire net had been tested for continuity. The probes would then move to the next network.

For Isolation tests, one of the moving probes would contact one network, while another would contact all of the nets on the product. The first probe would then move to the next network and the process would be repeated. This would require a large number of points to be probed and a considerable amount of time. A significant enhancement in moving probe tech-

FIGURE 26.12 Double-sided moving probe test system. *(Courtesy of Probot Inc.)*

nology was the development of adjacency software. *Adjacency* refers to other nets that come within some predetermined distance of the net being tested for isolation. The use of adjacency helps reduce the number of points probed by eliminating nets from each isolation test that, by design location, are unlikely to be shorted to the net being tested.

There is an additional measurement technique used by moving probe test systems, and that is a capacitive, discharge, or reference measurement method. This reference technique is not used so much for measuring capacitance, although it can; it is used in complement to or in place of the continuity and isolation tests. This technique further reduces the number of movements or points that the prober must contact.

A single probe makes contact with a network and applies a voltage, charging that network to a certain voltage level. The network is then discharged and the rate of discharge is measured. This value is stored or added, averaged, and stored as the reference value. The value may be stored as a time, voltage, or capacitive value, depending on approach and measurement method. The rate of discharge can be used to determine capacitance by the following formula, where i is the discharge current:

$$C = i\,\frac{t_2 - t_1}{V_2 - V_1}$$

The capacitance of a network is a rough measure of how much copper, tin, metal, or conductive material is present. The capacitance of a known good or golden board is self-learned, and a window or tolerance is added to allow for variations in plating, solder, thickness, etc. A network that shows a higher capacitance is likely to be shorted to another network because the additional conductive material added to the network being measured will make it a larger-value capacitor. Conversely, if the capacitance is lower than expected, it is likely that there is an open in the network and the reduction of conductive material being charged and discharged has resulted in a smaller-value capacitor (see Fig. 26.14).

FIGURE 26.13 Moving probes contacting board. *(Courtesy of Probot Inc.)*

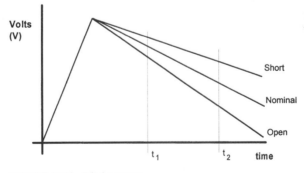

FIGURE 26.14 Discharge test.

There are some limitations to the capacitive technique. The dc voltage charge/discharge measurement is moderately accurate for low-value capacitances. In other words, it is less accurate as the nets become smaller or if they are single-point networks. It is possible that single-point and very small networks shorted to larger networks will not be detected. Opens in larger networks where the resulting network is still quite large and the portion isolated by the open is relatively small can also be missed. These small values of capacitance that indicate there is a fault can be swallowed up in the tolerance window programmed to allow for variations in trace width, plating, and solder thickness. Comparative measurements of adjacent nets can enhance the precision of the reference test. That is, if nets are shorted to one another, it is likely that two adjacent nets will show the same value.

Although the capacitance, discharge, or reference test method can help speed the moving probe test, it is best to combine this method with the Ohm's law or standard continuity and isolation test capabilities of the moving probe to ensure high fault coverage.

Regardless of the measurement technique used, each measurement requires some amount of mechanical motion to move the probes. The moving probe test system provides one of the slowest test methods as measured in boards-per-hour throughput compared to fixtured test systems. The primary benefit is that moving probe test systems do not require any type of fixturing or hardware dedicated to the board being tested. Therefore, there is no significant tooling cost or time associated with producing a test fixture. Data preparation and system setup are similar to other test approaches. Moving probe test system features would be as follows:

- Moderate to high system cost
- Very high technology capability
- Extremely low to no fixture and/or tooling costs
- Low boards-per-hour throughput
- Moderate data preparation time
- Quick setup time

In summary, no tooling cost, limited data preparation, low throughput, fine center, and high-density capabilities make the moving probe test system well suited to the test of short run, prototype board types and boards that contain high technology features.

26.5.2 Fixtured

The most common type of system used for electrical test, fixtured systems are flexible for testing prototype to high-volume and low- to high-technology boards. Fixtured test systems require the use of (interchangeably called) interface, translator, or test fixtures to assign the system's test points to the board. This means that each unique board design requires tooling or a fixture to test it. Spring probes or pins in the test fixture make contact with the board and complete the connection to the system.

26.5.2.1 Dedicated.   A dedicated test system is not called that because the system can test only one board type. It is called dedicated because the fixture type that the dedicated test system makes use of can test only one board type and is not reusable.

System.   A dedicated test system usually contains fewer test points than other fixtured test systems, because the system needs to have only enough total test points for the highest test point board intended for it. System test point counts between 1024 and 10,244 are typical. Other differences lie in the area of compression method, application, and, especially, fixturing methodology.

Fixture.   The interface on a dedicated test system is made up of a pattern of test points arranged to facilitate quick sequential wiring of the interface point to the spring probe used to contact the board. The interface point is usually referenced by test point number and is wired to a specific x-y coordinate via a road map (see Fixture Files section). The specific wiring sequence must be followed in order to match the data-driven program that was generated with the road map.

Compression Method.   Vacuum compression is the most common compression method used, but others are available, such as pneumatic and electronic compression. Matching the low-cost nature of dedicated systems with its relatively low point count, vacuum requires only that the system have a means to connect it, turn it on and off, and seal the fixture to create a cavity that can be evacuated. Pneumatic and electrical compression requires more hardware in the test system in the form of rams or motors. Figure 26.15 shows typical vacuum and pneumatic compression. Electrical and pneumatic compression systems use similar push-plate configurations.

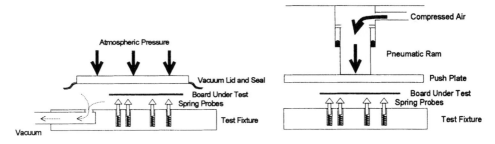

FIGURE 26.15   Vacuum and pneumatic compression.

Spring Probes.   The spring probes in the test fixture are what is being compressed. The contact under spring pressure provides good electrical contact with the board being tested. A variety of spring probe head styles are available for different applications, including different diameter heads to match different hole sizes and different diameter probes to match different surface-mount pad spacing (see Fig. 26.16).

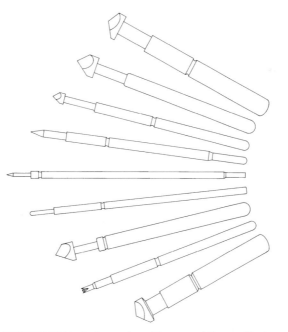

FIGURE 26.16   Spring probes. *(Courtesy of Everett Charles Technologies.)*

There are some limitations in the technology of product that can be tested on a dedicated test system. While the discrete placement of probes on fine centers is possible and there are no limitations on the density of test point placement, there are limitations on the pointing accuracy and ultimate miniaturization of a spring probe assembly. As the diameters of the spring probe assembly become smaller, in order to place them closer together, the materials become thinner and the assembly is more delicate. This makes the probes more expensive and causes them to have a shorter life. Tolerances between plunger and barrel, barrel and receptacle, and receptacle and hole when testing small-geometry surface-mount can severely limit success in hitting targets.

Specialization in wire-wrapping techniques, dedicated fixturing for fine centers, and low numbers of dedicated fixture builds (relative to universal grid) require most board fabricators to utilize third parties that specialize in this area. These third parties, or *fixture houses,* can realize the economies of fixture builds for many fabricators and, with the volume, maintain the specialized personnel necessary.

Usage. A summary of the dedicated test systems features is as follows:

- Inexpensive system
- Expensive and time consuming to build fixtures
- Fast test times, high throughput (board tests per hour)
- Moderate data preparation time
- Moderate to quick setup time
- Limitations on high technology

The applications appropriate for such features are test of boards being produced in medium to high volume, with a limited number of board types, and low to moderately high technology designs.

26.5.2.2 Universal Grid.
The most flexible and widely used electrical test solution, the universal grid test system revolutionized the testing of bare boards (see Fig. 26.17). In the 1980s, as product cycle times were reduced by an order of magnitude, the demand for prototype and short-production-run printed wiring boards grew astronomically. Initially, the primary test method was the dedicated test system. Although the systems were relatively low cost, the fixturing was very expensive for each new board type. The inexpensive and reusable universal grid fixturing helped make prototype production practical. As SMT became a larger portion of the board types, technology limitations were also realized with the dedicated fixture. The 1990s have shown considerable refinement in the universal grid, but most notably in the area of fixturing—not only in fixturing cost but in universal grid fixturing technical capabilities to address SMT.

System. The basic tenet of the universal grid test system is that it should contain a series of test points laid out on a standardized grid matrix or field (see Fig. 26.18). These test points provide a fixed density (100 points/in^2) available to be leaned or assigned to the points on the board requiring test.

The size of the universal grid is determined by the dimensions or product area of the largest board to be tested—to be more exact, the dimensions of the test area of the largest board to be tested. The test area is usually smaller than the product area, because most board designs have a margin or border around the edge. Therefore, an industry-standard full panel board of 18 in × 24 in with a 0.500-in margin around it would have a maximum test area of 17 in × 23 in. It is likely that the first testable feature within that margin would not be at the edge of the board, and the test area would be something more on the order of 16 in × 22 in.

When universal grids were first introduced in the 1970s, a considerable number of board designs were laid on a grid—specifically, a 0.100-in center grid. These boards were tested with the use of a mask. The mask was a sheet of phenolic or G-10 drilled with the pattern of the test points. All other points on the universal grid were blocked or masked from contacting the

FIGURE 26.17 Double-sided universal grid test system. *(Courtesy of Everett Charles Technologies.)*

FIGURE 26.18 Universal grid field. *(Courtesy of Everett Charles Technologies.)*

board. This type of testing is called *on-grid*. It does require some tooling in the form of the mask. It is the closest to a literal universal grid (see Fig. 26.19).

Smaller product sizes, faster clock speeds, and more complex products drove and are continuing to drive printed circuit board designs to SMT and finer lines and spaces. Although products have continued to be designed on grid, the spacing of the grid went from 0.100 in to 0.010 in to less than 0.001 in very rapidly. This produced designs that were off-grid relative to the 0.100-in centers of the test system. There were test points available to test the product, but it required a means to connect the off-grid or on-product locations to the universal grid. Fix-

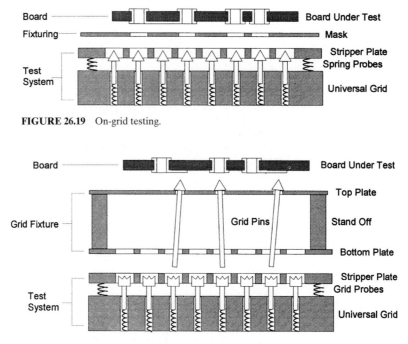

FIGURE 26.19   On-grid testing.

FIGURE 26.20   Off-grid testing.

turing was developed with pins that leaned or displaced from the grid location to the product location to make the connection between product and test system. This type of fixturing is called *grid fixturing* (see Fig. 26.20).

In addition to the requirement to test points that were off-grid, there are requirements to test points that are on the other side of the board. There are three ways to test boards that require double-sided access.

The first method is the *flip test.* Flip testing requires that either two fixtures, one with the top-side image and one with the bottom-side image, or one fixture with both images on it, be built. The board is then tested one side at a time. Although this does provide some fault coverage, it does not test the plated holes and would miss faults such as voided holes. Also, this type of testing requires that the fixture be built with redundant test points in it. Each side of the board is tested, pad to via. The via is pinned on both sides of the board. An additional reduction in fault coverage occurs if the vias are tented or have solder mask on them, preventing access. In this case, in addition to the nontested hole, there will be traces that go untested. Lastly, the additional testing reduces throughput (boards/hour) and increases handling and the likelihood of escapes.

Flip Testing

Advantages	Disadvantages
Inexpensive grid fixturing	Additional/redundant test points in fixture
Requires a single-sided grid	Does not test plated holes
Quick fixture build	May not test all traces
	Requires additional test time for multiple test
	Additional handling may cause escapes

The second method to gain double-sided access is by use of a *wired top-side fixture,* sometimes called a clamshell. In this scenario, a grid fixture is built for the bottom side of the board. The bottom side should be the most complex, in order to minimize the more costly wired top-side fixture (see Fig. 26.21). With this method as well as the flip test, there are redundant or additional test points. In this case, the additional test points are called *transfer points.* Transfer points are found outside the product area in the grid fixture and, on compression, they mate with contacts in the wired top fixture to complete the connection to the top-side points. Dual access with a wired top-side fixture provides excellent fault coverage, as it is simultaneously accessing all test points. Some of the drawbacks of the wired top fixture are expense, limitations on high-technology capabilities (the same limitations as the dedicated fixture), and the additional contact level at the transfer points. Additional contact levels provide opportunities for missed connections and increase the chances of having a false open test result.

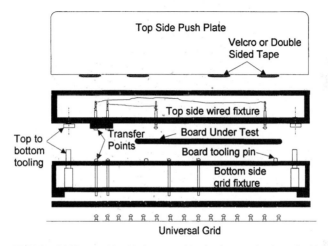

FIGURE 26.21   Double-sided access with wired top and universal grid bottom.

Double-Sided Access with a Wired Top Fixture

Advantages	Disadvantages
Inexpensive bottom grid fixture	Expensive wired top fixture
Requires a single-sided grid	Additional test points for transfer
Uncompromised fault coverage	Increased risk of false opens test result
Good throughput	Technology limitations in wired top fixture
	Wired fixture takes longer to build

The third method is the *double-sided universal grid.* The double-sided grid has active grid electronics on both top and bottom sides. Grid fixtures can then be used on both sides, providing economical fixturing, full fault coverage, good throughput, and high-technology capability.

Double-Sided Universal Grid

Advantages	Disadvantages
Inexpensive grid fixtures	Expensive test system
Uncompromised fault coverage	
High-technology capability	
Good throughput	
Quick fixture build	

Compression Method. Regardless of grid test method, there are a variety of compression methods. The three major ones are hydraulic, pneumatic, and electric. Hydraulic is probably the least used. Although it provides sufficient power to compress an entire grid probe field, it is slow and very difficult to provide location control. Also, hydraulics are difficult to keep from leaking. Leaks in close proximity to expensive electronics are unacceptable.

The electric compression is usually accomplished with one or more electronic motors driving belts or turn screws. Electric compression offers excellent location control and speed, but lacks power and uses a considerable amount of electricity. The lack of power is acceptable for most applications except the testing of high-point-count product or the compression of the entire grid field for diagnostics. Undercompression usually leads to poor contact and false opens test results.

Finally, there is pneumatics. Pneumatic compression is fast and powerful. Location control is good when used in combination with sensing devices such as optical encoders. Pneumatics require the least amount of maintenance.

The purpose of the compression is to overcome the force of the spring probes. The probes under compression can then apply a controlled amount of force to the fixture pin and thus to the board. Grid probe forces of 5 to 10 oz are typical. This may seem an insignificant force for such a large compression system, but keep in mind that a board requiring 5000 test points would require approximately 1900 lb of pressure. For diagnostics you may want to compress as many as 40,000 points or more. That would require a compression force of approximately 8 tons.

Fixture. Fixturing—and especially grid fixturing—has probably been the fastest evolving and changing area in electrical test to date. It would be difficult to cover the state of grid fixturing today and have the data be current for very long. Therefore, it is best that we look at grid fixturing in more of a historical sense. In this way, we can understand the key issues, items, and driving forces in the development, technology, and economics of grid fixturing.

Spring-Loaded Grid Fixture Pin.   Previously we discussed the need for off-grid testing and showed the basic concept in Fig. 26.25. Initially, the pin used to lean from the universal grid to the board was not a pin but a probe. The distinction between pin and probe is that a probe is spring-loaded and a pin is a singular, rigid component. This grid fixture probe interfaced to the grid system via a pad or contact on the surface of the grid field. This worked well, but the probes used in the fixture, although reusable, were expensive. Also, similar limitations to those found with spring probes in dedicated fixturing applications were encountered, i.e., limits on the ability to reduce the diameter of a spring probe assembly for higher-technology applications.

In the area of expense reduction, if the spring force could be moved out of the consumable and/or reusable grid fixture probe and into the test system, a considerable savings would be realized. Universal grid test systems then appeared with cassettes full of spring-loaded probes that sat on top of a grid made up of pads. This freed the fixture from the requirement to contain the spring force and allowed it to use the much less expensive rigid pins. There are a wide variety of pins available for use with different system types and for different applications (see Fig. 26.22).

Displacement and Pin Length.   The industry standard 1.1-in pin has features on it—changes in diameter and angle of cut—to extend its ability to lean. Later pin designs used longer length to achieve more ability to lean or greater pin displacement. Pin displacement is one of the more significant factors in a pin design's capacity to test higher-density and fine centers. With a relatively fixed rule of thumb of 10°, we can see from Fig. 26.23 that the longer the pin, the further the pin can be displaced from its on-grid location to its on-product

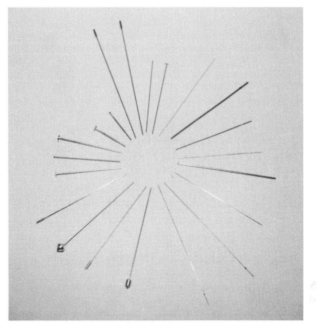

FIGURE 26.22 Universal grid fixture pins. *(Courtesy of Giese International.)*

requirement. Note that displacements in Fig. 26.23 are industry-accepted standards and are not exact to pin displacement trigonometry.

Binding. The rigid pins needed to lean some distance to connect the grid to the on-product location and, thus, the relationship between the plate thickness, hole diameter, and angle of displacement were and are critical. If these factors, plate thickness, hole diameter, and angle of displacement, are not correct, then binding can be the result.

Pin binding is a problem in that other pins in the fixture that can move freely will contact the board and hold it up off a pin that is bound (see Fig. 26.24). Normally, the pin would slide freely, or at least freely enough that the spring force of the grid could overcome the finding friction and push the pin into contact with the board. The relationship of pin displacement, plate thickness, and hole diameter is a trigonometric one. Minimum hole size HS_{min} in the fixture can be determined by taking the tangent of the angle of deflection θ times the plate thickness PT plus the diameter of the pin or shaft diameter SD:

$$HS_{min} = SD + PT(\tan\theta)$$

If θ is not known, it can be solved for by taking the inverse sine of the product of the pin deflection PD divided by the pin length PL:

$$\theta = \sin^{-1}\left(\frac{PD}{PL}\right)$$

If a calculator with trigonometric functions is not available, minimum hole size can be approximated by adding shaft diameter to the product of plate thickness times pin deflection divided by the pin length:

$$HS_{min} = SD + PT * \frac{PD}{PL}$$

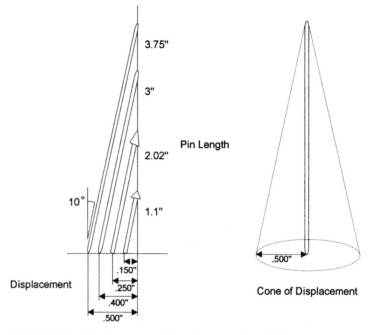

FIGURE 26.23 Displacement by pin length at approximately 10°.

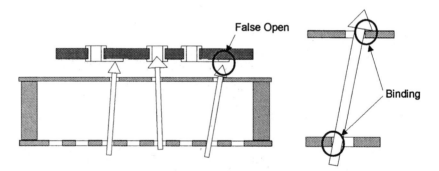

FIGURE 26.24 Pin binding.

These formulas are good for hole diameters less than 0.060 in. Note that the shaft diameter is an approximation of the cross-sectional diameter of the pin and assumes that the pin is not deflected (see Fig. 26.25).

This approximation error is not significant for small-diameter pins but becomes important as the shaft diameter increases. Thus, 0.001 to 0.002 in should be added to the hole size of pins over 0.060 in in diameter. In addition, the minimum hole size is usually not the drill size. The most common material used for grid fixtures is polycarbonate. Polycarbonate tends to have a finished hole size that is 0.001 in under the drill size. Therefore, 0.001 in should be added to minimum hole size for drill selection.

Pin Lean and Pointing Accuracy.   As the SMT found on boards advanced to finer and finer centers, headed pins that were longer were required (such as the 2.02 in). Greater pointing

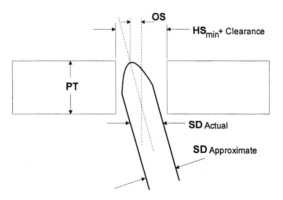

FIGURE 26.25 Shaft diameter approximation, where OS is *offset,* PT is *plate thickness,* HS_{min} is *minimum hole size,* and SD is *shaft diameter.*

FIGURE 26.26 Pointing accuracy.

accuracies were necessary. Pointing accuracy is defined as the pin's ability to hit a given target, usually described as a radial dimension. With the headed pin's head sitting on top of the top plate there was some loss of pointing accuracy (see Fig. 26.26). If the hole in the top plate were drilled exactly on pad center, then the tip of the pin would be somewhat off center. With larger targets, it is likely that the pin would still contact the pad. As pads became smaller—especially narrower—it became more likely that the pin would miss the pad. Some of this pointing accuracy problem can be improved in the fixturing software by compensating the top plate hole location. The software knows the pin displacement and can move the hole to compensate for the angle that the headed pin will be exiting the top plate and contacting the test pad.

Another method occasionally used is the use of a bent, curved, or flex pin. In this application, the pin is bent by means of additional fixture plates or the deformation of the pin such that the tip of the pin as it comes through the top plate is perpendicular to the test pad. This allows the top plate holes to remain on product and mirror the board under test and thus eliminates concerns about the effects of pin contact at an angle. Unfortunately, there are several problems induced. The first is that the bending of the pin increases the friction in the holes of the plates that are guiding the pin. This increased friction causes binding and increases the chances of false opens readings. Compensation can be made for some of the increased binding by increasing the spring force of the grid probe. The force required will vary with the diameter and material strength of the bent pin, leaving some pins binding. Further, some of the pins that have been assigned roughly on grid and are relatively straight up and down are driven into the test pad with this greater spring force, significantly increasing the dent or witness mark that is left on the test pad. At some level this marking causes difficulty at assembly, can expose copper, and, in severe cases, force enough material aside to cause a short to an adjacent pad. The final problem associated with the bent pin is in fixture assembly. Because the bent pin does not move freely, it is not as easy to load in the fixture and requires additional tools to provide a side force in guiding the pin through the grid fixture plates.

Offset Error Compensation.   We must return to trigonometry for a moment to discuss offset error and compensation. Figure 26.25 represents the problem associated with the deflection of a pin retained in the top plate and its ability to hit the center of the pad or target. The hole diameter must be oversized in order to allow the pin to pass through the hole at its angle of deflection without binding. This deflection also leaves the pin against one side of the hole and off center or offset from the pad center. This error is compensated for in most fixture design packages. Offset OS can be calculated by dividing the plate thickness PT by the product of 2 times the tangent of the angle of deflection θ:

$$OS = \frac{PT}{2\tan\theta}$$

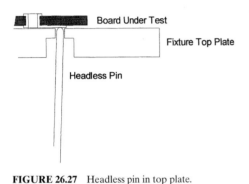

FIGURE 26.27 Headless pin in top plate.

Headless Retained Pins.   Returning to improvement of pointing accuracy, eventually the limits of the headed pin were reached and a better pin tip control method was developed. This was the headless pin. In a headless pin fixture design, the tip of the pin is retained in the top plate and protrudes only slightly if at all to hit the board (see Fig. 26.27). This significantly improved pointing accuracies but introduced a whole new area of problems. How do you retain the pin in the fixture? There is no head to rest on the top plate. Methods had to be developed to capture the pins in the fixture. In addition to these requirements, there was the requirement for grid fixtures for the top of double-sided universal grid systems. The headed pin fixtures could not be used in this double-sided grid application, because once the fixture was flipped over for the top, the pins would fall out. The headless, retained-pin grid fixture was the solution for improving pointing accuracy and providing a fixture for the top of double-sided universal grid systems.

There are a variety of headless pin retention methods. Figure 26.28 shows some of the more current methods in use. The development and change in this area has been rapid, with advancements and new methods appearing regularly. The following is a brief critique of each of the fixture designs pictured in Fig. 26.28.

Figure 26.28*a* represents a bent or curved pin design. Advantages are that pins hit the intended target perpendicularly. Hole diameter in the top plate can be tightened to improve pointing accuracy because all pins are passing through with little to no angle. Long pins allow for a greater degree of displacement, and retention method allows top and bottom grid fixturing to be identical.

Disadvantages are that hanging middle plates reduce the torsional stability of the fixture design, increasing chances of fixture distortion under compression and producing binding with false opens or loss of registration and/or pointing accuracy. The act of bending or curving pins necessitates binding in the fixture. Thicker-diameter pins that require bending do not

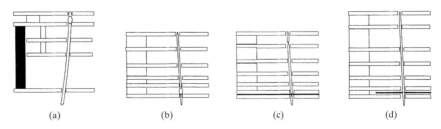

| (a) | (b) | (c) | (d) |

FIGURE 26.28 Headless pin retention methods.

bend easily. For this particular fixture style, additional test system spring force is required in the grid system to overcome this additional binding. While some pin binding can be overcome, some cannot producing false opens. In addition, some pins will not require bending or curving, because they are relatively straight up and down. These pins will transfer the test system's additional spring force directly to the board feature, potentially marking or gouging the board feature. Generally, this is undesirable. Further, this is a top-load design. Loaded with the top plate off, the crimp in the pin rests on the second plate. A pin cannot be removed without disassembling the fixture. When all the pins have been loaded, the top plate is put on with some difficulty, because the top plate hole is the tightest in the fixture, and because the top and second plates are drilled to the same pattern. Therefore, the bending or curving of the pin occurs with the mounting of the top plate. In high-point-count and high-density fixtures, the top plate can be difficult to put on. Pin crimps close to the top plate in close proximity under compression can touch and cause false shorts. One last item is that this fixture design is compressible. When the system compresses the board on the fixture, the fixture compresses as well, producing a dynamic pin displacement and pin curving/bending situation that is difficult to allow for in design and likely to produce loss of pointing accuracy, false opens, and shorting at the crimp point.

Figure 26.28b shows some significant improvements over Fig. 26.28a in that pins are not bent or curved. Pin binding is reduced significantly and requirements for additional spring force in the grid are eliminated by leaning the pins instead of bending them. The crimp is on the bottom of the fixture instead of the top, eliminating the possibility for shorting in the fixture. The fixture is loaded from the bottom side (the side of the fixture with the tighter plate spacing determines the load side). Bottom load significantly increases the pin load rate, because the bottom hole diameter is fairly loose and oversized relative to the tight hole requirement of the top plate, and the hole spacing on the bottom is fairly uniform due to the on-grid assignment. The fixture is rigid (noncompressible) and uniform in plate, and spacer locations provide a stable housing for the fixturing software to assign pins and lean or displace them. The dual top plate allows for top plate rigidity, while allowing maximum pin deflection. The first top plate is thin to allow a tightly sized hole diameter for accurate pin tip pointing without binding. The second top plate is thicker for top plate stability and flatness with an oversized hole to avoid pin binding while providing pin guidance.

Some shortcomings are the reduced pin length (3 in) loses some displacement and therefore slightly limits density and fine-pitch capability. Pins are still not removable without disassembling the fixture. There is a version available that uses a sheet of drilled mylar as the retaining plate for the crimp pin (similar to Fig. 26.28c). The mylar is sandwiched between standard polycarbonate plates and allows the pin to be pulled out from the bottom side without disassembling the fixture. The mylar version with the additional plates does require additional drilling.

The first of the dual top plates in Fig. 26.28b is very thin. This plate provides the pointing accuracy but is subject to material movement due to the drilling and inherent reduced stability of thin materials.

Figure 26.28c uses a grooved pin retained by a drilled mylar sandwich. Loading of the pins is improved by the nonoriented pin that is grooved on both ends. This allows handfuls of pins to be loaded into the fixture from the bottom side without having to orient them first. A countersunk top plate allows for even tighter top hole sizing for better pointing accuracy, while maintaining top plate flatness and thick material stability.

Unfortunately, pin motion under compression wears and distorts the mylar over time, causing the pins to slip or fall. Multiple loads and reloads of mylar-retained fixtures tends to further reduce retention life. Featured pins such as crimp or grooved music wire pins exhibit a weak point at the feature itself as pin diameters are reduced. Effective limits are somewhere around the 0.019-in diameter, at which material strength at the feature location under normal test system compression is insufficient. This fixture style incorporates additional plates for pin guiding throughout and most notably near the top plate. This plate under the top plate eases loading of especially fine or dense fixtures and reduces the opportunity for the pin to walk out of the hole during testing and catch under the top plate. This situation results in false opens and damaged pins.

Figure 26.28*d* represents some of the most advanced features to date, including nonoriented, nonfeatured pin design for maximum pin load rates and minimum pin cost, as well as maximum pin displacement and minimum pin diameter for fine center testing. The drilled latex is not sandwiched but floats, reducing wear on the latex and extending the retention life. Nonfeatured pins are available in finer diameters (no weak point) for closer center testing at higher densities. Additional drilling is offset by higher pin load rates and, thus, faster fixture build as well as higher-technology capability.

Headed Music Wire Pins.   There are occasions when pin tip diameters beyond the 0.051-in maximum of the music wire headless pins are required. In such cases as oversized plated holes, a head is attached to a standard pin diameter. A typical combination would be the attachment of a 0.078 or 0.125-in diameter head to a 0.031-in shaft. These headed music wire pins work in the fixture design much the same as the headless pin, i.e., flush in the top plate (see Fig. 26.29), with the exception that the headed pin must be loaded from the top individually.

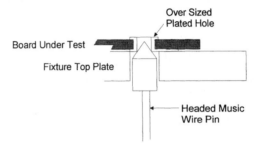

FIGURE 26.29   Headed pin in music wire fixture.

Usually, there are only a few features on a board requiring headed music wire pins, so that fixture build time and cost are not impacted significantly. In cases where there are a significant number of holes requiring headed pins (which are three to five times more expensive than straight music wire pins), using a smaller diameter music wire pin and offsetting the hole so that the pin hits the ring around the hole is the preferred method.

Multiple Plates.   There are several reasons for the use of multiplate fixtures. The two most significant are to make the fixture determined and to speed the fixture build by increasing the pin load rate. Determined fixtures ensure that a pin inserted into the fixture can end up in only one hole, the same hole. This facilitates the use of data-driven test programs, because the test program assumes a specific location for each of the test points. This determination of pin location must remain true if the fixture is taken apart or unloaded and then reloaded. In this way, the fixture can be reused with the same test program. Pin load rate is increased because the pin is guided into a single hole. Fixture assemblers do not have to pick between several possible holes and try to determine which provides the least deflection or at least acceptable deflection. This facilitates a variety of manual or even automatic pin shaking methods to load fixtures with pins.

Bottom and Top Load.   Typically, individual plates are spaced relatively closely on the side of the fixture that the pins are loaded from. The pin is inserted into the first plate and is quickly guided by the next plate. The third plate is spaced a little farther away and continues to guide the pin. Additional plates provide additional guidance to pin loading but also serve other functions. Fine-diameter music wire pins can flex under compression. Evenly spaced plates reduce the likelihood that pins will touch and short under compression. Additionally, plates located near the top of the fixture help keep the pin located in the tight top plate hole as the pin slides and moves under compression.

Top load fixtures may not require quite as many plates, but they do not load as fast because top holes are usually very tight and not spaced uniformly. Bottom load is preferred due to ease and speed of loading with the uniformity of the on-grid centers and relatively oversized hole diameters.

Usage.   The primary application for universal grids is in the testing of prototypes and medium-volume production. Advances in test system speed and mechanical cycle speed have extended the grid into higher-volume applications. Reductions in fixture cost and fixture build time have made grids more viable in short-run and quick-turn production applications as well.

26.5.3   Verification and Repair

The test system identifies faults on the board. Assuming that repaired boards are acceptable to the end user and it makes economical sense to repair boards, repair would normally follow testing. There is one intermediate step referred to as *verification.* This requires a technician to read the fault data and make some measurements on the failed board to determine if the faults indicated are real. It is possible due to poor fixture design, poor contact with the board, and a variety of other problems to have false test results. During verification, a technician will use an ohmmeter or the equivalent to determine if the indicated short, open, or leakage failure is valid. If the fault is valid, the board is then repaired or moves to the repair function. If the fault is not valid, the board may be retested or moved on, depending on customer requirements, in-house policy, etc.

In any of the cases just mentioned, there are several different methods for verification and repair. A relatively manual approach, and the simplest, would be use of an ohmmeter and possibly the artwork for the board. A piece of mylar with a 0.100-in grid is often used to locate the *x-y* coordinates of the fault provided by the test system. In the case of dedicated fixturing, the road map is used to locate the points indicated by the test system.

The next level of repair or verification adds a computer and is often referred to as *computer-automated repair* or CAR. At this level, a PC is used that contains a combination of board data and test program data generated by the fixturing software. The *x-y* coordinates are either entered manually via the keyboard or they are downloaded from the test system. Fail data is associated with a specific board via bar code or sequencing. Sequencing numbers the fault data sequentially, so that the first set of data is associated with the first failing board, the second set with the second board, etc. Sequencing requires that the failing boards be maintained in order so that fail data can be matched. PC-based CAR usually provides additional tools such as color coding of layers and highlight of failing nets, most likely short and open locations, and automatic stepping through faults.

An additional level of repair automation is provided by the CAR workstation (Fig. 26.30). CAR workstations provide an interactive means of overlaying the board trace and failure data on top of the actual board with operator activities by means of plasma displays or video cameras. Test points and faults are located more readily, increasing repair productivity.

Justifications for repair automation include reduction of scrap, increased repair productivity, and increased test system productivity. All too often, test system productivity is consumed by on-system fault verification and even repair.

26.5.4   Selection

Of the three major types of test systems—dedicated, universal grid, and moving probe—determinations must be made as to the most appropriate for a given application. Factors include board volume, number of part numbers, board technologies, and economics. There are many levels of complexity within these items, as well as many more factors. Figure 26.31 provides a basic picture of where the three system types fit within these basic factors. Note that Fig. 26.31 includes only the economics associated with the capital purchase and does not include impor-

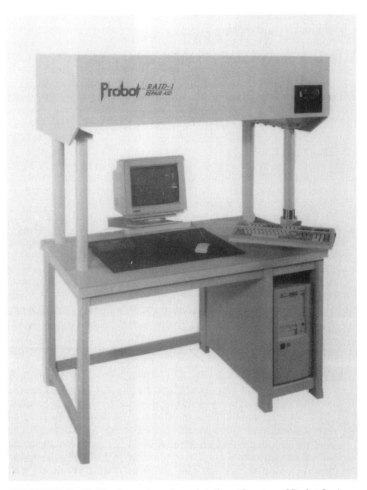

FIGURE 26.30   Verification and repair workstation. *(Courtesy of Probot Inc.)*

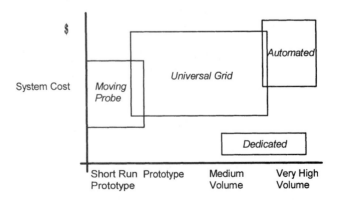

FIGURE 26.31   System type, cost, and production requirement.

tant economic issues such as fixturing costs, capacity requirements, and labor. Also, the system type marked "Automated" can be either dedicated or universal grid automation.

26.5.4.1 Production.   One of the first factors in selecting the appropriate system type is determining what type of production application the equipment will be used for. This may be based on the entire business type of the board manufacturer (quick turn, prototype, volume, etc.) or it can be based on the specific business segment or test area need that is most apparent (short runners, long runners, high technology boards, etc.).

Prototype.   Prototype board production has several segments. The first is *quick turn.* Quick turn requires that boards be produced in very short time frames, typically 24 to 72 h. Quick turn's unique requirement is that test be fast. This may mean a quick fixture build and a universal grid or no fixture build and a moving probe.

The second prototype segment is *short runners.* These are part numbers with quantities of 10 to 15 or less. Tooling costs are spread across a small number of parts, making tooling cost relatively large in comparison to the cost or price of the boards. Short runners require minimal tooling cost. This may require a moving probe system or very inexpensive grid fixturing.

The last and largest segment of prototype production is the typical prototype lots of 25 to 50 and sometimes upwards of 500. A significant portion of this business is not so much prototype but a result of manufacturing methodologies such as *just in time* (JIT), where a production order of 2000 pieces may be broken up into orders for lot sizes of 50 and 100. JIT demands minimum inventory and, as such, the board manufacturer cannot be sure of ultimate quantities or timing. This type of part number is, for all intents, prototype production.

What all three of these segments have in common is the need to minimize tooling costs because of the relatively small number of boards that the fixturing will be spread across.

The short time frame required for quick turn and prototype JIT production requires quick setup and changeover capabilities. These capabilities can be found on all three machine types. Although the moving probe system offers the fastest changeover and lowest tooling cost, it is limited in throughput and may simply not be able to test enough boards within a given shift, day, or week to meet requirements. The fixturing costs associated with dedicated systems is usually too much for small lots of boards to bear. Automated test systems are usually not well suited to many or quick changes and are generally not suited to prototype production.

Volume.   Where dedicated and automated systems are most suited is in volume production. Because dedicated systems require only enough test point electronics to meet the point count of the product being tested, the dedicated system cost is relatively low. The more expensive dedicated test fixture cost can be spread over a large quantity of boards and is thus not usually significant. Because system cost is low, additional systems are added to meet production requirements at a lower incremental capital cost than other system types.

Automated systems are simply versions of either dedicated or universal grid test systems with loading and/or unloading automation. The automation allows more boards per hour to be tested. Some of the benefits of automation are offset by increased fixture cost and significantly higher system cost.

Whether it's a dedicated or automated test system, the emphasis is on throughput. Fixturing cost and setup time are relatively minor factors, as volume production usually incorporates producing many parts and few part numbers.

Although maximizing throughput means testing the most boards in a given hour or shift, maximizing capacity adds an economic measure in which automation is traded off against labor and capital costs. Many board manufacturers look for flexibility in adding capacity, that is, the ability to add capacity quickly by adding automation to existing equipment or adding test capacity in small capital increments via the dedicated test system.

Mixed.   Many board manufacturers must meet a variety of requirements, including a mix of prototype and volume type production. If a single system is all that is required or possible, then the universal grid is the most versatile, with its low fixturing costs and moderate volume capability. If more than one system is required, then a combination of equipment may be feasible. For example, if a universal grid is in use but occasional high running part numbers consume a large portion of the test system availability, a dedicated test system can offload these few part numbers for a lower total system and tooling cost. This would free the grid for prototype work and utilize the dedicated system for the longer runners. There are, of course, many situations where an additional universal grid would be the appropriate solution.

Another example would be a universal grid in use with an excessive number of changeovers in a day or change time significantly exceeding actual time spent testing or some amount of short runners that cannot bear the burden of fixture costs. In this case, the universal grid could be offloaded with a moving probe system.

26.5.4.2 Technology. Technology of the boards produced adds another level of differentiation between appropriate systems or combinations of systems. Figure 26.32 represents basic test system type technology capability and does not include level of suitability in economics, capacity, or other ways to the respective levels of technology. It is notable that, although the moving probe can handle a wide range of technology, it is very limited in terms of throughput capability, as seen in Fig. 26.31.

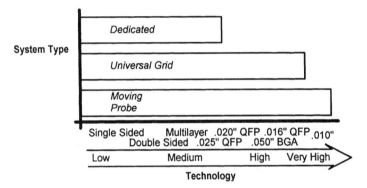

FIGURE 26.32 System type and technology capability.

As important as production type criteria are for selecting equipment, so is technology level. The technology of boards produced impacts equipment selection on several levels, including equipment type and cost, fixturing type and cost, and expected throughput.

Low—Single-Sided. The simplest type of printed wiring board produced is single-sided. Generally, they are produced in high volumes, usually for consumer or consumer-related products and presently are produced primarily in Asia. Technologies in this type of board are generally very simple: mostly through-hole and very simple surface-mount. Test methods are often visual inspection where labor rates are low. Visual inspection with this very low level of technology has a moderately high level of effectiveness. The alternative method is the use of very inexpensive dedicated test systems. Test parameters and test stringency is not deemed critical. The majority of this type of production is in areas of the world where labor is inexpensive and board prices are extremely low. Though automation might be appropriate, the expense for the equipment is often difficult to justify under such conditions.

Smaller quantities of low-technology single-sided work are suited to universal grids where some of the grids' most economical fixturing types (such as 1.1 in) can be applied in combination with lower-cost, single-sided grid systems. This method is especially effective if there are a large number of different parts and some higher technology is also produced. Moving probe systems can also be used, but the low cost of the board cannot usually bear the amortized cost of the prober for only this application, not considering that even moderate quantities will overburden prober capacity.

Medium—Double-Sided and Low-Layer-Count Multilayer. A very large portion of boards produced falls into this category. All of the major system types are appropriate for testing this type of product, moving probes for short runs, universal grids for prototype to medium volumes, dedicated and automated systems for high volumes. It is also noteworthy that many of the universal grid systems rival dedicated test systems in throughput capability and, as such, are often found testing boards in high volume.

Although some multilayer counts of 4 to 6 can be very high technology with fine lines and spaces, the medium-technology application for test systems refers to feature centers or pitch of 0.020 in and greater. In this category, equipment selection is driven by the economics of production type, prototype, or volume, or in between, and factors such as fixturing, equipment costs, and capacity.

High—Multilayer, Fine Lines and Spaces, and High Lead Densities. This category of board type includes features such as QFPs (quad flat packs) with centers of 0.020 in and less, BGAs (ball grid arrays) with centers of 0.050 in and less, and like features that present close centers, high densities, and small pad sizes. Moving probe systems are highly suited to testing this type of product in short runs. Dedicated test systems are somewhat limited on this type of product, especially on fine centers. The dedicated system issue is really in the technical limitations of dedicated fixtures. An interesting exception is in the area of BGAs where the dedicated system is not limited by density as a universal grid is. The limits again are related to the ability to put dedicated fixture probes on fine centers.

Universal grids are highly suited to this type of product. Dimensions of high-technology boards tend to be smaller than board dimensions; thus, the size of the universal grid required is less, reducing system cost. The music wire type grid fixture allows for very fine pin diameters to be placed on very close centers. For fixtured systems, the universal grid is the most technology capable. Limitation or additional system cost is encountered when lead densities exceed the standard 0.100-in single-density grid or 100 points/in^2. Although many components with lead densities higher than 100 points/in^2 can be tested on a 0.100-in grid with the use of long music wire pins (see Fig. 26.33), some require additional test system capabilities.

The example in Fig. 26.33 shows a QFP that requires a density of 130 test points/in^2, and its pin assignments to a 0.100-in or single-density grid. Note that if another feature were located within the area outside the device shown, this could increase the potential for conflict in the pin assignment.

In cases where high-technology board test point densities exceed the capability of both the single-density grid and the associated fixturing, higher densities are available. Figure 26.11 shows some common higher density configurations in double- and quad-density patterns. Determinations as to what density is required to test a specific board or board feature requires the use of fixturing software, a specific fixture design, and some trial assignments. The use of all available features of universal grids and grid fixturing can approach and surpass testing of 0.010-in centers. Ability to test prototype to volume, low technology to high, makes the universal grid extremely versatile.

The application of automated test systems to high-technology boards has some limitations. In particular, automation and automated systems tend to compromise some of the tooling tolerances in the fixturing, reducing the fixture's ability to hit accurately and repeatably fine SMT targets. In practice, test system operators use a variety of techniques to improve the pass rates of boards, including brushing them off and biasing them in a particular direction on the fixture. There are few features of automated systems that are comparable to these actions and the higher the technology of the product, the more likely some operator intervention and refinements will be invoked. An automated system will tend to fail the product, requiring that failed stacks of boards be put back through the system some number of times, allowing several opportunities to pass. This significantly reduces the effective throughput of the system and adds handling-induced test escapes and wear and tear on the boards. Also, the nature of automated systems is to run them with a minimum of changeovers. Changeovers are usually time consuming. To reduce changeover time, most automated system designs limit fixture types and board size. The limit to fixture type in particular may not allow the usage of advanced fixture types and methods and thus may reduce the level of technology that the system is capable of handling.

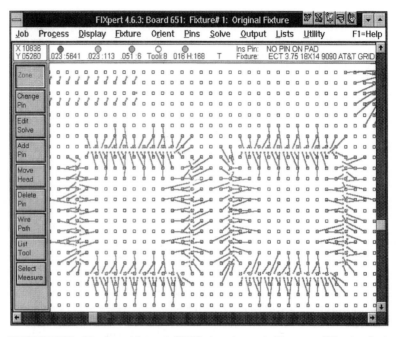

FIGURE 26.33 20-mil quad flat pack (QFP) pin assignment. *(Courtesy of Circuitest Inc.)*

Recent advancements in the area of registration and the use of optics seem likely to make automated systems more appropriate for high-technology product. Keep in mind that an automated system makes use of either a dedicated or universal grid fixturing system with all the associated capabilities and limitations.

26.5.4.3 Economics. It is impossible to discuss selecting appropriate equipment without considering economic factors. Equipment should be qualified on technical and production merit, but individual selections must include consideration of overall economics. That is the combination of costs associated with testing boards produced. There are many factors involved, and the following is only a discussion of the major ones.

Inside vs. Outside. An issue mostly for smaller operations is whether to test in-house or outside. The starting point is usually to have product tested outside as needed. There are many proven test services available. As testing outside becomes a more significant component of outside expenditures, it is time to start investigating the economics of testing inside. The simplest determination is to estimate the cost of equipment, fixturing, and labor inside for the operation's business type, technology, and capacity requirements and compare that estimate to outside expenditures.

In an ongoing board production facility where some test equipment is in place, there still may be outside expenditures for testing. Parts are often sent out to test services that have different equipment that will provide a lower cost of test or have a required capability not found in-house. An example might be a single-sided grid owner who sends short-run product to a test service with a moving probe system. The same single-sided system owner may send a product requiring double-sided test to a test service that has a double-sided universal grid for the same reason: lower cost of test. Another example may be a facility specializing in short runs and quick turn that uses moving probes and occasionally accepts production orders from its customers. Testing the production order on the moving probe would not allow time for the main business—short runs—to be tested. This might adversely affect the regular customers and thus threaten the business. In this case, it may be best to send the production order to a test service with the appropriate fixtured system. Finally, a facility may have a low-voltage test system and have customer-driven requirements for a high-voltage test or other test parameter not available in-house. Boards for those customers are sent out to a test service with a high-voltage test system.

System Cost. This is an important consideration, but not always the most important. For example, if capacity and throughput are important, a test system that can test twice as many boards per hour but is less than twice the cost would be a better value. If high-technology capability is most important, the system capable of testing the highest-technology product would have a longer useful life and a quicker return than a lower-cost system that is significantly limited. If cost is most important, cost for comparable throughput, system cost, labor cost, and especially fixturing cost must be included for a complete evaluation. It is important that all cost components be included.

Hidden system costs may be found in expansion and or options that may be added at a later date. If such throughput and high-technology capabilities cannot be added later, then true system cost may include an additional test system in a relatively short period of time.

Fixturing Cost. It is not unusual for total fixturing costs to exceed that of the equipment in just three to five years. Therefore, an inexpensive system with expensive fixtures is not likely to provide the best total cost picture. Material costs for fixturing include pins/probes, spacers, kit materials, and tools. Probably the most important cost element is in the assembly and pin load labor. Specifically how long does it take to build the fixture? The largest element in universal grid fixturing is usually pin loading. Pin load rates are determined not so much by operator skill as fixture design. Fixture design elements that facilitate higher load rates are nonoriented or bidirectional pins, bottom loading, and presence of multiple guide plates.

Pin loading can often be speeded by the use of shaker tables or pin loaders. Use of automated pin-loading systems or devices usually requires a much larger pin inventory (another cost consideration). Pin-loading automation should be considered a justification by itself. A conservative approach would suggest starting with a manual pin-load process and then gathering true in-house load rates and costs and using them to justify demonstrated pin-load automation later.

The last approach to fixturing cost may be to have the fixtures built outside by a third party. In comparing third parties, it is important to ensure that the fixture type supplied is appropriate to the board technology and volume level required. Arrangements can often be made to return fixtures that are no longer required so that the outside service may reuse components of it to help reduce total fixturing costs.

Data Prep and Programming. Usually a smaller component of the overall cost picture, cost of data preparation as the number of part numbers and level of technology rises is not insignificant. Data preparation usually requires a higher skill set than those of system operators or repair technicians in computer literacy. Technician- or engineer-level design expertise and often-overlooked test area and fixture design knowledge or expertise is preferred.

Capacity. A return look at capacity is important for board manufacturing facilities whose output will require more than one system presently or at some later date. Time spent maintaining, repairing, and setting up can reduce available test time and should be factored into a test system's capacity. Test system tools that speed setup and maintenance functions will considerably increase system output over the system's useful life. If multiple systems are or will be required, all cost components need to be factored for each system. For example, if capacity required three slower, lower-cost systems compared to two faster, higher-cost systems, it would be important to include the additional cost of operator labor on the slower systems as well as the possible requirement for duplicate fixtures to meet production turn time requirements. Added maintenance, power utilization, and floor space impacts may also be considered.

Capability. We must also return to capability for a moment. A system selected because it meets today's board technology may require another system purchase in a short period of time to meet next year's board requirements. Although predicting future requirements often includes some element of uncertainty, some risk may be hedged by observing market trends of market-leading bare-board manufacturers or the trends associated with bare-board customers in their respective markets.

Great advantages can be realized by systems on which technology and throughput capabilities can be added incrementally. This assumes that future requirements can be met with add-ons presently available or that will be available before the requirement emerges. This type of equipment reduces initial system cost while meeting present requirements. It reduces the risk that capability will be paid for and never used and that additional systems will be necessary to meet unforeseen requirements. In essence, the aim is to pay for what you need today and add only what you need later.

Other. There are many more factors to consider, such as vendor strength, longevity, support, and location. A system that is no longer supported can be considerably more expensive to own and operate than one that is. Large, healthy vendors tend to have more resources to produce new and innovative solutions. Cost of doing business with vendors located overseas may be subject to currency and/or political fluctuations.

Familiarity and compatibility should be considered. Additional systems from the same vendor may reduce training and spares requirements. Often, different test systems require changing to a different fixture type. This may be necessary to reduce costs or meet technology requirements. But many systems are limited in their ability to make use of other fixturing types. This puts additional burdens on test planning decisions when product must be fixtured for one system or the other, not either system. A system that offered fixturing compatibility to existing equipment and reduced cost and/or added higher-technology fixturing capabilities would present additional benefits.

26.5.5 Mixing Equipment

Often the technology and production makeup of a board-manufacturing operation is varied or mixed, requiring the implementation of multiple or complementary test strategies and test systems. The two most common combinations of equipment are universal grid with moving probe and universal grid with dedicated system.

26.5.5.1 Universal Grid with Moving Probe. There are two ways in which universal grids and moving probes are used together. The first is in prototype production where very short run product cannot justify a test fixture, or the number of short-run fixture builds and system setups degrades the universal grid system's productivity. The moving probe is then used to test short-run product while the grid tests the prototype and larger lot product. The second area is when the technology of a board requiring test exceeds the test system's density, fixturing, or general capability. In this case, the product could be tested entirely on the moving probe if the volume allows. To extend the usage of this complementary method without filling the capacity of the moving probe, a fixture can be built for the grid system that accesses what features it can, with the remainder accessed by the moving probe. Care must be taken to ensure that the combination test produces acceptable fault coverage.

26.5.5.2 Universal Grid with Dedicated System. The more expensive universal grid can become bogged down with higher running part numbers if an inexpensive dedicated test system is not available. Although the addition of automation to the grid or an additional grid system may be appropriate, a dedicated test system may supply more capacity at a lower total cost. That cost would include the lower-cost test system plus the appropriate number of the higher-cost test fixtures.

26.6 SURFACE-MOUNT TESTING

Surface-mount technology (SMT) provides a major challenge to the electrical test area. The challenge falls primarily in the area of fixturing. Test system capabilities and features can make the testing of SMT more or less difficult, as well as more or less expensive. Without good fixture design, SMT testing is very difficult and unproductive. This discussion focuses primarily on the application of double-sided universal grids to high-technology SMT boards.

26.6.1   Impact of Fine Lines, Spaces, and Densities on Test

What design elements or features of SMT impact test? Fine lines and spaces impact the complexity of the design and often reflect the fine width and pitch of SMT pads, but line width and spacing do not, of themselves, impact electrical test. Undoubtedly, the associated narrow pads and close pitch or pad center to center impact testability.

Density is a different measure all together. Density is not so much an issue of how closely pins can be placed together, but of how many can be placed in a given area. At the simplest level, the component level, higher-technology compact board designs will generally employ high-lead-density devices. Lead densities well in excess of the standard 100/in^2 are not uncommon. Devices as common as 0.025-in center QFPs often represent a lead density higher than 100 points/in^2. Yet they are usually testable, thanks to the grid fixture's ability to lean or displace pins. This allows grid points outside the area directly under the device to lean in and provide test access.

Testability of a particular package can be easily estimated. For a device with 196 pins and a device outline of 1 in^2, and a selected fixture and pin displacement capability of 0.400 in, we can determine testability on a single-density grid by the following:

$$\text{Available points} = 100 \times (\text{device outline} + \text{displacement capability})^2$$

$$= 100 \times (1 + 0.4)^2 = 196$$

Although this seems to work out as exactly testable, if there is such a thing, it is likely that the selected pin fixture combination would have to be displaced slightly over 0.400 in to fully assign test points to the site during data preparation. Test points drawn from the center area of the device may be more than 0.400 in away from the assigned location and, if limited to 0.400-in displacement, may not be usable. At the corners of the device, the assignment may be rather crowded and require displacements a little beyond 0.400 in to test the device.

A discussion of density goes well beyond an individual component site. The example previously given of a 1-in^2 device being tested with a fixture and pin design displacement of approximately 0.400 in assumes that no other features requiring test fall within the 0.400-in border around the device. The higher the technology and density of the board, the less likely this assumption will hold. This does not immediately imply a need for higher density, because there are higher displacement fixture and pin combinations than in this example.

We will discuss several methods of accessing high-density SMT features and fine pitch, including longer pins and increased density. But access to features requiring test has a few more elements. Solder mask can encroach or cover some portion of an SMT feature requiring test, effectively reducing the feature size. Some test methods require access to vias that can have solder mask very close or covering them, eliminating them as potential test point sites.

It is worth mentioning the impact of higher technology containing BGAs and fine-center QFPs on a test department that is not prepared or capable of handling them. Simply stated, it will be difficult to ship product. False test results, and especially false opens, are usually evidence of inadequate fixturing. Product can be shipped by manually verifying or invalidating test results. This would be very slow and extremely expensive in labor terms and is usually a sign of a need for new fixturing software, fixture design, or equipment.

In essence, the impact of higher-technology SMT features on test is that they drive fixturing considerations to a greater level of complexity. These considerations can increase fixturing cost, but they do not have to when considering the complete picture of the cost of testing.

26.6.2 Test Methods for Fine Centers

If a high-end fixture design is in place, the majority of success in fixturing for fine centers comes from the fixturing software. All of the subtleties of multiple plates, hole sizes, and angles of displacement come together there. The variety, complexity, and rapid advancements in high-end fixture designs cannot be assumed. They are something to be regularly worked with and improved. Here, we will examine the areas that require consideration as board technologies advance.

26.6.2.1 Fixturing. The most basic element of fixturing fine centers is the ability to place test pins close together. This implies that finer-diameter pins can be placed closer together. This is true with the limitation of the strength of the pin, that is, its ability to hold up under compression, during pin loading, storage, etc. Features in the pin may impact pin strength and the minimum usable pin diameter.

Assuming that the fixturing software has determined the best possible hole diameter relative to plate thickness and the amount of displacement, the hole that is drilled must be very good. Drill accuracy for the drilling of the top plate or the plate closest to the hole is paramount. Other plates in the fixture can actually be drilled on a less accurate drill, as their primary purpose is served once the fixture is loaded. The top plate holds the tip of the pin in position with the intent of hitting the center of the SMT pad. Any error in the drilling of this plate goes directly to the error tolerance stack-up associated with hitting SMT pads.

Additional tolerance is added by the tooling pins. The tooling pin diameter must be undersized relative to the tooling hole diameter to enable placement and removal of the board. It also must be tight enough to minimize slop or play in the location of the board. Spring-loaded tooling pins offer one of the least accurate tooling methods in that the pin in its spring-loaded housing adds additional tolerance to the tooling location. Hard-tooled tooling pins are preferred. Conical or bullet-nosed tooling taller than the thickness of the board offers additional benefits in ease of loading and placement. Hard-tooled tooling pins taller than the board must have clearance in the top fixture to allow for a place to accept the tooling pin under compression. This same discussion of tooling applies to tooling used for top-to-bottom fixture alignment, the emphasis being on making the tooling simple and rigid enough so as to introduce as few additional tolerances as possible.

The variety of high-technology fixture designs and the rate of development make statements about current high-end fixture technologies subject to obsolescence. One of the more common quick measures of the likelihood that a fixture will work well is how easily the pins move. The fixture should be laid on its side and, with a hand on each side of the fixture, the pins should be moved back and forth. If they do not move easily, it is likely that they are binding and will cause false opens and generally poor test results. This is usually because the holes are too tight or some parameter of the fixturing software is not appropriately sizing or locating holes.

Another measure is to compress a single board several times (three to seven) and then look at some of the finer pads on the board. All pin strikes or *witness marks* should be in the same spot. If the witness marks are not always in the same location on an individual site, this is called *pin scatter.* Pin scatter is a sign that top plate holes are too big and/or that tooling pins are too small. Both pin scatter and pin binding will result in inconsistent test results, such as false opens. It is especially frustrating when these false opens are not repeatable or move (sometimes called *walking*). Again, this is a result of inconsistent contact with the pad.

A third measure of fixturing accuracy is to compress an untested circuit board one time and then study the witness marks. A shift all in one direction may be a sign that the fixture tooling or drilling is shifted, but it is more likely that the board is exhibiting a shift. Therefore, the more important thing to look for is if the pins have hit the board consistently in the center of the pads or, if shifted in one direction, consistently in that direction. Keep in mind that a shift can be in $x, y,$ or θ (rotational). If the shift or location of witness marks relative to features is not consistent, then drill accuracy, fixturing software parameters, and or general fixture design are suspect.

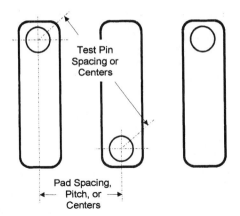

FIGURE 26.34 Test point spacing greater than pad spacing.

Test Centers.   Techniques are available for increasing pin-to-pin spacing, such as test point staggering, as shown in Fig. 26.12. Figure 26.34 shows the difference between pad centers and test pin centers. It is occasionally possible to do a triple stagger in order to further increase test pin centers relative to pad centers. This requires a long pad length.

One of the limiting factors in placing pins close together is hole breakout. At some point the holes for guiding the pins will open or break out into each other. Fixturing software will flag breakout. Although the top plate holes are the closest together, the breakout often occurs in the plates immediately following the top plate, because the hole diameters are larger and the pins are still fairly close together. Undetected hole breakout can cause pin shorting or binding.

There are some compromised methods for splitting up fine-center pads to make test easier. One method is called *split net testing.* A split net test would take every other pad on a fine-pitch device and put them on one fixture with the remainder on a second fixture. This would reduce the pin-to-pin spacing requirement. But the compromises are similar to those discussed in Sec. 26.4.2.1 for flip testing: possible reduced fault coverage, reduced throughput, additional handling and fixture costs, etc.

Pin Displacement.   The ability to place fine diameter pins close together is not the only issue in testing fine centers. The number of test pins required to be leaned or displaced into a given area to hit all of the SMT device pads can be quite high. This requires leaning pins in from well outside the outline of the device. There may be other features that border the device that also require test pins, although an outlying device may not require all of the pins within its outline. There may not be any devices on one or more sides of a fine-center device. The outline of the device may be very large, requiring a significant lean or displacement in order to access the pins at the center area. In all these cases, additional capability is acquired by a larger pin displacement. Although fixture design can limit displacement, generally, the longer the pin, the greater the displacement (see Fig. 26.28). Longer pins will add a surprisingly large degree of additional solving capability, which is the ability to assign pins in the fixturing software without having to manually assign or purchase a higher-density grid capability.

26.6.2.2 Registration Compensation.   With everything perfect in the fixture, it is possible to still see false opens, false shorts, and inconsistent test results due to registration shifts on the board. Registrations between the drilled features and the artwork or etched features of interest, as they represent the tooling pin site and the test pin site, respectively. The quickest way to site registration shift is to look at the vias on a board and note the registration between the drilled hole and the etched ring or annular ring. Registration shifts occur in many directions: *x, y,* θ, and top to bottom. Top to bottom is probably the least concern, as most boards have tougher features on one side. Since the tolerances for bottom-side testing are lower, the tougher side of the board should be placed down. Registration compensations made on the bottom often are appropriate for the top side or are within the tolerance range of the features on the top side.

Figure 26.35 shows registration shifts of 0.000 to 0.004 in on a 0.007-in-wide pad. The 0.004-in shift is clearly a marginal contact and would produce inconsistent test results. The dotted line around the test pin location in Fig. 26.35 represents the tolerance of the fixture and tooling pins, which can be 0.001 to 0.0035 in. Even the 0.002-in shift shows some marginality with the fixturing tolerance included.

The solution is first to have a fixture design that minimizes all tolerances. Only then is it appropriate to add registration compensation. Otherwise, while adjusting some points onto their pads, others are being adjusted off. Movable tooling pins are the most common means

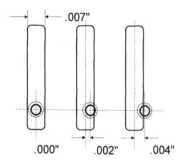

FIGURE 26.35 Registration shift.

and there are many schemes to accomplish this. It is important that the tooling pins be adjustable in *x, y,* and θ. Often, the shift found is the same for the entire lot requiring test. It can be compensated for at the beginning of the lot by moving the tooling manually and locking it in place. The addition of optics and vision recognition help speed the alignment process. Figure 26.36 is a typical fixture registration compensation instrument.

Registration shift in a single direction is the result of tooling error and the inherent tolerances of the two separate processes of imaging and drilling. Although this can be entirely compensated for, there is an additional registration factor encountered at very fine centers and in flex circuits that can only be optimized for. That is the consequence of material and artwork expansion and/or contraction, or "shrink and stretch." Because the fixture is rigid, it certainly cannot match the dynamics of shrink and stretch. At best, the effects can be halved or compensated for by adjusting tooling in such a fashion as to keep the test pins on the pads and leave the board testable.

26.6.3 Test Methods for High Density

Testing high-density product is not an issue of how closely the pins can be spaced, but instead, of how many pins can be placed in a given area. Figure 26.37 represents a BGA device

FIGURE 26.36 Registration compensation instrument. (*Courtesy of Everett Charles Technologies.*)

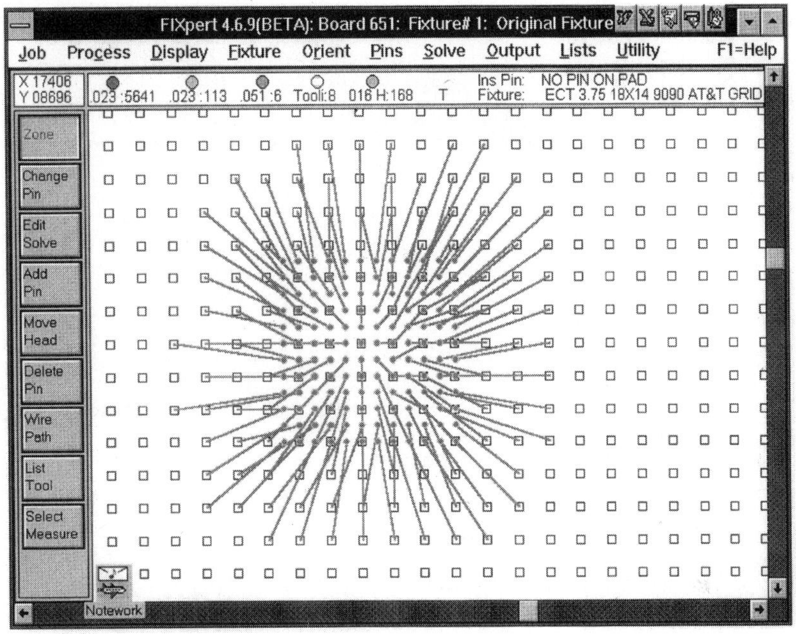

FIGURE 26.37   50-mil ball grid array (BGA) pin assignment. *(Courtesy of Circuitest Inc.)*

assigned to a single-density grid. Maximum displacement is 0.620 in. If several other devices were located in close proximity, there might not be enough test locations available.

26.6.3.1   Fixturing.   Many of the same items appropriate to testing fine centers are relevant here. Split net testing may be applied with the appropriate compromises. Longer pins with greater displacement capability provide more available test pin assignment locations. But what is different is that high density does not always mean fine test pin centers. This allows another fixturing method to be made use of: the dedicated or wired fixture. Dedicated fixtures are not as limited by density—more by fine-center capability. They can be used to test BGAs or in other high-density situations as long as it does not also include fine centers. Often fine centers and high density are found together, and one tends to lead to the other. As a result, making use of dedicated fixtures in high technology applications is relatively restricted. Moving probes can also be used for high density, but high density often means high test point count, further reducing moving probe throughput.

Displacement or longer pins again play a leading role in the resolution of high-density test problems. The longer the pin, the more the displacement and the greater the chance of resolving a density conflict.

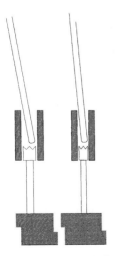

FIGURE 26.38   Pin displacement limitations for single- and double-density grids.

26.6.3.2   Additional Hardware.   Once fixture and pin solutions for high-density applications have been maximized, it is time to look into additional test system density

FIGURE 26.39   Increasing the density of a single-density test system with an adapter.

capability. Figure 26.11 displays the standard single-density grid and two higher-density configurations (double and quad). Additional density will provide more available test points within a given area. This may be the solution to the problem of a dense area of a board that was not previously testable in a single pass. It may take a board design requiring extreme pin displacements on single density and make it more reliable and repeatable on higher density.

In-System.   Test systems are available in configurations with higher-density universal grids. Keep in mind that doubling or quadrupling the test point count of a test system often does similar multiplication on the system price. Some single-density systems can have higher density added to them in the form of upgrades. Grids can be mixed density with a small central area of high density surrounded by a larger area of single density. In this configuration, the test system would be able to test small, high-density product and larger, less-dense product on the same system.

It is important to consider what is compromised when moving to higher density. For example, Fig. 26.38 shows a test point assigned to single density and double density. The smaller diameter of the stripper plate hole reduces the available pin displacement capability. For a 3.75-in pin, this reduction is approximately 0.500 to 0.300-in. In addition, this smaller hole may not allow the use of larger-diameter pins used for through-hole testing or found in existing test fixtures. If the larger pins are usable, they are subject to even more severe pin displacement limitations, increasing the likelihood that a fixture built and assigned to a single-density grid will contain pins displaced in excess of double-density limitations.

Adapters.   Another way to add additional density is through adapters (see Fig. 26.39). Single-density test systems can have adapters placed on top of them that convert the single-density grid centers to higher-density configurations. Larger boards can be tested by removing the adapter and accessing the single-density grid. Converting existing test points instead of adding new ones is significantly less expensive than the electronics upgrade and may put off the requirement for a new and more expensive test system.

P · A · R · T · 4

ASSEMBLY PROCESSES

CHAPTER 27
ASSEMBLY PROCESSES

Stephan A. Vickers
Universal Instruments Corp., Binghamton, New York

27.1 INTRODUCTION

Automated electronics assembly has come far since the first axial insertion machine was developed for IBM in Endicott, N.Y. in 1960. Since that time, a steady pace of machine development and component, board, and process standardization has helped to revolutionize the electronics industry, enabling a vast proliferation of electronic products. In the electronics market, characterized by ever-shorter product development and market life cycles, intense global competition, and rapidly evolving technology, understanding the assembly processes is not only desirable as a means of increasing profitability, but necessary as a means of ensuring survival. This chapter will cover:

- Basic principles employed in electronics assembly equipment
- Key considerations for selecting or specifying a piece of assembly equipment
- Board-level design issues which affect how efficiently the assembly processes may be performed

Electronics assemblies can be grouped into three basic categories: through-hole, surface-mount, and mixed technology, which is a combination of both through-hole and surface-mount on the same board (see Fig. 27.1a–c). In general, the category of assemblies which must be produced dictates the types of machines and processes which must be used.

Through-hole is the simplest of the three technology categories to manufacture. Most through-hole boards which are still being assembled are for products where overall board size is not a major concern (such as televisions, where the size of the picture tube dictates the overall size of the unit), for older product designs which are still in use (such as automotive engine controllers which must still be available to support older model cars), or for applications where certain components are required that are not available in surface-mount packages (such as power supplies, where large transformers or capacitors are used). No longer is it the case, however, that through-hole technology is selected for all low-cost products, as studies have shown that surface-mount is actually cheaper in some applications, especially when the cost of quality is also considered.

Surface-mount technology (SMT) assembly is far more complex than through-hole, resulting mostly from the size and complexity of SMT components, the need to place components on both sides of the board, and the problems caused by not mechanically securing component leads to the board before soldering. As a result of these differences, SMT really needs to be

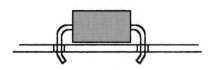

FIGURE 27.1a Through-hole components have leads which are inserted through holes in the board, are clinched (bent) below to mechanically secure the component in place, and are then wave soldered to provide reliable electrical connections.

FIGURE 27.1b Surface-mount components have leads or terminations which are placed into solder paste applied to pads on the board and are then reflow soldered to provide both the mechanical and electrical connections.

FIGURE 27.1c This circuit board predominantly uses surface-mount technology except for three through-hole connectors/headers.

thought of as an integrated assembly and soldering process and not just a series of individual component placement steps followed by a soldering step.

27.2 *THROUGH-HOLE ASSEMBLY*

Through-hole technology components can be classified as axial, radial, DIP (dual in-line package), or odd-form. Many standards have been developed since the mid 1950s governing the physical sizes of axial, radial, and DIP components and the methods by which they are packaged and presented to an assembly machine. As a result, these components can readily be assembled using standard machines available from a number of suppliers. However, odd-form components such as transformers, coils, switches, and connectors often are inserted by hand, although certain machines are available which are able to insert a wide variety of these types of components as well.

27.2.1 Axial Component Insertion

The first major innovation which enabled automatic component insertion to become practical was the sequential taping of axial components by their leads. Although body taping was also tried, lead taping provided the most uniform and consistent method of component packaging and presentation which, in turn, helped produce a more reliable insertion process. With the purchasing power of companies like IBM and AT&T (Western Electric) in those early years, lead taping soon became the standard method of packaging axial components for automatic assembly.

The earliest axial insertion machines cut components from their packaging tape, formed the leads in an upside-down U shape of a fixed span, inserted the component into one specific board location, and clinched (or bent) the leads below the board to secure the component in place. Machines soon evolved to include a Pantograph table, which allowed an operator to index manually through an entire board, inserting components at all the desired locations. This process could be performed at rates on the order of 2000 to 3000 insertions per hour. See Fig. 27.2.

Around 1965, NC (or numerical control) was becoming available, and it was a logical next step to replace the Pantograph table with an NC positioning table to speed up the insertion process and allow a greater number of components to be inserted by one machine. While it would still be some five years before servo positioning under direct computer control would be applied to component insertion, this development was a critical step forward toward developing a fully automated process.

Up to this point, axial insertion machines were set up and dedicated to one component part number for a given board to be assembled. The development of a *component sequencer* enabled a single machine to insert a variety of component types or values, provided that they all had the same lead span on the board. The sequencer automatically selected and cut a variety of components from their respective tapes and then retaped them in the proper sequence in which they would be needed to assemble a complete board. These sequenced tapes were prepared off-line and then loaded onto the insertion machine as needed. (See Fig. 27.3.)

The sequencer allowed one inserter to do the work of many, but each inserter was still limited to only one lead span. This precipitated the invention of a *variable center distance* (VCD) placement head, which could vary the span at which components were formed and inserted. The invention of the VCD head allowed a single machine to place all axial components on a single board. Multiple machines were required based only on production capacity requirements—not on board design.

Axial component insertion is still performed in very much the same way as in the late 1960s except that the level of automation has increased significantly. For example, sequencers have been combined with insertion machines, thus eliminating the separate step of preparing

FIGURE 27.2 Close-up of axial insertion tooling contacting the circuit board just after the leads have been formed (upside-down U shape captured by the outer tooling) and prior to pushing them down through the holes in the board (by the inner tooling).

the sequenced tape. The combined sequencer/inserter also greatly reduces the time required to change over from one product run to another by providing *random access* to the component supply. Changeover now takes the form of a program change instead of having to remove reels of taped components for one product and replace them with different reels required for the new product.

Insertion speed and reliability have also increased dramatically since those early days, as technology has advanced and assemblers have pushed machine suppliers for more capability. Today, insertion speeds of 32,000 components per hour are achievable by one machine with fewer than 50 defects every 1,000,000 insertion attempts. As insertion speeds began to climb into the tens of thousands per hour, it also became possible to build large quantities of scrap quickly if the wrong components were loaded onto the machine by mistake. To combat this possibility, on-line electrical verification of components was added to axial insertion machines to check each part immediately prior to insertion. Through over 30 years of standardization and machine developments like these, axial component insertion has become a well-defined and highly reliable assembly process.

27.2.2 DIP Component Insertion

The second major component type to move to automated assembly was DIP (dual in-line package) integrated circuits (ICs), and the first Pantograph DIP inserter debuted around 1966. DIPs were packaged end to end in plastic tubes, and standards were soon adopted which

FIGURE 27.3 Sequenced tape from an axial insertion machine showing a number of different component values ordered for sequential insertion into a circuit board.

governed the dimensions of the components (such as lead spans of 0.300, 0.400, or 0.600 in) and the associated packaging (such as maximum tube length and cross section). As DIP standards evolved through the 1970s, insertion machines became able to handle multiple lead spans and tens—even hundreds—of different part numbers in one machine.

DIP insertion contributed heavily to the beginning of the computer boom in the early 1980s, but DIP insertion is seldom utilized any longer as a mainstream assembly process. DIP components have been the hardest hit by the trend of conversion from through-hole to surface-mount. The emphasis on converting DIPs to surface mount was precipitated mainly by the large amount of board space the components consumed, especially when one considered the very small size of the die compared to the IC package. Since DIP ICs operated at low voltages where their large size was not required for thermal reasons, DIPs were ideal candidates for conversion to surface-mount. In the automated assembly processes of the 1990s, DIP component insertion, when it is necessary at all, is often treated more as an odd-form component process than a standard high-volume process.

27.2.3 Radial Component Insertion

In the early 1970s, radial lead components began coming out of Japan with their leads taped at a fixed span of 5.0 mm. Given this taping standard, radial lead insertion machines were developed to remove components from their packaging tape and insert the component leads into the board, maintaining the 5.0-mm span. (See Fig. 27.4.) Soon thereafter, additional taping spans were adopted as standards in order to increase the range of components which could be presented on radial tape. Insertion machine developers responded by providing the capability to reliably handle multiple lead spans in one machine.

Similar to axial and DIP inserters, radial insertion machines have undergone many years of development and improvement driven by the needs of electronics assemblers. To meet the demands of high-volume assemblers, components can be inserted by a single machine at rates

FIGURE 27.4 Close-up of radial insertion tooling contacting the circuit board just prior to pushing the leads down through holes in the board (the tooling holding the leads moves out from under the component at the same time).

approaching 10,000 cph. For high-mix environments, components can be loaded onto integrated sequencers or feeder carriages which provide random access to 100 or more unique part numbers. Given the requirements for high-quality products, radial components can be electrically verified immediately prior to insertion, and fewer than 50 defects per million insertions is achievable in real production.

The radial taping format has proven to be an effective means of packaging and delivering a wide variety of component types for automatic assembly. Devices such as tact switches, potentiometers, resistor networks, and fuse holders used to be available only in bulk and had to be inserted manually. These and many other components which were once considered odd-forms can be inserted reliably by radial insertion machines. This trend is expected to continue and cause machine suppliers to further expand the insertion capabilities of their machines.

27.2.4 Odd-Form Component Insertion

There has always been a desire to automate the entire board assembly process, but it has typically been practical only where component and packaging standards were established and proliferated. From a component supplier's point of view, volume component sales provide the motivation to make changes to the component design or to the packaging in which the components are sold. When it comes to transformers, connectors, switches, large capacitors, etc., they usually appear in small quantities relative to other components used on the board and there is often little commonality of parts used from one board to the next. Because of these factors, not to mention the large size and awkward shape of many of these components, there has been little drive toward standardization beyond the use of radial tape already discussed.

Odd-form components are thus appropriately named and have traditionally been inserted or placed by hand after the automatic assembly processes are completed. As robots became more functional and affordable in the 1980s, there was a move toward specialized robotic work cells which could insert or place a wide range of components. While many of these systems worked well and are still in production, it is arguable whether or not they proved to be cost-effective investments. Often components were purchased in bulk form and then manually loaded into tubes, matrix trays, or special tapes provided by third parties so that they could be handled reliably by the robotic work cell. This extra step obviously added cost to the process as well as another opportunity to damage the components. (See Fig. 27.5.)

Although advances in machine design continue to improve the capability and cost effectiveness of some odd-form assembly machines, there still is (and will be for some time) a fair degree of special engineering required in each odd-form assembly application. Early involvement of manufacturing engineers in the board design phase is wise in any case, but it is especially so where odd-form components are used. By involving them early on, manufacturing engineers can work with the equipment supplier applications engineers to provide valuable recommendations for improving the manufacturability of boards.

27.3 SURFACE-MOUNT ASSEMBLY

For most SMT boards, the bottom side contains only passive components while the top side contains both passive and active components. Most often, as the following flowcharts show, top-side components are placed first following the printing of solder paste onto the pads of the board, and then the board is moved through an oven which causes the solder paste to reflow and form the solder joints (see Fig. 26.7). If any through-hole components are used, they are inserted next. The board is then flipped over, an adhesive is applied on the board where the component bodies are to be located, the components are placed, and the board is then moved through an oven which cures the adhesive (sometimes ultraviolet light curing adhesives are used instead). The board is flipped over again and passed through a wave-soldering process which secures the through-hole and bottom-side surface-mount components in place.

Increasingly, assemblers of pure surface-mount boards are moving to a two-sided reflow process which uses solder paste with different reflow temperatures on each side of the board. The higher-temperature solder is used first so those components do not reflow again and fall off when the board is flipped and the second side is assembled and reflowed. This process

FIGURE 27.5   Close-up of an odd-form component placement machine showing the flexible servo-driven gripper tooling used to handle a wide range of component types.

eliminates the need for different top- and bottom-side assembly processes since there is no need for adhesive dispensing and wave soldering normally in a bottom-side line. Regardless of the specific process used, however, all machines in a surface-mount assembly line must work together as a well-integrated process to produce a quality product.

27.4   MACHINE VISION IN THE SURFACE-MOUNT PROCESS

The development and application of machine "vision" systems is one of the most important factors enabling the cost-effective proliferation of surface-mount electronics. Compared to other approaches available, vision provides a high level of accuracy and reliability without sacrificing flexibility and speed. The use of vision has been important in two areas primarily: component centering prior to each placement and board registration once a new board is located inside the placement machine.

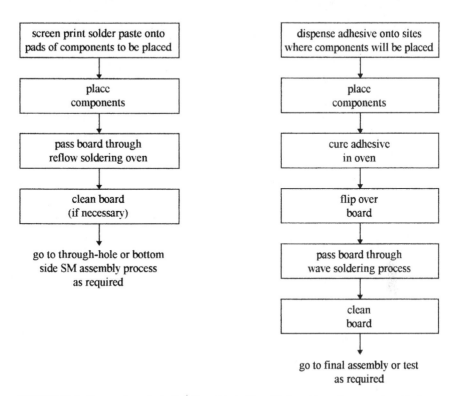

Top Side SM Assembly Process

- screen print solder paste onto pads of components to be placed
- place components
- pass board through reflow soldering oven
- clean board (if necessary)

go to through-hole or bottom side SM assembly process as required

Bottom Side SM Assembly Process

- dispense adhesive onto sites where components will be placed
- place components
- cure adhesive in oven
- flip over board
- pass board through wave soldering process
- clean board

go to final assembly or test as required

FIGURE 27.6   Process flows typically followed in bottom-side/top-side surface-mount applications.

27.4.1   How Machine Vision Works

Most vision systems take a standard black-and-white video image and digitize the signals into a matrix of pixels. Pixels are the individual elements which are assigned a digital value based on whether they are black, white, or a particular shade of gray. Often digital values range from 0 for pure black to 255 for pure white. Figure 27.7 illustrates this idea.

In Fig. 27.7, pixels which lie in the image area covered by the component body are assigned a very low value (e.g., 0) since they are black, pixels covered by the images of each of the component leads are assigned a medium value (e.g., 100) since they are gray, and pixels corresponding to the image background are assigned a high value (e.g., 255) since they are white. In real life, images are composed of many more shades of gray than this simple example illustrates, but the concepts are identical.

Once a particular image is captured and digitized, special computer algorithms can analyze the data and identify the locations of particular features of interest such as edges, corners, or centers of the component body or the individual

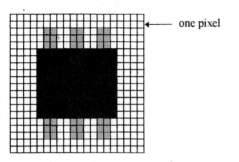

one pixel

FIGURE 27.7   Pixelized image of a surface-mount component ready for vision processing.

component leads (there are many different vision-processing approaches used by equipment suppliers). This information can then be compared with certain expected results to prevent unwanted actions from taking place (such as placing the wrong component on a board) or to make necessary corrections to ensure accurate processing of the circuit board.

Vision systems which analyze images where pixels may possess one of many discrete values are called *gray-scale* systems. To simplify and speed up the computational task of analyzing the image, some other systems *binarize* the image before analysis. Binarization is a process which reduces the many different discrete values representing various shades of gray into just two: 0 for black and 1 for white. In Fig. 27.7, all pixels with values below some threshold—for example, 150—would be assigned a value of 0, and all those with values above would be assigned a value of 1. The result is effectively a silhouette of the component against a white background. Systems such as these are called *binary* systems.

In general, binary vision processing works well for simpler applications where a high degree of precision is not needed. But as requirements for precision increase, such as the placement of fine-pitch surface-mount components (lead-to-lead spacing at or below about 0.025 in), gray-scale vision processing provides additional information which is often needed to ensure a high-yield process.

27.4.2   Vision-Assisted Component Placement

There are basically three methods for accurately placing components on a board.

Placement Method 1

1. Pick up component which has been precisely registered.
2. Transport it to the placement site being careful not to disturb its position on the nozzle.
3. Place it on the board.

Placement Method 2

1. Pick up a component which is only loosely registered.
2. Prior to or while transporting it to the placement site, physically contact the component on all four sides with mechanical jaws which move and center the component on the nozzle.
3. Place it on the board.

Placement Method 3

1. Pick up a component which is only loosely registered.
2. Prior to or while transporting it to the placement site, use a noncontact sensor (such as vision) to measure where the component is in relationship to the center of the nozzle.
3. Make a small positional correction corresponding to the offset between the component and nozzle centers.
4. Place it on the board.

The first method is undesirable since it requires that the component packaging, feeder, or both have additional features or capabilities to register each component repeatably before it is picked. This adds complexity and cost and may also slow down the overall process. The second placement method is undesirable because as components have become more fragile (small ceramic chip components or ICs with very fine leads), they cannot withstand the impact forces of the mechanical centering jaws. Furthermore, this approach does not offer the degree of accuracy required for many component types, and multiple sets of centering jaws are usually required to cover the complete range of components to be placed. The third placement method is superior since it allows component packaging and feeders to remain simple and inexpensive, but it also is a highly accurate approach, is flexible enough to handle a wide range of part types, and does not impart any potentially damaging forces to the components.

27.4.3 Vision-Assisted Board Registration

Screen printers, adhesive dispensers, and placement machines need to accurately align or compensate for the alignment of the PC board once it is brought into the machine. If this process is inaccurately performed, solder paste, adhesive, or components will not end up in the correct locations. There are basically two methods for accomplishing this in a machine.

Board Registration Method 1

1. Transfer the board into the machine (e.g., using a conveyor system).
2. Bring the board to a stop at approximately the right location.
3. Actuate a pair of conical tooling pins which engage corresponding tooling holes in the board and cause it to move (align) to a known position.

Board Registration Method 2

1. Transfer the board into the machine.
2. Bring the board to a stop at approximately the right location.
3. Use a noncontact sensor to locate special features on the board (called *fiducials*) and determine the actual position of the board.
4. Offset all programmed locations based on where the board actually was found.

In general, a board designer would do well to provide both tooling holes and fiducials in any design. This allows the assembler to use whatever equipment is already available to build the board. However, the use of tooling holes may not be practical for two main reasons:

1. *Board space may not be available for tooling holes.*   Tooling holes (usually two) are on the order of 3 to 4 mm in diameter, placed 5 to 10 mm from the edge of the board. No components may be placed in the area between the board edge and the tooling hole as well as within 1 to 2 mm of the tooling hole itself (actual numbers depend on the specific piece of equipment being used).
2. *Tooling pin registration may not provide sufficient accuracy.*   While the tooling pins themselves can register the board with sufficient repeatability (probably to better than 0.025 mm), there can be a large amount of variation between the location of the tooling holes and the pads on the board (ranging up to ±0.125 mm), resulting from the board fabrication process itself. Moreover, the amount of variation is not consistent from one lot of boards to the next. Unless the machine is able to detect the actual location of the artwork on the board, not just the board position, only a modest level of accuracy can be expected.

As a result of these factors, fiducial board registration is the preferred method in most applications.

27.5   *HIGH-SPEED VS. MODULAR COMPONENT PLACEMENT*

Basically, two competing concepts for SM component placement have evolved over the years: high-speed production lines and modular production lines.

27.5.1 High-Speed Production Lines

The high-speed concept was initially developed to manufacture high-volume products cost effectively—specifically, consumer electronics. High-speed lines consist of one or two types of placement machines in series, depending on whether bottom- or top-side board assembly is required. For bottom-side applications, one (sometimes more) high-speed turret-style *chip-shooter* places all SM components on the board (see Fig. 27.8). For top-side assembly, the chipshooter is often followed by a flexible/fine-pitch component placer to handle the larger leaded devices (at slower speeds) if they are used.

This concept relied on the chipshooter for placing the vast majority of the components on the board, so their placement speeds steadily increased along with the range of components they could handle and their purchase price. High-speed lines performed best when a single product or product family was run on the line every day. These lines efficiently placed large numbers of components, but that efficiency dropped off when they were used to assemble multiple dissimilar products within a given day. As high-speed lines were used more and more by assemblers who required flexibility, such as subcontract manufacturers, machine developers began to include many features and capabilities which greatly improved their efficiency in such high-mix environments. Most assemblers, in fact, find that high-speed production lines provide the best mix of speed and flexibility required for their production.

27.5.2 Modular Production Lines

The inherent inflexibility and high price of the early chipshooters were viewed as substantial constraints for the low- to medium-volume, high-mix assembler. Instead of high-speed lines, a

FIGURE 27.8 Close-up of a chipshooter turret showing six different nozzles (small numbers 1 through 6) on each of the placement heads (numbers 19 through 25 visible here).

preference developed for lines built up by a combination of smaller, modular, more flexible, and less expensive machines. An assembler could begin with one or two machines in the line and then add machines incrementally as capacity requirements increased. This concept offered scaleability and more flexibility than the high-speed line concept, but it presented assemblers with some different challenges: line balancing and system uptime.

Figure 27.9 compares a high-speed chipshooter at 14,400 components per hour (cph) and a modular line built up of placement machines of 4800 cph, each building a board with 300 components where the overall line uptime needs to be 90 percent.

To achieve the best possible production throughput with a modular system, each machine must share the placement load equally. Due to the number and types of component feeders required for a given product and various other issues, however, it is not always straightforward to equally balance the workload. Furthermore, with multiple machines in series required to place all the components, each machine must operate with a higher uptime than the single chipshooter so that the line as a whole yields the desired uptime. This is illustrated in Fig. 27.9 where three machines working together in the modular line each need to operate at 96.5 percent uptime in order for the entire line to reach 90 percent.

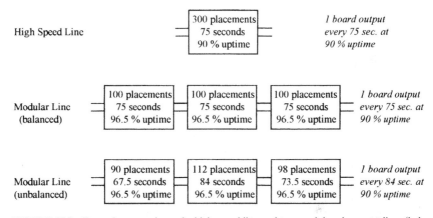

FIGURE 27.9   Example comparison of a high-speed line and two modular placement lines (balanced and unbalanced work loads) building the same board.

27.6 SURFACE-MOUNT ASSEMBLY EQUIPMENT

27.6.1 High-Speed Turret-Style Chipshooter

The chipshooter concept was developed in the early 1980s and can best be thought of as a pipeline architecture. Instead of picking the first part from a component feeder, centering the part on the nozzle, placing the part on the board, and then processing the second component in the same sequential way, the chipshooter breaks apart the process and performs the necessary elements in parallel with each other. This greatly increases machine throughput. The fastest chipshooters today can place parts onto a board at maximum rates of up to 40,000 cph. Figure 27.10 helps explain how a chipshooter works.

As a board enters the chipshooter, the turret starts to rotate. The turret has a number of heads on it (12 in this example) which each contain nozzles of different sizes so that a wide range of components can be handled. At head position 1, the first component needed at the board is picked from the corresponding feeder, which is brought into the proper position directly under head position 1. Once the component has been picked, the turret indexes for-

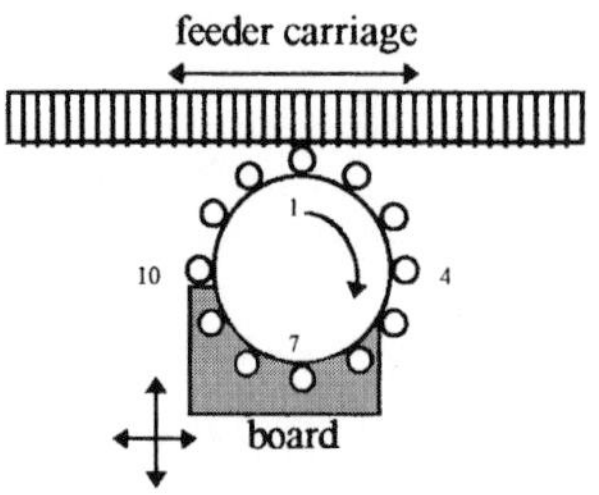

Head Position	Operation Performed
1	Pick component from feeder
2	Check if part is present
3	Rotate to nominal orientation
4	Perform vision inspection
5	No operation
6	Adjust theta based on vision
7	Place part on board
8	No operation
9	Dispose of part if bad
10	No operation
11	Select nozzle for next pick
12	No operation

FIGURE 27.10 Simplified illustration of how a turret-style chipshooter works.

ward so that a check can be performed to see if the component was picked successfully. This check is performed at head position 2 in parallel with the second component being picked by the next head now at position 1. This process continues until the first part picked makes it around to head position 7, where it is placed onto the board, which is positioned properly directly under that head position. At this point, the pipeline is full and a new part is placed each time the turret indexes.

The feeder carriage of a chipshooter is usually quite large and able to accept upwards of 160 individual tape feeders. The carriage moves from side to side under program control so as to bring the needed feeder directly under head position 1. Feeder carriages are usually split into two, sometimes four, separate sections. Each section can be set up for different products to be run, or they can be set up the same so that when a feeder runs out of parts, another section can quickly move into place so production can continue with minimal interruption.

Because the chipshooter can place a very high volume of components in a short period of time and because the feeder carriage continually moves back and forth, tape-fed components are the only types a chipshooter can accept. Reels of tape-fed parts hold up to 10,000 components and the packaging/feeder combination is robust enough to withstand the constant motion while reliably providing components. Any components fed in tubes, matrix trays, or other special forms of packaging need to be handled by the flexible/fine-pitch placer.

27.6.2 Flexible/Fine-Pitch Placer

Since the design of a chipshooter was optimized for placing small, tape-fed components quickly, there were usually a handful of complex components on the board which a chipshooter either could not handle or handled far too slowly. This fact precipitated the development of another machine type which was more flexible and could achieve much higher levels of accuracy but at slower speed.

The flexible/fine-pitch placer can generally cover the complete range of component and packaging types but at maximum speeds which are less than 20 percent of the maximum speed of a chipshooter. Most of the latest flexible machines are based on an overhead gantry positioning system (to allow for large x and y moves) on which is mounted the placement head (providing for z and rotational moves), often with multiple spindles. (See Fig. 27.11.) Components are picked from stationary feeders or feeder systems and then delivered to the board for placement. Component registration prior to placement can generally be accomplished in three ways:

FIGURE 27.11 Flexible placement machine showing tape- and tray-fed components, a four-spindle placement head, an upward-looking vision camera (shown in the center of the feeder bank), and a reject component station (to the right of the vision camera).

- Using mechanical centering jaws carried on the head
- Using a noncontact laser sensor carried on the head
- Using vision either carried on the head or using a stationary camera over which the head moves

The type of component registration employed is one of the most important characteristics of a flexible/fine-pitch placement machine as shown in Table 27.1.

Flexible/fine-pitch placers are used in the three ways listed as follows, and how the machine is to be used will largely influence what method of component registration is best.

- As a stand-alone machine to cover all component types needing to be placed
- As part of a high-speed line following a chipshooter
- As part of a modular placement line together with one or more similar placement machines

TABLE 27.1   Component Centering Methods—Strengths and Weaknesses

Method	Strengths	Weaknesses
Mechanical centering jaws	1. Speed—no time penalty since performed during travel to the board. 2. Price—the least expensive of all types of registration methods.	1. Impact forces on components, since jaws contact the component body and/or leads. 2. Time penalty due to tool changing, since different parts often require different centering jaws.
Laser centering	1. Speed—no time penalty since performed during travel to the board. 2. No impact forces on components, since noncontact.	1. Component range—cannot cover medium-large to large-size components. 2. Cannot detect bent leads—since the component profile (side view) is used, individual leads are not able to be seen.
Vision centering on the head	1. Speed—little time penalty since performed during travel to the board. 2. No impact forces on components, since noncontact. 3. Can detect bent leads—since the top or bottom view is used, individual leads can be seen.	1. Component range—may not be able to cover medium- to large-size components depending on implementation. 2. Complexity—often requires complex optics or mechanisms. 3. Price—vision is the most expensive of all types of registration.
Vision centering off the head	1. No impact forces on components, since noncontact. 2. Can detect bent leads—since the top or bottom view is used, individual leads can be seen. 3. Flexibility—can use multiple cameras or other techniques to cover the entire range of components. 4. Accuracy—most rigid/stable of all types of registration methods.	1. Speed—may impose a significant time penalty depending on part type and implementation. 2. Price—vision is the most expensive of all types of registration.

For example, in a modular line, most of the machines can perform well with only mechanical or laser centering on the head, since the larger components or those requiring more accuracy can be placed by some other machine in the line (one with vision). Following a chipshooter, full off-head vision capability is advisable since the machine will primarily need to handle large components or those requiring a high degree of accuracy. As a stand-alone, off-head vision is best from a flexibility point of view, but the particular component range to be handled may not require it.

The range of options available for flexible/fine-pitch placers is extensive, given the range of parts the machine is expected to handle. The following list is representative of the most common options, but it is not exhaustive:

1. *Random access matrix tray feeder*—accepts multiple trays, each of which can contain a different part number, and presents the placement machine with a component of the proper part number on demand.

2. *High-volume matrix tray feeder*—similar to above except only one part number is allowed in the multiple trays for higher-volume/lower-mix applications.

3. *Bank feeder changing carts*—allows a large group of feeders on the machine to be changed quickly.

4. *Coplanarity sensor*—measures the degree to which all leads on an IC will contact the same plane (i.e., so no leads will be lifted off their respective pads on the board).

5. *Adhesive dispensing head*—especially useful for low-volume applications where a separate adhesive dispenser purchase is not justifiable.

6. *Component verification system*—checks bar codes or electrically measures components to ensure that the proper components are loaded into the proper feeders in the proper location on the machine.

With these and other features and options available, the flexible/fine-pitch placer can be configured in many ways to handle a wide range of applications.

27.6.3 Adhesive Dispenser

Dispensing dots of adhesive, placing components, and then curing the adhesive is necessary in bottom-side applications where the board must be flipped over and passed through a wave-soldering system. For larger components, applying adhesive is a rather straightforward process with substantial margin for variation in dot placement accuracy and dot volume consistency. However, as surface-mount components have shrunk in size, especially for 0805 and smaller ceramic chip resistors and capacitors (0.08 in by 0.05 in), adhesive dispensing has become a more critical process step requiring more sophisticated dispensing machines. There are a number of different dispensing pump designs available in the market, and two are discussed here.

The simplest type of dispenser, often called an *air-over* system, applies air under pressure to a syringe of adhesive for a defined period of time. Under pressure, the adhesive in the syringe flows on to the board through a small nozzle. By controlling the duration that the high-pressure air is applied, dot volume can be varied. (See Fig. 27.12.)

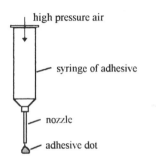

FIGURE 27.12 Simplified air-over adhesive dispensing head. High-pressure air is applied to the syringe of adhesive for a short duration to force adhesive onto the board through the nozzle.

This type of system is simple and quite inexpensive, and is fine for applications where precise dots are not needed. Problems can develop, however, as the application becomes more demanding. The biggest issue centers around changing viscosity of the adhesive. As ambient temperature changes, so does the viscosity of the adhesive, which alters the dot volume dispensed over a given time duration. Machines which utilize an air-over pump system usually also offer an environmental control option for the machine which helps maintain the ambient temperature and therefore produce more consistent dots.

Another type of pump technology is available which provides consistent dot volume independent of adhesive viscosity and is termed *positive displacement*. A positive displacement pump uses a piston moving through a chamber filled with adhesive to push controlled volumes of that adhesive out through a nozzle. Low-pressure air is applied continuously to keep the pump chamber full, but pressure and time are not critical control variables in the dispensing process. By controlling the stroke length of the piston, dot volume can be varied. (See Fig. 27.13.)

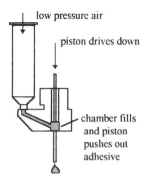

FIGURE 27.13 Simplified positive displacement adhesive dispensing head. Low-pressure air continually fills the chamber, and a piston is driven down through the chamber to push adhesive onto the board through the nozzle.

Positive displacement dispensing systems are a little more complex than air-over systems, but they do not need environmental control units because temperature does not affect dot volume—only the piston diameter and the stroke length determine how much adhesive is pushed out of the nozzle. When placing the smallest-chip components (such as 0603s and 0402s), precise dot control is very important. If the dot is slightly too large, adhesive may be pushed onto the board pads when the component is placed and, thereby, cause soldering defects. If the dot is slightly too small, insufficient adhesive may be present to hold the component securely on the board as it passes through the wave-soldering system.

27.6.4 Screen Printer

A screen printer is used to apply appropriate quantities of solder paste to each of the board pads where components are to be placed. The tacky solder paste holds components in position until the board passes through the reflow oven where the paste melts to form solder joints. Some early screen printers were actually modified silk screen printing machines used for applying ink to paper or cloth. In a screen printer, solder paste is pushed by a squeegee down through apertures in a screen which correspond to the component pads on a board which is located below the screen. In the early days of surface-mount, the aperture sizes were relatively large, and the screen helped support the squeegee as it passed over the openings. However, as surface-mount components became much smaller, so did the aperture sizes, and screens were largely replaced by stencils.

The application of solder paste on a surface-mount board is the most critical step in the assembly process and offers the greatest opportunities to generate defects. As evidence of this, the most widely used screen printers have become extremely sophisticated and can cost nearly as much as a placement machine in some cases. Due to the number and complexity of the issues surrounding screen printing of solder paste, they will not be dealt with here.

27.7 KEY MACHINE SELECTION CRITERIA

Beyond the range of features and options which must be evaluated when specifying or purchasing a piece of automated assembly equipment, there are a number of factors which must also be evaluated in order to determine how well the equipment will actually perform for a given product to be built. In fact, one could easily spend 80 percent of the evaluation time looking into these issues, and it would not be time wasted.

27.7.1 Throughput vs. Maximum Specified Speed

Machine suppliers specify a maximum insertion or placement rate, usually given as insertions per hour or placements per hour. The time required for a single placement is often referred to as *tact time*. These specifications correspond to the rate that can be achieved under highly optimized conditions which often are not achievable when building real boards. In practice, many overhead functions and other inefficiencies must be accounted for to determine what throughput a particular machine or system will yield. As a result, suppliers' speed specifications can be of little meaning when comparing different machine offerings.

27.7.1.1 Throughput Overhead Functions. Overhead functions can be defined as any actions or activities which must be performed and which consume time in a process but do not add value to the board being built. For example, time required to transfer a board into a screen printer or insertion machine is not a value-added action, but it is necessary to move the board into a position where value can be added (that is, apply solder paste or insert components). Time required to change tools or nozzles is also considered overhead and so is the time required to automatically retrieve another component if the first component is not picked successfully from the feeder.

27.7.1.2 Effective Throughput Example.   As a more specific example, assume placement machine A is specified at 5000 cph maximum speed, and machine B is specified at 4500 cph. To build a board with 30 components, machine A appears on the surface to be the best (fastest) choice. However, assume that board transfer time in machine A is 6 s, and board transfer takes 4 s in machine B. Furthermore, assume that machine A must perform a nozzle change to handle all types of components on the board, whereas machine B can place them all without requiring any nozzles be changed. The comparison of the two machines now looks much different (see Table 27.2).

TABLE 27.2   Effective Throughput Example

	A	B
Time to place 30 components	21.6 s	24.0 s
Board transfer time	6.0	4.0
Nozzle change time	3.0	0.0
Total time required	30.6 s	28.0 s
Effective production throughput	3529 cph	3857 cph

This may appear to be a trivial example, but it illustrates the impact that overhead times can have on the effective rate at which a particular board can be produced. From the perspective of a board designer, board panelization is about the only available method by which to minimize the effect of overhead times. If board transfer time is 4.0 s, for example, by grouping four boards together into one panel, the effective board transfer time can be reduced to 1.0 s by amortizing that time over four boards instead of one. But beyond overhead times, there are a number of other factors that can greatly reduce the effective throughput of a placement machine which are closely linked to the board design and are discussed in Sec. 27.8.

27.7.2 Accuracy and Repeatability

Lacking any industry-recognized standard definitions, trying to determine the accuracy or repeatability of a piece of assembly equipment and how these factors relate to the needs of the application can be difficult. Terms and specifications are often tossed about freely but have little significance to the real needs of the assembler. The best approach for anyone evaluating assembly equipment is to adopt a set of definitions and require all equipment suppliers to provide statistically valid data which can be used to fit those definitions. Furthermore, by comparing equipment based on process capability instead of accuracy and repeatability, a more equitable and meaningful comparison can be conducted.

27.7.2.1 Process Capability Index—C_{pk}.   Board design geometries and desired quality levels determine the capability (accuracy and repeatability) requirements for the assembly equipment in a given application. For example, consider Fig. 27.14, where a surface-mount component lead is to be placed on a particular board pad. Based on the geometries presented in the figure, the specification limits for the placement process (in the x dimension only) are $\pm\{(w_p - w_1)/2 + c\}$ around the ideal of a perfectly centered lead on the pad. That is, whenever the placement of the lead on the pad exceeds the specification limit in either the $+x$ (upper specification limit, or USL) or $-x$ (lower specification limit, or LSL) direction, the board would be rejected.

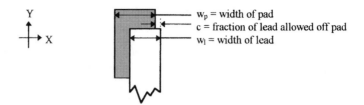

FIGURE 27.14   Surface-mount lead and pad geometry used in calculating the placement process capability (accuracy and repeatability) required in a given application.

Once the worst-case specification limits are determined for a particular board, statistical data provided by equipment suppliers can be put into the following form:

$$C_{pk} = \text{minimum of } \{(USL - \mu)/3\sigma, (\mu - LSL)/3\sigma\}$$

where μ and σ are the mean and standard deviation, respectively, that the equipment achieves over a large number of program-driven (not taught) trials. When asking a supplier for this data, it is wise to also ask for a detailed description of the test method by which the data was collected to ensure that the data may be legitimately compared to that provided by other suppliers.

The resulting value of the C_{pk}, or *process capability* index, describes the minimum number of standard deviations which fall between the mean of the distribution and the closest specification limit (upper or lower). For example, if the C_{pk} value equals 0.33, then only one standard deviation is between the mean and the closest specification limit. For every additional increment of 0.33, one more standard deviation falls between the mean and the closest specification limit. Therefore, a *six-sigma process* is one which has a C_{pk} equal to or greater than 2.0.

27.7.3   Uptime and Level of Automation

Uptime is roughly defined as the percentage of available time that a piece of equipment is actually producing product. Within the operation of the manufacturing facility itself, issues such as lack of production materials (boards and components) and operator breaks detract from uptime. However, there are also many aspects of the machine design which can greatly affect uptime and influence how valuable that piece of equipment proves to be. Machines which provide a high level of automation—that is, they automatically perform certain functions which must be performed manually on other pieces of equipment—may initially cost more to purchase but may actually pay back faster by generating more production output over a given time period.

27.7.3.1   Programming New Products   Obviously more important in a high-product-mix environment, the time required to program a machine to process a new product can be substantial, especially in the cases of surface-mount placement machines. Three main aspects of placement machine programming need to be evaluated: feeder locations, component centering data, and placement locations.

Feeder Locations.   Feeder locations can either be *taught* or *data-driven*. Taught feeder locations are programmed by the operator manually aligning the placement system to each feeder to be used, storing the individual locations along the way. Often, if the machine has a vision camera mounted alongside the placement head, the operator aligns a set of crosshairs on the vision monitor with each feeder pick point. Each time a new product is programmed, the feeders used have to be taught to the system. It is important that feeders locate in the feeder banks of the machine with a high degree of repeatability, otherwise reteaching will be required each time feeders are removed for reloading or between production runs. Data-driven feeder locations do not need to be taught but are instead established by identifying to the placement system which feeders are in which locations. This approach is much faster but requires a more sophisticated and mechanically precise system.

Component Centering Data.   Component centering data is usually stored in some type of library or database within the machine controller which contains all the necessary information for each component required by the machine. For each component, these dimensions are either hand entered by the user, taught to the machine using the vision system, or provided as defaults by the machine supplier and then edited by the user only as required. Editing the component library should be clear and easy and should be possible at the machine. If editing must be performed on an off-line computer system and then the updated program downloaded to the placement system, substantial time can be wasted. This is especially the case during the early production of a new product or when component lot or vendor changes occur.

Placement Locations.   Similar to feeder locations, placement locations which require teaching will take significantly more time to program than those which can accept board design (CAD) data and directly produce a program. The optimal case is when a CAD data file for the new board is loaded into the placement machine and a placement program is produced automatically, including all necessary linkages to the component library and optimal feeder locations. Again, regardless of how a program is produced, if the placement system is not highly accurate and stable, placement locations may need to be retaught or adjusted frequently, which can severely reduce uptime.

27.7.3.2 *Ease of Operation*   Since the first NC axial inserters back in the mid 1960s, there has been steady progress in using computers to control the actions of assembly machines in order to attain higher speeds and greater functionality. As machines became more complex in their actions, so did the programming required to make them run and the troubleshooting required to eliminate problems or malfunctions when they occurred. Utilizing the power available through the most advanced PCs, some equipment suppliers provide highly sophisticated machine interfaces which are also highly intuitive and easy to use.

The use of graphics has become extremely important as a way to reduce the complexity a machine operator must face. Graphical images replace the long lists of special commands required to operate a particular machine. This approach shortens the time required to learn the machine and reduces the potential for errors. In some cases, graphics can be used to help operators more quickly detect problems. For example, operators can more readily spot a misprogrammed component (wrong component type, location, or orientation) from a graphic of the board than from a list of component placement data. Graphics can also be a very powerful tool for maintenance personnel. On-line maintenance manuals and mechanical and electrical drawings are immediately available, complete, and current when needed.

27.7.3.3 *Product Changeover*   The time required to stop one production run and then start another run of a different board type is important for many assemblers. For every minute spent changing over between production runs, the machine or line stands idle and does not create value. Many different factors can affect the amount of time required to perform a changeover depending on the type of machine being discussed. However, the following general categories should be considered:

- Time to deactivate the previous program, load, and then activate the new program

- Time to change board holders or conveyors to accept the new board size

- Time to remove or clean up consumables from previous run (solder paste, components, etc.),

- Time to load consumables needed for new run

- Time to perform any other necessary setups or adjustments prior to new run

Many machine suppliers offer features and options which help to reduce the time needed for product changeover. Furthermore, setup verification options may also be available which can prove to be invaluable in environments where changeover is frequent. As an example, some surface-mount placement machines can be equipped with a feeder setup verification feature which ensures that the operator loads the proper feeders in the proper locations. Automatically verifying feeder setups can improve uptime and also eliminate the risk of building products incorrectly.

27.7.3.4 Machine Calibration Machine calibration is a critical and often overlooked machine procedure. Periodically throughout its lifespan, a machine will need to be recalibrated in order to correct for slight electromechanical changes that may occur through use (such as wear, electronics burn-in, or minor shifting or movement of certain subsystems) or if the machine is picked up and moved. If not recalibrated, accuracy could degrade to the point where desired process quality levels cannot be achieved. When evaluating a machine, calibration procedures should be considered from at least three points of view: level of automation, repeatability, and resulting accuracy.

Simple calibration routines for machines which are not designed for high levels of accuracy may be semiautomatic or even manual. The operator or maintenance technician may need to perform a number of key steps or even take certain measurements manually as part of a calibration procedure, but wherever human interaction is required, the opportunity for error is present. Calibration routines which are fully automatic can control every step of the process to a much greater degree of precision. However, this is not a complete guarantee either. The key requirement for a calibration routine is that it consistently produces the correct result every time it is run. If calibration is repeated multiple times in succession, the variation in machine performance between calibration runs should be negligible. For example, if evaluating a surface-mount placement machine (which is the most complex piece of equipment to calibrate), components placed after one calibration run should be in precisely the same relative location following another calibration run. If significant variation is detected, or if components are not placed precisely on their respective pads, then the calibration routine is not robust and may cause accuracy problems, which can lead to significant downtime while these problems are corrected.

27.7.3.5 Flexibility and New Technology Growth Capability While through-hole is a mature technology with few developments in the areas of components and packaging (except those discussed in Sec. 27.2.3, "Radial Component Insertion"), surface-mount technology is growing and changing rapidly to the point that it is difficult to predict what new assembly challenges will emerge in the next couple years. As such, there is a risk that certain assembly equipment specified or purchased for current needs may soon become obsolete. However, machine architectures based on modular subsystems and controlled interfaces offer considerable insurance against obsolescence by providing a growth path for future capabilities.

If a subsystem is designed as a stand-alone module (e.g., placement head, component feeder, vision camera) and its interface to the base machine is held constant, it becomes feasible to replace that subsystem with another which conforms to the same interface specification. In the best of cases, these upgrades can be performed at the customer site if and when it is determined that a new capability is needed. This approach relieves assemblers from having to predict future technology requirements at the time machines are specified or purchased or from suddenly discovering a recently purchased machine has become obsolete.

27.8 BOARD DESIGN FOR AUTOMATIC ASSEMBLY

From the point of view of automatic board assembly, optimal board design is very much linked to the architecture of the particular assembly machines which are to be used. Therefore, it is wise for a board designer to work closely with the manufacturing engineer to ensure that the appropriate equipment factors are considered. The following paragraphs identify some of these factors and their potential impacts on board design, although each factor discussed may not apply equally to all assembly machines either available or in use.

27.8.1 Axial and Radial Throughput Factors

In general, the distance between successive component insertions should be minimized. However, it is necessary to consider how large of a tooling footprint, clinch footprint, and above-board clearance zone exists, if any, before determining the minimum spacing allowed between adjacent components. Figure 27.15 shows the area around each component lead where the lead form and guide tooling is located at the time of insertion. For small components, this tooling footprint may be the limiting factor for component spacing in the x-y plane. Similarly below the board, the clinch tooling has a certain footprint which must also be considered. In the z dimension, the lead guide and clinch tooling usually require even greater clearance which can further constrain the minimum spacing next to tall components.

top view of board

FIGURE 27.15 Overhead view of a through-hole axial component showing the footprint of the insertion tooling on the board (dashed lines). This area needs to be clear of other components when the axial component is inserted.

Beyond minimizing the distance between successive component insertions, it is also advantageous to minimize the number of different component orientations and reduce the range of lead spans used (axial components only) on the board. Some insertion machines require additional time to rotate the board under the insertion head or to rotate the insertion head itself. If all components are able to be oriented at 0°, for example, no board or head rotations are necessary and throughput is increased. Furthermore, additional time may be required to move the VCD tooling on an axial machine from a very narrow span to a large span. By minimizing the number of times lead span must be changed or the amount of travel required, machine throughput should be improved.

27.8.2 Chipshooter Throughput Factors

For a chipshooter, the speed at which the turret rotates is influenced by basically three factors:

- Component type
- Where the next feeder is located in relation to the current feeder being used
- Where the next placement location is on the board in relation to the current placement location

If the component is large, or if the feeder carriage must move more than one or two feeder positions to access the next feeder, or if the board must be moved greater than some nominal distance (e.g., 10 mm) to reach the next placement location, the turret must slow down in order for all the necessary actions to occur in time. When all these real-world conditions are accounted for along with the required overhead functions, the practical throughput that a chipshooter will yield can derate by 10 to 50 percent from the specified maximum speed.

From the point of view of maximizing the throughput which can be achieved using a chipshooter, there are three aspects of a good board design.

1. *The number of unique part numbers required is minimized.*   Fewer part numbers translates into fewer component feeders which decreases the time required to set up a machine for a new production run and decreases the number of times the feeder carriage must move a new feeder into position. Minimizing the number of part numbers can have an even greater impact across a group of products to be manufactured. When common part numbers are used across multiple products, a chipshooter setup can be optimized such that little or no feeder changeover is required between production runs.

2. *Components used are available from component suppliers packaged in tape format.* Since the feeder carriage of a chipshooter moves, tube and matrix tray-fed parts cannot be placed by these machines. When a board designer selects a component which is not available in tape format, the component must be placed by a flexible/fine-pitch placer which constrains how the production line must be balanced and may in turn reduce the effective throughput of the line. Furthermore, if there is a choice, components packaged in narrower tape formats are preferable to those packaged in wider tape formats. In general, as the width of the tape increases, so do the component size and mass, and the turret must rotate at a slower speed to reliably handle these components. Effective throughput of a chipshooter is reduced appreciably when larger components must be placed.

3. *The distance on the board between components of the same part number is minimized.* When programming a chipshooter for maximum throughput, a serpentine path is defined such that the distance between successive placements is minimized and the number of times the feeder carriage must move is minimized. If a board is designed with large distances between components of the same part number, either large board moves or frequent back-and-forth moves of the feeder carriage are necessary, and these actions significantly reduce chipshooter throughput by requiring the turret to slow down its rotation.

27.8.3 Flexible/Fine-Pitch Throughput Factors

Flexible/fine-pitch machines tend to be less sensitive to the actual board design than chipshooters, although every different placement machine has certain special conditions under which it will perform best. But since these machines tend to place far fewer components on the board than do chipshooters, overhead functions can have a disproportionate impact on their effective production throughput. For example, a 4.0-s board transfer time has a greater impact on a machine running at 4000 cph placing only 15 components (18 percent reduction) than does a 6.0-s transfer time on a machine running at 22,000 cph placing 300 components (11 percent reduction). Moreover, nozzle changing and vision inspection of certain components on a flexible/fine-pitch machine can add many seconds of additional time, whereas the impact on a chipshooter may only be fractions of a second.

There is little that can be done in terms of board design to affect the throughput of the flexible/fine-pitch machines in general. Throughput versus speed is still a major issue, but it needs to be evaluated more in terms of the specific machine design issues than the board design. If a board is designed with the chipshooter guidelines in mind (refer to Sec. 27.8.2), throughput of the flexible/fine-pitch machine will tend to be improved, too. However, depending on the particular way a flexible/fine-pitch machine processes components and boards, including all overhead functions, large variations in throughput from one machine to the next can exist.

27.8.4 Board Panelization

Board panelization, or joining multiple boards of one type together so that they are processed as one panel, is a method which can be used to reduce the impact of board transfer time on effective throughput. As discussed in Secs. 27.7.1.2 and 27.8.3, board transfer time can greatly impact effective throughput, especially when the number of components to be inserted or placed is small. In such cases, by joining multiple boards together into a single panel (e.g., four boards) and processing them as one board, the impact of board transfer time is greatly reduced (i.e., reduced to $\frac{1}{4}$).

SOLDER AND SOLDERING

CHAPTER 28*
DESIGN FOR SOLDERING AND SOLDERABILITY

28.1 INTRODUCTION

This chapter deals with the specification of the materials system for the printed circuit and the design parameters which must be considered before a final circuit is laid out. The soldering operation must be considered from the inception of the board layout in order to ensure satisfactory performance. The rules are simple and straightforward; if they are followed, the operation should run smoothly and efficiently. If they are disregarded, however, the result is invariably recurring problems with bridges, icicles, and imperfectly formed fillets that will need handling by a large number of touch-up operators.

28.2 DESIGN CONSIDERATIONS

During the layout of the board, several soldering parameters should be carefully considered. They are (1) the wire-to-hole ratio, (2) the size and shape of the terminal areas, (3) the number and direction of extended parallel circuit runs, (4) the population density of the solder joints.

28.2.1 Wire-to-Hole Ratio

The wire-to-hole ratio represents a compromise between the ideal situation for assembly (large hole and small-diameter lead) and the ideal situation for soldering (smaller lead-to-wire ratio). The minimum hole size can be established by the rule of thumb that it should be no less than the lead diameter plus 0.004 in. The maximum hole diameter should be no more than 2.5 times the lead diameter. Of course, if the board is a plated-through-hole or a multilayer circuit board, the hole-to-wire ratio should be lower than 2.5 to encourage the capillary action of the flux and solder during the soldering operations.

28.2.2 Size and Shape of the Land Area

The pad area around the solder joint is normally either circular to slightly elongated (teardrop). It should not be more than 3 times the diameter of the hole in the board. There is

* Adapted from Coombs, *Printed Circuits Handbook, 3d ed., McGraw-Hill, New York, 1988, Chap. 23,* by Hugh Cole.

sometimes a tendency, particularly on low-density boards, to leave large irregular land areas around the holes. That should be avoided! Excessively large land areas expose too much copper to the solder pot, cause excessive quantities of solder to be used in joint formation, and promote bridging and webbing.

If the leads are to be clinched during assembly, the land should be so oriented that the clinched lead will be in the center of the elongated pad. Both the pad and the component should be so oriented that the clinched lead is parallel to the direction of solder flow in the solder wave and not perpendicular to it.

28.2.3 Number and Direction of Extended Parallel Lines

The use of automated printed board layout programs and the trend toward high-density circuit packaging have resulted in a tendency to group large numbers of circuit paths together and run them parallel to one another for long distances. If those paths are oriented perpendicularly to the direction of flow in the solder wave (i.e., at right angles to the direction of the conveyor), then they can contribute to bridging and webbing. Every effort should be made to maximize the spacing between lines which must be oriented perpendicular to the direction of the conveyor.

28.2.4 Population Distribution

An excessive number of joints in one area promotes bridging, icicling, and webbing. It may also cause a heat-sinking effect and interfere with the formation of a good solder joint.

28.3 MATERIAL SYSTEMS

In the soldering process there are two surfaces which must be considered before a solder flux is selected. They are the lead surface and the pad surface. The average printed circuit assembler has little control over the material systems used in component leads, since the selection is usually made by the component manufacturer. Furthermore, most components are mass-produced and supplied on large reels. It is not economically justifiable to treat each lead according to an individual assembly shop's specific requirement. Therefore, in selecting the components, care should be taken that the leads are solderable, and an incoming inspection should be established to ensure lead solderability.

The board itself, however, is a different story. Since each board is custom-manufactured, the assembly or soldering engineer can exercise a great deal of control over the material systems used on the board. Again, it is important, in order to keep defects to a minimum, that the board be made of a solderable material and that the solderability of the board be checked as a part of incoming material inspection. The next section will deal with some typical material systems encountered during the soldering process.

28.3.1 Common Metallic Surfaces

28.3.1.1 Bare Copper.   Because of its low cost and ease of processing, one of the most common metallic surfaces encountered is bare copper. Chemically clean copper is the easiest material to solder; it can be soldered with even the mildest fluxes. But unless it is protected with a rosin-based protective coating, its solderability will rapidly degenerate because of oxides and tarnishes. As we shall see later in this chapter, however, the solderability of tarnished copper surfaces is easily restored with surface conditioners. If boards with bare copper surfaces are used, care should be taken to maintain solderability during handling and storage (storage time should be minimal), and the boards should not be stored in the presence of sulfur-containing material such as paper, cardboard, or newsprint. Sulfur produces a tenaciously adhering tarnish on copper which seriously impairs the solderability.

28.3.1.2   Gold.   Gold is encountered most commonly on component leads and plug-in finger surfaces. It is a highly solderable material, but it is extremely expensive and it rapidly dissolves in the molten solder. Because it affects the properties of the solder joint, causing the joint to become dull and grainy, it is usually avoided or eliminated by pretinning the lead before soldering. Various studies have shown that all gold on a gold-plated lead can be dissolved in a solder pot of eutectic tin-lead solder within 2 s (plate thickness of about 50 μin). Therefore, pretinning is economical as well as easy.

28.3.1.3   Kovar.   Many dual in-line packages (DIPs) and related integrated circuitry are supplied with Kovar leads. Kovar is a very difficult metal to solder because it doesn't wet well. For that reason component manufacturers and/or assembly shops prefer to pretin Kovar. The pretinning is normally accomplished only with organic acid fluxes and certain proprietary acid cleaners.

28.3.1.4   Silver.   Although silver was once very popular in the electronics industry, it is not used on terminal areas or component leads. The reason is the problem of silver migration, a phenomenon discovered in the late 1950s and extensively researched during the early 1960s. Silver should be avoided. If it must be used, it is an easily soldered material and should be treated similarly to the bare copper surface (i.e., avoid sulfur-bearing materials and minimize storage and handling).

28.3.1.5   Immersion Tin.   Immersion tin coatings are electrolessly deposited coatings of tin metal on bare copper surfaces. When tin is initially deposited, the coating is extremely solderable. It does, however, deteriorate rapidly, and it becomes more difficult to solder than bare copper. Originally, immersion tin coatings were used to protect the solderability of bare copper surfaces and thereby extend the shelf life of the board. Experience has shown, however, that fused tin-lead plate is far superior for the purpose.

28.3.1.6   Tin-Lead.   Tin-lead coatings are put on printed boards and component leads to preserve the solderability of the material. They can be applied by electroplating, hot dipping, or roller coating. The mechanics of the processes are discussed elsewhere in this chapter. A properly prepared tin-lead surface should exhibit excellent solderability and long shelf life (about nine months to one year). Tin-lead coatings can be soldered with most rosin-based fluxes, even the nonactivated types. However, optimum results are obtained with the activated rosin fluxes.

28.4   WETTING AND SOLDERABILITY

Soldering is defined as a metallurgical joining technique involving a molten filler metal which wets the surface of both metals to be joined and, upon solidification, forms the bond. From the definition it is apparent that the materials to be soldered do not become molten and therefore the bonding occurs at the interface of the two metals and is strongly dependent on the wettability or solderability of the base metal by the molten alloy. Although the base metal does not become molten, some alloying can take place if the base metal is soluble in the filler metal. The bond which is formed is strictly metallic in nature, and no chemical reaction which covalently or ionically bonds the metal to the surface occurs.

To understand the basic mechanism of soldering, it is necessary to understand the thermo-dynamics of wetting. Fortunately, however, in order to understand wetting it is not necessary to understand thermodynamics. Wettability or solderability of two materials is a measure of how well one material "likes" the other. The property can be easily visualized by using a water drop resting on the surface, such as the one shown in Fig. 28.1. When the water drop doesn't like the surface on which it rests, it pulls up into a ball and touches the surface, in the idealized case, at only one point. The angle between the drop and the surface at the point of contact is called the dihedral angle. If the drop likes the surface, it spreads out all over the surface and comes in intimate contact with it. Various degrees of wettability are therefore related to the ability of the drop to spread out or wet the surface. Figure 28.2 shows the relation between the dihedral angle and the various wetting states. Wettability or solderability is related to the surface energy of the material. Wetting is substantially improved if the surface is clean and active (i.e., if all dirt and grease are removed and no oxide layer exists on the metal surface).

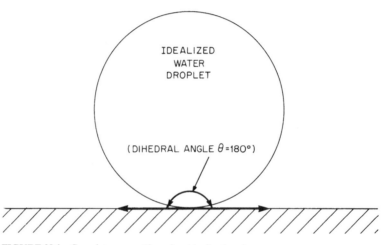

IDEALIZED
WATER
DROPLET

(DIHEDRAL ANGLE θ = 180°)

FIGURE 28.1   Complete nonwetting of an idealized surface.

Therefore, to form a solder bond efficiently, we must start with a material system which can be wet by the molten solder, and the cleanliness of the parts must be maintained.

28.5 SOLDERABILITY TESTING

Solderability testing is an important quality control procedure in the electronics industry. It is a simple procedure but problems can occur if the fundamental test principles are not under-stood thoroughly. *Solderability* is a measure of the ease (or difficulty) with which molten sol-der will wet the surfaces of the metals being joined. When molten solder leaves a continuous permanent film on the metal surface, it is said to wet the surface. Wetting is a surface phe-nomenon which depends on cleanliness. Fluxing facilitates wetting by cleaning the surface, and the degree of surface cleanliness depends on the activity of the flux.

However, there is often a limitation on the activity of the flux in the electronics industry. Most electronics soldering operations require relatively weak rosin-based fluxes to avoid the possibility of current leakage caused by flux residues remaining on the part. To enhance the

TOTAL NONWETTING (θ=180°)

PARTIAL WETTING (180°>θ>0)

TOTAL WETTING (θ=0°)

FIGURE 28.2 Relation between dihedral angle θ and the degree of wetting.

solderability of some surfaces and eliminate the need for active fluxes, electroplating often is employed to deposit a solderable coating over a base metal that tarnishes easily or is difficult to solder.

28.5.1 Testing Procedures

Testing for solderability can be a simple procedure of inspecting production parts or of dipping an appropriately fluxed lead or portion of a printed board in a solder pot and observing the results. Good and bad wetting are then identified visually. The problem is to recognize borderline cases which simulate effective solderability but quickly deteriorate. To alleviate borderline solderability, the mildest possible flux should be used at the lowest soldering time-temperature relations which will give adequate results.

An effective solderability test involves the use of water-white rosin flux and a solder pot. The surfaces to be checked are fluxed and immersed for 3 to 4 s in the solder pot, which is maintained at approximately 500°F. The solder is then permitted to solidify, and the components are cleaned of flux residues prior to visual examination. The inspection is usually performed with either no or low magnification (5 to 10×). Most solderability tests will permit up to a 5 percent imperfection of the total surface, provided the entire imperfection is not concentrated in one area.

More elaborate solderability tests are described in governmental and industrial specifications. Testing of component leads is covered by Electronic Industries Association (EIA) Test Method RS17814, which is similar to the solderability method described in Military Specification 202, Method 208. The test incorporates a dip fixture which provides identical dip ratio and immersion times (Fig. 28.3).

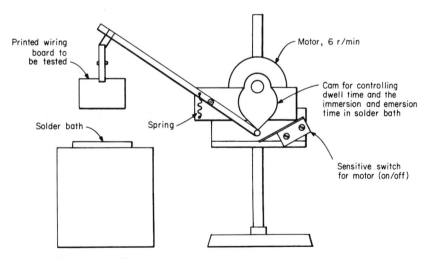

Printed wiring board to be tested

Motor, 6 r/min

Cam for controlling dwell time and the immersion and emersion time in solder bath

Solder bath

Spring

Sensitive switch for motor (on/off)

FIGURE 28.3 Solderability dip tester.

28.5.1.1 Dip Test.   For printed boards, the edge dip test, described in the EIA specification RS319 and by the IPC* in standard S801, often is employed. The edge of a printed board is dipped first in a mild flux and then in a solder pot for a predetermined time and temperature. After the flux residues are removed, the board is inspected visually for the quality of wetting. A similar test is employed to determine the solderability of solid wire leads, terminals, and conductive accessories of component parts normally joined by soft solder. Applicable test standards are EIA Standard RS178A, Solderability Test Standard, and MIL-STD-202C, Method 208 A, Solderability.

To perform the dip test, the operator places the item to be tested into a holding arm. The arm lowers the sample section into the solder pot. After the preset dwell time has elapsed, the arm automatically raises the sample. Then a visual determination of solderability is made. The dip test can also be performed as a manual operation, but that leaves too many variables to the discretion of the operator.

Since interpretation of results is based on a subjective judgment by the operator, it is essential that the operator be provided with examples of good, marginal, and poor solderability. It is imperative, too, that pot temperatures, cleaning and fluxing procedures, dwell times, and solder purity be controlled carefully to obtain meaningful results.

28.5.1.2 Globule Test.   This test is one that is prevalent throughout Europe and is mandatory for European suppliers whenever specifications dictate. It is described in the International Electrochemical Commission Publication 68-2 Test T, Solderability. The globule test provides a numerical designation for the solderability of wires and component leads. It measures the ability of the solder to wet the lead.

A lead wire, coated with a nonactivated rosin flux, is placed in a holding fixture. It is gripped and straightened and then lowered into a globule of molten solder. The volume and temperature of the globule are controlled. As the lead wire bisects the globule, the timer actuates and measures the time between the moment the wire contacts the solder and the moment the solder flows around and covers the lead. At this second point, the timer stops, and the elapsed time is registered on a read-out. Elapsed time is indicative of the solderability of the lead: the shorter the time, the greater the solderability.

This globule test method is completely automatic and is designed for continuous operation. Time is measured to $\frac{1}{100}$ s. Wires that are 0.008 to 0.062 in in diameter can be tested, and special heat regulators can hold solder temperature to ±2°F.

When wire plated with a soluble or fusible coating is tested, it is advisable to perform a dip test to supplement and verify the globule test findings. The reason is that, under certain conditions, the plated coating might be totally reflowed or dissolved during the soldering operation, which would give misleading results.

28.5.2 Standard Solderability Tests

Although many solderability tests are used throughout industry, the IPC has issued one described in its document IPC-S-804A that has been shown to give acceptable and repeatable results. If a printed board has a special surface treatment, a specifically designed test for that material may be required, but for copper, or solder surface boards this is an effective test.

Examples, and pictures, of standards of wetting, dewetting, and nonwetting are shown in Chapter 35 "Acceptability of Printed Boards," which can be used to evaluate the results of the IPC solderability test.

In addition to the preceding, Fig. 28.4 shows acceptable and nonacceptable examples of solder filling of plated-through-holes. This blow-hole formation is not a solderability issue, although it is often considered one. It is caused by moisture left from the plating process forming bubbles during the exposure to high temperature during soldering. This outgassing will usually leave voids in the hole after the solder solidifies. Often the reaction is to question the

---

* The Institute for Interconnecting and Packaging Electronic Circuits is referred to as IPC.

effectiveness of the solder process when, in fact, the drilling and/or plating processes most likely are the sources of the problem.

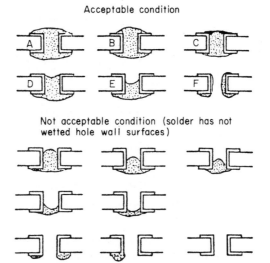

Acceptable condition

Not acceptable condition (solder has not wetted hole wall surfaces)

Note: Plated hole walls sometimes cause the formation of blow-holes by the evolution of gaseous products during the heating cycle of soldering. Such evolution is often visible during soldering and also after soldering as voids left in the solidified metal. This outgassing of material is a separate issue from the ability of the hole wall to be wet by solder. It is the responsibility of the supplier and user to agree on the acceptability of this outgassing condition.

FIGURE 28.4   Effectiveness of solder wetting of plated-through-holes. *(From IPC-5-804A.)*

28.6   PLATED COATINGS FOR PRESERVING SOLDERABILITY

The three commonly used types of plated coatings are generally referred to as fusible, soluble, and nonfusible and/or nonsoluble. Fusible electrodeposited coatings provide corrosion protection to a surface that has been activated for soldering. Whether the solder bond of a soluble electrodeposited coating is to the base metal or to the deposit depends on soldering conditions and coating thickness. Nonfusible and/or nonsoluble electrodeposited coatings are used frequently as barrier layers in electronic applications to prevent diffusion of solder and base metal.

28.6.1   Fusible Coatings

Tin and tin-lead electrodeposited coatings are commonly used in electronic applications to preserve solderability because they are fusible and do not contaminate the solder pot or fillet. Contamination can adversely affect tensile, creep, and shear strengths at a solder connection. Also, contamination of a part can reduce the flow and spread of the solder on the part.

If the coating operation is not closely controlled, an electrodeposited coating may be applied over a partially contaminated surface. If that happens, dewetting will occur in the contaminated areas because the electrodeposited coating is fused during soldering. Therefore, adequate cleaning prior to plating is essential to obtain good solderability. Figure 28.5 shows a surface which has dewet after a reflow operation.

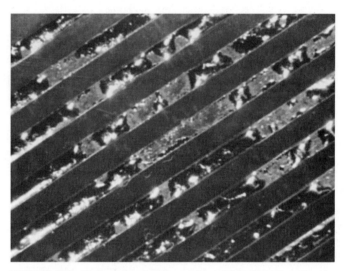

FIGURE 28.5   Tin-lead-plated surface which exhibits dewetting after the reflow operation. *(Alpha Metals, Inc.)*

Another point to remember is that plating thickness should be sufficient that porosity is virtually eliminated. Porosity and codeposited impurities will lower the protective value of the electrodeposited coating and will eventually cause poor solderability.

28.6.2 Soluble Coatings

Soluble coatings commonly used in electronic applications include gold, silver, cadmium, and copper. During soldering, these metal coatings are either completely or partially dissolved. The amount of dissolution depends on solubility of the coating metal, thickness of the deposit, and the soldering conditions. Silver and copper tend to tarnish, and if a mildly activated flux is called for, they should be protected with a thin rosin coating. Cadmium offers sacrificial corrosion protection which often necessitates the use of highly activated fluxes to promote effective soldering.

Soluble gold coatings provide excellent corrosion and chemical resistance. However, because of the high cost, fairly thin coatings are used. Moreover, care should be taken because gold coatings of under 50-μin thickness tend to be porous and, as a result, lower the protective value of the metal. Corrosion of the base metal or barrier plate via pores causes soldering problems because the gold usually dissolves completely during soldering and it is difficult to wet the corroded base metal. Also, solderability decreases with the amounts of alloying elements that are used to increase hardness and are often codeposited with the gold. Thicker gold coatings, on the other hand, may cause brittleness in a solder connection because of formation of gold-tin intermetallic compounds.

28.6.3   Nonfusible and Nonsoluble Coatings

Nickel and tin-nickel electrodeposited coatings are considered to be nonfusible and/or non-soluble because they provide an effective barrier to prevent alloying of solder to the base metal in electronic applications. They allow for effective soldering to such materials as aluminum and silicon. However, problems can occur from passivity, which is caused by code-posited impurities, or from some additional agents that are used in nickel plating to increase hardness and reduce internal stress. In such cases, nickel and tin-nickel electrodeposited coatings should be protected with tin or tin-lead to improve the shelf life of the soldered part.

Furthermore, nickel and tin-nickel have limited solubility in solder, and a flash coating is not an effective barrier. When electroless nickel is used as a barrier coating on aluminum, the required thickness will depend on soldering conditions. A thickness of 50 to 100 µin is sufficient for most operations.

28.6.4   Organic Coatings

Although the metallic coatings for preserving solderability are the most reliable and effective coatings, they are also the most expensive ones. For applications that do not require a long shelf life, considerable economies can be obtained by using an organic protective coating. There are several basic types of organic protective coatings: water-dip lacquers, rosin-based protective coating, and the benzotriazole-type coating. Organic protective coatings must be easily removable, and they must be compatible with the rosin-based fluxes normally used in the printed board industry.

Water-dip lacquers were once a very popular means of protecting the solderability of printed boards. However, they have fallen into disfavor because of their tendency to set up and polymerize with age. As they age, they become extremely difficult to remove. They also become insoluble in the flux solvent. If they are not properly removed after fluxing, they leave white residues which are not corrosive but are extremely unattractive.

Today, rosin-based protective coatings are much more prevalent than water-dip lacquers. They are applied by dip, spray, or roller coating, and, depending on the thickness, they will provide solderability protection for six weeks to four months. They are composed of the rosin solids material, and as such they are quite compatible with the rosin thinners and the normal cleaning method used to clean rosin fluxes. When those materials are used, it is important to ensure that adequate fluxing occurs and that the preheating time and temperature are sufficient to allow the protective coat to melt and be displaced by the flux. If the coat is not displaced, soldering will occur with a rosin nonactivated flux, no matter how active the solder flux really is.

A third alternative which some people have explored is the benzotriazole-type coating. Benzotriazole is an organic compound which is applied to the board surface during the final rinse operation of the plating line. It forms a thin nonporous film on the copper surface and prevents oxygen from reacting with the surface copper molecules. Benzotriazole films are very fragile, and they cannot be subjected to handling or scraping abuse.

28.7   TIN-LEAD FUSING

Fused coatings ordinarily are electrodeposited, low-melting metals or alloys that have been heated sufficiently above their melting points to become completely molten. In the molten state, alloying between the liquid and the basis metals is accelerated; on solidification, the deposit usually is dense and nonporous. The procedure is commonly known as *reflowing,* and it usually connotes tin or tin-lead electrodeposits. However, it can also apply to the remelting of hot-dipped coatings.

Fused coatings are employed to guarantee that the cleaning procedure prior to plating is adequate, to produce a slightly denser deposit with less porosity, and to improve the appearance of the coating. Reflowing leaves a bright deposit which has a definite sales appeal.

28.7.1 Thick Fused Coatings

Tin-lead electrodeposits that are reflowed are usually between 300 and 500 μin in thickness. That thickness provides adequate protection with a minimum of reflow problems. When printed boards are reflowed, the tin-lead deposit forms a meniscus on the conductor pad. For that reason the edges of the pad have a much thinner coating than the original plating, whereas the center is thicker. The average thickness is the same, but it is distributed differently. As the plating thickness increases over 500 μin, the surface forces are not always sufficient to hold the solder in the meniscus—especially on wide pads; the solder shifts upon solidification and the deposits appear uneven. On inspection, that may be mistaken for a dewetting condition, but it actually is a shifting of the molten solder before solidification.

When tin-lead with a thickness over 500 μin is reflowed, the boards must be in a horizontal position and withdrawn in a smooth manner. Otherwise, shifting of the molten solder is inevitable. Because of that problem, there is a practical limit on the coating thickness. In recent years, some military specifications have been calling for 0.001 to 0.0015 in (1000 to 1500 μin) in reflow tin-lead plating. The main objective is to obtain maximum corrosion protection. Deposits of that thickness have been reflowed, but not without processing difficulties.

Improvements in infrared reflow equipment have increased the use of thick fused coatings in recent years. Reflowed tin-lead electrodeposits offer several advantages. One advantage is that they provide a 100 percent quality control check immediately after etching. By examining the boards after reflow, problems in hole drilling, cleaning procedures, plating, and etching can be detected and corrective action can be taken immediately. The procedure has had a dramatic effect in improving printed board reliability.

Another benefit is that solder slivers are eliminated. During etching there is undercutting where the tin-lead coating overhangs the conductor pad. Under certain vibration conditions, the overhang can fall off and cause a short circuit. Fusing eliminates the condition and adds to board reliability.

28.7.2 Thin Fused Coatings

Thin fused coatings level the solder during fusing when they are applied by procedures such as roller coating, spin coating, and hydro-squeegeeing. The leveling is accomplished by means of a hot liquid ejected from spray nozzles. The techniques usually result in coatings under 50 μin, hardly enough for adequate corrosion protection. Also, thin coatings can mask poor solderability when tin-lead is plated over unsolderable copper. For those reasons, use of leveling techniques has diminished.

28.7.3 Problems in Reflowing Plated Coatings

Codeposited impurities, especially copper in tin-lead, can cause dewetting in a reflowed deposit. Variations in alloy composition raise the melting point and cause reflow problems. That is particularly true when organic contamination results in poor solution throwing power and consequent high lead deposit in the plated-through-holes. Heavy oxidation or tarnish films that result from chemical attack by etching solutions must be removed prior to reflowing. The films can act as insulating barriers and interfere with reflowing.

28.8   SOLDERABILITY AND THE PLATING OPERATION

Blowholes in plated-through-holes on printed boards normally are caused by solution entrapped in the hole, but they also can be caused by an excess of organics occluded in the electrodeposits. The heat involved in soldering causes moisture and entrapped chemicals in the laminate to build up in pressure and escape through voids or cracks in the plating. That results in blowholes. The problem can usually be alleviated by prebaking at 180 to 200°F.

In some cases blowholes can be caused by an excessive amount of occluded organics in the electrodeposit. The problem is more prevalent with bright plating deposits such as tin and tin-lead. When blowholes are caused by excessive organics occluded in the deposit, prebaking will not remedy the problem. The occluded material can be released only when the metal liquefies.

Figure 28.6 shows a cross section of a fused tin-lead surface that had an excessive amount of organic material. Note that the organic material tends to create voids in the plate which rise to the surface. The result is a grainy, pitted appearance after solidification.

FIGURE 28.6   Organic material from plating bath occluded in reflowed tin-lead deposit. *(Alpha Metals, Inc.)*

28.8.1   Effect of Organic Plating Additives

To solder successfully to electrodeposits that employ addition agents, it is extremely important that the additives be carefully controlled. Additives usually are essential to produce sound deposits of tin and tin-lead alloys. In electroplating, chemicals are added to the basic formulation of a plating solution to enhance the properties of the deposit. Some properties that can be improved by additives are throwing power, smoothness, hardness, leveling, brightness, and speed of deposition.

Normally, when foreign metals or organic materials are present in a plating solution, the properties of the deposit are adversely affected. In some rare cases, beneficial effects can be produced by codepositing small amounts of other metallic ions or occluding organic material. When that occurs, the materials are classified not as contaminates but as addition agents. When they produce a bright deposit, they are called brighteners. Strictly speaking, they are controlled impurities.

When organic additives are employed, some forms of the compounds are absorbed at the cathode surface during electrolysis. Often, the compound absorbed is a decomposition product of the original material. The amount that is absorbed is proportional to the nature and concentration of the compound and the time of electrolysis. Frequently, the organic decomposition products develop over a period of time and may affect the deposit adversely. Six months to a year may pass before critical concentrations are reached. If the breakdown products can be removed by an activated carbon treatment, the problem can be controlled. It always is a worthwhile practice to remove organic addition agents and their breakdown products by a carbon treatment at least two or three times a year. That assures continuous operation of the plating solution without unscheduled purification treatments during peak production.

28.8.2 Effect of the Plating Anode

When inorganic contaminants build up in a plating solution, increased concentrations of the additives are normally required to produce the desired effects. Poor-quality anodes constitute the major source of inorganic contaminants. In tin and tin-lead plating, at least a 99.9 percent purity anode is required. High-purity chemicals and efficient rinsing before plating are also essential to maintain a high-purity plating solution. Operation of tin-plating solutions at temperatures below 65°F can reduce the amount of organics occluded in the deposit.

When excess organics are occluded in a tin or tin-lead electrodeposit, bubbling is often observed during soldering. That often can be the cause of blowholes in soldering a printed board. However, it should be noted that the majority of blowholes are caused by entrapped plating or cleaning solutions. When postbaking does not alleviate the problem, occluded organics in the tin or tin-lead electrodeposits are a likely cause.

28.9   USE OF PRECLEANERS TO RESTORE SOLDERABILITY

In the electronics industry, a restriction is often placed on the activity of the flux that can be employed in soldering, because an assumption has been made that postsoldering cleaning may not always be 100 percent effective. If ionic residues are left on a printed board after cleaning, there is a possibility that voltage leaks could develop under high-humidity conditions. Because of that restriction, a situation in which effective soldering cannot be accomplished with the specified flux can arise. In that event, solderability must be restored or the parts must be scrapped.

28.9.1 Causes of Poor Solderability

It is important that the cause of poor solderability be understood. In some cases, oil, grease, or organic films may be responsible. A simple solvent or alkaline cleaning can remedy that situation. The most common cause of poor solderability, however, is heavy tarnish or oxidation on the surface of the metal being soldered. Precleaning in an acid cleaner usually will restore solderability. After acid cleaning, it is essential that the acid residues be thoroughly rinsed off. In critical applications, a neutralization step, followed by another rinse, is employed to ensure that all acid residues are removed. A quick, thorough drying is required after rinsing to prevent reoxidation.

It is also possible that the solderability problem may be a combination of the two situations. That would necessitate a solvent or alkaline cleaning to remove organic films and an acid cleaning to remove tarnish and oxidation. If the dual cleaning operation is impractical, then cleaning with an organic solvent containing acid should be considered. With that type of solution, effective cleaning can be performed in one operation followed by rinsing and thorough drying. That type of cleaning, which requires minimum space and equipment, is ideal when organic films on the surface are not extensive but do prevent 100 percent removal of oxides and tarnish.

A solvent containing acid cleaner is ideal for copper and brass, since it dissolves most organic films that could be on the surface and assures complete removal of tarnish and oxidation. Straight acid cleaners such as hydrochloric, sulfuric and fluoroboric acids, and sodium acid sulfate (sodium bisulfate) are completely effective only when organic films are removed in prior operations. In severe cases of copper oxidation, etching type cleaners such as ammonium persulfate sometimes are used. Although the solutions are very effective, it must be noted that they leave the metal in an active state so that it can easily reoxidize. Hence, it is a good practice to follow this procedure with a mild acid dip and thorough rinsing and drying.

28.9.2 Cleaning Tin-Lead Surfaces

Leads and printed boards are often coated with tin or tin-lead to preserve solderability. When that type of coating is applied by electroplating, it is extremely important that the deposit be applied on a solderable surface. Adequate cleaning prior to electroplating is essential. Tarnishing of the tin or tin-lead coating during etching or storage can detract from solderability. Acid cleaners for removing tarnish from tin or tin-lead usually contain thiourea, fluoboric acid, wetting, and complexing agents. If spray equipment having titanium heating coils or rollers is used, then an acid cleaner containing fluoboric acid cannot be used. However, there are available equivalent cleaners that do not contain fluoboric acid that will clean tin or tin-lead effectively in a spray operation. It should be noted that if the tin or tin-lead is plated over an unsolderable surface, then the only recourse is to strip the tin or tin-lead and replate. Solutions containing glacial acetic acid and hydrogen peroxide often are employed for the purpose. Stripping and replating can be a costly operation, and economic considerations may rule out the procedure in some cases.

CHAPTER 29
SOLDER MATERIALS AND PROCESSES

Gary M. Freedman
Digital Equipment Corporation, Maynard, Massachusetts

29.1 INTRODUCTION

Over the years soldering has become much more sophisticated. Surface-mount component insertions have rapidly replaced through-hole component onsertions. The changing nature of surface-mount technology, its evolving dominance, decreasing component pitches, along with the proliferation of mixed mount assembly, have forced many changes to printed wiring board design and manufacturing practices. Higher pin counts, introduction of the ball grid array, denser assemblies, increasing emphasis on no-clean processing, and the possibility of a move to lead-free solders have resulted in the onset of a dramatic industrial metamorphosis.

In addition, some non-mass-reflow techniques such as hot bar, laser bonding, and hot-gas soldering have been developed and matured considerably. Not necessarily meant to replace mass reflow per se, these newer soldering methods have found their way into niche production assembly and repair applications. The popularity of vapor phase soldering has ebbed due to potential harm to the ozone layer by its volatile organic-based reflow medium and it chlorofluorocarbon (CFC) cover vapor. Similarly, soldering flux selection has been radically altered because of cleaning considerations and the environmental impact of either CFCs or other harmful volatile organic compounds (VOCs) employed in solder paste formulation and used in larger volumes for postsoldering flux residue removal (circuit board cleaning). The face of the soldering industry is permanently changed, not only by environmental issues but also by process economics and increased demand for greater functionality in smaller and lighter products. All this has necessitated a rethinking of all process steps and materials. The changes have been catalyzed by new industry and governmental recommendations. In addition to concern over CFCs, which has hastened the quest for soldering processes requiring no postsolder cleaning, there is pending federal legislation which may provide incentive for industry to embrace non-lead-based solders. All these have caused a reexamination of soldering process basics, metallurgies, and circuit board cleaning methods.

This chapter will cover the fundamentals of soldering in a number of its most popular forms for modern printed circuit board (PCB) assembly. An overview of the chemical and physical aspects of soldering will be discussed. Additionally, specific processes and equipment descriptions will be offered to acquaint or update the reader. A review of fluxing agents and metallurgical considerations are provided along with the special needs mandated by the competitive migration to finer and finer pitch components, surface-mount, and through-hole.

While the thermodynamics of soldering can be a very complicated subject, the understanding needed to achieve desirable results in soldering is relatively simple. As with any technology, there is a plethora of information, including physical constants, material quirks, chemical peculiarities, and physical models. This chapter will cover only those fundamentals necessary for a clear understanding of the soldering process. This is not meant to be an end-all dissertation on the subject. It is written from the viewpoint of a user in the industrial world relying on off-the-shelf materials and process equipment. Outmoded techniques, for the most part, will not be dealt with in detail but may be referenced. Nor will the minutiae of physical modeling be covered. Sufficient bibliographic pointers have been included to provide a deeper probing of various facets of soldering technology. Observe the basics discussed here and the potential for high-yielding industrial soldering of printed circuit boards will be within grasp.

29.1.1 Designing for Process and Product

There are numerous considerations which are crucial for circuit assembly and solder joint success. The exposure environment must be understood:

1. What thermal conditions must it endure?
2. What mechanical shock and vibration will the assembly experience?
3. How many on-off cycles are expected of the product?
4. To what airborne contaminants and humidity regimes will the soldered assembly be exposed?

These considerations and others will have implications for materials, solder joint configuration, and assembly design rules. Unfortunately, design rules will be quite specific to these considerations, coupled to the bill-of-materials for the soldered product. So the notion of listing specific design criteria for broad use is not a simple or practical matter. Instead, it is necessary for the solderer to understand the basic phenomena which influence the soldering process and the finished assembly's reliability, which is the essence of this chapter. Additionally, there are certain key rules which one could follow for incoming printed circuit board cleanliness, solder purity, etc. These are best described in certain standards documents, such as those published by the IPC.*

The old-fashioned idea and trap of offering up generalized rules for all soldering process applications will be strictly avoided. The materials and solder properties for a desktop computer are vastly different from those for the ignition system printed circuitry under the hood of a car. Similarly, mobile electronics has added the need for mechanical shock-resistant assemblies for calculators, pocket pagers, etc. This, coupled with the reality of high-volume production for the mobile electronics market, has driven the industry to ever-increasing soldering yields, as well as better joint-to-joint and assembly-to-assembly reproducibility. The cost to repair, in some cases, may be steeper than the combined material and labor content of the as-assembled product. This further reinforces the need to solder properly the first time.

There are numerous rules of thumb which will become evident in discussions of metallurgies, fluxes, and processes which, if taken to heart, will result in best soldering yield and reliability. However, the only way to ensure that the assembly will endure its use and environment is to develop appropriate accelerated testing methods which can accurately predict product field reliability. This will be discussed in Chap. 37.

There are also abundant pitfalls in soldering. Too much gold in a tin-lead solder will cause catastrophic embrittlement of the solder joint. Too high a process time or temperature can have the same effect on tin-lead solder even in the absence of gold. The residues left by some

---

* Institute for Interconnecting and Packaging Electronic Circuits, 7380 N. Lincoln Ave., Lincolnwood, IL 60646-1705.

fluxes can cause electrochemical corrosion. These will be discussed in the various sections of this chapter.

Component-to-component spacing is a function of the materials, joint requirements, and soldering method applied. Component spacing from the edge of the circuit board may be a function of the soldering method chosen. There are no clear-cut, all-purpose rules for every soldering situation. The use of test builds to explore various layout configurations is highly recommended. Building these is crucial for a definitive understanding of the interactions of layout, materials, and process conditions. Although too often cliché, there is much to be said for design for manufacturing. With some forethought in layout and consideration for the processes which follow, the printed circuit board can become much less of a challenge to assemble.

29.1.2 Common Metal-Joining Methods

The three most popular techniques for joining metals are:

- Soldering
- Brazing
- Welding

While a rigorous review of the three techniques will be avoided, a cursory comparison of these metal-joining methods is useful in setting the stage for an in-depth discussion of circuit board soldering (see Fig. 29.1).

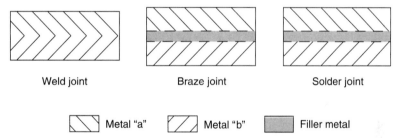

FIGURE 29.1 Welding involves heating of the metals to be joined to the point that they fuse into one another. Brazing and soldering involve the use of a filler material which is fluxed and combines metallurgically with the metals to be joined.

29.1.2.1 Soldering. In order for a metallurgical bond to result from the soldering process, the solder material has to be compatible with basis materials or any coatings applied to the underlying metals. The basis materials are those bulk metals which provide the shape and stiffness of the metallurgical structure, be it printed circuit board solder land, plated-through-hole, or component lead. The basis metal may be of single elemental composition such as copper or an alloyed metal such as Kovar. The basis metal may require a coated surface to permit, preserve, or enhance its solderability. Gold, tin, or solder over Kovar is a common example. Metal system alternatives will be discussed in subsequent sections.

29.1.2.2 Brazing. There are only subtle differences between soldering and brazing. The primary distinction is the temperature required for joint formation. Brazing is generally accomplished at relatively high-temperature regimes as compared to soldering. Most agree that when the filler metal has a melting temperature greater than about 500°C, it qualifies the process as brazing, although texts are not consistent on the cut-off temperature.

The filler metal is referred to as the solder or brazing alloy, depending on which process is being employed. Solders are generally thought of as soft, having low melting point, and ductile, while the opposite is generally true of the brazing alloys. The bulk metal being joined experiences only superficial metallurgical changes where in contact with the solder or brazing alloy. The bulk metals being joined, with the exception of any filler metal (solder or braze alloy), are never heated to their melting points, as is the case with welding.

Since circuit board assembly is done almost exclusively by means of soldering, this section will be devoted to that traditional joining method. The focus will be on the soft soldering process or soldering with relatively ductile, easily fused solders typified by the eutectic or near-eutectic tin-lead system with melting point in the range of ~180 to ~200°C. Compatibility with the circuit board materials and ease of processing dominate the list of reasons that soldering is chosen over brazing for circuit board assembly. This, along with discussions of alloy selection will be reviewed in subsequent sections.

29.1.2.3 Welding. Welding involves heating one or more compatible metals to the point that they join one another. They may be of the same material, in which case they merely melt into one another. Welding of two dissimilar materials is commonly accomplished where one metal alloys with another. Technically there is no need for the addition of a filler material for the welding process, since the bulk specimens being joined are altered to the point that they alloy or *wet* to one another. For various reasons, filler metals can be added. Welding may be highly localized or across entire mating metal surfaces. Welding is diametrically opposed to the soldering and brazing processes. In the latter two, a separate material, a filler metal, is necessarily sandwiched between the two metal surfaces to be joined. The filler metal must metallurgically combine, or *alloy*, with the surfaces of the parts to be joined. This fusible alloy, the filler, is the *cement* of the joint.

29.2 SOLDERING

When molten, the solder must wet to the materials in contact with it, forming a metallurgical bond by diffusion, dissolving, or alloying with the basis metal. To demonstrate this point, especially in the context of soldering for electronics, the most common example is the case of tin-lead solder joining the basis metal, copper. For this example, it is not necessary to discuss the exact alloy of tin-lead (Sn-Pb), but it is important to know how the materials involved alloy with the copper (Cu) basis. To develop an understanding of joint formation, one must examine the tenets of processes operant during soldering. Primary steps involved are as follows:

1. Intimate contact of the solder to materials being joined
2. Application of heat sufficient to melt the solder
3. Oxide removal from the basis and solder metallurgies
4. Solder wetting to basis metal(s) and intermetallic formation
5. Quenching of the solder liquidus

Each of these is summarized below.

29.2.1 Application of Heat to Solder

Heating is the one step that has the most bearing on the entire solder process. It should not be triavialized by merely associating thermal rise with the onset of solder liquidus. Warming solder will cause it to soften. Heating to the melting point will allow solder to flow which further enhances intimacy of the solder mass with the adjacent mating surfaces of parts to be joined. Note that at room temperature, eutectic tin-lead alloy (63 weight% Sn:37 weight% Pb) is already at 65 percent of the way to liquidus (183°C or 456°K) when referenced from absolute zero.

Thermal input is also responsible for imparting the necessary energy to activate the chemical processes which both aid and impede the soldering process. Most important, heating drives the metallurgical processes required for intermetallic formation. All of these concepts will be covered in this chapter.

29.2.2 Oxidation Formation

Most materials, when in equilibrium with our oxygen-rich environment, possess an oxidation coating. Upon heating, surfaces of the solder as well as the metallic surfaces of the basis metal will further and more thoroughly oxidize in our normal air environment. If a silver-bearing solder alloy is heated in the presence of a sulfur-containing ambient (sulfur-tainted air), sulfuration will occur and that tarnish will also inhibit soldering. Generally, the higher the soldering temperature or the longer the process time, the more oxidation or tarnish will be a problem. Oxides and tarnishes provide a physical barrier preventing alloy formation between the solder and the metal(s) to be joined by means of the solder process. Of course, in the case of gold (Au) there is insufficient oxidation to degrade soldering, but unless oxidation is removed from the solder itself, solder alloying will not be possible. Note that in most soldering processes, the ambient can be altered to mitigate the detrimental effects of oxygen or other airborne contaminants. More on that later.

29.2.3 Chemical Preparation of Solder Surfaces

The most generally applied remedy to the effects of oxidation and tarnish during soldering is the application of a chemical agent, *flux,* which attacks and removes tarnish and oxidation and, further, protects metal surfaces from reoxidation during the joining process. Flux comes from the Latin *fluxus,* which means flowing. It ensures that the solder, once molten, will flow over the surfaces to be bonded, unconstrained by oxide skins on the solder or the metals to be joined.

29.2.4 Solder Wetting/Intermetallic Formation

Intermetallic compound (IMC) formation is the key to soldering. It is a local alloying between the boundary of the solder liquidus and the surfaces of the basis metals to which it is in contact, which is the essence of soldering. There is much misinformation about IMCs. One thing is certain: Without intermetallic formation, there is no solder joint formation. This is stressed because some erroneously claim lack of IMC in such processes as laser soldering. In the case of that technology, the IMC can be exceptionally thin immediately after soldering, but it is and must be present for soldering to occur. The high temperature and the intimate contact of the liquid solder enhance the rate and area of intermetallic compound formation.

29.2.5 Solder Quenching

Once below the melting point again, the solder cools, intermetallic compound formation rate decreases significantly, and the solder joint is formed. It is critical that the solder attains its solid state at process completion and prior to circuit board handling to preclude accidental movement of the components in the molten solder.

29.3 SOLDER FILLETS

The solder fillet is an overt manifestation of surface tension and wetting. Figure 29.2*a* shows the formation when solder wets to the solder land and component lead. Figure 29.3 shows the cross sections of fillets for different solder joints.

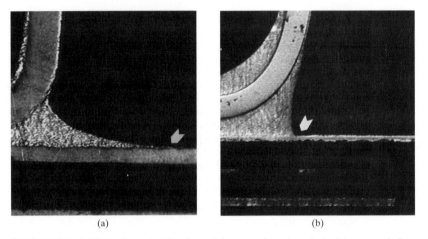

(a)   (b)

FIGURE 29.2   (*a*) Solder has set well to the pad (see arrow), as characterized by a very shallow contact angle; (*b*) wetting has been interfered with, as characterized by the steep dihedral angle (see arrow).

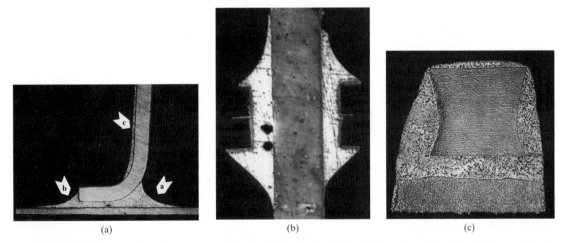

(a)   (b)   (c)

FIGURE 29.3   (*a*) Cross section of a surface-mount lead exhibiting heel and toe fillet formation, with solder wicking up the lead; (*b*) cross section of a plated-through-hole solder joint. Rich fillet formations extend from the barrel lands on both surfaces of the circuit board to the lead. (*c*) Transverse cross section of a surface-mount component lead to a circuit board pad, showing rich side fillets from pad to lead.

In Fig. 29.2, the menisci are easily discernible as anchored webs of solder extending from the bonding pad to the perimeter of the component lead. Looking at the side view, Fig. 29.3*a,* fillets are readily apparent at the heel and toe of the component lead. In Fig. 29.3*b* and 29.3*c,* side fillets between the bonding pad and the component lead are also quite distinct. The fillet is a reasonable indicator of the degree of wetting and, therefore, of process goodness. The higher the fillet, the better the joint. This can be confusing. When comparing two boards which were not processed simultaneously, a higher fillet may just indicate a longer time above liquidus. If this were the case, embrittlement of the solder joint may also result from intermetallic compound buildup. Intermetallic compounds are brittle and degrade joint strength. Large solder fillets may also be indicative of larger solder volumes. Therefore, fillet examination alone is not sufficient to accurately assess soldering process performance. But for a given time-temperature profile, solder alloy, species and conditions of metallurgical contacting surfaces, solder volume, flux, and soldering atmosphere, the solder fillets may provide a first-pass comparative assessment of the solderability of various parts of the bonded assembly. Too much solder wicking up the lead may cause solder shorting, particularly near the package body where the lead spacing may be finest. Excessive solder on the leads may reduce the flexibility of the lead and result in premature joint failure when thermally cycled through use in the field.

Note that up to this point in the discussion on the soldering process, the system has been treated as solid or liquid metal(s) interfacing with a gas; the soldering ambient. This simplistic view has been used to demonstrate the fundamentals of the process. However, the realities dictate a modified view. To keep the solder and surfaces to be joined bondable, they must be kept oxide free. Fluxes are therefore formulated to not only remove existing oxide on the room temperature solder, but to stem oxidation of the cleaned metal surfaces during the high-temperature excursions of the soldering process. This is accomplished by using fluxes which have a high enough molecular weight or configuration which prevents them from burning off entirely at solder alloying temperatures. Therefore, the solder flow and surface tension are influenced by a liquid-liquid interface, so solder spreading must be examined in terms of this liquid solder–liquid flux system.

29.4   INTERMETALLIC COMPOUNDS AND METALLURGY

At the boundary between the solder and the metal to which it is joined, there is an intermediate alloy phase of some or all of their contacting metal constituents. It is characterized by stoichiometric association and metallic bonding. This high-alloy-concentration region generally has properties which are vastly different from either the solder or the contacted base metal. It may be, and generally is, of brittle behavior. It may be electrically conducting or even semiconducting. This crystalline material is called *intermetallic compound* (IMC). IMC is also known as an *electron compound* or *Hume-Rothery compound.* Most people think of solder as a soft, forgiving material of low melting point. It is ironic that the essence of soldering—the actual bond, or more correctly, the bond's anchor—is, in fact, a brittle, high-melting-point composition of generally poor electrical conductivity. Without intermetallic formation, though, there is no solder joint.

29.5   SOLDERING TECHNIQUES

There have been many soldering methods devised over the millennia. The most common are the soldering torch and the soldering iron. These are direct outgrowths of the most ancient methods, but they are inadequate for printed circuit board soldering. The latter is characteristic of a *directed energy bonding* method where the heating is localized to a specific small piece of board real estate to accomplish soldering of one or a localized set of joints. Conversely, and hypothetically, the torch could be viewed as a means of *mass soldering,* encompassing a much larger area of heating than was possible by the iron. Thus, today's techniques are divided into categories according to area of heating or number of joints formed simultaneously.

The iron is too slow and clumsy for bonding the large number of fine-leaded components found on today's circuit cards. For the most part, a torch's flame is not controllable enough and is prone to damaging most circuit board substrate materials and component packages, but this technology has been reincarnated for fine circuit soldering, though it is not a popular choice. As the boards and components have matured, so have the soldering assembly methods. Although the tools of soldering for electronic assembly have changed dramatically over the last five decades, the dichotomy of methods persist. There are other terms applied to differentiate the two, such as flow soldering vs. reflow soldering. These will be explored later.

The topic of modern soldering methods can be divided into two distinct categories which encompass the following:

Mass soldering	*Directed energy methods*
Wave soldering	Hot-gas soldering
Oven reflow	Hot-bar soldering
Vapor phase reflow	Laser soldering
Wave soldering	Soldering iron
	Pinpoint torch

Each method has its place, purpose, and advantage. Techniques will have to be judged by their applicability, cost, and end result. Mass-soldering techniques are by far the most common for high-volume manufacturing circuit board assembly. Some of the directed energy soldering methods are now catching on in volume manufacturing and, as PCBs are miniaturized, suitability of the directed energy methods may become increasingly important.

29.5.1 Mass-Soldering Methods

The mass flow or reflow methods are suited for high-volume manufacturing. The entire board is heated and large numbers of components on the board are soldered at one time. The two most common of these methods are oven reflow soldering and wave soldering. A third technique, vapor phase reflow soldering, has dwindled in popularity due to environmental concerns regarding the use of chlorofluorocarbon-based solvents which were key to this process. These techniques will be reviewed along with mention of some other soldering methods in this chapter.

Choice of soldering method will lie in the types of components and boards being soldered, the required throughput rate, and requisite solder joint properties. There are no clear-cut rules. These days, some plated-through-hole components are being assembled along with surface-mount components in reflow ovens.

In that method, sometimes referred to as *intrusive reflow,* a generous amount of solder paste is deposited over the circuit board's plated-through-holes. The through-hole components (axially leaded, pin grid array, etc.) are inserted in the circuit board just before or after surface-mount component placement insertion. The paste-bearing board is then mass-reflowed in a reflow oven. Solder paste coalesces into liquid solder, which is drawn into the interstices between the through-holes and the inserted component leads concurrently with surface-mount component joint formation.

29.5.2 Component Types and Solder Methods

There are limitations in soldering which dictate the soldering method to be used. Most generally, these restrictions are clearly evident. Wave soldering seems to be limited to components with pitches greater than or equal to about 1.27 mm (0.05 in). Although slightly lower pitch soldering has been demonstrated, the capillarity which is dictated by lead spacing tends to dominate, and solder bridging is exceptionally difficult to avoid. Not long ago, oven reflow was a challenge at 0.635 mm (0.025 in), but with increased methods refinement, this pitch is now commonly soldered with high yields. The pitch barrier has been pushed lower and lower; each step beyond 0.635 mm (0.5 mm, 0.4 mm, 0.3 mm) has been demonstrated to be more and more difficult, not a mere scaling of the solder paste volume. Much of the difficulty lies not in the oven reflow method as much as in the paste deposition repeatability and mechanics of component placement. Given a solderable lead in contact with solid solder, flux, and a heating source, joint formation should be possible regardless of the heating technique. Following is a rough guide to methods for soldering various component types. The table applies to eutectic or near-eutectic tin-lead solder. Of course, there are exceptions, but it is meant to show current methodologies which are in use at the time of this writing.

Component type	Pitch limitations	Reflow method
Chip capacitors		Wave, oven reflow
Chip resistors		Wave, oven reflow
MELFs		Wave, oven reflow
J-bend	≥1.27 mm (0.05 in)	Wave, oven reflow
Gullwing	≥0.3 mm (0.0118 in)	Wave, oven reflow
Through-hole (axial, pin grid, D.I.P., etc.)		Wave
TAB		Hot bar, laser, hot gas

29.6 OVEN REFLOW SOLDERING

In reflow soldering, primarily used for surface-mount components, solder paste is forced through a metal stencil by either a metallic or polymeric squeegee. The paste contains both solder flux for preparing the metal surfaces for solder attachment and sufficient solder for joint formation. Components are placed in the solder paste on the board and the populated PCB is inserted into an oven for reflow. As in the wave-soldering machine, the boards are transported through the oven by means of a conveyor. The oven gradually raises the circuit board and component temperatures, activates the flux in the solder paste, and, finally, enough heat is imparted to cause the solder to flow (meaning to liquefy, also known as *reflow*). When built and implemented properly, the oven reflow process results in a controlled and predictable heating and cooling cycle, allowing reflow without spattering of the flux and volatiles which compose the solder paste. Rapid heating of the paste is widely known to be a source of solder ball formation. Solder balls, isolated spheres of solder not necessarily connected to the solder mass of the joint, can be problematic for printed circuit board assemblies. They can induce electrical shorts, especially with finer-pitch components where solder ball diameters may be on the order of component pad spacing. Too rapid a heating cycle or direct infrared irradiation of certain fluxes may cause flux charring or "caramelizing" which results in unsightly, difficult-to-clean flux residues. It also lessens the efficacy of the fluxing process.

The circuit board itself may also fall victim to the reflow process if temperatures are not maintained properly or evenly. It is for this reason that much development has ensued, resulting in an excellent selection of reflow ovens, accessories, and board-processing methodologies that are the mainstay of today's surface-mount manufacturing. Different approaches to reflow soldering will be discussed here which should help the reader to choose the best features when picking a reflow oven or identify or minimize problems in processing with new or existing reflow oven equipment.

29.6.1   Reflow Oven Subsystems

Even the simplest reflow ovens consist of several subsystems:

- Insulated tunnel
- Board conveyor
- Heater assemblies
- Cooling
- Venting

See Fig. 29.4.

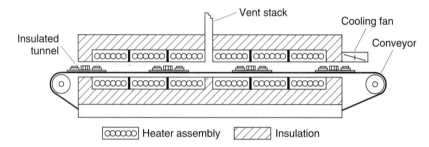

FIGURE 29.4   The five subassemblies of a reflow oven: heater assemblies with temperature controllers, insulated tunnel, conveyor, cooling fans, and venting system.

Reflow ovens have reached a high level of sophistication, and there are many other items which enhance oven suitability for the manufacturing floor. Those items, beyond the aforementioned reflow oven subsystems, are niceties, accessories, and gimmicks offered by oven manufacturers and will not be discussed in this section; however, those subsystems previously listed will be reviewed to allow readers an understanding of the basics of oven construction and operation as well as the most advantageous configuration for their applications.

29.6.1.1   Tunnel.   The tunnel is a thermally insulated passage through the length of oven that allows for a continuous reflow process. It serves to insulate the heaters and boards from the external (room) environment just as much as it is designed to maintain thermal conditions as prescribed by the process and demanded of the heaters. Boards are moved through the tunnel and past multiple heaters by a constant-speed conveyor. This permits controlled and gradual preheat, reflow, and post-reflow cooling of the circuit board. The heaters are controlled by means of closed-loop controllers which regulate their power. Each heater's thermal output is sensed via thermocouple, which is used to close the loop to the heater controller. In larger, production-worthy systems, heaters are located both above and below the plane of the circuit board and are at least as wide as the conveyor. Thermal uniformity across an 18-in tunnel width can be better than ±5°C on some top-of-the-line ovens. To a large extent, this is a function of the tunnel insulation, heater performance, and convective mixing of the heated air or gas.

Consideration of tunnel dimensions is critical for the application. Short tunnel ovens may not permit a profile adequate for attaining prescribed reflow temperature vs. time slopes for larger, thermally massive PCB assemblies. Tunnel height dimensions must also be adequate to accommodate the tallest components or component heat sinks.

29.6.1.2 *Conveyors.*

There are two main conveyor systems used in today's reflow ovens:

- Pin chain conveyor
- Mesh belt conveyor

One is required and both are recommended for any reflow machine. The pin chain conveyor, also known as an *edge-hold conveyor,* looks like a bicycle chain with a pin protruding inward from certain evenly spaced links, as shown in Fig. 29.5. There is one such chain on each side of the reflow oven. The two chains are driven from a common motor, appropriately geared to ensure that the circuit board is conveyed through the oven evenly and to preclude angling of the board and jamming of same in the oven. The board rests on the pin protrusions on the inner aspect of the chains. With board on pin, the chains transport the printed circuit board through the oven. The chains are slung on rails which parallel and run through the entire oven tunnel. Generally, one rail is fixed within the oven while the other one, parallel to the first, is adjustable with respect to the fixed rail and is movable across the width of the oven tunnel to accommodate various circuit board widths. The conveyors should have sufficient exposure area outside of the oven's tunnel to facilitate manual loading and unloading of the circuit boards.

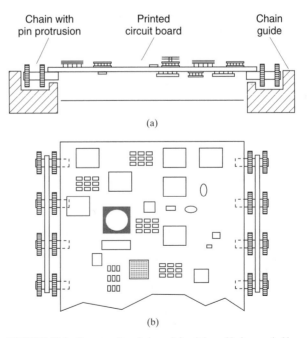

FIGURE 29.5 Cross-sectional view of circuit board being carried by pin chain conveyor: (*a*) The board is held on pin protrusions from the chain links; (*b*) plan view of pin chain conveyor.

Pin chain conveyors are best for circuit boards with components on both sides. Because the circuit board rests on its edges, and contact with the pins is minimal, there should be little thermal influence from the conveyor in a properly designed oven. Since the pin chain does not contact components on either side of the board, induced misregistration of to-be-reflowed or previously reflowed components on the opposite side of the board is minimized. This is sometimes a factor with the mesh conveyor system either through direct contact with the mesh conveyor on side two or from rocking around on the uneven surface of a mesh belt system. When the pin chain conveyor is absent, double-sided boards can be run in pallets to keep reverse-side components from contacting the mesh belt. Any mass added to the reflow process will have an effect on the time-temperature (thermal) profile. The pallet will have such an effect, so its impact will have to be gauged and accounted for.

When reflowing thin, large circuit boards, pin chain conveyance can enhance board sagging which will be quite noticeable after reflow. The sagging is due to thermal excursion above the glass transition temperature (T_g) of the circuit board epoxy during the reflow process. T_g is the temperature at which a partially crystalline polymer will change from a hard structure to a rubbery, viscous state as in the case of FR-4 and like laminate materials.

The T_g of most circuit board laminates is in the range of about 100 to 150°C, well below the peak process temperatures in the reflow of tin-lead solder. Sagging will be pronounced due to the fact that the board was unsupported at its middle as it surpassed its T_g while being supported only by edge hold conveyance. Copper traces within the board provide some support but often not enough to counter this. Sagging alone or together with rail-to-rail nonparallelisms, especially when the rails are at process temperature, can even lead to dropped boards. Many of today's oven manufacturers have suffered through numerous design changes to keep pin chain rails, the guides for the chains, from bowing or twisting when subjected to the differential heating incurred along the length of the tunnel. Most of the major vendors in the reflow oven market have conquered the rail twist problem, but hot testing with precisely toleranced test vehicles should be performed prior to final acceptance of an oven.

Board sagging can be mitigated, to some extent, by means of mechanical stiffeners affixed permanently or temporarily to the circuit board. It should be noted that stiffeners may affect the thermal mass of the board, making reflow more of a challenge. Care should be taken to ensure that the attachment of stiffeners does not interfere either mechanically or thermally with components that may be positioned close to the board edge. Design rules should preclude the use of reflow-challenging components or component fields too close to the circuit edges.

There are potential problems with some types of rail-based board conveyors. Some systems have been seen to be problematic in terms of apparent heat-sinking by the pin chain-rail combination. In some systems, the board is guided through slots on each rail and pushed along by either the conventional pin chain or by upward protruding pins or "fingers" on the chain. These edge-guided systems can have a dramatic impact on the thermal transfer at board edges overheating or heat-sinking, depending on the oven's performance and rail position. Some vendors offer rail heaters to counteract this effect. It is best to avoid this type of system because it adds further complexity to the oven and makes the job of process control all the more difficult.

This should not be a problem with the conventional pin chain conveyor because in actuality the pin chain is only point-contacting the circuit board. Thermal transfer through these points is very poor. Further, most of the newest reflow oven manufacturers have replaced carbon steel chains with stainless steel chains. Stainless steel has better wear characteristics and is a poorer thermal conductor than other commonly available chain materials.

Mesh belts used in reflow ovens are fabricated of coarsely woven stainless steel. The belt traverses the oven tunnel. Mesh belts offer exceptional versatility, as there is no need for adjustment for various board sizes. Mesh belt width is comparable to the full width of the oven's tunnel. Best yet, board dropping is mitigated completely.

The best situation, however, is a combination of conveyors with the pin chain running above a mesh belt. In this case, redundancy can save boards and maintenance time and perhaps can enhance personal safety. The mesh belt here serves as either an optional means of conveyance for boards populated on a single side or as a safety net to catch any boards which may fall off the pin chain conveyor. Were the mesh belt not used in conjunction with the pin chain, any dropped boards would "cook" on the heater assemblies. In doing so, there would be the release of noxious, irritating fumes. Additionally, the heater or heaters affected could become encrusted with the decomposed board laminate, which could impact their thermal performance. If a thermocouple, the sensing instrument for oven temperature control, is damaged or insulated by the laminate decomposition products, overheating of the zone could occur, causing oven damage and manufacturing downtime.

Reflow ovens with silicone edge belts should be strictly avoided as they have been seen to stretch unevenly with use. Being two different lengths, they will necessarily travel at two different speeds, even though propelled from a common motor drive and shaft. This can lead to board canting on the conveyor and eventually conveyor jamming by the board, as shown in Fig. 29.6

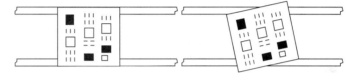

FIGURE 29.6   Plan view of board traveling on polymeric belt oven. If the belts are not traveling at the same speed, the boards will cant and may jam.

29.6.1.3 *Heaters.*   There are several heating schemes used in reflow ovens, the result of years of technological evolution. Focused infrared (IR) lamps have given way to secondary emission panel heaters and, finally, to forced hot-air convective ovens.

IR Heater Types.   Alternative IR heater types are shown in Fig. 29.7. Early ovens utilized focused and nonfocused IR lamps, mounted in the reflow oven tunnel. They bathed the solder paste-coated circuit boards and placed components with a broad spectrum of photonic energy heavily weighted to the IR end of the electromagnetic spectrum. The radiant energy absorbed by the circuit board materials caused the solder and the components on the PCB to heat eventually to the point required for sustained solder reflow and joint formation. As the board traveled beyond the last reflow heaters at the exit end of the oven, board heat was lost to the environment or the boards were actively cooled via forced, unheated air, permitting the molten solder to return to its solid state, completing the soldering cycle.

Since the materials which are introduced into the reflow process (component body materials, lead/pad metallurgies, solders, printed circuit board materials, solder paste fluxes, adhe-

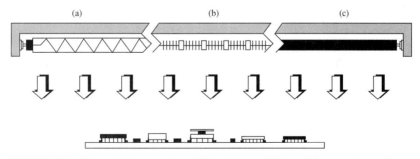

FIGURE 29.7   There are three prominent IR heater types: (*a*) lamp; (*b*) open resistance heater wire; (*c*) resistance rod (calrod-type heater).

sives) are constantly being reformulated by their manufacturers, the notion of a repeatable, predictable reflow process by direct radiation IR must be discarded. Hot spots due to localized IR absorption can result in overheating of some components and portions of the PCB, while other areas may not have seen enough heat to attain reflow. Worse yet, radiant IR heating has caused the loss of much circuit board product revenue through board charring and component body cracking, especially of plastic-packaged ICs. Nearly all major oven manufacturers have ceased building this type of reflow equipment.

IR Panel Heaters. The next evolutionary step in oven design came with secondary IR emitter panels lining the tunnel interior, as shown in Fig. 29.8. These are metal or ceramic platens heated either conductively via attached resistance heaters or by direct IR irradiation of the backside of the panel. During reflow, the circuit board is shielded from direct short-wavelength IR impingement from IR lamps or filament heaters. Instead, it is heated by black-body emission of the heated platen. This type of heating results in much longer wavelength IR emissions, allowing slower heating rates and more even heating, which is a significant improvement over direct IR lamp oven reflow soldering methods.

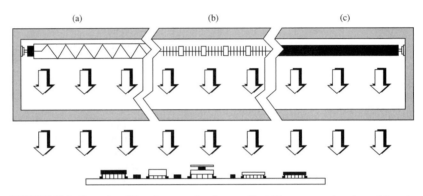

FIGURE 29.8 Secondary IR emitter panels rely on radiant IR sources such as lamp (*a*), resistance wire (*b*), or solid resistance heated rod (*c*). In the case of this type of heating panel, the broad spectrum IR radiation from these sources impinges on an absorbing platen, which itself becomes an emitter. The reemitted radiation is of longer wavelength and is prone to heating the circuit board and component materials more evenly.

A variant of this method is the convective IR oven. This technique also relies on radiant or panel IR heating, but the air in the oven is stirred by fans to enhance uniformity of heating. Today, however, techniques such as IR lamp, IR emitter, and combination convective units have been supplanted by a more favorable method: forced-air convection.

Other Heaters. There are two other heaters which are widely used in today's oven manufacture. The first is an enlarged version of a resistive cartridge heater embedded in a metal-finned or channeled thermal transfer jacket. The other is an open, coiled resistive wire, much as in older (and some new) kitchen ovens. Both of these are used in connection with the forced convection reflow oven, which will be examined next. The latter heater, being of considerably lower thermal mass, is much more responsive than the cartridge-type heater. This is advantageous if the heater control circuits and thermometry methods are suitably matched to this responsiveness. If not, an overtemperature condition can result, which can cause the in-process circuit boards to overheat. Conversely, the embedded cartridge-type heater may be too slow to respond to certain oven-loading conditions such as the first boards in a long queue, especially if the boards are thermally massive. The result is that those first into the oven may not be heated sufficiently, while those just upstream may be overheated, because the heaters respond to the increased thermal mass. In this case, the long time constant associated with the thermally massive, embedded cartridge-type heaters may work against the process goals.

29.6.2 Forced-Air Convection Reflow Oven

This method relies on heated air which is recirculated at high velocity in the oven tunnel. The only direct IR irradiation of the PCBs is by the longest IR wavelength. This radiation is incidental, resulting from blackbody radiation of heated oven components and accounts for only a small fraction of the total board heating. Instead, boards are bathed in heated air which is circulated at high velocity. This method has superior thermal uniformity and controllability of the reflow process. It precludes overheating of the circuit board and/or components caused by preferential absorption, which was a common problem with the old lamp IR reflow ovens. Although the combination IR/convective method has helped in this regard, it is no substitute for the hot-air convection technology which is now rapidly gaining dominance of the reflow oven market.

Top-of-the-line forced-air convection ovens have heating units mounted above and below the board conveyor. Air is heated by either passing the air stream over resistance heaters (such as the cartridge-type heater or the open resistance wire-type heater) through perforated resistance heated platens, or by using a combination of the two. These heaters are either well shielded from the board or the air circulation velocity is high enough to mitigate the effects of any direct or indirect IR impingement on the circuit board. The high-velocity air streams do a remarkable job of evening out the temperature of the air impinging on the PCB. The result is uniform thermal control all through the entire reflow process, as shown in Fig. 29.9, and the tightest process control of any of the heating methods.

29.6.3 Cooling

Some ovens rely upon passive cooling to lower the temperature of the PCB assembly below the solder liquidus point. The board would merely traverse a region of the oven devoid of heaters. This is generally adequate for thin, low-thermal-mass boards. But the reality of today's multilayer, densely packed circuit boards necessitates some means of cooling the board so that upon oven exit, the solder joints are solid. This calls for active cooling of the

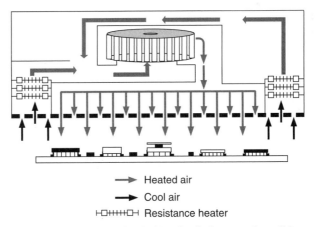

→ Heated air

➡ Cool air

⊢▢┼┼┼┼▢⊣ Resistance heater

FIGURE 29.9 Cross-sectional view of a single convection cell in a reflow oven. Cool air or nitrogen is drawn in from the oven tunnel ambient and passed through resistance heater elements. It is then forced through a diffuser, which baffles the flow and evens its velocity and temperature distribution. In this type of reflow environment, the board is predominantly heated by the forced air. This is an even heating and also avoids direct impingement of short-wavelength IR radiation.

board. Many silicon IC or passive component device manufacturers require a stringent thermal ramp rate that needs to be observed on heat-up or cooldown of the device. The ramp that is generally recommended ranges between 2 and 4°C/s.

Active cooling comes in many forms. Forced-air cooling by fans is the most common. Fans can be deployed on top, bottom, or in combination for board cooling. Among the most exotic but the most efficient is the water-to-gas heat exchanger found in some ovens. This provides a stream of temperature-controlled cool air at the exit end of the oven for board cooldown and has distinct advantages in inert reflow systems). This method can take advantage of whatever process gas is in the oven, cooling it and redirecting it onto the circuit board. This method does not require additional nitrogen for cooling, if running in an inert mode. Further, it precludes the need for cooling fans adjacent to the oven exit. This minimizes air turbulence at that end of the oven. Air turbulence can cause unwanted air entrainment into the oven's inerted environment. Water-to-gas cooling is efficient but it must be included in the reflow profile to ensure that thermal ramp rate is not exceeded.

Some ovens use polymeric "muffin" fans. These must be kept on at all times to prevent overheating of the fan blades and their motor's plastic fan support structure. Others use air rakes or even air amplifiers to direct a flow of cooling compressed air at the board.

29.6.4 Venting

An important and often overlooked reflow oven subsystem is exhaust venting, as shown in Fig. 29.10. This is most important from an industrial hygienic point of view, but it can also have a profound effect on the soldering process itself. There are three good reasons to insist on exhaust venting of any reflow soldering oven. During the soldering process, minute quantities of lead-rich dust may accumulate in the oven atmosphere or coat the oven surfaces. The dangers of prolonged exposure to microquantities of lead or lead salts are well understood, and necessitate venting of any soldering process.

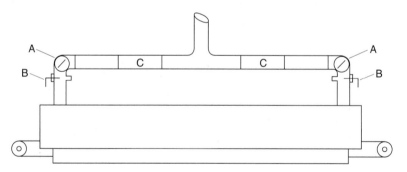

FIGURE 29.10 Oven with exhaust stacks at each end of the oven. Manometers (A) are mounted symmetrically on each branch of the line (C), with blast gates (B) mounted symmetrically in the branches.

29.6.4.1 *Volatiles and Fumes.*   During reflow, solder paste volatilizes and paste reaction products are given up. Since most solder pastes and fluxes are highly guarded proprietary formulations, the paste and flux vendors may neither accurately disclose the composition reagents nor report the decomposition products in the mandated Material Safety Data Sheet (MSDS). Additionally, if a PCB should fall off the pin-chain conveyor or a component should fall through the mesh belt, it may land on a high-temperature surface, either the heater itself or, in the case of forced-air convection reflow machines, on the perforated baffles above the heater assembly. Either board or plastic component will overheat, decompose, and release unpleasant or even dangerous fumes.

29.6.4.2   Venting and Performance.   Note that a high-velocity exhaust may have a profound influence on the performance of the oven. Too much exhaust will cause a significant end-to-end or end-to-middle flow through the oven, which can result in unwanted turbulence in a direction counter to the controlled convective flows established by the oven manufacturer. This will make temperature regulation much more difficult, decrease zone separation, decrease ease of profile establishment, and result in process variability. It is best to follow manufacturer exhaust requirements and recommendations. Further, one should install manometers or other exhaust pressure or exhaust velocity measuring analogs in the exhaust line(s) to monitor its setup and routine performance. This will ensure oven venting consistency for repeatable reflow processing and operator safety.

29.6.4.3   Oven Exhausting Schemes.   There are two types of reflow oven exhausting schemes in wide use today. These are passive and active exhaust systems.

A passive exhaust system comprises an outdoor vented exhaust duct without powered exhaust fan. This method relies upon the chimney effect to vent oven effluent, gaseous or particulate, skyward. Passive system performance is highly dependent on local weather conditions. Temperature inversions, rapid changes in barometric pressure, and wind vector changes will all contribute to a change in venting performance. The vagaries of this system make it undesirable for safe and repeatable oven operation.

Active exhaust denotes the use of some powered device to vent the oven to the outdoors. There are three types in use today:

* Eductor
* Oven-mounted exhaust fans
* Oven-mounted exhaust fans with powered exhaust duct

The eductor relies on a stream of compressed air to run a venturi device which actively draws on the tunnel's atmosphere. In this mode, as in most other exhaust methods, make-up air is entrained through the tunnel entrance and exit openings. The eductor is a noisy and inefficient method of exhausting waste products. Due to small orifice openings of the venturi itself, its performance can be affected by flux or paste residues and should be checked routinely as part of a preventive maintenance program. The eductor effluent is fed into a fanned or unfanned exhaust duct.

Some reflow ovens rely strictly on the fanned exhaust duct. This is one step above the passive system, since exhaust performance is still dependent on the vagaries of prevailing weather conditions. Another of the active exhaust systems is the oven-powered exhaust fan. An integral hood at each end of the oven contains a small fan which withdraws a small, controlled amount of atmosphere from the tunnel entrance and exit. This in turn is blown into the main powered exhaust vent line and pushed out of the building. This system is the most efficient and reliable of the exhaust methods and minimizes meteorological interferences.

Active exhaust systems should be checked to ensure that impeller blades are not being fouled by flux or flux decomposition product residues. Again, the installation of exhaust stack monitors should help pinpoint such problems.

29.6.5   Reflow Oven Characteristics

Reflow ovens are multizoned; i.e., they have multiple heating zones top and bottom, each independently controlled and settable to a different temperature. Some reflow ovens have as many as 24 heaters: 12 top and 12 bottom heater zones. Note that a zone here is the top and opposing bottom heater pair, as shown in Fig. 29.11.

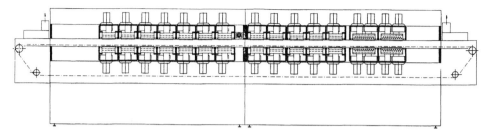

FIGURE 29.11 Forced hot air oven with 12 top and 12 bottom forced-air cells. Each cell is independently heated and controllable. The last two cells on the right are for active cooling of the circuit board as it exits. On this machine, cooling zones are aided by fans blowing over water-cooled radiators, and vent stacks are located at each end. *(Courtesy of Heller Industries.)*

Zone separation, the influence of one thermal zone upon another, is exceptionally important. The ability to separate the influence of one zone from another makes the job of profiling that much simpler and oven performance more predictable.

Temperature uniformity across the width of the tunnel is of primary importance. This will determine the quality and uniformity of the reflow and allows for controllable and consistent soldering. Better ovens will have rail-to-rail thermal uniformity better than ±5°C, even for board widths on the order of 20 in.

Another important characteristic of an oven that requires consideration is the responsiveness of the oven's heaters and accompanying thermal controller circuitry. As a board or multiple boards pass through the oven, the oven's heat is absorbed by those cooler boards on their way to reflow. The oven has to respond to that net loss. The thermocouples built into the oven sense the thermal impact to the tunnel's ambient. The heater controllers try to compensate for the thermal deficit by increasing energy to the heaters. Just as some oven heaters are more responsive than others, so, too, is the circuitry. Today's ovens have reached a high degree of sophistication, including computer-controlled thermostatic circuitry. If matched properly to the job and tuned accordingly, the oven should be able to reflow a train of closely spaced circuit boards just as well as a single board in its tunnel. It is important not to space the boards too closely together. This can fully segregate the top from the bottom heaters and thoroughly alter oven performance. The spacing between boards in a forced-air convection oven must be sufficient to obviate this top-to-bottom divisional isolation of the heater zones. The spacing will be dependent on the throughput and thermal mass dicta of the process line and product designs. Board separation may be as small as a couple of inches, but the effects of board loading and spacing need to be determined empirically and checked to detect any impact on the process temperature vs. time profile. Any assessment of new equipment ought to include load testing to ensure that the oven can handle anticipated process throughput and capacity. The oven's profile needs to be examined before, during, and after loading of the board train.

29.6.6 Reflow Profile

The reflow profile is of greatest importance in the oven soldering process. It is the relationship of temperature with respect to time required to bring a PCB assembly to solder liquidus and back to below the melting point of solder. This profile is dependent on many variables:

- Solder paste composition
- Circuit board composition
    Number of layers
    Board material

- Component types
- Component layout density

The profile in any soldering operation is largely dependent on the solder and flux in use. The solder will dictate the temperature regime, while the solder flux, or more commonly the flux contained in the solder paste, will impose its reflow requirements. Discussion once again will be restricted to reflow of eutectic or near-eutectic Sn-Pb solder, in this case Sn-Pb solder paste.

Paste manufacturers will generally provide a rough estimate of the profile required for each of their solder paste formulations. There is no universal profile recipe for reflow but it should be consistent from batch to batch of a single paste formulation for a given solder assembly or product. Each profile will be determined by the requirements of the solder paste in use. How well the profile is maintained will be dependent on the materials to be reflowed and the process equipment.

There are four distinct regions to a reflow oven to accommodate the requirements of the soldering profile. These are:

1. Preheat/drying
2. Thermal soak or activation
3. Reflow
4. Cooling

Refer to Fig. 29.12 for a depiction of a generalized profile.

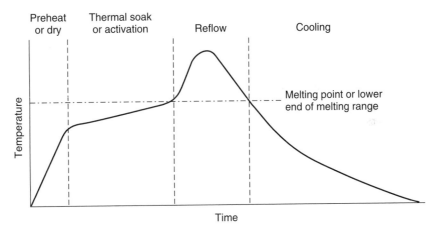

FIGURE 29.12   Generalized oven reflow time-temperature profile.

29.6.6.1 PreHeat/Drying.   The first is the preheat/drying zone in which the paste is relieved of vehicle volatiles. The vehicle regulates the paste viscosity, making it suitable for stenciling or dispensing. If the volatiles are given up too rapidly, then liquids in the paste will boil and cause the paste to spatter, resulting in unattached solder ball formation, as shown in Fig. 29.13. If there is enough explosive boiling, it may adversely affect the local volume of the solder and result in solder opens. If the spattered solder balls are very large or small but prolific, they may result in electrical shorts between two adjacent conductors.

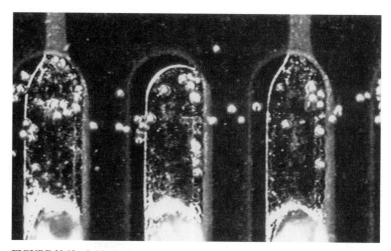

FIGURE 29.13   Solder balls may be loosely attached or they may be partially soldered to one another, with the potential for electric shorting.

Another consideration of presolder heating is that of oxidation. Naturally, the longer the board and devices to be soldered are held at elevated temperature, the greater the oxidation of the metals, including the solder, assuming that the reflow is conducted in an air ambient.

Ramp rate considerations are crucially important in this first step. The board sees its first large thermal differential in this step. The board is cold and is being ramped to about 100°C. There are restrictions, however, on the ramp rate aside from those imposed by the paste's propensity to boil and spatter. The electrical components and their packaging are heat sensitive and can be damaged if the heating rate is excessive. Device manufacturers generally restrict this ramp rate to between 2 and 4°C/s. A heating rate greater than that may cause component cracking, also know as *popcorning,* which is attributed to entrapped water which vaporizes internal to the package, stressing the packaging to its rupture point. This is particularly germane to plastic-encapsulated devices.

Other package types, such as ceramic, may be subjected to thermal shock and differential expansion which can cause packaging failure. Excessive ramps could also be deleterious to the IC itself, either causing it to delaminate from the packaging material, crack, or damage the electrical connections to the die. It is wise to check with the device vendors for the ramp rate specification for each of the devices being reflowed. Take time to measure and analyze the chosen time-temperature profile programmed into the oven to ensure that the heating and cooling ramp rates correspond with those recommendations. Last, qualify the packages for reflow to see that they are meeting the vendor's claims.

29.6.6.2 Thermal Soak.

29.6.6.2   Thermal Soak.   The next step, thermal soak, is a much slower, prolonged heating exposure. It is here that the flux is raised to a temperature sufficient to begin activation. Were the flux to activate very early in the process, it could be spent too soon. If its potency is lost, fluxed metal surfaces may begin to reoxidize in the critical moments before the onset of reflow. This would inhibit solder wetting (alloying) at liquidus, precluding effective solder joint formation. This region of the reflow profile has to be long enough and hot enough to ensure that the flux has time and energy to do its job in terms of stripping the metal surfaces of the component lead, pad, and solder of oxides and surface coatings which would otherwise interfere with the solder wetting process. Overheating the circuit board would stimulate intermetallic formation. This is especially true of copper pads previously treated by the HASL process or plated and reflowed solder or tin coatings. These surface finishes have begun to alloy with the copper which means that an intermetallic layer exists prior to the reflow soldering operation. During the reflow soldering process in which electrical devices are soldered to the circuit board, any intermetallic layer will be augmented by time and temperature, resulting in a yet thicker intermetallic compound buildup. This step also has to be at a low enough temperature and short enough time so as not to degrade the epoxy or other materials of the circuit board. The soak region is generally thought to begin at about 100°C and extend to about 160°C. It is wise to follow solder paste vendor recommendations and trial reflow runs. Those values are only rough guidelines to demonstrate the various aspects of the reflow time-temperature profile.

29.6.6.3 Spike.   The reflow spike is characterized by a rapid rise in temperature to and slightly beyond the liquidus point, as shown in Fig. 29.12 (reflow segment). For eutectic or near-eutectic tin-lead solder, liquidus onset is 183°C. The reflow spike is generally chosen to be well above the melting point of the solder chosen, generally on the order of 25 to 50°C. This temperature overage is to ensure that all the elements to be soldered, including the board, component, and solder, are heated sufficiently for reflow. It is meant to overcome variations in oven performance, compositional variations in the solder itself, and disparity in thermal mass of the board layout/loading. This high temperature also ensures that the solder's viscosity will be low, which will help it wet out on pads and leads, which is the essence of the reflow soldering process.

During this step, the component leads should be awash in liquid solder. If conditions of molten solder viscosity and wetting forces on the leads and pads are adequate, surface tension effects will draw component leads into best registration with circuit board pads.

As mentioned previously, the slope—the rise and fall of the reflow spike with respect to time—is critical. If exceeded, package integrity can be jeopardized, but high ramp rates in the spike step are less common than in the drying step.

29.6.6.4 Cooling.   The fourth and final stage is cooling. It is here that the board's temperature is lowered beyond that of solder liquidus prior to exiting the oven. Once again, recommendations for device heating/cooling ramp rates should be heeded. Most electronic packaging and board materials are reluctant to shed heat quickly. If the board is thick, the laminate, a relatively poor thermal conductor, will remain hot. It must be cooled to below solder liquidus prior to exiting the oven to preclude dislodging of any soldered components. On the other hand, with the trends of thinner circuit boards, slimmer components, and hot-fast profiles (to keep up with high-volume product demand), it is wise to ensure that thermal ramp requirements are considered for this step also.

As mentioned previously, the solder paste manufacturer will provide a recommended profile. This is a starting point only. The reflow engineer should optimize the profile based on actual product runs. Examining older textbooks and industrial references, they cite completeness of fillet formation and solder reflectivity as typical characteristics to examine. But these are subjective measures which may not be true indicators of joint quality. The best measure is tensile pull/peel testing.

If the reflow profile is too hot, i.e., if the the solder is maintained at liquidus for too long a time or at too high a temperature, the ensuing solder joints will be brittle owing to intermetallic buildup. These will be unreliable solder joints and will crack if subjected to either mechanical shock or thermal cycling.

29.6.7 Success in Reflow

There are several factors for successful oven reflow:

1. Adequately suitable, maintained and controlled reflow equipment

2. Good-quality solderable parts

3. Thermally balanced and process-in-mind board designs

4. Reliable solder (including solder paste) and proven thermal profile

5. Good thermometry techniques

29.6.7.1 Adequately Maintained and Controlled Reflow Equipment. The oven should have small thermal differentials across the width of the tunnel and should be capable of adequate heating and cooling ramps as well as adequate zone separation characteristics.

29.6.7.2 Good-Quality Solderable Parts. The best reflow equipment, profiles, and solder paste will not make up for inadequacies in part quality (lead form coplanity) or restore solderability. Extended storage should be avoided and parts should be kept cool and dry prior to use. Sufficient quality control methods should be established to ensure that the solder and components are solderable per vendor claims.

29.6.7.3 Thermally Balanced and Process-in-Mind Board Designs. It is a must for reliable and adequate reflow to ensure, when possible, that thermally massive components are not relegated to one portion of the board. Also, it is desirable to distribute smaller components rather than creating component fields to permit uniform thermal balance across the board. Components should be spaced adequately to prevent shadowing of smaller devices on the board by larger, neighboring components. This is particularly important in IR ovens without the forced convection option. If the oven is characterized by poor uniformity across the tunnel width, the board should be oriented, if possible, to take advantage of the imbalance; i.e., the board edge with greatest thermal mass should be aligned to the oven edge with the highest recorded process temperatures. Board components should be designed far enough away from board edges to preclude any pin-chain conveyor influence on the reflow.

29.6.7.4 Reliable Solder (Including Solder Paste) and Proven Thermal Profile. The profile provided by the solder paste vendor is only a recommended starting point which needs to be optimized for the reflow conditions and process time requirements. Also, recall that solder pastes with finer solder particles are more troublesome to flux owing to their greater total surface area and corresponding greater surface oxide volume per unit volume of solder.

It is important to limit exposure to high temperatures and particularly time above reflow temperature. It is in this regime that intermetallic formation occurs most vigorously for most of the common IMCs that accompany and distress the resulting solder joint. The thicker the IMC layer at the interface of a joint, the more likely the joint is to fail.

29.6.7.5 Good Thermometry Techniques. Understanding the thermal impact of the oven on the board and the board on the oven is critical for a controlled and reproducible reflow process. Thermometry is the only practical method for validating these influences. Some of the most important process nodes benefiting from or requiring adequate thermometric methods are:

- Identifying oven impact to the board as it traverses the oven length

  Heating/cooling ramps and ensuring that they are within the recommended bounds described by the IC and discrete device manufacturers

  Determining peak process temperature and duration

  Considering dependency on the heater types, quantities, cooling methods (whether active or passive), board and component materials, conveyor speed

- Determining how the heat is distributed along the oven's width

  Determining if center or one edge of board heats adequately for reflow while the other edge or center may not be heated sufficiently

- Determining rate at which the oven reacts to the board's presence
- Mimicking the preferred solder paste profile including paste manufacturer recommendations

29.6.8 Product Profile Board

All of the preceding and many more variables have dramatic impact on the soldering process. The only way to assess these is to accurately gauge the thermal energy distribution in the oven in the presence and absence of the board. Most process engineers trust their favorite profiling board to determine the health of their reflow oven or assess the performance of a new oven prior to purchase. The profiling board is simply a thermocouple-instrumented product board or test vehicle which is run through the oven. The thermocouples trace the temperature profile of the oven as seen by the lead or package as the board is conveyed through the oven for reflow.

However, reliance on a product board to determine oven performance may mask some inherent problems with the reflow oven. If the board is not thermally balanced in terms of componentry, it may not be able to detect a strong transverse (rail-to-rail) thermal differential. It is for this reason that a balanced oven diagnostic profiling device should be made and run to assess oven performance. That is not to say that the oven diagnostic board is a direct replacement for the product profiling board. The latter is to verify that the critical sectors of the board or, best yet, device leads are heating per set profile. Thermocouples for this board are deployed at the leading edge, trailing edge, center, and two sides, with the thermocouple beads ideally embedded within the solder joints of disparate component types. Additional thermocouples can be placed on unusually massive components as well as on adjacent smaller components to determine if the large component is thermally shadowing its miniature neighbor. The number of thermocouples deployed will be dependent on the package types, known oven characteristics, board thickness, board layout complexity, etc. The following sections will describe good thermometry practices and the oven diagnostic board, as well as some of the thermocouple measuring innovations which are now a mainstay of large-scale mass reflow manufacturing operations.

29.6.9 Oven Diagnostic Board

The oven diagnostic board can be a very simple or rather complex device. Its job is to probe the normal operating conditions of the oven and determine if all the heaters and circulating fans (if installed) are working to expectation. It is useful in assessing not only the oven's time-temperature profile parallel to the tunnel's long axis but also perpendicular to it at the rail edges. The profiles recorded by this board will not necessarily be translatable to the establishment of a product time-temperature profile. The diagnostic board, whether a product board or a separate test board, is balanced in design. It is designed to preclude thermal imbalance, high thermal conductivity and high thermal mass. These qualities may profoundly affect oven performance and diagnosis of its operating behavior. For this reason, materials are chosen which correspond to these properties. The ideal material will be thermally insulative. Attached to this are thermocouples mounted top-side and bottom in an evenly spaced array across the width of the material. They should be mounted close enough to the conveyor edges to determine how that region is influenced by such things as the conveyor rails or the lateral ends of the heater assemblies. Thermocouple beads should be identical in size and spacing from the insulating material. Further, they should also be mounted slightly off the insulating material such that the heated oven environment can freely swirl around them. The result of measuring with such a device will be the operational condition of the oven, a true picture of the oven's thermal environment.

29.6.10 Printed Circuit Board Thermometry

Knowledge of good thermometry practices and thermocouple use is key to acquiring accurate board time-temperature profiles and oven thermal performance information.

29.6.10.1 Good Thermocouple Practices. Thermocouples are nothing more than two atomically disparate metals in contact with one another. The contact is generally accomplished in one of two ways: twisting the wires tightly together or welding the two. Owing to the thermoelectric effect, when one thermocouple is tied to another held at constant temperature or electronically compensated, the EMF generated by the electronic difference between the two results in measurable voltage which is temperature dependent.

Although thermocouples can be simple to make, as shown in Fig. 29.14, they can also work against the reflow engineer. As previously mentioned, it is only sufficient for the two halves of the couple to touch one another to be useful for thermometry. If the two halves contact inadvertently, thermocouple output will be related to the temperature at that accidental juncture. This temperature may be vastly different from what is being experienced at the far end of the thermocouple pair where one is trying to measure temperature. Thermocouple wire should be welded to help preclude metric ambiguity. The two halves of the thermocouple pair should touch at only one point—that closest to the area desired for temperature measurement. Avoid the twisted pair.

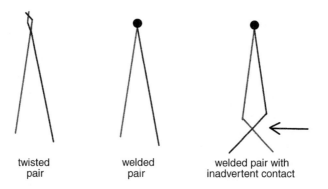

twisted pair   welded pair   welded pair with inadvertent contact

FIGURE 29.14 Diagram of welded pair vs. twisted pair, and welded pair with inadvertent contact.

The welded pair has a significant advantage in that the resulting weld bead can be made small and uniform in shape. As a rule of thumb, the bead diameter can be made as small as about 1.5 times the diameter of the individual conductors which compose the thermocouple. The temperature will be sensed only at the weld bead. The twisted pair output may not be so unambiguous and is rarely as small. Regardless of whether you are making your own welded bead assemblies or buying them, always check them, with a magnifier or microscope if necessary, to ensure that there are no other contacts between the legs of the thermocouple wires other than at the bead. During manufacture of a thermocouple assembly, it is usual practice to twist the thermocouple wires together prior to welding. Upon welding, the twisted material will fuse and melt back. It may be necessary to untwist the pair just behind the bead. Of course, this is risky because many of the thermocouple materials are brittle before welding and are even more so after. On the other hand, any twist below the bead will have the greatest influence on the measured temperature, regardless of how well the bead is formed or positioned.

The most common thermocouples used for mass reflow thermal assessment are of the K type. This is a Ni-Cr/Ni-Al or chromel/alumel couple and has a thermal measurement range which is well suited to that experienced in the reflow cycle of the most commonly used solder systems. There are two main devices in use for measuring the output of the thermocouple. The most primitive is the electronic (digital) thermometer with output tied to a chart recorder. The other—much more sophisticated—is the reflow profiler or tracker, an electronic package which can not only output the time-temperature plot of multiple thermocouples but can also make certain assessments of the data such as:

- Heating ramp rate
- Time below liquidus
- Time above liquidus
- Cooling ramp rate

Tracker systems are computer based and can generate detailed reports and graphs of a reflow cycle.

29.6.10.2 Thermocouple Deployment.   The size and deployment of the thermocouple is important, especially when trying to gauge the temperature of very small solder joints. There are many opinions and methods for securing the thermocouple bead to the PCB. Among those which have been suggested are:

- Adhesives
- High-temperature solders
- Tape
- Pressure contact

Recall that the goal is to ensure that all lead/solder/pad combinations are being exposed to enough thermal input for sufficient time to effect robust solder joints. Therefore, thermocouples adequately positioned on a product profile board should be able to monitor this process, ensuring an adequate profile. But there are numerous interferences which can preclude this from happening. Many items on the preceding list are, in fact, not adequate for the job. By examination of those suggested thermocouple hold-down techniques and materials, it is evident from a fundamental chemical and physical perspective that many on that list could be problematic.

As in every other facet of engineering, one should keep in mind the end goal and the fundamental phenomena that are operant in the process—even in a process as simple as thermometry of a circuit board. In fact, the board temperature is only one piece of the equation. Most important are the solder joints of the most demanding and disparate components on the circuit board. Let us start with the assumption that understanding the thermal behavior of a potential solder joint during the reflow process by thermocouple thermometry requires that certain criteria be met:

1. The thermocouple bead must be exposed to the same thermal conditions as for the solder joint reflow process.
2. There can be but one junction between the two legs of the thermocouple and that junction is closest to the object(s) to be measured.
3. The measuring technique must not interfere with the outcome of the measurement.

From the first assumption, it should be obvious that the thermocouple bead must be in the vicinity of the lead/pad combination. Where better than between the device lead and the circuit board bonding pad? After all, that is where the solder joint will result. The second has been described previously but should always be checked before and after measurement. In keeping with the third assumption, there are many factors which can confound the solder joint temperature measurement process, regardless of whether the thermocouple bead is properly deployed between lead and pad. Among these are the size of the bead and the thermal mass of the thermocouple assembly. In general, use fine-gauge thermocouples such as 20 to 36 AWG. See Table 29.1 for examples of wire size and bead diameter.

TABLE 29.1   AWG vs. Wire Diameter and Anticipated Thermocouple Bead Diameter

AWG	Wire diameter, in	Bead diameter, in
20	0.032	0.048
24	0.020	0.030
30	0.010	0.015
36	0.005	0.0075

Also strive for the shortest possible length of thermocouple wire pair which is practical for the application. This will be discussed later. The finer gauges such as 30 AWG will allow insertion between lead and pad even at very fine lead/pad pitches. Mechanically flattening the bead with a small hammer, vise, press or smooth-jaw pliers will enhance its placement between lead and pad.

If an adhesive is to be used to immobilize the thermocouple bead, its characteristics must be taken into account. It must be able to survive the reflow cycle. Were it to release the thermocouple bead during the process, then measurement data would be useless. Most adhesives will not tolerate the >200°C regime of a typical reflow cycle. Some of the UV curables will. Most of the fast-setting epoxies and adhesives (methyl methacrylate super glues) decompose below that temperature or at least soften to the point that they could not be trusted for bead hold-down. Further, it is important that if an adhesive is used that its thermal transfer properties must be understood. Some are characteristically insulative and inhibit exposure of the thermocouple to the true thermal environment. The best-case adhesive would be temperature compatible and filled with a fine, thermally conductive material such as some metals or high-thermal-fluence ceramic. There are few of these, though, which are both commercially available or affordable.

29.6.11 Reflow Profilers or Tracker

In tracker or profiler systems, the thermocouples on the circuit board are attached to a battery-powered, thermally insulated electronics box, the tracker, which accompanies the circuit board through the reflow cycle. Once a selected threshold temperature has been reached, such as 30°C, the tracker begins recording the experienced thermal environment per unit time. It samples and records the circuit board's thermocouples at short, programmable time intervals (several times per second) for the entire trip through the oven's tunnel. When the tracker emerges from the exit end of the oven's tunnel, it is removed from its protective thermal barrier and connected to the host computer following the reflow run. The data stored in the electronic tracker can be conditioned, displayed, reported, and printed for analysis. The user defines the reporting format, including the type of data sought, thermocouple plots, and other relevant, run-related data. One system is even able to output its data telemetrically as it is being recorded in the oven. Some systems are capable of making predictive corrections to the profile based on current measured conditions and recorded oven settings. This can further enhance the ease of adjusting a complex multizoned reflow oven to meet the requirements of a particular job. Whether simple or complex models are selected, these systems are invaluable for accurate reflow profiling and process repeatability.

When using an electronic tracker, its presence in the oven may have an impact on the resulting profile data. It may have an effect on the local aerodynamics within the oven. The tracker has thermal mass. Some are covered with insulative blankets while others may have a stainless steel cover with insulation beneath. In either case, one should determine empirically what influence the tracker has on the oven performance and measured reflow profile. To do this, use long thermocouple wires and, once the oven has warmed to a steady-state operating condition, run the profile tracker with the tracker a fixed distance behind the board.

Note: Trackers are usually placed to follow the board in reflow. Were it to precede, it may cause the heaters to ramp up as the oven attempts to compensate for the thermal mass of the tracker. Although that is what happens during a reflow cycle as a cooler board enters a heated zone of the oven, the oven would attempt to compensate for the board's thermal mass. The added thermal mass or disruption of the air flows from the profile tracker would not be a factor in the normal reflow process.

Once the profile is recorded, shorten the distance between the tracker and the board and once again record the oven's performance profile and compare it to the first in this series. Keep repeating this until the distance between the tracker can be standardized, adding some length as a safety factor.

29.6.12 Atmospheres for Reflow

The most common reflow atmosphere is ambient air. It is either passively entrained into the reflow tunnel or is heated and blown into the tunnel as in forced-air convection ovens. Air, especially at high temperatures, will cause most metals to oxidize, so the soldering flux in the system has to work very hard to remove native oxidation on the lead, pad, and solder as well as to prevent further oxidation at all phases of the reflow cycle until all elements of the joint (pad, lead) are wetted by the solder. Moist air is more of an oxidizing agent than dry air. Another item that can be subject to oxidation is the flux itself. Oxidation imparts a variability to the soldering process which is difficult to control except with the strongest solder-fluxing formulations. These highly activated fluxes are not generally used for electronic manufacturing. They are linked to reliability problems of the final electronic assembly; the main problem is corrosion from flux residues which have not been properly removed from the circuit board.

Were one to control the level of oxygen in the reflow process, weaker formulations of solder fluxes could be used with better success. Less oxidation would occur during the process. The flux could work on the oxides native to the metallurgy and would not be required to tackle an onslaught of atmospheric oxygen and its detrimental effect on the reflow process.

In many classical soldering texts there is discussion of how reflowing in an inert environment, such as nitrogen (N_2) can have profound effects on wetting. These texts describe the effect as surface-tension related. This is correct in a sense but seems to be widely misunderstood in the soldering community, because it is not that the surface tension of liquid solder varies much between an 80 percent N_2 atmosphere as in air and a pure (100 percent) N_2 ambient. Instead, the solder, when exposed to a mixture of N_2 and O_2 (~20 percent), rapidly develops a skin of oxide. This encapsulation has a profound effect on the underlying solder, preventing it from wetting and spreading unencumbered. It is not the same as water and ice having vastly different surface tension values. That is a one-material system. In the case of oxidized liquid solder, it is a two-material system. It is true that, even as the solder flux is working, there are rafts of predominantly tin-rich oxide afloat on the solder's surface. These can inhibit the solder from spreading and can even insulate it from wetting to adjacent metal surfaces.

In summary, the greatest effects of soldering in an inert or reduced oxygen atmosphere are as follows:

- The prevention of further oxidation of the metals component of the soldering system
- The elimination of oxidation of the flux itself
- Better fluxing action resulting in cleaner parts
- More thorough fluxing and dissolution of metal oxide rafts on the surface of the solder
- Lower level of residues when using no-clean solder paste formulations
- Reduction of tombstoning

- Better compensation for misalignment due to higher wetting forces
- Reduction of solder ball formation
- Fewer voids in the solder joint
- Less board discoloration

This last item is perhaps of little value, as board discoloration is rarely a concern. It used to be of much more concern in the older IR ovens where occasionally boards would char.

Unfortunately there is ambiguity in the reports as pertains to the reflow parameters, inerting levels, impact on manufacturing costs, and resultant soldering yields. There is, however, universal agreement that N_2 betters the soldering joint formation process.

Forced-air convection is, in a sense, the best and worst circumstance for reflow soldering. By far, it is the most uniform approach to heating a circuit board and has rapidly gained status as the preferrable machine. But it is the very nature of this reflow method which detracts from the process. As a metallurgical system is heated in the presence of air, it is more prone to oxidation. This method delivers a continuously replenished supply of air blown at the metal surfaces and the circuit board at high velocity. This ensures maximum oxidation of the soldering system elements. This may be in part counteracted by the thorough and uniform heating of the board by this type of oven.

Forced-convection systems are also notably hard to inert. In this type of oven, when specially configured for nitrogen convective recirculation, fresh air is not blown in. Instead, nitrogen is metered in lowering the oxygen content of the oven's atmosphere. The inherent turbulence internal to the oven can enhance entrainment of room ambient air. Special precautions are taken to prevent this from happening. Most oven manufacturers have inert reflow oven models, each with their own special inerting improvements installed.

Oven mass reflow will continue to dominate surface-mount manufacturing for many years to come. The sophistication of today's machines appears to be sufficient for future needs.

29.7 WAVE SOLDERING

Once the predominant method for mass assembly of circuit boards, this technique has taken a back seat to oven-based reflow. The rise in popularity of surface-mount along with a greater variety of surface-mountable packages, especially in the finer-pitch range {≤1.27 mm (0.05 in)}, has displaced much of the work done by this method. Nonetheless, through-hole componentry persists and mixed-mount (surface-mount plus through-hole) still may be the only alternative for some double-sided assemblies. It is unlikely that this soldering technique will disappear from PCB manufacturing.

Wave soldering utilizes a reservoir of molten solder pumped and circulated to form a standing wave. The circuit board with components affixed to it by means of adhesive for side #2 inserted, coarse-pitch surface-mounted components or with side #1 through-hole components inserted and clinched is fluxed, preheated, and passed over the molten solder wave with only the bottom surface of the board in contact with the wave's crest, as shown in Fig. 29.15.

Solder from the wave is accumulated on all solder-wettable surfaces and is drawn by capillary action into the through-hole barrels of the PCB. Once over the wave, the board temperature decreases, solidifying the solder and bonding components to the circuit board. Figure 29.16 shows the cross section of a through-hole pin which has been wave soldered.

29.7.1 Types of Wave-Soldering Systems

There are many types of wave-soldering systems, each with its unique advantage as claimed by the manufacturer. The soldering engineer has to assess these improvements as they relate to the type of assembly being soldered. The technology has matured significantly but the

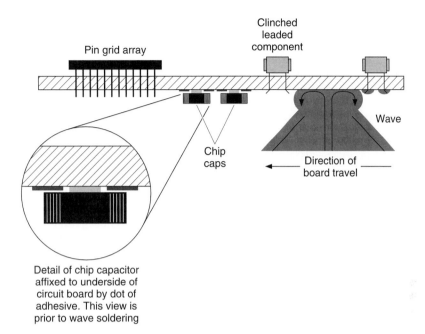

FIGURE 29.15 Diagram of combined SMT and through-hole board going over wave, with detail of glued chip capacitor and clinched leaded component.

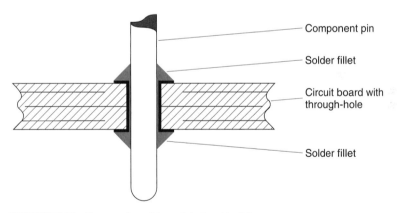

FIGURE 29.16 Cross section of through-hole solder joint.

degree of equipment complexity attests to the process complexity. There are many process variables associated with this operation. If not understood or properly controlled, wave-soldering defects such as skip soldering (electrical opens) and bridges (electrical shorts) will occur as in any other soldering operation. Another increasingly important defect is the influence of side #2 wave soldering on side #1 surface-mounted components. It is possible to re-reflow those side #1 SMDs, inducing opens or solder-starved joints. It is most commonly associated with thin, densely populated, double-sided, PWBs with fine-pitch surface-mount devices such as quad flat packs which are soldered on the opposite side from the wave. Thermal conduction from the wave through-vias and along electrical traces in and on the board provide enough heating to causes parts previously soldered to re-reflow. Solder can be drained away, wicked up side #1 surface-mount component leads or down traces and through-vias. This can result in an open or weakly soldered joint with an hour-glass shaped attachment of solder from the bottom of the lead to the bonding pad.

29.7.2 Flux Application for Wave Soldering

One of the key subprocesses of wave soldering is the application of flux. There have been many developments in this area. The most important criterion is the uniform application of a sufficient quantity and activity for the job at hand. Short preheat and liquidus times, characteristic of the wave-soldering process, may not meet the time-temperature requirements of some fluxes. This is particularly the case with no-clean fluxes, as they are generally the weakest of fluxing agents and may not have adequate time during the wave process to work at removing the metal oxides.

The flux must be heated to an ample temperature to permit best reactive conditions without drying it out or denaturing it. For the sake of economy, the thinnest application practicable is necessary such that the board will have sufficient flux to remove innate oxides on surfaces to be soldered but will be limited in quantity to minimize the remaining residues which may be difficult to clean. In the case of no-clean fluxes, thick applications of flux may leave unacceptably dense residues which may be difficult to penetrate when the boards are probed at the electrical test step.

Flux quantity may also be of concern in the wave-soldering process for yet another reason: fire hazard. Flux-laden boards are preheated going into the wave. If the flux application is too heavy, the flux may drip on to preheater elements. This may cause the flux to volatilize rapidly, combine with oxygen in the atmosphere, and provide the right conditions for flame initiation. Even if there is not direct exposure of the liquid flux to preheaters, if the quantity of volatile, flammable components is high enough in the vicinity of an ignition source, then an explosive condition may develop.

29.7.3 Flux Application Techniques

Wave and foam fluxing still seem to be the most popular techniques, although the number of proponents for other methods is steadily growing.

29.7.3.1 Foam Fluxers.   Foam fluxing is done by flowing and aerating a stream of liquid flux through a porous metal nozzle, a fritted glass, or porous stone. The nozzle, also called a chimney, shapes the flow of the aerated flux stream. The board to be soldered is run over the flux foam and then heated to activate the flux before reaching the solder wave. As it moves past the solder wave, the solder wets to solderable metals and solidifies to complete the soldering process. Foam fluxing is particularly effective for soldering of plated-through-hole assemblies. The foam, drawn into the plated-through-hole barrels, thinly and uniformly fluxes the walls of the plated barrel, on component leads in the barrel, and on any surface-mounted discrete components which are in contact with the foamed flux.

29.7.3.2 Wave Fluxers.   Wave fluxers work much as the solder wave itself. The printed circuit board is moved over a standing wave of solder flux. The height of the wave and depth of the board penetration into the wave are adjusted to allow for proper flux application thickness. Capillary action, as in all the fluxing methods for through-hole components, draws the flux into the space between the component lead and the barrel.

29.7.3.3 Spray Fluxers.   Spray fluxing has gotten to be an accurate technology. Precise amounts of a low-solids flux can be applied generally to a board or can be selectively delivered to small areas of the board to be soldered. One of the difficulties associated with this technique is the formulation and consistency of the flux. Very volatile flux solvents must be used to thin it sufficiently for spray application. Therefore, flux formulation and maintenance is much more critical. Fluxes meant for this method of deposit may be slightly more expensive than for other flux deposition methods. This method also brings with it the burden of more maintenance, especially in terms of system cleaning. It is messy, due mostly to the airborne mist and condensed volatiles which deposit wherever the air or process gases carry them. Fire hazard is also maximized. Ultrasonic methods minimize flux volumes consumed in manufacturing.

29.7.3.4 Fluxer Maintenance.   As fluxes are exposed to the atmosphere, they are vulnerable to evaporation of the volatile constituents. Of course, this is enhanced in systems such as wave, spray, or foam fluxers where the flux is open to the atmosphere or processing environment, have significant exposed flux surface area, and are constantly recirculated. This necessitates monitoring and maintenance of the flux. Although some automatic systems are now available, most require routine measurement and adjustment of the flux's specific gravity. A hydrometer is generally used for specific gravity determination. Flux thinner must be added to restore the specific gravity to compensate evaporative losses. In addition, the volume of the flux in the system must be adjusted to the proper level. The fluxer must be maintained to prevent impact to process yield. The flux manufacturer will provide information as to the target specific gravity per flux and will also recommend an appropriate thinning formulation.

It is wise to periodically empty the flux reservoir, clean it thoroughly, and refill with a fresh charge of flux. Sometimes the flux will develop a polymeric residue which will change its surface tension characteristics or clog nozzles or dispensing pores in foaming systems. In addition, it may become contaminated with debris carried in by the PCB to be soldered. These, too, will impact assembly quality. Since the plated-through-hole relies on a minute capillary to be filled first by flux and ultimately by solder from the solder-wave process, any small particulates entrained in the flux, or the solder for that matter, may be forced into the interstice between the through-hole component lead and the through-hole barrel, thus inhibiting solder filling of the barrel. Also, while the flux reservoir is empty, it is a good idea to inspect it to ensure that the materials of construction are holding up to the rigors of system operation and prolonged contact with fluxing agents which may be corrosive in the long term. An inspection of the materials of construction for the entire system should be made prior to committing to the purchase of a wave-soldering machine. Unfamiliar or untested materials should be avoided unless there is sufficient literature, test results, or experience to assure compatibility with fluxes which will be used in that system.

29.7.4 Preheat

As previously discussed in the fundamentals of soldering, heat is a significant component of the soldering process from three points of view:

1. The heat must be sufficient to melt the solder.
2. Materials (components and PCB) must be hot enough to permit alloying of the solder to the board.
3. The flux must reach a high enough temperature to allow its activation, reaction, and disruption of oxides and tarnishes on the metals of the materials to be soldered.

This last step, PCB/flux heating (part of the preheating stage), is exceptionally important to the wave-soldering process. A component's resident time in the solder wave is brief; in fact, its time at liquidus is 10 to 30 times shorter than for joint formation in a comparable oven reflow soldering cycle. By the time the circuit board and associated componentry hits the wave, it must be fluxed sufficiently to allow adequate solder joint formation. The preheater is responsible for this in the wave process. It brings metal surfaces up to a temperature at which the flux can start its work to remove the oxidation which can perturb soldering. There must be enough flux left on the circuit board after preheat to protect the newly fluxed surfaces to permit soldering when the assembly reaches the solder wave. As for any step in circuit board soldering, there are several process choices, although the method used for preheating will be dictated by the equipment and available options. Often the type of equipment purchased will limit types of preheaters available. Preheating is also critical in the avoidance of component cracking due to thermal shock when they contact the molten solder wave. In the case of thermally massive printed circuit boards, if not sufficiently preheated, they may soak up so much heat from the wave that rapid, localized solidification at the wave's surface may occur. This can cause widespread solder shorts because it affects the surface tension–defined meniscus from wave to board.

Just as in reflow soldering systems, there are two systems in prevalent use. These are radiant preheaters (direct and indirect IR) and forced-air convective preheaters. Both are effective, although the advantages of the latter are significant in terms of uniform heating of the components and board materials. An in-depth discussion and comparison of these two heating methods can be found in Sec. 29.6.

29.7.5 The Wave as a Process

There are numerous solder wave styles which are touted. A detailed discussion of each will not be presented here, but a basic overview of the process in relation to the wave will be presented. As previously mentioned, the molten solder is pumped to form a standing wave. This is accomplished by an impeller in the bottom or side of the solder reservoir. Once the solder is molten, the impeller motor is activated and the solder wells up between baffles and nozzle which reside within the solder reservoir, dictating overall wave dimensions. The nozzles and baffles are generally adjustable, as are impeller speed, molten solder temperature, board introduction angle, and board conveyor velocity. These, along with preheater settings, define the profile parameters or process variables which must be tamed to accomplish high-yield wave soldering.

Since the solder is a molten liquid, it is an excellent thermal conductor; therefore, uniformity of the wave temperature is generally not difficult to control. But hot solder is prone to rapid oxidation at the air-liquid solder interface. Although the wave is in constant motion, the solder is actually flowing beneath a stationary film. Thin and plastic, the skin is composed chiefly of tin oxide but also contains oxidized lead and other contaminants. These impurities which form on or float to the surface in the reservoir are broadly encompassed by the term *dross*. The skin has a beneficial aspect in that it helps to limit oxidation of the constantly recirculating wave. When adjusted properly, the board meets the crest of the wave disrupting this skin. In doing so, the fluxed components and board are immersed in the flowing, oxide-free molten solder. The solder will wet to these component leads, and solder joints will result on removal from the wave and cooling below the solder liquidus temperature.

29.7.6 Dross

The more the system is used to solder boards, the faster the contamination and dross buildup. The dross is of concern from three points of view:

1. *Economic*   Dross is solder lost from the manufacturing process. In high-volume manufacturing, it can mean hundreds of dollars of lost solder per week per machine. The dross can be returned to some solder founders for recycling, however.

2. *Process*   Excessive dross on the surface of the solder can disrupt normal wave dynamics. Since tin oxidizes more easily than lead, the solder can become tin depleted over the long term. This is known as *tin drift*.

3. *Hygienic*   Airborne tin and lead oxide fines are not healthy to breathe. Risks associated with lead oxide intake are well documented, but inhalation of any particulate should be considered potentially hazardous. Precautions should be taken, especially during system maintenance procedures, to preclude health-related problems. Donning a personal particulate mask and washable or disposable outergarment (contamination suit) is recommended. So too is proper hygienic venting of the work area, not only during maintenance procedures but for normal soldering operation.

Dross over the reservoir is predominantly tin-rich oxide accompanied by lead oxide. Molten solder droplets can become entrapped in the dross, a result of wave turbulence and mixing of the oxides with the liquid solder. Once oxidized, they are unable to rejoin solder in the reservoir. This thickened layer can impact wave-soldering results, especially if rafts of dross are entrained in the wave. They interfere by blocking the solder wave from effectively contacting land and lead. Opens result. They can also change the dynamics at the wave/land/lead interface, discouraging adequate pull-back of the solder and encouraging solder-induced electrical shorts (bridges). Various schemes have been devised to tame the dross, such as comixing the pumped solder with a mineral oil which floats to the surface, blanketing the solder from the atmosphere. Liquid reducing agents can be added to the solder, as well as fluxes. In the long term, none of these have proven popular. Inerting is effective in reducing dross formation and ensuring best fluxing from no-clean or other weakly activated fluxes. Nitrogen as a cover gas has become the most effective method of dross management.

Iman, et al.,[1] have explored the use of formic acid in gaseous form as an additive to the nitrogen atmosphere for the soldering process. The nitrogen-formic atmosphere not only prevents dross formation, but also thins and removes the oxide on the parts to be soldered and on the surface of the wave itself. In that work, formic's action was supplemented with adipic acid, a weak, water-soluble organic acid serving as a liquid flux. The fundamentals of this process were demonstrated by Hartmann[2] who had shown formic acid to be an effective gaseous fluxing agent for soldering.

29.7.7 Metals Contaminants

Metals contaminants can also have an effect on wave soldering. They are generally a result of the soldering process itself. As the circulating wave washes over component leads and PCB through-hole lands and pads, there is a leaching of their materials into the wave. Even if leads and pads are solder plated or coated, there is the opportunity for adulteration of the solder in the reservoir, dependent on coating composition, thickness, and underlying basis metals. Copper, gold, silver, additional tin or lead, as well as intermetallic compound precipitates are all common contaminants derived from the slight dissolution of lead and pad or coatings thereon during soldering. Of course, their contamination level is very small on a per-board basis, but in high-volume manufacturing the quantities can rapidly rise. Even in low-volume applications, if the solder pot contents are not changed frequently enough, the solder and resulting joints can be of inferior quality. Solder pot contamination can have significant process impact, eventually altering the liquidus temperature or melting range of a solder. This may lead to an increase in shorts or opens. It may also result in brittle solder joints. The composition of the wave reservoir can be assayed by a testing service to determine its impurity content. A small sample of the solder can be scooped out to check its solidus and liquidus points (melting range), although this is a less accurate method for contamination assessment and will not be adequate for assaying some impurities such as intermetallic precipitates.

Excessively high temperatures in the solder reservoir and low speeds through the wave should be avoided to limit dissolution of lead, pad, and through-hole metals. Note, though, that the solder wave is maintained at fairly high temperatures, often above 250°C. Board exposure is short (2 to 8 s). In fact, the board generally experiences less thermal impact than in the oven reflow process, where the entire board is maintained at solder reflow temperature for 30 to 120 s, typically. As in oven reflow, thermal shock in wave soldering can lead to component cracking or degradation problems. So the preheating rate should be tempered such that the maximum slope corresponds to that recommended by the component manufacturer, often in the range of 2 to 4°C/s.

29.7.8 Design for Wave Solder

In many plants, defect levels at the wave step are now higher than those of the oven mass reflow process. Although wave soldering has been around for a long time, it is still not very well understood, due mainly to the various machine configurations and number of process variables. There are numerous wave designs available from the various wave-solder machine manufacturers. There are wave machines which provide multiple, smaller, turbulent wave(s), which are best for leadless components such as surface-mount chip resistors and capacitors. Smoother flowing waves are recommended for leaded components, through-hole as well as coarse-pitch surface-mount devices. Wave dynamics are dictated by process values as well as the materials in contact with the wave. As the solder wets to the circuit board materials, solder wetting contact angle and solder viscosity will impose wave peel-off characteristics, as shown in Fig. 29.17. In extreme cases, the wave crest can be caused to collapse on itself or snap back and disrupt the process, promoting unwanted solder bridges (shorts).

Hot-air knives, jets of hot air directed at the wave-air-solder interface on the bottom side of the board, are sometimes deployed to help the solder drain from the components and separate from the board. This discourages solder bridge formation between adjacent leads/pads.

Pin fields in components such as pin grid arrays (PGAs), have grown large and pitches smaller. The introduction of the interstitial pin grid array (IPGA), also known as the staggered pin grid array, has caused a reexamination of wave dynamics. This device has pins positioned interstitial to the normal field of a PGA, as shown in Fig. 29.18). As the wave moves through this frustrated pin field, areas of fluid flow stagnation may occur and opens or insuf-

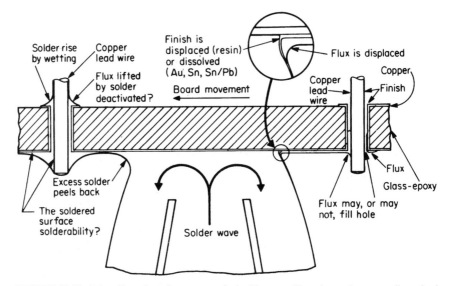

FIGURE 29.17   Printed board passing over a typical solder wave. Note the tendency to pull a web of solder from the wave as the board passes over. (*Alpha Metals, Inc.*)

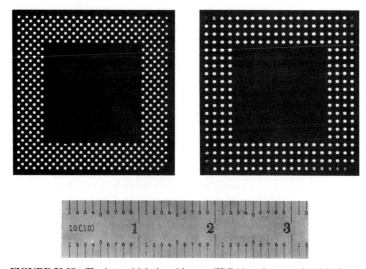

FIGURE 29.18   The interstitial pin grid array (IPGA) package on the right has a higher pin density than the orthogonal PGA, which frustrates solder flow, making it more prone to opens and bridges, and requiring a higher degree of process understanding and control.

ficient solder may result. In contrast, the IPGA may not drain solder well enough in other areas, causing solder bridge formation. There are numerous wave designs which are aimed at improving the soldering yields of these large packages, but the final choice is not yet clear.

In designing circuit boards for the wave-soldering process, it is important to anticipate the flow of the wave over the board. It is wise to avoid placing tall components in front of short component fields. Component spacing should be maximized. In both cases, the problem is the occlusion of solder from the wave. The taller component may shadow the flow of the wave, causing areas of flow eddying in the vicinity of shorter components behind it. Also, via placement should be as far away from the leads as is practical to avoid the aforementioned problems of re-reflow. This phenomenon has been known for a while but only recently reported.[3,4] Component spacing from the edge of the board will be dictated by wave flows and surrounding structure. There are no hard rules here, only hard lessons. Each machine is different, just as every wave has its own peculiarity and every PCB its own unique topography. System familiarity and experimentation with test boards are required to determine the efficacy of various circuit board design features and their impact on the wave process.

Kear's review of the thermal aspects of through-hole solder joint formation offers a glimpse of the physical phenomenon of the wave-soldering process.[5] A number of papers and patents have recently been written regarding this development.[6-9]

29.8   VAPOR PHASE REFLOW SOLDERING

Until very recently, vapor phase reflow was popular but not in as widespread use as oven reflow soldering. Because of safety and environmental concerns and compliance with the Montreal Protocol for the reduction of ozone-depleting chemicals, this soldering technique has fallen out of favor. Due to this diminished status, vapor phase reflow will be covered only in abbreviated fashion.

29.8.1 Basic Process

As in any other reflow technique, the board must be supplied with sufficient solder for joint formation. Most commonly, solder paste is stenciled onto circuit board pads. Components are placed onto the solder paste in preparation for reflow. The board is conveyed into the reflow chamber where it is exposed to the vapor phase of a boiling liquid. This liquid is inert with respect to the solder and board. It is a dense synthetic of high boiling point—slightly higher than that of solder liquidus but not high enough to damage the circuit board or components. Chlorofluorocarbons, hydrochlorocarbons, and hydrochlorofluorocarbons were used for this purpose. Some of these cost several hundred dollars per pound. In batch processors, a CFC was used as a cover gas to retard evaporation of the very expensive reflow medium. When conditions are optimized, the hot vapors begin to condense on the cooler PWB, heating it. As the process progresses, sufficient energy for sustained solder reflow results. Solder wets to lead and pad and, as the board is removed from the hot vapor, the molten solder solidifies, bonding component leads to circuit board pads.

29.8.2 Machine Subsystems

The vapor reflow soldering machine is composed of three main subsystems: conveyor, reservoir/vessel, and heaters. Most interesting to note is the fact that the vessel has cooling coils surrounding it, placed well above the level of the liquid in the reservoir. These condense the vapors, returning the majority to the reservoir, as shown in Fig 29.19.

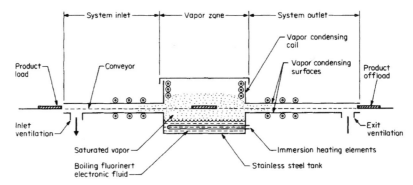

FIGURE 29.19 In-line single-vapor heating system schematic. (*Reprinted with permission from* Electronic Packaging and Production, *November 1982, p.63, Fig. 1.*)

29.8.3 Advantages/Disadvantages

The process has some distinct advantages. It is exceptionally uniform in heating and is also very precise in temperature. Problems associated with varying topologies and areas of high thermal mass are not a problem for this method of reflow as is the case in wave soldering or oven reflow. Since the reflow is occurring in a relatively inert atmosphere, joint quality can be excellent. Fluxes of lower activation levels are required than those for processing a comparable assembly in air-ambient oven reflow. Although vapor phase reflow has the appearance of being a fast process, there are some hidden time factors which must be considered. First, the use of solder paste dictates a preheat just as in other reflow processes. If the paste is heated too rapidly, paste volatiles may boil, resulting in explosive solder ball formation. Also, preheating is required to preclude damage to components. As in other soldering methods, the maximum heating ramp rate has to be commensurate with component manufacturer recommendations. Plastic package popcorning is pronounced with this method of reflow.

CFC restrictions top the list of negative attributes which, for the most part, have driven this technology off the manufacturing floor. The liquids used in vapor phase reflow are expensive. With their continued recycled use, there are toxic materials formed such as hydrofluoric acid and perfluorisobutylene. These must be neutralized and their by-products must be disposed of properly.

When massive, densely populated boards are introduced to the vapor reflow oven, another well-known problem can occur: vapor collapse. This is characterized by a condensation rate which outpaces that of vaporization. The result is that the internal atmosphere of the oven thins dramatically to the point that it cannot sustain adequate reflow. Vapor phase machines which relied on immersion heaters were prone to this phenomenon. More recent machines include massive heating element housings which provide sufficient thermal inertia to preclude this problem.

Increased incidence of tombstoning, solder ball formation, and component displacement have been noted in this method of reflow. Hutchins pointed out that the condensing vapor transfers heat directly to the surface of the board and, more particularly, to the leads of the components, the best thermal conductors on the surface.

Excessive solder wicking can occur, transporting solder from between the lead and pad up the lead where it is not needed. This can cause solder bridges proximal to the component body. The excess solder on the component lead also decrease the lead's flexural compliance, detracting from its reliability. Further, the lead–pad interface is now solder starved and an inferior solder joint has been formed. At worst, so much solder is depleted that an open can occur.

As previously noted, this soldering method does have some merit. The search is on by some vapor phase reflow machine manufacturers for safer, ecologically sound replacements for the CFC-based synthetics which compose the reflow medium.

Additional information can be gleaned from older reference books and other authoritative publications, including previous editions of this book.[10–12]

29.9   LASER REFLOW SOLDERING

The main features of the laser reflow soldering technique are its versatility, wide process window, and future promise.

29.9.1   Laser Soldering Applications

Laser soldering can accommodate soldering of the finest or coarsest peripherally leaded surface-mount packages. Device population density on the board, the thickness of the printed circuit board, the PCB materials, and the presence or absence of package heat sinks do not preclude the use of the laser for soldering. At the same time, lead, pad, or solder metallurgical systems do not necessarily preclude laser use either. It is ideal for a high mix of module manufacturing. When implemented properly, very high soldering yields are possible. Although it has much potential for manufacturing, very few manufacturers have realized its potential; its use is currently relegated mainly to low-volume, high-mix lines or niche applications. In order to use this technique successfully, it is necessary to use tooling to hold the component or, more specifically, component leads down to circuit board pads.

There are several advantages which distinguish laser bonding from other soldering techniques. Its biggest edge is the photonic advantage: the use of photons to do the bulk of the process work, more specifically, heating. While there are several ways of harnessing the photon to accomplish soldering, none possess the ease and elegance of laser-based manufacturing. Lasers offer a constancy in performance, predictability in behavior, and versatility in use that can be found in no other tool.

Photons—packets of electromagnetic energy—are massless and will not disrupt component lead position on a PCB bonding pad. Photons are focusable to small spot size and are easily moved around the circuit board. While it is true that other photon sources of a nonlaser variety can be used for soldering, the laser brings with it distinct advantages. It is constant in wavelength and therefore its effect on various materials is predictable—a necessity for ease of process setup and reproducibility. A laser's beam can be focused to smaller diameters more easily than other sources due to its monochromaticity. This quality permits its beam to be characterized easily as to spatial energy distribution and average power with off-the-shelf equipment. This facility to monitor is key to process control and consistent processing results.

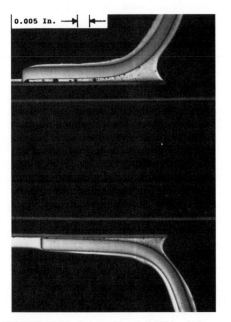

FIGURE 29.20   Laser-soldered, 0.025-in-pitch, surface-mount components bonded back to back on a 0.062-in printed circuit board. It has been shown that heating of the second side during laser soldering has no effect on the first side to board thickness of 0.016 in or less.

There are numerous myths surrounding laser soldering as regards price, safety, materials compatibility, and throughput. This section will help to unravel these. But first let us examine the essence of the laser and, most important, the methods associated with this form of bonding. Note that the plural "methods" was used. That is because laser bonding techniques are numerous and diverse in practice as well as application. Only the most notable examples will be studied here.

It should be noted that this is a highly specialized area and should not be attempted without the requisite knowledge of soldering, laser fundamentals, laser safety practices/regulations, and laser equipment. Although there seems to be much mystery associated with lasers and their application to the bonding space, the reader should find that the basic principles are quite simple.

Laser soldering requires no hot zones to profile or maintain, does not induce substrate warpage, and requires no substrate preheating to accomplish bonding. There is no heated bonding head which can degrade or vary with usage. Experience has shown that package configuration is of little consequence and the presence of component heat sinks is immaterial as long as it does not shadow the leads from the laser's bonding energy. Because its beam can be highly localized, current circuit board design wisdom can be successfully challenged. Components can be spaced exceptionally close to one another—closer than is currently permitted for other techniques. In addition, large active components can be placed on both sides of the printed circuit board since laser bonding on side #2 will have no influence on previously soldered side #1 components, as shown in Fig. 29.20.

29.9.2   Lasers

The word *laser* is derived from the acronym for "Light Amplification via Stimulated Emission Radiation." Although postulated by Einstein in 1917, the first practical demonstration of the laser took place in the late 1950s. Over the course of the 1960s and 1970s, they became ruggedized, capable of sustained use in manufacturing. Over the years they have proven to be an excellent production tool in many industries due to their versatility, simplicity, and high uptime. Although the PCB assembly industry has been slow to embrace lasers in manufacturing, there has been growing acceptance in terms of nonsoldering applications such as metrology and marking.

29.9.2.1 Laser Elements.   All lasers comprise three main subassemblies:

- Power supply
- Cavity or oscillator
- Beam delivery optics

Although there are many configurations and additional accessories which may enhance a laser's output, only the basics will be covered here. Figure 29.21 illustrates the basic laser sections.

29.9.2.2 Cavity/Oscillator.   Lasing, which is a laser photon generation and amplification process, occurs in the cavity, also known as the oscillator. The cavity contains the lasing medium, a material which is both the origin and the amplifier of the laser beam. Photons, electrons, or other high-energy sources are used to raise certain atoms or ions in the lasing medium to a temporarily stable electronic transition, a metastable state. When the medium is returned to its stable, ground state, energy is released in the form of heat and fluoresced pho-

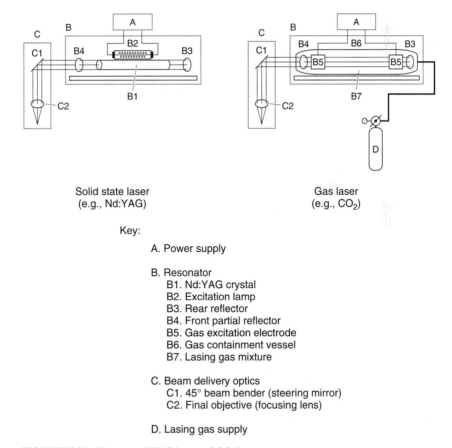

Solid state laser
(e.g., Nd:YAG)

Gas laser
(e.g., CO$_2$)

Key:

A. Power supply

B. Resonator
    B1. Nd:YAG crystal
    B2. Excitation lamp
    B3. Rear reflector
    B4. Front partial reflector
    B5. Gas excitation electrode
    B6. Gas containment vessel
    B7. Lasing gas mixture

C. Beam delivery optics
    C1. 45° beam bender (steering mirror)
    C2. Final objective (focusing lens)

D. Lasing gas supply

FIGURE 29.21   Diagrams of YAG laser and CO$_2$ laser

tons. These photons are, for the most part, reflected at the ends of the cavity and focused back through the lasing medium by the cavity optics.

There are always two types of reflectors which bound a laser's cavity. The rear- or retro-reflector focuses and returns nearly 100 percent of the emission wavelength photons back through the cavity, further stimulating the lasing medium to emit photons. The front reflector is a leaky mirror/lens, one which is reflective but somewhat transmissive also. It reflects most of the emission beam back into the oscillator for further stimulation of the lasing medium while allowing a small fraction of the laser beam to pass through it. The component of the beam which is transmitted by the front partial reflector is the working laser beam. It is monochromatic by virtue of the lasing medium, which limits photon emission to a set of discrete wavelengths, or laser lines, which are characteristic of the medium material and by the optical coatings on the front reflector which allow only one laser line through it.

29.9.2.3 Delivery Optics.   Delivery optics placed in the path of the laser beam direct it to the work piece. In the case of laser soldering, the work piece is the circuit board or, more specifically, the leads, pads, or lead/pad combinations. The beam can be easily steered by means of wavelength-appropriate mirrors and can be focused to the required spot size via a final objective lens to accomplish soldering. The delivery optics can be held fixed and the circuit board moved beneath, or, conversely, the optics can be moved to direct the beam as needed. Either can be done with great precision sufficient for any PCB soldering task. Moving beam or moving board, each has advantages. Moving the optics in any direction is very simple and will not interfere with any PCB or surface-mount device fixturing requirements. Also, moving the circuit board may cause misalignment of component leads to circuit board pads. Fixed optics are more stable and require fewer adjustments, although if engineered properly, moving optic beam delivery systems can be exceptionally stable and should not need frequent adjustment.

Fiber optics are in vogue for laser beam delivery, but it should be noted that, when dealing with high-energy-density laser beams as required for soldering, fibers are subject to damage if not precisely maintained. This maintenance requires cleaning and, most importantly, centering of an appropriately sized laser beam onto the face of the fiber optic or into the fiber optic coupling lens. Fiber diameter will dictate to some degree the ultimate minimum size of the laser beam. A good rule of thumb for delivered fiber optic beam size is that the resultant minimum beam diameter will be on the order of the diameter of the fiber bundle. Fixed optic systems require much less maintenance and are less expensive than fiber delivery systems. Of course, fiber delivery does have the advantage of allowing for easier steering of a beam in a complex machine which may preclude the use of orthogonal mirror and lens beam steering.

29.9.2.4 Beam Characteristics.   There are many key differences between a laser beam and other light sources. (The term *light* is generally reserved for those wavelengths that are part of the visible spectrum and detectable by the human eye, but for the purposes of this discourse, light and photonic emission will be used interchangeably.)

Laser beams have several distinctive characteristics. They are generally set to emit monochromatic radiation which is also coherent radiation. Coherence here relates to the synchronized propogation of photons; i.e., all waves of the emission radiation are in phase with one another. There are a number of other attributes which make the laser beam a useful manufacturing tool. These will be discussed in the context of laser soldering, also.

Although most lasing media are capable of emitting more than one wavelength, laser cavity optics are generally coated for an output emission which is restricted to a tightly distributed set of wavelengths—so tight that the beam is considered to be monochromatic. Coherence and monochromaticity are two important factors that permit fine focus of a beam. But that is not to say that a laser's emission has to be focused very finely to allow for soldering. This aspect of the soldering equation will be dealt with later.

29.9.3 Criteria for Lasers for Soldering

29.9.3.1 General Criteria.   The choice of laser for soldering is predicated on several criteria:

- Wavelength
- Required power
- Required beam diameter
- Reliability
- Price

29.9.3.2 Optical Properties Criteria.   The optical properties of the target material are of primary importance in the laser selection process. In the case of surface-mount soldering, the absorption, reflection, and transmission characteristics of the PCB laminate are important, as are the reflectivity and absorptivity of the metallics to be involved in the soldering process for leads, pads and solder. The vast majority of circuit boards produced today are composed of fiber-reinforced epoxy resin, although there are some MCMs of thin film, multilayer polyimide, ceramic, and polyimide over ceramic, among others. Each has its own unique optical properties and characteristic *laser damage threshold* (LDT). LDT can be defined as the energy required to cause denaturation or damage of the target material. In the case of an organic-based laminate PCB, it would be the laser energy necessary to char the board or cause the bonding pads to lift from the surface. In a ceramic MCM, it is the energy required to scribe, drill, or crack the ceramic.

29.9.4 Laser Alternatives

As in other sections of this chapter, discussion will be largely restricted to the bonding of eutectic, or near eutectic, tin-lead solder alloys on industry-standard substrate materials such as FR-4.

There are few practical choices for laser selection; only a few possess the characteristic energy and production-tested reliability necessary for PCB assembly. The most common are the neodymium drifted yttrium aluminum garnet (Nd:YAG) laser, an example of a solid-state laser, and the carbon dioxide laser, which has a gaseous lasing medium. These two types of laser are among the most common of the industrial machining lasers. Each has been on the manufacturing floor of various industries for at least a quarter of a century. They are versatile in terms of applications and capable of the output required to weld, braze, solder, cut, and mark. While there are other lasers that could be used for soldering, the aforementioned types are the most commonly available with proven track records and are also the most commonly reported in terms of application to soldering.

29.9.5 Carbon Dioxide (CO_2) Lasers

In the case of the CO_2 laser, there are mirrors at both ends of the tube which contains the lasing gas, a mixture of carbon dioxide, nitrogen, and helium. Each of the components of the mixture help in the lasing process. The CO_2 is the lasing medium per se, and electricity is discharged directly into this gaseous lasing medium. The discharge results in photons characteristic of the wavelength of the CO_2 gas or, more specifically, of that of the carbon-to-oxygen bonding. These photons are reflected back through the laser cavity to further stimulate the production of photons. As this process continues, the beam intensifies and emissions from the cavity compose the working laser beam. The introduction of N_2 helps in the transfer of energy to excite the CO_2 molecules into their metastable state. When the metastable state decays to its stable ground state, energy is released in the form of photons and heat. The helium, with its high thermal conductivity, helps to transfer some of this thermal energy to the laser's cooled cavity walls. Were the cavity gases to become too hot, the CO_2 would dissociate and would be less effective as a lasing medium. The majority of the photons generated are reflected back through the lasing medium which helps to stimulate further photon emissions. As previously indicated, one of the mirrors is a full reflector while the other is leaky, allowing a small fraction of the incident laser beam through it.

Known for their reliability and stability in manufacturing, the emission of the CO_2 laser is well into the IR spectrum at 10.6 µm (10,600 nm). It has limited use in PCB soldering since that wavelength is well absorbed by most organic materials (such as epoxy laminates) and is well reflected by most metallurgies. This is disadvantageous, since to get sufficient energy into a lead/pad combination, the CO_2 beam has to be kept to a small size to prevent it from spilling onto the FR-4. Were the FR-4 irradiated either directly or by errant reflection off of a specular surface, it would char and resultant carbon-rich residues may be electrically conductive enough to cause an electrical short circuit. Since the reflectivity of most metals is high at 10.6 µm, it is necessary to direct large amounts of energy at the solder target to start the heating process. As the temperature of a material increases, so does its optical absorption through a process known as *free-carrier* (free-electron) *absorption*. This is characterized as a runaway process. The hotter a solid metal or semiconductor is, the more absorptive it becomes. There are two other points which detract from the use of the CO_2 laser as the preferred tool for circuit board soldering. First, the minimum practical spot size is large—10 times that of an Nd:YAG laser. The theoretical diffraction limited spot size is directly proportional to wavelength. Since a laser's wavelength is fixed, one can calculate the spot size with the following formula:

$$S = \frac{f\lambda}{D} \qquad (29.1)$$

where
S = diffraction limited spot size
f = focal length of the lens
λ = wavelength of the laser
D = lens diameter

Thus, for a lens of 25-mm diameter and 100-mm focal length, in conjunction with CO_2 or YAG lasers, the spot sizes shown in Table 29.2 are theoretically possible.

TABLE 29.2   Theoretical Spot Size for Alternate Laser Type

Laser type	Emission wavelength, µm	Theoretical spot size, µm
CO_2	10.6 (10,600 nm)	42
Nd:YAG	1.064 (1064 nm)	4.2
Nd:YAG (frequency doubled)	0.532 (532 nm)	2.1

Imperfections in the lens or beam shape and other factors prevent practical achievement of these minimal spot sizes. Generally, the attainable focused beam diameter on the factory floor will be about two to three times larger than the ideally calculated spot size. Note that for an Nd:YAG laser, the spot size is at least a factor of 10 smaller than that of the CO_2, permitting a fine, high-energy-density spot for soldering.

Lastly, the CO_2 laser's output is not compatible with fiber optic delivery for all practical purposes. The wavelength is well absorbed by the most common fiber optic material, fused silica. Fibers for CO_2 wavelength of 10.6 μm is a topic of intense research. Despite these draw-backs, the use of CO_2 lasers for soldering has been widely reported in the literature.[13]

29.9.6 YAG Lasers

The Nd:YAG laser, commonly referred to as the YAG laser, has a solid-state medium. It relies on lamp excitation of a cut and polished yttrium-aluminum-garnet crystal which has been doped with neodymium. An intense broad-spectrum lamp is used to stimulate the YAG crystal solid-state lasing medium. The photons released by the solid-state lasing medium are used to stimulate more lasing medium–derived photons and the laser beam itself. Otherwise, the same lasing principles apply to the the operation of that laser as for the gaseous CO_2 laser. Nonlinear optical materials can be used in conjunction with the YAG laser to double the output frequency, halving the operating wavelength. This can be used to advantage when working with highly reflective materials such as gold and copper. As is the case with many metals, reflectivity is lower in visible and ultraviolet wavelengths than in the infrared. This, however, detracts from laser performance by decreasing available operating power, adding complexity to the system, as well as increasing maintenance requirements.

Both YAG and CO_2 lasers can be operated in a variety of modes, each of which can be used to advantage in soldering. Continuous wave operation, also referred to as CW, is a constant emission analogous to the continuous output of a light bulb which is powered by a direct current source. Diametrically opposed is the pulsed laser output and, furthering the light bulb analogy, is akin to a bulb operated by an alternating current or pulsating power supply—a strobe with intense bursts. The pulsing can be attained through a variety of methods, including a switched power supply, capacitive discharge, mechanical shutter, or by means of an optically manipulated shutter as by acoustooptic, electrooptic, or magneto-optic methods.

29.9.7 Laser-Soldering Fundamentals

There are relatively few variables associated with the laser in its application to soldering. This is one of the big advantages for laser processing. Beam wavelength, irradiation time, and beam power are important to the process, as are the properties of the materials being joined. Reflectivity, thermal conductivity, and laser damage threshold must be understood before attempting to solder. The wavelength will be fixed by the laser of choice, as shown in Table 29.3.

TABLE 29.3 Emission Wavelength for Alternative Laser Type

Laser type	Emission wavelength, nm
CO_2	10,600
Nd:YAG	1064
Nd:YAG (frequency doubled)	532

The shorter the wavelength, the smaller the theoretical spot size. This is important for single-point laser bonding of finest geometries. (More on that will follow.) Generally, the reflectivity of a metal is lower at shorter wavelengths. This means that a metal is more easily heated by an Nd:YAG laser as compared to a CO_2 laser. The converse is noticeably operant for many polymeric materials. Most are quite absorptive at longer wavelengths and prone to burning. Many polymeric materials are also absorptive at the UV end of the spectrum. Therefore, a carbon dioxide laser beam is more likely to impart damage to a circuit board than that of an Nd:YAG. Common circuit board laminates such as FR-4, G-10, and polyimide can be easily damaged by any laser beam if the energy is not regulated properly.

The reflectivity of metals varies widely with composition and surface condition. Every metal can be heated with a laser as long as the energy density of the beam is high enough and the dwell time of the beam sufficient to stimulate free-carrier absorption. This is also the case with laser-irradiated component leads, board pads, and solder during the laser bonding process. Measurements of the reflectivity of Sn-Pb solder show that a eutectic alloy can be as high as 74 percent at 10,600 nm versus 21 percent at 1060 nm. Therefore, in the case of the CO_2 laser at 10,600 nm on, say, a Sn-Pb-plated lead and solder-coated pad, much energy will have to be directed at the metals to start the absorption process, since only about 26 percent is being absorbed by the solder and converted to heat. This can be problematic owing to the specular reflectance of solder. The reflected or multiply reflected beam may impinge on adjacent components and damage package bodies or even the circuit board itself and cause it to char. That is why Nd:YAG is preferrable for circuit board soldering. CO_2 should be reserved for exceptionally large component bonding, such as board-mountable transformers and power supply tabs. Further discussion of laser soldering will be restricted to the Nd:YAG.

As mentioned previously, beam diameter is critical to laser processing. If the beam is larger than the target—in this case, the lead/pad combination—then the energy input must be compatible with the optical properties of the circuit board substrate. There are laser-soldering techniques where the beam is purposely large and does encroach on the circuit board laminate. That technique can be acceptable and successful. This technique as well as others will be discussed in a review of the most common laser-soldering methods.

29.9.8 Through-Lead vs. Through-Pad Bonding

Generally, the laser beam is directed at the component lead to accomplish soldering, but when the lead material is highly reflective, as would be the case with a gold-plated finish, heating would be slow and irradiation times impractically long. An alternative has been demonstrated whereby the beam is directed at the circuit board bonding pad. If there is leeway in design, the bonding pad can be extended to aid in this method, dubbed *through-pad bonding*. In contrast to the usual beam impingement on the component lead or *through-lead bonding,* the beam is directed at the more absorptive solder on the circuit board land, increasing process efficiency and locally melting the solder in the vicinity of beam impingement. Since the molten solder is about a hundred times more thermally conductive than the solid, the heat from the bonding process is rapidly transmitted down the pad to the lead. The process can result in soldering along the entire length of the component lead and circuit board pad with rich solder fillets evident if the process is conducted properly, as shown in Fig. 29.22.

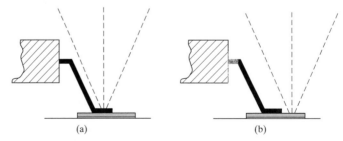

(a)   (b)

FIGURE 29.22 (*a*) For through-lead laser soldering, the laser's beam is directed at the foot of the component; (*b*) for through-pad laser soldering, the beam is directed at a pad extension; this heats the solder directly. This method can be used to solder leads coated with highly reflective materials such as gold.

29.9.8.1 Single-Point Laser Soldering. This method requires a laser beam which is smaller in diameter than the length or width of the component lead or bonding pad. The beam is stepped to each lead/pad, constrained to the single lead or pad, and left on long enough to cause the solder to flow. The beam can be continuous wave (CW), pulsed, or multiply pulsed to accomplish soldering as long as there is enough radiation delivered to cause the solder to undergo the phase change required for soldering.

Owing to the small beam diameter, as required by this technique for fine-pitch components, the energy density can be exceptionally high. If the lead is not in good contact with the bonding pad and if the energy density is too high, then the laser's beam can damage the lead, perhaps cutting through it rather than soldering it. Overly intense irradiation can also cause the bonding pad to delaminate from the PCB.

In this variation of laser soldering or in other methods where very small spot size is required, one must take precautions to precisely control the beam diameter. A very small variation in beam diameter, either through change in laser setup parameters or in working distance, will have a dramatic effect on the focused spot energy density. As an example, take the case of a 10-W Nd:YAG laser beam focused to a spot of 0.1 mm (~0.004 in) and 0.2 mm (~0.008 in). A seemingly small change in spot size will result in a large change in power density.

$$P = \frac{p}{d} \qquad (29.2)$$

where P = power density
        p = average power, W
        d = focused beam diameter

For this example, the power density would vary from 1273 W/mm^2 for the 0.1-mm beam to 318 W/mm^2 for the 0.2-mm beam diameter, a reduction factor of 4×. So, with finer spot sizes, it is crucial to maintain strict process control, because a small change in beam diameter will translate to a large change in delivered power.

It should be noted here that in most cases, a gaussian distribution of the beam's energy is assumed and in the optics world, it is customary to measure the beam at the $1/e^2$ point (13.5 percent of the peak height), so, in fact, the beam is impinging on a slightly larger area, but the most intense portion of the laser's beam is confined to the region bounded by the $1/e^2$ points in two dimensions, as shown in Fig. 29.23.

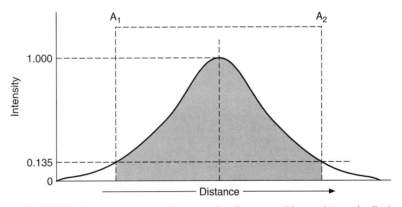

FIGURE 29.23   Laser output energy is conventionally measured from points on the distribution curve where the beam's intensity is $1/e^2$ (13.5 percent) of peak intensity, or between points A$_1$ and A$_2$ in this plot.

Single-point laser bonding has been applied to both inner lead bonding of a silicon die to TAB (tape-automated bonding) lead-frame, as well as for bonding TAB components to circuit boards. It has also been demonstrated for soldering conventional rigid leaded surface-mount packages to either a circuit board or multichip module.

29.9.8.2 Continuous-Wave Scanning. In sharp contrast to the single-point laser soldering, this technique relies on a larger, intense, moving beam to accomplish the heating. The beam may be many times larger than the narrowest lead or pad dimensions. The laser beam purposely spills over onto the substrate material, irradiating the lead, pad, or lead/pad combinations as well as the interpad board surfaces. Because larger beam diameters are used, longer-focal-length lenses can be employed. The longer-focal-length lens, along with the generous spot size, allow for much less stringent process control in terms of the final beam diameter and tolerances in terms of working distance of lens to circuit board surface. The laser spot is moved at a rate such that the beam exposure to the board is below the laser damage threshold limit. It heats the lead/pad combination, the solder flux, and the board sufficiently to cause the solder to change state.

A variation of this technique was reported by Raytheon for surface-mount soldering. It utilizes orthogonally mounted galvanometrically controlled scanners to move an Nd:YAG LASER beam around the periphery of a surface-mount device sitting atop solder lands on a circuit board. The beam is driven at high velocity repetitively around the surface-mount device until all leads are heated to the point of solder liquidus. As the beam is turned off, it solidifies and solder joints result.

29.9.8.3 Multiple Beam. One of the attractions of working with a laser is the fact that its beam can be split for multiple use within one station or even shared between two or more stations. The split can be accomplished by the use of bifurcated fibers or with beam splitters. The beam of a single laser cavity can be duplexed to solder two sides of a surface-mount component simultaneously. It is entirely possible to share a common beam between two or more soldering stations either simultaneously or in a time-shared manner.

29.9.8.4 Tooling. In all modes of laser bonding, the component leads must be in contact with solder lands on the PCB to accomplish joint formation. It is therefore necessary, in most cases, to use a specialized hold-down tool to ensure that leads do contact pads. This detracts from the ideal of noncontact bonding, but there are several methods that have been developed and reported. Much development work is continuing in this area. It is worthwhile to review a few of the reported methods.

Many investigators have used transparent hold-down media. Included are glass, quartz, and transparent high-temperature plastics. There are several significant problems associated with this type of approach, however, and it can result in an inconsistent soldering process. First, the materials are rigid, which is an impediment when trying to overcome lead-to-lead, pad-to-pad, or lead-to-pad coplanarity differences inherent in most circuit boards, components, and presoldered assemblies, as shown in Fig. 29.24.

Secondly, during the soldering cycle, the glass can accumulate spattered flux and flux by-products which may change the delivered laser beam intensity, adding variability to the process.

Comb or pin arrays have been applied which match the lead configuration of a package.

Probably the most common method for rigid-leaded surface-mount packages is the *body-push* method, where a force is applied to the component body, springing the leads just slightly. As the solder melts below the lead, the lead drops down to board level where it is frozen in the cooling solder. It is necessary to control the amount of push such that the solder joint is not stressed by a lead in compression. When board pads and component leads are reasonably coplanar, then this method is adequate for high-yield, high-reliability soldering.

A compliant hold-down method has been reported which is inexpensive to fabricate and easy to implement. This consists of a silicone rubber foot and an aperture which allows the

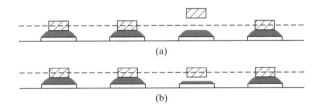

FIGURE 29.24   In order for laser soldering to be effective, it is necessary to have lead-to-lead, pad-to-pad, and lead-to-pad coplanarity: (*a*) non-coplanar leads on constant-volume solder pads; (*b*) coplanar lead array on non-coplanar PCB solder lands.

beam unobstructed access to the lead/pad combination. This has been proven effective for TAB as well as for rigid leaded surface-mount device bonding. It obviates the problems associated with transparent hold-down methods in terms of flux buildup. The compliant foot holds leads to pads and can accommodate lead-to-pad non-coplanarity differences.

29.9.8.5   *Bonding Rates.*   Lasers are capable of operating at very high speeds; even so, it is difficult to compete with mass reflow methods. It is anticipated that this will not be the case one day, especially as pitches decrease and mass reflow and ancillary processes such as placement and solder paste stenciling struggle to tackle finer and finer lead pitches. Bonding rates in laser soldering are very much dependent on the device pitch and outline. It can take as little as 10 μs to solder a lead, but the beam must be accurately translated to the next lead/pad combination. This translation can be orders of magnitude slower than the soldering itself. Practically speaking, for inner lead bonding, rates as high as 65 leads/s have been reported.*
Outer-lead soldering rates vary with package type, pitch, and footprint, but per-lead rates vary between about 15 to 60 joints per second. With exceptionally fine-pitch/leaded, small-outline packages such as TAB, bonding rates can be considerably higher.

29.9.8.6   *Flux for Laser Bonding.*   Requirements are much the same as for other reflow methods. It must be active enough to remove oxides from the lead and from the solder. Its optical charactistics in terms of reflection, absorption, and transmission must not interfere with the solder process. If too absorptive, it could caramelize or char and impart damage to the underlying circuit board.

In laser soldering, particularly in the scanned methods, the flux adds a path of heat transfer. The heated flux transfers its energy to the board, preheating the next joint to be soldered. In the absence of a liquid flux, there is more propensity for the board to char if the laser impingement is not stringently controlled.

During soldering, the laser beam's output is quick and intense. The high energy of the process results in exceptionally high processing temperatures for very short durations. The high-process temperature aids in flux activation, making even the mildest of no-clean fluxes quite an effective soldering aid.

There have been many reports of fluxless laser soldering. As used for inner-lead bonding to silicon die, these utilize a very high energy, short-duration pulse. Under these conditions, when the mass of the lead and the bonding pad are small enough, the process is more akin to welding. The component lead is reported to melt and alloy with an underlying metal such as tin.

However, to accomplish conventional reflow soldering by means of a laser, or any other technique, it is necessary to employ a liquid solder flux or gaseous analog pretreatment to per-

---

* See "Laser Based System for Tape Automated Bonding to Integrated Circuit," *Proceedings of IEEE/Electronic Components and Technology Conference,* May 1990, pp. 757–761. These rates are for TAB inner lead bonding of ultrafine leads in a small area.

mit effective bonding. Plasma cleaning and inert storage may be one such method. Ultrasonic assisted laser soldering can be effective but is slow, requiring precise placement of an ultrasonically agitated head and running the laser beam either through the ultrasonic tool or precisely adjacent to it. The ultrasonic agitation breaks up the oxide surrounding the molten solder and the lead, allowing joining of the liquidus to the lead metallurgy.

The author has demonstrated the use of gaseous phase carboxyllic acid fluxing in conjunction with laser bonding.[14] This precludes the use of conventional liquid fluxes and leaves no visible residues on the circuit board. No cleaning is required and the assembly reliability is not degraded from the use of a gaseous fluxing approach.

29.9.9   Laser-Solder Joint Characteristics

There are very few differences between solder joints prepared by laser as compared to those formed by other methods. Laser soldering results in intermetallic formation per usual but the layer is extremely thin if the laser-soldering cycle heating is kept to a minimum. It is much thinner than found in solder joints manufactured by more conventional methods. Upon cooling, which is very local and very rapid, the laser-soldered joint typically possesses exceptionally fine solder grain growth, distinctive of this process. The fine grain growth leads to greater joint strength initially. This strength advantage, although significant in magnitude, tapers off with age. After about a year of storage at room temperature, the metal grains coarsen and typical nonlaser solder joint metallurgical properties dominate.

Another characteristic of laser soldering is rich solder joint filleting. This is particularly true of joints prepared by the CW scanned method of laser bonding. The solder joints are generally full length and very strong compared to bonds made by conventional solder methods.

29.9.10   Solder Sources and Defects Associated with Laser Reflow

Solder requirements are the same as for any other process. There are no alloy composition requirements specific to laser soldering. It is possible, however, to use some of the more exotic materials such as 10:90 or 5:95 Sn-Pb with melting points of about 302 and 312°C, respectively.[15] These temperatures are generally considered too high for conventional reflow methods. The board will darken, burn, or warp in a reflow oven set high enough for the onset of high-lead-alloy liquidus. When single-point laser reflow is applied, the board quality and integrity is not compromised if parameters are chosen and adequately controlled.

The thickness of solder required on the board will be a function of the required product reliability and the component pitch. As the pitches decrease to about 0.5 mm and below, hot-air solder-leveled pads may bear sufficient solder for adequate joint formation. Electroplated reflowed or even unreflowed solder platings will be sufficient for laser soldering. Some of the new coatings such as SiPad® and Super Solder® have also been demonstrated as useful methods of solder deposition for laser reflow.

Laser soldering is not prone to defects if implemented correctly. Perhaps the most common characteristic defect unique to laser soldering is charring or burning of the circuit board. This can occur if too high an energy density is used and the laser damage threshold is exceeded. Charring or burning can also occur if the circuit board is grossly contaminated with grease or other organic contaminants. That is not to say that boards for laser soldering have extraordinary requirements for cleanliness. Requirements should be considered the same for this technique as for any other reflow process.

Another characteristic defect is the presence of solder balls when the laser's beam is focused onto a component lead embedded in solder paste or when the paste is irradiated directly. The use of raw solder paste is not recommended for laser soldering. Just as oven reflow of paste requires a gradually ramped drying of the solder paste, so the same is required of laser processing. If the paste is heated too rapidly, as would be the case with laser soldering, the solvents and vehicles in the paste would vaporize much too rapidly, causing explosive spattering of some of the paste mass. These volatile explosions are linked to solder ball formation. In general, laser soldering of plated or hot-air-leveled solder or other solid solder coatings will not result in appreciable solder ball formation.

Solder bridging is generally of little concern in laser soldering. In fact, if a solder bridge exists on the substrate prior to soldering, the laser-soldering process may relieve the bridging condition and cause the redistribution of the solder onto the component leads. This is particularly true with the scanned CW laser bonding method.

The occurence of solder opens will be proportional to the quality of the lead-frame of the component, its solderability, and the effectiveness of the component hold-down method. Very high yields are possible and, if implemented correctly, few opens will occur. Although some may feel that this technique is too futuristic or too slow, it is a technique which is ripe for commercial exploitation. Equipment costs can be modest, with the laser cavity available for about $30,000. Add about $5000 for each access and funds for a computer or CNC to drive the axes. An enclosure is easy to fabricate out of sheet metal.

29.9.11 Laser Safety Issues

Lasers are categorized by their safety hazard potential. A full review of these will not be provided, but suffice it to say that Class 1 is an intrinsically safe laser, posing no intraoccular danger, while Class 4 lasers pose the greatest eye hazard. All lasers considered for soldering use will be of the Class 4 variety. Because of this, they are generally embedded in appropriate cabinetry with laser-safe viewing ports or CCTV incorporation. Also, they are equipped with latches on all cabinet covers which are interlocked to the laser's safety. This precludes direct occular exposure to the laser's intense beam. When the Class 4 system is embedded in an interlocked cabinet as described, it is considered a Class 1 system. As such, it is poses no hazard to the immediate area; laser-safe eye wear need not be worn except on occasion for servicing the laser. As mentioned previously, lasers, especially Nd:YAG, are known for their high uptime and lack of required expendables.

As the need for finer bonding continues, lasers will continue to be scrutinized, because they are a method which exhibits much potential. Easy to automate, highly reproducible, extensible to bonding across the entire pitch spectrum, and without foreseeable limitation in pitch applicability, this technique is likely to persist and gain in acceptance.

There are numerous excellent supplemental texts available for additional detail and instruction in this technology. Those by Charschan, Hecht, and Ready are particularly useful.[16-19] Additional information on CO_2 lasers in the realm of soldering can be found in references provided.[20-24]

29.10 HOT-BAR SOLDERING

Specifically suited to surface-mount assembly of leaded packages, hot-bar soldering has been in use for several years. The technique relies on a resistance-heated element to push component leads into contact with solder and bonding pads, simultaneously reflowing the solder. Compression of the leads onto the circuit board lands is continued as the heat is ramped down. On cooling, the solder solidifies and the heating element is withdrawn from the newly formed solder joints. The heated element is commonly referred to as the *hot bar,* although the term *thermode* is also in widespread use.

29.10.1 Solder Application

The use of solder paste is discouraged because blade heat-up is fast and explosive solder ball formation, caused by rapidly volatilized paste constituents, will result. Also, the paste is likely to squeeze out from between component lead and circuit board pad which can cause the solder to bridge to adjacent joints. In fact, even with solid solder coatings on the circuit board, bridging can be problematic in hot-bar bonding. This is usually a function of the volume of solder on the pad, the quantity of flux and its degree of activity, and lead/pad pitch. As the solder is melted, it oozes out from between lead and pad in the rudimentary stages of solder wetting. This displaced solder may bulge laterally to the point that the solder masses of two or more adjacent pads may touch to one another, forming a solder bridge. Once the bridge has formed, the forces associated with lead/pad wetting and capillarity may not be strong enough to overcome the capillary conditions established during bridge formation. If that is the case, the bridging defect(s) will persist, as shown in Fig. 29.25.

Solid solder coatings such as hot-air-leveled pads or solder-plated boards are recommended for this bonding method.

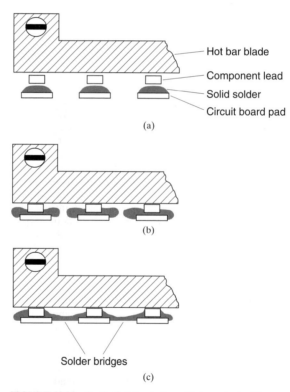

(a)

(b)

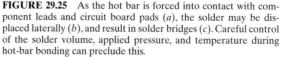

(c)

FIGURE 29.25 As the hot bar is forced into contact with component leads and circuit board pads (*a*), the solder may be displaced laterally (*b*), and result in solder bridges (*c*). Careful control of the solder volume, applied pressure, and temperature during hot-bar bonding can preclude this.

29.10.2 Fluxes and Fluxing

Liquid flux is applied just prior to soldering. Fluxes chosen should be tested to resist *caramelization,* the development of polymerized decomposition products, or lacquers, which adhere to both circuit board and hot bar. Residue buildup on the bar can adversely inhibit hot-bar performance by diminishing thermal transfer. It can also become thick enough to keep the hot bar from squarely contacting component leads. Baked-on residues make flux cleaning more difficult and also detract from the visual appearance of the printed circuit assembly.

29.10.3 Solder Operation

During the soldering operation, liquid solder is squeezed out from between the lead and pad unless a mechanical stop is employed to keep the bonding head from driving this far down. Of course, a thin film of solder remains which composes the solder joint. Solder-starved joints are notably weak, though, and it is preferable not to displace so much solder. One equipment vendor offers a system which automatically aligns the component to bonding pads and pushes component leads in contact with them, and, on reflow, the bond head and component are retracted several hundredths of a millimeter. This results in a thick coupling of solder between lead and land for robust joint formation. This retraction step is also claimed to discourage solder bridge formation.

As in any other soldering process, it is important to maintain proper reflow time-temperature characteristics. Most hot-bar systems are configured with a fine-gauge thermo-couple welded to the bar, an integral part of a closed-loop, temperature-control hot-bar heater system. Generally, hot-bar blades are relatively small in size; therefore, the thermal mass of the circuit board and components being bonded will have profound influence on its performance. Often they provide so much thermal conduction that accessory heaters must be utilized to augment the hot-bar heating process. This can be in the form of hot gas blowing on the top or bottom surface of the circuit board, but more commonly it is accomplished via substrate heating. The board is rested on a heated platen which raises the PCB to a nominal temperature well below that of solder liquidus. This permits circuit board bonding in a reasonable time period. Care must be taken to avoid overheating the circuit board so as not to re-reflow previously soldered components or otherwise damage the circuit board. It may also hinder bonding of the next sites as global preheating may hasten oxidation and intermetallic compound formation on pads which are not yet soldered. Also, this method of substrate heating is generally restricted to single-sided surface-mount assemblies.

29.10.4 Construction

A hot-bar bonding head can be composed of one or several hot bars. They are designed to solder one side, two sides, or all four sides of a component simultaneously. Each hot bar of the assembly is configured to accommodate the maximum span of a lead set; i.e., the bar's length is manufactured to be slightly longer than the lead array to be soldered. This permits concurrent bonding of all leads on a package side. The bar length is also generous enough to facilitate bar-to-component alignment. In the case of some very long connectors or other large packages, the thermal uniformity of a single blade may not be adequate to reflow all leads simultaneously without overheating some of the joints. This is sometimes remedied by using a smaller hot bar and stepping it along the length of the lead set until all leads are bonded. Bar thickness is somewhat dependent on the lead-form and should not interfere with same. It should sit flatly on the foot of the lead, neither contacting the radius area of the lead-form, nor overhanging the lead toe greatly, as shown in Fig. 29.26.

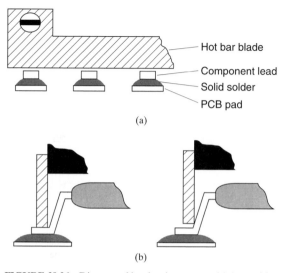

FIGURE 29.26   Diagram of hot bar in contact with leads: (*a*) a transverse view; (*b*) a lateral view. The hot bar must be positioned so as not to interfere with the leg of the formed lead. It should sit squarely on the foot of the lead.

29.10.5   Hot-Bar Design and Materials

The bar itself can be manufactured to nearly any dimension, but there are limitations on its size. The longer the blade, the worse its longitudinal thermal uniformity. Variations in blade temperature may cause it to distort due to differential thermal expansion/contraction. This will be discussed later. Thermal uniformity is critical for consistent lead-to-lead soldering and joint quality per component side. The tolerable variation in bar temperature will be limited by the component and board to be soldered, the solder itself, and product reliability requirements. As in any other soldering process, the variation in process temperature must be understood and controlled to assure highest board-assembly yields. The bonding head must also be able to shed heat rapidly to allow the solder to resolidify in a reasonable time frame.

There are numerous bar designs and materials of construction. Tungsten, titanium, and molybdenum are commonly chosen, not only for their electrical resistance and thermal conductivity, but for their impunity to flux damage and soldering wetting. Some ceramics are also used for blade construction.

The bar must be designed for uniform heating across its length. Additionally, it has to expand and contract uniformly throughout the soldering cycle. Some blades have been seen to develop a "frowning" or "smiling" profile in their *z* axis during heating, owing to differential thermal expansion or built-in stress in the metal, as shown in Fig. 29.27. For the same reasons, transverse warping of the blade is also commonplace.

The "smile" or "frown" will not provide full contact of blade to all lead/pad combinations. This can result in solder opens if the curvature is sufficiently large. There have been many solutions proposed in the realm of structure, materials of construction, and electrical input to permit highest uniformity of blade heating and contact to the bonding pads.*

---

* Waller, et al., have patented a rigid, molybdenum truss blade that has been found to be stable dimensionally and thermally uniform over long spans (in excess of 3 in).[25]

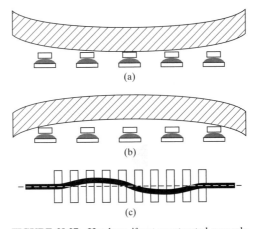

FIGURE 29.27 Hot bars, if not constructed properly, can develop a "smiling" profile (*a*), "frowning" profile (*b*), or may warp laterally along its length (*c*).

Other solutions include independently heated sectional bars and compliant ribbon blades. The former is a linear array composed of two or more hot-bar segments, each with their own heating control. This is more expensive to machine and maintain. It is also more difficult to use since its use includes an additional alignment of the bonding tool to ensure that interblade sections fall between and not on leads to be bonded.

Although the concept of a self-planarizing ribbon blade seems ideal to the task of accommodating variations in topography, these are also prone to distortion which can cause solder opens; this is especially true for long span ribbons.

Thermal uniformity along this blade is less controllable than for the conventional rigid hot bar. When comparing the options for electrical input for these two types of blades, the reason will become obvious. The ribbon can only be connected at its ends while the rigid hot bar can have multiple taps allowing adjustment of current to each section to establish a thermally balanced output.

Generally the hot-bar blade is attached to a self-leveling, spring-loaded bonding head which allows the blade to planarize itself in relation to the underlying circuit board. Nonetheless, variations in board contour, such as a localized high or low spot, can render the concept of self-planarization useless and solder opens can result.

Rigid-member hot bars are excellent for accommodating differences in lead coplanarity since the blade forces lead to pad. Driving a heavily sprung lead to pad can, however, build stress into the resultant solder joint since the solder is working to resist the spring force of the lead. This can detract from the joint quality and cause premature failure of same.

29.10.6 Maintenance and Diagnostic Methods

It is important to maintain the hot bar correctly. Check it frequently for distortion. Ensure that it is orthogonal to the circuit board to be bonded. Scrub the hot bar on a ceramic flat to release any flux residue scale or polymerized coating that may develop on it. This may need to be done every few bonding cycles, depending on the flux and the criticality of the assembly.

There are several diagnostic tools which can be applied to assessing hot-bar conditions, ranging from mundane to the exotic. The two most important characteristics which must be understood and monitored are thermal performance and planarity.

29.10.6.1 *Thermal Monitoring.* One of the most common methods of assessing hot-bar performance is the use of a thermocouple-instrumented board. Although true for all bonding methods, making one for thermode use has its own requirements. Fine-gauge thermocouples are attached to leads of the component or the bonding pad of the circuit board to be soldered. Best positioned at both ends of the lead set and also near its center, this will help quantify the thermal uniformity of the bar during soldering. It is also useful to deploy thermocouples on adjacent components to ensure that the hot-bar soldering process is not jeopardizing the integrity of previously soldered joints.

Since it is important that the coplanarity of the board and the component are not compromised, it is wise to avoid placing the thermocouple bead(s) between lead and pad. The added height of the bead would prevent the bar from contacting adjacent component leads and could result in point contact heating which is not indicative of the bar's normal operation. Instead, place the bead in the pad extension area either just in front of the lead foot or to the rear of the lead's heel. Attaching the thermocouple can be done with a small dot of high-temperature solder or thermally conductive epoxy. The amount of attachment material added must be kept small to minimize change to the thermal mass of the would-be joint. They also have to be restricted so that they do not interfere with the component seating plane, because leads must sit on pads absent of obstructive, nonfusible materials. It should be noted that the coplanarity of solder on the PCB pads does not have to be exact. The hot bar will be reflowing this solder and it will self-planarize, as does any liquid. It will remain so into the solid phase.

Once thermocouples are correctly installed, the component site on the board can be fluxed and subjected to a bonding trial. Thermocouple output can be directed to a calibrated strip chart recorder to assess the time-temperature profile of the bonding cycle.

IR cameras have been successful in allowing visualization of hot-bar thermal performance. This can be an excellent but expensive approach to evaluating bar-heating uniformity and its impact on the bonding operation.

29.10.6.2 *Planarity.* As stressed throughout this section, the orthogonality of the hot-bar blade or multiblade assembly with respect to the bonding surface is extremely important for the preclusion of solder opens. There are numerous measurement methods which can help diagnose this; unfortunately, though, they are meant for evaluation of the blade(s) at room temperature. As previously mentioned, a blade may distort temporarily or permanently during heating, but planarity measurements on hot blades are difficult and often not practical. So the majority of techniques encountered will be at room temperature. Wilkins suggests the use of a colorant, such as from a marking pen, applied to the cold bonding surface of a freshly cleaned thermode. Once the ink is dry, the blades are then scrubbed over a clean, flat ceramic plate. Low spots on the bar will be indicated by the presence of colorant remaining on the bar after several circular swipes on the ceramic flat. Regrinding of the blade(s) to restore flatness is recommended and the procedure repeated to ensure that the machining was effective.[26]

Driving the cold blade assembly down onto carbon paper is a another commonly used method. The carbon paper is sandwiched between a mechanical flat and a piece of thin, white paper. The carbon will leave an impression on the paper. The boldness of imprint will be a rough indicator of bar planarity. If nonplanar, the impression of the bar on the paper will run from dark on the low side of the blade to light on the high side. There are also pressure-sensitive papers which can be used to the same avail.

Single-bar and two- or four-sided blade assembly planarity can also be evaluated using an array of ground, leveled, rigidly mounted pressure transducers. Bar pressure differential, an indicator of blade planarity, can be adjusted so as to be uniform end to end and from blade to blade on the two-up or four-up hot-bar assembly. Of course, some hot-bar assemblies are self-leveling, but even these should be checked for planarity and force per blade to ensure best uniformity in bonding.

Hot-bar soldering is best suited for low-thermal-mass, single-sided surface-mount assemblies. Each component type requires its own hot-bar bonding head assembly. These can be expensive, costing a couple of hundred dollars to well over a thousand dollars per assembly. Price will be dependent on the complexity, materials of construction, precision required, and overall size of the head.

29.10.6.3 *Process-Induced Defects.*

Solder bridging is the most prevalent problem associated with this method of soldering. Recall that the solder can be squeezed out of the solder joint and conditions may favor solder bridge formation. Solder opens result from lack of coplanarity between the hot bar and the plane of the circuit board surface. Lead misalignment during the bonding cycle is another defect which detracts from this method. As pressure is applied to component leads by the hot bar prior to the onset of solder liquidus, leads are sometimes forced to slide down the solder domes. This displacement causes misregistration of component leads to bonding pads, and may build stress into soldered joints. If the forces are great enough, it may also cause the whole package to move and misregister the entire lead set.

Because the heating is rapid, the thermode temperature is necessarily well above the solder liquidus temperature. If the time-temperature cycle is not carefully controlled, intermetallic compound formation can be a problem. This is especially true in this process where the solder may be largely displaced from between lead and pad. Within the joint, the volume of intermetallic compound (hard and brittle) to the remaining solder (soft and compliant) may be large. If this is the case, solder joints will be less reliable and more susceptible to fracture failure.

All of these obstacles have prevented the widespread acceptance of hot-bar bonding in manufacturing. It is most useful for low-volume, fine-pitch surface-mount soldering and rework. Configured properly with a suction device to retain a surface-mount package, all four sides of a component can be reflowed simultaneously and the component removed. The addition of flux is helpful in the component removal process, since it serves as a heat spreader and also improves the contact area of the blade to the solder prior to reflow. After component removal, the pads are reconditioned (smoothed with a hand soldering iron, solder replenished, and fluxed). Braided copper wicking can be used to remove excess solder. A new component can be reinstalled via hot bar. Care must be taken once again to preclude intermetallic compound formation through the removal, dressing, and component resoldering process. Aside from the reliability risk imposed by a thickened intermetallic compound layer, the intermetallic layer is difficult to bond to and may require a more activated flux to complete the soldering.

29.11 HOT-GAS SOLDERING

Pressurized gas is heated and directed at component leads, solder, circuit board lands, and soldering flux. The thermal energy is absorbed by these four items, and if temperature rise is sufficient, melting of the solder will occur. Upon cooling, solder joints are formed. This noncontact, directed energy method is most suited to the bonding of surface-mount components. Although around for years and after numerous machine offerings in this vein, this technique is not a popular method for soldering despite its evolutionary improvements. Its most common incarnation, hot-gas soldering, is used for reworking components, i.e., removal of previously soldered devices (through-hole or surface-mount) from a circuit board and replacement of same.

One of the disadvantages of this soldering method is that the thermal energy is not very well localized. Most machines typically emit a hot-gas jet too large to be isolated to reflow only the lead or leads of interest. The gas jet, once impinged upon the board and component leads, is deflected and its backwash can be problematic. It may cause unwanted reflow of previously formed joints, especially on closely spaced, adjacent components. This problem is typically overcome by the use of baffles which are either applied to adjacent components or by a singular baffle which confines the gas jet to the component to be soldered.

As shown in Fig. 29.28, nozzles are available in a variety of forms. The simplest of nozzles is the single orifice. This can be translated around the entire periphery of a component. Some machines offer a double, translatable nozzle assembly which can solder two opposing sides of a component simultaneously. A plenum nozzle, comprising multiple gas ports, can solder or unsolder all sides of a component simultaneously without the need for nozzle translation except in the vertical direction. This last option relies on dedicated tooling per component type. The cost for inventorying numerous individual tools can be expensive.

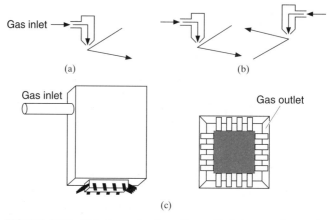

FIGURE 29.28   Hot air nozzles for reflow soldering or repair may be deployed singly (*a*) or multiply (*b*). In addition, a single plenum type assembly (*c*) can be used to reflow all sides of a component simultaneously.

The jetting gas, which is heated, is forced through a small nozzle orifice or nozzle array. It can be any pressurized gas compatible with the system and circuit board materials. Air is commonly employed for its economy, but it is an oxidizing medium and may preclude the use of weakly activated fluxes. Nitrogen is recommended because it is nonoxidizing, inexpensive, and safe. The use of hydrogen/nitrogen mixtures, argon, and other gases is also common to aid this method of reflow.

Solder can be applied to the board as a paste, solid preform, or solder-coated pad. If anything but solder paste is used, a means of component hold-down must be applied to ensure contact of component lead with bonding pad. Gas pressures must not be excessive, as this could move an unconstrained component during the reflow cycle. Proper gas pressure, temperature, nozzle translation speed, and flux are required to effect joint formation. Otherwise, the same reflow considerations are required of this technique as for any other. Heating ramp rate, solder paste preheating, peak temperature, liquidus duration, etc., must be observed for successful joint formation and for joint reliability considerations.

The use of thermocouples in the vicinity of reflow on anything but test boards is not practical, so sensing of the soldering temperature is not easily accomplished during a hot-gas soldering cycle on actual product. Therefore, a dummy board with thermocouple-instrumented component(s) is useful in determining the effects of the various operating parameters on the process performance and reflow profile. Additionally, thermocouples deployed in the solder joints of adjacent components is recommended to ensure that operating conditions chosen will not inadvertently re-reflow these neighboring devices. As in any soldering operation, care must be taken to prevent overheating of the component and circuit board during hot-gas soldering. Overheated circuit traces may delaminate, flux may char, and excessive intermetallic compound formation may result. All of these can impact product reliability.

29.12 *ULTRASONIC SOLDERING*

This method relies on a heated, ultrasonically vibrated soldering tip (see Fig. 29.29) which simultaneously melts and agitates the solder. The ultrasonic energy is transferred from the tip, through the molten solder droplet beneath it, and ultimately to the component lead and circuit board pad. This high-energy agitation of the solder droplet helps to cleanse bond-inhibiting materials from the solder and solder-metal interfaces. The integrity of metal oxides which encapsulate the solder, circuit board pad, and component lead are disrupted to the point that unoxidized, underlying metals are exposed and wetted by the solder. This precludes the need for the addition of chemical fluxing agents.

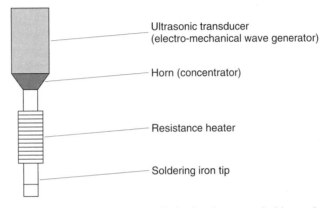

FIGURE 29.29 The ultrasonic soldering iron is composed of four main components: an ultrasonic transducer, a horn for concentrating and directing ultrasonic energy, a resistance heater, and the soldering tip which emits both thermal and ultrasonic energy.

Aluminum and other difficult-to-join metals can be soldered by this method. The viability of this technique has been well proven on a commercial scale, with the manufacture of air conditioner heat exchangers.[27,28] More important, this joining method has implications in the assembly of printed circuit boards.

Ultrasonic soldering has also been applied as a batch or continuous mass reflow process. In these instances, the molten solder is ultrasonically agitated while the assembly to be soldered is immersed in it. Similar arrangements have been made for ultrasonically vibrating the part while dipping it in a molten bath or wave of solder. These mass processes are more common for nonelectronic assembly.

Care must be taken in ultrasonic soldering to tune the tip amplitude and/or frequency to the mass of the system being soldered. Overagitation will result in excessive cavitation in the liquid solder, causing it to splash. This will generate solder balls, which could short finer-spaced leads or pads. Additionally, ultrasonic agitation will increase the dissolution rate of any soluble metals into the solder at any given temperature. This may degrade solder joint strength.

This technique can be useful for the repair of opens or the installation of new or change-order components onto completed circuit assemblies. Since no flux is required, a previously cleaned board will stay clean through repair or upgrade operation. This technique is applicable to all peripherally leaded surface-mount components. It can also accommodate through-hole device soldering. Equipment availability is limited, with only a few manufacturers worldwide. Several past and recent publications provide a comprehensive review of this technology's applicability and attributes.[29–32]

REFERENCES

1. R. Iman, et al., "Evaluation of a No-Clean Soldering Process Designed to Eliminate the Use of Ozone Depleting Chemicals," IWRP CRADA No. CR91-1026, issued by Sandia National Laboratories, 1991.

2. H. J. Hartmann, "Soft Soldering Under Cover Gas—a Contribution to Environmental Protections," *Elektr. Prod. und Prftechnik,* H.4, 1989, pp. 37–39; H. J. Hartmann, "Nitrogen Atmosphere Soldering," *Circuits Assembly,* Jan. 1991.

3. C. Hallmark, K. Langston, and C. Tulkoff, "Double Reflow: Degrading Fine Pitch Joints in the Wave Soldering Process," *Technical Proceedings of NEPCON-West,* 1994, pp. 695–705.

4. I. N. Sax, *Dangerous Properties of Industrial Materials,* 5th ed., Van Nostrand Reinhold, New York, 1979, pp. 766–769, 1032.

5. F. W. Kear, "The Dynamics of Joint Formation," *Circuits Assembly,* Oct. 1992, pp. 38–41.

6. S. Adams, "New Applications in Electronic Soldering," *Technology Magazine,* Oct. 1992.

7. R. Trovato, "Soldering Without Cleaning," *Circuits Magazine,* April 1990.

8. L. Hagerty, et al., "Wave Soldering in a Protective Atmosphere Enclosure Over a Solder Pot," U.S. Patent No. 5,121,875, June 1992.

9. Coombs, Jr., C. F. (ed.), *Printed Circuits Handbook,* 3d ed., McGraw-Hill, New York, pp. 27.18–27.20.

10. Manko, *Solders and Soldering,* 2d ed., McGraw-Hill, New York, 1979.

11. R. J. K. Wassink, *Soldering in Electronics,* Electrochemical Publications, Ltd., Ayre, Scotland, 1984.

12. C. L. Hutchins, "Soldering Surface Mount Assemblies," *Electronic Packaging & Production,* Supplement, August 1992, pp. 47–53.

13. P. J. Spletter and R. R. Goruganthu, "Bonding Metal Electrical Members with a Frequency Doubled Pulsed Laser Beam," U.S. Patent No. 5,083,007, January 1992.

14. G. Freedman, "Atmospheric Pressure Gaseous-Flux-Assisted LASER Reflow Soldering," U.S. Patent No. 5,227,604, July 1993.

15. "Properties of Lead and Lead Alloys," Lead Industries Association, Inc., 292 Madison Ave., New York, NY 10017.

16. S. Charschan, *LASERs in Industry,* LASER Institute of America, Toledo, Ohio, 1972, p. 116.

17. E. F. Lish, "LASER Attachment of Surface Mounted Components to Printed Wiring Boards," *6th Annual Soldering Technology Seminar,* Naval Weapons Center, China Lakes, Calif., Feb. 1982.

18. J. Hecht, *Understanding LASERs,* Howard W. Sams & Co., Indianapolis, 1988.

19. J. F. Ready, *Industrial Applications of LASERs,* Academic Press, New York, 1978.

20. F. Burns and C Zyetz, "LASER Microsoldering," *Electronic Packaging & Production,* May 1981, pp. 109–120.

21. D. U. Chang, "Analytical Investigation of Thick Film Ignition Module Soldering by LASER," *Proc. of ICALEO '85,* Nov., 1985, pp. 27–38.

22. M. Hartmann, et al., "Experimental Investigations in LASER Microsoldering," SPIE, vol. 1598, LASERs in Microelectronics Manufacturing, 1991, pp. 175–185.

23. S. Hernandez, "Wirebonding with CO_2 LASERs," *Surface Mount Technology,* March 1990, pp. 23–26.

24. E. Wright, "LASER vs. Vapor Phase Soldering," *Proc. of the 30th National SAMPE Symposium,* March 1985, pp. 194–201.

25. D. Waller, L. Colella, and R. Pacheco, "Thermode Structure Having Elongated, Thermally Stable Blade," July 1993.

26. J. A. Wilkins, "Heat Transfer Control for Hot Bar Soldering," *Proc. of Surface Mount International,* 1993, pp. 186–192.

27. R. Gunkel, "Solder Aluminum Joints Ultrasonically," *Welding Design and Fabrication,* vol. 52, no. 9, Sept. 1979, pp. 90–92.

28. J. L. Schuster and R. J. Chilko, "Ultrasonic Soldering of Aluminum Heat Exchangers (Air Conditioning Coils)," *Welding Journal (USA),* vol. 54, no. 10, Oct. 1975, pp. 711–717.

29. F. M. Hosking, D. R. Frear, P. T. Vianco, and D. M. Keicher, "SNL Initiatives in Electronic Fluxless Soldering," *Proc. of the 1st International Congress on Environmentally Conscious Manufacturing,* Santa Fe, N.M., Sept. 18, 1991.

30. P. T. Vianco, J. A. Rejent, and F. M. Hosking, "Applications-Oriented Studies in Ultrasonic Soldering," *Proc. of the American Welding Society Convention and Annual Meeting,* Cleveland, Ohio, 1993.

31. J. N. Antonevich, "Fundamentals of Ultrasonic Soldering," American Welding Society, *4th International Soldering Conference, Welding Journal, Research Supplement,* vol. 55, July 1976, pp. 200-s–207-s.

32. A. Shoh, "Industrial Applications of Ultrasound," *IEEE Transactions on Sonics and Ultrasonics,* vol. SU-22, March 1975, pp. 60–71.

CHAPTER 30
NO-CLEAN ASSEMBLY PROCESS

Paul W. Henderson
Hewlett-Packard Electronic Assembly Development Center,
Palo Alto, California

30.1 INTRODUCTION

Changes in environmental regulations governing the use of chlorine-containing solvents (particularly chloroflurocarbons or CFCs) forced the electronics industry to seek other methods of ensuring that printed circuit assemblies are free of harmful flux residues. Through 1992, the most common means of defluxing PCAs was to use some type of CFC defluxing process. When the laws changed, assemblers were faced with the choice of either converting to some other type of defluxing or changing their manufacturing processes in ways such that no defluxing of the finished assemblies would be required. The motivation behind the transition to no-clean processing continues to strengthen as environmental regulations for air, water, and waste discharge become progressively more stringent and opportunities to reduce costs are realized.

The transition to no-clean processing has been nearly as sweeping and traumatic as was the shift from through-hole to surface-mount assembly. Large electronics manufacturers spent tens of millions of dollars each on engineering, capital equipment, product requalification, and initial quality problems, all associated with the conversion to no-clean. The pain was also felt by printed circuit fabricators, flux, solder paste and solder mask suppliers, and equipment vendors who suddenly were called upon to meet new requirements imposed on them by their downstream customers. The lessons which were learned will allow others to avoid many of the pitfalls and expense which early adopters of the technology encountered.

This chapter will discuss some different approaches to no-clean processing, highlight some of the differences between no-clean and other processes which require cleaning, discuss the key success factors of no-clean implementation, and present a troubleshooting guide for no-clean. This chapter is intended to be of use to fabricators of printed circuit boards, assemblers, and those purchasing finished assemblies.

30.2 DEFINITION OF NO-CLEAN

The definition of a no-clean printed circuit assembly process is one in which the post-solder defluxing step has been eliminated. It does not mean, as the name implies, that cleaning is eliminated entirely. Wave-solder pallets, misprinted boards, and tools must still be cleaned.

Generally speaking, there are two main types of no-clean processes: low-residue processes and leave-on processes. There are some novel processes which deliver very low residue performance, but for various reasons (chiefly cost related), they have not become mainstream technologies.

30.2.1 Definition of a Low-Residue No-Clean Process

The low-residue category uses special fluxes, solder pastes, soldering atmospheres, and equipment all designed to minimize the amount of residue left on the board after assembly. The small amount of residue left from these materials can be difficult to detect without magnification. Low-residue materials interfere least with pin testing.

30.2.2 Definition of a Leave-On No-Clean Process

The leave-on category uses fluxes and solder pastes which are frequently low-activity versions of standard materials and have two to three times more residue than the low-residue materials. Leave-on materials do not require special soldering atmospheres or equipment but perform better in them. Leave-on materials have the advantage of being compatible with standard equipment and are usually more robust than the low-residue materials. The drawback of leave-on processes is that they produce flux residues that are readily detected by the naked eye and may interfere with pin probe testing. Because the activators are encapsulated in the residue, spot cleaning to enhance testability can be detrimental to reliability of the assembly, because those activators can be exposed. With leave-on materials it is best to clean thoroughly or not at all. Leave-on residues can also interfere with conformal coating.

30.3 CLEANING OR NO-CLEAN?

If the goal is to minimize cost on simple assemblies with no need for pin testing or concern for cosmetics, then a leave-on process is a good choice. Leave-on processes are attractive because they represent the least dramatic shift and are more tolerant to process variation. If there is no compelling reason to move to a low-residue process, the simpler and less expensive route is to use a leave-on process or some combination of low-residue and leave-on materials to achieve the optimal result. Unfortunately, committing to a leave-on process also means limiting the types of assemblies that can be built in the factory to ones which are compatible with a high-residue process.

Cleaning may be absolutely required in a very few circumstances. Choosing which type of process to implement depends mainly on the requirements of the assembly customer. In other cases, when the board is complex enough to require pin testing or cosmetics are an issue, a low-residue process may be the only choice that does not require cleaning. Assemblers frequently choose a low-residue process because they are forced to by the requirements of the product. To help select a strategy, consider the questions in Table 30.1 to identify the constraints which would direct the choice of one technology or another.

Replacing a mature, well-understood cleaning process can be expensive and requires a substantial effort by all parts of the supply chain. Most assemblers who have made the shift to no-clean have not done so out of environmental altruism alone, but have made the commitment to change only after a careful economic analysis of their operations indicated that no-clean would represent a lower overall cost of ownership.

Though it can be costly to implement, the shift to no-clean is frequently less expensive than aqueous or semiaqueous defluxing. The true cost of ownership can be evaluated only if the assemblers' cost models are detailed enough to provide a true understanding of the current and proposed processes. An accurate analysis must be total cost oriented and consider things that may not be reflected in the current cost model. Table 30.2 illustrates some examples of costs which may be eliminated and some new costs which are associated with changing to no-clean.

TABLE 30.1   Choosing Which Process to Use

Question:	If so, choose:
Will any residues have a negative effect on the electrical performance of the product during its functional life (e.g., corrosion or current leakage)?	For products with a long service life or products intended for a harsh service environment, cleaning or a more rigorous no-clean process qualification may be required.
Does the product operate at very high frequencies (e.g., over 50 MHz) or have very high impedance requirements ($>10^{12}$ $\Omega/\square$)?	A low-residue process or cleaning may be the only option to remove nonionic residues that can act as insulators, which can contribute to cross talk at high frequencies[1] and reduce the impedance between lines.
Does the product use guard traces to protect sensitive circuitry which could be rendered ineffective by residues?	If the guard traces are only on the wave-solder side of the board, a hybrid process using low-residue no-clean materials and a water or semiaqueous cleaning step would be effective for those assemblies. All other assemblies could be handled as no-clean.
Is the customer concerned about the cosmetic appearance of residues?	If so, a low-residue no-clean process may be preferable to a leave-on process.
Would residues have a negative effect on other downstream processes such as in-circuit test or conformal coating?	Cleaning or a low-residue no-clean process can be used with materials chosen, with particular emphasis on compatibility with test and coatings.
Is the assembly dense enough to require probing of solder pasted features (leads or pads)?	Cleaning or use of new types of test probes which rotate or use higher force have been shown to be effective with a low-residue process.

TABLE 30.2   Costs Eliminated and Added by No-Clean

Costs eliminated	Costs added
Floor space for defluxing and water purification equipment	New equipment for reflow and wave solder
Engineering and technical support for defluxing and water purification equipment	Process development
Less maintenance, material used, and waste generated from dross formation	Nitrogen facilities and material
Elimination of hand soldering of cleaner sensitive components	Better hand-soldering tools
Less nonvalue-added touchup	Operator training
	Product requalification

Other cost savings which are real but difficult to quantify are:

- Concerns about component compatibility with cleaning are eliminated.
- Water or solvent is entrapped in connectors or electrolytic capacitors.
- Flux deposits in connectors and switches are reduced.
- Contact poisoning by cleaning materials is eliminated.
- Many no-clean solder pastes are more robust than comparable water-clean pastes, resulting in fewer open solder joint defects and requiring less frequent replacement on the stencil.

No-clean processes are generally less expensive to operate than clean processes, given that the defluxing step and all of the associated operating, support, and occupancy costs are eliminated. However, the idea that all cleaning is eliminated from the process is not, strictly speaking, correct. There remains the need to wash some incoming PCBs or components if contaminated, remove solder balls from some assemblies, wash misprinted PCBs and stencils, and clean wave-solder fixtures. There are also several other new costs added by the switch to no-clean. For certain types of components, the stencil apertures are different for the no-clean process, requiring the replacement of stencils for existing designs. The stencil-washing operation may require a different chemistry (e.g., saponified water or semiaqueous), which may require different equipment. Some special provision must be made to deal with misprinted PCBs; previously, misprinted boards would simply be passed through the cleaning equipment. Facilities are required to support nitrogen storage or generation and have significant associated operating costs. Reflow is best accomplished in a nitrogen atmosphere, which requires that existing equipment be replaced or retrofitted. Wave solder performance is enhanced by nitrogen, which may require replacement, or at least a retrofit to existing equipment.

Whether a process is considered low-residue or leave-on is based on the amount of residual solids remaining in the flux after reflow, or wave, solder, as shown in Table 30.3.

TABLE 30.3 A Comparison of the Solids Content of Low-Residue and Leave-on Materials

Percent solids	Leave-on	Low-residue	Very low residue
Wave-solder flux	15–40%	1.5–4.0%	<1.5%
Solder paste	40–70%	20–30%	<20%

The role of the residues in the solder paste is very important. Rosin or resins serve to protect the solder particles in the paste from becoming oxidized in reflow, promote tack, activate the surfaces to be joined, and promote wetting. Other additives promote better rheology of the paste. All of the materials which do not volatilize in the reflow process are left behind on the assembly.

These categorizations are only meant to be representative. In practice, a wide variety of different combinations of materials may be used to achieve different results. For example, many assemblers will use a leave-on solder paste with a low-residue wave-solder flux to maximize the robustness of the SMT portion of the process and minimize the residues left on the wave-solder side of the assembly.

A few assemblers use a hybrid process where they use a leave-on solder paste and an organic acid wave-solder flux followed by DI water cleaning to compensate for components which are marginally solderable. The leave-on residues are unaffected by the DI water clean while the organic acid flux residues are removed. Other pure surface-mount products follow the same process with the exception of wave solder and cleaning.

30.4 IMPLEMENTING NO-CLEAN

Before beginning to implement no-clean, it is important to study the present cleaning equipment very carefully and log everything that goes into it. In addition to soldered assemblies, there are many other things that are routinely put through the cleaner: misprinted boards, parts in baskets, and reworked assemblies. There are many quality issues that can be hidden by cleaning: large numbers of misprinted boards, assemblies that are difficult to test, use of an aggressive flux to compensate for poor solderability, etc.

Nearly every assembly process step requires some adaptation to work successfully in the no-clean environment. Other parts of the organization not normally associated with production are also affected. Cost models will change to reflect differences in process. Procurement must get involved to control soldering materials coming into the factory. Materials engineering must determine which parts will be qualified and how; information systems and databases may change to include which parts are qualified and which are not. Inspection criteria and SPC procedures will change, requiring new training for operators and inspectors. Documentation must be updated to include new procedures to maintain ISO compliance.

30.4.1 Incoming Quality Assurance (IQA)

Procedures in IQA must be modified to include verification of solderability and cleanliness of incoming boards and components. If the assembler chooses not to conduct these tests in-house, the supplier's methods or other service must be evaluated. Additional resources may be required to work with component and PCB suppliers to bring their products into compliance.

30.4.2 Stencil Aperture Design and Stencil Finish

In order to prevent the formation of solder beads (small solder balls next to passive components on the solder-pasted side of the board), the stencil apertures must be modified to prevent the solder paste from being squeezed underneath the component during placement. An example of solder beading and several possible aperture modifications designed to eliminate them are shown in Fig. 30.1.

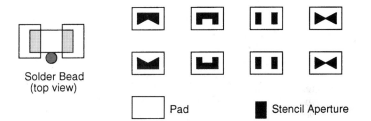

FIGURE 30.1   Stencil apertures used to eliminate solder beads.

The surface finish of the stencil can make a significant difference in the robustness of the stencil-printing process for pitches ≤0.65 mm. There are many materials and processes available to make stencils (plated Ni, molybdenum foils, laser etching, etc.), but the most important principle is that the walls of the aperture must be smooth in order to consistently release the paste. The least expensive way to accomplish this is to use a standard stencil material (e.g., alloy 42), with a subtractive etching process and electropolish the stencil afterward to smooth the surface. Electropolishing adds 10 to 20 percent to the cost of the stencil, but the result is well worthwhile.

30.4.3 Stencil Washing

The stencil-washing operation, which is a frequently overlooked part of the surface-mount process, is critical to the success of the process overall. If the stencil is inadequately cleaned, flux residues will adhere to the side walls of the apertures, making it difficult for the solder paste bricks to release from the stencil during printing. This problem causes insufficient solder joints and open solder joints on finer pitches, and is difficult to diagnose. It is extremely important to actively monitor the concentration of saponifier or the condition of the cleaning medium. If the saponifier concentration falls to an out-of-control low level, partially saponified flux residues will be left behind which are not visually obvious. These residues can be removed by applying alcohol liberally to the stencil and wiping dry with a clean, lint-free cloth. Scraping excess solder paste from the stencil with a polymer squeegee will aid in cleaning and help minimize the lead content of the effluent. Stencils should be washed as soon as possible after removing them from the stencil printer to prevent solder paste flux residues from drying in the stencil apertures.

30.4.4 Cleaning Misprinted PCBs

Cleaning misprinted boards requires some special consideration. Merely scraping the solder paste off and wiping the board with an alcohol wiper does not do an adequate job of removing the solder particles from between the lands and the solder mask. In some cases, the same equipment can be used for washing stencils and washing misprinted boards. With most solder pastes, misprinted boards should be washed within an hour of printing.

30.4.5 Stencil Printing

Low-residue solder paste rheology is more sensitive than most RMA pastes and anything that can be done to improve the consistency of stencil printing is worthwhile. The most important factor is to have a consistent process for setting up and operating the stencil printer which is followed by all of the operators.

Proper choice of squeegee material can have a significant impact on stencil-print process yield. Polymer squeegees have a tendency to deflect into stencil apertures in the direction perpendicular to squeegee travel and scoop out solder paste, leaving peaks of solder paste at the end of the printed bricks. This effect contributes to variability in the amount of solder paste deposited. This variability can be reduced dramatically by using metal squeegees which stay planar with the top surface of the stencil and do not scoop out the paste.[2]

Since low-residue solder pastes have more volatile components, the useful working time of the paste on the stencil is limited to 4 to 6 h. At the end of this time, the paste should be removed from the stencil and discarded, the stencil washed, and production resumed with fresh paste. The best indication that the paste is past its useful life is when insufficient paste defects suddenly begin to occur on 0.5-mm pitch patterns. Mixing fresh paste into the old paste on the stencil is not recommended; it only extends the usefulness of the paste for a few more prints. Humidity above 50 percent RH or below 10 percent RH will further reduce the life of the paste on the stencil. Making a plot of insufficients versus time will show at what point the material breaks down.

30.4.6 Pick and Place

The pick-and-place process itself is not significantly affected by no-clean, but queuing times before component placement can be limited with a low-residue process. Because the tack time is shorter with a low-residue process, there is less flexibility with printing a large number of boards and holding them in a buffer before pick and place. Similarly, tack will decrease after the component has been placed and before the board is reflowed. In practice, if a board has not been placed before 75 percent of the tack time has passed, it should be treated as a misprint, cleaned, and printed again. Humidity above 50 percent will reduce tack time significantly. See Table 30.4.

TABLE 30.4   Tack Times of Solder Pastes

Solder paste type	Average tack time, h
RMA/leave-on	>24
Low-residue no-clean	2–6
Water-clean	1–2

30.4.7   Nitrogen

Depending on the volume and purity of nitrogen required for the facility, nitrogen can be either delivered to the site in bulk liquid form or generated on-site through a variety of methods[3] (membrane separation, pressure swing absorption, etc.). Nitrogen promotes solder wetting by increasing the wetting force and decreasing the wetting time.[4] Since little oxygen is present, discoloration of laminates, light-colored plastic connectors, and flux residues is eliminated. The purity of nitrogen required is determined by the type of process. (See Table 30.5.)

TABLE 30.5   Nitrogen Purity Requirements

No-clean process type	Maximum allowable oxygen concentration
Leave-on	21% (air)
Low-residue	100–500 ppm
Very low residue	50–100 ppm

Nitrogen represents a significant operating cost ranging from $10 an hour per reflow oven or wave-solder machine in the United States to more than $80 in Singapore. For this reason alone, many assemblers in the Far East have chosen a leave-on process which can tolerate processing in air. However, in wave solder, it can be difficult to determine the difference in defect rates between soldering in a 5-ppm oxygen atmosphere and a 1000-ppm atmosphere. At 1000 ppm there is still a benefit of reduced dross formation, and on-site generation is a better alternative than not inerting the process.

30.4.8   Reflow

Many studies have indicated that reflow performance is significantly enhanced by the use of nitrogen.[5,6] Many assemblers use the transition to no-clean as an opportunity to upgrade their reflow equipment to fully convective ovens. A highly convective reflow environment enables better temperature control of the whole assembly with a smaller total temperature difference between the most and least dense parts of the assembly.

The penalty for this superior performance is more complicated, time consuming, and expensive maintenance of the equipment. The portion of the solder paste which volatilizes tends to redeposit on the cooler surfaces in the oven, requiring regular disassembly of the equipment for thorough cleaning, particularly if the oven uses a special cooling zone at the end. The lower the residue of the solder paste material, the more material there is to redeposit in the oven and exhaust. The volatile residues also tend to block the sampling ports of the oxygen analyzer, giving false readings (this can be readily diagnosed by checking the flow meter on the analyzer).

30.4.9 Wave Solder

Flux selection for wave solder depends primarily on the priority placed on different performance characteristics of the flux:

- Solder defect rate (skips, icicling, solder webbing, etc.)
- Visible residue level
- Compatibility with other process chemistries
- Compatibility with in-circuit test
- Surface insulation resistance
- Ionic contamination level
- Volatile organic compound (VOC) content
- Consistency of deposition

In many cases, one factor may dominate the decision-making process. For example, if a customer is very sensitive to any visible residues, residue level may be the driving factor. In locations where VOC emissions are strictly regulated, a VOC-free flux may be the only option. These fluxes use water instead of alcohol as a solvent and are not flammable. They do require additional preheating to evaporate the water. If any water remains on the bottom side of the board when it enters the solder wave, it will cause the molten solder to spatter, causing solder balls on the bottom surface of the board.

Flux can be applied with standard foam or wave fluxers, but most spray application methods are superior.[7] Foam and wave fluxing are difficult to control for most low-residue fluxes because of the high alcohol content (about 98 percent) and the rapid evaporation rate. Specific gravity monitoring is not possible for fluxes with a solids content of less than 5 percent. Instead, frequent titration is required to monitor the flux composition. The rapid evaporation of alcohol in the flux contributes significantly to VOC emissions. Foam fluxers require frequent cleaning, and contaminated flux must be disposed of as hazardous waste.

Spray fluxers may use a rotating mesh drum, an ultrasonic head, air spray, air-assisted airless spray, or other novel approaches. The most robust methods keep the flux in a sealed container so that the flux is never contaminated, composition does not vary, and it does not need to be controlled.[8] Spray fluxing offers more control over the quantity of flux deposited on the board, so that the minimum amount of flux needed may be applied. Spray flux methods can easily reduce flux and thinner usage by 70 to 90 percent compared to foam or wave fluxing. Table 30.6 illustrates some of the advantages and disadvantages of the different approaches to flux application.

The biggest difference in wave-solder equipment for no-clean is the addition of nitrogen inerting. Some benefits of inert wave soldering are 80 to 95 percent less dross formation, fewer solder skips, less icicling, solder webbing, and less makeup solder is required. Switching to inert wave soldering can often be justified on the basis of the reduced maintenance, downtime, and hazardous waste disposal associated with dross removal. Inert soldering will not, however, overcome poor design or solderability.[9] Dross formation is directly related to the amount of oxygen in the soldering atmosphere, as shown in Table 30.7.

Soldering equipment and retrofit options vary in the degree to which the equipment is inerted. The wave-solder machine may be fully inerted, have a short hood which covers a portion of the preheat and the solder pot, or only inerting the solder pot. Some of the advantages and disadvantages[10] of the different types of inerting are shown in Table 30.8.

Board design issues for no-clean are mostly generic to wave soldering. The biggest problems are solder skips on SOTs, ICs, Tantalums, and thick chip components. Component orientation is critical: The surfaces to be soldered must be perpendicular to the wave. Care must be exercised to prevent components from being shadowed by one another. Pad design is an important secondary effect.[11]

TABLE 30.6 Advantages and Disadvantages of Flux Application Methods

Flux application method	Advantages	Disadvantages
Foam or wave	Inexpensive equipment	Difficult to control flux composition and deposition quantity, high solvent evaporation loss, freqeuent cleaning required
Rotating drum spray	Simple, flux deposition quantity is more controllable than foam or wave	Same problems as foam and wave since the drum rotates in an open reservoir of flux
Ultrasonic spray	Good control of flux deposition quantity, excellent composition control	Sensitive to variations in exhaust, some variation from center to edge on large assemblies
Air spray	Good control of flux deposition quantity, good center-to-edge distribution control, excellent composition control, low maintenance	Significant overspray
Air-assisted airless spray	Good control of flux deposition quantity, good center-to-edge distribution control, excellent composition control, low maintenance	Significant overspray, more variation than airspray

TABLE 30.7 Dross Formation Rates as a Function of Oxygen Level

Oxygen level, ppm	Relative dross formation rate
5	1
50	2
500	4
1000	5.2
5000	9
10,000	10.8

TABLE 30.8 Advantages and Disadvantages of Inerting Methods

Wave-solder inerting method	Advantages	Disadvantages
Fully inerted	Prevents oxidation of board and components in preheat, lowest oxygen consumption (600–1200 SCFH)	Dedicated equipment—very expensive
Short hood retrofit	Reduces oxidation of board and components in preheat	Moderate oxygen consumption (>1400 SCFH)
Pot-only retrofit	Simple	Highest oxygen consumption (up to 2400 SCFH), does not prevent oxidation of board and components

30.4.10 Hand Soldering

Hand soldering and rework are made significantly more difficult by the use of low-residue no-clean materials. Leave-on rework fluxes and cored solders are similar to those which require cleaning, except that they are less active. The relatively high solids content of leave-on materials performs several important functions in soldering: it wets the surface to be soldered, activating it and providing good heat transfer between the tip of the soldering tool and the workpiece, it protects the tinned surface of the tip, and it provides protection against oxidation during the heating cycle. Because the flux residues remain on the workpiece, longer heating cycles can be used to overcome marginal solderability and less attention needs to be paid to soldering temperatures and tip maintenance.[12]

Low-residue hand soldering has none of these advantages. The low residues activate more quickly and at lower temperatures, volatilize while soldering, and require good solderability of the workpiece. The residue does not protect the tinned surface of the soldering tool well and requires that the tips be maintained much more frequently. Soldering must be done at the lowest possible temperature and as quickly as possible to prevent oxidation buildup on the tip. In addition to the flux in the cored solder, many instances will require a liquid flux to be applied with a fine brush to enable both the tip and the workpiece to be adequately cleaned. After soldering, some of the residues may be further volatilized by passing a stream of hot nitrogen over the hand-soldered joints with a hot-air pencil; this also ensures that all of the flux has been fully activated. Even so, some assemblies may require spot cleaning to enable testing and enhance cosmetics.

The key to successful implementation of low-residue hand soldering is training, discipline, use of appropriate soldering tools and rigorous maintenance. Even highly experienced hand-soldering operators will need to significantly change the way they work and will not readily accept the new materials without a good understanding of how they perform. Operators will need to:

- Learn to solder at the lowest possible temperature.
- Turn off soldering irons when not in use.
- Tin tips before storing them.
- Use tips that maximize contact between the tip and the workpiece (usually short, blunt ones).

Periodic review of soldering practices will help prevent operators from reverting to old practices. Trying to economize by purchasing cheap hand-soldering tools is a very bad idea. The better tools work by controlling the heat delivery to the tip and, though more expensive initially, last much longer and produce better quality results if maintained properly with tip tinners and tinning blocks.[13]

30.4.11 In-Circuit Testing

Test is one area which requires significant adaptation to be compatible with no-clean. In some cases, test pins should be replaced with high-force or rotating pins. In many cases where users of no-clean have had problems with test, the root cause was related to fixture design—rigorous adherence to fixture design rules is a must.

30.5 RELIABILITY OF NO-CLEAN PRODUCTS

The biggest concern related to no-clean processing is whether the assemblies will be reliable or not. But before discussing reliability, it is important to define the chemical nature of the residues which are left on the assembly after processing. The chemical nature of the residues will determine what tests to perform and what kind of results to expect. The most easily tested components of any residue left on the assembly are the residues contributed from the solder paste vehicle, wave-solder flux, rework flux, and the interactions of all of them. (See Table 30.9.) If a no-clean material is not fully activated (e.g., when flooding an area with liquid flux in a hand-soldering operation), the unreacted activators left behind can cause corrosion. The interactions between materials are important because two materials which are benign when separate can sometimes cause current leakage, corrosion, or dendritic growth when combined and exposed to high temperature or humidity, or are biased.[14,15] It is less easy to test other materials that may be present in the residue: ionic contamination from the PCB or components, lead and tin metallic salts which form when their oxides are removed, and organic byproducts which may be evolved when the PCB and components are elevated to reflow temperatures.

TABLE 30.9 Chemical Nature of No-Clean Residues

Residue type	Low-residue process	Leave-on process
Solder paste	Rheological agents, tackifiers, rosin or resin	Rosin, activators
Wave-solder flux	Adipic acid, succinic acid, surfactants	Rosin, activators
Rework flux	Adipic acid, succinic acid	Rosin, activators

Three of the most common reliability tests performed to qualify no-clean processes are surface insulation resistance testing (SIR), ionic contamination testing, and highly accelerated stress testing (HAST). In addition, product-specific reliability qualification testing which is appropriate to the intended service environment is essential to detect any unanticipated effects on the finished assembly. There are other methods for detecting residues (e.g., ion chromatography, high-performance liquid chromatography), but most are not well suited to a production environment because they are expensive to set up and operate and require highly trained people to operate and interpret them.

30.5.1 Surface Insulation Resistance Testing for No-Clean

Measuring SIR is probably the most effective and widely used method of determining if residues on an assembly are safe. One of the most accepted protocols is given in IPC-TM-650 section 2.6.3. It is particularly important to evaluate the interactive effect of the various materials used in the process. In some instances, incompatibilities have been found between solder paste flux and wave-solder flux, rework fluxes, and certain types of solder masks.

This test is commonly done by applying the material(s) to be tested to an IPC B-25 comb pattern, processing the test board or coupon through the normal process steps, and measuring the leakage current in an elevated temperature and humidity-controlled environment. Test conditions which are commonly used are 85°C, 85 percent RH and 40°C, 95 percent RH. It is important to choose a set of conditions to use and apply them consistently—it is very difficult to meaningfully compare results obtained at different temperature and humidity conditions. If a comb pattern is designed onto a sparse area of a production PCB, SIR can be used to monitor process performance.

30.5.2 Ionic Contamination Testing for No-Clean

Testing for ionic contamination via a solvent extraction (e.g., Omegameter, Ionograph or similar instrument) has long been used to monitor the effectiveness of cleaning processes used on organic acid fluxes. The methods used with each of the instruments are similar in that they rely on dissolving and dissociating any remaining flux residues in an alcohol/water solution and monitor the conductivity of the solution to estimate the level of contamination. Unfortunately, many no-clean materials do not dissociate well in the alcohol/water solution and the instruments are not able to detect them efficiently, rendering the current ICT standards largely irrelevant. The method may be useful for monitoring incoming materials (to evaluate the degree and consistency of solder mask cure, for example) and the baseline performance of the no-clean process, but will not, in fact, ensure that an assembly is acceptably clean.

30.5.3 Highly Accelerated Stress Testing (HAST) for No-Clean

Evaluating the effect of residues can be done with HAST[16] testing. This involves applying the flux material(s) of interest to SOT-23 diodes on a test board, processing the board normally, and exposing the board to an 85°C, 85 percent RH environment with a reverse 20-V bias for 1000 h. This method is sensitive to ionic residues, particularly chlorides and bromides. Since some flux formulations advertised as no-clean actually contain some amount of chloride activators, this test is particularly useful in evaluating their long-term effects.

30.6 THE IMPACT OF NO-CLEAN ON PRINTED CIRCUIT BOARD FABRICATION

Because the assembly is not intended to be cleaned again after the printed circuit board is fabricated, the bare board must be clean before it enters the assembly process. While the current mil-spec[17] for ionic contamination is aimed at the cleanliness of finished assemblies, it does not specify cleanliness levels for the raw board. The specific cleanliness level required varies depending on the instrument used to perform the test. A useful rule of thumb is to aim for a consistent bare-board cleanliness level of less than half the allowed level for the finished assembly. For example, if the specification for the finished assembly is 20 $\mu g/in^2$, the bare board should have no more than 10 $\mu g/in^2$ prior to assembly. This allows a reasonable margin for the additional contamination that is added to the assembly via flux residues, incoming contamination on components, and contamination from handling. The most effective way to implement this is for the printed circuit fabricator to sample the boards just prior to packing and shipment operations.

No-clean fluxes are significantly less active than fluxes which are intended to be removed by a cleaning operation. Poor solderability of the printed circuit board cannot be compensated for in a no-clean assembly process by using a stronger flux. The use of nitrogen in wave solder and reflow cannot promote wetting on inherently unsolderable surfaces. Unfortunately, no reliable, inexpensive method to quantify solderability has replaced the widely accepted "dip-and-look" method.[18] This test involves dipping a sample of the PCB coated with a standard flux into a solder pot and looking for any signs of nonwetting or dewetting of the solder. While far short of ideal, the dip-and-look test is better than no test at all and should be performed routinely by the printed circuit fabricator.

In the wave-solder process, it is common for small solder balls to adhere to the bottom of the board as it exits the solder wave. This is a phenomenon which has always occurred but was never specifically addressed because the solder balls were nearly always removed during postsolder cleaning. There are a variety of causes for solder balls that occur during wave soldering.[19] Some of the most common are:

- Solder mask material
- Solder mask surface roughness (can vary some depending on material surface treatment)
- Solder mask cure profile

- Type of flux used in hot-air leveling
- Type of wave-solder flux

The most significant factor is the choice of solder mask material. Some reduction in the number of solder balls can be made by experimenting with different combinations of wave solder and HAL flux types and solder mask cure profiles, but these measures offer only incremental improvements. Though troublesome and expensive, qualifying a new solder mask may be the only way to truly eliminate solder balls.

Hot-air-leveled solder has traditionally been applied to protect and promote solderability of the printed circuit board metallization. However, both fabricators and assemblers alike have been plagued with problems associated with the difficulty of applying a complete, even, and consistent thickness of solder to the board. An overly thin solder coating results in the copper-tin intermetallic layer being exposed, which is much more difficult to solder (largely negating the intended effect of ensuring a more solderable surface on the board). An overly thick or inconsistent solder coating makes assembly difficult because the bumpy topography of the board can hold the stencil away from the board, resulting in excess solder paste deposition on the board and bridging during reflow. Also, a thick solder coating results in crowned pads which are difficult to reliably place parts on. When a placement machine applies pressure to the part, the leads slide off of the crown, resulting in part misalignment and bridging.

To avoid the problems associated with hot-air-leveled solder surfaces, many assemblers have switched to organically coated bare copper boards. The metallization is perfectly flat, solders well, and has a lower ionic contamination level than similar hot-air-leveled boards.[20] The organic coating process is also vastly simpler and less expensive to operate than hot-air leveling. Most of the concerns about the solderability, shelf life, and robustness of the organically coated surface (e.g., imidazole) have turned out to be unfounded.

30.7 TROUBLESHOOTING THE NO-CLEAN PROCESS

See Table 30.10.

TABLE 30.10 Troubleshooting the No-Clean Process

Problem	Probable causes	Remedy
Poor wetting of solder paste to PCB	• Oxygen level in reflow oven too high (low-residue process)	• Check oven for leaks, check exhaust balance
	• PCB surface has poor solderability	• Test PCB for solderability
Solder beads next to passive components	• Full-sized apertures on stencil	• Check stencil apertures, modify stencil design if not updated to new design rules
Open solder joints on fine-pitch components	• Insufficient solder paste (clogged stencil apertures)	• Check stencil to see if apertures are clogged, clean stencil, discard solder paste and apply new paste to the stencil; if problem persists, check saponifier concentration in the stencil washer and correct
	• Poor component coplanarity	• Measure 30 components and calculate mean and standard deviation of coplanarity, if Cpk is <1.33, contact supplier

TABLE 30.10   Troubleshooting the No-Clean Process   (*Continued*)

Problem	Probable causes	Remedy
Solder shorts on solder paste side	• Excessive solder paste	• Check PCB for excess HASL
	• Component misalignment	• Check part alignment after placement and before reflow
Fine solder particles around pads on the paste side	• Stencil-to-board misalignment	• Check print alignment to see if solder paste is being printed in between the pad and the solder mask, correct alignment
	• Poor cleaning of a misprinted board	• Check to see if misprinted boards are being completely cleaned
	• Insufficient wiping of the underside of the stencil	• Wipe the bottom of the stencil with a dry wiper
Open solder joints on wave-solder side	• Assembly not in intimate contact with the solder wave	• Check wave height, board position in the conveyor, pallet condition
	• Incomplete flux coverage	• Run flux coverage test, check board position in the conveyor
Solder shorts on wave-solder side	• Component orientation	• Check component orientation with respect to the solder wave, rotate 90°
Components misaligned	• Tack failure of solder paste (low-residue process)	• Check to see if time between stencil print and placement has been more than 3 h; if so, clean pasted boards and reprint them.
		• Check to see if paste has been on the stencil for more than 6 h; if so, clean the stencil and use new paste
	• Crowned surface on PCB metallization (excess HASL)	• Rework bare PCBs
	• Placement machine error	• Check placement accuracy and correct if necessary
Poor print definition of solder paste	• Wiping	• Wipe bottom of the stencil with a dry, lint-free cloth
	• Alignment	• Check alignment of stencil to board
	• Stencil cleanliness	• Clean stencil
	• Saponifier concentration	• Check saponifier concentration
	• Old paste	• Paste on stencil more than 6 h—clean stencil and replace paste
Grainy solder joints	• Reflow profile too cool	• Check reflow profile
	• Oxygen level in oven too high	• Check oxygen level
		If the oxygen level reads OK, check to be sure that gas is flowing through the analyzer
		If the oxygen level is too high, check for changes to the oven setup and changes in the exhaust system from varying demands

TABLE 30.10 Troubleshooting the No-Clean Process (*Continued*)

Problem	Probable causes	Remedy
Large solder beads on top side of board next to passive components	• Stencil aperture shape	• Redesign stencil using an aperture shape that prevents solder from being squeezed underneath the component
Small solder particles on top side of the board between pad and solder mask	• Stencil alignment	• Check stencil printer alignment
	• Pad size on board less than stencil aperture size, paste is printed between the pad and the solder mask and may not coalesce with the rest of the joint during reflow	• Check to see if board feature size is within spec • Redesign stencil with slightly smaller apertures

REFERENCES

1. Allan Beikmohamadi, "Post-Reflow, No-Clean Solder Paste Residue and Electrical Performance," *Circuits Assembly,* March 1994.
2. Mark Curtin and Andrew Davis, "The Micro-Mechanics of Fine-Pitch Printing," *Circuits Assembly,* Aug. 1992.
3. Kevin McKean, "An Atmosphere-Purity Selection Guideline," *Surface Mount Technology,* Nov. 1994.
4. Mark Nowotarski, "Oxygen's Effect on the Surface of Solder," *Nepcon East,* Boston, June 1994.
5. Frank de Klein, "Open vs. Closed Reflow Soldering," *Circuits Assembly,* April 1993.
6. Steve Christensen, "An Observation of Nitrogen Atmospheres in a Convective IR Reflow System," *Proceedings of PWB Assembly Section of NEPCON East,* 1990, p. 655.
7. Brad Stoops, "Precision Application of No-Clean Fluxes," *Circuits Assembly,* March 1994.
8. Santiago Rodriguez-Sallaberry, "Spray Fluxing vs. Foam Fluxing," *Circuits Assembly,* June 1992.
9. Edward K. Chang, Mark T. Kirschner, and Sean M. Adams, "A Study of Several No Clean Fluxes under Different Atmospheres," *Circuits Assembly,* March 1994.
10. W. H. Down, "Wave Soldering Issues," *Circuits Assembly,* Nov. 1994.
11. John Maxwell, "Wave Soldering," *Surface Mount Technology,* Aug. 1994.
12. Edwin Oh, "Extending Soldering Iron Tip Life," *Circuits Assembly,* June 1994.
13. Kathi Johnson, "Hand Soldering and No-Clean Fluxes," *Circuits Assembly,* June 1994.
14. John Savi, Allan MacCormack, and Curt Gold, "No-Clean Flux Incompatibilities," *Circuits Assembly,* June 1992.
15. Chantal Hemens-Davis and Roy Sunstrum, "No-Clean: Material Compatibility Issues," *Circuits Assembly,* March 1993.
16. JEDEC Std. 22-A110.
17. MIL-P-28809 or IPC TM650.
18. MIL-STD-202F, Method 208F, or ASTM 0577.
19. Theo Langer and Torsten Reckart, "A Solder Ball Study, Part 2," *Printed Circuit Fabrication,* Dec. 1992.
20. Jerry Murray, "Beyond Anti-Tarnish: An SMT Revolution," *Printed Circuit Fabrication,* Feb. 1993.

CHAPTER 31
FLUXES AND CLEANING

Laura J. Turbini, Ph.D.
*Georgia Institute of Technology, School of Materials Science
and Engineering, Atlanta, Georgia*

31.1 INTRODUCTION

Computers, portable phones, and hand-held calculators have one thing in common. They each contain an electronic assembly composed of integrated circuits and discrete components soldered to a printed wiring board (PWB) to create an electrically functional circuit. In the past, printed circuit assemblies were made exclusively with through-hole components. Today's assemblies contain components that are both through-hole and surface-mount and some even contain unpackaged integrated circuit (IC) chips attached directly to the PWB. Except in the case of direct chip attachment by wire bonding, the use of a soldering flux to ensure good joining is almost universally practiced. Thus, soldering flux choice has become an important consideration in the manufacturing of electronic assemblies. As electronic product designs have moved to more densely packed printed wiring boards with fine lines and spacing, two-sided surface-mount technology, fine-pitch components, and ball grid array packages, the role of the soldering flux has become a critical link in the chain of events required for a successful manufacturing process.

Until recently, the soldering process was followed by a cleaning step to remove flux residues and to ensure the reliability of the assembly. This practice has been challenged by the elimination of a major class of cleaning materials which had been used for flux residue removal. The targeted cleaning agents include chlorofluorocarbons (CFCs) and methyl chloroform (1,1,1-trichloroethane) which have been shown to destroy stratospheric ozone.[1]

Twenty years ago, the predominant flux chemistry was rosin-based flux. Today, great advances have been made in fluxes, and a large variety of formulations with very different chemistries are being used. This chapter will review the assembly, soldering and cleaning processes; discuss the soldering flux in terms of its role in soldering; review the variety of flux chemistries available along with their advantages and disadvantages, and comment on the clean/no-clean options as they relate to flux choice. In addition, characterization techniques for soldering fluxes and pastes based on industry standards will be included.

31.2 ASSEMBLY PROCESS

The basic elements of an electronic assembly are the PWB, the components, and the interconnecting metallization. The majority of PWBs are made of epoxy-glass substrate with copper or solder-coated copper metallization. In many cases, there is a solder mask which covers most of the circuit traces, leaving exposed only those patterns where soldering will occur during assembly. Boards designed for through-hole components usually contain copper-plated through-holes which may be solder-coated; those designed for surface-mount components will have metallized pads for interconnecting the surface-mount parts to form the assembly.

Through-hole components and bottom-side surface-mount discrete components are soldered to the board in a wave-soldering machine. The process flow for this is diagrammed in Fig. 31.1. The PWB is populated with bottom-side discrete components which are placed on a small drop of adhesive. When the adhesive is cured, it holds the component to the board. Next, the board is turned over and the through-hole components are inserted. The assembled board is then placed on a conveyor which moves the assembly over (1) the flux applicator, (2) the preheat station, and (3) the solder wave. The most common flux application is by foam created when compressed air is forced through a porous stone immersed in liquid flux. As the assembled board passes over the fluxer, the foam flux covers the bottom surface of the board and penetrates up through the plated-through-holes. Spray fluxers which spray a fine mist of flux on the board are also used, particularly for applying the newer low-solids fluxes. A third type of flux application involves a wave fluxer in which flux is pumped up through a nozzle, producing a wave of liquid flux.

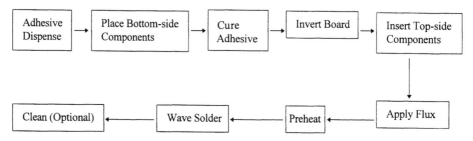

FIGURE 31.1 Traditional through-hole soldering involves the insertion of components, followed by flux application, a preheat step, wave soldering, and a final optional cleaning step. Today, bottom-side discrete components are also included in the wave solder process.

The preheater station is responsible for volatilizing the flux solvent and heating the flux ingredients to activate them. When the assembly moves on to the solder wave, the metallization on the board and components, having been cleaned through the action of the soldering flux, are bathed in molten solder which pushes up through the plated holes and metallurgically bonds the components to the board. In most instances, the solder alloy used in the solder wave is 63 percent Sn/37 percent Pb (melting point of 183°C) which is heated to as high as 260°C. Finally, the conveyor moves the assembly past the solder wave, allowing the molten solder to solidify upon cooling. In a high-volume manufacturing facility, the completed assembly frequently continues on a conveyor into an in-line cleaner.

Some assemblies are composed exclusively of surface-mounted components. In this case (Fig. 31.2) solder paste is stenciled onto the metallized pads of the PWB, the component leads are accurately placed into the solder paste, and the assembly is reflowed usually in a convection oven. As the conveyor carries the assembly through the oven, the first zone acts as a preheat zone where the solder paste becomes active in removing oxidation from the board and component metallization as well as the solder powder of the paste. The zones following the preheat zone allow the solder to melt, forming a bond between the metallization on the board and that on the component leads. The final zones allow cooling and solidification of the solder.

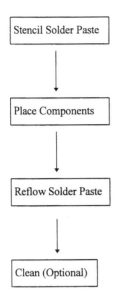

FIGURE 31.2 Surface-mount soldering requires stencil printing of solder paste, followed by component placement, reflow soldering, and a final optional cleaning step.

31.3 SOLDERING FLUX

Soldering[2] is defined as the process of joining metallic surfaces with solder without the melting of the basis metal. In order for this joining to take place, the metal surfaces must be clean of contamination and oxidation. This cleaning action is performed by the flux,[2] a chemically active compound which, when heated, removes minor surface oxidation, minimizes oxidation of the basis metal, and promotes the formation of an intermetallic layer between solder and basis metal. The soldering flux has several functions to perform. It must:

- React with or remove oxide and other contamination on the surface to be soldered.
- Dissolve the metal salts formed during the reaction with the metal oxides.
- Protect the surface from reoxidation before soldering occurs.
- Provide a thermal blanket to spread the heat evenly during soldering.
- Reduce the interfacial surface tension between the solder and the substrate in order to enhance wetting.

To perform these functions, soldering flux formulations contain the following types of ingredients: (1) vehicle, (2) solvent, (3) activators, and (4) other additives.

31.3.1 Vehicle

The vehicle is a solid or nonvolatile liquid which coats the surface to be soldered, dissolves the metal salts formed in the reaction of the activators with the surface metal oxides and, ideally, provides a heat transfer medium between the solder and the components or PWB substrate. Rosin, resins, glycols, polyglycols, polyglycol surfactants, and glycerine are among the major chemicals used. Rosin or resins are selected when more benign chemicals are required since their residues are less apt to cause reliability failures. Glycols, polyglycols, polyglycol surfactants, and glycerine are used in water-soluble flux formulations because they provide excellent wetting of the board surface and dissolve the more active materials used in these formulations.

31.3.2 Solvent

The solvent serves to dissolve the vehicle, activators, and other additives. It evaporates during the preheat and soldering process. Alcohols, glycols, glycol esters, and glycol ethers are common solvents used. The solvent chosen will depend on its ability to dissolve the flux constituents for a given formulation.

31.3.3 Activators

Activators are present in the flux formulation to enhance the removal of metal oxide from the surfaces to be soldered. They are reactive even at room temperature, but their activity is enhanced as the temperature is raised during the preheat step of the soldering process. Amine hydrochlorides, dicarboxylic acids such as adipic or succinic, and organic acids such as citric, malic, or abietic are among the common activators found in flux formulations. Halide- and amine-containing activators give excellent soldering yields but may cause reliability problems if not properly removed in a well-controlled cleaning step.

31.3.4 Other Additives

Soldering fluxes often contain small amounts of other ingredients which serve a specialized function. For example, a surfactant may be added to enhance the wetting properties. This constituent can also assist in the foaming characteristics required for foam flux application. Other additives may be included to lower the interfacial surface tension between the molten solder and the PWB as it exits the solder wave, decreasing the chance for solder bridges to form. Solder paste formulations require the presence of additives to provide good viscosity or flow characteristics, low slump during the preheat step, and good tack characteristics for holding the component in place until reflow occurs. Finally, cored-wire flux used for hand-soldering contains a plasticizer to soften the flux ingredients which are present in the core of the wire.

31.4 FLUX FORM VS. SOLDERING PROCESS

Although one usually thinks of soldering flux as a liquid, in fact, the soldering flux can exist in several different forms. *Liquid flux* is commonly used for wave-soldering or hand-soldering applications. *Paste flux,* a thick viscous flux, is used to hold components to the board prior to reflow of the already present solder. Direct attachment of a solder-bumped chip or ball grid array (BGA) packages to solder pads on a PWB is an example of its usefulness. *Solder paste* contains *solder-paste flux* which is the solder paste without the solder particles. Solder paste is used in surface-mount attachment of components such as chip carriers, TAB (tape-automated bonding) -leaded packages, and discrete resistors and capacitors. Finally, *flux-cored solder wire* is used for hand soldering and *flux-cored solder preforms* are used as the solder/flux source in some applications such as backplane connector pin reflow soldering.

Abietic Acid

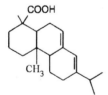

Pimaric Acid

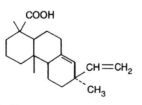

FIGURE 31.3 The two most common rosin isomers are abietic acid and pimaric acid.

31.5 ROSIN FLUX

Early flux formulations for electronics used rosin, which is a naturally occurring resin obtained from the sap of a pine tree. Its exact composition will vary depending on the part of the world where it originates as well as the time of the year. Rosin contains a mixture of resin acids, the two most common ones being pimaric acid and abietic acid (Fig. 31.3). Rosin has been a favorite material for soldering because it liquefies during the soldering process, dissolves the metal salts, and then solidifies when cooled, entrapping and, for the most part, immobilizing the contaminants. In addition, rosin has some innate fluxing activity since its molecular structure contains a weak organic acid. Finally, rosin-based fluxes work well in hand-soldering and repair operations because rosin provides good heat transfer characteristics.

The activity of a rosin-based flux will be determined by the activators and surfactants which are part of the formulation. Some activators help to remove metal oxide but also leave residues which are essentially noncorrosive. Halide-containing activators leave residues which could be corrosive if too much is left on the board. A variety of specifications are available which help to define the effect of flux residues, and one of these specifications will be detailed later in this chapter.

Military specifications[3] in the past have required the use of rosin-based fluxes. These were defined as R—pure rosin, RMA—rosin mildly activated, and RA—rosin activated, based on the level of halide activators they contained. Typically, only R or RMA fluxes were approved for high-reliability military applications.

In the 1970s, telecommunication companies in the United States and Europe predominantly used rosin fluxes for their wave-soldering requirements. These companies had their own internal sets of test methods for selecting noncorrosive rosin flux formulations. Using these selection criteria, they believed the fluxes to be sufficiently safe. For their applications they cleaned only the bottom side of the assembly where removal of rosin residues was needed to ensure good electrical contact during bed-of-nails testing.

31.6 WATER-SOLUBLE FLUX

Water-soluble fluxes have been called "organic acid" fluxes. This name is misleading since all fluxes used for electronic soldering contain organic ingredients and many contain organic acid activators. The term organic acid flux probably originated from the designation of water-soluble fluxes as "organic" and those activated with organic acid activators as "organic acid" fluxes. Other activators for these fluxes include halide-containing salts and amines. Although the correct name for this category of fluxes is *water-soluble* it should also be noted that the flux solvent is normally not water, but rather alcohols or glycols.

As the name implies, water-soluble fluxes are soluble in water and their soldering residues are also expected to be water soluble. These fluxes are much more active than rosin fluxes and they give a higher soldering yield with reduced defects. This means that the final assembly will require less touchup or repair. On the down side, water-soluble fluxes contain corrosive residues which, if not properly removed, will cause corrosion in the field and long-term reliability problems.

As indicated earlier, water-soluble fluxes usually contain glycols, polyglycols, polyglycol surfactants, glycerine, or other water-soluble organic compounds as the primary vehicle. These provide good solubility for the activators which are usually the more corrosive amines and halide-activators. With the onset of highly efficient cleaning equipment, this type of flux became popular for computer and telecommunication applications.

Concern was raised in the late 1970s by Zado[4] that water-soluble fluxes affect the electrical characteristics of the epoxy-glass laminate by reducing the insulation resistance. This reduction was due to the dissolution of the polyglycols of the flux formulation into the epoxy substrate during the soldering process. Later work by Brous[5] indicated that some polyglycols were much more deleterious than others. In general, polyglycol-containing fluxes (and fusing fluids used by board manufacturers to fuse tin-lead plating) can cause an increase in moisture absorbance of the epoxy-glass substrate.

There are several considerations the user must include in determining whether to use water-soluble fluxes in a given application. One important factor is the operating environment. If the assembly will experience extremes of temperature while under power, it is possible that localized condensation can occur and dendrites will form, shorting out some of the circuit elements. Assemblies of this nature should be conformally coated. A second critical factor is the use of a board design and cleaning process which assures that corrosive residues are removed. A third consideration is the voltage gradient in the electrical design of the circuit. Within reduced lines and spacings, a failure mechanism called conductive anodic filament formation (CAF)[6] has been associated with high-humidity and high-voltage gradients.

31.7 LOW-SOLIDS FLUX

Until the mid-1980s, liquid soldering fluxes were formulated in 25 to 35% (weight percent) solids or nonvolatile liquid. Then flux chemistries changed and new formulations which were lower in total solids content came on the scene. These fluxes are composed principally of weak organic acids which frequently contain a small amount of resin or rosin. Early formulations had 5 to 8% solids, but today's low-solids fluxes are 2 to 3% solids composition.

Nomenclature of these fluxes moved from *low-solids flux* to *low-residue flux* to *no-clean flux*. The thinking was that the amount of residue left by these fluxes after soldering was so minimal that, if the residues were noncorrosive, they did not need to be removed.

Flux application became a challenge. Guth[7] noted that when higher levels of these low-solids fluxes were applied to assemblies and soldered, dendritic growth could be observed later in field trials. Concern to limit the amount of flux applied to the assembly led to the increased use of carefully controlled spray fluxers. These could assure that flux was available in the through-holes of the PWB, but also limit the amount of flux which pushes up to the top side of the board during wave soldering.

Another challenge of low-solids fluxes is the processing window. Unlike water-soluble fluxes which give very low defect levels and have a wide processing window, the soldering process for low-solids fluxes must be carefully designed. To begin with, the recommended preheat temperatures are different from those for rosin flux and the preferred solder wave temperature is lower than that for rosin. Additionally, the solderability of incoming boards and components must be good. While water-soluble flux can cut through heavy oxide layers, the amount of fluxing ingredients in low-solids fluxes is not sufficient to accomplish the task.

Low-cost manufacturing can be achieved with low-residue fluxes if the cleaning step can be eliminated and if the soldering yield is high so that little or no touchup is required. This will require a flux whose residues are noncorrosive and one which will not impede or contaminate the electrical bed-of-nails test probes.

It should be noted here that a new category of low-solids fluxes was introduced in the early 1990s to meet the needs of localities where volatile organic compounds (VOCs) are regulated. These fluxes are marketed as VOC-free or low-VOC fluxes. The solvent in this case is 100% water or at least greater than 50% water. Use of these fluxes requires extreme care in the preheat step where the water solvent must be evaporated before the assembly reaches the solder wave.

31.8 CLEANING ISSUES

Flux removal is motivated by several factors, and the importance of these factors will vary with the end use of the product. In general, the purpose of cleaning is (1) to remove corrosive residues from the soldering process or handling operations (some fluxes have high levels of halide activators which would cause corrosion if they were not removed); (2) to remove rosin, resin, or other insulating residues which would interfere with bed-of-nails electrical testing; (3) to remove rosin, resin, or other residues which attract dust, dirt, and other airborne contaminants; (4) to ensure that the board is free of residues and contamination prior to conformal coating.

During the late 1970s there was a push to replace some of the chlorinated cleaning solvents used for rosin flux removal. Cleaning agents such as perchloroethylene and trichloroethylene were being listed as suspected carcinogens by the EPA and the allowed levels in the operator-breathing-zone was severely curtailed. At the same time, chlorofluorocarbon azeotropes with methyl alcohol, ethyl alcohol, and methylene chloride found increasing application as replacements.

31.8.1 Montreal Protocol

In September 1987, the Montreal Protocol on Substances that Deplete the Ozone Layer was signed by 24 countries at the United Nations Environment Program Conference in Montreal. The Protocol was the beginning of an international agreement on the reduction of chlorofluorocarbons (CFCs) which are considered to have a deleterious effect on the stratospheric ozone layer which protects us from harmful ultraviolet radiation. The initial Protocol covered CFCs 11, 12, 113, 114 and 115, and halons (bromine-containing CFCs) 1211, 1301 and 2402. In its initial form, a three-step reduction was proposed for CFCs:

1989   Freeze production at 1986 levels.

1994   Reduce production by 20 percent from 1986 levels.

1998   Reduce production by 50 percent from 1986 levels.

In June 1990, the Montreal Protocol signatories met in London to review the environmental data on CFCs and other ozone-depleting substances (ODS). At that meeting the restrictions on CFCs were increased. The parties agreed to the following:

1993   Reduce production by 20 percent based on 1986 levels.

1995   Reduce production by 50 percent based on 1986 levels.

1997   Reduce production by 85 percent based on 1986 levels.

2000   Eliminate CFC production.

In addition, methyl chloroform (1,1,1-trichloroethane) was regulated. This material is used extensively in metal degreasing and is also a constituent in solvent blends used for cleaning electronic assemblies. The regulations on methyl chloroform were as follows:

1993   Freeze at 1986 levels.

1995   Reduce production by 30 percent based on 1989 levels.

2000   Reduce production by 70 percent based on 1989 levels.

2005   Complete production phase-out.

Carbon tetrachloride (CCl_4), which had been used for dry cleaning in Europe, was to be reduced by 85 percent by 1995 and 100 percent eliminated by 2000.

In the initial days after the signing of the Montreal Protocol, solvent suppliers and others focused their development on azeotropes of hydrofluorochlorocarbons (HCFCs) as alternatives to CFCs. In the area of electronic assembly cleaning, formulations which included HCFC-141b and HCFC-123 were considered. However, toxicological studies indicated that HCFC-123 caused benign tumors in mice and its use was withdrawn. HCFC-141b fell into disfavor as a cleaning solvent when it was discovered that its ozone-depleting potential (ODP) was very similar to that of methyl chloroform which was being phased out. The London Amendment did not target HCFCs directly, but it did include a nonbinding intention to phase out these chemicals by 2040.

In November 1992, the Protocol signatories met in Copenhagen, Denmark, and made a final reduction in the timetable. CFCs were set for 75 percent reduction by 1994 and 100 percent elimination by 1996. Methyl chloroform was scheduled for 50 percent reduction by 1994 and complete elimination by 1996. Regulations on HCFCs were as follows:

1996   Freeze production based on 1989 consumption levels.*[8]

2004   Reduce production by 35 percent based on 1996 levels.

2010   Reduce production by 65 percent based on 1996 levels.

2020   Reduce production by 99.5 percent based on 1996 levels.

2040   Eliminate production.

In addition to the international agreements under the Montreal Protocol, the Clean Air Act provided the legal requirements in the United States. In February 1992, President Bush had set the end of 1995 as the deadline for eliminating CFCs and methyl chloroform in the United States. The 1990 Clean Air Act was modified to include this requirement. This regulation had already included a tax on the use of ozone-depleting chemicals based on their usage and potential for stratospheric damage, and a labeling requirement which went into effect on May 15, 1993, that required companies to label product which contained or was manufactured with CFCs or other defined ozone-depleting substances:

> *Warning: Contains [or Manufactured with] [insert name of substance], a substance which harms public health and environment by destroying ozone in the upper atmosphere.*

As this book goes to press, the elimination of CFCs is imminent.

31.8.2 Solvent Replacements

Until the Montreal Protocol dictated the reduction and later elimination of CFCs and methyl chloroform use, these chemicals were the major cleaning solvents for cleaning rosin residues from electronic assemblies. The elimination of their availability has forced manufacturers to rethink their flux and cleaning choices. Alternative cleaning agents were needed to remove flux residues left on the assembly after soldering. These alternatives must be capable of dissolving the particular chemical residues from a given flux formulation.

Solvent cleaning options for rosin fluxes have focused on semiaqueous cleaning and on aqueous detergent cleaning. Semiaqueous cleaning involves the use of an organic solvent capable of dissolving rosin or other residues. This solvent is usually sprayed onto the assemblies in its pure form. This step is followed by a rinse step which emulsifies the semiaqueous solvent and dissolves the ionic residues. Recent innovations[9] have shown that an aqueous emulsified solution of the solvent can also provide good cleaning. Semiaqueous cleaning agents are primarily used for rosin or resin-based fluxes because these cleaning materials require specialized capital equipment which is more costly than that needed for other cleaning chemicals.

Saponifying detergents have been used for removing rosin flux residues since the late 1970s. The detergent is diluted to a 4 to 10% aqueous solution which removes rosin in the form of a rosin-soap along with the ionic contaminants in a water-rinse step. A final blow-dry step using heated air ensures that the assembly is dry prior to electrical test. In addition to rosin flux, detergent cleaning can also be used to remove water-soluble flux or low-solids flux.

The environmental concerns related to these cleaning agents differ. In the case of semiaqueous systems, the solvent frequently has a relatively low flash point and the commercial cleaning equipment has specialized added features to assure safety. All organic cleaning

---

* Production would be capped at 3.1 percent of the ODP of the CFCs consumed in 1989.

agents are listed as VOCs by the EPA and their emissions are regulated. Closed-looped recycle systems exist for semiaqueous cleaning processes, and the spent solvent can be reused as an alternate fuel source.

In the case of detergents which are dissolved in water, their aqueous discharges are regulated. Detergents usually have a high pH (10 to 11) which exceeds the level acceptable for release to drain. Therefore, the spent solution and the rinse water must be neutralized prior to disposal. In addition to the pH level, detergents generally place a high biological oxygen demand (BOD) on the local municipality's waste treatment plant. In some parts of the United States, such as the Northeast, the BOD load associated with detergent cleaning exceeds the local EPA regulations. As a final environmental concern, heavy metals (Pb, Sn, Cu) can be dissolved in the detergent waste or in the rinse water from the aqueous process. These levels must be monitored and reported. Proper filtration units on the cleaner will remove undissolved solid solder residue and will help ensure that any dissolved heavy metals are well below those allowed by the regulations.

31.9 FLUX CHARACTERIZATION TEST METHODS

Soldering fluxes for electronics had traditionally been characterized by their chemical composition—i.e., rosin, resin or organic. Military specifications have, in the past, limited the manufacturer to rosin-based fluxes:

R   Pure rosin

RMA   Rosin mildly activated

RA   Rosin activated

The activation level of these has been defined, in part, by the use of a water extract resistivity test where the resistivity for RMA is greater than 100,000 Ω-cm and for RA is 50,000 to 100,000 Ω-cm. This characterization measurement developed as a means of controlling the amount of corrosive flux activators such as amine hydrohalides in fluxes used for military product.

In the early 1980s, the IPC developed a flux characterization criterion based on the flux and flux residue activity. Thus, fluxes were classified as:

L = Low or no flux/flux residue activity

M = Moderate flux/flux residue activity

H = High flux/flux residue activity

These designators were determined by a series of tests which include the copper mirror test, a qualitative silver chromate paper test for chlorides and bromides, a qualitative spot test for fluorides, a quantitative test for halides (chloride, bromide, and fluoride), a corrosion test for flux residue activity, and a surface insulation resistance test at accelerated temperature and humidity conditions. The latest industry standard, "Requirements for Soldering Fluxes" (J-STD-004), updates the earlier IPC-SF-818 solder flux specification and includes some international elements from the International Standards Organization (ISO-9454). In addition to defining the flux categories L, M, and H, it notes the absence or presence of halides by a 0 or 1, which is added to the descriptor. Fluxes are further classified by their chemical constituents in order to parallel the international standards. Thus, fluxes will be listed as RO (rosin), RE (resin), OR (organic), or IN (inorganic). The test methods for this specification are included at the end of the document and are also contained in the Test Methods Document (IPC-TM-650). A brief description of each of the test methods is included as follows. The test results are used to characterize the fluxes as L, M, or H. Table 31.1 summarizes the test results required for flux classification.

TABLE 31.1 Test Requirements for Flux Activity Classification

| Flux type | Copper mirror | Qualitative halide | | Quantitative halide | Corrosion test | Conditions for passing 100-MΩ SIR requirements |
		Silver chromate (Cl^-, Br^-)	Spot test F^-	Cl^-, Br^-, F^-		
L_0	No evidence of mirror	Pass	Pass	0.0%	None	Both cleaned and uncleaned
L_1	breakthrough	Pass	Pass	<0.5%		
M_0	<50% breakthrough	Pass	Pass	0.0%	Minor corrosion acceptable	Cleaned or uncleaned
M_1		Fail	Fail	0.5 to 2.0%		
H_0	>50% breakthrough	Pass	Pass	0.0%	Major corrosion acceptable	Cleaned
H_1		Fail	Fail	>2.0%		

31.9.1 Copper Mirror Test (TM 2.3.32)

In this test, a drop of flux is placed on one end of a glass slide with 5000 Å copper metal deposit. A drop of 25% water white (WW) rosin flux is placed on the other end. The fluxed slide is held at 25°C/50 percent RH for 24 h. Then the slide is rinsed with isopropyl alcohol. If there is no evidence of mirror breakthrough where the test flux was placed (no white showing through the slide when placed on white paper), this classifies the flux as L-type flux (provided that the flux passes all of the other tests for L-type fluxes). Breakthrough in less than 50 percent of the test area defines an M-type flux. Breakthrough in more than 50 percent of the test area classifies the flux as H-type.

31.9.2 Halide Content (TM 2.3.33)

The absence of chloride and bromide in a flux can be tested using the silver chromate paper test. When a drop of flux is applied to the test paper, the appearance of a yellow or white color will indicate the presence of these halides. This test is subjective but can reach sensitivity levels down to about 0.07 percent. If the flux fails this simple test, a titration test with silver nitrate can be used to determine the exact percent halides from chloride and bromide, based on the solids content of the flux. A total percent halide (including the fluoride component of the flux) of less than 0.5 classifies the flux as L-type; if it is between 0.5 and 2.0% the flux falls into the M-type category; and if the halide content is greater than 2%, the flux will be an H-type flux.

31.9.3 Fluoride Test (TM 2.3.35)

In the revised J-STD-004 document, a test for fluoride has been added. The qualitative test is a spot test using zirconium alizarin purple lake as the developing agent. A change in color from purple to yellow indicates the presence of fluoride. The presence of oxalate can give a false positive result. For quantitative analysis for fluoride, a fluoride-specific electrode is used to identify and quantify the fluoride present. The concentration of fluoride from this test is added to the aforementioned chloride/bromide concentration results to determine the total percent halides in the flux.

31.9.4 Corrosion Test (TM 2.6.15)

This test uses a small copper sheet which has a well (indentation) created in it with a ball peen hammer or other device. After the coupon is precleaned with sulfuric acid and ammonium persulfate to remove the metal oxide, a sample of flux solids and some solder wire is placed in the well. The coupon is then floated on a solder pot at $235 \pm 5°C$ (455°F) for 5 s after the solder has begun to reflow, creating flux residues. Then the coupon is cooled and placed in an oven set at 50°C/65 percent RH for 10 days. The absence of corrosion products indicates an L-type flux. Partial corrosion at the edges defines an M-flux. The presence of heavy corrosion places the flux in the H-category.

31.9.5 Surface Insulation Resistance (SIR) (TM 2.6.3.3)

The substrate of a printed wiring board has certain electrical properties which include a bulk and a surface resistivity. The test measuring the resistance to current flow between two surface conductors is termed a *surface insulation resistance test*. This is different from hole-to-hole resistance measurement which defines the bulk insulation resistance.

Frequently, interdigitated comb patterns are used to measure SIR. Here the comb patterns are electrically powered at a bias voltage and periodically measured for insulation resistance. This is done in a temperature/humidity chamber or in an oven with a bell-jar containing a saturated salt solution to provide the controlled humidity. When the humidity exceeds 65 to 70 percent, several molecular layers of water exist on the surface. This film of water can dissolve conductive ions, enhancing the rate of corrosion and degradation.

In the ANSI J-STD-004 document, the SIR test is performed at 85°C/85 percent RH. The IPC-B-24 coupon (Fig. 31.4) with 0.4-mm lines and 0.5-mm spaces is used for this test. A 45- to 50-V polarizing bias and a −100-V (reversed bias) test voltage is used. Test data is taken at 24, 96, and 168 h, but the 96- and 168-h reading must pass the minimum SIR level of 100 MΩ.

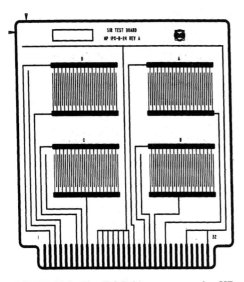

FIGURE 31.4 The IPC-B-24 test coupon for SIR testing contains four comb patterns with 0.4-mm lines and 0.5-mm spacing between conductors.

31.10   CRITERIA FOR CHOOSING A FLUX/CLEANING PROCESS

The elimination of CFCs and methyl chloroform as cleaning agents for rosin-based soldering fluxes has forced the electronics process engineer to evaluate new materials and processes. These evaluations should be based on a comparison with the material and process which it is replacing. There are a number of issues to be considered in making this choice.

31.10.1   Low-Solids/No-Clean

Cost effectiveness is always a major driving force. Thus, if a no-clean process can produce high yields and meet the end-point requirement of the customer, it is preferred, based on cost. To produce high yields with low-solids/no-clean fluxes, changes must be made in the preheat and soldering temperatures. If solder mask is used on the assembly, the compatibility of the chosen flux formulation with the solder mask is important. Solder balling, a common problem with low-solids flux formulations, can be minimized if a proper mating of the flux and solder mask is considered.

A no-clean flux philosophy requires a more carefully controlled approach to manufacturing. Incoming boards and components contain contaminants which are no longer removed when the cleaning process is eliminated. Thus, the manufacturer must work with the vendors to assure cleanliness of incoming parts. One must also consider the solderability of incoming parts. Low-solids/no-clean fluxes provide excellent soldering performance on solderable parts, but are far less tolerant of poor solderability. The process window for low-solids fluxes is much reduced from rosin or water-soluble fluxes. Thus, careful process control and consideration of these factors is important to a successful changeover.

A no-clean process also requires minimum handling of components and assemblies and careful control of contaminants introduced by the operators. The touchup and repair process will require an equivalent no-clean flux-cored solder. Operators will have to learn new techniques with the solder iron tip when using these new cored wires. There is very little flux to keep the tip clean, and the temperature of the tip may have to be lowered when the iron is not in use.

31.10.2   Rosin Flux/Semiaqueous or Detergent Cleaning

Rosin flux has been around for a long time and the reliability of electronics made with it is superior to other flux choices for extreme environments or for high-risk applications. When rosin flux is chosen, the cleaning alternatives are presently (1) semiaqueous cleaning and (2) saponifying detergent cleaning. Equipment costs for semiaqueous are higher, but the ability to provide good cleaning under fine-pitch components is superior. Aqueous detergent cleaning has been performed for a number of years and it is a proven technology. However, there are areas of the country where the effluents from this process would contain too high a BOD loading and the wastes would have to be placed in barrels and shipped to a hazardous waste site. In these areas of the country, detergent cleaning would not be applicable. Rosin flux soldering is not a low-cost choice because the defect level during the soldering process may be higher, but when reliability is the major criterion for the end product, it is the preferred material.

31.10.3   Water-Soluble Flux/Aqueous Cleaning

Water-soluble flux and aqueous cleaning have a lot of advantages. Soldering yields are high and the process window is broad. Thus, the manufacturing costs can be reduced because fewer repair operators are needed. When aqueous cleaning is performed without added detergent, the effluent stream can go out the drain or proceed through a closed recycle loop which lowers the total water usage. This can have cost savings even though additional equipment is required for the recycle step.

Water-soluble fluxes contain corrosive residues, making excellent cleaning equipment and process control paramount. Process checks using ionic contamination testers can assist the manufacturing floor in identifying problems at the fluxing or cleaning stations which could lead to corrosion in the field if not quickly corrected.

There are some applications where water-soluble flux usage should be tested for reliability before being chosen as an alternative. As mentioned earlier, some of the ingredients in some water-soluble fluxes have an affinity for the epoxy-glass and can absorb into it during the thermal cycling of the soldering process. This increases the potential moisture absorbance of these boards. Thus, if the end product is exposed to high-humidity conditions or severe temperature-cycling conditions and no conformal coating is used, problems could occur in the field. Those designs which have localized high-voltage gradients with low spacings can also cause field failures. For these applications, care should be exercised.

REFERENCES

1. D. A. Fisher, et al., "Relative Effects on Stratospheric Ozone of Halogenated Methanes and Ethanes of Social and Industrial Interest," *Scientific Assessment of Ozone: 1989,* vol. II, World Meteorological Organization Global Ozone Research and Monitoring Project—Report No. 20, pp. 301–377.

2. Terms and Definitions for Interconnecting and Packaging Electronic Circuits, (ANSI/IPC-T-50), published by the Institute for Interconnecting and Packaging Electronic Circuits (IPC), 7380 North Lincoln Avenue, Lincolnwood, IL 60646.

3. MIL-F-14256, Flux, Soldering, Liquid (Rosin Base).

4. F. M. Zado, "Effects of Non-Ionic Water Soluble Flux Residues," *The Western Electric Engineer,* vol. 27, no. 1, p. 40.

5. J. Brous, "Electrochemical Migration and Flux Residues Causes and Detection," *Proceedings of NEPCON West,* Feb. 1992, pp. 386–393.

6. J. P. Mitchell and T. L. Welsher, "Conductive Anodic Filament Growth in Printed Circuit Materials," *Printed Circuit World Convention II,* Munich, Germany, published as IPC Technical Report WC-2A-5, June, 1981.

7. L. A. Guth, "Low Solids Flux Technology for Solder Assembly of Circuit Packs," *Circuits Manufacturing,* vol. 29, no. 2, pp. 59–63.

8. Montreal Protocol on Substances That Deplete the Ozone Layer, a protocol to the Vienna Convention for the Protection of the Ozone Layer.

9. R. Breunsbach, "New Developments in Simplified, Low Cost, Semi-Aqueous Emulsion Cleaning Technology," *Proceedings of NEPCON West,* Feb. 1992, pp. 1217–1225.

CHAPTER 32
ASSEMBLY INSPECTION

Bruce Bolliger
Hewlett-Packard Company, Loveland, Colorado

32.1 INTRODUCTION

This chapter will cover the various reasons why manufacturers inspect printed circuit assemblies, how they have implemented and enhanced visual inspection, what automated process inspection systems they are using, and how they have implemented these automated systems. The scope of this chapter includes only inspection of printed circuit assemblies during the assembly process, as shown in Fig. 32.1. Thus, it includes inspection of solder paste after the paste printing process step, components after the component placement process step, and solder joints after the solder curing process step. Not included, however, is incoming inspection of components and the bare printed circuit board. The focus of this chapter is on production use of inspection, not the collection of measurements during process development in an R&D environment.

32.1.1 Visual Inspection

Manufacturers of printed circuit assemblies have always visually inspected their boards at various points in the assembly process. There are a variety of reasons for visual inspection of assemblies, including eliminating cosmetic defects, detecting obvious process defects quickly, and meeting military specifications. But with the advent and growth of surface-mount technology, visual inspection of printed circuit assemblies has also grown in importance and prevalence. SMT solder joints must carry a much bigger burden for mechanical or structural reliability than do plated-through-hole solder joints. The pin-in-through-hole solder joints carries much of the mechanical burden, helping to keep the component attached to the printed circuit board. But with SMT solder joints, it is often only the solder that keeps the component attached to the board. In many cases, only visual inspection could judge the mechanical reliability of an SMT solder joint.

As SMT geometries have continued to shrink and solder joints have become denser on printed circuit boards, visual inspection has become more difficult, so visual inspection results have become less consistent and reliable. In addition, new types of components, such as pin grid arrays or ball grid arrays, completely hide their solder joints from view. Yet, as Fig. 32.2 indicates, achieving a high assembly process yield is more important as the number of solder joints per assembly increases.

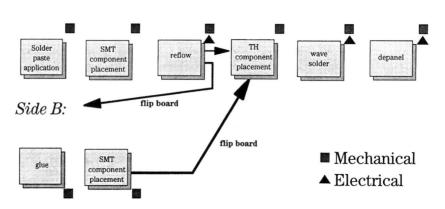

FIGURE 32.1   Generic manufacturing process for surface-mount technology printed circuit assemblies, including the possible locations within the process for inspection or test of mechanical or structural attributes and electrical characteristics of an assembly.

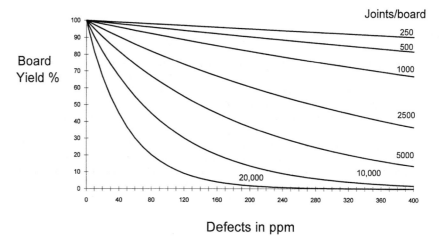

FIGURE 32.2   Printed circuit board yield decreases dramatically with increases in the number of solder joints per assembly if the defect rate per solder joint remains constant. For instance, at a 40-ppm defect rate, the yield drops from 96 percent at 1000 joints per assembly to 45 percent at 20,000 joints.

32.1.2   Automated Inspection

Inspection is an important source of process information, without which high yields are very difficult to obtain. Consequently, manufacturers have employed the following range of techniques to either simply enhance visual inspection or fully automate inspection:

- Microscopes, mono and stereoscopic, with magnification from 4× to 10×
- Real-time video images created using simple light or thermal or acoustic imaging
- Fully automated process test systems using light, laser, or x-ray imaging.

The automation of inspection has evolved into systems that resemble automated test equipment used to make electrical measurements and find electrical defects. These automated process test systems acquire real-time images, process the images to find and measure features within the image, and make accept/reject decisions based on this image processing. So these automated systems remove the human, and human judgment, from the inspection process altogether.

32.2 REASONS FOR INSPECTION

Manufacturers inspect printed circuit assemblies during their production for a variety of reasons. Most of these reasons fall into the following categories:

1. Improve process fault coverage.

2. Meet customer specifications.

3. Detect process defects as quickly after they occur as possible.

4. Decrease process defect rates through statistical process control (SPC).

32.2.1 Process Fault Coverage

The goal of higher fault coverage is the prevention of any defective printed circuit assemblies from reaching assembly of the board into its final product, whether final assembly is at the same site or at a separate customer site. Figure 32.3 shows a typical spectrum of SMT process defects. Some of these defects, such as misaligned solder joints and solder balls, can be discovered only by inspection, not by electrical testing, functional or in-circuit test. For instance, "marginal" solder joints are those that will pass electrical test just after assembly completion, but will eventually fail because of inferior mechanical strength. Insufficient solder and components partially misaligned with printed circuit pads are the two most common causes of low mechanical strength. Voids in solder joints and cosmetic defects, such as solder balls away from solder joints and "cold" or dull solder, are other examples of defects that can be found only by some kind of inspection.

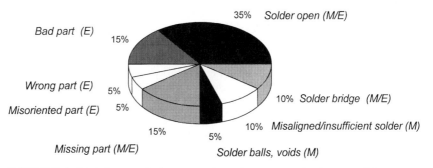

FIGURE 32.3 Typical process fault spectrum for surface-mount technology assemblies. Process faults marked E can be detected by electrical tests, those marked M can be detected by mechanical or structural inspection or test, and those marked both E and M can be detected by either method.

32.2.2 Customer Specifications

Many printed circuit assembly workmanship specifications, including MIL-STD-2000A, require visual inspection of solder joints. MIL-STD-2000A prescribes, for all defense and aerospace government contractors, the attributes of solder joints to be inspected and describes the conditions that result in nonconformance. Most commercial customers of contract manufacturers also have very specific solder-joint and cosmetic specifications that require the visual inspection of printed circuit assemblies. At the same time, there is growing preference for process control rather than 100 percent inspection, particularly for very fine pitch SMT. For instance, MIL-STD-2000A outlines acceptable sampling plans for using statistical process control (SPC) instead of 100 percent inspection. Nevertheless, customer specifications still often call for visual inspection. At the very least, customer specifications covering cosmetics normally require visual inspection.

32.2.3 Quick Defect Detection and Correction

Quick detection of process shifts or defects can lower rework costs in several different ways.

32.2.3.1 Prevent Defects. If a particular process step has drifted out of its control limits, discovering this fact as soon as possible will prevent more defects from occurring. If found quickly enough, and corrected immediately, perhaps no actual defects will occur.

32.2.3.2 Lower Rework Costs. Defects found earlier in the process often are easier to repair. For instance, if a defect in solder paste deposition is found before a component has been placed in the paste, it is fairly inexpensive to wipe the solder paste off and start over. If this same defect is found after the solder is reflowed, the solder joint itself will have to be touched up, a more difficult and expensive rework step. The same is true for repairing component placement defects before the solder is cured, particularly for missing or misaligned components.

32.2.3.3 Easier Defect Diagnosis. Finally, defects found earlier in the assembly process are often more easily diagnosed, shortening the overall repair time. An example is the inspection of solder joints. Inspection of solder joints will detect defects specific to the solder joints and will quickly determine the exact location and characteristic of the defect. Waiting until a later electrical test stage could make diagnosis more difficult because at that point, there could be several causes of the defect, such as a defective component and defects in other connections, in addition to the actual defective solder joint.

32.2.4 Statistical Process Control

Statistical process control requires reliable data that can be analyzed either in real time or historically. Visual inspection collects defect data, such as the number of solder joint defects per assembly right after the solder curing process, either reflow or wave soldering. Some manual and automated inspection techniques also take quantitative measurements of key assembly parameters, such as solder paste volume or solder-joint fillet height. To the extent that this data is repeatable, manufacturers use defect data or measurements to characterize the amount of process variation from assembly to assembly or from solder joint to solder joint. When the amount of variation starts to drift outside its normal range, outside its control limits, manufacturers can stop the assembly process until the process is adjusted to eliminate this drift. Historical analysis of the defect or measurement data also helps discover the cause of process variation. Eliminating the sources of process variation reduces the process defect rate, thus creating savings in rework costs and increasing product reliability.

32.3   VISUAL INSPECTION

Visual inspection is the visual comparison by a human of some attribute of the printed circuit assembly to specified standards that describe the acceptable range for that attribute. The inspector normally picks up the printed circuit assembly or places it under a microscope and carefully observes particular attributes, such as the condition or bend radius of component leads or the wetting of solder joints to a lead. Visual inspection always involves human judgment in comparing the attribute to its conditions of conformance to standards.

32.3.1   General Inspection Issues

As Fig. 32.1 indicated, visual inspection can occur after each of the several printed circuit assembly process steps. But visual inspection often has different purposes, depending on where in the assembly process it occurs. These purposes fall into the following three major categories:

1. Quick detection of an assembly process step that is not operating within its normal range
2. Detection of process defects as specified by the customer or industry or internal standards
3. Detection of cosmetic defects

Visual inspection after any process step other than reflow soldering and wave soldering usually has the purpose of quick detection of a process step out of its *control limits*. (Control limits may, in this case, be based just on operator judgment, not on any statistical analysis of process capability.) This type of visual inspection is usually done by a production line operator as only a small part of their normal responsibilities. The visual inspection is short, normally less than a minute, and consists of a quick scan of the assembly for obvious defects. After solder paste printing, the operator visually inspects for pads with very little solder paste or paste bricks that consistently do not line up with the pads adequately. After component placement, the operator visually inspects for missing components, pins not through holes, components grossly misaligned with the appropriate pads, and a number of other improper conditions. After glue deposition, the operator inspects for pads without glue dots or with excess glue and glue dots that are not aligned with the pads. If any of the defective conditions occurs more than is normal for that process step, the operator typically would stop the equipment for that process step and readjust the equipment or notify production engineering or management.

32.3.2   Solder Joint Inspection Issues

Visual inspection after the reflow and wave-soldering process steps can also be just a quick scan for obvious defects to detect a process condition outside of control limits. In this case, the operator visually inspects for solder bridges, large solder balls or solder splashes, lifted leads, and a number of other improper conditions. But more often, visual inspection after the soldering process steps is aimed at finding solder joints that do not meet their specification.

Visual inspection of solder joints against specification often covers 100 percent of the solder joints on an assembly. Inspecting samples of solder joint in conjunction with a documented process control system is also done, but 100 percent inspection is more common. So inspecting for this purpose can be a lengthy process, taking as long as a half hour for assemblies with 4000 solder joints being measured against military specifications. As a rule of thumb, this kind of visual inspection will have a throughput of about five joints per second. Thus, inspection of solder joints against specifications normally requires visual inspectors dedicated to this function with no other responsibilities.

The visual inspector must be very familiar with the specifications of the attributes for each solder joint type. Each solder joint can have as many as eight different criteria for defects, and each assembly typically has more than six or so different solder joint types corresponding to different component packages. As an example, Fig. 32.4 shows the specification attributes for one component type: rectangular passive chips. Table 32.1 gives the corresponding conformance criteria for each attribute for this component type. But more importantly, the visual inspector must be highly trained to make an accurate judgment of conditions on the borderline between good and bad. For instance, accurately determining whether a fillet height is one-quarter of the way up a component side that is only 0.05 mm high to begin with takes a lot of practice. Visual inspectors typically do not use any tools to help make these judgments. Rulers or calipers are very difficult or impossible to use to measure solder-joint dimensions or thicknesses. Using reticules in microscopes, in conjunction with coordinate measuring machines, is possible, but is usually much too time consuming to be done on a regular basis.

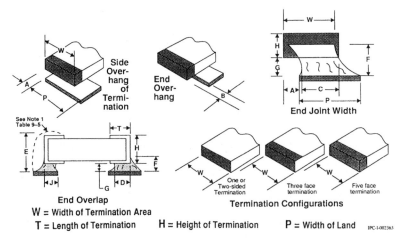

FIGURE 32.4 Inspection attributes for solder joints of surface-mounted rectangular passive chips.

Visual inspection for cosmetic defects often occurs at the end of the assembly process, or even after all of the electrical tests on the assembly have occurred. The visual inspector looks for scratches, partial delaminations, solder splashes or solder balls away from solder joints, and any other condition that does not affect assembly performance, but does make the assembly look like it may not be a high-quality product.

32.3.3 Standards for Visual Inspection

Many standards cover printed circuit board assemblies. Most major electronics manufacturers have their own internally developed workmanship standards. Several industry and military standards also exist. However, the Joint Industry Standard ANSI/J-STD-001, *Requirements for Soldered Electrical and Electronic Assemblies,* is the standard most often referenced for criteria defining reliable solder connections. This standard was jointly developed by the Institute for Interconnecting and Packaging Electronic Circuits, referred to as the IPC, and by the Electronic Industries Association, referred to as the EIA. IPC is headquartered in Lincolnwood, Illinois, and the EIA's Engineering Department is headquartered in Washington, D.C. The ANSI/J-STD-001 was first approved by ANSI on July 1, 1992.

TABLE 32.1 Dimensional Criteria—Rectangular or Square End Components
(Dimensions in mm)

Feature	Dim.	Class 1	Class 2	Class 3
Maximum side overhang	A	½W or ½P or 1.5, whichever is less	½W or ½P or 1.5, whichever is less	¼W or ¼P or 1.5, whichever is less
Maximum end overhang	B	Not permitted	Not permitted	Not permitted
Minimum end joint width	C	½W or ½P, whichever is less	½W or ½P, whichever is less	¾W or ¾P, whichever is less
Minimum side joint length	D	Not required	Not required	Not required
Maximum fillet height (see Note 1)	E	See Note 1	See Note 1	See Note 1
Minimum fillet height	F	*	G + ¼H or 0.5, whichever is less	G + ¼H or 0.5, whichever is less
Minimum thickness (see Note 2)	G	*	*	0.2 (See Note 2)
Minimum end overlap	J	Required	Required	Required

* Properly wetted fillet evident.
Notes:
1. The maximum fillet may overhang the land or extend onto the top of the end cap metallization; however, the solder shall not extend further onto the component body.
2. Unless satisfactory cleaning can be demonstrated with reduced clearance.

32.3.3.1 ANSI/J-STD-001 Requirements for Solder Joints.   The ANSI/J-STD-001 standard describes materials, methods, and verification criteria for producing quality solder connections on printed circuit assemblies. It covers criteria and methods for both pin-through-hole and surface-mount-technology solder connections. It also reflects requirements for three different classes of end products.

- Class 1 *General Electronic Products* includes consumer products and some computers and computer peripherals.
- Class 2 *Dedicated Service Electronic Products* includes communications equipment, critical business machines, and instruments where high performance is required and for which uninterrupted service is desirable.
- Class 3 *High-Performance Electronic Products* include commercial and military equipment where continued performance or performance on demand is imperative.

The Class 3 requirements of the ANSI-J-STD-001, except in isolated instances, match the requirements found in the MIL-STD-2000A covering the same specification areas. Table 32.1, which is taken from the ANSI/J-STD-001 standard, shows specifications for one type of surface-mount solder joint for all three classes of end products.

32.3.3.2 Supplementary IPC Standards.   The ANSI/J-STD-001 and MIL-STD-2000A standards can be augmented for use in printed circuit assembly by the following standards:

- IPC-A-620 *Acceptability of Printed Board Assemblies* for overall workmanship requirements.
- IPC-PC-90 *General Requirements for Implementation of Statistical Process Control* for establishing a process control plan. (EIA-557-1 also covers this topic.)

32.3.4 Capabilities of Visual Inspection

Visual inspection serves a number of important purposes well but also has several important limitations.

32.3.4.1   Advantages.   Visual inspection is really the only method of reliably detecting cosmetic defects. Visual inspection is an accurate and cost-effective method of defect detection for nonsubjective defects, such as missing components, wrong components, misoriented or reversed components, or solder bridges, which are clearly either defective or not. And when low volume or lack of technical resources prevents the use of automation or more sophisticated tools, visual inspection is the only alternative that finds many of the more subjective defects, such as solder joints with insufficient solder, lifted leads, or poor wetting. Finally, visual inspection can quickly detect when a process step has drifted significantly out of its control limits.

32.3.4.2   Disadvantages.   But visual inspection also has many limitations, including

- Low rate of solder joint defect detection repeatability, particularly for fine-pitch SMT, which result in high false accepts or defect escapes and high false reject rates
- Inability to see hidden solder joints in component types such as some connectors, pin grid arrays, and ball grid arrays
- Inability to collect quantitative measurements in addition to defect data

Repeatability Limitations.   Several studies have documented the low repeatability rate of visual inspection of solder joints. One such study was conducted by AT&T at its Federal Systems Division.[1] This study showed that even the same inspector inspecting the same assembly twice will have a defect call repeatability rate of only about 50 percent. Two different inspectors inspecting the same assembly will have a defect call repeatability rate of only about 28 percent. This study did not even include any very fine pitch SMT solder joints, which are more difficult to visually inspect.

To alleviate this severe limitation somewhat, manufacturers have implemented the use of microscopes with a magnification level of 10×. Often, stereoscopic microscopes are used to provide visual inspectors a better three-dimensional view. Not as frequently, manufacturers have implemented light sources and cameras to capture real-time magnified video images of the assembly being inspected. The lighting and high-resolution video images can make it easier for visual inspectors to see the acceptance criteria for which they are searching. These enhancements do improve the repeatability rate of visual inspection. But the requirement for subjective human calls and the tedium of carefully inspecting thousands of connections per hour still results in repeatability rates much lower than desired. Low repeatability means many missed defects that escape to final assembly or customers and wasted and possibly damaging rework of good connections.

Hidden Solder Joints.   Several component types used in printed circuit assemblies do not provide visual access to solder joints. These components include package arrays where the solder joints are distributed in a matrix under the entire component body, such as ball grid arrays. For these components, all of the joints except those on the edges of the array are completely hidden from view. Other packages, such as J-leaded components, where the connections are under the component body at the component edges, and 0.5-mm-pitch gullwing components, where the solder joint heel is only 0.08 mm high and behind the component leads, also make visual inspection more difficult. Some manufacturers have attempted to solve this problem by using a penetrating imaging technique, such as x ray, acoustics, or thermography, to acquire a live magnified video image that the visual inspector can look at to make a defect call. However, the images resulting from these techniques are either less consistent or less well defined than a visual image, still requiring the inspector to make a difficult judgment call. Therefore, a low repeatability rate persists.

No Quantitative Measurements.   Accurate quantitative measurements of dimensions ranging from 0.05 to 0.5 mm are not possible with visual inspection. Quantitative measurements provide much more information about a process step, allowing much tighter process control and providing insight into the causes of process variation, without which process improvement is a hit-or-miss proposition. Some manufacturers have implemented semiautomatic measurement tools to allow operators to take quantitative measurements. Examples include optical-focusing microscopes and semiautomatic laser triangulation equipment. These tools do collect useful quantitative measurements, but are typically limited to sampling of solder paste depositions. Sampling is required because they are very slow. Measurement of solder paste height, volume, and registration with pads is possible because of easy visual access to and the simple rectangular shape of solder paste depositions. Most solder joints do not have simple shapes with easy visual access. Therefore, these semiautomatic tools cannot obtain dimensional measurements of solder joints.

Automatic inspection techniques using automated process test equipment significantly overcome the repeatability and measurement limitations of visual inspection. It is for this reason that many manufacturers are implementing automatic inspection.

32.4 AUTOMATED INSPECTION

The automation of inspection has evolved into automated process test systems that resemble automated test equipment used to make electrical measurements and find electrical defects. Automated process test systems generate images of the item to be inspected, normally solder paste, components, or solder joints, digitally analyze the image to locate and measure key features, and based on these measurements, automatically decide whether a defect exists or not. Just like visual inspection, automated process test systems do not require physical contact with the printed circuit assembly to generate the desired images. Unlike visual inspection, automatic inspection removes all human subjectivity from defect detection, thereby increasing repeatability rates typically by an order of magnitude. Many of the automated process test systems also provide accurate, repeatable quantitative measurements that directly correspond to process parameters, thus providing the means for process control and improvement.[2]

32.4.1 Measurements by Automated Systems

Figure 32.5a, b, and c show examples of measurements made by automated process test systems.

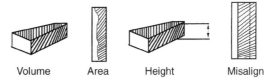

| Volume | Area | Height | Misalign |

FIGURE 32.5a Typical solder paste measurements made by automated process test systems, including the volume of paste deposition, the area of the pad covered by paste, the height of the paste deposition, and the offset of the paste from the pad.

32.4.1.1 Solder Paste Measurements.   Typical solder paste measurements, shown in Figure 32.5a, are volume, area of pad covered, height, and misalignment with the pad. These quantitative measurements provide information about the paste viscosity, stencil registration, cleanliness, and snap-off, and squeegee speed and pressure that can lead to improvement in the paste printing process.

32.4.1.2 Component Placement Measurements.   Typical component placement measurements, depicted in Fig. 32.5b, include whether or not the component is missing, misaligned, or skewed. These measurements are attribute measurements, just separating good from bad, rather than quantitative dimensional measurements. Component placement measurements provide information about the rate of placement accuracy.

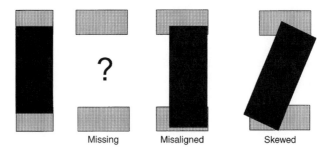

Missing   Misaligned   Skewed

FIGURE 32.5*b*   Typical component placement attributes inspected by automated process test systems, including missing component, components misaligned along or across the pads, and skewed components.

32.4.1.3 Solder Joint Measurements.   Solder joint measurements, such as fillet heights, average solder thickness across the pad, void volume, and pin-to-pad offsets, as shown in Fig. 32.5*c*, provide information about the paste-printing process, the component placement process, and the solder-curing process steps. For instance, the variation of heel fillet heights and void volume across an assembly provides insight into the oven temperature profile and spatial distribution. The variation of average solder thickness provides insight into squeegee speed and pressure and stencil cleanliness. And the pin-to-pad offsets measure the component placement accuracy.

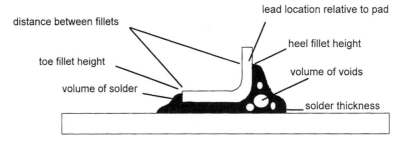

distance between fillets
lead location relative to pad
toe fillet height
heel fillet height
volume of voids
volume of solder
solder thickness

FIGURE 32.5*c*   Typical solder joint measurements made by automated process test systems, including volume of solder, toe and heel fillet heights, distance between fillets, void volume, average solder thickness across the solder joint, and the offset between solder joint and pad.

32.4.2 Types of Automated Process Test Systems

Automated process test systems normally are dedicated to one type of measurement capability: solder paste, component placement, or solder joint. For example, systems for solder paste measurements do not also make component placement measurements. The cost of combining different measurement capabilities into one system would typically make that system prohibitively expensive. But more important, to reduce manufacturing costs, manufacturers want to implement linear, sequential production lines where an assembly always flows in one direction and goes through each machine only once per assembly side. So automated process test systems fall into three major categories:

- Those that make solder paste measurements
- Those that make component placement measurements
- Those that make solder joint measurements

For all three types, the automated process test system will compare the measurements taken against a specified conformance range to automatically accept or reject a solder paste brick, component placement, or solder joint as being within specification.

32.5 SOLDER PASTE AUTOMATED PROCESS TEST SYSTEMS

32.5.1 Operating Principles

Automated process test systems designed for solder paste measurements use structured light sources and cameras or digital LED sensors to generate "three-dimensional" images of solder paste depositions. The structured light is normally either a sheet of light or a laser line or spot. As Fig. 32.6 shows, the structured light sweeps across a solder paste brick, creating discontinuities and other features in the image that are calibrated to actual physical dimensions, such as height and area.

32.5.1.1 View Magnification.   To achieve adequate accuracy, only a small portion, called a *view,* of the assembly is imaged at a single time. Magnification increases and digital quantization error decreases as the size of the view decreases. Views normally vary in size from 10 to 25 mm in diameter. So the automated process test system may use more than 100 views to

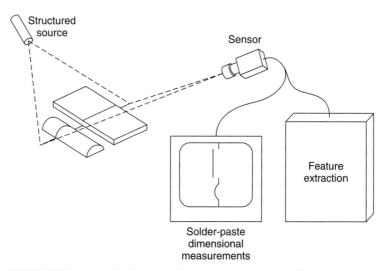

FIGURE 32.6   Schematic of automated process test system for solder paste measurement. The camera or LED sensor obtains images with discontinuities in the laser line scan; the image-processing software finds these discontinuities, measures them, and calibrates them to real physical dimensions.

cover a typical assembly. The system moves the assembly on a positioning stage from view to view. The sum of move time plus image acquisition time makes up most of the total inspection time for a particular assembly.

32.5.1.2 System Throughput.   The test speed for solder paste inspection systems varies anywhere from 5 to 25 paste depositions per second. Even the high end of this speed range is not fast enough to keep up with many automated printed circuit production lines with a typical speed of over 50 solder joints per second. So most manufacturers will inspect a specific subset of paste depositions on every assembly coming down the production line.

32.5.2 Application

Although defects found on a subset of depositions per assembly can be detected, the speed of these systems does not allow defect detection to be their main purpose. Instead, manufacturers use these systems to monitor the process by tracking the key quantitative solder paste measurements against control limits. The systems then alarm any condition where control limits are exceeded or definite drifts are detected, allowing the manufacturer to shut down the production line until appropriate adjustments have been made. (The alarm generated by the system is normally an obvious flashing message on a computer monitor.) Because the paste-printing process step causes at least half of all production defects, tight production control of this process step using quantitative measurements can significantly lower the process defect rate. In fact, automated solder paste inspection capability has been added to paste-printing systems, allowing not only process control, but also closed-loop feedback for automatic adjustment of paste-printing parameters based on the paste measurements.

32.5.3 Advantages and Disadvantages

Automated inspection of solder paste depositions has the following major advantages:

1. Real-time process control of paste printing to lower defect rates and rework costs
2. Quantitative measurements to help permanently eliminate the causes of paste defects
3. Defect detection where rework is easiest, before component placement and solder cure

Automated inspection of solder paste depositions has the following limitations:

1. Often too slow to cover all paste depositions on an assembly
2. Does not measure nor detect defects in component placement nor solder curing

32.6 COMPONENT PLACEMENT AUTOMATED PROCESS TEST SYSTEMS

32.6.1 Operating Principles

Automated process test systems designed for component placement measurement typically use optical techniques consisting of simple light sources and cameras to generate two-dimensional images of components. As Fig. 32.7 indicates, these systems compare the image of the components being inspected to a known good image. The systems' image-processing algorithms determine whether the current image is a close enough match to the known good image based on user inputs concerning the amount of variation from assembly to assembly. The system learns the known good image by inspecting a known good printed circuit assembly.

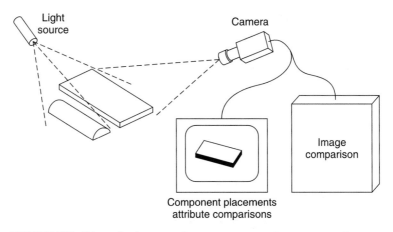

FIGURE 32.7 Schematic of automated process test system for component placement defect detection. The camera sensor obtains images of component positions relative to the printed circuit board; the image-processing software compares the image to a known good image and if the match is not close enough, flags the placement as defective.

Optical automated process test systems also image only a small portion, or view, of the assembly at a time. These systems normally can use bigger views than the structured-light systems because the features being detected do not require as much magnification as do measurements of solder paste depositions. So these systems are typically two to three times faster than structured light systems and range in inspection speed between 40 to 80 solder connections per second. Because of their simpler source and image detector subsystems, component placement automated process test systems are typically priced approximately one-half to two-thirds the price of the solder paste systems with the fastest inspection speed capability.

32.6.2 Application

The optical measurement technique of comparing the inspected component to a known good image does not generate quantitative measurements. Rather, these automated process test systems generate attribute—i.e., good vs. bad—data. For instance, these systems do not measure how far a component is misaligned from its proper placement, but instead they just determine whether or not the component is misaligned more than a predetermined amount. This attribute data is not as useful for process control and improvement, so manufacturers often resort to these systems strictly to detect defects in component placement, such as missing, skewed, or misaligned components. Often these systems do, however, alarm a condition where the same defect has occurred several times consecutively or within a specific number of assemblies. This systematic defect condition usually indicates improper setup or adjustment of the component placement equipment.

32.6.3 Advantages and Disadvantages

Automated inspection of component placement has the following major advantages:

1. Reduction of visual inspection labor costs and more accurate defect detection than visual inspection
2. Defect detection where rework is easier, before solder cure
3. Early detection of systematic process defects where equipment is out of adjustment

Automated inspection of component placement has the following limitations:

1. Does not generate quantitative measurements more useful for process control and continuous process improvement

2. Does not measure nor detect defects in solder paste printing nor solder curing

32.7 SOLDER JOINT AUTOMATED PROCESS TEST SYSTEMS

Solder joints have much more complex shapes than do solder paste depositions and components, so taking measurements of solder joints normally requires more complex imaging techniques than do solder paste and components. Automated process test systems for solder joints have tried a variety of imaging technologies, including optical, x ray, thermography, cooling profiles of laser-heated solder joints, and ultrasonic. But three technologies have dominated in these systems:

1. Optical imaging using multiple light sources and cameras

2. Transmission x-ray imaging

3. Cross-sectional x-ray imaging

32.7.1 Optical Imaging Systems

32.7.1.1 Operating Principles. Optical automated process test systems for solder joints are similar to, but more complex than, those for component placement. The multiple light sources and cameras create and detect shadows from various angles to detect features of solder joints of all types oriented in different directions on the printed circuit assembly. These optical systems for solder joints use smaller views, particularly for fine-pitch components, and therefore capture a smaller portion of the assembly at any one time. The smaller views allow more image pixels per solder joint feature, allowing a more accurate image processing and corresponding defect calls. The use of smaller views slows the throughput of these systems when compared to component placement systems.

32.7.1.2 Application. Similar to component placement inspection systems, these solder joint optical systems generate only attribute data. For instance, these systems will detect the existence of a solder bridge between two joints or the absence or presence of a heel fillet on solder joints. But they will not measure the height of the heel fillet nor the amount of solder in the solder joint. Optical systems also cannot inspect hidden solder joints, such as those for ball grid arrays, pin grid arrays, and J-leaded devices, and can have high false accept or reject rates for fine-pitch components, such as those at or below 0.5-mm pitch.

32.7.2 Transmission X-Ray Systems

32.7.2.1 Operating Principles. Transmission x-ray systems radiate x rays from a point source perpendicularly through the printed circuit assembly being inspected, as depicted in Fig. 32.8. An x-ray detector picks up a varying amount of x rays depending on the thickness of metals that the x rays are penetrating and converts the x rays to light photons for a camera to create a gray-scale image. The x-ray source is filtered so that metals of only a certain density range, that of lead, tin, gold, and silver, will absorb the x rays. The copper leads and frames of components sitting on top of solder joints do not absorb the x rays and are therefore practically invisible to the x ray detector. Thus, x-ray systems can easily see the entire solder joint, no matter what component material may be on top of the joint blocking its optical or visual access. The resulting x-ray image will be darker wherever the lead/tin solder is thicker in the solder joint. The image-processing capability of the systems then searches for features, such as the heel and toe fillets, the sides of the solder joint, and even voids internal to the joint based on gray-scale readings of the solder joint x-ray image. The systems then use predetermined decision rules to compare the gray-scale readings to acceptance criteria to automatically either accept or reject a solder joint as being good. For example, the system would compare the relative gray-scale reading for the heel fillet region, the center of the solder joint, and the toe fillet region. The acceptance criteria might state that the heel fillet reading should be twice that of the center and that the toe fillet reading should be 50 percent higher than that of the center. If the actual readings do not meet these criteria, then the solder joint is reported as being defective.

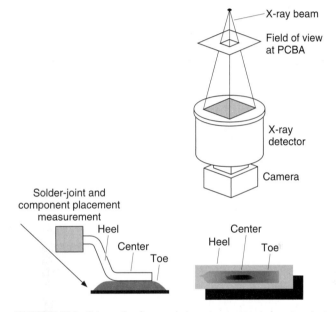

FIGURE 32.8 Schematic of transmission x-ray automated process test system for solder joint defect detection. The x-ray detector converts a varying amount of x rays to light, based on how much various parts of the solder joint absorbed; the camera converts the light photons to an image, which is then processed to find solder joint features and flag defects accordingly.

The bottom of Fig. 32.8 shows an x-ray image of a gullwing solder joint that shows the center of the joint as much darker than the heel fillet region. This solder joint is clearly defective as the heel fillet region should always be darker and with a higher gray-scale reading than the center of the joint, where the solder is thinnest for mechanically good solder joints. (The systems' image-processing capability is able to detect much more subtle changes in gray scales than can the human eye, allowing very accurate relative readings from one solder joint to the next.)

32.7.2.2 Application. Transmission x-ray technology works well for single-sided surface-mount assemblies. These automated process test systems will accurately detect solder joint defects such as opens, insufficient solder, excess solder, bridges, misalignment between pin and pad, and voids for most surface-mount solder joint types, including J-leads, gullwing, passive chip, and small-outline transistors. These systems also detect missing components and reversed tantalum capacitors. Based on trends in gray-scale readings, these systems also can accurately detect process drifts through real-time process control charting.

For double-sided assemblies, however, the transmission x-ray images of solder joints on the top side will overlap with the images of solder joints on the bottom side. The x rays are absorbed by any solder in their path through the printed circuit assembly from the source to the detector. These overlapping images make accurate solder joint measurement impossible. Transmission x-ray imaging also cannot easily distinguish between the top, bottom, and barrel of plated-through-hole (PTH) solder joints nor the top, bottom, and ball of ball-grid-array (BGA) solder joints. So transmission x-ray systems cannot be used for accurate measurement and defect detection of solder joints on double-sided assemblies nor for PTH and BGA solder joints. Manufacturers use cross-sectional x-ray systems instead for these applications.

32.7.3 Cross-Sectional X-Ray Systems

32.7.3.1 Operating Principles. Cross-sectional x-ray systems radiate x rays at an acute angle from vertical through the printed circuit assembly being inspected. As Fig. 32.9 indicates, images from all around the particular view being inspected are added together or inte-

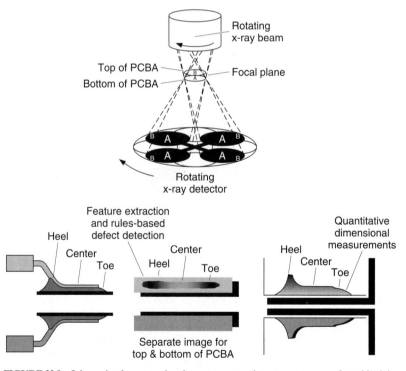

FIGURE 32.9 Schematic of cross-sectional x-ray automated process test system for solder joint measurement. Adding images around a circle from a rotating x-ray beam and detector creates a focal plane that captures just the solder joints of interest, nothing below or above. The image-processing software then finds and measures solder joint features and flags defects accordingly.

grated to essentially create an x-ray focal plane in space. This focal plane creates a cross-sectional image, approximately 0.2 to 0.4 mm in thickness, right at the focal plane by blurring everything above and below the focal plane into the background, or noise, of the image. By moving the top side of an assembly into the focal plane, cross-sectional images of only the solder joints on the top side are created. By moving the bottom side of an assembly into the focal plane, cross-sectional images of only the solder joints on the bottom side are created. Separate images of top and bottom sides are always created, preventing any image overlap from the two sides.

32.7.3.2 Application. Cross-sectional x-ray automated process test systems work well for all types of printed circuit assemblies, including single-sided and double-sided, surface-mount, through-hole, and mixed technology assemblies. These systems accurately detect the same solder joint and component defects as do transmission x-ray systems, but, in addition, the cross-sectional x-ray systems accurately detect insufficient solder conditions for ball grid array and pin-through-hole solder joints.

Some cross-sectional x-ray automated process test systems go beyond just gray-scale readings of specific solder-joint features. By carefully calibrating gray-scale readings to actual solder thickness, real-world measurements, in physical units rather than gray-scale numbers, of fillet heights, solder and void volume, and average solder thickness for the entire joint can be generated. Figure 32.10 shows an example of these calibrated measurements. This figure includes the actual cross-sectional x-ray image of tape-automated-bonded (TAB) solder joints. The profile shown at the top of the x-ray image is generated by the system in physical dimensional units by interpreting and calibrating the gray-scale readings of pin 193 in the x-ray image. The table below the x-ray image includes example measurements both for pin 193 and pin 194.

Analysis of these physical thickness measurements of solder joints provides the information required for process characterization and improvement. For instance, variations in average solder thickness or volume for the solder joints across a single assembly or from assembly to assembly provide insight into the quality level of and sources of defects in the paste-printing process.

32.7.4 Advantages and Disadvantages Summary

All three types of solder joint automated process test systems—optical, transmission x-ray, and cross-sectional x-ray—have faster test speeds than the solder paste inspection systems. Solder joint systems can reach average inspection speeds of around 40 to 50 joints per second. However, solder joint inspection systems also have higher prices, typically about 50 to 75 percent more than the price of the solder paste systems with the fastest inspection speed capability.

Automated inspection of solder joints has the following major advantages:

1. Eliminate visual inspection by automating solder joint defect detection, thereby also reducing unnecessary rework due to false reject calls.

2. Reduce rework analysis time by pinpointing defects to the exact solder joint.

3. Afford real-time process control of all three process steps—paste printing, component placement, and solder cure—to lower defect rates and rework costs.

X-ray automated inspection has the following additional advantages:

1. Quantitative measurements to help permanently eliminate the causes of defects from all three process steps

2. Reduction of failures at final assembly or in the field due to defective hidden solder joints and marginal solder joints due to insufficient solder, misalignment, or excessive voids

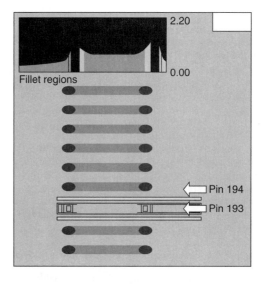

Good board (pin 6)

Reference designator	Inspection point	Thickness (in 0.001")
U1 pin 193	Pad	0.59
	Heel	1.18
	Center	0.69
	Toe	1.34
U1 pin 194	Pad	0.58
	Heel	1.20
	Center	0.68
	Toe	1.30

FIGURE 32.10 Cross-sectional x-ray image of tape-automated bond (TAB) solder joints. Image-processing software converts the gray-scale readings of the image for pin 193 into the side profile of solder thickness shown above the image. The actual calibrated measurements of average solder thickness across the pad, heel fillet height, center thickness, and toe fillet height processed from the images of pins 193 and 194 are shown in the table below the x-ray image. These measurements indicate that both of these solder joints are good.

Automated inspection of solder joints has the following limitations:

1. Not always fast enough test throughput to inspect all solder joints within the manufacturing cycle time for the printed circuit assembly
2. Requires a significant learning curve to become expert at developing solder joint tests with both low false accept and false reject rates

32.8 IMPLEMENTATION OF AUTOMATED PROCESS TEST SYSTEMS

Successful implementation of automated process test systems into printed circuit assembly production lines requires a significant investment in training, process analysis, and system integration. The implementation can be a lengthy process that requires concerted effort by engineers or skilled technicians. Listed here are highlights of what several manufacturers have learned are key aspects of successfully implementing automated inspection systems.

1. *Assess requirements carefully.*   Start by carefully assessing the requirements for automatic process test in the particular production environment into which the system will be integrated. Determine exactly what kind of defects are most important to detect by the inspection system, what measurements will most help with process improvement, and what benefits will generate the quickest financial return on investment.[3] This assessment must consider the test and measurement capability that already has been implemented as well as new requirements emanating from future printed circuit assembly designs.

2. *Evaluate select set of systems thoroughly.*   Select a small number of automated process test systems to evaluate thoroughly and compare against the system requirements. The evaluation should include a benchmark using printed circuit assemblies from production to determine system capability of accurately detecting the important defect types within the required false reject rate, repeatedly make the required measurements, and test time. Elements of cost of ownership should be well understood, including test development time, maintenance skills and cost, expected system downtime, and supplier maintenance services and prices.

3. *Plan for factory system interfaces.*   Consider and plan for interfaces to other factory systems carefully. These systems include board-handling equipment, barcode reading systems, CAD systems for automatic download of board layout and component package information, and quality-data management systems for statistical process control (SPC) and historical quality tracking.

4. *Focus on SPC measurements.*   Start with a focus on SPC measurements instead of defect detection. Until the process variation is reduced, most manufacturers will encounter either a false reject rate or a false accept rate that is higher than desired. By allowing one or the other rate to be too high while focusing on reducing the process variation first, time-consuming, unproductive tweaking of acceptance thresholds will be avoided. Reducing process variation requires correlating measurements to the process parameters that cause the process of variation and defects and then adjustment of these process parameters.[4]

5. *Define defects carefully.*   With an understanding of the selected systems capability, carefully define the defects that must be detected for product quality and reliability. Many of the visual inspection criteria used in the past are not appropriate for automated inspection systems because the system takes objective and different measurements.

6. *Invest enough resources.*   Do not under estimate the initial resource investment required to obtain optimum benefit from an automated process test system. The implementation plan should include dedicated technical support for the first six months of operation and test development. Developing a thorough understanding of the measurement results and correlating the data to process parameters is key to successful use of the system. Implementation should also address the fact that production personnel will have to be convinced of the accuracy of the system's test results before full benefit can be obtained from the system.

32.9   DESIGN IMPLICATIONS OF AUTOMATED PROCESS TEST SYSTEMS

Automated process test systems in general do not require many changes or limitations in the design of printed circuit assemblies. Since these systems use noncontact measurement techniques, fixturing requirements present very few design limitations, for instance. However, the following requirements will facilitate automatic inspection if they are considered during printed circuit design.

32.9.1   Automated Board-Handling Requirements

1. Parallel edges of the assembly or panel that have adequate clearance, typically at least 3 mm, to allow board-handling clamps or belts to grab the assembly.

2. Alignment fiducials on three corners of the assembly or panel. (For fiducials to be useful for x-ray systems, they should be tinned with solder at least 12.5 μm in thickness.)

3. Extra alignment fiducials near components with lead pitch less than 0.5 mm.

4. Barcode identification of assembly number and serial number at predefined location on each printed circuit assembly.

5. Adequate board rigidity to avoid need for fixture to prevent excessive board vibration during movement. Panels with prerouted, breakaway boards or bare boards less than 30 mil in thickness present the biggest challenge.

6. Component, heat-sink, or daughter-board height above or below the bare board that does not exceed the height clearance of the targeted automated process test system.

32.9.2   Test Development Ease of Use Requirements

1. As few as possible—ideally one—suppliers for each component type. Variation in lead and component package dimensions from supplier to supplier for the same component forces longer and more difficult development of inspection routines for each printed circuit assembly type.

2. Uniform pad shapes and sizes, particularly for each component package type. Variation in pad size and shape within a component package type forces longer and more difficult development of inspection routines for each printed circuit assembly type.

3. Clearly visible solder joints for optical and structured-light automated process test systems.

4. No components opposite or under dense structures, such as transformers, large capacitors, or thick steel heat sinks, for x-ray automated process test systems.

REFERENCES

1. A. J. Donnel, et al., *Visual Soldering Inspection Inconsistencies—Interpretation of MIL-SPEC Visual Acceptance Criteria,* AT&T Bell Laboratories, 1988.

2. Michael Lancaster, Ph.D., "Six Sigma in Contract Manufacturing," *Proceedings of Surface Mount International Conference,* San Jose, California, 1991.

3. Dennis L. Baird, "Using 3D X-ray Inspection for Process Improvement," *Proceedings of Nepcon West Conference,* Hughes Aircraft Company, Cahners Publishing, Des Plaines, Ill., 1993.

4. Thilo Sack, "Implementation Strategy for an Automated X-ray Inspection Machine," *Proceedings of Nepcon West Conference,* IBM Corporation, Cahners Publishing, Des Plaines, Ill., 1991.

P · A · R · T · 6

TEST AND REPAIR

CHAPTER 33
LOADED BOARD TESTING

Kenneth P. Parker
Hewlett-Packard Company, Loveland, Colorado

33.1 INTRODUCTION

Printed circuit boards, as with everything else in the electronics industry, have been undergoing rapid technological evolution. This is only natural since everything—from the boards themselves, to the CAD systems that create them, to the components that populate them, to the assembly methodologies used to fabricate them—has been undergoing similar changes. These changes have common themes: greater functional density, better performance, improved reliability, and lower cost.

The move towards surface-mount technology (SMT) has accelerated to the point that SMT designs are now the rule. SMT supplanted, in large part, the familiar 100-mil centered through-hole package technology. The change came slowly, embraced by leading-edge applications that needed the density improvements that came with SMT. Many held back since they did not have a need for higher densities and could not justify the risk of putting new processes in place to manufacture with SMT. The process of perfecting SMT brought to light a surprising fact: It was more efficient once the necessary automation was put in place and perfected. There are now applications using SMT that are not attracted by the density improvements, but rather, by the efficiencies. This is confirmed by the fact that many new devices cannot be obtained in the old-style through-hole packages.

Along with SMT came increases in lead pitch density. First there was 50-mil pitch; soon came 25-mil pitch; then came 15 mil, and so on. Other technologies such as tape-automated bonding (TAB), chip-on-board (COB), and multichip modules (MCM) are gaining interest. The industry is in the midst of a packaging revolution. This revolution has applied to boards as well. The average board now has more layers, finer lines and spaces, buried vias, devices mounted on both sides, and so forth. The net result is that loaded printed circuit boards are becoming incredibly densely packed with sophisticated components.

Testing has been impacted by all these changes. If perfect components were fed through perfect processes utilizing perfect machines run by perfect employees, testing would not be needed! Unfortunately, nearly perfect components are fed through processes that are subject to drift in many of the hundreds of variables that govern them, using machines that require careful calibration and preventive maintenance, by people who sometimes fail. For these reasons, testing is still an important part of loaded board manufacturing. However, as a result of the miniaturization brought on by the packaging revolution, our ability to gain physical and electrical access needed for testing purposes is increasingly hampered. Because *access* to a circuit is crucial for testing, accessibility difficulties make testing steadily more difficult to accomplish. On top of this, the electronics industry is expected to provide continued improvements in reliability and quality. Testing plays a crucial role towards these improvements, as will be seen.

33.2   FAULTS AND DEFECTS

Testing is a word often used in a vacuum. What are tests actually looking for? The answer to this question has a huge impact on how to go about testing effectively. It makes little sense to test for problems with low likelihood of occurring, as it makes little sense to inadequately test for likely problems.

The word *fault* is often used in testing discussions. What is a fault? Often, a fault is a manifestation of a *defect,* which is an undesirable deviation from a norm—for example, a missing bond wire in an IC. This defect may in turn be due to a problem (the root cause) in a wire-bonding machine, such as it is misfeeding wire. This defect then shows up as a fault; for example, an input to a logic gate sees a permanent logic 1 rather than a varying signal.*

An observed fault is not always a reliable pointer to a defect. For example, if an IC loaded on a board has defective solder on one input pin, causing an open circuit, this may appear to the IC to be a permanent, stuck-at-1 fault on that input. Under certain testing approaches, this faulty behavior is not readily apparent since the effect of the erroneous logic 1 must propagate through the internal workings of the IC before its effects (improper output behavior) are seen. When this faulty output behavior is observed, it can be a highly challenging task to relate this observed behavior to the input stuck-at fault caused by the solder defect. For this reason, it is important to utilize tests that target expected faults and that accurately resolve the underlying defects. When defects are resolved correctly, it is then much easier to find and correct the causal problems.

There are, in general, three categories of faults being tested for today: testing for performance faults, testing for manufacturing defects, and specification failures.

33.2.1   Performance Faults

A performance fault is a fault in the performance of a system that occurs due to a mismatch of important parameters among the system's components. This mismatch is the defect. As a common example, the path delay seen by a digital signal as it passes through several components may exceed the intended design value, causing a malfunction. No single component in the path is defective, but the cumulative contributions of several cause the performance fault. The fix for this defect is to replace one or more components in the path with new components specifically selected to give the proper delay.

There are several problems with testing for performance faults. First, the test developer must know about the circuit design in great detail. Second, it is difficult to set up a test that can resolve faults into specific defects (for example, the mismatch of parameters in several components). Third, it is difficult to avoid being fooled by unanticipated defects that produce behaviors similar to the defects of interest.

Solving these problems implies great knowledge and understanding of a board design. Indeed, in some instances in a carefully designed board, the designer may have specific knowledge of some critical parameter that has to be precisely managed and can alert those respon-

---

* Several other defects can produce this same fault behavior. For example, missing solder between the input pin and the board, an electrostatically damaged input buffer within the IC, or a broken printed circuit trace between the upstream driver and the input will all exhibit the same faulty behavior. It is the ultimate responsibility of the test process to first find the fault (this is called *detection*), then the underlying defect (this is called *diagnosis*), and in many cases, provide clues to the root cause for process improvement.

sible for test. However, much of the testing for performance faults carried out in the past was not done with this knowledge, but rather because of a *lack* of this knowledge. In the past, tools that could help control the key parameters of our design were unavailable, or designers were using components that were incompletely specified, or perhaps they were too trusting in their seat-of-the-pants instincts. It was expected that performance testing would give adequate coverage of any problems that might occur. In effect, performance testing was used to validate a design after the fact.

The expectation that performance testing will somehow protect our products from the effects of poor design is now obsolete. It amounts to wildly shooting in the dark against a well-hidden, stealthy enemy force of unknown size and distribution. With ever-increasing complexities of boards, it is simply not reasonable to expect that test engineers could stumble at random across effective tests for all possible design problems, and certainly not within the lifetime of the design. With the increase in effectiveness of our design tools, designers should no longer be relying on test for design validation. Testing for performance faults will still be important, but it must be used in its proper role—to verify that critical parameters identified in the design process are properly controlled.

33.2.2 Manufacturing Defects

A manufacturing defect is a defect resulting from a problem in the manufacturing process. Manufacturing defects tend to be fairly gross in nature. Table 33.1 gives a list of potential manufacturing defects.

Manufacturing defects are the result of the havoc inherent in manufacturing processes. These defects result in faults that may be very easy to detect and to correlate with their root cause, but this is a function of the test approach. Some manufacturing defects can still be difficult to detect and resolve, as illustrated by the previous example of a solder open on a device input pin.

33.2.3 Specification Failures

Specification failures are similar to performance faults. Performance specifications are checked against requirements for the full range of operating conditions expected, such as temperature, humidity, vibration, and electronic noise. Specification test is often a regulatory or contractual requirement. One may argue that they are largely unnecessary since, if a circuit design is robust, makes use of quality components, and is accurately assembled and tested, one

TABLE 33.1 Examples of Manufacturing Defects Seen at the Board Level, Source(s) of the Problem and Causes

Defect	Source(s)	Cause(s)
Solder shorts between pins	Wave/reflow soldering	Too much solder, solder screen defects, pin misregistration, bent pins
Solder open	Solder application, wave/reflow soldering	Too little solder, solder screen defects, tombstoning, bent pins
Missing component	Placement, solder	Shock, too little glue
Wrong component	Placement setup, inventory, handling	Handling error, mismarked, human error, wrong specification
Wrong component orientation	Placement setup	Handling error, human error
Dead component	Placement, solder	Dead on arrival, handling damage, electrostatic damage

does not have to make it perform all of its functions to know that it works. This is the *proof-by-construction* argument, used by successful flashbulb and bomb-detonator manufacturers. Full specification test may also be impossible in practical terms since there may be too many combinations of circuit functions versus operating ranges. If only a subset of combinations is to be checked, this begs the question of which subset.

If specification test is required nonetheless, such testing is usually carried out with custom tailored test equipment that can simulate the range of operational environments of interest. Such testing may be quite time consuming and the cost of the supporting test equipment may range from trivial to hyperexpensive. In one extreme, a manufacturer of I/O cards for personal computers may simply plug each one into a computer and see if it performs a simple loopback test. In the other extreme, a manufacturer of guidance computers for missiles may require a missile shot on a test range, full telemetry, and support from the Air Force and Navy.

33.3 TESTING APPROACHES

We have seen a spectrum of faults: performance faults, manufacturing defects, and specification faults. Each has evolved a test technology.

33.3.1 Testing for Performance Faults

Performance testers are often known as *edge connector functional testers*. They connect to the edge connectors of the board under test with mating connectors that are then adapted to the tester resources by a customized fixture called an *adapter*. In most cases, no other connections are made by the test fixturing to any internal nodes of the circuit. In essence, the board is tested in an environment that resembles its application to some degree.

Some performance testers have *guided probe* capability.[1,2] A guided probe is a manually positioned test probe with a measurement (and sometimes stimulus) capability and supporting software. It is used to temporarily gain access to internal nodes of a circuit, one at a time, where observations of circuit behavior during a test can be made and processed by software to provide enhanced fault resolution.

How does this software know what the nodes of a circuit are supposed to be doing during a test? One could enter all this data by hand if one knew the design of a circuit well, but this is quickly impossible for any circuit that consists of more than a handful of gates. The most popular way to get this data is by logic simulation of the circuit.[*2] *Good circuit simulation* is often used by designers to prove that the circuit behaves the way they expect it to under various input conditions (input vectors) they are interested in. *Fault simulation* is used to study how a circuit behaves when that circuit is perturbed by a modeled fault. An example of a modeled fault is a stuck-at-0 on a gate output, meaning no matter what the gate's inputs are, the output is 0. The "single stuck-at" model is the most prevalent fault model in existence. It assumes that only one stuck-at (either 0 or 1) may exist in a circuit at any one time. A fault simulator can be used to predict, for a given modeled fault, how the circuit will behave when stimulated with input (test) vectors. If the modeled fault causes one or more observation points (such as circuit output pins) to deviate from normal behavior, we can declare the fault

---

    * Logic simulation implies the treatment of the digital nature of the circuit, typically omitting any interaction with any analog portions of the circuit. Analog simulators do exist but are implemented in a very different technology from digital simulators. Mixed signal simulation is not anywhere near as viable as digital simulation, which presents a problem for test engineers.

detected by that vector. In the common case of sequential circuits, it is more accurate to say the fault was detected by all vectors up to and including the one that caused the observable deviation.

Another technology used by some performance testers is the *fault dictionary*.[2] Fault dictionaries are prepared with fault simulators. A fault dictionary is a three-dimensional data structure of boolean true/false bits. The first dimension is an enumeration of all test vectors. The second dimension is a list of modeled faults that are to be simulated. The third dimension is an enumeration of the circuit's output pins. A given bit is true if the corresponding output pin fails on the corresponding vector for a given fault.

For a given vector and fault, the output pins that are expected to fail can be looked up in this dictionary. In a testing scenario, we take a failing test vector and list of failed output pins, and attempt to look up a fault (or faults) that match the failed pin behavior for that vector. Fault dictionaries work well when actual defects that cause a circuit to fail closely match the fault model. When defects occur that vary from the modeled faults, then a dictionary lookup may come up empty (no matching fault), or matches are found but they point to the wrong faults, or so many matches are found that it is impractical to examine them all to see which (if any) are the actual problem. Dictionary generation is computationally intensive, dictionaries may consume huge amounts of storage space,* and dictionary lookups may not work. This technology was invented along with small-scale integrated bipolar technologies such as early TTL or ECL. The advent of large-scale integration and CMOS technology† has made fault dictionary technology essentially useless in practice.

Performance testers are intended to emulate the environment the board would encounter in its native application. This means that the tester itself needs to be carefully customized to supply this environment, or it must be a general-purpose tester with a great degree of flexibility. Flexibility brings cost, so commercial functional testers tend to be among the most expensive. Programming such machines is a complex task, due both to the flexibility of the tester and due to the nature of the test requirements. It is difficult at best to get automated support for functional test programming. Typically, such programming takes extreme patience and a high level of skill—again, two more costs. To compound this, any last-minute design changes to the board may cause expensive and time-consuming test modifications or invalidate the tests altogether.

33.3.2 Testing for Manufacturing Defects

Manufacturing defects can be detected by a functional test, but since functional testers are expensive and difficult to program, other techniques have arisen to test for them. These testers have one or more of the following advantages:

1. They are much easier to program, often requiring less than 10 to 20 percent of the time as functional test development.

2. Automatic test program generators that analyze the circuit design database do much of the work and relieve the skill required of the programmer.

---

* For example, say a circuit has 100,000 gates. The number of stuck-at faults to be simulated may easily be 200,000. A set of test vectors for these may easily exceed 500,000. If the circuit has a fairly normal complement of 250 outputs, then a fault dictionary for this example would consume the product of faults times vectors times outputs, 2.5×10^{13} bits, or about 3.125 terabytes (give or take a gigabyte). Fault simulation times lasting months, even on very fast computers, have been reported. Of course, larger circuits will need more!

† CMOS VLSI circuits have several defect modes that are inconvenient to model in popular fault simulators; thus, fault models are more likely not to match defects. Two of the offending defect modes are bridging faults (intermetal shorts), and metallization opens which may actually introduce capacitive memory into a circuit. These are difficult to model with traditional fault-modeling techniques.

3. Their programs are much less sensitive to design changes since they take a divide-and-conquer approach; the effects of design changes are localized requiring that only a portion of the test be reprogrammed.

4. They offer much better defect resolution for many defects because localized portions of the circuit are being analyzed, reducing diagnostic complexity.

The principal technology is the in-circuit tester. This tester utilizes a high degree of nodal access—that is, connection to printed circuit traces—to perform its work. Nodal access is provided by a unique fixture called the *bed of nails*. This fixture is composed of a platen that supports the board under test. The platen is drilled with holes below each target point for nodal access. In the holes are spring-loaded nails that contact the target points on the board. (Special clamshell fixtures allow nail access to both sides of a board.) The platen with board form the movable top layer of a vacuum chamber. When vacuum is actuated, the platen with board move down, depressing the nail springs and causing nail contact with board nodes. (Mechanical actuation in place of vacuum is also used sometimes.) The nails are wired (typically with wire-wrap technology) to the stimulus/measurement resources of the tester. See Fig. 33.1. These resources contain mechanical relays that allow connection of various tester functions to a given nail.

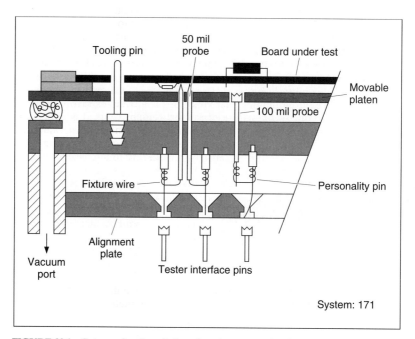

FIGURE 33.1 Cutaway drawing of a board resting on top of an in-circuit, vacuum-actuated test fixture: the bed of nails. The interface pins (the mechanical interface to the ATE pin electronics) are placed very close to reduce path lengths.

Once a tester has access to the nodes of a board, it can perform in-circuit (also called in-situ) tests. The idea is to test components as if they were standing alone, while they, in fact, are part of a board circuit. The problem of in-circuit testing can be subdivided into two main categories: analog in-circuit and digital in-circuit testing.

33.3.2.1 Analog In-Circuit Test. Analog in-circuit testing addresses the testing printed wiring circuits for short circuits. This includes analog components, which are typically passive devices such as resistors, inductors, and capacitors, as well as simple semiconductor components such as diodes and transistors.* Analog testing is conducted without applying power to the board.

Shorts—that is, unwanted connections between nodes—are tested for first, since subsequent testing will profit from the assumption that shorts are not a factor, and, since subsequent testing may need to apply power to the board. Unpowered shorts testing may be accomplished by applying a small DC voltage[†] to a node while all others are connected to ground. If current flow is observed that is below a computed threshold, then the node cannot be shorted to any of the grounded nodes. If the current flow is above the programmed threshold, there may be an unexpected path to at least one of the grounded nodes. The destination node(s) can be determined by linearly searching the grounded nodes for the current flow (this is slow) or by using half-splitting techniques (which are fast)[‡] to determine the other node(s) the current is flowing to. When the algorithm has finished stimulating all nodes sequentially, it can declare which nodes are shorted, and use *x-y* position data to show where to look for the problems. Typically, shorts are repaired before continuing with other tests since they may confuse the resolution of defects and may cause physical damage when the power is later turned on.

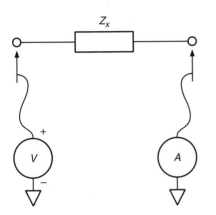

FIGURE 33.2   An analog component on a loaded board can be accessed by two in-circuit probes that connect its terminals with tester resources. In this case, a voltage source provides a current that is measured by a current meter.

Unpowered tests on analog components, such as resistors, capacitors, and inductors, are performed next. Again, low-stimulus voltages keep semiconductor junctions turned off. AC voltages are applied and phase-shifted currents are measured in order to deduce the values of reactive components (capacitors, inductors). For a simple measurement of a lone impedance[§] Z_x, apply a voltage to one terminal of the component (through the bed of nails) and connect a current-measuring device (conceptually, an ammeter with zero impedance to ground) to the other component terminal. The current flow observed due to the known stimulus voltage is related to Z_x by Ohm's law ($Z_x = V/I$). See Fig. 33.2.

However, some discrete analog components may be connected to one another in ways that prevent simple measurement of the current flowing through the component due to parallel pathways that sidetrack some of the current. In Fig. 33.3, when applying a voltage to one terminal of Z_x, a current also flows in a parallel path through Z_a and Z_b. The ammeter does not measure the true current through Z_x because current from the parallel path also gets to the ammeter.

The parallel path problem can be solved with a process called *guarding*. Guarding is accomplished by using a third nail to connect ground to the node marked *G*. When *G* is grounded, all the sidetracked current goes to ground because there is no voltage drop across Z_b to attract current to or from the ammeter. All the current seen by the ammeter comes through Z_x, so again, Ohm's law

---

* Complex analog devices such as analog or mixed-signal ICs are not very amenable to analog in-circuit testing since they require power to be applied to the board. Simple diodes and single transistors can be tested by in-circuit stimulus that essentially examines the characteristics of their semiconductor junctions.

[†] The reason for using a small stimulus voltage (typically less than 0.2 V) is to prevent current flow through semiconductor junctions that may exist between nodes. This voltage will not turn on a junction. These junctions may exist in parasitic form within ICs.

[‡] A half-splitting technique (also called a *binary chop*) is a fundamental algorithm of computer science. It works by successively considering half of a set of items (grounded nodes that are receiving current in this case) while removing the other half from consideration. It recursively divides sets repeatedly until only one item is left to consider. It has a complexity related to the log base 2 of the size of the original set of items. By comparison, a linear process has a complexity linearly related to the size of the original set.

[§] This component may not be alone in a physical sense, but since low-stimulus voltages are used, other connected devices such as ICs may be electrically quiescent so that the component is electrically alone.

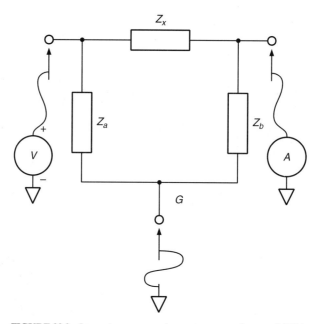

FIGURE 33.3 In most cases, an analog component to be tested (Z_x) is connected in a network with other devices such as Z_a and Z_b. The value of Z_x can still be measured by using additional tester resources to set up a guarded configuration to electrically isolate the measurement path.

gives the value of Z_x. This is a classic three-wire measurement. It turns out that for general component topologies, multiple guards (ground connections) may be required, but these are still considered three-wire measurements. In some cases where enhanced accuracies are needed or where there are extreme ratios of component values in a network, additional sense wires are used to eliminate errors that are due to small voltage drops in fixture nail, wire, and trace contributions. See Ref. 3 for a discussion of enhanced measurement accuracies.

33.3.2.2 Digital In-Circuit Test. Digital in-circuit test focuses on the digital components residing on a board and requires that power be applied to activate the digital logic contained within the ICs. Just as analog components can be tested without removing them from a board, so can digital components be tested. The key technology is *backdriving*. When applying digital stimuli to a digital device's inputs (via the bed of nails), a tester's driver must overcome the voltage levels that connected upstream devices are producing. This is done by equipping the digital in-circuit tester with powerful, low-impedance drivers that can backdrive upstream drivers with enough current to create the desired signal voltage in spite of their state. With tester receivers connected by nails to the device's outputs, the tester can monitor these outputs for expected responses to the stimuli. See Fig. 33.4.

A problem with backdriving is that the tester drivers are abusing the upstream drivers in other devices while testing the device of interest. Studies[4] have shown this is a legitimate concern and that damage to upstream devices may occur. For example, overdriven silicon junctions or device bond wires may heat up enough to be damaged. Sometimes this damage may occur surprisingly fast, within milliseconds. This problem can be solved by careful application of tests with an eye towards their duration. If backdrive testing can be done quickly, and/or with appropriate cooling intervals, then damage can be successfully avoided.[5] This has allowed digital in-circuit testing to be a dominant testing technology.

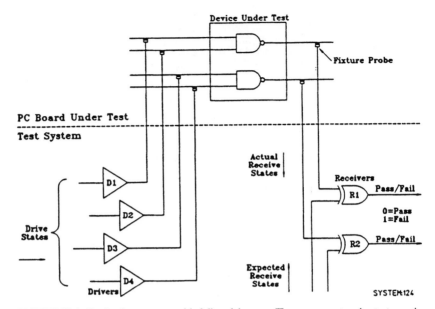

FIGURE 33.4 In-circuit test setup with full nodal access. The component under test may be embedded within a board and connected to other components.

A great advantage of digital in-circuit testing is that it is performed directly on the inputs and outputs of a targeted device. If the device should fail testing, this is seen directly, rather than having its identity masked by interactions with other devices. This is a major differentiation over functional testing. Faults typically can be resolved to two categories of defects: failed ICs or solder opens on I/O/power pins.

Another major differentiator is the ease—indeed, automation—of test programming that is possible with digital in-circuit testing. Tests for ICs can be prepared as if they were standing alone,* stored in a library, and recalled from a library when needed. Modern digital in-circuit testers may have library tests for tens of thousands of devices. For custom, one-of-a-kind ICs for which a library test may not exist (e.g., ASICs), it is still substantially easier to create a test for just the one device than it is for a collection of ICs.

33.3.2.3 *Manufacturing Defect Analyzer (MDA).* A manufacturing defect analyzer (MDA) is essentially a very low-end analog in-circuit tester. One way it maintains low equipment cost is by not having power supplies to power up a board. Another cost savings comes by having only rudimentary programming and operating software. Some amount of test accuracy and yield must be traded for this savings.

33.3.2.4 *General-Purpose In-Circuit Tester.* The workhorse of the electronics industry is the general-purpose in-circuit tester that merges support for analog and digital in-circuit tests. An example of a widely used system is shown in Fig. 33.5. It contains power supplies for powering boards and often contains sophisticated analog in-circuit programming tools and extensive libraries of digital tests. The typical test and repair flow for this tester is shown in Fig. 33.6.

---

* This assumes that the IC does not have any *topological constraints* on its I/O pins such as having an input pin connected directly to ground, or an output pin fed back to an input pin. In such cases, the prepared test may be incompatible with these constraints.

FIGURE 33.5 Example of a commercial in-circuit tester testhead and operator's terminal, with a printed circuit board mounted in the testing position on top of the bed-of-nails fixture.

Note the early exit to repair for boards that fail shorts testing. This avoids applying power to boards that contain shorts, since these may present hazards to the board and human operator, plus they also confuse the diagnosis of faults later in testing.

33.3.2.5 Combinational Tester. In situations where a manufacturing line has a variety of technologies in production, a need may exist for both functional and in-circuit testing. Thus, hybrid functional/in-circuit testers exist, commonly called *combinational* testers. These machines give test engineers a full complement of tools to address testing problems. They also allow one-stop testing where manufacturing defects and functional performance faults can be detected at one site in the production flow.

A combinational tester will utilize a bed of nails to perform in-circuit analog and digital tests. It may also utilize edge connector access to perform functional tests. In some cases, these approaches are hybridized by constructing a two-stage bed-of-nails fixture that has two lengths of nails used in the bed, and with a platen that has two stations of depression during operation. The first stage is full depression which brings all nails into contact with the circuit board for standard in-circuit access. The second stage is partial depression where only the longer nails still contact the board, perhaps at board edge, for functional testing. The removal of the shorter nails removes the electrical loading they present to internal circuit nodes that allows the board to operate in a more natural environment.

33.3.3 Unconventional Tests

Unconventional tests use radically different approaches to specifically address the resolution of defects. These may be needed to address blind spots in traditional electrical test methodologies. Two specific examples of defects that are difficult to resolve by traditional tests are given as examples.

First, consider a board with a large number of bypass capacitors. All of these capacitors are connected between power and ground so their parallel capacitances are summed. Using an

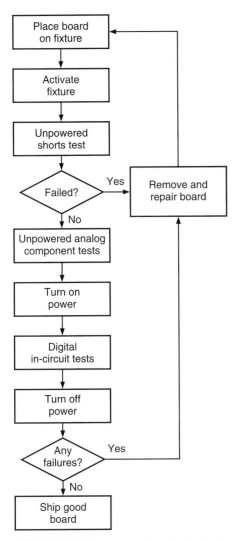

FIGURE 33.6 Typical test and repair flow for in-circuit tester.

analog in-circuit test, it is possible to test for this summed capacitance. However, if one capacitor is missing or tombstoned, the tester most likely will not notice, since the resulting decrement in capacitance will likely fall well within the summed tolerances of the summed capacitances. The performance of the board at higher operating frequencies may be adversely affected, however, due to a loss of noise immunity. This possibly could be detected by a performance test. However, if this performance test failed, it could be very difficult to resolve which capacitor was missing. One nontraditional way to test for this problem is to use human visual inspection to look for missing capacitors. This may not find solder opens, however. Another approach would be to use an automated x-ray laminographic tester to check for the existence and solder integrity of each capacitor. Even the orientation on polarized capacitors can be verified. (See Chap. 32 for a discussion of x-ray inspection.)

Second, consider again the open solder problem on a digital device input. This defect may manifest itself as improper device behavior, but it would be wrong to replace the device (which would also fix the solder open) since it is not at fault. Digital in-circuit testing has trouble resolving solder opens from bad devices.* Final resolution can be obtained either by visual inspection or by using a hand-held probe to see if board signals reach IC legs, but this is becoming increasingly difficult as packaging dimensions continue to shrink (e.g., TAB) or newer attachment technologies (e.g., ball grid arrays) are used that prohibit visual inspection or probing altogether.

An alternative approach to the open solder problem uses a capacitive coupling technique to look for opens. The technique exploits the fact that ICs have a lead frame that forms the conductive path from the legs of the device to the die bond wire pads. Using the bed of nails, all but one node attached to the IC can be grounded (this is an unpowered technique) and a small ac signal can be applied to the node that is left. An insulated metal plate pressed against the top of the IC forms the top plate of a capacitor, and the stimulated IC leg and lead frame conductor form the bottom plate. See Fig. 33.7. The capacitance may be on the order of 100 femtoFarads (100×10^{-15} F) which is small enough to require sophisticated detection electronics to measure in the face of environmental noise. Now, if the IC leg is soldered to the stimulated board node, the correct capacitance will be measured. If the solder joint is open, then a second capacitance now exists in series with the first. This may reduce the measured capacitance by a factor of 2 to 10. This technique allows testing of complex ICs for solder opens without knowing what the ICs actually do, requires no complicated programming, and gives accurate resolution of solder defects. The technique has been extended to allow testing of solder integrity for connectors and switches.† A fixture for capacitive opens testing is shown in Fig. 33.8.

---

*Ignore for the moment the possibility of using boundary-scan to solve this problem, which will be covered in Sec. 33.5.3 on standards-based test.

†This technique for detecting open solder connections is protected under U.S. Patent 5,254,953 and subsequent patents in the United States and other countries. The technology has been given the trademark TestJet by Hewlett-Packard Company.

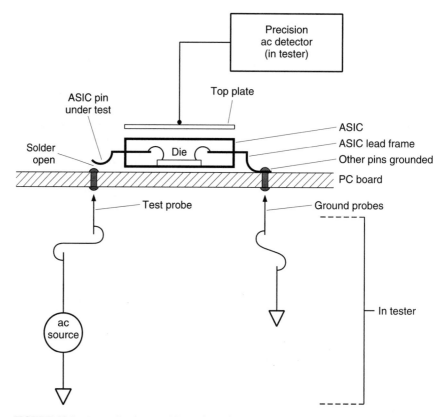

FIGURE 33.7   An application-specific IC (ASIC) contains a metallic leadframe and bond wires that interconnect the IC die to the printed circuit traces. The tester can drive an ac voltage signal onto that circuit trace and a top plate positioned above the IC can receive this signal through capacitive coupling with the leadframe. The presence of a solder open will greatly attenuate this signal, allowing its detection. Other IC pins are grounded by the tester to reduce noise and increase discrimination.

33.3.4   Tester Comparison

Table 33.2 summarizes the types of tester for comparative costs and capabilities.

33.4   *THE PROCESS OF TEST*

In the earliest years of the electronics industry—indeed, before anyone may have called it an industry—there was no concept of "test." A product was put together and shipped, because, inherent in the putting together was a basic appreciation for how it was supposed to look and behave. This crafting quickly gave way to mass production of somewhat more complicated items by workers who were not themselves experts in the craft. Of course, today, items of unbelievable complexity are produced by workers with little or no fathoming of what it is they are producing. If they had to know, it would undoubtedly be too expensive to make the product.

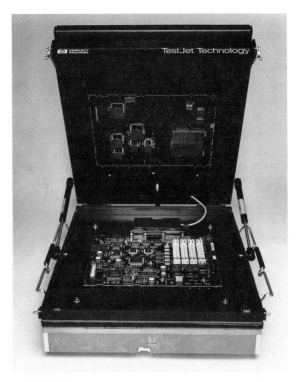

FIGURE 33.8 A test fixture with board on a bed of nails, with clamshell top fixture containing capacitive sensor plates. Notice eight closely spaced sensor plates (*right*) that test for opens in eight (white) connectors on the board.

TABLE 33.2 Costs and Capabilities of Various Testers

Tester	Typical cost, $	Program time	Diag. resol.	Fault cover	Comments
MDA	10^4–10^5	1–2 days	Fair	Poor	No digital coverage, requires known good board for programming
ICT	10^5–10^6	5–10 days	Best	Good	Fixturing a major portion of preparation time
Combo	10^5–10^6	10–30 days	Best	Best	Functional test a major portion of preparation time
Func	10^5–10^6	1–4 months	Fair	Good	Very high skill required
SpecV	10^3–10^7	days-months	Poor	?	High skill required for preparation and interpreting test results

It is also important to appreciate that boards are often themselves components of systems. Boards might have a respectable yield from a board test process of, say, 97 percent, which is to say, 3 of 100 still contain defects.* However, if 20 such boards are used in a sys-

---

* It is important to differentiate test yield from defect coverage of a test. The yield of the manufacturing process before test might be (say) 50 percent, and the yield after test may be 97 percent. This may be accomplished with a test that detects (covers) 90 percent of the important defects.

tem, the probability that the system will turn on is only 54 percent. Since debugging a system is usually far costlier and more difficult than testing a board, there is much interest in higher posttest yields. This is why yields are being pushed higher into the 99 percent and higher* levels.

Test has gone through three stages of evolution during this time. Test has been used as a sorting process, then as a repair driver, and finally as a process monitor.

33.4.1 Test as a Sorting Process

Test can be used to sort boards into two piles, good and bad. Essentially, such testing provides only one bit of information about a board. This one bit of information provides little clue as to what the problem is or how to repair it. If all we intend to do with a bad board is discard it, then one bit of information may be enough. In some applications—for example, making $2 digital watches by the million—it may be economically impossible to attempt to repair bad units. However, as will be seen soon, discarding bad boards may also discard valuable information about the health of our manufacturing process.

33.4.2 Test as a Repair Driver

It is very often economically justifiable to repair a bad board, if it can be done quickly and with little skilled analysis needed. This is where modern test systems begin to come into their own. More bits of information are needed per bad board; a diagnosis is needed that accurately resolves failures into defect reports that can be acted on to effect repairs. Since a freshly repaired board will need retesting to assure that it is now defect free, one also would like to find as many defects as feasible in each pass across a tester to avoid a glut of work-in-progress.

33.4.3 Test as a Process Monitor

When repairing boards, valuable information about the health of our board manufacturing process is at our fingertips. Indeed, the repair process may have the ultimate defect resolution, since faults detected by a tester may still not be perfectly correlated with defects. If one views test as a process monitor, one can gain valuable insight into what is happening upstream in many of the subprocesses that come together to produce boards. For example, one may see solder opens as a chronic problem. Further examination may show that they are happening in one area of a board more than any other. That may lead to the examination of the solder application process which shows that a solder screen squeegee has an uneven amount of paste on it. The root cause of this uneven distribution of paste can then be sought and corrected.

It is quite important for the tester to do a good job of resolving faults into defects. Using again the example of solder opens on digital devices, digital in-circuit test alone may indict devices as failing when it is really more of an open solder problem. The repair technician may notice this. However, it may well be overlooked since replacing the device "fixes" the problem. This pollutes the information about our process, causing one to call the IC vendor with complaints when one should be examining the solder process. If tests are focused more closely on defects than on faults, then one may be able to better trust tester-derived process information.

---

* Measuring yields in percentages is telling. In the IC industry, yields are measured in parts per million. One ppm corresponds to 99.9999 percent and 500 ppm, a good IC yield, equals 99.95 percent yield. Will the board industry ever get into these ranges? Will it make sense to try?

This requires test engineers to be students of their manufacturing process and available test technologies so that test techniques are kept in balance with the defects that are most important.

33.5 DESIGN FOR TEST

In the latter part of the 1970s, it became clear that forces of technology were causing an evolution in board complexity that was quickly outstripping test technology. It is quite possible to design boards that essentially cannot be tested. This will doom projects and products to failure. Even if boards can be tested, the question bears asking: Is there something a designer can do that will make testing easier, cheaper, more thorough, etc.? The answer is that there is a great deal a designer can do (or fail to do) that will affect the testability of a board. The technology that addresses this problem is called *design for testability,* or DFT.

In those same 1970s and into the 1980s, it was very common for a design department to be physically and organizationally removed from the test department. The nature of product life cycles dictates that by the time a test department starts ramping up test program development for a board, the design team is off on the next project and finds it distracting to go back and help the test engineers with testing problems. Thus, in those years, the designers were unknowing contributers to difficult test problems. Testing became a bottleneck in product development, which ultimately became severe enough that attention was paid to the effects that design has on testing, by the middle of the 1980s. A landmark survey on DFT technology by Williams and Parker[6] brought DFT out of common lore and into the design lexicon of the electronics industry. This paper is still remarkably current* years later. It coined the terms *ad-hoc testability* and *structured testability*. These are covered next.

33.5.1 Ad-Hoc DFT

Ad-hoc design for testability consists of a set of simple rules of the form "do this, don't do that," where "this" and "that" were often not motivated with reasons. For example, for ICs with preset or clear pins, a rule might read "tie unused preset/clear pins off through a 50-ohm resistor to a power rail; do not tie them directly." The first-level reason for this is that a test engineer might want to access the preset/clear functions during testing, even though these functions were not used by the designer. If they are tied through a resistor, a test engineer may still be able to manipulate them by applying a tester resource to them that can drive a signal in spite of the resistor. If these pins are tied directly to a power rail, the test engineer will never have that option.

The real reason for the various ad-hoc DFT rules is that to effectively and economically test a circuit, one must be able to *control* and *observe* the circuit's behavior. Most rules are related either to controllability or observability (or both) of the circuit. The rule cited here is a controllability rule. Observability rules typically suggest ways to monitor signals that are deeply embedded in combinatorial circuitry, or that are activated only rarely by deeply sequential events.

Ad-hoc DFT is essentially the only way many products could have improved testability, when those products were constructed with off-the-shelf merchant parts. Large, vertically integrated companies have the advantage of being able to customize testability into the heart of a design, including the very ICs themselves. Application-specific ICs (ASICs) allow more of this as well.

---

* This survey does not cover the topic of standards-based test, since the testability standardization work promulgated by the IEEE began in the later 1980s.

33.5.2 Structured DFT

Structured DFT was born in companies that had vertical control over their designs, from custom ICs through systems. They also were well aware of their test costs and realized that initial design decisions had a large impact on these downstream costs.

These companies studied the controllability and observability problems and instituted design rules into their design processes that, when followed, would guarantee that a circuit was testable. In the test department where they also had complete control, they could utilize these added features with customized test processes.

One of the earliest and most prominent structured DFT schemes was IBM's Level Sensitive Scan Design (LSSD) which was developed in the 1970s.[6] It is the precursor to what is called *full internal scan* technology now. In (greatly simplified) summary, the LSSD design discipline requires every memory element (flip-flop or latch) to be constructed such that it obeys a testability protocol. This protocol allows two modes of operation: first, the normal operation of being a memory element in a design, and, second, for testing purposes, all memory elements can be connected into a serial shift register that can be loaded and unloaded by serial shifting. This makes every memory element a control point and an observation point within a circuit. No other memory elements are allowed in the design; e.g., no asynchronous feedback is allowed.* This guarantees that circuitry between any control/observation point is combinatorial, not sequential.

The next piece of the puzzle was IBM's test generation software that was able to automatically construct complete tests for combinatorial circuits (known as the D-algorithm and its derivatives). By using LSSD discipline, IBM knew its designs would be completely testable, and those tests could be created by a computer program. Other companies such as Sperry Univac, Amdahl, and Hitatchi had similar proprietary structured approaches. Most smaller, nonintegrated companies were not able to participate in structured DFT—that is, until nonproprietary industry standards came into play.

33.5.3 Standards-Based Test

In the closing years of the 1980s, it became apparent that some sort of structured testability technology had to become accessible to the electronics industry at large. A small group of European companies lead by Philips formed the Joint European Test Action Group (JETAG) and began work on a testability standard. The effort quickly attracted the notice of North American companies, giving rise to the JTAG standard (and the "E" was dropped from the acronym). As the proposal took shape, it was turned over to the IEEE which ultimately produced IEEE Std. 1149.1-1990, "Standard Test Access Port and Boundary-Scan Architecture" in 1990.[†][7] A complete coverage of this standard is beyond the scope of this chapter (see Ref. 8), so a brief summary is given here for an overview.

The 1149.1 standard is a design discipline for digital ICs. It is a set of rules impressed primarily on the I/O structures of a device that allow two modes of operation: normal mode and test mode. In normal mode, the device performs its intended function. In test mode, the device obeys a protocol that has mandatory, optional, and customized elements. The mandatory elements must exist, with the others being left as design options. The principle mandatory element of interest is a test mode dedicated to *external test* or EXTEST. When an 1149.1 compliant device is in EXTEST mode, its I/O pins are divorced from their normal operation

---

* As might be imagined, these rules are looked upon by designers as restrictions of their creativity. Ed Eichelberger at IBM was a major proponent of LSSD and happens to be about 5.5 feet tall. When asked (in 1977) how designers received the LSSD rules, he quipped that at the start, he was over 6 feet tall. Structured testability is not easy to implement. It requires commitment from the whole organization, starting with management.

† An IEEE standard has as a suffix the year of its creation or last update. A standard must be updated and/or reaffirmed every five years. Up to two supplements to a standard may be issued within the five-year cycle. Users of a standard should keep up to date with it.

and all internal functions of the device. Instead, the inputs become observation resources and the outputs become control resources for test purposes. These resources are under control of the 1149.1 serial scan protocol. One can think of the I/O pins of the device being connected to shift register cells; states can be shifted in that will finally appear on all output pins (control) and the states of all input pins can be captured and shifted out (observe). This gives 1149.1-cognizant software a powerful tool for controlling and/or observing board level node states.

Figure 33.9 shows a simplified overview of the architecture. The normal content of the IC, called the internal logic, is surrounded by boundary-register cells interposed between the IC pins and the internal logic. A small state machine called the *test access port* (TAP) is used to control the test functions. Four mandatory test pins (test clock TCK, test mode select TMS, test data in TDI, and test data out TDO)* give standardized access to the test functions. All 1149.1 devices have a one-bit BYPASS register used to bypass the (much longer) boundary-register if it is not needed in a given testing activity. It is intended that collections of ICs (called *chains*) with 1149.1 be connected TDO-to-TDI so that they may form a long shiftable

---

* An optional fifth pin called test reset (TRST) is an asynchronous active low reset for the 1149.1 circuitry. Since any TAP can be reset by five clock pulses to TCK while TMS is held high, TRST is not actually needed for resetting an 1149.1 device. It is often included as a fail-safe measure with a board-level pull-down resistor providing a constant reset to the TAP. Many 1149.1-compliant ICs do not include the TRST pin since the extra pin required may be too costly.

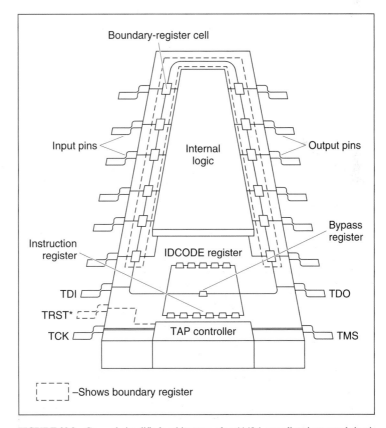

FIGURE 33.9   General, simplified architecture of an 1149.1-compliant integrated circuit.

register structure. The figure shows an optional IDCODE register that can be shifted out to uniquely identify the IC, its manufacturer, and revision.

The primary use for the 1149.1 EXTEST capability is to conduct board-level tests for shorts and opens. This is an example of how resources included in an IC design may be used to help with the testing problem at other levels in the manufacturing process. EXTEST can also be used during system test to see if there are any system integration problems such as bad connections in backplanes and cabling. An IC designer may not see much attraction in EXTEST, but the 1149.1 standard offers other test modes that will allow a designer to access internal scan paths, or, built-in self-test functions. The 1149.1 standard's name has two parts, "Standard Test Access Port" being the first and crucially important. It signifies that the standard anticipates being used as a standardized protocol for accessing *any* on-chip, board-level, or system-level testability scheme. In support of this, the standard is deliberately extensible, allowing clever designers to implement additional operational modes that can be used to solve unique testing problems.

The 1149.1 standard has proven itself to be quite useful and it has several contributions. First, it allows the creation of software that can automatically write tests for boards, where in the past, the same level of test effectiveness was nearly impossible to achieve, and only with weeks or even months of skilled labor. It is not uncommon to see a board test prepared in a single day, which otherwise might have taken weeks. Second, 1149.1 ICs can read their input pins and scan out the result. This allows diagnostic software to pinpoint the location of open solder problems, where in the past, an IC might falsely be indicted as faulty. Third, it allows one to perform tests on digital circuits without 100 percent accessibility to board nodes. With the trend toward miniaturization of components making it difficult to provide full nodal access, boundary-scan is allowing the elimination of many access points. Of course, not all points may be eliminated, so it must be understood which are still necessary. Finally, since many industry segments are affected by the test problem, a standard offers a way for everyone to benefit. A large number of applications and tools can be found to solve testing problems that would not have been possible without a standard.

Boundary-scan (1149.1) is a digital testability standard. However, there is also a trend in the superintegration of circuitry towards higher mixed-signal, digital/analog content in our designs. The IEEE is striving to develop a mixed-signal testability bus with a new proposed standard P1149.4, which, at the time of this writing, is in the definition stage.[9,10] This standard is envisioned* as a superset of 1149.1 boundary-scan, adding two additional analog test pins to the definition. The goal of the standard is to support opens and shorts testing of mixed-signal boards, and to provide the capability of making analog value measurements of discrete analog components such as resistors, inductors, and capacitors, without direct nodal accessibility. It has been likened to in-circuit test without a bed of nails, which is, again, not without caveats. The elimination of test access points will still have to be done with thoughtful deliberation. In the future, with these and other standards, test engineers may be able to do complex tests on superdense circuitry with far less nodal access than they were afforded in the past. This will be an enabling technology, since without it, the electronics industry may find it uneconomical to produce superdense designs except in very high-end applications.

REFERENCES

1. W. A. Groves, "Rapid Digital Fault Isolation with FASTRACE," *Hewlett-Packard Journal,* vol. 30, no. 3, March 1979.

2. K. P. Parker, *Integrating Design and Test: Using CAE Tools for ATE Programming,* Computer Society Press of the IEEE, Washington, D.C., 1987.

---

* The P1149.4 standard is in the draft stage and subject to change. The discussion given here represents the opinion of the author only and not the P1149.4 Working Group or the IEEE Standards Board.

3. D. T. Crook, "Analog In-Circuit Component Measurements: Problems and Solutions", *Hewlett-Packard Journal,* vol. 30, no. 3, March 1979.

4. G. S. Bushanam, et al., "Measuring Thermal Rises Due to Digital Device Overdriving," *Proceedings, International Test Conference,* Philadelphia Pa., Oct. 1984, pp. 400–407.

5. V. R. Harwood, "Safeguarding Devices Against Stress Caused by In-Circuit Testing," *Hewlett-Packard Journal,* vol. 35, no. 10, Oct. 1984.

6. T. W. Williams and K. P. Parker, "Design for Testability—A Survey," *Proceedings of the IEEE,* vol. 71, no. 1, Jan. 1983, pp. 98–112.

7. "IEEE Standard Test Access Port and Boundary-Scan Architecture," *IEEE Std. 1149.1-1990* (includes IEEE Std. 1149.1a-1993), IEEE Inc., 345 E. 47th St., New York, NY 10017.

8. K. P. Parker, *The Boundary-Scan Handbook,* Kluwer Academic Publishers, Norwell, Mass., 1992.

9. K. P. Parker, J. E. McDermid, and S. Oresjo, "Structure and Metrology for an Analog Testability Bus," *Proceedings, International Test Conference,* Baltimore, Md., Oct. 1993, pp. 309–322.

10. "IEEE Mixed-Signal Test Bus Standard," *IEEE Proposed Std. P1149.4,* IEEE Inc., 345 E. 47th St., New York, NY 10017.

P · A · R · T · 7

WASTE MINIMIZATION AND TREATMENT

CHAPTER 34
PROCESS WASTE MINIMIZATION AND TREATMENT

Joyce M. Avery
Avery Environmental Services, Saratoga, California

Peter G. Moleux, P.E
Peter Moleux and Associates, Newton Centre, Massachusetts

34.1 INTRODUCTION

In the past, manufacturers of printed circuit boards have relied on end-of-pipe treatment and disposal for hazardous wastes generated in the fabrication process. These technologies are no longer optimal strategies for managing waste for two reasons. First, the potential liabilities involved with the handling and disposal of waste have increased and will continue to increase, and second, waste disposal costs have gone up significantly due to restrictions placed on land disposal. As a result, the industry is faced with the challenge of finding alternative methods for managing hazardous waste. This chapter presents a brief overview of some of the alternatives available to address this challenge, as well as a summary of some of the issues involved in implementation.

34.2 REGULATORY COMPLIANCE

Fabricators of printed circuit boards today are faced with a complex set of environmental requirements. In the United States there are three basic environmental statutes impacting the fabrication and assembly of printed circuit boards.

- Clean Water Act
- Clean Air Act
- Resource Conservation and Recovery Act (RCRA)

34.2.1 Clean Water Act

The goals of the Clean Water Act are to "restore and maintain the chemical, physical, and biological integrity of the nation's waters." To accomplish these goals, discharges of industrial wastewater are subject to pretreatment requirements of federal, state, or municipal regulations. Industrial waste discharges are typically directed to a sewage treatment plant. Most sewage treatment plants use bacteria to biodegrade the organic matter present in the waste stream. Toxic materials such as copper, nickel, and lead from industrial discharges can pose a problem in two ways. These materials end up in the sludge from the sewage treatment process and can lead to disposal problems. Secondly, in high concentrations they can kill the bacteria in the treatment process, resulting in significant pollution of the receiving water. As a result, fabricators of printed circuit boards are required to pretreat their wastewater to specified levels prior to discharge to the sanitary sewer. The stringency of the requirements is ultimately determined by the use of the receiving water, as even minute amounts of toxics have been shown to have a negative impact on the aquatic environment. While the federal Clean Water Act specifies minimum pretreatment standards for fabricators of printed circuit boards, in most cases, state and local requirements may be more stringent. See Table 34.1 for an example of pretreatment requirements.

TABLE 34.1   Typical Pretreatment Requirements

Parameter	Limit, mg/l
pH	6.5–9.0
Copper	1.0
Nickel	0.5
Chromium	1.0
Silver	0.05
Cadmium	0.07
Zinc	0.5
Lead	0.2
Mercury	0.05
Aluminum	1.0
Selenium	0.2
Iron	2.0
Manganese	2.0
Tin	5.0
Cyanide	0.01
Phenol	0.05

34.2.2 Clean Air Act

The Clean Air Act established National Ambient Air Quality Standards (NAAQS) to achieve two goals:

1. Improve air quality in areas which fail to meet the standards.
2. Prevent significant deterioration of the air quality in clean air areas.

The states are responsible for achieving these standards by setting emission limitations and establishing timetables for compliance by sources. Printed circuit fabrication and assembly involves several processes that have an impact on air quality. Drilling, routing, sawing, and sanding create dust or airborne particulates. The plating process creates acid fumes and the etching process can generate ammonia if an ammoniacal etchant is used. Volatile organic compounds (VOCs) and lead particulates from the assembly process can pose a potential air pollution problem as well.

The technologies available for control of air pollutants include the following:

1. Electrostatic precipitators, baghouses (a type of dust collector with fabric bags mounted on frames), and cyclone separators are available to control airborne particulates.

2. Wet scrubbers containing a packed bed to provide surface area and water sprays are utilized for removing acid fumes. Addition of an acidic feed to the scrubbing liquid allows for the removal of ammonia. Addition of a caustic feed improves the scrubbing efficiency for other materials. Wet scrubbers are often used to prevent entrance of fumes back into the building from fresh air intakes.

3. Activated carbon filtration systems are utilized for removing chlorinated solvents and volatile organic compounds (VOCs). These can be regenerated on- or off-site.

34.2.3 Resource Conservation and Recovery Act

The Resource Conservation and Recovery Act (RCRA) goals are to protect human health and the environment by reducing or eliminating the generation of hazardous waste. To achieve this, the regulation mandates a system for managing hazardous wastes from cradle to grave. Anyone who generates, stores, treats, transports, or disposes of hazardous waste is subject to this regulation. The specific definitions of hazardous waste are spelled out in the federal statutes (40CFR Parts 260-280). Typically, however, the states have more stringent definitions. The states are responsible for the implementation and enforcement of RCRA. Wastes captured under this regulation in a printed circuit board fabrication facility include aqueous solutions with metals, acid or alkaline solutions with metals, sludges containing metals, etc. As a result, fabricators must comply with the following requirements.

1. Obtain an EPA identification number and apply for permits to generate, treat, store, or dispose of hazardous waste as appropriate.

2. Use appropriate containers for storage and disposal and approved manifests and labels for shipping.

3. Comply with technical requirements for on-site treatment of hazardous waste, including tank integrity standards, labeling, and secondary containment.

4. Keep records as appropriate for reporting to regulatory agencies.

A critical part of the regulation is to reduce and, where possible, eliminate the generation of hazardous waste. Waste minimization was specifically mandated in the 1984 Hazardous and Solid Wastes Amendments to the Resource Conservation and Recovery Act. This has had an enormous impact on the way waste is handled by printed circuit board facilities. Prevention of pollution has become the overriding goal in design with recycle and reuse technologies implemented only where pollution prevention is not feasible for technical and/or economic reasons. Chemical treatment of wastes should be utilized only where no other options exist.

34.3 MAJOR SOURCES AND AMOUNTS OF WASTEWATER IN A PRINTED CIRCUIT BOARD FABRICATION FACILITY

34.3.1 Major Sources of Waste

The following table indicates the major operations in the production of printed circuit boards with the waste streams they generate.

Source	Waste stream	Composition
1. Cleaning and surface preparation	Spent acid/alkaline baths Waste rinse waters	Metals, acids, alkalis
2. Electroless plating and deposition	Spent electroless copper bath Waste rinse water	Acids, palladium, complexed metals, chelating agents, formaldehyde
3. Pattern printing and masking	Spent stripper and developer solutions Waste rinse waters	Vinyl polymers, chlorinated solvents, organic solvents, alkalis
4. Electroplating	Spent plating bath Waste rinse waters	Metals, cyanide, sulfate
5. Etching	Spent etchant Waste rinse water	Ammonia, chromium, copper, iron, acids
6. Assembly	Aqueous and semiaqueous wastewaters	Lead, organics

34.3.2   Typical Amounts of Waste Materials

It is important to evaluate the waste generated in printed circuit board manufacturing in terms of the relative amounts of copper wasted from different processes in order to prioritize efforts at waste minimization. A waste audit should be performed to determine the types and amounts of waste generated. Figures 34.1 and 34.2 present two comparisons of copper-bearing wastes. The data presented are from two different printed circuit board fabrication facilities.

In Fig. 34.1, approximately 93 percent of the total amount of copper discharged was from the innerlayer and outerlayer etching process. The amount of copper discharged from the microetch baths (using sodium persulfate) was approximately the same as the copper contained in the rinses following acid copper and the microetch baths. That exact relationship is not always valid for every printed circuit board factory.

Figure 34.2 presents the results of an environmental audit at another printed circuit board facility in grams per hour of waste copper, excluding the large amounts of waste from I/L and O/L etching. The results presented in Fig. 34.2 closely resemble a "common" PCB factory.

The facility used to prepare Fig. 34.2 produced up to 1500 completed multilayer panels (18 in × 24 in) per 20-h day of production.

34.4   WASTE MINIMIZATION

34.4.1   Definitions

Waste minimization includes the procedures, operations, and equipment required to minimize the amount of waste produced. It includes anything that reduces the load on hazardous waste treatment or disposal facilities by reducing the quantity or toxicity of hazardous waste. Waste minimization should be approached as a hierarchy of options. The first step is *pollution prevention* or source reduction.

34.4.1.1   Pollution Prevention.   Pollution prevention is the use of materials, processes, or practices that reduce or eliminate the creation of pollutants or wastes. Pollution prevention is often cost effective because it may reduce raw material losses; reduce reliance on expensive end-of-pipe treatment technologies and disposal practices; conserve energy, water, chemicals, and other inputs; and reduce the potential liability associated with waste generation. Pollution

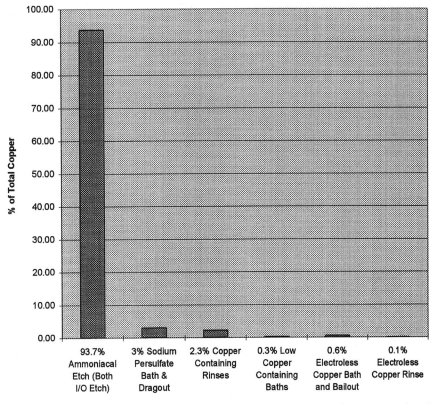

FIGURE 34.1 Amount of copper wasted for various waste streams expressed as a percent of total copper discharge.

prevention opportunities are intended to

1. Reduce the rinse water flow rate and volume.

2. Extend process bath life and reduce the dragout of a concentrated liquid (containing a contaminant such as copper).

3. Substitute materials where possible to eliminate or reduce the hazard of a particular waste.

34.4.1.2 Recycling and Recovery.   The next step in the hierarchy of waste minimization options is *recycling* or *recovery* of any waste that cannot be reduced or eliminated at the source. It includes reuse of waste in the process or recovery of metals from a waste before disposal. Recycling and recovery can occur both on- or off-site.

34.4.1.3 Alternative Treatment.   The last step in the waste minimization hierarchy is *alternative treatment.* Alternative treatments are selected to minimize the volume or hazard associated with a particular waste.

The benefits for implementing a waste minimization program can include savings in equipment and operating cost, recovery of natural resources, and significant reduction in risk of the liabilities associated with the disposal of hazardous waste. One measure of the effectiveness of a waste minimization project is the project's effect on the organization's cash flow. These projects should pay for themselves through reduced waste management and raw material costs.

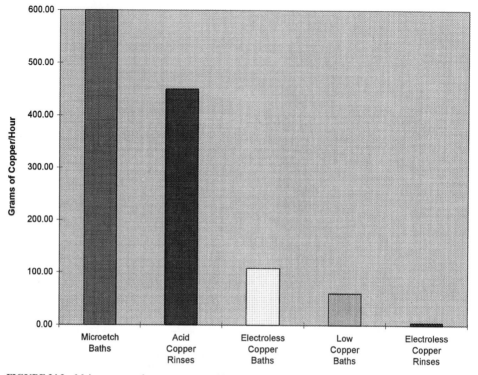

FIGURE 34.2   Major sources of copper expressed in grams per hour discharged. Inner- and outerlayer etching is excluded from this figure since it is so large in relation to the other contributors.

34.5   POLLUTION PREVENTION TECHNIQUES

Some common techniques available for pollution prevention in a printed circuit board fabrication facility are listed as follows. While this list is not all-inclusive, it provides an overview of the types of things that are important to consider. A brief description of each option is presented in the next section.

Rinse Water Reduction
1. Particulate filtration on deburr and panel-scrubbing operations with total or partial rinse water recycling
2. Etcher and conveyorized equipment design modifications
3. Immersion-type counterflow rinses
4. Alternating side spray rinses
5. Flexible orifice–type flow restrictors
6. DI and soft water for rinsing

Extend Bath Life
1. Filtration
2. Acid purification systems

3. In-tank electrolytic permanganate regeneration

4. Proper rack design and maintenance

5. Dragout recovery tanks

6. Monitor solution activity

Dragout Reduction
1. Etcher design

2. Automation

3. Rack design

4. DI and soft water for rinsing

Material Substitution
1. Acid tin as an etch resist

2. Eliminate thiourea from tin/lead stripping baths

3. Permanganate desmear

4. Direct metallization to eliminate electroless deposition and the use of formaldehyde

5. Nonaqueous waste resists

6. Use of nonproprietary chemistry to avoid chelating agents

34.5.1 Rinse Water Reduction

Most of the waste generated in the manufacture of printed circuit boards is from cleaning, plating, stripping, and etching. This section describes some of the techniques available for reducing the volume of rinse water used.

34.5.1.1 Particulate Filtration on Deburr and Panel-Scrubbing Operations. Deburrers are used to remove stubs of copper formed after the drilling of holes in double-sided and multilayer panels before they enter the copper deposition process where copper is deposited within the holes recently drilled in the panel. Scrubbers are used to remove oxides from printed circuit laminates, clean the surface prior to a surface coating to provide better adhesion, and remove residuals after etching or stripping. In deburring and board scrubbing, particulate materials are added to the water and are removed by various methods based on size and the weight of the copper particle such that the wash water becomes suitable for up to 100 percent recycle. The types of filtration available for this operation are cloth, sand, centrifugation, and gravity settling with filtration.

34.5.1.2 Etcher and Conveyorized Equipment Design Modifications. Use of recirculating rinse modules in the etcher and other conveyorized equipment will decrease the required flow rate of rinse water for that process step by about 50 percent without requiring significantly more floor space, compared to single-station spray rinse chambers (without recirculating rinses). In this application, fresh water is used for the final top and bottom nozzles in a rinse module. This water is collected in a sump located below the rinsing compartment. A pump recirculates this water through the first set of top and bottom nozzles (instead of using fresh water). As more fresh water enters the sump, the excess water overflows through a pipe fitting to drain. See Fig. 34.3.

Conveyorized equipment can also be used for, at least, innerlayer and outerlayer photoresist stripping and innerlayer and outerlayer photoresist developing, deburring, and panel scrubbing. Similar techniques to reduce water flow can be applied to these operations.

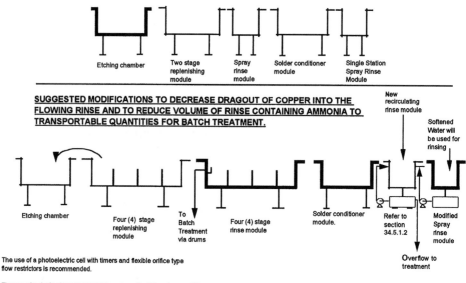

FIGURE 34.3   Suggested modifications to inner/outerlayer etching equipment.

34.5.1.3   Immersion-Type Counterflow Rinses.   Counterflow rinsing, employing several single-stage rinse tanks in series, is one of the most powerful waste reduction and water management techniques for innerlayer processing and in the electroless copper process. In counterflow rinsing, the plated part, after exiting the process bath, moves through several rinse contact stages, while water flows from stage to stage in the opposite direction. Over time, the first rinse reaches a steady-state concentration of process dragout contaminants that is lower than the process solution. The second rinse (away from the process bath) stabilizes at even a lower concentration. This enables less water to be used to produce the same cleanliness compared to a single-station rinse tank. The higher the number of rinse stations connected in series, the lower the rinse rate needed for adequate removal of the process solution from the panel. A reduction in rinse water use for a given process step of up to 90 percent over what would be used without counterflow rinsing can be achieved with this technique.

A multistage counterflow rinse system allows greater contact time between the panels and the rinse water, greater diffusion of the process chemicals into the rinse water, and more rinse water to come into contact with each panel. The disadvantage of multistage rinsing is that more steps are required and additional equipment and work space is required.

34.5.1.4   Alternating Side Spray Rinses.   Alternating side spray rinses can be used in place of or with immersion rinses in acid copper or solder plating lines. With this technique, rinse water pulsates on each side of a panel at different times so that penetration through holes can be achieved. The reduction in water consumption using an alternating side spray rinse for any given process step is about 85 to 90 percent of that consumed using single-stage immersion-type rinse. Another advantage of spray rinsing is that it will eliminate the need to dump the entire contents of an immersion-type rinse tank, for cleaning purposes, on a periodic basis.

Eventually, the concentration of the tank solution will increase to a point such that it provides an opportunity to

1. Recover metals.
2. Recycle a process bath since it is the same chemistry.

The disadvantage is that this opportunity may require additional production floor space.

A drip pan (also called a drain board) is one of the simplest methods for dragout recovery. The drip pan is located either under the rack while in transit or between tanks, and will capture drips of process solution from racks and panels as these are transferred between tanks. Drip pans not only save chemicals and reduce rinse water requirements, they also improve housekeeping by keeping the floor dry.

34.5.2.6 *Monitor Solution Activity.*   Bath life can be extended by monitoring the bath activity and replenishing stabilizers and reagents. This will reduce dump frequencies and result in a reduction in waste.

34.5.3 Dragout Reduction

Dragout reduction is desirable as a waste minimization step because it results in the saving of process chemicals as well as a reduction in sludge generation.

34.5.3.1 *Etcher Design.*   Etching machines can be the single largest source of copper waste in the discharge from a PCB facility. The amount of copper discharged and the rinse flow rate from that machine are a function of the machine design. An older etching machine often contains a single-stage etchant replenishing module positioned between the etching chamber and its continuously flowing single or multiple-stage water rinse chamber. Fresh etchant is fed to the replenishing module to wash the panels and that etchant (now containing copper washed off of the freshly etched panels), then flows (in a direction opposite to the direction of the panel movement) into the etching chamber. The continuous water rinse can contain from 100 to 500 mg/l or ppm of copper. Companies that use this type of equipment, with single-station rinse module, normally have floor space restrictions in their production area. See Fig. 34.3.

By way of comparison, adding a second stage replenisher station will reduce the range of copper concentration in the following rinse from 50 to 300 mg/l. Using a four-stage replenisher module and combination recirculating and then a single-stage rinse modules, will produce a rinse containing from less than 1.0 up to 2.0 mg/l of copper.

34.5.3.2 *Automation.*   Computerized process control systems can be used for panel handling and process bath monitoring to prevent unexpected decomposition of a process bath, controlled rinse flow, and uniform panel withdrawal from each process bath. Since these systems require a significant capital expense for initial installation, typically only large printed circuit board companies will find this to be a cost-effective alternative.

34.5.3.3 *Rack Design.*   Some plating rack designs allow the panels to be tilted to one side and the panel mounted at an angle (relative to the horizontal) to allow better solution drainage off of the panel. This will decrease the dragout.

34.5.3.4 *DI and Soft Water for Rinsing.*   Natural contaminants found in water used for production purposes can contribute to the volume of sludge produced in waste treatment because they precipitate as carbonates and phosphates. Another advantage is that pretreated rinse water is cleaner; therefore, the normal diffusion of contaminants from the panel into the rinse water occurs more quickly. As a result, water requirements for each rinse may be reduced since rinse efficiency is improved.

34.5.4 Material Substitution

Material substitution is a waste minimization technique that should result in a reduced hazard associated with a particular waste or a simplied means of waste treatment. It is important that all process impacts are thoroughly understood prior to instituting any material changes.

34.5.4.1 Acid Tin as Etch Resist. Acid solder baths are often used as an etch resist before final etching of an assembled multilayer printed circuit board. The lead and fluoride present in this bath must then be removed in the waste treatment process. Acid tin can be used as the etch resist in place of solder under certain circumstances. An advantage of this bath is that it does not contain lead ions or fluorides. Use of this bath will eliminate these materials from the discharge.

35.5.4.2 Eliminate Thiourea. Thiourea is a known carcinogen which has been used as a chelating agent in Sn/Pb stripping baths. A peroxide-based bath can be substituted when the etch resist is acid tin, thus eliminating this concern.

35.5.4.3 Permanganate Desmear. To reduce the amount and toxicity of waste, most printed circuit board factories in the United States use the alkaline permanganate process instead of chromic acid for desmear. This technique has gained favor due to the wastewater treatment equipment requirements to reduce the chromic acid and the control problems (especially in humid environments) of 96% sulfuric acid. The plasma desmear process produces the least amount of hazardous waste, but that technique is used primarily for small batch operations and not high-volume continuous operations.

35.5.4.4 Direct Metallization. Alternatives to the electroless copper process have emerged to avoid the use of formaldehyde, a toxic and carcinogenic material. The use of formaldehyde has recently (as of June 1993) required extensive in-plant air monitoring and will require employers to have their affected employees periodically checked by a medical doctor. This is an additional unwanted expense for each PCB factory owner.

One alternative to the electroless process utilizes conductive polymers. Polymer thick film (PTF) technology is a method of screening polymer conductors, resistors, dielectrics, and protective coatings on a substrate or printed wire board to create basic circuitry or interconnections. The use of screened-on conductive films in place of the formaldehyde-containing electroless copper process is gaining acceptance in Asia (more so than in the United States at this time).

Other technologies are being applied commercially which use palladium or graphite to provide conductive pathways in the holes of multilayer printed circuit boards.

34.5.4.5 Nonaqueous Waste Resists. One of the most exciting waste minimization techniques currently being tested is the elimination of the need for rinsing from both photoresist developing and stripping operations. This new process may eliminate spent developer wastes and will eliminate the spent resist stripper bath dump.

The photoresist, being demonstrated at Circuit Center (Dayton, Ohio) and at E. G. & G. Mound, is applied in a production process as a thin film from a liquid solution onto a circuit board and air dried. When exposed to a high-intensity ultraviolet light source, these photoresists will decompose and vaporize as inert gas. There appears to be no rinsing required for these operations. In fact, these operations, as we currently know them, will be eliminated, thus reducing the cost of waste treatment. The existing 30-month demonstration project is a cooperative effort between the University of Dayton Research Institute, the Air Force, the U.S. Environmental Protection Agency, and the Edison Materials Technology Center (EMTEC).

Depending on the actual chemistry used, the use of this new process may reduce the hazardous air emissions from these processes commonly produced with conventional semiaqueous and aqueous chemistries containing butyl cellosolve or butyl carbitol.

34.5.4.6 Use of Nonproprietary Chemistry to Avoid Chelating Agents. Chelating agents are molecules that form a charged complex with a metal ion such as copper. They are used to enhance solubility and keep the metal ions in solution. Typical chelating agents used in printed circuit board fabrication include ferrocyanide, ethylenediaminetetraacetic acid (EDTA), phosphates, and ammonia. Chelated baths are intended to enhance etching, cleaning, and electroless plating but make waste treatment much more difficult because the metals are tightly bound in the complex, which inhibits precipitation. Often ferrous sulfate must be added to wastewaters to break the chelators prior to precipitation of metal hydroxides. The iron is precipitated as well as other metals, thus increasing the amount of sludge produced. Use of nonchelated chemistry where possible will eliminate this problem. If some chelating chemistry is required in the process, proper waste segregation should be implemented to minimize the volume of any chelated waste streams.

34.6 RECYCLING AND RECOVERY TECHNIQUES

34.6.1 Copper Sulfate Crystallization

34.6.1.1 Theory of Operation. The sulfuric acid/hydrogen peroxide etching reaction is:

$$Cu + H_2O_2 + H_2SO_4 \longrightarrow CuSO_4 + 2H_2O \tag{34.1}$$

Systems employing crystallizers are designed to

1. Lower the solution temperature to lower the solubility of copper.
2. Then remove copper in the form of copper sulfate pentahydrate crystals ($CuSO_4 - 5H_2O$).
3. Then reheat the bath (to prevent copper from clogging the return pipe line if the bath temperature is lowered further) before transferring the bath back to its working tank.

An advantage, from a waste treatment point of view, is that the bath is recycled and not routinely dumped. Other microetchants must be dumped when the copper concentration increases. The most significant advantage, from a process point of view, is that a low copper concentration can be maintained and the printed circuit board factory will minimize its purchase of microetchant chemicals.

A disadvantage to this process is that, at the time of this writing, there are no outlets available to receive and recycle the crystals, so the only alternative for manufacturers using crystallizers is to dissolve the copper sulfate crystals in spent dilute (10%) sulfuric acid. After the copper has dissolved, this material can be pumped to another holding tank for recirculation through an electroplating cell for reclaim of the copper.

34.6.2 Rinse Water Recycling

Rinse waters can be treated and reused in the process. This can be accomplished in two ways. Rinse water recycling can be accomplished with a point-of-source system. In this system, the flow from selected rinses is recirculated through cation and anion exchange columns and then returned to the point of origin. It may be necessary to add a carbon filtration step for rinses containing organics.

The second method would involve a central system. Selected rinses could be run through an ion exchange system for copper removal. Following this step, these rinses would pass through a general resin for cation removal, a general resin for anion removal, systems for organic removal such as activated carbon, ozonation or UV peroxide, and final filtration. In some cases, reverse osmosis could be substituted for the general ion exchange steps. Given the complexity of this treatment process, it would be cost effective only for large printed circuit board facilities with high water use rates.

34.6.3   Copper Recovery via Electrowinning

34.6.3.1   Theory of Operation.   Electrowinning is the reduction of copper ions to solid metallic copper at a cathode. The following are the chemical reactions governing copper recovery in an acidic solution. The reduction reactions that occur at the *cathode* are:

$$Cu^{+2} + 2e^- \longrightarrow Cu \text{ (metal)} \tag{34.2}$$

$$2H^+ + 2e^- \longrightarrow H_2 \text{ (gas)} \tag{34.3}$$

The reaction that occurs at the *anode* is:

$$H_2O \longrightarrow \tfrac{1}{2}(O_2) + 2H^+ + 2e^- \tag{34.4}$$

The first reaction describes the principal objective of electroplating (the reduction of copper to its solid form on the cathode). As electroplating proceeds, the waste becomes more acidic, as noted in Eq. (34.4).

The speed of these reactions will be inhibited if oxidizing chemicals are present. Typical oxidizing agents include peroxides and persulfates, which are normal components of microetching baths. If these oxidizers are not chemically reduced in the solution entering an electroplating module, additional reaction time must be anticipated to reduce the oxidizers electrically. Following that, the reduction of copper will occur. For this reason, a chemical reduction step (addition of sodium bisulfite ($NaHSO_3$) or sodium metabisulfite ($Na_2S_2O_5$) is recommended before the waste is recirculated through an electroplating module.

34.6.3.2   Central Systems.   Copper can be recovered in a central system from the following sources:

1. Sulfuric acid regeneration of selective cation columns
2. Spent microetch baths
3. Dragout tanks
4. Copper sulfate electroplating bath bailout
5. Dissolved copper sulfate crystals from a crystallizer

The typical concentration of the preceding mixture (or any component of it) may range from 5 to 30 g of copper per liter. A central electrowinning system is shown in Fig. 34.4.

34.6.3.3   Parallel Plate Electrowinning Systems.   The purpose of parallel plating, in a central system, is to recover copper as a 99.9 percent pure metal sheet (for resale) and to reduce the copper concentration in the liquid being recirculated to 1.0 g/l, or less. The efficiency of the reaction drops significantly below 1.0 g of copper per liter, as observed by the generation of heat in the bath by the electroplating process.

Many factors affect the ability of an electrolytic cell to recover copper. Important design parameters center around improving the mass transport. These include solution agitation and cathode agitation. Air agitation of the waste within the electroplating cell is used to increase the efficiency of the cell. Control of the air inlet rate, bubble size, current density and distribution are all critical to maintaining high efficiency in each parallel plate cell. Particles (so-called *dendrites*) or fines of metal can be dislodged and accumulate in dead spots with the plating cell tank. Electrical shorting out of the anode to cathode can occur when particles accumulate, creating the possibility of isolated locations where burning of the cell may occur.

34.6.3.4   High-Surface-Area Electrowinning Systems (HSA).   HSA systems can be used to recover copper from a variety of solutions, including electroless copper concentrates and rinses. The use of high-surface-area cathodes improves the mass transport characteristics over flat plate cathodes. The HSA cathodes reduce electrode polarization potential and improve

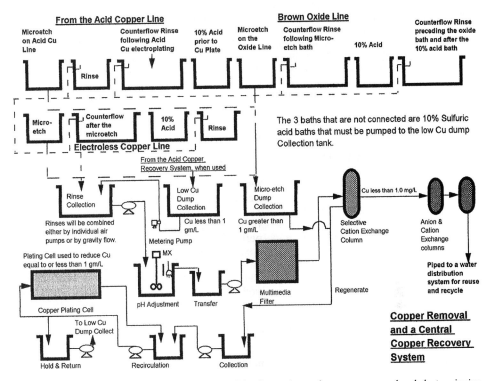

FIGURE 34.4 Central copper recovery system utilizing ion exchange for copper removal and electrowinning for copper recovery.

ion diffusion potential, allowing the copper to deposit rapidly on an HSA cathode from wastes with both high and low copper concentrations. HSA cathodes promote solution agitation by creating numerous bonding sites for copper. Expanded mesh carbon fibers or catalyzed foam are typical materials of construction in HSA cathodes. Some HSA systems require the purchase of new cathodes, while the cathodes in some systems can be regenerated for a period of time. To regenerate these cathodes they must be stripped of copper metal.

Stripping the cathode takes place in a second plating tank. The cathodes from the first tank must be manually removed and placed into the anodic position within the stripping tank. The copper is then recovered as a metal by electroplating the copper onto either a stainless steel or a copper laminate in a copper pyrophosphate electrolyte. The *reusable cathodes* are then available to be repositioned back to the first cell.

HSA systems can reduce the copper levels to low levels in an incoming waste stream, but it is important to note that copper is not recovered unless the stripping step takes place in the second plating tank.

34.6.3.5 *Point-of-Source Systems.*

Dragout tanks can be located between a process bath (for example, a copper-plating bath in the pattern-plating line) and its following rinse tank. Typically, dragout tanks are positioned *only* adjacent to the process tanks containing the most difficult wastes. These include the etching baths (if not conveyorized), the microetch baths (which produce the most copper), and the copper electroplating (usually sulfate-based) baths.

The contents of each dragout bath can be recirculated through its own plating cell for copper recovery, then back to the dragout tank. In this way, the concentration of copper is maintained at a low level. The plating cell, for this application, could be either a parallel plate or an HSA system.

If dedicated electroplating cells are not used to recover copper directly from a dragout bath, the dragout bath can periodically be discharged to a dilute (or concentrated) copper collection tank for recovery through an ion exchange system (or a central electroplating system, respectively).

34.7 ALTERNATIVE TREATMENTS

34.7.1 Selective Ion Exchange

Ion exchange is a process in which ions, which are held by electrostatic forces to charged functional groups on the surface of the ion exchange resin, are exchanged for ions of similar charge in a solution in which a resin is immersed. Ion exchange is classified as an adsorption process because the exchange occurs on the surface of a solid (a resin bead), and the exchanging ion must undergo a phase transfer from the solution phase to the surface of the solid. A single-pass selective cation exchange column can reduce the copper concentration in the influent stream to less than 1.0 mg/l. If two cation exchange columns are in series, as indicated in Fig. 34.4, the expected copper effluent concentration should be less than 0.5 mg/l. Organics present in the incoming waste can foul the resin and render it unusable; therefore, a carbon filtration step occurs ahead of the ion exchange column. Wastes with significant levels of organic material are not treated with this technology.

34.7.1.1 Theory of Operation.   Copper ions are normally present in their divalent (+2) state. The removal mechanism of divalent copper from an aqueous waste by ion exchange resins is:

$$Cu^{+2} + 2R\text{-}H \longrightarrow\!\!\!> 2H^+ + R_2\text{-}Cu \tag{34.5}$$

where R = a cation exchange resin. Here the copper is "attached" to the resin beads.

Ion exchange equipment suppliers will usually furnish a water meter that totalizes the quantity of waste processed through the column. After the system has been calibrated by the equipment supplier, the water meter will activate an alarm after a specified volume of waste has been processed. An alarm will sound if the system requires manual regeneration. If the system is supplied with automatic regeneration, the water meter will deactivate a column while regeneration takes place. Where multiple columns are included within a system, valves must be adjusted to accommodate regeneration. This will be accomplished by manual or automated (pneumatic-, electric-, or hydraulic-actuated) techniques.

34.7.1.2 Regeneration.   To recover the copper, the cation resins are first rinsed with water and then washed with 5 to 15% by volume sulfuric acid. This proceeds by the following reaction:

$$R_2\text{-}Cu + 2H^{+1} \longrightarrow\!\!\!> Cu^{+2} + 2R\text{-}H \tag{34.6}$$

where R = a cation exchange resin.

Copper is displaced from the resin by a proton (or hydrogen atom). The resulting sulfuric acid solution containing copper can be directed to an electroplating system to recover copper from the acidic solution. The remaining resin is washed with water to remove the residual sulfuric acid.

34.7.1.3 Spent Baths.   Certain spent baths can be bled into the ion exchange system. These typically include the copper sulfate electroplating dragout, acid cleaners, predips, microetch and rinses, rinses following cupric chloride and ammoniacal etchants, and copper waste from electrowinning after reduction to 1.0 ppm or less.

34.7.2 Removal of Copper from the Electroless Copper Bath

34.7.2.1 Theory of Operation.
It is well known that copper metal can be deposited onto metal (usually copper or palladium) within a PCB hole. Dissolved copper is automatically reduced (using formaldehyde as its reducing agent) to a solid metal and deposits itself onto the palladium inside of the hole while the panel is immersed in the electroless copper bath. The chemical reaction of copper deposition may be represented by

$$Cu\,(EDTA)^{-2} + 2HCHO + 4OH^{-1} \longrightarrow$$
$$Cu^0 + H_2 + 2H_2O + 2CHOO^{-1} + EDTA^{-4} \tag{34.7}$$

This process can be utilized to remove copper from the electroless copper baths and bailout. Products on the market include canisters or modules which contain a proprietary spongelike material deposited with palladium and copper. The electroless copper solution passes through the canister where the copper is autocatalytically reduced, trapped by the spongelike media and filtered out of the waste stream. See Fig. 34.5

Typically, a minimum of two canisters are connected in series. As the copper concentration in the first canister approaches 1.0 mg/l, the sponge material is replaced by the material in the second canister. New sponge material is added to the second canister.

34.7.3 Sodium Borohydride Reduction

Although not as common or as inexpensive as the autocatalytic method, one of the simplest methods for the treatment of electroless copper is by the use of another strong reducing

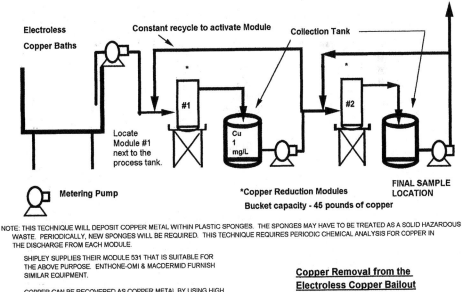

The copper concentration in the discharge
from this system should be equal to or less than 1 mg/L.

Electroless Copper Baths — Constant recycle to activate Module — Collection Tank

Locate Module #1 next to the process tank.

#1   Cu 1 mg/L   #2

Metering Pump

*Copper Reduction Modules
Bucket capacity - 45 pounds of copper

FINAL SAMPLE LOCATION

NOTE: THIS TECHNIQUE WILL DEPOSIT COPPER METAL WITHIN PLASTIC SPONGES. THE SPONGES MAY HAVE TO BE TREATED AS A SOLID HAZARDOUS WASTE. PERIODICALLY, NEW SPONGES WILL BE REQUIRED. THIS TECHNIQUE REQUIRES PERIODIC CHEMICAL ANALYSIS FOR COPPER IN THE DISCHARGE FROM EACH MODULE.

SHIPLEY SUPPLIES THEIR MODULE 531 THAT IS SUITABLE FOR THE ABOVE PURPOSE. ENTHONE-OMI & MACDERMID FURNISH SIMILAR EQUIPMENT.

COPPER CAN BE RECOVERED AS COPPER METAL BY USING HIGH SURFACE AREA CATHODES IN A TWO STEP MANUAL PROCESS OR BY ION EXCHANGE AND ELECTROPLATING.

Copper Removal from the Electroless Copper Bailout

FIGURE 34.5 Copper removal from electroless copper bailout using copper reduction.

agent, sodium borohydride ($NaBH_4$). This chemical is commercially available as a solution of 40% caustic soda containing 12% by weight of sodium borohydride. The chemical reaction can be represented by

$$8MX + NaBH_4 + 2H_2O => 8M + NaBO_2 + 8HX \qquad (34.8)$$

where M is the cation with +1 valence and X is the anion.

The spent electroless bath has to be in an active state for this method to work efficiently. Adding sodium hydroxide (NaOH) and/or formaldehyde (HCHO) to the bath will shift the equilibrium in the bath to this reactive stage. When this stage is reached, a small addition of sodium borohydride will catalyze the reaction, and reduced copper will precipitate out as metallic fines.

A typical process for using sodium borohydride requires the use of an open-top batch tank that is located in a well-ventilated area. Since $NaBH_4$ can react to release hydrogen as a side reaction, any source of flames or sparks must be eliminated. A 0.5 to 1%, by volume, $NaBH_4$ solution is added slowly to the batch reaction tank that contains the spent electroless copper solution. After a few minutes, the solution will effervesce vigorously and fine, pink copper particles will begin to form and become visible to the naked eye. Small bubbles of flammable hydrogen gas will also evolve from the solution, and these must be rapidly removed by appropriate exhausts. Usually within about one hour, the solution will turn clear and copper will precipitate from the solution. These fines will eventually settle to the bottom of the batch tank and the copper fines should be removed as soon as the reaction has been completed. Otherwise the copper fines may reoxidize and dissolve back into solution. More $NaBH_4$ will then be necessary to remove the copper. After the copper fines have been removed, hydrogen peroxide (H_2O_2) can be added to the clear solution to oxidize any excess formaldehyde to the less toxic formic acid.

This process can be used for other metal-bearing waste streams besides electroless copper. However, it is typically not a cost-effective means of treating nonchelated waste.

34.7.4 Aqueous and Semiaqueous Photoresist Stripping Bath Treatment

A significant volume of waste produced from PCB factory is from the stripping of resists. Resist stripping machines can utilize on-line or off-line equipment to remove semisolid photoresists on a continuous basis from the operating bath. Removing the suspended solids within the solution provides a longer life and more efficient usage.

In any case, there will be times when the bath becomes spent and must be dumped. Waste from this process should be segregated for treatment so that the sludge produced can be classified as nonhazardous. In addition, good engineering practice dictates that spent photoresist stripping baths not enter a continuous precipitation system since organic photopolymers may not always settle in a clarifier. Under some conditions (at certain temperatures or with certain organics) stratification of the organic material in the clarifier can occur. As a result, the organic solids can float and any metal hydroxide particles nearby may become attached to the floating material.

The treatment procedure for this waste uses chemical precipitation (caused by lowering the pH) and filtration (to remove the photoresist and residual metals). The treated wastes can be slowly discharged into the existing final pH adjustment tank. The specific treatment procedure follows.

The untreated pH of this waste is approximately 12.0 pH units. Sulfuric acid is slowly added to lower the pH to about 9.0. After a stable pH is achieved, the pH will be lowered to about 6.0 by the addition of acidic proprietary chemicals available at the time of this writing. At this low pH, the dissolved resist will precipitate out of solution and the solids formed can be removed by pumping the waste through a filter press.

34.8 CHEMICAL TREATMENT SYSTEMS

34.8.1 Definition

Chemical treatment of wastes involves the addition of chemicals to precipitate metals out of solution. This results in a sludge which must be disposed of. The sludge is then typically sent to a reclaimer for recovery of the metals or licensed disposal site. The latter option is becoming increasingly difficult and expensive. It should be avoided due to the unknown risks associated with the landfill of hazardous wastes. Chemical treatment of wastes should be utilized only when pollution prevention or recycling is not technically or economically feasible.

34.8.2 Treatment Process

Nonchelated metal rinses and dumps are typically treated in a two-stage process. In the first stage, rough pH control is accomplished with the addition of caustic soda and sulfuric acid. In the second stage, the pH is elevated with caustic to precipitate the metals in the hydroxide form. Lime has been used in this step in the past, but its use has been discouraged since it increases the sludge volume significantly.

Alternatively, the metals can be precipitated as in the sulfide form with the addition of FeS at pH 9. This process is more difficult to control and presents a potential hazard due to the possible evolution of H_2S. However, the lower solubility of the metal sulfides provides an advantage where discharge limits are more stringent.

Chelated metal rinses and dumps such as those from the electroless copper process provide more challenge in chemical treatment since the chelating agents bind the metals and keep them in solution. This problem is often addressed by the addition of ferrous sulfate to break down the chelated metal complexes, allowing the metal to precipitate as the hydroxide. It is often necessary to add large quantities of this reagent such that the ratio of iron to copper is 8:1. The disadvantage of this method is that iron will precipitate out as well, thus significantly increasing the volume of sludge produced.

Regardless of the specific treatment chemistry used, there are common components to all chemical treatment systems.

34.8.3 Collection System

The collection system is the tank or group of tanks where wastes are collected prior to treatment. The collection tanks should be sized to provide a minimum residence time of 20 min. Segregation of wastes can improve the efficiency of the waste treatment system. For example, process bath dumps can be collected in separate tanks and metered into the rinse waste stream at a low flow rate. Also, chelated wastes can be collected and treated separately from nonchelated streams, thus minimizing the use of ferrous sulfate.

34.8.4 pH Adjust

This is typically a dual-tank system where the pH is elevated and metals are precipitated as either the hydroxide or the sulfide, as previously described. Each stage must be adequately sized to provide adequate retention time (usually a minimum of 30 min) to ensure the completion of the reaction. Each tank is equipped with a mixer, pH probe, and controller. In addition, pH recorders should be provided to effectively monitor system performance.

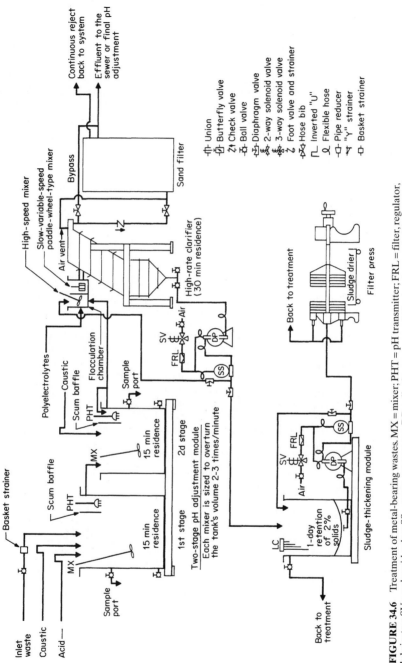

FIGURE 34.6 Treatment of metal-bearing wastes. MX = mixer; PHT = pH transmitter; FRL = filter, regulator, lubricator; SV = solenoid valve; SS = surge suppressor; DP = diaphragm pump; LC = level control. (*Courtesy of Baker Brothers/Systems.*)

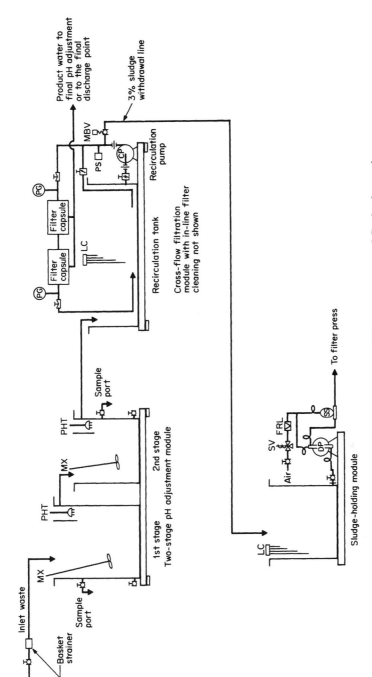

FIGURE 34.7 Cross-flow filtration. MX = mixer; PHT = pH transmitter; PG = pressure gauge; LC = level control; PS = pressure switch; MBV = motorized ball valve; CP = centrifugal pump; SV = solenoid valve; FRL = filter, regulator, lubricator; DP = diaphragm pump; SS = surge suppressor. (*Courtesy of Baker Brothers/Systems.*)

TABLE 34.2 Advantages and Disadvantages of Various PCB Wastewater Treatment Alternatives

Categories of major wastes	Category of waste minimization or treatment	Advantages	Disadvantages
1. Copper-containing acidic rinses.	Selective rinse water recycling with copper recovery.	Recovered copper metal can be sold. Recycling will reduce the quantity of waste being discharged. Reduced sewer use charges.	Most expensive. Requires flow control. Requires thorough and periodic bath analysis. Must address spent process baths.
	Copper removal from preselected rinses using selective ion exchange with copper recovery by electroplating.	Recovered copper metal can be sold. Minimizes the quantity of copper discharged.	More expensive equipment than used for chemical treatment. Requires expensive selective cation resins. Must address spent baths.
	Chemical treatment to precipitate copper.	Least capital cost. Requires clarification with filtration and proper pretreatment chemistry.	Produces sludge. Increasing liability. Requires intensive effort for labor. Must address spent process baths.
2. Copper-containing acidic spent process baths.	Bath purification with partial or total reuse using crystallization, ion exchange, filtration, and/or diffusion dialysis.	Reduce or eliminate the need to dump a bath. Recovered copper can be sold.	Requires through and periodic bath analysis. Optimum application is copper removal from rinse waters.
	Bleed spent bath into rinses for copper removal with copper recovery.	Recovered copper can be sold. Minimizes quantity of copper discharged.	More expensive equipment than used for chemical treatment.
	Allow a higher contaminant concentration before dumping.	Less frequent need to dump a process bath.	Requires through and periodic bath analysis.
	Copper recovery from microetchants.	Most copper recovery using least floor space and cost.	Requires that these wastes be collected and processed separately.
	Chemical treatment to precipitate copper.	Used to concentrate copper into sludge.	Produces sludge. Increasing liability. Requires intensive effort for labor.
3. Ammonium chloride etchants and rinses.	Recycle 95% etchant and rinse water.	Reduces fresh chemical and hauling purchases. Recovered copper can be sold. Reduces waste quantity.	May be justified only when both inner and outer layers are etched with this chemistry. Ammonium sulfate etchant requires a different method for recycling.
	Pipe rinse into copper removal with copper recovery system.	Recovered copper can be sold.	More expensive equipment than used for chemical treatment. Must continue to haul spent etchant.

Waste source	Pollution prevention method	Benefits	Limitations
4. Electroless copper bath growth.	Process chemistry substitution using palladium-based and/or graphite-based alternatives.	Eliminates formaldehyde.	May produce excess organic wastes. May not be suitable for all applications.
	Copper recovery.	Reduces copper discharge.	Expensive compared to other methods.
	Autocatalytic copper removal onto a sponge.	Effective removal of copper metal complexed with EDTA. Possible copper recovery.	Produces a waste to be transported. Continuous activation, heat, and monitoring are required.
	Chemical treatment.	Least capital cost.	Produces sludge. Chelating agents are still present in the treated waste.
5. Develop/Resist Strip.	Use resists which do not emit wastes.	Eliminates hauling solids.	May not be universally applicable.
	Chemical treatment to reduce volume compared to hauling spent process baths off-site for disposal or dumping waste to the sewer.	Reduces quantity of this material to be hauled for off-site disposal.	Solids handling could be a problem. Expensive proprietary chemicals. Minimal organic load reduction in treated waste. Requires segregation.
6. Other wastes including tin, tin/lead, nickel, and gold.	Recover metal and chemistry from dragout tank.	Bath and metal recovery and recycling are possible.	Requires space to install dragout tanks. Requires more waste segregation and can be expensive as more recycling and recovery is required.
	Chemical treatment and membrane filtration.	Least capital cost.	Produces sludge. Increasing liability. Requires intensive effort for labor.
7. Printed circuit assembly cleaning wastes.	Use of water-soluble solder mask and flux.	Eliminates toxic chemicals. Allows rinse recycling.	Not universally applicable.
	Use of semiaqueous or saponified cleaners for RMA fluxes.	Eliminates use of CFCs.	Possible chemical treatment of bath VOC emission from semiaqueous baths.

34.8.5 Settling Process

Following the second-stage pH adjust, waste flows to the flocculation chamber in a clarifier where polyelectrolytes and recycled sludge are added and rapidly mixed. The waste then enters a second stage where a slow-speed mixer is used to enlarge the hydroxides to make settling more effective. Finally, the flocculated waste will flow down the clarifier. The precipitated solids settle to the bottom of the clarifier and the clarified liquid is discharged to a final pH adjust system or in some cases to a sand filter prior to final pH adjust if required to meet discharge standards. (See Fig. 34.6.)

34.8.6 Cross-Flow Microfiltration

Cross-flow microfiltration systems are used in place of a clarifier and sand filter where the maximum discharge limit for copper is below 1.0 mg/l. Treated wastes are collected in a recirculation tank and pumped at turbulent flow and 10 to 35 psig through a series of capsules containing tubular filters. The majority of the recirculated wastewater plus all the suspended solids returns to the recirculation tank. The suspended solids free water will pass through the side walls of the tubular filter. Sludge is withdrawn near the discharge of the recirculation pump. The 3% (total suspended solids) sludge is pumped to a sludge holding tank and then pumped to a filter press. (See Fig. 34.7.)

34.8.7 Sludge Thickening and Dewatering

The purpose of the sludge thickening tank is to increase the concentration of the 1 to 2% sludge from the clarifier to approximately 3%. This is accomplished by continuously decanting the water from the sludge thickening tank and directing it back to the rinse collection tank. The solids from the sludge thickening or holding tanks are then pumped to a filter press for dewatering to reduce sludge volume.

The total suspended solids in the sludge can be increased to about 35% with a filter press. In addition, sludge dryers are available which increase the solids concentration to about 70% by adding heat to the sludge. This reduces the volume of sludge to be hauled away.

34.9 ADVANTAGES AND DISADVANTAGES OF VARIOUS TREATMENT ALTERNATIVES

All of the techniques described in this chapter have advantages and disadvantages. None of them are appropriate in all situations. Each potential application requires specific analysis and a thorough understanding of the technical and economic issues involved prior to implementation. Table 34.2 presents a summary of the advantages and disadvantages of some of the technologies discussed in this chapter.

QUALITY AND RELIABILITY OF PRINTED CIRCUIT PROCESSES

CHAPTER 35
ACCEPTABILITY OF FABRICATED CIRCUITS

A. D. Andrade
Sandia National Laboratories, Livermore, California

35.1 INSPECTION—IS IT NECESSARY?

The first printed wiring boards were fabricated out of inexpensive materials and were usually single- or double-sided, with the more expensive types having plated-through-holes. During this era, defective boards, found during assembly, were usually thrown away. Today the boards are usually multilayer or rigid-flex types with several layers of circuitry and high-density surface pattern circuitry. The cost of these boards can be compared to a building's structural foundation. Initial unit value is usually insignificant, compared to total building structure costs, however the value increases exponentially after the building construction is completed. The printed boards' value increase is dependent on type, design complexity, number and type of components, and replacement component availability. This increased value, like the structural foundation, should be considered when making a decision on inspection of whether to inspect or not to inspect.

35.2 INSPECTION OPERATIONS

Quality assurance operations are considered very costly; however, savings realized by reduced rework and improved customer relations greatly reduce the overall inspection cost. Customer relations improvements can be greatly enhanced by meeting with the customer prior to printed board fabrication and reviewing acceptable and rejectable attributes. One method is for both parties to review a common visual acceptance standard—for example, IPC-A-600—and agree on the target/nonconforming attributes by class designation. Then jointly mark up two copies of the acceptable attributes agreed to and list these documents in the procurement contract. Establish a team environment.

Quality assurance operations can be performed by the purchaser or they can be contracted out, partially or totally, to an independent company. Present printed wiring board fabrication technology is capable of conductor widths and spacing of less than 0.005 in (0.127 mm), reported down to 0.003 in (0.076 mm). Visual inspection of surface patterns on pattern densities less than 0.005 in (0.127 mm) is questionable. Many companies are replacing surface visual inspection of high-density patterns with automated electrical or image-scanning methods. Wherever the quality assurance operation is performed, however, there must be access to a facility equipped with the required types of mechanical gauges, as well as microsectioning, chemical analysis, dimensional measuring, and electrical and environmental testing.

Quality assurance requirements are usually met by one of the following methods:

1. Inspection data submitted by the fabricator are reviewed for compliance to design requirements.

2. Inspection data submitted by the fabricator are reviewed and a sample lot inspection is performed.

3. A complete inspection is performed to all design requirements including destructive testing.

Where and how the inspections are performed is a question of economics, required test equipment, and availability of experienced personnel. Prior to making a decision, management should review all aspects of the question, such as equipment cost and maintenance, work volume, time to and from quality assurance facility location, turnaround time, and qualified personnel availability.

35.3 USE OF TEST PATTERNS

The use of test patterns located outside the finished pattern contour area to monitor all processes and also for microsectioning is a controversial subject. Some state that test patterns located outside the contour area usually have greater plating thickness than the actual printed board pattern and, therefore, are not representative of the actual pattern. Others debate that the cost savings of not destroying actual circuits overshadow any slight differences in plating thickness. Test patterns are useful mechanisms for performing destructive tests such as peel strength, flammability, thermal stress, and solderability testing as an indication of the integrity of the finished printed boards. Multiple sets of test coupons are required on mil-standard fabricated printed boards. These coupons provide lot-to-lot process control and indirectly indicate printed board quality fabricated on the panels. An additional test coupon is suggested for solderability testing of multilayer or rigid-flex printed boards. The average multilayer or rigid-flex board has one or more planes internally, ground or voltage type. Plated-through-holes are usually connected to these planes through a thermal resistor–type interconnect to reduce thermal heat-sink effects during machine soldering assembly, thus providing a uniform thermal soldering environment. Several different thermal resistor designs are available through the different CAD programs. However, the designs are not usually created for functional purposes but for ease in CAD programming. Therefore it would be desirable to create a solderability test coupon which simulates your actual multilayer or rigid-flex board design with planes and thermal resistors. Solderability testing can then simulate actual solderability performance, indicating assembly machine soldering performance. If the fabrication panel allows placement of test patterns near the center of the panel, this would improve the acceptability confidence level.

The use of test patterns for the acceptance of printed boards is therefore an individual question and must be resolved for each design requirement and the economic advantage of various inspection operations.

35.4 DETERMINATION OF ACCEPTABILITY

The question of acceptability must be answered for individual printed board design functions. *Functionality through operational life* should be the ultimate criterion for acceptance. A printed board which will see extreme environmental conditions should not be inspected according to the same requirements applied to a printed board for an inexpensive toy or radio. Some of the characteristics normally inspected come under the heading of workmanship. In the majority of designs, those characteristics are cosmetic and pertain to how the printed board looks and not how it functions. In most cases, the characteristics are inspected to establish a confidence level for integrity of the finished PWB and materials. The inspection results should be used to establish a fabrication quality level and not to scrap parts that will meet the functional criteria. Scrapping functional parts has a considerable impact on unit cost. However, the same workmanship characteristics can have an effect on function of some designs, and the effects of the different characteristics will be discussed later in this chapter. The determination of printed boards that do not meet specified acceptance requirements but are functional should be made by a materials review board. The levels of acceptance have to be established by each company; they are dependent on the functional criteria to which the printed board will be subjected. The Institute for Interconnecting and Packaging Electronic Circuits (IPC) established recommended guidelines for acceptance categorized as classes 1, 2, and 3. The classes are defined as follows:

Class 1   Consumer products, including TV sets, toys, entertainment electronics, and noncritical consumer or industrial control devices

Class 2   General industrial, including computers, telecommunications equipment, sophisticated business machines, and instruments of certain noncritical military applications

Class 3   High reliability, including equipment where continued performance is critical, such as life-support equipment

Each group is then subdivided into three categories: target, minimum acceptable, and nonconforming. The acceptance guidelines in this chapter, however, utilize only two categories: preferred and nonpreferred. The illustrations in the nonpreferred category are typical examples of nonconforming conditions. They will guide individuals in establishing minimum acceptance levels applicable to their functional requirements.

35.5   THE MATERIALS REVIEW BOARD

The materials review board (MRB) usually comprises one or more representatives from the departments of quality, production, and design. The purpose of the materials review board is to effect positive corrective action within a short time period to eliminate the cause of recurring discrepancies and prevent occurrence of similar discrepancies. The board's responsibilities include:

1. Reviewing questionable printed boards or materials to determine compliance or noncompliance with quality and design requirements
2. Reviewing discrepant boards for effects on design functionality
3. Authorizing repair or rework of nonconforming materials, when appropriate
4. Establishing responsibility and/or identifying causes for nonconformance
5. Authorizing scrappage of excessive quantities of materials

35.6   VISUAL INSPECTION

Visual inspection is the inspection of characteristics which can be seen in detail with the unaided eye. Magnification, approximately 10×, is advantageous for viewing questionable characteristics after their initial location with the unaided eye or at low magnification, up to 4×. Note that large viewing screens are usually rated in diopters. One diopter is 0.25× magnification.

The viewing of printed board microsections for defects is the exception. Defects such as resin smear and plated-through-hole quality require magnifications of 50× to 500×, depending on the characteristic.

Note that the use of higher magnification for visual-type attributes can produce false results due to illumination and attribute contour effects. Visual inspection criteria are difficult to define grammatically, because individuals interpret words differently. An effective way to define visual inspection criteria is to use line illustrations and/or photographs. IPC utilized this method in the *Acceptability of Printed Boards Manual* to "visually standardize the many individual interpretations to specifications on printed boards." Another method is the use of an audiovisual aid projector. Slides of line illustrations and photographs, depicting visual inspection preferred and nonpreferred criteria along with the related description in audio, provide a reproducible inspection method. Pictorial standards and audiovisual aids are excellent methods for training inspectors, quality engineers, and design engineers.

Of the different types of inspection, surface visual inspection costs the least. Visual inspection by the unaided eye is usually performed on 100 percent of the printed boards or on a sample taken following an established sampling plan. MIL-STD-105, Sampling Procedures and Tables for Inspection by Attributes, is frequently used for this purpose. Inspection for visual defects, following a sampling plan, is done on the premise that the boards were 100 percent visually screened during the fabrication process. Defects which usually can be detected by visual inspection may be divided into three groups: surface defects, base material defects, and other defects.

35.6.1 Surface Defects

Surface defects include dents, pits, scratches, surface roughness, voids, pinholes, inclusions, and markings. Dents, pits, scratches, and surface roughness usually fall in the class of quality of workmanship. The defects, when minor, are normally considered to be cosmetic, and they usually have little or no effect on functionality. However, they can be detrimental to function in the edge board contact area (Fig. 35.1).

Voids in conductors, lands, and plated-through-holes can be detrimental to function, depending on the degree of defect. Pinholes and inclusions are in the same category. Voids or pinholes, either of which reduce the effective conductor width, reduce current-carrying capac-

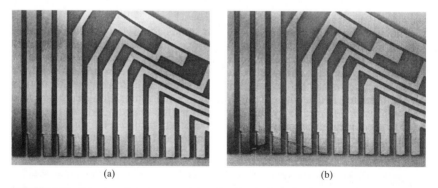

|(a)|(b)|

FIGURE 35.1 Edge-board contact area: (*a*) preferred: edge-board contact area free of delamination, pits, pinholes, dents, nodules, and scratches; (*b*) nonpreferred: (1) scratch depth at the contact area exceeds the microinch surface-roughness requirements; (2) delamination of one of the edge-board contacts. *(IPC.)*

ity and can effect other design electrical characteristics, such as inductance and impedance. Voids in the hole-wall plating area result in reduced conductivity, increased circuit resistance, and voids in plated-through-hole solder fillets. Large voids in plated-through-holes can result in hole barrel cracks during the assembly soldering operation. Soldering temperature, approximately 500°F, causes z-axis expansion, thus stressing weaker plating areas (Fig. 35.2).

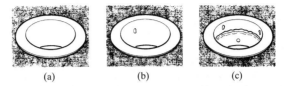

(a)   (b)   (c)

FIGURE 35.2   Voids in hole: (*a*) preferred: no voids in hole; (*b*) Acceptable: no more than three voids in the hole; total void area does not exceed 10 percent of the hole-wall area; (*c*) non-preferred: voids exceed 10 percent of the hole-wall plating area; circumferential void present. *(IPC.)*

Voids in lands are also detrimental to solderability. Pinholes or voids can undermine the top metal plate (Figs. 35.3 and 35.4). The degree of undermining depends on when during the fabrication process the defect occurred. The defects in this group are defined as follows:

1. *Dents.*   A smooth depression in the conductive foil which does not significantly decrease foil thickness.

2. *Pits.*   A depression in the conductive layer that does not penetrate entirely through it.

3. *Scratch.*   Slight surface marks or cuts.

4. *Surface roughness.*   Not smooth or level, having bumps, projections, etc.

5. *Voids.*   The absence of substances in a localized area.

6. *Pinhole.*   A small hole occurring as an imperfection which penetrates entirely through a layer of material.

7. *Inclusions.*   A foreign particle, metallic or nonmetallic, in a conductive layer, plating, or base material. Inclusions in the conductive pattern, depending on degree and material, can affect plating adhesion. Inclusions in a conductor, greater than 0.005 in (0.127 mm) in their greatest dimension, are usually cause for rejection, but inclusions less than 0.0001 in (0.00254 mm) in their largest dimension are usually allowed. Metallic inclusions in the base material reduce the electrical insulation properties and are not normally acceptable if minimum spacing requirements are violated.

8. *Markings (legend).*   A method of identifying printed boards with part number, revision letter, manufacturers date code, etc. The condition is usually considered minor, but if there are different revisions to the same part number, markings that are missing or partially obscured could have an effect on functionality (Fig. 35.5).

35.6.2   Base Material Effects/Defects

Visual inspection is also used to detect the following board material effects/defects: measling, crazing, blistering, delamination, weave texture, weave exposure, fiber exposure, and haloing (Fig. 35.6). These effects/defects have been a source of controversy as to what is good or what is bad. IPC formed a special committee in 1971 to consider base material defects and to better define them with illustrations and photographs. The conditions are defined and discussed here.

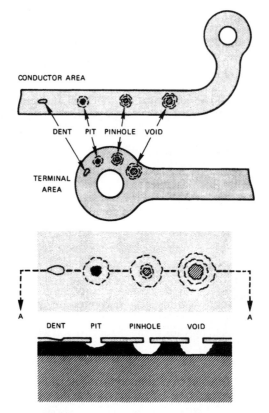

FIGURE 35.3 Pits, dents, pinholes, and voids. *(Sandia Laboratories.)*

FIGURE 35.4 Severe pitting and pinholing. *(IPC.)*

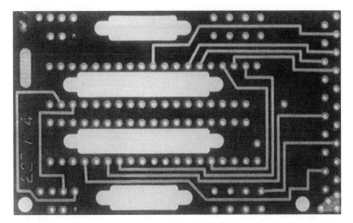

FIGURE 35.5   Part numbers partially obscured and missing. *(Sandia Laboratories.)*

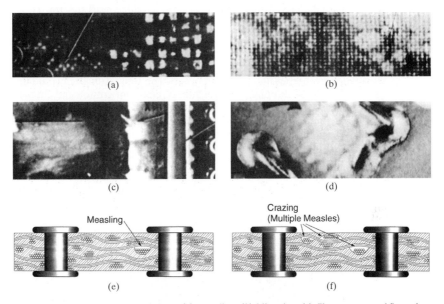

FIGURE 35.6   Base material defects: *(a)* measling; *(b)* blistering; *(c)* fiber exposure; *(d)* crazing; *(e)* measling; and *(f)* crazing (multiple measles). *(IPC.)*

1. *Measling.*   This is an internal condition occurring in laminated base material in which the glass fibers are separated from the resin at the weave intersection. This condition manifests itself in the form of discrete white spots or *crosses* below the surface of the base material. A report compiled by IPC, "Measles in Printed Wiring Boards," was released in November 1973, and stated that "measles may be objectionable cosmetically, but their effect on functional characteristics of finished products are, at worst, minimal and in most cases insignificant." The IPC Acceptability subcommittee readdressed the subjects of measles and crazing in 1994 and verified the 1973 findings. As of 1994 the IPC has not obtained any data indicating measles or crazing was detrimental to function. Therefore, starting with A-600 version E, all acceptance and/or rejection criteria were deleted. Measles and crazing were defined for information purposes only.

2. *Crazing.*   This is an internal condition occurring in the laminate base material in which the glass fibers are separated from the resin at the weave intersections. This condition manifests itself in the form of connected white spots or crosses below the surface of the base material. The 1994 Acceptability subcommittee examined the mechanics of crazing. It was determined that crazing visually looked like measling from the surface, but was not interconnected and was actually separated at each fiber junction (knuckle) and was actually multiple measles. The weave pattern actually alternates from one side of the fiber bundle knuckle to the other. If a continuous condition exists—for example, within a fiber bundle—it is termed *separation* (see Fig. 35.6e and f).

Confusion exists with the term *crazing*. Whereas printed wiring technology considers it an internal effect, most other technologies and the dictionary define crazing as a surface effect.

Note: If the measles or crazing condition exists in high-voltage circuits, the acceptance of the product should be reconsidered.

3. *Blistering.*   This is localized swelling and separation between any of the layers of a laminated base material or between base material and conductive foil. (It is a form of delamination.)

4. *Delamination.*   This is a separation between plies within the base material, between the base material and the conductive foil, or both. Blistering and delamination are considered to be major defects. Whenever a separation of any part of the board occurs, a reduction in insulation properties and adhesion occurs. The separation area could house entrapped moisture, processing solutions, contaminants, or electromigration and contribute to corrosion and other detrimental effects in certain environments (Fig. 35.7). There also is the possibility that the delamination or blister area will increase to the point of complete board separation normally during the assembly soldering operation.

Last is the question of solderability in plated-through-holes. Entrapped moisture, when subjected to soldering temperatures, has been known to create steam that blows holes through the plated side walls, exposing the resin and glass of the plated-through-holes and creating large voids in the solder fillet.

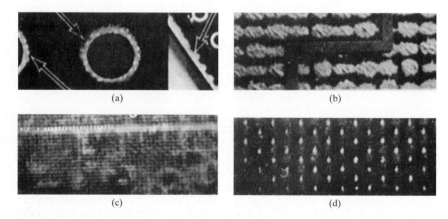

(a)   (b)

(c)   (d)

FIGURE 35.7 Base material defects: (*a*) haloing; (*b*) weave exposure; (*c*) delamination; and (*d*) weave texture. *(IPC.)*

5. *Weave Texture.*   This is a surface condition of base material in which a weave pattern of glass cloth is apparent, although the unbroken fibers of the woven cloth are completely covered with resin.

6. *Weave Exposure.*   This is a surface condition of base material in which the unbroken fibers of woven glass cloth are not completely covered by resin. Weave texture and weave exposure differ in the degree of defect (Fig. 35.7). A condition of weave texture after the board has been completely fabricated is considered a minor defect. However, if the condition materializes during processing, a judgment must be made concerning the possible attack of subsequent processing chemicals. Weave texture, usually caused by the lack of sufficient resin, can become weave exposure if processing chemicals do attack the thin resin layer. Weave exposure is considered a major defect. The exposed glass fiber bundles allow wicking of moisture and entrapment of processing chemical residues.

7. *Fiber exposure.*   This is a condition in which reinforcing fibers within the base material are exposed in machined, abraded, or chemically attacked areas. (See also Weave exposure.)

8. *Haloing.*   This is mechanically induced fracturing or delaminating on or below the surface of the base material; it is usually exhibited by a light area around holes, other machined areas, or both.

35.6.3 Resin Smear

Resin smear is transferred from the base material onto the surface or edge of the conductive pattern normally caused by drilling. Excessive heat generated during drilling softens the resin in holes and smears it over the exposed internal copper areas. The condition creates an insulator between the internal land and subsequent plated-through-holes, resulting in high resistance or *open circuits*. The defect is removed by chemical cleaning. Inspection for resin smear is performed by viewing vertical and horizontal microsections of plated-through-holes.

Chemical cleaning is the chemical process used in the manufacture of multilayer boards. Its purpose is to remove only resin from conductive surfaces exposed in the inside of the holes (Fig. 35.8). Sulfuric, chromic, and permanganate acid are some of the chemicals used in the chemical cleaning process. Subsequent inspection indicates whether it has fulfilled its purpose.

35.6.4 Registration, Layer-to-Layer X-Ray Method

The x-ray method provides a nondestructive way to inspect layer-to-layer registration of internal layers of multilayer boards. It utilizes an x-ray machine and, usually, Polaroid film.

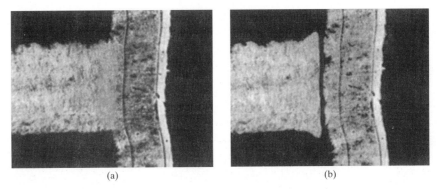

(a)   (b)

FIGURE 35.8   Resin smear: (*a*) Preferred: no evidence of resin smear between layer and plating in the hole; (*b*) nonpreferred: evidence of resin residue or resin between internal layer and plating in the hole. *(IPC.)*

The multilayer board is x-rayed in a horizontal position. The x-ray photos are then examined for hole breakout of the internal lands. The lack of an annular ring denotes severe misregistration (Fig. 35.9).

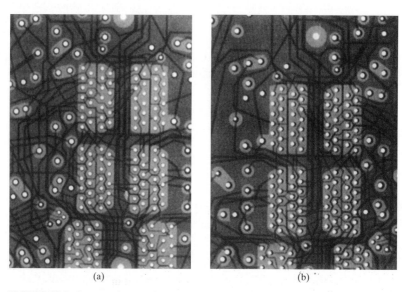

(a)   (b)

FIGURE 35.9   Layer-to-layer registration, x-ray method: (*a*) Preferred: all layers accurately registered; (*b*) nonpreferred: extreme misregistration; insufficient measurable annular ring exists on a segment of circumference. *(IPC.)*

35.6.5 Plated-Through Holes: Roughness and Nodulation

Roughness is an irregularity in the side wall of a hole; nodulation is a small knot or an irregular, rounded lump. Roughness and/or nodulation creates one or more of the following conditions:

1. Reduced hole diameter
2. Impaired lead insertion
3. Impaired solder flow through the hole
4. Voids in solder fillet
5. Possible entrapment of contaminants
6. Highly stressed areas in the plating

Although roughness and nodulation are not desirable, they are allowable in small amounts. Specifications have a tendency to use simple, generalized statements such as "good uniform plating practice" when defining acceptability criteria. Such statements require that a judgment be made by the inspector as to what is acceptable or rejectable. The use of visual aids allows judgment to be made by different inspectors within a close degree of consistency. Figure 35.10 illustrates the acceptance criteria recommended by the IPC.

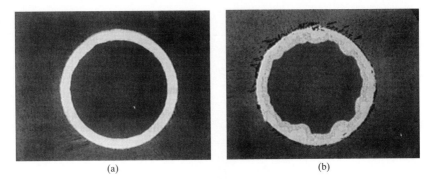

(a)   (b)

FIGURE 35.10   Plated-through-holes: roughness or nodulation. (*a*) Preferred: (1) plating is smooth and uniform throughout the hole; (2) there is no evidence of roughness or nodulation; (*b*) nonpreferred: (1) roughness or nodulation reduces plating thickness below minimum requirements; (2) roughness or nodulation reduces finished-hole size below minimum requirements; (3) excessive roughness or nodulation permits outgassing of the hole when it is solder-dipped. *(IPC.)*

35.6.6   Eyelets

Metallic tubes, the ends of which can be bent outward and over to fasten them in place, are called *eyelets*. Eyelets are used to provide electrical connections with mechanical strength on printed boards. Acceptability of eyeleted printed boards is based on eyelet installation. Eyeleted boards should be inspected for the following conditions:

1. Form of the flange and/or roll should be set in a uniform spread and be concentric to the hole.
2. Splits in the flange or roll should be permissible, provided they do not enter the barrel and provided they allow proper wicking of solder through the eyelet and around the setting.
3. Eyelets should be set sufficiently tight that they cannot move.
4. Eyelets should be inspected for improper installation, deformations, etc.
5. A sample lot of eyeleted holes should be microsectioned to inspect for proper installation. IPC acceptance criteria for roll and funnel flange eyelets are shown in Figs. 35.11 and 35.12.

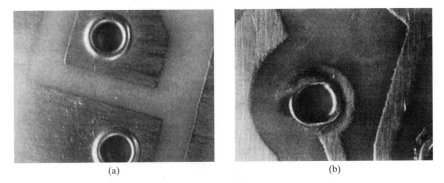

(a)   (b)

FIGURE 35.11   Roll-flange eyelets. (*a*) Preferred: (1) eyelet set uniformly to be concentric with hole; (2) strain or stress marks caused by rollover kept to a minimum; (*b*) nonpreferred: (1) eyelet flange uneven or crushed; (2) splits entering the barrel. *(IPC.)*

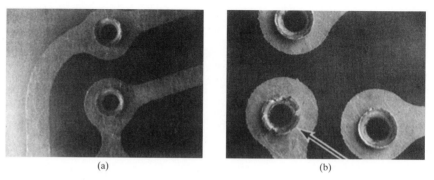

(a)
(b)

FIGURE 35.12   Funnel-flange eyelets. (*a*) Preferred: (1) funnel-flange eyelet (funnelet) set uniformly and concentric to hole; (2) strain or stress marks caused by setting kept to a minimum; (*b*) nonpreferred: (1) funnelet periphery uneven or jagged; (2) splits enter into barrel. *(IPC.)*

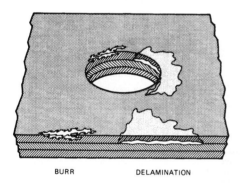

BURR   DELAMINATION

FIGURE 35.13   Base material edge roughness. *(Sandia Laboratories.)*

35.6.7   Base Material Edge Roughness

Base material edge roughness occurs on the printed board edge, cutouts, and nonplated through-hole edges (Fig. 35.13). It is classified as a quality of work condition, and it is created by dull cutting tools causing a tearing action instead of a clean cutting action.

35.6.8   Solder Mask

This is a coating material used to mask off or to protect selected areas of a pattern from the attachment of solder. Solder mask is also used as a conformal coating. Attributes inspected are registration, wrinkles, and delamination. Misregistration at land areas reduces or prevents adequate solder fillet formation. Minimum land area to obtain adequate solder fillets should be the minimum acceptance criteria. Wrinkles and delamination provide sites for moisture absorption and contaminates.

35.6.8.1   Visual Inspection.   The board attributes subjected to nondestructive and destructive visual inspection are listed in Table 35.1.

35.7   DIMENSIONAL INSPECTION

Dimensional inspection is the measurement of the printed board attributes such that dimensional values are necessary to determine compliance with functional requirements. The methods of inspection vary, but the basic inspection equipment consists of gauges and measuring microscopes. More sophisticated equipment is available, including comparators, numerical control measuring equipment, coordinate measuring systems, micro-ohm meters, and beta backscatter gauges and eddy current hand probes. Dimensional inspection is usually performed on a sampling plan basis. One such plan, termed *acceptable quality level* (AQL), is specified as the maximum percent of defects which, for the purpose of sampling, can be considered statistically satisfactory for a given product.

TABLE 35.1   Visual Inspection Chart

Subject	Nondestructive	Destructive
Dents	X	
Pits	X	
Scratches	X	
Voids	X	X
Pinholes	X	
Inclusions	X	
Surface roughness	X	
Markings	X	
Measling	X*	
Crazing	X*	
Blistering	X	
Delamination	X*	
Weave texture	X	
Weave exposure	X	
Haloing	X*	
Chemical cleaning		X*
Registration, layer-to-layer, x-ray method	X	
Plated-through-hole roughness and nodulation	X*	
Eyelets	X	X
Base material edge roughness	X	X*
Solder mask	X	

* Verification of many of the internal effects, visible from the surface, is done by microsection. However, microsection is a destructive method. Recent technology advances in x-ray inspection provide computer-enhanced laminography. The method allows inspection, in thin increments called slices; then the images are combined by computer graphics. This method is nondestructive; however, equipment costs are high. The method should be available at independent test laboratories.

The following attributes fall in the category of dimensional inspection.

35.7.1 Annular Ring

That portion of conductive material completely surrounding a hole is called the *annular ring* (Fig. 35.14). The primary purpose of the annular ring is that of a flange surrounding a hole; it provides an area for the attachment of electronic component leads or wires. Annular ring width of 0.010 in (0.254 mm) is a standard requirement, but some specifications have allowed rings as small as 0.005 in (0.127 mm). Figure 35.15 shows holes neatly centered in the land, holes on the extreme edge of the land, and holes breaking the edge.

Holes that extend beyond the land are generally not acceptable.

35.7.2 Registration, Pattern-to-Hole

The annular ring can also be used for determining registration between the pattern and the holes (Fig. 35.16). Some designers dimension a land to each datum on the master drawing. By

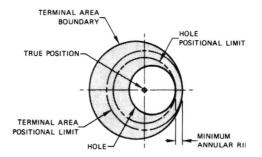

FIGURE 35.14   Annular ring. *(Sandia Laboratories.)*

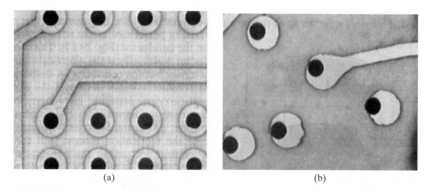

(a)   (b)

FIGURE 35.15   Land registration: (*a*) preferred: holes neatly centered in the land; (*b*) nonpreferred: holes not centered in the land. *(IPC.)*

verifying the dimensions on the printed boards and then verifying that the minimum widths of the annular rings on all other lands are within the drawing requirements, the pattern is considered to be in registration with the drilled hole location. Front-to-back registration is also inspected in this manner.

35.7.3   Conductor Width

The observable width of a conductor at any point chosen at random on the printed board, normally viewed from vertically above unless otherwise specified, is usually referred to as the *overall conductor width* (OCW). The conductor width affects the electrical characteristics of the conductor. A decrease in conductor width decreases the current-carrying capacity and increases electrical resistance. A significant difference in conductor width is realized by differences in fabrication process, panel versus pattern plating. As an example, a nominal conductor width of .010 in (0.25 mm) fabricated with 1 oz copper cladding 0.0014 in (0.03 mm) thickness and an additional 1 oz of copper electroplated on top of the cladding would have a cross-sectional area of 0.028 in (0.71 mm). Fabricating by the panel-plating process, the 0.010-in-wide (0.25-mm) conductor would be reduced to a cross-sectional area of 0.0214 in (0.54 mm) (78 percent of nominal) and if fabricated by the pattern-plate process the cross-sectional area would be 0.0260 in (0.66 mm) (93 percent of nominal). The fabrication process therefore has a significant effect on cross-section reduction.

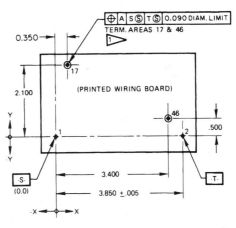

1 ▷ LOCATION OF PATTERN SHALL BE DETERMINED BY THE TWO INDICATED TERMINAL AREAS WITHIN THE TOLERANCES SPECIFIED.

FIGURE 35.16 Pattern-to-hole registration. *(Sandia Laboratories.)*

Most current-carrying capacity graphs take the fabrication process into consideration and adjust the current-carrying capacity to allow for a margin of safety. Although the conductor width definition is very basic, there are two different interpretations as to where on the conductor the measurement is performed: (1) The *minimum conductor width* (MCW) is measured at the minimum width of the conductor, and (2) the *conductor width* (OCW) is measured at the observable width (Fig. 35.17). The minimum conductor width usually can be measured only on a conductor cross section, and it is a destructive inspection. Plating outgrowth, during pattern plating, can prevent the minimum width from being seen unless a cross section is performed. The OCW is always nondestructive and easily measured; see Fig. 35.18, dimension C. (Note: New nondestructive equipment has recently been introduced to measure conductor resistance which can be related to cross-section area.)

The difference between the MCW and the OCW, which is measured from vertically above, can have an effect on the current-carrying capacity, inductance, and impedance. The difference can be significant on narrow conductors: 0.005 in (0.13 mm) or less, especially fabricated by the panel-plating process.

The IPC-RB-276 (Qualification and Performance Specification for Rigid Printed Boards) addresses conductor width requirements and allows added width reductions for edge roughness, nicks, pinholes, and scratches of 40 percent (Class 1), 30 percent (Class 2), and 20 percent (Class 3) from the minimum specified on the master drawing. The document states that this reduction applies to the minimum conductor width called out on the master drawing. However, if no minimum is specified, the minimum allowable default width shall be 0.004 in (0.10 mm). The cross-sectional area reduction could be tremendous, greater than 84 percent, if the designer intended for a 0.025-in-wide (0.64-mm) conductor but failed to specify this on the master drawing, even

FIGURE 35.17 Conductor width. *(Sandia Laboratories.)*

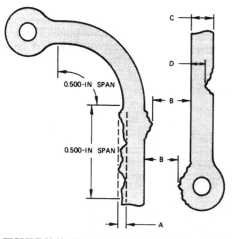

FIGURE 35.18 Edge definition. *(Sandia Laboratories.)*

though the supplied artwork reflected the 0.025-in (0.64-mm) width intent. Therefore, the minimum width requirement should be questioned if not stated on the master drawing, as a courtesy to the customer.

35.7.4 Conductor Spacing

This is the distance between adjacent edges (not centerline) of isolated conductive patterns to a conductive layer. The spacing between conductors and/or lands is designed to accommodate sufficient insulation between circuits. A reduction in the spacing can cause electrical leakage or affect the capacitance. The cross-sectional width of conductors is usually nonuniform; therefore, the spacing measurement is taken at the closest point between the conductors and/or land (see Fig. 35.18, dimension B).

35.7.5 Edge Definition

The fidelity of reproduction of pattern edge relative to the original master pattern is called *edge definition.* It falls in the cosmetic-effective category and does not normally affect functionality. It can, however, have an effect on high-voltage circuits: A corona discharge can be caused at the irregular conductor edges.

Measurement of edge definition is performed by measuring the distance from the crest to the trough (see Fig. 35.18, dimension A). A popular specification is 0.005 in (0.127 mm), crest to trough. Isolated indentations which do not reduce the conductor width by more than 20 percent are usually allowed (see Fig. 35.18, dimension D). Also allowed are isolated projections which do not reduce the conductor spacing below specification requirements. As previously stated, projections can produce corona discharge in high-voltage circuits. Figure 35.19 illustrates isolated indentation and projection and edge definition.

35.7.6 Hole Specifications

Hole size is the diameter of the finished plated-through- or unplated hole. A plated-through-hole is a hole in which electrical connection is made between internal or external conductive patterns, or both, by the deposition of metal on the wall of the hole. An unplated hole (*unsupported hole*) is a hole containing no conductive material nor any other type of reinforcement. The hole size measurement is performed to verify that the hole meets minimum and maximum drawing requirements. The size requirement is usually associated with a fit requirement of a component lead, mounting hardware, etc., plus adequate clearance for solder. Plated-through-holes providing layer-to-layer interconnection, where no components are soldered into the hole, are called *via holes.* Via holes do not have a fit requirement and therefore only the plating integrity is critical.

Two basic methods are used to measure hole size: (1) drill blank plug or suitable gauge (Fig. 35.20) and (2) optical. The latter method is utilized when soft coatings over the copper are used. The optical method prevents deformation of the soft coatings within the hole. When Kwik-Chek or drill blank plug gauges are used, the inspector should acquire a soft touch to prevent damage to the hole. The Kwik-Chek or drill blank gauges should be cleaned prior to use to prevent solderability degradation. Plating nodules are sometimes present in the hole

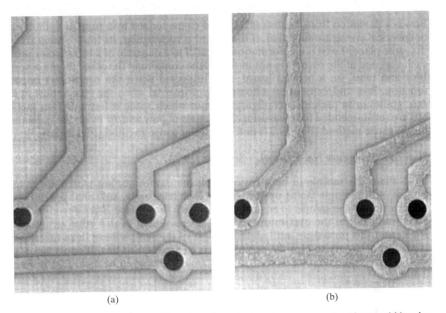

(a)   (b)

FIGURE 35.19   Edge definition: (*a*) preferred: conductor edges are smooth and even within tolerance; (*b*) nonpreferred: conductor edges are poorly defined and outside tolerance. *(IPC.)*

and restrict the penetration of the gauges. Forcing the gauges into the holes causes the nodules to be dislodged and that results in voids in the plated-through-hole side wall.

35.7.7   Bow and Twist

Bow is the deviation from flatness of a board characterized by a roughly cylindrical or spherical curvature such that, if the board is rectangular, its four corners are in the same plane. *Twist* is the deformation parallel to a diagonal of a rectangular sheet such that one of the corners is not in the plane containing the other three corners. Bow and twist, on a printed board, are inspected when the conditions impair function. Bow and/or twist on a board are detrimental when the board must fit in card guides or in packaging configurations in which space is limited. Two methods are recommended for measuring the degree of bow and/or twist: the indicator height gauge method (Fig. 35.21) and the feeler gauge method (Fig. 35.22).

35.7.7.1   *Procedure No. 1 (Bow).*   See Fig. 35.23.

1. Place the sample to be measured on the datum surface with the convex surface of the sample facing upwards. For each edge, apply sufficient pressure on both corners of the sample to insure contact with the surface. Take a reading with a dial indicator at the maximum vertical displacement of this edge denoted as R_1. Repeat this procedure until all four edges of the sample have been measured. It may be necessary to turn the sample over to accomplish this. Identify the edge with the greatest deviation from datum. This is the edge to be measured in steps 2 and 3.

2. Take a reading with the dial indicator at the corner of the sample contacting the datum surface, or determine R_2 by measuring the thickness of the sample with a micrometer (denoted R_2 in Fig. 35.24).

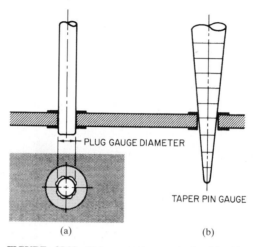

PLUG GAUGE DIAMETER

TAPER PIN GAUGE

(a)   (b)

FIGURE 35.20 Hole-measuring methods: (*a*) drill blank plug gauge method; (*b*) Kwik-Chek or taper-pin method. *(Sandia Laboratories.)*

3. Apply sufficient pressure so that the entire edge contacts the datum surface. Measure the length of the edge and denote as *L*.

4. Calculate bow for this edge as follows:

$$\text{Percent bow} = \frac{R_1 - R_2}{L} \times 100$$

The result of this calculation is the percent of bow.

Repeat the procedure for the other three edges and record the largest value percent of bow for the sample.

35.7.7.2 *Procedure No. 2 (Twist).* See Fig. 35.25.

1. Place the sample to be measured on the datum surface with any three corners of the sample touching the surface. Apply sufficient pressure to ensure that three corners are in contact with the datum surface. Take a measurement from the datum surface to the lifted corner and record the reading. Repeat this procedure until all four corners of the sample have been measured. It may be necessary to turn the sample over to accomplish this. Identify the corner with the greatest deviation from datum. This is the corner to be measured in steps 2 and 3.

2. Place the sample to be measured on the datum surface with three corners touching the surface; insert suitable shims under the raised corner so that it is just supported. When the correct shim thickness is used, the three corners will be in contact with the datum surface without applying pressure to any corner.

3. Without exerting any pressure on the sample, take a reading with the dial indicator at the maximum vertical displacement, denoted R_1 in Fig. 35.26, and record the reading. Without disturbing the sample, take a reading with the dial indicator on the top surface of the sample at the edge contacting the datum surface, or determine R_2 by measuring the thickness of the sample with a micrometer. Note: For fabricated boards, both readings must be made on base material.

4. Measure the diagonal of the sample (for rectangular boards) and record the reading. For nonrectangular boards, measure from the corners exhibiting displacement diagonally to the point on the opposite end of the board.

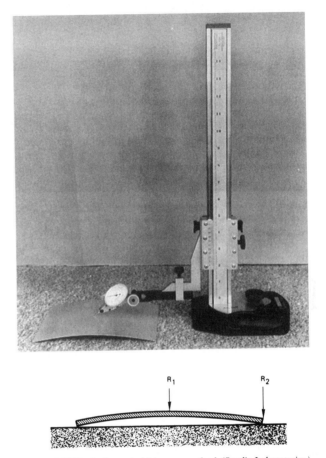

FIGURE 35.21   Indicator height gauge method. *(Sandia Laboratories.)*

Calculate as follows:

1. Deduct R_2 reading from R_1 reading and divide the result by 2.

$$\text{Deviation} = \frac{R_1 - R_2}{2}$$

2. Divide the measured deviation (step 1) by the recorded length and multiply by 100. The result of this calculation is the percent of twist.

$$\text{Percent twist} = \frac{R_1 - R_2}{\text{length}} \times 100$$

The presentation is expressed in a percentage allowable bow and twist and may be applied to either metric or customary dimensions; it is an expression of percentage per unit of measure. Thus, 1.5 percent allowable bow and twist translates to $0.015 \times$ inches or millimeters.

The maximum bow or twist allowed for the entire portion of the specimen or production board is 1.5 percent unless otherwise specified on the master drawing. The 1.5 percent allowable bow and twist is for standard printed wiring boards. Boards which will have surface-

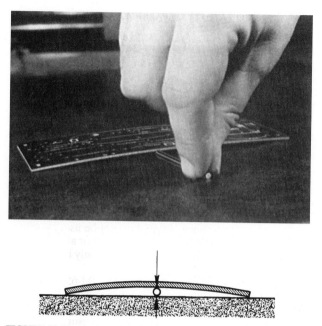

FIGURE 35.22 Feeler gauge method. *(IPC.)*

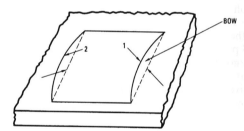

FIGURE 35.23 Bow. *(IPC.)*

FIGURE 35.24 Bow measurement. *(IPC.)*

mounted devices (SMDs) attached may require a tighter tolerance for SMD interconnection reliability. Check with the purchaser before fabrication and question the subsequent assembly requirements.

35.7.8 Conductor Pattern Integrity

Several methods are used to determine conductor pattern integrity—i.e., the quality or state of being complete. Some methods include the use of comparison equipment and overlays. The use of positive or negative overlays made from the master pattern is an inexpensive and effective method. By overlaying the film on the finished printed board, differences are easily detected. Overlays can also be used to determine if conductor widths are within tolerance and annular ring and contours are within drawing requirements.

35.7.9 Contour Dimensions

Contour dimensional inspection verifies that the outside border dimensions are within the drawing requirements. Contour dimension requirements can be considered a fit requirement. Both undersized and oversized printed boards can affect functionality, depending on the degree of requirement violation. Measuring methods vary from the use of a ruler or calipers to sophisticated numerical control equipment. The sophistication of the method is, naturally, dependent on the required dimensions and tolerances.

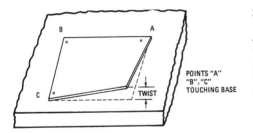

FIGURE 35.25 Twist. *(IPC.)*

35.7.10 Plating Thickness

35.7.10.1 Nondestructive Methods. The plating process is used in the fabrication of numerous printed board designs to produce plated-through-holes and conductive pattern circuitry. When the plating process is utilized, a plating thickness requirement is usually specified on the drawing or in the accompanying specifications. Verification of the plating thickness on the pattern and in the holes is usually required to assure circuit functionality. Two of the presently popular ways to measure plating thickness nondestructively are by the beta backscatter and micro-ohm methods.

Beta Backscatter Method. (Reference IPC-TM-650-2.2.13.2.) This method utilizes an energy source (a radioisotope) and a detector (a Geiger Muller tube). It functions on the beta radiation backscatter principle. It allows thickness measurements to be made within a short period of time, and it can be utilized on metallic, nonmetallic, magnetic, and nonmagnetic materials. The beta backscatter method can be used to measure plating thickness on the circuitry and in the plated-through-holes during or after the board fabrication process and prior to or after the etching operation. It is useful only in measuring the top metal thickness, and it reads the thickness as an average.

Micro-Ohm Method. (Reference IPC-TM-650, 2.2.13.1.) The micro-ohm method functions as a four-wire resistance bridge circuit that imposes a constant current across the area under measure and measures the voltage drop across the same area. The answer is given in micro-ohm units. In plated-through-hole measurements, it treats the hole as a cylindrical resistor. The method is effective only after the circuitry has been etched. When two different metals are used on top of one another, only the lowest-resistance metal thickness is detected. Like the beta backscatter method, the micro-ohm method reads the thickness only as an average. The probe configuration is available in two different configurations: a single-segment and a multiple-segment type. Using the single probe, several measurements are recommended (three or more) of each selected plated-through-hole. Average the measurements of each independent hole. The multiple-segment probe takes several measurements of each plated-through-hole electronically without requiring repositioning of the probe. The measurements of each independent hole are given as an average plating thickness. Check your equipment manual to determine if one or multiple readings are performed on each measurement operation.

35.7.10.2 Destructive Microsection Method. The verification of plating thickness on the surface and in the holes by the microsection method usually requires three measurements at three different locations on each plated-hole side wall (Fig. 35.27). The results are reported either individually or as an average. Care must be exercised to select locations free from

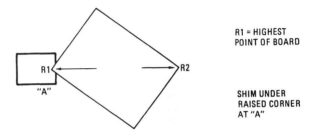

FIGURE 35.26 Twist measurement with shims. *(IPC.)*

voids; they are usually 0.010 in (0.254 mm) apart. Examples of plating thicknesses are shown in Fig. 35.28. Typical plating thickness requirements are as follows:

Copper	0.001 in (0.0254 mm) minimum
Nickel	0.0005 to 0.0010 in (0.0127 to 0.0254 mm)
Gold	0.000050 to 0.000100 in (0.00127 to 0.00254 mm)
Tin-lead	0.0003 in (0.00762 mm) minimum
Rhodium	0.000005 to 0.000020 in (0.000127 to 0.000508 mm)

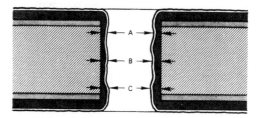

FIGURE 35.27 Verification of plating thickness in holes by use of vertical cross sections. *(Sandia Laboratories.)*

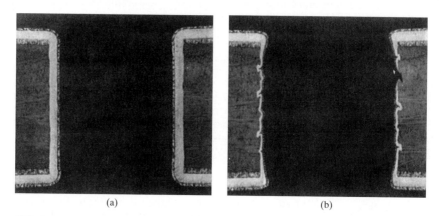

(a)	(b)

FIGURE 35.28 Examples of plating thickness. (*a*) Preferred: plating is uniform and meets thickness requirements; (*b*) nonpreferred: plating thickness less than requirements. *(Sandia Laboratories.)*

Polishing vertical plated-through-hole cross sections to the mean (center) of the hole is critical. If the hole is polished less than or greater than the mean of the hole, a plating thickness error is introduced. Horizontal plated-through-hole cross sections are recommended as references (Fig. 35.29). Although horizontal plated-through-hole cross sections are usually more accurate for plating thickness measurements, they do not allow adequate inspection of other attributes such as voids, plating uniformity, adhesion, etchback, and nodules. Surface plating thickness measurements are taken on vertical cross sections of conductor areas. Microsection mounts are usually etched with an appropriate etchant to show grain boundaries between the copper-clad foil and copper plating. Copper-plating surface measurements usually exclude the copper foil thickness unless otherwise specified.

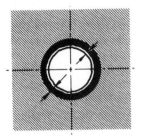

FIGURE 35.29 Verification of plating thickness in holes by use of horizontal cross sections. *(Sandia Laboratories.)*

35.7.10.3   Method of Preparing Microsections. (Institute for Interconnecting and Packaging Electronic Circuits, test method 2.1.1.) Cut from the printed board or test coupon a specimen for vertical evaluation that contains at least three of the smallest holes adjacent to the edge. Cut additional specimens from the board or test coupon for horizontal evaluation.

The test equipment and apparatus necessary for preparation of specimen is as follows:

1. Glass plate 5×7 in (127×177.8 mm)
2. Aluminum rings $1\frac{1}{4}$ in ID (31.75 mm)
3. Silicone release agent
4. Room temperature curing potting material
5. Wooden spatulas
6. Plastic cups (at least 6-oz cups)
7. Saw or shear
8. Engraver
9. 240-grit abrasive
10. Double-coated tape
11. Metallographic polishing tables
12. 240-, 320-, 400-, and 600-grit disks
13. Number 2 liquid alumina polish
14. Polishing cloths
15. Chemical etchants

For metallographic evaluation, the following equipment is necessary:

1. Microscope and camera accessories
2. Filar eyepieces or graduated reticle
3. Engraver
4. Photographic film or Polaroid film
5. Filter lens

The procedure* for preparing the specimen is as follows:

1. Clean glass plate and aluminum rings and dry thoroughly.
2. Apply strip of double-coated tape to plate to support specimen. Apply thin film of release agent to glass plate and ring.
3. Sand the long edge of the perpendicular specimen until the edges of the conductor pads appear and specimen will stand on edge on a flat surface. Use 240-grit abrasive.
4. When secondary plating thickness is being measured, overplate specimen with a harder electroplated metal. Specimens may be overplated as per ASTM method E3-58T.

---

* *Note:* Equipment and procedures are available from equipment manufacturers allowing multiple cross sections to be processed at the same time.

5. Measure inside diameter of plated-through-holes prior to encapsulation.

6. Stand specimen on edge on double-coated tape in aluminum ring with the plated-through-hole edge down. For parallel specimens, delete tape and lay specimen flat on glass plate inside ring.

7. Mix potting material and pour to one side of the specimen until flows through the holes. Support the specimen in the vertical position if necessary. Continue pouring until the ring is full. Avoid entrapment of air.

8. Allow specimen to cure at laboratory temperature. Accelerated curing at a higher temperature following manufacturer's instructions is permissible, provided cracking or deformation does not occur.

9. Identify specimen promptly by engraving.

10. If more than one specimen is potted in one ring, the specimens should be spaced apart to facilitate filling the holes. Specimens should be identified with a strip of paper marked with traceability information and molded into the mounting.

The grinding and polishing procedure is as follows:

1. Rough-grind the face of the specimen to the approximate center of the plated-through-holes by using 240-, 320-, 400-, and 600-grit disks in that order.

2. Flush away all residue by using tap water at room temperature. Wash hands repeatedly to avoid carrying over coarse grids.

3. Rotate specimen 360° about the axis of the wheel and opposite the direction of rotation of the wheel. Keep the face of the specimen flat on the wheel.

4. Micropolish by using a nylon disk and alumina polish number 2 until the specimen is smooth and free of sanding marks and a clear, sharp image of plating lines is evident.

5. Rinse specimen thoroughly and, while it is still wet, chemically etch by using a cotton swab to highlight plating boundaries.

6. Lightly rub twice across the specimen and immediately rinse in distilled water. Repeat if necessary.

7. Rinse thoroughly after etching to eliminate carryover of acids to the microscope.

8. Dry specimen prior to viewing through the microscope.

To make microscope examination, proceed as follows:

1. Place specimen on the microscope stage and adjust to get specimen centered with the eyepiece.

2. Focus and adjust lighting for best viewing; then scan specimen.

3. With filar micrometer or graduated reticle, make three thickness measurements of each plating on both walls of the plated-through-hole.

The following is the procedure for photo-micrographing (composite photographs):

1. Locate specimen, place flat on microscope stage, and mount camera to microscope tube. Insert film pack.

2. Set lighting and exposure time prearranged settings.

3. Focus on one part of one wall and push camera plunger.

4. Immediately remove negative from camera and develop.

5. Take sufficient photographs to illustrate the entire length of the wall.

6. Repeat steps 1 to 5 and photograph the opposite wall.

7. If defective junctions, voids, etc., appear, enlarged photographs may be made. Enlargements should be referenced to the photographs.

35.7.11 Undercut (After Fabrication)

This is the distance on one edge of a conductor measured parallel to the board surface from the outer edge of the conductor, excluding overplating and coatings, to the maximum point of indentation on the same edge. Measurement of the degree of undercut present is not usually required, because undercut is included in the minimum conductor width measurement. If, however, the undercut measurement is required separately, it is performed by first measuring the minimum conductor width and then subtracting that dimension from the design width of the conductor and dividing by 2 (see Fig. 35.30). For example:

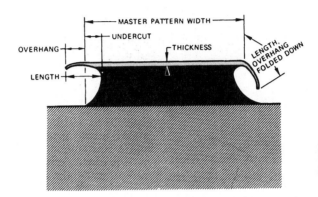

FIGURE 35.30   Undercut and outgrowth. *(Sandia Laboratories.)*

$$\frac{a - b}{2} = c$$

where a = design width of conductor dimension
        b = minimum conductor width dimension
        c = undercut dimension

35.7.12 Outgrowth

This is the increase in conductor width at one side of a conductor, caused by plating buildup, over that delineated on the production master. The measurement of the degree of outgrowth is required in some specifications. Excessive outgrowth can eventually lead to *slivering,* a thin metallic piece that breaks off of the conductive pattern.

Outgrowth length dimensions of 1½ times or less the outgrowth thickness, at the point where the outgrowth material extends beyond the main conductor configuration, are usually allowed. The degree of outgrowth is measured on a conductor cross section (Fig. 35.30).

An example of excessive outgrowth is depicted in Fig. 35.31. A method of determining if the outgrowth is prone to slivering utilizes an ultrasonic cleaner. The total printed board is suspended in water in an ultrasonic cleaner for 1 to 2 min. If the board is prone to slivering, metallic slivers will be evident along pattern edges (Fig. 35.32).

35.7.13 Etchback

A process for the controlled removal of nonmetallic materials from side walls of holes to a specified depth. It is used to remove resin smear and to expose additional internal conductor

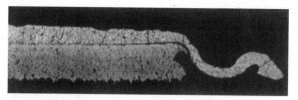

FIGURE 35.31 Outgrowth extension is approximately 10 times the thickness. *(Sandia Laboratories.)*

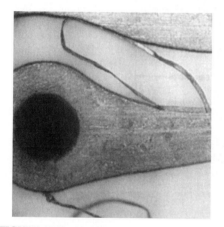

FIGURE 35.32 Metallic slivers present after ultrasonic test. *(Sandia Laboratories.)*

surfaces. The degree of etchback is critical to function. Too much etchback creates excessively rough hole side walls and causes weak plated-through-hole structures. Etchback requirements range from 0.0002 to 0.0030 in (0.00508 to 0.0762 mm); however, a maximum of 0.0015 to 0.0002 in (0.038 to 0.051 mm) is recommended. The requirement is usually specified as a minimum and a maximum. The degree of etchback is usually measured by utilizing vertical plated-through-hole cross sections of multilayer boards (Fig. 35.33).

Typical etchback acceptance criteria recommended by the IPC are shown in Fig. 35.34.

35.7.14 Registration, Layer to Layer

This is the degree of conformity of the position of a pattern, or portion thereof, with its intended position or with that of any other conductor layer of a board. It is required to ensure electrical connection between the plated-through-holes and the internal layers. Misregistration of internal layers increases electrical resistance and decreases conductivity. Severe misregistration creates an open-circuit condition, a complete loss of continuity. Two popular methods of measuring registration, layer to layer, are the x-ray method described in Sec. 35.6.4 and the microsection method, which is similar to the plating thickness inspection method.

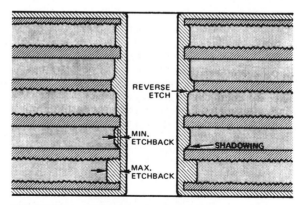

FIGURE 35.33 Etchback configurations. *(IPC.)*

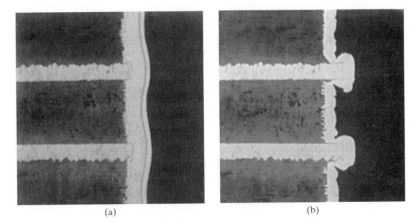

(a)   (b)

FIGURE 35.34 Etchback. (*a*) Preferred: uniform etchback of base laminate; uniform plating in the plated-through-hole; (*b*) nonpreferred: nonuniform and excessive etchback of base laminate results in unacceptable nonuniform plating in the hole. *(IPC.)*

The microsection method consists of measuring each internal land area on a vertical plated-through-hole cross section and determining the centerline. The maximum variation between centerlines is the maximum misregisteration (Fig. 35.35).

35.7.15 Flush Conductor, Printed Boards

This is a conductor whose outer surface is in the same plane as the surface of the insulating material adjacent to the conductor. Flush conductors are primarily used in rotating switches, commutators, and potentiometers. Common to those uses are brush or wiper and conductor pattern combinations. Making the conductors flush in these applications reduces wiper vibrations, wear, and intermittent or noisy signals. The height of the step allowed between pattern and base material is dependent on the relative wiper speed, the materials used, and the degree of signal error and electrical noise tolerable in the circuit. A commonly accepted height allowance is as follows:

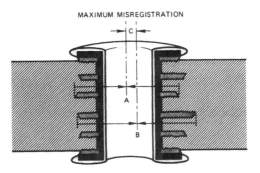

FIGURE 35.35 Layer-to-layer registration microsection method. *(IPC.)*

Up to 50 r/min   80–200 μin (2.032×10^{-4}–5.08×10^{-3} mm)
51–125 r/min   Better than 50 μin (1.27×10^{-4} mm)
126–500 r/min   Better than 30 μin (0.762×10^{-4} mm)

However, the IPC-RB-276 requirements document refers to requirements as stated on the master drawing.

Inspection of the degree of flushness is performed with height gauges or measuring microscopes (Fig. 35.36).

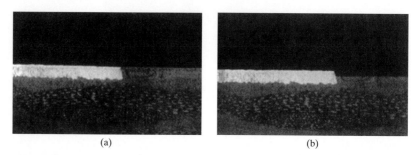

(a)   (b)

FIGURE 35.36   Flush printed circuits. (*a*) Preferred: conductor is flush to the board surface; (*b*) nonpreferred: conductor is not flush to the board surface and does not meet the specified tolerance. *(IPC.)*

35.7.16   Summary: Dimensional Inspection

The dimensional board attributes subjected to nondestructive and destructive inspection are listed in Table 35.2.

35.8   *MECHANICAL INSPECTION*

Mechanical inspection is applied to characteristics which can be verified with qualitative physical test. Mechanical inspection methods can be either nondestructive or destructive. The following methods are used to verify printed board fabrication integrity.

35.8.1   Plating Adhesion

A common method of inspecting for plating adhesion is the tape test, which is described in detail in the IPC Test Method IPC-TM-650, 2.4.1 and military specification MIL-P-55110. The basic test method is shown in Fig. 35.37.

Another method of determining plating adhesion is applied during the preparation and viewing of the microsection mounts. If adhesion is poor, the layers of plating will separate during the microsection specimen preparation or will indicate lack of adhesion at plating boundaries during microsection mount viewing. Figure 35.38 indicates lack of adhesion at the different plating boundaries, copper foil to copper plate and copper plate to tin-lead.

TABLE 35.2 Dimensional Inspection Chart

Subject	Nondestructive	Destructive
Annular ring	X	
Pattern-to-hole registration	X	
Conductor width	X	X
Conductor spacing	X	
Edge definition	X	
Hole size	X	
Bow and twist	X	
Conductor pattern integrity	X	
Contour dimensions	X	
Plating thickness	X	X
Undercut		X
Outgrowth		X
Etchback		X
Registration, layer to layer		X
Flush circuits	X	X

35.8.2 Solderability

Solderability inspection measures the ability of the printed pattern to be wetted by solder for the joining of components to the board. It involves the use of three terms: *wetting, dewetting,* and *nonwetting.* The terms are defined as follows.

1. *Wetting.* The formation of a relatively uniform, smooth, unbroken and adherent film of solder to a basis material, conductors, and land areas to form an adherent bond.

2. *Dewetting.* A condition which results when molten solder has coated a surface and recessed, leaving irregularly shaped mounds of solder separated by areas covered with a thin solder film; basis metal is not exposed. Most of the solder balls up at random locations on the surface.

3. *Nonwetting.* A condition whereby a surface has contacted molten solder, but the solder has not adhered to all of the surface; basis metal remains exposed.

Many methods for inspecting printed boards for solderability, both quantitatively and qualitatively, have been established. However, the most meaningful method is that which will be used in the assembly soldering operation hand soldering, wave soldering, drag soldering, etc. The IPC recently released an approved ANSI/J-STD-003 specification, Solderability Tests for Printed Boards. This specification addresses the fact that the recommended test methods and subsequent storage have had no adverse effect on the solderability of those portions of the printed wiring board intended to be soldered. Test coupons or product are submitted to accelerated aging to a length of time defined by a *coating durability* requirement called out on the master drawing or procurement contract, followed by solderability testing. The coating durability requirements are:

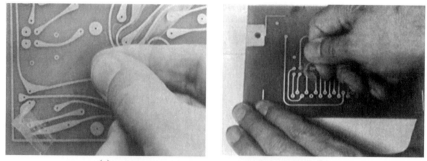

(a)   (b)

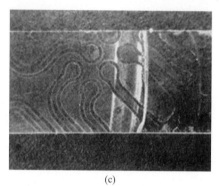

(c)

FIGURE 35.37   The tape test. (*a*) Step 1: Place transparent cellophane tape across the circuits to be tested, and press the tape onto the circuits. Eliminate all air bubbles with finger. (*b*) Step 2: Lift tape on one end enough to get a grip. Pull tape off the printed board at approximately 90° to the board. Use a rapid pull. (*c*) Step 3: A clear tape is the preferred test result. *(IPC.)*

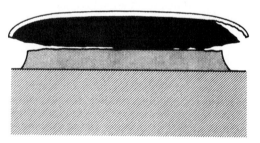

FIGURE 35.38   Plated metal adhesion. *(Sandia Laboratories.)*

Category 1	Minimum coating durability, intended to be soldered within 30 days from time of PB manufacture
Category 2	Average coating durability, intended for PB storage up to six months from time of manufacture
Category 3	Maximum coating durability, intended for PB storage over six months from time of manufacture

Categories 1 and 2 do not require accelerated aging; however, Category 1 requires nonactivated flux be used for surface testing. Category 2 requires nonactivated flux to be used for both surface and hole testing. Category 3 requires accelerated aging followed by nonactivated flux on the surface testing and nonactivated flux without accelerated aging for hole testing.

The IPC has adopted the criteria illustrated in Fig. 35.39 for printed board solderability acceptance.

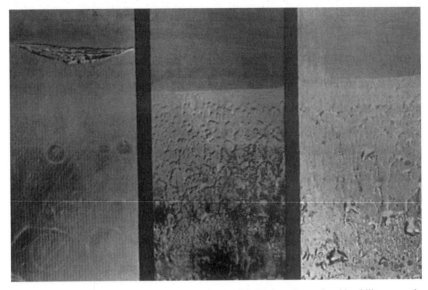

FIGURE 35.39 Solderability acceptance criteria. (*a*) Preferred: good solderability; smooth, bright, good wetted copper; and good solder coverage; (*b*) acceptable: some dewetting is visible at left surface; (*c*) nonpreferred: surface shows severe dewetting and nonwetting. (*IPC.*)

35.8.3 Alloy Composition

Two popular alloys used in printed board manufacture are tin-lead and tin-nickel. The composition of the tin-nickel bath is usually 65% tin and 35% nickel. The composition of the deposit, during electroplating, remains nearly constant despite fluctuations in bath composition and operation conditions. However, the composition of the tin-lead deposits can vary with bath composition and operation conditions and will influence the melting temperature of the alloy and affect solderability. Specifications usually require the tin content to be between 50 and 70%. Other finishes such as electroless nickel, rhodium, or paladium are used for specific projects but must be called out in the master drawing.

Methods available for analyzing the alloy composition on the plated printed board include wet analysis, atomic absorption, and the beta backscatter. The beta backscatter method is relatively new and is gaining in popularity because of the ease in obtaining the alloy composition nondestructively, but its results are not as precise as the other methods.

35.8.4 Thermal Stress, Solder Float Test

Temperature-induced strain or straining force that is exerted upon the printed board and tends to stress or deform the board shape can be a serious problem during the soldering oper-

FIGURE 35.40 Continuity, thermal stress, moisture resistance test pattern. *(IPC.)*

ation. Thermal stress inspection is performed to predict the behavior of the printed boards after soldering. Plated-through-hole degradation, separation of platings or conductors, or laminate delamination is detectable by the thermal stress test.

The printed board specimen is (1) conditioned at 250 to 300°F for 2 h minimum to reduce moisture; (2) placed in a dessicator, on a ceramic plate, to cool; (3) fluxed with type RMA flux; (4) floated in a solder bath ($63 \pm 5\%$ tin maintained at $550 \pm 10°F$) for 10 s; (5) after stressing, placed on an insulator to cool. Visual inspection for defects is followed by cross-sectioning the plated-through-holes and inspecting with magnification for integrity. Test patterns also are used for thermal stress inspection. (See Fig. 35.40 for a test pattern used in this and other connections.)

35.8.5 Peel Strength

This is the force per unit width required to peel the conductor or foil from the base material. It is usually associated with the acceptance testing of copper-clad laminate material upon receipt, but it is sometimes utilized to test the adhesion of the conductors to the finished board. Peel strength tests of conductors are usually performed after the specimens have been dip or flow soldered. Peel strength values in MIL-P-13949, after solder dip, also are used for printed board conductor peel strength tests. However, the values must be adjusted for the particular conductor width, because the peel strength values in MIL-P-13949 pertain to a 1.00-in (25.4-mm) conductor width. As an example:

Conductor width	= 0.050 in (1.27 mm)
Peel strength value in MIL-P-13949	= 10 lb
Conductor width in MIL-P-13949	= 1.00 in (25.4 mm)

$$\frac{0.050 \times 10.0}{1.00} = 0.5 \text{ lb}$$

A calculation with width in millimeters will, of course, yield the same results. Peel strength tests of conductors are a good method of assuring that the conductor-to-laminate adhesion is sufficient to withstand assembly soldering operations. Actual printed boards or test patterns can be utilized for the test. Figure 35.41 is an example of a typical peel strength test pattern.

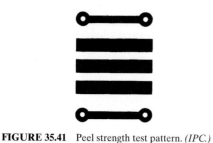

FIGURE 35.41 Peel strength test pattern. *(IPC.)*

35.8.6 Bond Strength (Terminal Pull)

The bond strength test is a test of the plating adhesion to the laminate in the hole. Poor adhesion in the holes can occur from the drilling, electroless copper deposition operations, and state of cleanliness in the hole being out of control or from the use of undercured laminate material. Whatever the cause, poor plating adhesion in the hole affects functionality.

Lack of plating adhesion to the laminate in the hole is detectable during microsection analysis; a terminal pull test should be performed to substantiate the condition (see Fig. 35.42).

FIGURE 35.42 Typical terminal pull test coupon. *(IPC.)*

35.8.7 Cleanliness (Resistivity of Solvent Extract)

The purpose of this is to verify the state of cleanliness. Printed boards are fabricated using wet chemistry and mechanical techniques. Some of the chemical baths have metallic salts or are corrosive in nature. These conditions could affect the functionality of the boards (i.e., reduced electrical insulation resistance, corrosion of the metal pattern, etc.). Another common problem is electromigration of metal between conductors. This condition is usually associated with low operating voltage, 10 V or less, and requires three components to be present: (1) moisture, (2) metallic contaminate, and (3) voltage.

The cleanliness test measures the resistivity of the wash solution that the board has been washed with. This test (Ref. MIL-P-55110) can be performed by open setup or with commercially available equipment.

35.8.7.1 Open Setup Procedure. Note that all laboratory ware must be scrupulously clean before use.

1. Position a convenient-size funnel over an electrolytic beaker.
2. Suspend the printed board within the funnel.
3. Prepare a wash solution of 75% by volume of ACS reagent-grade isopropyl alcohol and 25% by volume of distilled water. (Note: This wash solution must have a resistivity equal to or greater than 6×10^6 Ω-cm.)
4. Direct a fine stream of solution from a wash bottle onto both sides of the printed board until 100 ml of the wash solution are collected for each 10 in^2 of board surface (including both sides of the board). Wash activity time = 1 min minimum. (Note: The initial wash solution must be included in the sample to be measured for resistivity.)
5. Measure the resistivity of the collected wash solution with conductivity bridge or other instrument of equivalent range and accuracy. Minimum allowed resistivity of the collected wash solution is 2×10^6 Ω-cm.

35.8.7.2 Alternate Test Procedure. Commercial equipment is available to perform the cleanliness testing. Reference MIL-P-55110 for source and equipment listing. Note that when solder mask is required on printed wiring boards, the cleanliness test is performed on the uncoated boards before coating.

35.8.7.3 Mechanical Inspection. The mechanical board attributes subjected to nondestructive and destructive inspection are listed in Table 35.3.

35.9 ELECTRICAL INSPECTION

Electrical inspection is performed to verify circuit integrity after processing and also to substantiate that the electrical characteristics of the processed board meet design intent. Electrical inspection methods are both destructive and nondestructive. Nondestructive tests are usually performed on the actual printed boards. Destructive tests are performed on either printed circuit boards utilized for destructive acceptance testing or on test patterns fabricated outside the border of the board. Two popular nondestructive electrical tests are *insulation resistance* and *continuity*. They are usually performed on 100 percent of complex printed boards, especially multilayer ones. Care should be taken to prevent arcing as the probes approach the printed board pattern when the insulation resistance test is performed. An eas-

TABLE 35.3 Mechanical Inspection Chart

Subject	Destructive	Nondestructive
Plating adhesion	X	X
Solderability		X
Alloy composition	X	X
Thermal stress (solder float test)	X	
Peel strength, printed wiring conductor	X	
Bond strength (terminal pull)		X
Cleanliness	X	

ily activated switch in series with one of the probes allows the probes to make contact with the pattern prior to current flow. To prevent probe impressions on soft metal coatings, apply the same coating on the probe tips.

35.9.1 Continuity

Continuity tests are performed basically on multilayer circuits to verify that the printed circuit pattern is continuous. They can be performed with an inexpensive multimeter or with more elaborate equipment such as a computer-enhanced bed-of-nails tester. This type of tester can either be preprogrammed with all the circuit nets or use a known good multilayer board termed a *golden board*. The tester digitizes the golden board net circuits, then tests all subsequent boards to the digitized nets. In the printed circuits industry, the continuity test is performed in one of two ways: (1) as a go/no-go test to verify that the pattern is continuous, or (2) to verify that the pattern is continuous as well as to verify the integrity of the measured pattern. The latter results are reported in electrical resistance values (ohms). The preferred method is to perform the continuity test on all printed boards submitted for acceptance. This is especially recommended for multilayer circuitry, the internal patterns and interconnections of which cannot be inspected visually after fabrication.

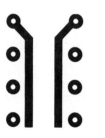

FIGURE 35.43 Insulation resistance, dielectric withstanding voltage, and moisture resistance test patterns. *(IPC.)*

Test coupons are sometimes used for the continuity test. See Fig. 35.43 for a pattern used on a typical coupon.

35.9.2 Insulation Resistance (Circuit Shorts)

The purpose of this test, as stated in MIL-STD-202, is to measure the resistance offered by the insulation members of a printed board to an impressed direct voltage that tends to produce a leakage of current through or on the surface of those members. Low insulation resistances can disturb the operation of circuits intended to be isolated by permitting the flow of large-leakage currents and the formation of feedback loops. The test also reveals the presence of contaminants from processing residues.

In printed circuitry, the test is performed by an open either between conductors on the same layer or between two different layers. The bed of nails allows all noncommon nets to be tested against each other. The test is also utilized before and after thermal shock and temperature cycling tests. Test voltages of 40 to 500 V_{dc} and minimum insulation resistances of 200 to 500 MΩ are popular. The insulation resistance test is performed on either the actual printed board or a test coupon fabricated on the same panel as the board (Fig. 35.43).

When special conditions such as isolation, low atmospheric pressure, humidity, and immersion in water are required, they should be specified in the test method instruction.

35.9.3 Current Breakdown (Plated-Through-Holes)

The current-breakdown test is used to determine if sufficient plating is present within the plated-through-hole to withstand a relatively high current potential. The time and current selected determine if this test is destructive or nondestructive. IPC test method TM-650-2.5.3 recommends a current of 10 A for 30 s. The test is performed as follows:

1. Place a load resistor of predetermined value across the negative and positive terminals of a current-regulated power supply.

2. Adjust the supply for a current of 10 A or any other desired value.

3. Remove one end of the resistor from the positive supply terminal.

4. Connect the desired plated-through-hole between the disconnected end of the resistor and the positive supply terminal.

5. Perform the test for the desired time. The test is performed either on an actual printed board or on a test pattern (Fig. 35.44).

FIGURE 35.44 Typical current-breakdown test pattern. *(IPC.)*

35.9.4 Dielectric Withstanding Voltage

This test is used to verify that the component part can operate safely at its rated voltage and withstand momentary overpotentials due to switching, surges, and similar phenomena. It also serves to determine whether insulating materials and spacings in the component part are adequate. It is thoroughly defined in MIL-STD-202, Electronic Components Method 301.

One of three different test voltages (500, 1000, and 5000 V) is usually specified. The test is performed on either an actual board or test coupon. Voltage is applied between mutually insulated portions of the specimen or between insulated portions and ground. The voltage is increased at a uniform rate until the specified value is reached. The voltage is held for 30 s at the specified value and then reduced at a uniform rate.

Visual examination of the part is performed during the test for evidence of flashover or breakdown between contacts. See Fig. 35.43 for a typical test pattern. The test can either be destructive or nondestructive depending on the degree of overpotential used.

35.9.5 Electrical Inspection

The electrical board attributes subjected to nondestructive and destructive inspection are listed in Table 35.4.

TABLE 35.4   Electrical Inspection Chart

Subject	Nondestructive	Destructive
Continuity	X	
Insulation resistance	X	
Current breakdown, plated-through-holes	X	X
Dielectric withstanding voltage	X	X

35.10   ENVIRONMENTAL INSPECTION

Environmental inspection consists of performing specific tests to ensure that the printed board will function under the influence of the climatic and/or mechanical forces to which it will be subjected during use. Environmental tests are performed on preproduction printed boards to verify design adequacy. Specific tests are sometimes specified as part of the printed board acceptance procedure to expose a prospective failure situation. Specific environmental tests, as part of the acceptance procedure, are prevalent in high-reliability programs.

Note: It is recommended to perform a component assembly soldering simulation preconditioning, two cycles, prior to performing environmental testing. Test information will then relate to actual conditions to which the printed wiring board will be subjected. Environmental tests are performed on either actual printed boards or coupon test patterns. This section briefly reviews some of the popular environmental tests. Specific details on performing the tests are referenced at the end of the chapter in Sec. 35.11.

35.10.1   Thermal Shock

The thermal shock test is particularly efficient in identifying (1) printed board designs with areas of high mechanical stress, and (2) the resistance of the printed board to exposure of high and low temperature extremes. This test is required in IPC-RB-276 for product acceptance for Class 3 and is also used for printed wiring board supplier qualification inspection, MIL-P-55110.

A thermal shock is induced on a printed board by exposure to severe and rapid differences in temperature. The test is usually performed by transferring the board from one temperature extreme (e.g., 125°C) to the other (e.g., –65°C) rapidly, usually within 2 min. A resistance difference in excess of 10 percent between the first and hundredth cycle is considered a reject. Thermal shock effects on the board include cracking of plating in the holes and delamination. See Fig. 35.46 for typical thermal shock test pattern (reference MIL-P-55110 for requirements and MIL-STD-202, method 107C, for procedure). (Note that continuous electrical monitoring during thermal shock cycling will display intermittent electrical circuits. Intermittent circuits usually occur at temperature transitions from cold to hot or hot to cold.)

35.10.2   Moisture and Insulation Resistance

The moisture resistance test is an accelerated method of testing the printed board for deteriorative effects of high humidity and heat conditions typical of tropical environments. The test conditions are usually at relative humidity of 90 to 98 percent at a temperature of 25 to 65°C. After the required

FIGURE 35.45   Typical thermal shock and moisture resistance test pattern. *(IPC.)*

test cycles are completed, the board is subjected to insulation resistance testing. Test specimens should exhibit no blistering, measling, warp, or delamination after the moisture resistance test. See Fig. 35.44 or 35.45 for typical test patterns.

35.11 SUMMARY

To select the printed board attributes to be inspected in an individual program, proceed as follows:

1. Review the environment in which the printed board will operate and the life expectancy of the board.
2. Review the electrical and mechanical parameters associated with functionality.
3. Consider the total assembly unit cost and the importance of the printed board before determining if a quality assurance program is economical.
4. Consider both functionality and economics in quality assurance program selection. Functionality should prevail, however.
5. Design the quality assurance program for at least a 90 percent confidence level by using sampling plans when they are appropriate.
6. Select for inspection the attributes which will satisfy requirements 1 and 2.
7. Select test methods which verify the printed board functionality and integrity. Test methods may require modification or creation to satisfy the quality assurance requirements.

35.12 TEST SPECIFICATIONS AND METHODS RELATED TO PRINTED BOARDS

Attributes	Method
Annular ring	IPC-TM-650, 2.2.1
Base material edge roughness	IPC-TM-650, 2.1.5
Blistering	IPC-TM-650, 2.1.5
Chemical cleaning	IPC-TM-650, 2.2.5 & 2.1.1
Conductor spacing	IPC-TM-650, 2.2.2
Conductor width	IPC-TM-650, 2.2.2
Crazing	IPC-TM-650, 2.1.5
Current breakdown, plated-through-hole	IPC-TM-650, 2.5.3
Dents	IPC-TM-650, 2.1.5
Dielectric withstanding voltage	IPC-TM-650, 2.5.7
	MIL-STD-202, 301
Edge definition	IPC-TM-650, 2.2.3
Etchback	IPC-TM-650, 2.2.5
Eyelets	IPC-TM-650, 2.1.5
Haloing	IPC-TM-650, 2.1.5
Hole size	IPC-TM-650, 2.2.6
Inclusions	IPC-TM-650, 2.1.5
Insulation resistance	IPC-TM-650, 2.5.9, 2.5.10, 2.5.11, MIL-STD-202, 302
Layer-to-layer registration, destructive	IPC-TM-650, 2.2.11
Markings	IPC-TM-650, 2.1.5
Measling	IPC-TM-650, 2.1.5
Microsections, methods of preparing	IPC-TM-650, 2.1.1

Moisture resistance	IPC-TM-650, 2.6.3, MIL-STD-202, 106C
Overhang	IPC-TM-650, 2.2.9
Pinholes	IPC-TM-650, 2.1.5
Pits	IPC-TM-650, 2.1.5
Plating adhesion	IPC-TM-650, 2.4.10
Plating thickness, Nondestructive	IPC-TM-650, 2.2.13.1, ASTM-B-567-72
Plating thickness, destructive	IPC-TM-650, 2.2.13, ASTM-B-567-58
Scratches	IPC-TM-650, 2.1.5
Solderability	IPC-TM-650, 2.4.12, 2.4.14
Surface roughness	IPC-TM-650, 2.1.5
Bond strength (terminal pull)	IPC-TM-650, 2.4.20, 2.4.21
Thermal shock	IPC-TM-650, 2.6.7, MIL-STD-202, 107C
Thermal stress	IPC-TM-650, 2.6.8
Voids	IPC-TM-650, 2.1.5
Warp and twist	IPC-TM-650, 2.4.22
Weave exposure	IPC-TM-650, 2.1.5
Weave texture	IPC-TM-650, 2.1.5

35.12.1 General Specifications Related to Printed Boards

The following printed board specifications are some of those used throughout the industry. The specifications usually cover both processing and acceptance requirements.

IPC Specifications

IPC-FC-250	Specifications for Double-Sided Flexible Wiring with Interconnections
ANSI/IPC-D-275	Design Standard for Rigid Printed Boards and Rigid Printed Board Assemblies
IPC-RB-276	Qualification and Performance Specification for Rigid Printed Boards
IPC-D-300	Printed Circuit Board Dimensions and Tolerances
IPC-MC-324	Performance Specification for Metal Core Boards
IPC-D-325	Documentation Requirements for Metal Core Boards
IPC-D-326	Information Requirements for Manufacturing Electronic Assemblies
ANSI/IPC-A-600	Acceptability of Printed Wiring Boards
IPC-SS/QE-605	Printed Board Quality Evaluation Slide Set and Handbook
IPC-TM-650	Test Methods Manual
IPC-OI-645	Standard for Visual Optical Inspection Aids
IPC-SM-840	Qualification and Performance of Permanent Polymer Coatings (Solder Mask) for Printed Boards

Military Specifications

MIL-Q-9858	Quality Assurance
MIL-P-55110	Printed Wiring
MIL-P-55640	Multilayer Printed Wiring
MIL-P-50884	Flexible Printed Wiring

MIL-STD-105	Sampling Procedure and Tables for Inspection by Attributes
MIL-STD-202	Test Methods for Electronic and Electrical Component Parts
MIL-STD-810	Environmental Test Methods
MIL-STD-1495	Multilayer Printed Wiring Boards for Electronic Equipment

Other Publications

ASTM-B-567-72	Measurement of Coating Thickness by the Beta Backscatter Principle
ASTM-A-226-58	Standard Method of Test for Local Thickness of Electrodeposited Coatings
EIA-RS-326	Solderability of Printed Wiring Boards
IEC No. 326	Performance Specification for Single- and Double-Sided Printed Wiring Boards
UL 796	Printed Wiring Boards

BIBLIOGRAPHY

Barr, V. C., Sandia National Laboratories, Livermore, Calif., private correspondence relating to tests of several thermal resistance design effects on solderability of plated-through-holes.

Draper, C. R., "The Production of Printed Circuits and Electronics Assemblies," Robert Draper, Ltd., London, 1969.

Estes, T. A., Conductor Analysis Technologies, Inc., private correspondence on the use of equipment to determine cross-sectional area of conductors.

Harper, C. A., Handbook of Electronic Packaging, McGraw-Hill, New York, 1969.

Kear, F. W., "The Design and Manufacture of Printed Circuits," part 14, *PCM-PCE Magazine,* Feb. 1970.

"Quality Assurance," *IPC-Design Guide,* sec. 9, Institute of Interconnection and Packaging Electronic Circuits.

Scarlett, J. A., *Printed Circuit Boards for Microelectronics,* Van Nostrand Reinhold, New York, 1970.

Shemilt, H. R., "Inspection of Printed Circuits," *Electronics Manufacturer Magazine,* vol. 15, 1971.

CHAPTER 36
ACCEPTABILITY OF PRINTED CIRCUIT BOARD ASSEMBLIES

Bruce Wooldridge
DSC Communications Inc., Plano, Texas

36.1 UNDERSTANDING CUSTOMER REQUIREMENTS

First and foremost in determining what acceptance criteria will be used to build or manufacture a printed circuit board assembly (PCBA) is to look at the contract between the supplier and the purchaser of the product. Always determine the needs and/or wants of the customer through contractual communications or, less formally, through talking to the customer if a contract is not detailed enough or a contract does not exist.

In some businesses, contracts are not the norms, such as for consumer electronics built for retail sale. In this case, the company must determine the level of quality desired based on company culture and goodwill, reputation for quality products, and the life cycle of the product. The company should decide to build product to an industry standard such as IPC-A-610, Acceptability of Electronic Assemblies, or develop their own workmanship manual that should closely match IPC-A-610 levels of quality. In any case, the workmanship manual must support the company's objectives to achieve customer satisfaction with their product.

Detailed specifications may be called out in a contract, such as in military specifications, or there may not be any documentation that identifies requirements. In the latter case, the recommendation is to revert to industry standards or an internal quality requirement such as a workmanship manual. Three common possibilities for acceptance criteria are discussed as follows.

36.1.1 Military, Telecommunications, and Consumer Specifications

Reference to these types of specifications are common in the applicable markets. No great amount of detail will be discussed; however, they are all worthy of some discussion.

36.1.1.1 Military Specifications. Generally, military specifications are not used in any market except for military products. There are a few exceptions to this, and the best example is MIL-STD-105, Sampling Procedures and Tables for Inspection by Attributes. This specification is used in many industries for multiple types of equipment. There are many military specifications that are applied to military electronics contracts. The ones with the most relevance to workmanship or acceptability criteria at the assembly level are MIL-STD-2000 and MIL-P-28809. There are many lower-level specifications for components and PCBs that can also be invoked. MIL-STD-2000 is titled Standard Requirements for Soldered Electrical and

Electronic Assemblies and MIL-P-28809 is titled Printed Wiring Assemblies. MIL-STD-2000 is used mainly for high-reliability requirements needed on military equipment and contains more stringent criteria than MIL-P-28809; therefore, this discussion focuses on MIL-STD-2000 criteria.

MIL-STD-2000 is a very detailed document and defines the defect types that must be reworked, repaired, or scrapped and cannot be used as is on government equipment. This, of course, takes away some flexibility from the manufacturer to evaluate a given defect type and make the decision to use the defect without rework or repair if it does not affect form, fit, or function.

MIL-STD-2000 also defines the assembly chemistry for a manufacturer in terms of solder composition, flux types, cleanliness, conformal coating, and solder mask. Any deviation from criteria specified in the document requires a qualification and procuring agency approval before use.

Solder connection characteristics for both plated-through-hole and surface-mount devices are defined by solder finish, physical attributes, fractures, voids, solder coverage, and wetting and filleting. The printed wiring board (PCB) requirements after assembly are detailed in terms of conductor finish and condition, conductor separation from the board, cleanliness of the assembly, PCB weave exposure, delamination, measles, haloing, and bow and twist. In addition, part markings must remain legible after assembly processing.

Also significant about MIL-STD-2000 requirements are the training of personnel and the subsequent certification that must be obtained in order to be authorized to work on product delivered under a MIL-STD-2000 contract. The specification also details methods for process control and defect reduction to be used in the assembly of PCBAs. One hundred percent inspection is required unless the following conditions are met, at which time a sample-based inspection may be utilized.

1. Training on utilization of process control and statistical methods is provided to personnel.
2. Quantitative evidence must be maintained that shows the process is in statistical control and is a capable process.
3. Sampling techniques must be statistically based and consistent with data collection requirements for maintaining process control.
4. Criteria for switching between sampling and 100 percent inspection must be defined. Sampling cannot be used if defect rates are above 2700 parts per million. If processes go out of control, 100 percent inspection must be instituted for the lot.
5. If defects are discovered in the sample, all hardware in that lot must be 100 percent inspected for other occurrences of the defect found.

36.1.1.2 Telecommunications-Bellcore TR-NWT-000078.[1] One of the most recognized requirements specifications in the telecommunications industry is Bell Communications Research (Bellcore) TR-NWT-000078, Generic Physical Design Requirements for Telecommunications Products and Equipment. This document was generated by Bellcore to be applied by their client companies for products to be used in the telecommunications network typical of a client company.

The specification is widely used by the Regional Bell Operating Companies (RBOC), and suppliers to the RBOCs are audited to the design and manufacturing requirements delineated within. Workmanship acceptability criteria are listed in some sections of the document; however, for the most part, TR-NWT-000078 does not show in any great detail the overall workmanship acceptability criteria for PCBAs.

36.1.1.3 Consumer Electronics. The key workmanship concerns for electronic assemblies for consumer products are the intended life cycle of the product and functionality of the unit. In many cases, the functionality can be achieved with less-than-acceptable workmanship attributes, but the product will lose some of its useful life since reliability of solder joints or mechanical strength may be affected. As stated earlier in this chapter, the company must determine the level of quality desired.

36.1.2 ANSI/J-STD and IPC-A-610 Industry Standards

The American National Standards Institute (ANSI) and the Institute for Interconnecting and Packaging Electronic Circuits (IPC) specifications are generally recognized as the standards for requirements and workmanship for PCB assemblies in many companies, both nationally and internationally. These specifications are gaining more recognition in the international arena and the trend to use them more is being seen.

36.1.2.1 ANSI/J-STD-001, Requirements for Soldered Electrical and Electronic Assemblies.

Another requirements document that is a little newer on the scene is the ANSI/J-STD-001, Requirements for Soldered Electrical and Electronic Assemblies,[2] which was first released in April 1992. This standard was a jointly developed document by the Electronics Industry Association (EIA) and the IPC.

ANSI/J-STD-001 classifies three levels of electronic assemblies based on end-item use. The three classifications were established to reflect differences in producibility, complexity, functional performance requirements, and verification frequency. The classes are as follows:

Class 1, General Electronic Products.   Includes consumer products, some computer and computer peripherals, and hardware suitable for applications where the major requirement is a function of the completed assembly.

Class 2, Dedicated Service Electronic Products.   Includes communications equipment, sophisticated business machines, and instruments where high performance and extended life are required, and for which uninterrupted service is desired but not critical. Typically the end-use environment would not cause failures.

Class 3, High-Performance Electronic Products.   Includes equipment for commercial and military products where continued performance or performance on demand is critical. Equipment downtime cannot be tolerated, end-use environment may be uncommonly harsh, and the equipment must function when required, such as in life-support systems and critical weapons systems.

ANSI/J-STD-001 addresses many of the same subjects as MIL-STD-2000,[3] but in most cases for Class 1 and 2 equipment, the requirements are less stringent. The Class 3 requirements in the majority of the subject areas are the same as MIL-STD-2000 requirements; however, there still remain a few areas that the military has not yet accepted. The IPC continues to try to get the joint military community to accept the ANSI/J-STD-001 specification as the military equipment standard and supersede all applicable military standards that currently exist.

36.1.2.2 ANSI/J-STD-002, Solderability Tests for Component Leads, Terminations, Lugs, Terminals and Wires.

The ANSI/J-STD-002,[4] Solderability Tests for Component Leads, Terminations, Lugs, Terminals and Wires, was released in April 1992 to complement the requirements of ANSI/J-STD-001. This standard prescribes the recommended test methods, defect definitions, acceptance criteria, and illustrations for assessing the solderability of electronic component leads, terminations, solid wire, stranded wire, lugs, and tabs.

Solderability evaluations are made to verify that the solderability of component leads and terminations meets the requirements established in ANSI/J-STD-002 and that subsequent storage has had no adverse effect on the ability to solder components to an interconnecting substrate. Determination of solderability can be made at the time of manufacture, at receipt of the components by the user, or just prior to assembly and soldering.

For a more detailed discussion of solderability issues refer to Sec. 36.5.

36.1.2.3   ANSI/J-STD-003, Solderability Tests for Printed Boards.   The ANSI/J-STD-003, Solderability Tests for Printed Boards,[5] was released in April 1992 to complement the requirements of ANSI/J-STD-001. This standard prescribes the recommended test methods, defect definitions and illustrations for assessing the solderability of printed board surface conductors, attachment lands, and plated-through-holes.

The solderability determination is made to verify that the PCB fabrication processes and subsequent storage have had no adverse effect on the solderability of those portions of the PCB intended to be soldered. This is determined by evaluation of the solderability specimen portion of a board or representative coupon which has been processed as part of the panel of boards and subsequently removed for testing per the method selected.

The objective of the solderability test methods described in ANSI/J-STD-003 is to determine the ability of printed board surface conductors, attachment lands, and plated-through-holes to wet easily with solder and to withstand the rigors of the PCB assembly processes.

For a more detailed discussion of solderability issues, refer to Sec. 36.5.

36.1.2.4   IPC-A-610, Acceptability of Electronic Assemblies.   As a companion document to ANSI/J-STD-001, a second document, IPC-A-610, Acceptability of Electronic Assemblies,[6] is used by many companies as the stand-alone workmanship standard for their products. The relationship of these two documents is that ANSI/J-STD-001 establishes the acceptability requirements for PCBA soldering, while IPC-A-610, when addressing soldering, is the complementary document. IPC-A-610 depicts the pictorial acceptability criteria for the requirements identified in the ANSI/J-STD-001 document. IPC-A-610 also addresses additional criteria which defines handling and mechanical workmanship requirements. A large percentage of the acceptability criteria defined in this chapter will be those criteria shown in the IPC-A-610.

The IPC-A-610 describes the acceptability criteria for producing quality soldering interconnections and assemblies. The methods used must produce a completed solder joint conforming to the acceptability requirements described in IPC-A-610. The IPC-A-610 document details the acceptance criteria for each class in three levels of quality: *target condition, acceptable,* and either *nonconforming defect* or *nonconforming process indicator.*

Target Condition.   This is a condition that is close to perfect and in the past has been labeled as preferred; however, it is a desirable condition and not always achievable and may not be necessary to ensure reliability of the assembly in its service environment.

Acceptable Condition.   This characteristic indicates a condition identified that, while not necessarily perfect, will maintain the integrity and reliability of the assembly in its service environment. Acceptable can be slightly better than the minimum end-product requirements to allow for shifts in the process.

Nonconforming Defect Condition.   A nonconforming defect is an identified condition that is insufficient to ensure the form, fit, or function of the assembly in its end-use environment. The manufacturer shall disposition (rework, repair, or scrap) the nonconforming product based on design, service, and customer requirements.

Nonconforming Process Indicator Condition.   Nonconforming process indicator is a condition which identifies a characteristic that does not affect the form, fit, or function of a product.

- Such condition *does* violate acceptance stated in IPC-A-610 or any other customer requirement.

- Such condition is a by-product of the process being out of control due to material, poor design, and operator- or machine-related causes.

- Such condition requires the manufacturer to get the process under control, identify causes, and take corrective action. The product affected will be dispositioned "Use as is."

If the manufacturer does not have a documented, customer-approved process control system, all nonconforming process indicators must be treated as nonconforming defects.

Nonconforming process indicators are characteristics that should be used to improve the process, because their occurrence signals a lack of good workmanship to the customer.

36.1.3 Workmanship Manuals

Many companies use a workmanship document of some sort. The IPC-A-610 is used frequently by manufacturing and quality personnel to determine acceptable quality levels of their product. There are companies that have developed very good workmanship manuals for their own use, but they also sell their manuals to any company that wishes to use them.

If a need exists to develop a unique workmanship manual, then this manual should be derived based on the contract requirements. It is desirable to use a manual already in existence since it can become very costly to develop your own.

36.2 HANDLING TO PROTECT THE PCBA

The handling of PCBs both before and after the soldering operation can be very important in terms of inducing possible damage to the board or contaminating the board such that subsequent operations are affected. There are three subjects that should be well thought out and controlled in an assembly operation for PCBAs: electrostatic discharge (ESD) protection, contamination prevention, and physical damage prevention.

36.2.1 ESD Protection

ESD is the rapid discharge of a voltage potential into an electronic assembly. ESD-sensitive components found on the assembly and the amount of current generated by the discharge will determine if electrostatic overstress or complete failure takes place.

Some electronic devices are more sensitive to electrostatic overstress (EOS) damage than others (Table 36.1). The degree of such sensitivity within a particular device is related directly to the manufacturing technology employed.

Where sensitive components are handled, protective measures must be taken to prevent component damage. Improper and careless handling accounts for a significant portion of ESD damage to components and assemblies. Before handling ESD-sensitive components, equipment should be carefully tested to ensure that it does not generate damage-causing spikes. The preferred workstation to be utilized in electronic assembly is shown in Fig. 36.1.

TABLE 36.1 Approximate EOS/ESD Damage Range for Some Components

Device type	Range of min. EOS/ESD susceptibility, V
VMOS	30–1800
MOSFET	100–200
GaAsFET	100–300
EPROM	100+
JFET	140–7000
SAW	150–500
Op-amp	190–2500
CMOS	250–3000
Schottky diodes	300–2500
Film resistors (thick, thin)	300–3000
Bipolar transistors	380–7800
ECL (PDC board level)	500–1500
SCR	680–1000
Schottky TTL	100–2500

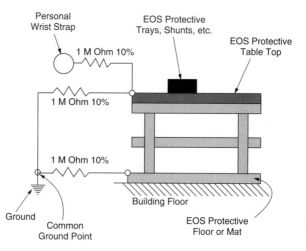

FIGURE 36.1 Target condition for EOS/ESD workstation. *(IPC.)*

Static charges are created when nonconductive materials are separated. Destructive static charges are often induced on nearby conductors, such as human skin, and discharged as sparks passing between conductors. This can happen when a PCBA is touched by a person having a static charge potential. The electronic assembly can be damaged as the discharge passes through the conductive pattern to a static-sensitive component. Static discharges may be too low to be felt by humans (less than 3500 V) and still damage ESD-sensitive components.

Sensitive components and assemblies must be enclosed in conductive, static-shielding bags, boxes, or wraps when not being worked on, unless otherwise protected. ESD-sensitive items must be removed from protective enclosures only at static dissipative or antistatic workstations. For ESD safety, a path-to-ground must be provided for static charges that would otherwise discharge on a device or board assembly. Provisions are made for grounding the worker's skin, preferably via a wrist strap or a heel strap, provided conductive flooring is used.

36.2.2 Contamination Prevention

The key to any contamination problem is to prevent it from happening. The cost of subsequent operations required to clean a product or rework a product are orders of magnitude more than any cost associated with preventing the contamination from occurring. These contaminants can cause soldering and solder mask or conformal coating problems. There are any number of possibilities of inducing contamination in an assembly environment, such as dirt, dust, machine oils, and process residues; however, in many cases, contamination is caused by the human body as salts and oils on the skin.

In a high percentage of assembly areas, good housekeeping will take care of contamination from the environment. It should be a common event on each shift to clean workstations, sweep floors, dust fixtures, empty trash, etc. This not only prevents contamination, but it also helps to keep personnel morale at a higher level. After all, we all desire to work in a nice, clean environment. It will also serve as a positive point if visitors or possible customers visit the assembly area.

To prevent contamination from the human body, every individual must be aware of the possibility of contaminating the PCBA. PCBAs should be touched only on the edges away from any edge connectors prior to the soldering operation (Fig. 36.2). Where a firm grip on the board is required due to any mechanical assembly procedures, gloves or finger cots should be worn. If the PCBA is to be conformal coated after the soldering operation, the handling of the

FIGURE 36.2   PCBA edge handling. *(IPC.)*

board is still very important to prevent contamination from fingerprints. In this case, gloves or finger cots should be worn until conformal coating is complete.

36.2.3 Physical Damage Prevention

Improper handling can damage components and assemblies. Typical defects associated with handling are cracked, chipped, or broken components, bent or broken terminals, scratched board surfaces, damaged traces or lands, fractured solder joints, and missing SMT components. Physical damage caused by handling can ruin assemblies and cause a high scrap rate of components or assemblies. Scrap is costly and must be avoided to have an efficient and high-quality operation.

Well-maintained handling equipment is also very important in preventing physical damage. One good example is conveyor systems when utilized. PCBAs can be caught in conveyors and damaged beyond rework or repair and, unless the area of operation is staffed, the conveyor system can damage multiple assemblies in a very short period of time.

36.3   PCBA HARDWARE ACCEPTABILITY CONSIDERATIONS

Most electronic assembly designs include a small percentage of mechanical assembly that uses hardware of various types to complete the assembly. Some of the more common component types and the acceptability criteria associated with each are discussed in the following sections.

36.3.1 Component Types

36.3.1.1 Threaded Fasteners.   Hardware stack-up for all threaded fasteners must be identified on engineering documentation. The stack-up can be critical, depending on the types of

material used for both the hardware and the PCB (Fig. 36.3). Any missing hardware is a problem that must be corrected for obvious reasons. Any damage to hardware that prevents it from accomplishing what it was designed to do is unacceptable. A good example of this is screws or nuts that have been stripped, cross-threaded, or damaged to the point that a screw or nut driver is no longer able to tighten or loosen the part (Fig. 36.4).

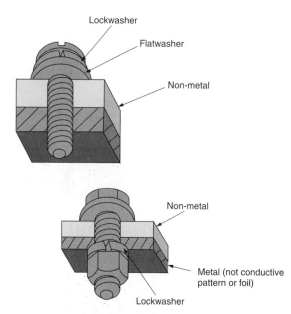

FIGURE 36.3   Hardware mounting for threaded fasteners. *(IPC.)*

FIGURE 36.4   PCBA hardware damage. *(IPC.)*

A minimum of 1½ threads shall extend beyond the threaded hardware unless the hardware could interfere with other components. The maximum extension of threaded hardware is 3 mm plus 1½ threads for hardware up to 25 mm long and 6.3 mm plus 1½ threads for hardware greater than 25 mm long.

Threaded fasteners shall be tight to the specified torque on engineering documentation. If torque is not specified on engineering documentation, a generic torque table should be available for use in the assembly environment. This is sometimes included in a workmanship manual.

36.3.1.2 Mounting Clips. Uninsulated metallic components, clips, or holding devices must be insulated from underlying circuitry. Minimum electrical spacing between land and uninsulated component body must not be violated (Fig. 36.5).

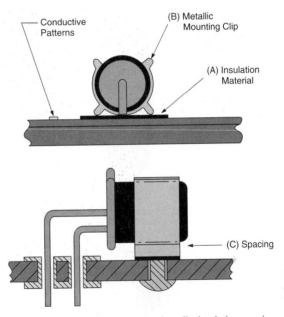

FIGURE 36.5 Component mounting clip insulation requirements. *(IPC.)*

The clip or holding device must make contact with the component sides on both ends of the component. The component must be mounted with its center of gravity within the confines of the clip or holding device. The end of the component may be flush or extend beyond the end of the clip or holding device if the center of gravity is within the confines of the clip or holding device (Fig. 36.6).

36.3.1.3 Heat Sinks. Visual inspection should include hardware security, component or hardware damage, and correct sequence of assembly. Heat sinks must be mounted flush (in contact) with the surface to provide for adequate thermal conductivity. The component must be in contact with three quarters of the mounting surface to be considered flush (Fig. 36.7). It is unacceptable to have the heat sink mounted on the wrong side of the board, a bent or cracked heat sink, or missing fins on the heat sink. Any hardware mounts must be tight enough to prevent the component from being moved.

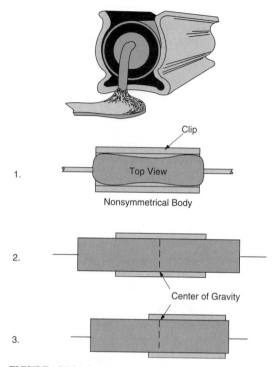

1. Clip

Top View

Nonsymmetrical Body

2.

Center of Gravity

3.

FIGURE 36.6 Component mounting clip orientation requirements. *(IPC.)*

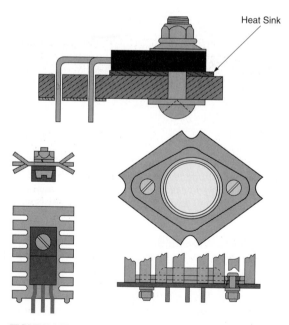

Heat Sink

FIGURE 36.7 Heat-sink acceptability requirements. *(IPC.)*

36.3.1.4   Terminals.   Terminals that are to be soldered to a land may be mounted such that they can be turned by hand, but should be stable in the *z* axis. Terminals may be bent if the top edge does not extend beyond the base and no other mechanical damage such as fractures or breakage to the terminal or the solder joint have occurred (Fig. 36.8). Ordinarily the terminals utilized are turret, bifurcated, hook, and pierced or perforated terminals.

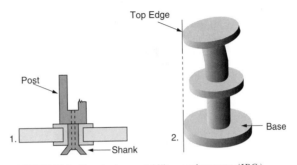

FIGURE 36.8   Terminal acceptability requirements. *(IPC.)*

36.3.1.5   Rivets and Funnels.   Rivet and funnel barrels that extend above the substrate should be swaged or rolled to create an inverted cone, uniform in spread and concentric to the hole being mechanically fastened. The swaged or rolled flange should not be split, cracked, or otherwise damaged to the extent that mechanical strength is compromised or allows contaminating materials to be entrapped in the rivet or funnel (Fig. 36.9).

FIGURE 36.9   Rivet swage. *(IPC.)*

After swage or roll of the rivet or funnel, the rolled area should be free of circumferential splits or cracks. It may have a maximum of three radial splits or cracks, provided that the splits or cracks are separated by at least 90° and do not extend into the barrel of the rivet or funnel (Fig. 36.10).

The rivet mandrel cannot be pulled below the seating plane that is defined as the surface of the substrate being mechanically fastened (Fig. 36.11). As long as the mandrel was captured

FIGURE 36.10 Rivet swage split into barrel. *(IPC.)*

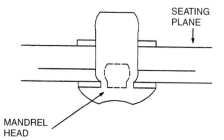

FIGURE 36.11 PCBA rivet—mandrel pulled below seating plane. *(DSC Communications.)*

long enough to form the rivet to secure the material, the mandrel need not be present; i.e., it may have fallen out of the rivet (Fig. 36.12). In all cases, the rivet or funnel must be mechanically secure in the z axis.

36.3.1.6 Rivet-Mounted Ejectors, Handles, and Connectors. Ejectors, handles, and connectors should not exhibit any cracks in the component material emanating from the roll pin or rivet that mounts the component to the PCBA. Roll pins should not protrude more than 0.015 in from the surface of the ejector, handle, or connector (Fig. 36.13). The major consideration for roll pins should be to ensure that any protrusion does not mechanically interfere with any other assembly. Damage to the part, PCB, or securing hardware is unacceptable.

Connector damage can also be the pins of the connector being pushed or bent out of specification. When connectors are mated there is the chance that the female portion of the connector pin will be pushed backwards and bent. This prevents adequate contact area between the male and female pins of the connector if it will mate at all. This circumstance is an unacceptable condition. There also exists the chance that the male connector pins can be bent. When the male pin is bent significantly, the mating of the female

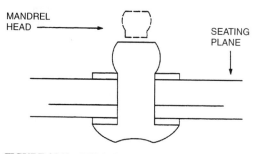

FIGURE 36.12 PCBA rivet—mandrel secured material correctly. *(DSC Communications.)*

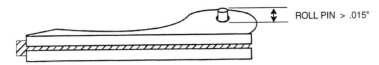

FIGURE 36.13 PCBA ejector roll—pin protrusion—nonconforming. *(DSC Communications.)*

and male connectors can cause mechanical damage to the connector casing due to the male pin being forced into the wrong female connector slot. In most cases, the damage is deformation, cracking, or breakage of the connector casing material, which are unacceptable.

When connector pins are installed (such as compliant pin, press fit), the pins must be straight within 50 percent of the pin thickness from the perpendicular. For Class 1 and 2 equipment, the PCB land may be lifted less than or equal to 75 percent of the annular ring width. Any land which is lifted across more than 75 percent of the annular ring or has been fractured is unacceptable (Fig. 36.14). For Class 3 equipment, no lifted or fractured lands are acceptable. For all classes, visibly twisted pins, damaged pins, or pins inserted such that there is a nonstandard pin height beyond a specified engineering tolerance is unacceptable.

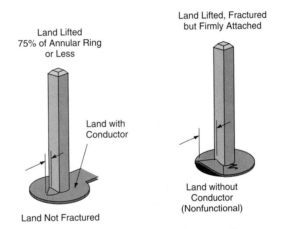

FIGURE 36.14 Connector pin installation requirements. *(IPC.)*

36.3.1.7 Faceplates. Faceplates must be clean and free of scratches or damage on the front surface. This is important since this is the surface that is commonly viewed by the customer and presents the cosmetic appeal to the product being purchased. An overexaggerated example of this is the purchase of an automobile. Few, if any, consumers would be willing to accept a new automobile with noticeable scratches in the painted surface.

A good rule of thumb for scratch criteria that some companies have adopted as a workmanship standard includes the following:

1. A scratch must be visible when viewed under the following conditions to be considered a defect:
   a. From a distance of 18 in
   b. No magnification utilized
   c. Normal room lighting used in the assembly area

2. A scratch must be visible from more than one angle to be considered a defect.

3. Metal or plastic faceplate scratches that exceed 0.125 in in length are considered a defect.

Surfaces exposed to frequent viewing should be free of blisters, runs, nicks, gouges, blemishes, or other abrasions that would detract from the general appearance of the finish. Faceplates must also be securely fastened to the PCB, i.e., tight enough to prevent physical movement.

36.3.1.8 Stiffeners. Stiffeners are commonly used on PCBA designs that are large in dimension to prevent warpage of the PCBA before, during, or after assembly operations. If a stiffener has kept a PCBA from warping outside acceptability criteria, it has done its job; however, the stiffener must meet the following criteria to be acceptable.

1. Any marking or color coatings must be permanent. Loss of marking such that it is not legible, or fading or loss of color outside the color standard being used, is unacceptable.

2. The stiffener must be properly seated and mechanically fastened. If the soldering operation is used to mechanically fasten the stiffener to the PCBA, then good wetting to the stiffener such that the stiffener is mechanically sound is required.

3. It is unacceptable to have a loose stiffener on a PCBA; i.e., the stiffener is not securely fastened to the PCBA.

36.3.2 Electrical Clearance

Electrical clearance of hardware to components or traces carrying current must be controlled by the design engineer. In the past, IPC-A-610 required that 0.030 in minimum be maintained between hardware and any current-carrying material. This is no longer felt to be a requirement since lower levels of currents and voltages are frequently used in some PCBA designs today (Fig. 36.15).

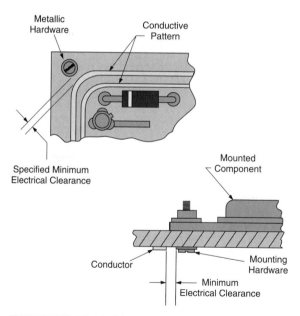

FIGURE 36.15 Electrical clearance—hardware to components. *(IPC.)*

It, therefore, becomes very important for the designer to identify the minimum electrical clearance required between hardware and current-carrying materials on the design documentation. For any given PCBA design, the electrical clearance should be verified by assemblers or inspectors to ensure that a shorting condition does not occur.

One example of a specification that has a definite requirement in this area is the Bellcore TR-NWT-000078 that requires a minimum of 0.005 in electrical clearance between uninsulated, noncommon conductive surfaces.

36.3.3 Physical Damage

Physical damage to hardware components in most cases refers to enough damage to a component to render it unusable in its application—for example, threads that are damaged to the point that mechanical fastening cannot be performed or a component that is fractured or broken such that it cannot perform the function for which it was intended.

Subjective judgments are common in this area since it is very much dependent on the application of the hardware in the given design, the environment in which the final product will be used, and life cycle expectations of the product.

36.4 COMPONENT INSTALLATION OR PLACEMENT REQUIREMENTS

Component installation or placement is the first step in the assembly of the PCBA. It may begin by preparation of the leads of a given package type in order to provide the correct lead protrusion, form the leads to fit the PCB plated-through-holes or pads, or put a bend in the leads which will serve as a standoff from the component to the PCB.

36.4.1 Plated-Through-Hole (PTH) Lead Installation

There are several requirements that apply to all PTH components. When using a polarized component, it must be oriented correctly. In all cases, the orientation must be correct or the board is unacceptable (Fig. 36.16), and when lead forming is required, the lead form must provide stress relief. Physical damage to the lead itself cannot exceed 10 percent of the diameter of the lead. Exposed basis metal as a result of lead deformation is a process indicator but does not render the board unacceptable.

36.4.1.1 Axial Leaded Components.   The target condition for axial components is that the entire body length of the component should be parallel and in contact with the board surface, provided the component dissipates less than 1 W of power. If the component dissipates more than 1 W of power, it must be mounted a minimum of 1.5 mm above the PCB surface to prevent burning or scorching the surface. The maximum space between the component and the PCB surface shall not violate the requirements for lead protrusion and cannot be greater than 3.0 mm for Class 1 and 2 and 0.7 mm for Class 3 equipment (Fig. 36.17).

Leads must extend from the component body at least one lead diameter (L) or thickness, but not less than 0.8 mm from the body or weld, before the start of the lead bend radius (Fig. 36.18).

No physical damage, such as chips or cracks to axial components, should be allowed; however, it is acceptable to allow minor damage. It becomes unacceptable if the insulating cover is damaged to the extent that the metallic element is exposed or the component shape is deformed (Fig. 36.19).

36.4.1.2 Radial Leaded Components.   The target condition for radial components is that the body is perpendicular to the PCB and the component base is parallel to the PCB. It is an

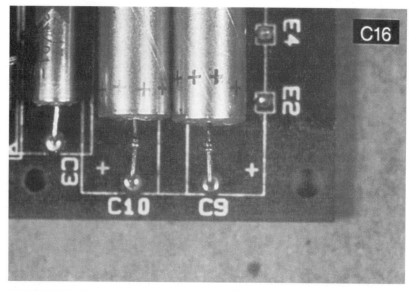

FIGURE 36.16 Component orientation—polarity. *(IPC.)*

FIGURE 36.17 Axial leaded component—above PCBA mounting. *(IPC.)*

acceptable condition to have the component tilt no more than 15° from the perpendicular. The space between the component base and PCB must be between 0.25 and 2.0 mm to be acceptable (Fig. 36.20). For components that have a coating meniscus, lack of visible clearance between the coating meniscus and the solder fillet is unacceptable but can be acceptable for Class 1 and 2 equipment under the following conditions:

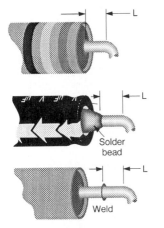

FIGURE 36.18 Lead extension from component body. *(IPC.)*

1. There is no risk of thermal damage to the component.

2. The component mass is less than 10 g.

3. The voltage is not greater than 240 V_{ac} RMS or 240 V_{dc} (Fig. 36.21).

Minor physical damage such as scratches, chips, or crazing to radial components is acceptable provided they do not expose the component substrate or active element and structural integrity is not compromised (Fig. 36.22).

36.4.2 Surface-Mount Technology (SMT) Placement

Coplanarity is very important in the placement of SMT components with leads. Occasionally, lead preparation to form the leads of SMT components is necessary to achieve the proper coplanarity for manual or automatic placement of components on the PCB. Most times, however, the components are purchased packaged with leads prepped and ready to be automatically placed by pick-and-place equipment. Another critical parameter for all surface-mounted components is the accuracy of the placement of the component onto the pads of the PCB.

36.4.2.1 Chip Components. Side overhang is acceptable up to one-half (one-quarter for Class 3) the width of the component end cap or PCB pad. End-cap overhang is not acceptable for all classes. The end-cap solder joint width is acceptable with a minimum solder joint length of one-half (three-quarters for Class 3) the component end cap or PCB land, whichever is less. A side solder joint length is not required; however, a properly wetted fillet must be evident.

FIGURE 36.19 Damaged axial leaded component. *(IPC.)*

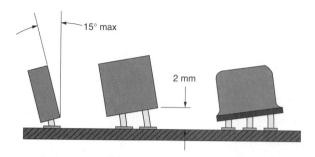

FIGURE 36.20   Radial leaded components—tilt and spacing. *(IPC.)*

FIGURE 36.21   Radial component coating meniscus in the PTH. *(IPC.)*

The maximum solder fillet height may overhang the land or extend onto the top of the end-cap metallization; however, the solder should not extend farther on the component body. The minimum solder fillet height must cover one-quarter the thickness, or height, of the component end cap. The component end cap must have overlap contact with the PCB pad. There is no minimum contact length specified (Fig. 36.23).

36.4.2.2   MELF or Cylindrical Components.   Side overhang is acceptable up to one-quarter the diameter of the end cap. End-cap overhang is not acceptable for all classes. The end-cap solder joint width is acceptable with a minimum solder joint length of one-half the diameter of the component end cap. A side solder joint length must be a minimum of one-half (three-quarters for Class 3) the end-cap thickness as measured from the end of the component toward the center of the component. The maximum solder fillet height may overhang the land or extend onto the top of the end-cap metallization; however, the solder should not extend farther on the component body. The minimum solder fillet height must cover one-quarter the thickness, or height, of the component end cap for Class 3 equipment and for Classes 1 and 2,

FIGURE 36.22   Damaged radial leaded component. *(IPC.)*

the minimum solder fillet must exhibit proper wetting. The component end cap must have overlap contact with the PCB pad. There is no minimum contact length specified (Fig. 36.24).

36.4.2.3 *Castellated Termination Leadless Chip Carrier Components.*   Side overhang is acceptable up to one-half (one-quarter for Class 3) the castellation width. End overhang of the castellation is not acceptable for all classes. The castellation end solder joint width is acceptable with a minimum solder joint length of one-half (three-quarters for Class 3) the castellation width. A minimum side solder joint length is one-eighth the castellation solder fillet height. The maximum solder fillet height is not a specified parameter for this type

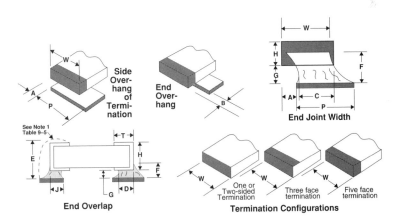

W = Width of Termination Area • T = Length of Termination • H = Height of Termination • P = Width of Land

FIGURE 36.23   Chip components—placement and soldering requirements. *(IPC.)*

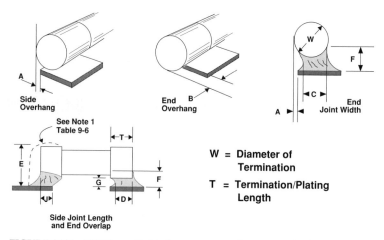

FIGURE 36.24 MELF or cylindrical components—placement and soldering requirements. *(IPC.)*

component. The minimum solder fillet height must cover one-quarter the castellation height (Fig. 36.25).

36.4.2.4 Gullwing Leaded Components. Side overhang is acceptable up to one-half (one-quarter for Class 3) the width of the component lead or 0.5 mm, whichever is less. Lead toe overhang is acceptable provided it does not violate minimum conductor spacing or solder joint fillet requirements for all classes. The end lead solder joint width is acceptable with a minimum solder joint length of one-half (three-quarters for Class 3) the component lead width. The lead side solder joint minimum length is one-half (three-quarters for Class 3) the component lead width. For maximum solder fillet height on *high*-profile devices such as QFPs

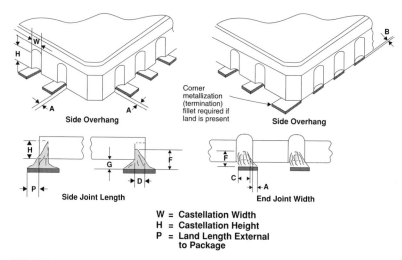

FIGURE 36.25 Castellated termination leadless chip carrier components—placement and soldering requirements. *(IPC.)*

and SOLs, the solder may extend to, but not touch, the package body or end seal. For maximum solder fillet height on *low*-profile devices such as SOICs and SOTs, the solder may extend to the package. The solder must not extend under the package in any case. The minimum solder fillet height must cover one-half the lead thickness (Fig. 36.26).

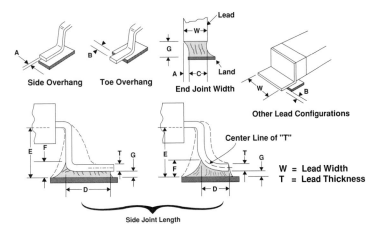

FIGURE 36.26 Gullwing leaded components—placement and soldering requirements. *(IPC.)*

The same criteria for acceptability of placement and soldering of gullwing components can be applied to round or coined (flattened) leaded components if utilized.

36.4.2.5 J-Leaded Components.   Side overhang is acceptable up to one-half (one-quarter for Class 3) the width of the component lead. Lead toe overhang is not specified for any class. The end lead solder joint width is acceptable with a minimum solder joint length of one-half (three-quarters for Class 3) the component lead width. A side solder joint length must be a minimum of 1½ times the lead width. The maximum solder fillet height is not specified; however, the solder fillet may not touch the component package body. The minimum heel solder fillet height must cover one-half the thickness of the component lead. The minimum solder thickness from PCB pad to component lead is not specified; however, there must be sufficient solder to form a properly wetted fillet (Fig. 36.27).

36.4.2.6 Ball Grid Array (BGA) Components.   BGA package components are relatively new types of components being used on PCBs. Although extremely desirable for the designers to use to get more function in a smaller space, this type of component package is virtually impossible to inspect visually. The prevailing thought on verifying compliance to workmanship standards is to verify the function through an in-circuit and/or functional test of the BGA circuit. If cost justification exists, due to volume or reliability requirements such as could be the case on Class 3 equipment, x-ray equipment can be used to verify the quality and integrity of the solder joints. This particular option is quite costly in terms of the upfront capital investment of the x-ray equipment but may pay for itself many times over in customer satisfaction.

36.4.3 Use of Adhesives

Adhesives can be used in surface-mount and PTH applications.

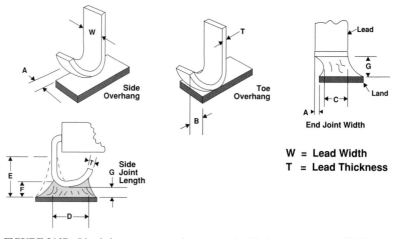

FIGURE 36.27   J-leaded components—placement and soldering requirements. *(IPC.)*

For SMT components, the most common use of adhesive is placing components onto the secondary side of the PCB, i.e., the side opposite the PTH components. In many process flows, the secondary-side SMT components are placed onto adhesive between PCB pads; the PCB is processed through an adhesive curing cycle; then the components are wave soldered onto the PCB along with the PTH components. The SMT components are acceptable as long as the adhesive has not contaminated the solder joint. If adhesive has contaminated the component solderable surface, lead or end cap, or the PCB pad such that an acceptable solder joint is not achieved, the PCBA is not acceptable.

Normally in PTH component application, adhesive is used to give large-profile and/or heavy components more mechanical stability. When used in this manner the following adhesive acceptance criteria apply:

- The adhesive must adhere to a *flush-mounted axial* component for 75 percent of the component length and 25 percent of its diameter on one side. The buildup of adhesive must not exceed 50 percent of the component diameter and adhesion to the mounting surface must be evident (Fig. 36.28).

- The adhesive must adhere to a *vertically mounted axial* component for 50 percent of the component length and 25 percent of its circumference, and adhesion to the mounting surface must be evident (Fig. 36.29).

- For components elevated from the PCB which weigh 7 g or more per lead, the component should be bonded to the mounting surface in at least four places and at least 20 percent of the total periphery of the component is bonded. The adhesion from component to mounting surface must be evident (Fig. 36.30).

36.5   COMPONENT AND PCB SOLDERABILITY REQUIREMENTS

Component solderability, which includes the solderability of the PCB, is probably the most important single characteristic to consider in building PCBAs. To be successful in soldering PCBAs, good wetting must be achieved. It is an ongoing effort to ensure that all PCBs and electrical components purchased and received from suppliers maintain good solderability.

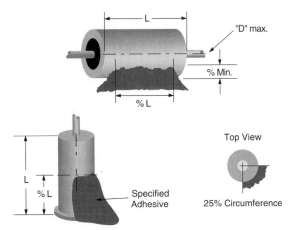

FIGURE 36.28   Adhesive bonding—axial components. *(IPC.)*

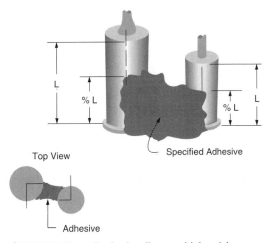

FIGURE 36.29   Adhesive bonding—multiple axial components. *(IPC.)*

The key to success in this all-important task is to have an excellent working relationship with the suppliers and manufacturers of the components to ensure good, solderable components. Until partnership relationships are achieved with suppliers, there should be a sample of each lot or batch of components received that are subjected to solderability testing. This testing should be conducted in accordance with ANSI/J-STD-002 and ANSI/J-STD-003. These documents were written to specifically address solderability requirements for electronic assembly components and PCBs.

Packaging and handling of components is important to maintain good solderability since many contaminants that could affect solderability can be transferred to solderable surfaces as a result of handling by equipment or personnel. Another possible problem that must be avoided is aging of the components. As tin-lead component lead finishes age, they will oxidize, and this oxidation will affect solderability of the component to the PCB. A rule of thumb used by many companies is to suspect solderability on components 2 or more years old. In some

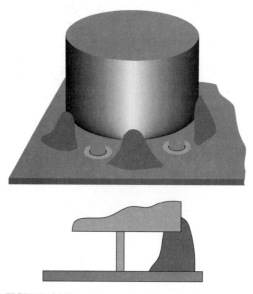

FIGURE 36.30 Adhesive bonding—elevated components >7 g per lead. *(IPC.)*

cases this can be tracked easily for components marked with a date code. Other components too small to mark or that for some other reason are not marked with a date code cannot be traced easily. Many times companies keep records on the date of receipt and base the age of the component on this date. Although not completely accurate, it serves the purpose. If components are known to be over 2 years old, a new solderability sample should be pulled to determine if the components are still usable. Many times, they are not usable due to oxidation or some other contaminant the component has been exposed to over time.

36.6 SOLDER-RELATED DEFECTS

All solder joints should exhibit wetting as shown by a concave meniscus between the component and PCB being soldered. The outline of the component being soldered should be easily determined. The most common solder defects produced by the soldering process are discussed in the following sections.

36.6.1 Plated-Through-Hole Solder Joint Minimum Acceptable Conditions

Table 36.2 shows the minimum acceptable plated-through-hole solder joint criteria.

36.6.2 Solder Balls or Solder Splash

Solder balls/splashes that violate minimum electrical design clearance, are not encapsulated in a permanent coating, or attached to a metal surface are unacceptable. Solder balls/splashes that are within 0.13 mm of lands or traces or exceed 0.13 mm in diameter are considered to be

TABLE 36.2   Minimum Acceptable PTH Solder Joint Criteria

Criteria	Class 1	Class 2	Class 3
Circumferential wetting on the primary side, including lead and barrel	Not specified	180°	270°
Vertical fill of solder*†	Not specified	*†	*†
Circumferential fillet, and wetting on the secondary side	270°	270°	330°
% of original land area covered with wetted solder, primary side	0	0	0
% of original land area covered with wetted solder, secondary side	75	75	75

    * A total maximum of 25 percent depression, including both solder source and destination sides, is permitted.
    † A total maximum of 50 percent depression, including both solder source and destination sides, is permitted on PTHs connected to voltage or ground planes. Solder must extend 360° around the lead and 100 percent wet PTH barrel walls to lead on the secondary side (Fig. 36.31).

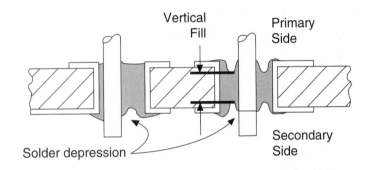

Minimum Acceptable for all Classes per Table 36.2

FIGURE 36.31   PTH solder fill requirements. *(IPC.)*

process indicators. Also considered as process indicators are more than five solder balls/splashes of a diameter of 0.13 mm or less in a 600-mm² area (Fig. 36.32).

36.6.3   Dewetting and Nonwetting

Dewetting is a condition that results when molten solder coats a surface and then recedes to leave irregularly shaped mounds of solder that are separated by areas that are covered with a thin film of solder and with the basis metal not exposed (Fig. 36.33). *Nonwetting* is the partial adherence of molten solder to a surface that it has contacted, while the basis metal remains exposed (Fig. 36.34).

    Dewetting and nonwetting of solder joints is generally caused by contaminants on either the component leads or on the PCB PTH or pads. A minimum of dewetting is allowed on solder joints assuming that the solder joint meets minimum requirements as defined in Table 36.2 and Sec. 36.4.2 by component package type, and good wetting is evident on the portion of the solder joint which does not display dewetting. Nonwetting is not acceptable since adequate wetting is not achieved and indicates a serious solderability problem on the component or the PCB.

FIGURE 36.32   Solder balls and solder splash requirements. *(IPC.)*

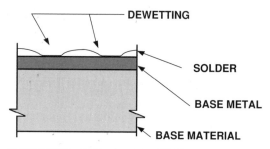

FIGURE 36.33   Solder dewetting. *(IPC.)*

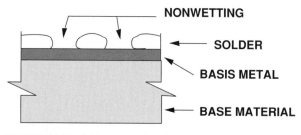

FIGURE 36.34   Solder nonwetting. *(IPC.)*

36.6.4   Missing and Insufficient Solder

Missing solder is an obvious unacceptable condition since solder provides electrical continuity and some measure of mechanical fastening of the component to the PCB.

Insufficient solder becomes an unacceptable condition for SMT components when minimum solder fillet requirements defined in Sec. 36.4.2 are not achieved. Insufficient solder becomes unacceptable for PTH components when the minimum requirements of Sec. 36.6.1 and Table 36.2 are not achieved.

36.6.5   Solder Webbing and Bridging

Solder bridged between electrically noncommon conductors creates a shorting condition and is an unacceptable condition. Solder webbing is a continuous film of solder that is parallel to, but not necessarily adhering to, a surface that should be free of solder. Solder webbing is also an unacceptable condition.

For components with leads, with the exception of criteria stated in Sec. 36.4.2.4, solder cannot come into contact with the component body or end seal. If solder contacts the component body or end seal it is an unacceptable.

36.6.6   Lead Protrusion Problems

Measurement of lead protrusion is defined as the distance from the top of the PCB land to the outermost part of the component lead, which can include any solder projection from the lead. Solder projections (icicles) are unacceptable if they violate lead protrusion maximum requirements or electrical clearance, or if they pose a safety hazard; otherwise, solder projections are an acceptable condition on both SMT or PTH components.

For single-sided PCBAs, lead or wire protrusion must be a minimum of 0.5 mm for all classes. For double-sided and multilayer PCBAs in all classes, the minimum lead protrusion is that the lead end be visible in the solder. The maximum lead protrusion for Class 1 is that there be *no danger of shorts* when the PCBA is used in its assembly application. For Class 2, the maximum lead protrusion is 2.5 mm and for Class 3 the maximum lead protrusion is 1.5 mm (Fig. 36.35).

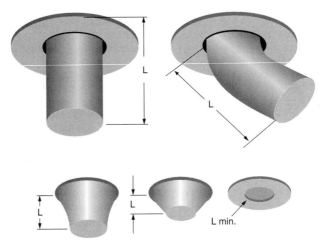

FIGURE 36.35   Lead protrusion requirements. *(IPC.)*

One notable exception to the lead protrusion requirement is for PCBs greater than 2.3 mm thick (nominal). For components with preestablished lead lengths—i.e., the leads are not cut to length by the board assembler—lead protrusion may not be visible and the PCBA is still considered to be acceptable. Some examples of components this may apply to are single/dual in-line packaged ICs (SIPs/DIPs), sockets, transformers/inductors, pin grid arrays (PGAs), and power transistors.

This relaxation of lead protrusion requirements is driven by the fact that some components are not offered in an array of different lead lengths by their manufacturers. When these types of components are used on PCBs of a thickness of 2.3 mm or greater, the lead will not protrude beyond the land by design. This exception should not be used as a license by the designer to select components on PCBAs which do not meet lead protrusion requirements. In many cases, components are available in longer lead lengths to accommodate the use of thick PCBs and should be utilized.

36.6.7   Voids, Pits, Blowholes, and Pinholes

Solder cavities (voids, pits, blowholes, pinholes, dewetting) are acceptable, provided the lead and land/pad are wetted and solder fillets meet requirements per Table 36.2. The areas adjacent to the solder cavity must be properly wetted and the bottom of the solder cavity must be visible with no basis metal exposed.

36.6.8 Disturbed or Fractured Solder Joints

Solder joints may be disturbed, i.e., rough, granular, or uneven in appearance, provided the wetting coverage criterion in Table 36.2 is met. Solder joints that have been fractured or cracked are unacceptable for all classes of equipment.

For solder joints in which leads have been trimmed after soldering, the solder joint cannot be damaged by the cutters due to physical shock. If lead cutting is required after solder, the solder joint shall be reflowed or visually inspected at 10× magnification to assure that the solder connection was not damaged as a result of the cutting operation. No fractures or cracks are allowed between the lead and solder (Fig. 36.36).

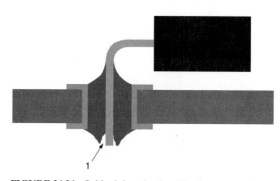

FIGURE 36.36   Solder joint—lead to fillet fracture. *(IPC.)*

36.6.9 Excess Solder

Excess solder conditions which produce a solder fillet that is slightly convex, or bulbous, and in which the lead is no longer visible are considered process indicator defects. This is an acceptable condition, assuming the condition is, indeed, excess solder and not the loss of lead protrusion due to component float, component tilt, or leads cut too short because of incorrect lead preparation. The exception for PCBs 2.3 mm or greater in thickness still applies (Fig. 36.37).

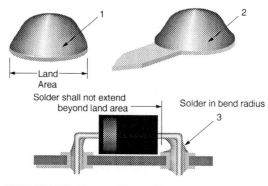

FIGURE 36.37   Excess solder requirements. *(IPC.)*

36.6.10 Solder Requirements for Vias

Plated-through-via-holes used only for interfacial connection do not need to be filled with solder if they were not exposed to a soldering process. This is usually achieved through temporary or permanent masks over the vias during the soldering process. Plated-through-holes or vias without leads when exposed to a soldering process should meet the acceptability requirements listed here.

1. The target condition is to have the holes completely filled with solder and the top of the lands show good wetting.
2. The minimum acceptable condition is the sides of the plated-through-hole are wetted with solder.
3. When solder has not wet the sides of the plated-through-hole, it will be considered a process indicator defect and product will not be rejected (Fig. 36.38).

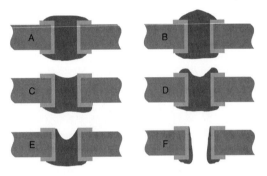

FIGURE 36.38 Via-hole solder fill requirements. *(IPC.)*

36.6.11 Soldering to Terminals

When soldering wire to terminals, the lead outline must be visible and good wetting between the wire and terminal must be evident to be acceptable. The wire insulation to terminal gap can be near zero if the insulation has not melted into the solder joint and a full 90° wrapped solder connection is evident. Slight melting of the insulation is acceptable. If the insulation gap is too large and allows potential shorting of wire to an electrically noncommon conductor, the joint is unacceptable. If the wire insulation is severely burned and the melt by-product intrudes into the solder joint, the joint is unacceptable (Fig. 36.39).

36.7 PCBA LAMINATE CONDITION, CLEANLINESS, AND MARKING REQUIREMENTS

36.7.1 Laminate Conditions

Laminate defect conditions may be caused by the laminator, PCB fabricator, or the assembly of the PCB. The major laminate conditions seen are measling, crazing, blistering, delamination, weave exposure, and haloing.

36.7.1.1 Measling and Crazing.   *Measling* is an internal condition occurring in laminated base material in which the glass fibers are separated from the resin at the weave intersections.

FIGURE 36.39 Soldering wire to a terminal. *(IPC.)*

This condition manifests itself in the form of white spots or crosses below the surface of the base material and is usually related to *thermally* induced stress.

Crazing is an internal condition occurring in laminated base material in which the glass fibers are separated from the resin at the weave intersections. This condition manifests itself in the form of connected white spots or crosses below the surface of the base material and is usually related to *mechanically* induced stress (Fig. 36.40).

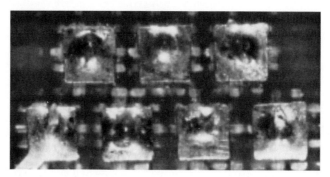

FIGURE 36.40 PCB crazing. *(IPC.)*

Measling or crazing that occurs as a result of an inherent weakness in the laminate is a warning of a potentially serious problem. If measling or crazing occur in the assembly process, they will usually not propagate further nor evolve into a more serious problem.

By the time a PCB enters an assembly process, the operator who observes measling or crazing cannot determine the source of the problem. This fact puts even more emphasis on getting high-quality PCBs from suppliers. This can be done through increased receiving inspection, source inspections, or a comprehensive qualification program and partnership with suppliers in which process control is utilized in the PCB fabrication and parametric data from the supplier is sent to the buyer to review for compliance to requirements. This kind of information can also be used to justify a dock-to-stock program if desired.

Evidence to date is that even boards with severe measles have functioned adequately over long periods of time and in harsh environments. In fact, the IPC has no data that shows a measled board has ever failed in the field in the absence of no other serious defects. The only acceptability criterion for measling and crazing is that the assembly be functional in its application.

36.7.1.2 Blistering and Delamination. *Blistering* is a localized swelling and separation between any of the layers of the base material or between the material and the metal cladding. *Delamination* is a separation between any of the layers of the base material or between the base material and the metal cladding.

Blistering/delamination cannot exceed 50 percent (25 percent for Class 3) of the distance between plated-through-holes or subsurface conductors.

36.7.1.3 Weave Exposure. *Weave exposure* is a surface condition of base material in which the unbroken fibers of woven glass cloth are not completely covered by resin. Weave exposure is acceptable if it does not reduce dielectric spacing as specified in engineering documentation between the weave exposure and a conductor. Class 3, however, does not accept any weave exposure.

37.6.1.4 Haloing and Edge Delamination. *Haloing* is a condition existing in the base material in the form of a light area around holes or other machined areas on or below the surface of the base material. Haloing is acceptable if the penetration of the haloing or edge delamination does not reduce edge spacing more than 50 percent of the distance to the nearest conductor or 2.5 mm maximum, whichever is less.

36.7.2 PCBA Cleanliness

Board cleanliness is needed to ensure that contaminants are sufficiently removed which could affect functionality at present or in the future. Some contaminants can actually promote growth of undesirable substances on the PCBA which can cause shorting or corrosion which would affect the PCBA functional integrity.

No visible residue from cleanable or any activated fluxes is allowed. Class 1 equipment suppliers may not be required to remove cleanable residues if qualification testing is performed which demonstrates no need for cleaning the PCBAs. No-clean or low-residue flux residues may be allowed if the PCBA is not conformal coated. If conformal coating is used, these residues are not acceptable since they will, in most cases, detrimentally affect the conformal coating ability to bond to the components or the PCB being coated.

For processes utilizing corrosive fluxes, the solvent extract conductivity (SEC) cleanliness test must be performed. When SEC is performed, the surface contamination level must meet 1.5 μg/cm^2 or less of NaCl equivalent in order for the PCBA cleaning process to be acceptable. In the event of failure, immediate process corrections must be made before any additional product is assembled.

Fluxes are considered to be noncorrosive if they meet the following criteria:

1. Copper mirror test as defined by flux type L requirements of IPC-SF-818, General Requirements for Electronic Soldering Fluxes, flux-induced corrosion test.

2. Halides test as defined by flux type L, Class 3 requirements of IPC-SF-818, General Requirements for Electronic Soldering Fluxes, presence of halides in flux test.

3. Surface insulation resistance must meet a minimum of 2×10^4 MΩ per IPC-B-25.

4. Electromigration resistance requirements must be met. The test sample shall be examined at 10× magnification with no evidence of filament growth that reduces conductor spacing by more than 20 percent.

Particulate matter such as dirt, lint, dross, lead clippings, etc., are not acceptable on PCBAs. Metallic areas or hardware on the PCBAs may not exhibit any crystalline white deposits, colored residues, or rusty appearance.

36.7.3 PCBA Marking Acceptability

Marking provides both product identification and traceability. It aids in assembly, in-process control, and field repairs. The methods and materials used in marking must serve the intended purposes and must be readable, durable, and compatible with the manufacturing processes as well as the end use of the product.

Fabrication and assembly engineering drawings should be the controlling documents for the locations and types of markings on PCBAs. Marking on components and fabricated parts should withstand all tests, cleaning, and assembly processes to which the item is subjected and shall remain legible (capable of being read and understood). Acceptability of marking is based on whether it is legible. If a marking is legible and cannot be confused with another letter or number, it is acceptable. Components and fabricated parts do not have to be installed so that reference designators are visible after installation. Missing, incomplete, or illegible characters in markings is unacceptable.

36.8 PCBA COATINGS

It should be noted that not all PCBA designs use conformal coating; however, when used, it must meet the following acceptability criteria. All PCBAs that utilize top- or bottom-layer etch (trace) runs have a solder mask over them if a solder wave or static solder bath process is used to solder components onto the PCB. Without solder mask, the solder would bridge between many solder wettable surfaces causing an uncontrollable problem.

36.8.1 Conformal Coating

Conformal coating is an insulating protective covering that conforms to the configuration of the objects coated when it is applied to a completed PCBA. Conformal coatings should be homogeneous, transparent, and unpigmented. The conformal coating should be properly cured and not exhibit tackiness. Defects associated with conformal coating are limited to those identified in Table 36.3.

Conformal coating thickness requirements for three types of coatings are listed as follows.

1. Types ER (epoxy), UR (urethane), and AR (acrylic)   0.05 to 0.08mm
2. Type SR (silicone)   0.08 to 0.13mm
3. Type XY (para-xylene)   0.01 to 0.05mm

The thickness may be measured on a coupon that has been processed with the assembly. No conformal coating on the tip of leads is required.

TABLE 36.3 Limits of Conformal Coating Defects
(Percentage of PCBA surface area)

Conformal coat defect	Class 1	Class 2	Class 3
Voids and bubbles	10	10	5
Adhesion loss	10	5	5
Foreign material	5	5	2
Dewetting	10	5	5
Ripples	15	10	5
Fisheyes	15	10	5
Orange peel	15	10	5

36.8.2   Solder Mask

Solder mask is a film coating used to provide dielectric and mechanical shielding during and after soldering operations. Solder mask material may be applied as a liquid or a dry film.

Cracking of solder mask after the soldering and cleaning operation is acceptable for Class 1 and 2 equipment but unacceptable for Class 3 equipment. After assembly soldering and cleaning operations, wrinkling of solder mask over tin-lead (SMOTL) plated traces is acceptable provided the solder mask has not been lifted or degraded to the point of flaking, peeling, or loose solder mask on the PCBA. Flaking, peeling, or loose solder mask on the PCBA is unacceptable. Wrinkling of solder mask over bare copper (SMOBC) traces is not acceptable

After assembly of SMOTL boards, any unacceptable flaking, peeling, or loose solder mask on the PCBA may be removed, leaving solder mask which is adequately adhered to the PCBA. The removal of this solder mask will render an acceptable PCBA.

36.9   SOLDERLESS WRAPPING OF WIRE TO POSTS (WIRE WRAP)

Many applications of wire wrap are still utilized in equipment design, and standards of acceptance should be used. Standards of acceptance in this area are shown in IPC-A-610 and in Bellcore TR-NWT-000078. The following is taken mainly from the Bellcore specification since it is slightly more detailed than the IPC specification.

36.9.1   Wrap Post

The wrap post cannot be bent or twisted before or after the wire is wrapped to the post. The wrap straightness will not exceed approximately 1 post diameter or thickness from its perpendicular position. The term "approximately" here implies that this is not a requirement that should be measured routinely and can be accepted based on visual observation and subjective judgment. After connection, the post must not be twisted more than 15° from its original position in order to be acceptable.

It should be noted that some wrap posts are used, stand-alone, as headers or test points and the question of tilt or post bend acceptability requirements continues to be raised. For this type of application, the tilt requirements should be loosened unless there are valid engineering concerns preventing it. Generally the tilt or bend will not exceed approximately 2 post diameters or thicknesses from its perpendicular position.

36.9.2   Wire Wrap Connection

Table 36.4 shows the number of wire wrap turns of insulated and uninsulated wire used on the wrapped connection. The connection is made using automatic or semiautomatic wire-wrapping devices. For this requirement, countable turns are those turns of bare wire or insulated wire in intimate contact with the corners of the terminals starting at the first contact with a terminal corner and ending at the last contact with a terminal corner (Fig. 36.41).

Maximum turns of bare and insulated wire are governed only by tooling configuration and space available on the ter-

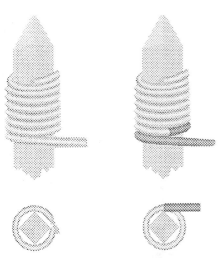

FIGURE 36.41   Wire wrap connection acceptability. *(IPC.)*

TABLE 36.4 Wire Wrap Turn Requirements

Wire gauge	Terminal size, in^2	Minimum number of turns	
		Uninsulated wire	Insulated wire
#20 and #22	0.025–0.045 in	5	None
#24	0.025–0.045	6	None
#26	0.025	6	None
#26	0.045	7	None
#28 and #30	0.025	7	¾

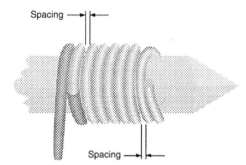

FIGURE 36.42 Single wire wrap spacing. *(IPC.)*

minal. Stripped ends of wires used for previous solderless wrapped connections shall not be reused. Electrical clearance between terminals as specified by engineering documentation must be maintained. Wire ends should in no case project to the extent that the required electrical clearance is compromised. In no case should the wire end project more than 0.125 in (1 wire diameter for Class 3) away from the terminal.

36.9.3 Single Wire Wrap Spacing

The wrapped conductors will be free of gaps (that is, each wrap will be in contact with the previous wrap) with turns not overlapping. The first insulated turn on a wrapped post cannot exceed a maximum of 0.050 in above the pin base of shoulder (wrappable surface of the pin). The first and last one-half-turns may have a space between turns, provided the space does not exceed 1 diameter of the uninsulated wire. Excluding the first and last one-half-turns, the wrapped conductors may have a single space between them, provided the opening does not exceed one-half the nominal diameter of uninsulated wire (Fig. 36.42).

36.9.4 Multiple Wire Wrap Spacing

Typically no more than three wires are wrapped to a single post. When more than one wrap is used on a single post the following requirements apply. The maximum spacing between consecutively wrapped wires is 2 uninsulated wire diameters with a preferred spacing of one-half the diameter of the uninsulated wire. The final wire wrap turn on a post must not extend to within 1 uninsulated wire diameter of the tapered portion of the wire wrap post's tip. The first insulated turn of a higher-level wire wrap may overlap the last turn of uninsulated wire on a lower-level wrap by a maximum of 1 turn (Fig. 36.43).

36.10 PCBA MODIFICATIONS

All modifications to PCBAs should be defined and detailed in approved engineering and/or methods documents. Jumper wires are considered as components and are defined by documentation for routing, termination, staking, and wire type.

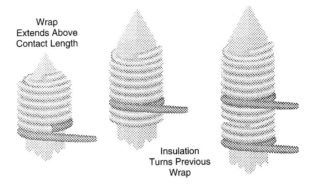

FIGURE 36.43 Multiple wire wrap requirements. *(IPC.)*

36.10.1 Cut Traces

Trace cuts should be at least 0.030 in in width as a minimum, with all loose material removed. Trace cuts should also be sealed with an approved sealant to prevent absorption of moisture. Care should be taken when removing etch from PCBs to prevent damaging the laminate material.

36.10.2 Lifted Pins

Lifted pins should be cut short enough to prevent the possibility of being shorted to the pad from which they were lifted should they be pushed back down. If the component hole from which the pad was lifted does not contain a jumper wire, it should be filled with solder.

36.10.3 Jumper Wires

Jumper wires may be used on all classes of equipment electronic assemblies and in thick-film hybrid technology. The wire may be terminated in plated-through-holes, on terminal stand-offs, on circuit lands, or on component leads. It should be noted here that Bellcore TR-NWT-000078 requires that wires be terminated only in plated-through-holes and that for Class 3 equipment a wire cannot be placed into the same plated-through-hole with a component lead.

Recommended jumper wire is solid insulated copper wire, tin-lead plated, 22 to 30 gauge with insulation capable of withstanding soldering temperatures. The insulation must have some resistance to abrasion and have a dielectric resistance equal to or better than the board insulation material. Jumper wire shall be insulated if greater than 1.0 in in length or it could possibly short between lands or component leads.

Jumper wires are to be routed in the shortest *x-y* route possible. Wire routing must be documented for each part number. Assemblies having the same part number must be routed in the same pattern (Fig. 36.44).

When jumper wires are used on the *primary side* of the PCBA, no wire is to pass over or under any components. The wire may pass over lands, provided the wire can be moved away from the land for component replacement. Care must be taken to avoid running wire near or in contact with heat sinks to prevent damage to the wire from excessive heat exposure (Fig. 36.45).

When jumper wires are used on the *secondary side* of the PCBA, the jumper wire should not pass through component footprints unless the layout of the assembly prohibits routing in

FIGURE 36.44 Jumper wire—*x-y* routing. *(IPC.)*

FIGURE 36.45 Jumper wire—routing over components. *(IPC.)*

other areas. If this condition occurs, it should be designated as a process indicator. The exception to this is for edge connectors on the PCBA. Jumper wires should not pass over test points or vias used as a test point.

Jumper wires should be staked to the base material with an approved adhesive. Uncured adhesive is unacceptable on the completed PCBA. The wire should be spot bonded along its route and must not be applied to lands, pads, or components. The interval of staking must be defined in the applicable engineering documentation but the wire must be staked at all changes in direction of the wire. Jumper wires must be staked or taut enough to prevent lifting the wire

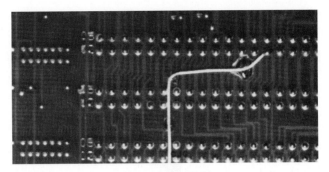

FIGURE 36.46   Jumper wire—staking. *(IPC.)*

FIGURE 36.47   Jumper wire installation requirements. *(IPC.)*

above the height of adjacent components. No more than two jumper wires may be stacked on a given route (Fig. 36.46).

When a jumper wire is attached to leads on the secondary side of the PCBA or to axial components on the primary side of the PCBA, it must form a full 180 to 360° loop around the component lead. When a jumper wire is soldered to other component package styles, the wire should be lap soldered to the component lead.

Jumper wires may be installed into a plated-through-hole with another component lead for Class 1 and 2 equipment;

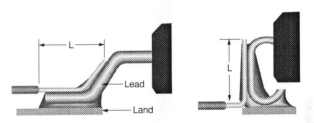

FIGURE 36.48   Jumper wire connection—leaded components. *(IPC.)*

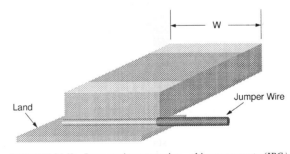

FIGURE 36.49   Jumper wire connection—chip components. *(IPC.)*

however, this is unacceptable for Class 3 equipment. Jumper wires may also be installed into via holes (Fig. 36.47).

For surface-mount components, the minimum length of the lap joint between the wire end and the lead or land must be the length *L* for leaded components and width *W* for leadless components (Figs. 36.48 and 36.49).

REFERENCES

1. TR-NWT-000078, *Generic Physical Design Requirements for Telecommunications Products and Equipment,* Bell Communications Research (Bellcore); Red Bank, N.J., issue no. 3, Dec. 1991.

2. ANSI/J-STD-001, *Requirements for Soldered Electrical and Electronic Assemblies,* Electronic Industries Association and Institute for Interconnecting and Packaging Electronic Circuits.

3. MIL-STD-2000, *Standard Requirements for Soldered Electrical and Electronic Assemblies.*

4. ANSI/J-STD-002, *Solderability Tests for Component Leads, Terminations, Lugs, Terminals and Wires,* Electronic Industries Association and Institute for Interconnecting and Packaging Electronic Circuits.

5. ANSI/J-STD-003, *Solderability Tests for Printed Boards,* Electronic Industries Association and Institute for Interconnecting and Packaging Electronic Circuits.

6. IPC-A-610, *Acceptability of Electronic Assemblies,* Institute for Interconnecting and Packaging Electronic Circuits.

CHAPTER 37
RELIABILITY OF PRINTED CIRCUIT ASSEMBLIES

Judith Glazer*

*Hewlett-Packard Company, Electronic Assembly
Development Center, Palo Alto, California*

This chapter describes the response of functional printed circuit board assemblies (PCAs) to environmental stresses—that is, their reliability in service—and the influence of design, materials, and manufacturing decisions on this behavior. A variety of stresses may be present in the service environment of the assembly. *Thermal* stresses come from fluctuations in the ambient temperature in the service environment of the assembly or from power dissipation of high-power devices mounted on the printed circuit board (PCB). There are also thermal stresses associated with assembly and rework. *Mechanical* stresses may be due to bending and flexing of the assembly during later assembly steps or in service, mechanical shock during transportation or use, or mechanical vibration, for example, from cooling fans. *Chemical* sources of environmental stresses include atmospheric moisture, corrosive gases (for example, smog or industrial process gases), and residual chemically active contaminants from the assembly processes (for example, from flux). These environmental stresses may act singly or in concert with one another and the electrical potential differences that exist when the assembly is functioning to cause electrical failures in the printed circuit assembly (PCA). This chapter will focus on the reliability of the PCB and the interconnects to it. Reliability of the electrical components themselves is beyond the scope of this chapter (see Fig. 37.1).

By defining reliability as the response of functioning assemblies to environmental stresses, we have excluded the large class of production defects that are detected in the testing processes immediately after manufacturing or that will cause the assembly to be nonfunctioning from the outset. This chapter will focus on the delayed effects of manufacturing defects and the wear-out mechanisms of properly manufactured product.

The remainder of this chapter is organized into six major sections:

37.1   Fundamentals of Reliability

37.2   Failure Mechanisms of PCBs and Their Interconnects

37.3   Influence of Design on Reliability

37.4   Impact of PCB Fabrication and Assembly on Reliability

---

* Significant portions of this chapter are drawn from T. A. Yager, "Reliability," chap. 30, *Printed Circuits Handbook,* 3d ed. (Coombs, ed.), 1988.

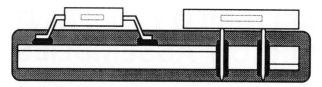

FIGURE 37.1 Schematic drawing of a printed circuit board assembly. This chapter focuses on the reliability of the printed circuit board and the interconnect between the printed circuit board and the components (shaded area in the drawing).

Where applicable, each section covers printed circuit boards, printed circuit board assemblies, and components and their packages, in turn. Section 37.2 is the core of the chapter; it covers the fundamental of the failure mechanisms and is the assumed underlying basis of the subsequent sections. The breadth of this chapter, the complexity of the failure mechanisms involved, and the rapid evolution of the field mean that this chapter can provide only a brief overview of important topics in PCB and PCA reliability, many of which are the subject of books in their own right. The reader is encouraged to refer to the references and suggestions for further reading given at the end of the chapter before attempting quantitative reliability predictions.

37.1 FUNDAMENTALS OF RELIABILITY

37.1.1 Definitions

The reliability of a component or system can be defined as the *probability* that a functioning product at time zero will function *in the desired service environment* for a *specified amount of time*. Without these three parameters, the question "Is x reliable?" cannot be answered yes or no. Since reliability describes the probability that the product is still functioning, it is related to the cumulative number of failures. Mathematically, the reliability of an object at time t can be stated as

$$R(t) = 1 - F(t)$$

where $R(t)$ is the reliability at time t (i.e., the proportion of parts still functioning) and $F(t)$ is the fraction of the parts or systems that have failed at time t. Time may be measured in calendar units or some other measure of service time such as on/off cycles or thermal or mechanical vibration cycles. The unit of time that makes sense depends on the failure mechanism. When several failure modes are present, it is often helpful to think in terms of several time scales.

A plot of the failure rate of a product as a function of time typically takes the shape of a "bathtub" curve (see Fig. 37.2). This curve illustrates the three phases that occur during the lifespan of a product from a reliability perspective. In the first, infant mortality phase, there is an initially high but rapidly declining failure rate caused by infant mortality. Infant mortality is typically caused by manufacturing defects that went undetected during inspection and testing and lead to rapid failure in service. Burn-in can be used to remove these units before shipment. The second phase, the normal operating life of the product, is characterized by a period of stable, relatively low failure rates.

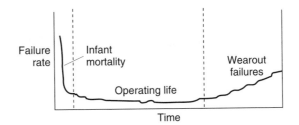

FIGURE 37.2 Classic bathtub reliability curve showing the three stages during the life of a product from a reliability perspective: infant mortality, steady-state, and wear-out.

During the operating life, failures occur apparently randomly and the failure rate r is roughly constant with time. An exponential life distribution is often assumed to describe the behavior in this region. In that case,

$$r = \left(\frac{N_t}{N_o} \right) \left(\frac{1}{\Delta t} \right)$$

and

$$R(t) = e^{-rt} = e^{\frac{-t}{\text{MTBF}}}$$

where N_t = number of failures in time interval Δt
            N_o = number of samples at the beginning of the interval
     MTBF = mean time between failures

During the third phase, the wear-out period, the failure rate increases gradually due to wear-out phenomena until 100 percent of the units have failed. For some systems, the second steady-state region may not exist; for solder joints, the wear-out region may extend over most of the life of the assembly. Understanding wear-out phenomena, which manifest themselves in properly manufactured parts after a period of service, and predicting when they will significantly affect the failure rate, are the primary focuses of this chapter.

Most wear-out phenomena can be characterized by cumulative failure distributions governed by either the Weibull or the log-normal distribution. Weibull distributions have been successfully used to describe solder joint and plated-through-hole fatigue distributions, while log-normal distributions are generally associated with electrochemical failure mechanisms. While these distributions may be quite narrow in some cases, their use should serve as a reminder that even with nominally identical samples, failures will be statistically distributed over time.

A practical use of fitting a distribution to reliability data is to extrapolate to smaller failure rates or other environmental conditions. To simplify the equations, the expressions in the text refer to the mean life of the relevant portion of the assembly. If the constants that define the failure distribution are known, the time to reach a smaller proportion of failures may be readily calculated. For example, for failure modes that are described by a Weibull distribution, the time t to reach $x\%$ failures is given by:

$$t(x\%) = t(50\%) \left[\frac{\ln(1 - 0.01x)}{\ln(0.5)} \right]^{1/\beta}$$

where β is the Weibull shape parameter, usually between 2 and 4 for solder joint failures.

37.1.2 Reliability Testing

Almost every reliability test program must solve the problem of determining whether an object is reliable in a calendar time period that is much shorter than the expected use period. Obviously, one cannot spend 3 to 5 years testing a personal computer that will be marketed for an even shorter time span or 20 years testing a military system. Depending on the failure mechanism, there are two approaches, which may be combined: (1) accelerate the frequency of the occurrence that causes failure and test the ability of the object to survive the expected number of events, or (2) increase the severity so that fewer occurrences are needed. Drop tests that simulate shock during transportation are an example of the first approach. Since the time between drops does not affect the amount of damage caused, a lifetime of drops can be conducted in rapid succession. However, the effect of temperature and humidity on corrosion over the lifetime of the product can be tested only by increasing the temperature, the humidity, or the concentration of contaminants, or some combination of these. The difficulty is ensuring that the test reproduces and/or correlates to the failure mechanism in service.

To use this data for making true reliability predictions—that is, *the probability of failures at a given time under given conditions*—testing must be continued until enough parts fail that a life distribution can be estimated. Unfortunately, this process can be time consuming and qualification tests are often substituted. Qualification test protocols specify a *maximum number of failures that may be observed in a specified period* in a sample of specified size. If few or no failures occur, a qualification test provides almost no information about the failure distribution; for example, the probability of failure during the next time interval is unknown. This limitation of qualification testing is minimized when the life distribution for properly manufactured samples is already known or can be estimated based on experience with similar designs. Many of the "reliability" tests described in Sec. 37.6 are actually qualification tests.

Many reliability or qualification testing schedules follow neither of these schemes. Instead, they test the ability of the product to survive a sequence of tests under extremely severe conditions for a short time or small number of exposures. Again, this type of testing may be adequate when it is supported by long experience with both the product type and its use environment; however, it is risky because it is not based on ensuring that probable failure modes will not occur in the life of the product. When new technologies or geometries are introduced, the old tests may not always be conservative. By the same token, irrelevant failure modes that would not occur in service may be introduced by the harsh test conditions.

37.2 FAILURE MECHANISMS OF PCBs AND THEIR INTERCONNECTS

This section will discuss the most important failure mechanisms of PCBs and the interconnects between PCBs and the components mounted on them. The discussion of PCB failure mechanisms will be more detailed since interconnect failures have been described far more extensively elsewhere. Whatever the environmental stress or the material response, these failures ultimately manifest themselves in terms of the functionality of the assembly, first as a change in electrical resistance between two points and then as electrical shorts or opens.

37.2.1 PCB Failure Mechanisms

PCB failure mechanisms fall into three groups: thermally induced failures, of which plated-through-holes are the most important example; mechanical failures; and chemical failure mechanisms, of which dendritic growth is the most important example.

37.2.1.1 *Thermally Driven Failure Mechanisms.*

PCBs are exposed to thermal stresses in a variety of situations. These may be either prolonged exposure to an elevated temperature or isolated or repeated temperature cycles. These temperature cycles can cause various PCB failures. The most important sources of thermal stress are:

- *Thermal shocks and thermal cycles during PCB manufacturing.* Thermal shocks are usually defined as temperature ramps faster than ~30°C/s, but include any ramp fast enough that temperature differentials play an important role. Examples include solder mask cure and hot-air solder leveling.
- *Thermal shocks and cycles during printed circuit assembly.* Examples are glue cure, solder reflow, wave soldering, and rework using a soldering iron, hot air, or molten solder pot.
- *Ambient thermal cycles in service.* Examples are going from inside to outside temperatures or ground to upper atmospheric temperatures, and elevation in box temperature due to heat dissipation from functioning electronic components.

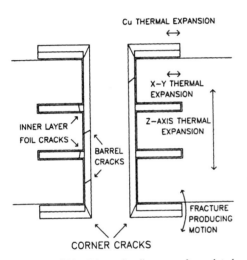

FIGURE 37.3 Schematic diagram of a plated-through-hole in a cross section of a four-layer printed circuit board showing common failure locations under thermal stress.

The primary PCB failure mechanisms accelerated by these thermal stresses are plated-through-hole cracking and delamination of the laminate.

Plated-Through-Hole Failures Due to Thermal Shocks or Cycling. Plated-through-holes (PTHs) are the most vulnerable features on PCBs to damage from thermal cycling and the most frequent cause of printed circuit board failures in service. PTHs include holes for through-hole (TH) components and vias that make electrical connections between layers. Figure 37.3 shows the common failure locations. Most organic resin-matrix substrate materials are highly anisotropic, with a much higher CTE above the glass transition temperature T_g in the through-thickness (z) direction than in the plane of the woven matrix cloth (the x-y plane of the board). Since above T_g the CTE climbs sharply, aggressive thermal cycles can result in large strains in the z direction and, consequently, on the PTHs (see Fig. 37.4[1]). The PTH acts like a rivet, which resists this expansion, but the Cu barrel is stressed and may crack, causing electrical failure. Figure 37.4 also illustrates the increasing strain on the barrel associated with a high temperature excursion. Failure may occur in a single cycle or may take place by initiation and growth of a fatigue crack over the course of a number of cycles. For high-aspect-ratio through-holes subject to repeated thermal shocks from room temperature to solder reflow temperatures (220 to 250°C) during board fabrication (e.g., hot-air solder leveling) and assembly (reflow, wave soldering, rework), it is not unheard of to encounter failures after 10 or fewer of these thermal cycles.

On a physical level, the number of thermal cycles to failure is affected by the strain imposed on the Cu in each cycle and the fatigue resistance of the copper. These factors are in turn controlled by a number of environmental, material, and manufacturing parameters. Low-cycle metal fatigue, in which most of the strain is plastic strain, can be treated approximately with the Coffin-Manson relation:

$$N_f \propto \frac{1}{2}\left(\frac{\varepsilon_f}{\Delta\varepsilon}\right)^m$$

where N_f = number of cycles to failure
  $\Delta\varepsilon$ = strain
  ε_f = strain ductility factor, which correlates closely with tensile ductility
  m = constant near 2.

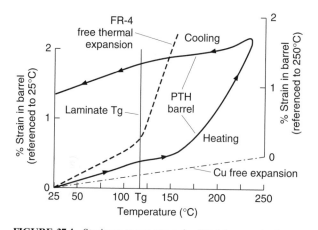

FIGURE 37.4 Strain vs. temperature for FR-4 (epoxy-glass), copper, and a PTH barrel in an FR-4 board during a single thermal cycle from 25 to 250 to 25°C. While the thermal expansion of the individual materials is fully reversible, much of the strain in the Cu PTH barrel is plastic, so most of the strain is not reversed during cooling. Note that the rate of thermal expansion of the FR-4 increases sharply at T_g. Results from Ref. 1.

This relation will significantly underestimate life for high cycle fatigue which can occur after repeated thermal cycling in service. The strain $\Delta \varepsilon$ can be estimated by finite element modeling or analytically. If no other data are available, ε_f for electroplated Cu can be approximated as 0.3.

The number of cycles to failure can be increased by increasing $\varepsilon_f / \Delta \varepsilon$, primarily by decreasing $\Delta \varepsilon$ by:

- Decreasing or eliminating thermal shocks by preheating the board before hot-air leveling, wave soldering, rework with a solder pot, etc.
- Decreasing the size of the thermal cycle (see Fig. 37.5[2]). Decreasing the size of the thermal cycle is the single most effective measure for increasing the life of the PTH, especially if the thermal cycle exceeds T_g.
- Decreasing the free thermal expansion of the laminate over the thermal cycle. The free thermal expansion can be reduced primarily by choosing a laminate material with a higher T_g, but also by choosing a laminate material (e.g., with Aramid fibers) with a low CTE below T_g (see Fig. 37.6).
- Decreasing the PTH aspect ratio (usually quoted as board thickness divided by finished hole size) by decreasing the board thickness or increasing the hole diameter (see Fig. 37.7). Aspect ratios tend to be higher in boards with eight or more layers because of their thickness and via density; aspect ratios greater than 3:1 require good-quality plating and aspect ratios higher than 5:1 are not recommended, in part because of the difficulty of achieving adequate plating thickness in the center of the barrel.
- Increasing the Cu plating thickness (see Fig. 37.8[2]). Increasing the plating thickness also increases the distance a fatigue crack must propagate to cause an electrical failure.
- Using Ni plating over the Cu (see Sec. 37.5.1.3 for more discussion).

The ratio $\varepsilon_f / \Delta \varepsilon$ can be increased by:

- Increasing the Cu ductility (increases ε_f) and yield strength (decreases ε). Cu strength and ductility are often inversely related, so these two factors must be balanced against one

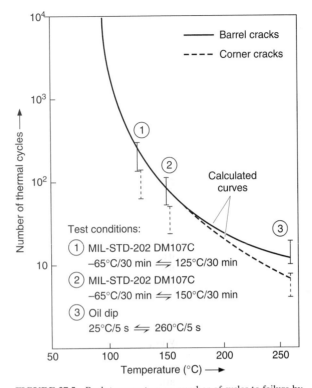

FIGURE 37.5 Peak temperature vs. number of cycles to failure by PTH barrel (solid bars) or corner (dashed bars) cracking in three different tests. Calculated lines are shown for comparison. Results are for pyrophosphate copper and FR-4. Other parameters are total strain energy required to cause fracture, 50 J/cm³; hole radius, 0.45 mm; distance from hole center to free end, 0.8 mm; plating thickness, 0.02 mm; distance from hole center to pad edge, 0.8 mm; board thickness, 2 mm. Results from Ref. 2.

another. However, the strength-ductility relationship can be altered by the choice of plating bath and plating conditions.

The number of cycles to failure can be dramatically decreased by defects in the hole wall or Cu plating in the hole or PTH knee that act as stress concentrations (increasing the local stresses and strains) and/or facilitate crack initiation. Because of the importance of this failure mode, it has been extensively studied experimentally and with analytical modeling techniques and more quantitative models are available.[3,4,5]

Laminate and Cu/Laminate Adhesion Degradation.   When a PCB is exposed to elevated temperatures for long periods of time, the adhesion between the Cu and the laminate and the flexural strength of the laminate itself will gradually degrade. Discoloration is usually an early symptom.

Several standards tests are used to compare the thermal resistance of different laminate materials. Cu adhesion is measured using a peel test.[6] Adhesion at elevated temperatures or after elevated temperature exposure gives some insight into the ability of the material to withstand rework and other high-temperature processes. Flexural strength stability is compared by measuring the times at 200°C before the flexural strength decreases to 50 percent of

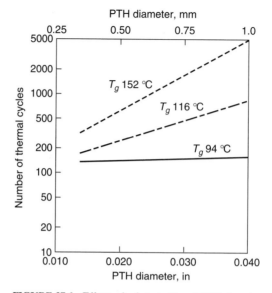

FIGURE 37.6 Effects of substrate T_g and PTH diameter on mean number of cycles to failure. The thermal cycle was 2-h cycle with extremes at −62 and +125°C. Multilayer printed circuit board thickness 0.10 in (2.5 mm); Cu in unfilled PTH is 1.2 mil (30 μm) thick. Results from Ref. 33.

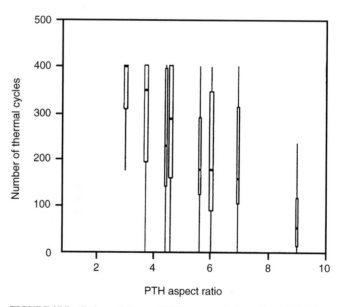

FIGURE 37.7 Cycles to failure vs. PTH aspect ratio for −65 to +125°C thermal shock cycles. Various hole diameters, board thicknesses, and board constructions. *(After Ref. 3.)*

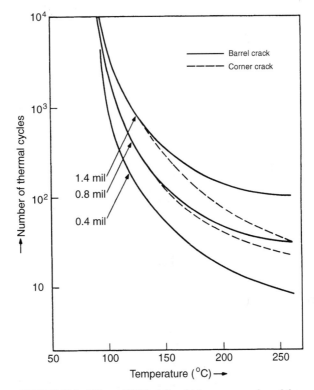

FIGURE 37.8 Effect of PTH plating thickness on number of thermal cycles to failure for thermal cycles with the indicated peak temperatures. For acid sulfate copper and FR-4 boards. Other hole parameters are the same as Fig. 37.5. *(After Ref. 2.)*

its original value. The quality of the bond between the resin and reinforcement is compared by measuring the time it takes for copper-clad laminate to blister during a solder float test at 290°C.[7]

37.2.1.2 Mechanically Induced Failures. PCBs may be mechanically loaded by test fixtures or processing equipment, when PCAs are loaded into card cages or fixtured into place with brackets, or when the assembly experiences mechanical shock or vibration in use. In general, once the PCA has been assembled, the interconnects to the components are the weak links in mechanical loading situations, not the boards themselves.

37.2.1.3 Electrochemical Failure Modes. The primary function of a printed circuit board is to provide electrical connections with the desired, stable, low-impedance and high-impedance insulation between them. A high surface insulation resistance (SIR) value is usually assumed by the circuit designer. Exposure to humidity, especially when ionic contaminants are present, is a common cause of insulation resistance failures that is accelerated by elevated temperatures and electrical bias. The impedance often decreases slowly over a long period of time. If the SIR value falls below the designed level, there will be cross talk between circuit elements that should be isolated, and the circuit may not function properly. Insulation resistance deterioration is particularly harmful for analog measurement circuits. If these circuits are used to measure low-voltage, high-impedance sources, changes in circuit impedance can result in the deterioration of instrument performance. Medical products that use sensors attached to a patient also pose special concerns, because deterioration of insulation resistance has the potential to cause electrical shock. For general applications, the surface resistivity is usually specified to exceed 10^8 $\Omega/\square$, but for these specialized applications higher values may be required. Electrochemical failures are usually accelerated by temperature, humidity, and applied bias.

High humidity is a significant cause of reliability problems because many corrosion mechanisms require water to operate. A humid environment is an excellent source of water, even when it is not condensing. Polymers commonly used in PCBs are hygroscopic; that is, they absorb moisture readily from the environment. This phenomenon is reversible; the moisture can be driven out of the PCB by baking it. The amount of moisture absorbed and the time to reach equilibrium with a humid environment depend on the laminate material, its thickness, the type of solder mask or other surface coating, and the conductor pattern.

The moisture absorbed by the PCB and ionic contaminants on or in the PCB play a role in a number of failure modes. Because the permittivity of water is much higher than that of most laminate materials, the increased water content can significantly affect the dielectric constant of the laminate, and thus may affect the electrical functionality of the board by increasing the capacitive coupling between traces. Absorbed and adsorbed water can lower SIR values, especially in the presence of ionizable contaminants (often from flux residues) and DC bias. The introduction of no-clean assembly processes has significantly increased the importance of measuring SIR values because contaminants left on the PCB remain there after assembly. Industrial pollutants can also be a source of ions that accelerate corrosion. In addition, typical industrial pollutants such as NO_2 and SO_2 can damage many materials used in PCAs, particularly elastomers and polymers. Some important mechanisms that cause failures due to low insulation resistance include dendritic growth and metal migration, galvanic corrosion, and conductive anodic filament growth. Whiskering can also cause electrical shorts, but neither electrical bias nor moisture is required.

Conductive Contaminant Bridging.   Bridging of circuits by conductive salts may occur if plating, etching, or flux residues remain on the board. These ionic residues are good conductors of electricity in a moist environment. They tend to migrate across both metallic and insulating surfaces to form shorts. Corrosive byproducts, such as chlorides and sulfides formed in industrial environments, are chemically similar and can also cause shorting. An example of this type of failure is shown in Fig. 37.9.[8]

Dendritic Growth.   Dendritic growth occurs by the electrolytic transfer of metal from one conductor to another; consequently, it is also termed *electrolytic metal migration*. It is also referred to as *electromigration,* although it should not be confused with the process that occurs in aluminum conductors in integrated circuits, which has a different mechanism. An example of a dendritic growth failure is shown in Fig. 37.10. Dendrites form on surfaces (including the interior surfaces of cavities) when the following conditions are met:

- Continuous liquid water film, a few molecules or more in thickness
- Exposed metals, especially Sn, Pb, Ag or Cu, that can be oxidized at the anode
- Low-current dc electrical bias

It is significantly accelerated by the presence of hydrolyzable ionic contaminants (for example, halides and acids from flux residues or extracted from polymers). Delaminations or voids that promote the accumulation of moisture or contaminants can promote dendritic growth. Conductive anodic filament growth (discussed later) is a special case of dendritic growth. Time to failure is inversely proportional to spacing squared and voltage. The failure mechanisms in accelerated tests have been reviewed.[9]

Dendritic growths usually form from cathode to anode. Metallic ions formed by dissolution at the anode are transported along a conductive path and reduced and deposited at the

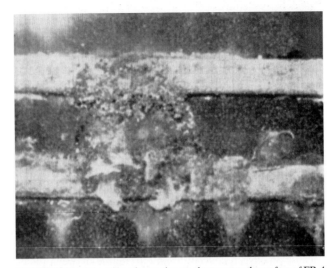

FIGURE 37.9   Migration of corrosion products across the surface of FR-4 bridging two conductors. From Ref. 11. *(From IPC-TR-476. Courtesy of Department of Defense.)*

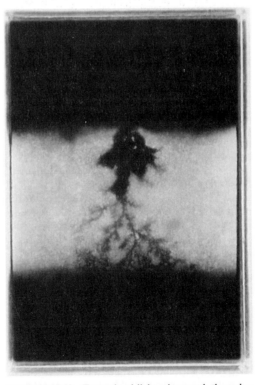

FIGURE 37.10   Transmitted light micrograph through a PCB that failed in the field. Dendritic growth has formed at the interface of a UV-cured screened solder mask and the FR-4 surface.

cathode. The dendrite resembles a tree, since it consists of a stalk with branches. When the growth touches the other conductor there is an abrupt rise in current, which sometimes destroys the dendrite but may also cause an electrical circuit to temporarily malfunction or damage a device.

It has been proposed that the absorption of moisture produces an electrochemical cell. The following electrode reactions for Cu are an example:

At the anode: $\qquad$ $Cu \rightarrow Cu^{n+} + ne^-$

$$H_2O \rightarrow \tfrac{1}{2}O_2 + 2H^+ + 2e^-$$

At the cathode: $\qquad$ $H_2O + e^- \rightarrow \tfrac{1}{2}H_2 + OH^-$

where the majority of the leakage is due to the electrolysis of water. Copper metal is dissolved at the anode and migrates to the cathode, where it is no longer soluble. The dendrite that forms follows the resulting pH gradient.[10] The voltage difference between the cathode and anode also affects the rate of dendrite growth. When the cathode and anode are the same metal (e.g., Cu), the voltage difference is determined primarily by the applied bias, although the access of moisture and air also has an effect. Corrosion can be accelerated in a crevice because an oxygen concentration differential between the anode and the cathode develops. When the metals are dissimilar, galvanic corrosion may occur without a bias voltage.

If there is an applied bias, dendritic growth will occur almost instantly if the cathode and anode are under water. A simple laboratory experiment can prove the point. A 6-V bias across two conductors is sufficient to induce rapid growth (readily observable with a low-power microscope) even when distilled or deionized water bridges the conductors, although growth will occur faster with tap water.[11]

Galvanic Corrosion. Galvanic corrosion occurs between dissimilar metals because they have differing affinities for electrons (i.e., they are more or less electronegative). Galvanic series have been compiled for many common metals and alloys (see Table 37.1). Metals near the top of the series (noble metals) do not corrode; those near the bottom corrode easily. When these metals are near each other, the more noble metal becomes the cathode, the less noble the anode. Moisture is required to couple the two metals electrically. Applied bias is generally not required, but may accelerate the reaction if the polarity is correct. When the anode is very small compared to the cathode, its corrosion can be very rapid. Conversely, if the anode is much larger than the cathode, corrosion is unlikely to be serious, particularly if the difference in electronegativity is small.

Conductive Anodic Filament Growth. Conductive anodic filament growth (CAF) causes electrical shorts when a metal that dissolves anodically is redeposited at the interface between the glass (or other) fibers and the resin matrix of a printed circuit board. Conductive anodic filament growth is promoted by delamination at the glass-polymer interface, which may in turn be promoted by various environmental stresses including high temperatures (greater than about 260°C for FR-4) and thermal cycling. Shorts seem to occur most rapidly when a single fiber bundle connects two pads. Once delamination has occurred, the metal migration that causes shorts to occur is promoted by increasing temperature, relative humidity, and applied voltage. Small conductor spacings also significantly decrease times to failure.[12] In multilayer boards, failures occur faster on outerlayers than innerlayers because the surface layer absorbs moisture more readily. By the same reasoning, solder mask and conformal coating both increase the time-to-failure because they slow the absorption of moisture from the atmosphere into the board.

Whiskers. Whiskers are faceted filament-like structures that grow spontaneously on the surface of a plated metal and can cause shorts between closely spaced conductors (see Fig. 37.11). Whiskering can be differentiated from other causes of shorts such as dendritic growth, because neither an electrical field nor moisture is required for whiskers to form. Whiskering is a particular problem with pure tin. The whiskers grow in response to internal stresses in the plating or external loads. Sn whiskers are commonly 50 μm long and 1 to 2 μm in diameter.

TABLE 37.1 Standard Electromotive Force Potential (Reductions Potentials) for Elements Commonly Found in Electronic Assemblies

	Reaction	Standard potential (Volts vs. standard hydrogen electrode)
Noble	$Au^{3+} + 3e^- = Au$	+1.498
	$Cl_2 + 2e^- = 2Cl^-$	+1.358
	$O_2 + 4H^+ + 4e^- = 2H_2O$ (pH 0)	+1.229
	$Pt^{3+} + 3e^- = Pt$	+1.2
	$Ag^+ + e^- = Ag$	+0.799
	$Fe^{3+} + e^- = Fe^{2+}$	+0.771
	$O_2 + 2H_2O + 4e^- = 4OH^-$ (pH 14)	+0.401
	$Cu^{2+} + 2e^- = Cu$	+0.337
	$Sn^{4+} + 2e^- = Sn^{2+}$	+0.15
	$2H^+ + 2e^- = H_2$	0.000
	$Pb^{2+} + 2e^- = Pb$	−0.126
	$Sn^{2+} + 2e^- = Sn$	−0.136
	$Ni^{2+} + 2e^- = Ni$	−0.250
	$Fe^{2+} + 2e^- = Fe$	−0.440
	$Cr^{3+} + 3e^- = Cr$	−0.744
	$2H_2O + 2e^- = H_2 + 2OH^-$	−0.828
	$Na^+ + e^- = Na$	−2.714
Active	$K^+ + e^- = K$	−2.925

Source: A. J. deBethune and N. S. Loud, *Standard Electrode Potentials and Temperature Coefficients at 25C,* Clifford A. Hampel, Skokie, Ill., 1964.

Once started, they may grow as fast as 1 mm per month. The tendency toward whisker growth is influenced by a variety of factors including plating conditions and the characteristics of the substrate. Growth may be inhibited by a Cu or Ni barrier layer beneath the tin coating. Pb seems to suppress whisker growth; eutectic Sn-Pb solder is considered almost immune. Whiskers do not cause the corrosion resistance or solderability of the tin coating to deteriorate, so tin may be used as a temporary finish. To avoid whiskering, plated pure Sn should not be used on closely spaced conductors that could short during service, such as connector terminations or component leads.[13,14]

37.2.2 Interconnect Failure Mechanisms

37.2.2.1 *Thermally Driven Failure Mechanisms*

Thermal Fatigue of Solder Joints. Thermal fatigue of solder joints has been extensively researched in the last decade. The mechanism of fatigue, accelerated testing methods, and methods for predicting life have all been described at length, although there is still much controversy about many of the details.[15–17] These references also illustrate how modern finite element methods can be used to model the strains in the solder under both operating and accelerated test conditions. This section briefly reviews some of the important principles underlying solder joint thermal fatigue.

The focus of the discussion is on surface-mount solder joints, which have been extensively researched; however, many of the same principles also apply to through-hole solder joints. Through-hole joints are generally less prone to solder joint fatigue failures, so long as the through-hole barrel is full of solder. Ideally, complete fillets should be observed on both surfaces of the board. Reviews of this topic can be found in Refs. 18 and 19.

Thermal fatigue in solder joints occurs because of the thermal expansion (CTE) mismatch between the PCB and the component interconnected by the solder joint (see Fig. 37.12). The

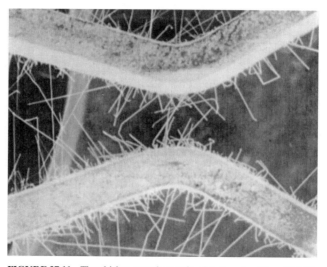

FIGURE 37.11 Tin whisker growth on a tin-plated surface. From Ref. 11. *(From IPC-TR-476. Courtesy of Burndy Corporation.)*

imposed thermal cycle ΔT results in an imposed cyclic strain $\Delta \varepsilon$ of the solder joint, which is generally the weakest part of the system. The relationship is simple under the assumptions that the part and substrate are rigid, the solder joints are relatively small, and that homogeneous shear deformation caused by the global CTE mismatch predominates:

$$\Delta \varepsilon = \frac{(\Delta T)(\Delta \alpha) l}{h} \qquad (37.1)$$

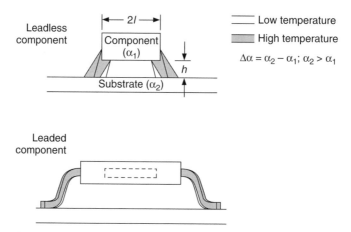

FIGURE 37.12 Schematic illustration of strains imposed on solder joints to leadless and leaded surface-mount components during a thermal cycle. Although the relative displacement of the substrate and component body is the same, the strain on the joint is reduced in the leaded case by the deflection of the lead.

where $\Delta\alpha$ = difference in thermal expansion coefficients of component and substrate
          l = distance between center of component and joint
          h = height of solder joint

If the component has leads or if the substrate is flexible, there will be some compliance in the system that will reduce the strain imposed on the solder joints. The local mismatch between the solder and the component lead or the pad or via metallization on the substrate can also contribute to the strains imposed on the solder.

Like plated-through-holes (PTHs), solder joints fail by a low-cycle-fatigue mechanism which can be crudely approximated by the Coffin-Manson relation

$$N_f = \frac{1}{2}\left(\frac{\varepsilon_f}{\Delta\varepsilon}\right)^m \qquad (37.2)$$

where, again, N_f is the number of cycles to failure, ε_f is the fatigue ductility, and m is an empirical constant near 2. However, unlike the PTH case, the number of cycles to failure also depends on the frequency at which the cycles are imposed and the hold time at each temperature extreme. The reason for this dependence is that, for solders, the primary deformation mechanism causing thermal fatigue failures is creep.

The phenomenon of creep and its connection to fatigue are fundamental to understanding thermal fatigue of solder. Creep is time-dependent deformation that occurs gradually in response to a fixed imposed stress or displacement (see Fig. 37.13). Creep occurs by a variety of thermally activated processes. These processes play an important role only when the temperature exceeds half the melting temperature (in degrees Kelvin) of the material and, even then, the rate of deformation increases strongly with increasing temperature. For electronic solders, even room temperature is well above half the melting temperature; consequently, creep is the most important deformation mechanism of solder. When a displacement is first imposed, the strain is a combination of elastic and plastic strain. The elastic deformation is reversible and damages the microstructure relatively little, while the plastic deformation is permanent and contributes more significantly to the initiation and propagation of fatigue cracks in the solder (see Fig. 37.14). Given time, the creep process relieves some or all of the elastic stress through further permanent deformation. This additional deformation does further microstructural damage and increases the amount of plastic strain imposed when the thermal cycle is reversed. Because there is less time for creep to occur, rapid thermal cycles are less damaging than slow cycles or cycles with long hold times at the temperature extremes, a fact which is important in designing accelerated reliability tests as well as in service. The importance of creep makes the fatigue behavior of solder different from structural metals, such as copper, aluminum, or steel.

In summary, the effects of the thermal cycling profile on solder joint thermal fatigue life are as follows:

- *Temperature extremes:*   Decreasing the size of the thermal excursion is the single most effective way to increase the life of the solder joints. Since creep occurs more rapidly at higher temperatures, decreasing the peak temperature of the thermal cycle further decreases the amount of creep deformation that occurs during the hold at high temperature.

- *Frequency:*   The thermal fatigue damage per cycle is greater at lower cycling frequencies because there is more time for creep to occur, increasing the amount of permanent deformation. (Recall that most of the damage is

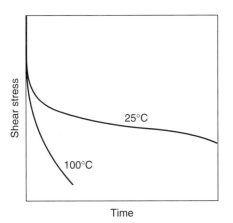

FIGURE 37.13 Typical behavior of solder in response to a constant applied displacement (for example, due to thermal expansion). The initial stress is relaxed over time as the solder elongates.

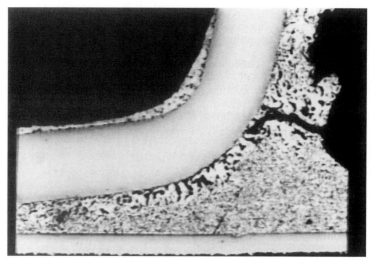

FIGURE 37.14 Thermal fatigue failure in eutectic Sn-Pb solder for a TSOP component. *(Photo courtesy K. Gratalo.)*

caused by the plastic deformation that occurs during each cycle, not by the cyclic stressing of the joint.)

- *Hold time:* As long as the stress on the solder joint remains nonzero, the thermal fatigue damage per cycle is increased if the hold time is lengthened, again because there is more time for creep to occur. Once the stress relaxation process has gone to completion, no further damage occurs and increasing the hold time further has no effect.

- *Thermal shock:* If the thermal cycle is extremely rapid, the components of the PCA may not be at the same temperature; consequently, the imposed strains may be larger or smaller than at slower rates.

Although the designer may be able to influence the peak temperature through cooling schemes, the thermal cycling profile and the frequency of thermal cycles in service are largely fixed by the application.

Solder joint fatigue life may be increased by decreasing the strain $\Delta\varepsilon$ imposed on the solder joint by:

- Choosing a package with a compliant attachment scheme. In this case, part of the strain is taken up by deflection of the lead, reducing the amount of strain in the solder. For these packages, the joint life can be further extended by decreasing the lead stiffness and increasing the joint area.

- Decreasing $\Delta\alpha$, the difference in the package and substrate thermal expansion coefficients, by carefully selecting the CTE of the package and substrate (see Secs. 37.5.3.1 and 37.5.1.1, respectively).

- Decreasing the size of the package, decreasing Δl.

- Increasing the height h of the solder joint.

Solder joint fatigue life may also be increased by:

- Decreasing the local CTE mismatch that occurs at the interfaces between the solder and the component lead and substrate metallization. While the substrate metallization is usually

Cu, which is moderately well matched to solder (17 vs. 25 ppm/°C), the leads may be made of a low-expansion metal such as Alloy 42 (~5 ppm/°C) or Kovar, as well as of Cu.

- Decreasing the mean stress imposed on the solder joint (for example, due to residual stress after assembly).

- Increasing ε_f or decreasing the creep rate of the solder by controlling the solder joint microstructure or by selecting an alternative solder. (Finer microstructures, which may be achieved by faster reflow cooling rates, have significantly greater fatigue lives because they are resistant to fatigue crack initiation and propagation. Unfortunately, solder microstructures coarsen over time, even at room temperature. Some solders, such as Sn-4Ag and 50In-50Pb, seem to have significantly improved fatigue lives over eutectic Sn-Pb; however, their higher reflow temperatures are not necessarily compatible with FR-4. See Sec. 37.5.2.2.)

Thermal Shock.   Thermal shocks (>30°C/s) cause failures because differential heating or cooling rates introduce large additional stresses into the assembly versus thermal cycling. Under thermal cycling conditions, it is a good assumption that all components of the assembly are at approximately the same temperature. (High-power components may be an exception.) Under thermal shock conditions, different portions of the assembly are temporarily at different temperatures because their heating or cooling rates are not the same. These temperature transients are caused by differences in thermal mass and thermal conductivity across the assembly; they are caused by component selection and placement decisions and by differences in the physical properties of the materials used in the assembly. The temperature differences across the assembly and any resulting warpage can enhance the stresses normally imposed during temperature changes due to differences in CTE. Thermal shocks can cause reliability problems, such as solder joint failures in overload and crazing in conformal coatings leading to corrosion failures, as well as a range of component failures. Because of the differential thermal stresses that may be induced, thermal shock can cause failures that do not occur during slower thermal cycling between the same temperature extremes. On the other hand, rapid thermal shock cycles actually cause less solder joint fatigue than slower thermal cycles; because little creep occurs, more cycles are needed to cause solder fatigue failure.

37.2.2.2 *Mechanically Induced Failures.*

PCAs can also fail in response to externally imposed mechanical stresses, for example, due to mechanical shock or vibration in shipping or in use. These failures can be divided into two categories: overload failures and mechanical fatigue failures, which are caused by mechanical shocks and vibration, respectively. Susceptibility to mechanical failures is closely linked to design of the PCA and the housing in which it is installed. The design determines the resonant frequency of the board, which in turn determines its response to external mechanical stresses. Cantilevers with low natural frequencies, such as an edge-mounted PCB with an unanchored large mass in the center, are particularly prone to failure. Depending on connector design and mounting scheme, solder joints to surface-mount connectors can also be vulnerable, particularly if there are many connector insertion cycles. See Ref. 20 for a more detailed discussion of design methodologies for mechanical durability.

Overload and Shock Failures of Solder Joints.   When a printed circuit assembly is flexed, jolted, or otherwise stressed, solder joint failures may occur. In general, solder is the weakest material in the assembly; however, when it connects a compliant structure such as a leaded component to the board, the lead flexes and the solder joint is not placed under much stress. Solder joints to leadless components will see large stresses since the board can bend and the components themselves are usually rigid. These stresses can occur if the assembly is mechanically shocked, for example, if the unit is dropped, or during further assembly processes if the PCB is bent through a significant radius. The primary method of eliminating this failure mode is through package selection; however, other factors also play a role, including PCB design, process control during printed circuit board fabrication and assembly, and the shear strength, tensile strength, and ductility of the solder. Solder joints are particularly prone to failure in tension because the brittle intermetallics at the interface between the solder and the substrate are stressed. Joints with thick intermetallic layers are more susceptible.

Mechanical (Vibration) Fatigue.   Vibration (a common source is an improperly mounted fan) can cause solder joint fatigue by repeatedly stressing the interconnects. Metal fatigue can occur even when this stress is well below the level that causes permanent deformation (that is, the yield stress). As for thermal fatigue of solder joints, the number of cycles to failure in mechanical vibration fatigue can be described by the Coffin-Manson relation. However, in contrast to thermal fatigue, failures usually occur after very large numbers of small, high-frequency cycles in which most of the strain in the solder is elastic ($\varepsilon = \sigma/E$, where σ is the stress and E is the elastic modulus of the solder). Consequently, creep does not play an important role in vibration fatigue. Although the damage per cycle is minimal, the number of cycles can be extremely high; they are often imposed at 50 or 60 Hz. Over time, a crack can nucleate, and subsequent cycles serve to propagate this crack. Again, the risk is much higher for joints to large leadless parts, since there is no compliant structure to take up part of the stress. The amount of damage to the solder joint depends on the imposed strain in each cycle, which depends largely on whether the excitation frequency is close to the natural frequency of the board. The mass of the component (including any heat sink) also plays an important role.

37.2.2.3   *Electrochemically Induced Failures.*   The electrochemical failure mechanisms accelerated by temperature, humidity, and electrical bias that were described in Sec. 37.2.1.3 for printed circuit boards also apply to the remainder of the PCA. The solder used for the interconnects and the metal component terminations and lead frame finishes can also be involved in the reactions. The large number of dissimilar metals increases the complexity of the situation and the possibility of galvanic corrosion in a humid environment. In addition, contaminants introduced during printed circuit assembly such as flux residues can contribute to the failures.

37.2.3   Components

Although the failure mechanisms of electronic components in general have been described in detail elsewhere[21–24] and are beyond the scope of this chapter, there are a few failure mechanisms that are specifically associated with electronic assembly. In addition, component de-rating for high-temperature service should be evaluated if the unit will be exposed to a severe service environment. Component failures due to thermal shock, exceeding the maximum allowable component temperatures, and plastic package cracking can occur during reflow or wave soldering. These assembly-related failure mechanisms are described briefly as follows.

37.2.3.1   *Thermal Shock.*   Multilayer ceramic capacitors may crack if exposed to thermal transients exceeding 4°C/s. These cracks are usually invisible, but may be the sites for dendritic growth in service, when the assembly is exposed to moisture under applied bias. Capacitors with high values and larger thicknesses are most susceptible. These failures can be avoided by following the manufacturer's requirements for maximum temperature excursion and rate of temperature change.

37.2.3.2   *Overtemperatures.*   Many components, including connectors, inductors, electrolytic capacitors, and crystals, cannot survive the SMT reflow process, although most will survive wave soldering. Problems can include melting of internal soldered connections, melting or softening of polymeric capacitor dielectrics, and expansion of elastomeric materials. These failures can be prevented by carefully following the manufacturer's recommendations for maximum processing temperature.[25]

37.2.3.3   *Molding Compound Delamination in Plastic SMT Packages.*   Plastic-packaged integrated circuits are generally transfer molded using a filled epoxy-based compound. The plastic can absorb moisture, which tends to accumulate at interfaces within the package, such as the die attach paddle. Subsequent heating can cause the moisture to vaporize, causing delamination at the interface, eventually leading to package failure. This delamination phenomenon is also termed package cracking or "popcorning." The newer thin SMT components (e.g., TSOPs and TQFPs) are more susceptible because the distance the moisture must diffuse through the plastic to reach internal interfaces is shorter. Delamination when these components are exposed to high temperature may be prevented by ensuring that the components are dry through dry storage and/or baking.[23]

37.3   *INFLUENCE OF DESIGN ON RELIABILITY*

Design has a major influence on the reliability of any product. The implications of the demands of the application and expected service environment on product design should be considered as early as possible, since they can influence a wide range of decisions, including integrated circuit partitioning, package and substrate selection (which will impose specific design rules and electrical performance characteristics), component layout and box design, and heat sinking and cooling. IPC Standard D-279, Design Guidelines for Reliable Surface Mount Technology Printed Board Guidelines, is a good place to start in considering these issues. Section 37.2 has already described how design can promote or hinder certain failure mechanisms. Section 37.4 discusses the influence of materials, which are selected during the design process, on PCB and interconnect failures. This section highlights the importance of good thermal and mechanical design.

The size of the thermal cycles imposed on the PCA during power on/off cycles can have an overwhelming influence on the reliability of integrated circuits, solder joints, and plated-though-holes, especially if the external service environment is not particularly severe; consequently, good thermal design is critical to reliability. The thermal cycles imposed on the assembly can come from joule heating from high-power components and from ambient heating. Integrated circuit reliability depends on maintaining low enough junction temperatures, usually below 85 to 110°C, depending on the IC technology. During continuous operation, solder joint temperatures should be kept below about 90°C to avoid the extensive intermetallic growth and grain coarsening that occur during long-term exposure to higher temperatures. As described under Sec. 37.2.1.1 and 37.2.2.1, the size and number of thermal excursions directly affect the fatigue life of both solder joints and plated-though-holes. Component spacings, orientations, air velocities, and enhancements such as thermally enhanced packages, heat sinks, and fans can all have major effects on the thermal cycle experienced by the assembly. PCBs can also be enhanced with metal cores to improve heat dissipation.

As mentioned in the earlier descriptions of specific failure modes, package selection and via and PTH specification can have a major effect on reliability. Although small holes can be desirable from a design density perspective, use of the smallest holes (aspect ratios of 5:1 or greater) should be minimized to minimize the risk of PTH failures. This is especially true if the design includes large through-hole parts which are likely to be reworked frequently (for example, due to test escapes). Similarly, some package styles are more susceptible to solder joint fatigue than others. The effect of integration on reliability can depend on the difference in package styles for the options under consideration. Integration can have a positive effect by reducing the total number of connections that could fail. On the other hand, if it requires a large package with a large CTE mismatch to the substrate, integration may reduce the reliability of the assembly.

The effect of externally imposed mechanical shock and vibration on PCA reliability is largely determined by design factors, although substrate and package selection also play a role. Component placement and PCA mounting in the box determine the natural frequency of the board and, consequently, the extent to which the board deflects. High-mass packages, often due to large heat sinks, are particularly susceptible, especially if there is a large lever arm.

37.4   IMPACT OF PCB FABRICATION AND ASSEMBLY ON RELIABILITY

37.4.1   Effect of PCB Fabrication Processes

37.4.1.1   Laminate and Lamination.   Delamination in PCBs may occur between the laminate materials or between the laminate material and the Cu foil. One cause of delamination is defective laminate material. Defects such as incomplete bonding at the resin/fiber interface can result in delamination due to formation of voids at these interfaces. Other common causes of delamination are excessive lamination pressure and/or temperature, contamination at interfaces, heavily oxidized copper foil surfaces, and lack of oxide treatment to enhance adhesion between copper innerlayers and prepreg. Debonding increases the risk of conductive anodic filament growth because it provides a place for moisture to accumulate. It can also result in increased stresses on the plated-through-holes (PTHs) during thermal cycling.

Laminate voids and resin recessions are separations of the laminate material from the copper conductor that may occur during multilayer PCB lamination. Most acceptability specifications prohibit voids larger than 0.076 mm (0.003 in); however, smaller voids are not generally considered to be detrimental to reliability. Some of the causes of laminate voids are entrapped air during lamination, improper flow of resin, and improper epoxy cure, perhaps due to improper lamination pressure and/or temperature, inappropriate heating rate, or too little prepreg.

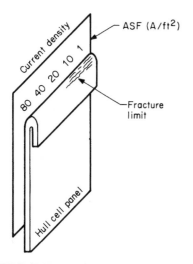

FIGURE 37.15   Ladwig panel ductility test. *(After Ref. 26.)*

37.4.1.2   Cu Foil.   The major cause of innerlayer foil cracks seems to be poor ductility of the Cu. Poor foil ductility can have a more significant effect on PTH reliability than such well-known culprits as insufficient plating thickness and excessive etchback. A minimum of 8 percent elongation is required for 1-oz foil to eliminate this problem. Foils plated in a Hull cell can be easily evaluated for room-temperature ductility using a 180° bend test. This technique is illustrated in Fig. 37.15, in which the sample panel is bent flat parallel to the axis along which current is varied.[26] Fractures occur at current densities producing low-ductility copper. This test can also be used to evaluate the influence of bath chemistry on ductility or as a bath monitor. Poor copper ductility can be correlated to the microstructure observed in metallographic cross sections.[27]

37.4.1.3   Drilling and Desmear.   Poor drilling and desmear (etchback) can cause PTH failures by providing stress concentrations that cause fatigue cracks to initiate. They can also cause voids and cracks at the interface to the copper plating, which can trap chemicals during plating and then contribute to conductive anodic filament growth. The following paragraphs describe the effects of poor desmear and some drilling defects which can cause poor plating, such as resin smear, rough walls, loose fibers, and burrs.

Resin smear can cause weak connections between plated-through-holes and innerlayer copper that fail under environmental stress. There is always some resin smear, which is removed by the desmear (etchback) process. If the desmear process is not effective, or if the resin smear is excessive, poor interconnection to the innerlayers can result. Possible causes of excessive smear are a dull drill or the wrong feed rate or drill speed, all of which can cause increased drill heating, resulting in more smear.

Similar errors in drilling setup can cause rough hole walls, loose fibers, or burrs. These defects are not serious in and of themselves, but can lead to rough plating or copper nodules, which introduce stress concentrations. Rough walls are typically associated with an incorrect feed rate or drill speed, or insufficiently cured material. Loose fibers may be caused by incorrect drilling parameters or improper cleaning. Burrs are usually associated with too fast a drill feed or a dull drill.

Poor drill registration can also decrease reliability of innerlayer via connections or the soldered connection to through-hole components. Poor registration can cause breakout on innerlayers; i.e., the drill hole may fall outside the pad on the innerlayer it is intended to connect to. Breakout increases the probability of PTH barrel failures. Breakout on outerlayers means that the solder fillet for a through-hole component will be partially missing, resulting in decreased reliability for some critical components.

Whether caused by excessive resin smear or not, poor etchback can result in a weak connection between the plating in the hole and the innerlayer copper. Etchback (see Fig. 37.16) removes laminate resin and woven glass in the hole so that the internal copper projects slightly into the hole, permitting the plating to make contact with the innerlayer foil on three sides. This strength is important to prevent cracking at the interface under thermal shock conditions. A review of innerlayer cracking in or around the electroless copper at the junction between the innerlayer foil and the electroplated Cu in the hole suggests that *negative* etchback, in which the electroplated Cu projects into the laminate may also give good results. Zero etchback, when innerlayer foil is flush with the hole wall, is the most dangerous case because the bond line between the foil and the plated copper is located at the point of maximum stress.[28] Causes of insufficient etchback include improper lamination and curing, hardened epoxy smear, a depleted smear removal bath, or a host of process control issues, including improper bath temperature, agitation, or time exposure.

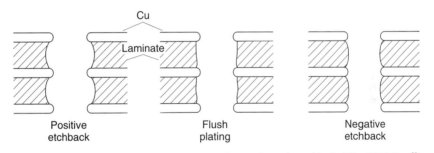

FIGURE 37.16   Schematic illustrations of positive, flush, and negative etchback. *(After M. W. Gray.[28])*

37.4.1.4 *Plating.*
Defects from the plating process can be responsible for a variety of PTH reliability problems; in addition, as previously described, problems in earlier process steps such as drilling and desmear often show up as plating defects.

Uniform coverage of the hole with electroless Cu is critical to the strength of the through-hole and the adhesion of the metallization to the laminate. Oxidation of the innerlayer copper prior to electroless Cu plating is one source of poor plating adhesion. Poor control of bath composition can have the same effect.

The adhesion of the electroplated Cu to the electroless Cu and the ductility of the electroplated Cu also strongly affect PTH reliability. If the adhesion between the layers is poor, this interface may be the weak point where failure initiates when the PTH is subjected to thermal stresses. Causes can include tarnished electroless copper that is insufficiently microetched, burning the electroless copper with too much current in electrolytic plating, and film contamination in the electrolytic copper.[28] Susceptibility to innerlayer cracks may be identified by looking for cracks in microsections after a solder float test. The fatigue life of the copper is directly related to its ductility. Plating process parameters and plating additives can strongly affect the plating ductility. For example, Mayer and Barbieri[29] found that good thermal shock resistance of electrodeposits of acid copper depended on proper concentrations of three additives:

1. A leveling agent, to smooth over surface imperfections. (Without the leveling agent imperfections are reproduced in the deposit.)

2. A ductility-promoting agent, which functions to produce the equiaxed grain structure.

3. A carrying agent, to guide the other two components to create the equiaxed structure. (Striations occurred with insufficient carrying agent.)

Additive levels below a certain threshold make the bath more susceptible to impurity effects. For example, iron contamination of 100 mg/L without the recommended concentration of ductility-promoting agents was found to produce a columnar grain structure at the hole corners. Similarly, organic contaminants such as photoresist can produce laminar deposits.

Insufficient plating thickness in the barrel also directly reduces PTH reliability because the stress and, consequently, the strain in the Cu are increased. Overall insufficient plating thickness can be caused by a depleted bath or insufficient plating time, among other things. Insufficient plating thickness in individual holes can also occur as a result of nonuniformities in plating current caused by nonuniform copper feature density. It is particularly difficult to obtain adequate plating thickness in the center of high-aspect-ratio PTHs; good process control is important for aspect ratios greater than 3:1. Good coverage is difficult to obtain for aspect ratios greater than 5:1 by electroplating.

What constitutes "sufficient" plating thickness in PTHs is a subject of some controversy. Specifications range from 0.5 to 1 mil (12 to 25 μm) Cu thickness in the barrel. There are at least two reasons why there is no one right specification. First, different applications provide different levels of thermal stress and demand different levels of reliability. Second, design factors such as the aspect ratio of the plated holes determine the susceptibility of the PTHs to thermal fatigue. The IPC recommends an average minimum copper-plating thickness of 0.5 mil for consumer products (Class 1) and 1.0 mil for general industrial and high-reliability applications (Classes 2 and 3).

Poor coverage at the PTH knee can significantly accelerate PTH failures because it means the plating is thin at a point of high stress. It can be caused by excessive concentration of the organic leveling agents added to an electroplating bath.

37.4.1.5 Solder Mask Application.   If it is properly applied, solder mask plays an important role in reducing the possibility of insulation resistance failures on PCBs. The solder mask protects the substrate from moisture and contaminants, which would otherwise promote shorting under electrical bias. The ability of the solder mask to perform this function depends on good conformity and adhesion of the solder mask to a clean, dry substrate. If solder mask conformity or adhesion is poor, moisture and other contaminants may accumulate at crevices or delaminations between the solder mask and the substrate. Substrate cleanliness is particularly critical, because in addition to causing poor solder mask adhesion, it can also provide the ionic species needed for rapid electromigration. When the laminate material absorbs moisture readily (e.g., polyimide, aramids), baking before reflow may be required to prevent solder mask delamination (as well as reinforcement/resin delamination). Other causes of poor adhesion or conformity include moisture on the board when the solder mask is applied, improper solder mask lamination or coating parameters, and improper solder mask cure parameters. Incomplete solder mask cure can create local soft pockets, which are common sites for delamination or contaminant entrapment. Solder mask over solder should also be avoided because delamination caused by reflow of the solder may allow contaminants to be entrapped.

37.4.2 Effects of Printed Circuit Assembly Processes

37.4.2.1 Stencil Printing and Component Placement. Stencil printing and component placement generally do not cause reliability problems; however, poor stencil design or stencil printing or placement process control can create issues with solder volume and component cracking. Very low solder volume can result in weak solder joints that fail rapidly in thermal fatigue or by overload. In some cases, excessive solder volume can also accelerate solder joint fatigue failures because the compliance of the lead is reduced. Assuming that the stencil was designed and manufactured correctly, low solder volumes are usually due to small or missing paste bricks caused by a clogged stencil aperture, a stencil that needs cleaning, or improper stencil-printing parameters. Paste bridging can cause low solder volumes on some joints and high volumes on others because one joint may rob solder from another. Paste bridging may be caused by improper stencil design or stencil-printing parameters or by excessive force when placing chip carriers (e.g., PLCCs) and quad flat packs (e.g., PQFPs). Excessive placement force can also cause component cracking, particularly for small leadless ceramic components.

37.4.2.2 Reflow. The reflow process attaches SMT and some TH components to the PCB by melting solder paste to form solder joints using an oven with a controlled thermal profile (see Fig. 37.17) and, in some cases, a controlled atmosphere (often N_2). Reliability problems that can arise due to improper reflow parameters can be grouped into three categories: damaged components, poor solder joints, and, for no-clean assemblies, cleanliness issues.

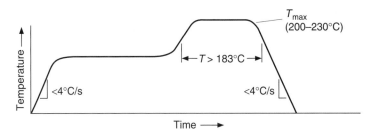

FIGURE 37.17 Schematic reflow profile for eutectic Sn-Pb solder paste, FR-4 substrate and typical surface-mount components illustrating key features from a reliability perspective.

Component Damage. The reflow process is responsible for most of the assembly-process-related component failures described in Sec. 37.2.3. These failures include molding compound delamination in plastic packages that have absorbed moisture (popcorning) and component failures due to overheating or thermal shock caused by excessive heating or cooling rates. All of these problems are preventable with good procedures and process controls.

Package cracking can be prevented by storing components in the unopened dry bags in which they are shipped and by baking the moisture out of components that have been exposed to ambient conditions for too long. The manufacturer's recommendations regarding bake-out conditions and maximum exposure times before reflow should be followed, but a good general guideline is that packages that have been exposed to the atmosphere for more than 8 h should be baked to a moisture content below 0.1 percent by weight immediately prior to use; a bake of 125°C for 24 h is usually safe, although shorter times may be acceptable. Note that the same concerns apply for rework and second-side reflow of double-sided boards; for example, if the boards are stored for several days between reflow steps, bake-out before the second reflow step may be required.

Component failures due to overheating or thermal shock can be prevented by monitoring the reflow temperature profile in several locations on the PCB to ensure that it meets the manufacturer's specifications for temperature-sensitive components. Measuring the board profile is important because temperatures on the board can differ significantly from oven panel temperatures and from the ambient temperature in each oven zone. Temperatures may also vary significantly across the board if there are large differences in the thermal mass of the components or in component density. Areas of the assembly that are devoid of components are particularly sensitive to overheating, which can damage the laminate as well as any small components in the area. Temperature variations across the assembly tend to be much smaller for ovens with predominantly convection heating than for ovens with predominantly infrared heating. A poor reflow profile can also cause a variety of other problems; some of the others that also affect reliability will be mentioned here.

Poor Solder Joints.   A sound solder joint wets both the component termination and the substrate well, does not contain large or numerous voids, and does not have excessively thick intermetallic layers at the interfaces. When using solder paste, the reflow profile is the dominant factor in achieving these goals. Good wetting requires solderable incoming materials, but it also requires a reflow profile that gives the flux sufficient time to act in the right temperature range. In addition, the profile should ensure that all parts of the board are at least 15°C over the melting temperature of the solder for at least several seconds. "Cold," improperly formed solder joints can occur if the solder does not fully melt or if oxidation prevents the solder balls in the paste from melting together. The latter problem can be caused by an improper reflow profile or the wrong reflow atmosphere. Voiding is generally caused by a reflow profile that does not permit enough time for the solvents in the paste to boil off before the solder melts. All of these problems can be avoided by ensuring that the reflow profile of the board and reflow atmosphere (e.g., O_2 level) correspond to the manufacturer's recommendations for the solder paste.

Excessively long reflow times (time above the solder liquidus) can cause thick intermetallic layers to form at the interface between the solder and the component termination or substrate. Formation of an intermetallic layer at the solder interface indicates good metallurgical bonding, but thick intermetallic layers are undesirable because intermetallics are brittle and prone to fracture, especially if the joint is stressed in tension rather than shear. Because solder joint fatigue takes place in the solder rather than in the intermetallics or at the solder/intermetallic interface, the basic mechanism is unaffected. Nonetheless long reflow times and the accompanying thick intermetallic layers should be avoided. Cross-sectioning can be used to judge the extent of intermetallic growth; as long as the intermetallic layer thickness is relatively small compared to the joint thickness, reliability should not be adversely affected.[30] (Note however that minimizing reflow time is still a good thing; the reliability of all the components on the board is adversely affected by time at elevated temperature, both during processing and in service. Unfortunately, in developing a reflow profile, there is often a tradeoff between reflow time and peak temperature.)

Cleanliness Issues.   An improper reflow profile can also cause solder balling and increase the amount of flux residue remaining on the board after reflow. The reliability concerns associated with these process issues are discussed in Sec. 37.4.2.4. Solder balls can be caused by a combination of improper paste storage or handling, incompatibility between the flux and reflow atmosphere and a reflow profile that does not conform to the manufacturer's specification.

37.4.2.3 *Wave-Soldering Process.*   Improper wave-soldering practice can cause reliability problems. The root cause is generally thermal shock, overheating of the top side of the board, or contamination of the solder bath.

Component Cracking.   Ceramic components such as resistors and capacitors will crack under thermal shock conditions. When they are located on the bottom of the board they can be heated rapidly by the solder wave. Prevention is relatively simple; the assembly must be preheated before it hits the solder wave. A temperature difference between the component and the solder wave of less than 100°C is recommended; a typical preheat temperature is 150°C.

Hot Cracking.   Hot cracking, also known as partial melting, can cause previously sound solder joints to fail during the wave-soldering process. A typical mixed TH/SMT assembly is manufactured by assembling the surface-mount components to the top side, inserting the through-hole components, and wave soldering these components to the board from the bottom side. The first step of the wave-soldering process usually involves preheating the entire board. During the wave-soldering process, the SMT joints on the top side will be further heated due to conduction of heat through the board, particularly if there are many vias. If these solder joints reach the melting temperature of the solder (usually 183°C), the joints will begin to melt. If the joints melt completely, the assembly may be intact after reflow; however, if they only begin to melt, the surface tension of the solder is insufficient to prevent cracks from forming between the portions that are still solid. This type of failure is often detected as an intermittent in the field, since in-circuit test fixtures may bring the two halves of the joint into mechanical contact, causing the joint to appear electrically good.

Solder Bath Contamination.   Solder bath contaminant levels should be regularly monitored and limited to levels found in IPC-S-815. Many metals found on component terminations will dissolve into molten eutectic Sn-Pb solder. High Cu concentration is a relatively common occurrence that is associated with a rough solder surface and causes poor solderability. High Au concentrations can embrittle solder joints (see Sec. 37.5.1.3 for a discussion of this phenomenon).

37.4.2.4 Cleaning and Cleanliness.

Improper handling procedures and improper selection and application of solder paste and wave-solder fluxes and their associated cleaning processes can cause ionic residues to be left on the board that result in low surface insulation resistance. Low SIR values can cause failures in and of themselves for some sensitive circuits and in other cases set up the conditions for further corrosion that eventually result in short circuits. Sodium and potassium ions and halide ions are the most commonly quoted culprits for these failures. The major source of sodium and potassium ions is handling, i.e., fingerprints. The primary sources of halide ions are soldering fluxes.

The elimination of chlorofluorocarbons (CFCs) mandated by the Montreal Protocol has caused most SMT manufacturers to switch to water cleaning or a no-clean process. Water cleaning has been used by most printed circuit board manufacturers for some time, but outgoing cleanliness was not carefully monitored since the boards were cleaned again after assembly. Both the no-clean and water-clean assembly approaches must meet certain criteria to provide reliable assemblies.

In a no-clean assembly process, there is no cleaning step after SMT or TH assembly. The finished assembly has whatever contaminants were present on the incoming board and components, plus any additional contaminants added during the assembly process. These contaminants are generally flux residues, both from the solder paste and the flux applied for wave soldering, although adhesives and fingerprints are other potential sources. A no-clean flux should have a low solids content so that it leaves little residue and be free of ionic contaminants such as halides that promote corrosion. Use of a flux that contains halides will result in low SIR readings and may result in shorting due to corrosion, particularly if the assembly is exposed to a humid environment. However the incoming components and boards are cleaned, it is important that they are also free of halides when they arrive for assembly. Although SIR testing provides the best correlation with reliability, an ionic contamination test may be used for statistical process control. The measurement method may be found in MIL-P-28809.

Solder balls may also be a problem on no-clean assemblies. Solder balls are formed during reflow of solder paste when some solder is left behind when the solder melts and beads up and by spattering during wave soldering. These solder balls are usually washed off by solvent or water cleaning; however, in a no-clean process they remain on the board. Solder balls can cause shorts by bridging the pads of small capacitors or resistors or the leads of fine-pitch quad flat packs.

In a water-clean assembly process, the assemblies are cleaned with jets of deionized or saponified water after SMT and TH assembly. This process will work only if the flux residues and other contaminants are sufficiently soluble in either water or saponified water. It also depends on good access to the residues; consequently, a minimum component standoff that permits cleaning is required if it is possible for flux to get underneath the component body during assembly. It is almost as important that the board be thoroughly dried because water is an excellent medium for galvanic corrosion. Proper drying can be quite difficult even with substantial air flow since water has a much lower vapor pressure than CFCs do. If the component standoff is low, capillary action holds water in the small gap. If water cleaning is done in midprocess (e.g., before a reflow or wave-soldering step), plastic components may absorb moisture; in this case, the board must be baked out to prevent package cracking in subsequent high-temperature processes (see Secs. 37.2.3 and 37.4.2.2).

The rework process should not be overlooked in planning a flux and cleaning strategy. Compared to the automated processes that proceed it, it is typical to use a more aggressive flux and more of it to do rework. Use of a halide-free flux or proper cleaning after rework is essential to prevent cleanliness-related reliability problems.

Finally, the cleaning process itself can damage the PCA. Ultrasonic cleaning can damage components with internal wire bonds or die attach. It has also been observed to cause fatigue cracking of solder joints to LEDs and SOT-23s when the energy density was high because these components have terminations that are mechanically resonant near the generator frequencies. Solvent cleaning can attack the polymers used in solder masks, PCBs, conformal coatings, and components. D-limonene (terpene)-based solvents should be tested carefully for compatibility with exposed plastics and metals.

37.4.2.5 *Electrical Test and Depanel.*

The electrical testing and depanel processes can impose large mechanical stresses on the PCB and its components. In-circuit electrical test utilizes a bed of nails or two beds in a clamshell arrangement to contact each electrical node on the board. The probes must contact the board with sufficient force to make good electrical contact. If the board is not properly fixtured or if the loading in a clamshell fixture is unbalanced, the resulting deflections can cause solder joint or component cracking. These cracks may cause electrical failures immediately or after some period of service. Depaneling, the process of separating individual images from a larger panel, is done by a variety of methods. The associated mechanical deflections or vibration can cause component cracking or solder joint fatigue.

37.4.2.6 *Rework.*

Rework, whether repair of open or shorted solder joints or replacement of defective components, has a significant negative effect on component reliability. If there were not enough other incentives for low process defect rates, the effect on product reliability would be enough. Reworking the quality in does not bring the board to the quality level that would have been reached if the boards were built right the first time. Some of the ways rework processes can adversely affect reliability are described here.

Thermal Shock During Rework. Thermal shock to components is a concern during rework as it is during reflow. The maximum heating or cooling rate is driven by the requirements for ceramic capacitors and should not exceed 4°C/s.[31]

Rework of large through-hole components, such as pin grid arrays (PGAs) and large connectors, poses special problems. If it is improperly done it can result in PTH failures. Because the damage during these large thermal cycles is cumulative, the number of rework operations at a given site should be monitored and limited to a safe number. The number of cycles that will cause a fatigue crack to initiate in the copper in the barrel and propagate to failure depends on the aspect ratio of the PTH, the type and thickness of plating in the hole, the substrate material, etc.

Due to the large number of joints that must be melted at once and the large thermal mass of the components, rework of large TH components is often done with a solder pot. The thermal shock caused when the molten solder hits the board can cause PTH cracking due to z-axis expansion. A preheat step (to about 100°C for FR-4) helps to reduce the damage. The time the board is in contact with the solder fountain should also be minimized since dissolution of the copper plating inside the PTH occurs during this time. Thinning the plating in the PTH tends to increase the strain in the Cu during thermal cycling, further accelerating failure. If the total time for part removal and replacement is kept under 25 s, little dissolution is measured.[32] Weakening of the PTH by copper dissolution during PGA rework can be essentially eliminated by using NiAu plating. Although the thin Au coating that protects the Ni dissolves almost instantly during soldering, Ni dissolves quite slowly and effectively prevents thinning of the PTH metallization.

Damage to Adjacent Components.   Rework can also damage components adjacent to the one being repaired or replaced. The hot cracking phenomenon during wave soldering can also occur in solder joints near the rework site if they reach the melting temperature of the solder. At slightly lower temperatures, rapid intermetallic growth can occur. Temperature-sensitive components can also be damaged. To prevent these problems, localized heating and shielding should be used and the temperature of adjacent components monitored. The generally recommended maximum temperature is 150°C. There are wide variations in the amount of heating of adjacent components among different types of rework equipment and between process protocols.[33]

Other Rework Concerns.   Rework can cause a host of moisture-related problems including measling and package cracking. Both of these problems can be prevented by baking the PCA beforehand to drive out moisture and by minimizing the peak temperature and time at elevated temperature during rework. Rework temperatures also weaken the adhesive bond between the copper conductors on the PCB and the laminate material; use of force to remove components when the solder is not completely molten can cause the pad to lift off the board. The latter can be a particular problem when using a soldering iron.[21,31]

37.5 INFLUENCE OF MATERIALS SELECTION ON RELIABILITY

37.5.1 PCB

37.5.1.1 Substrate.   Difunctional FR-4 is the workhorse material for high-reliability PCBs because its moderate z-axis expansion and moisture uptake characteristics are available at relatively low cost. Alternative substrate materials (see Table 37.2) are generally selected for more favorable properties in one or more of the following three areas: thermal performance, including maximum operating temperature and glass transition temperature; thermal expansion coefficient; and electrical properties, such as dielectric constant. Thermal performance characteristics and thermal expansion coefficient can have a significant effect on PCB and solder joint reliability. Other characteristics of these materials, such as moisture absorption, can also affect reliability.

PTH reliability can be improved by selecting a laminate with a lower z-axis CTE or a higher T_g. The damage caused to the PTH during a thermal cycle depends on the total z-axis expansion during the temperature change. Since the CTE is much lower below T_g than above,

TABLE 37.2 Physical Properties of Some Printed Circuit Board Laminate Materials

Material	CTE, x,y ppm/°C	CTE, z ppm/°C	T_g, °C
Epoxy glass (FR-4, G-10)	14–18	180	125–135
Modified epoxy glass (polyfunctional FR-4)	14–16	170	140–150
Epoxy aramid	6–8	66	125
Polyimide quartz	6–12	35	188–250

Source: After IPC-D-279.

the PTH strain can be reduced by increasing the T_g so that more or all of the cycle is below T_g (see Fig. 37.18a). Figure 37.18b shows that the increase in life can be quite significant. The strain imposed on the PTH can also be reduced by decreasing the CTE at temperatures below T_g, but the effect on total z-axis expansion is much smaller.

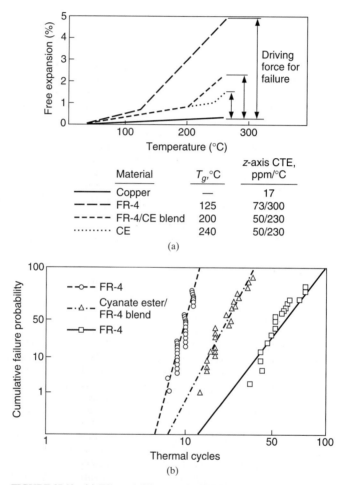

Material	$T_g,°C$	z-axis CTE, ppm/°C
—— Copper	—	17
– – – FR-4	125	73/300
– – – – FR-4/CE blend	200	50/230
· · · · · · · CE	240	50/230

(a)

(b)

FIGURE 37.18 (a) Effect of differences in CTE below T_g and T_g on the free z-axis expansion of FR-4 (epoxy-glass), cyanate ester (cyanate ester-glass) and a cyanate ester/epoxy blend. T_g and CTE for each material below/above T_g are indicated. Cyanate ester is abbreviated CE in the figure. Cu is shown for comparison. (b) Weibull plot of PTH failures for these substrates during thermal shock cycling between 25 and 260°C. PTHs are 0.029-in diameter on 0.100-in grid on 0.125-in-thick laminate. (*After Fehrer and Haddick.*[4])

A variety of specialty resins with increased T_g is available, albeit at higher prices. Modified FR-4 materials with higher functionality offer the best combination of improved T_g at a reasonable price. Further improvements in T_g and other characteristics can be obtained with bismaleimide triazine (BT), GETEK, cyanate ester, and polyimide, but at greater price penalties.

Interconnect failures due to thermal fatigue of solder joints can be reduced by closely matching the *x-y* plane thermal expansion properties of the substrate to at-risk components. Large leadless ceramic components that are used because of their hermeticity pose a particular risk. Possible approaches include altering the laminate reinforcement material, adding constraining metal cores or planes, and switching to a ceramic substrate. The first two approaches are discussed here. A more extensive discussion of these options can be found in Ref. 33.

A lower *x-y* plane thermal expansion coefficient laminate can be obtained by replacing the continuous-filament E-glass used in most FR-4 PCBs with an alternative material. The CTE decreases as the fraction of silica dioxide (SiO_2) decreases and the level of quartz (as well as the cost) increases in the progression E-glass, S-glass, D-glass, and finally quartz, which has a CTE about one-tenth of E-glass. Aramid (Kevlar) actually has a negative CTE, but it is available in only a few glass styles. Some of the disadvantages of aramid fibers are higher *z*-axis expansion and higher moisture absorption relative to glass fibers that can result in decreased susceptibility to PTH failures and corrosion-related insulation resistance failures, respectively. Aramid fiber is also used to make nonwoven paper fabric which has a lower modulus, but also a much smoother surface because there is no weave pattern. This form has better dimensional stability and reduced microcracking during thermal cycling.

Low-thermal-expansion metal cores or planes can also lower the overall substrate CTE because they constrain the expansion of the polymer material they are laminated to (see Fig. 37.19). Copper-Invar-copper (CIC) is the most widely used material for constraining metal cores (also termed polymer-on-metal or POM construction), followed by copper-molybdenum-copper (CMC). The PCB and core are bonded with a rigid adhesive, usually in a balanced construction to minimize warping. Other special processing is also required. The CTE of the assembly can be estimated using a simple model for composite structures most often written as

$$\text{CTE(overall)} = \frac{\Sigma E \alpha t}{\Sigma E t}$$

where *E*, α, and *t* are the elastic modulus, CTE, and thickness, respectively, of the various layers. A more sophisticated model can be found in Ref. 34.

An example of the low overall CTE that can be obtained using a CIC core is shown in Fig. 37.20. Unfortunately, the constrained *x-y* axis expansion results in increased *z*-axis expansion that can reduce PTH reliability to dangerously low levels, especially in an environment in which the full mil-spec thermal cycle of −55 to +125°C is imposed. Consequently, use of polyimide is recommended with CIC cores. Because of its high T_g and low CTE below T_g, polyimide imposes much lower strains on the PTH for a given thermal cycle than other dielectrics.

Constructions utilizing constraining low-CTE metal planes usually use CIC layers in place of ground and power planes in a standard multilayer board. The same PTH reliability concerns that hold for CIC core boards apply to these PCBs as well. PTH reliability can be improved by using polyimide resin and by using CuNiAu or CuNiSn metallization in the PTHs. These substrates are easier to manufacture than metal core boards because standard PCB fabrication techniques can be used for the most part.

Resin material can affect fiber/resin delamination, one of the prerequisites for conductive anodic filament growth. Measling occurs at about 260°C for FR-4, but may occur at lower temperatures for boards with more hygroscopic resins.

37.5.1.2 Solder Mask. The three major types of solder mask—liquid screen-printed, dry film, and liquid photoimageable (LPI)—come with different benefits and concerns from a reliability perspective. The solder mask material should be selected for its compatibility with the heat and solvent characteristics of the assembly process, its capability to provide good conformity over surface features on the PCB, and its ability to tent vias if required. Since many of these characteristics are product-specific, only a few general guidelines can be provided here. Where tenting of vias is required to keep solder, moisture, or flux from wicking up

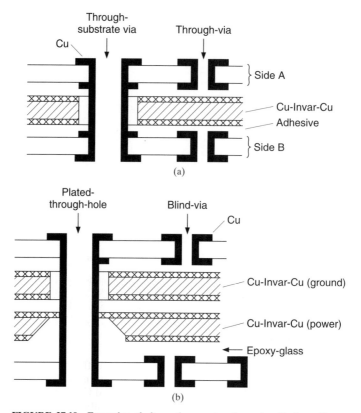

FIGURE 37.19 Examples of alternative construction using Cu-Invar-Cu to achieve low-*x-y* CTE: (*a*) metal core (sides A and B may be multilayer boards) and (*b*) metal plane constructions. (*After F. Gray.*[34])

under components, dry film solder mask should be used. However, excessively thick solder mask, particularly dry film over closely spaced traces, can result in crevices. If the solder mask cannot flow enough to adhere closely to the board, the resulting crevices can entrap contaminants such as flux that can accelerate corrosion later. LPI solder mask provides excellent coverage, resolution, and alignment to other features, but it generally cannot be used to tent vias. IPC-SM-840 defines the performance and qualification requirements for solder mask.

37.5.1.3 Metal Finish.   The metal finish on the SMT and TH pads can have an impact on PTH reliability and on the reliability of the solder joints made to these pads. Common metal finishes for solder-mask-over-bare-copper (SMOBC) boards include hot-air solder leveling (HASL or HAL), organic-coated copper (OCC), and electroless NiAu. Galvanically plated CuNiAu and CuNiSn made by another processing route are also available. These finishes provide a solderable finish for later printed circuit assembly. The pros and cons of the various finishes are discussed in turn.

Of the common metal finishes, HASL is the only one which can directly reduce reliability of the board. In a typical HASL process, the board receives a severe thermal shock when it is dunked into a bath of molten eutectic Sn-Pb solder. The PTHs can survive only a certain number of solder shocks without failure; this process uses up one of these thermal cycles before the board leaves the fabricator.

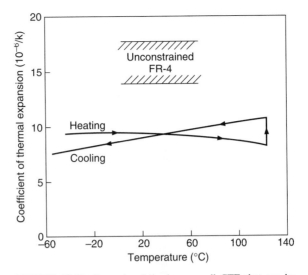

FIGURE 37.20 Example of the low overall CTE that can be achieved for a metal core construction similar to Fig. 37.19a. Two 0.055-in (1.4-mm)-thick multilayer FR-4 boards were bonded to a 0.085-in (2.2-mm)-thick copper-Invar-copper core. Data shown are for the third thermal cycle. (*After F. Gray.*)

Organic-coated copper provides a consistent, flat, solderable metal finish. Exposed copper after printed circuit assembly has been a persistent reliability concern, because it is generally not permitted on HASL boards. While exposed Cu on HASL boards is associated with poor solderability, which may be due to contaminants that were not removed before the HASL process, there is little evidence that exposed Cu on a properly processed OCC board causes reliability problems. Surface insulation resistance (SIR) testing shows that OCC boards have comparable or better performance than HASL boards in high-temperature, high-humidity storage tests.

CuNiAu boards fabricated either with the NiAu as the Cu etch resist or by the SMOBC process followed by electrolessly plating Ni and Au can confer improved PTH reliability. There are two mechanisms for the observed improvement: the enhanced rivet effect provided by the Ni and the elimination of Cu dissolution during solder shocks such as wave soldering or PGA rework. For high-aspect-ratio holes, electroless Ni confers an additional benefit because the plating thickness in the barrel is more consistent than for conventional electro-plating.

In the simple picture of PTH failure shown in Fig. 37.3, the comparatively low CTE metal-plated PTH acts as a rivet that resists the z-axis expansion of the PCB. Because Ni has a higher elastic modulus than Cu, it strains less under the stress imposed by the expanding PCB. Consequently, adding Ni plating lowers the strain imposed on the Cu and lessens the amount of fatigue damage. In this model, the Ni protects the Cu, increasing PTH life.

The ability of the Cu to withstand the forces imposed on it by thermal expansion of the PCB is also dependent on the thickness of the Cu in the PTH. Unfortunately, in the SMOBC process all subsequent steps after pattern or panel plating reduce the Cu thickness from the plated amount. Nickel plating is resistant to the etches and developers used in later processing steps, so it protects the underlying copper from thinning due to dissolution. The HASL process and rework of large through-hole connectors or pin grid arrays (PGAs) can have particularly negative effects. Cu dissolves rapidly into molten eutectic Sn-Pb solder. During the HASL process or component removal and replacement with a solder fountain, large amounts of Cu can dissolve from the knee of the PTH. Nickel barrier plating minimizes this effect because Ni dissolves far more slowly in eutectic Sn-Pb solder than Cu does.

Use of Au plating can embrittle the eutectic Sn-Pb solder most commonly used in electronic assembly. Gold plating of various thicknesses is used for a variety of reasons, including as a solderability preservative over nickel plating, for connector contacts, and to provide wire-bondable pads. Reliability problems can arise because Au has a high solubility in eutectic Sn-Pb solders at reflow temperatures and dissolves extremely rapidly. In most cases, the Au finish on a PCB or component termination will be completely dissolved into the solder. In a wave-soldering process, the Au will be washed into the bath, requiring monitoring and bath changes to maintain the Au concentration at a low level that does not affect the process. However, in a reflow process, this Au remains in the finished solder joint. To avoid embrittlement of the solder by the $AuSn_4$ and $AuSn_2$ intermetallics that can form, the Au concentration should be kept below a critical level that most authors set at 3 to 5 percent by weight.[35,36]

For most components used today, a nominal 5-μin (0.1-μm) thickness Au flash to preserve solderability is harmless. However, if thicker Au plating (e.g., for connector contacts or wire bonding) is used, if the component lead pitch is less than 0.5 mm, or if the component lead terminations are also Au-plated, care should be taken to ensure that the Au concentration remains below the 3 to 5 percent by weight limit. For some applications in which use of thick Au is unavoidable, 50In-50Pb solder, in which Au dissolves very slowly, has been used to get around this problem.[37] Selective thick Au plating is another option.

The Au concentration in the finished reflowed solder joint can be estimated using the following equation:

$$\text{Wt. \% Au} = \frac{(\text{Au volume})}{[(\text{Au volume}) + (\text{solder volume})(\rho_{solder/Au})]}$$

where $\rho_{solder/Au}$ is the ratio of the density of the solder to the density of Au (0.4552 for 63Sn-37Pb solder). If the Au is less than 1 μm thick, it is usually valid to assume that all of the Au on the joined surfaces has dissolved into the joint. The solder volume should include any solder plated on either the component or board termination as well as that applied by stencil printing. It is common to specify only a minimum Au plating thickness; it is important to use a representative value to calculate the expected Au content in the solder joint.

37.5.2 Interconnect Material

37.5.2.1 Eutectic Sn-Pb Solder.   Eutectic Sn-Pb solder, 63Sn-37Pb, and near-eutectic Sn-Pb solders, including 60Sn-40Pb and 62Sn-36Pb-2Ag, are used in the overwhelming majority of soldered electronic assemblies. From a reliability perspective, the most important characteristics of these solders are their susceptibility to creep and fatigue because ambient temperatures are so close to the metal temperature of the solder, their ability to dissolve common termination metals rapidly and in large amounts, and their tendency to form thick intermetallic layers with termination metals.

Although solder joint thermal fatigue is a major source of PCA field failures, the industry has used the same solder alloy for several decades. At present, there is no generally agreed-on alternative to eutectic Sn-Pb solder that has improved fatigue resistance as well as the favorable processing characteristics of eutectic Sn-Pb solder. However, there has been a tremendous surge in research into alternative solders, especially Pb-free solders, in the last decade and one can expect improved alloys in the future. There is some evidence that solders containing 2% Ag have improved properties in thermal cycling to high temperatures.

Many common termination metals dissolve rapidly in eutectic Sn-Pb solder, including Ag, Au, and Cu.[36] The dissolved metals can alter the properties of the solder. Reliability can also be impacted if the termination metal is dissolved entirely, the most notable case being Ag (or AgPd with less than 33% Pd) terminations on ceramic resistors and capacitors. If the entire termination thickness is dissolved, the solder will dewet from the ceramic part, leaving an open joint if the entire termination is dissolved, or a substantially weakened one if it is dissolved only in some areas. Use of 63Sn-36Pb-2Ag substantially reduces this problem, since the presence of Ag in the solder reduces the dissolution rate of the Ag forming the termination.

Finally, eutectic and near-eutectic Sn-Pb solders form intermetallics with the termination metals that influence the properties of the finished joints. On the most common termination metals, Cu and Ni, continuous intermetallic layers form: Cu_3Sn and Cu_6Sn_5 on copper, and Ni_3Sn_4, Ni_3Sn_2, and Ni_3Sn on nickel. These intermetallic layers are composed of compounds that are hard and brittle in comparison to both the solder and the termination metals. Although there have been few systematic comparisons made, it is general wisdom that when the intermetallic layers are very thick, solder joint reliability is reduced. While solder joint thermal fatigue mostly involves cracking in the solder, the intermetallics can affect their ability to withstand mechanical stresses, particularly in tension. The Ni-Sn intermetallics are particularly brittle. In every case, an effort should be made to minimize the total time the solder is molten during processing and to minimize the time above about 150°C once the solder joint is formed.

37.5.2.2 Other Solders.   A number of other solders are used in specialized applications, including 80Sn-20Pb for lead finishes, 50In-50Pb for solder on thick Au, high-Pb solders such as 95Pb-5Sn and 97Pb-3Sn for flip-chip assemblies (usually on ceramic substrates), and low-temperature solders such as 58Bi-42Sn and 52In-48In, where hierarchical soldering is desirable. Further information can be found in Refs. 23, 24, and 38.

37.5.2.3 Conductive Adhesives.   Electrically conductive adhesives are used today for specialized applications such as connections to LCD displays and attachment of small resistors and capacitors. These materials consist of conductive particles, usually silver flakes or carbon, suspended in a polymer matrix, most commonly epoxy. The electrical resistance of the contact to the PCB tends to be unstable over time, so these materials are not suitable for applications requiring a constant, low-resistance contact. The primary failure mechanism is moisture migration through the epoxy to the interface, resulting in oxidation of the contact metal. Adhesion strength is also a reliability concern. New materials suitable for a broader range of applications are under development. Further information can be found in Ref. 39.

37.5.3 Components

Components and their packages influence many of the field failures of electronic assemblies. Packages are primarily designed and selected for their ability to protect the electronic components inside; for example, ceramic packages may be selected over plastic ones for their greater hermeticity. This section will discuss the ways in which package selection can influence solder joint and cleanliness-related failures.

37.5.3.1 Package Selection to Minimize Solder Joint Thermal and Mechanical Failures.
Minimizing solder joint thermal and mechanical fatigue failures means minimizing the global and local mismatches in the system and introducing compliance that minimizes the stresses and strains transmitted to the solder joints. Figure 37.21 illustrates the important features of these systems. The following describes how component parameters can influence the incidence of solder joint failures.

Surface-Mount Technology vs. Through-Hole Components.   Although there is little compliance in the system, the reliability of through-hole solder joints generally exceeds that of surface-mount joints in thermal fatigue (assuming good solder fillets are present in both cases), because the loading geometry makes it difficult for a crack to propagate far enough to cause an electrical failure. However, the PTHs themselves may be susceptible to failure if they are exposed to even a few thermal cycles well above T_g.

Plastic vs. Ceramic Package. The global mismatch between the component body and substrate is minimized for most printed circuit boards if the package is plastic rather than ceramic. Most electronic ceramics have CTEs in the neighborhood of 4 to 10 ppm. Since the printed circuit board CTE is 14 to 18 ppm in-plane below T_g, the match to plastic packages which usually have average CTEs of 20 to 25 is better. The overall CTE of a plastic package can be significantly below that of the plastic if the die is large compared to the total package body. For example, TSOP components can have overall CTEs as low as 5.5 ppm. It is also worth recalling that component-level reliability must be considered; plastic packages suffer from other disadvantages versus ceramic packages, such as moisture absorption.

Leaded vs. Leadless Surface-Mount Components. Leadless surface-mount components with peripheral solder joints (e.g., leadless ceramic chip carriers, LCCCs) are more susceptible to solder joint failures due to thermal and mechanical stresses than leaded components because there is no compliance in the system (see Fig. 37.21). A compliant lead can take up relative displacement between the component body and the substrate during mechanical or thermal stressing. In doing so, it minimizes the stress and strain imposed on the solder joint, thus reducing the likelihood of failures. Large leadless components should be avoided whenever possible. If they must be used, the substrate must have as close a CTE mismatch as possible and be protected from mechanical stresses. A conformal coating should be considered.

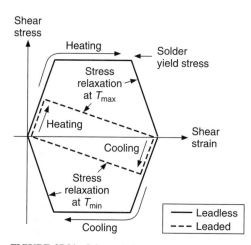

FIGURE 37.21 Schematic illustration of the strain in the solder during a thermal cycle for leaded and leadless surface-mount components. *(After W. Engelmaier)* (IPC-TP-797, Surface Mount Solder Joint Long-term Reliability: Design, Testing, Prediction.)

Ball grid arrays (BGAs) are a new style of leadless SMT component with an areal array of solder joints. The reliability of these components has come under intensive study. Plastic BGAs are less susceptible to solder joint fatigue failures than ceramic BGAs because the laminate and plastic body match the CTE of the PCB much better. At this time, it seems that there will be size and power limitations to ensure solder joint reliability.

Lead Compliance. As described, leadless components cause more reliability problems than leaded components because the entire displacement is imposed on the solder joint; however, there are also large differences in compliancy among leaded surface-mount components (see Fig. 37.22). Body height plays an important role because it determines the length of the

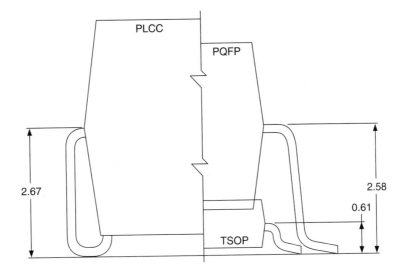

FIGURE 37.22 Schematic illustration of different surface-mount component lead types with widely differing compliance: (*left*) J-lead, (*right*) gullwing leads.

compliant beam. Other important lead characteristics that affect compliance are lead shape (e.g., J-lead vs. gullwing) and lead thickness (stiffness is proportional to thickness cubed).

Lead frame material also plays a role in determining solder joint life, although it is not as important as lead frame geometry. Common lead frame materials are Cu and Alloy 42 (Fe-42Ni); Alloy 42 has a better CTE match to silicon (and a greater mismatch to the solder), but it is much stiffer than Cu (see Table 37.3)

Thin small-outline packages (TSOPs), which are becoming increasingly common memory packages, pose the greatest solder joint reliability risks of any packages commonly used today. These packages generally have Alloy 42 lead frames and very low standoff from the PCB, resulting in a very stiff lead that transfers most of the relative displacement between the component and the substrate to the solder joint. The situation is exaggerated for this component because the overall CTE of the package is quite low. While adequate solder joint reliability can be achieved with TSOPs in many situations, some vendors have opted to encapsulate the solder joints with a filled epoxy to better distribute the stresses.[40]

37.5.3.2 Component Selection for Cleanliness. If fluid cleaning is used to remove flux residues after assembly, then a minimum component standoff (distance between the component body and the seating plane of the leads) is critical to ensuring proper cleaning and drying, and, therefore, resistance to corrosion and moisture-related failures. Industry standards for low standoff components permit the components to have 0–0.25 mm standoff from the board. These low standoffs permit corrosive residues and the cleaning fluid to be trapped

TABLE 37.3 CTE and Elastic Modulus at Room Temperature of Some Important Packaging Materials

	Cu	Alloy 42 (Fe-42Ni)	63Sn-37Pb Solder	Si
CTE, ppm/°C	17	5	25	3.5
E, GPa	130	145	~35	113

under the component. Poor fluid access can mean that flux residues are not removed. Drying is almost as important; it was not a major issue with highly volatile CFCs, but when the cleaning fluid is water, leaving it behind can promote moisture-driven failure mechanisms. Components which meet the standards for high standoff have a minimum standoff of 0.20 or 0.25 mm, which should be sufficient for cleaning and drying with water and most other cleaning fluids in use today. Using a no-clean process essentially eliminates these concerns about component standoff; however, an added concern is that any contamination of the external surface will remain. SIR testing should be conducted to ensure that the flux residues and other contaminants left on the board are not harmful.

37.5.3.3 Component Termination Selection for Joint Integrity

Surface-mount component termination finishes are generally tin-lead or tin, although other finishes are occasionally used. Good solderability is the foundation needed for forming a strong solder joint. Incoming cleanliness is another requirement that should go without saying, but has taken on increased importance with the advent of no-clean processes. With copper leads, formation of excessive quantities of Cu_3Sn and Cu_6Sn_5 intermetallics can occur if reflow times and temperatures are excessive. With pure tin, whisker growth can be a concern. When Au is used as a metal finish, the Au can be expected to dissolve rapidly into the solder joint. To avoid embrittling the solder, the finished joint should contain less than 3 to 5 weight percent Au (see Sec. 37.5.1.3).

Ceramic and ferrite components such as multilayer ceramic capacitors, chip resistors, and chip inductors are generally terminated with a fired-on silver or silver palladium paste. Because silver dissolves easily into molten Sn-Pb solder, a Ni/Sn or Ni/Au overplate is recommended.

37.5.4 Conformal Coatings

Conformal coatings are used for PCAs that require exceptional resistance to moisture, solvents, or abrasion. A wide variety of polymers are used to perform this function, including phenolic, silicone and urethane lacquers and silicone rubber, polystyrene, epoxy, and paraxylylene coatings. Epoxy and polyurethane-based coatings are the most commonly used. If conformal coatings are used in conjunction with a solder mask, they must be chemically compatible.[21,23]

Conformal coatings work by keeping contaminants away from the circuitry and preventing moisture from accumulating on the surface of the assembly. Since all conformal coatings are permeable to moisture, interfacial adhesion is essential to their function. Contaminants on the board that reduce the adhesion of the coating or trap moisture can cause the coating to fail, as can thermal stresses. When contaminants trap moisture, the coating will bubble up (vessicate), providing gaps where corrosion can occur. An ionograph is not always the right tool to detect the harmful level of ionic contamination; cleaning with both polar and nonpolar solvents before application is recommended.

A conformal coating that is not well matched to the use environment can actually promote new failure mechanisms that would not be found in the uncoated assembly. If it fills the gap beneath the component, the coating may place additional stresses on solder joints in thermal cycling by reducing or eliminating the compliance in the leads. It may also generate excessive stresses on the components if the service temperature drops below the T_g of the coating. Some coatings are not stable in hot, humid conditions.

37.6 BURN-IN, ACCEPTANCE TESTING, AND ACCELERATED RELIABILITY TESTING

This section reviews environmental stress testing procedures used to identify unacceptable parts or to estimate part life. These tests can be categorized by their intended goals: 100 percent screening to eliminate early failures (burn-in), acceptance testing on a sampling basis, and life distribution estimation (accelerated reliability estimation). Burn-in, more generally known as environmental stress screening (ESS), is an important subject in its own right that has been extensively written about; only its goals are described here. Acceptance or qualification testing and accelerated reliability testing are discussed together in sections covering testing of PCBs and PCAs under various environmental stresses.

Burn-in, also known as *environmental stress screening* (ESS), is used to eliminate early failures when infant mortality due to latent defects is a problem by exposing all parts to worst-case, but realistic, conditions. The conditions should not be too severe because burn-in decreases the useful life of the parts. On the other hand, in addition to increasing the reliability of the parts that are shipped, burn-in provides rapid feedback on process defects that can cause field failures. The most common use of burn-in in electronics is for integrated circuits, particularly memory chips, designed into leading-edge integrated circuit manufacturing processes.

Accelerated reliability tests are designed to cause failures that would occur by wear-out sometime during the service life of the part and provide the data for estimating the *life distribution* of the part. Estimating the life distribution requires that the test be continued until a large percentage of the parts fail. *Qualification tests* may be conducted under similar or even more severe conditions, but they are essentially pass/fail tests that are terminated after a specified period of time. Because there are few if any failures in a successful qualification, little new reliability information can be gained from this type of test. These tests should not be used routinely on all parts because they will greatly shorten the life of the parts.

Unfortunately, there is no standard suite of reliability tests in the industry, nor is there likely to be in the near future. There are several reasons for this. First, there are numerous service environments. The IPC has identified seven major application segments for electronic assemblies. Second, within these categories, the environment experienced by the assembly may differ from the external service environment, depending on product-specific design parameters, such as power dissipation and cooling efficiency, which influence the temperature and humidity in the vicinity of the assembly. Third, the desired product life and acceptable failure rates vary widely among applications and manufacturers. Finally, but of equal importance, as technology evolves, the tests must evolve, too. Use of reliability tests that once made sense but now are either unduly conservative or do not bring out potential failure modes of new designs has a high price in overdesigned assemblies that are larger or more costly than necessary and field failures that could have been predicted and prevented. This section describes some commonly used tests and methodologies for designing tests for new technologies or new applications.

As stated at the outset, reliability can be defined only after the service environment has been identified, and the acceptable failure rate over a specified service life is specified. If this environment proves unacceptable, the design can be modified by improving cooling, package hermeticity, cleaning, etc. If it is unclear whether the PCA will achieve the designed reliability goals, accelerated reliability tests should be designed to estimate the life distribution.

37.6.1 Design of Accelerated Reliability Tests

There are seven steps in accelerated reliability test design.

1. *Identify the service environment and the acceptable failure rate over a specified service life.*

2. *Identify actual environment of the PCA (modified service environment).*   The service environment should be translated into the ambient environment actually experienced by the PCA. For example, the temperature experienced by the PCA is influenced by both power dissipation and cooling. The mechanical environment is influenced by shock-absorbing material, resonances, and so on.

3. *Identify probable failure modes* (e.g., solder joint fatigue, conductive anodic filament growth). Accelerated reliability tests are based on the premise that the frequency and/or severity of the environmental exposure can be increased to accelerate the incidence of the failure that

occurs in service in a known way, i.e., that the data can be used to predict the life distribution in the in-service PCA environment. This assumption makes sense only if the same failure modes occur in the test as in real life. It cannot be overemphasized that the accelerated tests must be designed around the real failure modes. Probable failure modes may be identified from past service experience, the literature, or preliminary testing or analysis.

4. *For each failure mode, construct an acceleration model.*   An acceleration model that allows test data to be interpreted in terms of the expected service environment is crucial to life distribution estimation. It is also extremely helpful in designing good tests, so ideally the acceleration model should be developed before the accelerated reliability tests are carried out. Equation (37.2) for solder joint reliability plus Eq. (37.1) for strain in solder joints to rigid components is an example of an acceleration model. It predicts that increasing strain will decrease the number of cycles to failure in a specific way. Within a certain temperature range, increasing the temperature cycling range is a way of increasing the strain.

In general, the acceleration model should be based on the rate-controlling step in the failure process. In some cases, the rate will be determined by an Arrhenius type equation; for example, if diffusion is the rate-controlling process:

$$D = D_o \exp\left(\frac{-E_a}{kT}\right) \quad \text{and} \quad x \propto \sqrt{Dt} \tag{37.3}$$

$$t_2 = \left(\frac{D_1}{D_2}\right)t_1 = t_1 \exp\left(\frac{-E_a}{k}\left[\frac{1}{T_1} - \frac{1}{T_2}\right]\right)$$

where D = diffusion rate
D_o = diffusion constant
E_a = activation energy for the process
k = Boltzmann constant

and T_1 and T_2 and t_1 and t_2 are two temperatures and corresponding equivalent diffusion times

Note that even when temperature is an important factor, *an Arrhenius relationship may not exist;* in the preceding thermal cycling example, the failure rate is roughly proportional to $(\Delta T)^2$. Some acceleration models will be explored in the following sections.

The limits of applicability of an acceleration model are as important as the model itself. Increasing or decreasing the temperature too much may promote new failure modes that would not occur in service or invalidate the quantitative acceleration relationship. For example, if the temperature is elevated above the T_g of the board, the z-axis CTE increases sharply and the modulus decreases, which may actually lessen the strains imposed on solder joints, but may also promote PTH failures.

Finite element modeling (FEM) can be invaluable in developing and/or applying acceleration models for thermal and mechanical tests. Two-dimensional nonlinear modeling capability will usually be required in order to get meaningful results. Models can be constructed to estimate the stresses and strains in the material (e.g., the Cu in a PTH barrel or the solder in a surface-mount or through-hole joint) under operating conditions as well as under test conditions. These estimates will be far more accurate than the simple models provided in this overview because they can account for the interactions between materials in a complex structure and both elastic and plastic deformation.

5. *Design tests based on the acceleration models and accepted sampling procedures.*   Using the acceleration model and the service environment and life, select test conditions and test times that simulate the life of the product in a much shorter period of time. The sample size must be large enough that it is possible to determine whether the reliability goal (acceptable number of failures over the service life) has been met.[41] Ideally, the life distribution in the accelerated test should be determined, even when the test period must be extended to do so.

6. *Analyze failures to confirm failure mode predictions.* Since an accelerated test is based on the assumption that a particular failure mode in the accelerated test is the same one that occurs in service, it is important to confirm by failure analysis that this assumption is valid. If the failure mode in the accelerated test is different from the one expected, several possibilities should be considered. (1) The accelerated test is introducing a new failure mode different from the one that will occur in service. Usually this means that the acceleration of one parameter (e.g., frequency, temperature, humidity) was too severe. (2) The initial determination of the dominant failure mode was incorrect. In this case, to understand the significance of the test results, a new acceleration model must be developed for this failure mode. The new failure mode may be promoted more or less effectively by the test conditions than the mode originally assumed. (3) There may be several failure modes. In this case, the two failure distributions should be considered separately, so that life predictions will be meaningful. The difficulty in determining which of the above scenarios holds is that for genuinely new technologies or service environments, the failure mode in service may not be known. In these situations, it is desirable to conduct a parallel test with less aggressive acceleration for comparison.

7. *Determine life distribution from accelerated life distribution.* The accelerated life distribution should be determined by fitting the data with the appropriate statistical distribution, such as the Weibull or log-normal distribution. The life distribution in service can be determined by transforming the time axis of the life distribution using the acceleration model. This predicted life distribution in service can then be used to estimate the number of failures in the specified service life.

The following discussion of testing for some specific failures will provide examples of this methodology.

37.6.2 Printed Circuit Board Reliability Tests

37.6.2.1 Thermal. PTH failures are the predominant source of PCB failures in service and predicting them is the primary goal of PCB testing at elevated temperatures. PTH reliability testing should simulate the thermal excursions of a PTH throughout its life. Generally, the most severe thermal cycles are experienced during assembly and rework.

Two basic types of tests are conducted: thermal stress or solder float tests, and thermal cycling tests. Both of these tests are intended to be accelerated tests for the PTH, not for the laminate; the thermal stress test, in particular, is expected to severely degrade the laminate. The delamination test is similar to a solder float test, but is conducted at a lower temperature specified by the laminate manufacturer; typically, a different fluid is required.

The most commonly accepted thermal stress test is MIL-P-55110 (also found in IPC-TM-650). Following baking at 120 to 150°C (250 to 300°F), the specimens are immersed in an RMA flux and floated in a eutectic (or near-eutectic) Sn-Pb solder bath at 288°C (550°F) for 10 s. Other investigators use a bath at 260°C. Following the test, the samples are cross-sectioned and the PTHs are examined for cracks. This is a severe test that ensures that the sample will survive a single wave-soldering or solder pot rework cycle.

Most thermal cycling tests for PCBs cycle the PCB repeatedly over a wide temperature range; many are actually thermal shock tests using liquid-liquid cycling. The results of five accelerated tests with different temperature extremes, ramp rates, and dwell times have been compared by the IPC, which also provides a simplified analytical model to estimate PTH life.[3] The results of all tests suggest the same approaches for maximizing PTH reliability, but they do not all correlate well quantitatively. Two of the most common tests are (1) oven cycling from −65 to +125°C, and (2) thermal shock cycling between oil or fluidized sand baths at +25 to 260°C. Figure 37.23 shows a suitable test coupon that contains 3000 PTHs interconnected in series, several PTH sizes, and varying annular ring sizes. The PTHs can be monitored during the testing. Figure 37.18*b* shows the type of data that can be collected in this type of test.

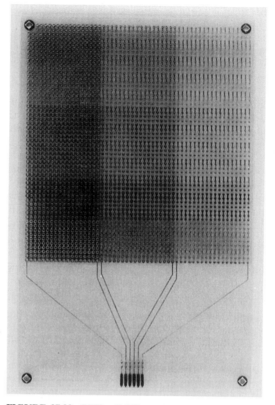

FIGURE 37.23   PTH reliability test coupon. This coupon contains three sets of 1000 PTHs interconnected in series on four layers. Each set is a different hole size. The pad size is also varied. Similar designs are available from the IPC.

37.6.2.2   Mechanical.   Printed circuit boards are rarely subjected to mechanical tests that could cause electrical failures; however, adhesion of both Cu and solder mask to the laminate is critical and is often tested. Loss of solder mask adhesion can provide a place for corrodants and moisture to accumulate, which can be the cause of electrical failures when the board is exposed to temperature and humidity.

Adhesion is commonly tested using the peel test described in IPC-TM-650, Method 2.4.28. The simplest version of this test is conducted by scribing the adherent and dividing it into small squares. If the Cu or solder mask pulls off with a piece of tape with strong adhesive, the adhesion is inadequate. More quantitative tests that measure the actual peel strength are performed primarily by laminate and solder mask suppliers.

37.6.2.3   Temperature, Humidity, Bias.   These tests are designed to promote corrosion on the PCB surface and conductive anodic filament growth, either of which can cause insulation resistance failures.

Surface insulation tests utilize two interleaved Cu combs with an imposed dc bias across the combs. These combs may be designed into existing boards or a coupon such as the IPC-B-25 test board shown in Fig. 37.24 may be used. The measured resistance (ohms) from the comb pattern can be converted to surface resistivity (ohms per square) by multiplying the measured

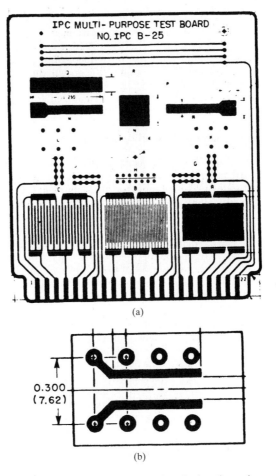

FIGURE 37.24 Test coupons used to check moisture, insulation, and metal migration resistance: (*a*) the IPC-B-25 test
board, used to qualify the process; (*b*) The Y coupon, designed
to be incorporated into production boards for statistical
process control. From IPC-SM-840.

resistance by the square count of the pattern. The square count is determined geometrically
by measuring the total length of the parallel traces between the anode and cathode and dividing by the separation distance. Special precautions are needed to make accurate measurements of insulation resistance.[42] Measurements of resistance above 10^{12} are very difficult and
require careful shielding. Measurements of resistance below 10^{12} can be conducted in most
laboratory environments if certain precautions are taken.

The actual tests are usually conducted at elevated temperature and humidity with an
applied dc bias. A test for moisture and insulation resistance of bare printed circuit boards is
included in IPC-SM-840A. The severity of the test depends on the intended use environment;
for typical commercial products (Class 2), the test is conducted at 50°C, 90% RH, and 100 V_{dc}
bias for 7 days. The minimum insulation resistance requirement is 10^8 Ω. The military test procedure for moisture and insulation resistance is specified in MIL-P-55110.[43] The moisture
resistance test should be conducted in accordance with MIL-STD-202, Method 106, with

applied polarization voltage (100 V_{dc}) and Method 402, Test condition A.[44] IPC-SM-840A also includes a test for electromigration resistance. The test is conducted at 85°C/90% RH at a 10 V_{dc} bias with a limiting current of 1 mA for 7 days. A significant change in current constitutes a failure. The samples are also microscopically inspected for evidence of electrolytic metal migration. A common test for dendritic growth due to flux residues is 85/85/1000 h at –20 V_{dc} bias. These tests are empirically based; however, several investigators have attempted to develop acceleration factors for these and similar tests.[45,46]

37.6.3 Printed Circuit Assembly Reliability Tests

37.6.3.1 Thermal.   Most thermal cycling of PCAs is intended to accelerate solder joint thermal fatigue failures. In spite of the existence of an IPC standard, there is no standard accelerated test today that is suitable for all component and substrate combinations and all service environments. There are several acceleration models in the literature, each of which seems to fit the data well in at least some situations. All are based on a combination of empirical observations and fundamental arguments under simplifying assumptions. This topic remains a subject of active research since in some cases the predictions are significantly different. There is also a move to replace thermal cycling tests with mechanical cycling tests, which could be conducted in a shorter period of time; however, these tests are even further from standardization. Finally, for some components which dissipate a significant amount of power (usually 1 W or more), cycling the ambient temperature (which heats from the outside) may give quite different results from power cycling (in which heating occurs from the inside); for example, the failure location may shift from corner joints (which see the largest displacements) toward solder joints located near the chip (because they are hotter). Consequently, while thermal cycling will be adequate for most ASICs, memory chips, etc., power cycling should be considered for microprocessors, particularly those that dissipate more than a few watts.

Thermal shock testing is commonly used to test components, but it is not necessarily a substitute for thermal cycling. Because the temperature ramp is extremely rapid and the dwell at the extremes is generally short, there is little time for creep; consequently, the number of cycles to failure is increased. Furthermore, the rapid temperature change can induce differential thermal stresses that may be larger than those experienced during thermal cycling. These stresses can induce early failures, particularly if the failure is not in the solder.

There are some principles for designing thermal cycling tests to accelerate solder fatigue that seem to be generally agreed on. The following guidelines apply to gradual temperature cycling due to ambient heating inside a unit (e.g., due to power dissipation). If the unit will be subjected to extreme temperatures or thermal shock in service, these generalizations may not apply. A sample cycling protocol is shown in Fig. 37.25.

- The maximum test temperature should be below the T_g of the printed circuit board, for FR-4 below about 110°C. At T_g, the CTE of the board increases rapidly, but many other properties also change; for example, the elastic modulus of the board decreases. To avoid approaching the melting temperature of the solder and changing the mechanism of solder creep, the maximum temperature should also be kept below about $0.9T_m$, where T_m is the melting temperature of the solder in Kelvin. For eutectic Sn-Pb solder, T_m is 137°C, well above T_g. But for printed circuit board materials with high T_g values or low-melting-temperature solders, this restriction may take precedence. Using a peak temperature above these limits results in unpredictable acceleration.

- The minimum temperature should be high enough that creep is still the primary deformation mechanism of the solder, that is, at least $0.5 T_m$, or –45°C for eutectic Sn-Pb solder. Many investigators prefer a higher minimum temperature (–20 or 0°C) to ensure that creep occurs fast enough to relieve the imposed shear stress during the allowed dwell time. Using too low a minimum temperature may seem to increase the acceleration factor (increased ΔT) while actually decreasing it (decreased $\Delta \varepsilon$), resulting in an overly optimistic life prediction.

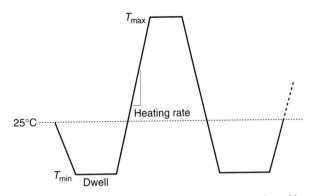

FIGURE 37.25 Schematic thermal cycling profile for testing solder joint thermal fatigue.

- The rate of temperature cycling should not exceed 20°C/min and the dwell time at the temperature extremes should be at least 5 min. The purpose of controlling the cycling speed is to minimize thermal shock and the stresses associated with differential heating or cooling. The dwell time at the temperature extremes is an absolute minimum needed to permit creep to occur. A longer dwell time is recommended, particularly at the minimum temperature.

As described here, there are several acceleration factors in the literature that may be applied to make life estimations from the accelerated test data that may be obtained using a thermal profile that fits the preceding criteria. One of the simplest expressions is due to Norris and Landzberg:

$$\frac{N_{op}}{N_{test}} = \left(\frac{v_{op}}{v_{test}}\right)^{1/3} \left(\frac{\Delta T_{test}}{\Delta T_{op}}\right)^{2} \left(\frac{\phi_{test}}{\phi_{op}}\right)$$

where N_{op} and N_{test} = life under operating and accelerated test conditions, respectively
v = cycling frequency
ϕ = mean temperature[47]

Another widely used expression may be found in IPC-SM-785. This expression tries to account for the effect of power cycling and the dwell time in the thermal profile; it also makes it possible to make predictions for one component or solder joint geometry based on data for another similar one. In its most simplified form, the acceleration factor for tests meeting the preceding criteria for FR-4 and eutectic Sn-Pb solder joints may be *approximated* as

$$\frac{N_{op}}{N_{test}} = \frac{\Delta T_{op}^{2.4}}{\Delta T_{test}} \qquad \text{for leadless surface-mount attachments}$$

$$\frac{N_{op}}{N_{test}} = \frac{\Delta T_{op}^{4}}{\Delta T_{test}} \qquad \text{for compliant-leaded surface-mount attachments}$$

assuming the test assemblies are nearly identical to the assemblies that will be put into service.

Mechanical fatigue cycling is increasingly being used as a quick way to induce solder joint failures. The goal is to *simulate* the thermal fatigue failure process in a much shorter test. The validity of this approach is still being investigated; although the imposed strain in each cycle is intended to be the same, the mechanical test eliminates thermomechanical effects (including creep) because the cycles are about two orders of magnitude faster. Nonetheless, mechanical cycling can certainly provide useful comparisons between different designs or package styles. The tests are usually conducted at a constant temperature with fixturing that puts the solder joints in shear when bending or tensile displacements are applied.

37.6.3.2   Mechanical.   Mechanical vibration and shock can cause solder joint failures, particularly for large, rigid components or components with large, heavy heat sinks. Mechanical shock tests are usually modeled after drops that may occur during transportation or use. The test drops are generally quite severe, but few in number, since the system is not expected to be subjected to repeated drops in service. One common test uses a maximum acceleration of about 600 g, a maximum velocity of about 300 in/s, and a shock pulse of about 2.5 ms duration. The test setup is shown schematically in Fig. 37.26.

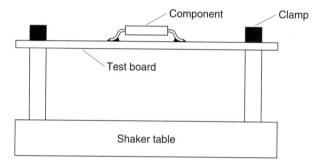

FIGURE 37.26   Schematic of setup used to test the resistance of printed circuit assemblies to out-of-plane mechanical vibration and shock.

On the other hand, the PCA may be exposed to millions of mechanical vibration cycles during its lifetime.[48] Depending on the application, both in-plane and out-of-plane vibration may play an important role. The damage done by these cycles depends primarily on whether the cycling frequency is near a natural frequency of the board, where large deflections can take place. For in-plane vibration, random vibration over a wide excitation frequency range is performed at a constant power spectral density. Most surface-mount components have high natural frequencies, and solder joint failures are rarely observed. For out-of-plane vibration, the following procedure is recommended:

- Design and fixture the test board so that each specimen is clamped at both ends and contains a single component at the center (see Fig. 37.26).
- Impose the vibration using a shaker table with sinusoidal excitation.
- Find the natural frequency of the sample by sweeping the frequency at a low amplitude (to prevent inadvertent damage before the start of the test). This natural frequency is near, but not the same as, the natural frequency at the larger amplitude that will be used for testing.
- Conduct the test by sweeping the frequency in a narrow range around the natural frequency previously determined. The amplitude can be set to correspond to a certain power spectral density or to achieve a desired deflection of the PCB.

37.6.3.3   Temperature, Humidity, Bias.   The primary purpose of these tests is to identify surface insulation resistance (SIR) degradation due to corrosive materials left on the board from the assembly process or due to galvanic couples set up in the assembly process. The usual test procedure is to use SIR comb patterns on the PCB like those described in Sec. 37.6.1.3 and to subject the assembly to 85°C/85% relative humidity/−20V_{dc} for 1000 h. The bias voltage is dependent on the test device or test vehicle chosen.

One acceleration model that is applied is the modified Eyring model, which was developed for moisture-induced corrosion in plastic packages:

$$t_{50\%} = \left[A \, \exp\left(\frac{E_a}{kT} \right) \right]\left[\exp\left(\frac{C}{H_r} \right) \right]\left[D\exp\left(\frac{-V}{B} \right) \right] \qquad (37.4)$$

where
$t_{50\%}$ = time at which 50 percent of parts have failed
$A, B, C,$ and D = empirical constants
E_a = thermal activation energy
k = Boltzmann constant
T = temperature in degrees Kelvin
H_r = relative humidity
V = reverse-biasing voltage[41,46]

The time to failure is also dependent on the concentration of ionic contaminants. The default industrial ionic contamination limit comes from MIL-STD-28809A; it is the equivalent of 3.1 μg/cm^2 of NaCl. For small plastic packages, enough data have been collected to show that an empirical acceleration factor for temperature and relative humidity AF$_{T,H}$r applies:

$$\mathrm{AF}_{T,H_r} = 2^{(T+Hr)\text{test} - (T+Hr)\text{service}} \qquad (37.5)$$

where
AF = acceleration factor
T = temperature in °C
H_r = relative humidity in percent[46,49]

The rule of thumb for the effect of reverse bias is very device-specific; the following relationship was established for 20-V Schottky diodes in SOT-23 packages:[46]

$$\mathrm{AF}_V = 7700 \, \exp\left(\frac{-V}{12.32} \right)$$

When both acceleration factors apply, the total acceleration factor is:

$$\mathrm{AF}_{\text{total}} = (\mathrm{AF}_{T,H_r})(\mathrm{AF}_V)$$

37.7 SUMMARY

Reliability of electronic assemblies is a complex subject. This chapter has touched on only one aspect of the problem: understanding the primary failure mechanisms of printed circuit boards and the interconnects between these boards and the electronic components mounted on them. This approach provides the basis for analyzing the impact of design and materials choices and manufacturing processes on printed circuit assembly reliability. It also provides the foundation for developing accelerated testing schemes to determine reliability. It is hoped that the fundamental approach will enable the reader to apply this methodology to new problems not yet addressed in mainstream literature.

REFERENCES

1. M. A. Oien, "Methods for Evaluating Plated-Through-Hole Reliability," *14th Annual Proceedings of IEEE Reliability Physics,* Las Vegas, Nev., April 20–22, 1976.

2. K. Kurosawa, Y. Takeda, K. Takagi, and H. Kawamata, "Investigation of Reliability Behavior of Plated-Through-Hole Multilayer Printed Wiring Boards," IPC-TP-385, IPC, Evanston, Ill., 1981.

3. IPC-TR-579, "Round Robin Reliability Evaluation of Small Diameter Plated Through Holes in Printed Wiring Boards," Institute of Interconnecting and Packaging Electronic Circuits, Lincolnwood, Ill. The IPC recently initiated a second round robin study, the results of which should be available in about 1996.

4. F. Fehrer and G. Haddick, "Thermo-mechanical Processing and Repairability Observations for FR-4, Cyanate Ester and Cyanate Ester/Epoxy Blend PCB Substrates," *Circuit World,* vol. 19, no. 2, 1993, pp. 39–44.

5. D. B. Barker and A. Dasgupta, "Thermal Stress Issues in Plated-Through-Hole Reliability," in *Thermal Stress and Strain in Microelectronics Packaging,* J. H. Lau (ed.), Van Nostrand Reinhold, 1993, pp. 648–683.

6. IPC-TM-650, Method 2.4.8.

7. L. D. Olson, "Resins and Reinforcements," in *ASM Electronic Materials Handbook, Vol. 1: Packaging,* ASM International, Materials Park, Ohio, 1989, pp. 534–537.

8. D. W. Rice, "Corrosion in the Electronics Industry," *Corrosion/85,* paper no. 323, National Association of Corrosion Engineers, Houston, 1985.

9. J. J. Steppan, J. A. Roth, L. C. Hall, D. A. Jeannotte, and S. P. Carbone, "A Review of Corrosion Failure Mechanisms during Accelerated Tests: Electrolytic Metal Migration," *J. Electrochemical Soc.,* vol. 134, 1987, pp. 175–190.

10. D. J. Lando, J. P. Mitchell, and T. L. Welsher, "Conductive Anodic Filaments in Reinforced Polymeric Dieletrics: Formation and Prevention," *17th Annual Proceedings of IEEE Reliability Physics Symposium,* San Francisco, April 24–26, 1979, pp. 51–63.

11. "How to Avoid Metallic Growth Problems on Electronic Hardware," IPC-TR-476, Sept. 1977.

12. B. Rudra, M. Pecht, and D. Jennings, "Assessing Time-of-Failure Due to Conductive Filament Formation in Multi-Layer Organic Laminates," *IEEE Trans. CPMT-Part B.,* vol. 17, August 1994, pp. 269–276.

13. J. W. Price, *Tin and Tin Alloy Plating,* Electrochemical Publications, Ayr, Scotland, 1983.

14. D. R. Gabe, "Whisker Growth on Tin Electrodeposits," *Trans. Institute of Metal Finishing,* vol. 65, 1987, p. 115.

15. C. Lea, *A Scientific Guide to Surface Mount Technology,* Electrochemical Publications, Ayr, Scotland, 1988.

16. J. H. Lau (ed), *Solder Joint Reliability: Theory and Applications,* Van Nostrand Reinhold, New York, 1991.

17. D. R. Frear, S. N. Burchett, H. S. Morgan and J. H. Lau, eds., *Mechanics of Solder Alloy Interconnects,* Van Nostrand Reinhold, New York, 1994.

18. J. H. Lau (ed.), *Thermal Stress and Strain in Microelectronics,* Van Nostrand Reinhold, New York, 1993.

19. S. Burchett, "Applications—Through-Hole," in *The Mechanics of Solder Alloy Interconnects, op. cit.,* pp. 336–360.

20. E. Suhir and Y.-C. Lee, "Thermal, Mechanical, and Environmental Durability Design Methodologies," in *ASM Electronic Materials Handbook, Vol. 1: Packaging, op cit.*

21. IPC-D-279, "Design Guidelines for Reliable Surface Mount Technology Printed Board Assemblies," to be published.

22. L. T. Manzione, *Plastic Packaging of Microelectronic Devices,* Van Nostrand Reinhold, New York, 1990.

23. *ASM Electronic Materials Handbook, Vol. 1: Packaging, op. cit.*

24. R. R. Tummala and E. J. Rymaszewski (eds.), *Microelectronic Packaging Handbook,* Van Nostrand Reinhold, New York, 1989.

25. For a more comprehensive list of components that may be at risk, see IPC-D-279, "Design Guidelines for Reliable Surface Mount Technology Printed Board Assemblies," App. C, to be issued.

26. L. Zakraysek, R. Clark, and H. Ladwig, "Microcracking in Electrolytic Copper," *Proceedings of Printed Circuit World Convention III,* Washington, D.C., May 22–25, 1984.

27. G. T. Paul, "Cracked Innerlayer Foil in High Density Multilayer Printed Wiring Boards," *Proceedings of Printed Circuit Fabrication West Coast Technical Seminar,* San Jose, Aug. 29–31, 1983.

28. M. W. Gray, "Inner Layer or Post Cracking on Multilayer Printed Circuit Boards," *Circuit World,* vol. 15, no. 2, pp. 22–29, 1989.

29. L. Mayer and S. Barbieri, "Characteristics of Acid Copper Sulfate Deposits for Printed Wiring Board Applications," *Plating and Surface Finishing,* March 1981, pp. 46–49.

30. J. L. Marshall, L. A. Foster, and J. A. Sees, "Interfaces and Intermetallics," in *The Mechanics of Solder Alloy Interconnects,* D. R. Frear, H. Morgan, S. Burchett, and J. Lau (eds.), *op. cit.,* pp. 42–86.

31. M. Economou, "Rework System Selection," *SMT,* February 1994, pp. 60–66.

32. J. Lau, S. Leung, R. Subrahmanyan, D. Rice, S. Erasmus, and C. Y. Li, "Effects of Rework on the Reliability of Pin Grid Array Interconnects," *Circuit World,* vol. 17, no. 4, pp. 5–10, 1991.

33. F. L. Gray, "Thermal Expansion Properties," in *ASM Electronic Materials Handbook, Vol. 1: Packaging, op. cit.*

34. P. M. Hall, "Thermal Expansivity and Thermal Stress in Multilayered Structures," in *Thermal Stress and Strain in Microelectronics Packaging,* J. H. Lau (ed), *op. cit.,* pp. 78–94.

35. J. Glazer, P. A. Kramer, and J. W. Morris, Jr., "The Effect of Gold on the Reliability of Fine Pitch Surface Mount Solder Joints," *Circuit World,* vol. 18, 1992, pp. 41–46.

36. G. Humpston and D. M. Jacobson, *Principles of Soldering and Brazing,* ASM International, Materials Park, Ohio, 1993, Chap. 3.

37. F. G. Yost, "Soldering to Gold Films," *Gold Bulletin,* vol. 10, 1977, pp. 94–100.

38. J. Glazer, "Metallurgy of Low Temperature Lead-free Solders: A Literature Review," *International Materials Review,* vol. 40, 1995, pp. 65–93.

39. H. L. Hvims, *Adhesives as Solder Replacement for SMT,* vols. I and II, Danish Electronics, Light and Acoutics, Hoersholm, Denmark, January 1994.

40. A. Emerick, J. Ellerson, J. McCreary, R. Noreika, C. Woychik, and P. Viswanadham, "Enhancement of TSOP Solder Joint Reliability Using Encapsulation," *Proceedings of the 43d Electronic Components and Technology Conference,* IEEE-CHMT, 1993, pp. 187–192.

41. P. Tobias and D. Trindade, *Applied Reliability,* Van Nostrand Reinhold, New York, 1986.

42. ASTM D 257-78, Standard Test Methods for DC Resistance or Conductance of Insulating Materials.

43. Military specification for Printed Wiring Boards.

44. Military standard test method for Electronic and Electrical Component Parts.

45. P. J. Boddy, R. H. Delaney, J. N. Lahti, E. F. Landry, and R. C. Restrick, "Accelerated Life Testing of Flexible Printed Circuits: Part I and II," *14th Annual Proceedings of the IEEE Reliability Physics Symposium,* Las Vegas, Nev., April 20–22, 1976.

46. K.-L. B. Wun, M. Ostrander, and J. Baker, "How Clean is Clean in PCA," *Proceedings of Surface Mount International,* San Jose, Calif., 1991, pp. 408–418.

47. K. C. Norris and A. H. Landzberg, *IBM Journal of Research and Development,* vol. 13, 1969, p. 266.

48. For example, see J. H. Lau, "Surface Mount Solder Joints Under Thermal, Mechanical, and Vibration Conditions," in *The Mechanics of Solder Alloy Interconnects,* D. R. Frear, H. Morgan, S. Burchett, and J. Lau (eds.), *op. cit.,* pp. 361–415.

49. E. B. Hakim, "Acceleration Factors for Plastic Encapsulated Semiconductors," *Solid State Technology,* Dec. 1991, pp. 108–109.

FURTHER READING

ASM Electronic Materials Handbook, Vol. 1: "Packaging," ASM International, Materials Park, Ohio, 1989.

Frear, D. R., H. Morgan, S. Burchett, and J. Lau, *The Mechanics of Solder Alloy Interconnects,* Van Nostrand Reinhold, New York, 1994.

IPC-A-600D, Acceptability of Printed Boards, August 1989.

IPC-A-610A, Acceptability of Electronic Assemblies, Feb. 1990.

IPC-D-279, Design Guidelines for Reliable Surface Mount Technology Printed Board Assemblies, to be issued.

IPC-SM-785, Guidelines for Accelerated Reliability Testing of Surface Mount Solder Attachments, Nov. 1992.

de Kluizenaar, E. E., "Reliability of Soldered Joints: A Description of the State of the Art," *Soldering and Surface Mount Technology,* Part I: no. 4, pp. 27–38; Part II: no. 5, pp. 56–66; Part III: no. 6, pp. 18–27, 1990.

Lau, J. H. (ed.), *Solder Joint Reliability,* Van Nostrand Reinhold, New York, 1991.

Lau, J. H. (ed.), *Thermal Stress and Strain in Microelectronics Packaging,* Van Nostrand Reinhold, New York, 1993.

Lea, C., *A Scientific Guide to Surface Mount Technology,* Electrochemical Publications, Ayr, Scotland, 1988.

Tummala, R. and E. J. Rymaszewski (ed.), *Microelectronic Packaging Handbook,* Van Nostrand Reinhold, New York, 1989.

CHAPTER 38
ELECTRONIC CONTRACT MANUFACTURING SUPPLIER SELECTION AND MANAGEMENT

Steven M. Allen
AVEX Electronics Inc., Fremont, California

38.1 INTRODUCTION

Intensified competition, short product life cycles, and budgetary constraints have caused electronics companies to create a boom to an emerging *electronic contract manufacturing* (ECM) industry. Electronic companies competing for a share of the world market rely a great deal on strategy, talent, and capital. With research and development costs to support up front, companies are hard pressed into dedicating a portion of their precious capital to justify a manufacturing facility along with the overhead that it requires.

Many *original equipment manufacturers* (OEMs) have adopted a strategy of focusing on core competencies in the areas of research and design, to ultimately develop patents that can be built by subcontractors whose goal is to manage capital utilization, inventory, and leading-edge manufacturing processes.

38.1.1 Development of the Electronic Manufacturing Services Industry

In the United States alone, the electronics industry will quadruple its outsourcing requirement from $7 billion to over $27 billion by 2000. EMSI sales for 1994 surpassed $10 billion, a 24 percent growth rate over 1993. Fueling a major portion of this growth is the advent of the OEM either selling off entire divisions to existing electronic manufacturing service providers, or subcontractors*, or actually jumping into the ECM business as a separate entity.

Lack of resources may make subcontracting an attractive choice; however, should an OEM fear the loss of control through outsourcing, risks may be minimized by putting together a thorough search for a competent and interested partner in the EMSI. The task of locating the "perfect" subcontractor may take a while, but by being prepared and making a thorough

---

* "Electronic Manufacturing Services Industry" is the general term established by the IPC to refer to all activities supporting the manufacture and assembly of electronic devices of original equipment manufacturers. For this chapter, however, we will use the terms *subcontractor* or *EMC* to denote *electronic manufacturing contractor* to describe an organization which provides either bare boards or loaded boards to higher-level users.

search, realistic expectations can be made by both parties to minimize risks and set the foundation for a long-term strategic relationship. In this chapter we will examine ways to evaluate a worthy ECM as well as to manage a relationship that is the lifeblood of the OEM.

38.2 BUSINESS PLAN

To understand what services an OEM requires to produce a quality product through the services of a contractor, a self-evaluation must first take place. The flowchart in Fig. 38.1 lists five basic stages in the life of a printed circuit board assembly (PCBA). By considering the major steps involved, a list can be put together to better understand which subcontractor is best suited to meet the needs of the OEM.

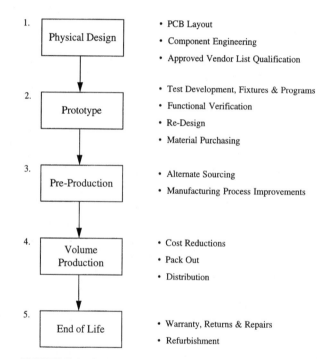

FIGURE 38.1 Customer requirements—five stages of product life.

38.2.1 Customer Requirements—Five Stages of Product Life

1. *Physical design:* Will the company need assistance in designing the PCBA or other engineering support? Is there a skilled PCBA design engineer available at the OEM? An experienced subcontractor will, at a minimum, have process/manufacturing engineers that can provide guidance in the areas of preferred location of tooling holes, fiducial markings, and test vias according to the requirements of the manufacturing equipment. But a skilled PCBA-designer will be necessary to ensure that the board can be manufactured in the most efficient way possible. As a *bill of materials* (BOM) list is developed, who will develop an *approved vendor list* (AVL)? A component engineer must be available to design-in vendors according to the board specifications. This is a job for which most subcontractors have limited resources. If a component engineer is not in-house (at the OEM), it may be necessary to render the services of a distributor to provide help.

2. *Prototype:* In the prototype stage, quick turns in manufacturing are necessary to confirm the functionality of the product. Are there skilled technicians available with the proper tools and work environment to produce prototypes in-house? Are there test engineers available that can set the test parameters and develop fixtures and programs. Is *in-circuit test* (ICT) or *functional test* (FVT) a skill that will be kept in-house while outsourcing the production? Most subcontractors prefer to test what they build in order to provide timely feedback to the manufacturing process with regard to failures. On the other hand, some OEMs prefer control over test to keep a closer watch over quality levels.

3. *Preproduction:* While prototype builds are meant to verify the functionality of a component, preproduction is intended to verify manufacturability. Quantities for a prototype build can range from 1 to 20 pieces and can be built by hand, while preproduction will require a *design for manufacturability* (DFM) verification on an automated line. If preproduction should remain in-house, skilled process engineers must be well versed in tracking yield information to avoid a second learning curve when moving to a subcontractor.

4. *Production:* At the higher volumes, can the OEM handle the ramp to production? Will the OEM share manufacturing with a subcontractor? Are there additional services/items required to ship the final product such as pack-out and/or software disk duplication?

5. *End of life:* Who will support the product at the end of its life as the quantities become minimal? Are there technicians in-house that can service returns, warranty support, refurbishment, or upgrades?

38.2.2 Supplier Requirements

Before visiting an ECM, keep in mind that they too have requirements of their prospects/customers. By understanding the needs of the ECM, time and effort can be saved by both parties before a substantial amount is invested. ECMs look at their customers as investments, and by understanding that their resources are limited, the OEM will be well advised to present itself as a worthy investment.

The largest risk any ECM will make is to purchase material to fulfill the turnkey requirements of the OEM. If a turnkey relationship is desired, ECMs will be interested in the company financials, how well an OEM is backed, and how their risk in exposure to inventory can be minimized. ECMs cannot survive if their customers become failures. Most ECMs survive on thin margins which leave little room for risk. Be objective in describing a business plan to an ECM, using an approach similar to the process of obtaining a loan from a bank, proving creditworthiness or reasons why the product and company are worth investing in. Be sure to include the product/company competitive advantage and marketplace. Partnerships require information to flow freely from both sides before determining whether or not to engage. With no written plan in place, information can easily be lost, forgotten, or made inconsistent. If the OEM product will experience an extended ramp to volume production, it will be necessary to get a buy-in from the ECM that it supports in the preproduction stage is critical. Another reason for the OEM to convince the ECM is to generate an unconditional interest in times of peak performance. It's easy for a subcontractor to fall into a pattern of emphasizing service to the largest customers in times of peak production. By convincing the ECM that the OEM has a promising future, the ECM is less likely to neglect its responsibilities in times of peak performance.

38.2.3 Presenting the Corporate Goals and Objectives

When approaching an ECM as a possible partner, being prepared to describe corporate goals and objectives will ensure that the candidate can best evaluate if the partnership makes sense from their point of view. It is also to the benefit of the OEM to best describe the corporate outlook in order to generate interest beyond the current requirements to emphasize both current and future opportunity. While some ECMs may desire any project, others may be selective for partners that minimize risk.

The OEM should set goals that are realistic in terms of volumes. If initial runs will be prototypes, be realistic about expecting a large shop to continually produce quick turns of small kits that can consume precious equipment time. Vendors look at customers as profit centers: If there is no volume shipping in the short term, then in the absence of revenue, it must be believed that volume production will definitely occur in the long term. This is not to say that some shops do not enjoy prototype (small-volume) manufacturing; however, it is more than likely that an ECM that specializes in small volumes will not be able to handle a quick ramp to higher volumes. Contractors with greater capacity to handle high-volume manufacturing can help avoid having to transfer a product when quantities exceed the capacity of a smaller shop. Being up-front and stating the requirements of the OEM from prototype to production with a time schedule will avoid the mistake of partnering with an ECM with short-term thinking.

38.2.4 Business Plan

- *Past:* How has the company or division evolved? Who are the founders? What has been the history of financials? What is the growth and profitability record?

- *Present:* What stage is the product in? What is changing; why the ECM search? What are the short-term goals? What are the main features, advantages, and benefits of the product? What is the competitive advantage that makes the product a winner? What are the requirements to build the product—both equipment and personnel? Describe the organization managing the product.

- *Future:* What forecast or goals does the company have and how does it plan on getting there? What is the anticipated market share? Describe the corporate line on outsourcing strategy. How does the product ramp up and what plans are in place for end-of-life support? What is the next-generation product?

Depending on the thoroughness of the OEM presentation, it will then be the task of the ECM to present to the OEM why a mutually beneficial partnership is viable and what services can be provided to fill the OEM needs. The better the OEM requirements can be described, the more customized an ECM's presentation can address specific needs.

38.3 SUPPLIER CAPABILITIES

38.3.1 Overall Capabilities

ECMs come in many shapes and sizes, some specializing in a few services and others attempting to offer the one-stop shop. Two main classes of ECM are those that are strictly consignment shops and those that are turnkey. For consignment ECMs there is also the option to use a third-party distributor to provide material.

38.3.1.1 Turnkey.   The ability to plan, purchase, receive, and inspect material as specified by the OEM-approved vendor list requirements.

38.3.1.2 Kitting.   This involves the same function as turnkey but using a third-party distributor to provide the service. While smaller ECMs lack the credit line to purchase three or more months of a customer's inventory, or they may not want the risks associated with turnkey manufacturing, many will use distributors as a third party to provide a kitting service. Although using a distributor (kitting service) adds another supplier to manage, this can provide an OEM the flexibility of keeping its buying power and allocation priority closer to the manufacturer of the components. Since distributors keep on hand many common components, they often have the ability to turn a kit, at a premium, with shorter lead times than an ECM.

38.3.1.3 Consignment Labor.   Provided the OEM has elected to purchase material on its own or use a distributor to provide a kitting service, a consignment shop will be a viable option. Consignment shops are generally smaller-run organizations that can provide a more personalized level of service. On the other hand, some smaller consignment shops do not have the resources or talent of larger turnkey ECMs.

38.3.2 Services Offered

38.3.2.1 PCB Layout.   Many ECMs can provide a service to take OEM schematics and lay out a PCBA with DFM and DFT in mind. In addition, fiducial markings and tooling-hole requirements may be specified in order to place the assembly on a particular type of manufacturing equipment.

38.3.2.2 Design for Manufacturability (DFM) and Testability (DFT).   In the rush to get a product to market, engineers and designers do not always adhere to volume manufacturing guidelines. To prepare the product for volume assembly, it may be necessary to make adjustments in lead spacing or surface-mount device land patterns. These changes may be intended to improve manufacturability and assure compatibility with automated systems. If the ECM was not involved in the layout of the PCBA, provide them with adequate time to evaluate DFM. Improvements made by experienced contractors can save a company thousands of dollars over the duration of the product. DFT is a service that should be integrated into the DFM study. A thorough DFM study will include the placement of test vias should ICT be required.

38.3.2.3 Testing Capability.   ECMs with experience in any of the three primary areas of test (ICT, FVT, and environmental stress screening, or ESS), can provide recommendations through experience with other current and past assemblies. ICT, the most commonly outsourced method of test, allows an ECM to verify for opens and shorts before shipping to the customer. Many ECMs will either develop ICT programs and fixtures or use a preferred third party to design the fixtures for a specific test base. An experienced test engineer will be able to recommend test point placement to maximize coverage and minimize test time. FVT requirements are generally developed by the OEM and then performed either at the site of the ECM or at the OEM. ESS testing depends largely on the application of the product and is dictated by the OEM's end use of the product. Some ECMs which offer ESS can provide assistance in developing fixtures to fit the needs of the OEM.

38.3.2.4 Material Procurement.   One of the clearest differentiators between the large and relatively small ECMs is the ability or desire to take on OEMs that require turnkey services, i.e., the ability to plan and purchase the raw material before assembly and delivery. While larger ECMs generally have more experience, capital equipment, talent, and customers, they may require a minimum volume of business from the OEM to make the partnership worth their time. Considering that the material cost in a PCBA may represent 80 to 90 percent of the total cost, with assembly labor, test, and packaging accounting for the remaining 10 to 20 percent, many ECMs consider turnkey manufacturing to be more profitable despite the inherent risks. Contractors' ability to provide turnkey services allows a single order to be placed for products that may have several hundred line items to order. While manufacturing lead times may take one to two weeks, the purchasing and receiving of material may take up to 20 or more weeks for hundreds of parts; thus, working in a turnkey relationship becomes a major factor in developing a strong relationship.

38.3.2.5 *Program and Fixture Support.*   Aside from test, other nonrecurring fixture costs include the development of a program to run automated manufacturing equipment and fixtures that enable the manufacturer to assemble the product during various stages of the process. Some fixture requirements may include:

Stencil	Solder paste application
Vacuum plate	To hold PCB in place during solder paste application
Surface-mount fixture	To hold PCB in place during component placement
Wave fixtures	To hold PCB if wave solder is required for pin-through-hole components

A contractor should be able to develop the requirements for fixtures, including quantities, according to the throughput required by the OEM. Most ECMs will use a third-party source to have fixtures developed and modified when changes occur.

38.3.3 Support Services

Aside from the core services, which include purchasing and assembly, there are many supporting roles that play a key role in ensuring that quality, communication, and delivery are not overlooked.

38.3.3.1 *Quality.*   Undoubtedly, all suppliers claim that their products are built with quality in mind. They may even boast of high first-pass yields at ICT, and share with the customer data that has been collected on a statistical level. While it's a great tribute that some ECMs can build dozens of different assemblies for a dozen different customers, it's not enough to just take their word for it. Quality does not happen by chance, and if a working model is not in place in every area and strictly adhered to, then there can be no assurance that a continuous improvement plan is working. If work is taking place at the ECM manufacturing site, quality measures should be evident at several checkpoints along the process, from solder paste application to pack-out. While a quality engineer should be able to clearly explain the quality process, each operator on the line should be able to explain what his or her contribution is to a quality product. In order to buy off on a quality system it must be understood how the ECM takes critical yield information and feeds it back to the process. If a closed-loop corrective action procedure is not in place to trace failures back to the source, then how is information compiled and constructively fed back to the source?

38.3.3.2 *Information Systems.*   When it comes time to transfer information, many tools are available to ensure that data is being received accurately and in timely fashion. Schedule and engineering changes, delivery schedules, shortage reports, and quality information are all forms of data that will be passed back and forth from the OEM to the ECM. Modern information systems that can be used by both parties can efficiently streamline the communication process, saving time and money. Although there is no substitute for meeting face to face with a supplier, leaving the office can be prohibitive at times. Information tools include *phone mail* to avoid playing phone tag or leaving lengthy messages with an operator; *pagers,* for when immediate accessibility of an individual is required; *facsimiles* (fax) to transfer written documentation; *electronic mail,* which is probably the most efficient means of communicating when several members need to be notified at the same time; and *EDI,* which allows users to transmit infinite amounts of data through a modem. Information systems can play an integral role not just in establishing efficient means of communication between the OEM and the ECM, but they also help individuals communicating in their own environments with other team members as well as other suppliers they have to manage. Even if an OEM is not able to utilize fully all the information tools offered initially by the ECM, the investment has been made to make communication more timely and accurate over the term of the relationship.

38.3.3.3 *Packaging/Shipping.* Before a finished good can be delivered, packaging specification must be met to ensure that no damage takes place during delivery. Most ECMs can assist in recommending bulk packaging requirements through a preferred third party. Proper packaging can prevent both *electrostatic discharge* (ESD) and physical damage. Bulk packaging may include an ESD bag and a carton with partitions, or a box that has been ESD-protected without a bag. For finished goods that require retail packaging, another assembly process must be added, which requires additional equipment and operators if shrinkwrap is necessary. If neither the OEM nor the ECM has the capability to provide finished packaging, a third party must be identified to take on the task.

For close-proximity shipping, it is useful to find out if the ECM is able to deliver finished goods to the OEM dock. Other options include third-party delivery or picking up product at the ECM dock. If the product is to be packaged for retail, then consider having product delivered directly to distribution or the end user.

38.3.4 Technical Capability

38.3.4.1 *Processes Offered/Equipment List.* Depending on the level of difficulty to manufacture a specific PCBA, certain process skills are necessary along with the appropriate equipment. If a PCBA has fine-pitch devices on both the top and bottom sides, then a proven process should be in place to ensure the OEM of the ECM's competence. Understand the ECM's experience relative to the technology at hand. Based on their customers' requirements, some ECMs can be way out in front of the learning curve. For technologies such as chip-on-board (COB), tape-automated bonding (TAB), and multichip module (MCM), special processes and equipment will be necessary. If the preferred supplier does not have the processes or equipment to place relatively sophisticated processes, then it must be determined if the OEM wants to invest in the learning of the process as well as the equipment with the ECM. A review of the equipment list can not only help identify if a current process is in place, but whether future technologies are being invested in, to stay ahead of the OEM requirements.

38.3.4.2 *Capacity.* Understanding the factors of capacity flexibility will provide guidance for avoiding growing pains. Most ECMs will run two to three shifts per day, five days per week, with the weekends available at a premium. Identify what the current capacity is for machine utilization, and then learn what measures the ECM can take to expand the current capacity. Is there room for additional manufacturing equipment? Are there sufficient cash or credit lines to support the cost of additional equipment? Are there other facilities in other locations that can provide the same service without altering the process?

38.3.4.3 *Engineers.* Engineers come with many different backgrounds with various levels of experience. Process, manufacturing, quality, and test engineering must be well represented in each area of the ECM to ensure that each process is well defined by qualified personnel to build a quality product. Look for examples from the ECM that exhibit experience which is relevant to the technology required by the OEM. What qualifications does the engineer require before being empowered as the lead engineer of a given OEM product?

38.4   *SUPPLIER QUALIFICATION*

In an effort to select the best ECM candidate, a qualification list should be developed to include services required and desired (see Fig. 38.2). Candidates can be scored based on how well they perform in the areas most desired, with less emphasis placed on areas that may add value at a later time.

By putting together a list of desired capabilities (see Fig. 38.2, Supplier Qualification Survey) an OEM can better understand the services as they are demonstrated by potential suppliers in the areas of importance to better choose a successful long-term strategic partner. One method of measuring a potential candidate might be to assign a score after each question/category on a scale of 1 to 4: 1=complete, 2=adequate, 3=incomplete, 4=inadequate. For preliminary questionnaires, to be filled out and returned by the proposed supplier, a simple yes or no is adequate to provide background information on the levels of service that are available. Categories may include technology, quality, responsiveness, delivery, cost, and business strategy. After the results have been tallied, suppliers can be ranked based on their respective scores.

38.5   *TIME-TO-MARKET ELEMENTS*

By understanding the process that must take place before a product is ready for delivery, an OEM can better commit to a realistic shipment date. The Gantt chart in Fig. 38.3 walks through many of the milestones that must be covered before a shipment can be made.

38.5.1   Specific Elements: Descriptions and Time Requirements

Quote.   A labor quotation, depending on the complexity, should take no longer than a week to complete. Turnkey quotation will add an additional 1 to 3 weeks, depending on the total number of line items of material to quote.

Manufacturing purchase agreement.   Before the order is placed, terms and conditions should be put in writing that specify payment terms, schedule flexibility, material liability, warranty, etc. Most ECMs will have a boilerplate agreement that can be modified per each OEM's requirements. A copy of the quote will become an attachment to the MPA.

Purchase order.   The official purchase order (PO) binds an agreement for the ECM to purchase material to meet a specified quantity to be delivered on a specified date at a specified price. An ECM may require 2 to 10 business days to verify acceptance of the OEM required delivery dates.

Material requirement planning.   Once the BOMs have been loaded onto the ECM's material requirement planning (MRP) system, the purchasing activity can take place. First-time MRP execution for a new assembly number may take two weeks to perform to compensate for the initial setup of the specific requirements. When recurring orders are placed, one week will suffice.

Purchase.   Through a quotation, it is advisable to identify all long-lead items—those that extend beyond 12 to 14 weeks. To avoid having to pay expedite charges or missing a target delivery date, buys should be placed, by the OEM in advance, for all long-lead items that may jeopardize a desirable delivery date. Purchase orders can be taken over by the ECM, or initial buys of long-lead items can be consigned to the ECM.

Receiving/inspection.   Receiving and inspection (RI) will add a week onto the lead time of components. If an ECM is handling the purchasing function, it is also their responsibility to verify that the components meet the specifications of the AVL. For a consignment mode, the ECM's responsibility is only to verify the count of the parts as supplied by the OEM or distributor.

FIGURE 38.2 Supplier Qualification Survey.

Technology

Item   1-2-3-4

1. Equipment in place is capable of meeting product need.   _____
2. Process is released and documented.   _____
3. Available technical support personnel are qualified to understand needs and provide required
   ongoing production/sustaining engineering: _____   Number of engineers   _____
                                                              Number of technicians   _____
4. A process development activity is in place and has defined goals.
   % for cost reduction   _____
   % for new processes   _____
   % for other _____   (describe) _____
5. Prototypes can be run on line that typifies production conditions.   _____
       1=Complete   2=Adequate   3=Incomplete   4=Inadequate

Quality Plans and Methods

Item   1-2-3-4

1. Quality control manual is available and can be shown to reflect actual shop practices.   _____
2. Process flowchart and operation documents are available.   _____
3. Process characterization is documented.   _____
       Process Capability Index derivation process clear   _____
       Other process capability measures (define) _____
4. Documented process for translating customer requirements.   _____
5. Process changes are under engineering control and communicated to the customer
   prior to implementation.   _____
6. Process documents are current.   _____
7. Process control plan is based on SPC principles.   _____
8. Process control points are determined with customer.   _____
9. SPC is used routinely in operations (control charts visible).   _____
10. Operators and technicians are trained in SPC methods.   _____
11. Control chart information is used to make adjustments to process
    (examples were shown).   _____
12. Defective material is identified, isolated, and recorded.   _____
13. Preventive maintenance program is documented and records show that it is followed.   _____
14. Tool calibration and traceability process is documented and shown to be in operation.   _____
        1=Complete   2=Adequate   3=Incomplete   4=Inadequate

Responsiveness

Item   1-2-3-4

1. Process exists for accepting and implementing engineering and schedule changes.   _____
2. Responsibility is defined for support of all customer issues.   _____
3. Problems are communicated to customer prior to detection by the customer.   _____
4. Process exists to provide price, schedule, and technical information in a time
   acceptable to the customer.   _____
5. Capacity exists to respond to short-term surges in demand.   _____
6. Prototype and small runs can be run inside regular lead time.   _____
       1=Complete   2=Adequate   3=Incomplete   4=Inadequate

Delivery

Item   1-2-3-4

1. Process exists that allow changes in delivery schedules.   _____
2. Demonstrated ability to deliver within an on-time window.   _____
       1=Complete   2=Adequate   3=Incomplete   4=Inadequate

FIGURE 38.2   Supplier Qualification Survey. *(Continued)*

Cost

Item	1-2-3-4
1. Total cost of ownership, including part price, inspection cost, warranty cost, inventory cost, and customer support cost is competitive.	_____
2. Cost improvement processes are in place that are coordinated with the customer.	_____
3. Quotation process ensures that costs reflect level of technology required by the customer.	_____

1=Complete   2=Adequate   3=Incomplete   4=Inadequate

Business Strategy

Item	1-2-3-4
1. Business strategies are consistent with customer's long-term needs.	_____
2. Business is financially sound.	_____
3. A process for disaster recovery is documented and evidence of its use is available.	_____

1=Complete   2=Adequate   3=Incomplete   4=Inadequate

Decision Criteria: The result of the survey process will be used in conjunction with the price quotation process (see Sec. 38.7.2) to make a final decision on whether a potential supplier should be further considered and what additional information is required prior to actually starting a business relationship.

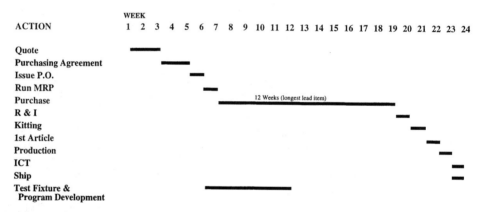

FIGURE 38.3   Typical timeline for starting a turnkey manufacturing relationship (assumes that long lead items beyond 12 weeks are ordered in advance).

Kitting.   Parts are assembled in kits and segregated by assembly number. Time will vary depending on the number of parts per assembly.

First article.   For first-time runs of new assemblies, an additional week may be necessary to verify the manufacturing process as well as the functionality of the product.

Production.   Lead times can vary from 1 to 10 days, depending on the complexity.

In-circuit test.   ICT can add an additional day or two, depending on complexity and first-pass yields. Failed units will have to be debugged and put through a rework process.

Ship.   Shipping can range from same day or overnight to one week, depending on proximity and method of transportation.

Test fixtures and program development.   Can take eight weeks or more, but should be accomplished within the materials lead time.

38.6   QUALITY SYSTEM

To understand how a particular product can be built to meet or exceed the expectation set by the OEM, ECMs must have in place a quality system that will aid the manufacturer information that can continuously improve the process. An effective quality system will not only ensure that a product's specification meets the needs of the end user, but can greatly contribute to the economic performance of the product.

38.6.1   Total Quality Management

Quality procedures and policies must be clearly written and understood by all employees who affect the outcome of a product's manufacturing cycle. In order to meet and/or exceed the customer's quality and reliability expectations, various quality policies must be in place and constantly managed by a quality management team or *total quality management* (TQM). This process will drive quality improvements based on a set of business and quality measurements that are reviewed at the highest level of the organization and then delivered to all employees through communication and/or action item meetings. Effective quality/continuous improvement will involve all personnel through meetings that solicit input from employees for improvements and problem resolutions.

38.6.2   ISO 9000

The International Standards Organization (ISO) has developed a list of procedures that enable corporations to adhere to guidelines that outline a method of demonstrating the adequacy of the quality system and its capability to achieve and service conformity with the specified requirements. ISO 9002 certification focuses on the manufacturing compliance per the specification as provided by another source while ISO 9001 certification focuses on compliance with regard to the design and the manufacturability of an assembly.

38.7   REQUEST FOR QUOTATION

38.7.1   Purpose

Aside from understanding what costs are associated with building a particular product, the quotation can serve as formal response from the ECM as to how efficiently it proposes to build the product, with any or all assumptions clearly documented. While some cost drivers can be assumed and built into the quote, others cannot be understood until several months' worth of production has gone by. Through a manufacturing agreement, terms should be discussed to identify and understand what costs are associated with the various cost drivers previously listed. Expectations should be put in writing to help avoid misunderstandings that will undoubtedly surface over the course of a relationship.

38.7.2   Contents and Sample

At a minimum, the information requested through a quotation should include assembly labor cost, test labor cost, material cost, nonrecurring expenditures, and all assumptions that may affect these categories. Figure 38.4 illustrates a quotation model.

FIGURE 38.4   Sample Quote.

Date
To: Customer Name   Bid # Revision
          Corporation
From: ECM
Re: Quote for Assembly #, Revision #, Assembly Name

Assembly # quantity/year	50 prototype	6,000	9,000	12,000
Assembly labor	$ 0.00	$ 0.00	$ 0.00	
Test labor	0.00	$ 0.00	$ 0.00	
Material cost	0.00	$ 0.00	$ 0.00	
Unit cost	$ 0.00	$ 0.00	$ 0.00	

Nonrecurring expenditures:

    Manufacturing startup: $0.00 (includes all setup costs)

    Router plate: $0.00

    PCB tooling: (if needed) $0.00

    ICT test fixture: $0.00

    ICT test program: $0.00

Notes and assumptions:

    Payment terms; build location; period of performance: 4/95–3/96; technology used; document baseline—*(date)*.

    Manufacturing assumptions: PCB will be panelized (*number of boards per panel*); quote assumes kit size (*minimum kit size*);

    Test assumptions: (*time standards, assumed first-pass yields*)

    Material assumptions: All components are quoted per customer AVL; minimum piece buys (*list part numbers and quantities*); list all long-lead items beyond 12 weeks; list alternate vendors that may cost less.

To accurately quote an OEM's manufacturing requirements, the following documentation is required:

Documentation needed	*Purpose*
Bill of material (BOM)	To quote materials and identify reference designators
Approved vendor list (AVL)	To quote material as specified by the customer
PCB fabrication drawings	To quote board fabrication costs
Assembly drawings	To quote assembly labor
Schematics	To quote test times, fixtures, and programs
	Other items of interest:
Gerber files, aperture list	To have PCB fab produced
Sample assemblies	To assist in DFM study and assembly labor quote

Quantities: After establishing an estimated annual forecast, the volumes required by the OEM to be quoted should represent both up-side and down-side possibilities, as well as prototype and preproduction quantities (see Fig. 38.4). Quantities may be quoted on an annual or monthly basis. Material prices are usually quoted on an annual usage basis, while assembly labor is quoted on a per-run basis in order to understand the amount of setups on a manufacturing line as well as material turns on inventory.

38.7.3 Responses Required

Unit cost: Total cost of final product including all services and materials as specified by the customer and/or specified by the supplier.

Assembly labor: The cost to manufacture a product, including the overhead and profit-related expenses, as specified by the customer and/or specified by the supplier.

Material cost: The cost of all materials, per unit, including overhead, profit, freight, and attrition. Depending on material value and location of vendor, freight and attrition may average 2 percent.

Test costs: The cost to test, per unit, as specified by the customer. Time standards, throughput, and first-pass yields, including estimated debug time per unit, should be understood up-front in order to verify time and yield estimates should they be grossly over- or underestimated.

Nonrecurring expenditures: The cost to develop all fixtures and programs proprietary to the customer's specific needs (See quotation model in Fig. 38.4).

In order to understand cost drivers, other information to gather that can be useful through the quote stage may include a costed BOM (by line item) and manufacturing processes and time standards. Suppliers may consider this information confidential, but depending on the relationship and/or the ability to leverage the supplier, an OEM may have access to virtually an unlimited amount of information.

38.8   *MANAGING THE RELATIONSHIP*

Because the vendor selection process can take a considerable amount of time and effort, managing the relationship effectively can prevent having to experience a learning curve in the manufacturing process as well as the relationship process. A failed partnership can mean disaster to the OEM—i.e., no product shipping.

38.8.1 Getting Started

A kick-off meeting should be assembled to introduce a program/product management team (see Fig. 38.5). In that meeting team members can explain their value-add or responsibilities to the program's success.

38.8.1.1 *Program Management Team.*   The *program manager* representing the ECM can be used as a focal point for all strategic information. Issuing purchase orders, engineering changes, and schedule changes should all be channeled through one individual to keep communication consistent. Surrounding team members should be looked on as support members who work in a tactical mode. Depending on the particulars of an ECM, the *manufacturing engineer* may be designated to develop the *manufacturing process instructions* (MPI). A *planner* will be responsible for assuring for the timing between manufacturing capacity and material availability. The *quality engineer's* responsibility may include collecting yield data and providing the information to the manufacturing engineer, who may need to fine-tune the process. The *test engineer* will provide timely yield information to the manufacturing engineer to point out areas of concern about failures. The *sales manager* may be responsible for processing quotations and proposals and/or

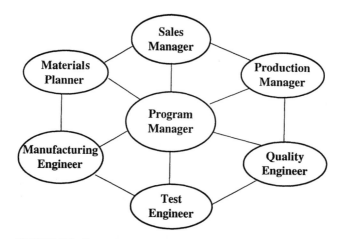

FIGURE 38.5 Example program management team.

Customer Satisfaction Survey

FROM: TO:
CUSTOMER: _____   PROGRAM MGR: _____
RESPONDENT: _____   FAX #: _____
FAX: _____   DATE: _____

4: Excellent at meeting and exceeding set requirements.
3: Generally meeting requirments most of the time.
2: Satisfactorily meeting requirements - could use improvement.
1: Generally missing requirements - needs development.
0: Unacceptable

Category	4	3	2	1	0
Quality					
Delivery					
Communication					
Service					
Overall					

COMMENTS:

SIGNED: _____   DATE: _____

FIGURE 38.6 Customer satisfaction survey.

monitoring the overall satisfaction level of the customer. While maintaining strategic information through the program manager, communication should be encouraged for each team member from all team members from both the ECM and the OEM. Meetings should be set on a regular basis either in person or by phone. The program manager, keeping an updated list of action items, can be in charge of seeing that all team members meet their obligations.

38.8.2 Evaluating Performance: Customer Satisfaction Survey (CSS)

By using a *customer satisfaction survey* (see Fig. 38.6) an OEM can quantify on a regular basis the level of service that is being provided by its supplier. The ECM can in turn use the CSS to provide guidance into the critical service areas as determined by their customer. ECMs can use the CSS report as a tool to provide corrective action plans as the customer identifies problems that have not been corrected through the day-to-day relationship. Although action items may be worked on and discussed on a regular basis, it's helpful for a supplier to understand exactly where they stand in the eyes of the customer. Depending on how frequent and heavy interaction is between a supplier and customer in relationship, a scorecard or CSS can be submitted weekly, monthly, or perhaps even quarterly.

Categories to score on a regular basis may include quality, delivery, communication, and service. A quality measurement may be based on first-pass yields at the site of the OEM at functional test. A goal for first-pass yield may be put in place based on a mutual agreement between the OEM and the ECM. As the ECM gains experience from manufacturing a particular OEM requirement, quality yields may be expected to increase. Scoring an ECM's ability to deliver product may be based on the requirements as stated on the PO, with consideration given to account for material that may have developed unusually long lead times due to shortages. Communication can be more of a subjective category when critiquing the performance of an ECM.

Poor marks in communication may mean anything from a lack of understanding between parties to a lack of response on a timely basis. Parameters can be set as to what kind of response time is required from an ECM for most recurring requests. Service can be another subjective category that lends the ECM an idea of how well the OEM feels it is being taken care of. When any category score depicts above or below what is expected in the relationship, it is imperative that the OEM describe in detail what it is experiencing. Specific comments will allow the ECM to respond to criticism in a constructive manner through the use of a corrective action plan. The CSS can also be used for appraisal, which can help motivate team members who deserve recognition. By using a CSS effectively, OEMs and ECMs can better define their objectives to work towards the same end result.

FLEXIBLE CIRCUITS

CHAPTER 39
MATERIALS FOR FLEXIBLE CIRCUITS*

Sheldahl Technical Staff[†]
Sheldahl Inc., Northfield, Minnesota

39.1 INTRODUCTION

Figure 39.1 shows the major material uses in flexible printed wiring.

39.1.1 Dielectric Substrates

The dielectric substrate is the base film on which the printed conductors are laid. The dielectric insulates conductors from each other and provides much of the circuit's mechanical strength. The choice of a *flexible* rather than a *rigid* dielectric is the main characteristic which distinguishes flexible printed wiring from rigid printed wiring boards.

Plastic films, synthetic papers, and resign-impregnated fabrics are used as dielectrics in FPW.

Dielectric films can be either *thermosetting* or *thermoplastic*. Thermosetting materials cure, set, or harden into shape when heated. Once cured, thermosetting materials cannot be resoftened by heating. Thermoplastic materials do not set or cure when heated. They soften to a flowable state when heated and harden when cooled.

Aramid paper is made from nylon fibers processed on conventional papermaking equipment. Aramid paper has a structure similar to heavy cellulose paper.

Reinforced dielectrics are glass or organic fibers, or both, impregnated with polymeric binders.

The important properties to consider when selecting dielectric substrates for FPW are:

- Mechanical strength
- Flexibility
- Dimensional stability
- Dielectric properties

---

* Includes material from Steve Gurley, "Flexible Circuit Design, Materials, and Fabrication," Chap. 35 in Clyde F. Coombs, Jr. (ed.), *Printed Circuits Handbook,* 3d ed., McGraw-Hill, New York, 1988.
[†] Adapted from "Flexible Circuitry Design Guide," published by Sheldahl Inc., 1984, used with permission.

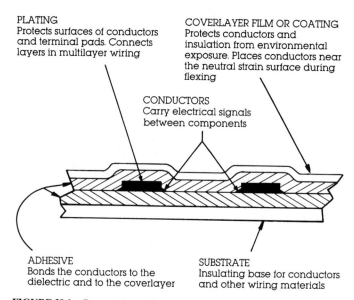

PLATING
Protects surfaces of conductors
and terminal pads. Connects
layers in multilayer wiring

COVERLAYER FILM OR COATING
Protects conductors and
insulation from environmental
exposure. Places conductors near
the neutral strain surface during
flexing

CONDUCTORS
Carry electrical signals
between components

ADHESIVE
Bonds the conductors to the
dielectric and to the coverlayer

SUBSTRATE
Insulating base for conductors
and other wiring materials

FIGURE 39.1 Cross section of flexible printed wiring showing material use.

- Thermal properties
- Chemical resistance
- Moisture absorption
- Cost

Table 39.1 gives a composition of FPW dielectrics.

39.1.2 Adhesives

FPW usually has distinct adhesive layers to bond layers together. Thermosetting, thermoplastic, and modified thermoplastic organic polymers are used as adhesives for flexible circuits. Modified thermoplastics form a structure similar to a thermosetting adhesive but with the flexibility of a thermoplastic.

The important properties to consider when selecting an FPW adhesive are:

- Adhesion
- Flexibility
- Chemical resistance
- Thermal resistance
- Moisture absorption
- Electrical properties
- Cost

Table 39.2 gives a comparison of FPW adhesives.

TABLE 39.1 Comparison of FPW Dielectrics

Property	Polyesters	Polyimides	Fluorocarbons	Aramid paper	Composites
Tensile strength	Excellent	Excellent	Fair	Good	Best
Flexibility	Excellent	Excellent	Excellent	Good	Fair/Good
Dimensional stability	Fair/Good	Good	Fair	Good	Excellent
Dielectric strength	Good	Good	Very good	Very good	Good
Solder withstand	Poor	Excellent	Fair	Excellent	Excellent
Continuous operating temperature (C)	105°	200—230°	150—180°	220°	105—180°
Thermal expansion	Low	Low	High	Moderate	Low
Chemical resistance	Good	Good	Excellent	Very good	Fair
Moisture absorption	Very low	High	Very low	Very high	Low
Cost	Low	High	High	Moderate	Moderate
Trade names	Mylar* Mellinex† Celanar‡	Kapton*	Teflon* Tedlar*	Nomex*	—

* Du Pont Trademark
† ICI™
‡ Celanese™

39.1.3 Conductors

Metals, metal alloys, and conductive inks are used as conductors in flexible circuits. Metal foils include copper, aluminum, nickel, silver, and gold. Metal alloys used include stainless steel, beryllium copper, phosphor bronze, INCONEL (copper-nickel), and MONEL (nickel-chromium). Polymer-thick films (PTF) are coatings containing conductive particles, usually silver or carbon, in an adhesive matrix.

Copper is the most commonly used conductor for FPW. Two general types of copper are used: electrolytically plated (ED) copper and rolled annealed (RA) copper. Rolled annealed copper has better flexibility than electrodeposited copper, but it is more expensive to process. The important properties to consider when selecting an FPW conductor are:

TABLE 39.2 Comparison of FPW Adhesives

Type	Temp. resistance	Chemical resistance	Electrical properties	Adhesion	Flexibility	Cost	Moisture absorption
Polyester	Fair	Good	Excellent	Excellent	Excellent	Low	Fair
Acrylic	Very good	Good	Good	Excellent	Good	Moderate	Poor
Modified epoxy	Good	Fair	Good/ Excellent	Excellent	Fair	High	Good
Polyimide	Excellent	Very good	Good	Very good*	Fair	Very high	Poor†
Fluorocarbon	Very good	Excellent	Good	Very good*	Excellent	Moderate	Excellent
Butyral phenolic	Good	Good	Good	Good	Good	Moderate	Fair

* Very difficult to process.
† Evolves water while curing.

- Current-carrying capacity
- Flexibility
- Types of interconnections
- Service temperature
- Chemical resistance
- Mechanical strength
- Cost

Table 39.3 gives a comparison of metals used for FPW conductors.

TABLE 39.3   Comparison of Metals Used for Flexible Printed Wiring Conductors

Conductor	Electrical properties	Thermal properties	Mechanical properties	Relative cost
Aluminum	Excellent	Fair	Good	Best
Copper	Excellent	Excellent	Good	Fair/Good
Gold	Good	Fair	Good	Excellent
Nickel	Good	Very good	Very good	Good
Silver	Excellent	Fair	Excellent	Excellent

39.1.4   Platings

Flexible circuit conductors are often selectively or completely plated with metal for protection against corrosion and to enhance electrical connection or mechanical bonding. The metallic platings used in flexible circuits include copper, nickel, tin, gold, and various solder materials, usually tin-lead alloys. (See Table 39.4.)

The properties to consider when selecting FPW plating are:

- Corrosion resistance
- Wear resistance
- Hardness
- Flexibility
- Soldering temperature
- Mechanical strength
- Electrical conductivity
- Thermal expansion
- Cost

39.1.5   Protective Cover Layers

Permanent insulating coatings are sometimes applied over the conductor side of flexible printed wiring to protect it from moisture, contamination, and damage and to reduce stress on the conductors during flexible. Three kinds of protective coatings are used:

- *Coverlays.*   Thin dielectric films laminated to the circuit with an adhesive
- *Covercoats.*   Liquid polymers coated onto the circuit and cured
- *Dry film solder masks.*   Transfer films vacuum-laminated to the circuit and photocured

TABLE 39.4   Plating Materials

Material	Applications
Copper	Most widely used plating Plating-through-holes between circuit layers
Tin-lead alloys (50–70% tin)	Contact materials Provide solderable surfaces Plated-through-holes and eyelet connectors Etchant resists
Nickel	Reinforcing plating in plated-through-hole fabrication Thermocompression of ultrasonic bonding of components Subplating to prevent copper migration into gold plating
Silver	Static pressure contacts and switch surfaces Tarnishes easily Migrates across dielectrics Less costly alternative to gold plating
Gold	Excellent corrosion protection Excellent resistance to processing chemicals Thicknesses over 80 millionths inch detrimental to soldering Best plating for good electrical contact to connectors Not for solder resist applications

Properties to consider when choosing a protective covering for a flexible circuit are:

- Adhesion
- Flexibility
- Electrical properties
- Thermal properties
- Abrasion resistance
- Chemical stability
- Environmental stability
- Cost

39.2   FILMS AND SUBSTRATES

One of the primary considerations in designing a flexible circuit is the selection of the proper base and cover film. (The cover film insulates the etched pattern of the circuit much as solder mask or resist does in rigid boards.) Although there are many substrates which could conceivably be used, there are only two kinds of film in general use for flexible circuits. These films are polyimide and polyester. Films such as Teflon and Ultem are also used, but they appear only in limited and very specialized applications.

39.2.1   Polyimide (Kapton)

The first choice of film in most circuit applications is polyimide film. Polyimide film can withstand the temperatures required in soldering operations. It has no known organic solvent, and it cannot be fused. This film is also used in wire insulation and transformer insulation, and as insulation in motors.

Polyimide films are offered in standard thicknesses of 0.0005, 0.001, 0.002, 0.003, and 0.005 in. Table 39.5 shows the various properties of this film and should be referred to when the operating and environmental requirements of the flexible circuit are established. (The trade name for the product used to generate this table is Kapton, which is a trademark of E. I. du Pont de Nemours & Company.)

TABLE 39.5 Typical Properties of Kapton Type H Film—25 μm (1 mil)

Physical	Typical values			Test method
	78K (−195°C)	296K (23°C)	473K (200°C)	
Ultimate (MD)* tensile Strength, MPa (lb/in²)	241 (35,000)	172 (25,000)	117 (17,000)	ASTM D-882-64T
Ultimate (MD) elongation	2%	70%	90%	ASTM D-882-64T
Tensile modulus, GPa (MD) (lb/in²)	3.5 (510,000)	3.0 (430,000)	1.86 (260,000)	ASTM D-882-64T
Tear strength—propagating (Elmendorf), g	—	8	—	ASTM D-1922-61T
Tear strength—initial (Graves), g(g/mil)	—	510 (510)	—	ASTM D-1004-61

Thermal	Typical values	Test condition	Test method
Zero strength temperature	1088K (815°C)	0.14MPa (20 lb/in²) load for 5 s	Du Pont Hot-bar test
Coefficient of linear expansion	2.0×10^{-5}m./m./K (2.0×10^{-5}in./in./°C)	259 to 311K (−14°C–38°C)	ASTM D-696-44
Flammability	94 VTM-O		UL-94 (1-24-80)
Limiting oxygen index	100H-38		ASTM D-2863-74

Electrical	Typical value	Test condition	Test method
Dielectric strength 25 μm (1 mil)	276 v/μm (7,000 v/mil)	60 Hz ¼-in electrodes	ASTM D-149-61
Dielectric constant 25 μm (1 mil)	3.5	1 kHz	ASTM D-150-59T
Dissipation Factor 25 μm (1 mil)	0.0025	1 kHz	ASTM D-150-59T

Chemical		
Chemical resistance	Excellent (except for strong bases)	
Moisture absorption 25 μm (1 mil)	1.3% type H 2.9% type H & V	50% RH at 296K (23°C) Immersion for 24 h at 296K (23°C)

* MD = machine direction.
Source: Du Pont, Polymer Products Division.

There are some very specialized versions of Kapton film, but these are available for use in applications requiring very special properties. Examples of these materials are designated as follows:

1. *Kapton XT.* Improved thermal conductivity for better heat dissipation as a dielectric insulator, or for higher speeds in thermal-transfer printers

2. *Kapton XC.* Film with conductive fillers providing a range of electrical conductivities for specific uses

While Kapton XT film is readily available, the Kapton XC products were still in experimental use only at the time of this writing, and the manufacturer of the film should be contacted for availability. Kapton XT properties are compared with standard HN film in Table 39.6.

TABLE 39.6 Kapton XT Properties

Description
Kapton polyimide film with alumina incorporated in the polymer to increase thermal conductivity

Major feature
Up to twice the heat-dissipating capacity of regular Kapton type H film

Intended uses

Magnet wire and motor coils
Semiconductor insulators
Thermal printer transfer substrate
Metal/XT composites for circuit substrates
Any application where more rapid heat dissipation improves performance

Property	Units	Typical values	
		200H	200XT
Tenacity, 23°C	kpsi	34	20
Elongation, 23°C	%	90	30
Shrinkage, 400°C	%	1	1
Moisture absorption, 23°C	%	3	5
Dielectric strength, 23°C	V/mil	5900	4000
Volume resistance, 200°C	$\Omega \cdot cm$	10^{14}	10^{14}
Dielectric constant, 23°C	—	3.4	3.4
Dissipation factor, 23°C*	—	0.0025	0.0024
Thermal conductivity, 23°C	$W/M \cdot K$	0.155	0.24

* At 1 kHz, 50% RH.
Note: Kapton type XT is a thermally conductive Kapton with up to twice the heat-dissipating capacity of Kapton type H film, which is an all-purpose, all-polyimide film that has been used successfully in application temperatures from −269°C to as high as 400°C. The high thermal conductivity of Kapton type XT is achieved by incorporating alumina in type H film.

Recent customer development programs have demonstrated the benefits of a heat-conducting, dielectrically insulating, thin film in several applications such as motor wire insulation, semiconductor insulating pads, electronic circuit substrates made from metal/XT composite, and thermal printers.

39.2.2 Polyester (Mylar)

Polyester film represents a good value for use in many flexible circuit applications. Technically, it is known as *polyethelyne terephthalate,* which is a polymer formed by the condensation reaction of ethylene glycol and terephthalic acid. One of the largest producers of this film is E. I. du Pont de Nemours & Company, which sells the product under the trade name of Mylar.

Polyester film is low in cost: about ¹⁄₂₀ the cost of polyimide film. It contains no plasticizers and therefore does not become brittle under normal conditions. It is very resistant to solvents and other chemicals and has a high tensile strength (25,000 lb/in²) and a good dielectric strength (7.5 kV/10⁻³ in for 0.001-in film).

The service temperature for this film ranges from 70 to 150°C. The low temperature resistance of the film is a drawback when the finished circuit must be exposed to soldering temperatures over 230°C, but with careful engineering of the product, even this problem can be circumvented by designing a circuit with a heavy 0.005-in base. It should have large solder pads and wide traces, and 2-oz* copper foil should be specified. This will result in a circuit which can be carefully hand soldered or even wave soldered using an appropriate mask or jig to keep the heat away from all parts of the circuit except the portions being soldered. Polyester is widely used in automotive and communications circuitry and is most cost effective in very large applications. See Table 39.7 for typical values of polyester (Mylar) film.

TABLE 39.7   Typical Property Values of Mylar* Polyester Film Type El for Printed Circuits

	Thermal
Melting point	Approx. 250°C (480°F) (Fisher Johns Method).
Coefficient of thermal expansion	1.7×10^{-6} in/in/°C (30°C · 50°C, ASTM D 696·44 modified).
Service temperature	−70–150°C (−100 to 300°F). (Soldering of circuits on Mylar can be done at solder temperatures up to about 275°C (530°F).
Strain relief	1.5% (30 min at 150°C (300°F)†
	Physical
Tensile strength	25,000 lb/in^2 (25°C, ASTM D 882·645T Method A).
Elongation	120% (25°C, ASTM D 882-64T Method A).
Tensile modulus	550,000 lb/in^2 (25°C, ASTM D 882·64T Method A).
Density	1.395 (25°C, ASTM D 1505·63T modified).
	Chemical
Moisture absorption	Less than 0.8% (ASTM D 570·63; 24-h immersion at 23°C).
	Electrical
Dielectric strength (1 mil)	7500 V/mil (25°C, 60 Hz, ASTM D 149·64).
Dielectric strength (1 mil)	5000 V/mil (150°C, 60 Hz, ASTM D 149·64).
Dielectric constant	3.0-3.7 (25–150°C, 60 Hz–1 MHz, ASTM D 150·65T).
Dissipation factor	0.005 (25°C, 1 kHz, ASTM D 150·65T).
Volume resistivity	10^{18} ohm·cm (25°C, ASTM D 257·66).
	10^{13} ohm·cm (150°C, ASTM D 257·66).

* Reg. U.S. Pat. Off.
† Typical strain relief for experimental low-shrink film is 1.0% at 150°C (300°F) for 30 min.
Source: Du Pont, Industrial Films Division, Polymer Products Department.

39.2.3   Aramid Material (Nomex)

Although the two films previously discussed are the most common ones in use, there are other base insulation materials which have attractive properties. Some of these include Nomex and Dacron-epoxy. Nomex is Du Pont's random-fiber aramid material. Nomex is a high-temperature paper which withstands soldering temperatures very well. Its main drawback in flexible circuit applications is that it is very hygroscopic and absorbs processing chemicals, which must be carefully removed from one wet-process point to the next. Nomex has fairly low initiation and propagation tear strengths. The material has a fairly low dielectric con-

---

* The expression *2-oz copper foil* refers to the standard technique of defining the thickness of copper laminated to an insulating substrate. The weight of copper per square foot of laminate area describes the thickness: for example, 2 oz/ft^2 equates to a thickness of 0.00275 in, and 1 oz defines a thickness of 0.001375 in.

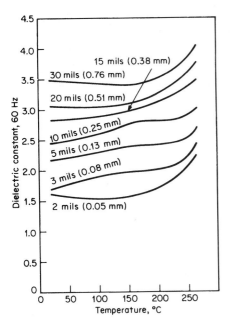

FIGURE 39.2 Dielectric constant vs. temperature for Nomex aramid paper type 410. *(Courtesy of E. I. du Pont de Nemours & Company, Wilmington, Del.)*

stant—about half that of Kapton. See Table 39.8 and Fig. 39.2 for typical properties of Nomex film.

39.2.4 Polyester-Epoxy (BEND/flex)

Dacron-epoxy-base insulation material is available in 0.005-, 0.0085-, 0.015-, 0.020-, and 0.030-in thicknesses. The material is manufactured using a nonwoven mat of Dacron polyester and glass fibers which is saturated with a B-stage epoxy. This saturated mat is then combined with copper foil and laminated into single- and double-clad material without using a separate adhesive system. One of the more interesting forms of this material is in a product called BEND/flex, which looks similar to rigid printed circuit materials but which can be bent into three-dimensional shapes without heating. The material will hold a set. This unique bendability is due to a low and broad glass transition temperature of the fully cured material. The general materials properties are shown in Table 39.9.

39.3 CONDUCTORS AND FOILS

Metal foils used to create the circuit patterns are usually made of copper. Copper foil is measured in ounces per square foot (see preceding), a carryover from the building trades industry. Copper foil is available in weights of ½, 1, and 2 oz, usually desired for most flexible circuit applications. It is also available in heavier weights if desired for high-current applications in which a larger cross section of material in the conductors is necessary.

There are two fundamental differences in the kinds of copper foils used in flexible printed circuitry. One product is produced by electrolytic deposition, and the other is produced by cold rolling.

39.3.1 Electrodeposited Copper

Electrodeposited (ED) copper is made by electroplating copper onto a stainless steel drum. The longer this plating action continues, the thicker the copper foil becomes. After the material is coated onto the drum, it is removed in coil form. The drum side of the material has a very smooth, shiny finish, whereas the outside, or dull side, of the material has a tooth which provides a very good surface for adhesion to take place with the adhesive. The grain structure of ED foil is very vertical in nature, and although this gives excellent bonds to various film bases, it is less ductile than the rolled, annealed product that is used primarily in dynamic, or moving applications. Typical ED foil properties are shown in Table 39.10.

39.3.2 Rolled Annealed Copper

Rolled annealed copper is manufactured by melting cathode copper, which is produced electrolytically, and then forming this copper into large ingots. This direct chill casting method allows for controlled solidification, which provides continuous purity monitoring and grain

TABLE 39.8 Typical Properties of Nomex Aramid Paper Type 410

Typical physical properties* of Nomex Aramid paper type 410 (MD = machine direction, XD = cross direction of paper)													
Nominal thickness	mils		2	3	5	7	10	12	15	20	24	29	30
	(mm)		(0.05)	(0.08)	(0.13)	(0.18)	(0.25)	(0.30)	(0.38)	(0.51)	(0.61)	(0.74)	(0.76)
Basis weight	oz/yd²		1.2	1.9	3.4	5.1	7.3	9.1	11	16	20	25	25
	(g/m)		(40)	(63)	(120)	(170)	(250)	(310)	(370)	(540)	(680)	(850)	(850)
Tensile strength (ASTM† D·828·60)	lb/in	MD	22	40	83	130	180	230	280	350	460	540	510
		XD	11	19	39	64	90	110	150	230	310	370	350
	(N/cm)	MD	(39)	(70)	(150)	(230)	(320)	(400)	(490)	(610)	(810)	(950)	(890)
		XD	(19)	(33)	(68)	(110)	(160)	(190)	(260)	(400)	(540)	(650)	(610)
Elongation	%	MD	9	12	16	20	21	21	21	21	19	17	20
		XD	7	9	13	16	18	18	18	18	14	13	16
Finch edge tear (ASTM D·827·47)	lb	MD	21	41	85	130	180	200	220	210	170	200	270
		XD	9	16	33	58	71	86	89	100	79	86	130
	(N)	MD	(93)	(180)	(380)	(580)	(800)	(890)	(980)	(930)	(760)	(890)	(1200)
		XD	(40)	(71)	(150)	(260)	(320)	(380)	(400)	(450)	(350)	(380)	(580)
Elmendorf tear (ASTM D·689)	g	MD	84	120	220	340	560	690	890	1200	—	—	—
		XD	160	250	580	750	1000	1200	1500	1900	—	—	—
	(N)	MD	(0.8)	(1.2)	(2.2)	(3.3)	(5.5)	(6.8)	(8.7)	(12)	—	—	—
		XD	(1.6)	(2.5)	(5.7)	(7.4)	(9.8)	(12)	(15)	(19)	—	—	—
Shrinkage at 300°C	%	MD	1.7	1.1	0.6	0.5	0.5	0.3	0.3	0.3	0.3	0.3	0.3
		XD	1.3	0.9	0.5	0.4	0.4	0.3	0.3	0.3	0.3	0.3	0.3
Limiting oxygen index (ASTM D·2863·70)								0.24–0.28					

* Not to be used for product specification purposes
† American Society for Testing and Materials, Philadelphia, PA

Typical electrical properties* of Nomex Aramid paper type 410 (Measured at 23°C, 50% RH)											
Nominal Thickness	mils	2	3	5	7	10	12	15	20	24	29	30
	(mm)	(0.05)	(0.08)	(0.13)	(0.18)	(0.25)	(0.30)	(0.38)	(0.51)	(0.61)	(0.74)	(0.76)
Dielectric strength ac rapid rise (ASTM D·149†)	V/mil	500	610	730	900	880	880	860	780	750	700	660
	(kV/mm)	(20)	(24)	(29)	(35)	(35)	(35)	(34)	(31)	(30)	(28)	(26)
Dielectric constant (ASTM D·150‡)	60 Hz	1.6	1.6	2.4	2.7	2.7	2.9	3.2	3.4	3.7	3.7	3.7
Dissipation factor (ASTM D·150‡)	60 Hz	0.004	0.005	0.006	0.006	0.006	0.007	0.007	0.007	0.007	0.007	0.007

* Not to be used for product specification purposes
† 2-in (51·mm) diameter electrodes
‡ 1-in (25·mm) diameter electrodes under 20 lb/in² (140 kPa) pressure
Source: E. I. du Pont de Nemours & Company, Wilmington, Del.

size selection and also eliminates existing defects, such as voids which would influence the quality of the foil when it is rolled into its final form.

The copper ingots are large and weigh several tons. They are hot-rolled to an intermediate gauge and then milled on all surfaces to ensure that there are no defects. After this milling operation, the copper is cold-rolled and annealed to specifications before being processed in a specially designed rolling mill called a Sendzimir mill.

Rolled copper is very flexible and should be used in dynamic applications requiring constant flexing. Figures 39.3 and 39.4 show the rolled copper foil's horizontal grain structure compared with the very vertical grain structure of electrodeposited foil. See Table 39.11 for typical specifications and properties of rolled copper. The horizontal grain allows the rolled copper, after being properly processed into a flexible circuit, to flex hundreds of millions of times with no conductor failures.

TABLE 39.9 BEND/flex 2400 Properties

Construction: 1 oz copper, (307 g/m²) 1 or 2 sides, insulation thickness (ASTM D-374A): 0.020 in (0.15 mm)*

	Test method	Units	Required value
	Physical properties		
Dimensional stability	IPC-TM-650, Section 2.2.4		
On etching MD		Max, %	±0.10
On etching TD			
On heat aging MD		Max, %	±0.15
On heat aging TD			
Peel strength	IPC-TM-650, Section 2.4.9, Method A	Min, lb$_f$/in., (KN/m)	8, (1.4)
Initiation tear strength	IPC-TM-650, Section 2.4.16		
MD		Min, lb$_f$, (N)	18, (80)
TD		Min, lb$_f$, (N)	18, (80)
Propagation tear strength	IPC-TM-650, Section 2.4.17.1		
MD		Min, lb$_f$, (N)	1.2, (53)
TD		Min, lb$_f$, (N)	1.3, (53)
	Electrical properties		
Insulation resistance	IPC-TM-650, Section 2.5.9	Min, MΩ	1×10^5
Dielectric strength	ASTM-D-149	Min, V/mil	300
	Chemical properties		
Flammability	IPC-TM-650, Section 2.3.8	Min, % O$_2$	28
U.L. 94 flame class	UL 94	—	94V-0
Solder float	IPC-TM-650, Section 2.4.13, Method A		Pass
	Environmental properties		
Moisture absorption	IPC-TM-650, Section 2.6.2	Max, %	1.0

* Required values for .015 and .030 in are available on request.

Note: BEND/flex™ material is easily processed using standard hardboard processing techniques and chemicals. It can be easily plated with tin or solder using standard roller coating or hot-air leveling processes.

When bending circuits into shape, it must have a minimum inside bend radius of 10 times the material thickness, and must be bent approximately 50 percent beyond the desired angle of set.

The circuit will then relax to its required angle of bend, or it can be manually positioned with little return force.

The information presented is, to the best of our knowledge, accurate. HOWEVER, values obtained are subject to handling and process variations. Rogers Corporation makes no warranties with respect to such data, and assumes no responsibility for performance characteristics resulting from conditions which differ from those used in laboratory tests. This data should not be used as specification limits.

Source: © 1985, Rogers Corporation, Rogers, Connecticut.

There are almost as many kinds of copper alloys as there are birds in the air. Flexible circuits, however, use only a few types. Some of the types are designated in hardness values. The temper of rolled copper can vary from ⅛ to ¾ hard (see Table 39.12), most commonly specified. These are also available as rolled and annealed copper (see Table 39.12). There is also a trademarked type available from the Thin Strip Brass Group, Sommers Division of Olin Corporation, called LTA copper. It is an alloy called 110 and is fairly hard when received by the flexible circuit materials laminator. It anneals at low temperatures which are the same as processing temperatures for laminations. This gives the laminator a copper which is easily handled without stretching or wrinkling and yet anneals into a very soft foil after it is combined with the film (see Table 39.13 for typical properties).

One other important feature to specify when using rolled annealed copper is a treatment which enhances the bond. The horizontal grain structure of the rolled copper is fairly smooth. An additional process which is similar to an electrolytic flash of copper on the surface enhances the bond without deteriorating the superior flexing characteristics of the rolled annealed copper.

TABLE 39.10 Mechanical Properties of Electrodeposited Copper

		At room temperature 23°C			At elevated temperature 180°C		
		Tensile		% Elongation (2.0 in GL)	Tensile		% Elongation (2.0 in GL)
Electrodeposited copper class	Copper weight oz.	lbs/in²	kgs/mm²	CHS 2 in/M	lbs/in²	kgs/mm²	CHS 0.05 in/M
1	½	15,000	10.55	2.0			
	1	30,000	21.09	3.0	Not applicable		
	2+	30,000	21.09	3.0			
2	½	15,000	10.55	5.0			
	1	30,000	21.09	10.0	Not applicable		
	2+	30,000	21.09	15.0			
3	½	15,000	10.55	2.0	—	—	—
	1	30,000	21.09	15.0	20,000	14.09	2.0
	2+	30,000	21.09	22.0	25,000	17.62	3.0
4	1	20,000	14.09	10.0	15,000	10.55	4.0

Foil specifications

Thickness by weight		Thickness by gauges	
oz/ft²	g/m²	Nom. in	Nom. mm
⅛	44	—	0.005
¼	80	—	0.009
⅜	106	—	0.012
½	153	0.0007	0.018
1	305	0.0013	0.035
2	610	0.0028	0.071
3	915	0.0042	0.106
4	1221	0.0056	0.143
5	1526	0.0070	0.178
6	1831	0.0084	0.213
7	2136	0.0098	0.246
10	3052	0.0140	0.353
14	4272	0.0196	0.492

Class description
1 Standard electrodeposited
2 High ductility electrodeposited (flexible applications with minor strain)
3 High temperature elongation electrodeposited (see special products section) (high reliability multilayer applications where severe stresses are imposed)
4 Annealed electrodeposited (high reliability multilayer and flexible applications where severe strains are imposed without high tensile requirements)
Source: Gould, Inc., Eastlake, Ohio.

Finally, Table 39.14 compares wrought annealed copper properties with those of electrodeposited flex-grade copper.

39.4 ADHESIVES

The third component of most flexible circuit materials is the adhesive system. There are many brand names available, but in the final analysis there are three major types of systems: poly-

FIGURE 39.3 Rolled copper grain structure. *(Courtesy of Olin Brass, Olin Corporation, Waterbury, Conn.)*

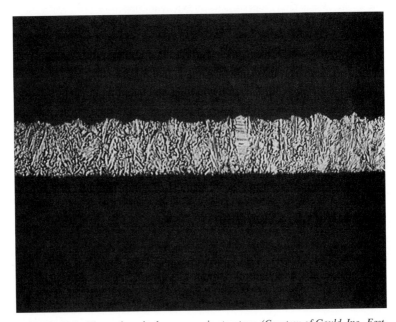

FIGURE 39.4 Electrodeposited copper grain structure. *(Courtesy of Gould, Inc., Eastlake, Ohio.)*

TABLE 39.11 Specifications and Physical Properties of Rolled Copper

Composition limits	Copper plus silver	99.9% Min
Applicable specifications	Oxygen ASTM B-451 Copper 110 MIL-F-55561 IPC-CF-150	0.03% Max

Physical properties		
	English units	Metric units
Melting point	1981°F	1083°C
Density	0.322 lb/in^3	8.91 g/cm^3
Coefficient of thermal expansion	0.0000098/°F (68-572°F)	0.0000177/°C (20-300°C)
Thermal conductivity (annealed)	226 Btu-ft/ft^2-h-°F @ 68°F	0.934 cal-cm/cm^2-s-°C @ 20°C
Electrical resistivity (annealed)	10.3 Ω circ mil/ft @ 68°F	1.71 μΩ-cm @ 20°C (volume) 0.152361 Ω-g/m^2 (weight)
Electrical conductivity (annealed)	101% I.A.C.S.* @ 68°F	0.586 mΩ/cm @ 20°C
Thermal capacity (specific heat)	0.092 Btu/lb/°F @ 68°F	0.092 cal/g/°C @ 20°C
Modulus of elasticity (tension)	17,000,000 lb/in^2	12,000 kg/mm^2
Modulus of rigidity	6,400,000 lb/in^2	4,500 kg/mm^2

* International Annealed Copper Standard.
Source: Olin Corporation, Sommers Brass Division, Waterbury, Conn.

TABLE 39.12 Mechanical Property Data for Wrought Copper

Annealed and as rolled tempers				
Temper name	Min. gauge, in	Max. width, in	Tensile strength, ksi (Min)	Elongation % in 2 in min.
Annealed	0.0007	24	15	5
	0.0014	28	20	10
	0.0028 or greater	28	25	20
As rolled	0.0007	24	50	½
	0.0014	28	50	½
	0.0028 or greater	28	50	1

Rolled tempers				
Temper name	Min. gauge, in	Max. width, in	Tensile strength, ksi	Elongation % in 2 in min.
⅛ hard	0.0095	12	32/40	17
¼ hard	0.0057	12	34/42	13
½ hard	0.003	12	37/50	5
¾ hard	0.002	12	40/55	3

Source: Olin Brass, Waterbury, Conn.

TABLE 39.13   Specific Properties of LTA Copper

	Properties as supplied ½ or 1 oz	
Temper	Tensile strength, lb/in^2	Elongation % in 2 in
As rolled	50,000 min	½ min

Properties following typical adhesive cure cycle for ½ oz foil			
Cure temperature and time, temp/min	Nominal tensile strength, lb/in^2	Nominal elongation % in 2 in	D_f*
350°F/15	15,000	5	25
350°F/45	15,500	7	32
350°F/180	17,000	7	34

Properties following typical adhesive cure cycle for 1-oz foil			
Cure temperature and time, temp/min	Nominal tensile strength, lb/in^2	Nominal elongation % in 2 in	D_f*
350°F/15	21,000	12	52
350°F/45	19,800	11	56
350°F/180	20,600	11	58

* Parallel (MD) and Transverse (XMD) average.
Source: *Olin Corporation, Sommers Brass Division, Waterbury, Conn.*

TABLE 39.14   General Comparison of Sommers Wrought Copper with Electrodeposited Flex Grade

	Wrought-annealed			Electrodeposited flex grade		
Gauge (weight)	0.0007 in (½ oz)	0.0014 in (1 oz)	0.0028 in (2 oz)	0.0007 in (½ oz)	0.0014 in (1 oz)	0.0028 in (2 oz)
Tensile strength, lb/in^2 (nominal)	23,000	25,000	34,100	39,000	40,000	44,000
Yield strength, lb/in^2 0.2% offset (nominal)	NA	11,100	13,600	NA	13,700	20,700
Elongation % in 2 in (nominal)	5	17	35	3	12	18
Mullens bulge height	0.175 in	0.292 in	0.363 in	0.140 in	0.197 in	0.267 in
Electrical resistivity (Weight: Ω g/m^2)		0.152361		<0.16359	<0.15940	NA

Source: *Olin Corporation, Sommers Brass Division, Waterbury, Conn.*

esters, epoxies, and acrylics. Each system and the dozens of modifications which exist offer properties suitable for a variety of applications.

39.4.1   Epoxy Adhesives

Epoxy systems include modified epoxies known as phenolic butyrals and nitrile phenolics. These systems are widely used and are generally lower in cost than acrylics but higher in cost than polyesters. Epoxy has good high-temperature resistance and remains in good condition in all approved soldering systems. It also has very long term stability at elevated temperatures in environmental conditions up to 250°F. (See Table 39.15 for typical properties of epoxy adhesives.)

TABLE 39.15   Flexible Adhesive Bonding Films—Epoxy
Material type: unsupported epoxy adhesive
Material designation: 000L

Property to be tested and test method	Class 1	Class 2	Class 3
1. Peel strength, min., lb/in—width IPC-TM-650, method 2.4.9			
As received	6.0*	7.0*	8.0*
Method A Method B			
After solder float	5.0*	6.0*	7.0*
Method C Method D			
After temp. cycling	6.0*	6.0*	8.0*
Method E Method F			
2. Low-temperature flexibility IPC-TM-650, method 2.6.18	NA	NA	Pass (5 cycles)
3. Flow, max. (squeeze out mil/mil of adhesive) IPC-TM-650, method 2.3.17.1	5	5	5
4. Volatile content (max. %) IPC-TM-650, method 2.3.37	4.0	3.0	2.0
5. Flammability, min. percent O_2 IPC-TM-650, method 2.3.8	15	18	20
6. Solder float Method A	NA	Pass	NA
IPC-TM-650, method 2.4.13 Method B	NA	NA	Pass
7. Chemical resistance, percentage IPC-TM-650, method 2.3.2 Method A	70	75	80
8. Dielectric constant, max. (at 1 MHz) IPC-TM-650, method 2.5.5.3	NA	4.0	4.0
9. Dissipation factor, max. (at 1 MHz) IPC-TM-650, method 2.5.5.3	NA	0.06	0.06
10. Vol. resistivity (damp heat), min. mΩ-cm IPC-TM-650, method 2.5.17	NA	10^6	10^6
11. Surface resistance (damp heat), min., mΩ IPC-TM-650, method 2.5.17	NA	10^3	10^4
12. Dielectric strength, min. V/mil ASTM-D-149	500	500	500
13. Insulation resistance, min., MΩ IPC-TM-650, method 2.6.3.2 at ambient	10^2	10^3	10^4
14. Moisture and insulation resistance, min., MΩ IPC-TM-650, method 2.6.3.2	NA	10^2	10^3
15. Moisture absorption, max., % IPC-TM-650, method 2.6.2	NA	4	4
16. Fungus resistance IPC-TM-650, method 2.6.1	NA	NA	Nonnutrient

NA = not applicable
* Represents values for peel with bonding to treated side of copper. Values are halved when bonding to untreated copper surfaces.
Source: *IPC, Lincolnwood, Ill., IPC-FC-233A/2, Feb. 1986.*

39.4.2 Polyester Adhesives

Polyesters are the lowest-cost adhesives used and the only adhesives which can be used properly with polyester films for base laminate and polyester cover film. The major drawback of this system is low heat resistance, which may not be a drawback at all if the application for the circuit does not require soldering, as in many automotive instrument cluster applications. (See Table 39.16 for typical properties of polyester adhesives.)

TABLE 39.16 Flexible Adhesive Bonding Films—Polyester
Material type: unsupported polyester adhesive
Material designation: 000N

Property to be tested and test method	Class 1	Class 2	Class 3
1. Peel strength, min., lb/in—width IPC-TM-650, method 2.4.9			
As received	NA	3.0	5.0
Method A Method B			
After solder float	NA	NA	NA
Method C Method D			
After temp. cycling	3.0	3.0	5.0
Method E Method F			
2. Low-temperature flexibility IPC-TM-650, method 2.6.18	NA	NA	Pass (5 cycles)
3. Flow, max. (squeeze out mil/mil of adhesive) IPC-TM-650, method 2.3.17.1	10	10	10
4. Volatile content (max. %) IPC-TM-650, method 2.3.37	2.0	1.5	1.5
5. Flammability, min. percent O_2 IPC-TM-650, method 2.3.8	15	18	20
6. Solder float Method A	NA	NA	NA
IPC-TM-650, method 2.4.13 Method B	NA	NA	NA
7. Chemical resistance, percentage IPC-TM-650, method 2.3.2 Method A	70*	80*	90*
8. Dielectric constant, max. (at 1 MHz) IPC-TM-650, method 2.5.5.3	NA	4.6	4.6
9. Dissipation factor, max. (at 1 MHz) IPC-TM-650, method 2.5.5.3	NA	0.13	0.13
10. Vol. resistivity (damp heat), min. MΩ-cm IPC-TM-650, method 2.5.17	NA	10^6	10^6
11. Surface resistance (damp heat), min., MΩ IPC-TM-650, method 2.5.17	NA	10^4	10^5
12. Dielectric strength, min. V/mil ASTM-D-149	1000	1000	1000
13. Insulation resistance, min., MΩ IPC-TM-650, method 2.6.3.2 at ambient	10^3	10^4	10^5
14. Moisture and insulation resistance, min., MΩ IPC-TM-650, method 2.6.3.2	NA	10^3	10^4
15. Moisture absorption, max., % IPC-TM-650, method 2.6.2	NA	2.0	2.0
16. Fungus resistance IPC-TM-650, method 2.6.1	NA	NA	Nonnutrient

NA = not applicable
* Except chlorinated solvents and ketones.
Source: *IPC, Lincolnwood, Ill., IPC-FC-233A/3, Feb. 1986.*

39.4.3 Acrylic Adhesives

Acrylic systems are most often used when the completed circuits are used in high-temperature soldering applications. They have the best resistance to short-term, high-temperature exposure. (See Table 39.17 for typical properties of acrylic adhesives.)

TABLE 39.17 Flexible Adhesive Bonding Films—Acrylic
Material type: unsupported acrylic adhesive
Material designation: 000M

Property to be tested and test method	Class 1	Class 2	Class 3
1. Peel strength, min., lb/in—width IPC-TM-650, method 2.4.9			
As received	6.0*	8.0*	8.0*
Method A Method B			
After solder float	5.0*	7.0*	7.0*
Method C Method D			
After temp. cycling	6.0*	7.0*	8.0*
Method E Method F			
2. Low-temperature flexibility IPC-TM-650, method 2.6.18	NA	NA	Pass (5 cycles)
3. Flow, max. (squeeze out mil/mil of adhesive) IPC-TM-650, method 2.3.17.1	5	5	5
4. Volatile content (max. percent) IPC-TM-650, method 2.3.37	4.0	3.0	2.0
5. Flammability, min. % O_2 IPC-TM-650, method 2.3.8	15	15	15
6. Solder float Method A	NA	Pass	NA
IPC-TM-650, method 2.4.13 Method B	NA	NA	Pass
7. Chemical resistance, percentage IPC-TM-650, method 2.3.2 Method A	70	75	80
8. Dielectric constant, max. (at 1 MHz) IPC-TM-650, method 2.5.5.3	NA	4.0	4.0
9. Dissipation factor, max. (at 1 MHz) IPC-TM-650, method 2.5.5.3	NA	0.05	0.05
10. Vol. resistivity (damp heat), min. MΩ-cm† IPC-TM-650, method 2.5.17	NA	10^6	10^4
11. Surface resistance (damp heat), min., MΩ† IPC-TM-650, method 2.5.17	NA	10^4	10^6
12. Dielectric strength, min., V/mil ASTM-D-149	1000	1000	1000
13. Insulation resistance, min., MΩ IPC-TM-650, method 2.6.3.2 at ambient	10^2	10^3	10^4
14. Moisture and insulation resistance, min., MΩ IPC-TM-650, method 2.6.3.2	NA	10^2	10^3
15. Moisture absorption, max., % IPC-TM-650, method 2.6.2	NA	6.0	6.0
16. Fungus resistance IPC-TM-650, method 2.6.1	NA	NA	Nonnutrient

N/A = not applicable

* Represents values for peel with bonding to treated side of copper. Values are halved when bonding to untreated copper surfaces.

† Data indicated is for 50% relative humidity and 73 ± 2°F. Data is being developed for damp heat.

Source: IPC, Lincolnwood, Ill., IPC-FC-233A/1, Feb. 1986.

39.5 PLATINGS AND COATINGS

Metallic platings are used in flexible circuits to:

- Provide interconnections between circuit layers.
- Protect exposed conductors.
- Permit joining of components to conductors during product assembly.

Solder plating is frequently the most cost-effective means of protecting exposed copper conductors from environmental extremes and for assuring solderability.

Through-hole plating is the most commonly used technique for interconnecting the layers of a multilayer circuit. Copper is plated on the walls of the circuit substrate openings, electrically joining the foil on two or more layers.

Some circuits must be selectively plated to permit electrical connection or mechanical bonding of components. Certain circuit applications call for solder plating of connector pads for later attachment of components.

39.5.1 Plating Methods

Table 39.18 compares common methods of plating FPW conductors.

TABLE 39.18 Comparison of FPW Plating Techniques

Plating technique	Characteristics	Disadvantages
Electroplating	Thicknesses: 0.0001 to 0.001 in. Uniformly enhanced by making plated and nonplated areas approximately equal. Close control of solder thickness (±0.0002 in). Very smooth, uniform surface, ideal for gas light interconnections. Moderate cost. Six-month shelf life. 39.20100% pad coverage.	Lower yields than unplated or roll tinned. Plating equipment can limit web widths. Requires treated copper. Requires conductors to be bused together if plated after covercoat is applied.
Solder coating	Faster and cheaper than electroplating. Cheaper than screen printing. Better yields than electroplating. Longer shelf life than electroplating. Better solderability Busing not required for pads. Does not require treated copper.	Large variations in thickness: 0.0001 to 0.009 in on the same circuit. Nonuniform surface. Less than 100% coverage of pads. Generally requires some rework. Requires better cleaning methods and very aggressive flux. High setup costs. Not suitable for low volume (<1000 circuits).
Screen printing	Typical thickness: 0.0015 in. Close control of solder thickness. Close control of coated areas.	More expensive than solder coating.

Electroplating: Metal deposition on the conductors by electrolysis using electric current as the driving force.

Electroless plating: Metal deposition in which a chemical oxidation-reduction reaction is used to reduce metal ions to metal on a nonconductive surface.

Solder coating: Metal deposition on a surface by direct contact with the molten metal.

Screen printing: Application of solder paste by printing through a screen or stencil, followed by fusion of the solder with IR radiation or heated gases.

When circuits must remain solderable for only a short time, during staging or inventory holds, the most economical coating is a hard, clear solder flux. Although flux coating has a shorter shelf life than solder coating, it is effective if circuits are sealed in plastic bags and stored in a cool, dry environment.

39.5.2 Conductive Coatings

Carbon or graphite filled, polymer-thick films (PTF) have been used to protect conductor surfaces from corrosion and oxidation and to inhibit metal migration, especially of silver PTF conductors. These coatings are particularly suited for pressure contacts like membrane switches and joints to components like liquid crystal displays (LCDs). PTF coatings are low in cost compared to plating. A typical 0.0005-in thick carbon coating adds about 1 to 10 mΩ to a pressure contact. PTF coatings are selectively applied by screen printing.

39.6   PROTECTIVE COVERLAYERS

A protective coverlayer is a permanent film or coating applied to the entire area of an FPW except for pad areas which are to be soldered. Protective coverlayers:

- Act as solder masks to prevent solder bridging during wave soldering.
- Provide long-term protection against moisture, contamination, and mechanical damage.
- Reduce stresses on the conductors during flexing by positioning them near the neutral strain surface.
- Reduce electromigration and high-voltage breakdown between adjacent conductors.
- Provide a cosmetically pleasing appearance.

Properties of protective coatings are compared in Table 39.19.

TABLE 39.19   Properties of FPW Protective Coatings

Coating method	Dynamic flexing	Electrical properties	Encapsulation	Cost
Coverlay films	Excellent	Excellent	Good	Medium
Liquid covercoats	Fair	Fair	Excellent	Low
Dry film solder mask	Fair	Excellent	Good	High

39.6.1 Coverlays

Coverlays consist of an insulating film coated with an adhesive. Pad access holes and registration holes are drilled or punched in the film. The coverlay is registered over the etched conductor pattern and laminated under heat and pressure.

In FPW, the thickness of the coverlay should be about the same as the thickness of the dielectric layer. This places the conductors near the neutral surface and reduces stress in the conductors during flexing.

The same material is often used for both the dielectric substrate and the coverlay of a flexible circuit. The most commonly used coverlay materials are polyester, polyimide, fluorocarbon films, aramid papers, and epoxies.

Coverlay films are available precoated with polyester, modified epoxy, acrylic, fluorocarbon, and butyral phenolic adhesives.

39.6.2 Covercoats

Covercoats are formed from solution or from liquid polymers. The material is screen printed onto the circuit, leaving pad areas exposed. The polymer resin is then cured either by infrared (IR) heating or by ultraviolet (UV) radiation, forming a permanent, thin, tough coating.

Acrylated epoxy, acrylated polyurethane, and thiolenes are used for flexible circuit covercoats. These materials are liquid polymers which require no solvents during coating. They are cured using ultraviolet radiation.

Good electrical insulating elastomers such as silicone, polyurethane, and butyl rubber have not been widely used on flexible circuits because they stretch and deform in service. Polyester and acrylic resins are sometimes used as liquid covercoats on polyester circuits.

39.6.3 Dry Film Solder Masks

Dry film solder masks are films in which conductor access holes are formed by photoprocessing. The films, mounted on release paper, are laminated to etched FPW using heat, pressure, and vacuum to achieve a very tight, uniform seal. They are then exposed to light through a photographic negative which leaves access holes and other unprotected areas unexposed. The film cures in photoexposed areas. Uncured film is chemically stripped, leaving a patterned covering.

The materials used for dry film solder masks are similar to the materials used for covercoats, except the materials are made photosensitive.

Advantages and disadvantages of protective coatings are compared in Table 39.20.

39.6.4 Photosensitive Liquid Solder Masks

Photosensitive liquid solder masks are applied in liquid form by roll, bar, or spray coating; cured with heat; and processed like dry film solder masks.

TABLE 39.20 Comparison of Protective Coatings

Protective coating	Advantages	Disadvantages
Coverlay films	Excellent dynamic flexibility. Free from pinholes. Nonporous. Highest dielectric strength.	Relatively expensive. Require precutting and prepunching operations. Heat and pressure during lamination may damage base circuit or cause dimensional changes. Susceptible to misregistration. Bridging or incomplete sealing of conductors.
Covercoats	Excellent encapsulation of circuit. Least expensive. Much wider range of suitable materials. Easy to repair by selective stripping and reapplication of covercoat. Low melting solder-through covercoats allow component attachment, new connections, or repair without prepunched holes in the covercoat. Better dimensional control by elimination of heat and pressure. Less damage to plated-through-holes.	Film porosity. Film defects leading to lowered dielectric strength. Relatively poor dynamic flexibility.
Dry film solder mask	Higher pattern resolution. Eliminates need for punching and drilling of access holes. Vacuum lamination provides excellent seal to base circuit.	Relatively poor dynamic flexibility. Expensive.

CHAPTER 40
DESIGN OF FLEXIBLE CIRCUITS

Sheldahl Technical Staff*

Sheldahl Inc., Northfield, Minnesota

40.1 INTRODUCTION

Flexible circuits are a unique type of interconnection system (see Fig. 40.1 for examples). Although many of the manufacturing processes for flexible circuits are similar to those for rigid boards, it is necessary to modify these processes to take into consideration such special factors as handling of thin films and foils. Specifications relating to adhesive systems are also important, since each type has different processing and electromechanical characteristics which must be tailored to the application. This chapter provides a general overview of the subject. However, for some detailed process descriptions it relies on material discussed in preceding, specialized chapters. By relying on this body of detailed information on the general techniques, it is fairly straightforward to relate to the differences in materials and processes presented here for an understanding of flexible circuits as a separate technology.

The Institute for Interconnecting and Packaging Electronic Circuits (IPC) publishes an industry guideline to technical terms for the printed circuit industry. In the document ANSI/IPC T-50 C, Rev. C, *flexible circuits* are defined as "a patterned arrangement of printed circuits and components utilizing flexible base materials with or without flexible cover layers." This definition may be accurate, but it leaves a lot to be desired relative to the actual use of flexible circuits and the proper choices of materials necessary for each and every application.

To understand flexible circuits, one must be familiar with metal foils, plastic films, and adhesive systems and must understand how all three are selected and used.

40.2 TYPES OF FLEXIBLE PRINTED WIRING (FPW)

Flexible printed wiring, like rigid PC boards, is often classified according to the various combinations of base, conductor, and cover layers used. (See Fig. 40.2.)

- *Single-sided,* having conductors on one side of a base layer.
- *Double-sided,* having conductors on both sides of a base layer. Conductors on opposite sides may be connected by plated-through-holes or other means.
- *Single access* having a given conductor layer accessible for external connection only from the side of the FPW on which that conductor lies.
- *Double access* (also called *back-bared*), having a given conductor layer accessible for external connection from either the conductor side or the base side of the FPW. Access is by

---

* Adapted from "Flexible Circuitry Design Guide," published by Sheldahl Inc., 1984, used with permission.

FIGURE 40.1 Examples of different kinds of flexible circuits. *(Courtesy of Rogers Corporation, Rogers, Conn.)*

means of holes formed in the base before conductors are bonded into place. Most double access FPW is single-sided.

- *Multilayer,* having more than two conductor layers laminated together with insulating base layers between them. Conductor layers are connected by plated-through-holes or by access holes provided in outerlayers for connection to innerlayers. The additional base and conductor layers tend to make multilayer printed wiring too rigid to bend without damaging the conductors.

- *Rigid-flex,* like multilayer except bonding and connections between layers are confined to restricted areas of the wiring plane. Between the rigid, laminated areas, each conductor layer is bonded to a single, thin base so the area remains flexible, like pages in a book, even though there may be many conductor layers.

- *Rigidized FPW,* having pieces of rigid sheet material selectively bonded to the FPW. Rigidizing is usually done to distribute mechanical stress, as from heavy components, over a larger area of the wiring.

40.2.1 Choosing the Best Wiring Method

Electrical interconnections for a product or system are too frequently an afterthought, chosen when many opportunities for effecting cost reductions have already been lost. The wiring methods should be selected early in the detail design phase, at the same time as the circuit design, components, and packaging configuration.

Alternative wiring methods should be evaluated considering circuit partitioning into subunits and cables, electrical joints to components, conductor and insulation requirements, and fabrication methods.

Most electrical or electronic wiring methods may be classified as one of the following:

- *Conventional, point-to-point.* Usually using round, insulated wire, soldered to terminals.
- *Wire wrap.* Using round wire with ends wrapped on an array of square posts.
- *Rigid, printed wiring board.* Most frequently used to support and connect small solid-state and passive components, often assembled and soldered by automated methods.
- *Flexible printed wiring.* Has many characteristics in common with rigid printed wiring.

TYPE	ADVANTAGES	LIMITATIONS	RELATIVE COST
SINGLE-SIDED 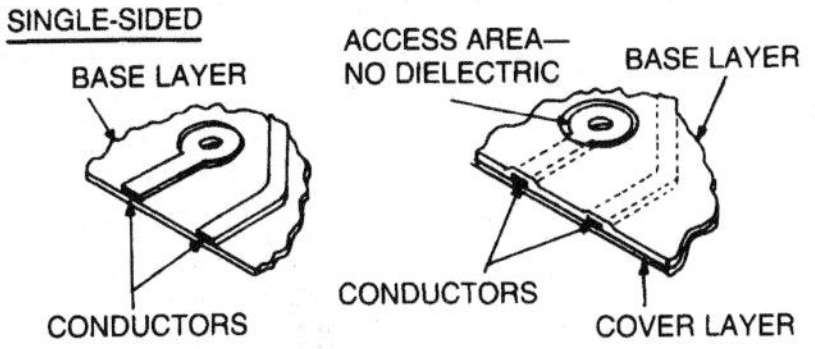 ACCESS AREA— NO DIELECTRIC BASE LAYER BASE LAYER CONDUCTORS CONDUCTORS COVER LAYER	LEAST EXPENSIVE	CONDUCTOR CROSSOVERS NOT POSSIBLE	1
DOUBLE-SIDED 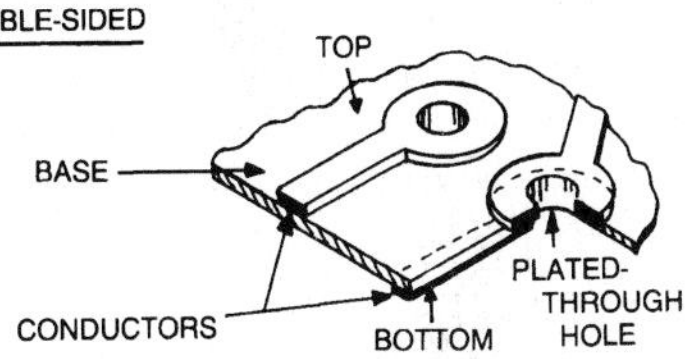 TOP BASE PLATED-THROUGH HOLE CONDUCTORS BOTTOM	HIGHER DENSITY REDUCED NUMBER OF SOLDER JOINTS	INCREASED COST REDUCED FLEXIBILITY	1.5-2
DOUBLE ACCESS 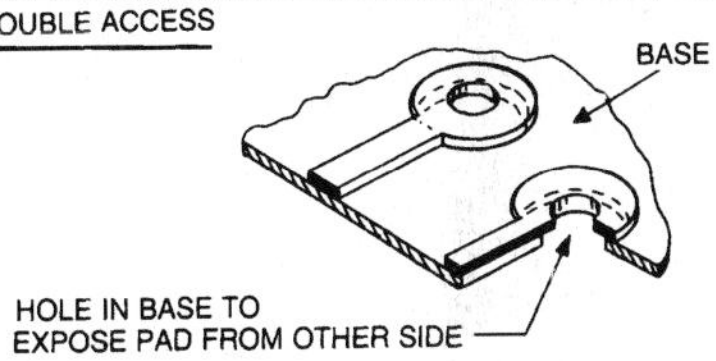 BASE HOLE IN BASE TO EXPOSE PAD FROM OTHER SIDE	MINIMUM NUMBER OF PARTS COMPONENT MOUNTING ON BOTH SIDES	MORE EXPENSIVE THAN SINGLE ACCESS	1.2-1.7
MULTI-LAYER 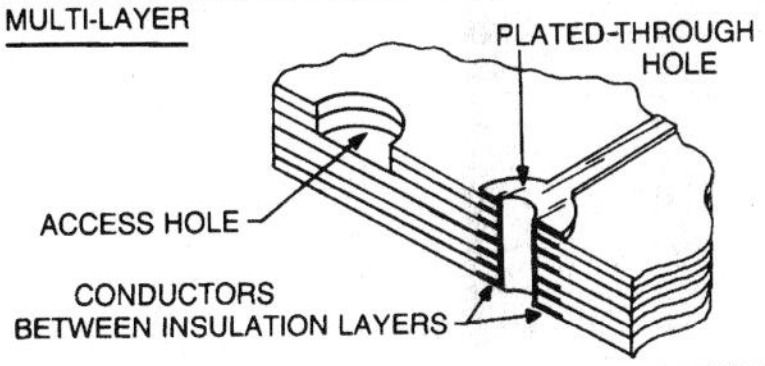 PLATED-THROUGH HOLE ACCESS HOLE CONDUCTORS BETWEEN INSULATION LAYERS	HIGH CONDUCTOR AND COMPONENT DENSITY INTEGRAL SHIELDING CONTROLLED IMPEDANCE	HIGH COST REDUCED RELIABILITY CANNOT BE REPAIRED NOT FLEXIBLE	3 to 20*
RIGID-FLEX 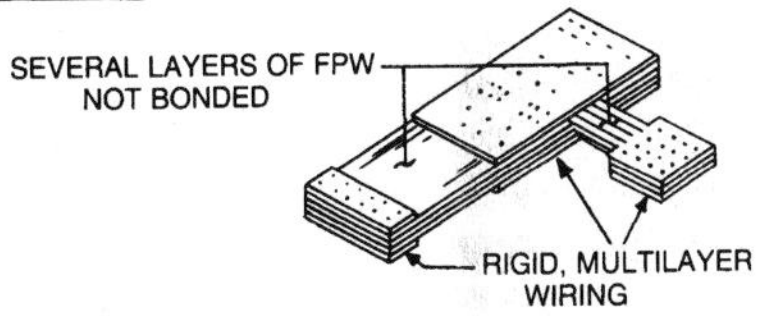 SEVERAL LAYERS OF FPW NOT BONDED RIGID, MULTILAYER WIRING	COMBINES MULTI-LAYER FEATURES WITH SELECTIVE FLEXIBILITY	(SAME AS MULTILAYER)	3 to 20*
RIGIDIZED FPW 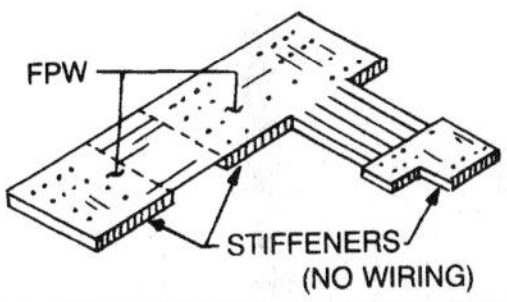 FPW STIFFENERS (NO WIRING)	STRAIN RELIEF AND COMPONENT SUPPORT	SOLDER ACCESS. RESTRICTED TO ONE SIDE	1.2-4
*DEPENDS ON NUMBER OF LAYERS			

FIGURE 40.2   Types of flexible printed wiring compared.

Table 40.1 provides a general comparison of the four wiring methods. Each method has advantages and disadvantages, and each is most suitable for particular types of interconnections. Many electronic systems use a combination of these methods.

Table 40.2 lists some characteristics of electronic packaging applications where flexible printed wiring is particularly appropriate.

40.3 ADVANTAGES AND LIMITATIONS OF FLEXIBLE PRINTED WIRING

Thorough familiarity with design alternatives is important in making an optimum wiring choice and in avoiding misapplications. After a wiring method is selected, success or failure often depends on how effectively the designer exploits the advantages of the method and minimizes its limitations.

Some of the advantages and limitations of FPW are summarized in Table 40.3 and discussed in the following paragraphs. The main considerations are *function, cost, reliability,* and *fabrication.* These considerations may overlap. For example, reliability enhancements can also reduce costs.

40.3.1 Functional Advantages and Limitations

Weight and volume of FPW arrays are typically less than 50 percent of equivalent round wire interconnections.

The flexibility of FPW permits:

- Connection of components which have motion relative to each other and allows up to one billion cycles of motion

- Component insertion, soldering, and testing while the assembly is flat, followed by bending or folding to conform to three-dimensional shapes of case or chassis

- Return to a flat configuration for service and repair

Better heat dissipation and ease of heat sinking increase the current-carrying capacity of FPW conductors. FPW temperature rise is typically 30 to 50 percent lower than rigid PW boards for the same conductor size and operating conditions.

Because FPW conductors are relatively thin (typically 0.001 to 0.005 in), on FPW of limited area it is often more effective to use separate round wire for conductors which will carry more than 5 or 10 A of current.

Consistent spacing and orientation of FPW conductors gives uniform mechanical and electrical characteristics from part to part compared with round wire cables. Characteristic impedance of FPW high-frequency transmission lines is more difficult to control than in rigid PW boards because of larger relative variations in thickness of dielectrics and adhesives. Compared to round wire interconnections, requirements for shielding are reduced with FPW because active lines can be physically separated from sensitive input signal lines. Integral connectors can be formed by folding edges or tabs of FPW around a stiffener.

FPW is cosmetically superior to round wire interconnections and adds product sales appeal for technically sophisticated customers. FPW can be flexed at assembly to adjust for misalignment between separate, rigidly mounted components. FPW cables between a chassis and moveable drawers or hinged panels can be designed with integral retractors.

Except for small-outline, surface-mounted devices, most components are not adequately supported against shock and vibration by the thin conductors and dielectrics in FPW.

TABLE 40.1 Comparison of Common Wiring Methods Used in Packaging Electronic Systems

Factor method	Conventional, point to point wiring	Wire wrap	Rigid printed wiring	Flexible printed wiring
Reliability	Good	Good, gas-tight connections. Requires more connections than PW	High	High, can minimize number of connections
Wiring accuracy	Lowest—requires careful test, inspection, and rework	Low for hand wrap; high for automatic	Consistently high and uniform	Consistently high and uniform
Design flexibility	Good for breadboarding and prototypes	Good for prototypes and limited quantities	Design must be fixed before tooling	Design must be fixed before tooling
Size and weight	Relatively heavy and space consuming	Moderate weight; wrap pins increase board depth	Good minimization of size and weight	Least where voltage drop not critical
Reproducibility of electrical characteristics	Can use coaxial, transmission lines for HF	Cumbersome transmission line technique; frequency limited	Can provide voltage and ground busing, transmission lines for HF	Can provide voltage and ground bussing, transmission lines for HF
Mechanical support for components	Requires chassis or rack to support components	Requires board or chassis to support components	Will support ICs and components of similar mass	Will support SMDs; heavier components need external support
Thermal capability	Heat dissipation limited, especially near cable core	Air flow around pins and wire gives good heat dissipation	Good heat dissipation in 1- and 2-layer form	Thin insulation gives best heat dissipation
Cost				
Nonrecurring	Low	High for automation	High	High
Recurring	High	Low for automation	Low	Low
Ease of manufacture	Requires high personnel skill level	Wiring and component assembly can be automated	Wiring, component insertion, and soldering can be automated	Wiring, component insertion, and soldering can be automated
Ease of inspection and test	Difficult to inspect visually; requires coding and marking of conductors	Effective tests are destructive; difficult to inspect	1- and 2-layer forms easy to inspect; multilayer forms difficult	1- and 2-layer forms easy to inspect; multilayer forms difficult
Ease of service and repair	Relatively easy to repair or change	More difficult to change than conventional wiring	Difficult, especially multilayer forms	Difficult, especially multilayer forms

TABLE 40.2 Characteristics of Electronic Packaging Applications Where Flexible Printed Wiring Is Appropriate

Characteristic	Reason
1. Folding or flexing required during assembly, installation, and servicing.	1. A flexible printed circuit can be designed to bend 360°.
2. Continuous or intermittent flexing required in application.	2. Flexible printed circuits can be designed to have flex lifetimes of up to a billion cycles.
3. Space savings and weight reduction desired.	3. Space and weight reductions of up to 75% compared to conventional wiring can be achieved.
4. Signal or logic-level power requirements.	4. Heavy power requirements necessitate larger conductors, which result in reduced flexibility.
5. High reliability required.	5. Flexible circuitry generally permits fewer solder joints and mechanical interconnects than conventional wiring.
6. Impedance control required.	6. Integral shielding layers can be added in close proximity to the conductors.
7. Wiring repeatability required.	7. Automatic circuit production assures error-free wiring and consistent electromechanical characteristics.

Adhesive-bonded stiffeners can be applied to component-mounting areas, or components can be supported by the product chassis or case.

40.3.2 Cost Advantages and Limitations

Flexible printed wiring can reduce assembly and installation costs by 20 to 50 percent compared to round wire interconnections:

TABLE 40.3 Advantages and Limitations of Flexible Printed Wiring

Advantages	Limitations
System cost reduction—because of reduced wiring errors and assembly effort.	*High nonrecurring cost*—compared to point-to-point wiring.
Simplified assembly—can be bent around components and bonded to chassis.	*Higher unit cost*—than equal area rigid PC boards.
	Difficult to change—design must be fixed before tooling to be cost effective.
Reduced weight and volume—up to 4:1 in weight, 7:1 in volume, compared to point-to-point wiring.	*Limited current capacity*—usually not practical above 10–20 A.
Flexibility—can connect moving machine elements and fold in 3 dimensions to fit after assembly and soldering.	*Requires stiffeners*—to support components.
Improved reliability—from reduced number of connections, reduced handling, reduced mass and stress on connections.	*Difficult to repair*—because of difficulty of insulation removal and hand soldering.
Uniform electrical characteristics—because of consistent spacing and orientation of conductors and insulation.	*Requires fixtures*—for automated assembly and mass soldering.
	Impedance less consistent—compared to rigid PC boards.
Better heat dissipation—from thin, flat conductors and thin insulation.	*Dimensionally less stable*—compared to rigid PC boards.

- Consistent, readily visible location and orientation of FPW conductors and terminals eliminate wiring errors. Simplified inspection, troubleshooting, and rework permits use of relatively unskilled assembly personnel.

- Measuring, cutting, stripping, tinning, routing, and lacing are eliminated.

Compared to rigid PW boards, the lower dimensional stability of many FPW dielectrics during manufacture requires additional process and tooling measures to control tolerances.

Costs of bare FPW boards are generally higher than costs of rigid PW boards of equal area. However, an FPW array can reduce product costs when used to replace a number of rigid circuit boards and interconnection cables. Integrating component-to-component and circuit board–to–circuit board interconnections in the same PW assembly reduces the number of terminals and solder joints.

Compared to round wire interconnections, the amount of conductor and insulation material can be reduced with FPW assemblies.

- Conductor cross sections can be smaller because of better heat dissipation from flat conductors.

- Signal lines can be reduced in cross section without reducing terminal size because of more efficient mechanical support of conductors.

- Service loops can be shorter because of the greater flexibility of FPW.

Although holes in FPW can be drilled, the thinner insulation permits mass punching of holes, including holes to be plated. This reduces hole formation costs in large quantities, compared to rigid PW boards.

Material flexibility permits economical, roll-to-roll material handling during processing of FPW arrays. The lower mass of FPW reduces the size and cost of cable restraints compared to round wire. FPW can be attached to surfaces with low-cost, pressure-sensitive adhesives or hook-and-loop fasteners. Consistent location of terminals reduces FPW assembly costs by permitting component placement, mass soldering, and crimping on conventional, automated equipment.

Nonrecurring costs and lead time for FPW design and tooling are similar to those for rigid PW boards, but are much higher than for point-to-point wiring. Changes may be costly to make after a PW design is tooled.

Because of the thin substrates used, FPW is more difficult to repair than rigid PW boards. It is usually more economical to replace damaged FPW rather than to repair it.

40.3.3 Reliability Advantages and Limitations

Combining component-mounting areas with interconnecting cables in a single FPW array reduces the number of terminals and solder joints. Plated-through-holes between conductor layers in FPW are more reliable than the solder joints and edge connectors which they can replace. When subject to shock and vibration, the greater flexibility and lower mass per length of FPW reduce strain on solder joints compared to round wire.

Terminal areas of FPW can be polarized and keyed to eliminate wiring errors during assembly. Compared to round wire, FPW has greater resistance to damage in flexure because conductor material can be positioned closer to the neutral surface and because the bond between conductors and insulation is uniformly distributed over a larger area.

Compared to round wire and rigid PW boards, FPW is more vulnerable to tearing when tension is applied to edges, particularly at notches and inside corners. This can be reduced or eliminated by proper package design and selective reinforcement of the FPW.

40.3.4 Fabrication Advantages and Limitations

FPW arrays are limited in width by process equipment to about 25 or 30 in, but roll-to-roll processing permits continuous lengths of up to several hundred feet where conductor image placement can be done in small increments. Unless the entire length is occupied by complex conductor patterns, it is usually less expensive to use a composite of smaller, flexible, or rigid PW boards connected by collated, flat flexible cable.

FPW can be hand or wave soldered using conventional equipment, but temperature and dwell time must be reduced compared to soldering conditions for rigid PW boards.

Unless an FPW design includes stiffeners for component support, special pallets or fixtures may be required to position FPW terminals during component placement, mass soldering, and testing.

40.4 FLEXIBLE CIRCUIT DESIGN

Flexible circuits are much different from their rigid board cousins in material composition, handling requirements, processing requirements, design rules, and interconnection technology.

40.4.1 Basic Rules

Several rules are almost universally true. (1) The material is less dimensionally stable than rigid material, so usually artwork must be developed to allow for material shrinkage during processing. (2) Retrofits almost never work. The design must be started from scratch. (3) All designs must be thought of in terms of a three-dimensional form, since the purpose of flexible circuits is to interconnect on multiplanar fields.

40.4.2 Applications

The two primary applications are static and dynamic. In static applications, the circuits are usually flexed once or bent into position, and they remain in that position for the life of the product. Dynamic applications must be specified differently to provide for maximum flex life, while using a combination of materials. Table 40.4 shows the different choices available by application. Figure 40.3 shows a typical static application.

Most dynamic flexing applications are designed with the copper in a neutral axis, with 1 oz of copper foil encapsulated on both sides with 0.001-in. Kapton film. Flexible circuits fabricated in this way have been known to operate for over 500 million cycles with no conductor

TABLE 40.4 Materials and Applications

Application	ED copper	Rolled copper	Polyimide film	Polyester film	Composites
Static	Best	Good	Good	Good	Good
Dynamic	Poor	Best	Best	Good	Poor
Instrument	Best	Good	Best	Good	Good
Automotive	Best	Good	Poor	Best	Poor
Telecommunication	Best	Good	Good	Best	Good

FIGURE 40.3 Typical static circuit application. *(Courtesy of Rogers Corporation, Rogers, Conn.)*

failures. Loop diameters in this kind of flexing application are always successful with ½-in diameters, and even diameters as small as ¼ in have a high level of flex life. Figure 40.4 shows a typical dynamic application.

40.4.3 Solderability Applications

If there is any question as to whether to specify polyester or polyimide in a flex circuit, the answer usually lies with solderability. If either hand soldering or wave soldering is a require-

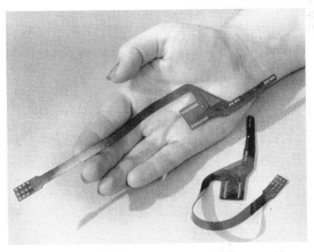

FIGURE 40.4 Typical disk drive flexible circuit. *(Courtesy of Rogers Corporation, Rogers, Conn.)*

ment in an application, then polyimide film most be specified to provide a good heat-resistant material which can be processed with few problems, such as delamination or distortion of the plastic film. The use of polyester will save a few cents per circuit in material cost, but the expense reduction does not justify the means except in very high volume applications (several hundred thousand per month).

40.4.4 Design for Processing

The best flexible circuit designs follow some rules which are unique to flexible circuits and not rigid printed circuits. One should always design traces by minimizing spaces. The more copper that is left on the circuit, the more stable it will be during process. It will also be easier to hold dimensional tolerances. All traces which cross a bend should cross at 90° to the bend. Tooling should be hard and sharp and designed so that the outline has no sharp inside corners where a tear could begin. This is especially true for dynamic circuit design. If components are to be mounted on the flexible circuit, then some reinforcement or rigidizing should be added to the circuit. This enforcement is commonly added before final drilling or punching, and the adhesive used is usually the same as or similar to that which is used in the circuit construction. If the circuit is to be bent against the rigid member in assembly, a strain relief, or at least a chamfer, on the rigid member should be employed to reduce the likelihood of trace breakage caused by sharp bending of the circuit against the reinforcing member.

40.4.4.1 Plating Considerations. Plating considerations should be made on the basis of a cost/need analysis. It would be simple to gold-plate everything and let it go at that; however, cost is important, so solder plating or tin plating is most commonly used. Roll-to-roll processing is impractical for all but the highest-volume applications, so panel plating is used in most cases. There are many methods of solder plating, and they vary between electrolytic pattern plating, where the plating becomes an etch resist, to molten roll soldering, which is usually applied to the exposed circuit pads only after a cover film is applied.

40.4.4.2 Imaging. Imaging a flex circuit laminate with etch resist can be done either with the classical silk screen method or with the more popular photoresist method discussed elsewhere in this book.

40.4.5 Specifications and Standards

Industry standards which will assist the designer are as follows.

40.4.5.1 General Specifications

MIL-STD-429	Printed wiring and printed circuits terms and definitions
IPC-T-50	Terms and definitions

40.4.5.2 Material Specifications

MIL-M-55627	Materials for flexible printed wiring
IPC-FC-231	Flexible bare dielectrics for use in flexible printed wiring
IPC-FC-232	Specifications for adhesive-coated dielectrics films for use as cover sheets for flexible printed wiring
IPC-FC-241	Metal-clad flexible dielectrics for use in fabrication of flexible printed wiring

40.4.5.3 General Circuitry Specifications

MIL-P-55110	Printed wiring boards
MIL-P-50884	Printed wiring, flexible

| IPC-FC-240 | Specification for single-sided flexible printed wiring |
| IPC-FC-250 | Specification for double-sided flexible wiring with interconnections |

40.4.5.4 *Testing Specifications*

MIL-STD-202	Test method for electronic and electrical component parts
MIL-STD-454	Standard general requirements for electronic equipment
MIL-STD-810	Environmental test methods

40.4.6 Critical Design Considerations

The most important design considerations in applications requiring FPW flexibility are

1. Fatigue life
2. Electrical resistance changes in the conductors
3. Tear resistance
4. Interconnections

40.4.6.1 *Fatigue Life.*

The fatigue life of copper conductors depends on the tensile and compressive strains applied during flexure. For a laminated circuit, the neutral (zero strain) surface may not be at the center of the conductors but shifted depending on the thickness and elasticity of the substrate and cover layer and on their adhesion to the copper foil. This tends to increase the strain and fatigue damage at each bending cycle.

Flexural fatigue in improperly designed FPW may cause conductors to fracture prematurely, resulting in an intermittent or continuous open circuit. If the flexibility is mostly in one direction, the wiring should be designed to put the copper in compression. Fatigue in compression will increase resistivity but is less likely to cause an open circuit.

40.4.6.2 *Resistance Changes.*

The resistance of copper increases with repeated flexure due to cold working, or work hardening. This effect is small and is important only for low-level circuits where a change in resistance could cause calibration drift.

40.4.6.3 *Tear Resistance.*

When tension is concentrated at the edge of FPW, it may tear or rupture, especially at inside corners or notches. Proper design and material selection can eliminate circuit tearing.

40.4.6.4 *Interconnections.*

As with any electronic system, one of the most important parts of a flexible circuit is the interconnections to other components. Flexible circuits can be terminated directly to connectors, lap-soldered to a rigid board, or incorporated directly into a rigid, multilayer board.

Adequate support must be provided to relieve stresses at junctions between flexible and rigid components. At solder joints, strains must be relieved with clamps or other devices between the joint and the first bend. Connectors terminating flexible circuits must have an adequate number of pins soldered to the circuit to provide vibration resistance.

FPW greatly reduces the problems associated with stripping, tinning, and properly joining discrete wiring to connectors and terminals. Assembly techniques are simplified, and troublesome errors encountered with conventional wiring are eliminated.

40.5 *FLEXIBILITY*

The ability of flexible printed wiring to bend or flex permits roll-to-roll manufacturing processes and simplifies large-volume production. The bend radii of packaging and service are typically much smaller than those experienced in roll processing.

Flexible printed wiring can be flexually formed during assembly and repair to assume complex, three-dimensional geometries and to sustain multiple bending cycles in service without damage.

The factors which affect circuit flexibility are:

- Final circuit geometry
- Number of flexures during functional life
- Assembly, adjustment, and repair procedures

The items which must be considered during the FPW design to ensure adequate flex performance are:

- Material selection
- Conductor location and orientation in the circuit plane
- Arrangement of material layers

Although these factors apply primarily to bend regions, their general application to flexible printed wiring arrays is good design practice. Figure 40.5 illustrates the different types of bending and shows how the radius varies.

40.5.1 Design for Flexibility

The behavior of simply shaped, homogeneous materials under cyclic bending depends on small-scale variables. Fatigue resistance can be very sensitive to minor variations in metallurgical or polymeric structure, manufacturing processes, testing techniques, and environmental conditions. The problem is compounded for FPW, since these are composites of different materials. Also, the components of interest—the conductors—are etched into complex forms.

Evaluation by testing the proposed FPW configuration is the most reliable design approach. For applications that require a large number of flex cycles, testing can be expensive. Long testing times are required to obtain a statistically valid amount of data. Flex life at one set of conditions cannot always be inferred from tests at different conditions. Even small design changes may require retesting. Accelerated cycling rates may cause failures from abrasion, heating, or other conditions not representative of actual service.

The *IPC Printed Wiring Design Guide* (section 6.2.1.2) describes an analytical method for predicting the number of flex cycles to failure for a flexible printed wiring array. This method is based on:

- The range of conductor strain, or relative changes in length, caused by tension and compression at the conductor surfaces
- The ductility (strain at fracture), tensile strength, and elastic modulus of the conductors

The method applies over a broad range of design conditions from high-strain, low-flex life configurations, which may be acceptable in static applications, to high-flex life conditions, where conductor strain must be minimized. The method requires finding statistical distributions for conductor ductility and for strain caused by thickness variations.

The flex life of conductors varies inversely with conductor strain at each bend cycle. Figure 40.6 indicates how material strain varies linearly from a maximum tensile value on the outside of the bend to a maximum compressive value inside the bend. The strain is zero at an interior "neutral" surface.

The strain at any interior point is equal to the distance from the neutral surface divided by the bend radius of the neutral surface. Providing for a larger bend radius in service or locating the conductors as near as possible to the neutral surface (part D of Figure 40.6) will increase flex life.

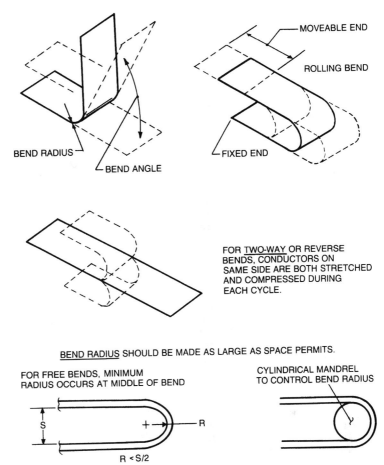

FOR <u>ONE-WAY</u> BENDS, CONDUCTORS ON SAME SIDE ARE EITHER STRETCHED OR COMPRESSED DURING EACH CYCLE.

MOVEABLE END

ROLLING BEND

FIXED END

BEND RADIUS

BEND ANGLE

FOR <u>TWO-WAY</u> OR REVERSE BENDS, CONDUCTORS ON SAME SIDE ARE BOTH STRETCHED AND COMPRESSED DURING EACH CYCLE.

<u>BEND RADIUS</u> SHOULD BE MADE AS LARGE AS SPACE PERMITS.

FOR FREE BENDS, MINIMUM RADIUS OCCURS AT MIDDLE OF BEND

CYLINDRICAL MANDREL TO CONTROL BEND RADIUS

S

R

$R < S/2$

FIGURE 40.5 Aspects of flexible printed wiring bending.

Double-sided laminates, as shown in part C of Figure 40.6, cause the largest conductor strains. For repeated 180° bends without reversal, part A is preferred over part B because conductors in compression have a longer flex life than conductors in tension.

To maximize flexibility, conductive shield layers for FPW in dynamic flex applications should be made of material like stainless steel or beryllium copper foil and not bonded to the FPW in the bend region.

The presence of discontinuities like nicks, pinholes, and other changes in cross section in FPW bend regions can significantly reduce flex life. The effect of conductor defects on available ductility of copper conductors is shown in Fig. 40.7. Defects smaller than 0.005 in are difficult to observe. Narrow conductors are more likely to fracture under bending, since defects not detected by inspection are a larger fraction of the width. Proper photoimaging techniques in controlled clean rooms during manufacture can reduce the size and frequency of etched conductor defects.

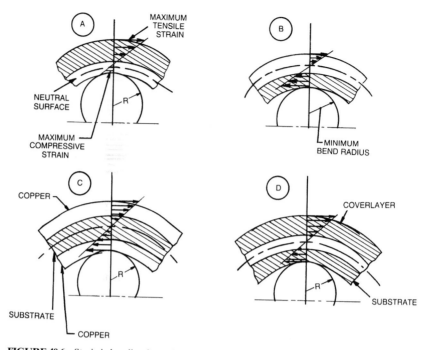

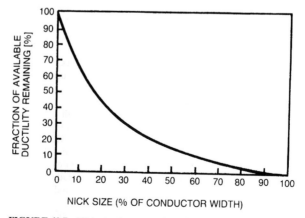

FIGURE 40.6 Strain in bending for various flexible printed wiring configurations: (*a*) and (*b*) single-sided without cover layer; (*c*) double-sided; (*d*) single-sided with cover layer.

Terminal pads, plated-through-holes, and abrupt changes in conductor width should be avoided in bend regions because these concentrate conductor strain. Conductors near the ends of bend regions should be formed in a U or L shape where they connect with terminal pads (Fig. 40.8).

In some applications, copper overplating of electrodeposited copper foil has improved flex life. Solder-plated circuits exhibit significantly better fatigue endurance when the solder is reflowed.

FIGURE 40.7 Nick size (percent of conductor width).

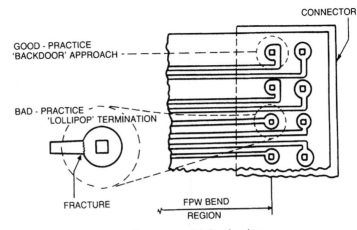

FIGURE 40.8 Joining conductors to pads in bend regions.

Table 40.5 summarizes a number of recommended design practices to prevent FPW conductor fractures in bend regions.

40.5.2 Flexing Modes in Flexible Circuits

40.5.2.1 Flexing to Reverse Terminals and Conductors. Terminal rows on a single-sided circuit can be moved from one side of the circuit to the other by folding the circuit in various configurations. This is usually less expensive than back-baring pads (providing double access). A small rod or wire inside the folds is recommended to control the bend radius. (See Fig. 40.9.)

40.5.2.2 Flexing in Packaging
The angle fold and its extension, the double-backfold, are used to fold a flexible circuit into its final package. The angle fold is used primarily for conformance to a three-dimensional configuration. High-vibration environments may require special mounting or other restriction of movement in the fold area.

TABLE 40.5 Design Practices to Maximize Flex Life of Flexible Printed Wiring in Bend Regions

- Minimize copper thickness.
- Minimize the number of conductor layers.
- Use rolled copper, if possible. Otherwise use high-ductility electrodeposited copper.
- Avoid plated-through-holes.
- Avoid narrow conductors.
- Avoid abrupt changes in conductor width.
- Avoid sharp changes in conductor direction.
- Distribute conductors evenly across the width of the bend region.
- Orient conductors perpendicular to the bend axis.
- Avoid locating conductors at the substrate edge.
- Use forming mandrels to control bend radius.
- Use strain relief between bend regions and soldered terminals.
- Prohibit repairs in bend regions.
- Prohibit etched legends and similar identifying features.

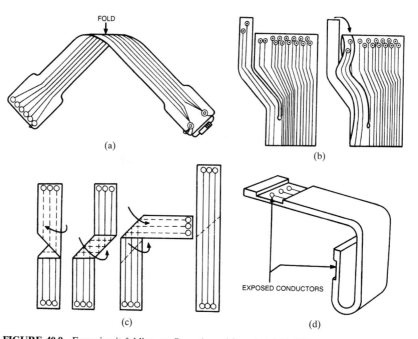

FIGURE 40.9   Four circuit folding configurations: (*a*) angled fold, 180° reversal; (*b*) cut and backfold 180° reversal of terminals; (*c*) multiple fold, 180° reversal of conductors and terminal areas; shape and orientation of circuit arm is maintained; a single-sided circuit can be folded on itself three times with a radius equal to its thickness if rolled annealed copper conductors are used; (*d*) double-backfold, 0 to 360° reversal of conductors and terminals; this can be used to form external connections by "baring" conductors at 180° fold.

The double-backfold is often used when rigid circuit boards are joined with flexible circuitry and arranged in a layer configuration in the final package.

Figures 40.10 through 40.13 illustrate recommended practices for folds and bends in static FPW applications.

40.5.3   Flexing Modes in Dynamic Flex Applications

40.5.3.1   Formable Circuits.   Creases, bends, or coils can be permanently formed into flexible circuitry. Polyester substrates can easily be heat-formed to retain shape memory. Polyimide-based circuits can be heat-formed to a degree, but the shape retention depends almost entirely on the conductors. Circuits with thick polyimide film tend to revert to their original flat shape over time. Formed circuits require special packaging to prevent damage and distortion during shipping.

40.5.3.2   Cable Flexing Modes.   Retractable cable-like flexible circuits are often used to interconnect sliding equipment drawers or other moveable elements.

In the *window-shade* configuration (Fig. 40.14), movement of the flexible circuit can be controlled either by a mechanical retractor or by a coil heat formed in the substrate. The most common application of the window-shade configuration is the connection of a sliding drawer to its cabinet, as used for equipment inspection and maintenance (see Fig. 40.15).

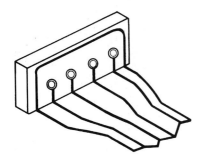

The *controlled fold* or *accordion* configuration (Fig. 40.16) can be used with dielectrics which have a weaker spring action or which cannot be heat-treated to retain plastic memory. The circuit can be made rigid at the folds and flexible in the straight sections, or flexible throughout.

The *controlled roll* configuration (Fig. 40.17) is sometimes used to control the position of flexible printed wiring within a narrow, enclosed conduit.

40.5.3.3   Other Flexing Modes.   Flexible circuits can be designed to flex about almost any axis with almost any circuit configuration of sufficient flex life.

40.6   TEAR RESISTANCE

The strength of FPW materials provides some resistance to both the initiation and propagation of tearing. However, it is good practice to provide tear resistance features, particularly in areas where large stresses may be applied to corners or notches in edges. Figures 40.18 through 40.21 illustrate tear resistance features.

40.7   VIBRATION AND SHOCK

FIGURE 40.10   Conductors perpendicular to fold-line. Conductors should approach and traverse a bend or fold perpendicular to the fold line.

The relatively low mass per unit area of flexible printed wiring reduces the stress applied to terminals and solder joints during shock and vibration compared to point-to-point round wiring. The distributed mass also simplifies the design of mechanical restraints. FPW can be provided with pressure-sensitive adhesive in selected areas for simplified bonding to interior surfaces of the package. Hook-and-pile fasteners or simple bar clamps can be used where the FPW assembly must be removed for servicing. Flexible printed wiring should not be allowed to rest against sharp edges on interior components in high-vibration conditions.

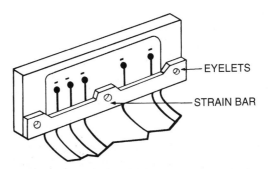

FIGURE 40.11   Strain relief bar. When bends must be made close to solder joints, especially if the bends have a sharp radius, a strain relief bar should be used to prevent strain from reaching solder joints.

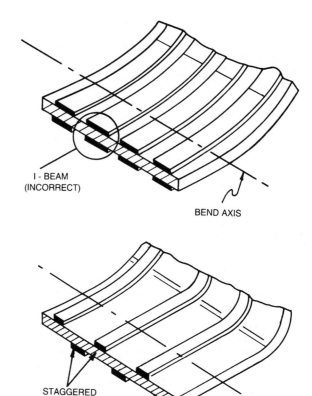

FIGURE 40.12   I-beam construction. Avoid I-beam effects with conductors in circuit bend areas.

40.8   FLEXIBLE CIRCUIT INTERCONNECTIONS

Interconnections are required in flexible circuits to:

- Connect conductors located on different layers.
- Attach electrical components to the circuit.
- Provide terminals and connector mounting.

40.8.1   Plated-Through-Holes

Connection of the conductors on different layers of a flexible circuit may be made using plated-through-holes (PTHs), a clinched wire soldered in place, or a mechanical device like an eyelet. A plated-through-hole connection is the most common and least costly technique. Plated-through-holes in FPW can be made in a continuous, roll-to-roll fabrication process. Plated-through-holes offer reliability equal to or better than solder joints and enhance component attachment by allowing soldering to the hole sides and to the area on both sides of the circuit.

Table 40.6 outlines the basic design considerations for plated-through-holes.

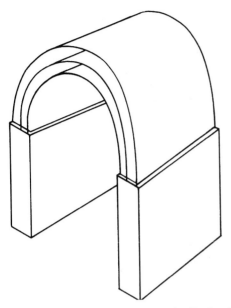

FIGURE 40.13 Book-binder construction. In a bend area with multiple circuit layers, the length of each subsequent layer should be increased by about 1.5 times the thickness, creating a book-binder effect. This minimizes bending stresses on multilayer circuits.

40.8.2 Other Interfacial Connection Methods

Rivets, eyelets, and tubelets are applied by inserting tubes of metal through-holes in the flexible circuit. These methods are used when the small number of connections does not justify the nonrecurring setup cost of plated-through-holes.

Two processes can be used to install tubular interconnections:

1. The circuit pattern is etched, the conductor pattern is solder coated, and tubes are placed in holes drilled through the solder-coated foil.
2. Eyelets are resistance-fused to the conductors.

40.9 EXTERNAL CONNECTIONS

Flexible printed wiring can be terminated by many methods and can be adapted to almost any conventional, round wire connector. External connection methods may be classified by the technique used to make electrical joints to the FPW conductors.

1. Mechanical crimping
     Tubular connectors
     Insulation piercing connectors
2. Pressure
     Edge connectors
     Clamps to PWB boards
     Conductive elastomeric pads
3. Soldering
     Lap soldering to PC boards
     Lap soldering to round wire solder pots on conventional connectors
     Soldering to pins passing through-holes in terminal pads on FPW

Table 40.7 lists flexible circuit connection techniques.

FIGURE 40.14 Window-shade construction issues: (1) Circuit extension forces are small; (2) circuit rolls up into compact cylinder; (3) it is important to allow enough room in the final package for circuit storage; (4) strain relief bars are required on each end of the circuit so tension and torsion forces do not reach solder terminations.

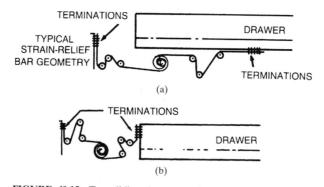

FIGURE 40.15 Two sliding drawer configurations: (*a*) under-the-drawer storage; (*b*) behind-the-drawer storage.

FIGURE 40.16 Controlled fold retraction issues: (1) Avoid sharp creases at fold line, and maintain minimum radius of curvature to distribute stress in the bend area; (2) use an external restriction member to control circuit position in the retracted condition; (3) do not allow flexing at circuit ends, as work hardening may significantly reduce copper flex life; (4) use strain relief bars on each end of the circuit so tension and torsion forces do not reach solder terminations.

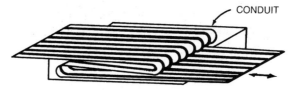

FIGURE 40.17 Controlled roll retraction.

40.9.1 Mechanical Crimp Terminations

40.9.1.1 Tubular Connectors. Rivets, eyelets, and snaps can be applied to flexible circuits by inserting tubular portions of the terminal through circuit holes. Rivets and eyelets can be used to reinforce pads soldered to heavy components.

Soldering is frequently used with inserted tubular connectors to enhance electrical reliability. When batteries or similar components are mated with flexible circuits using snaps, the circuit layout should include a pull tab located next to the terminal.

40.9.1.2 Insulation Piercing Connectors. Insulation piercing connections attach plated metal lugs, solder tabs, pins, or receptacles to flexible circuits by crimping staple-like prongs

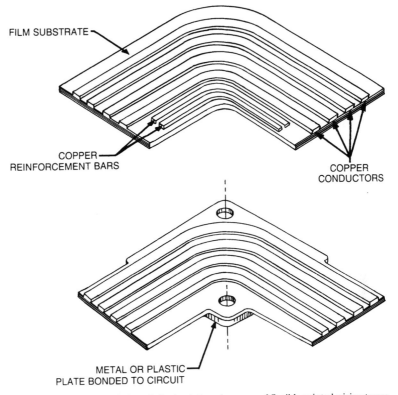

FILM SUBSTRATE

COPPER
REINFORCEMENT BARS

COPPER
CONDUCTORS

METAL OR PLASTIC
PLATE BONDED TO CIRCUIT

FIGURE 40.18   Methods for reinforcing internal corners of flexible printed wiring to prevent tearing.

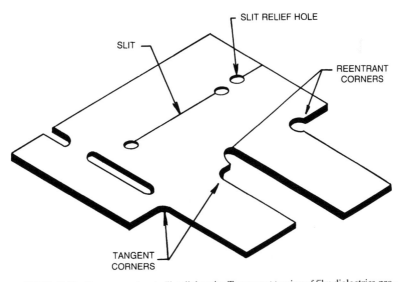

SLIT RELIEF HOLE

SLIT

REENTRANT
CORNERS

TANGENT
CORNERS

FIGURE 40.19   Tear prevention in film dielectrics. To prevent tearing of film dielectrics, provide generous radii at internal corners. Provide relief holes at ends of slits and narrow slots.

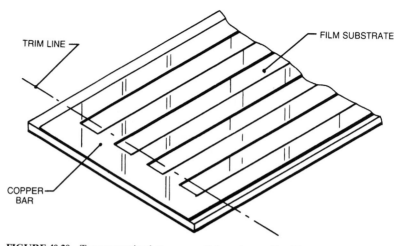

FIGURE 40.20 Tear prevention between parallel conductors. Provide a temporary copper bar across free ends of parallel conductors to protect the substrate from tears during assembly. The bar can be removed at any time before terminating the conductors.

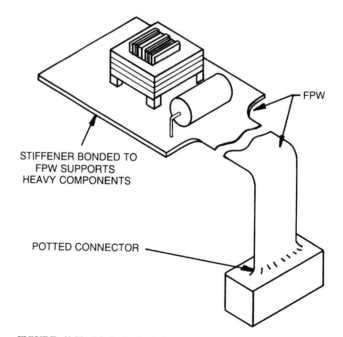

FIGURE 40.21 Methods for joining heavy components for flexible printed wiring to prevent tearing.

TABLE 40.6 Design Considerations for Plated-Through-Holes

Size	Any diameter hole made by practical sized (>0.025-in diameter) drills or punches can be plated.
Copper thickness in holes	A minimum hole wall thickness of 1 mil electroplated copper is generally specified. Smaller thicknesses are often adequate to carry the conductor current.
Plating	Solderable overplates such as tin-lead are generally used as resists. Tin-lead thicknesses of 0.2 to 0.3 mil are adequate.
Coverage	The metallization process does not always cover the hole interior completely. Some voids can be tolerated.
	Factors to consider are: • The amount of current being conducted • Whether component leads will be soldered in all holes

TABLE 40.7 Flexible Circuit Connection Techniques

For connections to interior conductors	
Direct to conductors	By separate devices
Pressure contacts	Insulation displacement connectors
Conductive elastomers	Inserted tubular connectors Gold dot connectors
For exterior connection to conductors at edges	
Direct to conductors	By separate devices
Conductors folded over	Zero insertion force connectors
Backbared or double access	Clincher connectors Soldered-on pins Crimped connectors

through the substrate and conductors to form a gas-tight connection. Terminals can be located anywhere in the interior or on the edges of the FPW. Terminals are available for installation on 0.100- and 0.050-in centers. (See Fig. 40.22.)

In-line arrays of pins or receptacles are available with housings having polarizing plugs or slots and strain relief fasteners for mating with standard connectors and pin headers (Fig. 40.23). Crimped lugs provide a rapid, low-cost way to connect leaded components to flexible circuits made of low-temperature materials and to make connections to conductors which cannot be soldered, like aluminum foil shields.

40.9.2 Pressure Termination

40.9.2.1 Edge Connectors. The edge of flexible printed wiring may be folded around a stiffener and inserted in a conventional PC edge connector (Fig. 40.24). The FPW conductors in the contact area should be plated with hard gold over nickel.

A number of edge connectors are manufactured specifically for flexible printed wiring in both spring-type and zero-insertion-force (ZIF) versions. Zero-insertion-force connectors are particularly effective for connecting to polymer–thick film FPW. The spring-type edge connectors tend to abrade the conductive coating and to limit the number of mating/unmating

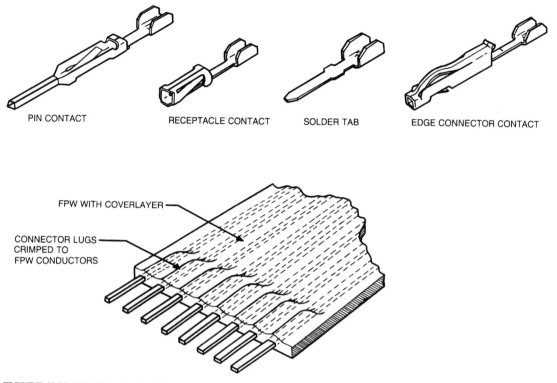

PIN CONTACT   RECEPTACLE CONTACT   SOLDER TAB   EDGE CONNECTOR CONTACT

FPW WITH COVERLAYER

CONNECTOR LUGS
CRIMPED TO
FPW CONDUCTORS

FIGURE 40.22   Flexible printed wiring terminals.

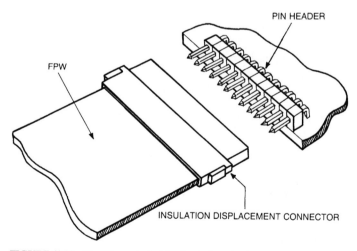

PIN HEADER

FPW

INSULATION DISPLACEMENT CONNECTOR

FIGURE 40.23   Flexible printed wiring insulation piercing connector for square pin header.

cycles. Copper conductors should be solder or gold plated in the contact area. Flexible printed wiring edge connectors are usually designed for mounting anywhere on a PC board by means of solder lugs.

40.9.2.2 *PWB Board Clamps for FPW Terminations*
Several proprietary devices are available which clamp conductors at the edge of flexible

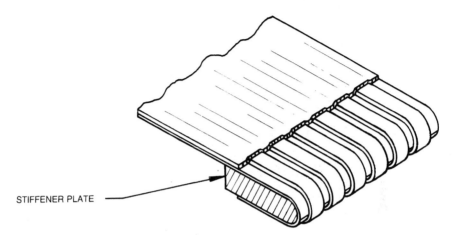

STIFFENER PLATE

FIGURE 40.24   Foldover with stiffener flexible printed wiring folded to form a male edge connector.

printed wiring to a matching in-line array of conductor pads on a PC board. These devices mount to a PC board, providing mechanical pressure, zero insertion force, and strain relief for the FPW.

Pressure contact pads on FPW are usually gold plated for corrosion resistance, but solder plating and graphite, polymer–thick film coatings have also been used successfully. Gold Dot pressure terminals for mating flexible printed wiring to PC boards are used for military and other high-reliability applications requiring a high terminal density (0.025 in center to center).

By using custom clamps, any array of pads on a component or PC board can be pressure-mated to a congruent array of FPW pads. Contact pressure may be equalized with rubber pads or metal springs to take up circuit thickness variations.

40.9.2.3 *Conductive Elastomeric Pads.*
Elastomeric pressure connectors are available in the form of strips or sheets having alternating bands of conductive and nonconductive rubber. The strips are placed between pads on the flexible printed wiring and mating pads on a PC board. Silicon rubber is the most widely used elastomer. It is made conductive with carbon or silver fillers. Elastomeric connectors exhibit higher contact resistance than most connectors. Their use is, therefore, restricted to high-impedance connector applications like liquid crystal displays, CMOS ICs, and other low-power devices.

40.9.3 Soldered Terminations

Flexible printed wiring conductors may be lap soldered to a PC board by hand, infrared heating, or a heated bar. Where terminal spacing and conductor size permit, flexible printed wiring can be lap soldered to round wire solder pots on connectors, such as mil-std cylindrical types. The flexible printed wiring should be potted into the connector shell for strain relief.

40.10   RELIABILITY

40.10.1   Reliability Considerations

The reliability of a system is the probability that it will operate in a specified manner in the environment for which it was designed for a specified period of time. The most common measure for reliability is the mean time between failures (MTBF). A high system reliability requires the MTBF to be significantly longer than the required operating time.

Reliability of electronic assemblies is inversely related to the number of connections between components. Products made with flexible printed wiring tend to be more reliable than those made with point-to-point or rigid printed wiring because of the significantly fewer interconnections made possible by flexible wiring media.

40.10.2   Failure Modes

FPW failures can be classified according to when they occur during service life.

- *Wear-out failures,* which occur at the end of the useful life of the circuit
- *Premature failures,* which occur prior to wear-out

Failures can be further classified by their cause:

- *Intrinsic failures,* which result from conditions existing within the wiring
- *Extrinsic failures,* which result solely from external factors

Extrinsic failures are due to random external events that cause failure regardless of wiring age or condition. Some of the principal causes of extrinsic circuit failures are:

- Overvoltage and overcurrent
- Corrosive atmospheres
- Contamination caused by handling and the precipitation of conductive particles, aerosols, etc.
- Uncontrolled ambient conditions resulting in water vapor condensation
- Mechanical damage from assembly and mishandling

The risk of extrinsic failures by these causes can be reduced by using a coverlayer to protect the conductors and insulation surfaces between them and providing overvoltage/overcurrent protection devices.

Intrinsic failures include both premature and wear-out failures. Common premature intrinsic failures of flexible printed wiring are:

- Open circuit failures caused by defective plating in through-holes, poor hole quality, or cuts and nicks in conductors
- Insulation resistance failures caused by incomplete removal of processing chemicals or defective raw materials

Premature intrinsic failures can be reduced by careful choice of raw materials and control of manufacturing processes.

Flexible printed wiring wear-out failure is usually related to conductor fatigue after repeated bending or to abrupt and catastrophic loss of insulation resistance caused by metal migration. Under normal conditions, with properly designed FPW, this process takes tens of years. Migration is the electrolytic growth of metal between conductors through the bulk or over the surface of the substrate and coverlayer insulation. The rate of metal migration depends on the amount of water, electrolyte, and dc voltage between conductors. The electrolyte may come from chemical breakdown of the insulation, handling, or airborne pollutants.

Metal migration wear-out failures may be controlled by:

- Use of a coverlayer to exclude moisture and contaminants
- Control of ambient humidity in service
- Choice of insulation free from constituents, like some flame retardants, which act as electrolytes
- Increased conductor spacing, particularly for sustained voltage differences
- Overvoltage protection for conductors

Table 40.8 shows some of the common failure modes for flexible printed wiring.

40.11 COST ANALYSIS

When making cost comparisons of wiring methods or design configurations, all applicable recurring and nonrecurring costs associated with a design should be determined using current procurement data. Manufacturing, engineering, and administrative time must be converted to equivalent dollars. (See Table 40.9.)

Flexible circuits generally have higher nonrecurring costs and lower recurring costs than other wiring methods. Flexible circuits are, therefore, generally less cost competitive at very low production volumes and more cost effective at high production volumes. (See Fig. 40.25.)

To determine the breakeven point, use the formula

$$N = NC_{fc} - \frac{NC_a}{R_a - R_{fc}}$$

where
N = breakeven number of units
NC_{fc} = nonrecurring costs, flexible circuit
NC_a = nonrecurring costs, alternative circuit
R_{fc} = recurring costs, flexible circuit
R_a = recurring costs, alternative circuit

Determining the cost of FPW is a complex subject because of the number of possible materials, configurations, and fabrication processes. Suppliers of FPW are the most accurate source for budgetary cost information.

40.12 UL LISTINGS FOR FLEXIBLE PRINTED WIRING

Electronic equipment which has been evaluated with respect to reasonably foreseeable hazards to life and property, and which incorporates safeguards against such hazards, may be granted a UL listing. Components which have been evaluated for use in end-product equipment covered by UL listing are granted UL recognition.

In order for equipment to be listed by UL

- Recognized components must be used
- Engineering designs must be approved by UL.
- Equipment production must be inspected periodically by a UL representative.

Some of the considerations for UL recognition of FPW are:

TABLE 40.8 Flexible Circuit Failure Modes

Failure mode	Cause	Corrective action
Loss of insulation resistance due to formation of conductive bridges between conductors	1. Shorts form through the substrate or between conductors on the same side of the substrate. 2. Substrate becomes contaminated with ionic material prior to application of covercoat, copper dendrites grow between conductors.	1. Use high quality, uniform dielectric materials not susceptible to hydrolysis. Use "buttercoat" layers with reinforced dielectrics. 2. Use hydrolytically stable substrates. Make sure that adhesive and coating additives, such as fire retardants, do not promote corrosion.
Conductor cracking during flexure	1. Dielectric substrate or adhesive not sufficiently flexible 2. Local defects in substrate or covercoat 3. Conductor irregularities 4. Conductors improperly placed in laminate 5. Copper embrittlement	1. Use laminate materials with adequate flexibility. 2. Properly select and handle laminate materials. Properly process and handle during coverlayer lamination. 3. Select high grade copper. Specify use of high-resolution imaging processes, performed in a clean room. 4. Put conductors in the neutral flexing plane. 5. Select proper copper type and grade for application. Control copper plating processes to avoid reducing copper flexibility.
Delamination of circuit layers	1. Inadequate adhesive bond 2. Differential thermal expansion of materials 3. Entrapment of contaminants	1. Use adhesives compatible with other circuit materials. 2. See "Solder joint cracking," below. 3. Use care in handling and processing prior to coverlayer lamination.

Defect	Cause	Corrective action
Solder joint cracking	1. Stress during flexing	1. Provide mechanical strain relief between soldered joints and flexed area. Reinforce solder joint terminations.
	2. Differential thermal expansion of materials	2. Select thermally compatible materials. Provide heat dissipation devices. Dissipate heat directly from component body, not through leads or terminations.
Damaged plated-through-holes	Improper punching or drilling	Use sharp drills. Control feed rate and rotational speed.
Cracked barrels of plated-through-holes	1. Low ductility of copper	1. Control copper-plating process to assure ductility.
	2. Copper thickness too small	2. Control copper-plating process to assure adequate copper thickness.
	3. Flexure near PTHs	3. Move PTHs to nonflexed areas.
Poor adhesion of through-hole barrels	Adhesive smear in through-holes	Use proper smear removal techniques.
Voids in conductors or plated areas	1. Over- or underetching	1. Control etching parameters and equipment.
	2. Faulty image placement	2. Specify high-resolution imaging process, performed in clean room.
Lifted pads	Differential thermal expansion of materials	See "Solder joint cracking."
Interlayer misregistration	1. Shifting during lamination	1. Adjust press parameters.
	2. Material dimensional changes	2. Use dimensionally stable substrates.

TABLE 40.9 Recurring and Nonrecurring Costs of Wiring Designs

Nonrecurring costs	Recurring costs
Design and development: • Circuit layout • Mock-up • Artwork • Material selection • Documentation	Procurement: • Wiring • Connectors • Terminals
Fabrication tooling	Incoming inspection
	Assembly fabrication
	Assembly inspection
	Assembly testing
	Assembly rework and retest
	Shipping
	Inventory and warehousing
	Administrative costs

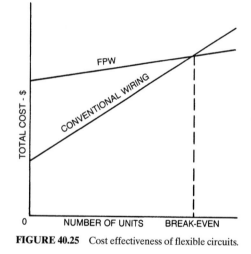

FIGURE 40.25 Cost effectiveness of flexible circuits.

• Solder shock temperature and time
• Operating temperature
• Copper weight
• Single- or double-sided applications
• Maximum conductor area
• Thickness
• Etchant type
• Flammability

UL also rates materials and constructions for flammability. UL flammability tests and three other commonly used flammability tests are listed in Table 40.10.

TABLE 40.10 Common Flammability Tests

Test	Method	Criteria
UL 94	Two 10-s applications of ¾-in Bunsen flame to a vertical material specimen	V-0 extinguish within 5 s and drips must not ignite surgical cotton V-1 extinguish within 25 s and drips must not ignite surgical cotton V-2 extinguish within 25 s and drips may ignite surgical cotton
FAA 25.853A	One 60-s application of 1-½-in Bunsen flame to a 4-½-in × 12-½-in vertical specimen	(Part A) average flame time—15 s, flaming drips must extinguish in 3 s, burned section 6 in.
ASTM D635-63	Two 60-second applications of 1″ Bunsen flame to horizontal specimen	NB nonburning—total extinguishing of part before reaching 1-in line SE, self extinguishing—total extinguishing of part before reaching 4-in line
ASTM D635-74	One 30-s application of 1-in Bunsen flame to horizontal specimen	Record average burn length in in/min minute

CHAPTER 41
FABRICATION AND ASSEMBLY OF FLEXIBLE CIRCUITS

Sheldahl Technical Staff*
Sheldahl Inc., Northfield, Minnesota

41.1 INTRODUCTION

Fabrication and assembly general processes for printed wiring boards are detailed in other parts of this book and in other references. A brief review, however, is in order here to show the differences in processing between rigid printed circuits and flexible circuits.

41.2 FABRICATION PROCESSES

41.2.1 Artwork Master

Imaging is much the same, with the exception that the artwork master must be checked to make sure it includes allowances for manufacturing tolerances present in flexible materials. To be absolutely the best, master art should be on glass, since it allows the least amount of dimensional change for a tightly toleranced circuit.

41.2.2 Tooling

Tooling is one of three basic types: hard-hard, hard-soft, and soft. The hard-hard tool provides the most accurate compound blanking and piercing, with tolerances as close as 0.003 to 0.005 in, depending on the feature. The soft tool, on the other hand, is usually a steel rule die with tolerances up to 5 times looser, or from 0.015 to 0.025 in. The circuit design usually dictates what kind of tooling is needed. The cost has a wide range, from as little as $300 to $500 for steel rule dies to $15,000 to $20,000 for hard-hard steel compound dies.

41.2.3 Indexing

Indexing, or sprocketing material with process guide holes, is used in many flexible circuit processes, especially in the large roll-to-roll production lines (see Fig. 41.1). The object is to

---

* Adapted from "Flexible Circuitry Design Guide," published by Sheldahl Inc., 1984, used with permission.

FIGURE 41.1 Etching flexible circuits in a continuous roll-to-roll etcher. *(Courtesy of Sheldahl Inc., Northfield, Minn.)*

have several very accurately punched holes, which will allow the manufacturer to align the tooling for through-holes and outlines with the artwork and image-placing processes.

41.2.4 Etching

Etching is done in standard spray etchers with a conveyor belt that pulls the circuitry through. Some very lightweight flexible circuitry panels require that they be taped to G-10 leader boards so they can be pulled through the etcher without being lost in the etchant spray turbulence. Many standard etchants are used, ranging from alkaline types to chlorides (cupric and ferric).

41.2.5 Lamination

After the circuit is etched, the resist is removed, and the surface is cleaned in preparation for the top layer of insulation (cover layer).

The next step in actual production is the lamination of cover film to the top of the circuit. The cover film is an adhesive (B-stage) coated film that is usually of the same type and thickness as the base film. The cover film is prepunched with holes for process and for solder pads. This material is then neat-tacked to the base circuit using pins and the punched holes for alignment. The resulting assembly is then put into a platen press, and the B-stage adhesive is cured under pressure of around 350 lb/in^2 at a temperature of about 350°F for 1 h or so and cooled under pressure for another 20 min.

The circuit then goes into a cleaning operation prior to solder application. The parts are coated with solder, cleaned again, and then moved to the blank and pierce or drilling area,

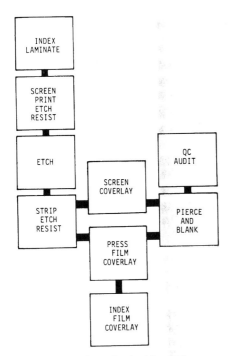

FIGURE 41.2   Print and etch with coverlay.

where holes are put in the exposed pads and, finally, where the outline or cutline of the circuit is created.

41.2.6   Process Flowcharts

Figures 41.2, 41.3, and 41.4 show different flexible circuit process charts.

41.3   COMPONENT ASSEMBLY

Almost any electric component can be attached to flexible printed wiring (FPW). Heavier components may require a stiffener element bonded to the FPW to distribute stresses during assembly, service, and repair. Components such as axial lead resistors, dual in-line IC packages, low- or medium-power transistors, and other components of similar mass and pin count have been mounted on unreinforced FPW arrays, but the product case or chassis is usually shaped to support the components after assembly. Components such as small-outline transistors and ICs, chip capacitors, and resistors may not require any mechanical support in low-vibration applications.

41.3.1   General Issues

Ease of component assembly and inspection depends on the circuit layout and the quality of the flexible printed wiring array. Components should be mounted parallel or perpendicular to common axes. Conventional component insertion and placement equipment has been adapted to FPW assembly by providing nests or fixtures to support the otherwise flexible wiring array during machine handling.

41.3.1.1   Attachment Methods.   Components may be attached to flexible circuits by soldering, mechanical joints, or with conductive adhesives.

41.3.1.2   Soldering.   Most flexible circuits are made with copper conductors. Component leads may be attached by conventional methods such as wave or reflow soldering. Soldering methods and techniques used for flexible circuits are discussed in detail later in this chapter (see Sec. 41.4).

41.3.1.3   Mechanical Connections.   Off-the-shelf connectors are available for flexible circuitry. Many of these form circuit connections by pressure contact or by piercing the conductors to form a gas-tight electrical joint. A detailed discussion of FPW connectors may be found near the end of this chapter.

41.3.1.4   Conductive Adhesives.   Components can be mounted to flexible circuits using adhesives filled with particles of silver, graphite, or other conductive materials. The adhesive is applied as a viscous liquid by screen printing or by precision dispensers. The components are placed in position, and the adhesive is cured in an oven. Conductive adhesives are preferred for circuits with polymer–thick film conductors, which are difficult to solder.

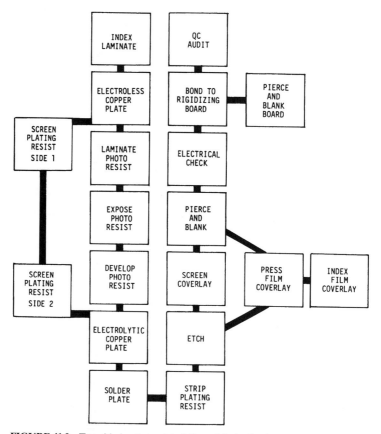

FIGURE 41.3 Two-sided pattern-plated through-hole circuit with coverlay.

41.3.2 Attachment Configurations

41.3.2.1 Straight-Through Attachment. Component leads are inserted into circuit holes and either left straight or crimped slightly. Actual connection is by dip or wave soldering. Plated-through-holes are recommended if the flexible printed wiring has more than one layer. (See Fig. 41.5.)

41.3.2.2 Clinched Lead Attachment. Component leads are inserted into circuit holes, bent by "wiping" the protruding leads and soldering. Clinched lead attachment can be used with unsupported holes, plated-through-holes, or eyeletted holes. Clinched lead attachment is recommended for multiple-lead components, such as integrated circuits, where greater lead strength is available and in systems where the extra lead length will not adversely affect performance. It may be necessary to support the FPW with fixtures from the component side during clinching.

41.3.2.3 Surface Mounting. Surface mounting is the only attachment method that provides access to conductive joints from the component side. Since components can be attached to both sides of the circuit, surface mounting allows maximum packaging density.

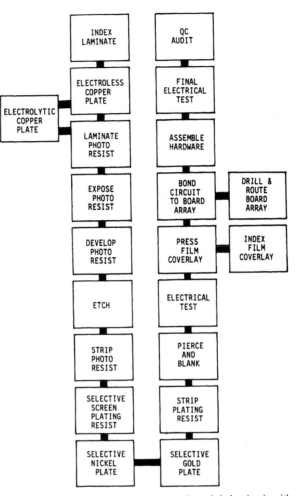

FIGURE 41.4 Two-sided panel-plated through-hole circuit with selective nickel-gold plating, film coverlay, rigid board array, and hardware.

In surface mounting, component leads are attached to the circuit by soldering in a *lap* configuration. Connection is by conventional or reflow soldering or by adhesive bonding to either or both sides of the circuit. (See Fig. 41.6.)

41.3.3 Soldering General Issues

41.3.3.1 Temperature Properties. The thermal properties of flexible printed wiring substrates, adhesives, coverlayers, and conductors all affect soldering. Soldering times and temperatures must be closely controlled to prevent melting or decomposition of the dielectric substrate and adhesive, blistering, or delamination of circuit layers, solder crazing, pad lifting, and separation of pads from plated-through-holes.

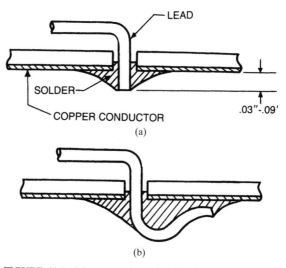

FIGURE 41.5 (*a*) Straight-through solder joints; (*b*) clinched lead solder joints.

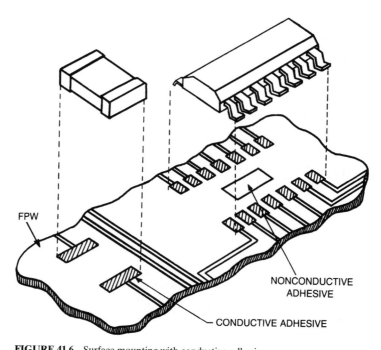

FIGURE 41.6 Surface mounting with conductive adhesive.

41.3.3.2 Water Absorption. At soldering temperatures, vaporization of moisture absorbed or trapped in the dielectric may cause blistering and delamination between the substrate and the conductors. Vinyl, polyesters, and fluorocarbon dielectrics do not absorb moisture. Dielectrics, like polyimide and aramid paper, are hygroscopic. They may require predrying for 1 to 2 h immediately before soldering to avoid outgassing of water vapor.

Predrying must be done immediately before soldering, since these materials can absorb substantial amounts of water in a short time. Polyimide can absorb up to 2½ percent of its weight in water in the first 15 min of exposure to air, depending on the relative humidity. At high relative humidity, it may absorb another 1 percent over 24 h. Long predrying cycles tend to oxidize exposed copper conductors. Normal rosin fluxes will dissolve the tarnish and adequately prepare the copper for soldering, provided the conductors are clean before heating.

41.3.3.3 Localizing Soldered Areas. Components and solder pads are often confined to a limited portion of a flexible circuit. Regions not to be soldered can be folded out of the soldering plane to conserve space in the soldering fixture.

41.3.3.4 Cleaning. Circuits must be cleaned after soldering to remove flux residues. Flexible printed circuit assemblies can be defluxed with common solvents like isopropyl alcohol, trichloroethylene, and commercial Freon-based materials. Chlorinated solvents are the least desirable, since prolonged exposure may soften some types of adhesives used in flexible circuits.

41.3.4 Soldering Methods

41.3.4.1 Manual Soldering. Most flexible circuit assemblies are soldered by automatic processes (hand soldering is used to rework defective joints) to replace components and to solder jumper connections. In hand soldering of flexible circuits, the contact time of the soldering iron to the work must be minimized. Recommended hand-soldering conditions are shown in Fig. 41.7.

41.3.4.2 Reflow Soldering. Solder may be predeposited at each joint as a preform, paste, or solder plating. The solder can be melted by resistance or hot-gas heating, forced-air oven, radiant heating, liquid immersion, or vapor phase condensation methods.

41.3.4.3 Wave Soldering. Wave soldering is a widely used and reliable method of soldering flexible circuits. Flexible printed wiring with polyimide film or epoxy-glass substrates can

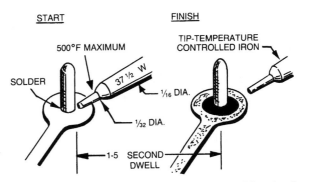

FIGURE 41.7 Hand-soldering conditions for flexible printed wiring.

be wave soldered by conventional techniques. If solder pads are small, conductors should be bonded to the substrate with high-temperature adhesives. Pad capture by coverlayer or solder masks will help protect the bond between pads and substrate. Solder plating under cover films or coatings is undesirable because the plating reflows during wave soldering and damages the coverlayer bond. For circuits with coverlayers, solder plating or hard flux coating on conductors should be restricted to the solder pads.

41.3.4.4 Fixturing for Wave Soldering. Unless rigid stiffeners are used to reinforce the areas of the FPW to be soldered, a carrier or fixture is usually required to hold the circuit flat during component insertion and passage over the wave. Fixtures should support the circuit to prevent sagging without applying strain which can cause distortion at solder temperatures. (See Figs. 41.8 and 41.9.)

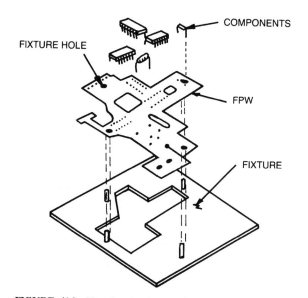

FIGURE 41.8 Fixturing for flexible printed wiring made of high-temperature materials. Flexible circuits made with high-temperature materials, such as polyimide, require no shielding over the solder wave. The circuit may be stretched between clamps in a frame or plate which is cut away to expose solder pads.

Experimentation on prototypes is recommended to establish solder process parameters for each circuit design. Usually, conventional wave-soldering equipment can be used without alteration. Fixtured circuits should be preheated. Solder pot temperatures should be below 260°C (500°F). Dwell time should be minimized, usually to less than 2 s.

41.4 EXTERNAL CONNECTIONS

41.4.1 General Issues

Flexible printed wiring can be terminated by many methods and can be adapted to almost any conventional, round wire connector. External connection methods may be classified by the technique used to make electrical joints to the FPW conductors.

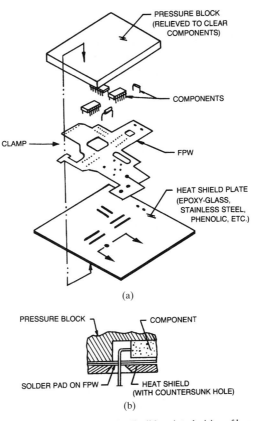

FIGURE 41.9 Fixturing for flexible printed wiring of low-temperature materials. (a) Flexible circuits made with low-temperature materials, such as polyesters, have relatively lower heat resistance and must be protected by the soldering fixture. Low-temperature circuits should be supported on the solder side by a thin plate of epoxy-glass, stainless steel, molded phenolic, or similar material. The plate should be provided with countersunk or beveled openings to expose the solder pads. A second clamping fixture is applied on the component side to prevent component float and to hold the circuit and plate in contact as they pass over the wave. (b) Shows a section through a component hole.

41.4.1.1 *Mechanical Crimping*
- Tubular eyelets, snaps
- Insulation piercing lugs

41.4.1.2 *Pressure*
- Edge connectors
- Clamps to PC boards
- Conductive elastomeric pads

41.4.1.3 *Soldering*
- Lap soldering to PC boards

- Lap soldering to round wire solder pots on conventional connectors
- Soldering to pins passing through holes in terminal pads on FPW

Table 41.1 lists flexible circuit connection techniques.

TABLE 41.1 Flexible Circuit Connection Techniques

For connections to interior conductors	
Direct to conductors	By separate devices
Pressure contacts	Insulation displacement connectors
Conductive elastomers	Inserted tubular connectors
	Gold dot connectors
For exterior connection to conductors at edges	
Direct to conductors	By separate devices
Conductors folded over	Zero insertion force connectors
Backbared or double access	Clincher connectors
	Soldered-on pins
	Crimped connectors

41.4.2 Mechanical Crimp Terminations

41.4.2.1 Tubular Connectors.

Rivets, eyelets, and snaps can be applied to flexible circuits by inserting tubular portions of the terminal through circuit holes. Rivets and eyelets can be used to reinforce pads soldered to heavy components.

Soldering is frequently used with inserted tubular connectors to enhance electrical reliability. When batteries or similar components are mated with flexible circuits using snaps, the circuit layout should include a pull tab located next to the terminal.

41.4.3 Insulation Piercing Connectors

Insulation piercing connections attach plated metal lugs, solder tabs, pins, or receptacles to flexible circuits by crimping staple-like prongs through the substrate and conductors to form a gastight connection. Terminals can be located anywhere in the interior or on the edges of the FPW. Terminals are available for installation on 0.100- and 0.050-in centers. (See Fig. 41.10.)

In-line arrays of pins or receptacles are available with housings having polarizing plugs or slots and strain relief fasteners for mating with standard connectors and pin headers (Fig. 41.11). Crimped lugs provide a rapid, low-cost way to connect leaded components to flexible circuits made of low-temperature materials and to make connections to conductors which cannot be soldered, like aluminum foil shields.

41.4.4 Pressure Termination

41.4.4.1 Edge Connections.

The edge of flexible printed wiring may be folded around a stiffener and inserted in a conventional PC edge connector (Fig. 41.12). The FPW conductors in the contact area should be plated with hard gold over nickel.

A number of edge connectors are manufactured specifically for flexible printed wiring in both spring-type and zero-insertion-force (ZIF) versions. (See Fig. 41.13.) Zero-insertion-force connectors are particularly effective for connecting to polymer–thick film FPW.

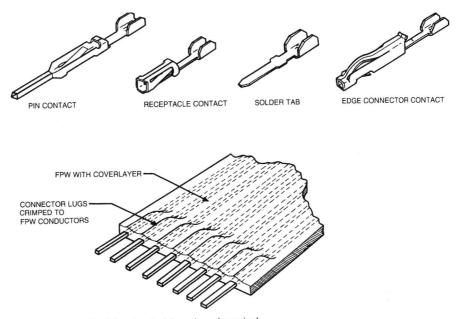

FIGURE 41.10   Flexible printed wiring crimped terminals.

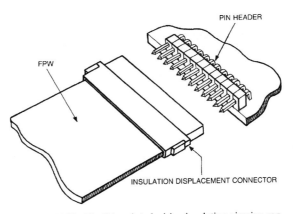

FIGURE 41.11   Flexible printed wiring insulation piercing connector for square pin header.

The spring-type edge connectors tend to abrade the conductive coating and to limit the number of mating/unmating cycles. Copper conductors should be solder or gold plated in the contact area. Flexible printed wiring edge connectors are usually designed for mounting anywhere on a PC board by means of solder lugs.

41.4.5   PC Board Clamps for FPW Terminations

Several proprietary devices are available which clamp conductors at the edge of flexible printed wiring to a matching in-line array of conductor pads on a PC board. These devices

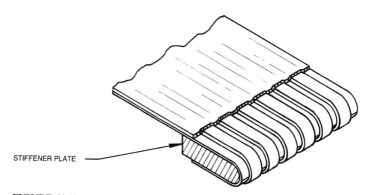

STIFFENER PLATE

FIGURE 41.12   Foldover with stiffener flexible printed wiring folded to form a male edge connector.

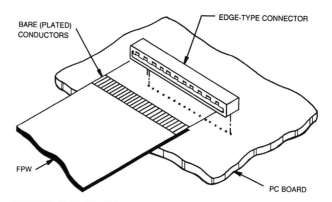

BARE (PLATED) CONDUCTORS

EDGE-TYPE CONNECTOR

FPW

PC BOARD

FIGURE 41.13   Flexible printed wiring edge connector for printed circuit board mounting.

mount to a PC board, providing mechanical pressure, zero insertion force, and strain relief for the FPW.

Pressure contact pads on FPW are usually gold plated for corrosion resistance, but solder plating and graphite, polymer–thick film coatings have also been used successfully. Gold Dot pressure terminals for mating flexible printed wiring to PC boards are used for military and other high-reliability applications requiring a high terminal density (0.025 in center to center). The technique has been applied to in-line contacts with up to 400 connections in a space 3 in × 0.3 in.

By using custom clamps, any array of pads on a component or PC board can be pressure-mated to a congruent array of FPW pads. Contact pressure may be equalized with rubber pads or metal springs to take up circuit thickness variations.

41.4.6 Conductive Elastomeric Pads

Elastomeric pressure connectors are available in the form of strips or sheets having alternating bands of conductive and nonconductive rubber. The strips are placed between pads on the flexible printed wiring and mating pads on a PC board. Silicone rubber is the most widely used elastomer. It is made conductive with carbon or silver fillers. Elastomeric connectors exhibit higher contact resistance than most connectors. Their use is, therefore, restricted to high-impedance connector applications like liquid crystal displays, CMOS ICs, and other low-power devices.

41.4.7 Soldered Terminations

Flexible printed wiring conductors may be lap soldered to a PC board by hand, infrared heating, or a heated bar. Where terminal spacing and conductor size permit, flexible printed wiring can be lap soldered to round wire solder pots on connectors, such as mil-std cylindrical types. The flexible printed wiring should be potted into the connector shell for strain relief. The soldering measures discussed in this chapter under "Component Assembly, General Issues" (see Sec. 41.3.1) should be followed.

CHAPTER 42
RIGID-FLEX CIRCUITS*

Steve Gurley

42.1 INTRODUCTION

Rigid-flex is a combination of rigid printed circuits and flexible printed circuits. The various combinations of layers are all laminated together. After lamination, the through-holes are drilled and then plated so that they connect the various layers together electrically. This kind of interconnect circuitry can be made with as many as 20 layers of material in panel sizes up to 16 × 20 in.

This circuitry is used when cumbersome wiring needs to be replaced with a simpler system to decrease weight, reduce assembly time, and improve reliability. Rigid-flex assemblies eliminate the need for jumpers and mother-daughter board combinations, and they reduce wiring errors while increasing package density.

42.2 PROCESS OVERVIEW

Figure 42.1 is a process chart showing the merger of flexible circuit technology and rigid board technology into rigid-flex technology. The two different technologies are brought together at the lamination step of the process.

42.3 MATERIALS

The selection of materials is very important and must be done very carefully, since all the component parts must withstand processing steps without damage. As discussed with flexible circuits, dimensional changes occur in the *x* and *y* axes of the product, but in rigid-flex, because of the thickness, a third, vertical stress comes into play called *z-axis expansion*. This distortion of materials can cause copper hole barrel cracking when the materials are exposed to final lamination and soldering temperatures. Tables 42.1 and 42.2 show some of the most popular material choices for rigid-flex assemblies.

---

* Adapted from Steve Gurley, "Flexible Circuit Design, Materials, and Fabrication," in Coombs (ed.), *Printed Circuits Handbook,* 3d ed., McGraw-Hill, New York, 1988, Chap. 35.

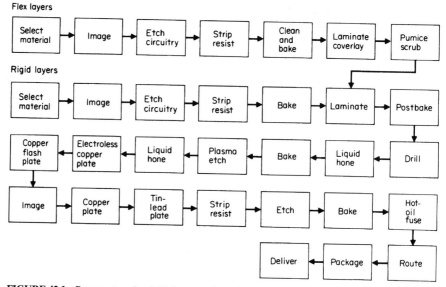

FIGURE 42.1 Process steps for rigid-flex manufacturing *(Courtesy of IPC.)*

TABLE 42.1 Rigid-Flex Material Combinations

Flexible section		
Copper-clad	Adhesive system	Cover layer
Polyimide	Modified epoxy	Polyimide
Polyimide	Acrylic	Polyimide
Rigid section		
Copper-clad	B-stage/bond plies	
Epoxy-glass	Epoxy-glass B-stage	
Epoxy-glass	Modified epoxy adhesive	
Epoxy-glass	Acrylic adhesive	
Polyimide-glass	Polyimide-glass B-stage	
Polyimide-glass	Modified epoxy adhesive	
Polyimide-glass	Acrylic adhesive	

42.4 PROCESS CONCERNS

The four most difficult areas of process in rigid-flex products are lamination, drilling to meet the center of all successive pads in all the layers, removing the adhesive deposited into the holes after drilling (smear removal), and the subsequent plating of the holes previously described after the adhesive smear is removed. These problem areas will cause anomalies such as adhesive smear from drilling, delamination, copper embrittlement, plated-through-hole cracking, and misregistration of the various layers. There is a multitude of reasons for these problems. Many can be overcome with careful processing.

Selection of materials is first. Polyimide materials are used in the flexible portions. The polyimide should be as stable as possible; Du Pont's type VN Kapton is very stable. Since

TABLE 42.2 Rigid-Flex System Combination

Copper-clad rigid material	Copper-clad flexible material	B-stage
Epoxy-glass	Polyimide Modified epoxy	Epoxy-glass
Epoxy-glass	Polyimide-acrylic	Epoxy-glass
Epoxy-glass	Polyimide Modified epoxy	Modified epoxy Cast film
Epoxy-glass	Polyimide-acrylic	Acrylic
Polyimide-glass	Polyimide-acrylic	Acrylic–cast film
Epoxy-glass	Polyimide Modified epoxy	Acrylic
Polyimide-glass	Polyimide Modified epoxy	Acrylic–cast film
Polyimide-glass	Polyimide-acrylic	Acrylic-glass
Polyimide-glass	Polyimide epoxy	Epoxy-glass
Polyimide-glass	Polyimide-acrylic	Modified epoxy Cast film

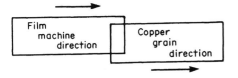

FIGURE 42.2 Grain orientations.

shrinkage of flexible polyimide materials is greater in the machine direction (MD) than in the transverse or cross-machine direction (TD), the artwork pattern should be placed on the material to take advantage of the more stable TD direction. Sheet-manufactured material is usually more stable than roll-manufactured material. All materials should be aligned so that the grain and stress orientation of the copper foils, polyimide films, and cover films are all aligned as shown in Fig. 42.2.

After the design is firm, it is easy to determine the center point of a circuit. Once the longest part of the circuit is determined, that dimension can be oriented in the transverse direction, which has the best dimensional stability. In addition, the designer should leave as much copper on the circuits as possible, including the borders. The copper left on the circuit after etching improves stability of the material.

42.5 RIGID-FLEX LAMINATION

When the innerlayer material is being prepared, the adhesive thickness should be called out to provide good fill-flow characteristics in the spaces between the copper traces. Usually 1-oz copper is combined with 0.001 in of adhesive, 2-oz with 0.002 in, 3-oz with 0.003 in, etc.

After all the component parts of the rigid-flex have been put together, the job of combining the flexible circuits to the rigid circuits is at hand. This is the most difficult part of the job, since most of the component parts are made of dissimilar materials.

Although many companies use standard platen presses for this job, the trend is toward vacuum lamination. There are as many steps in this final assembly portion of the job as there are in all the other steps combined. There are also a great number of process parameters and specifications for these steps. They differ widely because of the selection and processing characteristics of the materials. Only one type will be outlined here. Suppliers of flexible and rigid materials can give valued technical assistance when asked.

The steps for one process are as follows.

1. Bake all materials to remove moisture.
2. Arrange the stack-up of layers. (Pins can be used to keep layers aligned.)
3. Sandwich the lay-up between caul plates and laminating materials, which can include Teflon or Tedlar and glass-reinforced Teflon. Silicone rubber and kraft paper are also used.
4. Place in a vacuum press and draw down 28 to 30 in Hg.*
5. Bump the package a few times (add pressure and release several times) to help remove air trapped in the stack-up.
6. Put under full pressure of 325 to 350 lb/in^2 and a temperature of 350 to 375°F for 2 h, with a thermocouple at the load; make sure that the stack-up is at temperature for at least 1 h.
7. Cool the load while still under pressure for at least 20 min.
8. Remove the material from the press and immediately put in a postcure oven for 2 h at 250°F. Keep the pin tooling in place with its fixture to keep the package as stable as possible.

42.6 DRILLING

The next step is drilling the laminated package. Because many different materials will be drilled, feeds and speeds of the drill should be optimized for the cleanest drilled hole possible. This will save time and trouble during later steps.

Table 42.3 is from material published by the IP Further Rigid-Flex Workshop.

TABLE 42.3   Recommended Drilling Parameters for Rigid-Flex Printed Wiring Boards

Diameter range, in	Drill size range		Feed rate, in/min	r/min × 10^3
	No.	mm		
0.0135–0.0180	80–77	0.35–0.45	200	75
0.0197–0.0240	76–73	0.50–0.60	195	66
0.0250–0.0280	72–70	0.65–0.70	160	54
0.0292–0.0350	69–65	0.75–0.85	135	44
0.0354–0.0400	64–60	0.90–1.00	110	38
0.0410–0.0472	59–56	1.05–1.20	95	33
0.0492–0.0595	55–53	1.25–1.50	75	26
0.0610–0.0736	52–49	1.55–1.85	65	21
0.0748–0.0890	48–43	1.90–2.25	55	17
0.0906–0.1100	42–35	2.30–2.75	45	14
0.1102–0.1250	34–⅛ in	2.80–3.10	35	12

42.7 HOLE CLEANING

After the drilling process, the holes through the stacked materials must be cleaned so that the subsequent copper-plating process will yield a hole with no cracks or voids in the barrel.

---

* This applies when vacuum lamination is used.

Since most rigid-flex circuits are made with acrylic adhesive systems, the most popular etchback or hole-cleaning process in use is the plasma system. There are other methods in use, such as chromic sulfuric acid for epoxy-based systems. For the epoxy system, sulfuric acid relieves the excess epoxy resin, while the chromic portion enhances the action of the sulfuric. Fluorosulfonic acid is used to dissolve the exposed glass fibers left in the rigid portion of the stack-up. The actual process is more complex than described; information concerning the actual processes can be obtained elsewhere in this book and from the chemical manufacturers.

The plasma etchback system used with acrylic-based materials works with ionized gases (see Table 42.4). The gases are generated by a radio-frequency current which ionizes CF_4, (Freon) mixed with oxygen. It does a good job of desmearing the flexible circuit portion of the assembly but will not do anything to glass fibers that might be in the holes of the rigid portion. Proper drill speeds and feeds and *sharp* drills will minimize problems with the cleanliness of the holes. When only a few holes need to be desmeared, a mask-heat sink system is designed to expose the hole only. This can reduce the etchback time as well as keep the rigid-flex cool, since the mask protects the other polyimide surfaces and acts as a heat sink to protect the rest of the assembly during processing.

TABLE 42.4 Typical Plasma Etch Parameters

RF power	1.0–1.5 kW
Pressure	0.4 torr
Gas	70% O_2 and 30% CF_4
Time	12–15 min

After the plasma treatment, an organic residue is left in the holes. This is difficult to remove with ordinary cleaning, but it can be removed with an alkaline cleaner at 140°C for 2 to 3 min in an ultrasonic cleaner.

42.8 PLATING AND ETCHING

Now that the hole is drilled and cleaned, the holes are copper plated with an electroless copper. Etch-resist placement is next to provide the pattern for the top and/or bottom surfaces. The final surface and hole electrolytic plating is done, and then the panels are solder plated. The resist is then removed, allowing the solder plating to become the "new resist." Etching then removes the unwanted copper. The solder plating can be fused with hot oil. The panels are then cut (routed) into the final size and shape.

42.9 FINAL COVERLAYERS

The final coverlayers on the top and bottom of the finished rigid-flex assembly are applied. This process is very similar to that in a single-sided flexible circuit operation in that a prepunched or drilled cover-film panel complete with position registration holes is tacked down in a clean environment to the etched circuit. The resulting finished circuit is then laminated so the cover film is bonded and cured to the top and bottom etched circuits.

Some circuit manufacturers prefer not to deal with solder-plated circuitry, especially if it is to have a film or liquid cover coat on it. The problem with this kind of system is that when the final circuit is sent through a solder wave or IR reflow system, the solder on the traces melts and causes tunneling, which is a form of delamination. This means that the entire assembly is not a completely bonded homogeneous unit. The alternative approach is to use a positive etch resist, etch the copper, cover film the circuit, and then solder plate the pads only, prior to drilling out the final pad configuration.

42.10 MULTILAYER CONCERNS

The best rule for rigid-flex assemblies is to limit the number of layers as much as possible. The greater the number of individual layers, the more difficult it is to hold tolerances. There are increasing difficulties of dealing with larger coefficients of expansion and then resulting low yields, as layers increase in number. There is an exponentially increasing cost per square inch of circuitry as layers increase in number.

The very best way to start the package design is with a "paper-doll" layout of the circuit (see Fig. 42.3). In this way it is possible to anticipate what areas of difficulty there will be in fitting the finished circuit into its proper place in the electronic system chassis. Thicker circuit stack-ups also have problems forming around bends or corners. If this is a problem in the final design, make sure that a bookbinder approach is used in the design.

Design the circuit layers at the *outside* of the bend so they are slightly longer than the circuit layers of the *inside* of the bend. These layers must be kept separate and not bonded together unless the designer wants a permanent bend laminated into the assembly. Dimen-

FIGURE 42.3   An eight-layer rigid-flex board showing layers prior to lamination. (*Courtesy of Sheldahl Inc., Certel/Cerpac.*)

sional stability can be improved by leaving a copper pattern similar to a cross-hatch pattern etched into the copper. This will prevent excess shrinkage of the layers after the etching process.

There are many sources for design and processing information for flexible circuits. The best sources are always the producers of flexible circuits and/or the suppliers of process materials and chemicals. Using this information in combination with supplier information and some carefully designed experiments to prove process integrity, it is possible to fabricate dependable flexible and multilayer circuits to meet almost any need.

GLOSSARY

ACCELERATOR: A chemical that is used to speed up a reaction or cure, as cobalt naphthenate is used to accelerate the reaction of certain polyester resins. It is often used along with a catalyst, hardener, or curing agent. The term "accelerator" is often used interchangeably with the term "promoter."

ACCURACY: The ability to place the hole at the targeted location.

ADDITIVE PROCESS: A process for obtaining conductive patterns by the selective deposition of conductive material on an unclad base material.

ADHESIVE: Broadly, any substance used in promoting and maintaining a bond between two materials.

AGING: The change in properties of a material with time under specific conditions.

AMBIENT TEMPERATURE: The temperature of the cooling medium, such as gas or liquid, which comes into contact with the heated parts of an apparatus (or the normal temperature of the surrounding environment).

ANNULAR RING: The circular strip of conductive material that completely surrounds a hole.

ARC RESISTANCE: The time required for an arc to establish a conductive path in a material.

ARTWORK MASTER: An accurately scaled configuration used to produce the production master.

BACKUP MATERIAL: A material placed on the bottom of a laminate stack in which the drill terminates its drilling stroke.

BASE MATERIAL: The insulating material upon which the printed wiring pattern may be formed.

BASE MATERIAL THICKNESS: The thickness of the base material excluding metal foil cladding or material deposited on the surface.

BLISTERING: Localized swelling and separation between any of the layers of the base laminate or between the laminate and the metal cladding.

BONDING LAYER: An adhesive layer used in bonding other discrete layers during lamination.

BOND STRENGTH: The force per unit area required to separate two adjacent layers by a force perpendicular to the board surface; usually refers to the interface between copper and base material.

BOW: A laminate defect in which deviation from planarity results in a smooth arc.

B STAGE: An intermediate stage in the curing of a thermosetting resin. In it a resin can be heated and caused to flow, thereby allowing final curing in the desired shape.

B-STAGE LOT: The product from a single mix of B-stage ingredients.

B-STAGE RESIN: A resin in an intermediate stage of a thermosetting reaction. The material softens when heated and swells when in contact with certain liquids, but it may not entirely fuse or dissolve.

BURR: A ridge left on the outside copper surfaces after drilling.

CAPACITANCE: The property of a system of conductors and dielectrics which permits the storage of electricity when potential difference exists between the conductors.

CAPACITIVE COUPLING: The electrical interaction between two conductors caused by the capacitance between the conductors.

CARBIDE: Tungsten carbide, formula WC. The hard, refractory material forming the drill bits used in PWB drillings.

CATALYST: A chemical that causes or speeds up the cure of a resin but does not become a chemical part of the final product.

CERAMIC LEADED CHIP CARRIER (CLCC): A chip carrier made from ceramic (usually a 90–96% alumina or beryllia base) and with compliant leads for terminations.

CHIP CARRIER (CC): An integrated circuit package, usually square, with a chip cavity in the center; its connections are usually on all four sides. (See *leaded chip carrier* and *leadless chip carrier.*)

CHIP LOAD (CL): The movement of the drill downward per revolution; usually given in mils (thousandths of an inch) per revolution.

CHLORINATED HYDROCARBON: An organic compound having chlorine atoms in its chemical structure. Trichloroethylene, methyl chloroform, and methylene chloride are chlorinated hydrocarbons.

CIRCUIT: The interconnection of a number of electrical devices in one or more closed paths to perform a desired electrical or electronic function.

CLAD: A condition of the base material, to which a relatively thin layer or sheet of metal foil (cladding) has been bonded on one or both of its sides. The result is called a metal-clad base material.

CNC: Computer numerically controlled. Refers to a machine with a computer which stores the numerical information about location, drill size, and machine parameters, regulating the machine to carry out that information.

COAT: To cover with a finishing, protecting, or enclosing layer of any compound.

COLD FLOW: The continuing dimensional change that follows initial instantaneous deformation in a nonrigid material under static load. Also called creep.

COLLIMATION: The degree of parallelism of light rays from a given source. A light source with good collimation produces parallel light rays, whereas a poor light source produces divergent, nonparallel light rays.

COMPONENT HOLE: A hole used for the attachment and electrical connection of a component termination, including pin or wire, to the printed board.

COMPONENT SIDE: The side of the printed board on which most of the components will be mounted.

COMPOUND: A combination of elements in a stable molecular arrangement.

CONDUCTIVE FOIL: The conductive material that covers one side or both sides of the base material and is intended for forming the conductive pattern.

CONDUCTIVE PATTERN: The configuration or design of the electrically conductive material on the base material.

CONDUCTOR LAYER 1: The first layer having a conductive pattern, of a multilayer board, on or adjacent to the component side of the board.

CONDUCTOR SPACING: The distance between adjacent edges (not centerline to centerline) of conductors on a single layer of a printed board.

CONDUCTOR THICKNESS: The thickness of the copper conductor exclusive of coatings or other metals.

CONDUCTOR WIDTH: The width of the conductor viewed from vertically above, i.e., perpendicularly to the printed board.

CONFORMAL COATING: An insulating protective coating which conforms to the configuration of the object coated and is applied on the completed printed board assembly.

CONNECTOR AREA: The portion of the printed board that is used for providing external (input-output) electrical connections.

CONTACT BONDING ADHESIVE: An adhesive (particularly of the nonvulcanizing natural rubber type) that bonds to itself on contact, although solvent evaporation has left it dry to the touch.

COPOLYMER: See *polymer.*

CORE MATERIAL: The fully cured inner-layer segments, with circuiting on one or both sides, that form the multilayer circuit.

CORNER MARKS: The marks at the corners of printed board artwork, the inside edges of which usually locate the borders and establish the contour of the board.

COUPON: One of the patterns of the quality conformance test circuitry area. (See *test coupon.*)

CRAZING: A base material condition in which connected white spots or crosses appear on or below the surface of the base material. They are due to the separation of fibers in the glass cloth and connecting weave intersections.

CROSS-LINKING: The forming of chemical links between reactive atoms in the molecular chain of a plastic. It is cross-linking in the thermosetting resins that makes the resins infusible.

CROSS TALK: Undesirable electrical interference caused by the coupling of energy between signal paths.

CRYSTALLINE MELTING POINT: The temperature at which the crystalline structure in a material is broken down.

CTE: Coefficient of thermal expansion. The measure of the amount a material changes in any axis per degree of temperature change.

CURE: To change the physical properties of a material (usually from a liquid to a solid) by chemical reaction or by the action of heat and catalysts, alone or in combination, with or without pressure.

CURING AGENT: See *hardener*.

CURING TEMPERATURE: The temperature at which a material is subjected to curing.

CURING TIME: In the molding of thermosetting plastics, the time in which the material is properly cured.

CURRENT-CARRYING CAPACITY: Maximum current which can be carried continuously without causing objectionable degradation of electrical or mechanical properties of the printed board.

DATUM REFERENCE: A defined point, line, or plane used to locate the pattern or layer of a printed board for manufacturing and/or inspection purposes.

DEBRIS: A mechanically bonded deposit of copper to substrate hole surfaces.

DEBRIS PACK: Debris deposited in cavities or voids in the resin.

DEFINITION: The fidelity of reproduction of the printed board conductive pattern relative to the production master.

DELAMINATION: A separation between any of the layers of the base laminate or between the laminate and the metal cladding originating from or extending to the edges of a hole or edge of the board.

DIELECTRIC CONSTANT: The property of a dielectric which determines the electrostatic energy stored per unit volume for a unit potential gradient.

DIELECTRIC LOSS: Electric energy transformed into heat in a dielectric subjected to a changing electric field.

DIELECTRIC LOSS ANGLE: The difference between 90° and the dielectric phase angle. Also called the dielectric phase difference.

DIELECTRIC LOSS FACTOR: The product of dielectric constant and the tangent of dielectric loss angle for a material.

DIELECTRIC PHASE ANGLE: The angular difference in phase between the sinusoidal alternating potential difference applied to a dielectric and the component of the resulting alternating current having the same period as the potential difference.

DIELECTRIC POWER FACTOR: The cosine of the dielectric phase angle (or sine of the dielectric loss angle).

DIELECTRIC STRENGTH: The voltage that an insulating material can withstand before breakdown occurs, usually expressed as a voltage gradient (such as volts per mil).

DIMENSIONAL STABILITY: Freedom from distortion by such factors as temperature changes, humidity changes, age, handling, and stress.

DISSIPATION FACTOR: The tangent of the loss angle of the insulating material. Also called loss tangent or approximate power factor.

DRILL FACET: The surface formed by the primary and secondary relief angles of a drill tip.

DRILL WANDER: The sum of accuracy and precision deviations from the targeted location of the hole.

DUMMY: A cathode with a large area used in a low-current-density plating operation for the removal of metallic impurities from solution. The process is called "dummying."

DWELL POINT: The bottom of the drilling stroke before the drill bit ascends.

EDGE-BOARD CONTACTS: A series of contacts printed on or near an edge of a printed board and intended for mating with a one-part edge connector.

EDX: Energy dispersive x-ray fluorescent spectrometer.

ELASTOMER: A material which at room temperature stretches under low stress to at least twice its length but snaps back to its original length upon release of the stress. Rubber is a natural elastomer.

ELECTRIC STRENGTH: The maximum potential gradient that a material can withstand without rupture. It is a function of the thickness of the material and the method and conditions of test. Also called dielectric strength or disruptive gradient.

ELECTROLESS PLATING: The controlled autocatalytic reduction of a metal ion on certain catalytic surfaces.

ELEMENT: A substance composed entirely of atoms of the same atomic number, e.g., aluminum or copper.

EMULSION SIDE: The side of the film or glass on which the photographic image is present.

ENTRY MATERIAL: A material placed on top of a laminate stack.

EPOXY SMEAR: Epoxy resin which has been deposited on edges of copper in holes during drilling either as a uniform coating or as scattered patches. It is undesirable because it can electrically isolate the conductive layers from the plated-through-hole interconnections.

ETCHBACK: The controlled removal of all the components of the base material by a chemical process acting on the sidewalls of plated-through holes to expose additional internal conductor areas.

ETCH FACTOR: The ratio of the depth of etch to lateral etch.

EXOTHERM: A characteristic curve which shows heat of reaction of a resin during cure (temperature) vs. time. The peak exotherm is the maximum temperature on the curve.

EXOTHERMIC REACTION: A chemical reaction in which heat is given off.

FIBER EXPOSURE: A condition in which glass cloth fibers are exposed on machined or abraded areas.

FILLER: A material, usually inert, added to a plastic to reduce cost or modify physical properties.

FILM ADHESIVE: A thin layer of dried adhesive. Also, a class of adhesives provided in dry-film form with or without reinforcing fabric and cured by heat and pressure.

FLEXURAL MODULUS: The ratio, within the elastic limit, of stress to corresponding strain. It is calculated by drawing a tangent to the steepest initial straight-line portion of the load-deformation curve and using the equation $E_B = L^3 m/4bd^3$, where E_B is the modulus, L is the span (in inches), m is the slope of the tangent, b is the width of beam tested, and d is the depth of the beam.

FLEXURAL STRENGTH: The strength of a material subjected to bending. It is expressed as the tensile stress of the outermost fibers of a bent test sample at the instant of failure.

FLUOROCARBON: An organic compound having fluorine atoms in its chemical structure, an inclusion that usually lends stability to plastics. Teflon* is a fluorocarbon.

GEL: The soft, rubbery mass that is formed as a thermosetting resin goes from a fluid to an infusible solid. It is an intermediate state in a curing reaction, and a stage in which the resin is mechanically very weak.

GEL POINT: The point at which gelation begins.

GLASS TRANSITION POINT: The temperature at which a material loses properties and becomes a semiliquid.

GLASS TRANSITION TEMPERATURE: The temperature at which epoxy, for example, softens and begins to expand independently of the glass fabric expansion rate.

GLUE-LINE THICKNESS: Thickness of the fully dried adhesive layer.

GRID: An orthogonal network of two sets of parallel lines for positioning features on a printed board.

GROUND PLANE: A conducting surface used as a common reference point for circuit returns, shielding, or heat sinking.

GULL WING LEAD: A surface mounted device lead which flares outward from the device body.

HALOING: A light area around holes or other machined areas on or below the surface of the base laminate.

HARDENER: A chemical added to a thermosetting resin for the purpose of causing curing or hardening. A hardener, such as an amine or acid anhydride for an epoxy resin, is a part of the chemical reaction and a part of the chemical composition of the cured resin. The terms "hardener" and "curing agent" are used interchangeably.

HEAT-DISTORTION POINT: The temperature at which a standard test bar (ASTM D 648) deflects 0.010 in under a stated load of either 66 or 264 psi.

HEAT SEALING: A method of joining plastic films by simultaneous application of heat and pressure to areas in contact. The heat may be supplied conductively or dielectrically.

HOLE PULL STRENGTH: The force, in pounds, necessary to rupture a plated-through hole or its surface terminal pads when loaded or pulled in the direction of the axis of the hole. The pull is usually applied to a wire soldered in the hole, and the rate of pull is given in inches per minute.

HOOK: A geometric drill bit defect of the cutting edges.

HOT-MELT ADHESIVE: A thermoplastic adhesive compound, usually solid at room temperature, which is heated to fluid state for application.

---

*Trademark of E. I. du Pont de Nemours & Company.

HYDROCARBON: An organic compound containing only carbon and hydrogen atoms in its chemical structure.

HYDROLYSIS: The chemical decomposition of a substance involving the addition of water.

HYGROSCOPIC: Tending to absorb moisture.

I-LEAD: A surface mounted device lead which is formed such that the end of the lead contacts the board land pattern at a 90° angle. Also called a butt joint.

IMPREGNATE: To force resin into every interstice of a part, as of a cloth for laminating.

INHIBITOR: A chemical that is added to a resin to slow down the curing reaction and is normally added to prolong the storage life of a thermosetting resin.

INORGANIC CHEMICALS: Chemicals whose molecular structures are based on other than carbon atoms.

INSULATION RESISTANCE: The electrical resistance of the insulating material between any pair of contacts, conductors, or grounding devices in various combinations.

INTERNAL LAYER: A conductive pattern contained entirely within a multilayer board.

IPC: Institute for Interconnecting and Packaging Electronic Circuits. A leading printed wiring industry association that develops and distributes standards, as well as other information of value to printed wiring designers, users, suppliers, and fabricators.

IR: Infrared heating for solder-reflow operation.

J-LEAD: A surface mounted device lead which is formed into a "J" pattern folding under the device body.

JUMPER: An electrical connection between two points on a printed board added after the printed wiring is fabricated.

LAMINATE: The plastic material, usually reinforced by glass or paper, that supports the copper cladding from which circuit traces are created.

LAMINATE VOID: Absence of epoxy resin in any cross-sectional area which should normally contain epoxy resin.

LAND: See *terminal area.*

LANDLESS HOLE: A plated-through hole without a terminal area.

LASER PHOTOPLOTTER (laser photogenerator, or LPG): A device that exposes photosensitive material, usually a silver halide or diazo material, subsequently used as the master for creating the circuit image in production.

LAYBACK: A geometric drill bit defect of the cutting edges.

LAYER-TO-LAYER SPACING: The thickness of dielectric material between adjacent layers of conductive circuitry.

LAY-UP: The process of registering and stacking layers of a multilayer board in preparation for the laminating cycle.

LCCC: Leadless ceramic chip carrier.

LEADED CHIP CARRIER: A chip carrier (either plastic or ceramic) with compliant leads for terminations.

LEADLESS CHIP CARRIER: A chip carrier (usually ceramic) with integral metallized terminations and no compliant external leads.

LEGEND: A format of lettering or symbols on the printed board, e.g., part number, component locations, or patterns.

LOOSE FIBERS: Supporting fibers in the substrate of the laminate which are not held in place by surrounding resin.

MAJOR WEAVE DIRECTION: The continuous-length direction of a roll of woven glass fabric.

MARGIN RELIEF: The area of a drill bit next to the cutting edge is removed so that it does not rub against the hole as the drill revolves.

MASTER DRAWING: A document that shows the dimensional limits or grid locations applicable to any or all parts of a printed wiring or printed circuit base. It includes the arrangement of conductive or nonconductive patterns or elements; size, type, and location of holes; and any other information necessary to characterize the complete fabricated product.

MEASLING: Discrete white spots or crosses below the surface of the base laminate that reflect a separation of fibers in the glass cloth at the weave intersection.

MICROSTRIP: A type of transmission line configuration which consists of a conductor over a parallel ground plane separated by a dielectric.

MINOR WEAVE DIRECTION: The width direction of a roll of woven glass fabric.

MIXED ASSEMBLY: A printed wiring assembly that combines through-hole components and surface mounted components on the same board.

MODULUS OF ELASTICITY: The ratio of stress to strain in a material that is elastically deformed.

MOISTURE RESISTANCE: The ability of a material not to absorb moisture either from air or when immersed in water.

MOUNTING HOLE: A hole used for the mechanical mounting of a printed board or for the mechanical attachment of components to a printed board.

MULTILAYER BOARD: A product consisting of layers of electrical conductors separated from each other by insulating supports and fabricated into a solid mass. Interlayer connections are used to establish continuity between various conductor patterns.

MULTIPLE-IMAGE PRODUCTION MASTER: A production master used to produce two or more products simultaneously.

NAILHEADING: A flared condition of internal conductors.

NC: Numerically controlled. Usually refers to a machine tool, in this case a drilling machine. The most basic type is one in which a mechanical guide locates the positions of the holes. NC machines are usually controlled by punched tape.

NEMA STANDARDS: Property values adopted as standard by the National Electrical Manufacturers Association.

NOBLE ELEMENTS: Elements that either do not oxidize or oxidize with difficulty; examples are gold and platinum.

OILCANNING: The movement of entry material in the z direction during drilling in concert with the movement of the pressure foot.

ORGANIC: Composed of matter originating in plant or animal life or composed of chemicals of hydrocarbon origin, either natural or synthetic.

PAD: See *terminal area*.

PADS ONLY: A multilayer construction with all circuit traces on inner layers and the component terminal area only on the surface of the board. This construction adds two layers but may avoid the need for a subsequent solder resist, and since inner layers usually are easier to form, this construction may lead to higher overall yields.

pH: A measure of the acid or alkaline condition of a solution. A pH of 7 is neutral (distilled water); pH values below 7 represent increasing acidity as they go toward 0; and pH values above 7 represent increasing alkalinity as they go toward the maximum value of 14.

PHOTOGRAPHIC REDUCTION DIMENSION: The dimension (e.g., line or distance between two specified points) on the artwork master to indicate the extent to which the artwork master is to be photographically reduced. The value of the dimension refers to the 1:1 scale and must be specified.

PHOTOMASTER: An accurately scaled copy of the artwork master used in the photofabrication cycle to facilitate photoprocessing steps.

PHOTOPOLYMER: A polymer that changes characteristics when exposed to light of a given frequency.

PINHOLES: Small imperfections which penetrate entirely through the conductor.

PITS: Small imperfections which do not penetrate entirely through the printed circuit.

PLASTICIZER: Material added to resins to make them softer and more flexible when cured.

PLASTIC LEADED CHIP CARRIER (PLCC): A chip carrier packaged in plastic, usually terminating in compliant leads (originally "J" style) on all four sides.

PLATED-THROUGH HOLE: A hole in which electrical connection is made between printed wiring board layers with conductive patterns by the deposition of metal on the wall of the hole. (See *PTH*.)

PLATING VOID: The area of absence of a specific metal from a specific cross-sectional area: (1) When the plated-through hole is viewed as cross-sectioned through the vertical plane, it is a product of the average thickness of the plated metal times the thickness of the board itself as measured from the outermost surfaces of the base copper on external layers. (2) When the plated-through hole is viewed as cross-sectioned through the horizontal plane (annular method), it is the difference between the area of the hole and the area of the outside diameter of the through-hole plating.

PLOWING: Furrows in the hole wall due to drilling.

POLYMER: A high-molecular-weight compound made up of repeated small chemical units. For practical purposes, a polymer is a plastic. The small chemical unit is called a mer, and when the polymer or mer is cross-linked between different chemical units (e.g., styrene-polyester), the polymer is called a copolymer. A monomer is any single chemical from which the mer or polymer or copolymer is formed.

POLYMERIZE: To unite chemically two or more monomers or polymers of the same kind to form a molecule with higher molecular weight.

POTLIFE: The time during which a liquid resin remains workable as a liquid after catalysts, curing agents, promoters, etc., are added. It is roughly equivalent to gel time.

POWER FACTOR: The cosine of the angle between the applied voltage and the resulting current.

PRECISION: The ability to repeatedly place the hole at any location.

PREPRODUCTION TEST BOARD: A test board (as detailed in IPC-ML-950) the purpose of which is to determine whether, prior to the production of finished boards, the contractor has the capability of producing a multilayer board satisfactorily.

PRESS PLATEN: The flat heated surface of the lamination press used to transmit heat and pressure to lamination fixtures and into the lay-up.

PRESSURE FOOT: The tubelike device on the drilling machine that descends to the top surface of the stack, holding it firmly down, before the drill descends through the center of the pressure foot. The vacuum system of the drilling machine separates through the pressure foot to remove chips and dust formed in drilling.

PRINTED WIRING ASSEMBLY DRAWING: A document that shows the printed wiring base, the separately manufactured components which are to be added to the base, and any other information necessary to describe the joining of the parts to perform a specific function.

PRINTED WIRING LAYOUT: A sketch that depicts the printed wiring substrate, the physical size and location of electronic and mechanical components, and the routing of conductors that interconnect the electronic parts in sufficient detail to allow for the preparation of documentation and artowrk.

PRODUCTION MASTER: A 1:1 scale pattern used to produce one or more printed wiring or printed circuit products within the accuracy specified on the master drawing.

PROMOTER: A chemical, itself a feeble catalyst, that greatly increases the activity of a given catalyst.

PTH: Plated-through hole. Also refers to the technology that uses the plated-through hole as its foundation.

QUADPACK: Generic term for surface mount technology packages with leads on all four sides. Commonly used to describe chip carrier–like devices with gull wing leads.

QUALITY CONFORMANCE CIRCUITRY AREA: A test board made as an integral part of the multilayer printed board panel on which electrical and environmental tests may be made for evaluation without destroying the basic board.

RAW MATERIAL PANEL SIZE: A standard panel size related to machine capacities, raw material sheet sizes, final product size, and other factors.

REFRACTIVE INDEX: The ratio of the velocity of light in a vacuum to the velocity in a substance. Also, the ratio of the sine of the angle of incidence to the sine of the angle of refraction.

REGISTER MARK: A mark used to establish the relative position of one or more printed wiring patterns, or portions thereof, with respect to desired locations on the opposite side of the board.

REGISTRATION: The relative position of one or more printed wiring patterns, or portions thereof, with respect to desired locations on a printed wiring base or to another pattern on the opposite side of the base.

RELATIVE HUMIDITY: The ratio of the quantity of water vapor present in the air to the quantity which would saturate the air at the given temperature.

REPAIR: The correction of a printed wiring defect after the completion of board fabrication to render the board as functionally good as a perfect board.

RESIN: High-molecular-weight organic material with no sharp melting point. For current purposes, the terms "resin," "polymer," and "plastic" can be used interchangeably.

RESIST: A protective coating (ink, paint, metallic plating, etc.) used to shield desired portions of the printed conductive pattern from the action of etchant, solder, or plating.

RESISTIVITY: The ability of a material to resist passage of electric current through its bulk or on a surface.

RIFLING: Spiral groove or ridge in the substrate due to drilling.

ROCKWELL HARDNESS NUMBER: A number derived from the net increase in depth of an impression as the load on a penetrator is increased from a fixed minimum load to a higher load and then returned to minimum load.

ROUGHNESS: Irregular, coarse, uneven hole wall on copper or substrate due to drilling.

SCHEMATIC DIAGRAM: A drawing which shows, by means of graphic symbols, the electrical interconnections and functions of a specific circuit arrangement.

SEM: Scanning electron microscope.

SHADOWING: Etchback to maximum limit without removal of dielectric material from conductors.

SHORE HARDNESS: A procedure for determining the indentation hardness of a material by means of a durometer.

SINGLE-IMAGE PRODUCTION MASTER: A production master used to produce individual products.

SINGLE-IN-LINE PACKAGE (SIP): Component package system with one line of connectors, usually spaced 0.100 in apart.

SMC: Surface mounted component. Component with terminations designed for mounting flush to printed wiring board.

SMD: Surface mounted device. Any component or hardware element designed to be mounted to a printed wiring board without penetrating the board.

SMEAR: Fused deposit left on copper or substrate from excessive drilling heat.

SMOBC: Solder mask over bare copper. A method of fabricating a printed wiring board which results in the final metallization being copper with no other protective metal; but the non-soldered areas are coated by a solder resist, exposing only the component terminal areas. This eliminates tin-lead under the solder mask.

SMT: Surface mount technology. Defines the entire body of processes and components which create printed wiring assemblies without components with leads that pierce the board.

SOIC: Small-outline integrated circuit. A plastic package resembling a small dual-in-line package (DIP) with gull wing leads on two sides for surface mounting.

SOJ: SOIC package with J-leads rather than gull wing leads.

SOT: Small outline transistor. A package for surface-mounting transistors.

SPECIFIC HEAT: The ratio of the thermal capacity of a material to that of water at 15°C.

SPINDLE RUNOUT: The measure of the wobble present as the drilling machine spindle rotates 360°.

STORAGE LIFE: The period of time during which a liquid resin or adhesive can be stored and remain suitable for use. Also called shelf life.

STRAIN: The deformation resulting from a stress. It is measured by the ratio of the change to the total value of the dimension in which the change occurred.

STRESS: The force producing or tending to produce deformation in a body. It is measured by the force applied per unit area.

SUBSTRATE: A material on whose surface an adhesive substance is spread for bonding or coating. Also, any material which provides a supporting surface for other materials used to support printed wiring patterns.

SURFACE RESISTIVITY: The resistance of a material between two opposite sides of a unit square of its surface. It may vary widely with the conditions of measurement.

SURFACE SPEED: The linear velocity of a point on the circumference of a drill. Given in units of surface feet per minute—sfm.

TERMINAL AREA: A portion of a conductive pattern usually, but not exclusively, used for the connection and/or attachment of components.

TEST COUPON: A sample or test pattern usually made as an integral part of the printed board, on which electrical, environmental, and microsectioning tests may be made to evaluate board design or process control without destroying the basic board.

TETRA-ETCH*: A nonpyrophoric (will not ignite when exposed to moisture) proprietary etchant.

TETROFUNCTIONAL: Describes an epoxy system for laminates that has four cross-linked bonds rather than two and results in a higher glass transition temperature, or T_g.

T_g: Glass transition temperature. The temperature at which laminate mechanical properties change significantly.

THERMAL CONDUCTIVITY: The ability of a material to conduct heat; the physical constant for the quantity of heat that passes through a unit cube of a material in a unit of time when the difference in temperatures of two faces is 1°C.

THERMOPLASTIC: A classification of resin that can be readily softened and resoftened by repeated heating.

THERMOSETTING: A classification of resin which cures by chemical reaction when heated and, when cured, cannot be resoftened by heating.

---

*Trademark of W. L. Gore and Associates, Inc.

THIEF: An auxiliary cathode so placed as to divert to itself some current from portions of the work which would otherwise receive too high a current density.

THIXOTROPIC: Said of materials that are gel-like at rest but fluid when agitated.

THROUGH-HOLE TECHNOLOGY: Traditional printed wiring fabrication where components are mounted in holes that pierce the board.

THROWING POWER: The improvement of the coating (usually metal) distribution ratio over the primary current distribution ratio on an electrode (usually a cathode). Of a solution, a measure of the degree of uniformity with which metal is deposited on an irregularly shaped cathode. The term may also be used for anodic processes for which the definition is analogous.

TWIST: A laminate defect in which deviation from planarity results in a twisted arc.

UNDERCUT: The reduction of the cross section of a metal foil conductor caused by the etchant removing metal from under the edge of the resist.

VAPOR PHASE: The solder-reflow process that uses a vaporized solvent as the source for heating the solder beyond its melting point, creating the component-to-board solder joint.

VIA: A metallized connecting hole that provides a conductive path from one layer in a printed wiring board to another. (1) *Buried via*—connects one inner layer to another inner layer without penetrating the surface. (2) *Blind via*—connects the surface layer of a printed wiring board to an internal layer without going all the way through the other surface layer.

VOID: A cavity left in the substrate.

VOLUME RESISTIVITY: The electrical resistance between opposite faces of a 1-cm cube of insulating material, commonly expressed in ohm-centimeters. The recommended test is ASTM D 257 51T. Also called the specific insulation.

VULCANIZATION: A chemical reaction in which the physical properties of an elastomer are changed by causing the elastomer to react with sulfur or some other cross-linking agent.

WATER ABSORPTION: The ratio of the weight of water absorbed by a material to the weight of the dry material.

WEAVE EXPOSURE: A condition in which the unbroken woven glass cloth is not uniformly covered by resin.

WEAVE TEXTURE: A surface condition in which the unbroken fibers are completely covered with resin but exhibit the definite weave pattern of the glass cloth.

WETTING: Ability to adhere to a surface immediately upon contact.

WICKING: Migration of copper salts into the glass fibers of the insulating material.

WORKING LIFE: The period of time during which a liquid resin or adhesive, after mixing with catalyst, solvent, or other compounding ingredients, remains usable. (See *potlife.*)

INDEX

ABOUT THE EDITOR

Clyde F. Coombs, Jr., recently retired from Hewlett-Packard after a 30-year career in manufacturing and engineering. He has edited best-selling handbooks since the *Printed Circuits Handbook* was first published in 1967. His other books include two editions of *The Electronic Instrument Handbook* and the *Handbook of Reliability Engineering and Management,* for which he was co-editor, both available from McGraw-Hill.